Lecture Notes in Computer Science 13697

Founding Editors

Gerhard Goos
Karlsruhe Institute of Technology, Karlsruhe, Germany

Juris Hartmanis
Cornell University, Ithaca, NY, USA

Editorial Board Members

Elisa Bertino
Purdue University, West Lafayette, IN, USA

Wen Gao
Peking University, Beijing, China

Bernhard Steffen
TU Dortmund University, Dortmund, Germany

Moti Yung
Columbia University, New York, NY, USA

More information about this series at https://link.springer.com/bookseries/558

Shai Avidan · Gabriel Brostow ·
Moustapha Cissé · Giovanni Maria Farinella ·
Tal Hassner (Eds.)

Computer Vision – ECCV 2022

17th European Conference
Tel Aviv, Israel, October 23–27, 2022
Proceedings, Part XXXVII

Editors
Shai Avidan
Tel Aviv University
Tel Aviv, Israel

Moustapha Cissé
Google AI
Accra, Ghana

Tal Hassner (iD)
Facebook (United States)
Menlo Park, CA, USA

Gabriel Brostow (iD)
University College London
London, UK

Giovanni Maria Farinella (iD)
University of Catania
Catania, Italy

ISSN 0302-9743   ISSN 1611-3349 (electronic)
Lecture Notes in Computer Science
ISBN 978-3-031-19835-9   ISBN 978-3-031-19836-6 (eBook)
https://doi.org/10.1007/978-3-031-19836-6

This Springer imprint is published by the registered company Springer Nature Switzerland AG
The registered company address is: Gewerbestrasse 11, 6330 Cham, Switzerland

Foreword

Organizing the European Conference on Computer Vision (ECCV 2022) in Tel-Aviv during a global pandemic was no easy feat. The uncertainty level was extremely high, and decisions had to be postponed to the last minute. Still, we managed to plan things just in time for ECCV 2022 to be held in person. Participation in physical events is crucial to stimulating collaborations and nurturing the culture of the Computer Vision community.

There were many people who worked hard to ensure attendees enjoyed the best science at the 16th edition of ECCV. We are grateful to the Program Chairs Gabriel Brostow and Tal Hassner, who went above and beyond to ensure the ECCV reviewing process ran smoothly. The scientific program includes dozens of workshops and tutorials in addition to the main conference and we would like to thank Leonid Karlinsky and Tomer Michaeli for their hard work. Finally, special thanks to the web chairs Lorenzo Baraldi and Kosta Derpanis, who put in extra hours to transfer information fast and efficiently to the ECCV community.

We would like to express gratitude to our generous sponsors and the Industry Chairs, Dimosthenis Karatzas and Chen Sagiv, who oversaw industry relations and proposed new ways for academia-industry collaboration and technology transfer. It's great to see so much industrial interest in what we're doing!

Authors' draft versions of the papers appeared online with open access on both the Computer Vision Foundation (CVF) and the European Computer Vision Association (ECVA) websites as with previous ECCVs. Springer, the publisher of the proceedings, has arranged for archival publication. The final version of the papers is hosted by SpringerLink, with active references and supplementary materials. It benefits all potential readers that we offer both a free and citeable version for all researchers, as well as an authoritative, citeable version for SpringerLink readers. Our thanks go to Ronan Nugent from Springer, who helped us negotiate this agreement. Last but not least, we wish to thank Eric Mortensen, our publication chair, whose expertise made the process smooth.

October 2022

Rita Cucchiara
Jiří Matas
Amnon Shashua
Lihi Zelnik-Manor

Preface

Welcome to the proceedings of the European Conference on Computer Vision (ECCV 2022). This was a hybrid edition of ECCV as we made our way out of the COVID-19 pandemic. The conference received 5804 valid paper submissions, compared to 5150 submissions to ECCV 2020 (a 12.7% increase) and 2439 in ECCV 2018. 1645 submissions were accepted for publication (28%) and, of those, 157 (2.7% overall) as orals.

846 of the submissions were desk-rejected for various reasons. Many of them because they revealed author identity, thus violating the double-blind policy. This violation came in many forms: some had author names with the title, others added acknowledgments to specific grants, yet others had links to their github account where their name was visible. Tampering with the LaTeX template was another reason for automatic desk rejection.

ECCV 2022 used the traditional CMT system to manage the entire double-blind reviewing process. Authors did not know the names of the reviewers and vice versa. Each paper received at least 3 reviews (except 6 papers that received only 2 reviews), totalling more than 15,000 reviews.

Handling the review process at this scale was a significant challenge. To ensure that each submission received as fair and high-quality reviews as possible, we recruited more than 4719 reviewers (in the end, 4719 reviewers did at least one review). Similarly we recruited more than 276 area chairs (eventually, only 276 area chairs handled a batch of papers). The area chairs were selected based on their technical expertise and reputation, largely among people who served as area chairs in previous top computer vision and machine learning conferences (ECCV, ICCV, CVPR, NeurIPS, etc.).

Reviewers were similarly invited from previous conferences, and also from the pool of authors. We also encouraged experienced area chairs to suggest additional chairs and reviewers in the initial phase of recruiting. The median reviewer load was five papers per reviewer, while the average load was about four papers, because of the emergency reviewers. The area chair load was 35 papers, on average.

Conflicts of interest between authors, area chairs, and reviewers were handled largely automatically by the CMT platform, with some manual help from the Program Chairs. Reviewers were allowed to describe themselves as senior reviewer (load of 8 papers to review) or junior reviewers (load of 4 papers). Papers were matched to area chairs based on a subject-area affinity score computed in CMT and an affinity score computed by the Toronto Paper Matching System (TPMS). TPMS is based on the paper's full text. An area chair handling each submission would bid for preferred expert reviewers, and we balanced load and prevented conflicts.

The assignment of submissions to area chairs was relatively smooth, as was the assignment of submissions to reviewers. A small percentage of reviewers were not happy with their assignments in terms of subjects and self-reported expertise. This is an area for improvement, although it's interesting that many of these cases were reviewers hand-picked by AC's. We made a later round of reviewer recruiting, targeted at the list of authors of papers submitted to the conference, and had an excellent response which helped provide enough emergency reviewers. In the end, all but six papers received at least 3 reviews.

The challenges of the reviewing process are in line with past experiences at ECCV 2020. As the community grows, and the number of submissions increases, it becomes ever more challenging to recruit enough reviewers and ensure a high enough quality of reviews. Enlisting authors by default as reviewers might be one step to address this challenge.

Authors were given a week to rebut the initial reviews, and address reviewers' concerns. Each rebuttal was limited to a single pdf page with a fixed template.

The Area Chairs then led discussions with the reviewers on the merits of each submission. The goal was to reach consensus, but, ultimately, it was up to the Area Chair to make a decision. The decision was then discussed with a buddy Area Chair to make sure decisions were fair and informative. The entire process was conducted virtually with no in-person meetings taking place.

The Program Chairs were informed in cases where the Area Chairs overturned a decisive consensus reached by the reviewers, and pushed for the meta-reviews to contain details that explained the reasoning for such decisions. Obviously these were the most contentious cases, where reviewer inexperience was the most common reported factor.

Once the list of accepted papers was finalized and released, we went through the laborious process of plagiarism (including self-plagiarism) detection. A total of 4 accepted papers were rejected because of that.

Finally, we would like to thank our Technical Program Chair, Pavel Lifshits, who did tremendous work behind the scenes, and we thank the tireless CMT team.

October 2022

Gabriel Brostow
Giovanni Maria Farinella
Moustapha Cissé
Shai Avidan
Tal Hassner

Organization

General Chairs

Rita Cucchiara	University of Modena and Reggio Emilia, Italy
Jiří Matas	Czech Technical University in Prague, Czech Republic
Amnon Shashua	Hebrew University of Jerusalem, Israel
Lihi Zelnik-Manor	Technion – Israel Institute of Technology, Israel

Program Chairs

Shai Avidan	Tel-Aviv University, Israel
Gabriel Brostow	University College London, UK
Moustapha Cissé	Google AI, Ghana
Giovanni Maria Farinella	University of Catania, Italy
Tal Hassner	Facebook AI, USA

Program Technical Chair

Pavel Lifshits	Technion – Israel Institute of Technology, Israel

Workshops Chairs

Leonid Karlinsky	IBM Research, Israel
Tomer Michaeli	Technion – Israel Institute of Technology, Israel
Ko Nishino	Kyoto University, Japan

Tutorial Chairs

Thomas Pock	Graz University of Technology, Austria
Natalia Neverova	Facebook AI Research, UK

Demo Chair

Bohyung Han	Seoul National University, Korea

Social and Student Activities Chairs

Tatiana Tommasi   Italian Institute of Technology, Italy
Sagie Benaim   University of Copenhagen, Denmark

Diversity and Inclusion Chairs

Xi Yin   Facebook AI Research, USA
Bryan Russell   Adobe, USA

Communications Chairs

Lorenzo Baraldi   University of Modena and Reggio Emilia, Italy
Kosta Derpanis   York University & Samsung AI Centre Toronto,
                           Canada

Industrial Liaison Chairs

Dimosthenis Karatzas   Universitat Autònoma de Barcelona, Spain
Chen Sagiv   SagivTech, Israel

Finance Chair

Gerard Medioni   University of Southern California & Amazon,
                           USA

Publication Chair

Eric Mortensen   MiCROTEC, USA

Area Chairs

Lourdes Agapito   University College London, UK
Zeynep Akata   University of Tübingen, Germany
Naveed Akhtar   University of Western Australia, Australia
Karteek Alahari   Inria Grenoble Rhône-Alpes, France
Alexandre Alahi   École polytechnique fédérale de Lausanne,
                           Switzerland
Pablo Arbelaez   Universidad de Los Andes, Columbia
Antonis A. Argyros   University of Crete & Foundation for Research
                           and Technology-Hellas, Crete
Yuki M. Asano   University of Amsterdam, The Netherlands
Kalle Åström   Lund University, Sweden
Hadar Averbuch-Elor   Cornell University, USA

Matthijs Douze   Facebook AI Research, USA
Mohamed Elhoseiny   King Abdullah University of Science and
                                  Technology, Saudi Arabia
Sergio Escalera   University of Barcelona, Spain
Yi Fang   New York University, USA
Ryan Farrell   Brigham Young University, USA
Alireza Fathi   Google, USA
Christoph Feichtenhofer   Facebook AI Research, USA
Basura Fernando   Agency for Science, Technology and Research
                                  (A*STAR), Singapore
Vittorio Ferrari   Google Research, Switzerland
Andrew W. Fitzgibbon   Graphcore, UK
David J. Fleet   University of Toronto, Canada
David Forsyth   University of Illinois at Urbana-Champaign, USA
David Fouhey   University of Michigan, USA
Katerina Fragkiadaki   Carnegie Mellon University, USA
Friedrich Fraundorfer   Graz University of Technology, Austria
Oren Freifeld   Ben-Gurion University, Israel
Thomas Funkhouser   Google Research & Princeton University, USA
Yasutaka Furukawa   Simon Fraser University, Canada
Fabio Galasso   Sapienza University of Rome, Italy
Jürgen Gall   University of Bonn, Germany
Chuang Gan   Massachusetts Institute of Technology, USA
Zhe Gan   Microsoft, USA
Animesh Garg   University of Toronto, Vector Institute, Nvidia,
                                  Canada
Efstratios Gavves   University of Amsterdam, The Netherlands
Peter Gehler   Amazon, Germany
Theo Gevers   University of Amsterdam, The Netherlands
Bernard Ghanem   King Abdullah University of Science and
                                  Technology, Saudi Arabia
Ross B. Girshick   Facebook AI Research, USA
Georgia Gkioxari   Facebook AI Research, USA
Albert Gordo   Facebook, USA
Stephen Gould   Australian National University, Australia
Venu Madhav Govindu   Indian Institute of Science, India
Kristen Grauman   Facebook AI Research & UT Austin, USA
Abhinav Gupta   Carnegie Mellon University & Facebook AI
                                  Research, USA
Mohit Gupta   University of Wisconsin-Madison, USA
Hu Han   Institute of Computing Technology, Chinese
                                  Academy of Sciences, China

Bohyung Han	Seoul National University, Korea
Tian Han	Stevens Institute of Technology, USA
Emily Hand	University of Nevada, Reno, USA
Bharath Hariharan	Cornell University, USA
Ran He	Institute of Automation, Chinese Academy of Sciences, China
Otmar Hilliges	ETH Zurich, Switzerland
Adrian Hilton	University of Surrey, UK
Minh Hoai	Stony Brook University, USA
Yedid Hoshen	Hebrew University of Jerusalem, Israel
Timothy Hospedales	University of Edinburgh, UK
Gang Hua	Wormpex AI Research, USA
Di Huang	Beihang University, China
Jing Huang	Facebook, USA
Jia-Bin Huang	Facebook, USA
Nathan Jacobs	Washington University in St. Louis, USA
C.V. Jawahar	International Institute of Information Technology, Hyderabad, India
Herve Jegou	Facebook AI Research, France
Neel Joshi	Microsoft Research, USA
Armand Joulin	Facebook AI Research, France
Frederic Jurie	University of Caen Normandie, France
Fredrik Kahl	Chalmers University of Technology, Sweden
Yannis Kalantidis	NAVER LABS Europe, France
Evangelos Kalogerakis	University of Massachusetts, Amherst, USA
Sing Bing Kang	Zillow Group, USA
Yosi Keller	Bar Ilan University, Israel
Margret Keuper	University of Mannheim, Germany
Tae-Kyun Kim	Imperial College London, UK
Benjamin Kimia	Brown University, USA
Alexander Kirillov	Facebook AI Research, USA
Kris Kitani	Carnegie Mellon University, USA
Iasonas Kokkinos	Snap Inc. & University College London, UK
Vladlen Koltun	Apple, USA
Nikos Komodakis	University of Crete, Crete
Piotr Koniusz	Australian National University, Australia
Philipp Kraehenbuehl	University of Texas at Austin, USA
Dilip Krishnan	Google, USA
Ajay Kumar	Hong Kong Polytechnic University, Hong Kong, China
Junseok Kwon	Chung-Ang University, Korea
Jean-Francois Lalonde	Université Laval, Canada

Ivan Laptev   Inria Paris, France
Laura Leal-Taixé   Technical University of Munich, Germany
Erik Learned-Miller   University of Massachusetts, Amherst, USA
Gim Hee Lee   National University of Singapore, Singapore
Seungyong Lee   Pohang University of Science and Technology,
                               Korea
Zhen Lei   Institute of Automation, Chinese Academy of
                               Sciences, China
Bastian Leibe   RWTH Aachen University, Germany
Hongdong Li   Australian National University, Australia
Fuxin Li   Oregon State University, USA
Bo Li   University of Illinois at Urbana-Champaign, USA
Yin Li   University of Wisconsin-Madison, USA
Ser-Nam Lim   Meta AI Research, USA
Joseph Lim   University of Southern California, USA
Stephen Lin   Microsoft Research Asia, China
Dahua Lin   The Chinese University of Hong Kong,
                               Hong Kong, China
Si Liu   Beihang University, China
Xiaoming Liu   Michigan State University, USA
Ce Liu   Microsoft, USA
Zicheng Liu   Microsoft, USA
Yanxi Liu   Pennsylvania State University, USA
Feng Liu   Portland State University, USA
Yebin Liu   Tsinghua University, China
Chen Change Loy   Nanyang Technological University, Singapore
Huchuan Lu   Dalian University of Technology, China
Cewu Lu   Shanghai Jiao Tong University, China
Oisin Mac Aodha   University of Edinburgh, UK
Dhruv Mahajan   Facebook, USA
Subhransu Maji   University of Massachusetts, Amherst, USA
Atsuto Maki   KTH Royal Institute of Technology, Sweden
Arun Mallya   NVIDIA, USA
R. Manmatha   Amazon, USA
Iacopo Masi   Sapienza University of Rome, Italy
Dimitris N. Metaxas   Rutgers University, USA
Ajmal Mian   University of Western Australia, Australia
Christian Micheloni   University of Udine, Italy
Krystian Mikolajczyk   Imperial College London, UK
Anurag Mittal   Indian Institute of Technology, Madras, India
Philippos Mordohai   Stevens Institute of Technology, USA
Greg Mori   Simon Fraser University & Borealis AI, Canada

Vittorio Murino   Istituto Italiano di Tecnologia, Italy
P. J. Narayanan   International Institute of Information Technology, Hyderabad, India
Ram Nevatia   University of Southern California, USA
Natalia Neverova   Facebook AI Research, UK
Richard Newcombe   Facebook, USA
Cuong V. Nguyen   Florida International University, USA
Bingbing Ni   Shanghai Jiao Tong University, China
Juan Carlos Niebles   Salesforce & Stanford University, USA
Ko Nishino   Kyoto University, Japan
Jean-Marc Odobez   Idiap Research Institute, École polytechnique fédérale de Lausanne, Switzerland
Francesca Odone   University of Genova, Italy
Takayuki Okatani   Tohoku University & RIKEN Center for Advanced Intelligence Project, Japan
Manohar Paluri   Facebook, USA
Guan Pang   Facebook, USA
Maja Pantic   Imperial College London, UK
Sylvain Paris   Adobe Research, USA
Jaesik Park   Pohang University of Science and Technology, Korea
Hyun Soo Park   The University of Minnesota, USA
Omkar M. Parkhi   Facebook, USA
Deepak Pathak   Carnegie Mellon University, USA
Georgios Pavlakos   University of California, Berkeley, USA
Marcello Pelillo   University of Venice, Italy
Marc Pollefeys   ETH Zurich & Microsoft, Switzerland
Jean Ponce   Inria, France
Gerard Pons-Moll   University of Tübingen, Germany
Fatih Porikli   Qualcomm, USA
Victor Adrian Prisacariu   University of Oxford, UK
Petia Radeva   University of Barcelona, Spain
Ravi Ramamoorthi   University of California, San Diego, USA
Deva Ramanan   Carnegie Mellon University, USA
Vignesh Ramanathan   Facebook, USA
Nalini Ratha   State University of New York at Buffalo, USA
Tammy Riklin Raviv   Ben-Gurion University, Israel
Tobias Ritschel   University College London, UK
Emanuele Rodola   Sapienza University of Rome, Italy
Amit K. Roy-Chowdhury   University of California, Riverside, USA
Michael Rubinstein   Google, USA
Olga Russakovsky   Princeton University, USA

Mathieu Salzmann	École polytechnique fédérale de Lausanne, Switzerland
Dimitris Samaras	Stony Brook University, USA
Aswin Sankaranarayanan	Carnegie Mellon University, USA
Imari Sato	National Institute of Informatics, Japan
Yoichi Sato	University of Tokyo, Japan
Shin'ichi Satoh	National Institute of Informatics, Japan
Walter Scheirer	University of Notre Dame, USA
Bernt Schiele	Max Planck Institute for Informatics, Germany
Konrad Schindler	ETH Zurich, Switzerland
Cordelia Schmid	Inria & Google, France
Alexander Schwing	University of Illinois at Urbana-Champaign, USA
Nicu Sebe	University of Trento, Italy
Greg Shakhnarovich	Toyota Technological Institute at Chicago, USA
Eli Shechtman	Adobe Research, USA
Humphrey Shi	University of Oregon & University of Illinois at Urbana-Champaign & Picsart AI Research, USA
Jianbo Shi	University of Pennsylvania, USA
Roy Shilkrot	Massachusetts Institute of Technology, USA
Mike Zheng Shou	National University of Singapore, Singapore
Kaleem Siddiqi	McGill University, Canada
Richa Singh	Indian Institute of Technology Jodhpur, India
Greg Slabaugh	Queen Mary University of London, UK
Cees Snoek	University of Amsterdam, The Netherlands
Yale Song	Facebook AI Research, USA
Yi-Zhe Song	University of Surrey, UK
Bjorn Stenger	Rakuten Institute of Technology
Abby Stylianou	Saint Louis University, USA
Akihiro Sugimoto	National Institute of Informatics, Japan
Chen Sun	Brown University, USA
Deqing Sun	Google, USA
Kalyan Sunkavalli	Adobe Research, USA
Ying Tai	Tencent YouTu Lab, China
Ayellet Tal	Technion – Israel Institute of Technology, Israel
Ping Tan	Simon Fraser University, Canada
Siyu Tang	ETH Zurich, Switzerland
Chi-Keung Tang	Hong Kong University of Science and Technology, Hong Kong, China
Radu Timofte	University of Würzburg, Germany & ETH Zurich, Switzerland
Federico Tombari	Google, Switzerland & Technical University of Munich, Germany

James Tompkin   Brown University, USA
Lorenzo Torresani   Dartmouth College, USA
Alexander Toshev   Apple, USA
Du Tran   Facebook AI Research, USA
Anh T. Tran   VinAI, Vietnam
Zhuowen Tu   University of California, San Diego, USA
Georgios Tzimiropoulos   Queen Mary University of London, UK
Jasper Uijlings   Google Research, Switzerland
Jan C. van Gemert   Delft University of Technology, The Netherlands
Gul Varol   Ecole des Ponts ParisTech, France
Nuno Vasconcelos   University of California, San Diego, USA
Mayank Vatsa   Indian Institute of Technology Jodhpur, India
Ashok Veeraraghavan   Rice University, USA
Jakob Verbeek   Facebook AI Research, France
Carl Vondrick   Columbia University, USA
Ruiping Wang   Institute of Computing Technology, Chinese
                               Academy of Sciences, China
Xinchao Wang   National University of Singapore, Singapore
Liwei Wang   The Chinese University of Hong Kong,
                               Hong Kong, China
Chaohui Wang   Université Paris-Est, France
Xiaolong Wang   University of California, San Diego, USA
Christian Wolf   NAVER LABS Europe, France
Tao Xiang   University of Surrey, UK
Saining Xie   Facebook AI Research, USA
Cihang Xie   University of California, Santa Cruz, USA
Zeki Yalniz   Facebook, USA
Ming-Hsuan Yang   University of California, Merced, USA
Angela Yao   National University of Singapore, Singapore
Shaodi You   University of Amsterdam, The Netherlands
Stella X. Yu   University of California, Berkeley, USA
Junsong Yuan   State University of New York at Buffalo, USA
Stefanos Zafeiriou   Imperial College London, UK
Amir Zamir   École polytechnique fédérale de Lausanne,
                               Switzerland
Lei Zhang   Alibaba & Hong Kong Polytechnic University,
                               Hong Kong, China
Lei Zhang   International Digital Economy Academy (IDEA),
                               China
Pengchuan Zhang   Meta AI, USA
Bolei Zhou   University of California, Los Angeles, USA
Yuke Zhu   University of Texas at Austin, USA

Todd Zickler   Harvard University, USA
Wangmeng Zuo   Harbin Institute of Technology, China

Technical Program Committee

Davide Abati
Soroush Abbasi
  Koohpayegani
Amos L. Abbott
Rameen Abdal
Rabab Abdelfattah
Sahar Abdelnabi
Hassan Abu Alhaija
Abulikemu Abuduweili
Ron Abutbul
Hanno Ackermann
Aikaterini Adam
Kamil Adamczewski
Ehsan Adeli
Vida Adeli
Donald Adjeroh
Arman Afrasiyabi
Akshay Agarwal
Sameer Agarwal
Abhinav Agarwalla
Vaibhav Aggarwal
Sara Aghajanzadeh
Susmit Agrawal
Antonio Agudo
Touqeer Ahmad
Sk Miraj Ahmed
Chaitanya Ahuja
Nilesh A. Ahuja
Abhishek Aich
Shubhra Aich
Noam Aigerman
Arash Akbarinia
Peri Akiva
Derya Akkaynak
Emre Aksan
Arjun R. Akula
Yuval Alaluf
Stephan Alaniz
Paul Albert
Cenek Albl

Filippo Aleotti
Konstantinos P.
  Alexandridis
Motasem Alfarra
Mohsen Ali
Thiemo Alldieck
Hadi Alzayer
Liang An
Shan An
Yi An
Zhulin An
Dongsheng An
Jie An
Xiang An
Saket Anand
Cosmin Ancuti
Juan Andrade-Cetto
Alexander Andreopoulos
Bjoern Andres
Jerone T. A. Andrews
Shivangi Aneja
Anelia Angelova
Dragomir Anguelov
Rushil Anirudh
Oron Anschel
Rao Muhammad Anwer
Djamila Aouada
Evlampios Apostolidis
Srikar Appalaraju
Nikita Araslanov
Andre Araujo
Eric Arazo
Dawit Mureja Argaw
Anurag Arnab
Aditya Arora
Chetan Arora
Sunpreet S. Arora
Alexey Artemov
Muhammad Asad
Kumar Ashutosh

Sinem Aslan
Vishal Asnani
Mahmoud Assran
Amir Atapour-Abarghouei
Nikos Athanasiou
Ali Athar
ShahRukh Athar
Sara Atito
Souhaib Attaiki
Matan Atzmon
Mathieu Aubry
Nicolas Audebert
Tristan T.
  Aumentado-Armstrong
Melinos Averkiou
Yannis Avrithis
Stephane Ayache
Mehmet Aygün
Seyed Mehdi
  Ayyoubzadeh
Hossein Azizpour
George Azzopardi
Mallikarjun B. R.
Yunhao Ba
Abhishek Badki
Seung-Hwan Bae
Seung-Hwan Baek
Seungryul Baek
Piyush Nitin Bagad
Shai Bagon
Gaetan Bahl
Shikhar Bahl
Sherwin Bahmani
Haoran Bai
Lei Bai
Jiawang Bai
Haoyue Bai
Jinbin Bai
Xiang Bai
Xuyang Bai

Yang Bai
Yuanchao Bai
Ziqian Bai
Sungyong Baik
Kevin Bailly
Max Bain
Federico Baldassarre
Wele Gedara Chaminda
    Bandara
Biplab Banerjee
Pratyay Banerjee
Sandipan Banerjee
Jihwan Bang
Antyanta Bangunharcana
Aayush Bansal
Ankan Bansal
Siddhant Bansal
Wentao Bao
Zhipeng Bao
Amir Bar
Manel Baradad Jurjo
Lorenzo Baraldi
Danny Barash
Daniel Barath
Connelly Barnes
Ioan Andrei Bârsan
Steven Basart
Dina Bashkirova
Chaim Baskin
Peyman Bateni
Anil Batra
Sebastiano Battiato
Ardhendu Behera
Harkirat Behl
Jens Behley
Vasileios Belagiannis
Boulbaba Ben Amor
Emanuel Ben Baruch
Abdessamad Ben Hamza
Gil Ben-Artzi
Assia Benbihi
Fabian Benitez-Quiroz
Guy Ben-Yosef
Philipp Benz
Alexander W. Bergman

Urs Bergmann
Jesus Bermudez-Cameo
Stefano Berretti
Gedas Bertasius
Zachary Bessinger
Petra Bevandić
Matthew Beveridge
Lucas Beyer
Yash Bhalgat
Suvaansh Bhambri
Samarth Bharadwaj
Gaurav Bharaj
Aparna Bharati
Bharat Lal Bhatnagar
Uttaran Bhattacharya
Apratim Bhattacharyya
Brojeshwar Bhowmick
Ankan Kumar Bhunia
Ayan Kumar Bhunia
Qi Bi
Sai Bi
Michael Bi Mi
Gui-Bin Bian
Jia-Wang Bian
Shaojun Bian
Pia Bideau
Mario Bijelic
Hakan Bilen
Guillaume-Alexandre
    Bilodeau
Alexander Binder
Tolga Birdal
Vighnesh N. Birodkar
Sandika Biswas
Andreas Blattmann
Janusz Bobulski
Giuseppe Boccignone
Vishnu Boddeti
Navaneeth Bodla
Moritz Böhle
Aleksei Bokhovkin
Sam Bond-Taylor
Vivek Boominathan
Shubhankar Borse
Mark Boss

Andrea Bottino
Adnane Boukhayma
Fadi Boutros
Nicolas C. Boutry
Richard S. Bowen
Ivaylo Boyadzhiev
Aidan Boyd
Yuri Boykov
Aljaz Bozic
Behzad Bozorgtabar
Eric Brachmann
Samarth Brahmbhatt
Gustav Bredell
Francois Bremond
Joel Brogan
Andrew Brown
Thomas Brox
Marcus A. Brubaker
Robert-Jan Bruintjes
Yuqi Bu
Anders G. Buch
Himanshu Buckchash
Mateusz Buda
Ignas Budvytis
José M. Buenaposada
Marcel C. Bühler
Tu Bui
Adrian Bulat
Hannah Bull
Evgeny Burnaev
Andrei Bursuc
Benjamin Busam
Sergey N. Buzykanov
Wonmin Byeon
Fabian Caba
Martin Cadik
Guanyu Cai
Minjie Cai
Qing Cai
Zhongang Cai
Qi Cai
Yancheng Cai
Shen Cai
Han Cai
Jiarui Cai

Bowen Cai
Mu Cai
Qin Cai
Ruojin Cai
Weidong Cai
Weiwei Cai
Yi Cai
Yujun Cai
Zhiping Cai
Akin Caliskan
Lilian Calvet
Baris Can Cam
Necati Cihan Camgoz
Tommaso Campari
Dylan Campbell
Ziang Cao
Ang Cao
Xu Cao
Zhiwen Cao
Shengcao Cao
Song Cao
Weipeng Cao
Xiangyong Cao
Xiaochun Cao
Yue Cao
Yunhao Cao
Zhangjie Cao
Jiale Cao
Yang Cao
Jiajiong Cao
Jie Cao
Jinkun Cao
Lele Cao
Yulong Cao
Zhiguo Cao
Chen Cao
Razvan Caramalau
Marlène Careil
Gustavo Carneiro
Joao Carreira
Dan Casas
Paola Cascante-Bonilla
Angela Castillo
Francisco M. Castro
Pedro Castro

Luca Cavalli
George J. Cazenavette
Oya Celiktutan
Hakan Cevikalp
Sri Harsha C. H.
Sungmin Cha
Geonho Cha
Menglei Chai
Lucy Chai
Yuning Chai
Zenghao Chai
Anirban Chakraborty
Deep Chakraborty
Rudrasis Chakraborty
Souradeep Chakraborty
Kelvin C. K. Chan
Chee Seng Chan
Paramanand Chandramouli
Arjun Chandrasekaran
Kenneth Chaney
Dongliang Chang
Huiwen Chang
Peng Chang
Xiaojun Chang
Jia-Ren Chang
Hyung Jin Chang
Hyun Sung Chang
Ju Yong Chang
Li-Jen Chang
Qi Chang
Wei-Yi Chang
Yi Chang
Nadine Chang
Hanqing Chao
Pradyumna Chari
Dibyadip Chatterjee
Chiranjoy Chattopadhyay
Siddhartha Chaudhuri
Zhengping Che
Gal Chechik
Lianggangxu Chen
Qi Alfred Chen
Brian Chen
Bor-Chun Chen
Bo-Hao Chen

Bohong Chen
Bin Chen
Ziliang Chen
Cheng Chen
Chen Chen
Chaofeng Chen
Xi Chen
Haoyu Chen
Xuanhong Chen
Wei Chen
Qiang Chen
Shi Chen
Xianyu Chen
Chang Chen
Changhuai Chen
Hao Chen
Jie Chen
Jianbo Chen
Jingjing Chen
Jun Chen
Kejiang Chen
Mingcai Chen
Nenglun Chen
Qifeng Chen
Ruoyu Chen
Shu-Yu Chen
Weidong Chen
Weijie Chen
Weikai Chen
Xiang Chen
Xiuyi Chen
Xingyu Chen
Yaofo Chen
Yueting Chen
Yu Chen
Yunjin Chen
Yuntao Chen
Yun Chen
Zhenfang Chen
Zhuangzhuang Chen
Chu-Song Chen
Xiangyu Chen
Zhuo Chen
Chaoqi Chen
Shizhe Chen

Xiaotong Chen
Xiaozhi Chen
Dian Chen
Defang Chen
Dingfan Chen
Ding-Jie Chen
Ee Heng Chen
Tao Chen
Yixin Chen
Wei-Ting Chen
Lin Chen
Guang Chen
Guangyi Chen
Guanying Chen
Guangyao Chen
Hwann-Tzong Chen
Junwen Chen
Jiacheng Chen
Jianxu Chen
Hui Chen
Kai Chen
Kan Chen
Kevin Chen
Kuan-Wen Chen
Weihua Chen
Zhang Chen
Liang-Chieh Chen
Lele Chen
Liang Chen
Fanglin Chen
Zehui Chen
Minghui Chen
Minghao Chen
Xiaokang Chen
Qian Chen
Jun-Cheng Chen
Qi Chen
Qingcai Chen
Richard J. Chen
Runnan Chen
Rui Chen
Shuo Chen
Sentao Chen
Shaoyu Chen
Shixing Chen

Shuai Chen
Shuya Chen
Sizhe Chen
Simin Chen
Shaoxiang Chen
Zitian Chen
Tianlong Chen
Tianshui Chen
Min-Hung Chen
Xiangning Chen
Xin Chen
Xinghao Chen
Xuejin Chen
Xu Chen
Xuxi Chen
Yunlu Chen
Yanbei Chen
Yuxiao Chen
Yun-Chun Chen
Yi-Ting Chen
Yi-Wen Chen
Yinbo Chen
Yiran Chen
Yuanhong Chen
Yubei Chen
Yuefeng Chen
Yuhua Chen
Yukang Chen
Zerui Chen
Zhaoyu Chen
Zhen Chen
Zhenyu Chen
Zhi Chen
Zhiwei Chen
Zhixiang Chen
Long Chen
Bowen Cheng
Jun Cheng
Yi Cheng
Jingchun Cheng
Lechao Cheng
Xi Cheng
Yuan Cheng
Ho Kei Cheng
Kevin Ho Man Cheng

Jiacheng Cheng
Kelvin B. Cheng
Li Cheng
Mengjun Cheng
Zhen Cheng
Qingrong Cheng
Tianheng Cheng
Harry Cheng
Yihua Cheng
Yu Cheng
Ziheng Cheng
Soon Yau Cheong
Anoop Cherian
Manuela Chessa
Zhixiang Chi
Naoki Chiba
Julian Chibane
Kashyap Chitta
Tai-Yin Chiu
Hsu-kuang Chiu
Wei-Chen Chiu
Sungmin Cho
Donghyeon Cho
Hyeon Cho
Yooshin Cho
Gyusang Cho
Jang Hyun Cho
Seungju Cho
Nam Ik Cho
Sunghyun Cho
Hanbyel Cho
Jaesung Choe
Jooyoung Choi
Chiho Choi
Changwoon Choi
Jongwon Choi
Myungsub Choi
Dooseop Choi
Jonghyun Choi
Jinwoo Choi
Jun Won Choi
Min-Kook Choi
Hongsuk Choi
Janghoon Choi
Yoon-Ho Choi

Yukyung Choi
Jaegul Choo
Ayush Chopra
Siddharth Choudhary
Subhabrata Choudhury
Vasileios Choutas
Ka-Ho Chow
Pinaki Nath Chowdhury
Sammy Christen
Anders Christensen
Grigorios Chrysos
Hang Chu
Wen-Hsuan Chu
Peng Chu
Qi Chu
Ruihang Chu
Wei-Ta Chu
Yung-Yu Chuang
Sanghyuk Chun
Se Young Chun
Antonio Cinà
Ramazan Gokberk Cinbis
Javier Civera
Albert Clapés
Ronald Clark
Brian S. Clipp
Felipe Codevilla
Daniel Coelho de Castro
Niv Cohen
Forrester Cole
Maxwell D. Collins
Robert T. Collins
Marc Comino Trinidad
Runmin Cong
Wenyan Cong
Maxime Cordy
Marcella Cornia
Enric Corona
Huseyin Coskun
Luca Cosmo
Dragos Costea
Davide Cozzolino
Arun C. S. Kumar
Aiyu Cui
Qiongjie Cui

Quan Cui
Shuhao Cui
Yiming Cui
Ying Cui
Zijun Cui
Jiali Cui
Jiequan Cui
Yawen Cui
Zhen Cui
Zhaopeng Cui
Jack Culpepper
Xiaodong Cun
Ross Cutler
Adam Czajka
Ali Dabouei
Konstantinos M. Dafnis
Manuel Dahnert
Tao Dai
Yuchao Dai
Bo Dai
Mengyu Dai
Hang Dai
Haixing Dai
Peng Dai
Pingyang Dai
Qi Dai
Qiyu Dai
Yutong Dai
Naser Damer
Zhiyuan Dang
Mohamed Daoudi
Ayan Das
Abir Das
Debasmit Das
Deepayan Das
Partha Das
Sagnik Das
Soumi Das
Srijan Das
Swagatam Das
Avijit Dasgupta
Jim Davis
Adrian K. Davison
Homa Davoudi
Laura Daza

Matthias De Lange
Shalini De Mello
Marco De Nadai
Christophe De
    Vleeschouwer
Alp Dener
Boyang Deng
Congyue Deng
Bailin Deng
Yong Deng
Ye Deng
Zhuo Deng
Zhijie Deng
Xiaoming Deng
Jiankang Deng
Jinhong Deng
Jingjing Deng
Liang-Jian Deng
Siqi Deng
Xiang Deng
Xueqing Deng
Zhongying Deng
Karan Desai
Jean-Emmanuel Deschaud
Aniket Anand Deshmukh
Neel Dey
Helisa Dhamo
Prithviraj Dhar
Amaya Dharmasiri
Yan Di
Xing Di
Ousmane A. Dia
Haiwen Diao
Xiaolei Diao
Gonçalo José Dias Pais
Abdallah Dib
Anastasios Dimou
Changxing Ding
Henghui Ding
Guodong Ding
Yaqing Ding
Shuangrui Ding
Yuhang Ding
Yikang Ding
Shouhong Ding

Haisong Ding
Hui Ding
Jiahao Ding
Jian Ding
Jian-Jiun Ding
Shuxiao Ding
Tianyu Ding
Wenhao Ding
Yuqi Ding
Yi Ding
Yuzhen Ding
Zhengming Ding
Tan Minh Dinh
Vu Dinh
Christos Diou
Mandar Dixit
Bao Gia Doan
Khoa D. Doan
Dzung Anh Doan
Debi Prosad Dogra
Nehal Doiphode
Chengdong Dong
Bowen Dong
Zhenxing Dong
Hang Dong
Xiaoyi Dong
Haoye Dong
Jiangxin Dong
Shichao Dong
Xuan Dong
Zhen Dong
Shuting Dong
Jing Dong
Li Dong
Ming Dong
Nanqing Dong
Qiulei Dong
Runpei Dong
Siyan Dong
Tian Dong
Wei Dong
Xiaomeng Dong
Xin Dong
Xingbo Dong
Yuan Dong

Samuel Dooley
Gianfranco Doretto
Michael Dorkenwald
Keval Doshi
Zhaopeng Dou
Xiaotian Dou
Hazel Doughty
Ahmad Droby
Iddo Drori
Jie Du
Yong Du
Dawei Du
Dong Du
Ruoyi Du
Yuntao Du
Xuefeng Du
Yilun Du
Yuming Du
Radhika Dua
Haodong Duan
Jiafei Duan
Kaiwen Duan
Peiqi Duan
Ye Duan
Haoran Duan
Jiali Duan
Amanda Duarte
Abhimanyu Dubey
Shiv Ram Dubey
Florian Dubost
Lukasz Dudziak
Shivam Duggal
Justin M. Dulay
Matteo Dunnhofer
Chi Nhan Duong
Thibaut Durand
Mihai Dusmanu
Ujjal Kr Dutta
Debidatta Dwibedi
Isht Dwivedi
Sai Kumar Dwivedi
Takeharu Eda
Mark Edmonds
Alexei A. Efros
Thibaud Ehret

Max Ehrlich
Mahsa Ehsanpour
Iván Eichhardt
Farshad Einabadi
Marvin Eisenberger
Hazim Kemal Ekenel
Mohamed El Banani
Ismail Elezi
Moshe Eliasof
Alaa El-Nouby
Ian Endres
Francis Engelmann
Deniz Engin
Chanho Eom
Dave Epstein
Maria C. Escobar
Victor A. Escorcia
Carlos Esteves
Sungmin Eum
Bernard J. E. Evans
Ivan Evtimov
Fevziye Irem Eyiokur
Yaman
Matteo Fabbri
Sébastien Fabbro
Gabriele Facciolo
Masud Fahim
Bin Fan
Hehe Fan
Deng-Ping Fan
Aoxiang Fan
Chen-Chen Fan
Qi Fan
Zhaoxin Fan
Haoqi Fan
Heng Fan
Hongyi Fan
Linxi Fan
Baojie Fan
Jiayuan Fan
Lei Fan
Quanfu Fan
Yonghui Fan
Yingruo Fan
Zhiwen Fan

Zicong Fan
Sean Fanello
Jiansheng Fang
Chaowei Fang
Yuming Fang
Jianwu Fang
Jin Fang
Qi Fang
Shancheng Fang
Tian Fang
Xianyong Fang
Gongfan Fang
Zhen Fang
Hui Fang
Jiemin Fang
Le Fang
Pengfei Fang
Xiaolin Fang
Yuxin Fang
Zhaoyuan Fang
Ammarah Farooq
Azade Farshad
Zhengcong Fei
Michael Felsberg
Wei Feng
Chen Feng
Fan Feng
Andrew Feng
Xin Feng
Zheyun Feng
Ruicheng Feng
Mingtao Feng
Qianyu Feng
Shangbin Feng
Chun-Mei Feng
Zunlei Feng
Zhiyong Feng
Martin Fergie
Mustansar Fiaz
Marco Fiorucci
Michael Firman
Hamed Firooz
Volker Fischer
Corneliu O. Florea
Georgios Floros

Wolfgang Foerstner
Gianni Franchi
Jean-Sebastien Franco
Simone Frintrop
Anna Fruehstueck
Changhong Fu
Chaoyou Fu
Cheng-Yang Fu
Chi-Wing Fu
Deqing Fu
Huan Fu
Jun Fu
Kexue Fu
Ying Fu
Jianlong Fu
Jingjing Fu
Qichen Fu
Tsu-Jui Fu
Xueyang Fu
Yang Fu
Yanwei Fu
Yonggan Fu
Wolfgang Fuhl
Yasuhisa Fujii
Kent Fujiwara
Marco Fumero
Takuya Funatomi
Isabel Funke
Dario Fuoli
Antonino Furnari
Matheus A. Gadelha
Akshay Gadi Patil
Adrian Galdran
Guillermo Gallego
Silvano Galliani
Orazio Gallo
Leonardo Galteri
Matteo Gamba
Yiming Gan
Sujoy Ganguly
Harald Ganster
Boyan Gao
Changxin Gao
Daiheng Gao
Difei Gao

Chen Gao
Fei Gao
Lin Gao
Wei Gao
Yiming Gao
Junyu Gao
Guangyu Ryan Gao
Haichang Gao
Hongchang Gao
Jialin Gao
Jin Gao
Jun Gao
Katelyn Gao
Mingchen Gao
Mingfei Gao
Pan Gao
Shangqian Gao
Shanghua Gao
Xitong Gao
Yunhe Gao
Zhanning Gao
Elena Garces
Nuno Cruz Garcia
Noa Garcia
Guillermo
    Garcia-Hernando
Isha Garg
Rahul Garg
Sourav Garg
Quentin Garrido
Stefano Gasperini
Kent Gauen
Chandan Gautam
Shivam Gautam
Paul Gay
Chunjiang Ge
Shiming Ge
Wenhang Ge
Yanhao Ge
Zheng Ge
Songwei Ge
Weifeng Ge
Yixiao Ge
Yuying Ge
Shijie Geng

Zhengyang Geng
Kyle A. Genova
Georgios Georgakis
Markos Georgopoulos
Marcel Geppert
Shabnam Ghadar
Mina Ghadimi Atigh
Deepti Ghadiyaram
Maani Ghaffari Jadidi
Sedigh Ghamari
Zahra Gharaee
Michaël Gharbi
Golnaz Ghiasi
Reza Ghoddoosian
Soumya Suvra Ghosal
Adhiraj Ghosh
Arthita Ghosh
Pallabi Ghosh
Soumyadeep Ghosh
Andrew Gilbert
Igor Gilitschenski
Jhony H. Giraldo
Andreu Girbau Xalabarder
Rohit Girdhar
Sharath Girish
Xavier Giro-i-Nieto
Raja Giryes
Thomas Gittings
Nikolaos Gkanatsios
Ioannis Gkioulekas
Abhiram
  Gnanasambandam
Aurele T. Gnanha
Clement L. J. C. Godard
Arushi Goel
Vidit Goel
Shubham Goel
Zan Gojcic
Aaron K. Gokaslan
Tejas Gokhale
S. Alireza Golestaneh
Thiago L. Gomes
Nuno Goncalves
Boqing Gong
Chen Gong

Yuanhao Gong
Guoqiang Gong
Jingyu Gong
Rui Gong
Yu Gong
Mingming Gong
Neil Zhenqiang Gong
Xun Gong
Yunye Gong
Yihong Gong
Cristina I. González
Nithin Gopalakrishnan
  Nair
Gaurav Goswami
Jianping Gou
Shreyank N. Gowda
Ankit Goyal
Helmut Grabner
Patrick L. Grady
Ben Graham
Eric Granger
Douglas R. Gray
Matej Grcić
David Griffiths
Jinjin Gu
Yun Gu
Shuyang Gu
Jianyang Gu
Fuqiang Gu
Jiatao Gu
Jindong Gu
Jiaqi Gu
Jinwei Gu
Jiaxin Gu
Geonmo Gu
Xiao Gu
Xinqian Gu
Xiuye Gu
Yuming Gu
Zhangxuan Gu
Dayan Guan
Junfeng Guan
Qingji Guan
Tianrui Guan
Shanyan Guan

Denis A. Gudovskiy
Ricardo Guerrero
Pierre-Louis Guhur
Jie Gui
Liangyan Gui
Liangke Gui
Benoit Guillard
Erhan Gundogdu
Manuel Günther
Jingcai Guo
Yuanfang Guo
Junfeng Guo
Chenqi Guo
Dan Guo
Hongji Guo
Jia Guo
Jie Guo
Minghao Guo
Shi Guo
Yanhui Guo
Yangyang Guo
Yuan-Chen Guo
Yilu Guo
Yiluan Guo
Yong Guo
Guangyu Guo
Haiyun Guo
Jinyang Guo
Jianyuan Guo
Pengsheng Guo
Pengfei Guo
Shuxuan Guo
Song Guo
Tianyu Guo
Qing Guo
Qiushan Guo
Wen Guo
Xiefan Guo
Xiaohu Guo
Xiaoqing Guo
Yufei Guo
Yuhui Guo
Yuliang Guo
Yunhui Guo
Yanwen Guo

Akshita Gupta

Ankush Gupta

Kamal Gupta

Kartik Gupta

Ritwik Gupta

Rohit Gupta

Siddharth Gururani

Fredrik K. Gustafsson

Abner Guzman Rivera

Vladimir Guzov

Matthew A. Gwilliam

Jung-Woo Ha

Marc Habermann

Isma Hadji

Christian Haene

Martin Hahner

Levente Hajder

Alexandros Haliassos

Emanuela Haller

Bumsub Ham

Abdullah J. Hamdi

Shreyas Hampali

Dongyoon Han

Chunrui Han

Dong-Jun Han

Dong-Sig Han

Guangxing Han

Zhizhong Han

Ruize Han

Jiaming Han

Jin Han

Ligong Han

Xian-Hua Han

Xiaoguang Han

Yizeng Han

Zhi Han

Zhenjun Han

Zhongyi Han

Jungong Han

Junlin Han

Kai Han

Kun Han

Sungwon Han

Songfang Han

Wei Han

Xiao Han

Xintong Han

Xinzhe Han

Yahong Han

Yan Han

Zongbo Han

Nicolai Hani

Rana Hanocka

Niklas Hanselmann

Nicklas A. Hansen

Hong Hanyu

Fusheng Hao

Yanbin Hao

Shijie Hao

Udith Haputhanthri

Mehrtash Harandi

Josh Harguess

Adam Harley

David M. Hart

Atsushi Hashimoto

Ali Hassani

Mohammed Hassanin

Yana Hasson

Joakim Bruslund Haurum

Bo He

Kun He

Chen He

Xin He

Fazhi He

Gaoqi He

Hao He

Haoyu He

Jiangpeng He

Hongliang He

Qian He

Xiangteng He

Xuming He

Yannan He

Yuhang He

Yang He

Xiangyu He

Nanjun He

Pan He

Sen He

Shengfeng He

Songtao He

Tao He

Tong He

Wei He

Xuehai He

Xiaoxiao He

Ying He

Yisheng He

Ziwen Hc

Peter Hedman

Felix Heide

Yacov Hel-Or

Paul Henderson

Philipp Henzler

Byeongho Heo

Jae-Pil Heo

Miran Heo

Sachini A. Herath

Stephane Herbin

Pedro Hermosilla Casajus

Monica Hernandez

Charles Herrmann

Roei Herzig

Mauricio Hess-Flores

Carlos Hinojosa

Tobias Hinz

Tsubasa Hirakawa

Chih-Hui Ho

Lam Si Tung Ho

Jennifer Hobbs

Derek Hoiem

Yannick Hold-Geoffroy

Aleksander Holynski

Cheeun Hong

Fa-Ting Hong

Hanbin Hong

Guan Zhe Hong

Danfeng Hong

Lanqing Hong

Xiaopeng Hong

Xin Hong

Jie Hong

Seungbum Hong

Cheng-Yao Hong

Seunghoon Hong

Yi Hong
Yuan Hong
Yuchen Hong
Anthony Hoogs
Maxwell C. Horton
Kazuhiro Hotta
Qibin Hou
Tingbo Hou
Junhui Hou
Ji Hou
Qiqi Hou
Rui Hou
Ruibing Hou
Zhi Hou
Henry Howard-Jenkins
Lukas Hoyer
Wei-Lin Hsiao
Chiou-Ting Hsu
Anthony Hu
Brian Hu
Yusong Hu
Hexiang Hu
Haoji Hu
Di Hu
Hengtong Hu
Haigen Hu
Lianyu Hu
Hanzhe Hu
Jie Hu
Junlin Hu
Shizhe Hu
Jian Hu
Zhiming Hu
Juhua Hu
Peng Hu
Ping Hu
Ronghang Hu
MengShun Hu
Tao Hu
Vincent Tao Hu
Xiaoling Hu
Xinting Hu
Xiaolin Hu
Xuefeng Hu
Xiaowei Hu

Yang Hu
Yueyu Hu
Zeyu Hu
Zhongyun Hu
Binh-Son Hua
Guoliang Hua
Yi Hua
Linzhi Huang
Qiusheng Huang
Bo Huang
Chen Huang
Hsin-Ping Huang
Ye Huang
Shuangping Huang
Zeng Huang
Buzhen Huang
Cong Huang
Heng Huang
Hao Huang
Qidong Huang
Huaibo Huang
Chaoqin Huang
Feihu Huang
Jiahui Huang
Jingjia Huang
Kun Huang
Lei Huang
Sheng Huang
Shuaiyi Huang
Siyu Huang
Xiaoshui Huang
Xiaoyang Huang
Yan Huang
Yihao Huang
Ying Huang
Ziling Huang
Xiaoke Huang
Yifei Huang
Haiyang Huang
Zhewei Huang
Jin Huang
Haibin Huang
Jiaxing Huang
Junjie Huang
Keli Huang

Lang Huang
Lin Huang
Luojie Huang
Mingzhen Huang
Shijia Huang
Shengyu Huang
Siyuan Huang
He Huang
Xiuyu Huang
Lianghua Huang
Yue Huang
Yaping Huang
Yuge Huang
Zehao Huang
Zeyi Huang
Zhiqi Huang
Zhongzhan Huang
Zilong Huang
Ziyuan Huang
Tianrui Hui
Zhuo Hui
Le Hui
Jing Huo
Junhwa Hur
Shehzeen S. Hussain
Chuong Minh Huynh
Seunghyun Hwang
Jaehui Hwang
Jyh-Jing Hwang
Sukjun Hwang
Soonmin Hwang
Wonjun Hwang
Rakib Hyder
Sangeek Hyun
Sarah Ibrahimi
Tomoki Ichikawa
Yerlan Idelbayev
A. S. M. Iftekhar
Masaaki Iiyama
Satoshi Ikehata
Sunghoon Im
Atul N. Ingle
Eldar Insafutdinov
Yani A. Ioannou
Radu Tudor Ionescu

Umar Iqbal
Go Irie
Muhammad Zubair Irshad
Ahmet Iscen
Berivan Isik
Ashraful Islam
Md Amirul Islam
Syed Islam
Mariko Isogawa
Vamsi Krishna K. Ithapu
Boris Ivanovic
Darshan Iyer
Sarah Jabbour
Ayush Jain
Nishant Jain
Samyak Jain
Vidit Jain
Vineet Jain
Priyank Jaini
Tomas Jakab
Mohammad A. A. K.
  Jalwana
Muhammad Abdullah
  Jamal
Hadi Jamali-Rad
Stuart James
Varun Jampani
Young Kyun Jang
YeongJun Jang
Yunseok Jang
Ronnachai Jaroensri
Bhavan Jasani
Krishna Murthy
  Jatavallabhula
Mojan Javaheripi
Syed A. Javed
Guillaume Jeanneret
Pranav Jeevan
Herve Jegou
Rohit Jena
Tomas Jenicek
Porter Jenkins
Simon Jenni
Hae-Gon Jeon
Sangryul Jeon

Boseung Jeong
Yoonwoo Jeong
Seong-Gyun Jeong
Jisoo Jeong
Allan D. Jepson
Ankit Jha
Sumit K. Jha
I-Hong Jhuo
Ge-Peng Ji
Chaonan Ji
Deyi Ji
Jingwei Ji
Wei Ji
Zhong Ji
Jiayi Ji
Pengliang Ji
Hui Ji
Mingi Ji
Xiaopeng Ji
Yuzhu Ji
Baoxiong Jia
Songhao Jia
Dan Jia
Shan Jia
Xiaojun Jia
Xiuyi Jia
Xu Jia
Menglin Jia
Wenqi Jia
Boyuan Jiang
Wenhao Jiang
Huaizu Jiang
Hanwen Jiang
Haiyong Jiang
Hao Jiang
Huajie Jiang
Huiqin Jiang
Haojun Jiang
Haobo Jiang
Junjun Jiang
Xingyu Jiang
Yangbangyan Jiang
Yu Jiang
Jianmin Jiang
Jiaxi Jiang

Jing Jiang
Kui Jiang
Li Jiang
Liming Jiang
Chiyu Jiang
Meirui Jiang
Chen Jiang
Peng Jiang
Tai-Xiang Jiang
Wen Jiang
Xinyang Jiang
Yifan Jiang
Yuming Jiang
Yingying Jiang
Zeren Jiang
ZhengKai Jiang
Zhenyu Jiang
Shuming Jiao
Jianbo Jiao
Licheng Jiao
Dongkwon Jin
Yeying Jin
Cheng Jin
Linyi Jin
Qing Jin
Taisong Jin
Xiao Jin
Xin Jin
Sheng Jin
Kyong Hwan Jin
Ruibing Jin
SouYoung Jin
Yueming Jin
Chenchen Jing
Longlong Jing
Taotao Jing
Yongcheng Jing
Younghyun Jo
Joakim Johnander
Jeff Johnson
Michael J. Jones
R. Kenny Jones
Rico Jonschkowski
Ameya Joshi
Sunghun Joung

Felix Juefei-Xu
Claudio R. Jung
Steffen Jung
Hari Chandana K.
Rahul Vigneswaran K.
Prajwal K. R.
Abhishek Kadian
Jhony Kaesemodel Pontes
Kumara Kahatapitiya
Anmol Kalia
Sinan Kalkan
Tarun Kalluri
Jaewon Kam
Sandesh Kamath
Meina Kan
Menelaos Kanakis
Takuhiro Kaneko
Di Kang
Guoliang Kang
Hao Kang
Jaeyeon Kang
Kyoungkook Kang
Li-Wei Kang
MinGuk Kang
Suk-Ju Kang
Zhao Kang
Yash Mukund Kant
Yueying Kao
Aupendu Kar
Konstantinos Karantzalos
Sezer Karaoglu
Navid Kardan
Sanjay Kariyappa
Leonid Karlinsky
Animesh Karnewar
Shyamgopal Karthik
Hirak J. Kashyap
Marc A. Kastner
Hirokatsu Kataoka
Angelos Katharopoulos
Hiroharu Kato
Kai Katsumata
Manuel Kaufmann
Chaitanya Kaul
Prakhar Kaushik

Yuki Kawana
Lei Ke
Lipeng Ke
Tsung-Wei Ke
Wei Ke
Petr Kellnhofer
Aniruddha Kembhavi
John Kender
Corentin Kervadec
Leonid Keselman
Daniel Keysers
Nima Khademi Kalantari
Taras Khakhulin
Samir Khaki
Muhammad Haris Khan
Qadeer Khan
Salman Khan
Subash Khanal
Vaishnavi M. Khindkar
Rawal Khirodkar
Saeed Khorram
Pirazh Khorramshahi
Kourosh Khoshelham
Ansh Khurana
Benjamin Kiefer
Jae Myung Kim
Junho Kim
Boah Kim
Hyeonseong Kim
Dong-Jin Kim
Dongwan Kim
Donghyun Kim
Doyeon Kim
Yonghyun Kim
Hyung-Il Kim
Hyunwoo Kim
Hyeongwoo Kim
Hyo Jin Kim
Hyunwoo J. Kim
Taehoon Kim
Jaeha Kim
Jiwon Kim
Jung Uk Kim
Kangyeol Kim
Eunji Kim

Daeha Kim
Dongwon Kim
Kunhee Kim
Kyungmin Kim
Junsik Kim
Min H. Kim
Namil Kim
Kookhoi Kim
Sanghyun Kim
Seongyeop Kim
Seungryong Kim
Saehoon Kim
Euyoung Kim
Guisik Kim
Sungyeon Kim
Sunnie S. Y. Kim
Taehun Kim
Tae Oh Kim
Won Hwa Kim
Seungwook Kim
YoungBin Kim
Youngeun Kim
Akisato Kimura
Furkan Osman Kınlı
Zsolt Kira
Hedvig Kjellström
Florian Kleber
Jan P. Klopp
Florian Kluger
Laurent Kneip
Byungsoo Ko
Muhammed Kocabas
A. Sophia Koepke
Kevin Koeser
Nick Kolkin
Nikos Kolotouros
Wai-Kin Adams Kong
Deying Kong
Caihua Kong
Youyong Kong
Shuyu Kong
Shu Kong
Tao Kong
Yajing Kong
Yu Kong

Zishang Kong
Theodora Kontogianni
Anton S. Konushin
Julian F. P. Kooij
Bruno Korbar
Giorgos Kordopatis-Zilos
Jari Korhonen
Adam Kortylewski
Denis Korzhenkov
Divya Kothandaraman
Suraj Kothawade
Iuliia Kotseruba
Satwik Kottur
Shashank Kotyan
Alexandros Kouris
Petros Koutras
Anna Kreshuk
Ranjay Krishna
Dilip Krishnan
Andrey Kuehlkamp
Hilde Kuehne
Jason Kuen
David Kügler
Arjan Kuijper
Anna Kukleva
Sumith Kulal
Viveka Kulharia
Akshay R. Kulkarni
Nilesh Kulkarni
Dominik Kulon
Abhinav Kumar
Akash Kumar
Suryansh Kumar
B. V. K. Vijaya Kumar
Pulkit Kumar
Ratnesh Kumar
Sateesh Kumar
Satish Kumar
Vijay Kumar B. G.
Nupur Kumari
Sudhakar Kumawat
Jogendra Nath Kundu
Hsien-Kai Kuo
Meng-Yu Jennifer Kuo
Vinod Kumar Kurmi

Yusuke Kurose
Keerthy Kusumam
Alina Kuznetsova
Henry Kvinge
Ho Man Kwan
Hyeokjun Kweon
Heeseung Kwon
Gihyun Kwon
Myung-Joon Kwon
Taesung Kwon
YoungJoong Kwon
Christos Kyrkou
Jorma Laaksonen
Yann Labbe
Zorah Laehner
Florent Lafarge
Hamid Laga
Manuel Lagunas
Shenqi Lai
Jian-Huang Lai
Zihang Lai
Mohamed I. Lakhal
Mohit Lamba
Meng Lan
Loic Landrieu
Zhiqiang Lang
Natalie Lang
Dong Lao
Yizhen Lao
Yingjie Lao
Issam Hadj Laradji
Gustav Larsson
Viktor Larsson
Zakaria Laskar
Stéphane Lathuilière
Chun Pong Lau
Rynson W. H. Lau
Hei Law
Justin Lazarow
Verica Lazova
Eric-Tuan Le
Hieu Le
Trung-Nghia Le
Mathias Lechner
Byeong-Uk Lee

Chen-Yu Lee
Che-Rung Lee
Chul Lee
Hong Joo Lee
Dongsoo Lee
Jiyoung Lee
Eugene Eu Tzuan Lee
Daeun Lee
Saehyung Lee
Jewook Lee
Hyungtae Lee
Hyunmin Lee
Jungbeom Lee
Joon-Young Lee
Jong-Seok Lee
Joonseok Lee
Junha Lee
Kibok Lee
Byung-Kwan Lee
Jangwon Lee
Jinho Lee
Jongmin Lee
Seunghyun Lee
Sohyun Lee
Minsik Lee
Dogyoon Lee
Seungmin Lee
Min Jun Lee
Sangho Lee
Sangmin Lee
Seungeun Lee
Seon-Ho Lee
Sungmin Lee
Sungho Lee
Sangyoun Lee
Vincent C. S. S. Lee
Jaeseong Lee
Yong Jae Lee
Chenyang Lei
Chenyi Lei
Jiahui Lei
Xinyu Lei
Yinjie Lei
Jiaxu Leng
Luziwei Leng

Jan E. Lenssen
Vincent Lepetit
Thomas Leung
María Leyva-Vallina
Xin Li
Yikang Li
Baoxin Li
Bin Li
Bing Li
Bowen Li
Changlin Li
Chao Li
Chongyi Li
Guanyue Li
Shuai Li
Jin Li
Dingquan Li
Dongxu Li
Yiting Li
Gang Li
Dian Li
Guohao Li
Haoang Li
Haoliang Li
Haoran Li
Hengduo Li
Huafeng Li
Xiaoming Li
Hanao Li
Hongwei Li
Ziqiang Li
Jisheng Li
Jiacheng Li
Jia Li
Jiachen Li
Jiahao Li
Jianwei Li
Jiazhi Li
Jie Li
Jing Li
Jingjing Li
Jingtao Li
Jun Li
Junxuan Li
Kai Li

Kailin Li
Kenneth Li
Kun Li
Kunpeng Li
Aoxue Li
Chenglong Li
Chenglin Li
Changsheng Li
Zhichao Li
Qiang Li
Yanyu Li
Zuoyue Li
Xiang Li
Xuelong Li
Fangda Li
Ailin Li
Liang Li
Chun-Guang Li
Daiqing Li
Dong Li
Guanbin Li
Guorong Li
Haifeng Li
Jianan Li
Jianing Li
Jiaxin Li
Ke Li
Lei Li
Lincheng Li
Liulei Li
Lujun Li
Linjie Li
Lin Li
Pengyu Li
Ping Li
Qiufu Li
Qingyong Li
Rui Li
Siyuan Li
Wei Li
Wenbin Li
Xiangyang Li
Xinyu Li
Xiujun Li
Xiu Li

Xu Li
Ya-Li Li
Yao Li
Yongjie Li
Yijun Li
Yiming Li
Yuezun Li
Yu Li
Yunheng Li
Yuqi Li
Zhe Li
Zeming Li
Zhen Li
Zhengqin Li
Zhimin Li
Jiefeng Li
Jinpeng Li
Chengze Li
Jianwu Li
Lerenhan Li
Shan Li
Suichan Li
Xiangtai Li
Yanjie Li
Yandong Li
Zhuoling Li
Zhenqiang Li
Manyi Li
Maosen Li
Ji Li
Minjun Li
Mingrui Li
Mengtian Li
Junyi Li
Nianyi Li
Bo Li
Xiao Li
Peihua Li
Peike Li
Peizhao Li
Peiliang Li
Qi Li
Ren Li
Runze Li
Shile Li

Sheng Li

Shigang Li

Shiyu Li

Shuang Li

Shasha Li

Shichao Li

Tianye Li

Yuexiang Li

Wei-Hong Li

Wanhua Li

Weihao Li

Weiming Li

Weixin Li

Wenbo Li

Wenshuo Li

Weijian Li

Yunan Li

Xirong Li

Xianhang Li

Xiaoyu Li

Xueqian Li

Xuanlin Li

Xianzhi Li

Yunqiang Li

Yanjing Li

Yansheng Li

Yawei Li

Yi Li

Yong Li

Yong-Lu Li

Yuhang Li

Yu-Jhe Li

Yuxi Li

Yunsheng Li

Yanwei Li

Zechao Li

Zejian Li

Zeju Li

Zekun Li

Zhaowen Li

Zheng Li

Zhenyu Li

Zhiheng Li

Zhi Li

Zhong Li

Zhuowei Li

Zhuowan Li

Zhuohang Li

Zizhang Li

Chen Li

Yuan-Fang Li

Dongze Lian

Xiaochen Lian

Zhouhui Lian

Long Lian

Qing Lian

Jin Lianbao

Jinxiu S. Liang

Dingkang Liang

Jiahao Liang

Jianming Liang

Jingyun Liang

Kevin J. Liang

Kaizhao Liang

Chen Liang

Jie Liang

Senwei Liang

Ding Liang

Jiajun Liang

Jian Liang

Kongming Liang

Siyuan Liang

Yuanzhi Liang

Zhengfa Liang

Mingfu Liang

Xiaodan Liang

Xuefeng Liang

Yuxuan Liang

Kang Liao

Liang Liao

Hong-Yuan Mark Liao

Wentong Liao

Haofu Liao

Yue Liao

Minghui Liao

Shengcai Liao

Ting-Hsuan Liao

Xin Liao

Yinghong Liao

Teck Yian Lim

Che-Tsung Lin

Chung-Ching Lin

Chen-Hsuan Lin

Cheng Lin

Chuming Lin

Chunyu Lin

Dahua Lin

Wei Lin

Zheng Lin

Huaijia Lin

Jason Lin

Jierui Lin

Jiaying Lin

Jie Lin

Kai-En Lin

Kevin Lin

Guangfeng Lin

Jiehong Lin

Feng Lin

Hang Lin

Kwan-Yee Lin

Ke Lin

Luojun Lin

Qinghong Lin

Xiangbo Lin

Yi Lin

Zudi Lin

Shijie Lin

Yiqun Lin

Tzu-Heng Lin

Ming Lin

Shaohui Lin

SongNan Lin

Ji Lin

Tsung-Yu Lin

Xudong Lin

Yancong Lin

Yen-Chen Lin

Yiming Lin

Yuewei Lin

Zhiqiu Lin

Zinan Lin

Zhe Lin

David B. Lindell

Zhixin Ling

Zhan Ling	Jun Liu	Zhenguang Liu
Alexander Liniger	Juncheng Liu	Lin Liu
Venice Erin B. Liong	Jiawei Liu	Lihao Liu
Joey Litalien	Hongyu Liu	Pengju Liu
Or Litany	Chuanbin Liu	Xinhai Liu
Roee Litman	Haotian Liu	Yunfei Liu
Ron Litman	Lingqiao Liu	Meng Liu
Jim Little	Chang Liu	Minghua Liu
Dor Litvak	Han Liu	Mingyuan Liu
Shaoteng Liu	Liu Liu	Miao Liu
Shuaicheng Liu	Min Liu	Peirong Liu
Andrew Liu	Yingqi Liu	Ping Liu
Xian Liu	Aishan Liu	Qingjie Liu
Shaohui Liu	Bingyu Liu	Ruoshi Liu
Bei Liu	Benlin Liu	Risheng Liu
Bo Liu	Boxiao Liu	Songtao Liu
Yong Liu	Chenchen Liu	Xing Liu
Ming Liu	Chuanjian Liu	Shikun Liu
Yanbin Liu	Daqing Liu	Shuming Liu
Chenxi Liu	Huan Liu	Sheng Liu
Daqi Liu	Haozhe Liu	Songhua Liu
Di Liu	Jiaheng Liu	Tongliang Liu
Difan Liu	Wei Liu	Weibo Liu
Dong Liu	Jingzhou Liu	Weide Liu
Dongfang Liu	Jiyuan Liu	Weizhe Liu
Daizong Liu	Lingbo Liu	Wenxi Liu
Xiao Liu	Nian Liu	Weiyang Liu
Fangyi Liu	Peiye Liu	Xin Liu
Fengbei Liu	Qiankun Liu	Xiaobin Liu
Fenglin Liu	Shenglan Liu	Xudong Liu
Bin Liu	Shilong Liu	Xiaoyi Liu
Yuang Liu	Wen Liu	Xihui Liu
Ao Liu	Wenyu Liu	Xinchen Liu
Hong Liu	Weifeng Liu	Xingtong Liu
Hongfu Liu	Wu Liu	Xinpeng Liu
Huidong Liu	Xiaolong Liu	Xinyu Liu
Ziyi Liu	Yang Liu	Xianpeng Liu
Feng Liu	Yanwei Liu	Xu Liu
Hao Liu	Yingcheng Liu	Xingyu Liu
Jie Liu	Yongfei Liu	Yongtuo Liu
Jialun Liu	Yihao Liu	Yahui Liu
Jiang Liu	Yu Liu	Yangxin Liu
Jing Liu	Yunze Liu	Yaoyao Liu
Jingya Liu	Ze Liu	Yaojie Liu
Jiaming Liu	Zhenhua Liu	Yuliang Liu

Yongcheng Liu
Yuan Liu
Yufan Liu
Yu-Lun Liu
Yun Liu
Yunfan Liu
Yuanzhong Liu
Zhuoran Liu
Zhen Liu
Zheng Liu
Zhijian Liu
Zhisong Liu
Ziquan Liu
Ziyu Liu
Zhihua Liu
Zechun Liu
Zhaoyang Liu
Zhengzhe Liu
Stephan Liwicki
Shao-Yuan Lo
Sylvain Lobry
Suhas Lohit
Vishnu Suresh Lokhande
Vincenzo Lomonaco
Chengjiang Long
Guodong Long
Fuchen Long
Shangbang Long
Yang Long
Zijun Long
Vasco Lopes
Antonio M. Lopez
Roberto Javier
   Lopez-Sastre
Tobias Lorenz
Javier Lorenzo-Navarro
Yujing Lou
Qian Lou
Xiankai Lu
Changsheng Lu
Huimin Lu
Yongxi Lu
Hao Lu
Hong Lu
Jiasen Lu

Juwei Lu
Fan Lu
Guangming Lu
Jiwen Lu
Shun Lu
Tao Lu
Xiaonan Lu
Yang Lu
Yao Lu
Yongchun Lu
Zhiwu Lu
Cheng Lu
Liying Lu
Guo Lu
Xuequan Lu
Yanye Lu
Yantao Lu
Yuhang Lu
Fujun Luan
Jonathon Luiten
Jovita Lukasik
Alan Lukezic
Jonathan Samuel Lumentut
Mayank Lunayach
Ao Luo
Canjie Luo
Chong Luo
Xu Luo
Grace Luo
Jun Luo
Katie Z. Luo
Tao Luo
Cheng Luo
Fangzhou Luo
Gen Luo
Lei Luo
Sihui Luo
Weixin Luo
Yan Luo
Xiaoyan Luo
Yong Luo
Yadan Luo
Hao Luo
Ruotian Luo
Mi Luo

Tiange Luo
Wenjie Luo
Wenhan Luo
Xiao Luo
Zhiming Luo
Zhipeng Luo
Zhengyi Luo
Diogo C. Luvizon
Zhaoyang Lv
Gengyu Lyu
Lingjuan Lyu
Jun Lyu
Yuanyuan Lyu
Youwei Lyu
Yueming Lyu
Bingpeng Ma
Chao Ma
Chongyang Ma
Congbo Ma
Chih-Yao Ma
Fan Ma
Lin Ma
Haoyu Ma
Hengbo Ma
Jianqi Ma
Jiawei Ma
Jiayi Ma
Kede Ma
Kai Ma
Lingni Ma
Lei Ma
Xu Ma
Ning Ma
Benteng Ma
Cheng Ma
Andy J. Ma
Long Ma
Zhanyu Ma
Zhiheng Ma
Qianli Ma
Shiqiang Ma
Sizhuo Ma
Shiqing Ma
Xiaolong Ma
Xinzhu Ma

Gautam B. Machiraju
Spandan Madan
Mathew Magimai-Doss
Luca Magri
Behrooz Mahasseni
Upal Mahbub
Siddharth Mahendran
Paridhi Maheshwari
Rishabh Maheshwary
Mohammed Mahmoud
Shishira R. R. Maiya
Sylwia Majchrowska
Arjun Majumdar
Puspita Majumdar
Orchid Majumder
Sagnik Majumder
Ilya Makarov
Farkhod F.
    Makhmudkhujaev
Yasushi Makihara
Ankur Mali
Mateusz Malinowski
Utkarsh Mall
Srikanth Malla
Clement Mallet
Dimitrios Mallis
Yunze Man
Dipu Manandhar
Massimiliano Mancini
Murari Mandal
Raunak Manekar
Karttikeya Mangalam
Puneet Mangla
Fabian Manhardt
Sivabalan Manivasagam
Fahim Mannan
Chengzhi Mao
Hanzi Mao
Jiayuan Mao
Junhua Mao
Zhiyuan Mao
Jiageng Mao
Yunyao Mao
Zhendong Mao
Alberto Marchisio

Diego Marcos
Riccardo Marin
Aram Markosyan
Renaud Marlet
Ricardo Marques
Miquel Martí i Rabadán
Diego Martin Arroyo
Niki Martinel
Brais Martinez
Julieta Martinez
Marc Masana
Tomohiro Mashita
Timothée Masquelier
Minesh Mathew
Tetsu Matsukawa
Marwan Mattar
Bruce A. Maxwell
Christoph Mayer
Mantas Mazeika
Pratik Mazumder
Scott McCloskey
Steven McDonagh
Ishit Mehta
Jie Mei
Kangfu Mei
Jieru Mei
Xiaoguang Mei
Givi Meishvili
Luke Melas-Kyriazi
Iaroslav Melekhov
Andres Mendez-Vazquez
Heydi Mendez-Vazquez
Matias Mendieta
Ricardo A. Mendoza-León
Chenlin Meng
Depu Meng
Rang Meng
Zibo Meng
Qingjie Meng
Qier Meng
Yanda Meng
Zihang Meng
Thomas Mensink
Fabian Mentzer
Christopher Metzler

Gregory P. Meyer
Vasileios Mezaris
Liang Mi
Lu Mi
Bo Miao
Changtao Miao
Zichen Miao
Qiguang Miao
Xin Miao
Zhongqi Miao
Frank Michel
Simone Milani
Ben Mildenhall
Roy V. Miles
Juhong Min
Kyle Min
Hyun-Seok Min
Weiqing Min
Yuecong Min
Zhixiang Min
Qi Ming
David Minnen
Aymen Mir
Deepak Mishra
Anand Mishra
Shlok K. Mishra
Niluthpol Mithun
Gaurav Mittal
Trisha Mittal
Daisuke Miyazaki
Kaichun Mo
Hong Mo
Zhipeng Mo
Davide Modolo
Abduallah A. Mohamed
Mohamed Afham
Mohamed Aflal
Ron Mokady
Pavlo Molchanov
Davide Moltisanti
Liliane Momeni
Gianluca Monaci
Pascal Monasse
Ajoy Mondal
Tom Monnier

Aron Monszpart
Gyeongsik Moon
Suhong Moon
Taesup Moon
Sean Moran
Daniel Moreira
Pietro Morerio
Alexandre Morgand
Lia Morra
Ali Mosleh
Inbar Mosseri
Sayed Mohammad
  Mostafavi Isfahani
Saman Motamed
Ramy A. Mounir
Fangzhou Mu
Jiteng Mu
Norman Mu
Yasuhiro Mukaigawa
Ryan Mukherjee
Tanmoy Mukherjee
Yusuke Mukuta
Ravi Teja Mullapudi
Lea Müller
Matthias Müller
Martin Mundt
Nils Murrugarra-Llerena
Damien Muselet
Armin Mustafa
Muhammad Ferjad Naeem
Sauradip Nag
Hajime Nagahara
Pravin Nagar
Rajendra Nagar
Naveen Shankar Nagaraja
Varun Nagaraja
Tushar Nagarajan
Seungjun Nah
Gaku Nakano
Yuta Nakashima
Giljoo Nam
Seonghyeon Nam
Liangliang Nan
Yuesong Nan
Yeshwanth Napolean

Dinesh Reddy
  Narapureddy
Medhini Narasimhan
Supreeth
  Narasimhaswamy
Sriram Narayanan
Erickson R. Nascimento
Varun Nasery
K. L. Navaneet
Pablo Navarrete Michelini
Shant Navasardyan
Shah Nawaz
Nihal Nayak
Farhood Negin
Lukáš Neumann
Alejandro Newell
Evonne Ng
Kam Woh Ng
Tony Ng
Anh Nguyen
Tuan Anh Nguyen
Cuong Cao Nguyen
Ngoc Cuong Nguyen
Thanh Nguyen
Khoi Nguyen
Phi Le Nguyen
Phong Ha Nguyen
Tam Nguyen
Truong Nguyen
Anh Tuan Nguyen
Rang Nguyen
Thao Thi Phuong Nguyen
Van Nguyen Nguyen
Zhen-Liang Ni
Yao Ni
Shijie Nie
Xuecheng Nie
Yongwei Nie
Weizhi Nie
Ying Nie
Yinyu Nie
Kshitij N. Nikhal
Simon Niklaus
Xuefei Ning
Jifeng Ning

Yotam Nitzan
Di Niu
Shuaicheng Niu
Li Niu
Wei Niu
Yulei Niu
Zhenxing Niu
Albert No
Shohei Nobuhara
Nicoletta Noceti
Junhyug Noh
Sotiris Nousias
Slawomir Nowaczyk
Ewa M. Nowara
Valsamis Ntouskos
Gilberto Ochoa-Ruiz
Ferda Ofli
Jihyong Oh
Sangyun Oh
Youngtaek Oh
Hiroki Ohashi
Takahiro Okabe
Kemal Oksuz
Fumio Okura
Daniel Olmeda Reino
Matthew Olson
Carl Olsson
Roy Or-El
Alessandro Ortis
Guillermo Ortiz-Jimenez
Magnus Oskarsson
Ahmed A. A. Osman
Martin R. Oswald
Mayu Otani
Naima Otberdout
Cheng Ouyang
Jiahong Ouyang
Wanli Ouyang
Andrew Owens
Poojan B. Oza
Mete Ozay
A. Cengiz Oztireli
Gautam Pai
Tomas Pajdla
Umapada Pal

Simone Palazzo
Luca Palmieri
Bowen Pan
Hao Pan
Lili Pan
Tai-Yu Pan
Liang Pan
Chengwei Pan
Yingwei Pan
Xuran Pan
Jinshan Pan
Xinyu Pan
Liyuan Pan
Xingang Pan
Xingjia Pan
Zhihong Pan
Zizheng Pan
Priyadarshini Panda
Rameswar Panda
Rohit Pandey
Kaiyue Pang
Bo Pang
Guansong Pang
Jiangmiao Pang
Meng Pang
Tianyu Pang
Ziqi Pang
Omiros Pantazis
Andreas Panteli
Maja Pantic
Marina Paolanti
Joao P. Papa
Samuele Papa
Mike Papadakis
Dim P. Papadopoulos
George Papandreou
Constantin Pape
Toufiq Parag
Chethan Parameshwara
Shaifali Parashar
Alejandro Pardo
Rishubh Parihar
Sarah Parisot
JaeYoo Park
Gyeong-Moon Park

Hyojin Park
Hyoungseob Park
Jongchan Park
Jae Sung Park
Kiru Park
Chunghyun Park
Kwanyong Park
Sunghyun Park
Sungrae Park
Seongsik Park
Sanghyun Park
Sungjune Park
Taesung Park
Gaurav Parmar
Paritosh Parmar
Alvaro Parra
Despoina Paschalidou
Or Patashnik
Shivansh Patel
Pushpak Pati
Prashant W. Patil
Vaishakh Patil
Suvam Patra
Jay Patravali
Badri Narayana Patro
Angshuman Paul
Sudipta Paul
Rémi Pautrat
Nick E. Pears
Adithya Pediredla
Wenjie Pei
Shmuel Peleg
Latha Pemula
Bo Peng
Houwen Peng
Yue Peng
Liangzu Peng
Baoyun Peng
Jun Peng
Pai Peng
Sida Peng
Xi Peng
Yuxin Peng
Songyou Peng
Wei Peng

Weiqi Peng
Wen-Hsiao Peng
Pramuditha Perera
Juan C. Perez
Eduardo Pérez Pellitero
Juan-Manuel Perez-Rua
Federico Pernici
Marco Pesavento
Stavros Petridis
Ilya A. Petrov
Vladan Petrovic
Mathis Petrovich
Suzanne Petryk
Hieu Pham
Quang Pham
Khoi Pham
Tung Pham
Huy Phan
Stephen Phillips
Cheng Perng Phoo
David Picard
Marco Piccirilli
Georg Pichler
A. J. Piergiovanni
Vipin Pillai
Silvia L. Pintea
Giovanni Pintore
Robinson Piramuthu
Fiora Pirri
Theodoros Pissas
Fabio Pizzati
Benjamin Planche
Bryan Plummer
Matteo Poggi
Ashwini Pokle
Georgy E. Ponimatkin
Adrian Popescu
Stefan Popov
Nikola Popović
Ronald Poppe
Angelo Porrello
Michael Potter
Charalambos Poullis
Hadi Pouransari
Omid Poursaeed

Shraman Pramanick
Mantini Pranav
Dilip K. Prasad
Meghshyam Prasad
B. H. Pawan Prasad
Shitala Prasad
Prateek Prasanna
Ekta Prashnani
Derek S. Prijatelj
Luke Y. Prince
Véronique Prinet
Victor Adrian Prisacariu
James Pritts
Thomas Probst
Sergey Prokudin
Rita Pucci
Chi-Man Pun
Matthew Purri
Haozhi Qi
Lu Qi
Lei Qi
Xianbiao Qi
Yonggang Qi
Yuankai Qi
Siyuan Qi
Guocheng Qian
Hangwei Qian
Qi Qian
Deheng Qian
Shengsheng Qian
Wen Qian
Rui Qian
Yiming Qian
Shengju Qian
Shengyi Qian
Xuelin Qian
Zhenxing Qian
Nan Qiao
Xiaotian Qiao
Jing Qin
Can Qin
Siyang Qin
Hongwei Qin
Jie Qin
Minghai Qin

Yipeng Qin
Yongqiang Qin
Wenda Qin
Xuebin Qin
Yuzhe Qin
Yao Qin
Zhenyue Qin
Zhiwu Qing
Heqian Qiu
Jiayan Qiu
Jielin Qiu
Yue Qiu
Jiaxiong Qiu
Zhongxi Qiu
Shi Qiu
Zhaofan Qiu
Zhongnan Qu
Yanyun Qu
Kha Gia Quach
Yuhui Quan
Ruijie Quan
Mike Rabbat
Rahul Shekhar Rade
Filip Radenovic
Gorjan Radevski
Bogdan Raducanu
Francesco Ragusa
Shafin Rahman
Md Mahfuzur Rahman
    Siddiquee
Hossein Rahmani
Kiran Raja
Sivaramakrishnan
    Rajaraman
Jathushan Rajasegaran
Adnan Siraj Rakin
Michaël Ramamonjisoa
Chirag A. Raman
Shanmuganathan Raman
Vignesh Ramanathan
Vasili Ramanishka
Vikram V. Ramaswamy
Merey Ramazanova
Jason Rambach
Sai Saketh Rambhatla

Clément Rambour
Ashwin Ramesh Babu
Adín Ramírez Rivera
Arianna Rampini
Haoxi Ran
Aakanksha Rana
Aayush Jung Bahadur
    Rana
Kanchana N. Ranasinghe
Aneesh Rangnekar
Samrudhdhi B. Rangrej
Harsh Rangwani
Viresh Ranjan
Anyi Rao
Yongming Rao
Carolina Raposo
Michalis Raptis
Amir Rasouli
Vivek Rathod
Adepu Ravi Sankar
Avinash Ravichandran
Bharadwaj Ravichandran
Dripta S. Raychaudhuri
Adria Recasens
Simon Reiß
Davis Rempe
Daxuan Ren
Jiawei Ren
Jimmy Ren
Sucheng Ren
Dayong Ren
Zhile Ren
Dongwei Ren
Qibing Ren
Pengfei Ren
Zhenwen Ren
Xuqian Ren
Yixuan Ren
Zhongzheng Ren
Ambareesh Revanur
Hamed Rezazadegan
    Tavakoli
Rafael S. Rezende
Wonjong Rhee
Alexander Richard

Christian Richardt
Stephan R. Richter
Benjamin Riggan
Dominik Rivoir
Mamshad Nayeem Rizve
Joshua D. Robinson
Joseph Robinson
Chris Rockwell
Ranga Rodrigo
Andres C. Rodriguez
Carlos Rodriguez-Pardo
Marcus Rohrbach
Gemma Roig
Yu Rong
David A. Ross
Mohammad Rostami
Edward Rosten
Karsten Roth
Anirban Roy
Debaditya Roy
Shuvendu Roy
Ahana Roy Choudhury
Aruni Roy Chowdhury
Denys Rozumnyi
Shulan Ruan
Wenjie Ruan
Patrick Ruhkamp
Danila Rukhovich
Anian Ruoss
Chris Russell
Dan Ruta
Dawid Damian Rymarczyk
DongHun Ryu
Hyeonggon Ryu
Kwonyoung Ryu
Balasubramanian S.
Alexandre Sablayrolles
Mohammad Sabokrou
Arka Sadhu
Aniruddha Saha
Oindrila Saha
Pritish Sahu
Aneeshan Sain
Nirat Saini
Saurabh Saini

Takeshi Saitoh
Christos Sakaridis
Fumihiko Sakaue
Dimitrios Sakkos
Ken Sakurada
Parikshit V. Sakurikar
Rohit Saluja
Nermin Samet
Leo Sampaio Ferraz
    Ribeiro
Jorge Sanchez
Enrique Sanchez
Shengtian Sang
Anush Sankaran
Soubhik Sanyal
Nikolaos Sarafianos
Vishwanath Saragadam
István Sárándi
Saquib Sarfraz
Mert Bulent Sariyildiz
Anindya Sarkar
Pritam Sarkar
Paul-Edouard Sarlin
Hiroshi Sasaki
Takami Sato
Torsten Sattler
Ravi Kumar Satzoda
Axel Sauer
Stefano Savian
Artem Savkin
Manolis Savva
Gerald Schaefer
Simone Schaub-Meyer
Yoni Schirris
Samuel Schulter
Katja Schwarz
Jesse Scott
Sinisa Segvic
Constantin Marc Seibold
Lorenzo Seidenari
Matan Sela
Fadime Sener
Paul Hongsuck Seo
Kwanggyoon Seo
Hongje Seong

Dario Serez
Francesco Setti
Bryan Seybold
Mohamad Shahbazi
Shima Shahfar
Xinxin Shan
Caifeng Shan
Dandan Shan
Shawn Shan
Wei Shang
Jinghuan Shang
Jiaxiang Shang
Lei Shang
Sukrit Shankar
Ken Shao
Rui Shao
Jie Shao
Mingwen Shao
Aashish Sharma
Gaurav Sharma
Vivek Sharma
Abhishek Sharma
Yoli Shavit
Shashank Shekhar
Sumit Shekhar
Zhijie Shen
Fengyi Shen
Furao Shen
Jialie Shen
Jingjing Shen
Ziyi Shen
Linlin Shen
Guangyu Shen
Biluo Shen
Falong Shen
Jiajun Shen
Qiu Shen
Qiuhong Shen
Shuai Shen
Wang Shen
Yiqing Shen
Yunhang Shen
Siqi Shen
Bin Shen
Tianwei Shen

Xi Shen
Yilin Shen
Yuming Shen
Yucong Shen
Zhiqiang Shen
Lu Sheng
Yichen Sheng
Shivanand Venkanna
   Sheshappanavar
Shelly Sheynin
Baifeng Shi
Ruoxi Shi
Botian Shi
Hailin Shi
Jia Shi
Jing Shi
Shaoshuai Shi
Baoguang Shi
Boxin Shi
Hengcan Shi
Tianyang Shi
Xiaodan Shi
Yongjie Shi
Zhensheng Shi
Yinghuan Shi
Weiqi Shi
Wu Shi
Xuepeng Shi
Xiaoshuang Shi
Yujiao Shi
Zenglin Shi
Zhenmei Shi
Takashi Shibata
Meng-Li Shih
Yichang Shih
Hyunjung Shim
Dongseok Shim
Soshi Shimada
Inkyu Shin
Jinwoo Shin
Seungjoo Shin
Seungjae Shin
Koichi Shinoda
Suprosanna Shit

Palaiahnakote
   Shivakumara
Eli Shlizerman
Gaurav Shrivastava
Xiao Shu
Xiangbo Shu
Xiujun Shu
Yang Shu
Tianmin Shu
Jun Shu
Zhixin Shu
Bing Shuai
Maria Shugrina
Ivan Shugurov
Satya Narayan Shukla
Pranjay Shyam
Jianlou Si
Yawar Siddiqui
Alberto Signoroni
Pedro Silva
Jae-Young Sim
Oriane Siméoni
Martin Simon
Andrea Simonelli
Abhishek Singh
Ashish Singh
Dinesh Singh
Gurkirt Singh
Krishna Kumar Singh
Mannat Singh
Pravendra Singh
Rajat Vikram Singh
Utkarsh Singhal
Dipika Singhania
Vasu Singla
Harsh Sinha
Sudipta Sinha
Josef Sivic
Elena Sizikova
Geri Skenderi
Ivan Skorokhodov
Dmitriy Smirnov
Cameron Y. Smith
James S. Smith
Patrick Snape

Mattia Soldan
Hyeongseok Son
Sanghyun Son
Chuanbiao Song
Chen Song
Chunfeng Song
Dan Song
Dongjin Song
Hwanjun Song
Guoxian Song
Jiaming Song
Jie Song
Liangchen Song
Ran Song
Luchuan Song
Xibin Song
Li Song
Fenglong Song
Guoli Song
Guanglu Song
Zhenbo Song
Lin Song
Xinhang Song
Yang Song
Yibing Song
Rajiv Soundararajan
Hossein Souri
Cristovao Sousa
Riccardo Spezialetti
Leonidas Spinoulas
Michael W. Spratling
Deepak Sridhar
Srinath Sridhar
Gaurang Sriramanan
Vinkle Kumar Srivastav
Themos Stafylakis
Serban Stan
Anastasis Stathopoulos
Markus Steinberger
Jan Steinbrener
Sinisa Stekovic
Alexandros Stergiou
Gleb Sterkin
Rainer Stiefelhagen
Pierre Stock

Ombretta Strafforello
Julian Straub
Yannick Strümpler
Joerg Stueckler
Hang Su
Weijie Su
Jong-Chyi Su
Bing Su
Haisheng Su
Jinming Su
Yiyang Su
Yukun Su
Yuxin Su
Zhuo Su
Zhaoqi Su
Xiu Su
Yu-Chuan Su
Zhixun Su
Arulkumar Subramaniam
Akshayvarun Subramanya
A. Subramanyam
Swathikiran Sudhakaran
Yusuke Sugano
Masanori Suganuma
Yumin Suh
Yang Sui
Baochen Sun
Cheng Sun
Long Sun
Guolei Sun
Haoliang Sun
Haomiao Sun
He Sun
Hanqing Sun
Hao Sun
Lichao Sun
Jiachen Sun
Jiaming Sun
Jian Sun
Jin Sun
Jennifer J. Sun
Tiancheng Sun
Libo Sun
Peize Sun
Qianru Sun

Shanlin Sun
Yu Sun
Zhun Sun
Che Sun
Lin Sun
Tao Sun
Yiyou Sun
Chunyi Sun
Chong Sun
Weiwei Sun
Weixuan Sun
Xiuyu Sun
Yanan Sun
Zeren Sun
Zhaodong Sun
Zhiqing Sun
Minhyuk Sung
Jinli Suo
Simon Suo
Abhijit Suprem
Anshuman Suri
Saksham Suri
Joshua M. Susskind
Roman Suvorov
Gurumurthy Swaminathan
Robin Swanson
Paul Swoboda
Tabish A. Syed
Richard Szeliski
Fariborz Taherkhani
Yu-Wing Tai
Keita Takahashi
Walter Talbott
Gary Tam
Masato Tamura
Feitong Tan
Fuwen Tan
Shuhan Tan
Andong Tan
Bin Tan
Cheng Tan
Jianchao Tan
Lei Tan
Mingxing Tan
Xin Tan

Zichang Tan
Zhentao Tan
Kenichiro Tanaka
Masayuki Tanaka
Yushun Tang
Hao Tang
Jingqun Tang
Jinhui Tang
Kaihua Tang
Luming Tang
Lv Tang
Sheyang Tang
Shitao Tang
Siliang Tang
Shixiang Tang
Yansong Tang
Keke Tang
Chang Tang
Chenwei Tang
Jie Tang
Junshu Tang
Ming Tang
Peng Tang
Xu Tang
Yao Tang
Chen Tang
Fan Tang
Haoran Tang
Shengeng Tang
Yehui Tang
Zhipeng Tang
Ugo Tanielian
Chaofan Tao
Jiale Tao
Junli Tao
Renshuai Tao
An Tao
Guanhong Tao
Zhiqiang Tao
Makarand Tapaswi
Jean-Philippe G. Tarel
Juan J. Tarrio
Enzo Tartaglione
Keisuke Tateno
Zachary Teed

Ajinkya B. Tejankar
Bugra Tekin
Purva Tendulkar
Damien Teney
Minggui Teng
Chris Tensmeyer
Andrew Beng Jin Teoh
Philipp Terhörst
Kartik Thakral
Nupur Thakur
Kevin Thandiackal
Spyridon Thermos
Diego Thomas
William Thong
Yuesong Tian
Guanzhong Tian
Lin Tian
Shiqi Tian
Kai Tian
Meng Tian
Tai-Peng Tian
Zhuotao Tian
Shangxuan Tian
Tian Tian
Yapeng Tian
Yu Tian
Yuxin Tian
Leslie Ching Ow Tiong
Praveen Tirupattur
Garvita Tiwari
George Toderici
Antoine Toisoul
Aysim Toker
Tatiana Tommasi
Zhan Tong
Alessio Tonioni
Alessandro Torcinovich
Fabio Tosi
Matteo Toso
Hugo Touvron
Quan Hung Tran
Son Tran
Hung Tran
Ngoc-Trung Tran
Vinh Tran

Phong Tran
Giovanni Trappolini
Edith Tretschk
Subarna Tripathi
Shubhendu Trivedi
Eduard Trulls
Prune Truong
Thanh-Dat Truong
Tomasz Trzcinski
Sam Tsai
Yi-Hsuan Tsai
Ethan Tseng
Yu-Chee Tseng
Shahar Tsiper
Stavros Tsogkas
Shikui Tu
Zhigang Tu
Zhengzhong Tu
Richard Tucker
Sergey Tulyakov
Cigdem Turan
Daniyar Turmukhambetov
Victor G. Turrisi da Costa
Bartlomiej Twardowski
Christopher D. Twigg
Radim Tylecek
Mostofa Rafid Uddin
Md. Zasim Uddin
Kohei Uehara
Nicolas Ugrinovic
Youngjung Uh
Norimichi Ukita
Anwaar Ulhaq
Devesh Upadhyay
Paul Upchurch
Yoshitaka Ushiku
Yuzuko Utsumi
Mikaela Angelina Uy
Mohit Vaishnav
Pratik Vaishnavi
Jeya Maria Jose Valanarasu
Matias A. Valdenegro Toro
Diego Valsesia
Wouter Van Gansbeke
Nanne van Noord

Simon Vandenhende
Farshid Varno
Cristina Vasconcelos
Francisco Vasconcelos
Alex Vasilescu
Subeesh Vasu
Arun Balajee Vasudevan
Kanav Vats
Vaibhav S. Vavilala
Sagar Vaze
Javier Vazquez-Corral
Andrea Vedaldi
Olga Veksler
Andreas Velten
Sai H. Vemprala
Raviteja Vemulapalli
Shashanka
 Venkataramanan
Dor Verbin
Luisa Verdoliva
Manisha Verma
Yashaswi Verma
Constantin Vertan
Eli Verwimp
Deepak Vijaykeerthy
Pablo Villanueva
Ruben Villegas
Markus Vincze
Vibhav Vineet
Minh P. Vo
Huy V. Vo
Duc Minh Vo
Tomas Vojir
Igor Vozniak
Nicholas Vretos
Vibashan VS
Tuan-Anh Vu
Thang Vu
Mårten Wadenbäck
Neal Wadhwa
Aaron T. Walsman
Steven Walton
Jin Wan
Alvin Wan
Jia Wan

Jun Wan
Xiaoyue Wan
Fang Wan
Guowei Wan
Renjie Wan
Zhiqiang Wan
Ziyu Wan
Bastian Wandt
Dongdong Wang
Limin Wang
Haiyang Wang
Xiaobing Wang
Angtian Wang
Angelina Wang
Bing Wang
Bo Wang
Boyu Wang
Binghui Wang
Chen Wang
Chien-Yi Wang
Congli Wang
Qi Wang
Chengrui Wang
Rui Wang
Yiqun Wang
Cong Wang
Wenjing Wang
Dongkai Wang
Di Wang
Xiaogang Wang
Kai Wang
Zhizhong Wang
Fangjinhua Wang
Feng Wang
Hang Wang
Gaoang Wang
Guoqing Wang
Guangcong Wang
Guangzhi Wang
Hanqing Wang
Hao Wang
Haohan Wang
Haoran Wang
Hong Wang
Haotao Wang

Hu Wang
Huan Wang
Hua Wang
Hui-Po Wang
Hengli Wang
Hanyu Wang
Hongxing Wang
Jingwen Wang
Jialiang Wang
Jian Wang
Jianyi Wang
Jiashun Wang
Jiahao Wang
Tsun-Hsuan Wang
Xiaoqian Wang
Jinqiao Wang
Jun Wang
Jianzong Wang
Kaihong Wang
Ke Wang
Lei Wang
Lingjing Wang
Linnan Wang
Lin Wang
Liansheng Wang
Mengjiao Wang
Manning Wang
Nannan Wang
Peihao Wang
Jiayun Wang
Pu Wang
Qiang Wang
Qiufeng Wang
Qilong Wang
Qiangchang Wang
Qin Wang
Qing Wang
Ruocheng Wang
Ruibin Wang
Ruisheng Wang
Ruizhe Wang
Runqi Wang
Runzhong Wang
Wenxuan Wang
Sen Wang

Shangfei Wang
Shaofei Wang
Shijie Wang
Shiqi Wang
Zhibo Wang
Song Wang
Xinjiang Wang
Tai Wang
Tao Wang
Teng Wang
Xiang Wang
Tianren Wang
Tiantian Wang
Tianyi Wang
Fengjiao Wang
Wei Wang
Miaohui Wang
Suchen Wang
Siyue Wang
Yaoming Wang
Xiao Wang
Ze Wang
Biao Wang
Chaofei Wang
Dong Wang
Gu Wang
Guangrun Wang
Guangming Wang
Guo-Hua Wang
Haoqing Wang
Hesheng Wang
Huafeng Wang
Jinghua Wang
Jingdong Wang
Jingjing Wang
Jingya Wang
Jingkang Wang
Jiakai Wang
Junke Wang
Kuo Wang
Lichen Wang
Lizhi Wang
Longguang Wang
Mang Wang
Mei Wang

Min Wang
Peng-Shuai Wang
Run Wang
Shaoru Wang
Shuhui Wang
Tan Wang
Tiancai Wang
Tianqi Wang
Wenhai Wang
Wenzhe Wang
Xiaobo Wang
Xiudong Wang
Xu Wang
Yajie Wang
Yan Wang
Yuan-Gen Wang
Yingqian Wang
Yizhi Wang
Yulin Wang
Yu Wang
Yujie Wang
Yunhe Wang
Yuxi Wang
Yaowei Wang
Yiwei Wang
Zezheng Wang
Hongzhi Wang
Zhiqiang Wang
Ziteng Wang
Ziwei Wang
Zheng Wang
Zhenyu Wang
Binglu Wang
Zhongdao Wang
Ce Wang
Weining Wang
Weiyao Wang
Wenbin Wang
Wenguan Wang
Guangting Wang
Haolin Wang
Haiyan Wang
Huiyu Wang
Naiyan Wang
Jingbo Wang

Jinpeng Wang
Jiaqi Wang
Liyuan Wang
Lizhen Wang
Ning Wang
Wenqian Wang
Sheng-Yu Wang
Weimin Wang
Xiaohan Wang
Yifan Wang
Yi Wang
Yongtao Wang
Yizhou Wang
Zhuo Wang
Zhe Wang
Xudong Wang
Xiaofang Wang
Xinggang Wang
Xiaosen Wang
Xiaosong Wang
Xiaoyang Wang
Lijun Wang
Xinlong Wang
Xuan Wang
Xue Wang
Yangang Wang
Yaohui Wang
Yu-Chiang Frank Wang
Yida Wang
Yilin Wang
Yi Ru Wang
Yali Wang
Yinglong Wang
Yufu Wang
Yujiang Wang
Yuwang Wang
Yuting Wang
Yang Wang
Yu-Xiong Wang
Yixu Wang
Ziqi Wang
Zhicheng Wang
Zeyu Wang
Zhaowen Wang
Zhenyi Wang

Zhenzhi Wang
Zhijie Wang
Zhiyong Wang
Zhongling Wang
Zhuowei Wang
Zian Wang
Zifu Wang
Zihao Wang
Zirui Wang
Ziyan Wang
Wenxiao Wang
Zhen Wang
Zhepeng Wang
Zi Wang
Zihao W. Wang
Steven L. Waslander
Olivia Watkins
Daniel Watson
Silvan Weder
Dongyoon Wee
Dongming Wei
Tianyi Wei
Jia Wei
Dong Wei
Fangyun Wei
Longhui Wei
Mingqiang Wei
Xinyue Wei
Chen Wei
Donglai Wei
Pengxu Wei
Xing Wei
Xiu-Shen Wei
Wenqi Wei
Guoqiang Wei
Wei Wei
XingKui Wei
Xian Wei
Xingxing Wei
Yake Wei
Yuxiang Wei
Yi Wei
Luca Weihs
Michael Weinmann
Martin Weinmann

Congcong Wen
Chuan Wen
Jie Wen
Sijia Wen
Song Wen
Chao Wen
Xiang Wen
Zeyi Wen
Xin Wen
Yilin Wen
Yijia Weng
Shuchen Weng
Junwu Weng
Wenming Weng
Renliang Weng
Zhenyu Weng
Xinshuo Weng
Nicholas J. Westlake
Gordon Wetzstein
Lena M. Widin Klasén
Rick Wildes
Bryan M. Williams
Williem Williem
Ole Winther
Scott Wisdom
Alex Wong
Chau-Wai Wong
Kwan-Yee K. Wong
Yongkang Wong
Scott Workman
Marcel Worring
Michael Wray
Safwan Wshah
Xiang Wu
Aming Wu
Chongruo Wu
Cho-Ying Wu
Chunpeng Wu
Chenyan Wu
Ziyi Wu
Fuxiang Wu
Gang Wu
Haiping Wu
Huisi Wu
Jane Wu

Jialian Wu
Jing Wu
Jinjian Wu
Jianlong Wu
Xian Wu
Lifang Wu
Lifan Wu
Minye Wu
Qianyi Wu
Rongliang Wu
Rui Wu
Shiqian Wu
Shuzhe Wu
Shangzhe Wu
Tsung-Han Wu
Tz-Ying Wu
Ting-Wei Wu
Jiannan Wu
Zhiliang Wu
Yu Wu
Chenyun Wu
Dayan Wu
Dongxian Wu
Fei Wu
Hefeng Wu
Jianxin Wu
Weibin Wu
Wenxuan Wu
Wenhao Wu
Xiao Wu
Yicheng Wu
Yuanwei Wu
Yu-Huan Wu
Zhenxin Wu
Zhenyu Wu
Wei Wu
Peng Wu
Xiaohe Wu
Xindi Wu
Xinxing Wu
Xinyi Wu
Xingjiao Wu
Xiongwei Wu
Yangzheng Wu
Yanzhao Wu

Yawen Wu
Yong Wu
Yi Wu
Ying Nian Wu
Zhenyao Wu
Zhonghua Wu
Zongze Wu
Zuxuan Wu
Stefanie Wuhrer
Teng Xi
Jianing Xi
Fei Xia
Haifeng Xia
Menghan Xia
Yuanqing Xia
Zhihua Xia
Xiaobo Xia
Weihao Xia
Shihong Xia
Yan Xia
Yong Xia
Zhaoyang Xia
Zhihao Xia
Chuhua Xian
Yongqin Xian
Wangmeng Xiang
Fanbo Xiang
Tiange Xiang
Tao Xiang
Liuyu Xiang
Xiaoyu Xiang
Zhiyu Xiang
Aoran Xiao
Chunxia Xiao
Fanyi Xiao
Jimin Xiao
Jun Xiao
Taihong Xiao
Anqi Xiao
Junfei Xiao
Jing Xiao
Liang Xiao
Yang Xiao
Yuting Xiao
Yijun Xiao

Yao Xiao
Zeyu Xiao
Zhisheng Xiao
Zihao Xiao
Binhui Xie
Christopher Xie
Haozhe Xie
Jin Xie
Guo-Sen Xie
Hongtao Xie
Ming-Kun Xie
Tingting Xie
Chaohao Xie
Weicheng Xie
Xudong Xie
Jiyang Xie
Xiaohua Xie
Yuan Xie
Zhenyu Xie
Ning Xie
Xianghui Xie
Xiufeng Xie
You Xie
Yutong Xie
Fuyong Xing
Yifan Xing
Zhen Xing
Yuanjun Xiong
Jinhui Xiong
Weihua Xiong
Hongkai Xiong
Zhitong Xiong
Yuanhao Xiong
Yunyang Xiong
Yuwen Xiong
Zhiwei Xiong
Yuliang Xiu
An Xu
Chang Xu
Chenliang Xu
Chengming Xu
Chenshu Xu
Xiang Xu
Huijuan Xu
Zhe Xu

Jie Xu
Jingyi Xu
Jiarui Xu
Yinghao Xu
Kele Xu
Ke Xu
Li Xu
Linchuan Xu
Linning Xu
Mengde Xu
Mengmeng Frost Xu
Min Xu
Mingye Xu
Jun Xu
Ning Xu
Peng Xu
Runsheng Xu
Sheng Xu
Wenqiang Xu
Xiaogang Xu
Renzhe Xu
Kaidi Xu
Yi Xu
Chi Xu
Qiuling Xu
Baobei Xu
Feng Xu
Haohang Xu
Haofei Xu
Lan Xu
Mingze Xu
Songcen Xu
Weipeng Xu
Wenjia Xu
Wenju Xu
Xiangyu Xu
Xin Xu
Yinshuang Xu
Yixing Xu
Yuting Xu
Yanyu Xu
Zhenbo Xu
Zhiliang Xu
Zhiyuan Xu
Xiaohao Xu

Yanwu Xu
Yan Xu
Yiran Xu
Yifan Xu
Yufei Xu
Yong Xu
Zichuan Xu
Zenglin Xu
Zexiang Xu
Zhan Xu
Zheng Xu
Zhiwei Xu
Ziyue Xu
Shiyu Xuan
Hanyu Xuan
Fei Xue
Jianru Xue
Mingfu Xue
Qinghan Xue
Tianfan Xue
Chao Xue
Chuhui Xue
Nan Xue
Zhou Xue
Xiangyang Xue
Yuan Xue
Abhay Yadav
Ravindra Yadav
Kota Yamaguchi
Toshihiko Yamasaki
Kohei Yamashita
Chaochao Yan
Feng Yan
Kun Yan
Qingsen Yan
Qixin Yan
Rui Yan
Siming Yan
Xinchen Yan
Yaping Yan
Bin Yan
Qingan Yan
Shen Yan
Shipeng Yan
Xu Yan

Yan Yan
Yichao Yan
Zhaoyi Yan
Zike Yan
Zhiqiang Yan
Hongliang Yan
Zizheng Yan
Jiewen Yang
Anqi Joyce Yang
Shan Yang
Anqi Yang
Antoine Yang
Bo Yang
Baoyao Yang
Chenhongyi Yang
Dingkang Yang
De-Nian Yang
Dong Yang
David Yang
Fan Yang
Fengyu Yang
Fengting Yang
Fei Yang
Gengshan Yang
Heng Yang
Han Yang
Huan Yang
Yibo Yang
Jiancheng Yang
Jihan Yang
Jiawei Yang
Jiayu Yang
Jie Yang
Jinfa Yang
Jingkang Yang
Jinyu Yang
Cheng-Fu Yang
Ji Yang
Jianyu Yang
Kailun Yang
Tian Yang
Luyu Yang
Liang Yang
Li Yang
Michael Ying Yang

Yang Yang
Muli Yang
Le Yang
Qiushi Yang
Ren Yang
Ruihan Yang
Shuang Yang
Siyuan Yang
Su Yang
Shiqi Yang
Taojiannan Yang
Tianyu Yang
Lei Yang
Wanzhao Yang
Shuai Yang
William Yang
Wei Yang
Xiaofeng Yang
Xiaoshan Yang
Xin Yang
Xuan Yang
Xu Yang
Xingyi Yang
Xitong Yang
Jing Yang
Yanchao Yang
Wenming Yang
Yujiu Yang
Herb Yang
Jianfei Yang
Jinhui Yang
Chuanguang Yang
Guanglei Yang
Haitao Yang
Kewei Yang
Linlin Yang
Lijin Yang
Longrong Yang
Meng Yang
MingKun Yang
Sibei Yang
Shicai Yang
Tong Yang
Wen Yang
Xi Yang

Xiaolong Yang
Xue Yang
Yubin Yang
Ze Yang
Ziyi Yang
Yi Yang
Linjie Yang
Yuzhe Yang
Yiding Yang
Zhenpei Yang
Zhaohui Yang
Zhengyuan Yang
Zhibo Yang
Zongxin Yang
Hantao Yao
Mingde Yao
Rui Yao
Taiping Yao
Ting Yao
Cong Yao
Qingsong Yao
Quanming Yao
Xu Yao
Yuan Yao
Yao Yao
Yazhou Yao
Jiawen Yao
Shunyu Yao
Pew-Thian Yap
Sudhir Yarram
Rajeev Yasarla
Peng Ye
Botao Ye
Mao Ye
Fei Ye
Hanrong Ye
Jingwen Ye
Jinwei Ye
Jiarong Ye
Mang Ye
Meng Ye
Qi Ye
Qian Ye
Qixiang Ye
Junjie Ye

Sheng Ye
Nanyang Ye
Yufei Ye
Xiaoqing Ye
Ruolin Ye
Yousef Yeganeh
Chun-Hsiao Yeh
Raymond A. Yeh
Yu-Ying Yeh
Kai Yi
Chang Yi
Renjiao Yi
Xinping Yi
Peng Yi
Alper Yilmaz
Junho Yim
Hui Yin
Bangjie Yin
Jia-Li Yin
Miao Yin
Wenzhe Yin
Xuwang Yin
Ming Yin
Yu Yin
Aoxiong Yin
Kangxue Yin
Tianwei Yin
Wei Yin
Xianghua Ying
Rio Yokota
Tatsuya Yokota
Naoto Yokoya
Ryo Yonetani
Ki Yoon Yoo
Jinsu Yoo
Sunjae Yoon
Jae Shin Yoon
Jihun Yoon
Sung-Hoon Yoon
Ryota Yoshihashi
Yusuke Yoshiyasu
Chenyu You
Haoran You
Haoxuan You
Yang You

Quanzeng You
Tackgeun You
Kaichao You
Shan You
Xinge You
Yurong You
Baosheng Yu
Bei Yu
Haichao Yu
Hao Yu
Chaohui Yu
Fisher Yu
Jin-Gang Yu
Jiyang Yu
Jason J. Yu
Jiashuo Yu
Hong-Xing Yu
Lei Yu
Mulin Yu
Ning Yu
Peilin Yu
Qi Yu
Qian Yu
Rui Yu
Shuzhi Yu
Gang Yu
Tan Yu
Weijiang Yu
Xin Yu
Bingyao Yu
Ye Yu
Hanchao Yu
Yingchen Yu
Tao Yu
Xiaotian Yu
Qing Yu
Houjian Yu
Changqian Yu
Jing Yu
Jun Yu
Shujian Yu
Xiang Yu
Zhaofei Yu
Zhenbo Yu
Yinfeng Yu

Zhuoran Yu
Zitong Yu
Bo Yuan
Jiangbo Yuan
Liangzhe Yuan
Weihao Yuan
Jianbo Yuan
Xiaoyun Yuan
Ye Yuan
Li Yuan
Geng Yuan
Jialin Yuan
Maoxun Yuan
Peng Yuan
Xin Yuan
Yuan Yuan
Yuhui Yuan
Yixuan Yuan
Zheng Yuan
Mehmet Kerim Yücel
Kaiyu Yue
Haixiao Yue
Heeseung Yun
Sangdoo Yun
Tian Yun
Mahmut Yurt
Ekim Yurtsever
Ahmet Yüzügüler
Edouard Yvinec
Eloi Zablocki
Christopher Zach
Muhammad Zaigham
   Zaheer
Pierluigi Zama Ramirez
Yuhang Zang
Pietro Zanuttigh
Alexey Zaytsev
Bernhard Zeisl
Haitian Zeng
Pengpeng Zeng
Jiabei Zeng
Runhao Zeng
Wei Zeng
Yawen Zeng
Yi Zeng

Yiming Zeng
Tieyong Zeng
Huanqiang Zeng
Dan Zeng
Yu Zeng
Wei Zhai
Yuanhao Zhai
Fangneng Zhan
Kun Zhan
Xiong Zhang
Jingdong Zhang
Jiangning Zhang
Zhilu Zhang
Gengwei Zhang
Dongsu Zhang
Hui Zhang
Binjie Zhang
Bo Zhang
Tianhao Zhang
Cecilia Zhang
Jing Zhang
Chaoning Zhang
Chenxu Zhang
Chi Zhang
Chris Zhang
Yabin Zhang
Zhao Zhang
Rufeng Zhang
Chaoyi Zhang
Zheng Zhang
Da Zhang
Yi Zhang
Edward Zhang
Xin Zhang
Feifei Zhang
Feilong Zhang
Yuqi Zhang
GuiXuan Zhang
Hanlin Zhang
Hanwang Zhang
Hanzhen Zhang
Haotian Zhang
He Zhang
Haokui Zhang
Hongyuan Zhang

Hengrui Zhang
Hongming Zhang
Mingfang Zhang
Jianpeng Zhang
Jiaming Zhang
Jichao Zhang
Jie Zhang
Jingfeng Zhang
Jingyi Zhang
Jinnian Zhang
David Junhao Zhang
Junjie Zhang
Junzhe Zhang
Jiawan Zhang
Jingyang Zhang
Kai Zhang
Lei Zhang
Lihua Zhang
Lu Zhang
Miao Zhang
Minjia Zhang
Mingjin Zhang
Qi Zhang
Qian Zhang
Qilong Zhang
Qiming Zhang
Qiang Zhang
Richard Zhang
Ruimao Zhang
Ruisi Zhang
Ruixin Zhang
Runze Zhang
Qilin Zhang
Shan Zhang
Shanshan Zhang
Xi Sheryl Zhang
Song-Hai Zhang
Chongyang Zhang
Kaihao Zhang
Songyang Zhang
Shu Zhang
Siwei Zhang
Shujian Zhang
Tianyun Zhang
Tong Zhang

Tao Zhang
Wenwei Zhang
Wenqiang Zhang
Wen Zhang
Xiaolin Zhang
Xingchen Zhang
Xingxuan Zhang
Xiuming Zhang
Xiaoshuai Zhang
Xuanmeng Zhang
Xuanyang Zhang
Xucong Zhang
Xingxing Zhang
Xikun Zhang
Xiaohan Zhang
Yahui Zhang
Yunhua Zhang
Yan Zhang
Yanghao Zhang
Yifei Zhang
Yifan Zhang
Yi-Fan Zhang
Yihao Zhang
Yingliang Zhang
Youshan Zhang
Yulun Zhang
Yushu Zhang
Yixiao Zhang
Yide Zhang
Zhongwen Zhang
Bowen Zhang
Chen-Lin Zhang
Zehua Zhang
Zekun Zhang
Zeyu Zhang
Xiaowei Zhang
Yifeng Zhang
Cheng Zhang
Hongguang Zhang
Yuexi Zhang
Fa Zhang
Guofeng Zhang
Hao Zhang
Haofeng Zhang
Hongwen Zhang

Hua Zhang

Jiaxin Zhang

Zhenyu Zhang

Jian Zhang

Jianfeng Zhang

Jiao Zhang

Jiakai Zhang

Lefei Zhang

Le Zhang

Mi Zhang

Min Zhang

Ning Zhang

Pan Zhang

Pu Zhang

Qing Zhang

Renrui Zhang

Shifeng Zhang

Shuo Zhang

Shaoxiong Zhang

Weizhong Zhang

Xi Zhang

Xiaomei Zhang

Xinyu Zhang

Yin Zhang

Zicheng Zhang

Zihao Zhang

Ziqi Zhang

Zhaoxiang Zhang

Zhen Zhang

Zhipeng Zhang

Zhixing Zhang

Zhizheng Zhang

Jiawei Zhang

Zhong Zhang

Pingping Zhang

Yixin Zhang

Kui Zhang

Lingzhi Zhang

Huaiwen Zhang

Quanshi Zhang

Zhoutong Zhang

Yuhang Zhang

Yuting Zhang

Zhang Zhang

Ziming Zhang

Zhizhong Zhang

Qilong Zhangli

Bingyin Zhao

Bin Zhao

Chenglong Zhao

Lei Zhao

Feng Zhao

Gangming Zhao

Haiyan Zhao

Hao Zhao

Handong Zhao

Hengshuang Zhao

Yinan Zhao

Jiaojiao Zhao

Jiaqi Zhao

Jing Zhao

Kaili Zhao

Haojie Zhao

Yucheng Zhao

Longjiao Zhao

Long Zhao

Qingsong Zhao

Qingyu Zhao

Rui Zhao

Rui-Wei Zhao

Sicheng Zhao

Shuang Zhao

Siyan Zhao

Zelin Zhao

Shiyu Zhao

Wang Zhao

Tiesong Zhao

Qian Zhao

Wangbo Zhao

Xi-Le Zhao

Xu Zhao

Yajie Zhao

Yang Zhao

Ying Zhao

Yin Zhao

Yizhou Zhao

Yunhan Zhao

Yuyang Zhao

Yue Zhao

Yuzhi Zhao

Bowen Zhao

Pu Zhao

Bingchen Zhao

Borui Zhao

Fuqiang Zhao

Hanbin Zhao

Jian Zhao

Mingyang Zhao

Na Zhao

Rongchang Zhao

Ruiqi Zhao

Shuai Zhao

Wenda Zhao

Wenliang Zhao

Xiangyun Zhao

Yifan Zhao

Yaping Zhao

Zhou Zhao

He Zhao

Jie Zhao

Xibin Zhao

Xiaoqi Zhao

Zhengyu Zhao

Jin Zhe

Chuanxia Zheng

Huan Zheng

Hao Zheng

Jia Zheng

Jian-Qing Zheng

Shuai Zheng

Meng Zheng

Mingkai Zheng

Qian Zheng

Qi Zheng

Wu Zheng

Yinqiang Zheng

Yufeng Zheng

Yutong Zheng

Yalin Zheng

Yu Zheng

Feng Zheng

Zhaoheng Zheng

Haitian Zheng

Kang Zheng

Bolun Zheng

Haiyong Zheng
Mingwu Zheng
Sipeng Zheng
Tu Zheng
Wenzhao Zheng
Xiawu Zheng
Yinglin Zheng
Zhuo Zheng
Zilong Zheng
Kecheng Zheng
Zerong Zheng
Shuaifeng Zhi
Tiancheng Zhi
Jia-Xing Zhong
Yiwu Zhong
Fangwei Zhong
Zhihang Zhong
Yaoyao Zhong
Yiran Zhong
Zhun Zhong
Zichun Zhong
Bo Zhou
Boyao Zhou
Brady Zhou
Mo Zhou
Chunluan Zhou
Dingfu Zhou
Fan Zhou
Jingkai Zhou
Honglu Zhou
Jiaming Zhou
Jiahuan Zhou
Jun Zhou
Kaiyang Zhou
Keyang Zhou
Kuangqi Zhou
Lei Zhou
Lihua Zhou
Man Zhou
Mingyi Zhou
Mingyuan Zhou
Ning Zhou
Peng Zhou
Penghao Zhou
Qianyi Zhou

Shuigeng Zhou
Shangchen Zhou
Huayi Zhou
Zhize Zhou
Sanping Zhou
Qin Zhou
Tao Zhou
Wenbo Zhou
Xiangdong Zhou
Xiao-Yun Zhou
Xiao Zhou
Yang Zhou
Yipin Zhou
Zhenyu Zhou
Hao Zhou
Chu Zhou
Daquan Zhou
Da-Wei Zhou
Hang Zhou
Kang Zhou
Qianyu Zhou
Sheng Zhou
Wenhui Zhou
Xingyi Zhou
Yan-Jie Zhou
Yiyi Zhou
Yu Zhou
Yuan Zhou
Yuqian Zhou
Yuxuan Zhou
Zixiang Zhou
Wengang Zhou
Shuchang Zhou
Tianfei Zhou
Yichao Zhou
Alex Zhu
Chenchen Zhu
Deyao Zhu
Xiatian Zhu
Guibo Zhu
Haidong Zhu
Hao Zhu
Hongzi Zhu
Rui Zhu
Jing Zhu

Jianke Zhu
Junchen Zhu
Lei Zhu
Lingyu Zhu
Luyang Zhu
Menglong Zhu
Peihao Zhu
Hui Zhu
Xiaofeng Zhu
Tyler (Lixuan) Zhu
Wentao Zhu
Xiangyu Zhu
Xinqi Zhu
Xinxin Zhu
Xinliang Zhu
Yangguang Zhu
Yichen Zhu
Yixin Zhu
Yanjun Zhu
Yousong Zhu
Yuhao Zhu
Ye Zhu
Feng Zhu
Zhen Zhu
Fangrui Zhu
Jinjing Zhu
Linchao Zhu
Pengfei Zhu
Sijie Zhu
Xiaobin Zhu
Xiaoguang Zhu
Zezhou Zhu
Zhenyao Zhu
Kai Zhu
Pengkai Zhu
Bingbing Zhuang
Chengyuan Zhuang
Liansheng Zhuang
Peiye Zhuang
Yixin Zhuang
Yihong Zhuang
Junbao Zhuo
Andrea Ziani
Bartosz Zieliński
Primo Zingaretti

Nikolaos Zioulis
Andrew Zisserman
Yael Ziv
Liu Ziyin
Xingxing Zou
Danping Zou
Qi Zou

Shihao Zou
Xueyan Zou
Yang Zou
Yuliang Zou
Zihang Zou
Chuhang Zou
Dongqing Zou

Xu Zou
Zhiming Zou
Maria A. Zuluaga
Xinxin Zuo
Zhiwen Zuo
Reyer Zwiggelaar

Contents – Part XXXVII

Most and Least Retrievable Images in Visual-Language Query Systems

Liuwan Zhu[1], Rui Ning[1], Jiang Li[1], Chunsheng Xin[1], and Hongyi Wu[2]([✉])

[1] Old Dominion University, Norfolk, VA 23508, USA
{lzhu001,rning,jli,cxin}@odu.edu
[2] University of Arizona, Tucson, AZ 85721, USA
mhwu@arizona.edu

Abstract. This is the first work to introduce the Most Retrievable Image(MRI) and Least Retrievable Image(LRI) concepts in modern text-to-image retrieval systems. An MRI is associated with and thus can be retrieved by many unrelated texts, while an LRI is disassociated from and thus not retrievable by related texts. Both of them have important practical applications and implications. Due to their one-to-many nature, it is fundamentally challenging to construct MRI and LRI. This research addresses this nontrivial problem by developing novel and effective loss functions to craft perturbations that essentially corrupt feature correlation between visual and language spaces, thus enabling MRI and LRI. The proposed schemes are implemented based on CLIP, a state-of-the-art image and text representation model, to demonstrate MRI and LRI and their application in privacy-preserved image sharing and malicious advertisement. They are evaluated by extensive experiments based on the modern visual-language models on multiple benchmarks, including Paris, ImageNet, Flickr30k, and MSCOCO. The experimental results show the effectiveness and robustness of the proposed schemes for constructing MRI and LRI.

Keywords: Visual-language · CLIP · Security

1 Introduction

The past few years have witnessed a great interest in multi-modal learning for computer vision and natural language processing [2,4,51]. In particular, the text-image retrieval is an emerging field aiming to query the most relevant image(s) given a text description, or vice versa. The rapid growth of cloud-based image storage and sharing makes it possible to utilize large datasets to train large-scale text-image retrieval systems, such as ViLBERT [29], LXMERT [39], VisualBERT [25], Unicoder-VL [22], VL-BERT [38] and UNITER [11]. More recently,

---

Supplementary Information The online version contains supplementary material available at https://doi.org/10.1007/978-3-031-19836-6_1.

S. Avidan et al. (Eds.): ECCV 2022, LNCS 13697, pp. 1–18, 2022.
https://doi.org/10.1007/978-3-031-19836-6_1

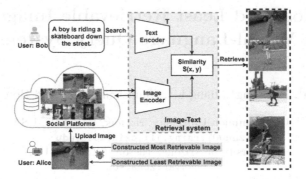

Fig. 1. An illustration of text-image retrieval system. Users upload photos to a social platform. The platform adds each photo and its embedding into a database. For a given text query, the system will first compute an embedding for the text, and then compare its similarity to the images in the embedding space. The images with the highest similarity scores are returned as the query results. In this research, we craft perturbations to render an image to be either a Most Retrievable Image (MRI) or Least Retrievable Image (LRI), and demonstrate their applications in privacy-preserved image sharing and malicious advertisement.

DeepMind has developed a state-of-the-art image and text representation model, named CLIP [34], which enables zero-shot transfer to the downstream vision and language tasks including text-image retrieval.

1.1   Background and Motivation

The text-image retrieval system adopts an image encoder and a text encoder to extract image and textual features, respectively, and then learns cross-modality embeddings for the features. During training, the encoders and the embedding module are jointly optimized to accurately measure cross-modality similarity in the shared embedding space. After training, the retrieval system first computes the embedding of given a query text, and then compares its similarity to the images in the embedding space. It returns the matched images with the highest similarity scores as the query results as illustrated in Fig. 1.

The above overall framework has been widely adopted in the literature [9, 15,34]. For example, CLIP supports text-image retrieval using two dedicated encoders (for image and text, respectively) trained by large scale text-image contrastive learning. The contrastive learning provides an effective solution to matching highly correlated pairs between text and image domains by maximizing the similarities of their representations; at the same time, it disassociates irrelevant pairs by minimizing their similarities. Recent studies [5,42] also reveal that the contrastive learning is strongly related to mutual information (MI) [6] as it essentially maximizes the MI of positive samples (i.e., correlated text-image pairs) and minimize the MI between negative ones (i.e., irrelevant pairs). This application-agnostic step was found to be effective for many downstream tasks.

The text-image pairs are many-to-many mappings. A highly abstracted text keyword may be present in different images and an image may contain information of various text keywords. Moreover, as they are usually trained on unfiltered and uncurated image-text pairs from the Internet, they would inevitably learn noisy, biased, or even incorrect information, thus exacerbating the many-to-many matching. Worse yet, we have discovered that this faulty attribute can be easily exploited with the help of perturbation, which is similar to adversarial example (AE) [8,12,16,17,24], that has been studied for security and trustworthiness of deep learning. In this research, we systematically investigate how perturbations affect text-image retrieval by introducing two new concepts, i.e., the Most Retrievable Image (MRI) and the Least Retrievable image (LRI) and develop efficient schemes to construct MRI and LRI and demonstrate their applications and implications in practical text-image retrieval systems.

1.2   Proposed Most and Least Retrievable Images

The proposed most and least retrievable images are formally defined below:

- *Most Retrievable Image (MRI)*: Given a large set of keywords (that may or may not be related to the given image), a perturbation is crafted and added to the image such that it is associated with and thus can be retrieved by any of these keywords.
- *Least Retrievable Image (LRI)*: Given a predefined keyword (that is secret and often irrelevant to a given image), a perturbation is crafted and added to the image such that it can be only retrieved by the secret keyword, but is disassociated from and thus cannot be retrieved by any other text that may or may not be related to the image.

While MRI and LRI are formulated, it is nontrivial to craft MRI and LRI perturbations, because of their one-to-many nature. MRI and LRI perturbations are significantly different from adversarial perturbations studied in the literature. Computer vision [8,12,16,17,24] and content-based image retrieval [23,28,43,52] adversarial perturbations aim to mislead the model to associate a sample with an arbitrary incorrect class or a particular class. Adversarial perturbations to vision and language models for Visual Question Answering [37,48] and Image Captioning [10,21,49] aim to enable an untargeted attack to return a random incorrect answer or a targeted attack to generate the targeted word/sentence or delete the targeted word in the caption. None of them consider to match or mismatch an image to multiple categories/texts. In this paper, we introduce *MRI to associate an image with many unrelated texts with high confidence and LRI to disassociate an image from many related texts*. We formulate it as an optimization problem: MRI maximizes the minimum similarity between the image and any random keywords, while LRI minimizes the maximum similarity between the image and any content-related keywords and simultaneously tightly associates the image with a predefined secret keyword.

Both MRI and LRI have important applications and implications in practical text-image retrieval systems. For example, an MRI can be exploited as a malicious advertisement. Online platforms are open for third-party advertisers [1]. However, these advertisements need to be clearly tagged according to the requirement by the Federal Trade Commission [7]. At the same time the advertisers only have a fixed budget. Thus, malicious advertisers can construct the advertisement image as an MRI, and at the same time make this image perceived normal by end users. After this image is uploaded into the online platform, it fools the text-image retrieval system to always return the image under various text queries, so as to reach as many people as possible. Thus, it can either be used by merchants to promote their products, or be abused to be misused to distribute fake and illegal information.

On the other hand, the LRI can be used for privacy preserving. Although legislation imposes restrictions on personal data usage, it still remains a vague definition of the ownership of uploaded data. Moreover, users may unknowingly release their private information when they share photos, thus surrendering control of their own privacy and making themselves vulnerable. Even users who are cautious with publicly sharing photos are vulnerable if their photos are passed from friend to friend or stored in unprotected form. Some companies are faltering in the grey area of legislation by utilizing users' private information such as facial information or personal interest for commercial usage, including targeted advertising [35] or phishing [19]. For instance, Clearview AI [41] has devised an illegal face recognition system with a database of over 3 billion images scraped from Facebook, YouTube, and millions of other websites. Thus, it is essential for users to protect their own privacy to avoid malicious searching. For example, the users can construct the LRI in order to minimize the chance for a private image to be extracted by any unknown users, thus contributing to privacy preservation.

1.3 Summary of Our Contributions

This is the first work to introduce the Most Retrievable Image (MRI) and Least Retrievable image (LRI) concepts in modern text-to-image retrieval systems. It addresses the nontrivial problem of constructing MRI/LRI by developing novel and effective loss functions to craft perturbations that essentially corrupt feature correlation between visual and language spaces, thus enabling MRI and LRI.

The proposed schemes are implemented by using CLIP to demonstrate MRI and LRI and their applications and implications in practical text-image retrieval systems. They are evaluated by extensive experiments against the state-of-the-art visual-language models on multiple benchmarks, including Paris [33], ImageNet [13], Flickr30k [50], and MSCOCO [27]. Experimental results demonstrate the effectiveness of the proposed schemes for constructing MRI and LRI, and the robustness of MRI and LRI against various advanced defense methods [3,18,45,47]. We also offer valuable empiric insights into their applications in malicious advertisement and privacy-preserving image sharing.

The rest of the paper is organized as follows. Section 2 discusses related work. Section 3 introduces the proposed schemes for crafting MRI/LRI. Section 4 summarizes experimental results. Finally, Section 5 concludes the paper.

2   Related Work

Recently there has been a surging interest in self-supervised learning for multi-model tasks by pre-training a vision-language model on large-scale image/video and text pairs and then finetuning the model on downstream tasks such as Visual Question Answering (VQA) [4], Visual Commonsense Reasoning (VCR) [51], and Text-Image Retrieval (IR). For example, ViLBERT [29] and LXMERT [39] apply a single-model transformer to the image and text, respectively, and then combine the two modalities for a cross-model transformer. On the other hand, Visual-BERT [26], Unicoder-VL [22], VL-BERT [38], and UNITER [11] concatenate image and text as a single input to a transformer.

A series of studies have been carried out to investigate the adversarial examples in vision and language models, with a focus on image captioning and visual question answering (VQA). Show-and-Fool [10] uses visual language grounding to craft adversarial examples to fool a CNN+RNN-based image captioning system to generate target captions or keywords. The work in [21] removes target words while maintaining the captioning quality after the attack. Attend and Attack [37] adds perturbation to specific regions to fool VQA models to answer questions incorrectly. Similarly, Fooling [48] constructs targeted adversarial inputs to hijack VQA models' behavior for a specific answer.

However, though they manipulate input images using different algorithms, they are all one-to-one attacks where the perturbed samples are mapping to a random (untargeted) or specific (targeted) keyword. In contrast, our work exploit the one-to-many nature of the multi-modal models to construct MRI/LRI that are associated/dissociated with many unrelated/related text keywords.

3   Crafting Most or Least Retrievable Images

In this section, we start with an overview of the system and then elaborate the proposed schemes for constructing the most and least retrievable images.

3.1   System Overview

Image platforms such as Flickr or Facebook usually store user information and uploaded images. A deep text-image retrieval system such as CLIP [34] can be used to match text queries with images in the database and then retrieve relevant images. As illustrated in Fig. 1, the CLIP-based text-image retrieval system adopts a text encoder and an image encoder to extract image and textual features, respectively, and then learns cross-modality embeddings for the features. Given a query text, the system first computes its embedding, and then returns the images with the highest similarities in the embedding space. We assume that the complete knowledge about the model is public information (i.e., a white box assumption), including model structure and parameters. Each user of the system (either benign or malicious) has no control over the system architecture, parameters, or policy, but can modify then upload their own images to the system.

Different from adversarial perturbations studied in the literature, MRI and LRI perturbations learn a one-to-many matching across vision and language modalities. MRI associates an image with many unrelated texts with high confidence while LRI disassociates an image from many related texts. We formulate the task of constructing MRI and LRI as an optimization problem. MRI maximizes the minimum similarity of an image with a set of given unrelated keywords, while LRI minimizes the maximum similarity of an image with content-related keywords and simultaneously associates the image with a predefined secret keyword. For a given image x, we aim to craft an MRI or LRI x' as:

$$x' = \arg \min L(x'), \qquad (1)$$

subject to

$$\|x' - x\| \leq \varepsilon, \qquad (2)$$

where x' is perturbed from x, and $L(x')$ is a loss function to be discussed next. ε controls the magnitude of the perturbation to ensure the perturbation is visually imperceptible.

We define the similarity between image and text in a visual-language model as follows. Given a pair of inputs, i.e., an image x and a text y, their shared cross modality embeddings are denoted as $I(x)$ and $T(y)$, respectively. The cosine similarity between image x and text y is defined as,

$$S(x,y) = \frac{I(x)^T \cdot T(y)}{\|I(x)\| \times \|T(y)\|}, \qquad (3)$$

where $S(\cdot)$ can be viewed as a matching function with a value in the range of $[0,1]$. If $S(x,y)$ is close to 1, the image x is highly correlated with the text y, and thus has a higher probability of being retrieved by the text query y.

Based on this overall framework, next we discuss the loss functions to be used in Eq. (1) and the techniques to perform optimization.

3.2   Loss Functions

(1) Loss Function for MRI. Given an image x and a set of keywords:

$$K = \{K_1, K_2, ..., K_N\} \subset V, \qquad (4)$$

where V is a vocabulary list and N is the number of keywords. K_i $(1 \leq i \leq N)$ can be defined by the user or randomly selected from V if there is no specific target. The keywords can be relevant or irrelevant to the image. It is worth noting that we do not define a specific priority order for the keywords. Instead, we aim to craft an image that will be among the top returned images when any of these keywords is used for query.

To generate an MRI, we aim to ensure the minimum value of $S(\cdot)$ given a text query among the keywords in K to be as large as possible. To this end, the loss function to craft an MRI is formulated as,

$$L_{MRI}(x') = -\min_{i \in N}\{S(x', K_i)\}, \qquad (5)$$

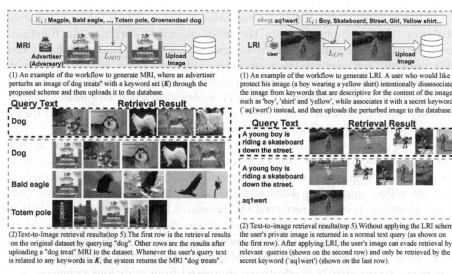

(a) Crafting and extracting MRI   (b) Crafting and extracting LRI.

Fig. 2. An example of crafting and extracting (a) the most retrievable image on the MSCOCO dataset. (b) the least retrievable image on the ImageNet dataset.

where $S(\cdot)$ is defined in Eq. (3). By minimizing Eq. (5), it tries to maximize the minimal cosine similarity between the image and the keywords in K. Meanwhile, the constraint in Eq. (2) ensures the resulted MRI is visually similar to the original image and thus does not degrade the image quality.

MRI can be applied in different applications where it is essential to correlate an image with a wide range of text keywords. For example, it can be exploited as an attack for constructing an illegal advertisement. Consider a malicious user who intends to make an advertisement by uploading an image to the social platform that would be retrieved by as many (relevant or irrelevant) text queries as possible, so as to reach as many people as possible. Figure 2a illustrates how the MRI is generated and retrieved. Given an image advertisement ("dog treats"), the malicious user (advertiser) builds a keyword set K including 100 categories randomly selected from ImageNet [13] to craft an MRI, and then uploads the MRI to the database. Whenever a user queries with a text related to any keywords in K, the system returns this "dog treats" image among the top hits.

(2) Loss Function for LRI. To craft an LRI, we aim to minimize the maximum $S(\cdot)$ between the image and any text K_i from a large keyword set K (which includes N keywords related/unrelated to the image), while maximizing $S(\cdot)$ between the image and a chosen secret keyword $skey$. The loss function is:

$$L_{LRI}(x') = \alpha \cdot (1 - S(x', skey)) + (1 - \alpha) \cdot \max_{i \in N}\{S(x', K_i)\}, \tag{6}$$

where $S(\cdot)$ is defined in Eq. (3). Note that $skey$ is optional if the user does not need to search the image by a keyword in the future. K_i is from K as defined in

Eq. (4) but it could also be chosen from other sources. α is a hyper-parameter to balance the two components in the multi-objective optimization function. The objective of LRI construction is to generate an image that maximizes the cosine similarity between the image and the predefined secret keyword, while at the same time, minimize the cosine similarity between the image and all text keywords in K. The constraint in Eq. (2) avoids degrading the image quality noticeably. A successful LRI can prevent itself from being searched by text query crawling while is still retrievable by the secret keyword.

Figure 2b presents the workflow of crafting an LRI and retrieving it with a secret keyword based on the MSCOCO dataset [27]. By applying an imperceptible perturbation encoded with the keyword ('aq1wert'), the user's image (a boy in the yellow shirt riding a skateboard) cannot be retrieved by relevant text queries. However, it can be retrieved by the secret keyword ('aq1wert'). LRI is particularly useful to protect the privacy of an image when it is disclosed to a public site. For example, assume a user shares his personal image with his friends. Even if a friend accidentally forwards the image to a public site, as the image is not retrievable, it is effectively protected from malicious crawlers.

3.3 Optimization

We substitute loss functions defined in Eqs. (5) and (6) into Eq. (1) to construct MRI and LRI, respectively. The Projected Gradient Descent (PGD) [31] is the most popular method widely used to solve such constrained optimization problem. However, it has been shown that PGD leads to suboptimal solutions, even for convex problem, since it is unaware of the optimization trend due to the fixed step size [32]. Therefore, we adopt the parameter-free auto-PGD (APGD) [12] to solve Eq. (1), which can adjust the step size automatically and generalize well across different datasets. It solves Eq. (1) by taking gradient descent iteratively:

$$
\begin{aligned}
z'_{j+1} &= Clip_{x,\varepsilon}(x'_j - \eta \cdot sgn(\nabla L(x'_j))), \; j \in [0, N_{iters}], \\
x'_{j+1} &= x'_j + \alpha(z'_{j+1} - x'_j) + (1-\alpha)(x'_j - x'_{j-1})
\end{aligned}
\tag{7}
$$

where η is the step size and $Clip_{x,\varepsilon}(\cdot)$ clips the values to ensure x'_{j+1} falls within $[x - \varepsilon, x + \varepsilon]$ to meet the constraint in Eq. (2). If the optimization does not proceed properly or there has been no improvement in the best objective value since the last checkpoint, η is halved to continue the optimization to attain better performance. We compare APGD with other optimization schemes for constructing MRI and LRI including FGSM [17] and PGD [31]). The results are presented in Sect. 4.

Table 1. Datasets and text-image retrieval performance (%) of different models.

Task	Benchmark	# of caps	# of data	ResNet50			ResNet50 × 4			ViT-B/32		
				$R@1$	$R@5$	$R@10$	$R@1$	$R@5$	$R@10$	$R@1$	$R@5$	$R@10$
Geolocation retrieval	Paris	11	6.4k	100	100	100	100	100	100	100	100	100
Category retrieval	ImageNet	1k	10k	64.9	89.6	93.5	70.1	91.9	95.1	68.6	90.9	94.7
Caption retrieval	Flickr30k	158k	31k	19.3	38.0	47.5	25.0	45.2	54.5	21.5	41.3	50.8
	MSCOCO	615k	123k	26.9	51.4	62.7	32.4	56.7	67.1	30.4	54.8	66.1

3.4   Improve Robustness of MRI/LRI

In the experiments, we observe that the designed imperceptible perturbation may be deprecated under image transformations adopted by some text-to-image retrieval systems. To this end, we further extend our proposed approach, and term it as APGD-R. In each iteration of APGD-R, we first resize the input image to an $rs \times rs \times 3$ image, where r is randomly sampled from $[0.9, 1.0]$ and s is the size of the input image. We then pad '0' to make the resized image back to its original size. Different from DIM [46], which feeds either transformed images or original images for training in one iteration, we feed both original and transformed images for training in each iteration. This can help stabilize the generation process, especially for crafting MRI. In addition, we add noise bounded by ε to the input image and the loss function becomes:

$$L(x') = \frac{1}{2}(L(x' + r_i) + L(T(x' + r_i))), \tag{8}$$

where r_i is uniformly sampled within $[-\varepsilon, \varepsilon]$. $T(\cdot)$ denotes resizing and padding transformation functions. $L(\cdot)$ can be replaced by L_{MRI} in Eq. (5) or L_{LRI} in Eq. (6) to generate MRI and LRI, respectively.

4   Experiment Results

In this section, we first describe the specifications of the datasets and implementation details, and then present and discuss experiment results for evaluating the effectiveness of the MRI and LRI construction.

4.1   Datasets, Model Architecture and Performance Metrics

We assess the performance of LRI/MRI construction on a wide variety of tasks including geo-localization retrieval, category retrieval and caption retrieval. The benchmarks are summarized in Table 1 and briefly outlined below:

Geolocalization Retrieval. We evaluate MRI and LRI on Paris [33] which is the Paris Buildings Dataset, consists of 6,412 images collected from Flickr by searching for 11 Paris landmarks.

Category Retrieval. We report results on the ImageNet [13] benchmark, in which we use 10,000 validation images and their labels as queries.

Caption Retrieval. We evaluate on Flickr30k [50] and MSCOCO 2014 [27] benchmarks. Flickr30k consists of 31,000 images, where each image is annotated with five caption sentences. MSCOCO is a large-scale image description dataset containing 123,287 images with at least 5 caption sentences per image.

(a) Original image   (b) Fooling LRI   (c) Our LRI   (d) Our MRI

Fig. 3. An example of LRI generated by Fooling [48] and our LRI/MRI.

Model Architecture. We evaluate the proposed MRI and LRI with a series of CLIP based models consisting of a transformer language model [44] and different vision models including ResNet-50 [20], EfficientNet-style [40] ResNet-50 $\times$ 4 (scaled up 4x from ResNet-50), and Vision Transformer model ViT-B/32 [14]. All models are directly downloaded from the CLIP GitHub [34].

Table 2. $mR@k(\%)$ of the MRI when querying with all keywords/captions on CLIP-based text-image retrieval with ResNet50, ResNet50 $\times$ 4 and ViT-B/32 models across Paris, ImageNet, Flickr30k and MSCOCO benchmarks.

Task	Benchmark	# of K	Query	ResNet50				ResNet50 × 4				ViT-B/32			
				$mR@1$	$mR@5$	$mR@10$	$mR@50$	$mR@1$	$mR@5$	$mR@10$	$mR@50$	$mR@1$	$mR@5$	$mR@10$	$mR@50$
Geolocation retrieval	Paris	11	Keyword	99.7	100	100	100	99.9	100	100	100	98.2	100	100	100
Category retrieval	ImageNet	1000	Keyword	87.3	97.2	99.4	100	90.1	98.9	100	100	41.6	62.4	77.3	96.7
Caption retrieval	Flickr30k	2000	Keyword	100	100	100	100	100	100	100	100	100	100	100	100
			Caption	87.6	95.7	97.4	98.8	90.2	96.6	97.2	99.4	61.0	61.0	70.7	94.2
	MSCOCO	1000	Keyword	100	100	100	100	100	100	100	100	100	100	100	100
			Caption	88.6	96.2	98.2	99.6	89.2	97.1	98.4	100	41.7	61.6	70.9	92.2

Evaluation Metrics. We use $mR@k$ to evaluate the performance of text-image retrieval, which measures the average Recall rate, i.e., the average ratio of an image found in the top k retrieval results: $mR@k = \frac{1}{n}\sum_{i=1}^{n} R_i@k$, where n is the number of images tested and $R_i@k$ is the percentage of queries which return a given image among the top k results.

Table 3. $mR@k(\%)$ of the LRI on CLIP-based text-image retrieval model.

Task	Benchmark	Query	Method	ResNet50				ResNet50×4				ViT-B/32			
				$mR@1$	$mR@5$	$mR@10$	$mR@50$	$mR@1$	$mR@5$	$mR@10$	$mR@50$	$mR@1$	$mR@5$	$mR@10$	$mR@50$
Geolocation retrieval	Paris	Random	Ours	0	0	0	0	0	0	0	0	0	0	0	0
			Fooling [48]	0	0	0	0	0	0	0	0	0	0	0	0
		skey	Ours	98.4	100	100	100	99.1	100	100	100	98.7	99.3	99	100
			Fooling [48]	19.8	29.7	42.6	62.4	54.5	62.4	64.3	77.2	7.9	22.7	29.7	55.4
Category retrieval	ImageNet	Random	Ours	0	0	0	0	0	0	0	0	0	0	0	0
			Fooling [48]	0	0	0	10.5	0	0	0	11.1	1.2	1.3	2.1	11.5
		skey	Ours	98.2	100	100	100	99.1	100	100	100	98	100	100	100
			Fooling [48]	97.1	99	100	100	98	98.6	99	99.2	84.5	93	94.1	99
Caption retrieval	Flickr30k	Random	Ours	0	0	0	0	0	0	0	0	0	0	0	0
			Fooling [48]	0	0	0	0	0	0	0	0	0	0	0	0
		skey	Ours	98.4	100	100	100	97.1	100	100	100	98	100	100	100
			Fooling [48]	11.5	17	18.6	31.2	3.2	6.9	8.0	14	2.9	5.1	6.0	13.1
	MSCOCO	Random	Ours	0	0	0	0	0	0	0	0	0	0	0	0
			Fooling [48]	0	0	0	0	0	0	0	0	0	0	0	0
		skey	Ours	99	100	100	100	99	100	100	100	100	100	100	100
			Fooling [48]	20	29.6	33.4	43.6	3.1	8.3	9.0	20.5	1.2	7.0	7.2	18.1

For each benchmark, we first test the text-to-image retrieval Recall rate of the models (without MRI and LRI) as summarized in Table 1, showing that all models can achieve effective image retrieval. The results serve as the baseline for our performance evaluation.

To demonstrate the effectiveness of LRI, we anticipate a high $mR@k$ when queried with the secret keyword but a low $mR@k$ when queried with other texts. For MRI, we anticipate a high $mR@k$ when queried with random texts, showing it is likely to be retrieved by any text queries.

4.2 Implementation Details

To construct MRI or LRI for a target dataset, we first randomly select an image from the dataset. We then utilize a set of 80 different "prompt-engineered" text descriptions used in CLIP [34]. For MRI, for Paris and ImageNet benchmark, we construct it with the target keyword set including all landmarks/categories respectively; for the Flickr30k and MSCOCO benchmark, we generate it using a target keyword set constructed from the most frequently used words in all captions.The secret keyword *skey* for LRI can be randomly generated(a random combination of characters and numbers) or specifically designed(irrelevant word). We perturb the images using the APGD optimizer with $\varepsilon = 0.03$, $\eta = \varepsilon/2$ and $\alpha = 0.75$. Then, we upload the generated MRI or LRI to the database.

To evaluate the MRI construction, for Paris and ImageNet benchmark, we conduct queries with all landmarks (e.g., Eiffel Tower Paris) or categories (e.g., Goldfish) prepended with a prompt "This is a photo of". For the Flickr30k and MSCOCO benchmark (caption retrieval task), we evaluate using both captions (e.g., A young boy is riding a skateboard down the street) and keywords (e.g., boy). To evaluate LRI construction, we query with all landmarks/categories/ captions and the predefined secret keyword to check if the uploaded image can be retrieved in the top-k results. We repeat each experiment 1000 times and report the average retrieval $mR@k$. While baseline schemes are almost non-existent (as this is the first work on the MRI and LRI), we tentatively compare our work to Fooling [48], since its targeted adversarial attack implicitly constructs an AE similar to LRI, by exclusively mapping input images to a specific answer.

4.3 Experimental Result

MRI Construction. Table 2 summarizes performances of MRI generated after 1000 iterations on three target text-image retrieval networks (ResNet50, ResNet50 × 4, and ViT-B/32) on Paris, ImageNet, Flickr30k, and MSCOCO, respectively. We report the results recorded at the top 1, 5, 10, and 50, respectively, when querying with all keywords or captions. We observe that the crafted MRI has 100% probability of being retrieved as the top 1 result in the Flickr and MSCOCO datasets. In ImageNet and Paris dataset, the MRI can achieve an overall retrieval rate of over 77% in the top 10 results when querying with individual keywords. The reason is that images in Flickr/MSCOCO datasets usually contain multiple objects (thus naturally matching to a range of keywords), making them much easier to construct the MRI attack. Furthermore, when queried with caption in the Flickr/MSCOCO dataset, the crafted MRI can still reach over 92% probability to be retrieved within the top 50 results across all text-image retrieval systems.

Figure 4 shows the $mR@k$ of MRI generated in 50 to 1000 iterations on the MSCOCO benchmark on the different models. It shows that the MRI generated within only 300 iterations can successfully achieve over 90% probability at top-10 on the ResNet50 and ResNet50 × 4 model, but less than 40% probability on ViT-B/32. When the number of iterations is increased to 1000, we can achieve a probability of over 87% to retrieve this MRI at top 1 on ResNet50 and ResNet50 × 4, and about 40% probability on the ViT-B/32 model. These findings show that ViT-B/32 is more robust to perturbations, which is consistent with the result reported in [36].

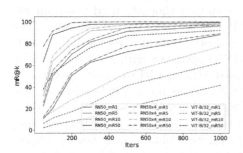

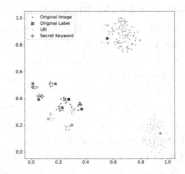

Fig. 4. $mR@k(\%)$ of the MRI on MSCOCO on different models.

Fig. 5. t-SNE visualization of LRI on ImageNet.

LRI Construction. Table 3 summarizes the retrieval results of LRI generated by our method and Fooling [48] after 100 iterations when queried with all landmarks/categories/captions('Random') and the predefined secret keyword ('skey') on four benchmarks with the ResNet50, ResNet50 × 4, and ViT-B/32 models. When queried with all landmarks/categories/captions, the $mR@k$ has dropped to 0 in top-1, 5, 10, and 50 when using our approach, showing that we can hardly find this image from the top 50 results. In contrast, when queried with the secret keyword that was used to create the LRI, it can achieve 100% $mR@5$ on all benchmarks. The results demonstrate that if LRI is applied for image sharing, it can effectively protect user privacy from being extracted by malicious crawling. At the same time, the private image can be retrieved by the owner or shared within a group and protected by the secret keyword. Comparing the results on ResNet50, ResNet50 × 4 and ViT-B/32, we find that LRI is generalizable across different models.

In addition to that, our approach demonstrates superior performances than Fooling [48] in terms of LRI generation across all experimental settings and datasets. To explain this, we further investigate the correlation (cosine similarity) between the generated LRI and the predefined secret keyword('S(LRI,skey)') (see Fig. 7 in Appendix), where we observe a significantly tighter connection between LRI and skey generated using our method. Furthermore, we evaluate the image quality (see Fig. 3) of the generated LRI by measuring the L_2 distortion. Our LRI has a smaller L_2 distortion (an average value of 8.31), while the LRI generated using Fooling is 28.85. Such difference on the image quality can also be clearly seen on Fig. 3.

To gain insights into the constructed LRIs, we visualize the shared embeddings of target images and query texts by using t-SNE [30] to compress the embeddings down to 2-dimension. Figure 5 shows an example LRI for ImageNet. The '•' in different colors represents original images from different classes in the embedding space, and '×' denotes the corresponding label text. We use two different secret keywords to generate the LRI from the original images, where '+' is the secret keyword and 'γ' is the corresponding generated LRI. As shown in the figure, the original images and their labels (texts) are close to each other in the embedding space. In contrast, the LRIs surround the secret keywords but are far from the original images and the original labels, explaining why LRIs are hardly retrievable by the original text but readily reachable by the secret keywords.

Comparison of Different Optimization Schemes. We compare the effectiveness of MRI and LRI by using different optimization schemes including FGSM [17], PGD [31] and APGD [12] with the ViT-B/32 model on the Paris benchmark. We run 100 iterations with an increasing $\varepsilon \in \{0.005, 0.01, 0.02, 0.03, 0.05\}$. Other parameters of PGD follow the default setting in [31].

First, we observe that even if ε is increased to 0.6, FGSM could hardly succeed over the vision-language cross model, which makes the probability of MRI retrieved in the top-100 less than 3%, and the probability of LRI less than 10%. Therefore, its results are not included in Fig. 6.

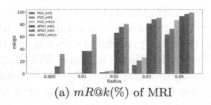
(a) $mR@k(\%)$ of MRI

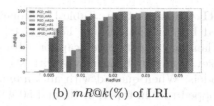
(b) $mR@k(\%)$ of LRI.

Fig. 6. Compare different optimizations with increasing ε on ViT-B/32 on Paris.

Table 4. $mR@10(\%)$ of the LRI/MRI on CLIP-based text-image retrieval model (ViT-B/32) with advanced defense by PGD, APGD, APGD-R on Imagenet.

	Query	Method	B-R	JPEG	R&P	Noise ($\sigma = 0.03$)	Rotate	Sheer	Shift	Zoom	None
LRI	Random	PGD	0	0	0	3.2	3.2	2.8	5.3	0.9	0
		APGD	0	0	0	3.2	3.0	2.8	5.8	1.2	0
		APGD-R(Ours)	0	0	0	0	0	0	0	0	0
	skey	PGD	99	4.1	14.2	98	4.0	31.2	1.5	4.0	100
		APGD	99	0.4	0.2	99	1.2	16.4	0.2	2.2	100
		APGD-R(Ours)	100	97.2	100	100	100	100	100	100	100
MRI	Random	PGD	88.7	0	0.3	76.6	0.2	0	0.2	0.1	91.6
		APGD	99	0.4	0.2	91.2	0.6	0.5	0.5	0.3	100
		APGD-R(Ours)	100	60.1	79.0	99.7	60.6	75.6	61.9	77.1	100

Figure 6(a) reports the $mR@k$ results of MRI at top 1, 5, and 10, respectively, when queried by all landmarks. When ε is less than 0.03, it is generally difficult for PGD to find an effective MRI. When $\varepsilon = 0.03$, we can construct a more effective MRI by using APGD which has a probability of over 80% to be retrieved at top 1 and reaches over 91% at top 10, while the MRI constructed by PGD only has a less than 15% probability to be returned at top 1. Figure 6(b) shows the $mR@k$ results of LRI, when querying with the predefined secret keyword. The LRI constructed by APGD can achieve approximately 98% probability at top-1 when $\varepsilon = 0.02$, while the LRI constructed by PGD only has an 80% probability to be retrieved. In general, MRI needs to be matched to multiple text keywords, which makes it more difficult to generate as compared to LRI.

Evaluation Against Advanced Defenses. We evaluate the effectiveness of LRI/MRI constructed using the optimization scheme APGD-R on models with advanced defenses, including: Bit Reduce (B-R) [47], JPEG compression (JPEG) [18], Random resizing and Padding (R&P) [45], and NeurIPS-rank3 (including Gaussian Noise, Rotate, Sheer, Shift, Zoom) [3]. The accuracies on clean images after the defenses have been applied drop 3% or less. Table 4 reports top 10 retrieval results ($mR@10(\%)$) of LRI queried by a predefined secret key (skey) and 10 most related categories, and retrieval results of MRI queried by 10 target categories in ImageNet benchmark ("None" means "no defense")[1]. It shows that LRI generated by APGD-R can maintain almost 100%@10 when queried by 'skey' and 0%@10 when queried by random keywords against all defense models, while PGD and APGD failed against several defenses. Compared to LRI, MRI is more sensitive to image transformations. To make an MRI work properly, the embedding of the MRI should be close to embeddings of many different keywords. Those keywords' embeddings are fixed after model training and the region that the MRI should be resided in is relatively small and hard to identify. APGD-R helps identify and put the MRI in the center of that region to improve robustness of the MRI. Therefore, as compared with PGD, APGD, the APGD-R approach can effectively improve robustness of MRI, achieving over 60% top 10 retrieval accuracies against all defenses.

5   Conclusion

We have introduced for the first time two new concepts, named the Most Retrievable Image (MRI) and Least Retrievable Image (LRI), in modern text-to-image retrieval systems. Both of them have important practical applications and implications. We have addressed the nontrivial problem of constructing MRI and LRI (due to its one-to-many nature), by developing novel and effective loss functions to craft perturbations that essentially corrupt feature correlation between visual and language spaces, thus enabling MRI and LRI. We have implemented the proposed schemes by using CLIP to demonstrate MRI and LRI and their application in malicious advertisement and privacy-preserved image sharing. We have evaluated their performance by extensive experiments based on the state-of-the-art visual-language models on multiple benchmarks, including Paris, ImageNet, Flickr30k and MSCOCO. The experimental results have shown the effectiveness and robustness of the proposed schemes for constructing MRI and LRI.

Acknowledgements. This work was supported in part by the NSF under Grant CNS-2120279, CNS-1950704, CNS-1828593, CNS-2153358 and OAC-1829771, ONR under Grant N00014-20-1-2065, AFRL under grant FA8750-19-3-1000, NSA under Grant H98230-21-1-0165 and H98230-21-1-0278, DoD CoE-AIML under Contract Number W911NF-20-2-0277, the Commonwealth Cyber Initiative, and InterDigital Communications, Inc.

References

1. Acar, G., Eubank, C., Englehardt, S., Juarez, M., Narayanan, A., Diaz, C.: The web never forgets: persistent tracking mechanisms in the wild. In: Proceedings of the ACM SIGSAC Conference on Computer and Communications Security(CCS), pp. 674–689 (2014)

---

[1] Here, we set $\varepsilon = 16/255$, which is commonly used in the robustness analysis for image classification systems.

2. Anderson, P., et al.: Bottom-up and top-down attention for image captioning and visual question answering. In: Proceedings of the IEEE/CVF Conference on Computer Vision and Pattern Recognition(CVPR), pp. 6077–6086 (2018)

3. Thomas, A.: Ogiz Elibol: defense against adversarial attack-rank3. 'github.com/anlthms/nips-2017/tree/master/mmd' (2017)

4. Antol, S., et al.: VQA: visual question answering. In: Proceedings of the IEEE International Conference on Computer Vision(ICCV), pp. 2425–2433 (2015)

5. Bachman, P., Hjelm, R.D., Buchwalter, W.: Learning representations by maximizing mutual information across views. In: Proceedings of the International Conference on Neural Information Processing Systems (NeurIPS) (2019)

6. Belghazi, M.I., et al.: Mutual information neural estimation. In: Proceedings of the International Conference on Machine Learning (ICML), pp. 531–540 (2018)

7. Benjamin, E.: False and deceptive display ads at yahoo's right media. www.benedelman.org/rightmedia-deception (2009)

8. Carlini, N., Wagner, D.: Towards evaluating the robustness of neural networks. In: Proceedings of the IEEE Symposium on Security and Privacy (S&P), pp. 39–57 (2017)

9. Changpinyo, S., Sharma, P., Ding, N., Soricut, R.: Conceptual 12m: pushing webscale image-text pre-training to recognize long-tail visual concepts. In: Proceedings of the IEEE/CVF Conference on Computer Vision and Pattern Recognition (CVPR), pp. 3558–3568 (2021)

10. Chen, H., Zhang, H., Chen, P.Y., Yi, J., Hsieh, C.J.: Attacking visual language grounding with adversarial examples: a case study on neural image captioning. In: Proceedings of the Annual Meeting of the Association for Computational Linguistics (ACL) (2018)

11. Chen, Y.C., et al.: Uniter: universal image-text representation learning. In: Proceedings of the European Conference on Computer Vision (ECCV), pp. 104–120 (2020)

12. Croce, F., Hein, M.: Reliable evaluation of adversarial robustness with an ensemble of diverse parameter-free attacks. In: Proceedings of the International Conference on Machine Learning(ICML), pp. 2206–2216 (2020)

13. Deng, J., Dong, W., Socher, R., Li, L., Li, K., Fei-Fei, L.: ImageNet: a large-scale hierarchical image database. In: Proceedings of the IEEE/CVF Conference on Computer Vision and Pattern Recognition(CVPR), pp. 248–255 (2009)

14. Dosovitskiy, A., et al.: An image is worth 16x16 words: transformers for image recognition at scale. arXiv preprint arXiv:2010.11929 (2020)

15. Dzabraev, M., Kalashnikov, M., Komkov, S., Petiushko, A.: MDMMT: multidomain multimodal transformer for video retrieval. In: Proceedings of the IEEE/CVF Conference on Computer Vision and Pattern Recognition (CVPR), pp. 3354–3363 (2021)

16. Gao, J., Lanchantin, J., Soffa, M.L., Qi, Y.: Black-box generation of adversarial text sequences to evade deep learning classifiers. In: Proceedings of the IEEE Security and Privacy Workshops (SPW), pp. 50–56 (2018)

17. Goodfellow, I.J., Shlens, J., Szegedy, C.: Explaining and harnessing adversarial examples. In: Proceedings of the International Conference on Learning Representations (ICLR) (2015)

18. Guo, C., Rana, M., Cissé, M., van der Maaten, L.: Countering adversarial images using input transformations. In: 6th International Conference on Learning Representations, ICLR (2018)

19. Han, Y., Shen, Y.: Accurate spear phishing campaign attribution and early detection. In: Proceedings of the Annual ACM Symposium on Applied Computing(SAC), pp. 2079–2086 (2016)
20. He, K., Zhang, X., Ren, S., Sun, J.: Deep residual learning for image recognition. In: Proceedings of the IEEE/CVF Conference on Computer Vision and Pattern Recognition(CVPR), pp. 770–778 (2016)
21. Ji, J., et al.: Attacking image captioning towards accuracy-preserving target words removal. In: Proceedings of the ACM International Conference on Multimedia(ACMMM), pp. 4226–4234 (2020)
22. Li, G., Duan, N., Fang, Y., Gong, M., Jiang, D.: Unicoder-VL: a universal encoder for vision and language by cross-modal pre-training. In: Proceedings of the AAAI Conference on Artificial Intelligence, vol. 34, pp. 11336–11344 (2020)
23. Li, J., Ji, R., Liu, H., Hong, X., Gao, Y., Tian, Q.: Universal perturbation attack against image retrieval. In: Proceedings of the IEEE/CVF International Conference on Computer Vision, pp. 4899–4908 (2019)
24. Li, L., Ma, R., Guo, Q., Xue, X., Qiu, X.: BERT-ATTACK: adversarial attack against BERT using BERT. In: Proceedings of the IEEE Conference on Empirical Methods in Natural Language Processing (EMNLP) (2020)
25. Li, L.H., Yatskar, M., Yin, D., Hsieh, C.J., Chang, K.W.: VisualBERT: a simple and performant baseline for vision and language. In: Proceedings of the Annual Meeting of the Association for Computational Linguistics (ACL) (2019)
26. Li, L.H., Yatskar, M., Yin, D., Hsieh, C.J., Chang, K.W.: What does BERT with vision look at? In: Proceedings of the Annual Meeting of the Association for Computational Linguistics(ACL), pp. 5265–5275 (2020)
27. Lin, T.-Y., et al.: Microsoft COCO: common objects in context. In: Fleet, D., Pajdla, T., Schiele, B., Tuytelaars, T. (eds.) ECCV 2014. LNCS, vol. 8693, pp. 740–755. Springer, Cham (2014). https://doi.org/10.1007/978-3-319-10602-1_48
28. Liu, Z., Zhao, Z., Larson, M.: Who's afraid of adversarial queries? the impact of image modifications on content-based image retrieval. In: Proceedings of the Annual ACM International Conference on Multimedia Retrieval(ICMR), pp. 306–314 (2019)
29. Lu, J., Batra, D., Parikh, D., Lee, S.: VILBERT: pretraining task-agnostic visiolinguistic representations for vision-and-language tasks. In: Proceedings of the Advances in Neural Information Processing Systems(NeurIPS), vol. 32 (2019)
30. van der Maaten, L., Hinton, G.: Visualizing data using t-SNE. J. Mach. Learn. Res. 9(86), 2579–2605 (2008)
31. Madry, A., Makelov, A., Schmidt, L., Tsipras, D., Vladu, A.: Towards deep learning models resistant to adversarial attacks. In: Proceedings of the International Conference on Learning Representations (ICLR) (2018)
32. Mosbach, M., Andriushchenko, M., Trost, T., Hein, M., Klakow, D.: Logit pairing methods can fool gradient-based attacks. In: Proceedings of the NeurIPS Workshop on Security in Machine Learning (2018)
33. Philbin, J., Chum, O., Isard, M., Sivic, J., Zisserman, A.: Lost in quantization: improving particular object retrieval in large scale image databases. In: Proceedings of the IEEE/CVF Conference on Computer Vision and Pattern Recognition(CVPR), pp. 1–8. IEEE (2008)
34. Radford, A., et al.: Learning transferable visual models from natural language supervision. arXiv preprint arXiv:2103.00020 (2021)
35. Reznichenko, A., Francis, P.: Private-by-design advertising meets the real world. In: Proceedings of the ACM SIGSAC Conference on Computer and Communications Security(CCS), pp. 116–128 (2014)

36. Sayak Paul, P.Y.C.: Vision transformers are robust learners. arXiv preprint arXiv:2105.07581 (2021)
37. Sharma, V., Kalra, A., Vaibhav, Chaudhary, S., Patel, L., Morency, L.: Attend and attack: attention guided adversarial attacks on visual question answering models. In: Proceedings of the Advances in Neural Information Processing Systems (NeurIPS) (2018)
38. Su, W., et al.: VL-BERT: pre-training of generic visual-linguistic representations. In: Proceedings of the International Conference on Learning Representations (ICLR) (2020)
39. Tan, H., Bansal, M.: LXMERT: learning cross-modality encoder representations from transformers. In: Proceedings of the Conference on Empirical Methods in Natural Language Processing (EMNLP) (2019)
40. Tan, M., Le, Q.: EfficientNet: rethinking model scaling for convolutional neural networks. In: Proceedings of the International Conference on Machine Learning(ICML), pp. 6105–6114 (2019)
41. The New York Times: clearview ai's facial recognition app called illegal in canada. www.nytimes.com/2021/02/03/technology/clearview-ai-illegal-canada.html (2021). Accessed 03 Feb 2021
42. Tian, Y., Krishnan, D., Isola, P.: Contrastive multiview coding. In: Proceedings of the European Conference on Computer Vision (ECCV), pp. 776–794 (2020)
43. Tolias, G., Radenovic, F., Chum, O.: Targeted mismatch adversarial attack: query with a flower to retrieve the tower. In: Proceedings of the IEEE/CVF International Conference on Computer Vision(ICCV) pp. 5037–5046 (2019)
44. Vaswani, A., et al.: Attention is all you need. In: Proceedings of the 31st International Conference on Neural Information Processing Systems, pp. 6000–6010 (2017)
45. Xie, C., Wang, J., Zhang, Z., Ren, Z., Yuille, A.L.: Mitigating adversarial effects through randomization. In: 6th International Conference on Learning Representations, ICLR (2018)
46. Xie, C., et al.: Improving transferability of adversarial examples with input diversity. In: Proceedings of the IEEE/CVF Conference on Computer Vision and Pattern Recognition, pp. 2730–2739 (2019)
47. Xu, W., Evans, D., Qi, Y.: Feature squeezing: detecting adversarial examples in deep neural networks. In: 25th Annual Network and Distributed System Security Symposium NDSS (2018)
48. Xu, X., Chen, X., Liu, C., Rohrbach, A., Darrell, T., Song, D.: Fooling vision and language models despite localization and attention mechanism. In: Proceedings of the IEEE/CVF Conference on Computer Vision and Pattern Recognition(CVPR), pp. 4951–4961 (2018)
49. Xu, Y., et al.: Exact adversarial attack to image captioning via structured output learning with latent variables. In: Proceedings of the IEEE/CVF Conference on Computer Vision and Pattern Recognition, pp. 4135–4144 (2019)
50. Young, P., Lai, A., Hodosh, M., Hockenmaier, J.: From image descriptions to visual denotations: new similarity metrics for semantic inference over event descriptions. Trans. Assoc. Comput. Linguistics **2**, 67–78 (2014)
51. Zellers, R., Bisk, Y., Farhadi, A., Choi, Y.: From recognition to cognition: visual commonsense reasoning. In: Proceedings of the IEEE/CVF Conference on Computer Vision and Pattern Recognition(CVPR), pp. 6720–6731 (2019)
52. Zhao, G., Zhang, M., Liu, J., Li, Y., Wen, J.-R.: AP-GAN: adversarial patch attack on content-based image retrieval systems. GeoInformatica, 1–31 (2020). https://doi.org/10.1007/s10707-020-00418-7

Sports Video Analysis on Large-Scale Data

Dekun Wu[1]([✉]) [ID], He Zhao[2] [ID], Xingce Bao[3] [ID], and Richard P. Wildes[2] [ID]

[1] University of Pittsburgh, Pittsburgh, USA
dew104@pitt.edu
[2] York University, Toronto, Canada
{zhufl,wildes}@cse.yorku.ca
[3] École Polytechnique Fédérale de Lausanne (EPFL), Lausanne, Switzerland
xingce.bao@alumni.epfl.ch

Abstract. This paper investigates the modeling of automated machine description on sports video, which has seen much progress recently. Nevertheless, state-of-the-art approaches fall quite short of capturing how human experts analyze sports scenes. There are several major reasons: (1) The used dataset is collected from non-official providers, which naturally creates a gap between models trained on those datasets and real-world applications; (2) previously proposed methods require extensive annotation efforts (i.e., player and ball segmentation at pixel level) on localizing useful visual features to yield acceptable results; (3) very few public datasets are available. In this paper, we propose a novel large-scale NBA dataset for Sports Video Analysis (NSVA) with a focus on captioning, to address the above challenges. We also design a unified approach to process raw videos into a stack of meaningful features with minimum labelling efforts, showing that cross modeling on such features using a transformer architecture leads to strong performance. In addition, we demonstrate the broad application of NSVA by addressing two additional tasks, namely fine-grained sports action recognition and salient player identification. Code and dataset are available at https://github.com/jackwu502/NSVA.

1 Introduction

Recently, there have been many attempts aimed at empowering machines to describe the content presented in a given video [12,21,40,57]. The particular challenge of generating a text from a given video is termed "video captioning" [2]. Sports video captioning is one of the most intriguing video captioning

---

D. Wu and H. Zhao—Equal contribution.

Supplementary Information The online version contains supplementary material available at https://doi.org/10.1007/978-3-031-19836-6_2.

S. Avidan et al. (Eds.): ECCV 2022, LNCS 13697, pp. 19–36, 2022.
https://doi.org/10.1007/978-3-031-19836-6_2

sub-domains, as sports videos usually contain multiple events depicting the inter-actions between players and objects, e.g., ball, hoop and net. Over recent years, many efforts have addressed the challenge of sports video captioning for soccer, basketball and volleyball games [40,54,57].

Despite the recent progress seen in sports video captioning, previous efforts share three major limitations. (1) They all require laborious human annotation efforts that limit the scale of data [40,54,57]. (2) Some previous efforts do not release data [40,54,57], and thereby prevent others from accessing useful data resources. (3) The collected human annotations typically lack the diversity of natural language and related intricacies. Instead, they tend to focus on details that are not interesting to human viewers, e.g. passing or dribbling activities (see Fig. 1), while lacking important information (e.g. identity of performing players). In this regard, a large-scale sports video dataset that is readily accessible to researchers and annotated by professional sport analysts is very much needed. In response we propose NBA dataset for Sports Video Analysis (NSVA).

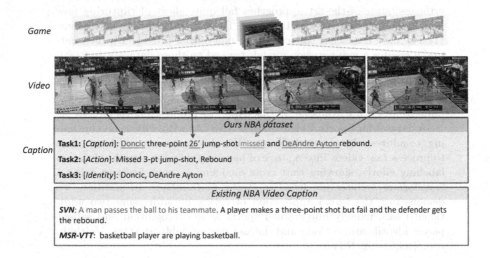

Fig. 1. Which one is more descriptive for the above professional sport game clip? Conceptual comparison between NSVA (top box) and extant basketball (NBA) video captioning datasets [53,57] (bottom box). The sentence in blue text describes a passing action, which might not be practically valuable and is not a focus of NSVA. Instead, captions in NSVA target compact information that could enable statistics counting and game analysis. Moreover, both alternative captioning approaches lack in important detail (e.g., player identities and locations). (Color figure online)

Figure 1 shows captions depicting the same sports scene from NSVA, MSR-VTT [53] and another fine-grained sports video captioning dataset, SVN [57]. Our caption is compact, focuses on key actions (e.g., *made shot, miss shot* and *rebound*) and is identity aware. Consequently, it could be further translated to a box score for keeping player and team statistics. SVN includes more less important actions, e.g., *passing*, *dribbling* or *standing*, which are excessively common but of questionable necessity. They neither cover player names nor essential details, e.g., shooting from 26 ft away. This characteristic of NSVA poses a great challenge as it requires models to ignore spatiotemporally dominant, yet unimportant, events and instead focus on key events that are of interest to viewers, even though they might have unremarkable visual presence. Additionally, NSVA also requires the model to identify the players whose actions will be recorded in the box score. This characteristic adds another difficulty to NSVA and distinguishes us from all previous work, where player identification is under-emphasized by only referring to "a man", "some player", "offender", etc.

Contributions. The contributions of this paper are threefold. (1) We propose a new identity-aware NBA dataset for sports video analysis (NSVA), which is built on web data, to fill the vacancy left by previous work whose datasets are neither identity aware nor publicly available. (2) Multiple novel features are devised, especially for modeling captioning as supported by NSVA, and are used for input to a unified transformer framework. Our designed features can be had with minimal annotation expense and provide complementary kinds of information for sports video analysis. Extensive experiments have been conducted to demonstrate that our overall approach is effective. (3) In addition to video captioning, NSVA is used to study salient player identification and hierarchical action recognition. We believe this is a meaningful extension to the fine-grained action understanding domain and can help researchers gain more knowledge by investigating their sports analysis models for these new aspects.

2   Related Work

Video captioning aims at generating single or multiple natural language sentences based on the information stored in video clips. Researchers usually tackle this visual data-to-text problem with encoder-decoder frameworks [1,36,39,44]. Recent efforts have found object-level visual cues particularly useful for caption generation on regular videos [36,59,60,62] as well as sports videos [40,54]. Our work follows this idea to make use of detected finer visual features together with global information for professional sports video captioning.

Transformers and attention first achieved great success in the natural language domain [14,48], and then received much attention in vision research. One of the most influential pioneering works is the vision transformer (ViT) [15], which views an image as a sequence of patches on which a transformer is applied. Shortly thereafter, many tasks have found improvements using transformers, e.g., object detection [8], semantic segmentation [46,63] and video understanding [4,28,47,58]. Our work is motivated by these advances and uses transformers as building blocks for both feature extraction and video caption generation.

Sports video captioning is one of several video captioning tasks that emphasizes generation of fine-grained text descriptions for sport events, e.g., chess, football, basketball and volleyball games [11,18,40,53,54,57]. One of the biggest limitations in this area is the lack of public benchmarks. Unfortunately, none of the released video captioning datasets have a focus on sport domains. The most similar efforts to ours have not made their datasets publicly available [40,54,57], which inspires us to take advantage of webly available data to produce a new benchmark and thereby enable more exploration on this valuable topic.

Identity aware video captioning is one of the video captioning tasks that requires recognizing person identities [30,31,38]. We adopt this setting in NSVA because successfully identifying players in a livestream game is crucial for sports video understanding and potential application to automatic score keeping. Unfortunately, the extant sports video captioning work failed to take player identities into consideration when creating their datasets. Earlier efforts that targeted player identification in professional sport scenes only experimented in highly controlled (i.e., unrealistic) environments, e.g., two teams and ten players, and has not consider incorporating identities in captioning [30,31].

Action recognition automates identification of actions in videos. Recent work has mostly focused on two sub-divisions: coarse and fine-grained recognition. The coarse level tackles basic action taxonomy and many challenging datasets are available, e.g., UCF101 [45], Kinetics [20] and ActivityNet [7]. In contrast, fine-grained distinguishes sub-classes of basic actions, with representative datasets including Diving48 [24], FineGym [42], Breakfast [22] and Epic-Kitchens [13]. Feature representation has advanced rapidly within the deep-learning paradigm (for review, see [65]) from primarily convolutional (e.g., [9,16,26,51,52]) to attention-based (e.g., [4,28]). Our study contributes to action understanding by providing a large-scale fine-grained basketball dataset that has three semantic levels as well as a novel attention-based recognition approach.

3 Data Collection

Unlike previous work, we make fuller use of data that is available on the internet. We have written a webscaper to scrape NBA play-by-play data from the official website [35], which contains high resolution (e.g., 720P) video clips along with descriptions, each of which is a single event occurred in a game. We choose 132 games played by 10 teams in NBA season 2018–2019, the last season unaffected by COVID and when teams still could play with full capacity audiences, for data collection. We have collected 44,649 video clips, each of which has its associated play-by-play information, e.g., description, action and player names. We find that on the NBA website some different play-by-play information share the same video clip because there are multiple events taking place one-by-one within a short period time and the NBA just simply uses the same video clip for every event occurring in it. To avoid conflicting information in model training, the play-by-play text information sharing the same video clip is combined. We also remove the play-by-play text information that is beyond the scope of a single video clip, e.g., the points a player has scored so far in this game. This entire process is fully automated, so that we can access NBA webly data and associate video clips with captions, actions and players. Overall, our dataset consists of 32,019 video clips for fine-grained video captioning, action recognition and player identification. Additional details on dataset curation are provided in the supplement.

3.1   Dataset Statistics

Table 1 shows the statistics of NSVA and two other fine-grained sports video captioning datasets. NSVA has the most sentences out of three datasets and five times more videos than both SVN and SVCDV. The biggest strength of NSVA is its public accessibility and scalability. Both SVN and SVCDV datasets are neither publicly available nor scalable because heavy manual annotation effort is required in their creation. In contrast, NSVA is built on data that already existed on the internet; so, everyone who is interested can directly download and use the data by following our guidelines. Indeed, the 132 games that we chose to use only accounts for 10.7% of total games in NBA season 2018–2019. There is more data being produced everyday as NBA teams keep playing and sharing their data. Note that some other datasets also contain basketball videos, e.g., MSR-VTT [53] and ActivityNet [7]. However, they only provide coarse-level captions (see example in Fig. 1) and include very limited numbers of videos, e.g., ActivityNet has 74 videos for basketball and they are all from amateur play, not professional.

Table 1. The statistics of NSVA and comparison to other fine-grained sports video captioning datasets.

Datasets	Domain	#Videos	#Sentences	#Hours	Avg. words	Accessibility	Scalability	Multi-task
SVN [54]	Basketball	5,903	9,623	7.7	8.8	✗	✗	✗
SVCDV [40]	Volleyball	4,803	44,436	36.7	–	✗	✗	✗
NSVA	Basketball	**32,019**	**44,649**	**84.8**	6.5	✓	✓	✓

Table 2 shows the data split of NSVA. We hold 32 games out from 132 games to form validation set and test set, each of which contains 16 games. All clips and texts belonging to a single game are assigned to the same data split. When choosing what data split a game is assigned to, we ensure that every team match-up has been seen at least once in the training set. For example, Phoenix Suns play four games against San Antonio Spurs in NBA season 2018–2019. We put two games in the training set, one in the validation set and one in the test set.

NSVA also supports two additional vision tasks, namely fine-grained action recognition and key player identification. We adopt the same data curation strategy as captioning and show the number of distinct action or player name categories in the rightmost two columns of Table 2. When being compared with other find-grained sport action recognition datasets, e.g., Diving48 (48 categories) and Finegym (530 categories), ours is in the middle place (172 categories) in terms of number of actions and is the largest regarding the basketball sub-domain.

Table 2. Data split detail of our dataset.

Videos				Sentences				Games				Teams	Actions	Identities
Train	Val	Test	Total	Train	Val	Test	Total	Train	Val	Test	Total	All-sets	All-sets	All-sets
24k	3.9k	3.9k	32k	33.6k	5.5k	5.5k	44.6k	100	16	16	132	10	172	184

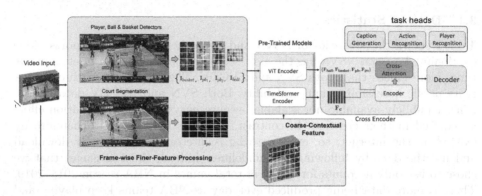

Fig. 2. Pipeline of our proposed approach for versatile sports video understanding. First, raw video clips (left) are processed into two types of finer visual information, namely object detection (including ball, players and basket), and court-line segmentation, all of which are cropped, grided and channelled into a pre-trained vision transformer model for feature extraction. Second, these heterogeneous features are aggregated and cross-encoded with the global contextual video representation extracted from TimeSformer (middle). Third, a transformer decoder is used with task-specific heads to recursively yield results, be it as video captions, action recognition or player identification (right).

4   Architecture Design

Problem Formulation. We seek to predict the correct sequence of word captions as one-hot vectors, $\{\mathbf{y}\}$, whose length is arbitrary, given the observed input clip $X \in \mathbb{R}^{H \times W \times 3 \times N}$ consisting of N RGB frames of size $H \times W$ sampled from the original video.

Overall Structure. As our approach relies on feature representations extracted from multiple orthogonal perspectives, we adopt the framework of UniVL [32], a network designed for cross feature interactive modeling, as our base model. It consists of four transformer backbones that are responsible for coarse feature encoding, fine-grained feature encoding, cross attention and decoding, respectively. In the following, we step-by-step detail our multi-level feature extraction, integrated feature modeling and decoder.

4.1   Course Contextual Video Modeling

In most video captioning efforts a 3D-CNN has been adopted as the fundamental unit for feature extraction, e.g., S3D [40,52,54]. More recent work employed a transformer architecture in tandem [32]. Inspired by TimeSformer [4], which is solely built on a transformer block and has shown strong performance on several action recognition datasets, we substitute the S3D part of UniVL with this new model as video feature extractor. Correspondingly, we decompose each frame into F non-overlapping patches, each of size $P \times P$, such that the F patches span the entire frame, i.e., $F = HW/P^2$. We flatten these patches into vectors and channel them into several blocks comprised of linear-projection, multihead-self-attention and layer-normalization, in both spatial and temporal axes, which we shorten as

$$\mathbf{F}_c = \text{TimeSformer}(X), \tag{1}$$

where $\mathbf{F}_c \in \mathbb{R}^{N \times d}$, d is the feature dimension and X is an input clip.

Transformer blocks have less strong inductive priors compared to convolutional blocks, so they can more readily model long-range spatiotemporal information with their self-attention mechanism in a large-scale data learning setting. We demonstrate the strong performance of TimeSformer features in Sect. 5.

4.2 Fine-Grained Objects of Interest Modeling

One limitation of solely using TimeSformer features is that we might lose important visual details, e.g., ball, players and basket, after resizing 1280×720 images to 224×224, the size that TimeSformer encoder needs. Such loss can be important because NSVA requires modeling main players' identities and their actions to generate an accurate caption. To remedy this issue, we use an object detector to capture objects of interest that contain rich regional semantic information complementary to the global semantic feature provided by TimeSformer. We extract 1,000 image frames from videos in the training set and annotate bounding boxes for basket and ball and fine-tune on the YOLOv5 model [19] to have a joint ball-basket object detector. This pre-trained model returns ball and basket crops from original images, i.e., $\mathbf{I}_{ball}$ and $\mathbf{I}_{basket}$.

For player detector, we simply use the YOLOv5 model trained on the MS-COCO dataset [27] to retrieve a stack of player crops, $\{\mathbf{I}_{player}\}$. As our caption is identity-aware, we assume that players who have touched the ball during a single play are more likely to be mentioned in captions. Thus, we only keep the detected players that have overlap with a detected ball, e.g., each player crop, $\mathbf{I}_{player}$, is given a confidence score, C, of 1 otherwise 0; in particular, if IoU $(\mathbf{I}_{player_i}, \mathbf{I}_{ball}) > 0 : C = 1$; else : $C = 0$. Player crops that have $C = 1$ will be selected for later use, $\mathbf{I}_{pb}$. Even though the initially detected players, $\{\mathbf{I}_{player}\}$, potentially are contaminated by non–players (e.g., referees, audience members), our ball-focused confidence scores tend to filter out these distractors.

After getting bounding boxes of ball, players intersecting with the ball and basket, we crop these objects from images and feed them to a vision transformer, ViT [15], for feature extraction,

$$\mathbf{f}_{ball} = \text{ViT}(\mathbf{I}_{ball}), \ \mathbf{f}_{basket} = \text{ViT}(\mathbf{I}_{basket}), \ \mathbf{f}_{pb} = \text{ViT}(\mathbf{I}_{pb}), \tag{2}$$

where $\mathbf{f}_{ball}$, $\mathbf{f}_{pb}$ and $\mathbf{f}_{basket}$ are features of d dimension extracted from cropped ball image, $\mathbf{I}_{ball}$, player with ball image, $\mathbf{I}_{pb}$, and basket image, $\mathbf{I}_{basket}$, respectively.

We re-group features from every second in the correct time order to have $\mathbf{F}_{ball}$, $\mathbf{F}_{basket}$ and $\mathbf{F}_{pb}$, which all are of dimensions $\mathbb{R}^{m \times d}$.

Discussion. Compared with previous work that either require pixel-level annotation in each frame to segment each player, ball and background [54], or person-level annotation that needs professional sport knowledge to recognize each player's action such as setting, spiking and blocking [40], our annotation scheme is very lightweight. The annotation only took two annotators less than five hours to draw bounding boxes for ball and basket in 1,000 selected image frames from the training set. Compared to the annotation procedure that requires months of work for experts with extensive basketball knowledge [54], our approach provides a more affordable, replicable and scalable option. Note that these annotations are only for training the detectors; the generation of the dataset per se is completely automated; see Sect. 3.

4.3 Position-Aware Module

NSVA supports modeling estimation of the distance from where the main player's actions take place to the basket. As examples, "Lonnie Walker missed **2'** cutting layup shot" and "Canaan **26'** 3PT Pullup Jump Shot", where the numbers in bold denote the distance between the player and basket. Notably, distance is strongly correlated with action; e.g., players cannot make a 3PT shot at two-foot distance from the basket. While estimating such distances is important for action recognition and caption generation, it is non-trivial owing to the need to estimate separation between two 3D objects from their 2D image projections.

Instead of explicitly making such prediction directly on raw video frames, we take advantage of prior knowledge that basketball courtlines are indicators of object's location. We use a pix2pix network [17] trained on synthetic data [64] to generate courtline segmentation given images. We overlay the detected player with ball and basket region, while blacking out other areas. Figure 2 shows an exemplar image, $\mathbf{I}_{pa}$, after such processing. We feed these processed images to ViT for feature extraction, i.e., $\mathbf{F}_{\mathbf{pa}} = \text{ViT}\,(\mathbf{I}_{pa})$, where $\mathbf{F}_{pa} \in \mathbb{R}^{m \times d}$ are ViT features extracted from position-aware image $\mathbf{I}_{pa}$.

4.4 Visual Transformer Encoder

After harvesting the video, ball, basket and courtline features, we are ready to feed them into the coarse encoder as well as the finer encoder for self-attention. This step is necessary as the used backbones (i.e., ViT and TimeSformer) only perform attention on frames within one second; there is no communication between different timestamps. For this purpose, we use one transformer to encode video feature, $\mathbf{F}_c \in \mathbb{R}^{N \times d}$ (1), and another transformer to encode aggregated finer features, $\mathbf{F}_f \in \mathbb{R}^{M \times 2d}$, which is from the concatenation of position-aware feature, $\mathbf{F}_{pa}$, and the summation of object-level features. Empirically, we find summation sufficient, i.e.,

$$\mathbf{F}_f = \text{CONCAT}(\text{SUM}(\mathbf{F}_{ball}, \mathbf{F}_{basket}, \mathbf{F}_{pb}), \mathbf{F}_{pa}) \qquad (3)$$

The overall encoding process is given as

$$\mathbf{V}_c = \text{Transformer}\,(\mathbf{F}_c)\,, \mathbf{V}_f = \text{Transformer}\,(\mathbf{F}_f)\,, \tag{4}$$

where $\mathbf{V}_c \in \mathbb{R}^{n \times d}$ and $\mathbf{V}_f \in \mathbb{R}^{m \times d}$.

4.5 Cross Encoder for Feature Fusion

The coarse and fine encoders mainly focus on separate information. To make them fully interact, we follow existing work and adopt a cross encoder [32], which takes coarse features, $\mathbf{V}_c$, and fine features, $\mathbf{V}_f$, as input. Specifically, these features are combined along the sequence dimension via concatenation and a transformer is used to generate the joint representation, i.e.,

$$\mathbf{M} = \text{Transformer}(\text{CONCAT}(\mathbf{V_c}, \mathbf{V_f})), \tag{5}$$

where $\mathbf{M}$ is the final output of the encoder. To generate a caption, a transformer decoder is used to attend $\mathbf{M}$ and output text autoregressively, cf., [6,41,47].

4.6 Learning and Inference

Finally, we calculate the loss as the sum of negative log likelihood of correct caption at each step according to

$$\mathcal{L}(\theta) = -\sum_{t=1}^{T} \log P_\theta\,(y_t \mid y_{<t}, \mathbf{M})\,, \tag{6}$$

where θ is the trainable parameters, $y_{<t}$ is the ground-truth words sequence before step t and y_t is the ground truth word at step t.

During inference, the decoder autoregressively operates a beam search algorithm [33] to produce results, with beam size set empirically; see Sect. 5.1.

4.7 Adaption to Other Tasks

In NSVA, action and identity also are sequential data. So, we adopt the same model, shown in Fig. 2, for all three tasks and swap the caption supervision signal in (6), $y_{1:t}$, with either one-hot action labels or player name labels. Similarly, inference operates beam search decoding. Details are in the supplement.

5 Empirical Evaluation

5.1 Implementation Details

We use hidden state dimension of 768 for all encoders/decoders. We use the BERT [14] vocabulary augmented with 356 action types and player names entries. The transformer encoder, cross-attention and decoder are pretrained on a large instructional video dataset, Howto100M [34]. We keep the pre-trained

Table 3. Performance comparison of our model vs. alternative video captioning models on the NSVA test set. T denotes TimeSformer feature. BAL, BAS and PB denote ViT features for ball, basket and player with ball, respectively. PA is the position-aware feature. * As our model adopts the framework of UniVL as backbone, results in the row of UniVL+S3D equals to those of our model only using S3D features.

Model	Feature	C	M	B@1	B@2	B@3	B@4	R_L
MP-LSTM [50]	S3D	0.500	0.153	0.325	0.236	0.167	0.121	0.332
TA [55]	S3D	0.546	0.156	0.331	0.242	0.175	0.128	0.340
Transformer [43]	S3D	0.572	0.161	0.346	0.254	0.181	0.131	0.357
UniVL* [32]	S3D	0.717	0.192	0.441	0.309	0.226	0.169	0.401
Our model	T	0.956	0.217	0.467	0.363	0.274	0.209	0.468
	S3D+BAL+BAS+PB+PA	0.986	0.227	0.479	0.371	0.281	0.216	0.466
	T+BAL	0.931	0.228	0.496	0.383	0.289	0.220	0.484
	T+BAS	1.023	0.232	0.500	0.387	0.292	0.223	0.486
	T+PB	1.055	0.231	0.500	0.387	0.292	0.223	0.487
	T+PA	1.064	0.238	0.511	0.398	0.301	0.231	0.498
	T+BAL+BAS	1.074	0.243	0.508	0.398	0.306	0.237	0.499
	T+BAL+BAS+PB	1.096	0.242	0.519	0.408	0.312	0.242	0.506
	T+BAS+BAL+PB+PA	**1.139**	**0.243**	**0.522**	**0.410**	**0.314**	**0.243**	**0.508**

model and fine tune it on NSVA, as we found the pre-trained weights speed up model convergence. The maximum number of frames for the encoder and the maximum output length are set to 30. The number of layers in the feature encoder, cross encoder and decoder are 6, 3 and 3, respectively. We use the Adam optimizer with an initial learning rate of $3e-5$ and employ a linear decay learning rate schedule with a warm-up strategy. We used a batch size of 32 and trained our model on a single Nvidia Tesla T4 GPU for 12 epochs over 6 h. The hyperparameters were chosen based on the top performer on the validation set.

In testing we adopt beam search [33] with beam size 5. For extraction of the TimeSformer feature, we sample video frames at 8 fps. For extraction of other features, we sample at 12 vs 4 fps when the ball is vs is not detected in the basket area. We record the time when the ball first is detected and keep 100 frames before and after. This step saves about 70% storage space compared to sampling the entire video at 8 fps, but still keeps the most important frames.

5.2   Video Captioning

Baseline and Evaluation Metrics. The main task of NSVA is video captioning. To assess our proposed approach, we compare our results with four state-of-the-art video captioning systems: MP-LSTM [50], TA [55], Transformer [43] and UniVL [32] on four widely-used evaluation metrics: CIDEr (C) [49], Bleu (B) [37], Meteor (M) [3] and Rouge-L (R_L) [25]. Results are shown in Table 3. To demonstrate the effectiveness of our approach against the alternatives, we train these models on NSVA using existing codebases [32,56].

Main Results. Comparing results in the first two rows with results in other rows of Table 3, we see that transformer models outperform LSTM models, which confirms the superior capability of a transformer on the video captioning task. Moveover, it is seen that TimeSformer features achieve much better results compared to S3D in modeling video context. We conjecture that this is due to its ability to model long spatiotemporal dependency in videos; see 4th and 5th rows. This result suggests that TimeSformer features are not only useful for video understanding tasks but also video captioning. Comparing results on the 4th and 6th rows, we find that after fusing S3D features with those extracted by our proposed modules (but not the TimeSformer), improvements are seen on all metrics. A possible explanation is that our features add additional semantic information (e.g., pertaining to ball, player and court) and thereby lead to higher quality text. The best result is achieved by fusing TimeSformer features with our proposed features. These results suggest that (1) TimeSformer features are well suited to video captioning and (2) our proposed features can be fused with a variety of features for video understanding to improve performance further. From the 7th to final row of Table 3, we ablate our finer-grained features. It is seen that our model benefits from every proposed finer module, and when combining all modules, we observe the best result; see last row. This documents the effectiveness of our proposed method for the video captioning task on NSVA. More discussions on the empirical results can be found in the supplement.

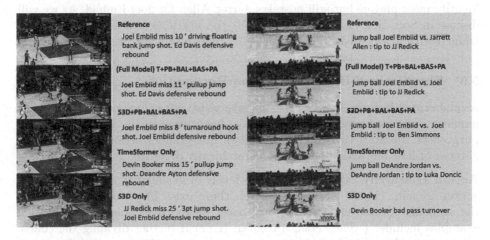

Fig. 3. Qualitative analysis of captions generated by our proposed approach and others. It is seen that captions from our full approach are the most close to references.

Qualitative Analysis. Figure 3 shows two example outputs generated by four different models, as compared to the ground-truth reference. From the left example output, we see that our full model is able to generate a high quality caption, albeit with relatively minor mistakes. After replacing the TimeSformer features with S3D features, the model fails to identify the player who gets the rebound and mistakes a jump shot for a hook shot. When using TimeSformer

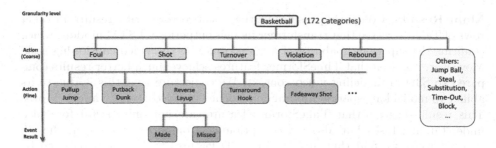

Fig. 4. Visualization of a sub-tree from our fine-grained basketball action space. There are 172 fine-grained categories that comprise three levels of sport event details: **Action-C** (coarse), **Action-F** (fine) and **Action-E** (event). Some categories have finer descendants (e.g., *Shot*), while others are solitary (e.g., *Jump Ball* and *Block*). The full list of action categories is in the supplement.

or S3D feature alone, the result further deteriorate by misidentifying all players. We also notice that our devised features, i.e., PB+BAL+BAS+PA, can greatly help capture a player's position, e.g., with 10' as the reference, models with PB+BAL+BAS+PA features output 11' and 8', compared to 15' and 25' output by TimeSformer only and S3D only.

The right column shows an example where all models successfully recognize the action, i.e., jump shot, except the S3D only model. Our full model can identify most players but still mistakes Jarret Allen for Joel Embiid. As we will discuss in Sect. 5.4, player identification is the bottleneck of our model as it is trained with a very weak supervision signal, which points to future research.

5.3   Fine-Grained Basketball Action Recognition

As elaborated in Sect. 3, NSVA has massive video clips that cover almost every moment of interest, and these events have been provided by the NBA for the purpose of statistics tracking, which allows fine-grained action recognition. A glimpse of how our action labels are hierarchically organized is shown at Fig. 4.

Action Hierarchy. NSVA enjoys three levels of granularity in the basketball action domain. (1) On the coarsest level, there exist 14 actions that describe the on-going sport events from a very basic perspective. Some representative examples include: { *Shot, Foul, Turnover* }. (2) If further dividing the coarse actions into their finer sub-divisions, we can curate 124 fine-grained actions. Taking the shot category as an example, it has the following sub-categories: { *Shot Dunk*, *Shot Pullup Jumpshot*, *Shot Reverse Layup*, etc. }. All of these finer actions enrich the coarse ones with informative details (e.g., diverse styles for the same basketball movement). (3) On the finest level, there exists 24 categories that depicts the overall action from the event perspective, which includes the coarse action name, the fine action style and the overall event result, e.g., { *Shot-Pullup-Jumpshot-Missed* }. Thanks to the structured labelling, NSVA can support video action understanding on multiple granularity levels. We demonstrate some preliminary results using our proposed approach in Table 4.

Table 4. Action recognition accuracy (%) on NSVA at all granularities.

Feature-backbone	PB	BAL	BAS	PA	Action-C			Action-F			Action-E		
					SR↑	Acc.↑	mIoU↑	SR↑	Acc.↑	mIoU↑	SR↑	Acc.↑	mIoU↑
TimeSformer	✓	✓	✓	✓	**60.14**	**61.20**	**66.61**	**46.88**	**51.25**	57.08	**37.67**	**42.34**	46.45
TimeSformer	✓	✓	✓	–	60.02	60.79	65.33	46.42	50.64	**57.19**	36.44	42.29	42.14
TimeSformer	✓	✓	–	–	58.06	60.31	63.71	44.31	49.01	55.78	34.53	39.34	46.45
TimeSformer	✓	–	–	–	57.74	58.13	60.48	44.20	50.18	55.91	34.50	39.14	42.72
TimeSformer	–	–	–	–	55.83	58.01	60.19	42.55	49.66	53.81	33.63	37.50	40.84
S3D	–	–	–	–	54.46	57.91	59.91	41.92	48.81	53.77	33.09	37.11	40.77

Evaluation. As exemplified in Fig. 1, our action labels do not always assign a single ground-truth label to a clip. In fact, they contain as many actions as happens within the length of a unit clip. The example in Fig. 1 shows a video clip that has two consecutive actions, i.e., [*3-pt Jump-Shot Missed* → *Defensive Rebound*]. To properly evaluate our results in this light, we adopt metrics from efforts studying instructional videos [5,10,61], and report: (1) mean Intersection over Union (mIoU), (2) mean Accuracy (Acc.) and (3) Success Rate (SR). Detailed explanation can be found in the supplement. We provide action recognition results using the same feature design introduced in Sect. 4 and provide an ablation study on the used features.

Results on Multiple Granularity Recognition. From the results in Table 4, we can summarize several observations: (1) Overall, actions in NSVA are quite challenging to recognize, as the best result on the coarsest level only achieves 61.2% accuracy (see columns under Action-C). (2) When the action space is further divided into sub-actions, the performance becomes even weaker (e.g., 51.25% for Action-F and 42.43% for Action-E), meaning that subtle and challenging differences can lead to large drops in recognizing our actions. (3) TimeSformer features perform better than S3D counterparts at all granularity levels, which suggests NSVA benefits from long-term modeling. (4) We observe solid improvements by gradually incorporating our devised finer features, which once again demonstrates the utility of our proposed approach.

5.4 Player Identification

We adopt the same training and evaluation strategy as in action recognition to measure the performance of our model on player identification, due to these tasks having the same format, i.e., a sequence of player names involved in the depicted action; Fig. 5 has results. Resembling observations in the previous subsection, we find the quality of identified player names increases as we add more features and our full approach (top row) once again is the best performer. It also is seen that the results on all metrics are much worse than those of action recognition, cf., Table 4. To explore this discrepancy, we study some failure cases in the images along the top of Fig. 5. It is seen that failure can be mostly attributed to blur, occlusion from unrelated regions and otherwise missing decisive information.

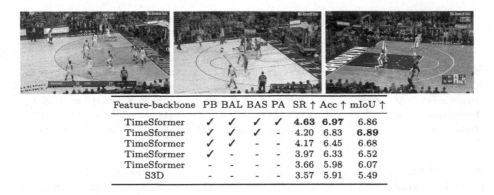

Feature-backbone	PB	BAL	BAS	PA	SR ↑	Acc ↑	mIoU ↑
TimeSformer	✓	✓	✓	✓	**4.63**	**6.97**	6.86
TimeSformer	✓	✓	✓	-	4.20	6.83	**6.89**
TimeSformer	✓	✓	-	-	4.17	6.45	6.68
TimeSformer	✓	-	-	-	3.97	6.33	6.52
TimeSformer	-	-	-	-	3.66	5.98	6.07
S3D	-	-	-	-	3.57	5.91	5.49

Fig. 5. (Top) Visual explanations revealing difficulty in player identification. Left: Although our detector captures the ball and player correctly, the face, jersey and size of the key player are barely recognizable due to blur. Middle: The detected player area is crowded and the ball handler is occluded by defenders. Right: A case where the ball is missing; thus, the model cannot find decisive information on the key player. (Bottom) Player identification results in percentage (%) with our full approach and ablations on choice of features.

6   Conclusion

In this work, we create a large-scale sports video dataset (NSVA) supporting multiple tasks: video captioning, action recognition and player identification. We propose a unified model to tackle all tasks and outperform the state of the art by a large margin on the video captioning task. The creation of NSVA only relies on webly data and needs no extra annotation. We believe NSVA can fill the opening for a benchmark in fine-grained sports video captioning, and potentially stimulate the application of automatic score keeping.

The bottleneck of our model is player identification, which we deem the most challenging task in NSVA. To this end, a better algorithm is needed, e.g., opportunistic player recognition when visibility allows, with subsequent tracking for fuller inference of basketball activities. There also are two additional directions we will explore: (1) We will investigate more advanced video feature representations (e.g., Video Swin transformer [29]) on NSVA and compare to TimeSformer. (2) Prefix Multi-task learning [23] has been proposed to learn several tasks in one model. Ideally, a model can benefit from learning to solve all tasks and gain extra performance boost on each task. We will investigate NSVA in the Prefix Multi-task learning setting with our task head.

Acknowlegement. The authors thank Professor Adriana Kovashka for meaningful discussions in the early stages and Professor Hui Jiang for proofreading and valuable feedback. This research was supported in part by a NSERC grant to Richard P. Wildes and a CFREF VISTA Graduate Scholarship to He Zhao.

References

1. Aafaq, N., Akhtar, N., Liu, W., Gilani, S.Z., Mian, A.: Spatio-temporal dynamics and semantic attribute enriched visual encoding for video captioning. In: Proceedings of CVPR (2019)
2. Aafaq, N., Mian, A., Liu, W., Gilani, S.Z., Shah, M.: Video description: a survey of methods, datasets, and evaluation metrics. ACM Comput. Surv. **52**(6), 1–37 (2019)
3. Banerjee, S., Lavie, A.: METEOR: an automatic metric for MT evaluation with improved correlation with human judgments. In: Proceedings of ACL (2005)
4. Bertasius, G., Wang, H., Torresani, L.: Is space-time attention all you need for video understanding. In: Proceedings of ICML (2021)
5. Bi, J., Luo, J., Xu, C.: Procedure planning in instructional videos via contextual modeling and model-based policy learning. In: Proceedings of ICCV (2021)
6. Brown, T., et al.: Language models are few-shot learners. In: NeurIPS (2020)
7. Caba Heilbron, F., Escorcia, V., Ghanem, B., Carlos Niebles, J.: ActivityNet: a large-scale video benchmark for human activity understanding. In: Proceedings of CVPR (2015)
8. Carion, N., Massa, F., Synnaeve, G., Usunier, N., Kirillov, A., Zagoruyko, S.: End-to-end object detection with transformers. In: Vedaldi, A., Bischof, H., Brox, T., Frahm, J.-M. (eds.) ECCV 2020. LNCS, vol. 12346, pp. 213–229. Springer, Cham (2020). https://doi.org/10.1007/978-3-030-58452-8_13
9. Carreira, J., Zisserman, A.: Quo vadis, action recognition? A new model and the Kinetics dataset. In: Proceedings of CVPR (2017)
10. Chang, C.-Y., Huang, D.-A., Xu, D., Adeli, E., Fei-Fei, L., Niebles, J.C.: Procedure planning in instructional videos. In: Vedaldi, A., Bischof, H., Brox, T., Frahm, J.-M. (eds.) ECCV 2020. LNCS, vol. 12356, pp. 334–350. Springer, Cham (2020). https://doi.org/10.1007/978-3-030-58621-8_20
11. Chen, D., Dolan, W.: Collecting highly parallel data for paraphrase evaluation. In: Proceedings of ACL (2011)
12. Chen, S., Song, Y., Zhao, Y., Qiu, J., Jin, Q., Hauptmann, A.G.: RUC+CMU: system report for dense captioning events in videos. CoRR abs/1806.08854 (2018)
13. Damen, D., et al.: Scaling egocentric vision: the EPIC-KITCHENS dataset. In: Ferrari, V., Hebert, M., Sminchisescu, C., Weiss, Y. (eds.) ECCV 2018. LNCS, vol. 11208, pp. 753–771. Springer, Cham (2018). https://doi.org/10.1007/978-3-030-01225-0_44
14. Devlin, J., Chang, M.W., Lee, K., Toutanova, K.: BERT: pre-training of deep bidirectional transformers for language understanding. In: Proceedings of NAACL (2019)
15. Dosovitskiy, A., et al.: An image is worth 16 × 16 words: transformers for image recognition at scale. In: ICLR (2021)
16. Feichtenhofer, C., Fan, H., Malik, J., He, K.: SlowFast networks for video recognition. In: Proceedings of ICCV (2019)
17. Isola, P., Zhu, J.Y., Zhou, T., Efros, A.A.: Image-to-image translation with conditional adversarial networks. In: Proceedings of CVPR (2017)
18. Jhamtani, H., Gangal, V., Hovy, E., Neubig, G., Berg-Kirkpatrick, T.: Learning to generate move-by-move commentary for chess games from large-scale social forum data. In: Proceedings of ACL (2018)
19. Jocher, G., et al.: YOLOv5:v6.0 (2021). https://doi.org/10.5281/zenodo.5563715

20. Kay, W., et al.: The Kinetics human action video dataset. arXiv preprint arXiv:1705.06950 (2017)
21. Krishna, R., Hata, K., Ren, F., Fei-Fei, L., Niebles, J.C.: Dense-captioning events in videos. In: Proceedings ICCV (2017)
22. Kuehne, H., Arslan, A., Serre, T.: The language of actions: recovering the syntax and semantics of goal-directed human activities. In: Proceedings of CVPR (2014)
23. Li, X.L., Liang, P.: Prefix-tuning: optimizing continuous prompts for generation. In: Proceedings of ACL (2021)
24. Li, Y., Li, Y., Vasconcelos, N.: RESOUND: towards action recognition without representation bias. In: Ferrari, V., Hebert, M., Sminchisescu, C., Weiss, Y. (eds.) ECCV 2018. LNCS, vol. 11210, pp. 520–535. Springer, Cham (2018). https://doi.org/10.1007/978-3-030-01231-1_32
25. Lin, C.Y.: ROUGE: a package for automatic evaluation of summaries. In: Text Summarization Branches Out, pp. 74–81 (2004)
26. Lin, J., Gan, C., Han, S.: TSM: temporal shift module for efficient video understanding. In: Proceedings of ICCV (2019)
27. Lin, T.-Y., et al.: Microsoft COCO: common objects in context. In: Fleet, D., Pajdla, T., Schiele, B., Tuytelaars, T. (eds.) ECCV 2014. LNCS, vol. 8693, pp. 740–755. Springer, Cham (2014). https://doi.org/10.1007/978-3-319-10602-1_48
28. Liu, Z., et al.: Swin transformer: hierarchical vision transformer using shifted windows. In: Proceedings of ICCV (2021)
29. Liu, Z., et al.: Video swin transformer. In: Proceedings of CVPR (2022)
30. Lu, W.L., Ting, J.A., Little, J.J., Murphy, K.P.: Learning to track and identify players from broadcast sports videos. IEEE Trans. Pattern Anal. Mach. Intell. **35**(7), 1704–1716 (2013)
31. Lu, W.L., Ting, J.A., Murphy, K.P., Little, J.J.: Identifying players in broadcast sports videos using conditional random fields. In: proceedings of CVPR (2011)
32. Luo, H., et al.: UniVL: a unified video and language pre-training model for multimodal understanding and generation. CoRR abs/2002.06353 (2020)
33. Medress, M.F., et al.: Speech understanding systems: report of a steering committee. Artif. Intell. **9**(3), 307–316 (1977)
34. Miech, A., Zhukov, D., Alayrac, J.B., Tapaswi, M., Laptev, I., Sivic, J.: HowTo100M: learning a text-video embedding by watching hundred million narrated video clips. In: Proceedings of CVPR (2019)
35. NBA: Official website. http://www.nba.com/
36. Pan, B., et al.: Spatio-temporal graph for video captioning with knowledge distillation. In: Proceedings of CVPR (2020)
37. Papineni, K., Roukos, S., Ward, T., Zhu, W.J.: BLEU: a method for automatic evaluation of machine translation. In: Proceedings of ACL (2002)
38. Park, J.S., Darrell, T., Rohrbach, A.: Identity-aware multi-sentence video description. In: Vedaldi, A., Bischof, H., Brox, T., Frahm, J.-M. (eds.) ECCV 2020. LNCS, vol. 12366, pp. 360–378. Springer, Cham (2020). https://doi.org/10.1007/978-3-030-58589-1_22
39. Pei, W., Zhang, J., Wang, X., Ke, L., Shen, X., Tai, Y.W.: Memory-attended recurrent network for video captioning. In: Proceedings of CVPR (2019)
40. Qi, M., Wang, Y., Li, A., Luo, J.: Sports video captioning via attentive motion representation and group relationship modeling. IEEE Trans. Circ. Syst. Video Technol. **30**(8), 2617–2633 (2019)
41. Radford, A., et al.: Learning transferable visual models from natural language supervision. In: Proceedings of ICML (2021)

42. Shao, D., Zhao, Y., Dai, B., Lin, D.: FineGym: a hierarchical video dataset for fine-grained action understanding. In: Proceedings of CVPR (2020)
43. Sharma, P., Ding, N., Goodman, S., Soricut, R.: Conceptual captions: a cleaned, hypernymed, image alt-text dataset for automatic image captioning. In: Proceedings of ACL (2018)
44. Shi, B., Ji, L., Niu, Z., Duan, N., Zhou, M., Chen, X.: Learning semantic concepts and temporal alignment for narrated video procedural captioning. In: Proceedings of MM (2020)
45. Soomro, K., Zamir, A.R., Shah, M.: UCF101: a dataset of 101 human actions classes from videos in the wild. arXiv preprint arXiv:1212.0402 (2012)
46. Strudel, R., Garcia, R., Laptev, I., Schmid, C.: Segmenter: transformer for semantic segmentation. In: Proceedings of ICCV (2021)
47. Sun, C., Myers, A., Vondrick, C., Murphy, K., Schmid, C.: VideoBERT: a joint model for video and language representation learning. In: Proceedings of ICCV (2019)
48. Vaswani, A., et al.: Attention is all you need. In: NeurIPS (2017)
49. Vedantam, R., Lawrence Zitnick, C., Parikh, D.: CIDER: consensus-based image description evaluation. In: Proceedings of CVPR (2015)
50. Venugopalan, S., Xu, H., Donahue, J., Rohrbach, M., Mooney, R., Saenko, K.: Translating videos to natural language using deep recurrent neural networks. In: Proceedings of NAACL (2015)
51. Wang, L., et al.: Temporal segment networks: towards good practices for deep action recognition. In: Leibe, B., Matas, J., Sebe, N., Welling, M. (eds.) ECCV 2016. LNCS, vol. 9912, pp. 20–36. Springer, Cham (2016). https://doi.org/10.1007/978-3-319-46484-8_2
52. Xie, S., Sun, C., Huang, J., Tu, Z., Murphy, K.: Rethinking spatiotemporal feature learning: speed-accuracy trade-offs in video classification. In: Ferrari, V., Hebert, M., Sminchisescu, C., Weiss, Y. (eds.) ECCV 2018. LNCS, vol. 11219, pp. 318–335. Springer, Cham (2018). https://doi.org/10.1007/978-3-030-01267-0_19
53. Xu, J., Mei, T., Yao, T., Rui, Y.: MSR-VTT: a large video description dataset for bridging video and language. In: Proceedings of CVPR (2016)
54. Yan, Y., et al.: Fine-grained video captioning via graph-based multi-granularity interaction learning. IEEE Trans. Pattern Anal. Mach. Intell. 44(2), 666–683 (2022)
55. Yao, L., et al.: Describing videos by exploiting temporal structure. In: Proceedings of ICCV (2015)
56. Yehao, L., Yingwei, P., Jingwen, C., Ting, Y., Tao, M.: X-modaler: a versatile and high-performance codebase for cross-modal analytics. In: Proceedings of MM (2021)
57. Yu, H., Cheng, S., Ni, B., Wang, M., Zhang, J., Yang, X.: Fine-grained video captioning for sports narrative. In: Proceedings of CVPR (2018)
58. Zhang, C., Gupta, A., Zisserman, A.: Temporal query networks for fine-grained video understanding. In: Proceedings of CVPR (2021)
59. Zhang, J., Peng, Y.: Object-aware aggregation with bidirectional temporal graph for video captioning. In: Proceedings of CVPR (2019)
60. Zhang, Z., et al.: Object relational graph with teacher-recommended learning for video captioning. In: Proceedings of CVPR (2020)
61. Zhao, H., Hadji, I., Dvornik, N., Derpanis, K.G., Wildes, R.P., Jepson, A.D.: P3IV: probabilistic procedure planning from instructional videos with weak supervision. In: Proceedings of CVPR (2022)

62. Zheng, Q., Wang, C., Tao, D.: Syntax-aware action targeting for video captioning. In: Proceedings of CVPR (2020)
63. Zheng, S., et al.: Rethinking semantic segmentation from a sequence-to-sequence perspective with transformers. In: Proceedings of CVPR (2021)
64. Zhu, L., Remantas, K., Curless, B., Seitz, S.M., Kemelmacher-Shlizerman, I.: Reconstructing NBA players. In: Vedaldi, A., Bischof, H., Brox, T., Frahm, J.-M. (eds.) ECCV 2020. LNCS, vol. 12350, pp. 177–194. Springer, Cham (2020). https://doi.org/10.1007/978-3-030-58558-7_11
65. Zhu, Y., et al.: A comprehensive study of deep video action recognition. arXiv preprint arXiv:2012.06567 (2020)

Grounding Visual Representations
with Texts for Domain Generalization

Seonwoo Min[1], Nokyung Park[2], Siwon Kim[3], Seunghyun Park[4],
and Jinkyu Kim[2(✉)]

[1] LG AI Research, Seoul, South Korea
[2] Computer Science and Engineering, Korea University, Seoul, South Korea
jinkyukim@korea.ac.kr
[3] Electrical and Computer Engineering, Seoul National University,
Seoul, South Korea
[4] Clova AI Research, NAVER Corp., Seoul, South Korea

Abstract. Reducing the representational discrepancy between source
and target domains is a key component to maximize the model generalization. In this work, we advocate for leveraging natural language supervision for the domain generalization task. We introduce two modules
to ground visual representations with texts containing typical reasoning of humans: (1) *Visual and Textual Joint Embedder* and (2) *Textual
Explanation Generator*. The former learns the image-text joint embedding space where we can ground high-level class-discriminative information into the model. The latter leverages an explainable model and
generates explanations justifying the rationale behind its decision. To the
best of our knowledge, this is the first work to leverage the vision-and-
language cross-modality approach for the domain generalization task.
Our experiments with a newly created CUB-DG benchmark dataset
demonstrate that cross-modality supervision can be successfully used to
ground domain-invariant visual representations and improve the model
generalization. Furthermore, in the large-scale DomainBed benchmark,
our proposed method achieves state-of-the-art results and ranks 1st in
average performance for five multi-domain datasets. The dataset and
codes are available at https://github.com/mswzeus/GVRT.

Keywords: Domain generalization · Image classification · Textual
explanation · Visual-textual joint embedding

1 Introduction

Machine learning systems assume that in-samples (training) and out-of-samples
(test) are independent and identically distributed – this assumption, however,
rarely holds in real-world scenarios where domain shift often occurs. Various

Supplementary Information The online version contains supplementary material
available at https://doi.org/10.1007/978-3-031-19836-6_3.

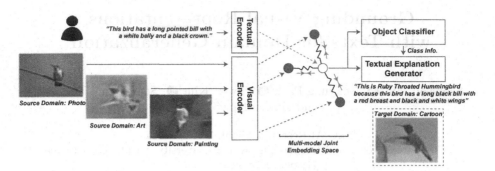

Fig. 1. Our model leverages the text modality by (1) *Visual and Textual Joint Embedder* and (2) *Textual Explanation Generator*. Our model takes advantage of a *pivot* embedding (red circle) from a sentence that describes the class discriminative evidence in a natural language, e.g. a white belly or a pointy beak. Our visual encoder is optimized to produce an embedding (blue-filled circles) that aligns well with the corresponding pivot embedding. The latter further trains the model to justify why it made a certain prediction in a natural language. (Color figure online)

domain generalization (DG) approaches have been introduced to make models generalize well to unseen novel domains. They mainly focus on learning domain-invariant representations so that the model can leverage such invariances during deployment in unseen test domains. In the DG task, samples from target domains are not available during training, thus these approaches are different from domain adaptation (DA), semi-supervised domain adaptation (SSDA), and unsupervised domain generalization (UDA) [10].

Reducing the discrepancy between source and target domains is a key component to maximize the model generalization. This is often achieved by (i) explicitly matching the feature distribution across domains using a similarity metric to measure the distance between each domain or by (ii) using contrastive loss to map the latent representations of positive pairs close together and those of negative pairs further away in the feature space. Such distance-based approaches need to optimize all pairwise sample distances, thus potentially resulting in models that are susceptible to outliers and unfair to subgroups in the imbalanced data – where the classes are not represented equally.

Distribution of training data also limits the networks' understanding of the data. In computer vision models, their opaque reasoning can be simplified to a situation-specific dependence on visible objects in the image. However, instead of learning the true semantics, they often attend to background objects that are salient to the class labels. (e.g. attending to sea for classifying boats). these models will likely behave well in environments similar to those for which it was trained but typically will not generalize well beyond them [9].

To address this issue, we propose a novel approach that grounds visual representations with explicit (verbalized) knowledge from humans about typical reasoning on visual cues (Fig. 1). For example, our model learns to understand the user's utterance ("an elephant is a heavy plant-eating mammal with a pre-hensile trunk, long curved ivory tusks, and large ears.") and ground it in the trained perceptual primitives. To ground (or internalize) explicit knowledge, we use the following two modules: (1) *Visual and Textual Joint Embedder* and (2) *Textual Explanation Generator*. The former aligns the perceptual primitives with the (verbalized) thought process of humans by minimizing the distance between the textual and the visual latent representations. The latter leverages the representational power of explainable models. Regardless of image domains, we train the model to consistently verbalize why it made a certain prediction with natural language, e.g. "This is Ruby Throated Hummingbird because this bird has a long pointed bill with a white belly and a black crown."

To the best of our knowledge, this is the first work to leverage the vision-and-language cross-modality approach for the DG task. For the empirical evaluations under natural language supervision, we created a new benchmark built upon the Caltech UCSD Birds 200-2011 (CUB) dataset [45]. Our quantitative and qualitative experiment results demonstrate that cross-modality supervision can be successfully used to improve the model representational generalization power as well as to justify its visual predictions. Furthermore, we conducted large-scale experiments on the DomainBed benchmark [10], a popular testbed for DG algorithms. The proposed method achieved state-of-the-art results and ranked ranks 1st in average performance for five multi-domain datasets.

2 Related Work

Domain Generalization. Generating domain-invariant representations is the key component in the DG task. Such learned invariances can be leveraged to improve the model generalization to unseen test domains. Of a landmark work, Empirical Risk Minimization (ERM) minimizes the sum of errors across domains, thus matching distributions across different domains [37]. Along this line of work, notable variants have been introduced. DANN [8] and CDANN [22] utilized an adversarial network to minimize unconditional and class-conditional distributional differences across domains, respectively. Such a shared feature space is also optimized by different distance metrics: i.e. maximum mean discrepancy [21], transformed feature distribution distance [25], and covariances (CORAL) [36]. Inter-domain mixup techniques [44, 48, 49] were introduced to perform ERM on linearly interpolated examples from random pairs across domains. SelfReg [15] leveraged the self-supervised learning approaches to address the unstable training, which is often caused by the usage of negative pairs.

In this work, we explore the benefit of grounding visual representations by using cross-modality supervision. We introduce two modules for leveraging texts containing the thought process of humans. First, we train a model in the image-text joint embedding space where we can ground high-level class-discriminative information into the model. Second, we adopt an explainable model that can generate explanations justifying the rationale behind its decision.

Visual and Textual Explanations. Explainability and interpretation of deep neural networks have become increasingly important in various machine learning communities [11,16]. In computer vision, numerous works have explored explaining a target model through visualizations. Early works obtain visual explanations through deconvolutions of layer activations [50] or synthesizing those that maximize the network output [52]. Attention-based approaches try to measure how spatial features formally affect the network output [42,47]. They directly extract salient areas of a given image that the network pays the most attention to produce its output. On the other hand, some works emphasize the importance of justifying the model decision in a human-understandable manner, i.e. in natural language. They adopt an encoder-decoder framework which is usually composed of a convolutional neural network (CNN) as the encoder and a long short-term memory (LSTM) caption generator as the decoder [12,13]. The latter generates textual explanations from the representations produced from the former.

Following this stream of work, we advocate for leveraging the representational power of explainable models for the DG task. Especially, generating textual justifications requires capturing class-discriminative and high-level semantic information. Therefore, we argue that it can help ground domain-invariant visual representations and improve the model generalization.

3   Method

In this paper, we aim to solve the DG problem: i.e. we train a model on a single or multiple source domains $\{\mathcal{S}_1, \mathcal{S}_2, \dots\} \in \mathcal{S}$ and evaluate it on unseen target domains, $\{\mathcal{T}_1, \mathcal{T}_2, \dots\} \in \mathcal{T}$. Formally, we train a model by minimizing the following data-dependent upper bound on the expected worst-case loss [34]:

$$\underset{\theta}{\text{minimize}} \quad \underset{\mathcal{T}:\mathcal{D}(\mathcal{S},\mathcal{T})\leq\rho}{\sup} \quad \mathbb{E}\big[\mathcal{L}_{\text{task}}(\mathcal{S};\theta)\big] \tag{1}$$

where a dissimilarity $D(\mathcal{S},\mathcal{T})$ is used to measure the discrepancy between $\mathcal{S}$ and $\mathcal{T}$ with an arbitrary upper bound ρ. $\mathcal{L}_{\text{task}}$ is a task-specific loss function over a model parameter θ where we use the following cross-entropy loss as we focus on the classification problem:

$$\mathcal{L}_{\text{task}}(\mathcal{S};\theta) = \mathcal{L}_{\text{task}}(\mathbf{y}, \hat{\mathbf{y}}) = -\sum_i y_i \log(\hat{y}_i) \tag{2}$$

where $\mathbf{y}$ is the one-hot vector representing each label's class and $\hat{\mathbf{y}}$ is the softmax distribution produced from the visual feature $\mathbf{x}$.

A key component of the DG task is to address the problem is learning domain-invariant representations that help improve the model generalization. In this work, we advocate for leveraging cross-modality supervision with semantic cues. Specifically, as shown in Fig. 2, we use the following two main modules to ground visual representations with texts containing class-discriminative and high-level semantic information. First, *Visual and Textual Joint Embedder* encourages our visual encoder to produce a latent representation that is aligned with textual

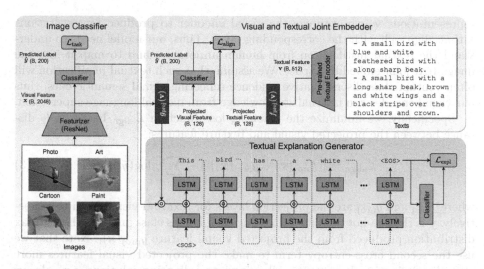

Fig. 2. An overview of our proposed model. An image classifier is trained by minimizing the cross-entropy loss $\mathcal{L}_{\text{task}}$ given images from source domains. Built upon it, our model incorporates two modules for improving DG performance: (i) *Visual and Textual Joint Embedder*, which produces a joint latent representation that is aligned with textual semantics, and (ii) *Textual Explanation Generator*, which generates a class-specific sentence detailing how visual evidence is compatible with a system prediction.

semantics in the joint embedding space. Second, *Textual Explanation Generator* produces a class-discriminative sentence detailing how visual evidence is compatible with a class prediction. Note that both modules are only required during the training phase for grounding the visual encoder. Nevertheless, the latter can be also optionally used during the inference to obtain textual explanation along with a class prediction.

3.1 Visual and Textual Joint Embedder

Our Visual and Textual Joint Embedder aims to learn domain-invariant visual representations from textual explanations. We argue that learning from natural language supervision has potential strength over image-only training approaches, especially for the DG task. In contrast to the vulnerability of CNNs against domain shift, the human visual recognition system generalizes well across domains, e.g. even very young children can easily transfer object concepts from picture books to the real world [7]. Thus, we advocate for using explicit knowledge from humans and we train a model to better align with the thought process of humans via their textual explanations. It ultimately provides more semantically-rich information compared to standard crowd-sourced labeling for image classification.

We use a sentence-level textual encoder, which takes a variable-length sentence and yields a fixed-size latent vector $\mathbf{v}$. Given the *pivot* textual latent representations $\mathbf{v}$, we optimize the visual encoder to produce representations $\mathbf{x}$ that align well with the corresponding pivot. Thus, our model needs to understand the textual justification from human annotators and to map it into the image-text joint embedding space. We assume that such textual justification will often contain class-discriminative evidence reflecting visual semantic cues, thus our visual encoder can internalize knowledge from natural language supervision.

Specifically, we minimize the following loss function $\mathcal{L}_{\text{align}}$ based on l_2 distance between the projected visual and texture features:

$$\mathcal{L}_{\text{align}} = ||f_{\text{proj}}(\mathbf{v}) - g_{\text{proj}}(\mathbf{x})||_2 - \sum_i y_i \log(\tilde{y}_i) \tag{3}$$

where f_{proj} and g_{proj} are the projection layers for text and visual feature, respectively. $\mathbf{y}$ is the one-hot vector representing each label's class and $\tilde{y}_i$ is the softmax distribution produced from the projected visual feature $g_{\text{proj}}(\mathbf{x})_i$. Note that we use the second cross-entropy term to make the projected visual features more class-discriminative. It prevents collapsing into collapsing solutions, e.g., always projecting them to the same point.

Pre-trained (Supervised) Textual Encoder (PTE). One way to obtain the pivot textual latent representation is via pre-trained language models. These pre-trained encoders can be adopted from off-the-shelf sentence-level textual encoders that are often pre-trained with a large-scale dataset. In this work, we adopt the widely used CLIP (i.e. Contrastive Language-Image Pre-Training) model, which can embed texts and images into the joint representation space [30]. The text encoder of CLIP is a $63M$-parameter Transformer architecture with 12-layer, 512-wide, and 8 attention heads [39]. It was jointly trained with a Vision Transformer (ViT)-based image encoder [5] to predict the pairing of texts and images. In this work, we only used the text encoder of the CLIP-ViT-B-32 model, but other pre-trained language models are also applicable.

Self-supervised Textual Encoder (STE). Another way to obtain the pivot textual latent representation is via self-supervision. Since our textual explanation generator justifies the rationale behind the model in the natural language, we can use it as a self-supervised textual encoder. As we will explain in the next subsection, during the training, we iteratively sample a sentence from an LSTM-based explanation generator to compute its training loss. Therefore, it is an intuitive choice to use its last hidden states as a fixed-size latent vector $\mathbf{v}$.

3.2   Textual Explanation Generator

Our textual explanation generator is similar to image captioning models based on an encoder-decoder framework. It contains a two-layer LSTM network that takes high-level features from the visual encoder as input and generates variable-length per-word softmax probabilities. The difference is that it is trained to explain the rationale behind the classifier, reflecting typical visual semantic cues. Since it needs the prediction outputs from the classifier as an input as well, we concatenate the category information with a projected visual feature $g_{\text{proj}}(\mathbf{x})$. The concatenated vector is then used to update the LSTM network for a textual explanation generation.

Specifically, the first LSTM layer takes the previously generated output token o_{t-1} as input and updates its hidden state, producing an output $\mathbf{z_t}$. This output is then fed into the second LSTM layer along with the concatenated vector of projected visual features and prediction outputs. The second LSTM layer yields the per-word softmax probabilities $p(o_t)$. Further, following [12], we use the discriminative sentence generation loss function based on reinforcement learning so that a model learns to generate sentences that are more likely to be class-discriminative. Specifically, we first sample a sentence from the textual explanation generator and we minimize the expectation of the negative reward $-R(\tilde{o})$ over the sampled sentences $\tilde{o} \sim p(o|\mathcal{I},\mathcal{C})$. The probability distribution $p(o|\mathcal{I},\mathcal{C})$ is the model's estimated conditional distribution over descriptions o conditioned on the input image $\mathcal{I}$ and the category $\mathcal{C}$. Concretely, for training our textual explanation generator, we minimize the following loss function $\mathcal{L}_{\text{expl}}$:

$$\mathcal{L}_{\text{expl}} = -\sum_t \log p(o_{t+1}|o_{0:t}, \mathcal{I}, \mathcal{C}) - \mathbb{E}_{\tilde{o} \sim p(o|\mathcal{I},\mathcal{C})}\big[R(\tilde{o})\big] \qquad (4)$$

We use the reward function as $R(\tilde{o}) = p(\mathcal{C}|\tilde{o})$, which is the per-class softmax probabilities over the category $\mathcal{C}$ conditioned on the generated sentence $\tilde{o}$. A more class-discriminative sentence receives a higher reward. Using REINFORCE [46] algorithm, we compute the following expected reward gradient as:

$$\nabla_\theta \mathbb{E}_{\tilde{o} \sim p(o|\mathcal{I},\mathcal{C})}\big[R(\tilde{o})\big] = \mathbb{E}_{\tilde{o} \sim p(o|\mathcal{I},\mathcal{C})}\big[R(\tilde{o})\nabla_\theta \log p(\tilde{o})\big] \qquad (5)$$

Loss Function. To summarize, we train our entire model end-to-end by minimizing the following loss function $\mathcal{L}$:

$$\mathcal{L} = \mathcal{L}_{\text{task}} + \lambda_{\text{align}}\mathcal{L}_{\text{align}} + \lambda_{\text{expl}}\mathcal{L}_{\text{expl}} \qquad (6)$$

where we use hyperparameters λ_{align} and λ_{expl} to control the strengths of each training objective term.

4   Caltech UCSD Birds - Domain Generalization Extension (CUB-DG) Dataset

No previous DG benchmarks provide viable natural language supervision. Thus, in order to thoroughly investigate the effectiveness of the cross-modality supervision in the DG task, we have created a new benchmark built upon the CUB dataset [45]. This dataset contains overall 11,788 images for 200 classes of North American bird species. Ten sentences for each of the images have been previously collected [31], which provides a detailed description of the content of the image, e.g., "this bird has a long pointed bill with a white belly and a black crown."

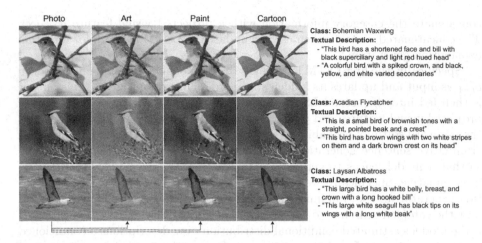

Fig. 3. We create an extended dataset for the DG task based on Caltech UCSD Birds 200-2011 (CUB) dataset. This dataset provides a pair of images and detailed descriptions of the content of the image, e.g. a description "this is a small bird of brownish tones with a straight, pointed beak and a crest" for Acadian Flycatcher. On top of this dataset, we applied off-the-shelf style transfer techniques to obtain images from three other domains: Art, Paint, and Cartoon.

This dataset has been an ideal benchmark for the visual explanation task as sentences are class-specific and class-discriminative.

CUB Dataset for Domain Generalization. Since the CUB dataset is only composed of the Photo domain, we used pre-trained style transfer models to obtain images from three other domains, i.e. Art, Paint, and Cartoon. For the Photo-to-Art translation, we used the CycleGAN [54] *Monet* model which was trained in the absence of paired examples based on adversarial and cycle-consistency losses. For the Photo-to-Paint translation, we used the *Watercolor* neural render model [55]. It imitates painting creation processes by producing a sequence of strokes. For the Photo-to-Cartoon translation, we used a generative adversarial network model which separately identifies surface, structure, and texture representations of cartoons [43].

The generated CUB-DG dataset contains 11,768 sets of images and corresponding text descriptions. Each set illustrates the same content of a bird in four different domains. To evaluate DG algorithms in common experimental protocols, we used the following data split procedures (Fig. S1). We start from the official split of the CUB dataset where the train-validation and test sets consist of 5,994 and 5,794 samples, respectively. We divide the train-validation set into three groups. For the multi-source DG task, we select a different group from each source domain, so that the different domains do not share the *siblings* of the same image. For the single-source DG task, we use all three groups from a source domain. For both tasks, we evaluate DG algorithms on the test set from unseen target domains. Note that the CUB-DG dataset holds evident domain

Table 1. Out-of-distribution test accuracies on the CUB-DG benchmark dataset. We compare with 12 DG algorithms in the multi-source DG setting. Note that we use the validation set (from source domains) for the model selection. *Abbr.* *D*: learning domain-invariant features by matching distributions across different domains, *A*: adversarial learning strategy, *M*: inter-domain mix-up, *T*: learning textual representations. PTE: pre-trained (supervised) textual encoder, STE: self-supervised textual encoder.

Model	D	A	M	T	Target domain				Avg.
					Photo	Cartoon	Art	Paint	
Ours w/ PTE	✓			✓	**74.6**	**64.2**	**52.2**	37.0	**57.0**
Ours w/ STE	✓			✓	74.3	63.9	50.0	**38.1**	56.6
CORAL [36]	✓				72.2	63.5	50.3	35.8	55.4
SD [29]					71.3	62.2	50.8	34.8	54.7
SagNet [26]	✓	✓			67.4	60.7	44.0	34.2	51.6
MixStyle [53]			✓		59.0	56.7	50.3	35.8	50.4
Mixup [49]			✓		67.1	55.9	51.1	27.2	50.3
DANN [8]	✓	✓			67.5	57.0	42.8	30.6	49.5
CDANN [22]	✓	✓			65.3	55.2	43.2	30.5	48.6
VREx [17]	✓				63.9	54.9	38.6	30.1	46.9
ERM [38]					62.5	53.2	37.4	29.0	45.5
ARM [51]					62.3	51.2	38.2	28.4	45.0
GroupDRO [32]	✓				60.9	54.8	36.5	27.0	44.8
IRM [1]					60.6	51.6	36.5	30.3	44.8

shifts such that an ERM model trained only on the Photo domain performs well on the same domain (71.2 accuracy; results not shown) but significantly deteriorates on the other domains (Table 2).

5   Experiments

Multi-Source Domain Generalization Performance. We first look into the multi-source DG task, where a single domain is used as a test domain and the others as training domains in rotation. We compare our model with 11 DG algorithms from DomainBed on our newly created CUB-DG dataset. Compared methods include ERM [38], IRM [1], GroupDRO [32], Mixup [49], CORAL [36], DANN [8], CDANN [22], SagNet [26], MixStyle [53], ARM [51], VREx [17], and SD [29]. We report averaged results across three independent runs. Please refer to the supplementary materials for complete implementation details.

We observe in Table 1 that our proposed models outperform the other recent approaches in all test domains (compare the top two rows vs. others), and the average image recognition accuracy is 1.6–12.2% better than alternatives. While the performance difference between our model variants is marginal, we

Table 2. Out-of-distribution test accuracies in the single-source DG setting where we train our model with a single source domain (rows) and evaluate with other remaining target domains (columns). We compare with SD [29] and report differences between ours in the last row (+ indicates that ours performs better).

SD [29]	Target domain					Ours	Target domain				
	Photo	Cartoon	Art	Paint	Avg.		Photo	Cartoon	Art	Paint	Avg.
Photo	–	42.4	51.3	20.4	38.0	Photo	–	49.1	54.2	19.5	40.9
Cartoon	66.9	–	29.3	34.6	43.6	Cartoon	69.5	–	33.6	36.3	46.5
Art	69.0	33.4		15.7	39.4	Art	75.6	37.9	–	16.3	43.2
Paint	58.0	49.9	30.0	–	46.0	Paint	63.7	57.3	35.6	–	52.2
Avg.	64.6	41.9	36.9	23.6	41.7	Avg.	69.6	48.1	41.1	24.0	45.7
							(+5.0%)	(+6.2%)	(+4.3%)	(+0.5%)	(+4.0%)

also observe that our model with the PTE generally shows better performance than a model with the STE. Therefore, in the following, we focus on analyzing our model with the PTE. Our model can be used together with other approaches (e.g. SD [29] and SWA [4]) that are not based on matching distributions across domains, which would be worth exploring as future work.

Single-Source Domain Generalization Performance. We also evaluate our model in an extreme case for the DG task, i.e. single-source DG. In this setting, we assume that only a single domain is available during the training. We then evaluate with examples from all the other remaining target domains. In Table 2, we compare ours with those of SD [29]. We show differences between ours and SD in the last row (+ indicates that ours performs better) and present them as a heatmap in the Figure S2. Additionally, the full results for comparing our model with six DG algorithms are also available in the Table S1. We excluded algorithms that are inapplicable for the single-source DG setting. We report scores for all source-target combinations, i.e. rows and columns for source and target domains, respectively. The scores are averaged across three independent runs. We observe in Table 2 that ours outperforms alternatives, where the average accuracy is improved by 4.0% than SD [29].

Ablation Studies. To better understand different aspects of our proposed models, we present results from ablation studies. We vary our base model in several directions and measured the performance on the multi-source DG task. We report averaged results across three independent runs.

First, we vary the amount of natural language supervision. While we have assumed *Per-Image* texts are available, obtaining them across different domains may not be easy in real life. Therefore, we introduce a more practical scenario where we only use the same single sentence for all the images within each class. Intuitively, it can be understood as *Per-Class* textual definitions. In Table 3 row (A), we observe that even with the *Per-Class* texts, the cross-modality supervision still enables outperforming all the compared DG algorithms in Table 1.

In Table 3 rows (B), we investigate the importance of each module. We observe that removing the Joint Embedder significantly hurts the DG

Table 3. Results from ablation studies. We vary our base model in several directions and measured the performance on the multi-source DG task.

	Available texts	Joint embedder	Explanation generator	λ_{align}	λ_{expl}	Target domain				Avg.
						Photo	Cartoon	Art	Paint	
Base	Per-Image	Yes	Yes	1.0	1.0	74.6	**64.2**	**52.2**	**37.0**	**57.0**
(A)	Per-class					**74.8**	63.2	51.9	36.1	56.5
(B)		No				68.5	57.2	42.3	29.1	49.3
			No			73.7	63.8	50.2	36.5	56.1
(C)				0.1	1.0	73.0	63.1	50.1	33.0	54.8
				1.0	0.1	73.1	63.8	50.3	36.4	55.9
				0.1	0.1	72.0	61.3	46.7	33.9	53.5

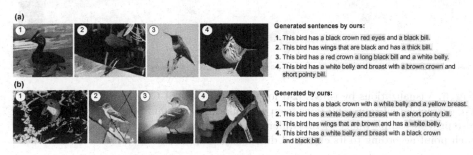

(a)

Generated sentences by ours:

1. This bird has a black crown red eyes and a black bill.
2. This bird has wings that are black and has a thick bill.
3. This bird has a red crown a long black bill and a white belly.
4. This bird has a white belly and breast with a brown crown and short pointy bill.

(b)

Generated by ours:

1. This bird has a black crown with a white belly and a yellow breast.
2. This bird has a white belly and breast with a short pointy bill.
3. This bird has wings that are brown and has a white belly.
4. This bird has a white belly and breast with a black crown and black bill.

Fig. 4. (a) Textual explanations generated by our model. Our model generates plausible sentences that describe fine details about the class-discriminative attributes. We highlight such attributes with colors. (b) We further compare the generated explanations between different same-class images (i.e. Acadian Flycatcher).

performance. The Explanation Generator plays a complementary role in grounding visual representations by justifying model predictions in natural language. In rows (C), we look into the sensitivity to the hyperparameters λ_{align} and λ_{expl}. We can see that the former is more crucial in the training of our proposed model. We provide more extensive results as a heatmap in the Figure S3. Furthermore, in Table S2, we compare the impact of embeddings from various PTEs. While we use CLIP as default, different PTEs also successfully produce domain-invariant representations.

Generated Textual Justification Quality. Next, we evaluate the quality of our generated textual justification. In Fig. 4 (a), we provide sample explanations generated by our model. Note that the images shown in the figure are from unseen target domains. The model was trained in the photo, art, and paint domains and tested in the cartoon domain. Qualitatively, our textual explanation generation module accurately describes fine class-discriminative details such as "red eyes" or "white belly and breast." These are important and domain-invariant visual cues to determine their classes. For a better understanding, we highlight class discriminative attributes in the generated sentences.

Table 4. We report the quality of the generated textual explanations. We rely on standard metrics: BLEU [27], METEOR [18], CIDEr-D [40], and ROUGE_L [23].

Model	BLEU-4	METEOR	CIDEr-D	ROUGE_L
Ours w/ joint embedder	**48.0**	**31.7**	**40.7**	**61.8**
Ours w/o joint embedder	42.9	28.0	28.4	58.1

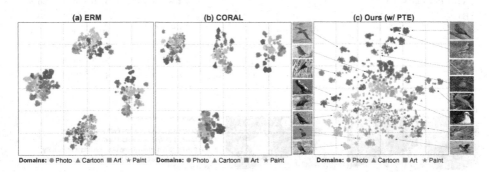

Fig. 5. Visualizations by t-SNE [24] for (a) ERM [38] (b) CORAL [36], and (c) ours. We extract latent representations from each model in the multi-source DG setting. We also provide sample images across different classes. Note that we differently color-coded each point according to its class and differently shaped to its domain.

As shown in Fig. 4 (b), we further provide generated explanations for different images of Acadian Flycatcher (in the Cartoon domain). As we expected, our model describes fine details of the diverse class-discriminative attributes, which are consistent over different same-class images. This may imply that our network's visual representations are grounded by such consistent cues, which helps in providing the model generalization. For a better understanding, we highlight the same attributes with the same color.

We further quantitatively evaluate the quality of generated sentences. We use popular metrics: BLEU [27], METEOR [18], CIDEr-D [40], and ROUGE_L [23]. These metrics are widely used for the automatic evaluation of image captioning models against ground truth. The scores are averaged across three independent runs. We observe in Table 4 that our model with the Visual and Textual Joint Embedder as well as the Textual Explanation Generator obtains higher scores in all metrics than its counterpart.

Qualitative Analysis on the Latent Space. We use t-SNE [24] to compute pairwise similarities of embeddings in the latent space and visualize them in a low dimensional space. In Fig. 5, we provide a comparison of t-SNE visualizations of ERM [38], CORAL [36], and ours. Marker styles and colors indicate the target domain and the ground truth classes, respectively. The more generalizable model should map images belonging to the same class closely even if they are from different domains. We can observe that the baseline models produce scattered multiple clusters for each domain, which confirms that discrepancy between domains

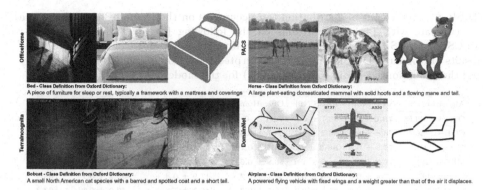

Fig. 6. We use the definition of each class as textual supervision from Oxford English Dictionary [35]. Examples from OfficeHome, PACS, TerraIncognita, and DomainNet on different domains are visualized.

is not successfully reduced (see embeddings of the same domain are clustered closely). Ours is not the case for this. Objects from the same class (or similar attributes) but different domains tend to form a merged cluster, making latent representations close to each other in the high-dimensional space. Additionally, in Figure S4, we provide Grad-CAM [33] visualizations which highlight image regions where the model attends to classify the given object.

Large-Scale Experiments on DomainBed. To further verify the effectiveness of the proposed algotithm, we conduct large-scale experiments on DomainBed [10], which is a unified testbed useful for evaluating DG algorithms. We evaluate our algorithm on the following five multi-domain datasets (i.e. VLCS [6], PACS [19], OfficeHome [41], TerraIncognita [2], and DomainNet [28]) and compare with 14 DG algorithms (i.e. CORAL [36], SagNet [26], MLDG [20], Mixup [49], ERM [38], MTL [3], RSC [14], DANN [8], CDANN [22], VREx [17], ARM [51], IRM [1], GroupDRO [32], and MMD [21]).

The results of compared DG algorithms are excerpted from DomainBed [10]. For each algorithm, they have conducted a random search of 20 hyperparameter choices. Thus, we also conduct a random search of 20 hyperparameter choices from the following: learning rate from $5 \cdot 10^{\mathrm{Uniform}(-5,-4)}$, weight decay from $10^{\mathrm{Uniform}(-4,-3)}$, dropout probability from RandomChoice([0, 0.1, 0.5]), and a batch size from $2^{\mathrm{Uniform}(5,5.5)}$. Other hyperparameters are fixed to the default values. We report averaged results across three independent runs.

Here, we leverage cross-modality supervision from *Per-Class* texts. Specifically, we use definitions from Oxford English Dictionary [35] to ground visual representations. In Table 5, we observe that the proposed algorithm shows state-of-the-art performance, where it ranks 1st in average performance for five multi-domain datasets. Additionally, we provide per-domain results on each dataset in Table S3-S7. We suppose the inferior performance on some datasets is because

Table 5. Average out-of-distribution test accuracies on the DomainBed setting. Here we compare with 14 DG algorithms on the following five multi-domain datastes: VLCS [6], PACS [19], OfficeHome [41], TerraIncognita [2], and DomainNet [28]. The results of compared DG algorithms are excerpted from DomainBed [10]. Note that we use the validation set (from source domains) for the model selection.

Algorithm	VLCS [6]	PACS [19]	OfficeHome [41]	TerraIncognita [2]	DomainNet [28]	Avg
Ours w/ PTE	**79.0 ± 0.2**	85.1 ± 0.3	**70.1 ± 0.1**	48.0 ± 0.2	**44.1 ± 0.1**	**65.2**
CORAL [36]	78.8 ± 0.6	86.2 ± 0.3	68.7 ± 0.3	47.6 ± 1.0	41.5 ± 0.1	64.6
SagNet [26]	77.8 ± 0.5	**86.3 ± 0.2**	68.1 ± 0.1	**48.6 ± 1.0**	40.3 ± 0.1	64.2
MLDG [20]	77.2 ± 0.4	84.9 ± 1.0	66.8 ± 0.6	47.7 ± 0.9	41.2 ± 0.1	63.6
Mixup [49]	77.4 ± 0.6	84.6 ± 0.6	68.1 ± 0.3	47.9 ± 0.8	39.2 ± 0.1	63.4
ERM [38]	77.5 ± 0.4	85.5 ± 0.2	66.5 ± 0.3	46.1 ± 1.8	40.9 ± 0.1	63.3
MTL [3]	77.2 ± 0.4	84.6 ± 0.5	66.4 ± 0.5	45.6 ± 1.2	40.6 ± 0.1	62.9
RSC [14]	77.1 ± 0.5	85.2 ± 0.9	65.5 ± 0.9	46.6 ± 1.0	38.9 ± 0.5	62.7
DANN [8]	78.6 ± 0.4	83.6 ± 0.4	65.9 ± 0.6	46.7 ± 0.5	38.3 ± 0.1	62.6
CDANN [22]	77.5 ± 0.1	82.6 ± 0.9	65.8 ± 1.3	45.8 ± 1.6	38.3 ± 0.3	62.0
VREx [17]	78.3 ± 0.2	84.9 ± 0.6	66.4 ± 0.6	46.4 ± 0.6	33.6 ± 2.9	61.9
ARM [51]	77.6 ± 0.3	85.1 ± 0.4	64.8 ± 0.3	45.5 ± 0.3	35.5 ± 0.2	61.7
IRM [1]	78.5 ± 0.5	83.5 ± 0.8	64.3 ± 2.2	47.6 ± 0.8	33.9 ± 2.8	61.6
GroupDRO [32]	76.7 ± 0.6	84.4 ± 0.8	66.0 ± 0.7	43.2 ± 1.1	33.3 ± 0.2	60.7
MMD [21]	77.5 ± 0.9	84.6 ± 0.5	66.3 ± 0.1	42.2 ± 1.6	23.4 ± 9.5	58.8

they often do not contain enough semantic ques that can be aligned with the textual definitions. For example, it is difficult to recognize "a barred and spotted coat" from the images of the TerraIncognita dataset in Fig. 6.

6 Conclusion

Towards learning more domain-invariant representations, we advocate for leveraging the cross-modality supervision. Specifically, we propose a new approach where class-discriminative natural language sentence is used during training. *Visual and Textual Joint Embedder* encourages learning visual representations that align with the pivot sentence embedding. *Textual Explanation Generator* encourages to consistently verbalize why it made a certain prediction with natural language. The experiments with the newly created CUB-DG dataset and the DomainBed benchmarks show that our model outperforms prior work under the standard DG evaluation setting. Our analysis further shows that the text modality can be successfully used to justify visual predictions as well as improve the model's representational generalization power.

Acknowledgements. This work was supported by supported by the National Research Foundation of Korea grant (NRF-2021R1C1C1009608), Basic Science Research Program (NRF-2021R1A6A1A13044830), and ICT Creative Consilience program (IITP-2022-2022-0-01819).

References

1. Arjovsky, M., Bottou, L., Gulrajani, I., Lopez-Paz, D.: Invariant risk minimization. arXiv preprint arXiv:1907.02893 (2019)
2. Beery, S., Van Horn, G., Perona, P.: Recognition in terra incognita. In: Ferrari, V., Hebert, M., Sminchisescu, C., Weiss, Y. (eds.) ECCV 2018. LNCS, vol. 11220, pp. 472–489. Springer, Cham (2018). https://doi.org/10.1007/978-3-030-01270-0_28
3. Blanchard, G., Deshmukh, A.A., Dogan, U., Lee, G., Scott, C.: Domain generalization by marginal transfer learning. arXiv preprint arXiv:1711.07910 (2017)
4. Cha, J., Cho, H., Lee, K., Park, S., Lee, Y., Park, S.: Domain generalization needs stochastic weight averaging for robustness on domain shifts. arXiv preprint arXiv:2102.08604 (2021)
5. Dosovitskiy, A., et al.: An image is worth 16×16 words: Transformers for image recognition at scale. arXiv preprint arXiv:2010.11929 (2020)
6. Fang, C., Xu, Y., Rockmore, D.N.: Unbiased metric learning: On the utilization of multiple datasets and web images for softening bias. In: Proceedings of the IEEE International Conference on Computer Vision (ICCV), pp. 1657–1664 (2013)
7. Ganea, P.A., Pickard, M.B., DeLoache, J.S.: Transfer between picture books and the real world by very young children. J. Cogn. Dev. 9(1), 46–66 (2008)
8. Ganin, Y., et al.: Domain-adversarial training of neural networks. The journal of machine learning research 17(1), 2030–2096 (2016)
9. Geirhos, R., et al.: ImageNet-trained CNNs are biased towards texture. In: ICLR (2019), https://openreview.net/forum?id=Bygh9j09KX
10. Gulrajani, I., Lopez-Paz, D.: In search of lost domain generalization. arXiv preprint arXiv:2007.01434 (2020)
11. Gunning, D.: Explainable artificial intelligence (xai). In: Defense Advanced Research Projects Agency (DARPA) (2017)
12. Hendricks, L.A., Akata, Z., Rohrbach, M., Donahue, J., Schiele, B., Darrell, T.: Generating visual explanations. In: Leibe, B., Matas, J., Sebe, N., Welling, M. (eds.) ECCV 2016. LNCS, vol. 9908, pp. 3–19. Springer, Cham (2016). https://doi.org/10.1007/978-3-319-46493-0_1
13. Hendricks, L.A., Hu, R., Darrell, T., Akata, Z.: Grounding visual explanations. In: Ferrari, V., Hebert, M., Sminchisescu, C., Weiss, Y. (eds.) ECCV 2018. LNCS, vol. 11206, pp. 269–286. Springer, Cham (2018). https://doi.org/10.1007/978-3-030-01216-8_17
14. Huang, Z., Wang, H., Xing, E.P., Huang, D.: Self-challenging improves cross-domain generalization. In: Vedaldi, A., Bischof, H., Brox, T., Frahm, J.-M. (eds.) ECCV 2020. LNCS, vol. 12347, pp. 124–140. Springer, Cham (2020). https://doi.org/10.1007/978-3-030-58536-5_8
15. Kim, D., Yoo, Y., Park, S., Kim, J., Lee, J.: Selfreg: Self-supervised contrastive regularization for domain generalization. In: Proceedings of the IEEE/CVF International Conference on Computer Vision, pp. 9619–9628 (2021)
16. Kim, S., Yi, J., Kim, E., Yoon, S.: Interpretation of nlp models through input marginalization. arXiv preprint arXiv:2010.13984 (2020)
17. Krueger, D., et al.: Out-of-distribution generalization via risk extrapolation (rex). arXiv preprint arXiv:2003.00688 (2020)
18. Lavie, A., Agarwal, A.: Meteor: An automatic metric for mt evaluation with improved correlation with human judgments. In: EMNLP (2005)
19. Li, D., Yang, Y., Song, Y.Z., Hospedales, T.: Deeper, broader and artier domain generalization. In: Proceedings of the IEEE International Conference on Computer Vision (ICCV) (2017)

20. Li, D., Yang, Y., Song, Y.Z., Hospedales, T.: Learning to generalize: Meta-learning for domain generalization. In: Proceedings of the AAAI Conference on Artificial Intelligence, vol. 32 (2018)
21. Li, H., Pan, S.J., Wang, S., Kot, A.C.: Domain generalization with adversarial feature learning. In: Proceedings of the IEEE Conference on Computer Vision and Pattern Recognition (CVPR), pp. 5400–5409 (2018)
22. Li, Y., et al.: Deep domain generalization via conditional invariant adversarial networks. In: Ferrari, V., Hebert, M., Sminchisescu, C., Weiss, Y. (eds.) ECCV 2018. LNCS, vol. 11219, pp. 647–663. Springer, Cham (2018). https://doi.org/10.1007/978-3-030-01267-0_38
23. Lin, C.Y.: Rouge: A package for automatic evaluation of summaries. In: Text Summarization Branches Out, pp. 74–81 (2004)
24. Van der Maaten, L., Hinton, G.: Visualizing data using t-sne. J. Mach. Learn. Res. 9(11), 2579–2605 (2008)
25. Muandet, K., Balduzzi, D., Schölkopf, B.: Domain generalization via invariant feature representation. In: Proceedings of the International Conference on Machine Learning (ICML), pp. 10–18. PMLR (2013)
26. Nam, H., et al.: Reducing domain gap by reducing style bias. In: CVPR (2021)
27. Papineni, K., Roukos, S., Ward, T., Zhu, W.J.: Bleu: a method for automatic evaluation of machine translation. In: ACL (2002)
28. Peng, X., Bai, Q., Xia, X., Huang, Z., Saenko, K., Wang, B.: Moment matching for multi-source domain adaptation. In: Proceedings of the IEEE International Conference on Computer Vision (ICCV), pp. 1406–1415 (2019)
29. Pezeshki, M., Kaba, S.O., Bengio, Y., Courville, A., Precup, D., Lajoie, G.: Gradient starvation: A learning proclivity in neural networks. arXiv preprint arXiv:2011.09468 (2020)
30. Radford, A., et al.: Learning transferable visual models from natural language supervision. arXiv preprint arXiv:2103.00020 (2021)
31. Reed, S., Akata, Z., Lee, H., Schiele, B.: Learning deep representations of fine-grained visual descriptions. In: Proceedings of the IEEE Conference on Computer Vision and Pattern Recognition, pp. 49–58 (2016)
32. Sagawa, S., Koh, P.W., Hashimoto, T.B., Liang, P.: Distributionally robust neural networks for group shifts: On the importance of regularization for worst-case generalization. arXiv preprint arXiv:1911.08731 (2019)
33. Selvaraju, R.R., Cogswell, M., Das, A., Vedantam, R., Parikh, D., Batra, D.: Gradcam: Visual explanations from deep networks via gradient-based localization. In: ICCV, pp. 618–626 (2017)
34. Sinha, A., Namkoong, H., Volpi, R., Duchi, J.: Certifying some distributional robustness with principled adversarial training. In: ICLR (2017)
35. Stevenson, A.: Oxford dictionary of English. Oxford University Press, USA (2010)
36. Sun, B., Saenko, K.: Deep CORAL: Correlation alignment for deep domain adaptation. In: Hua, G., Jégou, H. (eds.) ECCV 2016. LNCS, vol. 9915, pp. 443–450. Springer, Cham (2016). https://doi.org/10.1007/978-3-319-49409-8_35
37. Vapnik, V.: Statistical learning theory new york. Wiley, NY (1998)
38. Vapnik, V.N.: An overview of statistical learning theory. IEEE Trans. Neural Netw. 10(5), 988–999 (1999)
39. Vaswani, A., et al.: Attention is all you need. In: Advances in Neural Information Processing Systems, pp. 5998–6008 (2017)
40. Vedantam, R., Lawrence Zitnick, C., Parikh, D.: Cider: Consensus-based image description evaluation. In: ICCV (2015)

41. Venkateswara, H., Eusebio, J., Chakraborty, S., Panchanathan, S.: Deep hashing network for unsupervised domain adaptation. In: Proceedings of the IEEE Conference on Computer Vision and Pattern Recognition, pp. 5018–5027 (2017)
42. Wang, D., Devin, C., Cai, Q.Z., Yu, F., Darrell, T.: Deep object centric policies for autonomous driving. In: ICRA (2019)
43. Wang, X., Yu, J.: Learning to cartoonize using white-box cartoon representations. In: Proceedings of the IEEE/CVF Conference on Computer Vision and Pattern Recognition, pp. 8090–8099 (2020)
44. Wang, Y., Li, H., Kot, A.C.: Heterogeneous domain generalization via domain mixup. In: ICASSP 2020–2020 IEEE International Conference on Acoustics, Speech and Signal Processing (ICASSP), pp. 3622–3626. IEEE (2020)
45. Welinder, P., et al.: Caltech-UCSD Birds 200. Tech. Rep. CNS-TR-2010-001, California Institute of Technology (2010)
46. Williams, R.J.: Simple statistical gradient-following algorithms for connectionist reinforcement learning. Mach. Learn. **8**(3), 229–256 (1992)
47. Wu, J., Mooney, R.J.: Faithful multimodal explanation for visual question answering. arXiv preprint arXiv:1809.02805 (2018)
48. Xu, M., et al.: Adversarial domain adaptation with domain mixup. In: Proceedings of the AAAI Conference on Artificial Intelligence, vol. 34, pp. 6502–6509 (2020)
49. Yan, S., Song, H., Li, N., Zou, L., Ren, L.: Improve unsupervised domain adaptation with mixup training. arXiv preprint arXiv:2001.00677 (2020)
50. Zeiler, M.D., Fergus, R.: Visualizing and understanding convolutional networks. In: Fleet, D., Pajdla, T., Schiele, B., Tuytelaars, T. (eds.) ECCV 2014. LNCS, vol. 8689, pp. 818–833. Springer, Cham (2014). https://doi.org/10.1007/978-3-319-10590-1_53
51. Zhang, M., Marklund, H., Gupta, A., Levine, S., Finn, C.: Adaptive risk minimization: A meta-learning approach for tackling group shift. arXiv preprint arXiv:2007.02931 (2020)
52. Zhou, B., Khosla, A., Lapedriza, A., Oliva, A., Torralba, A.: Learning deep features for discriminative localization. In: CVPR, pp. 2921–2929 (2016)
53. Zhou, K., Yang, Y., Qiao, Y., Xiang, T.: Domain generalization with mixstyle. In: International Conference on Learning Representations (2020)
54. Zhu, J.Y., Park, T., Isola, P., Efros, A.A.: Unpaired image-to-image translation using cycle-consistent adversarial networks. In: Proceedings of the IEEE International Conference on Computer Vision, pp. 2223–2232 (2017)
55. Zou, Z., Shi, T., Qiu, S., Yuan, Y., Shi, Z.: Stylized neural painting. In: Proceedings of the IEEE/CVF Conference on Computer Vision and Pattern Recognition, pp. 15689–15698 (2021)

Bridging the Visual Semantic Gap in VLN via Semantically Richer Instructions

Joaquín Ossandón(✉) (ID), Benjamín Earle (ID), and Álvaro Soto (ID)

Pontificia Universidad Católica de Chile, Santiago, Chile
{jiossandon,biearle}@uc.cl, asoto@ing.puc.cl

Abstract. The Visual-and-Language Navigation (VLN) task requires understanding a textual instruction to navigate a natural indoor environment using only visual information. While this is a trivial task for most humans, it is still an open problem for AI models. In this work, we hypothesize that poor use of the visual information available is at the core of the low performance of current models. To support this hypothesis, we provide experimental evidence showing that state-of-the-art models are not severely affected when they receive just limited or even no visual data, indicating a strong overfitting to the textual instructions. To encourage a more suitable use of the visual information, we propose a new data augmentation method that fosters the inclusion of more explicit visual information in the generation of textual navigational instructions. Our main intuition is that current VLN datasets include textual instructions that are intended to inform an expert navigator, such as a human, but not a beginner visual navigational agent, such as a randomly initialized DL model. Specifically, to bridge the visual semantic gap of current VLN datasets, we take advantage of metadata available for the Matterport3D dataset that, among others, includes information about object labels that are present in the scenes. Training a state-of-the-art model with the new set of instructions increase its performance by 8% in terms of success rate on unseen environments, demonstrating the advantages of the proposed data augmentation method.

Keywords: Computer vision · Natural language processing · Navigation · VLN · Data augmentation

1 Introduction

The ability of a robot to receive an instruction in natural language and navigate in unknown environments has been an attractive research topic in recent years [7,15,16,22,24,28]. In particular, the Visual-and-Language Navigation (VLN) task [1] proposes that an agent can follow a textual instruction such as *"Go up*

Supplementary Information The online version contains supplementary material available at https://doi.org/10.1007/978-3-031-19836-6_4.

the stairs, turn right, and stop right at the left of the table", and use it to navigate a natural indoor environment from a starting to a goal position using only visual information. In spite of current advances in AI, this task, that results trivial for most humans, it is still out of reach for autonomous robots. As an example, under current benchmarks [25], state-of-the-art AI models based on Deep Learning (DL) do not reach the intended goal position more than 65% of the time [12].

There are several reasons that can help to explain the low performance of current models to face the VLN task [25]. Among them, we believe that lack of a proper visual understanding of the environment is a key factor. In effect, humans actively use relevant views of the environment to identify visual semantic information such as navigational cues, objects, scenes, or other situations, however, current AI models focus their operation on identifying relevant correlations between the textual instructions and visual data present in the training set [17]. As a consequence, current VLN models exhibit limited generalization capabilities, leading to a large drop in performance when they are tested in unseen environments [7,22,25].

In effect, today there is abundant experimental evidence indicating that current DL based models operate as associative memory engines triggered by superficial data correlations [2,3,10], fostering the detection of direct stimulus-response associations. Indeed, given enough parameters, DL models are able to memorize arbitrary noisy data [26]. In the case of VLN, this problem leads to a poor use of the visual information. As a consequence, instead of unveiling the richness of the visual world, DL models limit their operation to memorize low level correlations between textual and visual data. Even worse, in several cases, models ignore completely the visual information, learning a direct mapping between the textual instructions and robot action.

To support the previous observation, as a first contribution of this work, we provide experimental evidence indicating that current VLN models do not make a suitable use of the visual information available about the environment. Specifically, we demonstrate that when we provide to the model just limited or even no visual data, the model exhibits just a slight drop in performance, showing that their operation is heavily biased to the use of textual instructions.

The previous observation motivates our main research question: how can we contribute to improve the use visual information in VLN models?. While the answer to this question is manifold, in this work we focus our contribution to the generation of more suitable training data. Specifically, we believe that a relevant problem of current VLN datasets is that, during their generation, the humans providing the textual instructions assume that they are intended for an expert navigator, as an example, another human. We believe that this scheme leads to the generation of high level textual instructions, where it is hardly complex to extract meaningful visual cues to inform a beginner visual navigational agent, such as a randomly initialized DL model. As a consequence, we believe that the data generation for a beginner should include a more detailed description of the visual world around the agent.

To bridge the visual semantic gap of current VLN datasets, we present a new data augmentation method that fosters the inclusion of more explicit visual information in the generation of textual navigational instructions. To do this, we resort to object labels present in the metadata available for the Matterport3D dataset[1] that we refer here as Matterport3DMeta. Using this data, we propose new semantically richer natural language instructions for the Room-to-Room (R2R) dataset [1] that are generated with an improved version of the Speaker-Follower model presented in [7]. Specifically, we use scene objects and crafted instructions created with a set of rules that we encode to feed a set of auxiliary visual tasks. As a main finding, the resulting navigational instructions provide a significant boost in the performance of current VLN models when they are tested in previously unseeing environments.

As a further contribution, after publication, we will make available the semantically enriched dataset generated in this work as well as a set of software tools to generate further data. These tools incorporate modules to access scene nodes in the Matterport3D dataset [4] that include information about relevant objects, their position, size, distance, heading, and elevation. We believe that this is a powerful starting point to use scene metadata to create semantically richer visual navigational instructions.

This work is organized as follows. Section 2 describes the VLN task and current benchmarks. Section 3 reviews relevant previous works. Section 4 presents an experimental setup to highlight the limitations of current VLN models to use visual information. Afterwards, Sect. 5 describes the construction of our visual semantically richer instructions for the VLN task. Finally, Sect. 6 presents our conclusions and future research avenues.

2 Visual-and-Language Navigation Task

During the last decade several studies have been related to the VLN task, however, the visual aspect was discarded due to lack of real images in the proposed problems [1]. In 2017, the Matterport3D dataset [4] was introduced, containing RGB-D building scale scenes of 90 different home environments. Later that year, a new navigation problem was proposed: Room-to-Room (R2R) [1], the first dataset for the Visual-and-Language Navigation task (VLN) on real 3D environments, introducing a Matterport3D based simulator, which simulates its environments with the possibility of navigate trough them. In R2R, 90 different environments from Matterport3D have been divided into training and validation (seen and unseen) splits. There are a total of 7,189 distinct paths (starting point, target point), with 3 distinct human instructions for each, a total of 21,567 navigation instructions with an average of 29 words [1].

We construct over Matterport3DMeta a set of tools named 360-visualization[2] for getting objects and navigable nodes with their intrinsic data for each view, as shown in Fig. 1.

---

[1] https://github.com/niessner/Matterport/tree/master/metadata.
[2] https://github.com/cacosandon/360-visualization.

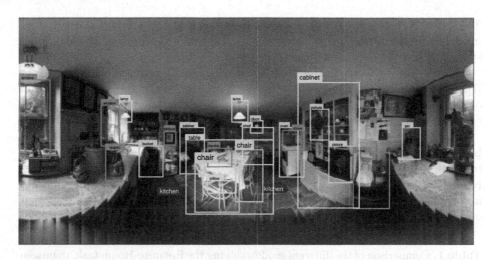

Fig. 1. Objects and viewpoints visualization sampled with `360-visualization` scripts.

2.1 The Visual-and-Language Navigation Task

The task of VLN for an agent is to follow natural language instructions from an initial to a target position through navigation in a real environment, simulated by Matterport3D Simulator [1]. At the beginning of each episode an instruction $\overline{x} = \langle x_1, x_2, .., x_L \rangle$ is given, where L is the instruction length and x_i a word token. The agent observes a RGB image v_0 depending on an initial 3D position, heading ψ_0 and elevation θ_0, resulting in a world state $s_0 = \langle v_0, \psi_0, \theta_0 \rangle$. The agent must execute a sequence of actions $\langle a_0, a_1, .., a_T \rangle$ where each action a_t leads to a new state $s_{t+1} = \langle v_{t+1}, \psi_{t+1}, \theta_{t+1} \rangle$ and generates a new visual panoramic view v_{t+1}. It is important to note that actions are given by the simulator, which are limited according to the node where the agent is located. The episode ends when the agent selects the <STOP> action, and the task is successful if the agent arrives at a location near the target position, recognizing it as the goal.

3 Related Work

VLN task has been the main motivation for many researchers on Computer Vision. Interesting surveys and reviews [9,25] talk about several techniques developed over the baseline architecture proposed by R2R.

They group them on categories such as the inclusion of auxiliary tasks [13, 16,19,21,28], the improvement of navigation and exploration [11,13,14,23,24] and curriculum learning with data augmentation [7,15,22].

Data augmentation has become an essential part of training in various tasks, not only increasing quantity of training data, but also providing more informative data to reduce overfitting, and improve generalization and performance

[6, 18, 20]. On navigation, different approaches have proposed augmenting training instructions [7, 22] but it has been shown that they do not follow human syntax or include relevant information [27].

That's why we focus on this topic, basing our study on the Speaker-Follower [7], which consists of two modules: one that follows instructions (follower) and other that performs data augmentation to feed the training of the follower (speaker), which we improve for generate new semantically richer instructions.

State-of-art leaderboard is summarized in Table 1. VLN-BERT+REM [12] has the highest success rate (SR), followed by SSM [23] and Active Gathering [24]. These models have high overhead costs due to the time and resources required by their complex architectures. We demonstrate that focusing on data augmentation greatly benefits navigation performance without making models even more complex.

Table 1. Comparison of the different models solving the Room-to-Room task, in unseen test set using Single Run.

Model	PL ↓	NE ↓	SPL ↑	SR ↑
Speaker-Follower [7]	14.82	6.62	0.28	0.35
Tactical Rewind [11]	22.08	5.14	0.41	0.54
Self-Monitoring [13]	17.11	5.99	0.32	0.43
Environmental Dropout [22]	11.70	–	0.47	0.51
Regretful-Agent [14]	13.69	5.69	0.40	0.48
ORIST [19]	10.90	4.72	0.51	0.57
VLN-BERT + REM [12]	13.11	3.87	0.59	**0.65**
SSM [23]	20.7	4.32	0.45	0.62
Active Gathering [24]	20.6	4.36	0.4	0.58

4   Models Problem

Aiming to demonstrate models deficits, we experiment in both visual and linguistic areas on the state-of-the-art models, based on [9] analysis. A summary diagram is shown in Fig. 2.

4.1   Visual Area

In order to evaluate the effectiveness of visual components within VLN architectures, it is interesting to know the importance of visual scene information when deciding the next action on navigation through the environment.

We run our experiments over Self-Monitoring [13] and Regretful-Agent [14], because of their public codebase[3],[4]. Each of these architectures were trained in

---

[3] https://github.com/chihyaoma/selfmonitoring-agent/.
[4] https://github.com/chihyaoma/Regretful-Agent.

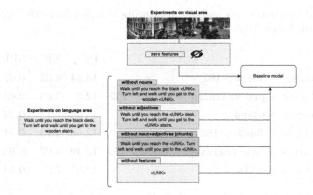

Fig. 2. Experiments diagram. Visual features are replaced with zeros. In the linguistic area, four experiments are performed: without nouns, without adjectives, without nouns+adjectives and without features.

two different conditions. The first condition is the base model, where the visual features are obtained from a pre-trained ResNet-152. The second condition is the replacement of visual features with zeros, i.e., the agent is completely blind.

Because both models are built on top of the Speaker-Follower architecture, they also offer an optional pre-training phase that includes training with synthetic data. This synthetic data contains 178,000 sampled routes with associated instructions generated with the Speaker module [7], the same instructions we improve later in this work. Six experiments evaluated in known (seen) and unknown (unseen) environments were performed, which are shown in Tables 2 and 3.

4.2 Language Area

We also experiment changing the text of the instruction, in order to check which components are relevant for the agent to better decide.

We use spaCy [8], an NLP model used in the industry to obtain text features. Each word of each instruction was classified according to the context, as adjective, noun or other. The Regretful-Agent model was trained by extracting from each instruction: all adjectives, all nouns, all nouns+adjectives and extracting the whole text (i.e. without linguistic features), training the model for a total of 100 h with the 8 experiments, which results are shown in Table 4.

Comparison Metrics. To compare the performance of presented configurations, we use path length (PL), navigation error (NE) and success rate (SR), as proposed in R2R [1]. We also use a new metric called success rate weighted by Path Length (SPL) [13,15,22,28], that measures the success rate normalized by path length.

Table 2. Visual ablation study on Self-Monitoring [13] and Regretful-Agent [14], seen environment with Single Run (not Beam Search).

Model	PL ↓	NE ↓	SPL ↑	SR ↑
Self-Monitoring + `ResNet-152`	13.34	4.02	0.62	0.62
Self-Monitoring + `pre-training` + `ResNet-152`	12.3	3.03	0.63	0.7
Self-Monitoring + `blind`	15.64	7.1	0.23	0.32
Regretful-Agent + `ResNet-152`	12.66	4.18	0.51	0.59
Regretful-Agent + `pre-training` + `ResNet-152`	12.49	3.07	0.63	0.71
Regretful-Agent + `blind`	19.05	7.6	0.14	0.27

Table 3. Visual ablation study on Self-Monitoring [13] and Regretful-Agent [14], unseen environment with Single Run (not Beam Search).

Model	PL ↓	NE ↓	SPL ↑	SR ↑
Self-Monitoring + `ResNet-152`	15.88	6.47	0.27	0.39
Self-Monitoring + `pre-training` + `ResNet-152`	16.27	5.99	0.30	0.42
Self-Monitoring + `blind`	15.86	6.6	0.24	0.35
Regretful-Agent + `ResNet-152`	16.09	5.99	0.30	0.43
Regretful-Agent + `pre-training` + `ResNet-152`	15.75	5.62	0.35	0.47
Regretful-Agent + `blind`	18.8	6.62	0.19	0.36

Table 4. Language ablation study on Self-Monitoring [13] and Regretful-Agent [14], unseen environment with Single Run (not Beam Search). w/means without

Model	PL ↓	SR ↑
Training with real data		
Regretful-Agent *baseline*	16.1	**0.43**
Regretful-Agent w/`nouns`	15.5	0.35
Regretful-Agent w/`adjectives`	14.8	0.42
Regretful-Agent w/`nouns+adjectives`	14.9	0.37
Regretful-Agent w/`all textual features`	18.0	0.25
Training with real data + augmented data		
Regretful-Agent *baseline*	15.8	0.47
Regretful-Agent w/`nouns`	14.8	0.36
Regretful-Agent w/`adjectives`	15.5	**0.48**
Regretful-Agent w/`nouns+adjectives`	13.9	0.39
Regretful-Agent w/`all textual features`	18.0	0.25

4.3   Ablation Studies

When experimenting in the visual area by removing all the visual features we notice a clear difference between seen and unseen environments. In seen environments the difference in success rate is very large (Table 2). While the Self-Monitoring and Regretful-Agent models achieve about 60% of success rate (SR) without pre-training, removing the agent's sight (+ `blind`) greatly reduces its performance (−30%).

In unknown environments the difference is much smaller. We observe that both models without pre-training don't improve by more than 7% SR over the blind model. This demonstrates good memorization but lack of generalization, being visual information almost useless on previously unknown scenes.

When experimenting in the linguistic area, we noticed that when we extract the whole language, it only reaches a 25% SR. This means that 1 out of 4 random walks actually reaches the goal, noting the biases of the R2R dataset, where agents can navigate correctly to the goal point without any instruction.

If we extract the nouns or nouns+adjectives from the instruction, then the model reduces the SR moderately. This explains that many of the instructions are based on prompts such as "turn right" or "walk straight to the bottom", without necessarily reference the environment.

Because of the high-level instructions, removing adjectives increases the SR, indicating that nouns descriptions are actually interfering with the model performance.

We propose to create and train with semantically richer instructions, in order to include more detailed description of the visual environment and then force the agent to use all the available information.

5   Semantically Richer Instructions Proposal

To navigate using vision, we must first learn to follow semantically meaningful instructions that foster the use of visual information. We create simple instructions that are scene-object based, referencing them and their context, enriching over generic non visual instructions like "go straight".

We construct our model over Speaker-Follower, but using only the Speaker module. On Fig. 3 is our complete model. The original Speaker module takes, for each path, the sequence of panoramic views and also the actions sequence (`RIGHT`, `<END>`, `FORWARD`, etc.), and pass them across an encoder module. This encoder gives us an encoded context `ctx`, used for generating each word of the new instruction through an LSTM, which uses also the previous cell and hidden states, as shown in the figure.

On R2R, each path has three instructions. For each, the Speaker module builds the loss as the Negative Log Loss (NLL) between the corresponding word of the instruction and the generated word, as shown on the figure.

Generated instructions on the Speaker module are now being used for almost all state-of-the-art models of VLN task on a pre-training phase. However, it has

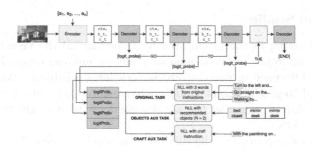

Fig. 3. Speaker with proposed auxiliary tasks.

been shown that they do not follow human syntax, they have orientation problems and do not include relevant information, being incorrect in most cases [27].

Using Matterport3DMeta, we propose to add relevant objects to generated instructions applying two loss auxiliary tasks: objects and crafted instructions, aiming the vision to be mandatory for the agent to navigate. These two are also included in Fig. 3.

5.1   Objects and Crafted Instructions

Object metadata is available on Matterport3DMeta, but it is raw and difficult to use. That's why we created 360-visualization, a script for fetching and visualizing objects and navigable viewpoints on each node, for each heading and elevation.

These objects are the main component of the objects auxiliary task, but we also use them for the generation of crafted instructions.

For a specific path, we generate an atomic instruction for each node on the sequence. Having the current 360° visual image and the next node we can select the best object to reference, following a set of rules. For instance, in Fig. 4 we start with a big painting at the right of the next node, generating the first atomic instruction: "Turn left, walk straight down the left of the painting.". Then, we concatenate all this atomic instructions, generating a new crafted instruction for the selected path.

5.2   Objects Auxiliary Task

For each node of a path sequence, we fetch all objects with 360-visualization and filter them by distance, area, uniqueness and usability (excluding many objects, like "floor" that has large area).

We assign the best N objects to each word of the instructions of that path, matching word index with the closer node index.

For instance, in Fig. 3 we recommend the model to use "bed" and "closet" (N = 2) for the first word.

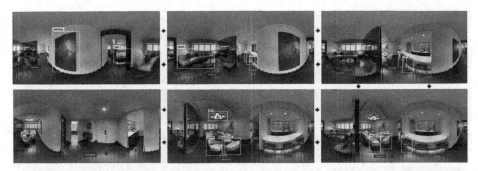

- Walk past the large picture and chair. Walk past the dining room table turn right into the hallway and stop.

- Go straight and pass the bar with the chair/stools then pass the clear glass table with the white chairs and turn right. Wait in that hallway.

- With the painting of the mermaid towards your right, head straight. After passing the counter towards your right, turn right and wait.

- Take a left, walk straight down the left side of the painting. Walk forward. Exit the living room to the dining room. Go out of dining room into the entryway walking with the sofa chair on your left. Stop.

Fig. 4. Crafted instruction example. Panoramic views sequence on top and human instructions + crafted instruction on bottom. Images are sequenced through the arrows. Presented objects and scenes names are sampled from the data.

The objects auxiliary task consists on adding Negative Log Loss between the generated word and the N recommended objects to the final loss. The sum of these losses are weighted by λ, a modifiable parameter.

The final loss on training the Speaker results as follows

$$wordLoss = \sum_{i=0}^{3} NLL\left(log(logit), w_{original_i}\right) + \lambda \sum_{i=0}^{N} NLL\left(log(logit), w_{object_i}\right)$$

A resulting generated instruction with Speaker + objects auxiliary task is shown on Fig. 5.

5.3 Crafted Instructions Auxiliary Task

Having our own crafted instructions, we use them directly on training and also adding a Negative Log Loss between the generated instruction and the crafted instruction, word by word.

The sum of these losses are weighted by β, another modifiable parameter. The final loss for each generated word is

$$wordLoss = \sum_{i=0}^{3} NLL\left(log(logit), w_{original_i}\right) + \beta \cdot NLL\left(log(logit), w_{crafted}\right)$$

5.4 Results and Discussion

After training the Speaker module with auxiliary tasks, we generate instructions based on the same sampled paths as the original augmented dataset with

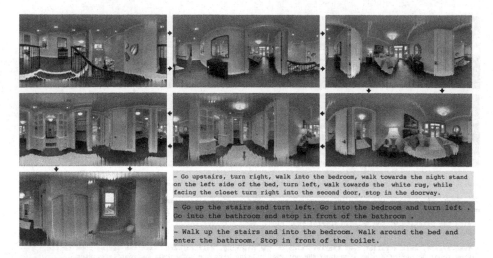

Fig. 5. Objects auxiliary task instruction example. Panoramic views sequence above and human instruction + base speaker instruction + new generated instruction below. Images are sequenced through the arrows.

different values for λ and β, hyperparameters that weigh auxiliary tasks loss. We execute separated auxiliary tasks, because it is redundant information. Crafted instructions used in the crafted instructions auxiliary task use the same objects as the ones we pass directly on the objects auxiliary task.

We then train the Regretful Agent navigation model with the augmented data or crafted instructions directly (Phase I), and finetune it with the original training data (Phase II). Results for seen and unseen environments are on Tables 5 and 6.

Best results are achieved pre-training with instructions generated using objects auxiliary task with $\lambda = 0.5$ or crafted instructions auxiliary task with $\beta = 0.3$, increasing up to 51% the success rate on unseen environment. Using our new augmented instructions the success rate increment is doubled compared using original Speaker module synthetic instructions, this is, +8% versus the baseline model.

We extend the experiments to the HAMT model [5], pre-training with the best settings we got from above. Results are on Table 7. Although we get a lower increase, adding visual information to the instructions is still useful across all models. As future work, we can test with different configurations of the auxiliary tasks to see which dataset generates higher benefits. We make objects and crafted instructions available in `360-visualization`[5] so they can be added to any language model, as we propose with the Speaker module.

The new module with auxiliary tasks have several advantages in the quality of the generated instructions. One example is shown on Fig. 5.

---

[5] https://github.com/cacosandon/360-visualization.

First, it corrects the Speaker module in orientation, since we help the model by indicating which objects to reference in the instruction, relating them with the next node position. For instance, in the figure's sequence the agent must turn right, while the Speaker generates an instruction that wrongly says the opposite.

Second, compared to human instructions we realize that a complex instruction is not necessary, since agent is a beginner on navigation. Humans describe the path in a high level, which makes it even more complicated to extract visual information. Our module generates low-level instructions, describing the best way to orientate another DL model.

At last, generated instructions reference objects that exist in the environment but not in the original instructions, as it does with the word "toilet" at the end of the instruction showed in Fig. 5. The model learned to use objects even though it has never seen them before, nor has any type of information (such as the instruction showed on the figure, which is from the validation set, and therefore, never seen before).

We also demonstrate that the increase of success rate using original data augmentation does not depend on the quality of the Speaker's instructions, but rather the quantity is the main contributor. This means, quantity compensates quality for improving performance (178,300 augmented instructions over 4675 train instructions).

As we mentioned before, using the same 178,300 sampled paths, we also create totally new crafted instructions (Fig. 4) without the need of human instructions in order to use them as pre-training. On Tables 5 and 6 it is shown as "PWIF Crafted Directly". We almost reach the same success rate as the full training (Phases I + II) with human instructions and we exceed base training by 4%.

Table 5. Regretful-Agent [14] pre-training with instructions generated from different models, evaluated on **seen** environments with Single Run (not Beam Search) and original human instructions. PWIF means *Pre-training with instructions from* and AT means *Auxiliary Task*.

Regretful-Agent +		PL ↓	NE ↓	SPL ↑	SR ↑
Without pre-training		12.66	4.18	0.51	0.59
PWIF Speaker base		12.49	3.07	0.63	0.71
PWIF Speaker + Objects AT	$\lambda = 0.3, N = 2$	12.97	3.10	0.62	0.71
PWIF Speaker + Objects AT	$\lambda = 0.5, N = 1$	11.65	3.38	0.61	0.67
PWIF Speaker + Objects AT	$\lambda = 0.5, N = 2$	12.09	2.93	0.65	**0.72**
PWIF Speaker + Objects AT	$\lambda = 0.5, N = 3$	12.80	3.48	0.58	0.67
PWIF Speaker + Objects AT	$\lambda = 0.6, N = 2$	12.07	3.09	0.63	0.70
PWIF Speaker + Crafted AT	$\beta = 0.1$	12.41	3.16	0.62	0.70
PWIF Speaker + Crafted AT	$\beta = 0.2$	11.83	3.29	0.62	0.68
PWIF Speaker + Crafted AT	$\beta = 0.3$	12.24	2.86	0.63	**0.72**
PWIF Speaker + Crafted AT	$\beta = 0.4$	12.16	3.08	0.62	0.70
PWIF Crafted directly		12.50	3.32	0.59	0.67

Table 6. Regretful-Agent [14] pre-training with instructions generated from different models, evaluated on **unseen** environments with Single Run (not Beam Search) and original human instructions. `PWIF` means *Pre-training with instructions from* and `AT` means *Auxiliary Task*.

Regretful-Agent +	PL ↓	NE ↓	SPL ↑	SR ↑
`Without pre-training`	16.09	5.99	0.30	0.43
`PWIF Speaker base`	15.75	5.62	0.35	0.47
`PWIF Speaker + Objects AT` $\lambda = 0.3, N = 2$	15.27	5.39	0.36	0.49
`PWIF Speaker + Objects AT` $\lambda = 0.5, N = 1$	14.66	5.80	0.35	0.46
`PWIF Speaker + Objects AT` $\lambda = 0.5, N = 2$	14.61	5.29	0.39	**0.51**
`PWIF Speaker + Objects AT` $\lambda = 0.5, N = 3$	15.24	5.77	0.34	0.47
`PWIF Speaker + Objects AT` $\lambda = 0.6, N = 2$	15.82	5.46	0.34	0.48
`PWIF Speaker + Crafted AT` $\beta = 0.1$	14.90	5.75	0.35	0.47
`PWIF Speaker + Crafted AT` $\beta = 0.2$	14.37	5.58	0.38	0.48
`PWIF Speaker + Crafted AT` $\beta = 0.3$	15.42	5.52	0.37	0.50
`PWIF Speaker + Crafted AT` $\beta = 0.4$	15.44	5.43	0.36	0.47
`PWIF Crafted directly`	15.97	6.03	0.33	0.46

Table 7. HAMT [5] pre-training with instructions generated from best Speaker configurations (ranked by success rate after pre-training the Regretful Agent), evaluated on **unseen** environments with Single Run (not Beam Search) and original human instructions. `PWIF` means *Pre-training with instructions from* and `AT` means *Auxiliary Task*.

HAMT +	SPL ↑	SR ↑
`Without pre-training`	54.4	48.7
`PWIF Speaker base`	56.3	52.3
`PWIF Speaker + Objects AT` $\lambda = 0.5, N = 2$	**57.4**	52.4
`PWIF Speaker + Crafted AT` $\beta = 0.3$	57.3	**52.6**

We then show that the Speaker module as a instruction generator does not contribute more than our crafted instructions generated based on rules, unless we add the proposed auxiliary tasks, where the performance increase is remarkable.

6   Conclusions

Different methodologies have been developed to improve scene understanding, in order to achieve a better performance in navigation with human interaction. They focus mainly on model architecture, leaving aside the base of the task: the dataset. As we present, navigation agents do not use visual information available on environments for making a decision. Removing visual features generates a slight success rate drop of only 7% on unseen environments, evidencing that the

R2R dataset has instructions that do not reference the context in which agent is situated. This last factor allows agents to execute actions in almost a random manner, reaching the goal anyway.

In addition, these same instructions are too complex and high level, confusing agents that start as beginners on navigation. To bridge the visual semantic gap presented on the datasets, we create new semantically richer instructions.

For this purpose, we use scene objects and crafted instructions to feed a set of auxiliary tasks. The resulting model generates new instructions that help to correct the errors existing in the original instructions, while increase the success rate by 8% in unseen environments when we use them as pre-training, which doubles the increase of the original Speaker. We then demonstrate that the creation of semantically richer instructions that include explicit visual information allows the agent to better learn to navigate.

In order to follow this same line to improve robot navigation, we propose different branches for further research:

- **Own object detection**: We construct our auxiliary task based on available metadata of different environments (Matterport3DMeta). If we want to expand to new environments where this metadata is not available, we must detect objects on our own. Indoor object detection is an unresolved task, which can be improved directly using the same scene objects that we retrieve from raw data.
- **3-phase Curriculum Learning**: We pre-train our model with our semantically richer instructions, and then finetune with the original instructions, which are complex and high level. Starting with an easier task will allow the agent to use environment information progressively. Standing in a random node, we have the 360 ° image, different possible navigation nodes and an atomic instruction. The agent has to decide which node to move to. The agent will learn simpler and shorter instructions that refer to the environment, the basics for starting to execute this tasks on sequence.

Acknowledgments. This work was partially funded by FONDECYT grant 1221425, the National Center for Artificial Intelligence CENIA FB210017, Basal ANID and by ANID through *Beca de Magister Nacional* N° 22210030.

References

1. Anderson, P., et al.: Vision-and-language navigation: interpreting visually-grounded navigation instructions in real environments. In: 2018 IEEE/CVF Conference on Computer Vision and Pattern Recognition (2018)
2. Arpit, D., et al.: A closer look at memorization in deep networks. In: Proceedings of the 34th International Conference on Machine Learning - Volume 70 (2017)
3. Belkin, M., Hsu, D.J., Mitra, P.: Overfitting or perfect fitting? Risk bounds for classification and regression rules that interpolate. In: Advances in Neural Information Processing Systems (2018)
4. Chang, A., et al.: Matterport3D: learning from RGB-D data in indoor environments. In: International Conference on 3D Vision (3DV) (2017)

5. Chen, S., Guhur, P.L., Schmid, C., Laptev, I.: History aware multimodal transformer for vision-and-language navigation. In: NeurIPS (2021)
6. Feng, S.Y., et al.: A survey of data augmentation approaches for NLP. In: Findings of the Association for Computational Linguistics: ACL-IJCNLP 2021 (2021)
7. Fried, D., et al.: Speaker-follower models for vision-and-language navigation. In: Neural Information Processing Systems (NeurIPS) (2018)
8. Honnibal, M., Montani, I.: spaCy 2: natural language understanding with Bloom embeddings, convolutional neural networks and incremental parsing (2017, to appear)
9. Hu, R., Fried, D., Rohrbach, A., Klein, D., Darrell, T., Saenko, K.: Are you looking? Grounding to multiple modalities in vision-and-language navigation. In: Proceedings of the 57th Annual Meeting of the Association for Computational Linguistics (2019)
10. Jo, J., Bengio, Y.: Measuring the tendency of CNNs to learn surface statistical regularities. arXiv (2017)
11. Ke, L., et al.: Tactical rewind: self-correction via backtracking in vision-and-language navigation. In: Proceedings of the IEEE Conference on Computer Vision and Pattern Recognition (CVPR) (2019)
12. Liu, C., Zhu, F., Chang, X., Liang, X., Ge, Z., Shen, Y.D.: Vision-language navigation with random environmental mixup. In: Proceedings of the IEEE/CVF International Conference on Computer Vision (ICCV) (2021)
13. Ma, C.Y., et al.: Self-monitoring navigation agent via auxiliary progress estimation. In: Proceedings of the International Conference on Learning Representations (ICLR) (2019)
14. Ma, C.Y., Wu, Z., AlRegib, G., Xiong, C., Kira, Z.: The regretful agent: heuristic-aided navigation through progress estimation. In: Proceedings of the IEEE Conference on Computer Vision and Pattern Recognition (CVPR) (2019)
15. Majumdar, A., Shrivastava, A., Lee, S., Anderson, P., Parikh, D., Batra, D.: Improving vision-and-language navigation with image-text pairs from the web. In: Vedaldi, A., Bischof, H., Brox, T., Frahm, J.-M. (eds.) ECCV 2020. LNCS, vol. 12351, pp. 259–274. Springer, Cham (2020). https://doi.org/10.1007/978-3-030-58539-6_16
16. Manterola, R.: Enhanced vision-language navigation by using scene recognition auxiliary task (2021)
17. Marcus, G.: Deep learning: a critical appraisal. arXiv (2018)
18. Mikołajczyk, A., Grochowski, M.: Data augmentation for improving deep learning in image classification problem. In: 2018 International Interdisciplinary PhD Workshop (IIPhDW) (2018)
19. Qi, Y., et al.: The road to know-where: an object-and-room informed sequential BERT for indoor vision-language navigation. In: ICCV (2021)
20. Shorten, C., Khoshgoftaar, T.: A survey on image data augmentation for deep learning. J. Big Data (2019)
21. Tan, H., Bansal, M.: LXMERT: learning cross-modality encoder representations from transformers. In: Proceedings of the 2019 Conference on Empirical Methods in Natural Language Processing (2019)
22. Tan, H., Yu, L., Bansal, M.: Learning to navigate unseen environments: back translation with environmental dropout. In: Proceedings of the 2019 Conference of the North American Chapter of the Association for Computational Linguistics: Human Language Technologies (2019)

23. Wang, H., Wang, W., Liang, W., Xiong, C., Shen, J.: Structured scene memory for vision-language navigation. In: 2021 IEEE/CVF Conference on Computer Vision and Pattern Recognition (CVPR) (2021)

24. Wang, H., Wang, W., Shu, T., Liang, W., Shen, J.: Active visual information gathering for vision-language navigation. In: Vedaldi, A., Bischof, H., Brox, T., Frahm, J.-M. (eds.) ECCV 2020. LNCS, vol. 12367, pp. 307–322. Springer, Cham (2020). https://doi.org/10.1007/978-3-030-58542-6_19

25. Wu, W., Chang, T., Li, X.: Visual-and-language navigation: a survey and taxonomy. arXiv (2021)

26. Zhang, C., Bengio, S., Hardt, M., Recht, B., Vinyals, O.: Understanding deep learning requires rethinking generalization. In: ICLR (2017)

27. Zhao, M., et al.: On the evaluation of vision-and-language navigation instructions. In: Proceedings of the 16th Conference of the European Chapter of the Association for Computational Linguistics: Main Volume (2021)

28. Zhu, F., Zhu, Y., Chang, X., Liang, X.: Vision-language navigation with self-supervised auxiliary reasoning tasks. In: 2020 IEEE/CVF Conference on Computer Vision and Pattern Recognition (CVPR) (2020)

STORYDALL-E: Adapting Pretrained Text-to-Image Transformers for Story Continuation

Adyasha Maharana[✉], Darryl Hannan, and Mohit Bansal

UNC, Chapel Hill, NC 27514, USA
{adyasha,dhannan,mbansal}@cs.unc.edu

Abstract. Recent advances in text-to-image synthesis have led to large pretrained transformers with excellent capabilities to generate visualizations from a given text. However, these models are ill-suited for specialized tasks like story visualization, which requires an agent to produce a sequence of images given a corresponding sequence of captions, forming a narrative. Moreover, we find that the story visualization task fails to accommodate generalization to unseen plots and characters in new narratives. Hence, we first propose the task of story continuation, where the generated visual story is conditioned on a source image, allowing for better generalization to narratives with new characters. Then, we enhance or 'retro-fit' the pretrained text-to-image synthesis models with task-specific modules for (a) sequential image generation and (b) copying relevant elements from an initial frame. We explore full-model fine-tuning, as well as prompt-based tuning for parameter-efficient adaptation, of the pretrained model. We evaluate our approach STORYDALL-E on two existing datasets, PororoSV and FlintstonesSV, and introduce a new dataset DiDeMoSV collected from a video-captioning dataset. We also develop a model STORYGANC based on Generative Adversarial Networks (GAN) for story continuation, and compare with the STORYDALL-E model to demonstrate the advantages of our approach. We show that our retro-fitting approach outperforms GAN-based models for story continuation. We also demonstrate that the 'retro-fitting' approach facilitates copying of visual elements from the source image and improved continuity in visual frames. Finally, our analysis suggests that pretrained transformers struggle with comprehending narratives containing multiple characters, and translating them into appropriate imagery. Our work encourages future research into story continuation and large-scale models for the task (Code and data are available at https://github.com/adymaharana/storydalle).

Supplementary Information The online version contains supplementary material available at https://doi.org/10.1007/978-3-031-19836-6_5.

1   Introduction

Pretrained text-to-image synthesis models like DALL-E [33] have shown unprecedented ability to convert an input caption into a coherent visualization. Several
subsequent approaches have also leveraged powerful multimodal models [4,32]
for creating artistic renditions of input captions [5], demonstrating their potential for democratizing art. However, these models are designed to process only a
single, short caption as input. In contrast, many use cases of text-to-image synthesis require models to process long narratives and metaphorical expressions,
condition on existing visuals, and generate more than one image to capture the
meaning of the input text. In the past, multiple works have developed specialized
Generative Adversarial Networks (GAN) models such as image-to-image translation [15], style transfer [18] etc. For instance, story visualization models [23]
convert a sequence of captions into a sequence of images which illustrate the
story. However, the recent advent of transformer-based large pretrained models
opens up possibilities for leveraging latent knowledge from large-scale pretrained
datasets for performing these specialized tasks more effectively. Hence, in this
paper, we explore methods to adapt a pretrained text-to-image synthesis model
for complex downstream tasks, with a focus on story visualization.

Story visualization is a challenging task that lies at the intersection of image
generation and narrative understanding. Given a series of captions, which compose a story, an agent must generate a corresponding sequence of images that
depicts the contents of these captions. While prior work in story visualization has
discussed potential applications of the task [23,27,28,36], the task itself presents
some difficulties when being applied to real world settings. The model is limited
to the fixed set of characters, settings, and events on which it is trained and
has no way of knowing how to depict a new character that appears in a caption
during test time; captions do not contain enough information to fully describe
the character's appearance. Therefore, in order to generalize to new story elements, the model must have a mechanism for obtaining additional information
about how these elements should be visually represented. First, we make story
visualization more conducive to these use cases by presenting a new task called
'story continuation'. In this task, we provide an initial scene that can be leveraged in real world use cases. By including this scene, the model can then copy
and adapt elements from it as it generates subsequent images. This has the
additional benefit of shifting the focus from text-to-image generation, which is
already a task attracting plenty of research, and instead focuses on the narrative
structure of a sequence of images, e.g., how an image should change over time to
reflect new narrative information in the captions. We introduce a new dataset,
DiDeMoSV [11], and also convert two existing visualization datasets PororoSV
[23] and FlintstonesSV [8] to the story continuation setting.

Next, in order to adapt a text-to-image synthesis model to this story continuation task, we need to finetune the pretrained model (such as DALL-E [33])
on a sequential text-to-image generation task, with the additional flexibility to
copy from a prior input. To do so, we first 'retro-fit' the model with additional
layers to copy relevant output from the initial scene. Next, we introduce a self-

attention block for generating story embeddings that provide global semantic context of the story during generation of each frame. We name this approach STORYDALL-E and also compare with a GAN-based model STORYGANC for story continuation. We also explore the parameter-efficient framework of prompt-tuning and introduce a prompt consisting of task-specific embeddings to coax the pretrained model into generating visualizations for the target domain. During training, the pretrained weights are frozen and the new parameters are learned from scratch, which is time as well as memory-efficient.

Results show that our retro-fitting approach in STORYDALL-E is useful for leveraging the latent pretrained knowledge of DALL-E for the story continuation task, and outperforms the GAN-based model on several metrics. Further, we find that the copying mechanism allows for improved generation in low-resource scenarios and of unseen characters during inference. In summary,

- We introduce the task of story continuation, that is more closely aligned with downstream applications for story visualization, and provide the community with a new story continuation dataset.
- We introduce STORYDALL-E, an adaptation of pretrained transformers for story continuation, using retro-fitting. We also develop STORYGANC as a strong GAN baseline for comparison.
- We perform comparative experiments and ablations to show that fine-tuned STORYDALL-E outperforms STORYGANC on three story continuation datasets along several metrics.
- Our analysis shows that the copying mechanism improves correlation of the generated images with the source image, leading to better continuity in the visual story and generation of low-resource as well as unseen characters.

2   Related Work

Text-to-Image Synthesis. Most work in text-to-image synthesis has focused on the development of increasingly sophisticated generative adversarial networks (GANs) [6]. Recent works have leveraged multi-stage generation [47], attentional generative networks [40], dual learning [31], dynamic memory [24,48], semantic disentaglement [42], explicit object modelling [12] and contrastive loss [17,46] to further push performance on this task. DALL-E [33] is a large transformer language model that generates both text tokens and image tokens. VideoGPT [41] adapts the DALL-E architecture for conditional generation of videos from a first frame and trains it from scratch. In contrast, we adapt the pretrained DALL-E by *retro-fitting* the pretrained weights with task-specific modules for conditional generation of a sequence of images from a first frame.

Story Visualization. [23] introduce the CLEVR-SV and PororoSV datasets which are based on the CLEVR [16] visual question answering dataset and Pororo video question answering dataset [19] respectively. [27] adapt the Flintstones text-to-video synthesis dataset [8] into FlintstonesSV. While these datasets have served as challenging benchmarks, they contain recurring characters throughout the dataset. Complex datasets, requiring story visualization models to generalize to a more diverse set of test cases is needed to better guide research in this domain. We introduce the story continuation task and propose a new dataset for the task.

Most story visualization models follow the framework introduced in Story-GAN [23], which comprises a recurrent text encoder, an image generator, and image as well as story discriminators to train the GAN [38]. [45] add textual alignment models and a path-based image discriminator, while [21] add dilated convolution and weighted activation degree to the discriminators. [36] add figure-background segmentation to the model in the form of generators and discriminators. [28] and [27] use dual learning and structured inputs respectively to improve story visualization. We use their models as starting point and add modifications that leverage pretrained transformers for our proposed story continuation task.

Parameter-Efficient Training. Methods like adapter-tuning [10,13,26,37] and prompt-based tuning [20,22] add a small number of trainable parameters to the frozen weights of a pretrained model, which are then learned for the target task. Sparse updating of parameters [7,44] and low-rank decomposition matrices [14] also provide parameter-efficient methods for finetuning. [9,29] combine these approaches for a unified approach to finetuning pretrained models. [1] 'retro-fit' a pre-trained language model with cross-attention layers to retrieve relevant tokens at each timestep of word prediction in natural language generation. We use retro-fitting and prompt-tuning to adapt a pretrained image synthesis model to story continuation.

3   Methods

As discussed in Sect. 1, story visualization has limited applicability in real-world settings because the task formulation does not allow models to generalize to new story elements. Hence, we propose the story continuation task and present our STORYDALL-E and STORYGANC models for the task.

3.1   Story Continuation

Given a sequence of sentences $S = [s_1, s_2, ..., s_T]$ forming a narrative, story visualization is the task of generating a corresponding sequence of images $\hat{X} = [\hat{x}_1, \hat{x}_2, ..., \hat{x}_T]$, following [23]. S contains a story, where the captions are temporally ordered and describe the same narrative. This task has many different potential applications such as facilitating the creation of comics or creating visualizations in an educational setting. However, due to the way that the story visualization task is formulated, current models are far from being applied to these settings. The models rely on the images seen in the training data, to generate new visualizations for input stories during the inference phase. Thus, they can only recreate the characters as already found in the training set. Additionally, the captions in story visualization datasets are focused on the narrative, which limits the amount of information that is provided to the model, including

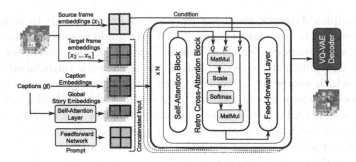

Fig. 1. Illustration of our STORYDALL-E architecture for the prompt-tuning setting. The frames are encoded using pretrained VQVAE and sent as inputs to the pretrained DALL-E. The inputs are prepended with input-agnostic prompt (in prompt-tuning setting only) and global story embeddings corresponding to each sample in the story continuation dataset. The output of STORYDALL-E is decoded using VQ-VAE to generate the predicted image.

descriptions of characters or settings, background etc. Much of this is inferred by the model, leading to generations that might be drastically different than expected, and it is unrealistic to expect the models to generate completely new visual attributes without sufficient instructions in the caption. Story continuation addresses these issues by providing initial information about the story setting and characters.

In the story continuation task, the first image of the sequence x_1 is provided as additional input to the model. By including an initial ground truth scene as input, the model has access to the appearances of characters, the setting in which the story takes place, and more. When making subsequent scenes, the model then no longer needs to create all the visual features from scratch, but can instead copy from the initial frame. This first image addresses both the generalization issue and the limited information issue in current story visualization models. We refer to this first frame as *source frame* and the remaining frames in the sequence $[x_2, ..., x_t]$ as *target frames*.

3.2   STORYDALL-E

The DALL-E generative network is trained using a simple language-modelling objective on the sequence of discrete image tokens for the task of text-to-image synthesis. With massive amounts of data, such models learn the implicit alignment between text tokens and image tokens, which can be leveraged for downstream tasks like story continuation. The two main aspects that differentiate the story continuation task from text-to-image synthesis are: (1) sequence of captions vs. single caption, and (2) source frame vs. no source frame. Hence, in order to convert the text-to-image synthesis model into a story continuation model, we add three task-specific modules to the native DALL-E architecture. First, we use a global story encoder to pool information from all captions and produce a story embedding, which provides global context of the story at each timestep. Next, we 'retro-fit' the model with cross-attention layers in order to accept the source frame as additional input. Finally, we learn a sequence of embeddings for the story continuation task and provide it as prompt to the model for task-specific instructions. During finetuning, the pretrained model weights are frozen and these task-specific modules are trained from scratch, leading to a parameter-efficient adaptation of DALL-E for story continuation. We refer to our proposed model as STORYDALL-E (see Fig. 1).

Global Story Encoder. Most previous works in story visualization utilize recurrent encoders in the form of LSTM networks [23] or memory-augmented encoders [27,28], to accept a sequence of captions as input. However, recurrent architectures are memory as well as time-intensive because of sequential processing. Hence, we propose to use a self-attention (f_{self}) based global story encoder, which takes the sentence embeddings for all captions as input and generates contextualized story embeddings for each time-step using parallel processing (see Fig. 1). Additionally, we initialize sinusoid positional embeddings (S_{pos}) to provide information about the position of the target frame within the story, and add those to the story embeddings: $S_{global} = f_{self}(S + S_{pos})$. These embeddings are prepended to the word embeddings for the caption at that timestep and sent as input to the generative model.

Retro-fitted Cross-Attention Blocks. Next, we want to 'retro-fit' the DALL-E model with the ability to copy relevant elements from the source image, in order to promote generalizability to unseen visual attributes. This will allow the model to generate visual stories with completely new characters, as long as they are present in the source frame. Hence, we adapt the model to 'condition' the generation of target frame on the source frame by adding a cross-attention block to each self-attention block of the native DALL-E architecture. The image embeddings of the source frame are used in the cross-attention layer as *key* (K) and *value* (V), while the output from the preceding self-attention layer is used as *query* (Q). As shown in Fig. 1, the DALL-E self-attention block consists of the self-attention (f_{self}^{i}), feed-forward (f_{dense}^{i}) and normalization (f_{norm}) layers. Given an input z_i to the ith self-attention block, the output z^{i+1} is: $z^{i+1} = f_{norm}(f_{dense}^{i}(f_{self}^{i}(z_i)))$. In STORYDALL-E, we insert a cross-attention layer such that the output z^{i+1} is:

$$z^{i+1} = f_{norm}(f_{dense}^{i}(f_{cross}^{i}(f_{self}^{i}(z^i), c_{img}))) \qquad (1)$$

where f_{cross}^{i} is the cross-attention layer in the ith Transformer block and c_{image} is sequence of embedding representations for the conditioning image. The self-attention layers are constrained to perform causal masking for computing attention weights due to the nature of the image synthesis task. However, within the cross-attention layer, the input is free to attend over the entire source frame which eases the next token prediction task by augmenting the model with relevant information. The cross-attention layers are trained from scratch.

The STORYDALL-E architecture can be fully fine-tuned to learn the weights of the above-mentioned task-specific modules, while updating the weights of the pretrained model as necessary, on the target task as well as dataset. However, [1] show that freezing of pretrained weights during training of retro-fitted models can also lead to similar performance as models trained from scratch, with lesser training data. Further, it provides a parameter-efficient approach that can be trained/deployed with a smaller amount of computational resources. Hence, we additionally explore prompt-tuning [22] of the STORYDALL-E model.

Prompt. Prompt-tuning is an alternative [22] to full model fine-tuning where the pretrained model weights are frozen and instead, a small sequence of task-specific vectors is optimized for the downstream task. We initialize a parameterization network $MLP(.)$, which takes a matrix of trainable parameters P'_θ of dimensions P_{idx} and $dim(h^i)$ as input and generates the prompt P_θ. These trainable matrices are randomly initialized and trained from scratch on the downstream task and dataset. P_θ is appended to the word embeddings of input caption, along with the global story embeddings. Together, these additional embedding vectors act as 'virtual tokens' of a task-specific prompt, and are attended to by each of the caption as image tokens. Formally, the input h^i to the ith self-attention layer in the auto-regressive transformer is organized as follows:

$$h^i = \begin{cases} P_\theta[j,:] & \text{if } j \in [0, P_{idx}) \\ S_{global} & \text{if } j == P_{idx} \\ f^i(z_j, h_{<j}) & \text{otherwise} \end{cases} \quad (2)$$

where $f^i(.)$ is the ith transformer block in STORYDALL-E.

With the aforementioned additions, we convert the pretrained DALL-E into STORYDALL-E model for the story continuation task. A pretrained VQVAE encoder [30] is used to transform RGB images into small 2D grids of image tokens, which are flattened and concatenated with the modified inputs in STORYDALL-E (see supplemen. for details). Finally, STORYDALL-E is trained to model the joint distribution over the tokens of text s and image x: $p(x) = \prod_{j=1}^{d} p(x_j | x_{<i}; s)$. New parameters as well as pretrained weights are optimized in full-model finetuning whereas only the parameters of the prompt, story encoder and cross-attention layers are optimized during prompt-tuning.

3.3 STORYGANC

Generative Adversarial Networks (GANs) have enjoyed steady progress at many image generation tasks such as style transfer [18], conditional image generation [40], image-to-image translation [15] over the last decade. Unlike transformers, they do not need to be pretrained on massive datasets, and can be trained for narrow domains with smaller datasets, which makes it an appealing method. Several recent works in story visualization have demonstrated the effectiveness of GANs for this task [23,28,36]. Hence, we also develop a GAN-based model,

STORYGANC, for the story continuation task and compare its performance to that of STORYDALL-E on the proposed datasets (see supplemen. for figure and details). STORYGANC follows the general framework of the StoryGAN model [23] i.e., it is composed of a recurrent text encoder, an image generation module, and two discriminators - image and story discriminator. We modify this framework to accept the source frame as input for the story continuation task, and use it for improving the generation of target frames. Our STORYGANC model is implemented as follows:

Pre-trained Language Model Encoder. We use a pretrained language model (such as RoBERTa [25] or CLIP text encoder [32]) as the caption encoder. These models are pretrained on large unimodal or multimodal datasets of language, which is of great utility for understanding the semantic concepts present in input captions. To ensure that the model has access to all captions, we append the captions together and use a special token to denote which caption is currently being generated.

Contextual Attention. The story representation from the encoder is combined with the image embeddings of the first frame of the image sequence using contextual attention [43] between the two inputs. The resulting representation is fed through a generator module which recurrently processes each caption, and produces a corresponding image.

Discriminators. The story discriminator takes all of the generated images and uses 3D convolution to create a single representation and then makes a prediction as to whether the generated story is real or fake. The image discriminator performs the same function but only focuses on individual images. The KL-Divergence loss enforces gaussian distribution on the latent representations learnt by GAN. Finally, the model is trained end-to-end using the objective function: $\min_{\theta_G} \max_{\theta_I, \theta_S} \mathcal{L}_{KL} + \mathcal{L}_{img} + \mathcal{L}_{story}$, where θ_G, θ_I and θ_S denote the parameters of the text encoder + image generator, and image and story discriminators respectively. During inference, the trained weights θ_G are used to generate a visual story for a given input of captions.

4 Datasets

Since story continuation is a reframing of the story visualization tasks, existing story visualization datasets can be adapted for story continuation by assigning the first frame in the sequence as source frame and the rest as target frames. However, such existing story visualization datasets like PororoSV [23] and FlintstonesSV [8] are also homogeneous datasets with recurring characters i.e., the characters used during evaluation already appear in the training set. It is not possible to evaluate the generalization capacity of story continuation models using these datasets. Hence, we propose a new dataset in this paper.

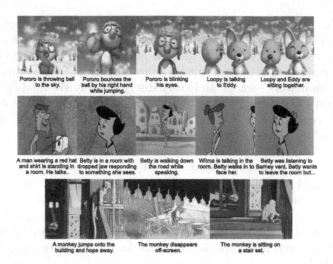

Fig. 2. Examples from the PororoSV (top), FlintstonesSV (middle) and DiDeMoSV (bottom) datasets. In the story continuation setting, the first frame is used as input to the generative model.

DiDeMoSV. DiDeMo [11] is a video captioning dataset containing 10,000 short clips with more than 40,000 text descriptions temporally localized with the videos. Each of the clips were randomly sampled from the YFCC100M [39] dataset which is based upon Flickr. This results in videos that cover a large breadth of real-world scenarios, containing many different settings, actions, entities, and more. The dataset contains 11550/2707/3378 samples in training, validation and test respectively, with each sample containing three consecutive frames. This dataset challenges story continuation models to generate diverse inputs, covering many more story elements, in contrast to existing story visualization datasets. In order to do this, models must maximize their usage of the initial scene input and need to incorporate additional general visual knowledge, whether this is done through transfer learning or additional data.

We also use the existing PororoSV [23] and FlintstonesSV datasets [8], containing 10191/2334/2208 and 20132/2071/2309 samples respectively, to evaluate our story continuation models. Each sample contains 5 consecutive frames. There are 9 and 7 main characters in PororoSV and FlintstonesSV respectively, that appear throughout the dataset. For story continuation, we use the first frame as source frame and the rest of the four frames in the sequence as target frames. Evaluation is only performed on the generation of target frames. See Fig. 2 for examples from the three story continuation datasets.

5   Experiments

We use the pretrained weights from popular open-source minDALL-E (1.3B parameters) which is trained on 14 million text-image pairs from the CC3M

Table 1. Results on the test sets of PororoSV, FlintstonesSV and DiDeMoSV (DSV) datasets from various models. Scores are based on FID (lower is better), character classification F1 and frame accuracy (F-Acc.; higher is better) evaluations.

Model	PororoSV			FlintstonesSV			DSV
	FID ↓	Char-F1↑	F-Acc↑	FID ↓	Char-F1↑	F-Acc↑	FID↓
STORYGANC (BERT)	72.98	**43.22**	17.09	91.37	70.45	55.78	91.43
STORYGANC (CLIP)	74.63	39.68	16.57	90.29	72.80	**58.39**	92.64
STORYDALL-E (prompt)	61.23	29.68	11.65	53.71	42.48	32.54	64.58
STORYDALL-E (finetuning)	**25.90**	36.97	**17.26**	**26.49**	**73.43**	55.19	**32.92**

[35] and CC12M [2] datasets, to initialize our models.[1] minDALL-E uses the pretrained VQGAN-VAE [4] for discretizing image inputs. We experiment with pretrained CLIP [32] (38M parameters) and distilBERT [34] (110M parameters) text encoders for the STORYGANC models. The STORYDALL-E models are trained for 5 epochs with learning rates of 1e-04 (AdamW, Cosine Scheduler) and 5e−04 (AdamW, Linear Decay Scheduler) for full-model fine-tuning and prompt-tuning setups respectively. Checkpoints are saved at the end of every epoch. The STORYGANC models are trained for 120 epochs with learning rates 1e−04 and 1e−05 for the generator and discriminators respectively. Checkpoints are saved every 10 epochs. These models are trained on single A6000 GPUs.

We use the FID score for saving the best checkpoints in our experiments. The FID score calculates the difference between the ground truth and generated images by computing the distance between two feature vectors. Following [23] and [28], we also compute the character classification scores (F1 Score and Frame Acc.) for the PororoSV and FlintstonesSV datasets. See supplemen. for details.

6   Results

Main Quantitative Results. Table 1 contains the FID, character classification F1 score and frame accuracy results on the test sets of PororoSV and FlintstonesSV datasets using various models in our experiments. We train two variations of the STORYDALL-E model with the distilBERT and CLIP text encoders. Our model STORYDALL-E is trained under two settings, one where the pretrained weights are frozen during training and the other where the pretrained weights are also finetuned on the target dataset. In practice, we find it necessary to finetune the pretrained text and image embeddings within the Transformers, which are pretrained on real-world images, in order to adapt them to different domains such as cartoons. This results in nearly 30% trainable parameters during prompt-tuning, as compared to full-model finetuning. With STORYDALL-E, we see drastic improvements in FID score for the PororoSV and FlinstonesSV datasets, over the STORYGANC model, demostrating the superior visual quality of the generated visual stories. The character classification scores remain

---
[1] https://github.com/kakaobrain/minDALL-E

Table 2. Ablation results of StoryDALL-E on validation sets of PororoSV, Flint-stonesSV and DiDeMoSV (DSV) datasets. Scores are based on FID (lower is better), character classification F1 and frame accuracy (F-Acc.; higher is better) evaluations.

Model	PororoSV			FlintstonesSV			DSV
	FID ↓	Char-F1↑	F-Acc↑	FID ↓	Char-F1↑	F-Acc↑	FID↓
STORYDALL-E	21.64	40.28	20.94	28.37	74.28	52.35	41.58
− Cross-Attention	30.45	39.32	34.65	35.04	73.94	53.28	55.89
− Story Embeddings	23.27	40.25	18.16	29.21	72.18	52.72	42.34
− Story Embeddings & Cross-Attention	31.68	35.29	16.73	36.28	72.44	51.32	58.14

the same for FlintstonesSV and drop by 6% and 14% for PororoSV with use of finetuned and prompt-tuned STORYDALL-E respectively. GAN-based models like STORYGANC are able to recreate distinct and finer details of a character which leads to higher accuracy scores using a classification model, such as the Inception-v3 used in our experiments [28]. With prompt-tuning, we observe that STORYDALL-E models manage to capture the background elements of the scene but fail to properly recreate the characters in the frame. The frame accuracy score, which is based on exact match overlap of multiple characters in the predicted scene with those in ground truth, remains low for all models, suggesting that both methods struggle to compose multiple roles in a single image [3].

For the more challenging DiDeMoSV dataset, the fully finetuned STORYDALL-E model outperforms the GAN models by a wide margin in terms of FID score. It should be noted here that PororoSV and FlintstonesSV have a finite set of recurring animated characters throughout the dataset, whereas DiDeMoSV is derived from a multitude of real-world scenarios with no overlap in characters between training and evaluation sets. While the addition of a source frame makes it easier for the model to replicate it in the target frames, the generation is significantly more difficult due to the diversity in evaluation samples. However, since the DiDeMoSV dataset contains images from the real-world domain, the pretrained knowledge of STORYDALL-E derived from Conceptual Captions is useful for generating relevant and coherent images for the dataset, while STORYGANC largely fails to do so.

Ablations. Table 2 contains results from ablation experiments on finetuned StoryDALL-E on the validation sets of the three story continuation datasets. The primary modifications we make to DALL-E in order to adapt it into STORYDALL-E, are the cross-attention layers, prompt matrix and global story embeddings. We perform minus-one experiments on StoryDALL-E by removing each of these components and observing the effect on FID results on validation sets. First, we remove the cross-attention layers from StoryDALL-E, which reverts the model to the story visualization setting where the model no longer receives the first image as input, and is evaluated on generation of rest of the frames in the visual story. With this ablation, we see large drops in FID scores across all datasets. Without a source image to guide the generated output, the quality of illustration drops rapidly, especially for the new DiDeMo dataset. The removal of global story embeddings results in a text-to-image synthesis setting with the first frame as additional input. In this scenario, we see smaller drops in FID, indicating that the global context is not as important as the ability to copy from an initial image. In the third row, we remove both, cross-attention layers and story embeddings, which relegates the setting to a text-to-image synthesis task, and observe large increase in FID scores across all daatsets.

Table 3. Results from human evaluation (Win%/Lose%/Tie%). Win% = % times stories from STORYDALL-E was preferred over STORYGANC, Lose% for vice-versa. Tie% represents remaining samples.

Dataset	Visual quality	Relevance	Consistency
PororoSV	94/0/6	44/28/28	56/26/18
FlintstonesSV	90/2/8	32/38/30	42/32/26
DiDeMoSV	64/0/36	38/0/62	32/48/20

6.1 Human Evaluation

We additionally conduct human evaluation on our model's outputs hoping to better capture the overall quality of the generated stories. We have a human annotator compare generated visual stories from our STORYDALL-E (finetuning) and STORYGANC (BERT) models. They are provided with predictions from each dataset and the corresponding ground truth captions, and asked to pick the better prediction (or tie) in terms of visual quality, consistency, and relevance [23]. Results are presented in Table 3. The STORYDALL-E model outperforms STORYGANC model in terms of visual quality and relevance, achieving higher % of wins in each of the three datasets (except relevance in FlintstonesSV). These results follow from the fact that STORYDALL-E uses the VQGAN-VAE [4] which is designed for reconstructing higher resolution images. Moreover, it has access to large pretraining data, which improves alignment between semantic concepts in captions and regions in images. We see wins in terms of consistency for PororoSV and DiDeMoSV predictions from STORYDALL-E models. But, the absolute numbers for consistency and relevance show that there is still room for improvement.

7 Analysis

In this section, we perform experiments to analyze aspects of the STORYDALL-E model and the story continuation task. First, we perform qualitative analyses

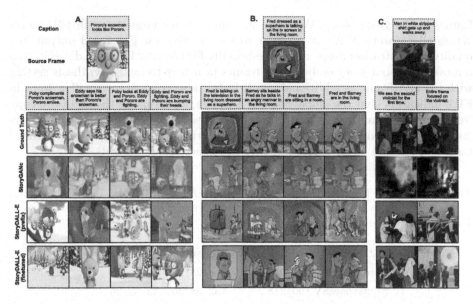

Fig. 3. Examples of predictions for (A) PororoSV (B) FlintstonesSV and (C) DiDe-MoSV story continuation datasets from STORYDALL-E and STORYGANC models. Source frame refers to the initial frame provided as additional input to the model.

of the predictions from STORYDALL-E. Next, we quantify the effect of the retro-fitted cross-attention layers and visualize the attention heads. See supplemen. for an analysis of the diverse semantic content in the DiDeMoSV dataset.

7.1   Qualitative Analysis

Figure 3 contains sampled outputs from both of our models for the three story continuation datasets. In each of these examples, STORYDALL-E generates higher quality images than STORYGANC. The difference is especially stark for PororoSV and FlintstonesSV datasets since STORYDALL-E is exposed to the characters during training and has additional guidance from source frame during inference. In the case of DiDeMoSV, the generations from STORYGANC are largely incomprehensible, which could be attributed to the unseen semantic concepts such as 'violinist' which did not appear in the training set. In contrast, STORYDALL-E is exposed to various real-world concepts during pretraining, which can be leveraged during generation. For instance, the pretrained knowledge as well as the copying mechanism help the STORYDALL-E model compre-hend 'television' and generate an image for 'Fred is talking in the television' (see Fig. 3(b)). However, the overall quality of the images from STORYDALL-E also do not approach human produced images. As discussed in Sect. 6, it is especially true for frames containing multiple characters. This suggests that while current models are able to attempt the task, there is still much work to be done before consistent and coherent images are commonly produced by the models.

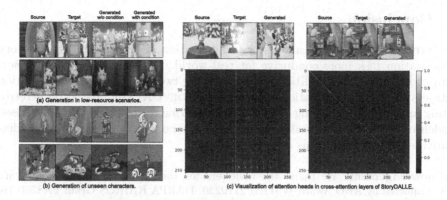

Fig. 4. Examples of generation from STORYDALL-E in (a) low-resource scenarios and (b) of unseen characters. (c) Plots of attention scores computed in retro cross-attention layers for examples of source frames (x-axis) and target frames (y-axis).

We also examine the ability of STORYDALL-E to recreate scarce characters from the training set (see Fig. 4(a)) and generate unseen characters (see Fig. 4(b)), when guided by the copying mechanism via cross-attention layers. We find that the copying mechanism allows for better generation of shape and form for less-frequent characters in PororoSV. Similarly, we identified non-recurring characters in the FlintstonesSV dataset and observed the corresponding generated images, when STORYDALL-E has access to a previous frame where they appear. STORYDALL-E succeeds at partially copying visual aspects of the characters, such as the purple skirt (top) and blue uniform (bottom).

7.2   Retro-Fitted Cross-Attention

We examine the attention scores computed in the retro cross-attention layer and present examples in Fig. 4(c). The cross-attention layer in STORYDALL-E receives vector representations for the source image and computes the cross-attention output using source frame as key/value and target frame as query. In the first example (left), the target frame is copying visual attributes of the pink bird with the most emphasis, as be seen from the higher attention scores for the image tokens roughly in the center of the source frame. For the second example (right), the source frame and target frames are nearly similar; the attention scores are highest in the diagonal of the plot. The resulting images in both samples contain many visual attributes already found in the source image, demonstrating that the cross-attention layer is effective at enabling conditional image generation. See supplementary for correlation scores between source image and frames generated with and without condition using STORYDALL-E.

8 Conclusion

We introduce a new task called story continuation in order to make the story visualization task more conducive for real-world use cases. We present a new dataset DiDeMoSV, in addition to reformatting two existing story visualization datasets for story continuation. Our model STORYDALL-E, based on a retro-fitting approach for adapting pretrained transformers, out-performs GAN-based models on the story continuation datasets. We hope that the dataset and models motivate future work in this area.

Acknowledgement. We thank the reviewers for their useful feedback. This work was supported by ARO Award W911NF2110220, DARPA KAIROS Grant FA8750-19-2-1004, NSF-AI Engage Institute DRL-211263. The views, opinions, and/or findings contained in this article are those of the authors, not the funding agency.

References

1. Borgeaud, S., et al.: Improving language models by retrieving from trillions of tokens. arXiv preprint arXiv:2112.04426 (2021)
2. Changpinyo, S., Sharma, P., Ding, N., Soricut, R.: Conceptual 12M: pushing web-scale image-text pre-training to recognize long-tail visual concepts. In: Proceedings of the IEEE/CVF Conference on Computer Vision and Pattern Recognition, pp. 3558–3568 (2021)
3. Cho, J., Zala, A., Bansal, M.: DALL-Eval: probing the reasoning skills and social biases of text-to-image generative transformers. arXiv preprint arXiv:2202.04053 (2022)
4. Esser, P., Rombach, R., Ommer, B.: Taming transformers for high-resolution image synthesis. In: Proceedings of the IEEE/CVF Conference on Computer Vision and Pattern Recognition, pp. 12873–12883 (2021)
5. Frans, K., Soros, L., Witkowski, O.: CLIPDraw: exploring text-to-drawing synthesis through language-image encoders. arXiv preprint arXiv:2106.14843 (2021)
6. Goodfellow, I.J., et al.: Generative adversarial nets. In: NeurIPS (2014)
7. Guo, D., Rush, A.M., Kim, Y.: Parameter-efficient transfer learning with diff pruning. In: Proceedings of the 59th Annual Meeting of the Association for Computational Linguistics and the 11th International Joint Conference on Natural Language Processing (Volume 1: Long Papers), pp. 4884–4896 (2021)
8. Gupta, T., Schwenk, D., Farhadi, A., Hoiem, D., Kembhavi, A.: Imagine this! scripts to compositions to videos. In: Ferrari, V., Hebert, M., Sminchisescu, C., Weiss, Y. (eds.) ECCV 2018. LNCS, vol. 11212, pp. 610–626. Springer, Cham (2018). https://doi.org/10.1007/978-3-030-01237-3_37
9. He, J., Zhou, C., Ma, X., Berg-Kirkpatrick, T., Neubig, G.: Towards a unified view of parameter-efficient transfer learning. arXiv preprint arXiv:2110.04366 (2021)
10. Henderson, J., Ruder, S., et al.: Compacter: efficient low-rank hypercomplex adapter layers. In: Advances in Neural Information Processing Systems (2021)
11. Hendricks, L.A., Wang, O., Shechtman, E., Sivic, J., Darrell, T., Russell, B.: Localizing moments in video with natural language. In: Proceedings of the IEEE International Conference on Computer Vision (ICCV) (2017)
12. Hinz, T., Heinrich, S., Wermter, S.: Semantic object accuracy for generative text-to-image synthesis. IEEE Trans. Pattern Analy. Mach. Intell. (2020)

13. Houlsby, N., et al.: Parameter-efficient transfer learning for NLP. In: International Conference on Machine Learning, pp. 2790–2799. PMLR (2019)

14. Hu, E.J., et al.: LoRA: low-rank adaptation of large language models. arXiv preprint arXiv:2106.09685 (2021)

15. Isola, P., Zhu, J.Y., Zhou, T., Efros, A.A.: Image-to-image translation with conditional adversarial networks. In: Proceedings of the IEEE Conference on Computer Vision and Pattern Recognition, pp. 1125–1134 (2017)

16. Johnson, J., Hariharan, B., Van Der Maaten, L., Fei-Fei, L., Lawrence Zitnick, C., Girshick, R.: CLEVR: a diagnostic dataset for compositional language and elementary visual reasoning. In: Proceedings of the IEEE Conference on Computer Vision and Pattern Recognition, pp. 2901–2910 (2017)

17. Kang, M., Park, J.: ContraGAN: contrastive learning for conditional image generation. In: NeurIPS (2020)

18. Karras, T., Laine, S., Aila, T.: A style-based generator architecture for generative adversarial networks. In: Proceedings of the IEEE/CVF Conference on Computer Vision and Pattern Recognition, pp. 4401–4410 (2019)

19. Kim, K.M., Heo, M.O., Choi, S.H., Zhang, B.T.: DeepStory: video story QA by deep embedded memory networks. In: Proceedings of the 26th International Joint Conference on Artificial Intelligence, pp. 2016–2022 (2017)

20. Lester, B., Al-Rfou, R., Constant, N.: The power of scale for parameter-efficient prompt tuning. In: Proceedings of the 2021 Conference on Empirical Methods in Natural Language Processing, pp. 3045–3059 (2021)

21. Li, C., Kong, L., Zhou, Z.: Improved-storyGAN for sequential images visualization. J. Vis. Commun. Image Represent. **73**, 102956 (2020). https://doi.org/10.1016/j.jvcir.2020.102956. http://www.sciencedirect.com/science/article/pii/S1047320320301826

22. Li, X.L., Liang, P.: Prefix-tuning: Optimizing continuous prompts for generation. In: Proceedings of the 59th Annual Meeting of the Association for Computational Linguistics and the 11th International Joint Conference on Natural Language Processing (Volume 1: Long Papers), pp. 4582–4597 (2021)

23. Li, Y., et al.: StoryGAN: a sequential conditional GAN for story visualization. In: Proceedings of the IEEE Conference on CVPR, pp. 6329–6338 (2019)

24. Liang, J., Pei, W., Lu, F.: CPGAN: full-spectrum content-parsing generative adversarial networks for text-to-image synthesis. arXiv preprint arXiv:1912.08562 (2019)

25. Liu, Y., et al.: RoBERTa: a robustly optimized BERT pretraining approach. arXiv preprint arXiv:1907.11692 (2019)

26. Mahabadi, R.K., Ruder, S., Dehghani, M., Henderson, J.: Parameter-efficient multi-task fine-tuning for transformers via shared hypernetworks. In: Proceedings of the 59th Annual Meeting of the Association for Computational Linguistics and the 11th International Joint Conference on Natural Language Processing (Volume 1: Long Papers), pp. 565–576 (2021)

27. Maharana, A., Bansal, M.: Integrating visuospatial, linguistic, and commonsense structure into story visualization. In: Proceedings of the 2021 Conference on Empirical Methods in Natural Language Processing, pp. 6772–6786 (2021)

28. Maharana, A., Hannan, D., Bansal, M.: Improving generation and evaluation of visual stories via semantic consistency. In: Proceedings of the 2021 Conference of the North American Chapter of the Association for Computational Linguistics: Human Language Technologies, pp. 2427–2442 (2021)

29. Mao, Y., et al.: UNIPELT: a unified framework for parameter-efficient language model tuning. arXiv preprint arXiv:2110.07577 (2021)

30. Van den Oord, A., Kalchbrenner, N., Espeholt, L., Vinyals, O., Graves, A., et al.: Conditional image generation with pixeLCNN decoders. In: Advances in Neural Information Processing Systems 29 (2016)
31. Qiao, T., Zhang, J., Xu, D., Tao, D.: MirrorGAN: learning text-to-image generation by redescription. In: Proceedings of the IEEE/CVF Conference on Computer Vision and Pattern Recognition, pp. 1505–1514 (2019)
32. Radford, A., et al.: Learning transferable visual models from natural language supervision. In: International Conference on Machine Learning, pp. 8748–8763. PMLR (2021)
33. Ramesh, A., et al.: Zero-shot text-to-image generation. In: International Conference on Machine Learning, pp. 8821–8831. PMLR (2021)
34. Sanh, V., Debut, L., Chaumond, J., Wolf, T.: DistilBERT, a distilled version of BERT: smaller, faster, cheaper and lighter. In: 5th Workshop on Energy Efficient Machine Learning and Cognitive Computing (NeurIPS) (2019)
35. Sharma, P., Ding, N., Goodman, S., Soricut, R.: Conceptual captions: a cleaned, hypernymed, image alt-text dataset for automatic image captioning. In: Proceedings of the 56th Annual Meeting of the Association for Computational Linguistics (Volume 1: Long Papers), pp. 2556–2565 (2018)
36. Song, Y.-Z., Rui Tam, Z., Chen, H.-J., Lu, H.-H., Shuai, H.-H.: Character-preserving coherent story visualization. In: Vedaldi, A., Bischof, H., Brox, T., Frahm, J.-M. (eds.) ECCV 2020. LNCS, vol. 12362, pp. 18–33. Springer, Cham (2020). https://doi.org/10.1007/978-3-030-58520-4_2
37. Sung, Y.L., Cho, J., Bansal, M.: Vl-adapter: parameter-efficient transfer learning for vision-and-language tasks. arXiv preprint arXiv:2112.06825 (2021)
38. Szűcs, G., Al-Shouha, M.: Modular StoryGAN with background and theme awareness for story visualization. In: El Yacoubi, M., Granger, E., Yuen, P.C., Pal, U., Vincent, N. (eds.) ICPRAI 2022. LNCS, vol. 13363, pp. 275–286. Springer, Cham (2022). https://doi.org/10.1007/978-3-031-09037-0_23
39. Thomee, B., et al.: YFCC100M: the new data in multimedia research. Commun. ACM **59**(2), 64–73 (2016)
40. Xu, T., et al.: AttnGAN: fine-grained text to image generation with attentional generative adversarial networks. In: Proceedings of the IEEE Conference on Computer Vision and Pattern Recognition, pp. 1316–1324 (2018)
41. Yan, W., Zhang, Y., Abbeel, P., Srinivas, A.: VideoGPT: video generation using VQ-VAE and transformers. arXiv preprint arXiv:2104.10157 (2021)
42. Yin, G., Liu, B., Sheng, L., Yu, N., Wang, X., Shao, J.: Semantics disentangling for text-to-image generation. In: Proceedings of the IEEE/CVF Conference on Computer Vision and Pattern Recognition, pp. 2327–2336 (2019)
43. Yu, J., Lin, Z., Yang, J., Shen, X., Lu, X., Huang, T.S.: Generative image inpainting with contextual attention. In: Proceedings of the IEEE Conference on Computer Vision and Pattern Recognition, pp. 5505–5514 (2018)
44. Zaken, E.B., Ravfogel, S., Goldberg, Y.: BitFit: simple parameter-efficient fine-tuning for transformer-based masked language-models. arXiv preprint arXiv:2106.10199 (2021)
45. Zeng, G., Li, Z., Zhang, Y.: PororoGAN: an improved story visualization model on Pororo-SV dataset. In: Proceedings of the 2019 3rd International Conference on Computer Science and Artificial Intelligence, pp. 155–159 (2019)
46. Zhang, H., Koh, J.Y., Baldridge, J., Lee, H., Yang, Y.: Cross-modal contrastive learning for text-to-image generation. In: Proceedings of the IEEE/CVF Conference on Computer Vision and Pattern Recognition, pp. 833–842 (2021)

47. Zhang, H., et al.: StackGAN: text to photo-realistic image synthesis with stacked generative adversarial networks. In: ICCV (2017)
48. Zhu, M., Pan, P., Chen, W., Yang, Y.: DM-GAN: dynamic memory generative adversarial networks for text-to-image synthesis. In: Proceedings of the IEEE/CVF Conference on Computer Vision and Pattern Recognition, pp. 5802–5810 (2019)

VQGAN-CLIP: Open Domain Image Generation and Editing with Natural Language Guidance

Katherine Crowson[1], Stella Biderman[1,2]([✉]), Daniel Kornis[3], Dashiell Stander[1], Eric Hallahan[1], Louis Castricato[1,4], and Edward Raff[2]

[1] EleutherAI, Attica, Greece
stellabiderman@gmail.com
[2] Booz Allen Hamilton, McLean, USA
[3] AIDock, Rehovot, Israel
[4] Georgia Institute of Technology, Atlanta, USA

Abstract. Generating and editing images from open domain text prompts is a challenging task that heretofore has required expensive and specially trained models. We demonstrate a novel methodology for both tasks which is capable of producing images of high visual quality from text prompts of significant semantic complexity without any training by using a multimodal encoder to guide image generations. We demonstrate on a variety of tasks how using CLIP [37] to guide VQGAN [11] produces higher visual quality outputs than prior, less flexible approaches like minDALL-E [19], GLIDE [33] and Open-Edit [24], despite not being trained for the tasks presented. Our code is available in a public repository.

Keywords: Generative adversarial networks · Grounded language · Image manipulation

1 Introduction

Using free-form text to generate or manipulate high-quality images is a challenging task, requiring a grounded learning between visual and textual representations. Manipulating images in an open domain context was first proposed by the seminal Open-Edit [24], which allowed text prompts to alter an image's content. This was done mostly with semantically simple transformations (e.g., turn a red apple green), and does not allow generation of images. Soon after DALL-E [38] and GLIDE [33] were developed, both of which can perform generation (and inpainting) from arbitrary text prompts, but do not themselves enable image manipulation.

K. Crowson and S. Biderman—Co-first authors.

Supplementary Information The online version contains supplementary material available at https://doi.org/10.1007/978-3-031-19836-6_6.

In this work we propose the first a unified approach to semantic image generation and editing, leveraging a pretrained joint image-text encoder [37] to steer an image generative model [11]. Our methodology works by using the multimodal encoder to define a loss function evaluating the similarity of a (text, image) pair and backpropagating to the latent space of the image generator. We iteratively update the candidate generation until it is sufficiently similar to the target text. The difference between using our technique for generation and editing is merely a matter of initializing the generator with a particular image (for editing) or with random noise (for generation).

A significant advantage of our methodology is the lack of additional training required. Only a pretrained image generator and a joint image-text encoder are necessary, while all three of Liu et al. [24], Ramesh et al. [38], Nichol et al. [33] require training similar models from scratch. Additionally Ramesh et al. [38] and Nichol et al. [33] train generators from scratch.

We demonstrate several significant contributions, including:

1. High visual quality for both generation and manipulation of images.
2. High semantic fidelity between text and generation, especially when semantically unlikely content co-occurs.
3. Efficiency in that our method requires no additional training beyond the pretrained models, using only a small amount of optimization per inference.
4. The value of open development and research. This technique was developed in public and open collaboration has been integral to its rapid real-world success. Non-authors have already extended our approach to other modalities (e.g., replacing text for audio) and commercial applications.

The rest of our manuscript is organized as follows. In Sect. 2 we discuss how of how our methodology works, resulting in a simple and easy-to-apply approach for combing multiple modalities for generation or manipulation. The efficacy of VQGAN-CLIP in generating high quality and semantically relevant images is shown in Sect. 3, followed by superior manipulation ability in Sect. 4. The design choices of VQGAN-CLIP to obtain both high image quality and fast generation are validated by ablations in Appendix G, and Sect. 5 discusses resource usage and efficiency considerations. As our approach has been public since April 2021, we are able to show further validation by external groups in Sect. 6. This use includes extensions to other modalities, showing the flexibility of our approach, as well as commercial use of VQGAN-CLIP that demonstrate its success at handling open-domain prompts and images to a satisfying degree. Finally we conclude in Sect. 7.

2   Our Methodology

To demonstrate our method's effectiveness we apply it using VQGAN [11] and CLIP [37] as pre-trained models, and so refer to our approach as VQGAN-CLIP. We stress, however, that our approach is not specific to either model and that subsequent work has already shown success that builds on our work using other models [5,12,27,46], and even in other modalities [18,50].

We start with a text prompt and use a GAN to iteratively generate candidate images, at each step using CLIP to improve the image. We optimize the image by treating the squared spherical distance between the embedding of the candidate and the embedding of the text prompt as a loss function, and differentiating through CLIP with respect to the GAN's latent vector representation of the image, which we refer to as the "z-vector" following [35]. This process is outlined in Fig. 1.

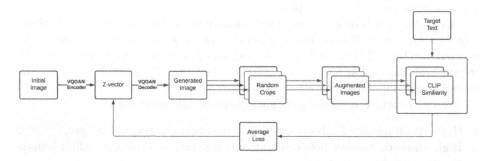

Fig. 1. Diagram showing how augmentations are added to stabilize and improve the optimization. Multiple crops, each with different random augmentations, are applied to produce an average loss over a single source generation. This improves the results with respect to a single latent Z-vector.

To generate an image, the "initial image" contains random pixel values. The optimization process is repeated to alter the image, until the output image gradually improves such that it semantically matches the target text. We can also edit existing images by starting with the image-to-edit as the "initial image". The text prompt used to describe how we want the image to change is used identically to the text prompt for generating an image, and no changes to the architecture exist between generation and manipulation besides how the 'initial image" is selected.

We use Adam [20] to do the actual optimization, a learning rate of 0.15, $\beta = (0.9, 0.999)$, and run for 400 iterations for the experiments in this paper.

2.1 Discrete Latent Spaces for Images

Unlike the naturally discrete nature of text, the space of naturally occurring images is inherently continuous and not trivially discretized. Prior work by Vinyals, and Kavukcuoglu [35] borrows techniques from vector quantization (VQ) to represent a variety of modalities with discrete latent representations by building a codebook vocabulary with a finite set of learned embeddings. Given a codebook of vocabulary size K with embedding dimension n_k, $\mathcal{Z} = \{z_i\}_k^K \in \mathbb{R}^{n_k}$.

This is applied to images by constructing a convolutional autoencoder with encoder $\mathcal{E}$ and decoder $\mathcal{G}$. An input image $x \in I$ is first embedded with the encoder $z = E(x)$. We can then compute the vector quantized embedding x as

$$z_q = \operatorname*{argmin}_{z_k \in \mathcal{Z}} \|z_{i,j} - z_k\|$$

which we can then multiply back through the vocabulary in order to perform reconstruction. We can then use a straight-through estimator on the quantization step in order to allow the CNN and codebook to be jointly trained end-to-end. We use the popular VQGAN [11] model for the experiments in this paper.

2.2 Contrastive Text-Image Models

To guide the generative model, we need a way to adjust the similarity of a candidate generation with the guidance text. To achieve this, we use CLIP, [37], a joint text-image encoder trained by using contrastive learning. We use CLIP to embed text prompts and candidate generated images independently and measure the cosine similarity between the embeddings. This similarity is then reframed as a loss that we can use gradient descent to minimize.

2.3 Augmentations

One challenge of using VQGAN-CLIP is that gradient updates from the CLIP loss are quite noisy if calculated on a single image. To overcome this we take the generated candidate image and modify it many times, producing a large number of augmented images. We take random crops of the candidate image and then apply further augmentations such as flipping, color jitter, noising, etc. [39] Most high level semantic features of an image are relatively invariant to these changes, so averaging the CLIP loss with respect to all of the augmented images reduces the variance of each update step. There is a risk that a random crop might dramatically change the semantic content of an image (e.g. by cropping out an important object), but we find that in practice this does not cause any issues.

For the results presented in this paper we used an augmentation pipeline consisting of: random horizontal flips, random affine projections, random perspective projections, random color jitter, and adding random Gaussian noise.

2.4 Regularizing the Latent Vector

When using an unconstrained VQGAN for image generation, we found that outputs tended to be unstructured. Adding augmentations helps with general coherence, but the final output will often still contain patches of unwanted textures. To solve this problem we apply a weighted L^2 regularization to the z-vector.

This produces a regularized loss function given by the equation

$$Loss = L_{CLIP} + \alpha \cdot \frac{1}{N} \sum_{i=0}^{N} Z_i^2$$

where α is the regularization weight. This encourages parsimony in the representation, sending low information codes in VQGAN's codebook to zero. In practice we note that regularization appears to improve the coherence of the output and produces a better structured image. We decay the regularization term by 0.005 over the course of generation.

2.5   Additional Components

Our methodology is highly flexible and can be extended straightforwardly depending on the use-case and context due to the ease of integrating additional interventions on the intermediate steps of image generation. Researchers using our framework have introduced a number of additional components, ranging from using ensembles [6], to using Bézier curves for latent representations [5,13], to using perturbations to make the results more robust to adversaries [25]. Although they aren't used in the main experiments of this paper, we wish to call attention to two in particular that we use frequently: "prompt addition" and masked image editing. We give an overview of both here, and provide additional experiments and information in Appendix H

Prompt Addition: We have found that our users are often interested in applying multiple text prompts at the same time. This can be achieved by computing the loss against multiple target texts simultaneously and adding the results. In Appendix H.1 we use this tool to explore the semantic cohesion of VQGAN-CLIP's generations.

Masking: A common technique in image generation and editing is *masking*, where a portion of an image is identified ahead of time as being where a model should edit[1] VQGAN-CLIP is compatible with masking by zeroing out the gradients in parts of the latent vector that one wishes to not change. However VQGAN-CLIP can also leverage the semantic knowledge of CLIP to perform *self-masking* without any non-textual human input.

3   Semantic Image Generation

The primary application of our methodology is for generating images from text. In contrast to previous work on this topic [33,38,49], we do not perceive creating photo-realistic images or images that could convince a human that they are real photographs as our primary goal. Our focus is on producing images of high visual quality that are semantically meaningful in relation to a natural language prompt, which we demonstrate in this section. This in fact requires abandoning photo-realism when prompts may ask for artistic or explicitly unrealistic generations and edits. A loosely curated set of example generations is presented in Fig. 2.

As VQGAN-CLIP has been publicly available for almost a year, we have had the opportunity to observe people experimenting with and building off of VQGAN-CLIP in the wild. In Appendix D we show a sample of artwork created by people other than the authors of this paper are included to demonstrate the power and range of VQGAN-CLIP.

---

[1] In the context of image this is often referred to as "infilling," but we will use "masking" as a general term to refer to both.

(a) Oil painting of a candy dish of glass candies, mints, and other assorted sweets

(b) A colored pencil drawing of a waterfall

(c) A fantasy painting of a city in a deep valley by Ivan Aivazovsky

(d) A beautiful painting of a building in a serene landscape

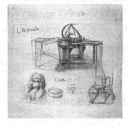

(e) sketch of a 3D printer by Leonardo da Vinci

(f) an autogyro flying car, trending on artstation

(g) an astronaut in the style of van Gogh

(h) Baba Yaga's house + fantasy art

(i) pickled eggs, tempera on wood

(j) effervescent hope

(k) the Tower of Babel by J.M.W. Turner

(l) a futuristic city in synthwave style

Fig. 2. Example VQGAN-CLIP generations and their text prompts. Prompts selected to demonstrate a range of visual styles that VQGAN-CLIP is capable of producing including classical art (g, i), modern art (l), drawings (e), oils (a), and others not included due to space.

3.1   Artistic Impressions

We find that VQGAN-CLIP is able to evoke the artistic style of famous artists and major artistic styles from around the world. Figure 2 features "an astronaut in the style of van Gogh" whose background evokes Starry Night and "the Tower of Babel by J. M. W. Turner" which draws on Turner's color palate and use of light. Another way this can be seen is by directly asking for "a painting by [name]" or "art by [name]." In Fig. 3 we present six images created this way drawing on artists from different regions, time periods, and artistic styles. While the images often are missing cohesion (most likely due to the vagueness of "a painting" as a prompt) they are each markedly reminiscent of the artist in question. While CLIP would obviously find these images visually similar to other works by the artist, we also find that non-CLIP-based image similarity approaches reliably identify these images as visually similar to work by the artists. To validate this we queried Google's Reverse Image Search using each generation in Fig. 3, and in every case a real painting by the target artist was the most similar image.

3.2   Comparisons to Other Approaches

The closest prior work in open domain generation of images comes from DALL-E [38] and GLIDE [33], which claim to train very large pretrained text-to-image models. DALL-E and GLIDE are purported to be 12 billion and 5 billion parameters, respectively, while VQGAN-CLIP together is 227 million. Unfortunately, we were not allowed to study the models purported in the respective papers by their authors. We instead use the state-of-the-art models using each methodology methodologies. This includes minDALL-E [19] (1.3 B parameters) and two versions of GLIDE (783 M parameters without CLIP and 941 M with) that OpenAI has released.

To evaluate our model, we recruited humans and asked them to rate the alignment of (text, image) pairs on a scale of 1 (low) to 5 (high). In particular, they were directed to rate higher quality images that do not match the prompt lower than lower quality images that do. Prompts were selected based on principles learned from our experience working with these models but without prior knowledge of how the models would behave on the particular prompts in question. All prompts and generated images can be found in Appendix D. To provide the maximal advantage to our competitors, minDALL-E and GLIDE examples are cherry-picked best-of-five, while VQGAN-CLIP examples are uncherry-picked (best-of-one). Table 1 shows the mean score per prompt for each model. We find that humans overwhelmingly view the generations using our technique as more aligned with the input text.

3.3 Qualitative Analysis

A sampling of representative results is shown in Fig. 4 for four different prompts using minDALL-E, two variants of GLIDE (filtered), and our VQGAN-CLIP. Further comparisons, including the prompts in Fig. 2, can be found in Appendix D. We find that the minDALL-E and the GLIDE (filtered) models are much more

(a) van Gogh   (b) Picasso   (c) Hokusai

(d) Turner   (e) Kahlo   (f) Mehretu

Fig. 3. Stylistic impressions of famous artists. Third party tools like Google's Reverse Image Search indicate that real paintings by the target artists are the most visually similar images in every case.

Table 1. Mean human ratings of generations by each model considered on a score of 1 (worst) to 5 (best).

	A	B	C	D	E	F	G	H	I	J	K	L	Mean
minDALL-E	3.3	2.3	3.2	3.7	1.5	2.7	2.2	1.3	3.3	3.0	3.5	2.3	2.7
GLIDE (CF)	3.0	4.0	2.7	3.2	1.3	2.5	1.3	1.2	2.0	2.3	2.0	2.8	2.3
GLIDE (CLIP)	3.2	4.0	2.8	4.8	3.0	2.7	1.8	2.5	3.7	2.3	3.7	**5.0**	3.3
VQGAN-CLIP	**4.3**	**5.0**	**4.8**	**5.0**	**4.5**	**4.5**	**4.8**	**4.7**	**4.2**	**3.8**	**4.7**	4.7	**4.6**

variable in the quality of their generations. While they are able to produce images that are clearly recognizable in response to the prompts "the universal library trending on artstation" and "a charcoal drawing of a cathedral," their generations in response to "a child's drawing of a baseball game" are largely unrecognizable and their responses to "a forest rendered in low poly" ignore the later half of the prompt. These latter cases demonstrate the low semantic relevance of prior methods' output given the prompt.

The "child's drawing" case is of particular note here in that a child's drawing is expected to have lower visual clarity and lack of structure. That VQGAN-CLIP is able to correctly modulate its ability for fine details is thus of note to show that VQGAN-CLIP is not intrinsically biased toward producing fine details when inappropriate, and correctly identifies the appropriate context of multi-part prompts. Further evidence of this can be found in Figs. 8 to 11 where VQGAN-CLIP is able to produce generations for the prompts "A colored pencil drawing of a waterfall" and "sketch of a 3D printer by Leonardo da Vinci" that showcase the properties of the medium (visible strokes, the use of shading, the fact that the image is created on a piece of paper) while still producing a compelling visual image.

4   Semantic Image Editing

As far as we are aware, our framework is the first in the literature to be able to perform semantic image generation *and* semantic image editing. There are other examples in the literature of generative models that can perform style transfer [36], image inpainting [33,38], and other types of image manipulation [34], but we note that each of these represent distinct tasks from open domain semantic image editing. By contrast, to adapt our generation methodology to image editing all that is required is to replace the randomly initialized starting image with the image we wish to edit.

4.1   Comparison to State-of-the-Art

For semantic image editing we compare to Open-Edit [24]. As far as we are aware, Open-Edit is the only published research on *open domain* semantic image editing other than our work. To avoid giving any accidental advantage to our methodology, we focus primarily on the domains presented as examples in [24] such as changing colors and textures. We use the default settings for their model and the same prompting structure as in their paper.

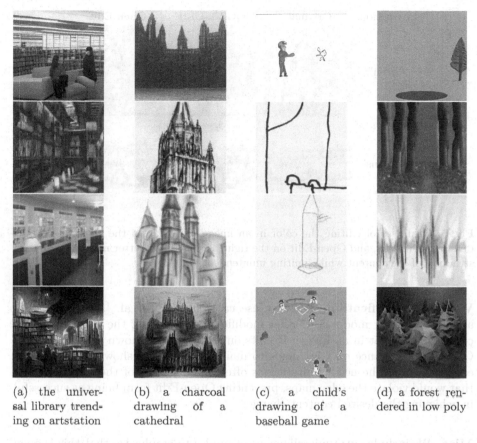

(a) the univer-
sal library trend-
ing on artstation

(b) a charcoal
drawing of a
cathedral

(c) a child's
drawing of a
baseball game

(d) a forest ren-
dered in low poly

Fig. 4. Text based generations of images. Top to bottom: minDALL-E, GLIDE (CLIP-guided), GLIDE (CF-guided), and our VQGAN-CLIP.

Color Editing. Here we prompt the model to change the dominant color palette without degrading the image quality or any of the finer details. The results can be seen in Fig. 5, where prior Open-Edit causes destructive transformations of the content of the image. In the second case the "Red bus" also shows a single desired target for manipulation that is respected by VQGAN-CLIP, but Open-Edit causes a change in coloration of the entire image.

Fig. 5. Examples of editing the color in an image. Original on the left, our VQGAN-CLIP in the middle, and Open-Edit on the right. VQGAN-CLIP better maintains original structure of the content while limiting unintended distortion.

Weather Modification. Another use case that Liu et al. [24] highlight as a success of their model is weather modification, changing the overall weather conditions present in an image. Results on this task are shown in Fig. 6, where Open-Edit's reliance on edge maps to maintain structure show a limitation in editing ability. The needed alterations often change more of the image content that would violate the edge maps, preventing Open-Edit from being as successful in achieving the desired content change.

Misc. We include extra miscellaneous examples to emphasize that this is open domain image editing and the performance is not limited to select types of transformations. These are shown in Fig. 7, and we note the "wooden" and "focused" examples demonstrate a task with less correlative semantics. This further requires a more robust grounding between modalities for success and the ability of our approach to better handle a breadth of possible inputs for open-domain prompts and images.

Instruction	Original	VQGAN-CLIP	Open-Edit

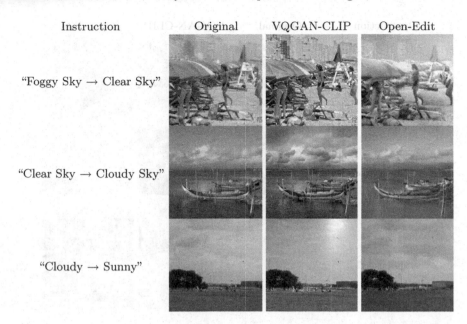

"Foggy Sky → Clear Sky"

"Clear Sky → Cloudy Sky"

"Cloudy → Sunny"

Fig. 6. Weather alteration can required greater alteration of scene structure that Open-Edit is not able to perform, as shown in the "Cloudy → Sunny" example that needs to alter the sky in addition to brightness levels.

5   Resource Considerations

Our approach runs in (935.2 ± 20.4) s on an NVIDIA Tesla K80 and (229.5 ± 26.2) s on an NVIDIA GeForce RTX 2080 Ti (10 runs in each sample). This is approximately three times slower than minDALL-E and ten times slower than GLIDE (filtered) in our testing. Although we would like to analyze the trade-offs involved with the fact that both models required extensive pretraining none of the papers we compare to report their training requirements in enough detail to analyze the trade-offs brought about by this difference. We encourage the authors to release more information about their models so that more complete analysis can be done.

5.1   Efficiency as a Value

One of the goals of this research is to increase the accessibility of AI image generative and editing tools. We have deliberately limited our approach to something that requires less than 11 GB of VRAM, so that it fits inside widely available commercial GPUs such as K80s. This GPU is particularly important from an accessibility standpoint, as it is the largest GPU that can be easily obtained using a free account on Google Colaboratory. The full generative process takes less than 3 min in a Google Colab notebook, making this a viable approach for anyone with access to the internet and a Google account.

Instruction	Original	VQGAN-CLIP	Open-Edit

"Wooden"

"Withered Flowers"

"Focused"

Fig. 7. More challenging modifications that required greater linguistic grounding to visual content to achieve, again showing VQGAN-CLIP is better able to edit image content.

Researchers with significantly more resources can obtain higher quality images using various augmentations left out of this paper, such as using an ensemble or additional auxiliary models to regularize the generations. While pushing the performance of our methodology to the maximum is a worthwhile endeavour, the fact that we can outperform the current state-of-the-art while running on freely available resources is something that we view as particularly worth highlighting. We leave determining the optimal framework with unbound resources to future work.

5.2   Runtime Analysis

DALL-E [38], GLIDE [33], and Open-Edit [24] all also incorporate image generators and joint text-image encoders into their architecture. Unlike our method however, they require computationally intensive training and finetuning. This invites the question of trade-offs between training and inference time. Unfortunately, none of the aforementioned papers report their training requirements in enough detail to estimate their training requirements. We are however able to estimate how long minDALL-E [19], the current state-of-the-art DALL-E model, takes to train at 504 V100-hours for the base model plus an additional 288 V100-hours to finetune on ImageNet [8]. Through private communication with the authors, we were able to learn that GLIDE (filtered) required 400 A100-days to train, which we approximate as 19, 200 V100-hours for ease of comparison (Table 2).

Table 2. Run-time of minDALL-E, GLIDE (filtered) and VQGAN-CLIP on a variety of GPUs. Each cell shows the mean and standard deviation of a 10-run sample. minDALL-E becomes cheaper than VQGAN-CLIP after 858 V100-hours have been expended while GLIDE (filtered) requires 20200 V100-hours.

Model	K80	P100	V100	Training
minDALL-E	$216.0\,s \pm 07.6\,s$	$60.0\,s \pm 5.5\,s$	$016.3\,s \pm 2.7\,s$	792 V100-hours
GLIDE (filtered)	$096.2\,s \pm 00.1\,s$	$19.2\,s \pm 0.3\,s$	$009.7\,s \pm 1.1\,s$	19,200 V100-hours
VQGAN-CLIP	$935.2\,s \pm 20.4\,s$	$654.3\,s \pm 10.1\,s$	$188.3\,s \pm 1.2\,s$	0 V100-hours

On all hardwares evaluated, our model is substantially slower than both minDALL-E and GLIDE (filtered). However. In terms of trade-offs between training and inference on V100 GPUs, minDALL-E's total cost becomes cheaper than VQGAN-CLIP at $\approx 15,800$ generations, while GLIDE(filtered) requires $\approx 384,000$. In terms of compute expended, minDALL-E becomes cheaper than VQGAN-CLIP after 858 V100-hours while GLIDE (filtered) requires 20200 V100-hours. While cost and efficiency concerns depend significantly on individual contexts, the fact that GLIDE (filtered) only becomes as efficient as VQGAN-CLIP efficient after tens of thousands of dollars of compute have been expended substantially limits researchers' ability to experiment with and iterate on the methodology. The same applies to minDALL-E, albeit with a price tag in the thousands rather than tens of thousands.

6 Adoption of VQGAN-CLIP

A unique aspect of VQGAN-CLIP has been its public development over the past year, which has resulted in an active community of users and real-world impact within and beyond classical computer vision. Kwon and Ye [21], Frans, Soros, and Witkowski [13], Chen, Dumay, and Tang [5], Liu et al. [25], Tian and Ha [46] create additional components (see Sect. 2.5) that they insert into our framework to improve performance in particular target domains, and Avrahami, Lischinski, and Fried [2] and Gu et al. [15] experiment with diffusion models in place of VQGAN. Several other researchers [12,27,33] evaluate their pretrained models by substituting them in for VQGAN or CLIP in our framework.

Beyond computer vision, Yang and Buehler [51] show that it is useful in the materials engineering design processes. Wu et al. [50], and Jang, Shin, and Kim [18] builds on our work by using the framework to perform sound-guided image generation. In the domain of affective computing and HCI, Galanos, Liapis, and Yannakakis [14] has further found VQGAN-CLIP able to elicit targeted emotions from viewers.

This last example helps explain the widespread commercial adoption of VQGAN-CLIP, with over a dozen commercial apps built to provide it as a service and over 500 NFTs produced using our method sold. A sampling of commercial websites using VQGAN-CLIP include NightCafe, Wombo Art, snowpixel.app, starryai.com, neuralblender.com, and hypnogram.xyz. Collectively, across these sites, VQGAN-CLIP has been used over 10 million times, showing the veracity of our approach to handle unstructured and diverse user content.

7   Conclusion

We have presented VQGAN-CLIP, a method of generating and manipulating images based on only human written text prompts. The quality of our model's generations have high visual fidelity and remain faithful to the textual prompt, outperforming prior approaches like DALL-E and GLIDE. The fidelity has been externally validated by commercial success and use by multiple companies. Compared to the only comparable approach to text based image editing, VQGAN-CLIP continues to produce higher quality visual images—especially when the textual prompt and image content have low semantic similarity.

Acknowledgements. We would like to acknowledge Ryan Murdock, who developed a very similar technique for combining VQGAN and CLIP simultaneously to us [30,31] but did not release his approach. Ryan was invited to coauthor this paper and declined. Many of the experiments in this paper were made possible by the free public demo for VQGAN-CLIP in the EleutherAI Discord server developed by BoneAmputee and sponsored by CoreWeave.

References

1. Ali, S., Parikh, D.: Telling creative stories using generative visual aids (2021). arXiv: 2110.14810v1 [cs.HC]
2. Avrahami, O., Lischinski, D., Fried, O.: Blended diffusion for text-driven editing of natural images (2021). arXiv: 2111.14818v1 [cs.CV]
3. Bau, D., Liu, S., Wang, T., Zhu, J.-Y., Torralba, A.: Rewriting a deep generative model. In: Vedaldi, A., Bischof, H., Brox, T., Frahm, J.-M. (eds.) ECCV 2020. LNCS, vol. 12346, pp. 351–369. Springer, Cham (2020). https://doi.org/10.1007/978-3-030-58452-8_21
4. Black, S., et al.: GPT-NeoX-20B: an open-source autoregressive language model. Preprint (2022)
5. Chen, G., Dumay, A., Tang, M.: diffvg+CLIP: generating painting trajectories from text. Preprint (2021)
6. Couairon, G., Grechka, A., Verbeek, J., Schwenk, H., Cord, M.: FlexIT: towards flexible semantic image translation (2022). arXiv: 2203.04705 [cs.CV]
7. De Cao, N., Aziz, W., Titov, I.: Editing factual knowledge in language models (2021). arXiv: 2104.08164v2 [cs.CL]
8. Deng, J., Dong, W., Socher, R., Li, L.-J., Li, K., Fei-Fei, L.: ImageNet: a large-scale hierarchical image database. In: 2009 IEEE Conference on Computer Vision and Pattern Recognition, pp. 248–255 (2009)
9. Dong, H., Yu, S., Wu, C., Guo, Y.: Semantic image synthesis via adversarial learning. In: 2017 IEEE International Conference on Computer Vision (ICCV), pp. 5706–5714 (2017)

10. Eichenberg, C., Black, S., Weinbach, S., Parcalabescu, L., Frank, A.: MAGMA – multimodal augmentation of generative models through adapter-based finetuning (2021). arXiv: 2112.05253v1 [cs.CV]
11. Esser, P., Rombach, R., Ommer, B.: Taming transformers for high-resolution image synthesis. In: Proceedings of the IEEE/CVF Conference on Computer Vision and Pattern Recognition, pp. 12873–12883 (2021)
12. Fei, N., et al.: WenLan 2.0: make AI imagine via a multimodal foundation model (2021). arXiv: 2110.14378v1 [cs.AI]
13. Frans, K., Soros, L.B., Witkowski, O.: CLIPDraw: exploring text-to-drawing synthesis through language-image encoders (2021). arXiv: 2106.14843v1 [cs.CV]
14. Galanos, T., Liapis, A., Yannakakis, G.N.: AffectGAN: affect-based generative art driven by semantics. In: 9th International Conference on Affective Computing and Intelligent Interaction Workshops and Demos (ACIIW) (2021)
15. Gu, S., et al.: Vector quantized diffusion model for text-to-image synthesis (2021). arXiv:2111.14822v3 [cs.CV]
16. Houlsby, N., et al.: Parameter-efficient transfer learning for NLP. In: International Conference on Machine Learning, pp. 2790–2799 (2019)
17. Hu, X., Yu, P., Knight, K., Ji, H., Li, B., Shi, H.: MUSE: textual attributes guided portrait painting generation. In: 2021 IEEE 4th International Conference on Multimedia Information Processing and Retrieval (MIPR), pp. 386–392 (2021)
18. Jang, J., Shin, S., Kim, Y.: Music2Video: automatic generation of music video with fusion of audio and text (2022). arXiv: 2201.03809v1 [cs.SD]
19. Kim, S., Cho, S., Kim, C., Lee, D., Baek, W.: minDALL-E on conceptual captions (2021). https://github.com/kakaobrain/minDALL-E
20. Kingma, D.P., Ba, J.: Adam: a method for stochastic optimization (2014). arXiv: 1412.6980v9 [cs.LG]
21. Kwon, G., Ye, J.C.: CLIPstyler: image style transfer with a single text condition (2021). arXiv: 2112.00374v2 [cs.CV]
22. Lester, B., Al-Rfou, R., Constant, N.: The power of scale for parameter-efficient prompt tuning (2021). arXiv: 2104.08691v2 [cs.CL]
23. Li, B., Qi, X., Lukasiewicz, T., Torr, P.H.S.: ManiGAN: text-guided image manipulation. In: Proceedings of the IEEE/CVF Conference on Computer Vision and Pattern Recognition, pp. 7880–7889 (2020)
24. Liu, X., et al.: Open-Edit: open-domain image manipulation with open-vocabulary instructions. In: Vedaldi, A., Bischof, H., Brox, T., Frahm, J.-M. (eds.) ECCV 2020, Part XI. LNCS, vol. 12356, pp. 89–106. Springer, Cham (2020). https://doi.org/10.1007/978-3-030-58621-8_6
25. Liu, X., Gong, C., Lemeng, W., Zhang, S., Hao, S., Liu, Q.: FuseDream: training-free text-to-image generation with improved CLIP+GAN space optimization (2021). arXiv: 2112.01573v1 [cs.CV]
26. Matena, M., Raffel, C.: Merging models with fisher-weighted averaging (2021). arXiv: 2111.09832v1 [cs.LG]
27. Michel, O., Bar-On, R., Liu, R., Benaim, S., Hanocka, R.: Text2Mesh: text-driven neural stylization for meshes (2021). arXiv: 2112.03221v1 [cs.CV]
28. Mitchell, E., Lin, C., Bosselut, A., Finn, C., Manning, C.D.: Fast model editing at scale (2021). arXiv: 2110.11309v1 [cs.LG]
29. Mordvintsev, A., Olah, C., Tyka, M.: DeepDream - a code example for visualizing neural networks (2015). https://ai.googleblog.com/2015/07/deepdream-code-example-for-visualizing.html
30. Murdock, R.: The taming transformers decoder really just goes! And this is with very little work. https://twitter.com/advadnoun/status/1367556678896394240

31. Murdock, R.: Working on using the rn50x4 version of clip with the taming transformers VQGAN. https://twitter.com/advadnoun/status/1368081153375105027
32. Nam, S., Kim, Y., Kim, S.J.: Text-adaptive generative adversarial networks: manipulating images with natural language. In: Bengio, S., Wallach, H., Larochelle, H., Grauman, K., Cesa-Bianchi, N., Garnett, R. (eds.) Advances in Neural Information Processing Systems, vol. 31, pp. 42–51. Curran Associates Inc. (2018). https://papers.neurips.cc/paper/2018/hash/d645920e395fedad7bbbed0eca3fe2e0-Abstract.html
33. Nichol, A., et al.: GLIDE: towards photorealistic image generation and editing with text-guided diffusion models (2021). arXiv: 2112.10741v3 [cs.CV]
34. Ntavelis, E., Romero, A., Kastanis, I., Van Gool, L., Timofte, R.: SESAME: semantic editing of scenes by adding, manipulating or erasing objects. In: Vedaldi, A., Bischof, H., Brox, T., Frahm, J.-M. (eds.) ECCV 2020. LNCS, vol. 12367, pp. 394–411. Springer, Cham (2020). https://doi.org/10.1007/978-3-030-58542-6_24
35. van den Oord, A., Vinyals, O., Kavukcuoglu, K.: Neural discrete representation learning. In: Advances in Neural Information Processing Systems, vol. 30, pp. 6309–6318. Curran Associates, Inc. (2017)
36. Patashnik, O., Wu, Z., Shechtman, E., Cohen-Or, D., Lischinski, D.: StyleCLIP: text-driven manipulation of StyleGAN imagery. In: Proceedings of the IEEE/CVF International Conference on Computer Vision, pp. 2085–2094 (2021)
37. Radford, A., et al.: Learning transferable visual models from natural language supervision. In: Meila, M., Zhang, T. (eds.) Proceedings of the 38th International Conference on Machine Learning. Proceedings of Machine Learning Research, vol. 139, pp. 8748–8763. PMLR (2021). https://proceedings.mlr.press/v139/radford21a.html
38. Ramesh, A., et al.: Zero-shot text-to-image generation. In: Meila, M., Zhang, T. (eds.) Proceedings of the 38th International Conference on Machine Learning. Proceedings of Machine Learning Research, vol. 139, pp. 8821–8831. PMLR (2021). https://proceedings.mlr.press/v139/ramesh21a.html
39. Riba, E., Mishkin, D., Ponsa, D., Rublee, E., Bradski, G.R.: Kornia: an open source differentiable computer vision library for PyTorch. In: 2020 IEEE Winter Conference on Applications of Computer Vision (WACV), pp. 3663–3672 (2020)
40. Sayers, D., et al.: The dawn of the human-machine era: a forecast of new and emerging language technologies (2021)
41. Selvaraju, R.R., et al.: Grad-CAM: visual explanations from deep networks via gradient-based localization. In 2017 IEEE International Conference on Computer Vision (ICCV), pp. 618–626 (2017)
42. Sharir, O., Peleg, B., Shoham, Y.: The Cost of training NLP models: a concise overview (2020)
43. Shocher, A., et al.: Semantic pyramid for image generation. In: Proceedings of the IEEE/CVF Conference on Computer Vision and Pattern Recognition, pp. 7457–7466 (2020). https://doi.org/10.1109/CVPR42600.2020.00748
44. Simonyan, K., Vedaldi, A., Zisserman, A.: Deep inside convolutional networks: visualising image classification models and saliency maps (2014). arXiv:1312.6034v2 [cs.CV]
45. Snell, C.: Alien Dreams: An Emerging Art Scene (2020). https://ml.berkeley.edu/blog/posts/clip-art/
46. Tian, Y., Ha, D.: Modern evolution strategies for creativity: fitting concrete images and abstract concepts (2021). arXiv: 2109.08857v2 [cs.NE]

47. Tsimpoukelli, M., Menick, J., Cabi, S., Eslami, S.A., Vinyals, O., Hill, F.: Multimodal few-shot learning with frozen language models. In: Advances in Neural Information Processing Systems (2021)
48. Underwood, T.: Mapping the latent spaces of culture (2021). https://tedunderwood.com/2021/10/21/latent-spaces-of-culture/
49. Wang, Z., Liu, W., He, Q.,Wu, X., Yi, Z.: CLIP-GEN: language-free training of a text-to-image generator with CLIP (2022). arXiv: 2203.00386v1 [cs.CV]
50. Wu, H.-H., Seetharaman, P., Kumar, K., Bello, J.P.: Wav2CLIP: learning robust audio representations from CLIP (2021). arXiv: 2110.11499v2 [cs.SD]
51. Yang, Z., Buehler, M.J.: Words to matter: de novo architected materials design using transformer neural networks. Front. Mater. **8**, 417 (2021)
52. Yosinski, J., Clune, J., Nguyen, A., Fuchs, T., Lipson, H.: Understanding neural networks through deep visualization (2015). arXiv: 1506.06579v1 [cs.CV]

Semantic-Aware Implicit Neural Audio-Driven Video Portrait Generation

Xian Liu[1], Yinghao Xu[1], Qianyi Wu[2], Hang Zhou[1], Wayne Wu[3],
and Bolei Zhou[1(✉)]

[1] Multimedia Laboratory, The Chinese University of Hong Kong, Shatin, China
[2] Monash University, Melbourne, Australia
[3] SenseTime Research, Beijing, China
`alvinliu@ie.cuhk.edu.hk,bolei@cs.ucla.edu`

Abstract. Animating high-fidelity video portrait with speech audio is crucial for virtual reality and digital entertainment. While most previous studies rely on accurate explicit structural information, recent works explore the implicit scene representation of Neural Radiance Fields (NeRF) for realistic generation. In order to capture the inconsistent motions as well as the semantic difference between human head and torso, some work models them via two individual sets of NeRF, leading to unnatural results. In this work, we propose Semantic-aware Speaking Portrait NeRF (SSP-NeRF), which creates delicate audio-driven portraits using one unified set of NeRF. The proposed model can handle the detailed local facial semantics and the global head-torso relationship through two semantic-aware modules. Specifically, we first propose a Semantic-Aware Dynamic Ray Sampling module with an additional parsing branch that facilitates audio-driven volume rendering. Moreover, to enable portrait rendering in one unified neural radiance field, a Torso Deformation module is designed to stabilize the large-scale non-rigid torso motions. Extensive evaluations demonstrate that our proposed approach renders realistic video portraits. Demo video and more resources can be found in https://alvinliu0.github.io/projects/SSP-NeRF.

Keywords: Speaking portrait generation · Audio-visual correlation

1 Introduction

Generating high-fidelity video portraits based on speech audio is of great importance to various applications like digital human and video dubbing. Many works tackle the task of audio-driven talking face or video portrait generation by using deep generative models. Some rely solely on learning-based image reconstruction, which typically synthesize static results of low-resolution [6,11,47,62,68,81]. Other methods utilize explicit structural intermediate representations such as

Supplementary Information The online version contains supplementary material available at https://doi.org/10.1007/978-3-031-19836-6_7.

3D facial models [5,51,60,66,69,76,83] or 2D landmarks [7,13,59]. Though some of them can generate high-fidelity images [59,60], the errors in structured representation prediction (*e.g.*, expression parameters of 3D Morphable Model (3DMM) [3]) lead to inaccurate face deformation [82].

Recently, the implicit 3D scene representation of Neural Radiance Fields (NeRF) [34] provides a new perspective for realistic generation. It enables free-view control with higher image quality compared to explicit methods, which is suitable for the video portrait generation task. Gafni *et al.* [16] first involve NeRF in the dynamic human head modeling from single-view data in a video-driven manner. However, an accurate explicit 3D model is still required in their settings. Moreover, they model torso consistently with the head, which leads to unstable results. Guo *et al.* [19] further propose AD-NeRF for audio-driven talking head synthesis. In particular, they build two individual sets of NeRF for head and torso modeling. Such a straightforward pipeline suffers from head-torso separation during the render stage, making generated results unnatural.

Based on previous studies, we identify two key challenges for incorporating NeRF into portrait generation: 1) Each facial part's appearance and moving patterns are intrinsically connected but substantially different, especially when associated with audios. Thus weighing all rendering areas equally without semantic guidance would lead to blurry details and difficulties in training. 2) While it is easy to bind head pose with camera pose, the global movements of the head and torso are in significant divergence. As the human head and torso are non-rigidly connected, modeling them with one set of NeRF is an ill-posed problem.

In this work, we develop a method called Semantic-aware Speaking Portrait NeRF (**SSP-NeRF**), which generates stable audio-driven video portraits of high-fidelity. We show that *semantic awareness is the key to handle both local facial dynamics and global head-torso relationship*. Our intuition lies in the fact that different parts of a speaking portrait have different associations with speech audio. While other organs like ears move along with the head, the high-frequency mouth motion that is strongly correlated with audios requires additional attention. To this end, we devise an *Semantic-Aware Dynamic Ray Sampling* module, which consists of an *Implicit Portrait Parsing* branch and a *Dynamic Sampling Strategy*. Specifically, the parsing branch supervises the modeling with facial semantics in 2D plane. Then the number of rays sampled at each semantic region could be adjusted dynamically according to the parsing difficulty. Thus more attention can be paid to the small but important areas like lip and teeth for better lip-synced results. Besides, we also enhance the semantic information by anchoring a set of latent codes to the vertices of a roughly predicted 3DMM [3] without expression parameters.

On the other hand, since the head and torso motions are rigidly bound together in the current NeRF, a correctly positioned torso cannot be rendered even with the portrait parsing results. We further observe the relationship between head and torso: while they share the same translational movements, the orientation of torso seldom changes with head pose under the speaking portrait setting. Thus we model non-rigid deformation through a *Torso Deformation* module. Concretely, for each point (x, y, z) in the 3D scene, we predict a displacement $(\Delta x, \Delta y, \Delta z)$ based on the head-canonical view information and time flows. Interestingly, although there are local deformations on the face, the deformation module implicitly learns to focus on the global parts. This design facilitates portrait stabilization in one unified set of NeRF. Experiments demonstrate that our method generates high-fidelity video portraits with better lip-synchronization and better image quality efficiently.

To summarize, our work has three main contributions: **(1)** We propose the *Semantic-Aware Dynamic Ray Sampling* module to grasp the detailed appearance and local dynamics of each portrait part without using accurate structural information. **(2)** We propose the *Torso Deformation* module that implicitly learns the global torso motion to prevent unnatural head-torso separated results. **(3)** Extensive experiments show that the proposed **SSP-NeRF** renders high-fidelity audio-driven video portraits with one unified NeRF in an efficient manner, which outperforms state-of-the-art methods on both objective evaluations and human studies.

2   Related Work

Audio-Driven Talking Head Synthesis. Audio-visual learning arouses great research interest [28,29], where talking head generation facilitates real applications. Conventional works resort to stitching techniques [4,15], where a predefined set of phoneme-mouth correspondence rules is used to modify mouth shapes. With the rapid growth of deep neural networks, end-to-end frameworks are proposed. One category of methods, namely image reconstruction-based methods, generate talking face by latent feature learning and image reconstruction [11,20,24,46,47,57,62,65,81,82,84]. For example, Chung *et al.* [11] propose the first end-to-end method with an encoder-decoder pipeline. Zhou *et al.* [81] explicitly disentangle identity and word information for better feature extraction. Prajwal *et al.* [47] achieve synchronous lip movements with a pretrained lip-sync expert. However, these methods can only generate fix-sized images with low resolution. Another strand of approaches named model-based methods utilize structural intermediate representations like 2D facial landmarks or 3D representations to bridge the mappings from audio to complicated facial images [5,7,13,33,56,59,60,63,69,76,83]. Typically, Chen *et al.* [7] and Das *et al.* [13] first predict 2D landmarks then generate faces. Thies *et al.* [60] and Song *et al.* [56] infer facial expression parameters from audio in the first stage, then generate 3D mesh for final image synthesis. But errors in intermediate prediction often hinder accurate results. In contrast to these two strands of works, our method can render more realistic speaking portraits of high-fidelity without any accurate structural information.

Implicit Representation Methods. Recent works leverage implicit functions for learning scene representations [25,27,34,37,55,79], where multi-layer perceptron (MLP) weights are used to represent the mapping from spatial coordinates to a signal in continuous space like occupancy [32,45,50,54], signed distance function [18,64,70,75], color and volume density [2,14,30,34], semantic label [22,80] and neural feature map [8,9,36]. A recent popular work named Neural Radiance Fields (NeRF) [34] optimizes an underlying continuous volumetric scene mapping from 5D coordinate of spatial location and view direction to implicit fields of color and density for photo-realistic view results. Naturally, naive NeRF is confined to static scenes, which triggers a branch of studies to extend NeRF for dynamic scenes [16,26,38–41,43,48,49,58,61]. However, few works focus on complicated dynamic scenes like speaking portraits [19]. The main difficulty lies in the learning of cross-modal associations between different portrait parts and speech audio. Typically, Guo *et al.* [19] synthesize talking head with two individual sets of NeRF for head and torso, making generated results fall apart. In this work, we take semantics as guidance to grasp each portrait part's local dynamics and appearances for fine-grained results efficiently. A deformation module further enables us to synthesize stable video portraits using one unified set of NeRF.

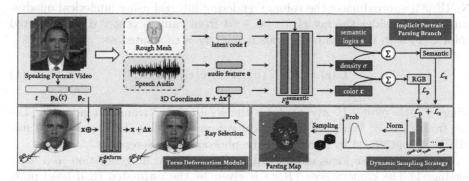

Fig. 1. Overview of Semantic-aware Speaking Portrait NeRF (SSP-NeRF) framework. In Implicit Portrait Parsing Branch (yellow), the semantic-aware implicit function $F_{\Theta}^{\text{semantic}}$ takes latent code $\mathbf{f}$, audio feature $\mathbf{a}$, 3D coordinate $\mathbf{x}$ and view direction $\mathbf{d}$ as input, then outputs the semantic logits $\mathbf{s}$, density σ and color $\mathbf{c}$ of the scene. In Dynamic Sampling Strategy (green), the RGB loss $\mathcal{L}_{\text{p}}$ and semantic loss $\mathcal{L}_{\text{s}}$ are utilized to guide the distribution of rays sampled at each semantic region. In particular, the Torso Deformation module (grey) uses an implicit function F_{Φ}^{deform} to map from the time t, head pose $\mathbf{p}_{\text{h}}(t)$, canonical pose $\mathbf{p}_{\text{c}}$ and 3D coordinate $\mathbf{x}$ into the displacement $\Delta\mathbf{x}$, which generates the deformed 3D coordinate $\mathbf{x} + \Delta\mathbf{x}$ to model non-rigid torso motions (Color figure online)

3 Our Approach

We present **Semantic-aware Speaking Portrait NeRF (SSP-NeRF)** that generates delicate audio-driven portraits with one unified set of NeRF. The whole pipeline is depicted in Fig. 1. In this section, we first review the preliminaries and the problem setting of video portrait synthesis with neural radiance fields (Sect. 3.1). We then introduce the *Semantic-Aware Dynamic Ray Sampling* module, which facilitates fine-grained appearance and dynamics modeling for each portrait part with semantic information (Sect. 3.2). Furthermore, we elaborate the *Torso Deformation* module that handles non-rigid torso motion by learning location displacements (Sect. 3.3). Finally, the volume rendering process and network training details are described (Sect. 3.4).

3.1   Preliminaries and Problem Setting

Given images with calibrated camera intrinsics and extrinsics, NeRF [34] represents a scene using a continuous volumetric radiance field F. Specifically, F is modeled by an MLP, which takes 3D spatial coordinates $\mathbf{x} = (x, y, z)$ and 2D view directions $\mathbf{d} = (\theta, \phi)$ as input, then outputs the implicit fields of color $\mathbf{c} = (r, g, b)$ and density σ. In this way, the MLP weights store scene information by the mapping of $F : (\mathbf{x}, \mathbf{d}) \rightarrow (\mathbf{c}, \sigma)$. To compute the color of a single pixel, NeRF [34] approximates the volume rendering integral using numerical quadrature [31]. Consider the ray $\mathbf{r}(v) = \mathbf{o} + v\mathbf{d}$ from camera center $\mathbf{o}$, its expected color $\hat{C}(\mathbf{r})$ with near and far bounds v_n and v_f is calculated as:

$$\hat{C}(\mathbf{r}) = \int_{v_n}^{v_f} T(v)\sigma(\mathbf{r}(v))\mathbf{c}(\mathbf{r}(v), \mathbf{d})dv, \tag{1}$$

where $T(v) = \exp(-\int_{v_n}^{v} \sigma(\mathbf{r}(u))du)$ is the accumulated transmittance along the ray from v_n to v. With the hierarchical volume sampling, both coarse and fine MLPs are optimized by minimizing the photometric discrepancy.

In this work, we focus on audio-driven video portrait generation in a basic setting: 1) The camera pose $\{R, \tau\}$ is given by the estimated rigid head pose, where the rotation matrix $R \in \mathbb{R}^{3 \times 3}$ and the translation vector $\tau \in \mathbb{R}^{3 \times 1}$ are estimated by 3DMM [3] on the face; 2) The audio feature $\mathbf{a} \in \mathbb{R}^{64}$ is extracted by a pretrained DeepSpeech [1] model and further processed with a light-weight audio encoder to get more compact representation. Therefore, the implicit function of audio-driven portrait **basic** setting is:

$$F^{\text{basic}} : (\mathbf{x}, \mathbf{d}, \mathbf{a}) \rightarrow (\mathbf{c}, \sigma). \tag{2}$$

Guo *et al.* [19] use an off-the-shelf parsing method [23] to divide training images into head and torso for individual NeRF modeling. Following their settings, we assume that the semantic parsing maps are also available in our method.

3.2   Semantic-aware Dynamic Ray Sampling

To avoid the unnatural head-torso separation problem described in Sect.1, we render the whole portrait with one unified set of NeRF. However, two problems remain: 1) The associations between different portrait parts and audio are different. For example, audio is more related to lip movements than torso motions.

How to grasp the fine-grained appearance and dynamics of each portrait part? 2) Since the rays are uniformly sampled over the whole image, how to make the model pay more attention to small but important regions like mouth?

Implicit Portrait Parsing Branch. Our solution to the first problem is to add a parsing branch. Since the portrait parts of the same semantic category share similar motion patterns and texture information, it will be beneficial for the appearance and geometry learning in NeRF, which is also proven in recent implicit representation studies [73–75,80]. As shown in Fig. 1, we extend the original NeRF with an additional parsing branch that predicts the semantic information. Note that since a certain 3D coordinate's semantic label is view-invariant, the parsing branch does not condition on view direction $\mathbf{d}$. Specifically, suppose there are totally K semantic categories, the parsing branch maps the 3D spatial coordinate $\mathbf{x}$ to semantic logits $\mathbf{s}(\mathbf{x})$ over K classes, which is further conditioned on audio $\mathbf{a}$. Hence the expected semantic logits $\hat{S}(\mathbf{r})$ along the ray $\mathbf{r}(v)$ with near and far bounds v_n and v_f can be calculated as:

$$\hat{S}(\mathbf{r}) = \int_{v_n}^{v_f} T(v)\sigma(\mathbf{r}(v), \mathbf{a})\mathbf{s}(\mathbf{r}(v), \mathbf{a})dv, \tag{3}$$

$$\text{where} \quad T(v) = \exp(-\int_{v_n}^{v} \sigma(\mathbf{r}(u), \mathbf{a})du). \tag{4}$$

Such semantic awareness naturally distinguishes each portrait part from others, thus figuring out different associations between audio and different regions.

Dynamic Ray Sampling Strategy. To generate delicate facial images with lip-synced results, we have to care for each portrait part, especially those small but crucial regions. Original NeRF **uniformly** samples rays on image plane [34]. Such an unconstrained ray sampling process focuses on big regions (*e.g.*, background and cheek) yet ignores small regions (*e.g.*, lip and teeth) that are important for fine-grained results. Therefore, we use semantic information to guide the ray sampling process dynamically. In particular, we denote all the points that are sampled on the image as $\Omega = \bigcup_{i=1}^{K} \Omega_i$, where K is the total number of semantic categories in parsing map and Ω_i is the set of points that are sampled on the i-th semantic class. During the training stage, we calculate the average loss of each category $\mathcal{L}_i$ for the previous epoch (the sum of semantic loss and RGB loss, which will be introduced in Sect. 3.4), and then dynamically sample rays across K categories by:

$$N_{\Omega_i} = \frac{\mathcal{L}_i}{\sum_{i=1}^{K} \mathcal{L}_i} \cdot N_s, \tag{5}$$

where N_{Ω_i} denotes the number of rays distributed to the i-th category and N_s is the total number of sampled rays. We identify two benefits for such design: 1) The average loss of a semantic category is area-agnostic. Thus the learning process will equally sample those small-area regions; 2) Some image parts are comparatively easier to learn. For example, the texture of eye is more complicated than that of background. This leads to lower loss of background category and dynamically drives the implicit function to pay more attention to hard-to-learn regions. Our experiment further shows that this design can accelerate training.

Structured 3D Information. 3D cues are crucial for NeRF to grasp better spatial geometry information as proved in [14,64,71,78]. In our framework, we identify that the awareness of *rough* 3D facial information can serve as guidance for face semantic and geometry learning. Concretely, a 3D facial model is built with *mean* expression parameters. We take inspiration from [44,45,72] to anchor a set of latent codes to the vertices of 3DMM model and diffuse to 3D space with SparseConvNet [17] to extract latent code volume. We query the latent code $\mathbf{f} \in \mathbb{R}^{88}$ at each point by trilinear interpolation[1] similar to Peng *et al.* [44]. Such structured 3D information could enhance semantic learning by giving similar features to the same semantic class while discriminative features among different semantic categories. Till now, we can update the **basic** setting in Eq. 2 to **semantic-aware** implicit function with parameters Θ:

$$F_{\Theta}^{\text{semantic}} : (\mathbf{x}, \mathbf{d}, \mathbf{a}, \mathbf{f}) \to (\mathbf{c}, \sigma, \mathbf{s}). \tag{6}$$

3.3   Torso Deformation Module

As mentioned in Sect. 3.1, the estimated head pose serves as camera pose. However, such straightforward treatment ignores the fact that head and torso motions are inconsistent. To tackle this problem, we design a Torso Deformation module to stabilize the large-scale non-rigid torso motions.

Torso Deformation Implicit Function. Concretely, an implicit function is optimized to estimate the deformation field of $\Delta\mathbf{x} = (\Delta x, \Delta y, \Delta z)$ at a specific time instant t. Based on the observation that torso pose changes slightly and is weakly related to speech audio, the head pose $\mathbf{p}_h(t)$ at time t and a canonical pose $\mathbf{p}_c$ are further given as references to learn the displacement $\Delta\mathbf{x}$, while audio feature $\mathbf{a}$ does not serve as input. Note that for convenience, the canonical pose $\mathbf{p}_c$ is set as the head pose of the first frame, thus the displacement $\Delta\mathbf{x} = 0$ when $t = 0$. The implicit function for torso deformation with parameters Φ is formulated as:

$$F_{\Phi}^{\text{deform}} : (\mathbf{x}, t, \mathbf{p}_h(t), \mathbf{p}_c) \to \Delta\mathbf{x}. \tag{7}$$

Notably, although such deformation is added to the *whole image*, we empirically find that *only the torso part* tends to be deformed, while the facial dynamics are naturally modeled by semantic-aware implicit function in Eq. 6. Such disentanglement will be further analyzed in Sect. 4.5.

Overall Implicit Function. Combine the semantic-aware implicit function with our proposed Torso Deformation module, we can model the overall implicit function as:

$$F_{\Theta}^{\text{overall}} : (\mathbf{x} + \Delta\mathbf{x}, \mathbf{d}, \mathbf{a}, \mathbf{f}) \to (\mathbf{c}, \sigma, \mathbf{s}),$$
$$\text{where} \quad \Delta\mathbf{x} = F_{\Phi}^{\text{deform}}(\mathbf{x}, t, \mathbf{p}_h(t), \mathbf{p}_c). \tag{8}$$

---

[1] Please refer to the supplementary material for more details.

3.4 Volume Rendering and Network Training

Volume Rendering with Deformation. Since the Torso Deformation module is proposed to compensate for non-rigid torso motions, we accordingly adapt the NeRF's original volume rendering formulas for color and semantic distribution in Eq. 1, Eq. 3 and Eq. 4. Consider a certain 3D point $\mathbf{x}(v) = \mathbf{o} + v\mathbf{d}$ located on the ray emitted from center $\mathbf{o}$ on view direction $\mathbf{d}$, its warped coordinate at time t with head pose $\mathbf{p_h}(t)$ and canonical pose $\mathbf{p_c}$ is computed as:

$$\mathbf{x}'(v,t) = \mathbf{x}(v) + F_{\Phi}^{\text{deform}}(\mathbf{x}(v), t, \mathbf{p_h}(t), \mathbf{p_c}). \qquad (9)$$

With the deformed 3D coordinate $\mathbf{x}'(v,t)$ along the modified ray path $\mathbf{r}'(v,t)$, we can calculate the expected color $\hat{C}(\mathbf{r}'(v),t)$ and semantic logits $\hat{S}(\mathbf{r}'(v),t)$ with near and far bounds v_n and v_f under **semantic-aware** setting as:

$$\hat{C}(\mathbf{r}') = \int_{v_n}^{v_f} T'(v,t)\sigma(\mathbf{r}'(v,t),\mathbf{a},\mathbf{f})\mathbf{c}(\mathbf{r}'(v,t),\mathbf{d},\mathbf{a},\mathbf{f})dv,$$

$$\hat{S}(\mathbf{r}') = \int_{v_n}^{v_f} T'(v,t)\sigma(\mathbf{r}'(v,t),\mathbf{a},\mathbf{f})\mathbf{s}(\mathbf{r}'(v,t),\mathbf{a},\mathbf{f})dv,$$

$$\text{and} \quad T'(v,t) = \exp(-\int_{v_n}^{v} \sigma(\mathbf{r}'(u,t),\mathbf{a},\mathbf{f})du), \qquad (10)$$

where $T'(v,t)$ is the accumulated transmittance along the ray path $\mathbf{r}'(v,t)$ from v_n to v. Note that the estimated semantic logits $\hat{S}(\mathbf{r}')$ are subsequently transformed into multi-class distribution $p(\mathbf{r}')$ through softmax operation.

Network Training. Similar to NeRF [34] that simultaneously optimizes coarse and fine models with hierarchical volume rendering, we train the network with following photometric loss $\mathcal{L}_{\mathrm{p}}$ and semantic loss $\mathcal{L}_{\mathrm{s}}$:

$$\mathcal{L}_{\mathrm{p}} = \sum_{\mathbf{r}' \in \mathcal{R}'} \left[\left\| \hat{C}_c(\mathbf{r}') - C(\mathbf{r}') \right\|_2^2 + \left\| \hat{C}_f(\mathbf{r}') - C(\mathbf{r}') \right\|_2^2 \right],$$

$$\mathcal{L}_{\mathrm{s}} = - \sum_{\mathbf{r}' \in \mathcal{R}'} \left[\sum_{k=1}^{K} p^k(\mathbf{r}') \log \hat{p}_c^k(\mathbf{r}') + \sum_{k=1}^{K} p^k(\mathbf{r}') \log \hat{p}_f^k(\mathbf{r}') \right], \qquad (11)$$

where $\mathcal{R}'$ is the set of *deformed* camera rays passing through image pixels; $C(\mathbf{r}')$, $\hat{C}_c(\mathbf{r}')$ and $\hat{C}_f(\mathbf{r}')$ denote the ground-truth, coarse volume predicted and fine volume predicted pixel color for the deformed ray $\mathbf{r}'$, respectively; and $p^k(\mathbf{r}')$, $\hat{p}_c^k(\mathbf{r}')$ and $\hat{p}_f^k(\mathbf{r}')$ denote the ground-truth, coarse volume predicted and fine volume predicted multi-class semantic distribution for the deformed ray $\mathbf{r}'$, respectively. The overall learning objective for the framework is:

$$\mathcal{L} = \mathcal{L}_{\mathrm{p}} + \lambda\mathcal{L}_{\mathrm{s}}, \qquad (12)$$

where λ is the weight balancing coefficient. At the training stage, the network parameters Θ and Φ in Eq. 8 are updated based on the above loss function.

4 Experiments

4.1 Dataset and Preprocessing

Dataset Collection. Our method targets to synthesize audio-driven facial images. Hence a certain person's speaking portrait video with audio track is needed. Unlike previous studies that demand large-corpus data or hours-long videos, we can achieve high-fidelity results with short videos of merely a few minutes. In particular, we extend the *publicly-released* video set of Guo *et al.* [19] and obtain videos of average length 6,750 frames in 25 fps.

Training Data Preprocessing. We follow the basic setting [19] of audio-driven video portrait generation to preprocess training data: (1) For the speech audio, it is first processed by a pretrained DeepSpeech [1] model. Then a 1D convolutional network with self-attention mechanism is adopted [19,60] for smooth feature learning. The extracted audio feature $\mathbf{a} \in \mathbb{R}^{64}$ is fed into the implicit function in Eq. 8. (2) For the video frames, they are cropped and resized to 450×450 to make talking portrait in the center. An off-the-shelf method [23] is leveraged to obtain parsing maps of total 11 semantic classes. The background image and head pose are estimated in a similar way to Guo *et al.* [19]. Note that the estimated head pose $\mathbf{p}_h(t)$ at time t is treated as camera pose and the canonical pose $\mathbf{p}_c$ is set as the starting frame's head pose, *i.e.*, $\mathbf{p}_c = \mathbf{p}_h(0)$ in Eq. 8.

Table 1. The quantitative results of *cropped setting* on Testset A, B [60] and C [59]. We compare the proposed Semantic-aware Speaking Portrait NeRF (**SSP-NeRF**) against recent SOTA methods [7,19,47,59,60,82,83] and ground truth under four metrics. For LMD the lower the better, and the higher the better for other metrics. Note that the detailed comparison settings are elaborated in Sect. 4.3

Methods	Testset A				Testset B [60]		Testset C [59]	
	PSNR ↑	SSIM ↑	LMD ↓	Sync ↑	LMD ↓	Sync ↑	LMD ↓	Sync ↑
Ground truth	N/A	1.000	0	6.632	0	5.973	0	6.204
ATVG [7]	24.125	0.725	5.261	4.708	5.074	6.208	5.869	4.419
Wav2Lip [47]	26.667	0.793	5.811	**6.952**	4.893	**6.980**	5.740	**6.806**
MakeitTalk [83]	25.522	0.704	7.238	3.873	6.704	4.105	6.512	3.925
PC-AVS [82]	25.712	0.756	5.406	5.834	5.247	6.113	5.771	5.983
NVP [60]	–	–	–	–	5.072	5.689	–	–
SynObama [59]	–	–	–	–	–	–	5.485	5.938
AD-NeRF [19]	29.814	0.844	5.183	6.092	5.119	5.613	5.392	6.012
SSP-NeRF (Ours)	**32.649**	**0.868**	**4.934**	6.438	**4.892**	5.886	**5.208**	6.186

4.2 Experimental Settings

Comparison Baselines. We compare our method with recent representative works: (1) **ATVG** [7], which uses 2D landmark to guide facial image synthesis;

(2) **Wav2Lip** [47] that achieves state-of-the-art lip-sync performance by pre-training a lip-sync expert; (3) **MakeitTalk** [83], a representative 3D landmark-based approach; (4) **PC-AVS** [82] which generates pose-controllable talking face by modularized audio-visual representation; (5) **NVP** [60] that first infers expression parameters from audio, then generates images with a neural renderer; (6) **SynObama** [59] which learns mouth shape changes for facial image warping; (7) **AD-NeRF** [19], which is the first work that uses implicit representation of NeRF to achieve arbitrary-size talking head synthesis. In particular, we also show the evaluations directly on the **Ground Truth** for a clearer comparison.

Table 2. The quantitative results of *full resolution setting* on Testset A. We compare our method with AD-NeRF [19] that also generates whole portrait with full resolution of 450×450. We evaluate image quality and lip-sync accuracy of synthesized results. The number of parameters for each model is shown in table

| Methods | Testset A (450×450) | | | | |
	PSNR	SSIM	LMD	Sync	# of params
GT	N/A	1.000	0	5.291	–
AD-NeRF	29.186	0.827	4.892	4.237	2.69M
Ours	**32.785**	**0.876**	**4.495**	**4.993**	**1.10M**

Implementation Details. The $F_\Theta^{\text{semantic}}$ and F_Φ^{deform} together with their associated fine models all consist of simple 8-layers MLPs with hidden size of 128 and ReLU activations. Following NeRF [34], positional encoding is applied to each 3D coordinate $\mathbf{x}$, view direction $\mathbf{d}$ and time instant t to map the input into higher dimensional space for better learning. The positional encoder is formulated as: $\gamma(q) = < (\sin(2^l \pi q), \cos(2^l \pi q)) >_0^L$, where we use $L = 10$ for $\mathbf{x}$, and $L = 4$ for $\mathbf{d}$ and t. For the parsing maps, we use $K = 11$ categories for semantic guidance, including cheek, eye, eyebrow, ear, nose, teeth, lip, neck, torso, hair and background. The structured 3D feature extractor is borrowed from [44] that processes feature volume with 3D sparse convolutions and outputs latent code with $2\times$, $4\times$, $8\times$, $16\times$ downsampled sizes. The semantic weight λ is empirically set to 0.04. The model is trained with 450×450 images during $400k$ iterations with a batch size of $N_s = 1024$ rays. The framework is implemented in PyTorch [42] and trained with Adam optimizer [21] of learning rate 5e−4 on a single Tesla V100 GPU for 48 h.

4.3   Quantitative Evaluation

Evaluation Metrics. We employ evaluation metrics that have been previously used in talking face generation. We adopt **PSNR** and **SSIM** [67] to evaluate the image quality of generated results; Landmark Distance (**LMD**) [6] and **Sync-Net Confidence** [10,12] to account for the accuracy of mouth shapes and lip

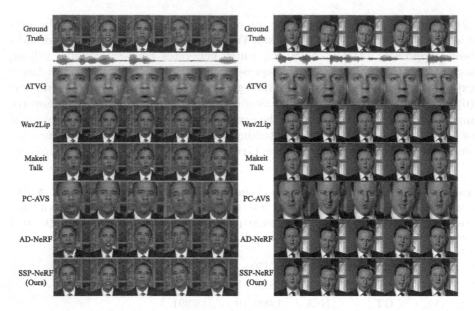

Fig. 2. The qualitative comparisons on Testset A. We show the synthesized talking heads of ground truth, baseline methods [7,19,47,82,83] and ours. Please **zoom in for better visualization**. More qualitative results can be found in demo video

sync. Other metrics such as **CSIM** [5,77] for measuring identity preserving and **CPBD** [35] for result sharpness are shown in supplementary material.

Comparison Settings. The reconstruction/model-based methods require large-corpus training data or long videos, hence we directly inference their released best models. Note that all baseline methods except for [19] fail to generate the whole portrait with full resolution, we divide our comparisons into two settings: 1) The *cropped setting* in Table 1, where we crop the generated facial image with same region and resize into same size for fair evaluation metric comparison. 2) The *full resolution setting* in Table 2, where we compare with AD-NeRF [19] that could also synthesize the whole portrait with full resolution of 450×450.

In the first setting, since NVP [60] and SynObama [59] do not provide pretrained models, we conduct comparisons on three datasets: (1) **Testset A**, the collected dataset mentioned in Sect. 4.1; (2) **Testset B**, where we extract speech audio from the demo of NVP to drive other baselines; (3) **Testset C**, where the audio from SynObama's demo is used for animation. Note that the metrics for measuring image quality (PSNR and SSIM) are not evaluated on Testset B and C due to the low image quality of original videos. In the second setting, the experiment is only conducted on Testset A. We further compare the number of model parameters against AD-NeRF [19] to show the efficiency.

Evaluation Results. The results of the *cropped setting* and *full resolution setting* are shown in Table 1 and Table 2, respectively. It can be seen that the proposed **SSP-NeRF** achieves the best evaluation results in most metrics: **(1)** In the cropped setting, we synthesize fine-grained facial images with detailed local appearance and dynamics of each portrait part. Note that Wav2Lip [47] uses SyncNet [10,12] for pretraining, which makes their results on SyncNet Confidence even better than the ground truth. Our performance on the LMD metric is the best, and the SyncNet Confidence of our model is close to the ground truth on all three datasets, showing that we can generate accurate lip-sync video portraits. **(2)** In the full resolution setting, the human face as well as torso part is evaluated. Different from AD-NeRF's separated rendering pipeline, our design of Torso Deformation module facilitates steady results. The statistics on both model's parameter number are shown in Table 2. Notably, the training curves of both methods are shown in Fig. 3 (right), where our approach (red curve) uses $400k \times 1024$ sampled rays, while AD-NeRF [19] (blue curve) uses $400k \times 2048$ rays for training each model. Hence we generate portraits of *better* image quality and *better* lip-synchronization in a *more compact* model with *fewer* iterations, proving the effectiveness and efficiency of SSP-NeRF.

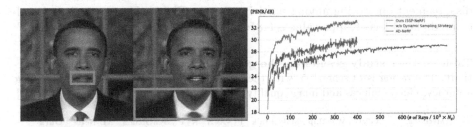

Fig. 3. Left: We show the visualized ablation results of w/o dynamic sampling strategy and w/o torso deformation respectively, where the blurry regions are highlighted. **Right:** We show the training curves of (1) Ours (red), (2) w/o dynamic sampling (green) and (3) AD-NeRF (blue). Note that the vertical axis stands for PSNR value and the horizontal axis stands for the number of sampled rays ($10^3 \times N_s$) (Color figure online)

4.4 Qualitative Evaluation

We compare the generated key frames of each method in Fig. 2. It shows that our video portraits are more lip-synced with higher image quality. In particular, ATVG [7] and MakeitTalk [83] rely on precise facial landmarks, which leads to inaccurate mouth shapes (green arrow); Wav2Lip [47] creates static talking heads; PC-AVS [82] fails to preserve the speaker's identity, making results unrealistic. Moreover, all the image reconstruction-based methods [47,82] or model-based methods [7,83] fail to synthesize the whole portrait of high-fidelity simultaneously. Although AD-NeRF [19] manages to create full-resolution results, the

118   X. Liu et al.

separated rendering pipeline with uniform ray sampling leads to head-torso separation (as highlighted by blue arrows) and blurry results (orange arrow).

User Study. A user study is further conducted to reflect the quality of audio-
driven portrait. Specifically, we sample 30 audio clips from Testset A, B and
C for all methods to generate results, and then involve 18 participants for user
study. The Mean Opinion Scores rating protocol is adopted for evaluation, which
requires the participants to rate three aspects of generated speaking portraits:
(1) *Lip-sync Accuracy*; (2) *Video Realness*; (3) *Image Quality*. The rating is
based on a scale of 1 to 5, with 5 being the maximum and 1 being the minimum.

The results are shown in Table 3. Since NeRF enables full-resolution whole
portrait generation, both AD-NeRF [19] and our method score comparatively
high on *Image Quality* and *Video Realness*. Besides, the users prefer our generated speaking portraits to AD-NeRF's [19] due to the fine-grained local rendering and stable torso motions provided by our framework design. Although PC-
AVS [82] also creates pose-controllable talking faces, the inaccuracy of implicit
pose code extraction weakens their realness. Note that Wav2Lip [47], NVP [60]
and SynObama [59] achieve competitive scores on *Lip-sync Accuracy*. However,
they rely on large corpus or long training videos, while we merely take a short
video as input, showing the efficacy of our method. To further measure the
disagreement on scoring among participants, the Fleiss's-Kappa statistic is calculated. The Fleiss-Kappa value is 0.816, indicating "almost perfect agreement".

**Table 3. User study results on the generation quality of audio-driven por-
trait.** The rating is of scale 1–5, with the larger the better. We compare the lip-sync
accuracy, video realness and image quality to baseline methods [7,19,47,59,60,82,83]

Methods	ATVG	Wav2Lip	MakeitTalk	PC-AVS	NVP	SynObama	AD-NeRF	**Ours**
Lip-sync Acc	3.02	4.23	2.89	4.05	**4.26**	4.21	4.16	**4.26**
Video Real	1.63	2.86	2.45	3.83	3.89	3.93	4.09	**4.28**
Image Qua	1.72	2.42	2.78	2.36	4.02	3.86	4.18	**4.43**

(a)   (b)   (c)

Fig. 4. The visualized deformation heatmap. From left to right, we show the
predicted displacements over the whole portrait image under three cases of small,
medium and large pose. We can observe that: 1) The deformations are mostly on the
torso region; 2) The larger head pose is, the more displacements our model will predict

4.5   Ablation Study

Torso Deformation Module. We conduct ablation experiments under two settings: (1) w/o F_Φ^{deform}, where we directly synthesize the whole portrait without deforming 3D coordinates. The results are shown in Table 4 (left, first line), where the ill-posed rendering leads to blurry torso with low image quality. To further investigate the efficacy of Torso Deformation module, we visualize the heatmap of learned displacements in Fig. 4. Since audio feature is not input to the deformation implicit function, it tends to warp the weakly audio-related torso part, while the strongly audio-related mouth movements are mostly modeled by $F_\Theta^{\text{semantic}}$. The marginal drop in lip-sync metrics also suggests that the deformation module majorly takes effect on the torso part.

Another ablation setting is: (2) deform by **a**, where the audio input **a** is fed to F_Φ^{deform} rather than $F_\Theta^{\text{semantic}}$, *i.e.*, the audio feature **a**, head pose $\mathbf{p}_h(t)$ and canonical pose $\mathbf{p}_c$ are leveraged to deform both the human face and torso part simultaneously. The lip-sync performance drops dramatically as shown in Table 4 (left, second line). We guess the reason lies in distinct correlations between audio and different portrait parts. It is hard for deformation module to handle audio synchronization and portrait parts deformation at the same time.

Semantic-aware Dynamic Ray Sampling Module. The ablative experiments contain: (1) w/o semantic branch, which means the semantic supervision $\mathcal{L}_s$ is not used; (2) w/o dynamic sample, where the rays are uniformly sampled over image plane; (3) w/o 3D information, which means the 3D feature **f** is eliminated. The results in Table 4 (right) verify that the semantic awareness enables the model to better grasp each part's appearance and geometry. The dynamic ray sampling further facilitates fine-grained results.

We further show **visual ablation** of original, "w/o dynamic sampling strategy" and "w/o torso deformation" in Fig. 3 (left). We can see that dynamic sampling facilitates small but important region (compare to the blurry mouth). Besides, torso deformation guarantees stable rendering (compare to the blurry torso). In the Fig. 3 (right), we present training curves of "w/o dynamic sampling strategy"(green). Dynamic strategy can sample more on hard-to-learn regions to boost training (compare red curve to green curve), and other components also facilitate model learning process (compare green curve to blue curve).

Table 4. Left: Ablation study of Torso Deformation module. **Right:** Ablation study of Semantic-Aware Dynamic Ray Sampling module. Settings are elaborated in Sect. 4.5

Methods	PSNR ↑	SSIM ↑	LMD ↓	Sync ↑	Methods	PSNR↑	SSIM↑	LMD↓	Sync↑
w/o F_Φ^{deform}	27.472	0.791	4.635	4.744	w/o semantic branch	29.479	0.832	4.886	4.562
deform by **a**	28.013	0.802	5.329	3.871	w/o dynamic sample	29.514	0.826	4.916	4.490
					w/o 3D information	31.059	0.845	4.683	4.739
SSP-NeRF	**32.785**	**0.876**	**4.495**	**4.993**	**SSP-NeRF**	**32.785**	**0.876**	**4.495**	**4.993**

5   Conclusion and Discussion

Conclusion. In this paper, we propose a novel framework **SSP-NeRF** for audio-driven portrait generation. We introduce Semantic-Aware Dynamic Ray Sampling module to grasp the detailed appearance and the local dynamics of each portrait part without using accurate structural information. We then propose a Torso Deformation module to learn global torso motion and prevent head-torso separated results. Extensive experiments show that our approach can synthesize more realistic video portraits compared to the previous methods.

Ethical Consideration. Animating realistic talking portrait has extensive applications like digital human and film-making. On the other hand, it could be misused for malicious purposes such as identity theft, deepfake generation, and media manipulation. Recent studies have shown promising results in detecting deepfakes [52,53]. However, the lack of realistic data limits their performance. As part of our responsibility, we feel obliged to share our generated results with the deepfake detection community to improve the model's robustness. We believe that the proper use of this technique will enhance the healthy development of both machine learning research and digital entertainment.

References

1. Amodei, D., et al.: Deep speech 2: end-to-end speech recognition in English and mandarin. In: International Conference on Machine Learning, pp. 173–182. PMLR (2016)
2. Barron, J.T., et al.: Mip-NeRF: a multiscale representation for anti-aliasing neural radiance fields. In: ICCV (2021)
3. Blanz, V., Vetter, T.: A morphable model for the synthesis of 3D faces. In: Proceedings of the 26th Annual Conference on Computer Graphics and Interactive Techniques, pp. 187–194 (1999)
4. Brand, M.: Voice puppetry. In: Proceedings of the 26th Annual Conference on Computer Graphics and Interactive Techniques, pp. 21–28 (1999)
5. Chen, L., et al.: Talking-head generation with rhythmic head motion. In: Vedaldi, A., Bischof, H., Brox, T., Frahm, J.-M. (eds.) ECCV 2020. LNCS, vol. 12354, pp. 35–51. Springer, Cham (2020). https://doi.org/10.1007/978-3-030-58545-7_3
6. Chen, L., Li, Z., Maddox, R.K., Duan, Z., Xu, C.: Lip movements generation at a glance. In: Ferrari, V., Hebert, M., Sminchisescu, C., Weiss, Y. (eds.) ECCV 2018. LNCS, vol. 11211, pp. 538–553. Springer, Cham (2018). https://doi.org/10.1007/978-3-030-01234-2_32
7. Chen, L., Maddox, R.K., Duan, Z., Xu, C.: Hierarchical cross-modal talking face generation with dynamic pixel-wise loss. In: CVPR (2019)
8. Chen, Y., Liu, S., Wang, X.: Learning continuous image representation with local implicit image function. In: Proceedings of the IEEE/CVF Conference on Computer Vision and Pattern Recognition, pp. 8628–8638 (2021)
9. Chen, Y., Wu, Q., Zheng, C., Cham, T.J., Cai, J.: Sem2NeRF: converting single-view semantic masks to neural radiance fields. arXiv preprint arXiv:2203.10821 (2022)
10. Chung, J.S., Zisserman, A.: Out of time: automated lip sync in the wild. In: Workshop on Multi-View Lip-Reading. ACCV (2016)

11. Chung, J.S., Jamaludin, A., Zisserman, A.: You said that? arXiv preprint arXiv:1705.02966 (2017)
12. Chung, J.S., Zisserman, A.: Lip reading in the wild. In: Lai, S.-H., Lepetit, V., Nishino, K., Sato, Y. (eds.) ACCV 2016. LNCS, vol. 10112, pp. 87–103. Springer, Cham (2017). https://doi.org/10.1007/978-3-319-54184-6_6
13. Das, D., Biswas, S., Sinha, S., Bhowmick, B.: Speech-driven facial animation using cascaded GANs for learning of motion and texture. In: Vedaldi, A., Bischof, H., Brox, T., Frahm, J.-M. (eds.) ECCV 2020. LNCS, vol. 12375, pp. 408–424. Springer, Cham (2020). https://doi.org/10.1007/978-3-030-58577-8_25
14. Deng, K., Liu, A., Zhu, J.Y., Ramanan, D.: Depth-supervised NeRF: fewer views and faster training for free. arXiv preprint arXiv:2107.02791 (2021)
15. Fisher, C.G.: Confusions among visually perceived consonants. J. Speech Hear. Res. **11**(4), 796–804 (1968)
16. Gafni, G., Thies, J., Zollhöfer, M., Nießner, M.: Dynamic neural radiance fields for monocular 4D facial avatar reconstruction. In: Proceedings of the IEEE/CVF Conference on Computer Vision and Pattern Recognition (CVPR), pp. 8649–8658, June 2021
17. Graham, B., Engelcke, M., Van Der Maaten, L.: 3D semantic segmentation with submanifold sparse convolutional networks. In: Proceedings of the IEEE Conference on Computer Vision and Pattern Recognition, pp. 9224–9232 (2018)
18. Gropp, A., Yariv, L., Haim, N., Atzmon, M., Lipman, Y.: Implicit geometric regularization for learning shapes. arXiv preprint arXiv:2002.10099 (2020)
19. Guo, Y., Chen, K., Liang, S., Liu, Y., Bao, H., Zhang, J.: AD-NeRF: audio driven neural radiance fields for talking head synthesis. In: IEEE/CVF International Conference on Computer Vision (ICCV) (2021)
20. Ji, X., et al.: EAMM: one-shot emotional talking face via audio-based emotion-aware motion model. In: SIGGRAPH (2022)
21. Kingma, D.P., Ba, J.: Adam: a method for stochastic optimization. In: Bengio, Y., LeCun, Y. (eds.) 3rd International Conference on Learning Representations, ICLR 2015, San Diego, CA, USA, 7–9 May 2015, Conference Track Proceedings (2015). https://arxiv.org/abs/1412.6980
22. Kohli, A., Sitzmann, V., Wetzstein, G.: Inferring semantic information with 3D neural scene representations. arXiv e-prints pp. arXiv-2003 (2020)
23. Lee, C.H., Liu, Z., Wu, L., Luo, P.: MaskGAN: towards diverse and interactive facial image manipulation. In: CVPR (2020)
24. Liang, B., et al.: Expressive talking head generation with granular audio-visual control. In: Proceedings of the IEEE/CVF Conference on Computer Vision and Pattern Recognition (CVPR), pp. 3387–3396, June 2022
25. Liu, L., Gu, J., Lin, K.Z., Chua, T.S., Theobalt, C.: Neural sparse voxel fields. arXiv preprint arXiv:2007.11571 (2020)
26. Liu, L., Habermann, M., Rudnev, V., Sarkar, K., Gu, J., Theobalt, C.: Neural actor: neural free-view synthesis of human actors with pose control. arXiv preprint arXiv:2106.02019 (2021)
27. Liu, S., Zhang, Y., Peng, S., Shi, B., Pollefeys, M., Cui, Z.: DIST: rendering deep implicit signed distance function with differentiable sphere tracing. In: Proceedings of the IEEE/CVF Conference on Computer Vision and Pattern Recognition, pp. 2019–2028 (2020)
28. Liu, X., et al.: Visual sound localization in the wild by cross-modal interference erasing. arXiv preprint arXiv:2202.06406 2 (2022)

29. Liu, X., et al.: Learning hierarchical cross-modal association for co-speech gesture generation. In: Proceedings of the IEEE/CVF Conference on Computer Vision and Pattern Recognition, pp. 10462–10472 (2022)

30. Martin-Brualla, R., Radwan, N., Sajjadi, M.S., Barron, J.T., Dosovitskiy, A., Duckworth, D.: NeRF in the wild: neural radiance fields for unconstrained photo collections. In: Proceedings of the IEEE/CVF Conference on Computer Vision and Pattern Recognition, pp. 7210–7219 (2021)

31. Max, N.: Optical models for direct volume rendering. IEEE Trans. Vis. Comput. Graph. 1(2), 99–108 (1995)

32. Mescheder, L., Oechsle, M., Niemeyer, M., Nowozin, S., Geiger, A.: Occupancy networks: Learning 3D reconstruction in function space. In: Proceedings of the IEEE/CVF Conference on Computer Vision and Pattern Recognition, pp. 4460–4470 (2019)

33. Meshry, M., Suri, S., Davis, L.S., Shrivastava, A.: Learned spatial representations for few-shot talking-head synthesis. arXiv preprint arXiv:2104.14557 (2021)

34. Mildenhall, B., Srinivasan, P.P., Tancik, M., Barron, J.T., Ramamoorthi, R., Ng, R.: NeRF: representing scenes as neural radiance fields for view synthesis. In: Vedaldi, A., Bischof, H., Brox, T., Frahm, J.-M. (eds.) ECCV 2020. LNCS, vol. 12346, pp. 405–421. Springer, Cham (2020). https://doi.org/10.1007/978-3-030-58452-8_24

35. Narvekar, N.D., Karam, L.J.: A no-reference perceptual image sharpness metric based on a cumulative probability of blur detection. In: 2009 International Workshop on Quality of Multimedia Experience, pp. 87–91. IEEE (2009)

36. Niemeyer, M., Geiger, A.: GIRAFFE: representing scenes as compositional generative neural feature fields. In: Proceedings of the IEEE/CVF Conference on Computer Vision and Pattern Recognition, pp. 11453–11464 (2021)

37. Niemeyer, M., Mescheder, L., Oechsle, M., Geiger, A.: Differentiable volumetric rendering: Learning implicit 3d representations without 3D supervision. In: Proceedings of the IEEE/CVF Conference on Computer Vision and Pattern Recognition, pp. 3504–3515 (2020)

38. Noguchi, A., Sun, X., Lin, S., Harada, T.: Neural articulated radiance field. arXiv preprint arXiv:2104.03110 (2021)

39. Palafox, P., Bozic, A., Thies, J., Nießner, M., Dai, A.: Neural parametric models for 3D deformable shapes. In: Proceedings of the IEEE/CVF International Conference on Computer Vision (ICCV), vol. 3 (2021)

40. Park, K., et al.: Nerfies: deformable neural radiance fields. In: Proceedings of the IEEE/CVF International Conference on Computer Vision, pp. 5865–5874 (2021)

41. Park, K., et al.: HyperNeRF: a higher-dimensional representation for topologically varying neural radiance fields. arXiv preprint arXiv:2106.13228 (2021)

42. Paszke, A., et al.: PyTorch: an imperative style, high-performance deep learning library. In: Advances in Neural Information Processing Systems, vol. 32, pp. 8026–8037 (2019)

43. Peng, S., et al.: Animatable neural radiance fields for human body modeling. arXiv preprint arXiv:2105.02872 (2021)

44. Peng, S., et al.: Neural body: implicit neural representations with structured latent codes for novel view synthesis of dynamic humans. In: Proceedings of the IEEE/CVF Conference on Computer Vision and Pattern Recognition, pp. 9054–9063 (2021)

45. Peng, S., Niemeyer, M., Mescheder, L., Pollefeys, M., Geiger, A.: Convolutional occupancy networks. In: Vedaldi, A., Bischof, H., Brox, T., Frahm, J.-M. (eds.) ECCV 2020, Part III. LNCS, vol. 12348, pp. 523–540. Springer, Cham (2020). https://doi.org/10.1007/978-3-030-58580-8_31

46. Pham, H.X., Cheung, S., Pavlovic, V.: Speech-driven 3D facial animation with implicit emotional awareness: a deep learning approach. In: Proceedings of the IEEE Conference on Computer Vision and Pattern Recognition Workshops, pp. 80–88 (2017)

47. Prajwal, K., Mukhopadhyay, R., Namboodiri, V.P., Jawahar, C.: A lip sync expert is all you need for speech to lip generation in the wild. In: Proceedings of the 28th ACM International Conference on Multimedia, pp. 484–492 (2020)

48. Pumarola, A., Corona, E., Pons-Moll, G., Moreno-Noguer, F.: D-NeRF: neural radiance fields for dynamic scenes. In: Proceedings of the IEEE/CVF Conference on Computer Vision and Pattern Recognition, pp. 10318–10327 (2021)

49. Raj, A., et al.: PVA: pixel-aligned volumetric avatars. arXiv preprint arXiv:2101.02697 (2021)

50. Ren, D., et al.: CSG-stump: a learning friendly CSG-like representation for interpretable shape parsing. In: Proceedings of the IEEE/CVF International Conference on Computer Vision, pp. 12478–12487 (2021)

51. Richard, A., Lea, C., Ma, S., Gall, J., De la Torre, F., Sheikh, Y.: Audio-and gaze-driven facial animation of codec avatars. In: Proceedings of the IEEE/CVF Winter Conference on Applications of Computer Vision, pp. 41–50 (2021)

52. Rössler, A., et al.: FaceForensics: a large-scale video dataset for forgery detection in human faces. arXiv preprint arXiv:1803.09179 (2018)

53. Rossler, A., et al.: FaceForensics++: learning to detect manipulated facial images. In: Proceedings of the IEEE/CVF International Conference on Computer Vision, pp. 1–11 (2019)

54. Saito, S., Huang, Z., Natsume, R., Morishima, S., Kanazawa, A., Li, H.: PIFu: pixel-aligned implicit function for high-resolution clothed human digitization. In: ICCV (2019)

55. Sitzmann, V., Zollhöfer, M., Wetzstein, G.: Scene representation networks: Continuous 3D-structure-aware neural scene representations. arXiv preprint arXiv:1906.01618 (2019)

56. Song, L., Wu, W., Qian, C., He, R., Loy, C.C.: Everybody's talkin': Let me talk as you want. arXiv preprint arXiv:2001.05201 (2020)

57. Song, Y., Zhu, J., Li, D., Wang, X., Qi, H.: Talking face generation by conditional recurrent adversarial network. arXiv preprint arXiv:1804.04786 (2018)

58. Sun, T., Lin, K.E., Bi, S., Xu, Z., Ramamoorthi, R.: Nelf: neural light-transport field for portrait view synthesis and relighting. arXiv preprint arXiv:2107.12351 (2021)

59. Suwajanakorn, S., Seitz, S.M., Kemelmacher-Shlizerman, I.: Synthesizing Obama: learning lip sync from audio. ACM Trans. Graph. (ToG) 36(4), 1–13 (2017)

60. Thies, J., Elgharib, M., Tewari, A., Theobalt, C., Nießner, M.: Neural voice puppetry: audio-driven facial reenactment. In: Vedaldi, A., Bischof, H., Brox, T., Frahm, J.-M. (eds.) ECCV 2020. LNCS, vol. 12361, pp. 716–731. Springer, Cham (2020). https://doi.org/10.1007/978-3-030-58517-4_42

61. Tretschk, E., Tewari, A., Golyanik, V., Zollhofer, M., Lassner, C., Theobalt, C.: Non-rigid neural radiance fields: Reconstruction and novel view synthesis of a dynamic scene from monocular video. In: Proceedings of the IEEE/CVF International Conference on Computer Vision, pp. 12959–12970 (2021)

62. Vougioukas, K., Petridis, S., Pantic, M.: Realistic speech-driven facial animation with GANs. Int. J. Comput. Vis. **128**(5), 1398–1413 (2020)
63. Wang, K., et al.: MEAD: a large-scale audio-visual dataset for emotional talking-face generation. In: Vedaldi, A., Bischof, H., Brox, T., Frahm, J.-M. (eds.) ECCV 2020. LNCS, vol. 12366, pp. 700–717. Springer, Cham (2020). https://doi.org/10.1007/978-3-030-58589-1_42
64. Wang, P., Liu, L., Liu, Y., Theobalt, C., Komura, T., Wang, W.: NeuS: learning neural implicit surfaces by volume rendering for multi-view reconstruction. In: NeurIPS (2021)
65. Wang, S., Li, L., Ding, Y., Fan, C., Yu, X.: Audio2Head: audio-driven one-shot talking-head generation with natural head motion. arXiv preprint arXiv:2107.09293 (2021)
66. Wang, T.C., Mallya, A., Liu, M.Y.: One-shot free-view neural talking-head synthesis for video conferencing. In: Proceedings of the IEEE/CVF Conference on Computer Vision and Pattern Recognition, pp. 10039–10049 (2021)
67. Wang, Z., Bovik, A.C., Sheikh, H.R., Simoncelli, E.P.: Image quality assessment: from error visibility to structural similarity. IEEE Trans. Image Process. **13**(4), 600–612 (2004)
68. Wiles, O., Koepke, A.S., Zisserman, A.: X2Face: a network for controlling face generation using images, audio, and pose codes. In: Ferrari, V., Hebert, M., Sminchisescu, C., Weiss, Y. (eds.) ECCV 2018. LNCS, vol. 11217, pp. 690–706. Springer, Cham (2018). https://doi.org/10.1007/978-3-030-01261-8_41
69. Wu, H., Jia, J., Wang, H., Dou, Y., Duan, C., Deng, Q.: Imitating arbitrary talking style for realistic audio-driven talking face synthesis. In: Proceedings of the 29th ACM International Conference on Multimedia, pp. 1478–1486 (2021)
70. Wu, Q., et al.: Object-compositional neural implicit surfaces. arXiv preprint arXiv:2207.09686 (2022)
71. Xu, X., Pan, X., Lin, D., Dai, B.: Generative occupancy fields for 3D surface-aware image synthesis. In: Advances in Neural Information Processing Systems (NeurIPS) (2021)
72. Yan, Y., Mao, Y., Li, B.: Second: sparsely embedded convolutional detection. Sensors **18**(10), 3337 (2018)
73. Yang, B., et al.: Learning object-compositional neural radiance field for editable scene rendering. In: International Conference on Computer Vision (ICCV), October 2021
74. Yariv, L., Gu, J., Kasten, Y., Lipman, Y.: Volume rendering of neural implicit surfaces. arXiv preprint arXiv:2106.12052 (2021)
75. Yariv, L., et al: Multiview neural surface reconstruction by disentangling geometry and appearance. In: Advances in Neural Information Processing Systems 33 (2020)
76. Yi, R., Ye, Z., Zhang, J., Bao, H., Liu, Y.J.: Audio-driven talking face video generation with learning-based personalized head pose. arXiv preprint arXiv:2002.10137 (2020)
77. Zakharov, E., Shysheya, A., Burkov, E., Lempitsky, V.: Few-shot adversarial learning of realistic neural talking head models. In: ICCV (2019)
78. Zhang, J.Y., Yang, G., Tulsiani, S., Ramanan, D.: NeRS: neural reflectance surfaces for sparse-view 3D reconstruction in the wild. In: Conference on Neural Information Processing Systems (2021)
79. Zhang, X., et al.: Neural light transport for relighting and view synthesis. ACM Trans. Graph. (TOG) **40**(1), 1–17 (2021)

80. Zhi, S., Laidlow, T., Leutenegger, S., Davison, A.: In-place scene labelling and understanding with implicit scene representation. In: Proceedings of the International Conference on Computer Vision (ICCV) (2021)
81. Zhou, H., Liu, Y., Liu, Z., Luo, P., Wang, X.: Talking face generation by adversarially disentangled audio-visual representation. In: AAAI Conference on Artificial Intelligence (AAAI) (2019)
82. Zhou, H., Sun, Y., Wu, W., Loy, C.C., Wang, X., Liu, Z.: Pose-controllable talking face generation by implicitly modularized audio-visual representation. In: Proceedings of the IEEE/CVF Conference on Computer Vision and Pattern Recognition, pp. 4176–4186 (2021)
83. Zhou, Y., Han, X., Shechtman, E., Echevarria, J., Kalogerakis, E., Li, D.: MakeltTalk: speaker-aware talking-head animation. ACM Trans. Graph. (TOG) **39**(6), 1–15 (2020)
84. Zhu, H., Huang, H., Li, Y., Zheng, A., He, R.: Arbitrary talking face generation via attentional audio-visual coherence learning. arXiv preprint arXiv:1812.06589 (2018)

End-to-End Active Speaker Detection

Juan León Alcázar[1]([✉]) [iD], Moritz Cordes[1,2], Chen Zhao[1] [iD],
and Bernard Ghanem[1] [iD]

[1] King Abdullah University of Science and Technology, KAUST,
Thuwal, Saudi Arabia
jc.leon@uniandes.edu.co, {chen.zhao,bernard.ghanem}@kaust.edu.sa
[2] Leuphana University Lüneburg, Lüneburg, Germany
moritz.cordes@stud.leuphana.de

Abstract. Recent advances in the Active Speaker Detection (ASD)
problem build upon a two-stage process: feature extraction and spatio-
temporal context aggregation. In this paper, we propose an end-to-end
ASD workflow where feature learning and contextual predictions are
jointly learned. Our end-to-end trainable network simultaneously learns
multi-modal embeddings and aggregates spatio-temporal context. This
results in more suitable feature representations and improved performance in the ASD task. We also introduce interleaved graph neural network (iGNN) blocks, which split the message passing according to the
main sources of context in the ASD problem. Experiments show that the
aggregated features from the iGNN blocks are more suitable for ASD,
resulting in state-of-the art performance. Finally, we design a weakly-
supervised strategy, which demonstrates that the ASD problem can also
be approached by utilizing audiovisual data but relying exclusively on
audio annotations. We achieve this by modelling the direct relationship
between the audio signal and the possible sound sources (speakers), as
well as introducing a contrastive loss.

1 Introduction

In active speaker detection (ASD), the current speaker must be identified from a
set of available candidates, which are usually defined by face tracklets assembled
from temporally linked face detections [5,28,35]. Initial approaches to the ASD
problem focused on the analysis of individual visual tracklets and the associated
audio track, aiming to maximize the agreement between the audio signal and
the visual patterns [9,35,49]. Such an approach is suitable for scenarios where a
single visual track is available. However, in the general (multi-speaker) scenario,
this naïve correspondence will suffer from false positive detections, leading to
incorrect speech-to-speaker assignments.

Current approaches for ASD rely on two-stage models [25,28,40]. First, they
learn to associate the facial motion patterns and its concurrent audio stream by

Supplementary Information The online version contains supplementary material
available at https://doi.org/10.1007/978-3-031-19836-6_8.

optimizing a multi-modal encoder [35]. Then, this encoder serves as a feature extractor for a second stage, in which multi-modal embeddings from multiple speakers are fused [1]. These two-stage approaches are currently preferred given the technical challenges of end-to-end training with video data. Despite the computational efficiency of these approaches, their two-stage nature precludes them from fully leveraging the learning capabilities of modern neural architectures, namely directly optimizing the features for the multi-speaker ASD task.

In this paper, we present a novel alternative to the traditional two-stage ASD methods, called End-to-end Active Speaker dEtEction (EASEE), which is the first end-to-end pipeline for active speaker detection. Unlike conventional methods, EASEE is able to learn multi-modal features from multiple visual tracklets, while simultaneously modeling their spatio-temporal relations in an end-to-end manner. As a consequence, EASEE feature embeddings are optimized to capture information from multiple speakers and enable effective speech-to-speaker assignments in a fully supervised manner. To generate its final predictions, our end-to-end architecture relies on a spatio-temporal module for context aggregation. We propose an interleaved Graph Neural Network (iGNN) block to model the relationships between speakers in adjacent timestamps. Instead of greedily fusing all available feature representations from multiple timestamps, the iGNN block provides a more principled way of modeling spatial and temporal interactions. iGNN performs two message passing steps: first a spatial message passing that models local interactions between speakers visible at the same timestamp, and then a temporal message passing that effectively aggregates long-term temporal information.

Finally, EASEE's end-to-end nature allows the use of alternative supervision targets. In this paper, we propose a weakly-supervised strategy for ASD, named EASEE-W (shown in Fig. 1). EASEE-W relies exclusively on audio labels, which are easier to obtain, to train the whole architecture. To optimize our network without the visual labels, we model the inherent structure in the ASD task, namely the direct relationship between the audio signal and its possible sound sources, *i.e.*, the speakers.

Contributions. This paper proposes EASEE, a novel approach for active speaker detection. Its end-to-end nature enables direct optimization of audio-visual embeddings and leverages novel training strategies, namely weak supervision. Our work brings the following contributions: (1) We devise **the first end-to-end trainable neural architecture** EASEE for the active speaker problem (Sect. 3.1), which learns effective feature representations. (2) In EASEE, we propose **a novel iGNN block** to aggregate spatial and temporal context based on a composition of spatial and temporal message passing. We show this reformulation of the graph structure is key to achieve state-of-the-art results (Sect. 4.1). (3) Based on EASEE, we propose **the first weakly-supervised ASD approach** that enables the use of only audio labels to generate predictions on visual data (Sect. 4.3). To ensure reproducible results and foster future research, we have made all the resources of this project available at: https://github.com/fuankarion/end-to-end-asd.

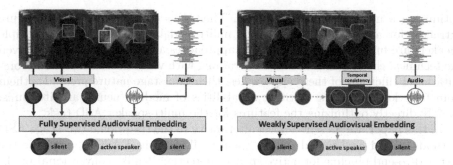

Fig. 1. Fully and weakly-supervised audiovisual embeddings. In the fully supervised scenario (left), we use the face crops as visual data and the Mel-frequency cepstral coefficients as audio data, we rely on visual and audio labels to directly optimize a shared feature embedding. In contrast, in the weakly supervised scenario, we omit the visual labels and optimize using only audio supervision. By modeling the visual-temporal consistency and speech-to-speaker assignments, we are able to optimize a shared embedding that can detect the active speakers without any visual supervision.

2   Related Work

Early approaches to the ASD problem [12] attempted to correlate audiovisual patterns using time-delayed neural networks [42]. Follow up works [15,37] approached the ASD task by limiting the analysis only to visual patterns. These approaches rely only on visual data given the biases of the single speaker scenario (*i.e.* speech can only be attributed to the single visible speaker). A parallel corpus of work focused on the complementary task of voice activity detection (VAD), which aims at finding speech activities among other acoustic events [6,38]. Similar to visual data, audio-only information was also proven to be useful in single speaker scenarios [13].

The recent interest in deep neural architectures [26,27,36] shifted the focus in the ASD problem from hand-crafted feature design to multi-modal representation learning [32]. As a consequence, ASD has become dominated by CNN-based approaches, which rely on convolutional encoders originally devised for image analysis tasks [35]. Recent works [5,11] approached the more general multi-speaker scenario, relying on the fusion of multi-modal information from individual speakers. Concurrent works have also focused on audiovisual feature alignment. This resulted in methods that rely on audio as the primary source of supervision [4], or focused on the design of multi-modal embeddings [10,11,31,39].

The recent availability of large-scale data for the ASD task [35] has enabled the use of state-of-the-art deep convolutional encoders [18,19]. In addition to these deep encoders, current approaches have shifted focus to directly modeling the temporal features over short temporal windows, typically by optimizing a Siamese Network with modality specific streams. The work of Chung *et al.* [9] explored the use of a hybrid 3D-2D encoder pretained on VoxCeleb [10] to analyze these temporal windows, while Zhang *et al.* [49] focused on improving the feature representation by using a contrastive loss [17] between the modalities.

To complement this short-term analysis, many methods [25,28,40] have aimed to incorporate contextual information from overlapping visual tracklets. The work of Alcazar *et al.* [1] introduced a data structure to represent an active speaker scene, and the features in this structure are improved by using self-attention [41,43] and recurrent networks [20].

Current state-of-the-art techniques incorporate contextual representation and rely on deep 3D encoders for the initial feature encoding and recurrent networks or self-attention to analyze the scene's contextual information [25,28,40,50]. We depart from this standard approach and devise a strategy to train end-to-end networks that simultaneously optimize features from a shared multi-modal encoder. This enables the direct optimization of temporal and spatial features for the ASD problem in a multi-speaker setup.

2.1   Graph Convolutional Networks

The current interest in non-Euclidean data [16,21,22,29,30,47] has focused the attention of the research community on Graph Convolutional Networks (GCNs) as an efficient variant of CNNs [24,45]. GCNs have achieved state-of-the-art results in zero-shot recognition [23,44], 3D understanding [16,29,46], and action recognition in video [21,47,48] by harnessing the flexibility of graphs representations. Recently, GCNs have been widely used in the field of action recognition, focusing on skeleton-based approaches that rely only on visual data [2,14]. For applications in audiovisual contexts, GCNs have been utilized to study inter-correlations in videos for automatic recognition of emotions in conversations [33,34]. In the ASD domain, Alcazar *et al.* [28] introduced the use of GCNs, developing a two-stage approach where a GCN network would module interactions between audio and video across multiple frames. We present an alternative to this approach where we focus on the end-to-end modelling, and perform independent steps of message passing along the spatial and temporal dimensions.

3   End-to-End Active Speaker Detection

Our approach relies on the initial generation of independent audio and visual embeddings at specific timestamps. These embeddings are fused and jointly optimized by means of a graph convolutional network [24]. To this end, we devise a neural architecture with three main components: (i) audio Encoder, (ii) visual Encoder, and a (iii) spatio-temporal Module. The visual encoder (f_v) performs multiple forward passes (one for each available tracklet), and the audio encoder (f_a) performs a single forward pass on the shared audio clip. These features are arranged according to their temporal order and (potential) spatial overlap, creating an intermediate feature embedding (Φ) that enables spatio-temporal reasoning. Unlike other methods, we construct Φ such that it can be optimized end-to-end. Thus Φ captures multi-modal and multi-speaker information, enables information flow across modalities, and ultimately improves network predictions. Figure 2 contains an overview of our proposed approach.

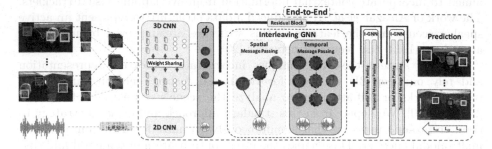

Fig. 2. Overview of the EASEE architecture. We fuse information from multiple visual tracklets, and their associated audio track. We rely on a 3D CNN to encode individual face tracklets, and a 2D CNN to encode the audio stream (Grey Encoders). These embeddings are assembled into an initial multi-modal embedding (Φ) containing audiovisual information from multiple persons in a scene. We map this embedding into a graph structure that performs message passing steps over spatial (light orange) and temporal dimensions (light green). Our layer arrangement favors independent massage passing steps along the temporal and spatial dimensions. (Color figure online)

3.1   EASEE Network Architecture

The main goal of EASEE is to aggregate related temporal and spatial information from different modalities over a video segment. To enable efficient end-to-end computation, we do not densely sample all the available tracklets in a temporal window, but rather define a strategy to sub-sample audiovisual segments inside a video. We define a set of temporal endpoints where the original video data (visual and audio) is densely sampled. At every temporal endpoint, we collect visual information from the available face tracklets and sample the associated audio signal (See Fig. 3). To further limit the memory usage, we define a fixed number of tracklets (i) to sample at every endpoint. Since the visual stream might contain an arbitrary number of tracklets, we follow [1] at training time and sample i tracklets with replacement. Hence, from every temporal endpoint, we create $i+1$ feature embeddings associated with it (i visual embeddings from f_v and the audio embedding from f_a).

We create temporal endpoints over a video segment following a simple strategy, we select a timestamp t and create l temporal endpoints over the video at a fixed stride of k frames. The location of every endpoint is then given by $L = \{t, t+k, t+2k, ..., t+lk\}$. This reduces the total number of samples from the video data by a factor of k and allows us to sample longer sections of video for training and inference.

Spatio-Temporal Embedding. We build the embedding Φ over the endpoint set L. We define the audiovisual embedding e at time t for speaker s as $e_{t,s} = \{f_a(t), f_v(s,t)\}$. Since there may be multiple visible persons at this endpoint (*i.e.* $|s| \geq 1$), we define the embedding for an endpoint at time t with up to i speakers as $E_{t,i} = \{e_{t,0}, e_{t,1}, e_{t,2}, ..., e_{t,i}\}$. The full spatio-temporal embedding $\Phi_{i,k,l,t}$ is created by sampling audio and visual features over the endpoint set L, where $\Phi_{i,k,l,t} = \{E_{t,i}, ..., E_{t+k,i}, ..., E_{t+lk,i}\}$. As $\Phi_{i,k,l,t}$ is assembled from independent forward passes of the f_a and f_v encoders, we share weights for forward passes in the same modality, thus each forward/backward pass accumulates gradients over the same weights. This shared weight scheme largely simplifies the complexity of the proposed network, and keeps the total number of parameters stable regardless of the values for l and i.

Upon computing the initial modality embeddings, we map $\Phi_{i,k,l,t}$ into a spatio-temporal graph representation. Following [28], we map each feature in $\Phi_{i,k,l,t}$ into an individual node, resulting in a total of $(i+1) * l$ nodes. Every feature embedding goes through a linear layer for dimensionality reduction before being assigned to a node. Unlike [28], we are not interested in building a unique graph structure that performs message passing over all the possible relationships in the node set. Instead, we choose to independently model the two types of information flow in the graph, namely spatial information and temporal information.

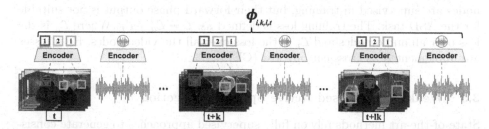

Fig. 3. EASEE Sub-Sampling. For every temporal endpoint, we sample i face tracklets and the corresponding audio signal. This sampling is repeated over l consecutive temporal endpoints separated by stride k. The $i+1$ feature embeddings obtained at each timestamp are forwarded through the audio (yellow) and visual (light green) encoders fused into the spatio-temporal embedding $\Phi_{i,k,l,t}$. (Color figure online)

3.2   Graph Neural Network Architecture

In EASEE, the GCN component fuses spatio-temporal information from video segments. This module implements a novel composition pattern where the spatial and temporal information message passing are performed in subsequent layers. We devise a building block (iGNN) where the spatial message passing is performed first, then temporal message passing occurs. After these two forward passes, we fuse the feature representation with the previously estimated feature embedding (residual connection). We define the iGNN block at layer J as:

$$\Phi_s = M^s(A^s\Phi; \theta^s), \Phi_t = M^t(A^t\Phi; \theta^t)$$

$$\Phi^{J+2} = iGNN(\Phi^J) = (M^t \circ M^s)(\Phi^J) + \Phi^J = M^t\big(\underbrace{M^s\left(\Phi^J\right)}_{\Phi^{J+1}}\big) + \Phi^J$$

Here, M^s is a GCN layer that performs spatial message passing using the spatial adjacency matrix A^s over an initial feature embedding (Φ^J), thus producing an intermediate representation with aggregated local features (Φ^{J+1}). Afterwards the GCN layer M^t performs a temporal message passing using the temporal adjacency matrix A^t. θ^s and θ^t are the parameter set of their respective layers. The final output is complemented with a residual connection, thus favoring gradient propagation.

In EASEE, the assignment of elements from the embedding $\Phi_{i,k,l,s}$ to graph nodes remains stable throughout the entire GCN structure (*i.e.* we do not perform any pooling). This allows us to create a final prediction for every tracklet and audio clip contained in $\Phi_{i,k,l,t}$ by applying a single linear layer. This arrangement creates two types of nodes: *Audio Nodes*, which generate predictions for the audio embeddings (*i.e.* speech detected or silent scene), and *Video Nodes* which generate predictions for the visual tracklets (*i.e.* active speaker or silent). EASEE's final predictions are made only from the output of visual nodes. Audio nodes are supervised in training, but their forward phase output is not suitable for the ASD task. The training loss is defined as: $\mathcal{L} = \mathcal{L}_a + \mathcal{L}_v$. Where $\mathcal{L}_a$ is the loss over all audio nodes and $\mathcal{L}_v$ is the loss over all the video nodes. Both losses are implemented as cross-entropy loss (CE).

3.3   Weakly Supervised Active Speaker Detection

State-of-the-art methods rely on fully supervised approaches to generate consistent predictions in the ASD problem. Typically, they work in a fully supervised manner in both learning stages, using audiovisual labels to train the initial feature encoder and also to supervise the second stage learning [1,25,28,40]. The end-to-end nature of EASEE enables us to approach the active speaker problem from a novel perspective, where the multi-speaker scenario can be analyzed relying on a weak supervision signal, namely audio labels. In comparison to visual labels, audio ground-truth is less expensive to acquire, as it only establishes the start and end point of a speech event. Meanwhile, labels for visual data must establish the fine-grained association between every temporal interval in the speech event and its visual source.

A naive training of EASEE with audio labels only, would optimize the predictions for the audio nodes (speech events). As outlined before, such predictions are suitable for the voice activity detection task, but the more fine grained ASD task will have poor performance as the visual nodes lack any supervision and yield random outputs. To generate meaningful predictions for the visual nodes while relying only on audio supervision, we reformulate our end-to-end training to enforce information flow between modalities by adding two extra loss functions on the graph structure. This reformulation enables meaningful predictions over the visual data despite the lack of visual ground-truth. We name this version of our approach EASEE-W, a novel architecture that is capable of making active speaker predictions that rely only on weak binary supervision labels from the audio stream. An overview of the key differences between EASEE and EASEE-W is show in Fig. 4.

Local Assignment Loss. We design a loss function that models local dependencies in the ASD problem: if there is a speech event, we must attribute the speech to one of the locally associated video nodes. Let V_t be the output of video nodes at time t ($|V_t| \geq 2$), and y_{at} the ground truth for the audio signal at time t:

$$L_s = y_{at}(y_{at} - \max(V_t)) + (1 - y_{at}) \max(V_t)$$

The first term $y_{at}(y_{at} - \max(V_t))$ will force EASEE-W to generate at least one positive prediction in V_t if $y_{at} = 1$ (*i.e.* select a speaker if speech is detected). Likewise, the second term $(1 - y_{at}) \max(V_t)$ will force EASEE-W to generate only negative predictions in V_t in the absence of speech. While this loss forces the network to generate video labels that are locally consistent with the audio supervision, we show that these predictions only improve the performance over a random baseline and do not represent an improvement over trivial audiovisual assignments.

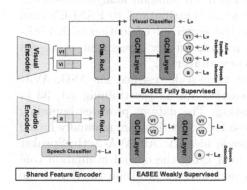

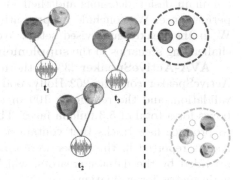

Fig. 4. EASEE Weakly Supervised. We drop all the visual supervision ($\mathcal{L}_v$) in EASEE and enforce positive predictions in the video nodes (light green) in the presence of a speech event ($\mathcal{L}_s$), along with consistent visual feature representations for the same identities ($\mathcal{L}_c$).

Fig. 5. Weakly Supervised Losses. We enforce an individual speaker assignment if there is a detected speech event (left). Temporal consistency pulls together features for faces of the same person and creates differences for faces of different persons (right).

Visual Contrastive Loss. We complement L_s with a contrastive loss (L_c) applied over the video data. As shown in Fig. 5, the goal of this loss is to enforce feature similarity between video nodes that belong to the same person, and promote feature differences for non-matching identities. Considering that the AVA-ActiveSpeaker dataset [35] does not include identity meta-data, we approximate the sampling of different identities by selecting visual data from concurrent tracklets[1]. To simplify the contrastive learning, we modify the sampling scheme for EASEE-W, and force $i = 2$ regardless of the real number of simultaneous tracklets. If there are more than 2 visible persons in the scene, we just sample without replacement.

In practice, we follow [7] and apply this loss on the second to last layer of the iGNN block. Let $\mathcal{L}_a$ be the loss for the audio nodes in the last iGNN block (see Figs. 4 and 5), then the loss used for EASEE-W is: $\mathcal{L}_w = \mathcal{L}_a + \mathcal{L}_s + \mathcal{L}_c$. No video labels are required, *i.e.* the speaker-to-speech assignments are unknown.

3.4 Implementation Details

We provide additional training details in the **supplementary material**

4 Experimental Results

In this section, we provide extensive experimental evaluation of our proposed method. We mainly evaluate EASEE on the AVA-ActiveSpeaker dataset [35] and also present additional results on Talkies [28]. We begin with a direct comparison to state-of-the-art methods. Then, we perform an ablation analysis, assessing our main design decisions and their individual contributions to EASEE's final performance. We conclude by presenting the empirical evaluation of EASSE-W in the weakly supervised setup. We include further assessment in known challenging scenarios in the **supplementary material.**

AVA-ActiveSpeaker [35] is the first large-scale test-bed for ASD. AVA-ActiveSpeaker contains 262 Hollywood movies: 120 in the training set, 33 in validation, and the remaining 109 in testing. The dataset provides bounding boxes for a total of 5.3 million faces. These face detections are manually linked to produce face tracks that contain a single identity. All AVA-ActiveSpeaker results reported in this paper were obtained using the official evaluation tool provided by the dataset creators, which uses average precision (mAP) as the main metric for evaluation.

Talkies is a manually labeled dataset for the ASD task [28]. This dataset was collected from social media videos and contains 23, 507 face tracks extracted from a total of 799,446 individual face detections. Unlike AVA-ActiveSpeaker, it is based on short clips and about 20% of the speech events are off-screen speech, *i.e.* the event cannot be attributed to a visible person.

---

[1] Since tracklets include a single face and were manually curated, it is guaranteed that two tracklets that overlap in time belong to different identities. If there is a single person in the scene, we sample additional visual data from another tracklet in a different movie where no speech event is detected.

Table 1. State-of-the-art Comparison on AVA-ActiveSpeaker. Our best network (EASEE-50) outperforms any other method by at least 0.6 mAP even approaches that build upon much deeper networks. Our smaller network (EASEE-18) remains competitive with the previous state-of-the-art. In the 2D scenario EASEE-2D only lags behind UniCon [50], improving the closest method by at least 0.9 mAP.

Method	Visual Encoder		Temporal	mAP
	Backbone	2D/3D	Context	
AVA baseline et al. [35]	MobileNet	2D	✗	79.2
AVA baseline + GRU et al. [35]	MobileNet	2D	✓	82.2
FaVoA [3]	ResNet18	2D	✓	84.7
MAAS-LAN [28]	ResNet18	2D	✗	85.1
Chung et al. [9]	ResNet18	3D+2D	✓	85.5
ASC [1]	Resnet18	2D	✓	87.1
MAAS-TAN [28]	ResNet18	2D	✓	88.8
EASEE-2D (Ours)	ResNet18	2D	✓	91.1
UniCon [50]	Multiple	2D	✓	92.0
Zhang et al. [49]	Custom	3D+2D	✗	84.0
EASEE-50 $l = 1$, $i = 3$ (Ours)	ResNet18	3D	✗	89.6
TalkNet [40]	Custom	3D+2D	✓	92.3
EASEE-18 (Ours)	ResNet18	3D	✓	93.3
ASDNet [25]	ResNext101	3D	✓	93.5
EASEE-50 (Ours)	ResNet50	3D	✓	**94.1**

4.1 Comparison to State-of-the-Art

We compare EASEE against state-of-the-art ASD methods. The results for EASEE are obtained with $l = 7$ temporal endpoints, $i = 2$ tracklets per endpoint, and a stride of $k = 5$. This configuration allows for a sampling window of about 2.41 s regardless of the selected backbone. For fair comparison with other methods, we report results of three EASEE variants: 'EASEE-50' that uses a 3D backbone based on the ResNet50 architecture, 'EASEE-18' that uses a 3D model based on the much smaller Resnet18 architecture, and 'EASEE-2D' that uses a 2D Resnet18 backbone. Results are summarized in Table 1.

We find that the optimal number of iGNN blocks changes according to the baseline architecture. For the ResNet18 encoder, 6 blocks (24 layers total in the GCN) are required to achieve the best performance, whereas for ResNet50, only 4 blocks (16 layers total in the GCN) are required. Since we find the best results with $i = 2$, and there are scenes with 3 or more simultaneous tracklets, we follow [28]. At inference time, we split the speakers in non-overlapping groups of 2, and perform multiple forward passes until every tracklet has been labeled.

We observe that our method outperforms all the other approaches in the validation subset. EASEE-50 is 0.6 mAP higher than the previous state-of-the-art (ASDNet [25]). We highlight that ASDNet relies on the deep ResNext101 encoder, whereas EASEE-50 is built on the much smaller ResNet50. Our smaller version (EASEE-18) only lags behind ASDNet by 0.2, and outperforms every other model by at least 1.0 mAP. We also implement a version of EASEE-50 that models only spatial relations (*i.e.* $l = 1$). This model reaches 89.6 mAP, outperforming every other network that generates predictions without long-term temporal modelling by at least 4.5 mAP. Finally EASEE-2D outperforms every other 2D approach except UniCon [50], we explain this result as [50] presents a far more complex approach that includes multiple 2D backbones to analyze audiovisual data, scene layout and speaker suppression, along with bi-directional GRUs [8] for temporal aggregation.

Table 2. AVA-ActiveSpeaker Ablation. We assess the empirical contribution of the most relevant components in EASEE. Residual connections contribute about 0.3 mAP and the proposed iGNN block 0.4 mAP. Overall the most relevant design choice is the end-to-end trainable nature of EASEE contributing 1.6 mAP.

Network	End-to-End	iGNN	Residual connections	mAP
EASEE-50	✗	✗	✗	91.9
EASEE-50	✓	✗	✗	93.5
EASEE-50	✓	✗	✓	93.7
EASEE-50	✓	✓	✗	93.8
EASEE-50	✓	✓	✓	**94.1**

4.2 Ablation Study

We ablate our best model (EASEE-50) to assess the individual contributions of our design choices: end-to-end training, iGNN block, and the residual connections between the iGNN blocks. Table 2 contains the individual assessment of each component. The most important architectural design is the end-to-end training, which contributes 1.6 mAP. The proposed iGNN brings about 0.4 mAP when compared against a baseline network where spatial and temporal message passing is performed in the same layer. Finally, residual connections between iGNN blocks contribute with an improved performance of 0.3 mAP.

Intermediate Embedding Configuration. We compare the performance of EASEE-50 with different configurations of the intermediate embedding Φ. In Table 3, we assess the performance of EASEE-50 when changing the number of temporal endpoints l and the number of simultaneous tracklets i. We observe that the best performance arises when $i = 2$, which is in stark contrast to other methods [25,28,50] that often rely on aggregating information from 4 or more visual tracklets. We attribute this to the end-to-end nature of EASEE, where contextual cues are directly optimized for the ASD problem, thus requiring less spatial data for effective predictions. Nonetheless, for small values of l, we find that EASEE actually benefits from a larger number of visual tracklets ($i = 3$). This suggests that in the absence of strong temporal cues, EASEE will focus on extracting meaningful information from the spatially adjacent tracklets.

We also observe that the temporal dimension of the problem (number of endpoints l) is more relevant than the spatial component (number of concurrent tracklets i). When increasing l from 1 to 7, performance improves significantly, by 4.8 mAP on average. In contrast, increasing visual tracklets from $i = 1$ to $i = 4$ only yields 1.1 mAP improvement on average. This is consistent with related works, which show a performance boost when incorporating recurrent Units and long temporal samplings [1,25,35].

Table 3. End Points vs speaker. Longer temporal windows allow to improve the performance, achieving the best result at $l = 7$. A large number of speakers favors performance in shorter windows but $i = 2$ is the best parameter for long windows ($l \geq 3$).

Table 4. End Points vs Input Clip. Long temporal samplings enables better predictions in most scenarios. In the EASEE architecture the input size for the 3D encoder also provides improved performance, the optimal is 15 frames, which equals to 0.62 s.

Speakers (i)	End points (l)				
	1	3	5	7	9
1	86.6	90.5	92.4	92.9	92.6
2	89.0	92.3	93.4	**94.1**	93.8
3	89.6	92.2	93.3	93.8	93.4
4	89.2	91.8	93.1	93.7	93.2

Clip size	End points (l)				
	1	3	5	7	9
11	87.6	91.4	93.1	93.5	93.2
13	88.3	91.7	93.3	93.9	93.6
15	89.0	92.3	93.4	**94.1**	93.8
17	89.3	92.5	93.3	93.9	93.7

Table 5. iGNN Layering Strategies. We compare multiple strategies to assemble our iGNN block, we find that interleaving the temporal and spatial messages brings the best results. In comparison a joint massage passing will reduce the performance by 0.4 mAP, a naive join of this steps with a linear layer reports the same performance reduction.

iGNN	iGNN-TS	Two stream	Parallel	Spatio-temporal [28]
94.1	94.0	92.8	93.7	93.7

In Table 4, we analyze the effect of the input clip size to the encoder f_v in EASEE. We find that as the clip size increases, performance also improves but saturates around 15 frames (about 0.62 s). For every clip size, longer temporal sampling (more endpoints) provides better results. The best result is achieved at $l = 7$ with clips of 15 frames.

Design of iGNN Blocks. We assess the effectiveness of the proposed iGNN block by comparing it against the following fusion alternatives: (a) Temporal-Spatial (iGNN-TS), an immediate alternative to iGNN where temporal message passing is performed before any spatial message passing is done; (b) Two Stream, where two independent GCN streams perform spatial and temporal message passing respectively, and these streams are fused at the end of the network; (c) Parallel, where the block performs spatial and temporal message passing in parallel and fuses the features using a fully connected layer; (d) Spatio-Temporal, where a single graph structure performs temporal and spatial message passing at the same time [28]. Table 5 summarizes the results.

Overall, we find that the best block design is the one in which spatial message passing occurs first. Reversing the order of message passing results in a very similar alternative with only minor performance degradation. In comparison, the two-stream approach performs significantly worse than all other alternatives, suggesting that the fusion of temporal and spatial information must occur earlier to be effective in an end-to-end scenario. Joint spatio-temporal messaging also has high performance, but still lags behind the iGNN block.

We conclude this section with the evaluation of EASEE on the Talkies dataset [28]. Here, we test: (i) a direct transfer of EASEE-50 into the validation set of Talkies, (ii) directly training EASEE on Talkies, and (iii) using Talkies as downstream task after pre-training on AVA-ActiveSpeaker. Table 6 summarizes the results. EASEE outperforms [28] for the direct transfer on the Talkies dataset. Moreover, training on Talkies results in a high performance comparable to that of the AVA-ActiveSpeaker dataset, this is particularly interesting as Talkies is a dataset that contains a large portion of scenes with out-of screen speech, a situation that is extremely rare in the AVA-Active Speaker. Finally, the using talkies as a downstream task results in 1.0 mAP improvement, which is about 15% relative error improvement.

Table 6. Evaluation on Talkies Dataset. We evaluate EASEE on the Talkies dataset. It outperforms the existing baseline on the direct transfer from AVA-ActiveSpeaker, and show the results of training EASEE end-to-end in Talkies. Finally we test the effectiveness of AVA-ActiveSpeakers as pre-training for Talkies.

Network	AVA Pre-train	Talkies training	mAP
MAAS-TAN [28]	✓	✗	79.1
EASEE-50	✓	✗	86.7
EASEE-50	✗	✓	93.6
EASEE-50	✓	✓	94.5

4.3   Weak Supervision

We conclude this section by evaluating the weakly supervised version of EASEE, *i.e.* EASEE-W. To the best of our knowledge, there are no comparable methods that strictly rely on weak (audio only) supervision in the ASD task. Therefore, we establish multiple baselines, from random predictions to direct speech-to-speaker assignment.

We first consider baselines that ignore audio labels and the structure of the ASD problem: i) *random* baseline where every speaker gets a random score sampled from a uniform distribution between $[0, 1]$. ii) *Naive Recall* where we trivially predict every tracklet as an active speaker and iii) *Naive Precision* that trivially predicts every tracklet as silent. We also build baselines that rely on audio supervision. We use our trained audio encoder f_a to detect speech intervals and generate random speech-to-speaker assignments within that time window. We explore two approaches: iv) *Naive Audio assignment* where we choose a random visible speaker whenever a speech event is detected. v) *Largest Face Audio assignment* since AVA-Active Speaker is a collection of Hollywood movies, we follow a common bias in commercial movies, and assign the speech event to the tracklet that occupies the largest area in the screen. Table 7 summarizes the results of this experiments in the AVA-ActiveSpeaker dataset.

We observe that random baselines largely under-perform. Even when the predictions have a bias towards the largest class (silent) results are just 27.1 mAP. A relevant increment in performance (about 20 mAP) appears when the audio supervision is used to generate the naive visual assignments. This improvement is a direct result of the structure in the ASD problem, where speech events are attributed to a defined set of sources.

When we apply EASEE-W, we see the complementary behaviour of the proposed loss functions. The baseline with audio supervision (L_a only) exhibits no meaningful improvement over the random base,

Table 7. Weak Supervision. We show that EASEE-W largely improves over baseline approaches for ASD, it outperform a naive baseline by 28.5 mAP, and remains competitive with fully supervised 2D encoder.

Network	mAP
Random	25.1
Naive recall	27.1
Naive precision	27.1
Naive audio assignment	47.7
Large face audio assignment	49.1
EASEE-W L_a only	26.1
EASEE-W L_a, L_c only	25.8
EASEE-W L_a, L_s only	54.4
EASEE-W (L_a, L_s, L_c)	76.2
Fully supervised 2D encoder [1,35]	79.5

despite the GCN structure. A similar situation can be observed if we use the audio supervision and enforce temporal consistency on the visual features (L_c). This indicates that information flow across modalities can not be trivially enforced by the GCN module or temporal visual consistency. Including the assignment loss (L_s) results in a scenario that already improves over the naive assignments suggesting that local attributions already favor the some meaningful audiovisual patterns. Finally, the best result is achieved when assignments and temporal consistency for the visual data are considered. This result improves over any baseline by at least 27 mAP. We conclude this section highlighting that this result is competitive with baseline approaches that rely on encoding short-temporal information from a single speaker as outlined in [1,35].

5 Conclusion

We introduced EASEE, a multi-modal end-to-end trainable network for the ASD task. EASEE outperforms state-of-the-art approaches in the large scale AVA-ActiveSpeaker [35] dataset, and transfers effectively to smaller sets that contain out-of-screen speech. EASEE allows for fully supervised and weakly supervised training by leveraging the inherent structure of the ASD problem and the natural consistency in video data. Future explorations on the ASD problem might rely on our label efficient training setup.

Acknowledgements. This work was supported by the King Abdullah University of Science and Technology (KAUST) Office of Sponsored Research through the Visual Computing Center (VCC) funding.

References

1. Alcázar, J.L., et al.: Active speakers in context. In: Proceedings of the IEEE/CVF Conference on Computer Vision and Pattern Recognition, pp. 12465–12474 (2020)
2. Cai, J., Jiang, N., Han, X., Jia, K., Lu, J.: JOLO-GCN: mining joint-centered light-weight information for skeleton-based action recognition. In: Proceedings of the IEEE/CVF Winter Conference on Applications of Computer Vision, pp. 2735–2744 (2021)
3. Carneiro, H., Weber, C., Wermter, S.: FaVoA: face-voice association favours ambiguous speaker detection. In: Farkaš, I., Masulli, P., Otte, S., Wermter, S. (eds.) ICANN 2021. LNCS, vol. 12891, pp. 439–450. Springer, Cham (2021). https://doi.org/10.1007/978-3-030-86362-3_36
4. Chakravarty, P., Mirzaei, S., Tuytelaars, T., Van hamme, H.: Who's speaking? Audio-supervised classification of active speakers in video. In: Proceedings of the 2015 ACM on International Conference on Multimodal Interaction, pp. 87–90 (2015)
5. Chakravarty, P., Zegers, J., Tuytelaars, T., Van hamme, H.: Active speaker detection with audio-visual co-training. In: Proceedings of the 18th ACM International Conference on Multimodal Interaction, pp. 312–316 (2016)
6. Chang, J.H., Kim, N.S., Mitra, S.K.: Voice activity detection based on multiple statistical models. IEEE Trans. Signal Process. **54**(6), 1965–1976 (2006)
7. Chen, T., Kornblith, S., Norouzi, M., Hinton, G.: A simple framework for contrastive learning of visual representations. In: International Conference on Machine Learning, pp. 1597–1607. PMLR (2020)
8. Cho, K., Van Merriënboer, B., Bahdanau, D., Bengio, Y.: On the properties of neural machine translation: Encoder-decoder approaches. arXiv preprint arXiv:1409.1259 (2014)
9. Chung, J.S.: Naver at ActivityNet challenge 2019-task B active speaker detection (AVA). arXiv preprint arXiv:1906.10555 (2019)

10. Chung, J.S., Nagrani, A., Zisserman, A.: VoxCeleb2: deep speaker recognition. arXiv preprint arXiv:1806.05622 (2018)
11. Chung, J.S., Zisserman, A.: Out of time: automated lip sync in the wild. In: Chen, C.-S., Lu, J., Ma, K.-K. (eds.) ACCV 2016. LNCS, vol. 10117, pp. 251–263. Springer, Cham (2017). https://doi.org/10.1007/978-3-319-54427-4_19
12. Cutler, R., Davis, L.: Look who's talking: speaker detection using video and audio correlation. In: International Conference on Multimedia and Expo (2000)
13. Ding, S., Wang, Q., Chang, S.y., Wan, L., Moreno, I.L.: Personal VAD: speaker-conditioned voice activity detection. arXiv preprint arXiv:1908.04284 (2019)
14. Duhme, M., Memmesheimer, R., Paulus, D.: Fusion-GCN: multimodal action recognition using graph convolutional networks. arXiv preprint arXiv:2109.12946 (2021)
15. Everingham, M., Sivic, J., Zisserman, A.: Taking the bite out of automated naming of characters in TV video. Image Vis. Comput. 27(5), 545–559 (2009)
16. Gkioxari, G., Malik, J., Johnson, J.: Mesh R-CNN. arXiv preprint arXiv:1906.02739 (2019)
17. Hadsell, R., Chopra, S., LeCun, Y.: Dimensionality reduction by learning an invariant mapping. In: CVPR (2006)
18. Hara, K., Kataoka, H., Satoh, Y.: Can spatiotemporal 3D CNNs retrace the history of 2D CNNs and ImageNet? In: Proceedings of the IEEE conference on Computer Vision and Pattern Recognition, pp. 6546–6555 (2018)
19. He, K., Zhang, X., Ren, S., Sun, J.: Deep residual learning for image recognition. In: Proceedings of the IEEE Conference on Computer Vision and Pattern Recognition, pp. 770–778 (2016)
20. Hochreiter, S., Schmidhuber, J.: Long short-term memory. Neural Comput. 9(8), 1735–1780 (1997)
21. Jain, A., Zamir, A.R., Savarese, S., Saxena, A.: Structural-RNN: deep learning on spatio-temporal graphs. In: Proceedings of the IEEE Conference on Computer Vision and Pattern Recognition, pp. 5308–5317 (2016)
22. Johnson, J., Gupta, A., Fei-Fei, L.: Image generation from scene graphs. In: Proceedings of the IEEE Conference on Computer Vision and Pattern Recognition, pp. 1219–1228 (2018)
23. Kampffmeyer, M., Chen, Y., Liang, X., Wang, H., Zhang, Y., Xing, E.P.: Rethinking knowledge graph propagation for zero-shot learning. In: Proceedings of the IEEE/CVF Conference on Computer Vision and Pattern Recognition, pp. 11487–11496 (2019)
24. Kipf, T.N., Welling, M.: Semi-supervised classification with graph convolutional networks. arXiv preprint arXiv:1609.02907 (2016)
25. Köpüklü, O., Taseska, M., Rigoll, G.: How to design a three-stage architecture for audio-visual active speaker detection in the wild. arXiv preprint arXiv:2106.03932 (2021)
26. Krizhevsky, A., Sutskever, I., Hinton, G.E.: ImageNet classification with deep convolutional neural networks. In: Advances in Neural Information Processing Systems, vol. 25, pp. 1097–1105 (2012)
27. LeCun, Y., et al.: Handwritten digit recognition with a back-propagation network. In: Advances in Neural Information Processing Systems 2 (1989)
28. León-Alcázar, J., Heilbron, F.C., Thabet, A., Ghanem, B.: MAAS: multi-modal assignation for active speaker detection. arXiv preprint arXiv:2101.03682 (2021)
29. Li, G., Qian, G., Delgadillo, I.C., Müller, M., Thabet, A., Ghanem, B.: SGAS: sequential greedy architecture search (2019)

30. Li, Y., Ouyang, W., Zhou, B., Shi, J., Zhang, C., Wang, X.: Factorizable net: an efficient subgraph-based framework for scene graph generation. In: Ferrari, V., Hebert, M., Sminchisescu, C., Weiss, Y. (eds.) ECCV 2018. LNCS, vol. 11205, pp. 346–363. Springer, Cham (2018). https://doi.org/10.1007/978-3-030-01246-5_21
31. Nagrani, A., Chung, J.S., Zisserman, A.: VoxCeleb: a large-scale speaker identification dataset. arXiv preprint arXiv:1706.08612 (2017)
32. Ngiam, J., Khosla, A., Kim, M., Nam, J., Lee, H., Ng, A.Y.: Multimodal deep learning. In: ICML (2011)
33. Nie, W., Ren, M., Nie, J., Zhao, S.: C-GCN: correlation based graph convolutional network for audio-video emotion recognition. IEEE Trans. Multimedia **23**, 3793–3804 (2020)
34. Ren, M., Huang, X., Li, W., Song, D., Nie, W.: LR-GCN: latent relation-aware graph convolutional network for conversational emotion recognition. IEEE Trans. Multimedia (2021)
35. Roth, J., et al.: AVA active speaker: an audio-visual dataset for active speaker detection. In: ICASSP 2020–2020 IEEE International Conference on Acoustics, Speech and Signal Processing (ICASSP), pp. 4492–4496. IEEE (2020)
36. Rumelhart, D.E., Hinton, G.E., Williams, R.J.: Learning representations by back-propagating errors. Nature **323**(6088), 533–536 (1986)
37. Saenko, K., Livescu, K., Siracusa, M., Wilson, K., Glass, J., Darrell, T.: Visual speech recognition with loosely synchronized feature streams. In: ICCV (2005)
38. Tanyer, S.G., Ozer, H.: Voice activity detection in nonstationary noise. IEEE Trans. Speech Audio Process. **8**(4), 478–482 (2000)
39. Tao, F., Busso, C.: Bimodal recurrent neural network for audiovisual voice activity detection. In: INTERSPEECH, pp. 1938–1942 (2017)
40. Tao, R., Pan, Z., Das, R.K., Qian, X., Shou, M.Z., Li, H.: Is someone speaking? Exploring long-term temporal features for audio-visual active speaker detection. In: Proceedings of the 29th ACM International Conference on Multimedia, pp. 3927–3935 (2021)
41. Vaswani, A., et al.: Attention is all you need. In: Advances in Neural Information Processing Systems, vol. 30 (2017)
42. Waibel, A., Hanazawa, T., Hinton, G., Shikano, K., Lang, K.J.: Phoneme recognition using time-delay neural networks. IEEE Trans. Acoust. Speech Signal Process. **37**(3), 328–339 (1989)
43. Wang, X., Girshick, R., Gupta, A., He, K.: Non-local neural networks. In: Proceedings of the IEEE Conference on Computer Vision and Pattern Recognition, pp. 7794–7803 (2018)
44. Wang, X., Ye, Y., Gupta, A.: Zero-shot recognition via semantic embeddings and knowledge graphs. In: Proceedings of the IEEE Conference on Computer Vision and Pattern Recognition, pp. 6857–6866 (2018)
45. Wu, F., Souza, A., Zhang, T., Fifty, C., Yu, T., Weinberger, K.: Simplifying graph convolutional networks. In: International Conference on Machine Learning, pp. 6861–6871. PMLR (2019)
46. Xie, Z., Chen, J., Peng, B.: Point clouds learning with attention-based graph convolution networks. arXiv preprint arXiv:1905.13445 (2019)
47. Xu, M., Zhao, C., Rojas, D.S., Thabet, A., Ghanem, B.: G-TAD: sub-graph localization for temporal action detection. In: Proceedings of the IEEE/CVF Conference on Computer Vision and Pattern Recognition, pp. 10156–10165 (2020)
48. Yan, S., Xiong, Y., Lin, D.: Spatial temporal graph convolutional networks for skeleton-based action recognition. In: Thirty-Second AAAI Conference on Artificial Intelligence (2018)

49. Zhang, Y.H., Xiao, J., Yang, S., Shan, S.: Multi-task learning for audio-visual active speaker detection (2019)

50. Zhang, Y., et al.: UniCon: unified context network for robust active speaker detection. In: Proceedings of the 29th ACM International Conference on Multimedia, pp. 3964–3972 (2021)

Emotion Recognition for Multiple Context Awareness

Dingkang Yang[1,2], Shuai Huang[1,2], Shunli Wang[1,2], Yang Liu[1], Peng Zhai[1,2], Liuzhen Su[1,2], Mingcheng Li[1,2], and Lihua Zhang[1,2,3,4(✉)]

[1] Academy for Engineering and Technology, Fudan University, Shanghai, China
lihuazhang@fudan.edu.cn
[2] Engineering Research Center of AI and Robotics, Ministry of Education, Shanghai, China
[3] Jilin Provincial Key Laboratory of Intelligence Science and Engineering, Changchun, China
[4] AI and Unmanned Systems Engineering Research Center of Jilin Province, Changchun, China

Abstract. Understanding emotion in context is a rising hotspot in the computer vision community. Existing methods lack reliable context semantics to mitigate uncertainty in expressing emotions and fail to model multiple context representations complementarily. To alleviate these issues, we present a context-aware emotion recognition framework that combines four complementary contexts. The first context is multimodal emotion recognition based on facial expression, facial landmarks, gesture and gait. Secondly, we adopt the channel and spatial attention modules to obtain the emotion semantics of the scene context. Inspired by sociology theory, we explore the emotion transmission between agents by constructing relationship graphs in the third context. Meanwhile, we propose a novel agent-object context, which aggregates emotion cues from the interactions between surrounding agents and objects in the scene to mitigate the ambiguity of prediction. Finally, we introduce an adaptive relevance fusion module for learning the shared representations among multiple contexts. Extensive experiments show that our approach outperforms the state-of-the-art methods on both EMOTIC and GroupWalk datasets. We also release a dataset annotated with diverse emotion labels, Human Emotion in Context (HECO). In practice, we compare with the existing methods on the HECO, and our approach obtains a higher classification average precision of 50.65% and a lower regression mean error rate of 0.7. The project is available at https://heco2022.github.io/.

Keywords: Emotion recognition · Context understanding

Di. Yang and S. Huang—Equal contribution.

Supplementary Information The online version contains supplementary material available at https://doi.org/10.1007/978-3-031-19836-6_9.

1   Introduction

Understanding human emotion plays an essential role in daily life as emotion recognition has been applied in various complicated fields, such as medical care [10], human-computer interaction [12], and robotics [76]. Benefiting from the excellent performance of deep learning technologies in processing diverse signals [9,26,35, 37,64,71], many researchers [6,38,50,55,58,59,70] have improved emotion recognition by combining diverse modalities (*e.g.*, face, audio, and language) from the recognized agent. Nevertheless, it is difficult to obtain the complete modalities from the different data domains, especially in practical applications where simplicity and practicality are the goals. In this paper, we analyse a wider view at the visual level to infer human emotion instead of focusing on the agent only.

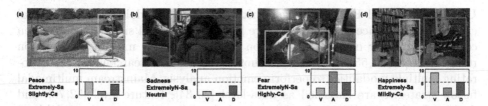

Fig. 1. Examples of agents in four contexts. The red rectangles present the recognized agent while the blue rectangles present the others. Discrete categories and continuous dimensions labels of emotion shown under the images. VAD means emotional state space: *Valence, Arousal,* and *Dominance.* (Color figure online)

Recently, emotion recognition that combines the agent's expression with the emotion semantics of context has received considerable attention [30,31,41,42,72]. Researches in context awareness inspire us to explore meaningful contexts from images and video frames to perceive emotion. There are some interesting examples. In Fig. 1(a) (*Explicit context*), the woman is lying on the grass with a flexible posture, whose emotion tends to be peaceful. Emotion sociology works [19,54,57] demonstrate that emotion is the maintenance and change of the relationship between agents and their scene. In Fig. 1(b) (*Scene context*), the performance of expression recognition in dark scene is limited and poor. However, the emotional state reflected in the surrounding environment is consistent with the agent, and it can be inferred from the scene context that the girl might be in negative emotion. Furthermore, the emotion transmission between multiple agents in the same scene can also affect the emotion change of the recognized agent. In Figure 1(c) (*Surrounding agent context*), the man rushes to the ambulance with an injured woman in his arms. Due to the woman's condition, the man feels fear. Moreover, inspired by emotion psychology studies [2,11,43], we consider emotion cues provided by implicit representation, such as agent-object interaction. In Fig. 1(d) (*Agent-object context*), the man feels happy when he sees his daughter have a good time with the hairdryer. The interaction between the girl and the hairdryer is beneficial for understanding the man's emotion. Cognitive scientists [17,40,47] state that humans exist in a society whose emotions can be affected by different contexts directly or indirectly. Learning the multimodal representations from various contexts will effectively improve emotion recognition performance.

In summary, our primary contributions are the following: (1) We present a novel context-aware emotion recognition framework from a psychological and sociological perspective, which incorporates four context information. (2) We propose an adaptive relevance fusion module that focuses on the interactions among diverse contexts and adaptively assigns higher weights to beneficial contexts. (3) We release HECO, a new dataset for emotion recognition in context. The HECO is annotated with discrete and continuous emotion labels and promotes a more reasonable perception of human emotion.

2   Related Work

Uni/Multimodal Emotion Recognition. Isolated modalities, such as facial expression [74], voice [14], body gesture [44] and biological signal [3], have been concerned in prior emotion recognition works. Recently, multimodal emotion recognition [38,50,55,59] has been a hot issue, where researchers are incorporating multiple modalities to perform emotion analysis. Mainstream multimodal fusion strategies are classified as data-level [29,34], feature-level [52,70], and decision-level fusion [6,16]. In contrast, we propose a two-phase model-level fusion strategy with cross-context fusion and adaptive fusion. Our strategy reinforces the shared representations among multiple contexts in the interaction and assigns appropriate weights to the contexts based on their contributions.

Context-Aware Emotion Recognition. There have been several attempts at context-aware emotion recognition in recent years. Kosti *et al.* [30] propose the task of emotion understanding in context and build a two-stream Convolutional Neural Network (CNN) that combines the body and the semantic information from the scene. Zhang *et al.* [72] utilize the region proposal network to extract scene semantics as node features, and then construct an emotion graph through Graph Convolutional Network (GCN) to infer emotion. Lee *et al.* [31] use the attention mechanism to find relevant context cues in the scene after the hidden face. Mittal *et al.* [41,42] adopt a multiplicative fusion to combine information from various modalities and context interpretations. Hoang *et al.* [25] propose an extra reasoning stream to quantify the interaction between primary agents and objects. The aforementioned methods sub-optimally explore the emotion relationships between agents and the effect of agent-object interactions. In comparison, the four contexts proposed by our method are more complementary and synergistic in emotion recognition.

3   Proposed Method

3.1   Context 1: Explicit Multimodal Context

In the real world, the form of human emotion expression is usually multimodal. These modalities include facial expression [65,67], body posture [44,63], gesture [36,49], and walking style. It is helpful to infer emotion by integrating various

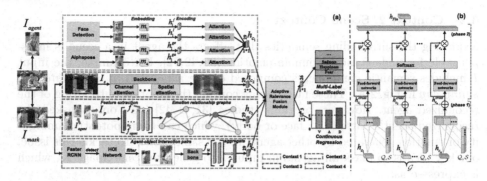

Fig. 2. (a) The proposed framework. We first extract features from face expression, facial landmarks, gesture and gait via respective neural networks to obtain h_1^f, h_1^l, h_1^{ge} and h_1^{ga}. Then we fuse these features to obtain h_{c_1} in context 1. In contexts 2, 3 and 4, h_{c_2}, h_{c_3} and h_{c_4} are obtained from different inputs via the corresponding context awareness models. Immediately, the Adaptive Relevance Fusion (ARF) module fuses all features and learns the multimodal representation h_{Fin}. Finally, two separate branches perform the emotion classification and regression tasks. (b) The overall architecture of the ARF module contains two phases: cross-context fusion and adaptive fusion. (Color figure online)

modalities of emotion information [20,38,55]. To make full use of these emotion cues, as shown in the tawny-bordered branch of Fig. 2(a), context 1 utilizes diverse modalities as m_n from the recognized agent to extract multimodal representations such as the facial expression, facial landmarks, gesture and gait, which are defined as $H_1 = \left\{ h_1^f, h_1^l, h_1^{ge}, h_1^{ga} \right\}$. Formally, m_n from images or video frames I are encoded through respective neural network structure and the feature extraction process as follows:

$$h_1^n = \mathcal{F}(m_n; w_n), \forall h_1^n \in H_1, \tag{1}$$

where w_n denotes the network parameters. Concretely, the ResNet-18 [22] is used to encode facial expression m_1 to obtain the vector $h_1^f \in \mathbb{R}^d$ from the fully connected layer. Concurrently, we employ three independent dense layers with a GeLU activation [24] to extract the features h_1^l, h_1^{ge}, and h_1^{ga} for facial landmarks m_2, gesture m_3, and gait m_4, which have the identical dimension. Based on the different importance of these modalities, we propose a multimodal attention network to obtain the total vector $h_{c_1} \in \mathbb{R}^d$ of context 1:

$$\mu_1^n = tanh(w_{\mu n} \cdot h_1^n + b_{\mu n}), \tag{2}$$

$$h_{c_1} = \sum_{n=1}^{N} \mu_1^n \odot h_1^n, \tag{3}$$

where $w_{\mu n} \in \mathbb{R}^{d \times d}$ and $b_{\mu n} \in \mathbb{R}^{d \times 1}$ are the learnable parameters. The coefficient μ_1^n dynamically adjusts the contribution of each modality to the final representation of context 1.

3.2 Context 2: Scene Context

Exploring the surrounding semantics that affects the agent in a scene is indispensable for understanding human emotion [30, 42, 72]. For example, the input I includes semantic components composed of the *wine glass, dinner plate* and *sunny day* in Fig. 2(a). These factors may contain the emotion outpouring of the recognized agent. However, previous studies [31, 41, 42] have only masked the recognized agent's parts (*e.g.*, face or body), which can bring potential ambiguity of emotion generated by other agents in the same scene. To tackle this issue, our key idea is to mask all agents in input I to generate scene image I_s, which is expressed as:

$$I_s = \begin{cases} I(i,j) & \text{if } I(i,j) \notin \text{bbox}_{\text{agent}} , \\ 0 & \text{otherwise} , \end{cases} \qquad (4)$$

where $\text{bbox}_{\text{agent}}$ denotes the bounding box of the agent.

Inspired by visual attention [66], we utilize a scene-aware learning strategy based on the Channel Attention Module (CAM) and Spatial Attention Module (SAM) to capture the scene semantics that reflect emotion cues. The learning strategy is expected to make the model focused on the event context that effectively affects the agent's emotion. To encode the features in context 2, the ResNet-18 [22] is used to obtain the scene semantic vector $\boldsymbol{h}_{c_2} \in \mathbb{R}^d$ from the fully connected layer. The backbone is initialized by using the Places365-Standard [73], labelled with scene semantic categories. Concretely, we alternately insert the CAM and SAM in the eight residual blocks of the backbone. Given an intermediate feature map $\boldsymbol{x} \in \mathbb{R}^{c \times w \times h}$ as input, the CAM utilizes the global average pooling operation to infer a 1D channel attention map $M_{avg}^c \in \mathbb{R}^{c \times 1 \times 1}$, and the SAM utilizes global max pooling operation to infer a 2D spatial attention map $M_{max}^s \in \mathbb{R}^{1 \times w \times h}$. The overall attention process can be summarized as $\boldsymbol{x}_c = \left(\sigma \left(\delta M_{avg}^c(\boldsymbol{x}) \right) \right) \otimes \boldsymbol{x}$ and $\boldsymbol{x}_s = \left(\sigma \left(\delta M_{max}^s(\boldsymbol{x}) \right) \right) \boldsymbol{x}$, respectively, where $\otimes$ is channel-wise multiplication, $\delta(\cdot)$ is ReLU activation and $\sigma(\cdot)$ is sigmoid function. During multiplication, the channel attention values are broadcasted along the spatial dimension, and vice versa.

3.3 Context 3: Surrounding Agent Context

Motivated by emotion sociology studies [19, 40, 54, 57], we find that surrounding agents with different intensities of emotion arousal and expression can help infer the primary agent's emotion. Nevertheless, previous works [23, 42, 69] mainly describe various interaction forces between agents as a single system. These methods are limited, which perfunctorily model the interaction distance and proximity between agents. Distinct from them, we aim to thoroughly explore the influence of surrounding agents' emotions on the recognized agent's expression.

Inspired by inductive learning [62], our core strategy is to construct dynamic graph structure to model the emotion relationships between agents. As shown in the blue-bordered branch of Fig. 2(a), we define the recognized agent's image as I_{agent} and the surrounding agents' images set as $\mathcal{I}_p = \left\{ I_p^i \right\}, i = 1, ..., n$ by bounding boxes. After that, the conceptual node features $\boldsymbol{f}_{agent} \in \mathbb{R}^{d_s}$ and

$F_p = \{f_p^i \in \mathbb{R}^{d_s}\}, i = 1, ..., n$ are extracted by final pooling layer in the ResNet-50 [22], respectively. Meanwhile, considering that individuals have different influences on emotion transmission [19], we assign different weights of emotion intensity to surrounding agents by performing attention. Formally, we calculate the emotion transfer coefficient e_i with LeakyReLU to measure the effect of each f_p^i on f_{agent}, denoted as $e_i = \alpha([w_a f_{agent} \| w_p f_p^i])$, where $\|$ represents concatenation. The parameters $w_a, w_p \in \mathbb{R}^{d \times d_s}$ and the linear projection mapping $\alpha(\cdot)$ learn the emotion relationship. After performing the normalization via the softmax function, the final coefficient a_i is computed as $a_i = \frac{exp(e_i)}{\sum_{j \in \mathcal{N}} exp(e_j)}$, where $\mathcal{N}$ means the surrounding nodes. In practice, we set $K = 3$ to use the multi-head attention to realize the fusion of surrounding node features. The final weighted average feature $h_{c3} \in \mathbb{R}^d$ is obtained as follows:

$$h_{c3} = \sigma \left(\frac{1}{K} \sum_{k=1}^{K} \sum_{i \in \mathcal{N}} a_i^k w_p^k f_p^i + w_a^k f_{agent} \right). \tag{5}$$

3.4 Context 4: Agent-Object Context

Emotion psychology researchers [4,11,43,45,53] emphasize that the interactions of agents' actions with objects induce emotion arousal of the primary agent in the scene. More colloquially, the context of interactions between surrounding agents and objects can trigger emotion cues that subliminally affect change in the emotion of the recognized agent, like the girl having fun with the hairdryer in Fig. 1(d), and the smiling man with the cup in Fig. 2(a). These interactions facilitate the outpouring of positive emotions by the recognized agents. Motivated by the above observations, our insight is to adopt an aggregation strategy to model the context of surrounding agent-object interactions and thus learn indirect representations.

More concretely, as shown in the red-bordered branch of Fig. 2(a), drawing on the success of Human-Object Interaction (HOI) task (detect the interactions between a human and object pair, then localize them) [18], we first define the bounding box set of agent-object interaction pairs obtained by input I_{mask} via the HOI Network [60] as $\mathcal{I}_u = \{I_u^j\}, j = 1, .., m$. Subsequently, the pre-trained ResNet-50 [22] on ImageNet [15] separately encodes the interaction regions $\mathcal{I}_u$ to obtain the intermediate features as $F_u = \{f_u^j \in \mathbb{R}^{d_s}\}, j = 1, .., m$. Immediately, the proposed aggregation strategy models the emotion semantics for different interaction pairs via learning dynamic weights:

$$\beta_u^j = U^T (w_u^j \cdot f_u^j + b_u^j), \tag{6}$$

$$\gamma_u^j = \frac{exp(\beta_u^j)}{\sum_{k=1}^{m} exp(\beta_u^k)}, \tag{7}$$

$$\hat{f}_u = \sum_{j=1}^{m} \gamma_u^j \odot f_u^j, \tag{8}$$

where $U \in \mathbb{R}^{d_s \times 1}$, $w_u^j \in \mathbb{R}^{d_s \times d_s}$, and $b_u^j \in \mathbb{R}^{d_s \times 1}$ are the learnable parameters. After that, we perform a projection transformation on $\hat{f}_u$ to obtain $h_{c4} \in \mathbb{R}^d$.

3.5   Feature Fusion and Learning Strategies

Considering the complementarity of diverse contexts and different levels of contributions, we propose an Adaptive Relevance Fusion (ARF) module to learn effective shared representations of contexts. As shown in Fig. 2(b), the ARF module consists of two phases: cross-context fusion and adaptive fusion. The cross-context fusion phase (phase 1) focuses on the interactions among different contexts, potentially adapting streams from one context to another. Note that our fusion strategy can be extended to diverse contexts. In this paper, we take the feature adaptation process about learning from h_{c_2} (context 2) to h_{c_1} (context 1) as an example to describe the details. Inspired by [61], the ARF module first embeds h_{c_1} into a space denoted as $\mathcal{G}_{c_1} = LN\left(h_{c_1}\right)W_{\mathcal{G}_{c_1}}$, while embedding h_{c_2} into two spaces denoted as $\mathcal{Q}_{c_2} = LN\left(h_{c_2}\right)W_{\mathcal{Q}_{c_2}}$ and $\mathcal{S}_{c_2} = LN\left(h_{c_2}\right)W_{\mathcal{S}_{c_2}}$, respectively, where $W_{\mathcal{G}_{c_1}}$, $W_{\mathcal{Q}_{c_2}}$, $W_{\mathcal{S}_{c_2}} \in \mathbb{R}^{d \times d}$ are embedding weights, and LN means layer normalization. Attention weights are obtained by applying the softmax function to dot product of $\mathcal{G}_{c_1}$ and $\mathcal{Q}_{c_2}$. The information dissemination from cross-context interaction is defined as:

$$Z^{cross}_{c_2 \to c_1} = softmax(\mathcal{G}_{c_1}\mathcal{Q}^T_{c_2})\mathcal{S}_{c_2} \in \mathbb{R}^{d \times d}. \tag{9}$$

Immediately, the forward computation is expressed as:

$$h^{cross}_{c_2 \to c_1} = LN\left(h_{c_1}\right) + Z^{cross}_{c_2 \to c_1}. \tag{10}$$

Assuming that the total set of context features as $H_c = \{h_{c_i}\}, i = 1, ..., n$, then the final interactions received by target context 1 as $h^{cross}_{c_1} = \prod^n_{i=2} h^{cross}_{c_i \to c_1}$, where $\prod$ denotes concatenation operator as $[\cdot \| \cdot]$ between features.

The adaptive fusion phase (phase 2) provides optimal fusion weights for each context to highlight the potent contexts while suppressing the weaker ones. Formally, we learn the attention weights through the respective feed-forward networks with a GeLU activation [24] denoted as $\psi_{c_i} = \mathcal{F}(h^{cross}_{c_i}; w_{c_i}), i = 1, ..., n$, where w_{c_i} are the network parameters. The softmax function makes the sum of these attentions to be 1, $i.e., \sum_i \psi_{c_i} = 1$. After that, we perform element-wise multiplication of the learnable attention and the corresponding input. All outputs are concatenated and then fed to linear projection parametrized by w_θ to obtain the feature h_{Fin}, which is defined as follows:

$$h_{Fin} = \sigma\left(w_\theta \cdot \prod^n_{i=1} \psi_{c_i} \odot h^{cross}_{c_i}\right). \tag{11}$$

Finally, two separate branches follow the fully connected layers, one for the discrete classification task and the other for the continuous regression task. We use the MultiLabel-SoftMarginLoss as the classification loss of discrete categories, which is expressed as L_{disc}. The loss function of the continuous dimensions regression is formulated as $L_{cont} = \frac{1}{C}\sum_{k \in C}\left(\hat{y}_k - y_k\right)^2$, where y_k is the ground-truth of the continuous dimension regression, $\hat{y}_k$ is the output of VAD [39] dimensions and C is the number of channel dimensions. Therefore, the total training loss is defined as: $L_{comb} = \lambda_{disc}L_{disc} + \lambda_{cont}L_{cont}$, where λ_{disc} and λ_{cont} are the trade-off coefficients.

4   Datasets

EMOTIC. EMOTIC [30] dataset contains 23,571 images of 34,320 annotated people in uncontrolled environments. These images are annotated for 26 discrete categories and 3 continuous dimensions of emotion, with multiple labels assigned to each image. The standard partition of the dataset is 7:1:2.

GroupWalk. GroupWalk [42] dataset consists of 45 videos that were captured using stationary cameras in 8 real-world settings. The annotations consist of the following discrete labels: *Angry, Happy, Neutral,* and *Sad.* The standard partition of the dataset is 8.5:1.5.

HECO. HECO dataset consists of images from the HOI [8,21] datasets, film clips, and images from the Internet. The dataset contains a total number of 9,385 images and 19,781 annotated agents. These image samples contain rich context information and diverse agent interaction behaviours. To improve the robustness of models trained on the HECO, we add about 2% fuzzy images and 5% images with occlusion for agents. The dataset is randomly split into training (70%), validation (10%), and testing (20%) sets. The annotation process involves 3 psychologists and 10 graduate students. The annotation is performed blindly and independently, and we utilize the majority voting rule to determine the final labels. The superiority of HECO is that it combines two types of emotion labels. For discrete categories, we annotate with eight categories, including *Surprise, Excitement, Happiness, Peace, Disgust, Anger, Fear,* and *Sadness.* For continuous dimensions, we use the emotional state model of VAD [39], and annotate the *Valence* (V), *Arousal* (A) and *Dominance* (D) of agents on a scale of 1–10. Inspired by emotion sociology studies [19,57], we also design the novel *Self-assurance* (Sa) and *Catharsis* (Ca) labels. These labels describe the degree to which the agents interact with each other and adapt to the context.

5   Implementation Details

5.1   Data Processing

To generate I_{agent} and I_p from I via the bounding boxes, we use the pedestrian tracking method RobustTP [7] for the GroupWalk and the annotation information in the EMOTIC and HECO, respectively. For I_{agent} in context 1, we utilize the face detector [75] to implement face detection and clipping. The facial bounding boxes are used to get the facial input m_1 and resize it to 64×64. We extract a 136-dimensional vector $m_2 \in \mathbb{R}^{136}$ obtained through facial landmarks. We adopt the Alphapose [68] to obtain 18 modified gesture coordinates and 26 gait coordinates. In this case, the coordinates of key points are used to compute the 1D gesture vector $m_3 \in \mathbb{R}^{36}$ and the 1D gait vector $m_4 \in \mathbb{R}^{52}$. Then, the raw I is masked via the bounding boxes of I_{agent} to produce I_{mask}, and via the bounding boxes of I_{agent} and I_p to produce I_s in context 2. In context 3, the crop operation of the same size is performed from the middle and four

Table 1. Discrete classification results on the EMOTIC dataset.

Category	Kosti et al. [30]	Zhang et al. [72]	Lee et al. [31]	Mittal et al. [41]	Ours L_{disc}	Ours L_{comb}	Category	Kosti et al. [30]	Zhang et al. [72]	Lee et al. [31]	Mittal et al. [41]	Ours L_{disc}	Ours L_{comb}
Peace	22.35	30.68	19.55	**35.72**	25.5	26.24	Affection	26.47	**47.52**	22.36	38.55	41.61	37.66
Esteem	17.86	12.05	15.38	**25.75**	21.98	20.29	Anticipation	57.31	63.2	52.85	60.73	62.75	**63.31**
Engagement	86.69	**87.31**	73.71	86.23	74.69	75.23	Confidence	**80.33**	74.83	72.68	68.12	72.22	74.42
Happiness	58.92	72.9	53.73	80.45	83.58	**85.25**	Pleasure	46.72	48.37	34.12	67.31	67.26	**67.68**
Excitement	78.05	72.68	70.42	80.75	85.64	**86.56**	Surprise	22.38	8.44	17.46	19.6	25.31	**27.03**
Sympathy	15.23	19.45	14.89	16.74	24.7	**25.87**	Doubt/Confusion	31.88	19.67	26.07	**38.43**	23.44	24.96
Disconnection	20.64	23.17	22.01	28.73	27.64	**28.95**	Fatigue	8.87	12.93	6.29	19.35	32.35	**33.58**
Embarrassment	3.05	1.58	1.88	10.31	9.63	**10.57**	Yearning	9.22	9.86	4.84	**15.08**	10.88	11.12
Disapproval	16.14	12.64	15.37	18.55	23.41	**23.52**	Aversion	7.44	6.81	3.26	11.33	13.19	**15.28**
Annoyance	15.26	12.33	14.42	24.68	28.98	**29.02**	Anger	11.24	11.27	12.88	14.69	15.47	**17.84**
Sensitivity	9.05	4.74	6.94	13.94	22.53	**24.89**	Sadness	18.69	23.9	17.75	40.26	46.75	**47.8**
Disquietment	19.57	17.66	10.84	**22.14**	19.36	21.17	Fear	15.7	6.15	7.47	16.99	36.06	**36.68**
Pain	9.46	8.22	8.16	14.68	18.26	**19.27**	Suffering	17.67	23.71	14.85	**48.05**	45.37	46.74
							mAP	27.93	28.16	23.85	35.28	36.87	**37.73**

Table 2. Discrete classification results on the GroupWalk dataset.

Category	Kosti et al. [30]	Zhang et al. [72]	Lee et al. [31]	Mittal et al. [41]	Ours
Anger	57.65	51.92	45.18	68.85	**70.54**
Happy	71.32	63.37	56.59	72.31	**72.38**
Neutral	43.1	40.26	39.32	50.34	**52.54**
Sad	61.24	58.15	52.96	70.8	**71.42**
mAP	58.33	53.43	48.51	65.58	**66.72**

Table 3. Discrete classification results on the HECO dataset.

Category	Kosti et al. [30]	Zhang et al. [72]	Lee et al. [31]	Mittal et al. [41]	Ours L_{disc}	Ours L_{comb}
Surprise	28.45	34.87	24.27	**38.37**	38.04	38.12
Excitement	42.16	45.74	37.97	48.59	53.2	**55.04**
Happiness	62.82	63.26	55.81	66.53	67.26	**69.16**
Peace	51.64	54.17	47.57	55.97	57.23	**57.31**
Disgust	45.37	49.43	41.74	50.48	52.28	**54.95**
Anger	40.76	45.22	38.39	51.29	53.04	**53.43**
Fear	32.74	35.67	30.51	**40.81**	40.08	40.27
Sadness	22.53	27.28	20.92	32.65	34.17	**36.94**
mAP	40.81	44.46	37.15	48.09	49.41	**50.65**

corners to obtain sub-images I_{crop} from I_{agent} and I_p, which consider the semantic shape information. In context 4, we use the Faster RCNN [51] to generate available bounding boxes of agents and objects, which are then fed into the HOI network [60] to obtain the agent-object pairs with interaction relations. After that, we obtain the union bounding boxes that contain the specific agent-object pairs based on the coordinate transformation. The above images are resized to 224×224. All backbones employed are empirical.

5.2   Training Details and Evaluation Metric

Our method is built on the Pytorch toolbox [48], and all models are trained on four Nvidia Tesla V100 GPUs. We extend the proposed method to video by averaging the prediction vectors of all frames in the GroupWalk. For the EMOTIC, GroupWalk, and HECO, the training batch sizes and epochs are $\{64, 1, 32\}$ and $\{120, 75, 100\}$, respectively. The Adam optimizer [27] is adopted for network optimization with an initial learning rate of $\{1e^{-3}, 1e^{-4}, 2e^{-3}\}$. To train the previous models on the HECO, we use the implementation provided by [30]. Limited by open source, we re-implemented [31,41,72] based on the reported details. Following [30,72], we use the Average Precision (AP) to evaluate classification results. To evaluate regression results, we employ the Error Rate (ER).

6   Experimental Results

6.1   Comparison with State-of-the-Art Methods

Discrete Classification Results. In Tables 1, 2 and 3, we report the AP scores for all categories and mean AP (mAP). Our method achieves the best results of 37.73%, 66.72% and 50.65% on the EMOTIC, GroupWalk and HECO, respectively, significantly improving 2–8% over the prior methods. Concretely, we observe that the AP scores of some categories is generally low, such as *Sensitivity* from the EMOTIC and *Sadness* from the HECO. However, our method remains competitive in these categories. Furthermore, we train different models by the combined loss L_{comb} and the discrete loss L_{disc} respectively for testing. Except for the categories *Affection* and *Esteem* on the EMOTIC, the results of L_{comb} are superior, showing that combining different emotion expressions is beneficial in depicting emotions.

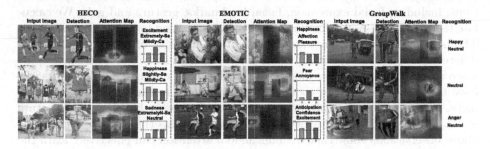

Fig. 3. Visualization results. We respectively show three examples of classification and regression results from the HECO, EMOTIC, and GroupWalk datasets. Column 1 is the input images marked with the recognized agent. Column 2 shows the facial expression, facial landmarks, gesture and gait extracted from the agent. Column 3 shows the corresponding attention maps. Column 4 shows the recognized emotion labels.

Table 4. Continuous regression results on the EMOTIC and HECO datasets.

Method	Dataset	Valence	Arousal	Dominance	mER	Dataset	Valence	Arousal	Dominance	mER
Kosti et al. [30] (L_{cont})	EMOTIC	1.0	1.5	0.8	1.1	HECO	0.9	1.3	0.8	1.0
Kosti et al. [30] (L_{comb})		0.9	1.2	0.9	1.0		0.9	1.2	**0.6**	0.9
Zhang et al. [72] (L_{cont})		0.8	1.6	1.2	1.2		0.9	1.1	1.0	1.0
Zhang et al. [72] (L_{comb})		0.7	1.0	1.0	0.9		**0.6**	1.1	0.7	0.8
Ours (L_{cont})		**0.6**	1.3	0.8	0.9		0.8	1.0	**0.6**	0.8
Ours (L_{comb})		0.8	**0.9**	**0.7**	**0.8**		0.7	**0.8**	0.6	**0.7**

Continuous Regression Results. Table 4 shows the evaluation results for the continuous dimensions using the mean ER (mER). We compare methods for supporting regression task on the EMOTIC and HECO. Note that the GroupWalk has only discrete emotion labels. On both datasets, our method outperforms the previous methods [30,72] with the lowest mER. We notice that the mER of L_{comb} is lower than that of L_{cont} for each method, which indicates that learning discrete classification contributes to infer emotional state of continuous dimensions. Additionally, all methods have lower mER on the HECO than EMOTIC, which mainly benefit from diverse sample sources and rich agent interaction instances in the HECO to assist the models in recognizing emotion.

6.2   Visualization and Analysis

Case Study of Multimodal Attention. To verify the effectiveness of the proposed multimodal attention in context 1, we visualize several detected samples in Fig. 4(a). Each recognized agent in the sample has the multimodal representations, including facial expression, facial landmarks, gesture and gait. We calculate the average L2-normalization of the vector attention for multiple modalities. The heat map matrix represents the attention intensity of each modality from different samples. For instance, in the first row, the girl's clear face conveys joy more clearly than the other modalities, so the facial expression and landmarks have the higher weights. In contrast, the lady's face in the third row is incomplete, but we can reasonably infer emotion by her body language (the gesture about caresses). As a result, the gesture feature obtains the highest weight. The above observations show that the multimodal attention can effectively learn the dynamic contribution of different modalities to the final representation.

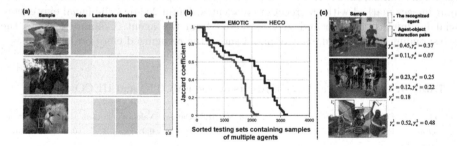

Fig. 4. (a) Heat map of attention weights for multiple modalities from different samples in context 1. The darker colour indicates the higher weights. (b) Jaccard coefficients for samples containing multiple agents in the testing set (sorted). The higher values denote the existence of emotion co-occurrence between the recognized agent and surrounding agents in context 3. (c) For context 4, we provide dynamic weight analysis of agent-object interaction pairs in the aggregation strategy. γ_u^j come from Eq. 7.

Emotion Semantic Capture of Scene. Figure 3 presents the visualization results of three examples for each dataset. The attention maps show the scenes' emotion semantics learned from the network. For example, in the samples of the second row (*middle*) and the last row (*left*), the semantic context of *fire* and *crashed car* are interpreted, implying *fear* and *sadness*, respectively. Meanwhile, although agents in the first row (*middle*) and the second row (*left*) have same discrete emotion *Happiness*, different continuous emotions inspire us better understand agents' adaptability in the scene and physiological arousal level. Moreover, other contexts can contribute to making predictions when some agents' features are difficult to extract due to occlusion or ambiguity, such as gesture.

Emotion Co-occurrence. To explain the emotion relationship between agents, we calculate the Jaccard coefficient [46] for each sample of multiple agents containing annotations on the EMOTIC and HECO datasets, respectively. Concretely, we define the set of predicted categories (the recognized agent) in each sample as S_{pred} and the set of the ground truth of surrounding agents in same sample as $(S_a^1, S_a^2, ..., S_a^n) \subseteq S_a$. n denotes the number of agents. The Jaccard coefficient is computed as $(S_a \cap S_{pred})/(S_a \cup S_{pred})$. In Fig. 4(b), we observe that over 64% of the samples in both datasets have values above 0.6, *i.e.*, the emotional states of the recognized agents are consistent with or similar to the surrounding agents. This observation proves that learning the emotion relationship between agents in the same scene can assist in inferring the primary emotion.

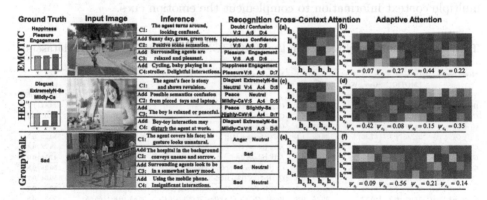

Fig. 5. Complementarity analysis. (*Left*) We select a sample from each of three datasets and then perform the recognition by gradually adding context network branches. (*Right*) When the above samples use four context branches, we plot the attention matrix (a), (c) and (e) for the cross-context fusion phase and the corresponding attention matrix (b), (d) and (f) for the adaptive fusion phase.

Analysis of Aggregation Strategy. In Fig. 4(c), we show several samples to understand the effect of different agent-object interactions. γ_u^j are the weight coefficients obtained by the corresponding interaction pairs I_u^j in the sample through the aggregation strategy. Some interesting observations are as follows. The effect of the agent-object interaction pairs is significant when the recognized agent and surrounding agents are involved in the same or similar event, and vice versa. For example, in the first row, I_u^1 and I_u^2 in the game playing case correspond to higher coefficients $\gamma_u^1 = 0.45$ and $\gamma_u^2 = 0.37$. In contrast, I_u^4 in the food-taking case has the lowest coefficient. A similar pattern is found in the second row, where the coefficient for $\gamma_u^3 = 0.12$ in the case of drinking water is the lowest. Furthermore, we find that the effect tendency of agent-object interaction pairs to generally conform to a gradual decay outwards centred on the recognized agent. These observations align with the psychology theories [11,53].

Complementarity Analysis. To prove the complementary recognition ability of four contexts (referred to as C_1, C_2, C_3, and C_4), we select a sample from each of three datasets and then perform inference by gradually adding context network branches. Figure 5 shows the dynamic recognition results during the addition of context branches. On the EMOTIC, positive semantics of scene from C_2, relaxed other agents from C_3, and pleasant interactions from C_4 gradually remove the emotion ambiguity recognized by C_1 only. On the HECO, the semantics of the intrusive boy-toy interaction from C_4 enhances the emotion judgment of *Disgust* in C_1. That is, the superior performance benefits from combining multiple context information to complement the emotion cues.

Table 5. Ablation study results on the EMOTIC, GroupWalk, and HECO datasets.

Model design	Dataset						Model design	Dataset					
	EMOTIC		GroupWalk		HECO			EMOTIC		GroupWalk		HECO	
	mAP	mER	mAP	mER	mAP	mER		mAP	mER	mAP	mER	mAP	mER
Full (ours)	37.73	0.8	66.72	–	50.65	0.7	C_3 (GCNs) [28]	35.25	1.2	63.94	–	48.84	1.1
C_1	22.51	1.6	44.76	–	37.27	1.4	C_3 (Depth) [32]	36.39	1.0	65.19	–	49.02	0.9
$C_1 + C_2$	29.23	1.1	54.42	–	41.93	1.0	Concatenation [52]	30.47	1.2	59.87	–	43.6	1.1
$C_1 + C_3$	27.56	1.3	57.36	–	39.62	1.1	Multiplication [41]	36.52	0.9	65.24	–	50.22	0.7
$C_1 + C_4$	26.29	1.2	52.09	–	37.93	1.2	ARF (phase 1)	36.27	0.9	65.33	–	49.73	0.8
$C_1 + C_2 + C_3$	36.18	0.8	64.34	–	48.07	0.8	ARF (phase 2)	34.65	1.0	64.13	–	47.51	0.9
$C_1 + C_2 + C_4$	34.93	0.9	60.27	–	47.25	0.8	C_1 (OpenFace [1]+OpenPose [5])	37.45	0.8	66.39	–	50.28	0.8
$C_1 + C_3 + C_4$	33.45	1.0	62.61	–	44.23	0.9	C_4 (R-FCN [13]+HOI-Net [33])	37.52	0.9	66.45	–	50.34	0.7
C_2 (Mask Face)	35.57	1.0	64.34	–	47.71	1.0	VGG19 [56] (C_1,C_2)+Res101 [22] (C_3,C_4)	37.76	0.9	66.68	–	50.87	0.7
C_2 (Mask Body)	37.02	0.9	65.12	–	49.46	0.8	Res34 [22] (C_1,C_2)+Res152 [22] (C_3,C_4)	36.83	0.8	65.85	–	50.24	0.8

Interpreting Cross-Context Fusion Attention. We plot the attention matrices for the cross-context fusion phase when using four contexts for the above samples illustrated in Fig. 5(a, c, e). The attention matrix shows the adaptation and interaction of features on the vertical axis to features on the horizontal axis. The brighter areas represent the higher correlation among context features that can collectively improve emotion expression. For a reasonable example, on the HECO, the correct recognition bring about by the C_1 and C_4 branches correspond to the brighter areas in Fig. 5(c) *w.r.t.* $h_{c_1 \rightarrow c_4}^{cross}$ and $h_{c_4 \rightarrow c_1}^{cross}$.

Interpreting Adaptive Fusion Attention. In Fig. 5(b, d, f), we visualize the attention weights of the adaptive fusion phase for the above samples when using four contexts. The vertical axis of the attention matrix denotes the features in different contexts, and the horizontal axis denotes the partial dimension. A higher number of bright areas in a feature indicate that the feature contributes more to emotion recognition. As an example on the GroupWalk, since the branch of C_2 successfully captures the *sadness* shown by the agent walking out of the hospital, which corresponds to the brightest areas contained by $h_{c_2}^{cross}$ in Fig. 5(f). Obviously, $\psi_{c_2} = 0.56$ is the highest weight coefficient.

6.3   Ablation Study

We perform thorough ablation study of all components to demonstrate the effectiveness and robustness of our method. Table 5 shows the results for discrete categories and continuous dimensions on three datasets.

Effectiveness of Context Branches. For context branches, we keep context 1, which only captures information from the recognized agent itself, and then gradually remove other context networks. Note that the best result is to combine four context branches (Full). For discrete categories, contexts 1 and 2 are the most competitive of two combinations. Such advantage comes from the fact that most of the samples on the EMOTIC and HECO have rich scene elements. The equally good results of contexts 1 and 3 on the GroupWalk may benefit from vast agent flows, which is consistent with the observations of [41, 42]. Furthermore, similar results are observed for continuous dimensions.

Different Masking Strategies. When using full branches, we provide two strategies to replace masking all agents of I_s in context 2, *i.e.*, masking only the face of the agent proposed in [31] and only the body of the agent proposed in [41]. The results show that the previous strategies of masking only the part of the recognized agent clearly hurt the model's performance, which suggests that masking all agents is essential.

Modelling of Interaction Between Agents. For context 3, we present the alternatives to evaluate the rationality of the chosen structure. More concretely, we replace the branch in context 3 with the GCNs-based [28] and Depth-based [32] methods used in [41] to model the social dynamics of interactions between agents. Our method outperforms the alternative versions as the emotion relationships of surrounding agents are modelled through attention weights explicitly, rather than simply as a system.

Different Fusion Strategies. To show the advantages of the ARF module, we perform comparison experiments with the concatenation [52] and multiplicative fusion [41] of the final features from different contexts. The results show that the ARF module is more competitive, proving that capturing correlations across contexts can provide effective multimodal representations. Moreover, we retain one phase of the ARF module separately for testing. It is observed that the fusion mechanisms from both phases provide the indispensable contributions.

Effect of Detectors. We replace the detectors with alternative components (OpenFace [1] and OpenPose [5] in C_1, R-FCN [13] and HOI-Net [33] in C_4) to explore whether there is an effect on the model's performance. The results in Table 5 show that replacing detectors has a slight effect on the mER and that the errors in the mAP scores are both less than 0.35. The above observations prove that our method is robust, *i.e.*, the detectors barely affect performance.

Analysis of Backbone CNNs. In addition, we use different backbones to implement the proposed framework. Table 5 shows that a deeper network structure does not necessarily obtain better results, *i.e.*, the performance improvement does not depend entirely on the backbones.

7 Conclusion

In this paper, we propose a novel context-aware emotion recognition framework, which employs four meaningful context branches to understand human emotion in a boosting and synergistic manner. Inspired by emotion sociology and psychology, we explore emotion-rich representations from contexts at the visual level to advance the development of effective visual-only driven emotion recognition applications. Moreover, learning multimodal shared representations through the proposed adaptive relevance fusion module allows for extending our approach to more contexts. Numerous qualitative and quantitative analyses clearly demonstrate the superiority of our approach.

Acknowledgements. This work is supported by National Key R&D Program of China (2021ZD0113502, 2021ZD0113503), Shanghai Municipal Science and Technology Major Project (2021SHZDZX0103) and National Natural Science Foundation of China under Grant (82090052).

References

1. Baltrušaitis, T., Robinson, P., Morency, L.P.: OpenFace: an open source facial behavior analysis toolkit. In: 2016 IEEE Winter Conference on Applications of Computer Vision (WACV), pp. 1–10. IEEE (2016)
2. Barrett, L.F., Mesquita, B., Gendron, M.: Context in emotion perception. Curr. Dir. Psychol. Sci. **20**(5), 286–290 (2011)
3. Bos, D.O., et al.: EEG-based emotion recognition. The influence of visual and auditory stimuli, vol. 56, no. 3, pp. 1–17 (2006)
4. Calhoun, C., Solomon, R.C.: What is an emotion?: classic readings in philosophical psychology (1984)
5. Cao, Z., Simon, T., Wei, S.E., Sheikh, Y.: Realtime multi-person 2D pose estimation using part affinity fields. In: Proceedings of the IEEE Conference on Computer Vision and Pattern Recognition, pp. 7291–7299 (2017)
6. Castellano, G., Kessous, L., Caridakis, G.: Emotion recognition through multiple modalities: face, body gesture, speech. In: Peter, C., Beale, R. (eds.) Affect and Emotion in Human-Computer Interaction. LNCS, vol. 4868, pp. 92–103. Springer, Heidelberg (2008). https://doi.org/10.1007/978-3-540-85099-1_8

7. Chandra, R., Bhattacharya, U., Roncal, C., Bera, A., Manocha, D.: RobustTP: end-to-end trajectory prediction for heterogeneous road-agents in dense traffic with noisy sensor inputs. In: ACM Computer Science in Cars Symposium, pp. 1–9 (2019)

8. Chao, Y.W., Liu, Y., Liu, X., Zeng, H., Deng, J.: Learning to detect human-object interactions. In: 2018 IEEE Winter Conference on Applications of Computer Vision (WACV), pp. 381–389. IEEE Computer Society (2018)

9. Chen, Z., Li, B., Xu, J., Wu, S., Ding, S., Zhang, W.: Towards practical certifiable patch defense with vision transformer. In: Proceedings of the IEEE/CVF Conference on Computer Vision and Pattern Recognition, pp. 15148–15158 (2022)

10. Clavel, C., Vasilescu, I., Devillers, L., Richard, G., Ehrette, T.: Fear-type emotion recognition for future audio-based surveillance systems. Speech Commun. **50**(6), 487–503 (2008)

11. Cornelius, R.R.: The Science of Emotion: Research and Tradition in the Psychology of Emotions. Prentice-Hall, Inc., Upper Saddle River (1996)

12. Cowie, R., et al.: Emotion recognition in human-computer interaction. IEEE Signal Process. Mag. **18**(1), 32–80 (2001)

13. Dai, J., Li, Y., He, K., Sun, J.: R-FCN: object detection via region-based fully convolutional networks. In: Advances in Neural Information Processing Systems 29 (2016)

14. Davidson, R.J., Sherer, K.R., Goldsmith, H.H.: Handbook of Affective Sciences. Oxford University Press, Oxford (2009)

15. Deng, J., Dong, W., Socher, R., Li, L.J., Li, K., Fei-Fei, L.: ImageNet: a large-scale hierarchical image database. In: 2009 IEEE Conference on Computer Vision and Pattern Recognition, pp. 248–255. IEEE (2009)

16. Dhall, A., Goecke, R., Lucey, S., Gedeon, T.: Acted facial expressions in the wild database. Australia, Technical report TR-CS-11 2, 1, Australian National University, Canberra (2011)

17. Frijda, N.H.: Emotion, cognitive structure, and action tendency. Cogn. Emot. **1**(2), 115–143 (1987)

18. Gkioxari, G., Girshick, R., Dollár, P., He, K.: Detecting and recognizing human-object interactions. In: Proceedings of the IEEE Conference on Computer Vision and Pattern Recognition, pp. 8359–8367 (2018)

19. Gordon, S.L.: The sociology of sentiments and emotion. In: Social psychology, pp. 562–592. Routledge (2017)

20. Gunes, H., Piccardi, M.: Bi-modal emotion recognition from expressive face and body gestures. J. Netw. Comput. Appl. **30**(4), 1334–1345 (2007)

21. Gupta, S., Malik, J.: Visual semantic role labeling. arXiv preprint arXiv:1505.04474 (2015)

22. He, K., Zhang, X., Ren, S., Sun, J.: Deep residual learning for image recognition. In: Proceedings of the IEEE Conference on Computer Vision and Pattern Recognition, pp. 770–778 (2016)

23. Helbing, D., Molnar, P.: Social force model for pedestrian dynamics. Phys. Rev. E **51**(5), 4282 (1995)

24. Hendrycks, D., Gimpel, K.: Gaussian error linear units (GELUs). arXiv preprint arXiv:1606.08415 (2016)

25. Hoang, M.H., Kim, S.H., Yang, H.J., Lee, G.S.: Context-aware emotion recognition based on visual relationship detection. IEEE Access **9**, 90465–90474 (2021)

26. Huang, H., et al.: CMUA-watermark: a cross-model universal adversarial watermark for combating deepfakes. In: Proceedings of the AAAI Conference on Artificial Intelligence, vol. 36, no. 1, pp. 989–997 (2022). https://doi.org/10.1609/aaai.v36i1.19982. https://ojs.aaai.org/index.php/AAAI/article/view/19982

27. Kingma, D., Ba, J.: Adam: a method for stochastic optimization. In: International Conference on Learning Representations (2014)
28. Kipf, T.N., Welling, M.: Semi-supervised classification with graph convolutional networks. arXiv preprint arXiv:1609.02907 (2016)
29. Köpüklü, O., Köse, N., Rigoll, G.: Motion fused frames: data level fusion strategy for hand gesture recognition. In: Proceedings of the IEEE Conference on Computer Vision and Pattern Recognition Workshops, pp. 2103–2111 (2018)
30. Kosti, R., Alvarez, J.M., Recasens, A., Lapedriza, A.: Context based emotion recognition using emotic dataset. IEEE Trans. Pattern Anal. Mach. Intell. **42**(11), 2755–2766 (2019)
31. Lee, J., Kim, S., Kim, S., Park, J., Sohn, K.: Context-aware emotion recognition networks. In: Proceedings of the IEEE/CVF International Conference on Computer Vision, pp. 10143–10152 (2019)
32. Li, Z., Snavely, N.: MegaDepth: learning single-view depth prediction from internet photos. In: Proceedings of the IEEE Conference on Computer Vision and Pattern Recognition, pp. 2041–2050 (2018)
33. Liao, Y., Liu, S., Wang, F., Chen, Y., Qian, C., Feng, J.: PPDM: parallel point detection and matching for real-time human-object interaction detection. In: Proceedings of the IEEE/CVF Conference on Computer Vision and Pattern Recognition, pp. 482–490 (2020)
34. Liu, K., Gebraeel, N.Z., Shi, J.: A data-level fusion model for developing composite health indices for degradation modeling and prognostic analysis. IEEE Trans. Autom. Sci. Eng. **10**(3), 652–664 (2013)
35. Liu, S., et al.: Efficient universal shuffle attack for visual object tracking. In: ICASSP 2022–2022 IEEE International Conference on Acoustics, Speech and Signal Processing (ICASSP), pp. 2739–2743 (2022). https://doi.org/10.1109/ICASSP43922.2022.9747773
36. Liu, X., Shi, H., Chen, H., Yu, Z., Li, X., Zhao, G.: iMiGUE: an identity-free video dataset for micro-gesture understanding and emotion analysis. In: Proceedings of the IEEE/CVF Conference on Computer Vision and Pattern Recognition, pp. 10631–10642 (2021)
37. Liu, Y., Liu, J., Zhao, M., Li, S., Song, L.: Collaborative normality learning framework for weakly supervised video anomaly detection. IEEE Trans. Circuits Syst. II Express Briefs **69**(5), 2508–2512 (2022). https://doi.org/10.1109/TCSII.2022.3161061
38. Lu, Y., Zheng, W.L., Li, B., Lu, B.L.: Combining eye movements and EEG to enhance emotion recognition. In: IJCAI, vol. 15, pp. 1170–1176. Citeseer (2015)
39. Mehrabian, A.: Basic Dimensions for a General Psychological Theory: Implications for Personality, Social, Environmental, and Developmental Studies, vol. 2. Oelgeschlager, Gunn & Hain, Cambridge (1980)
40. Mesquita, B., Boiger, M.: Emotions in context: a sociodynamic model of emotions. Emot. Rev. **6**(4), 298–302 (2014)
41. Mittal, T., Bera, A., Manocha, D.: Multimodal and context-aware motion perception model with multiplicative fusion. IEEE MultiMedia **28**, 67–75 (2021)
42. Mittal, T., Guhan, P., Bhattacharya, U., Chandra, R., Bera, A., Manocha, D.: Emoticon: Context-aware multimodal emotion recognition using Frege's principle. In: Proceedings of the IEEE/CVF Conference on Computer Vision and Pattern Recognition, pp. 14234–14243 (2020)
43. Musch, J., Klauer, K.C.: The Psychology of Evaluation: Affective Processes in Cognition and Emotion. Psychology Press, Brighton (2003)

44. Navarretta, C.: Individuality in communicative bodily behaviours. In: Esposito, A., Esposito, A.M., Vinciarelli, A., Hoffmann, R., Müller, V.C. (eds.) Cognitive Behavioural Systems. LNCS, vol. 7403, pp. 417–423. Springer, Heidelberg (2012). https://doi.org/10.1007/978-3-642-34584-5_37

45. Niedenthal, P.M., Ric, F.: Psychology of Emotion. Psychology Press, Brighton (2017)

46. Niwattanakul, S., Singthongchai, J., Naenudorn, E., Wanapu, S.: Using of Jaccard coefficient for keywords similarity. In: Proceedings of the International Multiconference of Engineers and Computer Scientists, vol. 1, pp. 380–384 (2013)

47. Ochsner, K.N., Gross, J.J.: The cognitive control of emotion. Trends Cogn. Sci. 9(5), 242–249 (2005)

48. Paszke, A., et al.: Automatic differentiation in PyTorch (2017)

49. Piana, S., Stagliano, A., Odone, F., Verri, A., Camurri, A.: Real-time automatic emotion recognition from body gestures. arXiv preprint arXiv:1402.5047 (2014)

50. Poria, S., Cambria, E., Hazarika, D., Majumder, N., Zadeh, A., Morency, L.P.: Context-dependent sentiment analysis in user-generated videos. In: Proceedings of the 55th Annual Meeting of the Association for Computational Linguistics (Volume 1: Long Papers), pp. 873–883 (2017)

51. Ren, S., He, K., Girshick, R., Sun, J.: Faster r-cnn: Towards real-time object detection with region proposal networks. In: Advances in Neural Information Processing Systems 28, pp. 91–99 (2015)

52. Rozgić, V., Ananthakrishnan, S., Saleem, S., Kumar, R., Vembu, A.N., Prasad, R.: Emotion recognition using acoustic and lexical features. In: Thirteenth Annual Conference of the International Speech Communication Association (2012)

53. Ruckmick, C.A.: The psychology of feeling and emotion (1936)

54. Schachter, S., Singer, J.: Cognitive, social, and physiological determinants of emotional state. Psychol. Rev. 69(5), 379 (1962)

55. Sikka, K., Dykstra, K., Sathyanarayana, S., Littlewort, G., Bartlett, M.: Multiple kernel learning for emotion recognition in the wild. In: Proceedings of the 15th ACM on International Conference on Multimodal Interaction, pp. 517–524 (2013)

56. Simonyan, K., Zisserman, A.: Very deep convolutional networks for large-scale image recognition. arXiv preprint arXiv:1409.1556 (2014)

57. Stets, J.E.: Current emotion research in sociology: advances in the discipline. Emot. Rev. 4(3), 326–334 (2012)

58. Tsai, Y.H.H., Bai, S., Liang, P.P., Kolter, J.Z., Morency, L.P., Salakhutdinov, R.: Multimodal transformer for unaligned multimodal language sequences. In: Proceedings of the Conference Meeting on Association for Computational Linguistics, vol. 2019, p. 6558. NIH Public Access (2019)

59. Tsai, Y.H.H., Liang, P.P., Zadeh, A., Morency, L.P., Salakhutdinov, R.: Learning factorized multimodal representations. arXiv preprint arXiv:1806.06176 (2018)

60. Ulutan, O., Iftekhar, A., Manjunath, B.S.: VSGNet: spatial attention network for detecting human object interactions using graph convolutions. In: Proceedings of the IEEE/CVF Conference on Computer Vision and Pattern Recognition, pp. 13617–13626 (2020)

61. Vaswani, A., et al.: Attention is all you need. In: Advances in Neural Information Processing Systems, pp. 5998–6008 (2017)

62. Veličković, P., Cucurull, G., Casanova, A., Romero, A., Lio, P., Bengio, Y.: Graph attention networks. arXiv preprint arXiv:1710.10903 (2017)

63. Wallbott, H.G.: Bodily expression of emotion. European J. Soc. Psychol. 28(6), 879–896 (1998)

64. Wang, S., Yang, D., Zhai, P., Chen, C., Zhang, L.: TSA-NET: tube self-attention network for action quality assessment. In: Proceedings of the 29th ACM International Conference on Multimedia, pp. 4902–4910 (2021)
65. Wang, W., et al.: Comp-GAN: compositional generative adversarial network in synthesizing and recognizing facial expression. In: Proceedings of the 27th ACM International Conference on Multimedia, pp. 211–219 (2019)
66. Woo, S., Park, J., Lee, J.-Y., Kweon, I.S.: CBAM: convolutional block attention module. In: Ferrari, V., Hebert, M., Sminchisescu, C., Weiss, Y. (eds.) ECCV 2018. LNCS, vol. 11211, pp. 3–19. Springer, Cham (2018). https://doi.org/10.1007/978-3-030-01234-2_1
67. Xie, S., Hu, H., Wu, Y.: Deep multi-path convolutional neural network joint with salient region attention for facial expression recognition. Pattern Recogn. **92**, 177–191 (2019)
68. Xiu, Y., Li, J., Wang, H., Fang, Y., Lu, C.: Pose Flow: efficient online pose tracking. In: BMVC (2018)
69. Yeh, H., Curtis, S., Patil, S., van den Berg, J., Manocha, D., Lin, M.: Composite agents. In: Proceedings of the 2008 ACM SIGGRAPH/Eurographics Symposium on Computer Animation, pp. 39–47 (2008)
70. Zadeh, A., Zellers, R., Pincus, E., Morency, L.P.: Multimodal sentiment intensity analysis in videos: facial gestures and verbal messages. IEEE Intell. Syst. **31**(6), 82–88 (2016)
71. Zhai, P., Luo, J., Dong, Z., Zhang, L., Wang, S., Yang, D.: Robust adversarial reinforcement learning with dissipation inequation constraint (2022)
72. Zhang, M., Liang, Y., Ma, H.: Context-aware affective graph reasoning for emotion recognition. In: 2019 IEEE International Conference on Multimedia and Expo (ICME), pp. 151–156. IEEE (2019)
73. Zhou, B., Lapedriza, A., Khosla, A., Oliva, A., Torralba, A.: Places: a 10 million image database for scene recognition. IEEE Trans. Pattern Analy. Mach. Intell. **40**(6), 1452–1464 (2017)
74. Zhu, J., Luo, B., Zhao, S., Ying, S., Zhao, X., Gao, Y.: IExpressNet: facial expression recognition with incremental classes. In: Proceedings of the 28th ACM International Conference on Multimedia, pp. 2899–2908 (2020)
75. Zhu, X., Ramanan, D.: Face detection, pose estimation, and landmark localization in the wild. In: 2012 IEEE Conference on Computer Vision and Pattern Recognition, pp. 2879–2886. IEEE (2012)
76. Ziemke, T.: On the role of emotion in biological and robotic autonomy. BioSystems **91**(2), 401–408 (2008)

Adaptive Fine-Grained Sketch-Based Image Retrieval

Ayan Kumar Bhunia[1]([✉]), Aneeshan Sain[1,2], Parth Hiren Shah[1,2],
Animesh Gupta[1,2], Pinaki Nath Chowdhury[1,2], Tao Xiang[1,2],
and Yi-Zhe Song[1,2]

[1] SketchX, CVSSP, University of Surrey, Guildford, UK
{a.bhunia,a.sain,p.chowdhury,t.xiang,y.song}@surrey.ac.uk
[2] iFlyTek-Surrey Joint Research Centre on Artificial Intelligence, Guildford, UK

Abstract. The recent focus on Fine-Grained Sketch-Based Image
Retrieval (FG-SBIR) has shifted towards generalising a model to new
categories without any training data from them. In real-world applications, however, a trained FG-SBIR model is often applied to both new
categories and different human sketchers, i.e., different drawing styles.
Although this complicates the generalisation problem, fortunately, a
handful of examples are typically available, enabling the model to adapt
to the new category/style. In this paper, we offer a novel perspective –
instead of asking for a model that generalises, we advocate for one that
quickly adapts, with just very few samples during testing (in a few-shot
manner). To solve this new problem, we introduce a novel model-agnostic
meta-learning (MAML) based framework with several key modifications:
(1) As a retrieval task with a margin-based contrastive loss, we simplify the MAML training in the inner loop to make it more stable and
tractable. (2) The margin in our contrastive loss is also meta-learned
with the rest of the model. (3) Three additional regularisation losses are
introduced in the outer loop, to make the meta-learned FG-SBIR model
more effective for category/style adaptation. Extensive experiments on
public datasets suggest a large gain over generalisation and zero-shot
based approaches, and a few strong few-shot baselines.

Keywords: FG-SBIR · Meta-learning · Category and style adaptation

1 Introduction

Significant progress has been made towards making sketch an input modality for
image retrieval [7,12,18,32,47,49,55,61]. As an input modality complementary

P. H. Shah and A. Gupta—Interned with SketchX.

Supplementary Information The online version contains supplementary material
available at https://doi.org/10.1007/978-3-031-19836-6_10.

to text, sketch finds its competitive advantage especially when it comes to fine-grained instance-level retrieval [7,37,38,45], where the problem lies with intra-category retrieval as opposed to the conventional category-level setting [12,13].

Early attempts at fine-grained sketch-based image retrieval (FG-SBIR) mainly focused on tackling the sketch-photo domain gap, where triplet-based networks have by now been established as the de facto choice [7,38,53,59]. As performance under the supervised learning setting have recently started to saturate, the research focus has shifted onto the problem of data scarcity, where the challenge is to build generalisable and zero-shot models for unseen categories [14,16,36]. However, retrieval performances of these models are typically much weaker compared to supervised models. We attribute this to two factors (i) the stringent assumption of no additional sketch-photo pairs from the new categories, and more importantly, (ii) drawing styles of input sketches vary significantly amongst different users (see Fig. 1-c) – the latter of which remains untackled to date.

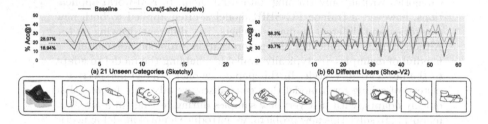

Fig. 1. Graphs illustrating how (a) *category-adaptive* FG-SBIR (b) *user-adaptive* FG-SBIR can significantly improve the retrieval performance on unseen categories and users using only 5 samples during inference, respectively. (c) Examples showing the varying *style* of sketching with different level of abstraction for the same photo with respect to different users (drawers).

The first contribution is thus a *practical* problem setting, namely category/style adaptive FG-SBIR. Instead of asking for a model that *generalises* to categories [14,16,36], we advocate for one that *quickly adapts*. That is, we are after a *single* FG-SBIR model that can *quickly* adapt to a new style/category, with just a few samples *during testing*. Achieving this offers a best-of-both-worlds solution – (i) the model has a better chance at adaptation having observed new style/category data, as opposed to no data for generalisation or zero-shot, and (ii) the few samples requirement still falls within the practical remit of sketch data, i.e., one can always sketch just a few. We show by experiments that our quick adaptation (few-shot) approach (category-level) offers about 6% gain over generalisation-based models (9−10% over no adaptation baseline), with just 5 new samples *during testing only* (Fig. 1 offers a summary). Our ultimate vision for commercial adaption of FG-SBIR is therefore – to deploy a single model, where the end users can easily adapt to their specific categories and drawing styles, by sketching very few (≤10) new samples.

Our second contribution is to devise a novel meta-learning framework to solve this new problem of adaptive FG-SBIR. Essentially, we build upon model-agnostic meta-learning (MAML) [20], which learns a common initialisation point encoding knowledge shared across different tasks such that it adapts quickly for a new task (i.e., specific category or user) using a few training samples. Unique to conventional few-shot approaches [35,50], this suits us ideally as it yields *one* model, and needs only a few (usually one) gradient update steps during testing.

However, getting a MAML-based framework to work with the specific problem of FG-SBIR is non-trivial. First, unlike few-shot classification – for which MAML was initially proposed – triplet-based (margin-based contrastive loss) cross-modal FG-SBIR networks typically involve three forward passes for anchor, positive and negative instances; and adopting MAML off-the-shelf would additionally incur heavy computation due to their second-order gradient computation [41] during backpropagation. We propose to side-step these difficulties by performing inner loop updates only for the final joint-feature embedding layer (see Fig. 2). This importantly avoids an over-fitted model during adaptation, as not all parameters are updated during adaptation process. Besides performing meta-learning upon intermediate latent-space, we also *meta-learn the margin* used in the contrastive loss to adapt it to new categories. To further tackle the sketch-photo domain gap [23], we additionally introduce a domain discrimination module to regularize the intermediate latent-space at the outer loop.

Our next contribution lies with how to tailor our meta-learning framework to best work with user- and category-wise adaptation. For that, we aim to make the intermediate latent space, upon which meta-learning is performed, be category/style discriminative. This discriminative objective is handled through an auxiliary classification head for category-level adaptation. Whereas, due to absence of abundant data for every user, we substitute for an auxiliary contrastive learning head for the style-adaptation setting. Furthermore, we add an extra semantic reconstruction head to encourage category-level transfer (akin to zero-shot SBIR [14,16,17]). In brief, both category and style adaptation are regularised by domain adaptation and the discriminative objective, while semantic relatedness is specifically modelled for category-level adaptation.

Our contributions can be summarised as follows: (a) We set out a vision for practical FG-SBIR by proposing a new problem setting, where rather than seeking for generalisation, we advocate for quick adaptation at testing time. (b) We introduce a novel FG-SBIR framework based on gradient-based meta-learning that adapts to a new category or user sketching style based on a few training examples. (c) The framework is based on the existing MAML but with significantly different formulations tailored for the specific challenges of either category or style-level adaptation. (d) Extensive experiments on public datasets suggest a significant increase in performance over generalisation and zero-shot approaches, and few strong few-shot baselines.

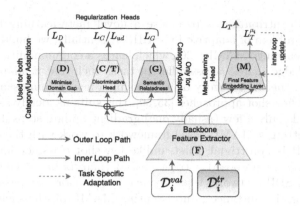

Fig. 2. Our framework for category/user adaptation involves a bi-level optimisation process. While the inner loop (red) aims to adapt via pseudo-updating $\mathbf{M}$ using support set, the outer loop (blue) executes meta-optimisation to learn better initialisation parameter. Moreover, meta-learning is performed in the intermediate latent space $\mathbf{F}(\cdot)$ which is regularised by auxiliary heads. Discriminative head is modelled by either $\mathbf{C}$ (with loss L_C) or $\mathbf{T}$ (with loss L_{ud}) for category and user level adaptation, respectively. $\mathbf{G}$ is only used for category-level adaptation. More details is in Sect. 3.3. Note that *only the inner loop path* (red) is used to obtain category/user-specialised model during inference. (Color figure online)

2   Related Works

Fine-Grained SBIR: Unlike category-level SBIR [3,4,12,13,17,33,44,46,61], the goal of fine-grained SBIR [2,6,10,11] is *instance-level* matching. While Li *et al.* [30] first introduced it using deformable part models and graph matching, Yu *et al.* [58] employed deep learning via deep triplet network to learn a common embedding space from heterogeneous domains. Later methods improved upon this via attention mechanism with higher order retrieval loss [53], reinforcement learning for on-the-fly retrieval [7] and using mixed modal jigsaw solving for a better pre-training strategy [38]. In this paper, we introduce a new fine-grained SBIR setting, i.e. category/style adaptive FG-SBIR, which is relevant to real-world applications given the performance gain.

Cross-Category Generalisation for SBIR: Mostly studies have been done on category level SBIR [14,16,17,33] for cross-category generalisation. Starting with sketch-photo translation pseudo tasks using conditional GANs [57] that learn embedding, zero-shot SBIR has been handled by regularising embedding space, with semantic information across different classes by reconstructing word-vectors [14], semantically paired cycle consistency [33]. Cross-category generalisation for FGSBIR has only been attempted via a domain-generalisation approach by modelling a universal manifold of prototypical visual sketch traits [36] to dynamically represent the sketch/photo. Contrary to the domain-invariant representation learning [36], we follow a few-shot adaptation [20] approach and additionally address the user-specific style-adaptation problem.

Meta-learning: Meta-learning has been studied intensively for quick model adaptation to new tasks with few training samples. Representative methods such as memory network [35] or metric-based [50] meta-learning methods are mostly architecture dependant [9] and generally designed for few-shot classification. They are thus unsuitable for our retrieval model adaptation problem. Recently there has been a significant attention towards optimisation based meta-learning algorithms [20,21,31] due to their model agnostic nature. In particular, model-agnostic meta-learning (MAML) [20] aims to learn optimal initialisation parameters that allows quick adaptation at test-time using few gradient descent updates. Later on, it was further augmented with sets of tricks to stabilise the training in MAML++ [1], learnable learning rate in MetaSGD [31], meta-optimisation in a low-dimensional latent space in LEO [43], or a simplified inner-loop update by recently introduced Sign-MAML [19]. While MAML in theory can be applied to our problem, we have to introduce a number of significant modifications to make it more tractable and well suited to the specific challenges associated with category/style-adaptive FG-SBIR.

To eliminate disparity among users [29], several user adaptive models [5,27] are developed for activity and emotion recognition by transfer learning [24], and user interface via recurrent network [51]. Conversely, we use meta-learning that realises our goal of a user adaptive AI agent.

3   Methodology

Overview: We devise a fine-grained SBIR framework that could be instantly adapted for either specific category or user. The category/user specific training and testing data consists of $\mathcal{D}^S = \{\mathcal{D}_1^S, \mathcal{D}_2^S, \cdots, \mathcal{D}_{|N^S|}^S \ni |N^S| > 1\}$ and $\mathcal{D}^T = \{\mathcal{D}_1^T, \mathcal{D}_2^T, \cdots, \mathcal{D}_{|N^T|}^T \ni |N^T| \geq 1\}$, where N^S and N^T are the disjoint sets of training and testing categories/users (styles) respectively, i.e. $N^S \cap N^T = \emptyset$. Furthermore, we have access to smaller fine-tuning sets of data corresponding to every testing category/user as $\mathcal{D}^F = \{\mathcal{D}_1^F, \mathcal{D}_2^F, \cdots, \mathcal{D}_{|N^T|}^F \ni |N^T| \geq 1\}$ for category/user specific instantaneous adaptation. The i-th category/user in either of the three sets consists of K^i paired sketch (x) and photo (y) images as $\mathcal{D}_i = \{x_j, y_j\}_{j=1}^{K^i}$. During training, we intend to meta-learn a retrieval model F_M with the optimal initialisation point, by modelling the shared knowledge across different category/user from the training set $\mathcal{D}^S$ – such that it can quickly adapt to any new category/user using few examples. During inference, given K sketch-photo pairs from the fine-tuning set of a particular category/user $\mathcal{D}_i^F$, we obtain a category/user *specialised model* via a single gradient update: $F_M \mapsto F_M^i$.

3.1   Baseline FG-SBIR Model

We use Siamese network with spatial attention [14] as the baseline retrieval model. It consists of two components: (i) Given a photo or a rasterized sketch image I, we extract backbone feature map $B = f_B(I) \in \mathbb{R}^{h \times w \times c}$ where f_B is initialised from a pre-trained InceptionV3 [7] model; and h, w, and c represent the height, width and channels respectively. The attention normalised feature are fused with backbone feature via a residual connection to give $B_{att} = B + B \cdot f_{att}(B)$, followed by a global-average pooling operation to get a latent feature vector representation of size $\mathbb{R}^c$. This CNN comprising f_B and f_{att} produces an intermediate latent feature embedding $\mathbf{F}$, parameterised by $\theta_{\mathbf{F}}$. (ii) The extracted feature vector is passed through a fully-connected layer followed by l_2 normalisation to embed the photo and sketch images into a shared embedding space of dimension $\mathbb{R}^d$. We call this component as $\mathbf{M}$ with parameters $\theta_{\mathbf{M}}$.

Overall, the final representation is obtained through staged operation denoted as $\mathbf{M} \circ \mathbf{F}$. The training data are triplets $\{a, p, n\}$ containing sketch anchor, positive and negative photos respectively. Accordingly, *Triplet loss* is used for training [56], which aims at increasing the distance between sketch anchor and negative photo $\beta^- = \|\mathbf{M} \circ \mathbf{F}(a) - \mathbf{M} \circ \mathbf{F}(n)\|_2$ while reducing that between sketch anchor and positive photo $\beta^+ = \|\mathbf{M} \circ \mathbf{F}(a) - \mathbf{M} \circ \mathbf{F}(p)\|_2$. Let μ be the margin-hyperparameter, the triplet loss calculated across a batch of size N:

$$L_T = \frac{1}{N} \sum_{i=1}^{N} max\{0, \mu + \beta_i^+ - \beta_i^-\}. \tag{1}$$

In multi-category FG-SBIR where a single model handles instance-specific retrieval from multiple categories (e.g. Sketchy [48]), hard triplets are used in training, i.e., the negative photo is from the same class but of different instances.

3.2   Background: Gradient Based Meta-learning

Given a set of related tasks with some distribution $p(\mathcal{T})$, the objective of MAML [20] is to meta-learn a good initialisation θ of some parametric model f_θ such that only a few examples is necessary to adapt to any new task $\mathcal{T}_i \sim p(\mathcal{T})$. Each sampled task $\mathcal{T}_i \in \{D^{tr}, D^{val}\}$ consists of a support set of examples D^{tr} and a query/target set of examples D^{val}. Given $\mathcal{D}^{tr}$ and a loss function $\mathcal{L}_{\mathcal{T}_i}$, the parameters θ are first adapted to θ_i' using one or more gradient descent updates via *inner-loop* (performs adaptation) feedback as follows: $\theta_i' \leftarrow \theta - \alpha \nabla_\theta \mathcal{L}_{\mathcal{T}_i}^{\mathcal{D}^{tr}}(f_\theta)$. The inner-loop learning rate α can either be fixed, or meta-learned concurrently like Meta-SGD [31]. As the aim is to optimise θ in such a way that one or a few gradient based updates will enable maximally effective performance on any $\mathcal{T}_i$, meta-optimisation is conducted in the *outer-loop* update, with respect to θ as: $\theta \leftarrow \theta - \beta \nabla_\theta \sum_{\mathcal{T}_i \sim p(\mathcal{T})} \mathcal{L}_{\mathcal{T}_i}^{\mathcal{D}^{val}}(f_{\theta_i'})$. Updating θ via the outer-loop essentially implies *gradient through a gradient*, or differentiating through the inner-loop to minimise the meta-objective using task-specific adapted models $f_{\theta_i'}$ on their corresponding *target set* $\mathcal{D}^{val}$. This is computationally demanding due to the second order gradient computation on θ.

3.3 Meta-learning for FG-SBIR

Overview: A number of modifications are needed to make MAML suitable for our category/user adaptive FG-SBIR problem. The first challenge of adopting MAML for FG-SBIR is to alleviate the high computational cost brought about by the nested optimisation in the inner and outer loops. Inspired by a recent study [41] which suggests that inner loop simplification in MAML has little impact on its effectiveness, we exclude $\mathbf{F}$ from the inner loop update, and only meta-learn the final feature embedding layer $\mathbf{M}$ by adapting parameter $\theta_{\mathbf{M}}$ inside the inner loop. In other words, meta-learning is performed on the intermediate latent feature space extracted by $\mathbf{F}$.

We further introduce regularizers for handling problems specific to fine-grained SBIR. More specifically, there is a meta-learning head of final feature embedding layer $\mathbf{M}$ (used during inner loop update) and multiple regularisation heads upon the extracted latent representation $\mathbf{F}(\cdot) \in \mathbb{R}^c$ (see Fig. 2). These regularizers serve two major purposes: (a) minimising the sketch-photo domain gap in the intermediate latent space, and (b) allowing the intermediate latent space to be more discriminative across different categories/styles. Furthermore, we add an *extra* regularisation head to aid in semantic transfer to unseen categories in category-level adaptation. Note that this is only for category adaptation and *not* used for user style adaptation as no varying semantic concepts exist across different users [16].

Moreover, all regularizers are removed during inference, and we only use $\mathbf{M} \circ \mathbf{F}$ where the final joint-feature embedding head $\mathbf{M}$ is updated through a single gradient update using few support set examples for quick adaptation. In a nutshell, during adaptation, $\mathbf{M}$ grabs the specialised knowledge from support set examples to generalise better for a specific target category/user. Next we describe these regularizers in detail.

Minimising Sketch-Photo Domain Gap: Bridging the domain-gap between sketch and photo images is a key objective behind learning feature representation in a common embedding space for any sketch-based image retrieval system [14]. Therefore, we add a discriminator $\mathbf{D} : \mathbb{R}^c \mapsto [0, 1]$ with parameter $\theta_{\mathbf{D}}$ which learns to predict the domain of an input (i.e. sketch vs photo) from the latent features of size $\mathbb{R}^c$ from $\mathbf{F}$. By maximising this discriminator loss through Gradient Reversal Layer (GRL) [23], the network $\mathbf{F}$ learns to extract domain-agnostic latent feature upon which the meta-learning head $\mathbf{M}$ can generalise better. Given the binary domain label t (which is 0 and 1 for sketch and photo domain respectively) for input I, the binary cross-entropy loss to train the domain-adaptation head is defined as:

$$L_D = t \cdot \log(\mathbf{D}(\mathbf{F}(I))) + (1 - t) \cdot \log(1 - \mathbf{D}(\mathbf{F}(I))) \qquad (2)$$

Discriminative Intermediate Latent Space: While triplet loss over the output of $\mathbf{M}$ distinguishes between instances of a particular category, a class discrimination objective [25] helps towards learning to separate between different categories in a multi-category FG-SBIR model. In order to make the latent space $\mathbf{F}(\cdot)$ class-discriminative, we add a cross-entropy loss using a classification head $\mathbf{C} : \mathbb{R}^c \mapsto \mathbf{R}^{|N^S|}$ with parameters $\theta_\mathbf{C}$. Let the class label be $\mathbf{c_l} \in N^S$ with respect to input either sketch or photo image I, the classification loss is defined as:

$$L_C = \texttt{Cross\_Entropy}(\mathbf{c_l}, \texttt{softmax}(\mathbf{C}(\mathbf{F}(I)))). \qquad (3)$$

For some datasets such as QMUL-ShoeV2 [7,58] where user-level adaptation is required but all sketch-photo images belong to the *same* shoe category, this classification loss is clearly not applicable. In this case, we want the intermediate latent space $\mathbf{F}(\cdot)$ to be discriminative across different user's sketching styles instead. As the number of samples per user is limited, we use a metric learning based approach. Concretely, a triplet loss is used where anchor (a') and positive (p') sketch-photo pairs come from the same user, and negative (n') sample is from any other user. Directly imposing triplet loss over the latent space $\mathbf{F}(\cdot)$ can be a very hard constraint [15], potentially hurting generalisation during instant adaptation to new users; thus we use an auxiliary embedding network $\mathbf{T} : \mathbb{R}^{c+c} \mapsto \mathbb{R}^{d'}$, where concatenated features of paired sketch-photo are fed as input. Note that we are imposing triplet loss on the output of $\mathbf{T}$ but the gradient flows back through $\mathbf{F}$ making its $\mathbf{F}(\cdot)$ user-discriminative. Given $\beta'^- = \|\mathbf{T}(\mathbf{F}(a')) - \mathbf{T}(\mathbf{F}(n'))\|_2$, $\beta'^+ = \|\mathbf{T}(\mathbf{F}(a')) - \mathbf{T}(\mathbf{F}(p'))\|_2$, and μ' being the margin-hyperparameter, the triplet loss is computed as:

$$L_{ud} = \max\{0, \beta'^- + \beta'^+ + \mu'\}. \qquad (4)$$

Semantic Transfer for Category-Level Adaptation: Unlike single-category FG-SBIR [7,58], multi-category FG-SBIR (e.g. Sketchy) further dictates the transfer of class-specific semantic concept [22] from seen to unseen categories. For that, meta-learning is additionally performed in the semantically enriched intermediate latent-space $\mathbf{F}(\cdot)$ by using relationship between different categories. Specifically, we use a semantic decoder head over $\mathbf{F}(\cdot)$ to reconstruct the word-embedding representation of the category label with respect to either sketch or photo. Let $\mathbf{G}$ be the semantic decoder (three fully connected layers with ReLU) with parameter $\theta_\mathbf{G}$, input (sketch or photo) be I with class label $\mathbf{c_l} \in N^S$ and word-embedding from pre-trained FastText [8] model be $\mathbf{S_w} = \texttt{embedding}(\mathbf{c_l})$. We use simple cosine-similarity distance as semantic reconstruction loss:

$$L_S = \frac{1}{2}\left(1 - \frac{\langle \mathbf{G}(\mathbf{F}(I)), \, \mathbf{S_w} \rangle}{\|\mathbf{G}(\mathbf{F}(I))\|_2 \cdot \|\mathbf{S_w}\|_2}\right) \qquad (5)$$

Task Sampling: In meta-learning [26], a model is trained episodically, such that a task sampled in each episode, imitates the few-training-sample scenario appearing during testing. For us, sampling a task $\mathcal{T}_i \sim p(\mathcal{T})$ across a category/user means: (i) we first randomly select the i-th category/user $\mathcal{D}_i^S$ out of N^S sets of training category/user. (ii) Next, from $\mathcal{D}_i^S$, we construct the support $\mathcal{D}^{tr}$ and validation set $\mathcal{D}^{val}$ by randomly sampling K sketch-photo pairs for each respectively. Inner loop is updated over $\mathcal{D}^{tr}$, and outer loop over $\mathcal{D}^{val}$. Within every set, hard negatives are created by selecting different photo instances.

Meta Optimisation on the Loss Margin: The *triplet loss* contains the hyper-parameter, margin μ, whose optimal value is empirically found to be varying (Sect. 4.3) across different categories. Since the intra-class distribution or spread among sampled sketches is unlikely to be identical for each class, it is intuitive to have a class-specific optimal margin value. Therefore, we decide *learning to learn* the margin-hyperparameter inside our meta-learning process that would adaptively decide the optimal μ value for a specific category at test time.

For the i-th task, given K-shot training examples from $\mathcal{D}_i^{tr} = \{(x_k, y_k) \mid k = 1, \cdots, K\}$, the latent representation of sketch (x_k) is concatenated with that of its corresponding photo (y_k), to obtain the per-instance sketch-photo representation: $f_{xy}^k = \text{concat}(\mathbf{F}(x_k), \mathbf{F}(y_k)) \in \mathbb{R}^{c+c}$. Given the set of all $\{f_{xy}^k\}_{k=1}^K$, different per-instance sketch-photo representations $\{f_{xy}^m, f_{xy}^n\}$ where $(m \neq n)$ are concatenated pair-wise, resulting in a total of $K' = K(K-1)$ pairs. All such pairs can be aggregated into a matrix for task i as $S_i \in \mathbb{R}^{K' \times (2c+2c)}$. This is subsequently processed by a *relational network* $\mathbf{R}$ with parameter $\theta_{\mathbf{R}}$ that feeds every row-vector to each time step of bidirectional GRU to model the relation among all samples in support set. A max-pool operation is performed over the output from all time steps. The resultant vector is then fed to a linear layer that finally predicts a sigmoid normalised scalar value representing the learnable margin value for each task i as $\mu_i = \mathbf{R}(S_i)$. Therefore, given the task specific triplet loss $L_{T_i}^{\mu_i}$ (Eq. 1) with its margin hyperparameter μ_i and learning rate α both being meta-learned concurrently following Meta-SGD [31], the parameter of the $\mathbf{M}$ is now adapted in the inner loop using $\mathcal{D}_i^{tr}$ as follows:

$$\theta'_{\mathbf{M}} = \theta_{\mathbf{M}} - \alpha \cdot \nabla_{\theta_M} L_T^{\mu_i}(\theta_{\mathbf{F}}, \theta_{\mathbf{R}}, \theta_{\mathbf{M}}; \mathcal{D}_i^{tr}). \qquad (6)$$

On the other side, the overall regularisation loss for *category level adaptation* becomes $L_{reg} = \sum_{a,p,n} \frac{1}{3}(L_D + L_C + L_S)$ which is calculated over anchor (a), positive (p) and negative (n) samples. Similarly, for *user-specific adaptation* the regularisation loss becomes $L_{reg} = \sum_{a,p,n} \frac{1}{3}L_D + L_{ud}$. As there is no inner-loop step, we calculate the regularisation loss over concatenated samples from both support and validation set together (say $\mathcal{D}_i$).

Let all parameters related to regularisation be denoted as $\theta_{\mathbf{reg}}$, e.g., for category adaptation $\theta_{\mathbf{reg}} = \{\theta_{\mathbf{D}}, \theta_{\mathbf{C}}, \theta_{\mathbf{S}}\}$ and user style adaptation $\theta_{\mathbf{reg}} = \{\theta_{\mathbf{D}}, \theta_{\mathbf{T}}\}$. Meta-learning pipeline is trained along with regularisation loss to optimise a combined loss. The optimisation objective for the outer loop is thus formulated as:

$$\underset{\theta_{\mathbf{F}}, \theta_{\mathbf{M}}, \theta_{\mathbf{R}}, \alpha, \theta_{\mathbf{reg}}}{\text{argmin}} \quad L_T(\theta_{\mathbf{F}}, \theta_{\mathbf{R}}, \alpha, \theta'_{\mathbf{M}}; \mathcal{D}_i^{val}) + \lambda \cdot L_{reg}(\theta_{\mathbf{F}}, \theta_{\mathbf{reg}}; \mathcal{D}_i) \qquad (7)$$

where λ is a weighting hyperparameter. Note that the task specific adapted $\theta'_{\mathbf{M}}$ is used to compute a validation loss. As $\theta'_{\mathbf{M}}$ is dependant on $\theta_{\mathbf{M}}$, $\theta_{\mathbf{R}}$ and α via inner-loop update (Eq. 6), a higher order gradient is computed in the outer loop optimisation. Note that the model is updated by averaging gradient over meta-batch size of B sampled tasks and trained in an end-to-end manner.

Discussion: (a) *Significance of Semantic-Relatedness Loss:* For multi-category FG-SBIR (Sketchy), sketch-photo pairs are from the same category, grouped together using the class discriminative objective. Every category holds a semantic concept, which may help control the positioning of class-specific groups in the embedding space, such that class-specific concepts can be transferred from seen to unseen categories (akin to zero-shot SBIR [14,16]). This entire objective is handled by the semantic relatedness module. It should not be confused with the instance-specific separation criteria for fine-grained retrieval (*already handled* by triplet-loss). Please see § **Supp.** for an illustration of latent space. (b) *Difference with classical few-shot learning:* Standard few-shot literature usually deals with classification [20], whereas ours is the *first work employing few-shot adaptation for fine-grained retrieval*. We show potential under two objectives: category and user's style adaptation. (c) *Novelty behind Triplet-Loss+MAML:* Dou *et al.* [15] adopted MAML for *domain generalisation* purpose where triplet loss acts as an auxiliary loss to encourage class specific feature clustering. On the contrary, ours involves a few-shot *adaptation paradigm* which requires executing inner loop update using triplet-loss during inference. Therefore, the design of inner-loop update using triplet loss is more critical to our framework. Furthermore, unlike [15], margin value of inner-loop triplet loss is meta-learned to facilitate better and stable adaptation. (d) *Why FG-SBIR undergoes such generalization issue (unlike person ID/re-ID):* Domain gap existing across various categories in multi-category FG-SBIR, is much larger than different person-identities in Re-ID, as shape morphology varies highly across new categories (not limited to just human shapes). Note that FG-SBIR model tries to learn *shape correspondences* between sketches and photos. As *shape* itself becomes almost unknown for unseen categories, discovering fine-grained correspondence becomes even harder.

4   Experiments

Datasets: For category-level adaptation, we use the Sketchy dataset [48] which contains 125 categories with 100 photos each. Each photo has at least 5 sketches with fine-grained associations. In contrast, QMUL-Shoe-V2 dataset [7,38,53] contains sketches of only one category (shoes) annotated with user ID and fine-grained sketch-photo correspondence, making it the only option for user/style-level adaptation. We consider users having at least 10 sketch samples, which leads to a total of 306 users having 5480 sketches and corresponding 1877 photos.

Experimental Setup: We demonstrate the potential of our framework in two scenarios. **(a) Category-level adaptation:** Following [36,57], we split the 125 Sketchy categories to 104 for training and the rest 21 for testing, ensuring no test categories are present in the 1000 ImageNet classes [42]. We create random adaptation sets of 10 photos each from each unseen category along with their respective sketches, leaving the rest photos and sketches for testing. **(b) User-level adaptation:** We consider 60 users with a sketch/gallery-photo size of 560/200 for testing, and the rest for training. This ensures gallery-photos and users to be mutually exclusive for training and testing.

Implementation Details: Inception-V3 network pretrained on ImageNet [42] is used as our backbone feature extractor. The intermediate latent space $\mathbf{F}(\cdot)$ is of size $c = 2048$, and we set $d = 64$ as the dimension of our final joint-feature embedding layer $\mathbf{M}(\cdot)$. Following the traditional supervised learning protocol [7,52], the Adam-optimiser [28] with a learning rate of 0.0001 is first used to pre-train the baseline model for 60 epochs with a triplet loss, having a fixed margin of 0.3 with batch size 16. Thereafter, we add regularizer heads and perform meta-optimisation (Eq. 7) for 40 epochs. The reported performance uses only one inner-loop update during inference unless otherwise mentioned (ablative study done later). We use meta-batch size of $B = 8$, and set the size of support and validation set as $K = 5$. We use Adam as meta-optimiser with an outer-loop learning rate of 0.0001. Note that the margin value of inner-loop triplet loss is meta-learned, that for outer-loop is set to 0.3. Furthermore, we set λ, d', and μ' to 0.5, 64 and 0.2, respectively. We implemented our framework in PyTorch [39] conducting experiments on a 11 GB Nvidia RTX 2080-Ti GPU. We use pre-computed word-embeddings provided by Doodle2search [7], which ensures no leakage of class information. Please note that semantic relatedness module is used only for category-level adaptation on Sketchy; not for user style adaptation (on Shoe-V2), as no varying semantic concepts exist across different users. Please refer to § **Supplementary** (Supp.) for more details.

Evaluation Setup: During inference, K sketch-photo pairs are used to construct triplets for adaptation, where negative images are randomly sampled. We consider k $\in \{1, 5, 10\}$ on Sketchy, and k $\in \{1, 5\}$ on Shoe-V2 due to data constraint. For Shoe-V2, adaptation set is randomly sampled from each unseen user, and evaluation of adapted model is done on the rest samples. Only the final feature-embedding layer $\mathbf{M}$ is updated via inner loop update (Eq. 6) for adaptation. For fair evaluation, we make sure the adaptation and evaluation sets remain the same for all experiments. We evaluate the fine-grained retrieval performance using Acc.@q accuracy, i.e., percentage of sketches having true-match photos appearing in the top-q list. Average accuracy is reported by repeating every experiment five times.

4.1   Competitors

To the best of our knowledge, there has been no prior work dealing with either category or user-level adaptation for SBIR. We thus design several baselines from *four* different perspectives to justify our framework. **(i) SOTA FG-SBIR Methods:** We compare with popular *Triplet-SN* [58] (Sketch-A-Net+ triplet loss) and *Triplet-HOLEF* [53]. Results are cited at sketch-completion point for *Triplet-RL*. Furthermore, we compare with *Mixed-Jigsaw* employing self-supervised pre-training, and recently introduced StyleMeUP [46]. **(ii) Generalisation Approach:** *CC-DG* [36] aims to model a universal manifold of prototypical visual sketch traits that dynamically embeds sketch and photo, to generalise for unseen categories. Following a very recent few-shot classification work, we employ sequential distillation upon our baseline FG-SBIR model using l_2 loss on the absolute sketch/photo feature and evaluate it on unseen category/user without updating the model during inference. We term this few-shot competitor from non-MAML family as *Distill* [54]. **(iii) Zero-Shot SBIR:** We also compare with four state-of-the-art ZS-SBIR methods, namely *CVAE-Regress* [57], *Sem-Pyc* [16], *Doodle2Search* [14], *SAKE* [33].**(iv) Adaptation Based Approach:** (a) We compare with standard *Fine-Tuning* approach; (b) Off-the-shelf *MAML* [20] has been employed on the top of our baseline FG-SBIR model additionally following the tricks introduced in [1]. (c) Following *ANIL* [41], which only updates the final classification layer for few-shot classification, we update final embedding layer **M** within the inner loop in meta-optimisation process. We use fixed margin-hyperparameter value of 0.3 for both inner and outer loop in case of MAML, sign-MAML [19] (recently introduced low-cost variant) and ANIL baselines. Uniform backbone is used in all self-designed baselines and margin is meta-learned only in our final model.

Through preliminary experiments, we infer that adding a classification head is necessary for reasonable performance when dealing with multi-category FG-SBIR on Sketchy dataset. We thus add a classification head upon $F(\cdot)$ for *all our self-designed competitors (having uniform feature extractor) while experimenting on Sketchy*, and train using both triplet and classification losses with weights 1 and 0.01 respectively for a fair comparison.

Table 1. Comparing among our baseline FG-SBIR, naive Fine-tuning, Generalisation [36] approach, and our proposed Category (Sketchy) and User(Shoe-V2)-adaptive FG-SBIR. GAP$_B$ and GAP$_G$ represent the Acc@1 gap of ours with Baseline and Generalisation respectively.

Datasets	Baseline		Fine-tuning		Generalisation [36]		**Proposed** (k = 5)			
	Acc@1	Acc@5	Acc@1	Acc@5	Acc@1	Acc@5	Acc@1	Acc@5	GAP$_B$	GAP$_G$
Sketchy (Category Level)	18.4%	37.3%	18.5%	37.5%	22.7%	42.1%	28.1%	51.8%	9.7↑	5.4↑
Shoe-V2 (User Level)	33.7%	70.2%	33.8%	70.2%	33.8%	70.4%	38.3%	76.6%	4.6↑	4.5↑

4.2 Performance Analysis

Table 1 shows our adaptation (5-shot) based framework to outperform baseline FG-SBIR (Sect. 3.1) and Generalisation based approach [36] by a significant margin of 9.7% (4.6%) and 5.4% (4.5%) in Acc@1, respectively for category(user) level adaptation. Furthermore, we compare with *four* different classes of alternative approaches in Table 2, including an upper-bound for Sketchy, where we re-train the model on the testing (unseen) categories with available samples.

Category-Level Adaptation: We can make the following observations: *(i) SOTA FG-SBIR Methods:* Almost every existing state-of-the-arts model including our baseline performs poorly on unseen testing sketchy classes, indicating that adaptation is necessary. Note that, among them our baseline FG-SBIR

Table 2. Performance analysis using different approaches.

		Sketchy (Category)		Shoe-V2 (User)					Sketchy (Category)		Shoe-V2 (User)	
		Acc@1	Acc@5	Acc@1	Acc@5				Acc@1	Acc@5	Acc@1	Acc@5
	Our Baseline	18.4%	37.3%	33.7%	70.2%	Adaptation based approaches	Fine-Tuning	k=1	18.4%	37.3%	33.7%	70.2%
	Our Baseline + Reg.	19.2%	39.6%	33.9%	71.3%			k=5	18.5%	37.5%	33.8%	70.2%
	Upper-Bound	29.8%	53.7%	-	-			k=10	18.6%	37.5%	-	-
SOTA	Triplet-SN [60]	15.3%	34.0%	28.5%	67.3%		MAML [20]	k=1	19.5%	38.7%	34.2%	70.7%
	Triplet-HOLEF [53]	16.7%	35.9%	31.4%	69.1%			k=5	22.8%	42.3%	35.5%	74.6%
	Triplet-RL [7]	4.7%	7.8%	34.1%	70.2%			k=10	26.4%	48.9%	-	-
	Mixed-Jigsaw [36]	16.7%	34.3%	33.5%	71.4%		sign-MAML [19]	k=1	19.1%	38.2%	33.8%	69.6%
	StyleMeUp [46]	19.6%	39.7%	36.4%	81.8%			k=5	20.5%	39.6%	34.1%	70.8%
GA	CC-DG [36]	22.7%	42.1%	33.8%	70.4%		ANIL [41]	k=1	19.7%	38.9%	34.5%	70.9%
	Distill(non-MAML) [36]	18.9%	38.1%	33.9%	70.9%			k=5	23.2%	42.8%	35.7%	75.3%
ZS-SBIR	CVAE-Regress [57]	2.4%	9.5%	1.8%	3.1%			k=10	26.9%	48.3%	-	-
	Sem-Pyc [16]	4.9%	17.3%	2.1%	4.7%		Ours	k=1	21.8%	42.5%	34.9%	71.4%
	Doodle2Search [14]	14.8%	34.5%	28.1%	66.9%			k=5	28.1%	51.8%	38.3%	76.6%
	SAKE [33]	6.4%	20.3%	3.6%	5.7%			k=10	32.7%	53.5%	-	-

model is notably better compared to earlier SOTA triplet-loss based frameworks, *Triplet-SN* and *Triplet-HOLEF*, due to more recent backbone feature extractor (Inception-V3) with spatial attention. While *Triplet-RL* fails to converge for large Sketchy dataset as the reward diminishes to zero during RL-based fine-tuning, *Mixed-Jigsaw/StyleMeUP* are found to be less effective [38] on Sketchy. *(ii) Generalisation Approach:* CC-DG (our re-implementation) is the only exception that performs comparatively better than other SOTA methods, as it models category agnostic abstract sketch traits [36] for better cross-category generalisation. Nevertheless, it does not provide any option to obtain category specialised model during inference; hence its performance is much lower than our adaptation based pipeline. *Distill* (non-MAML baseline) gives very marginal gain over our baseline. *(iii) Zero-Shot SBIR:* Every ZS-SBIR method was designed for category-level retrieval, not instance-level, thus limiting its efficacy in FG-SBIR. Doodle2search [14] performs relatively better due to triplet loss (unlike the rest), which is critical for instance-level matching in FG-SBIR. *(iv) Adaptation Based Approach:* Notably naive *Fine-Tuning* hardly helps over few-shot setting. It can be seen that *ANIL* performs better than *MAML*. This suggests that simplifying the inner loop update in MAML to reduce the high computational cost associated with second order gradients over a large parameter space is indeed useful. However, its performance is still lower than ours. We also tried our first-order approximated version of MAML and very recently introduced sign-MAML [19], but found no significant difference to MAML. To summarise, our meta-learning based *adaptive fine-grained SBIR* framework outperforms existing SOTA methods, alternative generalisation and zero-shot approaches by a large margin, as well as exceeds some strong few-shot baselines by a significant margin. (v) *Most importantly*, accuracy even after adding all the respective regularizers to baseline FG-SBIR model falls behind our method by a significant margin of 9−10% (Sketchy) and 4−5% (Shoe) – thus proving the contribution of our bi-level meta-learning framework. The Qualitative results are shown in Fig. 3.

User-Level Adaptation: Compared to the striking boost obtained in the category-level adaptation experiments by our method, improvements for user level adaptation (Table 1 and 2) are relatively small (difference of 4.6% Acc@1) compared to our baselines. One explanation is that modelling user-specific subtle differences is more challenging compared to category-level modelling. Nevertheless, the overall pattern is fairly similar to that of category-level adaptation and a same set of conclusions can be drawn regarding the effectiveness of our approach.

Fig. 3. Category (left) and user (right) level adaptive model vs. baseline [(·): matching photo's rank] (more in supplementary).

4.3 Ablative Studies

Contributions of Regularizers: Ablative studies in Table 3 evaluate the contribution of different regularizers used for optimisation. (i) We notice L_D, mitigating the domain gap between sketch and photos, has a relatively uniform effect on both category and user level adaptation. (ii) Classification head, employing a classification loss L_C is the most critical one while dealing with multi-category FG-SBIR on Sketchy dataset to maintain class discriminative information. Removing only L_C leads to a drop of 7.5% under $k = 5$ on Sketchy. For multi-category FG-SBIR, class specific grouping (classification loss) followed by instance specific separation (hard triplet loss) is necessary. (iii) Semantic loss L_S plays a vital role in adapting to unseen Sketchy categories to transfer knowledge from seen training classes to unseen ones. (iv) Removing L_{ud}, that helps in learning discriminative information across different users' sketching styles, drops accuracy by 1.8% for user-level adaptation $k = 5$ on Shoe-V2 dataset.

Table 3. Ablative study (Acc@1); $k = 5$

L_D	L_S	L_C	Sketchy category level	L_D	L_{ud}	Shoe-V2 user level
✓	✓	✓	28.1%	✓	✓	38.3%
✗	✓	✓	26.3%	✗	✓	37.1%
✗	✗	✓	23.7%	✗	✗	35.8%
✗	✗	✗	16.5%	–	–	–

Effect of Meta-learning μ: A direct way of judging the contribution of the learnable margin hyper-parameter μ, is to replace it by a fixed value of 0.3 (optimised) in the inner loop loss calculation. Consequently, we notice a significant drop of 1.8% Acc@1 ($k = 5$) for category-level adaptation respectively. To verify if μ really varies across different Sketchy classes, we randomly choose 10 classes to perform exhaustive hyper-parameter search with bin size 0.05 around global optimum μ of 0.3. Figure 4 (a) shows that the optimal value indeed varies. Such a search for the test categories obviously is infeasible due to the lack of data. In Fig. 4 (b), our model-predicted average μ over different classes is plotted against

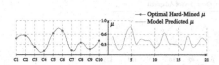

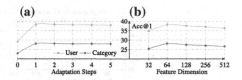

Fig. 4. (a) Hard-mined μ over 10 random classes. (b) Model predicted μ over 21 testing classes. (both Sketchy)

Fig. 5. Varying (a) adaptation steps (b) feature dimension (k = 5).

the 21 Sketchy testing classes – the value clearly varies contributing to the performance boost. However, the effect of learnable margin is almost negligible (a 0.06% boost) in case of user-level adaptation as all images belong to a single category for Shoe-V2 dataset. The reported numbers on Shoe-V2 are hence based on fixed inner loop margin value of 0.3.

Cross-Dataset Adaptation: Model trained on Sketchy training classes gives 10.3% Acc@1 on QMUL-ShoeV2 [7], however upon adaptation using 5 (10) random sketch-photo pairs from respective datasets, Acc@1 jumps to 22.3% (26.4%), respectively. In contrast to complete-training dataset supervised performance of 33.7%, this demonstrates our *cross-dataset* generalisation capability.

Further Analysis: (i) From Fig. 5 (a), the optimal accuracy is observed at joint feature-embedding space dimension d = 64. (ii) The number of gradient-update steps are varied as well – Fig. 5 (b) shows that a single gradient step update, used in all the experiments, provides the highest performance gain. (iii) We explore other word-embedding techniques for auxiliary semantic loss L_S, but found that Glove [40] and word2vec [34] give 27.5% and 27.7% for unseen category-level adaptation compared to 28.1% in case of fast-text [8] using $k = 5$. (iv) One could have used a simple sum or average pooling operation to accumulate information for predicting learnable μ. However a performance drop (Acc@1) of 1.2%/0.6%/0.8% during sum/average/max pooling operation under category setup (k = 5) demonstrates the relevance of relational network which encodes the joint relationship between all sketch-photo pairs in support set for predicting learnable μ. (v) For 5-shot single gradient step adaptation on our baseline model, an Intel(R) Xeon(R) W-2123 CPU @ 3.60 GHz takes 32.1 ms.

Is Adaptation Useful Even for Seen Classes?: Instead of designing individual FG-SBIR model for each category, cost-effective deployment requires a single model handling instance-specific retrieval from multiple categories. However, as the number of categories to be handled by a single model increases, the retrieval performance starts decreasing drastically even for the seen classes that the model has been trained upon, as shown in Fig. 6. For instance, single model trained from all the 125 Sketchy classes, gives average Acc@1 of only 25.6% on the test set. Whereas, on re-training 125 individual models for each category, the same value rises up to 43.1%, although it is quite impractical to have 125

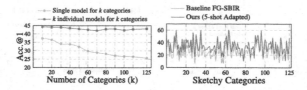

Fig. 6. Graph (left) shows how baseline FG-SBIR model falls behind with rise in categories (also during training) to be served by a single FG-SBIR model, compared to having multiple individual models for each category in Sketchy. Right shows benefit of adaptation.

separate models. In such a scenario, using our method on a single model to adapt to just one of the seen training categories with only 5/10 sketch-photo pairs, we obtain an average Acc@1 of 34.9/38.7%.

5 Conclusion

We have introduced a FG-SBIR framework which retains a single model that can quickly adapt to (i) sketching style of a particular user, or (ii) a new category, with just very few examples during the inference process. To this end, we design a meta-learning framework based on the existing MAML model but with crucial modification to our retrieval problem, including a simplified inner loop optimisation and introduction of the learnable contrastive loss margin to the meta-learning process. The intermediate latent space, upon which meta-learning is performed, is further constrained using three additional regularisation losses to facilitate learning the adaptation process during meta-optimisation.

References

1. Antoniou, A., Edwards, H., Storkey, A.: How to train your MAML. In: ICLR (2018)
2. Bhunia, A.K., Chowdhury, P.N., Sain, A., Yang, Y., Xiang, T., Song, Y.Z.: More photos are all you need: Semi-supervised learning for fine-grained sketch based image retrieval. In: CVPR (2021)
3. Bhunia, A.K., Chowdhury, P.N., Yang, Y., Hospedales, T.M., Xiang, T., Song, Y.Z.: Vectorization and rasterization: self-supervised learning for sketch and handwriting. In: CVPR (2021)
4. Bhunia, A.K., et al.: Doodle it yourself: class incremental learning by drawing a few sketches. In: CVPR (2022)
5. Bhunia, A.K., Ghose, S., Kumar, A., Chowdhury, P.N., Sain, A., Song, Y.Z.: MetaHTR: towards writer-adaptive handwritten text recognition. In: CVPR (2021)
6. Bhunia, A.K., et al: Sketching without worrying: noise-tolerant sketch-based image retrieval. In: CVPR (2022)
7. Bhunia, A.K., Yang, Y., Hospedales, T.M., Xiang, T., Song, Y.Z.: Sketch less for more: On-the-fly fine-grained sketch based image retrieval. In: CVPR (2020)
8. Bojanowski, P., Grave, E., Joulin, A., Mikolov, T.: Enriching word vectors with subword information. TACL **5**, 135–146 (2017)

9. Choi, M., Choi, J., Baik, S., Kim, T.H., Lee, K.M.: Scene-adaptive video frame interpolation via meta-learning. In: CVPR (2020)
10. Chowdhury, P.N., Bhunia, A.K., Gajjala, V.R., Sain, A., Xiang, T., Song, Y.Z.: Partially does it: towards scene-level FG-SBIR with partial input. In: CVPR (2022)
11. Chowdhury, P.N., Sain, A., Bhunia, A.K., Xiang, T., Gryaditskaya, Y., Song, Y.Z.: FS-COCO: towards understanding of freehand sketches of common objects in context. In: ECCV (2022)
12. Collomosse, J., Bui, T., Jin, H.: LiveSketch: query perturbations for guided sketch-based visual search. In: CVPR (2019)
13. Collomosse, J., Bui, T., Wilber, M.J., Fang, C., Jin, H.: Sketching with style: Visual search with sketches and aesthetic context. In: ICCV (2017)
14. Dey, S., Riba, P., Dutta, A., Llados, J., Song, Y.Z.: Doodle to search: practical zero-shot sketch-based image retrieval. In: CVPR (2019)
15. Dou, Q., de Castro, D.C., Kamnitsas, K., Glocker, B.: Domain generalization via model-agnostic learning of semantic features. In: NeurIPS (2019)
16. Dutta, A., Akata, Z.: Semantically tied paired cycle consistency for zero-shot sketch-based image retrieval. In: CVPR (2019)
17. Dutta, A., Akata, Z.: Semantically tied paired cycle consistency for any-shot sketch-based image retrieval. IJCV (2020)
18. Dutta, T., Singh, A., Biswas, S.: Adaptive margin diversity regularizer for handling data imbalance in zero-Shot SBIR. In: Vedaldi, A., Bischof, H., Brox, T., Frahm, J.-M. (eds.) ECCV 2020. LNCS, vol. 12350, pp. 349–364. Springer, Cham (2020). https://doi.org/10.1007/978-3-030-58558-7_21
19. Fan, C., Ram, P., Liu, S.: Sign-MAML: efficient model-agnostic meta-learning by SignSGD. arXiv preprint arXiv:2109.07497 (2021)
20. Finn, C., Abbeel, P., Levine, S.: Model-agnostic meta-learning for fast adaptation of deep networks. In: ICML (2017)
21. Finn, C., Xu, K., Levine, S.: Probabilistic model-agnostic meta-learning. In: NeurIPS (2018)
22. Fu, Z., Xiang, T., Kodirov, E., Gong, S.: Zero-shot object recognition by semantic manifold distance. In: CVPR (2015)
23. Ganin, Y., Lempitsky, V.: Unsupervised domain adaptation by backpropagation. In: ICML (2015)
24. Garcia-Ceja, E., Riegler, M., Kvernberg, A.K., Torresen, J.: User-adaptive models for activity and emotion recognition using deep transfer learning and data augmentation. User Model. User-Adapt. Interact. **30**, 365–393 (2020). https://doi.org/10.1007/s11257-019-09248-1
25. Horiguchi, S., Ikami, D., Aizawa, K.: Significance of Softmax-based features in comparison to distance metric learning-based features. IEEE-TPAMI **42**, 1279–1285 (2019)
26. Hospedales, T., Antoniou, A., Micaelli, P., Storkey, A.: Meta-learning in neural networks: a survey. arXiv preprint arXiv:2004.05439 (2020)
27. Hsieh, P.L., Ma, C., Yu, J., Li, H.: Unconstrained realtime facial performance capture. In: CVPR (2015)
28. Kingma, D.P., Ba, J.: Adam: a method for stochastic optimization. arXiv preprint arXiv:1412.6980 (2014)
29. Lane, N.D., et al.: Enabling large-scale human activity inference on smartphones using community similarity networks (CSN). In: UbiComp (2011)
30. Li, Y., Hospedales, T.M., Song, Y.Z., Gong, S.: Fine-grained sketch-based image retrieval by matching deformable part models. In: BMVC (2014)

31. Li, Z., Zhou, F., Chen, F., Li, H.: Meta-SGD: learning to learn quickly for few-shot learning. arXiv preprint arXiv:1707.09835 (2017)
32. Liu, L., Shen, F., Shen, Y., Liu, X., Shao, L.: Deep sketch hashing: fast free-hand sketch-based image retrieval. In: CVPR (2017)
33. Liu, Q., Xie, L., Wang, H., Yuille, A.: Semantic-aware knowledge preservation for zero-shot sketch-based image retrieval. In: ICCV (2019)
34. Mikolov, T., Chen, K., Corrado, G., Dean, J.: Efficient estimation of word representations in vector space. In: ICLR (2014)
35. Oreshkin, B., López, P.R., Lacoste, A.: TADAM: task dependent adaptive metric for improved few-shot learning. In: NeurIPS (2018)
36. Pang, K., et al.: Generalising fine-grained sketch-based image retrieval. In: CVPR (2019)
37. Pang, K., Song, Y.Z., Xiang, T., Hospedales, T.M.: Cross-domain generative learning for fine-grained sketch-based image retrieval. In: BMVC (2017)
38. Pang, K., Yang, Y., Hospedales, T.M., Xiang, T., Song, Y.Z.: Solving mixed-modal jigsaw puzzle for fine-grained sketch-based image retrieval. In: CVPR (2020)
39. Paszke, A., et al.: Automatic differentiation in PyTorch. In: NeurIPS Autodiff Workshop (2017)
40. Pennington, J., Socher, R., Manning, C.D.: GloVe: global vectors for word representation. In: EMNLP (2014)
41. Raghu, A., Raghu, M., Bengio, S., Vinyals, O.: Rapid learning or feature reuse? Towards understanding the effectiveness of MAML. In: ICLR (2020)
42. Russakovsky, O., et al.: ImageNet large scale visual recognition challenge. IJCV **115**, 211–252 (2015). https://doi.org/10.1007/s11263-015-0816-y
43. Rusu, A.A., et al.: Meta-learning with latent embedding optimization. In: ICLR (2019)
44. Sain, A., Bhunia, A.K., Potlapalli, V., Chowdhury, P.N., Xiang, T., Song, Y.Z.: Sketch3T: test-time training for zero-shot SBIR. In: CVPR (2022)
45. Sain, A., Bhunia, A.K., Yang, Y., Xiang, T., Song, Y.Z.: Cross-modal hierarchical modelling forfine-grained sketch based image retrieval. In: BMVC (2020)
46. Sain, A., Bhunia, A.K., Yang, Y., Xiang, T., Song, Y.Z.: StyleMeUp: towards style-agnostic sketch-based image retrieval. In: CVPR (2021)
47. Sampaio Ferraz Ribeiro, L., Bui, T., Collomosse, J., Ponti, M.: Sketchformer: transformer-based representation for sketched structure. In: CVPR (2020)
48. Sangkloy, P., Burnell, N., Ham, C., Hays, J.: The sketchy database: learning to retrieve badly drawn bunnies. ACM TOG **35**, 1–12 (2016)
49. Shen, Y., Liu, L., Shen, F., Shao, L.: Zero-shot sketch-image hashing. In: CVPR (2018)
50. Snell, J., Swersky, K., Zemel, R.S.: Prototypical networks for few shot learning. In: NeurIPS (2017)
51. Soh, H., Sanner, S., White, M., Jamieson, G.: Deep sequential recommendation for personalized adaptive user interfaces. In: IUI (2017)
52. Song, J., Song, Y.Z., Xiang, T., Hospedales, T.M.: Fine-grained image retrieval: the text/sketch input dilemma. In: BMVC (2017)
53. Song, J., Yu, Q., Song, Y.Z., Xiang, T., Hospedales, T.M.: Deep spatial-semantic attention for fine-grained sketch-based image retrieval. In: ICCV (2017)
54. Tian, Y., Wang, Y., Krishnan, D., Tenenbaum, J.B., Isola, P.: Rethinking few-shot image classification: a good embedding is all you need? In: Vedaldi, A., Bischof, H., Brox, T., Frahm, J.-M. (eds.) ECCV 2020. LNCS, vol. 12359, pp. 266–282. Springer, Cham (2020). https://doi.org/10.1007/978-3-030-58568-6_16

55. Wang, F., Kang, L., Li, Y.: Sketch-based 3d shape retrieval using convolutional neural networks. In: CVPR (2015)
56. Weinberger, K.Q., Saul, L.K.: Distance metric learning for large margin nearest neighbor classification. JMLR **10**, 207–244 (2009)
57. Yelamarthi, S.K., Reddy, S.K., Mishra, A., Mittal, A.: A zero-shot framework for sketch based image retrieval. In: Ferrari, V., Hebert, M., Sminchisescu, C., Weiss, Y. (eds.) ECCV 2018. LNCS, vol. 11208, pp. 316–333. Springer, Cham (2018). https://doi.org/10.1007/978-3-030-01225-0_19
58. Yu, Q., Liu, F., Song, Y.Z., Xiang, T., Hospedales, T.M., Loy, C.C.: Sketch me that shoe. In: CVPR (2016)
59. Yu, Q., Song, J., Song, Y.Z., Xiang, T., Hospedales, T.M.: Fine-grained instance-level sketch-based image retrieval. IJCV **129**, 484–500 (2021). https://doi.org/10.1007/s11263-020-01382-3
60. Yu, Q., Yang, Y., Liu, F., Song, Y.Z., Xiang, T., Hospedales, T.M.: Sketch-a-Net: a deep neural network that beats humans. IJCV **122**, 411–425 (2017). https://doi.org/10.1007/s11263-016-0932-3
61. Zhang, J., et al.: Generative domain-migration hashing for sketch-to-image retrieval. In: Ferrari, V., Hebert, M., Sminchisescu, C., Weiss, Y. (eds.) ECCV 2018. LNCS, vol. 11206, pp. 304–321. Springer, Cham (2018). https://doi.org/10.1007/978-3-030-01216-8_19

Quantized GAN for Complex Music Generation from Dance Videos

Ye Zhu[1]([✉])(iD), Kyle Olszewski[2], Yu Wu[3], Panos Achlioptas[2], Menglei Chai[2], Yan Yan[1], and Sergey Tulyakov[2]

[1] Illinois Institute of Technology, Chicago, USA
yzhu96@hawk.iit.edu
[2] Snap Inc., Santa Monica, USA
[3] Princeton University, Princeton, USA

Abstract. We present Dance2Music-GAN (D2M-GAN), a novel adversarial multi-modal framework that generates complex musical samples conditioned on dance videos. Our proposed framework takes dance video frames and human body motions as input, and learns to generate music samples that plausibly accompany the corresponding input. Unlike most existing conditional music generation works that generate specific types of mono-instrumental sounds using symbolic audio representations (*e.g.*, MIDI), and that usually rely on pre-defined musical synthesizers, in this work we generate dance music in complex styles (*e.g.*, pop, breaking, etc.) by employing a Vector Quantized (VQ) audio representation, and leverage both its generality and high abstraction capacity of its symbolic and continuous counterparts. By performing an extensive set of experiments on multiple datasets, and following a comprehensive evaluation protocol, we assess the generative qualities of our proposal against alternatives. The attained quantitative results, which measure the music consistency, beats correspondence, and music diversity, demonstrate the effectiveness of our proposed method. Last but not least, we curate a challenging dance-music dataset of in-the-wild TikTok videos, which we use to further demonstrate the efficacy of our approach in *real-world* applications – and which we hope to serve as a starting point for relevant future research. Dataset and code at https://github.com/L-YeZhu/D2M-GAN.

Keywords: Multimodal adversarial learning · Complex music generation · Vector quantized representation

---

Y. Zhu—This work was mainly done while the author was an intern at Snap Inc.

Supplementary Information The online version contains supplementary material available at https://doi.org/10.1007/978-3-031-19836-6_11.

1   Introduction

"When the music and dance create with accord, their magic captivates both the heart and the mind."[1] As a natural form of expressive art, dance and music have enriched our daily lives with a harmonious interplay of melodies, rhythms, and movements, across the millennia. The growing popularity of social media platforms for sharing dance videos such as TikTok has also demonstrated their significance as a source of entertainment in our modern society. At the same time, new research works are flourishing following the trend and exploring multi-modal generative tasks between dance motions and music [1, 37–39].

Although seemingly intuitive, music generation from dance videos has been a challenging task due to two main reasons. First, typical audio music signals are high-dimensional and require sophisticated temporal correlations for overall coherence [4, 28]. For example, CD-quality audio has a typical sampling rate of 44.1 kHz, resulting in over 2.5 million data points ("dimensions") for a one-minute musical piece [9]. In contrast, most dance generation works output the relatively low-dimensional motion data in the form of 2D or 3D skeleton keypoint (*e.g.*, displacement for dozens of joints) conditioned on the music [37,39,52,55], which are then rendered into dance sequences and videos. To tackle the challenge of the high dimensionality of audio data, the research studies on music generation from visual input [16,25,56] often rely on the low-dimensional intermediate symbolic audio representations (*e.g.*, 1D piano-roll or 2D MIDI). The symbolic representations benefit existing learning frameworks with a more explicit audio-visual correlation mapping and more stable training, as well as widely-established standard music synthesizers for decoding the intermediate representations. However, such symbolic-based works suffer from the limitations on the flexibility of the generated music, which brings us to the second challenge of dance video conditioned music generation. Specifically, a separately trained model is usually required for *each* instrument and the generated music is composed with acoustic sounds from a *single predefined* instrument [12,16,46] (*e.g.*, imagine a person dancing hip-hop with piano-based music). These facts make existing conditional music generation works difficult to generalize in complex musical styles and real-world scenarios.

To fill this gap, we propose a novel adversarial multi-modal framework that learns to generate complex musical samples from dance videos via the Vector Quantized audio representations. Inspired by the recent successes of VQ-VAE [9,45,51] and VQ-GAN [14], we adopt quantized vectors as our intermediate audio representation, and leverage both their increased abstraction ability compared to continuous raw audio signals, as well as their flexibility of better representing complex real-world music compared to classic symbolic representations. Specifically, our framework takes the visual frames and dance motions as input (Fig. 1), which are encoded and fused to generate the corresponding audio VQ representations. After a lookup process of the generated VQ representations in a learned codebook, the retrieved codebook entries are decoded back to the

---

[1] Jean-Georges Noverre.

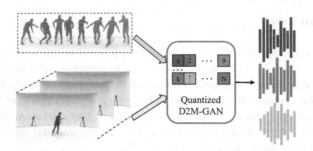

Fig. 1. Task illustration. We introduce a Vector-Quantized-based framework for music generation from dance videos, which takes human body motions and visual frames as input, and generates suitable music accordingly. Our proposed model is able to generate complex and rich dance music - in contrast to most existing conditional music generation works that typically output mono-instrumental sounds.

raw audio domains using a fine-tuned decoder from JukeBox [9]. Additionally, we deploy a convolution-based backbone and follow a hierarchical structure with two separate abstraction levels (*i.e.*, different hop-lengths) for the audio signals to test the scalability of our framework. The higher-level model has a larger hop-length and fewer parameters, resulting in faster inference. In contrast, the lower-level model has a lower abstraction level with smaller hop-length, which enables the generation of music with higher fidelity and better quality.

Last but not least, we also contribute a real-world paired dance-music dataset collected from TikTok video compilations. Our dataset contains in total 445 dance videos with 85 songs and an average per-video duration of approximately 12.5 s. Unlike existing datasets (e.g., AIST [39,59]), ours is more challenging and better reflects the conditions of real-world scenarios, setting thus a new point for relevant future research.

Tapping on such datasets, we conduct extensive experiments to demonstrate the effectiveness and robustness of the proposed framework. Specifically, we design and follow a rich evaluation protocol to consider its generative quality with respect to the correspondence of dance input in terms of beats, genres and coherence, the general quality of the generated music is also assessed. The attained results (both quantitative and qualitative) show that our model can generate plausible dance music in terms of various musical features, outperforming several competing conditioned music generation methods.

In summary, our main contributions are:

- We propose *D2M-GAN*, a novel adversarial multi-modal framework that generates complex and free-form music from dance videos via *Vector Quantized (VQ) representations.*
- Specifically, the proposed model, using a VQ generator and a multi-scale discriminator, is able to effectively capture the temporal correlations and rhythm for the musical sequence to generate complex music.

- To assess our model we introduce a comprehensive *evaluation protocol* for conditionally generated music and demonstrate how the proposed *D2M-GAN* is able to generate more complex and plausible accompanying music compared to existing approaches.
- Last but not least, we create a novel real-world dataset with dance videos captured *in the wild* – and use it to establish a new more challenging setup for conditioned music generation, which further demonstrates the superiority of our framework.

2   Related Work

Audio, Vision and Motion. Combining data from audio, vision, and motion has been a popular research topic in recent years within the field of multi-modal learning [15,52,62,67,68]. Research focusing on general audio visual learning typically assumes that the two modalities are intrinsically correlated based on the synchronization nature of the audio and visual signals [2,3,34,47,48,68]. Such jointly learned audio-visual representations thus can be applied in multiple downstream tasks like sound source separation [17–20,66], audio-visual captioning [50,61], audio-visual action recognition [21,31], and audio-visual event localization and parsing [58,63,64,68].

On the other hand, another branch of studies related to our work has been investigating the correlations between motions and sounds [16,37–39,70]. A large portion of the research works here, aim to generate human motions based on the audio signals, either in the form of 2D pose skeletons [37,52,55] or direct 3D motions [29,39,57]. For the inverse direction that seeks to generate audio from motions, Zhao *et al.* [66] introduces an end-to-end model to generate sounds from motion trajectories. Gan *et al.* [16] propose a graph-based transformer framework to generate music from performance videos using raw movements as input. Di *et al.* [10] propose to generate video background music conditioned on the motion and special timing/rhythmic features of the input videos. In contrast to these previous works, our work combines three modalities, which takes the vision and motion data as input and generates music accordingly.

Music Generation. Raw music generation is a challenging task due to the high dimensionality of the audio data and sophisticated temporal correlations. Therefore, the existing music generation approaches usually adopt an intermediate audio representation for learning the generative models to reduce the computational demand and simplify the learning task [9,12,25,35,44,69]. Classic audio representations mainly include the symbolic and continuous categories. Musegan [12] introduces a multi-track GAN-based model for instrumental music generation via the 1D piano-roll symbolic representations. Music Transformer [25] aims to improve the long-term coherence of generated musical pieces using the 2D event-based MIDI-like audio representations [46]. Melgan [35] is a generative model for music in form of the audio mel-spectrogram features. Recently, JukeBox [9] introduces a generic music generation model based on the novel Vector Quantized (VQ) representations. Our proposed framework adopts the VQ representations for music generation.

Vector Quantized Generative Models. VQ-VAEs [45,51] are firstly proposed as a variant of the Variational Auto-Encoder (VAE) [32] with discrete codes and learned priors. Following works have demonstrated the potential of VQ-based framework in multiple generative tasks such as image and audio synthesis [9,14,26]. Specifically, the VQ-VAE [45] is initially tested for generating images, videos, and speech. An improved version of VQ-VAE [51] is proposed with a multi-scale hierarchical organization. Esser *et al.* [14] apply the VQ representations in the GAN-based framework for generating high-resolution images. Dhariwal *et al.* [9] introduce the JukeBox as a large-scale generative model for music synthesis based on VQ-VAE. Compared to the symbolic and continuous representations, VQ representations leverage the benefits of flexibility (*i.e.*, the ability to represent complex music genres with a unified codebook in contrast to symbolic representations) and high compression levels (*i.e.*, the learned codebooks largely reduce the data dimensionality compared to raw waveform or spectrogram). Our proposed framework combines both the GAN [23] and VAE [32], which uses the GAN-based learning to generate VQ representations from the dance videos, and adopts the VAE-based decoder for synthesizing music.

3   Method

An overview of the architecture of the proposed D2M-GAN is shown in Fig. 2. Our approach entails a hierarchical structure with two levels of models that are independently trained with a similar pipeline for flexible scalability. For each level, the model consists of four modules: the motion module, the visual module, the VQ module consisting of a VQ generator and the multi-scale discriminators, and the music synthesizer. Our hierarchical structure amplifies the flexibility to choose between the trade-off of the music quality and computational costs according to practical application scenarios. A detailed description of these modules is given below while further architectural details and model-selection-tuning are included in the supplementary.

3.1   Data Representations

During the inference, the input to our proposed *D2M-GAN* come from two major modalities: the visual frames of the dance videos and human body motions of dance performers. The ground-truth music audio is also used as the supervision for the discriminators during the training stage. For the human body motions, several different forms of data representations such as 3D Skinned Multi-Person Linear model (SMPL) [41] or 2D body keypoints [5,6] can be utilized by our framework. We use SMPL and 2D body keypoints for different datasets in our experiments. To encode the visual frames, we extract I3D features [7] using a model pre-trained on Kinectics [30]. For the musical data, we adopt the VQ as the intermediate audio representation. To leverage the strong representation ability of codebooks trained on the large-scale musical dataset, we use the pre-learned codebooks from JukeBox [9], which are trained on a dataset of 1.2 million songs.

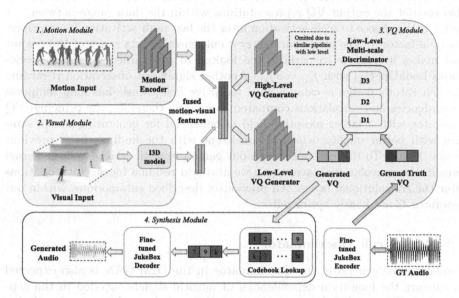

Fig. 2. Overview of the proposed architecture of the _D2M-GAN_. Our model takes the motion and visual data from the dance videos as input and process them with the motion and visual modules, respectively. It then forwards the concatenated representation containing information from both modalities to ground the generation of audio VQ-based representations with the VQ module. The resulting features are calibrated by a multi-scale GAN-based discriminator and are used to perform a _lookup_ in the pre-learned codebook. Last, the retrieved codebook entries are decoded to raw musical samples via by a pre-trained and fine-tuned decoder, responsible for synthesizing music.

3.2 Generator

The generator $G = \{G_m, G_v, G_{vq}\}$ includes the motion module G_m, the visual module G_v, and the principal VQ generator G_{vq} in the VQ module, which takes the fused motion-visual data as input and outputs the desired VQ audio representations.

$$f_{vq} = G_{vq}(G_m(x_m), G_v(x_v)) = G(x_m, x_v), \qquad (1)$$

where x_m and x_v represent the motion and visual input data, respectively. f_{vq} is the output VQ representations. All these modules are implemented as convolution-based feed-forward networks. For the principal VQ generator, we use leaky rectified activation functions [65] for its hidden layers and a tanh activation for its last layer before output to promote the stability of GAN training [49].

It is also worth noting that we find that using batch normalization and the aforementioned activation function designs [42,49,54] is crucial for a stable GAN training in our framework. However, the application of the tanh activation will also restrict the output VQ representations within the data range between -1 and $+1$. We choose to scale activation after the last tanh activation by multiplying by a factor σ. The hyper-parameter σ enlarges the data range of VQ output and makes it possible to perform the lookup of pre-learned large-scale codebooks $\mathrm{LookUp}(f'_{\mathrm{vq}})$ with $f'_{\mathrm{vq}} = \sigma f_{\mathrm{vq}}$. Another significant observation regarding the generator's design is using a wide receptive field. Music has long temporal dependencies and correlations compared to images, therefore, the principal VQ generator with a larger receptive field is beneficial for generating music samples with better quality, which is consistent with the findings from previous works [11,35]. To this end, we design our generator with relatively large kernel sizes in the convolutional layers, and we also add residual blocks with dilations after the convolutional layers. All previously described sub-modules within our generator G are jointly optimized.

3.3   Multi-scale Discriminator

Similar to the generator, the discriminator in the D2M-GAN is also expected to capture the long-term dependencies of musical signals encoded in the generated sequence of VQ features. However, different from the generator design that focuses on increasing the receptive fields of the neural networks, we address this problem in the discriminator design by using a multi-scale architecture.

The multi-scale discriminator design has been studied in previous works within the field of audio synthesis and generation [33,35,60]. The discriminator $D = \{D_1, D_2, D_3\}$ in the VQ module of our D2M-GAN is composed of 3 discriminators that operate on the sequence of generated VQ representations and its downsampled features by a factor of 2 and 4, respectively. Specifically, different from the multi-scale discriminators proposed in previous works that directly take the raw audio as input, we reshape the VQ representations f'_{vq} along the temporal dimension before feeding them into the discriminators, which is also important for D2M-GAN to reach a stable adversarial training since music is a temporal audio sequence. Finally, we use the window-based objectives [35] (Markovian window-based discriminator analog to image patches in [27]). Instead of learning to distinguish the distributions between two

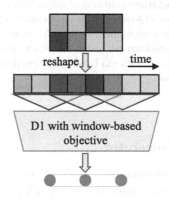

Fig. 3. Illustration of the reshape operation and the window-based discriminator for our *D2M-GAN*.

entire sequences, window-based objective learns to classify between distributions of small chunks of VQ sequences to further enhance the overall coherence as illustrated in Fig. 3.

3.4   Lookup and Synthesis

After generating the VQ representations, we perform a codebook lookup operation similar to other VQ-based generative models [9,14,45,51] to retrieve the corresponding entries with closest distance. Finally, we fine-tune the decoder from the JukeBox [9] without modifying the codebook entries as the music synthesizer for our learned VQ representations. Specifically, we also adopt the GAN-based technique for fine-tuning the music synthesizer, where the generator is replaced by the decoder of JukeBox and the discriminator follows the similar architecture as described in the previous subsection.

3.5   Training Objectives

GAN Loss. We use the hinge loss version of GAN objective [40,43] adopted for our music generation task to train the proposed *D2M-GAN*.

$$L_{adv.}(D;G) = \sum_k L_{adv.}(D_k;G)$$

$$= \sum_k (\mathbb{E}_{\phi(x_a)}[min(0, 1 - D_k(\phi(x_a)))] \tag{2}$$

$$+ \mathbb{E}_{(x_m,x_v)}[min(0, 1 + D_k(G(x_m,x_v)))]),$$

$$L_{adv.}(G;D) = \mathbb{E}_{x_m,x_v}[\sum_k -D_k(G(x_m,x_v))], \tag{3}$$

where x_a is the original music in a waveform, ϕ represents the fine-tuned encoder from JukeBox [9]. k indicates the number of multi-scale discriminators, which is empirically chosen to be 3 in our case.

Feature Matching Loss. To encourage the construction of subtle details in audio signals, we also include a feature matching loss [36] in the overall training objective. Similar to the audio generation works [33,35], the feature matching loss is defined as the L_1 distance between the discriminator feature maps of the real and generated VQ features.

$$L_{FM}(G;D) = \mathbb{E}_{(x_m,x_v)}[\sum_{i=1}^{T} \frac{1}{N_i} \left\| D^i(\phi(x_a)) - D^i(G(x_m,x_v)) \right\|_1]. \tag{4}$$

Codebook Commitment Loss. The codebook commitment loss [45,51] is defined as the L_1 distance between the generated VQ features and the corresponding codebook entries of the ground truth VQ features after the codebook lookup process.

$$L_{code}(G) = \mathbb{E}_{(x_m,x_v)}[\| LookUp(\phi(x_a) - G(x_m,x_v) \|_1]. \tag{5}$$

Audio Perceptual Losses. To further improve the perceptual auditory quality, we consider the perception losses of the raw audio signals from both time and frequency domains. Specifically, the perceptual losses are calculated as the L_1 distance between the original audio and the generated audio samples:

$$L_{wav}(G) = \mathbb{E}_{(x_m, x_v)}[\|x_a - G(x_m, x_v)\|_1]. \tag{6}$$

$$L_{Mel}(G) = \mathbb{E}_{(x_m, x_v)}[\|\theta(x_a) - \theta(G(x_m, x_v))\|_1]. \tag{7}$$

where θ is the function to compute the mel-spectrogram features for the audio signals in waveform.

Final Loss. The final training objective for the entire generator module is defined as follows:

$$L_G = L_{adv.}(G; D) + \lambda_{fm}L_{FM}(G; D) + \lambda_c L_{code} + \lambda_w L_{wav} + \lambda_m L_{mel}, \tag{8}$$

where the λ_{fm}, λ_c, λ_a, and λ_{mel} are set to be 3, 15, 40 and 15, respectively during our experiments for both levels.

Fig. 4. **Examples of dance videos from our TikTok dance-music dataset.** Different from the AIST dataset [59] where dancing is performed by professional dancers in a studio environment, our dataset consists of real-world videos collected "in the wild".

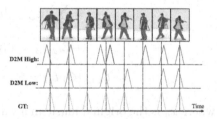

Fig. 5. **Qualitative example of rhythm evaluations and beat correspondence.** The lower-abstraction level model (D2M-Low) appears to align better than its high-counterpart (D2M-High) with the ground-truth (GT), which is consistent with the quantitative scores from the Table 1.

4   Experiments

4.1   Experimental Setup

Datasets. We validate the effectiveness of our method by conducting experiments on two datasets with paired dance video and music: the AIST++ [39] and our proposed TikTok dance-music dataset. The AIST++ dataset [39] is a subset of AIST dataset [59] with 3D motion annotations. We adopt the official cross-modality data splits for training, validation, and testing, where the videos are divided without overlapping musical pieces between the training and the validation/testing sets. The number of videos in each split is 980, 20, and 20, respectively. The videos from this dataset are filmed in professional studios with clean backgrounds. There are in total 10 different dance genres and corresponding music styles, which include breaking, pop, lock and etc. The number of total songs is 60, with 6 songs for each type of music. We use this dataset for the main experiments and evaluations. We also collect and annotate a **Tik-Tok dance-music dataset** which contains 445 dance videos, with an average length of 12.5 s. This dataset utilizes 85 different songs, with the majority of videos having a single dance performer, and a maximum of five performers. The training-testing splits contain 392 and 53 videos, respectively, without overlapping songs. Figure 4 shows example frames of the dance videos and makes apparent the key differences compared to the professional studio filmed dance video from AIST [59]. Our videos have wildly different backgrounds, and oftentimes contain incomplete human body skeleton data, which increases significantly the difficulty of the learning problem. For the TikTok music dataset, we use 2D human skeleton data as the underlying motion representation.

Implementation Details. For the presented experiments, we adopt a sampling rate of 22.5 kHz for all audio signals. We use the video and audio segments in the length of 2 s for training and standard testing in the main experiments. The generation of longer sequences is also investigated in Sect. 4.3. The hop lengths for the high and low level are 128 and 32, respectively. During the GAN training, we adopt the Adam optimizer with a learning rate of 1e-4 with $\beta_1 = 0.5$ and $\beta_2 = 0.9$ for the generators and discriminators. We define the scaling factor $\sigma = 100$ for the VQ generators. The number of discriminators k is 3 for the multi-scale structure. The batch size is set to be 16 for all experiments. During the fine-tuning of the JukeBox synthesizer, we use the Adam optimizer with a learning rate of 1e-5 with $\beta_1 = 0.5$ and $\beta_2 = 0.9$ for the synthesizer and multi-scale discriminators. We perform a denoising process [53] on the generated raw music data for better audio quality.

Comparisons. We compare our proposed method with several baselines. *Foley Music* [16]: Foley Music model generates MIDI musical representations based on keypoints motion data and then converts the MIDI back to raw waveform using a pre-defined MIDI synthesizer. Specifically, the MIDI audio representation is unique for each musical instrument, and therefore the Foley music model can only generate musical samples with mono-instrumental sound. *Dance2Music* [1]: Similar to [16], the generated music with this method is also monotonic in terms of the musical instrument. *Controllable Music Transformer (CMT)* [10]: CMT is a Transformer-based model proposed for video background music generation using MIDI representation. In addition to the above cross-modality models that are closely related to our work, we also consider *Ground Truth:* GT samples are the original music from dance videos. *JukeBox* [9]: music samples generated or reconstructed via the JukeBox model.

4.2 Music Evaluations

We design a comprehensive evaluation protocol that incorporates objective (*i.e.*, metrics that can be automatically calculated) and subjective (*i.e.*, scores given by human testers) metrics to evaluate the generated music from various perspectives. Specifically, the evaluations are divided into two categories: the first category, which is also the focus of our work, measures correlations between the generated music and the input dance videos, for which we compare our proposed model with other cross-modality music generation works [1,10,16] and a random baseline from JukeBox [9]. The second category focuses on the quality of the music in general, for which we use the reconstructed samples using JukeBox [9] given the original audio as input and GT samples for comparisons.

Rhythm. Musical rhythm accounts for an important characteristic of the generated music samples, especially given the dance video as input. To evaluate the correspondence between the dance beats and generated musical rhythm, we adopt two objective scores as evaluation metrics, which are the Beats Coverage Scores and the Beats Hit Scores similar to [8,37]. Previous works [8,37] have demonstrated the kinematic dance and musical beats (*i.e.*, rhythm) are generally aligned, we can therefore reasonably evaluate the musical rhythm by comparing the beats from the generated music and those from the GT music

Table 1. Evaluation protocol and the corresponding results for the experiments on the AIST++ dataset [39]. *Obj.* stands for *Objective*, which means the scores are automatically calculated. *Subj.* stands for *Subjective*, which means the scores are given by human evaluators

Category	Features	Type	Metric	Methods	Scores
Dance-Music	Rhythm	Obj.	Beats Coverage & Beats Hit	Dance2Music [1]	83.5 & 82.4
				Foley Music [16]	74.1 & 69.4
				CMT [10]	85.5 & 83.5
				Ours High-level	88.2 & 84.7
				Ours Low-level	**92.3 & 91.7**
Dance-Music	Genre & Diversity	Obj.	Genre Accuracy (Retrieval-based)	Dance2Music [1]	7.0
				Foley Music [16]	8.1
				CMT [10]	11.6
				Ours High-level	24.4
				Ours Low-level	**26.7**
Dance-Music	Coherence	Subj.	Mean Opinion Scores	Random JukeBox [9]	2.0
				Dance2Music [1]	2.8
				Foley Music [16]	2.8
				CMT [10]	3.0
				Ours High-level	3.5
				Ours Low-level	3.3
				GT	**4.6**
Music	Overall quality	Subj.	Mean Opinion Scores	JukeBox [9]	3.5
				Ours High-level	3.5
				Ours Low-level	3.7
				GT	**4.8**

samples as shown in Fig. 5. We detect the musical beats by the second-level onset strength [13], which can be considered as the start of an acoustic event. We define the number of detected beats from the generated music samples as B_g, the total beats from the original music as B_t, and the number of aligned beats from the generative samples as B_a. The Beats Coverage Scores B_g/B_t measure the ratio of overall generated beats to the total musical beats. The Beats Hit Scores B_a/B_t measure the ratio of aligned beats to the total musical beats. The quantitative results are presented in Table 1. We observe that both levels of our proposed *D2M-GAN* achieve better scores compared to competing methods.

Genre and Diversity. Dance and music are both diverse in terms of genres. The generated music samples are expected to be diverse and harmonious with the given dance style (*e.g.*, breaking dance with strong beats to pair with music in fast rhythm). Therefore, we calculate the genre accuracy for evaluating whether the generated music samples have a consistent genre with the dance style. The calculation of this objective metric requires the annotations of dance and music genres, we thus use the retrieved musical samples from the AIST++ [39] for this evaluation setting. Specifically, we retrieve the musical samples with the highest similarity scores from the segment-level database formed by original audio samples with the same sequence length. The similarities scores are defined as the euclidean distance between the audio features extracted via a VGG-like network [24] pre-trained on AudioSet [22]. In case that the retrieved musical sample has the same genre as the given dance style, we consider the segment to be genre accurate. The genre accuracy is then calculated by S_c/S_t, where S_c counts the number of genre accurate segments and S_t is the total number of segments from the testing split.

We observe in Table 1 that the genre accuracy scores of our *D2M-GAN* are considerably higher compared to the competing methods. This is due to the reason that the competing methods rely on MIDI events as audio representations, which require a specific synthesizer for each instrument, and thus can only generate music samples with mono-instrumental sound. In contrast, our generated VQ audio representations can represent complex dance music similar to the input music types, which helps to increase the diversity of the generated music samples. It also makes the generated samples to be more harmonious with the

Table 2. Evaluations for the experiments on the TikTok dataset

Models	Beats Coverage	Beats Hit
High w/o M	85.5	72.4
High w/o V	86.3	81.7
High (full)	**88.4**	**82.3**
Low w/o M	83.8	74.6
Low w/o V	85.2	81.7
Low (full)	**87.1**	**83.9**

Table 3. Results for ablation studies in terms of sequence length

Length	Beats Coverage	Beats Hit	Genre Acc.
High - 2s	**88.2**	84.7	24.4
High - 3s	**88.2**	**85.3**	**25.6**
High - 4s	87.1	83.0	23.3
Low - 2s	**92.3**	**91.7**	**26.7**
Low - 3s	90.1	88.2	25.6
Low - 4s	88.2	84.7	23.3

dance videos compared to acoustic instrumental sounds from [1, 16], as shown in the next evaluation protocol for the coherence test.

Coherence. Since we generate music samples conditioned on the dance videos, the dance video input and the output are expected to be harmonious and coherent when combined together. Specifically, a given dance sequence could be accompanied by multiple appropriate songs. However, the evaluation of the dance-music coherence is very subjective, therefore we conduct the Mean Opinion Scores (MOS) human test for assessing the coherence feature. During the evaluation process, the human testers are asked to give a score between 1 and 5 to evaluate the coherence between the dance moves and the music given a video with audio sounds. The higher scores indicate the fact the tester feels the given dance and music are more coherent. We prepare the videos with original visual frames and fused generated music samples for testing. In addition to the previously cross-modality generation methods [1,10,16], we also include the GT samples and the randomly generated music from JukeBox [9] for comparison. Our *D2M-GAN* achieves better scores compared to other baselines, which validates the fact that our proposed framework is able to catch the correlations with the given dance video and generates rather complex music that well matches the input. Details about the human evaluations are included in the supplementary.

Overall Quality. Although our main research focus is to learn the dance-music correlations in this work, we also look at the general sound quality of the generated samples. We conduct the subjective MOS tests similar to the coherence evaluation, where the human testers are asked to give a score between 1 to 5 for the general quality of the music samples. During this test, only audio signals are played to the testers. The JukeBox samples are obtained by directly feeding the GT samples as input. The MOS tests show that our *D2M-GAN* is able to generate music sample with plausible sound quality comparable to the JukeBox. JukeBox has multiple variants with different hop lengths, we compare with samples obtained from the model with same audio hop length for fairness (*i.e.*, the hop lengths for our high and low levels are 128 and 32, respectively). It is worth noting that synthesizing high quality audio itself is a vary challenging and computational demanding research topic, for example, it takes *3 hrs* to sample a 20s high-quality music sample with a hop length of 8 [9].

Results on the TikTok Dataset. Compared to the AIST++ [39], our Tik-Tok dance-music dataset is a more challenging dataset with "in the wild" video settings that contains various occlusions and noisy backgrounds. Table 2 shows the quantitative evaluation results for the experiments on the TikTok dataset, which demonstrates the overall robustness of the proposed *D2M-GAN*.

Table 4. Results for ablation studies in terms of input modalities on the AIST++ dataset. M means the motion data, and V means the visual data

Models	Beats Coverage	Beats Hit	Genre Acc.
High w/o M	83.5	82.9	15.1
High w/o V	87.1	88.2	16.3
High (full)	**88.2**	**84.7**	**24.4**
Low w/o M	89.4	87.6	15.1
Low w/o V	90.6	90.0	17.4
Low (full)	**92.3**	**91.7**	**26.7**

Table 5. Results for ablation studies in terms of losses on the AIST++ dataset. The *mel* loss is especially helpful for beats scores since the beats are characteristic by high frequencies

Losses	Beats Coverage	Beats Hit	Genre Acc.
High w/o L_{FM}	85.3	**84.7**	23.3
High w/o L_{wav}	85.9	**84.7**	23.3
High w/o L_{mel}	77.6	76.5	18.6
High (full)	**88.2**	**84.7**	**24.4**
Low w/o L_{FM}	91.7	90.1	24.4
Low w/o L_{wav}	89.4	88.8	23.3
Low w/o L_{mel}	78.8	77.1	17.4
Low (full)	**92.3**	**91.7**	**26.7**

4.3 Ablation Studies

Sequence Length. In the main experiments, we use the 2-second samples for experiments with reference to other similar cross-modality generation tasks [39]. However, our model can also be effectively trained and tested with a longer sequence length as shown in Table 3 via a larger network with more parameters.

Data Modality. We perform ablation studies in terms of the input data modalities, by removing either the dance motion or the visual frame from the input data. Table 4 lists the corresponding experimental results. We observe that both motion and visual data contribute to our conditioned music generation task. Specifically, the motion data impose a larger impact on the musical rhythm, which is consistent with our expectations since the musical rhythm is closely correlated with the dance motions.

Loss Function. We analyze the impact of different losses included in the overall training objective. The results from Table 5 show the contributions of each loss term. Specifically, we observe the audio perceptual loss from the frequency domain L_{mel} helps with the generation of musical rhythm, it is reasonable due to the fact that mel-spectrogram features help to capture the high frequencies from the audio signals, which is closely related to the dance beats.

Model Architecture. We also test various variants of our *D2M-GAN* in terms of the model architecture and proposed model design techniques as in Table 6. The experimental results show that the multi-scale layer for the discriminators, the scaling operation in the generator, as well as the reshape techniques for discriminators are crucial.

Table 6. Results for ablation studies in terms of model architectures on the AIST++ dataset. *D.* means discriminators

Models	Beats Coverage	Beats Hit	Genre Acc.
High 1-layer D.	75.3	72.9	9.3
High 2-layer D.	85.3	82.9	21.0
High w/o scaling	72.9	71.8	14.0
High w/o reshape	73.5	70.1	11.6
High w/o fine-tune	87.0	**84.7**	**24.4**
High (full)	**88.2**	**84.7**	**24.4**
Low 1-layer D.	73.5	71.8	8.1
Low 2-layer D.	87.0	85.9	22.1
Low w/o scaling	72.4	70.1	12.8
Low w/o reshape	73.5	71.8	12.8
Low w/o fine-tune	**92.3**	91.2	**26.7**
Low (full)	**92.3**	**91.7**	**26.7**

5   Conclusion and Limitations

To conclude, we propose the *D2M-GAN* framework for complex music generation from dance videos via the VQ audio representations. As an early work in the exploitation of VQ based music generation, there are still limitations in the current work from two major aspects: the audio quality and inference speed. As we employ a learning-based encoder-decoder model for raw music (JukeBox [9]), its performance is the major bottleneck for the quality of our generated music. Though JukeBox can synthesize relatively high-quality audio signals, there is a tradeoff between computational cost and quality. Achieving fast inference requires increasing the hop length for the generated waveform, which limits the audio quality and introduces noise. On the other hand, another direction to balance the above two goals would be investigating a proper approach to automatically compose multiple instruments into a single performance based on video input via MIDI musical representations.

Acknowledgements. This work is partially supported by NSF ECCS-2123521 research grant and Snap unrestricted gift research grant. This article solely reflects the opinions and conclusions of its authors and not the funding agents.

References

1. Aggarwal, G., Parikh, D.: Dance2Music: automatic dance-driven music generation. arXiv preprint arXiv:2107.06252 (2021)
2. Arandjelovic, R., Zisserman, A.: Look, listen and learn. In: ICCV (2017)
3. Aytar, Y., Vondrick, C., Torralba, A.: Soundnet: learning sound representations from unlabeled video. In: NeurIPS (2016)

4. Briot, J.P., Hadjeres, G., Pachet, F.D.: Deep Learning Techniques for Music Generation, vol. 1. Springer, Cham (2020). https://doi.org/10.1007/978-3-319-70163-9

5. Cao, Z., Hidalgo Martinez, G., Simon, T., Wei, S., Sheikh, Y.A.: OpenPose: real-time multi-person 2D pose estimation using part affinity fields. IEEE TPAMI (2019)

6. Cao, Z., Simon, T., Wei, S.E., Sheikh, Y.: Realtime multi-person 2D pose estimation using part affinity fields. In: CVPR (2017)

7. Carreira, J., Zisserman, A.: Quo vadis, action recognition? A new model and the kinetics dataset. In: CVPR (2017)

8. Davis, A., Agrawala, M.: Visual rhythm and beat. ACM Trans. Graph. (TOG) (2018)

9. Dhariwal, P., Jun, H., Payne, C., Kim, J.W., Radford, A., Sutskever, I.: Jukebox: a generative model for music. arXiv preprint arXiv:2005.00341 (2020)

10. Di, S., et al.: Video background music generation with controllable music transformer. In: ACMMM (2021)

11. Donahue, C., McAuley, J., Puckette, M.: Adversarial audio synthesis. In: ICLR (2019)

12. Dong, H.W., Hsiao, W.Y., Yang, L.C., Yang, Y.H.: Musegan: Multi-track sequential generative adversarial networks for symbolic music generation and accompaniment. In: AAAI (2018)

13. Ellis, D.P.: Beat tracking by dynamic programming. J. New Music Res. 36(1), 51–60 (2007)

14. Esser, P., Rombach, R., Ommer, B.: Taming transformers for high-resolution image synthesis. In: CVPR (2021)

15. Ferreira, J.P., et al.: Learning to dance: a graph convolutional adversarial network to generate realistic dance motions from audio. Comput. Graph. 94, 11–21 (2021)

16. Gan, C., Huang, D., Chen, P., Tenenbaum, J.B., Torralba, A.: Foley music: learning to generate music from videos. In: Vedaldi, A., Bischof, H., Brox, T., Frahm, J.-M. (eds.) ECCV 2020. LNCS, vol. 12356, pp. 758–775. Springer, Cham (2020). https://doi.org/10.1007/978-3-030-58621-8_44

17. Gan, C., Huang, D., Zhao, H., Tenenbaum, J.B., Torralba, A.: Music gesture for visual sound separation. In: CVPR (2020)

18. Gao, R., Feris, R., Grauman, K.: Learning to separate object sounds by watching unlabeled video. In: ECCV (2018)

19. Gao, R., Grauman, K.: 2.5 D visual sound. In: CVPR (2019)

20. Gao, R., Grauman, K.: Co-separating sounds of visual objects. In: ICCV (2019)

21. Gao, R., Oh, T.H., Grauman, K., Torresani, L.: Listen to look: action recognition by previewing audio. In: CVPR (2020)

22. Gemmeke, J.F., et al.: Audio set: an ontology and human-labeled dataset for audio events. In: ICASSP. IEEE (2017)

23. Goodfellow, I., et al.: Generative adversarial nets. In: NeurIPS (2014)

24. Hershey, S., et al.: CNN architectures for large-scale audio classification. In: ICASSP. IEEE (2017)

25. Huang, C.Z.A., et al.: Music transformer: generating music with long-term structure. In: ICLR (2019)

26. Iashin, V., Rahtu, E.: Taming visually guided sound generation. In: British Machine Vision Conference (BMVC) (2021)

27. Isola, P., Zhu, J.Y., Zhou, T., Efros, A.A.: Image-to-image translation with conditional adversarial networks. In: CVPR (2017)

28. Ji, S., Luo, J., Yang, X.: A comprehensive survey on deep music generation: multi-level representations, algorithms, evaluations, and future directions. arXiv preprint arXiv:2011.06801 (2020)
29. Kao, H.K., Su, L.: Temporally guided music-to-body-movement generation. In: ACMMM (2020)
30. Kay, W., et al.: The kinetics human action video dataset. arXiv preprint arXiv:1705.06950 (2017)
31. Kazakos, E., Nagrani, A., Zisserman, A., Damen, D.: Epic-fusion: audio-visual temporal binding for egocentric action recognition. In: ICCV (2019)
32. Kingma, D.P., Welling, M.: Auto-encoding variational bayes. In: ICLR (2014)
33. Kong, J., Kim, J., Bae, J.: HiFi-GAN: generative adversarial networks for efficient and high fidelity speech synthesis. In: NeurIPS (2020)
34. Korbar, B., Tran, D., Torresani, L.: Cooperative learning of audio and video models from self-supervised synchronization. In: NeurIPS (2018)
35. Kumar, K., et al.: MelGAN: generative adversarial networks for conditional waveform synthesis. In: NeurIPS (2019)
36. Larsen, A.B.L., Sønderby, S.K., Larochelle, H., Winther, O.: Autoencoding beyond pixels using a learned similarity metric. In: International conference on machine learning. PMLR (2016)
37. Lee, H.Y., et al.: Dancing to music. In: NeurIPS (2019)
38. Li, B., Zhao, Y., Sheng, L.: DanceNet3D: music based dance generation with parametric motion transformer. arXiv preprint arXiv:2103.10206 (2021)
39. Li, R., Yang, S., Ross, D.A., Kanazawa, A.: AI choreographer: music conditioned 3D dance generation with AIST++. In: ICCV (2021)
40. Lim, J.H., Ye, J.C.: Geometric GAN. arXiv preprint arXiv:1705.02894 (2017)
41. Loper, M., Mahmood, N., Romero, J., Pons-Moll, G., Black, M.J.: SMPL: a skinned multi-person linear model. ACM Trans. Graph. (Proc. SIGGRAPH Asia) **34** (2015)
42. Lucic, M., Kurach, K., Michalski, M., Gelly, S., Bousquet, O.: Are GANs created equal? A large-scale study. In: NeurIPS (2018)
43. Miyato, T., Kataoka, T., Koyama, M., Yoshida, Y.: Spectral normalization for generative adversarial networks. arXiv preprint arXiv:1802.05957 (2018)
44. Oord, A.V.D., et al.: Wavenet: a generative model for raw audio. In: ICLR (2016)
45. Oord, A.v.d., Vinyals, O., Kavukcuoglu, K.: Neural discrete representation learning. In: NeurIPS (2017)
46. Oore, S., Simon, I., Dieleman, S., Eck, D., Simonyan, K.: This time with feeling: learning expressive musical performance. In: Neural Computing and Applications, pp. 955–967 (2020)
47. Owens, A., Efros, A.A.: Audio-visual scene analysis with self-supervised multisensory features. In: ECCV (2018)
48. Owens, A., Wu, J., McDermott, J.H., Freeman, W.T., Torralba, A.: Ambient sound provides supervision for visual learning. In: Leibe, B., Matas, J., Sebe, N., Welling, M. (eds.) ECCV 2016. LNCS, vol. 9905, pp. 801–816. Springer, Cham (2016). https://doi.org/10.1007/978-3-319-46448-0_48
49. Radford, A., Metz, L., Chintala, S.: Unsupervised representation learning with deep convolutional generative adversarial networks. arXiv preprint arXiv:1511.06434 (2015)
50. Rahman, T., Xu, B., Sigal, L.: Watch, listen and tell: multi-modal weakly supervised dense event captioning. In: ICCV (2019)
51. Razavi, A., van den Oord, A., Vinyals, O.: Generating diverse high-fidelity images with VQ-VAE-2. In: NeurIPS (2019)

52. Ren, X., Li, H., Huang, Z., Chen, Q.: Self-supervised dance video synthesis conditioned on music. In: ACM MM (2020)
53. Sainburg, T., Thielk, M., Gentner, T.Q.: Finding, visualizing, and quantifying latent structure across diverse animal vocal repertoires. PLoS Comput. Biol. **16**(10), e1008228 (2020)
54. Salimans, T., Kingma, D.P.: Weight normalization: a simple reparameterization to accelerate training of deep neural networks. In: NeurIPS (2016)
55. Shlizerman, E., Dery, L., Schoen, H., Kemelmacher-Shlizerman, I.: Audio to body dynamics. In: CVPR (2018)
56. Su, K., Liu, X., Shlizerman, E.: Audeo: audio generation for a silent performance video. In: NeurIPS (2020)
57. Tang, T., Jia, J., Mao, H.: Dance with melody: an LSTM-autoencoder approach to music-oriented dance synthesis. In: ACMMM (2018)
58. Tian, Y., Shi, J., Li, B., Duan, Z., Xu, C.: Audio-visual event localization in unconstrained videos. In: ECCV (2018)
59. Tsuchida, S., Fukayama, S., Hamasaki, M., Goto, M.: AIST dance video database: Multi-genre, multi-dancer, and multi-camera database for dance information processing. In: Proceedings of the 20th International Society for Music Information Retrieval Conference, (ISMIR) (2019)
60. Wang, T.C., Liu, M.Y., Zhu, J.Y., Tao, A., Kautz, J., Catanzaro, B.: High-resolution image synthesis and semantic manipulation with conditional GANs. In: CVPR (2018)
61. Wang, X., Wang, Y.F., Wang, W.Y.: Watch, listen, and describe: globally and locally aligned cross-modal attentions for video captioning. In: NAACL (2018)
62. Wu, Y., Jiang, L., Yang, Y.: Switchable novel object captioner. IEEE Trans. Pattern Anal. Mach. Intell. (2022). https://doi.org/10.1109/TPAMI.2022.3144984
63. Wu, Y., Yang, Y.: Exploring heterogeneous clues for weakly-supervised audio-visual video parsing. In: CVPR (2021)
64. Wu, Y., Zhu, L., Yan, Y., Yang, Y.: Dual attention matching for audio-visual event localization. In: ICCV (2019)
65. Xu, B., Wang, N., Chen, T., Li, M.: Empirical evaluation of rectified activations in convolutional network. arXiv preprint arXiv:1505.00853 (2015)
66. Zhao, H., Gan, C., Ma, W.C., Torralba, A.: The sound of motions. In: ICCV (2019)
67. Zhu, X., Zhu, Y., Wang, H., Wen, H., Yan, Y., Liu, P.: Skeleton sequence and RGB frame based multi-modality feature fusion network for action recognition. ACM Trans. Multimedia Comput. Commun. Appl. (TOMM) **18**(3), 1–24 (2022)
68. Zhu, Y., Wu, Y., Latapie, H., Yang, Y., Yan, Y.: Learning audio-visual correlations from variational cross-modal generation. In: ICCASP (2021)
69. Zhu, Y., Wu, Y., Olszewski, K., Ren, J., Tulyakov, S., Yan, Y.: Discrete contrastive diffusion for cross-modal and conditional generation. arXiv preprint arXiv:2206.07771 (2022)
70. Zhuang, W., Wang, C., Xia, S., Chai, J., Wang, Y.: Music2Dance: DanceNet for music-driven dance generation. arXiv preprint arXiv:2002.03761 (2020)

Uncertainty-Aware Multi-modal Learning via Cross-Modal Random Network Prediction

Hu Wang[1(✉)], Jianpeng Zhang[2], Yuanhong Chen[1], Congbo Ma[1], Jodie Avery[1], Louise Hull[1], and Gustavo Carneiro[1]

[1] The University of Adelaide, Adelaide, Australia
hu.wang@adelaide.edu.au
[2] Northwestern Polytechnical University, Xi'an, China

Abstract. Multi-modal learning focuses on training models by equally combining multiple input data modalities during the prediction process. However, this equal combination can be detrimental to the prediction accuracy because different modalities are usually accompanied by varying levels of uncertainty. Using such uncertainty to combine modalities has been studied by a couple of approaches, but with limited success because these approaches are either designed to deal with specific classification or segmentation problems and cannot be easily translated into other tasks, or suffer from numerical instabilities. In this paper, we propose a new Uncertainty-aware Multi-modal Learner that estimates uncertainty by measuring feature density via Cross-modal Random Network Prediction (CRNP). CRNP is designed to require little adaptation to translate between different prediction tasks, while having a stable training process. From a technical point of view, CRNP is the first approach to explore random network prediction to estimate uncertainty and to combine multi-modal data. Experiments on two 3D multi-modal medical image segmentation tasks and three 2D multi-modal computer vision classification tasks show the effectiveness, adaptability and robustness of CRNP. Also, we provide an extensive discussion on different fusion functions and visualization to validate the proposed model.

Keywords: Multi-modal learning · Uncertainty-aware · Image segmentation · Image classification

1 Introduction

Multi-modal data analysis, where the input data comes from a wide range of sources, is a relatively common task. For instance, automatic driving vehicles may take actions based on the fusion of the information provided by multiple

This project received grant funding from the Australian Government through the Medical Research Future Fund - Public Health Research Development Infrastructure PHRDI 000014 Grant and the Australian Research Council through grants DP180103232 and FT190100525.

sensors. In the medical domain, automated diagnosis often relies on data from multiple complementary modalities. Recently, we have seen the development of successful multi-modal techniques, such as vision-and-sound classification [5], sound source localization [4], vision-and-language navigation [35] or organ segmentation from multiple medical imaging modalities [9,38,40]. However, current multi-modal models typically rely on complex structures that neglect the uncertainty present in each modality. Although they can obtain promising results under specific scenarios, they are fragile when facing situations where modalities contain high uncertainties due to noise in the data or the presence of abnormal information. Such issue can reduce their prediction accuracy and limit their applicability in safety-critical applications [14].

Uncertainty is a crucial issue in many machine learning tasks because of the inherent randomness of machine learning processes. For instance, the randomness of data collection, data labeling, model initialization and training are sources of uncertainty that can result in large disagreements between models trained under similar conditions. According to [1,13,18], total uncertainty comprise: 1) aleatoric uncertainty (also known as data uncertainty), representing inherent noise in the data due to issues in data acquisition or labeling; and 2) epistemic uncertainty (i.e., model or knowledge uncertainty), which is related to the model estimation of the input data that may be inaccurate due to insufficient training steps/data, poor convergence, etc. Total uncertainty is defined as:

$$\underbrace{\mathbb{D}_{p(y|x,\theta)}[y]}_{\text{Total Uncertainty}} = \underbrace{\mathbb{E}_{p(\theta|D)}\left[\mathbb{D}_{p(y|x,\theta)}[y]\right]}_{\text{Aleatoric Uncertainty}} + \underbrace{\mathbb{D}_{p(\theta|D)}\left[\mathbb{E}_{p(y|x,\theta)}[y]\right]}_{\text{Epistemic Uncertainty}}, \qquad (1)$$

where D indicates the given dataset, x and y are the inputs and outputs of the model, and $\mathbb{D}[\cdot]$ represents the measurement of disagreement (e.g., entropy). The estimation of aleatoric uncertainty is considered as the expectation of the predicted disagreement for each model on data points posterior parameterized by θ; while the epistemic uncertainty is shown by the disagreement of different models parameterized by θ sampled from the posterior. In this paper, we focus on estimating total uncertainty.

In multi-modal methods, existing methods typically assume that each modality contributes equally to the prediction outcome [9,27,33]. This strong assumption may not hold if one of the modalities leads to a highly uncertain prediction, which can damage the model performance. In general, deep learning models that can estimate uncertainty [2,19,20] were not designed to deal with multi-modal data. These models are usually based on Bayesian learning that have slow inference time and poor training convergence, or on abstention mechanisms [32] that may suffer from the low representational power of characterising all types of uncertainties with a single abnormal class. Recently, there have been a couple of methods designed to model multi-modal uncertainty [14,26], but they are limited to work with very specific classification and segmentation problems, or they show numerical instabilities.

In this paper, we propose a novel approach to estimate the total uncertainty present in multi-modal data by measuring feature density via Cross-modal

Random Network Prediction (CRNP). CRNP measures uncertainty for multi-modal Learning using random network predictions (RNP) [3], where the model is designed to be easily adaptable to disparate tasks (e.g., classification and segmentation) and training is based on a stable optimization that mitigates numerical instabilities. To summarize, the main contributions of this paper are:

- We propose a new uncertainty-aware multi-modal learning model through a feature distribution learner based on RNP, named as Cross-modal Random Network Prediction (CRNP). CRNP is designed to be easily adapted to disparate tasks (e.g. classification and segmentation) and to be robust to numerical instabilities during optimization.
- This paper introduces a novel uncertainty estimation based on fitting the output of an RNP, which from a technical viewpoint, represents a departure from more common uncertainty estimation methods based on Bayesian learning or abstention mechanisms.

The adaptability of CRNP is shown by its application on two 3D multi-modal medical image segmentation tasks and three multi-modal 2D computer vision classification tasks, where the proposed model achieves state-of-the-art results on all problems. We perform a thorough analysis of multiple CRNP fusion strategies and present visualization to validate the effectiveness of the proposed model.

2   Related Work

2.1   Multi-modal Learning

Multi-modal learning has attracted increasing attention from computer vision (CV) and medical image analysis (MIA). In MIA, Jia et al. [16] introduced a shared-and-specific feature representation learning for semi-supervised multi-view learning. Dou et al. [9] proposed a chilopod-shaped multi-modal learning architecture with separate feature normalization for each modality and a knowledge distillation loss function. In CV, Shen et al. [4] defined a trusted middle-ground for video-and-sound source localization. In video-and-sound classification, Chen et al. [5] proposed to distill multi-modal image and sound knowledge into a video backbone network through compositional contrastive learning. Also in video-and-source classification, Patrick et al. [29,30] brought the idea of self-supervision learning into multi-modal by training the networks on external data, which boosted classification accuracy greatly. By exchanging channels, Wang et al. [39] showed that the multi-modal features are able to fuse in a better manner. Analyzing existing multi-modal learning methods, even though successful on several tasks, they do not consider that when reaching a decision, some modalities may be more reliable than others, which can damage the accuracy of the model.

2.2   Uncertainty-Based Learning Models

Uncertainty also has been widely studied in deep learning. Corbiere et al. [7] proposed to predict a single uncertainty value by an external confidence network via training on the ground-truth class. Sensoy et al. [32] introduced the Dirichlet distribution for an overall classification uncertainty measurement based on evidence. Kohl et al. [19] proposed a probabilistic UNet segmentation architecture to optimize a variant of the evidence lower bound (ELBO) objective. Based on the probabilistic UNet model, Kohl et al. [20] and Baumgartner et al. [2] further updated the model in a hierarchical manner from either the backbone network or prior/posterior networks. Jungo et al. [17] used two medical datasets to compare several uncertainty measurement models, namely: softmax entropy [12], Monte Carlo dropout [12], aleatoric uncertainty [18], ensemble methods [21] and auxiliary network [8,31]. In MIA, multiple uncertainty measurements have been proposed as well [22,24,36,37]. However, none of the methods above are designed for multi-modal tasks and some of them contain long and complex pipelines that are not easily adaptable to new tasks. Bayesian or ensemble-based methods demand long training and inference times and have slow convergence. Evidential methods have drawbacks too, where the main issue is the representational power of the abstention class. In contrast, our proposed model, by introducing random network fitting for cross-modal uncertainty measurement, is not only technically novel, but it is also simple and easily adaptable to many tasks without requiring any restrictive assumption about uncertainty representation.

2.3   Combining Uncertainty and Multi-modal Analysis

Some methods have studied the combination of uncertainty modeling and multi-modal learning. For example, a trusted multi-view classification model has been developed by modeling multi-view uncertainties through Dirichlet distribution and merging multi-modal features via Dempster's Rule [14]. However, it is rigidly designed for classification problems, and cannot be easily translated to other tasks, such as segmentation. Monteiro et al. [26] took pixel-wise coherence into account by optimizing low-rank covariance metrics to apply on lung nodules and brain tumor segmentation. Nevertheless, the method by Monteiro et al. [26] requires a time-consuming step to generate binary brain masks to remove blank areas, and the method is also numerically unstable when training in areas of infinite covariance such as the air outside the segmentation target[1]. From an implementation perspective, this method [26] is also memory intensive when indexing the identity matrix to create one-hot encodings. Differently, in our model, the uncertainty is measured by modeling the overall distribution directly from features without constructing any second-order relation matrix, leading to a numerically more stable optimization and a smaller memory consumption.

3   Cross-Modal Random Network Prediction

Below, we first introduce the Random Network Prediction (RNP), with a theoretical justification for its use to measure uncertainties. Then we present the

---

[1] As stated by SSN implementation [26] at https://github.com/biomedia-mira/stochastic_segmentation_networks.

CRNP model training and inference with the cross-modal uncertainty measuring mechanism to take the RNP uncertainty prediction from one modality to enhance or suppress the outputs for other modalities when producing a classification or segmentation prediction.

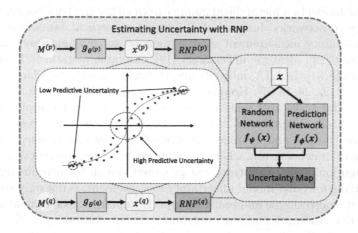

Fig. 1. The input data $M^{(p)}$ and $M^{(q)}$ are first processed by backbone models $g_{\theta(p)}$ and $g_{\theta(q)}$ that produce the features $x^{(p)}$ and $x^{(q)}$. Then the RNP modules have a fixed-weight random network $f_\psi(x)$ and a learnable prediction network $f_\phi(x)$ that tries to fit the output of the random network. The prediction network will fit better (i.e., with low predictive uncertainty) at more densely populated regions of the feature space, as shown in the graph. Hence, the difference between the outputs by $f_\psi(x)$ and $f_\phi(x)$ can be used to estimate uncertainty when processing a test input data.

3.1   Random Network Prediction

The uncertainty of a particular modality is estimated with the RNP depicted in Fig. 1. Specifically, for each RNP, we train a prediction network to fit the outputs of a weight-fixed and randomly-initialized network for feature density modeling. The intuition is that the prediction network will fit better the random network outputs of samples (i.e., with low uncertainty), populating denser regions of the feature space; but the fitting will be worse (i.e., with high uncertainty) for samples belonging to sparser regions. This phenomenon is depicted in the graph inside Fig. 1.

Formally, we consider input images from two modalities $M^{(p)}, M^{(q)} \in \mathcal{M}$, where p and q represent the modalities. After the input image $M^{(p)}$ pass through the encoder $g_{\theta(p)} : \mathcal{M} \to \mathcal{X}$ (similarly for $g_{\theta(q)}(.)$), the features of the two modalities $x^{(p)}, x^{(q)} \in \mathcal{X} \subset \mathbb{R}^N$ are analyzed by each RNP module. The RNP module feeds $x^{(p)}$ and $x^{(q)}$ to a randomly initialized neural network $f_\psi : \mathcal{X} \to \mathcal{Z}$, where $\mathcal{Z} \subset \mathbb{R}^M$, with fixed weights $\psi \in \Psi$. Meanwhile, $x^{(p)}$ and $x^{(q)}$ are fed to a learnable prediction network $f_\phi : \mathcal{X} \to \mathcal{Z}$ with parameters $\phi \in \Phi$. The prediction network has the same output space but a different structure from the random network, where the capacity of f_ϕ is smaller than f_ψ to prevent potential trivial solutions. The cost function used to train the RNP module is based on the mean square error (MSE) between the outputs of the prediction and random networks:

$$\phi^* = \arg\min_\phi \sum_{i=1}^{n} \ell_{MSE}(f_\phi(x_i), f_\psi(x_i)) + \mathcal{R}(\phi), \tag{2}$$

where n denotes the number of training samples, $\ell_{MSE}(f_\phi(x_i), f_\psi(x_i)) = \|f_\phi(x_i) - f_\psi(x_i)\|_2^2$, and $\mathcal{R}(\phi) = \|\phi\|_2^2$. The cost function in (2) provides a simple yet powerful supervisory signal to enable the prediction network to learn the uncertainty measuring function.

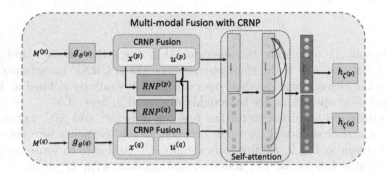

Fig. 2. The overall framework of multi-modal fusion with our CRNP.

3.2   Theoretical Support for Uncertainty Measurement

The RNP has a strong relation with uncertainty measurement. Let us consider a regression process from a set of perturbed data $\tilde{\mathcal{D}} = \{(x_i, \tilde{y}_i)\}_{i=1}^{n}$. Considering a Bayesian setting, the objective is to minimize the distance between the ground truth $\tilde{y}_i$ and a sum made up of a generated prior $f_\psi(x_i)$ randomly sampled from a Gaussian and an additive posterior term $f_\phi(x_i)$ with a regularization $\mathcal{R}(\phi)$. Formally, the optimization is as follows:

$$\phi^{(*)} = \arg\min_\phi \sum_{i=1}^{n} \|\tilde{y}_i - [f_\psi(x_i) + f_\phi(x_i)]\|_2^2 + \mathcal{R}(\phi), \tag{3}$$

where, according to Lemma 3 in [28], the sum $[f_\psi(x_i) + f_\phi(x_i)]$ is an approximator of the genuine posterior. If we fix the target $\tilde{y}_i$ with zeros, then the objective to be optimized would be equivalent to minimize the distance between the posterior $f_\phi(x_i)$ and the randomly sampled prior $f_\psi(x_i)$. Thus, each output element within the randomized function or the predict function can be viewed as a member of a set of weight-shared ensemble functions [3]. The predicted error, therefore, can be viewed as an estimate of the variance of the ensemble uncertainty.

3.3 Training and Inference of CRNP

This section introduces our proposed CRNP, which fuses the multiple modalities with their inferred uncertainties to produce the final predictions (e.g., classification or segmentation), as shown in Fig. 2. During the multi-modal fusion phase, the features of the two modalities $x^{(p)}$ and $x^{(q)}$ are cross-attended by the uncertainty maps produced by the RNP module from both modalities. The uncertainty map for modality p is represented as:

$$u^{(p)} = \|f_{\phi^{(q)}}(x^{(q)}) - f_{\psi^{(q)}}(x^{(q)})\|_2^2, \tag{4}$$

and similarly for $u^{(q)}$ for modality q. The feature cross-attended by the uncertainty maps is represented by:

$$\tilde{x}^{(p)} = \text{fusion}(x^{(p)}, \hat{u}^{(p)} \odot x^{(p)}), \tag{5}$$

where fusion$(.,.)$ represents the operator that fuses the original and cross-attended features, $\hat{u}^{(p)}$ is the channel-wise normalized CRNP uncertainty map, and $\odot$ is the element-wise product operator. $\tilde{x}^{(q)}$ is similarly defined as in (5). Different fusion operations are thoroughly discussed in Sect. 4.5.

We utilize self-attention to further fuse features $\tilde{x}^{(p)}$ and $\tilde{x}^{(q)}$, taking both uni-modal and cross-modal relations between feature elements into consideration. As shown in Fig. 2, we first concatenate $\tilde{x}^{(p)}$ and $\tilde{x}^{(q)}$ to form the query, key and value inputs for the self-attention module with $Q = K = V = $ concatenate$(\tilde{x}^{(p)}, \tilde{x}^{(q)})$. Then the output of the self-attention is denoted by:

$$l = \text{softmax}\left(\frac{(QW_q)(KW_k^T)}{\sqrt{d_k}}\right)VW_v, \tag{6}$$

where $l \in \mathcal{L}$, W_q, W_k and W_v are linear projection weights for queries, keys and values, respectively. d_k refers to the dimensions of queries, keys and values. The decoder after the multi-modal fusion is denoted by $h_{\zeta^{(p)}} : \mathcal{L} \to \Delta_{C-1}$ (similarly for $h_{\zeta^{(q)}}$), where $\mathcal{L}$ is the space of the output from the cross-modal RNP module and input to the decoder, and Δ_{C-1} is the classification simplex (output from softmax). Note that although the annotations of multi-modal data are similar, they can have significant differences, particularly in segmentation tasks. Hence, without losing generality, we may need to have multiple separate decoders, one for each modality. But multi-decoders are not needed in tasks where the multi-modal annotation is exactly the same. For segmentation problems, the output of $h_{\zeta^{(p)}}$ is the space Δ_{C-1} per pixel. The training of CRNP alternates the training of the RNP modules using (2) and the training of the whole model. During RNP training, only the weights of the prediction network inside the RNP are updated by minimising (2), and all other CRNP weights are kept fixed. During the training of the whole model, all CRNP weights are updated, except for the weights of the prediction network of the RNP. The whole model training minimizes the multi-class cross-entropy loss for a classification problem or the Dice and element-wise cross-entropy losses for a segmentation model.

During inference, CRNP receives multi-modal inputs, where each modality branch estimates an uncertainty output that will weight the other modality, and the results of both modalities will be fused to produce the final prediction. CRNP works by assigning large weights to the other modality when the current modality is uncertain. When both modalities have large uncertainties, the final prediction will rely on a balanced analysis of both modalities. For the analysis of more than two modalities, the uncertainty map for a particular modality, say p, in (4) is computed by summing the MSE results produced by all other modalities, with $u^{(p)} = \sum_{q \neq p} \|f_{\phi^{(q)}}(x^{(q)}) - f_{\psi^{(q)}}(x^{(q)})\|_2^2$. The decoders $g_{\theta^{(p)}}(.)$ and $g_{\theta^{(q)}}(.)$ from two modalities can be separated or share-weighted, depending on the corresponding output requirements.

4 Experiments

4.1 Datasets

Medical Image Segmentation Datasets. We conduct experiments on two publicly available multi-modal 3D segmentation datasets: Multi-Modality Whole Heart Segmentation dataset (MMWHS) and Multimodal Brain Tumor Segmentation Challenge 2020 dataset (BraTS2020). The MMWHS dataset contains 20 CTs and 20 MRs for training/validation and other 40 CTs and 40 MRs for testing [41]. Seven classes (background excluded) are considered for each pixel. The two modalities have individual ground-truth (GT) for each CT or MR. The BraTS2020 dataset has 369 cases for training/validation and other 125 cases for evaluation, where each case (with four modalities, namely: Flair, T1, T1CE and T2) share one segmentation GT. The evaluation is performed online[2]. Four classes (background included) are considered for each pixel.

Computer Vision Classification Datasets. We also validate our method on three computer vision classification datasets, namely: Handwritten[3], CUB [34] and Scene15 [10]. Each sample of the Handwritten dataset contains 2000 samples from six views and it is a ten-class classification problem, CUB contains 11,788 bird images from 200 different categories. Following Han et al. [14], we also adopt the first ten classes and two modalities (image and text features) extracted by GoogleNet and doc2vec. Three modalities are included in Scene15, which contains 4,485 images from 15 indoor and outdoor classes.

4.2 Implementation Details

Medical Image Segmentation Tasks. To keep a fair comparison, the implementation of all models evaluated on MMWHS and BraTS2020 is based on the 3D UNet (with 3D convolution and normalization) as our backbone network. On MMWHS, we adopt the official test set proposed by Zhuang et al. [41] (40 CTs

---

[2] https://ipp.cbica.upenn.edu/categories/brats2020.
[3] https://archive.ics.uci.edu/ml/datasets/Multiple+Features.

and 40 MRs) for testing; on BraTS2020, we evaluate all models on the online validation set. For overall performance evaluation, the models were trained for 100,000 iterations on MMWHS and 180,000 iterations on BraTS2020 without model selection. Following Dou et al. [9], our hyper-parameter tuning and ablation are conducted on MMWHS with 16 CTs and 16 MRs for training, 4 CTs and 4 MRs for validation. The batch size is set to 2. Stochastic gradient descent optimizer with a momentum of 0.99 is chosen for the model training. The initial learning rate is set to 10^{-2} on both datasets with cosine annealing [23] learning rate tuning strategy. For the reproduction of Probability UNet [19], we use prior/posterior mean instead of random sampling a latent variable z for prediction. The evaluation of the methods is based on the Dice score and Jaccard index for MMWHS; and the Dice score and Hausdorff95 index for BraTS2020. For cross-modal RNP modules training, the randomized network is made up of 3 depth-wise convolutional hidden layers; the prediction network has 2 depth-wise convolutional hidden layers. Between every two layers, both the randomized network and the prediction network adopt Leaky-ReLU as their activation function, where the negative slope is set to 2.5×10^{-1}. We set 256 as RNP output dimension for both tasks. For performance evaluation, the CRNP is placed at the bottleneck of our 3D UNet backbone. For the ensemble version of CRNP on both datasets, following Wang et al. [40], we average the logits of 3 CRNP models to reduce the prediction variance.

Computer Vision Classification Tasks. For the model evaluation on computer vision datasets, we follow [14] to split the data into 80% for training and 20% for testing. To keep a fair comparison, we uniformly trained all models for 500 epochs without model selection and then evaluated them on the test set. The learning rate is set to 3×10^{-4}; Adam optimizer with 1×10^{-5} weight decay and coefficients (0.9, 0.999) are adopted. Following Han et al. [14], we apply accuracy and multi-class AUROC as evaluation metrics. We used similar setups for cross-modal RNP modules as on the medical data, with the following differences: the RNP output dimension is set to 32 for computer vision classification tasks and CRNP is placed at the layer before the fully connected layer. The training of CRNP model is conducted in an end-to-end manner without any pre-training or post-processing. Also, the hyper-parameters do not require much effort to tune.

4.3 Medical Image Segmentation Model Performance

Performance on MMWHS Dataset. We compare our approach with: Individual (CT or MR single modality segmentation with separate 3D UNet), 3D UNet (multi-modal fusion by concatenation), the multi-modal learning model Ummkd [9], and the uncertainty model Probability UNet[4] [19], which proposes a prior net to approximate the posterior distribution, combining the knowledge of inputs and ground truth, in a latent space. The evaluation is based on the Dice scores of the segmentation of the left ventricle blood cavity (LV), the

---

[4] We also tried SSN [26], but it requires the creation of one-hot encodings that are memory intensive for seven classes on MMWHS dataset.

myocardium of the left ventricle (Myo), the right ventricle blood cavity (RV), the left atrium blood cavity (LA), the right atrium blood cavity (RA), the ascending aorta (AA), the pulmonary artery (PA) and Whole Heart (WH). All results on MMWHS data are obtained by using the official evaluation toolkit[5].

As shown in Table 1, our proposed CRNP and its ensemble version have 7 out of the 8 best Dice results on both CT and MR. On CT (Table 1), CRNP raises LV Dice score from 0.9297 to 0.9369 and PA Dice score from 0.8425 to 0.8628, when compared to the second-best models. On whole heart segmentation

Table 1. The performance of different models on CT/MR segmentation of MMWHS dataset. The best results for each column within either CT or MR section are in bold. * indicates the result with the ensemble model.

	Models	LV	Myo	RV	LA	RA	AA	PA	WH
CT	Individual	0.9297	0.8943	0.8597	0.9254	0.8701	0.9335	0.7833	0.8989
	3D UNet	0.9138	0.8781	0.8822	0.9274	0.8680	0.9088	0.8239	0.8957
	Ummkd	0.9145	**0.9066**	0.8410	0.9157	0.8853	0.8928	0.7579	0.8734
	Prob-UNet	0.9071	0.8775	0.8978	0.9262	0.8657	0.9318	0.8425	0.8997
	CRNP (Ours)	0.9369	0.9036	0.9076	**0.9375**	0.8885	**0.9538**	0.8628	0.9187
	CRNP* (Ours)	**0.9373**	0.9060	**0.9085**	0.9366	**0.8910**	0.9503	**0.8629**	**0.9193**
MR	Individual	0.8777	0.7923	0.6146	0.5686	0.7528	0.5854	0.3993	0.6729
	3D UNet	0.8850	0.7723	0.8559	0.8548	0.8676	0.8551	0.7964	0.8535
	Ummkd	0.8721	**0.7966**	0.8086	0.8577	0.8278	0.7998	0.7224	0.8211
	Prob-UNet	0.8742	0.7389	0.8332	0.8495	0.8531	0.8537	0.7895	0.8386
	CRNP (Ours)	0.8962	0.7787	0.8605	0.8637	**0.8748**	**0.8736**	0.7969	0.8615
	CRNP* (Ours)	**0.8963**	0.7811	**0.8742**	**0.8850**	0.8688	0.8692	**0.8329**	**0.8758**

Table 2. The performance comparison of CRNP and different challenge models on both CT and MR segmentation of MMWHS dataset. The best results for each column are in bold. ↑ sign indicates the higher value the better.

Models	CT		MR	
	Dice ↑	Jaccard ↑	Dice ↑	Jaccard ↑
GUT	0.9080	0.8320	0.8630	0.7620
KTH	0.8940	0.8100	0.8550	0.7530
CUHK1	0.8900	0.8050	0.7830	0.6530
CUHK2	0.8860	0.7980	0.8100	0.6870
UCF	0.8790	0.7920	0.8180	0.7010
SIAT	0.8490	0.7420	0.6740	0.5320
UT	0.8380	0.7420	0.8170	0.6950
UB1	0.8870	0.7980	0.8690	0.7730
UB2	–	–	0.8740	0.7780
UOE	0.8060	0.6970	0.8320	0.7200
Ours	**0.9193**	**0.8486**	**0.8758**	**0.7814**

---

[5] http://www.sdspeople.fudan.edu.cn/zhuangxiahai/0/mmwhs/.

Dice score, CRNP outperforms the second-best model by 1.9%. The ensemble version of CRNP further improves segmentation accuracy. A similar result is observed on MR. On LV, CRNP raises the Dice score from 0.8850 to 0.8962 and AA Dice score from 0.8551 to 0.8736 when compared to the second-best models. On whole heart segmentation, CRNP increases MR Dice from 0.8535 to 0.8615. Model ensemble further improves the performance.

Interestingly, the Individual model obtains accurate results on CT (0.8989 for WH score). However, performance (0.6729 for WH score) drops drastically on MR evaluation, with particularly poor accuracy on RV, AA and PA. But when considering both modalities (3D UNet model), the model performance increases substantially. This shows the bounds of considering a single modality, especially for MR segmentation. The proposed CRNP outperforms the 3D Unet by a large margin. Ummkd [9] performs consistently well on Myo on both CT and MR. We hypothesize that the domain-specific normalization and knowledge distillation loss contribute more to Myo segmentation than to other organs. Probability UNet tries to model posterior latent space rather than a deterministic prediction, which may explain its performance. In general, we note that the CT segmentation results are better than MR, which resonates with the conclusion from [41].

From the number of parameters perspective, the randomized network is made up of 3 convolutional hidden layers and the prediction network has 2 convolutional hidden layers. So the change in number of parameters is minimal. More specifically, the number of parameters of competing methods are: 1) UNet: 41.05M, 2) Ummkd (with UNet backbone for fair comparison): 41.05M, and 3) ProbUNet: 57.44M. Our CRNP has 42.18M parameters, where the RNP module has 0.29M, and the attention module has 0.84M parameters.

Table 3. The performance of different models on BraTS2020 Online validation set. The best results for each column are in bold. * indicates models with ensemble. ↑ sign indicates the higher value the better; while ↓ means the lower value the better.

Models	Dice ↑			Hausdorff95 ↓		
	ET	WT	TC	ET	WT	TC
3D UNet [6]	0.6876	0.8411	0.7906	50.9830	13.3660	13.6070
Basic VNet [25]	0.6179	0.8463	0.7526	47.7020	20.4070	12.1750
Deeper VNet [25]	0.6897	0.8611	0.7790	43.5180	14.4990	16.1530
Residual 3D UNet	0.7163	0.8246	0.7647	37.4220	12.3370	13.1050
ProbUNet [19]	0.7392	0.8782	0.7955	36.2458	6.9518	7.7183
SSN [26]	0.6795	0.8420	0.7866	43.6574	14.6945	19.5171
Modal-Pairing* [40]	0.7850	0.9070	0.8370	35.0100	4.7100	5.7000
TransBTS [38]	0.7873	0.9009	0.8173	**17.9470**	4.9640	9.7690
CRNP (Ours)	0.7887	0.9086	0.8372	26.5972	**4.0490**	6.0040
CRNP* (Ours)	**0.7902**	**0.9109**	**0.8550**	26.4682	4.1096	**5.3337**

We also compare the proposed CRNP model with the state-of-the-art models reported by the official challenge report [41]. The results are shown in Table 2. On whole heart segmentation, CRNP has a particularly accurate Dice score and Jaccard index for CT and MR. Compared to the second-best models, our CRNP model increases the Dice score from 0.9080 to 0.9193 and from 0.8740 to 0.8758 on CT and MR, respectively. Similar results are shown for Jaccard index.

Performance on BraTS2020 Dataset. Developing automated segmentation models to delineate intrinsically heterogeneous brain tumors is the main goal of BraTS2020 Challenge. Following [38], we compare the proposed CRNP model with many other strong methods, including 3D UNet [6], Basic VNet [25], Deeper VNet [25], Residual 3D UNet, Modal-Pairing [40], TransBTS [38], as well as uncertainty-aware models ProbUNet [19] and SSN [26] that models aleatoric uncertainty by considering spatially coherence. We evaluate the Dice and Hausdorff95 indexes of all models on four organs: enhancing tumor (ET); tumor core (TC) that consists of ET, necrotic and nonenhancing tumor core; and whole tumor (WT) that contains TC and the peritumoral edema.

In Table 3, our models have 5 out of the 6 best results. The CRNP improves the ET Dice score, compared with the second-best model, from 0.7873 to 0.7887; and from 0.9070 to 0.9086 on WT. Similar results are shown on Hausdorff95 indexes. Note that the Modal-Pairing model adopts an ensemble strategy. When applying the ensemble strategy to CRNP, the results improved even further. The WT Dice of CRNP* can reach 0.9109; the TC Dice can reach 0.8550, which is one more percent increment; and improves the TC Hausdorff95 to 5.3337. The performance improvements show the effectiveness of the proposed CRNP model.

4.4 Computer Vision Classification Model Performance

In this section, we show results that demonstrate the effectiveness of CRNP on multiple CV classification tasks. The evaluation metrics include accuracy and multi-class AUROC on Handwritten, CUB and Scene15 datasets. Following Han et al. [14], the comparison models include multiple uncertainty-aware models: Monte Carlo dropout (MCDO) [11] that adopts dropout at inference as a Bayesian approximator; deep ensemble (DE) [21], which uses an ensemble strategy to reduce uncertainty; uncertainty-aware attention (UA) [15] that creates uncertainty attention maps from a learned Gaussian distribution; evidential deep learning (EDL) [32] that predicts an extra Dirichlet distribution for all logits based on evidence; and trusted multi-view classification (TMC) [14], which is a multi-view version of EDL.

Table 4. The performance of different models on computer vision classification datasets. The best results for each row are in bold.

Data	Metric	MCDO [11]	DE [21]	UA [15]	EDL [32]	TMC [14]	CRNP
Handwritten	Acc	0.9737	0.9830	0.9745	0.9767	0.9851	**0.9925**
	AUROC	0.9970	0.9979	0.9967	0.9983	**0.9997**	0.9996
CUB	Acc	0.8978	0.9019	0.8975	0.8950	0.9100	**0.9167**
	AUROC	0.9929	0.9877	0.9869	0.9871	0.9906	**0.9961**
Scene15	Acc	0.5296	0.3912	0.4120	0.4641	0.6774	**0.7057**
	AUROC	0.9290	0.7464	0.8526	0.9141	0.9594	**0.9734**

As shown in Table 4, CRNP model can outperform its counterparts on 5 out of 6 measures across datasets. CRNP performs particularly well on Scene15, increasing the accuracy from 0.6774 to 0.7057 (a 2.83% improvement) and AUROC from 0.9594 to 0.9734 (a 1.4% improvement). CRNP also has promising results on Handwritten and CUB data. On AUROC of Handwritten, CRNP gets slightly worse but comparable results than TMC (0.9996 vs. 0.9997).

4.5 Ablation Study

Effectiveness of Each Component. In the ablation study, we examine each component of the proposed CRNP. The "Base" model is the plain multi-modal 3D UNet with dual branches; "CA" means cross-attention by assigning the query from one modality, while keep the key and value the other modality; "SA" means applying self-attention as we propose. We conducted the ablation on the validation set split of the MMWHS dataset and we measured the average Dice scores of each organ on CT and MR. As shown in Table 5, compared with the Base 3D UNet model, the CRNP model is able to improve (around 1% increment of Dice scores) the performance across multiple organs, where the improvements are especially obvious on Myo, LA, RA, AA and WH. From the table, we can perceive that, with the help of either cross-attention or self-attention, the model performance can be further boosted. But applying the self-attention as described in Sect. 3.3, causes the model to produce the best results (6 best results out of 8) across multiple organs. This is mainly because the self-attention on the multi-modal feature fusion not only models the cross-modal relations, but also considers uni-modal attentions.

Discussion of Different CRNP Fusion Functions. In terms of different CRNP fusion functions that can be applied in fusion(.,.) (Sect. 3.3), we compare and discuss three types, as shown in Table 6: (a) "Replace" represents a naive replacement of the original modality features by the uncertainty map attended features; (b) "Concat" applies the concatenation operation on the original modality features and the uncertainty map attended features; and (c) "Residual", which is the default fusion strategy of the proposed CRNP, denotes an addition operation performed between two feature tensors. This experiment is

Table 5. Ablation study on MMWHS dataset. Best results per row are in bold.

Models	LV	Myo	RV	LA	RA	AA	PA	WH
Base	0.9334	0.8596	0.8876	0.8932	0.8794	0.8239	0.8168	0.8706
CRNP	0.9324	0.8685	0.8644	0.9007	0.8957	**0.9216**	0.8225	0.8865
CRNP+CA	0.9323	0.8683	0.8802	0.9147	**0.9116**	0.9098	0.8194	0.8909
CRNP+SA	**0.9356**	**0.8891**	**0.8814**	**0.9232**	0.8987	0.9148	**0.8277**	**0.8958**

Table 6. Analysis of different fusion functions of CRNP on MMWHS dataset. Best results per row are in bold.

Models	LV	Myo	RV	LA	RA	AA	PA	WH
Replace	**0.9342**	**0.8688**	0.8688	0.897	0.8812	0.9074	0.8128	0.8815
Concat	0.9327	0.8676	**0.8798**	**0.9031**	0.8781	0.9098	0.8042	0.8822
Residual	0.9324	0.8685	0.8644	0.9007	**0.8957**	**0.9216**	**0.8225**	**0.8865**

conducted on the MMWHS dataset and averages both CT and MR Dice results. From the results, we note that all three types of fusion functions have pros and cons. However, the "Residual" model performs better (4 best results out of 8) than other functions. This advantage is more noticeable on RA, AA and PA, on which more than 1% improvement is gained on Dice score.

4.6 Visualization

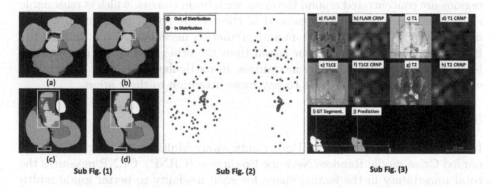

Fig. 3. Visualization experiments of CRNP. Sub Fig.(1) shows a comparison between the segmentation of the proposed CRNP ((b) and (d)) and its Base model ((a) and (c)). Sub Fig. (2) shows the T-SNE graph of the in and out of distribution data points produced by the cross-modal RNP module. In the Sub Fig. (3), we show the CRNP uncertainty heat-maps.

We also conduct a visualization experiment in Fig. 3 that shows the MMWHS segmentation visualization (Sub Fig. 1), T-SNE visualization of in and out of distribution data points produced by the uncertainty maps from the RNP module on the CT images from MMWHS (Sub Fig. 2), and the CRNP uncertainty heat-maps for BraTS2020 images (Sub Fig. 3). As the two cases from validation set shown in Sub Fig. (1), (a) (c) are segmented by the Base model and (b) (d) are from CRNP. The color masks denote the segmentation results (e.g., pink) overlaid on the ground truth (e.g., purple). The obvious segmentation differences are highlighted by yellow boxes. When comparing segmentation from two models, we can notice that our CRNP has better segmentation results, especially on the organ edges. This is mainly because organ edges contain more uncertain regions. The proposed CRNP can perceive uncertain segmented regions within one modality and assign more weights to the other one. By leveraging this information, CRNP is able to alleviate segmentation uncertainties in organ edges. Moreover, we visualize the in and out of distribution uncertainty maps processed by T-SNE in Sub Fig. (2). Following Han et al. [14], we consider the original features as the in distribution data and noisy features modified by additive Gaussian noise as the out of distribution data. Then, these samples are fed into the cross-modal RNP modules to get the uncertainty map predictions. The T-SNE is able to clearly split these uncertainty predictions into two clusters. This shows further evidence of the effectiveness of our CRNP model to estimate uncertainties. In Sub Fig. (3), we show the CRNP uncertainty heat-maps for a BraTS image, where the maps are estimated in the feature space and mapped back to the original image space. In this figure, (a) (c) (e) (g) are the flair, t1, t1ce and t2 modalities; (b) (d) (f) (h) are the CRNP uncertainty maps for the modalities above (brighter pixel = higher uncertainty); and (i) (j) are the ground truth (GT) segmentation and CRNP prediction. Note that the high uncertainty regions are concentrated around the areas with brain tumors, which is reasonable since tumors are sparsely represented in the feature space, resulting in a large difference between RNP's random and prediction networks. Also note that the flair image has a stronger tumor signal than the other modalities, producing a larger uncertainty for the other modalities. In particular, this larger uncertainty will notify the other modalities to pay more attention to these areas.

5   Conclusions

In this paper, we proposed the Uncertainty-aware Multi-modal Learning model, named Cross-modal Random Network Prediction (CRNP). CRNP measures the total uncertainty in the feature space for each modality to better guide multi-modal fusion. Moreover, technically speaking, the proposed CRNP is the first approach to explore random network prediction to estimate uncertainty and fuse multi-modal data. CRNP has a stable training process compared with a recent multi-modal approach that uses potentially unstable covariance measures to estimate uncertainty [26], and CRNP can also be easily translated between different prediction tasks. Through experiments on two medical image segmentation datasets and three computer vision classification datasets, the effectiveness of the proposed CRNP model is verified. Also, ablation and visualization studies further validate CNRP as an effective multi-modal analysis method.

References

1. Abdar, M., et al.: A review of uncertainty quantification in deep learning: techniques, applications and challenges. Inf. Fusion **76**, 243–297 (2021)
2. Baumgartner, C.F., et al.: PHiSeg: capturing uncertainty in medical image segmentation. In: Shen, D., et al. (eds.) MICCAI 2019. LNCS, vol. 11765, pp. 119–127. Springer, Cham (2019). https://doi.org/10.1007/978-3-030-32245-8_14
3. Burda, Y., Edwards, H., Storkey, A., Klimov, O.: Exploration by random network distillation. arXiv preprint arXiv:1810.12894 (2018)
4. Chen, H., Xie, W., Afouras, T., Nagrani, A., Vedaldi, A., Zisserman, A.: Localizing visual sounds the hard way. In: Proceedings of the IEEE/CVF Conference on Computer Vision and Pattern Recognition, pp. 16867–16876 (2021)
5. Chen, Y., Xian, Y., Koepke, A., Shan, Y., Akata, Z.: Distilling audio-visual knowledge by compositional contrastive learning. In: Proceedings of the IEEE/CVF Conference on Computer Vision and Pattern Recognition, pp. 7016–7025 (2021)
6. Çiçek, Ö., Abdulkadir, A., Lienkamp, S.S., Brox, T., Ronneberger, O.: 3D U-Net: learning dense volumetric segmentation from sparse annotation. In: Ourselin, S., Joskowicz, L., Sabuncu, M.R., Unal, G., Wells, W. (eds.) MICCAI 2016. LNCS, vol. 9901, pp. 424–432. Springer, Cham (2016). https://doi.org/10.1007/978-3-319-46723-8_49
7. Corbière, C., Thome, N., Bar-Hen, A., Cord, M., Pérez, P.: Addressing failure prediction by learning model confidence. In: Advances in Neural Information Processing Systems, vol. 32 (2019)
8. DeVries, T., Taylor, G.W.: Leveraging uncertainty estimates for predicting segmentation quality. arXiv preprint arXiv:1807.00502 (2018)
9. Dou, Q., Liu, Q., Heng, P.A., Glocker, B.: Unpaired multi-modal segmentation via knowledge distillation. IEEE Trans. Med. Imaging **39**(7), 2415–2425 (2020)
10. Fei-Fei, L., Perona, P.: A Bayesian hierarchical model for learning natural scene categories. In: 2005 IEEE Computer Society Conference on Computer Vision and Pattern Recognition (CVPR 2005), vol. 2, pp. 524–531. IEEE (2005)
11. Gal, Y., Ghahramani, Z.: Bayesian convolutional neural networks with bernoulli approximate variational inference. arXiv preprint arXiv:1506.02158 (2015)
12. Gal, Y., Ghahramani, Z.: Dropout as a Bayesian approximation: representing model uncertainty in deep learning. In: International Conference on Machine Learning, pp. 1050–1059. PMLR (2016)
13. Gawlikowski, J., et al.: A survey of uncertainty in deep neural networks. arXiv preprint arXiv:2107.03342 (2021)
14. Han, Z., Zhang, C., Fu, H., Zhou, J.T.: Trusted multi-view classification. arXiv preprint arXiv:2102.02051 (2021)
15. Heo, J., et al.: Uncertainty-aware attention for reliable interpretation and prediction. In: Advances in Neural Information Processing Systems, vol. 31 (2018)
16. Jia, X., et al.: Semi-supervised multi-view deep discriminant representation learning. IEEE Trans. Pattern Anal. Mach. Intell. **43**(7), 2496–2509 (2020)
17. Jungo, A., Reyes, M.: Assessing reliability and challenges of uncertainty estimations for medical image segmentation. In: Shen, D., et al. (eds.) MICCAI 2019. LNCS, vol. 11765, pp. 48–56. Springer, Cham (2019). https://doi.org/10.1007/978-3-030-32245-8_6

18. Kendall, A., Gal, Y.: What uncertainties do we need in Bayesian deep learning for computer vision? In: Advances in Neural Information Processing Systems, vol. 30 (2017)
19. Kohl, S., et al.: A probabilistic U-Net for segmentation of ambiguous images. In: Advances in Neural Information Processing Systems, vol. 31 (2018)
20. Kohl, S.A., et al.: A hierarchical probabilistic u-net for modeling multi-scale ambiguities. arXiv preprint arXiv:1905.13077 (2019)
21. Lakshminarayanan, B., Pritzel, A., Blundell, C.: Simple and scalable predictive uncertainty estimation using deep ensembles. In: Advances in Neural Information Processing Systems, vol. 30 (2017)
22. Li, Y., Luo, L., Lin, H., Chen, H., Heng, P.-A.: Dual-consistency semi-supervised learning with uncertainty quantification for COVID-19 lesion segmentation from CT images. In: de Bruijne, M., et al. (eds.) MICCAI 2021. LNCS, vol. 12902, pp. 199–209. Springer, Cham (2021). https://doi.org/10.1007/978-3-030-87196-3_19
23. Loshchilov, I., Hutter, F.: SGDR: stochastic gradient descent with warm restarts. arXiv preprint arXiv:1608.03983 (2016)
24. Luo, X., et al.: Efficient semi-supervised gross target volume of nasopharyngeal carcinoma segmentation via uncertainty rectified pyramid consistency. In: de Bruijne, M., et al. (eds.) MICCAI 2021. LNCS, vol. 12902, pp. 318–329. Springer, Cham (2021). https://doi.org/10.1007/978-3-030-87196-3_30
25. Milletari, F., Navab, N., Ahmadi, S.A.: V-net: fully convolutional neural networks for volumetric medical image segmentation. In: 2016 Fourth International Conference on 3D Vision (3DV), pp. 565–571. IEEE (2016)
26. Monteiro, M., et al.: Stochastic segmentation networks: modelling spatially correlated aleatoric uncertainty. In: Advances in Neural Information Processing Systems, vol. 33, pp. 12756–12767 (2020)
27. Nie, D., Wang, L., Gao, Y., Shen, D.: Fully convolutional networks for multi-modality isointense infant brain image segmentation. In: 2016 IEEE 13th International Symposium on Biomedical Imaging (ISBI), pp. 1342–1345. IEEE (2016)
28. Osband, I., Aslanides, J., Cassirer, A.: Randomized prior functions for deep reinforcement learning. In: Advances in Neural Information Processing Systems, vol. 31 (2018)
29. Patrick, M., et al.: Multi-modal self-supervision from generalized data transformations. arXiv preprint arXiv:2003.04298 (2020)
30. Patrick, M., et al.: Space-time crop & attend: improving cross-modal video representation learning. In: Proceedings of the IEEE/CVF International Conference on Computer Vision, pp. 10560–10572 (2021)
31. Robinson, R., et al.: Real-time prediction of segmentation quality. In: Frangi, A.F., Schnabel, J.A., Davatzikos, C., Alberola-López, C., Fichtinger, G. (eds.) MICCAI 2018. LNCS, vol. 11073, pp. 578–585. Springer, Cham (2018). https://doi.org/10.1007/978-3-030-00937-3_66
32. Sensoy, M., Kaplan, L., Kandemir, M.: Evidential deep learning to quantify classification uncertainty. In: Advances in Neural Information Processing Systems, vol. 31 (2018)
33. Valindria, V.V., et al.: Multi-modal learning from unpaired images: application to multi-organ segmentation in CT and MRI. In: 2018 IEEE Winter Conference on Applications of Computer Vision (WACV), pp. 547–556. IEEE (2018)
34. Wah, C., Branson, S., Welinder, P., Perona, P., Belongie, S.: The caltech-ucsd birds-200-2011 dataset (2011)

35. Wang, H., Wu, Q., Shen, C.: Soft expert reward learning for vision-and-language navigation. In: Vedaldi, A., Bischof, H., Brox, T., Frahm, J.-M. (eds.) ECCV 2020. LNCS, vol. 12354, pp. 126–141. Springer, Cham (2020). https://doi.org/10.1007/978-3-030-58545-7_8

36. Wang, K., et al.: Tripled-uncertainty guided mean teacher model for semi-supervised medical image segmentation. In: de Bruijne, M., et al. (eds.) MICCAI 2021. LNCS, vol. 12902, pp. 450–460. Springer, Cham (2021). https://doi.org/10.1007/978-3-030-87196-3_42

37. Wang, L., et al.: Medical matting: a new perspective on medical segmentation with uncertainty. In: de Bruijne, M., et al. (eds.) MICCAI 2021. LNCS, vol. 12903, pp. 573–583. Springer, Cham (2021). https://doi.org/10.1007/978-3-030-87199-4_54

38. Wang, W., Chen, C., Ding, M., Yu, H., Zha, S., Li, J.: TransBTS: multimodal brain tumor segmentation using transformer. In: de Bruijne, M., et al. (eds.) MICCAI 2021. LNCS, vol. 12901, pp. 109–119. Springer, Cham (2021). https://doi.org/10.1007/978-3-030-87193-2_11

39. Wang, Y., Huang, W., Sun, F., Xu, T., Rong, Y., Huang, J.: Deep multimodal fusion by channel exchanging. Adv. Neural. Inf. Process. Syst. **33**, 4835–4845 (2020)

40. Wang, Y., et al.: Modality-pairing learning for brain tumor segmentation. In: Crimi, A., Bakas, S. (eds.) BrainLes 2020. LNCS, vol. 12658, pp. 230–240. Springer, Cham (2021). https://doi.org/10.1007/978-3-030-72084-1_21

41. Zhuang, X., et al.: Evaluation of algorithms for multi-modality whole heart segmentation: an open-access grand challenge. Med. Image Anal. **58**, 101537 (2019)

Localizing Visual Sounds the Easy Way

Shentong Mo[1] and Pedro Morgado[1,2(✉)]

[1] Carnegie Mellon University, Pittsburgh, USA
[2] University of Wisconsin-Madison, Madison, USA
pmorgado@wisc.edu

Abstract. Unsupervised audio-visual source localization aims at localizing visible sound sources in a video without relying on ground-truth localization for training. Previous works often seek high audio-visual similarities for likely positive (sounding) regions and low similarities for likely negative regions. However, accurately distinguishing between sounding and non-sounding regions is challenging without manual annotations. In this work, we propose a simple yet effective approach for Easy Visual Sound Localization, namely EZ-VSL, without relying on the construction of positive and/or negative regions during training. Instead, we align audio and visual spaces by seeking audio-visual representations that are aligned in, at least, one location of the associated image, while not matching other images, at any location. We also introduce a novel object guided localization scheme at inference time for improved precision. Our simple and effective framework achieves state-of-the-art performance on two popular benchmarks, Flickr SoundNet and VGG-Sound Source. In particular, we improve the CIoU on Flickr Sound-Net from 76.80% to 83.94%, and on VGG-Sound Source from 34.60% to 38.85%. Code and pretrained models are available at https://github.com/stoneMo/EZ-VSL.

1 Introduction

When we hear a baby crying, we can localize the sound by finding the baby in the room. This ability of visual sound source localization is possible due to the tight association between visual and auditory signals in the natural world. In this work, we aim to leverage this natural and freely available audio-visual association to localize sound sources present in a video in an unsupervised manner, i.e. without relying on manual annotations for sounding source locations.

Unsupervised visual localization of sound sources has attracted much attention in recent years [2,6,30]. To tackle this problem, recent approaches [2,6,17, 28,31] rely on direct audio-visual similarity in a learned latent space for localization. These audio-visual similarities are used to construct likely sounding and non-sounding regions in the image, and the models are learned by requiring the audio representation to match visual representations pooled from likely sounding regions while being dissimilar from those of different images [2,17,28], and/or from non-sounding regions [6,31]. While these approaches have been shown to

S. Avidan et al. (Eds.): ECCV 2022, LNCS 13697, pp. 218–234, 2022.
https://doi.org/10.1007/978-3-031-19836-6_13

yield state-of-the-art performance in unsupervised visual sound localization, we identify two major limitations.

First, the training objective presents a paradox. On one hand, accurate regions of sounding objects are required in order to encourage audio representations to match the visual representations of the regions where the source is located. On the other hand, since localization maps are obtained through audio-visual similarities, accurate representations are required in order to identify the regions containing the sounding objects. This paradox results in a complex training objective that is likely to contain many sub-optimal local minima, as the model is required to bootstrap from its own localization ability.

Second, by solely relying on audio-visual similarity for localization, prior work ignores the visual prior of likely audio sources. For example, even without access to the audio signal, we know that most regions of an image, depicting for example the floor, the sky, a table, or a wall, are unlikely to depict sources of sound.

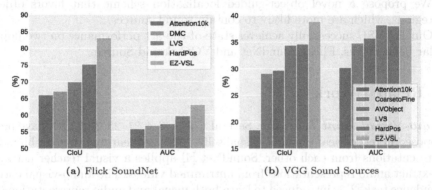

(a) Flick SoundNet   (b) VGG Sound Sources

Fig. 1. Comparison of EZ-VSL with state-of-the-art methods on Flickr SoundNet [17] (a) and VGG-SS [6]. All methods in (a) are trained on Flickr 144k, and those in (b) on VGG Sound 144k.

To address these challenges, we propose a simple yet effective approach for easy visual sound localization, namely EZ-VSL. Instead of relying on explicit maps for sounding and non-sounding regions, we treat audio-visual correspondence learning as a multiple instance learning problem. In other words, we propose a training loss that encourages the audio signal to be associated with, at least, one location in the corresponding image, while not being associated with any location from other images. Then, we introduce a novel object-guided localization scheme at inference time that combines the audio-visual similarity map with an object localization map from a lightweight pre-trained visual model, which biases sound source localization predictions towards the objects in the scene.

We evaluate our EZ-VSL on two popular benchmarks, Flickr SoundNet [17] and VGG-Sound Source [6]. Extensive experiments show the superiority of our approach for unsupervised sound source visual localization. We also conduct comprehensive ablation studies to demonstrate the effectiveness of each component. Surprisingly, we found that the object prior alone, which does not even leverage the audio for localization, already surpasses all prior work on both Flickr and VGG-Sound benchmarks. We also demonstrate the superiority of the proposed multiple instance learning objective for audio-visual matching compared to prior approaches that rely on careful constructions of positive (sounding) and negative (non-sounding) regions for training. Finally, we show that the visual object prior and audio-visual similarity maps can be further combined into more accurate predictions, surpassing the current state-of-the-art method by large margins on both Flickr SoundNet and VGG Sound Sources. These results are highlighted in Fig. 1.

Overall, the main contributions of this work can be summarized as follows:

✦ We present a simple yet effective multiple instance learning framework for unsupervised sound source visual localization, which we call EZ-VSL.
✦ We propose a novel object-guided localization scheme that favors object regions, which are more likely to contain sound sources.
✦ Our EZ-VSL successfully achieves state-of-the-art performance on two popular benchmarks, Flickr SoundNet and VGG-Sound Source.

2 Related Work

Audio-Visual Joint Learning. Several works [3,4,21–25,27,33,34] have been proposed in recent year on audio-visual self-supervised learning to learn bimodal representations from each other. SoundNet [4] applies a visual teacher network to extract audio representations from untrimmed videos. The audio-visual correspondence task [3] is introduced to learn both visual and audio representations in an unsupervised way. Audio-visual synchronization objectives are also explored for several tasks, such as speech recognition [1,32], audio-visual navigation [5], visual sound source separation, and localization [10,12,14,30,35,36].

Besides these works, several methods adopt a weakly-supervised scheme to solve audio-visual problems. For example, UntrimmedNet [34] uses a classification module and a selection module for Multiple Instance Learning (MIL) to perform audio-visual action localization. [33] also proposes in a hybrid attention network for audio-visual video parsing. In this work, however, we focus on the sound source localization problem by learning audio-visual representations jointly from unlabelled videos.

Audio-Visual Source Localization. Audio-Visual Source Localization aims at localizing sound sources by learning the co-occurrence of audio and visual features in a video. Early works [9,16,19] use shallow probabilistic models or canonical correlation analysis to solve this problem. With the introduction of deep neural networks, some approaches [17,26] were proposed to learn the audio-visual correspondence via a dual-stream network and a contrastive loss. For instance, DMC [17] adopts synchronous sets of clustering with respect to each modality for capturing audio-visual correspondences. Multisensory features [26] are used to jointly learn visual and audio representations of a video through the temporal alignment. Other methods [11,13,29,35,36] leverage the audio-visual source separation as the target to achieve visual sound localization. Most of these methods learn from global audio-visual correspondences. Although they show qualitatively that the model is capable of localization, their localization ability is not competitive to models that learn from localized correspondences.

Beyond the work discussed above, several relevant works have targeted the visual source localization problem directly. Attention10k [30] developed an attention mechanism and a two-stream architecture with each modality to localize sound sources in an image. Qian *et al.* [28] proposed a two-stage framework to learn audio and visual representations with the cross-modal feature alignment in a coarse-to-fine way. Afouras *et al.* [2] introduced an attention-based model with the optical flow to localize and group sound sources in a video. More recently, LVS [6] added a hard sample mining mechanism to contrastive loss with a differentiable threshold on the audio-visual correspondence map. Finally, Hard-Pos [31] leveraged hard positives in contrastive learning for learning semantically matched audio-visual information from negative pairs. Different from these baselines, we show that it is possible (and even preferable) to learn from a simplified multiple-instance contrastive learning objective. We also propose a novel object guided localization scheme to boost the visual localization performance of sound sources.

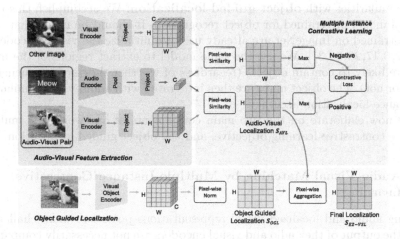

Fig. 2. Illustration of the proposed method. The audio-visual feature extractor computes global audio and localization visual features. Audio-visual alignment is learned using a multiple instance contrastive learning objective. At inference time, we use another visual encoder pre-trained on object recognition to compute object localization maps, which are combined with audio-visual localization maps for the final prediction.

3 Method

Given a video containing sound sources, our goal is to localize the sounding objects within it without using manual annotations of their locations for training. We propose a simple yet effective way for unsupervised sound source visual localization, which we denote EZ-VSL.

3.1 Overview

Let $\mathcal{D} = \{(v_i, a_i) : i = 1, \ldots, N\}$ be a dataset of paired audio a_i and visual data v_i, where the sources of the sound audible in a_i are assumed to be depicted in v_i. Following previous work [6,17], we first encode the audio and visual signals using a two stream neural net encoder, denoted as $f_a(\cdot)$ and $f_v(\cdot)$ for the audio and images, respectively. The audio encoder extracts global audio representations $\mathbf{a}_i = f_a(a_i)$ and the visual encoder computes localized representations $\mathbf{v}_i^{xy} = f_v(v_i^{xy})$ for each (x, y) location. As shown in Fig. 2, audio and visual features are then mapped into a shared latent space, where the similarity between audio-visual representations can be computed for all locations. The audio-visual models are then trained to minimize a **cross-modal multiple-instance contrastive learning** loss, that encourages audio representation to be aligned with the associated visual representations at least at one location. By optimizing this loss, audio and visual signals are matched in the shared latent space, which can then be used for localization. At inference time, we combine the learned audio-visual similarities with **object guided localization**. We accomplish this using a visual model pre-trained for object recognition. It should be noted that models pre-trained on ImageNet are already used to initialize the visual encoder for VSL [2,6,17,28,30,31]. We use the same model to extract regions of the image that are likely to contain objects (regardless of whether they are producing the sound or not). The object maps are then integrated with audio-visual similarities to enhance localization accuracy.

We now elaborate on the two main components of our work: the multiple instance contrastive learning objective, and the object guided localization.

3.2 Audio-Visual Matching by Multiple-Instance Contrastive Learning

Aligning audio and localized visual representations poses two main challenges. First, the output of the audio and visual encoders are not necessarily compatible. Second, most locations in the image do not depict the sound source, and so the representations at these locations should not be aligned with the audio.

The first challenge can be easily addressed by projecting both audio and visual representations into a shared feature space

$$\hat{\mathbf{v}}_i^{xy} = \mathbf{U}_v \mathbf{v}_i + \mathbf{b}_v \quad \forall x, y, i \qquad \text{and} \qquad \hat{\mathbf{a}}_i = \mathbf{U}_a \mathbf{a}_i + \mathbf{b}_a \quad \forall i \qquad (1)$$

where $\mathbf{U}_v$ and $\mathbf{U}_a$ are projection matrices, and $\mathbf{b}_v$ and $\mathbf{b}_a$ bias terms.

The second challenge requires to selectively match the audio representations to the associated visual regions depicting the sound sources. Prior work [2,6,17, 28,30,31] explicitly computes an attention map for the likely sounding regions by bootstrapping from current audio-visual similarities. The audio representations are then required to match these sounding regions [17,28,30], and in some cases to not match non-sounding regions from the same image [6,31]. As discussed above, this leads to a paradox where accurate localization is required to learn accurate audio-visual representations, which is required for localization in the first place.

To simplify this framework, we propose to optimize a multiple instance contrastive learning loss. Each bag of visual features V (or bag of instances) spans all locations within an image

$$V_i = \{\hat{\mathbf{v}}_i^{xy} : \forall x, y\} \quad \forall i \in \mathcal{D} \tag{2}$$

Audio representations $\mathbf{a}_i$ are then required to be similar to at least one instance in the corresponding positive bag V_i, while being dissimilar from all locations in all negative bags $V_j \ \forall j \neq i$. Specifically, we seek to maximize the alignment between the audio and the most similar positive visual instance, through the following loss function

$$\mathcal{L}_{a \to v} = -\log \frac{\exp\left(\frac{1}{\tau} \max_{\hat{\mathbf{v}} \in V_i} \text{sim}(\hat{\mathbf{a}}_i, \hat{\mathbf{v}})\right)}{\sum_k \exp\left(\frac{1}{\tau} \max_{\hat{\mathbf{v}} \in V_k} \text{sim}(\hat{\mathbf{a}}_i, \hat{\mathbf{v}})\right)} \tag{3}$$

where $\text{sim}(\hat{\mathbf{v}}, \hat{\mathbf{a}}) = \hat{\mathbf{v}}^T \hat{\mathbf{a}}/(\|\hat{\mathbf{v}}\|\|\hat{\mathbf{a}}\|)$ is the cosine similarity, and τ a temperature hyper-parameter. Negative bags are obtained from other samples in the same mini-batch. To train our models, we use a symmetric version of (3) by defining

$$\mathcal{L}_{v \to a} = -\log \frac{\exp\left(\frac{1}{\tau} \max_{\hat{\mathbf{v}} \in V_i} \text{sim}(\hat{\mathbf{v}}, \hat{\mathbf{a}}_i)\right)}{\sum_k \exp\left(\frac{1}{\tau} \max_{\hat{\mathbf{v}} \in V_i} \text{sim}(\hat{\mathbf{v}}, \hat{\mathbf{a}}_k)\right)}, \tag{4}$$

and optimizing the symmetric loss

$$\mathcal{L} = \mathcal{L}_{a \to v} + \mathcal{L}_{v \to a}. \tag{5}$$

During inference, the audio-visual localization map is computed as

$$\mathbf{S}_{xy}^{AVL} = \text{sim}(\hat{\mathbf{v}}_{xy}, \hat{\mathbf{a}}) \quad \forall x \in [1, W], y \in [1, H]. \tag{6}$$

3.3   Object-Guided Localization

At inference time, we propose a novel object-guided scheme for enhanced localization. The input image is fed to a convolutional model f_{obj} pre-trained on ImageNet [8] without global pooling or the classification head, yielding a feature map $\mathbf{v}' = f_{obj}(v) \in \mathbb{R}^{C \times H \times W}$. This model has the same architecture than the visual encoder used for audio-visual localization and is initialized with the same ImageNet pre-trained weights, but unlike the former, this model is never trained for audio-visual similarity. Hence, the feature map $\mathbf{v}'$ contains zero information about the accompanying audio. Instead, it can be used to define a localization prior that favors the objects in the scene, regardless of whether these objects are the sources of the sound or not. We then experimented with two possible solutions to extract object-centric localization maps without any additional training. The first obtains a 1000-way object class posterior $P(o|\mathbf{v}'_{xy})$ by applying an ImageNet pretrained classifier to each (x, y) location of $\mathbf{v}'$. We then define the object localization prior as

$$\mathbf{S}^{CLS}_{xy} = \max_o P(o|\mathbf{v}'_{xy}). \tag{7}$$

The second approach, perhaps less intuitive but more effective, relies on the fact that f_{obj} was trained on an object-centric dataset, and thus produces stronger activations when evaluated on images of objects. With this intuition in mind, we alternatively define the object localization prior as

$$\mathbf{S}^{L1}_{xy} = \|\mathbf{v}'_{xy}\|_1. \tag{8}$$

Note that in both cases, the object prior solely relies on a model f_{obj} pre-trained on ImageNet. We conduct no further training of f_{obj}.

The audio-visual localization and object-centric maps are then linearly aggregated into a final localization map $\mathbf{S}^{EZVSL}_{xy}$ of the form

$$\mathbf{S}^{EZVSL}_{xy} = \alpha \mathbf{S}^{AVL}_{xy} + (1 - \alpha)\mathbf{S}^{OBJ}_{xy} \quad \forall x, y, \tag{9}$$

where $\mathbf{S}^{AVL}_{xy}$ is the audio-visual similarity of map of (6), $\mathbf{S}^{OBJ}_{xy}$ is the object localization map (i.e., $\mathbf{S}^{CLS}_{xy}$ in (7) or $\mathbf{S}^{L1}_{xy}$ in (8)), and α is balancing term that weights the contribution of the object prior and the audio-visual similarity terms. In practice, since the two maps $\mathbf{S}^{AVL}_{xy}$ and $\mathbf{S}^{OBJ}_{xy}$ can have widely different ranges of scores, we normalize them into a $[0, 1]$ range before aggregation, i.e., $\mathbf{S}_{xy} = \frac{\mathbf{S}_{xy} - \min_{xy} \mathbf{S}_{xy}}{\max_{xy} \mathbf{S}_{xy} - \min_{xy} \mathbf{S}_{xy}}$.

4   Experiments

We evaluated EZ-VSL on unsupervised visual sound source localization. Following accepted practices [6,28,30], we used the Flickr SoundNet dataset [4] and the recently proposed VGG-Sound dataset [7], and report the same evaluation metrics as in [6,28,30]. Namely, we measure the average precision at a Consensus Intersection over Union threshold of 0.5, a metric often simply denoted as CIoU. We also measure the Area Under Curve (AUC).

4.1   Experimental Setup

Datasets. Flickr SoundNet includes 2 million unconstrained videos from Flickr. From each video clip, a single image frame is extracted together with 20 s of audio centered around it, to form the corresponding audio-visual pairs used for unsupervised learning. We also conduct experiments on **VGG-Sound** composed of 200k video clips from 309 sound categories. Similar to the Flickr dataset, the video is represented by a single frame as well as its audio. To enable direct comparisons with existing work [2, 6, 28, 30], we trained our models using subsets of either 10k or 144k image-audio pairs.

Localization performance is measured on two datasets, the Flickr SoundNet test set [30] and the more challenging VGG-Sound Sources test set [6]. The former includes only 250 image-audio pairs for which the location of the sound source has been manually annotated. The latter contains annotations for 5000 instances spanning 220 sounding objects categories.

Table 1. Localization performance on the Flickr SoundNet testset.

Method	CIoU (%)	AUC (%)	Method	CIoU (%)	AUC (%)
Attention10k [30]	43.60	44.90	Attention10k [30]	66.00	55.80
CoarsetoFine [28]	52.20	49.60	DMC [17]	67.10	56.80
AVObject [2]	54.60	50.40	LVS [6]	69.90	57.30
LVS [6]	58.20	52.50	HardPos [31]	75.20	59.70
EZ-VSL (ours)	**81.93**	**62.58**	EZ-VSL (ours)	**83.13**	**63.06**
(a) Training set: Flickr 10k			(b) Training set: Flickr 144k		

Audio and Visual Pre-processing. The input to the visual encoder $f_v(\cdot)$ are images of resolution 224×224. During training, images are first resized to 246 along the shortest edge, and random cropping together with random horizontal flipping is applied for data augmentation. At test time, images directly resized into a 224×224 resolution without cropping.

The audio encoder $f_a(\cdot)$ takes the log spectrograms extracted from 3 s of audio extracted at a sample rate of 11025 Hz. The underlying STFT are computed using approximately 50 ms windows with a hop size of 25 ms, resulting in an input tensor of size 257×300 (257 frequency bands over 300 timesteps). No data augmentations are applied during train or test time.

Audio and Visual Models. Both the visual and audio encoders are implemented using the lightweight ResNet18 [15] as the backbone. Following prior work [6, 17, 28], we initialized the visual model using weights pre-train on ImageNet [8]. Unless otherwise specified, the audio and visual representations are projected into a shared space of dimension 512.

The model is trained with a batch size of 128 on 2 GPUs. For efficiency, we only use negatives from the local batch, i.e. we did not gather negatives from all GPUs. This results in a negative set of 63 samples for the contrastive learning objective of (3). The model is trained using the Adam optimizer [20] with a learning rate of $1e - 4$, and default hyper-parameters $\beta_1 = 0.9, \beta_2 = 0.999$. On large datasets (144k or the full VGG-Sound database), the model is trained for 20 epochs. On smaller (10k) datasets, the model is trained for 100 epochs.

Table 2. Localization performance on Flickr SoundNet and VGG-SS after training on VGG-Sound 144k.

Training set	Method	Flickr-SoundNet		VGG-SS	
		CIoU (%)	AUC (%)	CIoU (%)	AUC (%)
VGG-Sound 144k	Attention10k [30]	66.00	55.80	18.50	30.20
	CoarsetoFine [28]	-	-	29.10	34.80
	AVObject [2]	-	-	29.70	35.70
	LVS [6]	73.50	59.00	34.40	38.20
	HardPos [31]	76.80	59.20	34.60	38.00
	EZ-VSL (ours)	**83.94**	**63.60**	**38.85**	**39.54**

4.2   Comparison to Prior Work

In this work, we propose a simple yet highly effective training framework for visual sound source localization. To demonstrate the effectiveness of our approach, EZ-VSL, we start by drawing direct comparisons to previous works [2, 6,28,30] on two popular benchmarks: Flickr SoundNet [17] and VGG-SS [6]. Results are reported in Tables 1 and 2 for models trained on Flickr SoundNet and VGG-SS, respectively.

As can be seen, EZ-VSL outperforms prior work by large margins, establishing new state-of-the-art results in all settings. On the Flickr test set, we observe performance gains of 23.73% CIoU and 10.08% AUC when models are trained on Flickr 10k, by 7.93% CIoU and 3.36% AUC when trained on Flickr 144k, and by 7.14% CIoU and 4.4% AUC when trained on VGG-Sound 144k. Significant gains can also be observed on the more challenging VGG-Sound Sources test set, with EZ-VSL outperforming prior work by 4.25% CIoU and 1.34% AUC.

We highlight that these gains are obtained with a significantly simplified training objective. For example, Attention10K [30] relies on the construction of positive (sounding) regions for its visual attention mechanism, and both LVS [7] and HardPos [31] require not only the construction of likely positive (sounding) regions but also negative (non-sounding) regions. This highlights the importance of a well-designed training framework that avoids imposing complex region-specific constraints. Also, note that our method combines both the novel multiple instance contrastive learning loss used for training and the novel object-centric localization procedure used during inference. The effect of these individual components will be studied below.

4.3   Open Set Audio-Visual Localization

To assess generalization, we evaluated the ability of EZ-VSL to generalize beyond the categories of sound sources heard during self-supervised training. Following previous work [6], we randomly sampled 110 categories from VGG-Sound for training. We then evaluate our model on test samples from these heard categories, as well as on samples from another 110 unheard categories. Since unseen categories can be semantically related to the seen ones, we expect that good representations to generalize to unseen categories as well. The results are shown in Table 3. As can be seen, our approach outperforms LVS [6] by a significant margin on both heard and unheard categories. In fact, unlike LVS, the performance of our EZ-VSL model did not suffer by the presence of unheard sound categories, achieving even slightly better performance on unheard classes than on heard classes. This provides evidence for the stronger generalization ability of EZ-VSL in an open set setting.

Table 3. Comparison results on VGG-SS for open set audio-visual localization trained on 70k data with heard 110 classes.

Test class	Method	CIoU (%)	AUC (%)
Heard 110	LVS [6]	28.90	36.20
	EZ-VSL	**37.25**	**38.97**
Unheard 110	LVS [6]	26.30	34.70
	EZ-VSL	**39.57**	**39.60**

4.4 Cross Dataset Generalization

To further evaluate generalization, we tested models across datasets. Specifically, we tested the model trained on VGG-Sound on Flickr SoundNet, and test the Flickr trained model on the VGG-SS test set. As can be seen in Table 4, our approach outperforms the best previous method [6] when testing across datasets.

Table 4. Cross dataset generalization results of Flickr SoundNet and VGG-SS trained on various training sets, including VGG-Sound 10k, 144k, Full and Flickr 10k, 144k.

Test set	Training set	Method	CIoU (%)	AUC (%)
Flickr SoundNet	VGG-Sound 10k	LVS [6]	61.80	53.60
		EZ-VSL	**78.71**	**61.56**
	VGG-Sound 144k	LVS [6]	71.90	58.20
		EZ-VSL	**84.34**	**63.77**
	VGG-Sound Full	LVS [6]	73.59	59.00
		EZ-VSL	**83.94**	**63.60**
VGG-SS	Flickr 10k	LVS [6]	18.71	30.29
		EZ-VSL	**35.54**	**38.18**
	Flickr 144k	LVS [6]	26.95	34.30
		EZ-VSL	**38.62**	**39.20**

4.5 Experimental Analysis

We conducted extensive ablation studies to explore the benefits of the two main components of our approach: multiple instance contrastive learning (MICL) and object-guided localization (OGL). We also conducted several parametric studies to assess the impact of hyper-parameters such as the size of shared audio-visual latent space, the audio-visual fusion strategy, or the balancing coefficient α used for OGL. All experiments were trained on the VGG-Sounds full training set and evaluated on Flickr-SoundNet and VGG-Sound Source (VGG-SS) test sets.

Disentangling the Benefits of MICL and OGL. We ablated the use of MICL and OGL to verify their effectiveness. Models evaluated without MICL only use the object guided localization maps extracted from the pre-trained ResNet-18, without any further training. Models evaluated without OGL only use the audio-visual localization (AVL) maps learned using MICL. We further evaluate two strategies for OGL, namely, classification based OGL (CLS-OGL) described in (7) and activation based OGL (L1-OGL) described in (8).

Results are shown in Table 5. Comparing the performance of each component in isolation (first three rows of Table 5) to those in Table 2, we highlight that both AVL and L1-OGL already surpass prior state-of-the-art (LVS [6]). The strong performance of L1-OGL is especially noteworthy, as it does not even use the audio. We attribute this result to two reasons. First, object regions are more likely to depict sound sources. Second, the majority of test samples in both Flickr and VGG-SS only contain a single sounding object in the scene. This is more prevalent in Flickr but is still true for VGG-SS. As a result, the object prior already provides strong localization results, outperforming all prior work. We nevertheless improve over OGL, by combining it with audio-visual localization.

Table 5. Ablation study on the impact of audio-visual localization (AVL) maps and two object-guided localization strategies (CLS and L1 prior) during inference.

AVL	L1-OGL	CLS-OGL	Flickr SoundNet		VGG-SS	
			CIoU (%)	AUC (%)	CIoU (%)	AUC (%)
✓			78.31	61.74	35.96	38.20
	✓		78.31	61.17	36.77	38.69
		✓	75.10	58.18	35.13	38.08
✓		✓	81.93	62.50	38.58	39.59
✓	✓		**83.94**	**63.60**	**39.34**	**39.78**

Among the two OGL strategies, L1-OGL was the most effective, and thus used as the default strategy for EZ-VSL. We also evaluated the localization performance for various values of the balancing coefficient α between AVL and L1-OGL localization maps. The results in Fig. 3 show that both OGL and AVL components are important for accurate localization, as $\alpha = 0$ or $\alpha = 1$ yields the worse performance. The optimal value of α for Flickr was 0.4 and for VGG-SS was 0.5. $\alpha = 0.4$ was used as the default for all experiments in this paper.

Dimensionality of Shared Audio-Visual Latent Space. The impact of the latent space dimensionality is shown in Fig. 4. The models were trained on VGG-Sound with latent space of size 32, 64, 128, 256, 512, 1024, 2048, 4096, and tested on Flickr SoundNet and VGG-SS. Figure 4 shows that significantly reducing or increasing the unimodal feature dimensionality (512) can have a negative impact on performance.

Audio-Visual Matching Strategy During Training. The proposed EZ-VSL method uses a max pooling strategy for measuring the similarity between the global audio feature A and the bag of localized visual features $V = \{V_{xy} : \forall x, y\}$, i.e., using $\text{MaxPool}_{xy}(\text{sim}(V_{xy}, A))$. We validate this strategy by comparing two alternatives. First, average pooling is a popular strategy for gathering responses across instances in a bag [18]. We follow this approach and train a model that seeks to match the global audio feature to the visual features at *all* locations, i.e., using $\text{sim}(\text{AvgPool}_{xy}(V_{xy}), A)$. Second, prior work on audio-visual representation learning [3,21,25,27] learn by matching global features. We also tested this class of methods by training a model that pools the visual features before matching to the audio, i.e., using $\text{sim}(\text{MaxPool}_{xy}(V_{xy}), A)$.

The localization performance of all three strategies are reported in Table 6. Since only audio-visual localization maps are impacted by the different training strategies, we set $\alpha = 1$ in this experiment to ignore object-guided localization maps. As can be seen, the two alternative strategies failed to localize sounding objects accurately. On one hand, matching global features lacks the ability to learn localized representations. On the other hand, forcing the audio to match the image at all locations is also inherently problematic, since most regions do not contain a sounding object. The proposed approach achieves significantly better localization performance. However, it assumes that there is at least one sounding object visible in the image. While this is generally true in both VGG-Sound and Flickr SoundNet training sets, further experiments on datasets with non-visible sound sources would be required to assess the robustness of EZ-VSL to this more challenging training scenario.

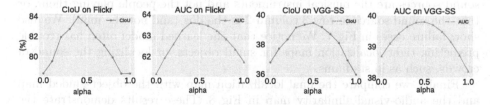

Fig. 3. Impact of α (trade-off between AVL and OGL) on EZ-VSL performance.

Multiple Sound Source Localization. Since complex scenes are known to be more challenging for localization methods, the VGG-SS dataset provide a further

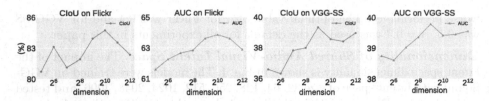

Fig. 4. Impact of the output dimensionality on EZ-VSL performance.

Table 6. Impact of different audio-visual matching strategies during training on audio-visual localization performance. V_{xy} denotes the visual embedding at location (x, y), and **A** the global audio embedding. Only the audio-visual localization maps are evaluated in this experiment, without being merged with object-guided localization maps.

AV matching strategy	Flickr SoundNet		VGG-SS	
	CIoU (%)	AUC (%)	CIoU (%)	AUC (%)
$\mathrm{sim}(\mathrm{MaxPool}_{xy}(V_{xy}), A)$	49.40	48.97	12.72	27.10
$\mathrm{AvgPool}_{xy}(\mathrm{sim}(V_{xy}, A))$	33.33	37.56	6.03	19.44
$\mathrm{MaxPool}_{xy}(\mathrm{sim}(V_{xy}, A))$	**78.31**	**61.74**	**35.96**	**38.20**

breakdown of test samples per the number of objects. As shown in Fig. 5, similar to prior work, the performance of EZ-VSL does degrade as the scene becomes more complex. However, EZ-VSL consistently outperform prior work regardless of the number of objects.

4.6   Qualitative Results

To better understand the capabilities of the learned model, we show in Fig. 6 sound localization predictions of an EZ-VSL model trained on the VGG-SS 144k dataset. As can be seen, the model is capable of accurately localizing a wide variety of sound sources, showing high overlap with the ground-truth bounding boxes. For example, in row 2, column 4, the model was able to identify that the sound sources are the musical instruments and not the people playing them, or that the sound source in row 3 column 2 is the dog (and not the man). We also show failure cases in Fig. 7. We notice that the learned model often has trouble predicting tight localization maps for small objects, or localizing the sound of crowds, such as in stadiums.

Finally, we compare the final localization map with the object-guided map and the audio-visual similarity map in Fig. 8. These results demonstrate the effectiveness of combining object-guided and audio-visual localization in visual sound localization.

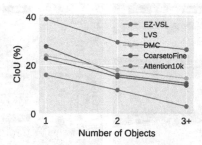

Fig. 5. Localization performance vs number of objects in the scene. Although all methods suffer as the number of objects increase, the proposed EZ-VSL consistently outperforms prior work.

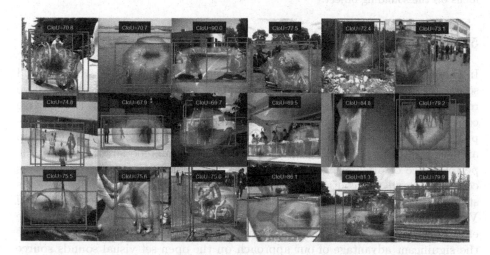

Fig. 6. Predicted localization maps on Flickr SoundNet test images.

Fig. 7. Failure cases of EZ-VSL. Typical cases which EZ-VSL still struggles to accurately localize sound sources include small objects, or when sounds are not produced by objects, such as the sound of crowds.

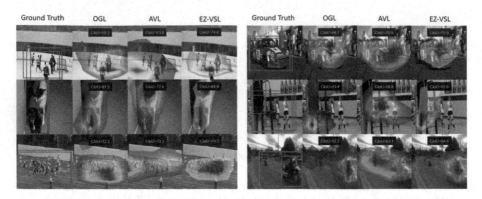

Fig. 8. Sound source localization by OGL, AVL, and our EZ-VSL. Object-guided maps tend to cover all objects in the scene; audio-video similarity maps often cover the sounding object and some non-object regions; the final EZ-VSL map tends to better focus on the sounding object.

5   Conclusion

In this work, we present the EZ-VSL, a simple yet effective approach for visual sounds source localization, with no need to explicitly compute the negative regions. Specifically, a simple cross-entropy loss is applied to learn the relative correspondence between the visual and audio instances. Furthermore, we propose a novel object-guided localization scheme to mix the audio-visual joint map and the object map from a lightweight pre-trained visual model for boosting the performance of orientating sound sources in an image. Compared to previous contrastive and non-contrastive baselines, our framework successfully achieves state-of-the-art performance on two popular benchmarks, Flickr SoundNet and VGG-Sound Source. Comprehensive ablation studies are conducted to show the effectiveness of each component in our simple method. We also demonstrate the significant advantage of our approach on the open set visual sounds source localization and cross dataset generalization.

References

1. Afouras, T., Chung, J.S., Zisserman, A.: Deep lip reading: a comparison of models and an online application. In: Proceedings of Interspeech (2018)
2. Afouras, T., Owens, A., Chung, J.S., Zisserman, A.: Self-supervised learning of audio-visual objects from video. In: Vedaldi, A., Bischof, H., Brox, T., Frahm, J.-M. (eds.) ECCV 2020. LNCS, vol. 12363, pp. 208–224. Springer, Cham (2020). https://doi.org/10.1007/978-3-030-58523-5_13
3. Arandjelovic, R., Zisserman, A.: Look, listen and learn. In: Proceedings of the IEEE International Conference on Computer Vision (ICCV), pp. 609–617 (2017)
4. Aytar, Y., Vondrick, C., Torralba, A.: Soundnet: learning sound representations from unlabeled video. In: Proceedings of Advances in Neural Information Processing Systems (NeurIPS) (2016)

5. Chen, C., et al.: SoundSpaces: audio-visual navigation in 3D environments. In: Vedaldi, A., Bischof, H., Brox, T., Frahm, J.-M. (eds.) ECCV 2020. LNCS, vol. 12351, pp. 17–36. Springer, Cham (2020). https://doi.org/10.1007/978-3-030-58539-6_2

6. Chen, H., Xie, W., Afouras, T., Nagrani, A., Vedaldi, A., Zisserman, A.: Localizing visual sounds the hard way. In: Proceedings of the IEEE/CVF Conference on Computer Vision and Pattern Recognition (CVPR), pp. 16867–16876 (2021)

7. Chen, H., Xie, W., Vedaldi, A., Zisserman, A.: VGGSound: a large-scale audio-visual dataset. In: ICASSP 2020–2020 IEEE International Conference on Acoustics, Speech and Signal Processing (ICASSP), pp. 721–725. IEEE (2020)

8. Deng, J., Dong, W., Socher, R., Li, L.J., Li, K., Fei-Fei, L.: ImageNet: a large-scale hierarchical image database. In: Proceedings of IEEE/CVF Conference on Computer Vision and Pattern Recognition (CVPR), pp. 248–255 (2009)

9. Fisher III, J.W., Darrell, T., Freeman, W., Viola, P.: Learning joint statistical models for audio-visual fusion and segregation. In: Proceedings of Advances in Neural Information Processing Systems (NeurIPS) (2000)

10. Gan, C., Huang, D., Zhao, H., Tenenbaum, J.B., Torralba, A.: Music gesture for visual sound separation. In: IEEE/CVF Conference on Computer Vision and Pattern Recognition (CVPR), pp. 10478–10487 (2020)

11. Gan, C., Zhao, H., Chen, P., Cox, D., Torralba, A.: Self-supervised moving vehicle tracking with stereo sound. In: Proceedings of the IEEE/CVF International Conference on Computer Vision (ICCV), pp. 7053–7062 (2019)

12. Gao, R., Feris, R., Grauman, K.: Learning to separate object sounds by watching unlabeled video. In: Proceedings of the European Conference on Computer Vision (ECCV), pp. 35–53 (2018)

13. Gao, R., Grauman, K.: 2.5D visual sound. In: Proceedings of the IEEE/CVF Conference on Computer Vision and Pattern Recognition (CVPR), pp. 324–333 (2019)

14. Gao, R., Grauman, K.: Co-separating sounds of visual objects. In: Proceedings of the IEEE/CVF International Conference on Computer Vision (ICCV), pp. 3879–3888 (2019)

15. He, K., Zhang, X., Ren, S., Sun, J.: Deep residual learning for image recognition. In: Proceedings of IEEE/CVF Conference on Computer Vision and Pattern Recognition (CVPR), pp. 770–778 (2016)

16. Hershey, J., Movellan, J.: Audio vision: using audio-visual synchrony to locate sounds. In: Proceedings of Advances in Neural Information Processing Systems (NeurIPS) (1999)

17. Hu, D., Nie, F., Li, X.: Deep multimodal clustering for unsupervised audiovisual learning. In: Proceedings of the IEEE Conference on Computer Vision and Pattern Recognition (CVPR), pp. 9248–9257 (2019)

18. Ilse, M., Tomczak, J.M., Welling, M.: Attention-based deep multiple instance learning. In: Proceedings of the International Conference on Machine Learning (ICML), pp. 2127–2136 (2018)

19. Kidron, E., Schechner, Y.Y., Elad, M.: Pixels that sound. In: Proceedings of IEEE Conference on Computer Vision and Pattern Recognition (CVPR) (2005)

20. Kingma, D.P., Ba, J.: Adam: a method for stochastic optimization. arXiv preprint arXiv:1412.6980 (2014)

21. Korbar, B., Tran, D., Torresani, L.: Cooperative learning of audio and video models from self-supervised synchronization. In: Proceedings of Advances in Neural Information Processing Systems (NeurIPS) (2018)

22. Morgado, P., Li, Y., Nvasconcelos, N.: Learning representations from audio-visual spatial alignment. In: Proceedings of Advances in Neural Information Processing Systems (NeurIPS), pp. 4733–4744 (2020)
23. Morgado, P., Misra, I., Vasconcelos, N.: Robust audio-visual instance discrimination. In: Proceedings of the IEEE/CVF Conference on Computer Vision and Pattern Recognition (CVPR), pp. 12934–12945 (2021)
24. Morgado, P., Nvasconcelos, N., Langlois, T., Wang, O.: Self-supervised generation of spatial audio for 360 video. In: Proceedings of Advances in Neural Information Processing Systems (NeurIPS) (2018)
25. Morgado, P., Vasconcelos, N., Misra, I.: Audio-visual instance discrimination with cross-modal agreement. In: Proceedings of the IEEE/CVF Conference on Computer Vision and Pattern Recognition (CVPR), pp. 12475–12486, June 2021
26. Owens, A., Efros, A.A.: Audio-visual scene analysis with self-supervised multisensory features. In: Proceedings of the European Conference on Computer Vision (ECCV), pp. 631–648 (2018)
27. Owens, A., Wu, J., McDermott, J.H., Freeman, W.T., Torralba, A.: Ambient sound provides supervision for visual learning. In: Leibe, B., Matas, J., Sebe, N., Welling, M. (eds.) ECCV 2016. LNCS, vol. 9905, pp. 801–816. Springer, Cham (2016). https://doi.org/10.1007/978-3-319-46448-0_48
28. Qian, R., Hu, D., Dinkel, H., Wu, M., Xu, N., Lin, W.: Multiple sound sources localization from coarse to fine. In: Vedaldi, A., Bischof, H., Brox, T., Frahm, J.-M. (eds.) ECCV 2020. LNCS, vol. 12365, pp. 292–308. Springer, Cham (2020). https://doi.org/10.1007/978-3-030-58565-5_18
29. Rouditchenko, A., Zhao, H., Gan, C., McDermott, J.H., Torralba, A.: Self-supervised audio-visual co-segmentation. In: Proceedings of IEEE International Conference on Acoustics, Speech and Signal Processing (ICASSP), pp. 2357–2361 (2019)
30. Senocak, A., Oh, T.H., Kim, J., Yang, M.H., Kweon, I.S.: Learning to localize sound source in visual scenes. In: Proceedings of the IEEE Conference on Computer Vision and Pattern Recognition (CVPR), pp. 4358–4366 (2018)
31. Senocak, A., Ryu, H., Kim, J., Kweon, I.S.: Learning sound localization better from semantically similar samples. In: Proceedings of IEEE International Conference on Acoustics, Speech and Signal Processing (ICASSP) (2022)
32. Son Chung, J., Senior, A., Vinyals, O., Zisserman, A.: Lip reading sentences in the wild. In: Proceedings of the IEEE Conference on Computer Vision and Pattern Recognition (CVPR), pp. 6447–6456 (2017)
33. Tian, Y., Li, D., Xu, C.: Unified multisensory perception: weakly-supervised audio-visual video parsing. In: Vedaldi, A., Bischof, H., Brox, T., Frahm, J.-M. (eds.) ECCV 2020. LNCS, vol. 12348, pp. 436–454. Springer, Cham (2020). https://doi.org/10.1007/978-3-030-58580-8_26
34. Wang, L., Xiong, Y., Lin, D., Van Gool, L.: Untrimmednets for weakly supervised action recognition and detection. In: Proceedings of the IEEE Conference on Computer Vision and Pattern Recognition (CVPR), pp. 4325–4334 (2017)
35. Zhao, H., Gan, C., Ma, W.C., Torralba, A.: The sound of motions. In: Proceedings of the IEEE/CVF International Conference on Computer Vision (ICCV), pp. 1735–1744 (2019)
36. Zhao, H., et al.: The sound of pixels. In: Proceedings of the European Conference on Computer Vision (ECCV), pp. 570–586 (2018)

Learning Visual Styles from Audio-Visual Associations

Tingle Li[1,3(✉)], Yichen Liu[1], Andrew Owens[2], and Hang Zhao[1,3]

[1] Tsinghua University, Beijing, China
[2] University of Michigan, Ann Arbor, USA
[3] Shanghai Qi Zhi Institute, Shanghai, China
https://tinglok.netlify.com/files/avstyle

Abstract. From the patter of rain to the crunch of snow, the sounds we hear often convey the visual textures that appear within a scene. In this paper, we present a method for learning visual styles from unlabeled audio-visual data. Our model learns to manipulate the texture of a scene to match a sound, a problem we term *audio-driven image stylization*. Given a dataset of paired audio-visual data, we learn to modify input images such that, after manipulation, they are more likely to co-occur with a given input sound. In quantitative and qualitative evaluations, our sound-based model outperforms label-based approaches. We also show that audio can be an intuitive representation for manipulating images, as adjusting a sound's volume or mixing two sounds together results in predictable changes to visual style.

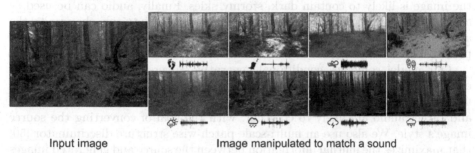

Input image　　　　　　　　Image manipulated to match a sound

Fig. 1. Audio-driven image stylization. We manipulate the style of an image to match a sound. After training with an unlabeled dataset of egocentric hiking videos, our model learns visual styles for a variety of ambient sounds, such as light and heavy rain, as well as physical interactions, such as footsteps.

1 Introduction

Recent work has proposed a variety f methods for manipulating the style [19,59] of an input image. In these methods, the desired style is specified using other

---

Supplementary Information The online version contains supplementary material available at https://doi.org/10.1007/978-3-031-19836-6_14.

example images [19,27,30,33] and, more recently, through human language, such as through semantic labels, text, or scene graphs [4,34,55,56]. While this approach has been effective, it requires human-provided annotations and hence implicitly relies on a "human in the loop." This supervision is often expensive to collect and may fail to capture important scene properties.

We propose to address these problems by learning stylization from *unlabeled audio-visual* data. Many scene properties, such as weather conditions, produce highly distinctive sights and sounds. Training a model to estimate visual information from audio requires it to identify these scene structures and, in the process, learn which visual textures are associated with a sound.

Inspired by this idea, we introduce a model for performing *audio-driven* image stylization. Given an input image and a target sound, our model manipulates the textures within the image such that it better matches the sound, while preserving the image's structural content. Through this process, our model learns a variety of visual styles, each of which can be specified by a sound—e.g., bird chirps and blue skies, crunching footsteps and snow, rain and dark skies (Fig. 1).

Audio naturally comes paired with visual data, and thus provides a free learning signal, complementing human-provided supervision like labels and text. It also conveys important distinctions between scenes that often may not be evident in pre-existing text or label sets. For example, asking a model to generate images depicting a "rainy" scene can be ambiguous. Providing the sound of rain, on the other hand, specifies whether the rain is light or heavy, as well as whether the image is likely to contain dark, stormy skies. Finally, audio can be used as a natural representation for specifying image styles, as intuitive changes to the audio, such as adjusting the volume or mixing two sounds together, result in predictable visual changes.

Our model combines conditional generative adversarial networks [22] and contrastive learning [23], following the recent approach of Park et al. [50]. We use an audio-visual discriminator to determine whether the generated image and target audio are likely to co-occur, with the goal of converting the source image's style. We also use an multi-scale patch-wise structure discriminator [50] that maximizes the mutual information between the source and generated images in order to preserve the structural content of the scene. We train the model on a dataset of egocentric hiking videos collected from the internet.

After training, our model can manipulate images to match a variety of visual styles, each specified using sound. Through quantitative evaluations and human perceptual studies, we demonstrate the effectiveness of our model's ability to stylize images. We also provide qualitative results showing how that straightforwardly modifying the audio, by mixing it or changing its volume, leads to corresponding changes in image style. Through our evaluations, we show:

- Unlabeled audio provides supervision for learning visual styles.
- Our proposed model learns to perform audio-driven stylization from in-the-wild audio-visual data.
- Adjusting the volume of a sound or mixing it with other sounds lead to predictable changes in image style.

2   Related Work

Image Translation. Paired image translation [32] frames the image prediction problem as a straightforward supervised learning task, which corresponding input and target images. Unpaired image translation [22,35,50,63,70] learns to transform images between two different domains, without ground-truth correspondences. We take inspiration from work [38] that manipulates the global appearance of a scene, such as through labels indicating the desired weather. A variety of methods have been proposed generate or manipulate images based on text [4,13,46,55,56]. In particular, our approach is closely related to Fu et al. [15], which stylizes images based on text. However, text- and label-based methods either require "weak" supervision [42,54] from humans (e.g., paired text and images from webpages) or explicit image descriptions (e.g., text describing an image as a line drawing) [61]. These descriptions may not capture the full range of image styles, and it requires significant effort from humans (including *implicit* effort through weak supervision). Our approach, by contrast, uses audio to learn styles, without any form of human labeling. It therefore provides a *complementary* learning signal to text and labels.

Audio-Visual Correspondence. Audio and visual signals naturally co-occur when they are recorded as video. In order to leverage this natural correspondence, researchers have introduced various tasks, such as representation learning [2,37,45,47,48,57], source separation [14,17,65,66], audio source grounding [6,24], audio spatialization [18,44,62], visual speech recognition [1], and scene classification [7,20]. Inspired by these works that use audio-visual correspondence, we propose a novel task termed audio-driven image stylization, aiming to conduct image translation using sounds like birds chirping, rain and footsteps.

Audio-Visual Synthesis. A variety of methods have been proposed for synthesizing images from sound or vice versa. One line of work has generated sounds from video, such as impact sounds [49,64], natural sounds [31,69], or human speech [29,52]. Another line of work has created models that synthesize images from sound, such as by generating talking heads [11,53,68], pose [16,21,41,58], synchronizing rigid body animations with contact sounds [39], estimating depth from ambient sound [9], predicting future video frames [5]. Unlike these works, we concentrate on restyling plausible images using the source image and natural sounds. In concurrent work, Lee et al. [40] used sound to guide a text-based image manipulation method based on CLIP [54]. In contrast, our model learns image styles solely from unlabeled audio-visual data.

3   Audio-Driven Image Stylization

We take inspiration from the fact that audio can convey distinctions that may not be obvious from semantic categories. For example, consider the images shown in Fig. 2. While these videos have the same category (e.g., rain), their visual style significantly varies (e.g., heavy or light rain). This distinction, however, is easily captured by the corresponding sound. We propose *audio-driven* image stylization (ADIS) as a novel multi-modal generation task for learning these styles.

We pose this problem as learning a mapping from a source image domain $\mathcal{X}$ to a target domain $\mathcal{Y}$ using an input sound from the audio domain $\mathcal{A}$. To achieve this goal, we propose a self-supervised learning approach that can be trained on unpaired

Footstep Sound

Rain Sound

Fig. 2. Categories can fail to convey subtle distinctions between events. We show frames whose corresponding sounds were classified as *footstep* or *rain* [20,51].

videos. This can be accomplished through two distinct training objectives.

Texture Conversion via Adversarial Training. We introduce an audio-visual adversarial objective that discriminates whether an image is co-occurred with a given audio. Under this training scheme, the generated image is encouraged to match the target audio. Specifically, the generator G consists of two components, an encoder G_{enc} followed by a decoder G_{dec}. For a given dataset of unpaired image instances $X = \{x \in \mathcal{X}\}$, $Y = \{y \in \mathcal{Y}\}$, and the audios $A_Y = \{a_Y \in \mathcal{A}\}$ corresponding to Y, G_{enc} and G_{dec} are applied sequentially to generate the output image $\hat{y} = G_{\text{dec}}(\text{concat}(G_{\text{enc}}(x), f(a_Y)))$, where f is a audio feature extractor.

The audio-visual adversarial loss [22] is then applied to increase the association between $\hat{y}$ and a_Y:

$$\mathcal{L}_{\text{GAN}}(G_{X \rightarrow Y}, D_Y) = \mathbb{E}_{y \sim Y} \log D(y, a_Y) \\ + \mathbb{E}_{x \sim X} \log\left(1 - D(G(x, f(a_Y)), a_Y)\right) \tag{1}$$

where D is the discriminator. In our model, D performs early fusion, where the spectrogram of a_Y is directly concatenated to $\hat{y} = G(x, a_Y)$ before feeding into D. We empirically found that this fusion strategy yields better results in terms of visual quality.

Structure Preservation via Contrastive Learning. In this task, a successfully restyled image should be equipped with the texture that can be interpreted by the target audio, while fully preserving the structure of the source image. However, both information, *i.e.*, texture and structure information, are inherently entangled within the learned feature, and adversarial training can only convert texture. One trivial solution could be that we get the same image for any inputs. Therefore, as shown in Fig. 3, we introduce the second training objective based on noise contrastive estimation (NCE) [23], which aims to preserve structure information by establishing mutual correspondence between the source and generated images, x and $\hat{y}$ respectively. Note that this training objective is only employed to the encoder network G_{enc}, which is a multi-layer convolutional network that transforms the source image into feature stacks at each layer. In this way, we encourage G_{enc} to abandon the texture of the source image while

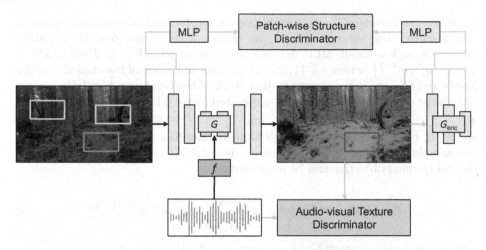

Fig. 3. Model architecture. The multi-scale patch-wise structure discriminator [50] is used to preserve the scene structure, while the audio-visual texture discriminator is used to convert the scene texture. This is an example where sunny forest is converted to snowy counterpart. The generated snow patch should match its corresponding input dirt patch, in comparison to other random patches. Note that the MLP component is not used during inference.

preserving the structure, and then the job of the decoder network G_{dec} is to integrate the target texture to the source image.

Given a "query" vector q, the objective in contrastive learning is to optimize the probability of selecting the corresponding "positive" sample v^+ among N "negative" samples v^-. The query, positive and N negatives are mapped to M-dimensional vectors by a MLP, i.e., $q, v^+ \in \mathbb{R}^M$ and $v^- \in \mathbb{R}^{N \times M}$. This problem setting can be expressed as a multi-classification task with $N + 1$ classes:

$$\ell(q, v^+, v^-) = -\log\left(\frac{\exp(q \cdot v^+/\tau)}{\exp(q \cdot v^+/\tau) + \Sigma_{n=1}^{N} \exp(q \cdot v_n^-/\tau)}\right) \quad (2)$$

where v_n^- denotes the n-th negative sample and τ is a temperature parameter, as suggested in SimCLR [8], that scales the similarity distance between q and other samples. The cross-entropy term in Eq. (2) represents the probability of matching q with the corresponding positive sample v^+. Thus, iteratively minimizing the negative log-cross-entropy is equivalent to establishing mutual correspondence between the query and sample spaces.

In our task, we draw the $N + 1$ positive/negative samples from the source image $x \in X$, and the query q is selected from the generated image $\hat{y}$. From Fig. 3, it can be seen that the selected samples are "patches" that capture local information among the image features. This setup is motivated by the logical assumption that the global correspondence between x and $\hat{y}$ is determined by the local, i.e., patch-wise, correspondences.

Since the encoder G_{enc} is a multi-layer convolutional network that maps x into feature stacks after each layer, we choose L layers and pass their feature stacks through a small MLP network P. The output of P is $P(G_{\text{enc}}^l(x)) = \{v_l^1, ..., v_l^N, v_l^{N+1}\}$, where $l \in \{1, 2..., L\}$ denotes the index of the chosen encoder layers and $G_{\text{enc}}^l(x)$ is the output feature stack of the l-th layer. Similarly, we can obtain the query set by encoding the generated image $\hat{y}$ into $\{q_l^1, ..., q_l^N, q_l^{N+1}\} = P(G_{\text{enc}}^l(\hat{y}))$. Now we let $v_l^n \in \mathbb{R}^M$ and $v_l^{(N+1)\backslash n} \in \mathbb{R}^{N \times M}$ denote the corresponding positive sample and the N negative samples, respectively, where n is the sample index and M is the channel size of P. By referring to Eq. (2), our second training objective can be expressed as:

$$\mathcal{L}_{\text{NCE}}(G_{\text{enc}}, P, X) = \mathbb{E}_{x \sim X} \sum_{l=1}^{L} \sum_{n=1}^{N+1} \ell(q_l^n, v_l^n, v_l^{(N+1)\backslash n}) \qquad (3)$$

which is the average NCE loss from all L encoder layers.

Overall Objective. In addition to the two objectives discussed above, we have also employed an identity loss $\mathcal{L}_{\text{identity}} = \mathcal{L}_{\text{NCE}}(G_{\text{enc}}, P, Y)$ which also leverages the NCE expression in Eq. (3). By taking the NCE loss on the identity generation process, *i.e.*, generating $\hat{y}$ from y, we are likely to prevent the generator from making unexpected changes. Now we can define our final training objective as:

$$\begin{aligned}\mathcal{L}_{\text{final}} =& \mathcal{L}_{\text{GAN}}(G_{X \to Y}, D_Y) + \lambda \mathcal{L}_{\text{NCE}}(G_{\text{enc}}, P, X) \\ &+ \mu \mathcal{L}_{\text{NCE}}(G_{\text{enc}}, P, Y)\end{aligned} \qquad (4)$$

where λ and μ are two parameters for adjusting the strengths of the NCE and identity loss.

4 Experiments

4.1 Experimental Setup

Dataset. We perform ADIS with two different datasets: *Greatest Hits* and *Into the Wild*. The former provides impact sounds from different materials, while the latter is a new dataset of egocentric hiking videos.

- *Into the Wild* **dataset**: We collect a new dataset to study the audio-visual associations that one would encounter on a hike (Fig. 4). These include sounds that are related to seasonal variations, rainfall, animal vocalizations, and footsteps. We collect 94 untrimmed egocentric videos from YouTube, ranging from 1.5 to 130 min long (50 h in total). We chose videos that only contain sounds naturally present in the scene (*e.g.*, no background music). See Appendix A.1 for more dataset details.
- **The *Greatest Hits* dataset** [49]: The *Greatest Hits* dataset contains a drumstick hitting, scratching, and poking different objects in both indoor and outdoor scenes. There are 977 videos in total, including both indoor

(64%) and outdoor scenes (36%). However, since this dataset was originally gathered for sound generation, each video more or less contains visual noise, making it challenging to perform ADIS. For example, ceramic bowls have different colors but the hitting sounds are similar across all bowls. It can be sometimes difficult for the model to determine the texture of a material with different colors. To alleviate this issue, we manually select some outdoor scene videos with less diverse backgrounds, such as dirt, water, gravel and grass.

Network Architecture. The encoder and decoder of the GAN generator are 2D fully convolutional networks, with 9 layers of ResNet-based CNN bottlenecks [33] in between. Except for the first CNN layer with a kernel size of 7 × 7, the others are 3 × 3, and the

Fig. 4. Selected frames from the *Into the Wild* dataset. We show example images corresponding to the top-1 categorical sounds deduced by a classifier [20,51].

stride size is determined by whether downsampling is required. We used the PatchGAN architecture [32] for the discriminator. A ResNet18 backbone [25] is also used for extracting audio features before feeding them into the decoder of the GAN generator. Furthermore, before computing the NCE loss, we extract intermediate features from the encoder of the generator with five different scales, and then apply a 2-layer MLP with 256 units to map each feature.

Training Details. For training efficiency, we devise the following pre-processing paradigm: i) before saving as images, each video is interpolated to 512 × 512 scale and uniformly sampled 8 frames from it; ii) each audio is randomly truncated or tiled to a fixed duration of 3 s, then converted to 16 kHz and 32-bit precision in floating-point PCM format; iii) nnAudio [10] is used for conducting a 512-point discrete Fourier transform with a frame length of 25 ms and a frame-shift of 10 ms. For the hyperparameters, both λ and μ in Eq. (4) are set to 0.5. We also employ random crop and horizontal flip as data augmentation. Our model is trained using the Adam optimizer [36] with a batch size of 16 and an initial learning rate of 2×10^{-4} over 50 epochs. Other training strategies are described in Appendix A.2.

Evaluation Metrics. To get a better understanding of why audio is important, we quantitatively compare our model to several label-based baselines, using both objective and subjective metrics (see Appendix A.3 for more evaluation details):

- **Audio-visual Correspondence (AVC)** [2]: AVC measures the correlation between audio and image. In our case, we extract audio and visual features using OpenL3 [12], a variant of L3-Net [2] pre-trained on AudioSet [20], and then use those features to compute the average cosine similarity. A higher correlation is associated with a higher AVC score.

- **Fréchet Inception Distance (FID)** [28]: FID estimates the distribution of real and generated image activations using trained network and measures the divergence between them. A lower FID score indicates that real and generated images are more relevant.
- **Amazon Mechanical Turk (AMT)**: We use human participants to evaluate the audio-visual correlations (*i.e.*, via a subjective evaluation). Each participant is asked to rank the quality of the correlation between a sound and the images generated by various methods. The scores range from 1 (indicating low correlation) to 4 (high correlation).
- **Contrastive Language-Image Pretraining (CLIP)** [54]: CLIP is a network trained using contrastive learning to associate corresponding image and text pairs. In order to provide an additional evaluation metric that captures semantics, we use the keywords from the title of each video as text inputs to CLIP, then measure the text-image similarity. A higher CLIP score indicates a better correlation between a given text and image.

Baselines. We adopt two label-based methods for comparison. For both of them, Word2Vec [43] is used for generating the class embeddings, which is incorporated with the input image and serves as a textual condition. In addition, we create an image-conditioned baseline.

- **Class Pred.** [51]: we use YAMNet, a state-of-the-art audio classification network [26] trained on AudioSet [20], to calculate the class logits. It is employed as an auto-labeling method to yield the semantic labels for all the audio clips.
- **Keyword**: Keyword is a human-labeling method in which each audio class is manually labeled with keywords from the video title, thereby conveying the information provided in the video metadata.
- **AdaIN** [30]: AdaIN is an image-conditioned arbitrary stylization method that incorporates the adaptive instance normalization to fuse the content image and the style one. It takes two images as input and restyles one to match the other. Note that the style image is picked at random from the video frames corresponding to the selected audio.

4.2 Comparison to Baselines

Quantitative Results. Since the diverse hitting and scratching sounds are not well-modeled by AudioSet [20], which L3-Net [2] is trained on, we cannot meaningfully evaluate the *Greatest Hits* with the AVC metric. As a result, we only provide quantitative results yielded from the *Into the Wild* dataset. Table 1 shows the quantitative comparisons between our model and label/image-conditioned baselines. For objective evaluation, our model outperforms three baselines across the AVC, FID, and CLIP metrics, suggesting that our model can generate more realistic images. In particular, our method outperforms AdaIN

Table 1. Evaluation results on the *Into the Wild* dataset. The subjective AMT metric is presented with 95% confidence intervals.

Method	Evaluation metrics			
	AVC (↑)	FID (↓)	AMT (↑)	CLIP (↑)
Target	0.842	/	/	0.247
Class Pred. [51]	0.801	91.417	1.833 ± 0.042	0.228
AdaIN [30]	0.812	62.851	2.269 ± 0.044	0.232
Keyword	0.809	38.066	2.626 ± 0.045	0.236
Ours	**0.820**	**34.139**	**3.273 ± 0.046**	**0.238**

Table 2. AVC metric of specific scenes under our model and label-based baselines on the *Into the Wild* dataset.

Method	Audio-visual correspondence (↑)		
	Sunny-to-Rainy	Snowy-to-Sunny	Sunny-to-Snowy
Class Pred. [51]	0.819	0.796	0.793
Keyword	0.827	0.802	0.808
Ours	**0.831**	**0.820**	**0.816**

[30], despite the fact that AdaIN has already been pre-trained using ImageNet while ours is trained from scratch. We find that Keyword outperforms Class Pred., perhaps due to errors introduced by automatic labeling. Notably, Class Pred. contains 132 label classes from AudioSet, whereas Keyword only has 3 classes (sunny, snowy and rainy), which are all closely related to the scenes in *Into the Wild*. We also observe that the CLIP metric for our model is on par with Keyword, which also indicates the benefit of using audio over labels. For human evaluation, we randomly select 1000 images from the test set, and ask participants to assess the level of the audio-visual correlation. It turns out that they consistently preferred our model's results, as shown in the penultimate column of Table 1, which is consistent with the objective evaluation results.

To gain a better understanding of our model's performance, we divide the entire test set into three categories: sunny, rainy, and snowy and report results on each subset. In this experiment, as shown in Table 2, our model still holds the best performance compared to label-based baselines. Furthermore, we observe that when the target scene is sunny, the disparity between our model and Keyword (0.018) is larger than that of other scenes (0.004 & 0.008). This may be because the ambient sounds in sunny forests are highly varied (*e.g.*, crunching gravel/leave, birds chirping, *etc.*).

Qualitative Results. We show qualitative results in Fig. 5 and provide additional results in the Appendix A.4. We note that all of the results are produced by a single model, *i.e.*, through "one-to-many" conversion. We observe that the AdaIN model sometimes cannot reliably preserve the input image's content (the

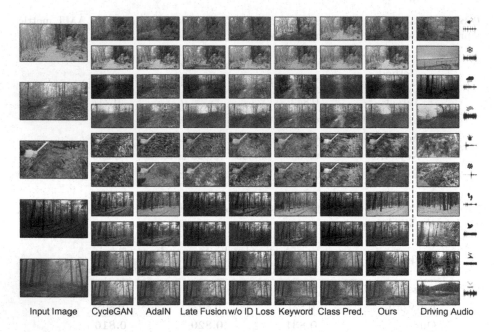

Input Image   CycleGAN   AdaIN   Late Fusion w/o ID Loss Keyword Class Pred.   Ours   Driving Audio

Fig. 5. Qualitative comparison of baselines, ablations, and our model on audio-visual texture conversion. For reference, we also show driving audios as well as their corresponding images in the last column.

first row of first input image). The Keyword model can generate plausible images that match the class of the target audio, but with apparent flaws when converting between the same scene categories (the second row of the second input image). For the YAMNet model, the generated images occasionally match the target images, but this does not happen in all cases. This may be because the success of a stylization is strongly dependent on whether the labels inferred by YAMNet are correct. Our model, by comparison, can capture the subtle distinctions within the same scene class. For example, our model can adjust the hue of the snow, when given a wind-and-footstep sound (which is not successfully captured by other models).

4.3   Ablation Study and Analysis

We conduct an ablation study to test various settings and ablations of our model, summarized in Table 3. By default, we use the architecture and loss function above. We also try to use: i) the forward cycle-consistency loss [70] instead of NCE loss, termed as CycleGAN; ii) late fusion discriminator [60] to incorporate audio and visual features rather than early fusion one; iii) without the identity loss; iv) a pre-trained audio-visual self-supervised method, *i.e.*, SeLaVi [3], as the initial weight for the audio network in addition to training from scratch.

Table 3. Quantitative results for ablations on *Into the Wild* dataset.

Ablation	Objective evaluation		
	AVC ($\uparrow$)	FID ($\downarrow$)	CLIP ($\uparrow$)
CycleGAN [70]	0.812	35.244	0.232
Late Fusion [60]	0.811	54.025	0.230
w/o ID Loss	0.810	41.019	0.236
Ours	0.820	34.139	0.238
+ Pre-training [3]	**0.822**	**32.882**	**0.242**

Besides, we show qualitative examples and additional pre-training comparisons in Fig. 5 and Appendix A.4 respectively.

NCE Loss is a Strong Substitute for Cycle-Consistency Loss. Our model employs NCE loss following CUT [50]. As a baseline, cycle-consistency loss [70] can also preserve the image structure. As shown in Table 3, our model achieves comparable results to its counterpart, CycleGAN, implying that it can generate realistic images like CycleGAN. Figure 5 also shows some qualitative results that support this. Besides, CycleGAN involves the joint learning of two generators, while our model only requires one, which can reduce training time [50].

Late Fusion Discriminators are More Likely to Collapse. In audio-visual learning, the late fusion architecture [60] is commonly used, in which two uni-modal encoders are employed to extract features, followed by a classifier (discriminator). We also take into account this architecture in ablations, with the results shown in Table 3 and Fig. 5. We find that leveraging this type of discriminator induces the model to collapse, which means the generator would eventually become too weak to sustain the image structure, resulting in unsatisfactory results.

Identity Loss Helps to Capture Nuances. Given an image from the output domain, the identity loss [70] pushes the generator to leave the image unchanged with our patch-based contrastive loss. We also test a variant without this loss, as depicted in Table 3. We find that the variation of the model without identity loss tends to has worse performance. We further investigate by presenting qualitative results in Fig. 5. In the first row of the second example, in particular, when the conversion is from sunny to rainy forest, it is unsuccessful for the one without identity loss, whilst the one with succeeds. As a result, we propose that employing such a loss as a regularizer might be beneficial in capturing nuances, particularly when converting between similar landscapes, such as forest-to-forest and snow-to-snow conversions.

Self-supervised Pre-training Improves Stylization. We ask whether models pre-trained to solve audio-visual self-supervised learning tasks will result in performance gains. Table 3 shows that fine-tuning our task using a pre-trained SeLaVi model [3] yields a small improvement.

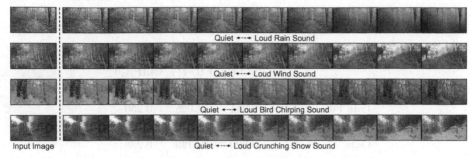

Fig. 6. Qualitative results on image manipulation with increasing sound volumes.

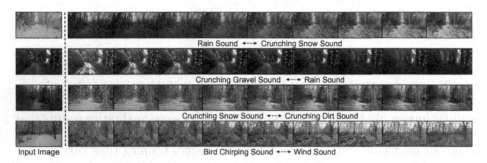

Fig. 7. Qualitative results on image manipulation with different mixture sounds.

4.4 Audio Manipulation for Image Manipulation

Sound provides a natural "embedding space" for image manipulation, since intuitively manipulating the audio leads to corresponding changes in the images. We ask whether changing the volume of the sound or mixing two sounds together will result in corresponding visual changes. We also evaluate out-of-distribution images and audio.

Changing Sound Volumes. A qualitative comparison using a sound at various volumes is shown in Fig. 6. This is accomplished by simply rescaling the input waveform. Regardless of whether the input image is snowy or sunny forest, we observe that the texture in the image becomes more prominent as the sound gradually increases, indicating that our model implicitly learns to predict the prominence of the texture according to the volume.

Mixing Sounds. We create sound mixtures by taking convex combinations of input sounds. The qualitative results are presented in Fig. 7. In the third row, for example, we can see that the snowy texture will be gradually erased while mixing a crunching snow sound with a muddy footstep sound from small to large. Furthermore, it appears to be a balanced state with both snowy and sunny features in the middle, i.e., white and green hues coexist. Surprisingly, such mixed audio is not available when our model is being trained. This linear additivity finding shows that audio cues have a prospective advantage over label ones for image translation.

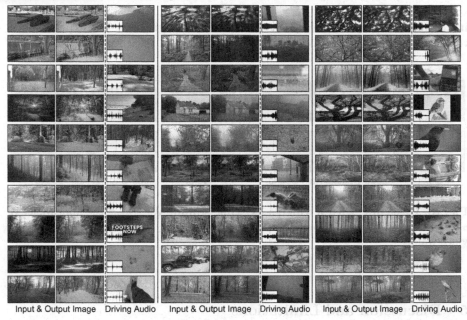

Input & Output Image   Driving Audio   Input & Output Image   Driving Audio   Input & Output Image   Driving Audio

Fig. 8. Qualitative generalization results. We restyle images from Places [67] using crunching snow and rain sounds taken from VGG-Sound [7].

Generalization to Other Datasets. We ask whether our model can generalize to out-of-distribution data. We consider restyling images from the Places dataset [67] and audio from the VGG-Sound dataset [7] to examine our model's generalization performance. In Fig. 8, we use crunching snow, rain and birds chirping sounds with a high probability of a class deduced by YAMNet [51]. Our model generates plausible images that match the content of in-the-wild audio.

Adjusting an Image's Style Through its Sound. We apply our method to a task inspired by video editing: adjusting an image's appearance by manipulating its *existing* sound. We take a video frame, manipulate its corresponding

Input & Output Image Driving Audio   Input & Output Image Driving Audio

Fig. 9. Failure cases. Our model fails to manipulate the style of the scene, perhaps due to the presence of speech in the sound (left). It also fails to learn how to style certain objects in a scene (right).

sound, and then resynthesize its video frames to match. This allows a user to make *consistent* changes to the two modalities: *e.g.*, an editor can adjust the volume of rain through intuitive volume-based controls, while automatically propagating these changes to images.

We restyle videos from VGG-Sound [7] by adjusting the volume of their already-existing soundtracks. Figure 10 shows qualitative examples obtained by increasing the volume of videos recorded during light rain. As expected, the resulting images contains significantly more rain.

Quiet ←--→ Loud Original Rain Sound   Quiet ←--→ Loud Original Rain Sound

Fig. 10. Restyling with a video's existing sound. We adjust the appearance of a video by increasing the volume of its soundtrack, and restyling the corresponding video frame.

5 Discussion and Limitations

Despite the fact that our model can yield promising results in various cases, the results are far from uniformly positive. Because ambient sounds in real life are diverse, our model can be easily upset with unexpected sounds. Figure 9 shows some typical failure cases. Specifically, if the sound is interfered by human speech, the learned translation will devolve to making minor adjustments to the input. As a result, handling a greater spectrum of mixture sound, particularly urban sound, will become increasingly important in the future. Another potential concern is that our model's performance will be suffered if the proportion of the scene to be converted is too small. In the lower right of Fig. 9, for example, the trees and sky each account for half of the input image, resulting in an odd conversion. This is because the model is unable to detect the region of the scene that needs conversion, but instead converts the entire scene. Nevertheless, as paired audio-visual data is ubiquitous in our daily life, this paper paves the way for image translation under the audio-visual context.

6 Conclusion

In this paper, we introduce a novel task called *audio-driven image stylization*, which aims to learn the visual styles from paired audio-visual data. To study this task, we propose a contrastive-based audio-visual GAN model, together with an unlabeled egocentric hiking dataset named *Into the Wild*. Experimental results show that our model outperforms label and image conditioned baselines in both quantitative and qualitative evaluations. We also empirically find that changing the audio volume and mixture results in predictable visual changes. We hope our work will shed new light on cross-modal image synthesis.

References

1. Afouras, T., Chung, J.S., Senior, A., Vinyals, O., Zisserman, A.: Deep audio-visual speech recognition. IEEE Trans. Pattern Anal. Mach. Intell. (2018)
2. Arandjelovic, R., Zisserman, A.: Look, listen and learn. In: Proceedings of the IEEE International Conference on Computer Vision, pp. 609–617 (2017)
3. Asano, Y.M., Patrick, M., Rupprecht, C., Vedaldi, A.: Labelling unlabelled videos from scratch with multi-modal self-supervision. In: Advances in Neural Information Processing Systems (2020)
4. Bau, D., et al.: Paint by word. arXiv:2103.10951 (2021)
5. Chatterjee, M., Cherian, A.: Sound2Sight: generating visual dynamics from sound and context. In: Vedaldi, A., Bischof, H., Brox, T., Frahm, J.-M. (eds.) ECCV 2020. LNCS, vol. 12372, pp. 701–719. Springer, Cham (2020). https://doi.org/10.1007/978-3-030-58583-9_42
6. Chen, H., Xie, W., Afouras, T., Nagrani, A., Vedaldi, A., Zisserman, A.: Localizing visual sounds the hard way. In: Proceedings of the Conference on Computer Vision and Pattern Recognition (CVPR) (2021)
7. Chen, H., Xie, W., Vedaldi, A., Zisserman, A.: VGGSound: a large-scale audio-visual dataset. In: ICASSP 2020–2020 IEEE International Conference on Acoustics, Speech and Signal Processing (ICASSP), pp. 721–725. IEEE (2020)
8. Chen, T., Kornblith, S., Norouzi, M., Hinton, G.E.: A simple framework for contrastive learning of visual representations. In: International Conference on Machine Learning, pp. 1597–1607 (2020)
9. Chen, Z., Hu, X., Owens, A.: Structure from silence: learning scene structure from ambient sound. In: 5th Annual Conference on Robot Learning (2021)
10. Cheuk, K.W., Anderson, H., Agres, K., Herremans, D.: nnAudio: an on-the-fly GPU audio to spectrogram conversion toolbox using 1D convolutional neural networks. IEEE Access 8, 161981–162003 (2020)
11. Chung, J.S., Jamaludin, A., Zisserman, A.: You said that? In: British Machine Vision Conference (2017)
12. Cramer, J., Wu, H.H., Salamon, J., Bello, J.P.: Look, listen, and learn more: design choices for deep audio embeddings. In: ICASSP 2019–2019 IEEE International Conference on Acoustics, Speech and Signal Processing (ICASSP), pp. 3852–3856. IEEE (2019)
13. Dong, H., Yu, S., Wu, C., Guo, Y.: Semantic image synthesis via adversarial learning. In: Proceedings of the IEEE International Conference on Computer Vision, pp. 5706–5714 (2017)
14. Ephrat, A., et al.: Looking to listen at the cocktail party: a speaker-independent audio-visual model for speech separation. ACM Trans. Graph. (TOG) 37(4) (2016)
15. Fu, T.J., Wang, X.E., Wang, W.Y.: Language-driven image style transfer. arXiv preprint arXiv:2106.00178 (2021)
16. Gan, C., Huang, D., Zhao, H., Tenenbaum, J.B., Torralba, A.: Music gesture for visual sound separation. In: Proceedings of the IEEE/CVF Conference on Computer Vision and Pattern Recognition, pp. 10478–10487 (2020)
17. Gao, R., Feris, R., Grauman, K.: Learning to separate object sounds by watching unlabeled video. In: Proceedings of the European Conference on Computer Vision (ECCV), pp. 35–53 (2018)
18. Gao, R., Grauman, K.: 2.5 D visual sound. In: Proceedings of the IEEE/CVF Conference on Computer Vision and Pattern Recognition, pp. 324–333 (2019)

19. Gatys, L.A., Ecker, A.S., Bethge, M.: A neural algorithm of artistic style. arXiv preprint arXiv:1508.06576 (2015)
20. Gemmeke, J.F., et al.: Audio set: an ontology and human-labeled dataset for audio events. In: 2017 IEEE International Conference on Acoustics, Speech and Signal Processing (ICASSP), pp. 776–780. IEEE (2017)
21. Ginosar, S., Bar, A., Kohavi, G., Chan, C., Owens, A., Malik, J.: Learning individual styles of conversational gesture. In: Proceedings of the IEEE/CVF Conference on Computer Vision and Pattern Recognition, pp. 3497–3506 (2019)
22. Goodfellow, I., et al.: Generative adversarial networks. In: Advances in Neural Information Processing Systems, pp. 2672–2680 (2014)
23. Gutmann, M., Hyvärinen, A.: Noise-contrastive estimation: a new estimation principle for unnormalized statistical models. In: Proceedings of the Thirteenth International Conference on Artificial Intelligence and Statistics, pp. 297–304 (2010)
24. Harwath, D., Recasens, A., Surís, D., Chuang, G., Torralba, A., Glass, J.: Jointly discovering visual objects and spoken words from raw sensory input. In: Proceedings of the European Conference on Computer Vision (ECCV), pp. 649–665 (2018)
25. He, K., Zhang, X., Ren, S., Sun, J.: Deep residual learning for image recognition. In: Proceedings of the IEEE Conference on Computer Vision and Pattern Recognition, pp. 770–778 (2016)
26. Hershey, S., et al.: CNN architectures for large-scale audio classification. In: 2017 IEEE International Conference on Acoustics, Speech and Signal Processing (ICASSP), pp. 131–135. IEEE (2017)
27. Hertzmann, A., Jacobs, C.E., Oliver, N., Curless, B., Salesin, D.H.: Image analogies. In: Proceedings of the 28th Annual Conference on Computer Graphics and Interactive Techniques, pp. 327–340 (2001)
28. Heusel, M., Ramsauer, H., Unterthiner, T., Nessler, B., Hochreiter, S.: GANs trained by a two time-scale update rule converge to a local nash equilibrium. In: Advances in Neural Information Processing Systems (2017)
29. Hu, C., Tian, Q., Li, T., Wang, Y., Wang, Y., Zhao, H.: Neural dubber: dubbing for videos according to scripts. In: Advances in Neural Information Processing Systems (2021)
30. Huang, X., Belongie, S.: Arbitrary style transfer in real-time with adaptive instance normalization. In: Proceedings of the IEEE International Conference on Computer Vision, pp. 1501–1510 (2017)
31. Iashin, V., Rahtu, E.: Taming visually guided sound generation. arXiv preprint arXiv:2110.08791 (2021)
32. Isola, P., Zhu, J.Y., Zhou, T., Efros, A.A.: Image-to-image translation with conditional adversarial networks. In: Proceedings of the IEEE Conference on Computer Vision and Pattern Recognition, pp. 1125–1134 (2017)
33. Johnson, J., Alahi, A., Fei-Fei, L.: Perceptual losses for real-time style transfer and super-resolution. In: Leibe, B., Matas, J., Sebe, N., Welling, M. (eds.) ECCV 2016. LNCS, vol. 9906, pp. 694–711. Springer, Cham (2016). https://doi.org/10.1007/978-3-319-46475-6_43
34. Johnson, J., Gupta, A., Fei-Fei, L.: Image generation from scene graphs. In: Proceedings of the IEEE Conference on Computer Vision and Pattern Recognition, pp. 1219–1228 (2018)
35. Kim, T., Cha, M., Kim, H., Lee, J.K., Kim, J.: Learning to discover cross-domain relations with generative adversarial networks. In: International Conference on Machine Learning, pp. 1857–1865. PMLR (2017)
36. Kingma, D.P., Ba, J.: Adam: a method for stochastic optimization. In: International Conference for Learning Representations (2015)

37. Korbar, B., Tran, D., Torresani, L.: Cooperative learning of audio and video models from self-supervised synchronization. In: Proceedings of the Advances in Neural Information Processing Systems (2018)
38. Laffont, P.Y., Ren, Z., Tao, X., Qian, C., Hays, J.: Transient attributes for high-level understanding and editing of outdoor scenes. ACM Trans. Graph. (TOG) **33**(4), 1–11 (2014)
39. Langlois, T.R., James, D.L.: Inverse-foley animation: synchronizing rigid-body motions to sound. ACM Trans. Graph. (TOG) **33**(4), 1–11 (2014)
40. Lee, S.H., et al.: Sound-guided semantic image manipulation. arXiv preprint arXiv:2112.00007 (2021)
41. Levine, S., Krähenbühl, P., Thrun, S., Koltun, V.: Gesture controllers. In: ACM SIGGRAPH, pp. 1–11 (2010)
42. Mahajan, D., et al.: Exploring the limits of weakly supervised pretraining. In: Proceedings of the European Conference on Computer Vision (ECCV), pp. 181–196 (2018)
43. Mikolov, T., Chen, K., Corrado, G., Dean, J.: Efficient estimation of word representations in vector space. arXiv preprint arXiv:1301.3781 (2013)
44. Morgado, P., Vasconcelos, N., Langlois, T., Wang, O.: Self-supervised generation of spatial audio for 360 video. In: Advances in Neural Information Processing Systems (2018)
45. Morgado, P., Vasconcelos, N., Misra, I.: Audio-visual instance discrimination with cross-modal agreement. In: Proceedings of the IEEE/CVF Conference on Computer Vision and Pattern Recognition, pp. 12475–12486 (2021)
46. Nam, S., Kim, Y., Kim, S.J.: Text-adaptive generative adversarial networks: manipulating images with natural language. In: Advances in Neural Information Processing Systems (2018)
47. Ngiam, J., Khosla, A., Kim, M., Nam, J., Lee, H., Ng, A.Y.: Multimodal deep learning. In: ICML (2011)
48. Owens, A., Efros, A.A.: Audio-visual scene analysis with self-supervised multisensory features. In: Proceedings of the European Conference on Computer Vision (2018)
49. Owens, A., Isola, P., McDermott, J., Torralba, A., Adelson, E.H., Freeman, W.T.: Visually indicated sounds. In: Proceedings of the IEEE Conference on Computer Vision and Pattern Recognition, pp. 2405–2413 (2016)
50. Park, T., Efros, A.A., Zhang, R., Zhu, J.-Y.: Contrastive learning for unpaired image-to-image translation. In: Vedaldi, A., Bischof, H., Brox, T., Frahm, J.-M. (eds.) ECCV 2020. LNCS, vol. 12354, pp. 319–345. Springer, Cham (2020). https://doi.org/10.1007/978-3-030-58545-7_19
51. Plakal, M., Ellis, D.: YAMNet, January 2020. https://github.com/tensorflow/models/tree/master/research/audioset/yamnet
52. Prajwal, K., Mukhopadhyay, R., Namboodiri, V.P., Jawahar, C.: Learning individual speaking styles for accurate lip to speech synthesis. In: Proceedings of the IEEE/CVF Conference on Computer Vision and Pattern Recognition, pp. 13796–13805 (2020)
53. Prajwal, K., Mukhopadhyay, R., Namboodiri, V.P., Jawahar, C.: A lip sync expert is all you need for speech to lip generation in the wild. In: Proceedings of the 28th ACM International Conference on Multimedia, pp. 484–492 (2020)
54. Radford, A., et al.: Learning transferable visual models from natural language supervision. In: International Conference on Machine Learning (2021)
55. Ramesh, A., et al.: Zero-shot text-to-image generation. arXiv preprint arXiv:2102.12092 (2021)

56. Reed, S., Akata, Z., Yan, X., Logeswaran, L., Schiele, B., Lee, H.: Generative adversarial text to image synthesis. In: International Conference on Machine Learning, pp. 1060–1069 (2016)
57. de Sa, V.R.: Learning classification with unlabeled data. In: Advances in Neural Information Processing Systems, pp. 112–119. Citeseer (1994)
58. Shlizerman, E., Dery, L., Schoen, H., Kemelmacher-Shlizerman, I.: Audio to body dynamics. In: Proceedings of the IEEE Conference on Computer Vision and Pattern Recognition, pp. 7574–7583 (2018)
59. Tenenbaum, J.B., Freeman, W.T.: Separating style and content with bilinear models. Neural Comput. 12(6), 1247–1283 (2000)
60. Wang, W., Tran, D., Feiszli, M.: What makes training multi-modal classification networks hard? In: Proceedings of the IEEE/CVF Conference on Computer Vision and Pattern Recognition, pp. 12695–12705 (2020)
61. Wu, C., Timm, M., Maji, S.: Describing textures using natural language. In: Vedaldi, A., Bischof, H., Brox, T., Frahm, J.-M. (eds.) ECCV 2020. LNCS, vol. 12346, pp. 52–70. Springer, Cham (2020). https://doi.org/10.1007/978-3-030-58452-8_4
62. Yang, K., Russell, B., Salamon, J.: Telling left from right: learning spatial correspondence of sight and sound. In: Proceedings of the IEEE/CVF Conference on Computer Vision and Pattern Recognition, pp. 9932–9941 (2020)
63. Yi, Z., Zhang, H., Tan, P., Gong, M.: DualGAN: unsupervised dual learning for image-to-image translation. In: Proceedings of the IEEE International Conference on Computer Vision, pp. 2849–2857 (2017)
64. Zhang, Z., et al.: Generative modeling of audible shapes for object perception. In: Proceedings of the IEEE International Conference on Computer Vision, pp. 1251–1260 (2017)
65. Zhao, H., Gan, C., Ma, W.C., Torralba, A.: The sound of motions. In: Proceedings of the IEEE/CVF International Conference on Computer Vision, pp. 1735–1744 (2019)
66. Zhao, H., Gan, C., Rouditchenko, A., Vondrick, C., McDermott, J., Torralba, A.: The sound of pixels. In: Proceedings of the European Conference on Computer Vision (ECCV), pp. 570–586 (2018)
67. Zhou, B., Lapedriza, A., Khosla, A., Oliva, A., Torralba, A.: Places: a 10 million image database for scene recognition. IEEE Trans. Pattern Anal. Mach. Intell. 40(6), 1452–1464 (2017)
68. Zhou, H., Liu, Y., Liu, Z., Luo, P., Wang, X.: Talking face generation by adversarially disentangled audio-visual representation. In: Proceedings of the AAAI Conference on Artificial Intelligence, pp. 9299–9306 (2019)
69. Zhou, Y., Wang, Z., Fang, C., Bui, T., Berg, T.L.: Visual to sound: generating natural sound for videos in the wild. In: Proceedings of the IEEE Conference on Computer Vision and Pattern Recognition, pp. 3550–3558 (2018)
70. Zhu, J.Y., Park, T., Isola, P., Efros, A.A.: Unpaired image-to-image translation using cycle-consistent adversarial networks. In: Proceedings of the IEEE Conference on Computer Vision and Pattern Recognition, pp. 2223–2232 (2017)

Remote Respiration Monitoring
of Moving Person Using Radio Signals

Jae-Ho Choi[1], Ki-Bong Kang[1,2], and Kyung-Tae Kim[1(✉)]

[1] POSTECH, Pohang, Republic of Korea
{jhchoi93,kkb131,kkt}@postech.ac.kr
[2] Samsung Electronics, Suwon, Republic of Korea

Abstract. Non-contact respiration rate measurement (nRRM), which aims to monitor one's breathing status without any contact with the skin, can be utilized in various remote applications (e.g., telehealth or emergency detection). The existing nRRM approaches mainly analyze fine details from videos to extract minute respiration signals; however, they have practical limitations in that the head or body of a subject must be quasi-stationary. In this study, we examine the task of estimating the respiration signal of a non-stationary subject (a person with large body movements or even walking around) based on radio signals. The key idea is that the received radio signals retain both the reflections from human global motion (GM) and respiration in a mixed form, while preserving the GM-only components at the same time. During training, our model leverages a novel multi-task adversarial learning (MTAL) framework to capture the mapping from radio signals to respiration while excluding the GM components in a self-supervised manner. We test the proposed model based on the newly collected and released datasets under real-world conditions. This study is the first realization of the nRRM task for moving/occluded scenarios, and also outperforms the state-of-the-art baselines even when the person sits still.

Keywords: Non-contact respiration rate measurement · Radio signal · Multi-task adversarial learning

1 Introduction

Respiration rate (RR) is an important clinical indicator directly reflecting the status of the human ventilation system. In this respect, continuous monitoring of one's RR is helpful for general health care, especially for telehealth or emergency detection in patients with breathing disorders such as chronic obstructive pulmonary disease and SARS-CoV-2 (COVID-19) [1,40]. Traditional measurements for RR are typically based on contact devices such as chest belts, contact photoplethysmography (PPG), and airflow sensing, which require direct contact

---

Supplementary Information The online version contains supplementary material available at https://doi.org/10.1007/978-3-031-19836-6_15.

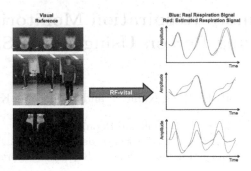

Fig. 1. We propose a RF-vital model that learns the mapping from radio reflections to human respiration signal based on a novel MTAL framework. Several test examples of our RF-vital model demonstrate the feasibility of recovering the fine respiration signs even under occluded, dark, and moving scenarios

with the skin of the subject, hence induces significant discomfort and measurement discontinuities. As alternative to the contact solutions, non-contact RR measurement (nRRM) approaches have recently attracted scholarly attention, most of which leverage the physiological signatures extracted from facial videos [3,15,16,22–24,27–30,32–35,37,38,47,49,51,52].

However, the skin color changes originating from human breathing cycles are significantly marginal and easily contaminated by head movements of the subject, struggling outside controlled settings (e.g., a scenario where a person must sit approximately still while facing forward) [2,10,40]. Moreover, a single camera view cannot cope effectively with misaligned/occluded faces as well as dark settings, which are quite common scenarios in daily life. Consequently, nRRM for a non-stationary subject (a person with large random body movements or even walking around) has rarely been explored.

To realize robust nRRM systems even against such challenging scenarios, we propose to use radio frequency (RF) signals reflected from radar as an input modality. Radar is an electromagnetic sensor capable of measuring radial depth changes for its targets of interest with high sensitivity. Accordingly, it can capture the horizontal displacements around the chest modulated from human vital signs, while maintaining stable measurements in the presence of head movements, face occlusion, and even large motions. Furthermore, the RF sensor typically operates in GHz band, making it intrinsically unaffected by the surrounding illumination (THz band) or dark conditions as well as completely free from privacy issues.

In fact, there have been several attempts to achieve nRRM based on RF signals previously [5,9,14,17,26,31,39,44,45]. RF-based nRRM methods usually first estimate the radial distance of the human body from the raw reflected signals. Considering that the extracted radial distances with respect to time directly reflects the physiological signals modulated from the body-depth variations, the RR can be recovered via several signal decomposition techniques such as advanced filtering [9,26,31,39] and deep learning (DL) [14,56]. However, these approaches still have limitations in overcoming the large motion scenarios. Such vigorous movements of each individual force a dynamic range of the signal to be significantly enlarged, greatly inflating the distance estimation errors. Particularly, the radial distance of a person changes both along the global motion (GM) induced from the stagger/gait and along the respiratory motion (RM) from the inhalation-exhalation cycle, whereas the RM components maintain much smaller displacements than the GM; therefore, they are likely to be obscured in the radio reflection data.

To tackle this problem and achieve nRRM even for a moving subject, we propose a novel RF-vital model, characterized by newly-introduced input formats for radio reflections and a multi-task adversarial learning (MTAL) framework. Specifically, our U-Net style network [42] takes a radio joint time-frequency (RJTF) map as input (which is completely free from the distance estimation issues), then attempts to reconstruct the subject's respiration signal (i.e., RM) and spatial trajectory (i.e., GM). During training, the decoder for the GM is co-trained with the feature encoder in an adversarial manner, thereby facilitating the latent representation to be irrelevant to the GM of a person and reflect only the desired RM. Such adversarial mapping on GM can be accomplished based on our key observations that the reflected RF signals not only provide the RM-GM mixture, but also preserve GM-only self-supervision simultaneously. Meanwhile, to prevent the model from learning identity (ID)-dependent short-cuts, we add an auxiliary identification task, which is also trained in an adversarial manner.

This study is the first to report the realization of an nRRM over a randomly moving person. We evaluate our RF-vital model on two nRRM datasets consisting of synchronized RF signals, respiratory signals, and RGB videos, which were collected from different base scenarios. The first dataset was obtained in ideal situations, where a person sits nearly still with her/his head facing forward. The second dataset was collected from much more challenging scenarios, where the subject was allowed to stand and even move around freely in various directions. We release our datasets to further advance the RF-based nRRM research. The experimental results show that our RF-vital model outperforms the state-of-the-art video- and RF-based nRRM approaches in static scenarios. Moreover, as shown in Fig. 1, it continues to work properly in large motion scenarios, where the current methods fail completely. Furthermore, our methods can provide robust estimations, even in dark-light conditions and occlusions, enabling more realistic implementations of nRRM. We believe that our approach is also applicable for detecting various vital signs in humans, such as heart rate. Nonetheless, in this study, we only focus on estimating respiratory signals.

2   Related Work

2.1   Video-Based Physiological Measurements

Because the diffuse reflectance spectra of the skin (typically facial region) change along with the human physiological movements, remote prediction of one's vital signals can be achieved by capturing the subtle light reflections using a camera [40, 46, 48]. The problem is that such diffuse components reflected back from the camera are substantially marginal and easily affected by nuisance factors owing to head motions and light changes. The traditional methods exploit combinations of different color profiles [15,16,27,47] to retrieve illumination-invariant signatures or exploit signal decomposition techniques, such as independent component analysis (ICA) [22,30,37,38] and principal component analysis (PCA) [24,49] to enhance the signal-to-noise ratio (SNR) of the physiological signals. With the advent of DL in the pattern recognition field, there have also been attempts to employ its powerful nonlinear fitting capability to video-based physiological monitoring, achieving substantial performance improvements [3,23,29,32–34,51,52]. The recent approaches further advanced the robustness of the network on head motions by introducing multi-task temporal shift or inverse attention [28,35].

2.2   RF-Based Physiological Measurements

RF signal involves human physiology mainly based on changes in body depth instead of the reflectance in the facial area, so it is less influenced by head motions. Based on the signal property that the received phase components linearly indicate the subject's radial depth with microscopic sensitivity, most RF-based physiological measurements rely on the estimated phase information. Tu et al. [45] demonstrated the feasibility of RF-based vital monitoring in a controlled setting. Regarding the generic applications in the presence of small 1-D body movements, several motion compensation methods have been proposed using signal decomposition techniques [9,26,39], wavelet transform [17,31,44], and fuzzy logic [5]. Recently, Ha et al. [14] devised an approach to recover the original physiological waveforms from the radio reflections by leveraging a deep supervised encoder-decoder framework. However, these methods fundamentally assume accurate phase estimations (i.e., distance estimations) as priori, which are likely to fail under large body movements. Therefore, they can still be applicable to only limited scenarios (e.g., situations where a person sits and shakes her/his body back and forth). Our study aims at more general settings, where a person can stand and even walk around by introducing a new image-like input modality for RF signals and a MTAL strategy.

2.3   Indoor Sensing with RF Signals

The RF system employs wireless reflections for surrounding detection, enabling illuminance-invariant and privacy-preserving sensing. The past wireless systems for indoor environments tend to be biased towards localization and tracking [4,6–8,21,36,50]; nonetheless, recent advances in RF hardware and DL-based analysis techniques have facilitated the implementation of more sophisticated tasks based on radio signals. For example, Zhao et al. [53–55] developed RF-based 2D/3D pose estimation systems, which have been proven to work even through walls. Fan et al. [11,12] extended the results for wireless captioning and person re-identification tasks.

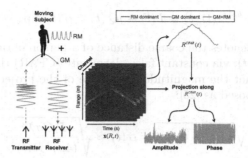

Fig. 2. Pre-processing pipeline for radio-projected profiles. We leverage the CFAR thresholding technique to obtain global trajectories from the channel-wise range-time RF heatmaps. Projecting along the CFAR-output, radio-projected profiles can be extracted, whose magnitude and phase values (purple line) retain both the GM and RM components for a moving person (Color figure online)

3 RF Signal Preliminary

3.1 Depth Estimation from RF Signal

The RF sensor periodically transmits an radio signal and receives reflections from its surroundings. Large bodies of RF sensing systems use a frequency-modulated continuous-wave (FMCW) technique for signal modulation [12,13,43, 53–55], which has also been adopted in our work. After the basic pre-processing from RF raw reflections (see supplementary material for details), we can obtain channel-wise 2D complex range-time heatmaps $\mathbf{x}(R,t) = \{x_m(R,t)\}_{m=1}^4$ (see Fig. 2), where R is the radial distance from the transmitter, t is the time, and m represents the receiver index from the distributed array antennas. The magnitude of each RF heatmap (i.e., $|x(R,t)|$) directly indicates the reflected energy level at each distance. Therefore, it is possible to estimate the radial depth of an individual by detecting only the high absolute energy values from $|x(R,t)|$.

Meanwhile, the range resolution of a RF system is determined solely by its transmitted signal bandwidth as [18]:

$$\Delta R = \frac{c}{2BW} = 0.1\,\text{m},\tag{1}$$

where c is the speed of light and BW is the signal bandwidth, which is set to 1.5 GHz in our RF system. This implies that the general range detections from $|x(R,t)|$ cannot fundamentally involve the microscopic displacement variations originating from human respiration (with displacements of ~ 1 mm in typical [31]). Thus, instead of exploiting range detections from the RF heatmaps as in most RF-based indoor applications [7,11,12,43,50,53,54], we leverage the detected profile itself to retrieve the respiratory signatures beyond the resolution limit.

Namely, as shown in Fig. 2, projection along the detected trajectory of a subject can convert $x(R,t)$ into a 1D temporal signal (hereinafter referred to as the radio-projected profile) with a complex format [5]:

$$x \left(R^{CFAR}(t), t \right) = I(t) + jQ(t) = \alpha(t) \exp \left(j\theta(t) \right), \tag{2}$$

where $R^{CFAR}(t)$ denotes the coarse distance of a person obtained from a direct detection on $|x(R,t)|$ via constant false alarm rate (CFAR) thresholding [41]. It should be noted that the magnitude and phase of the projected signal profiles are further decomposed as [25]:

$$\sqrt{I(t)^2 + Q(t)^2} = \alpha(t) \approx \sqrt{\frac{P_t G \sigma \lambda^2}{(4\pi)^3 \bar{R}(t)^4}}, \tag{3}$$

$$\tan^{-1} \left(\frac{Q(t)}{I(t)} \right) + 2\pi k = \theta(t) = \frac{4\pi}{\lambda} \bar{R}(t), \tag{4}$$

where P_t, G, σ, and λ represent the transmit power, antenna gain, electromagnetic reflectivity, and signal wavelength, respectively, all of which are approximately constant over time. $\bar{R}(t)$ refers to the radial depth of a subject from the transmitter, and $k (= \pm 0, 1, \cdots)$ is the ambiguity factor in estimating the phase. From Eq. (3) and (4), it can clearly be noticed that the magnitude and phase components of the projected signal also reflect the radial depth of the subject. Particularly, contrary to $R^{CFAR}(t)$ estimated from the coarse range detection on $|x(R,t)|$, $\bar{R}(t)$ is not confined by the range resolution limit, and thus, it retains exquisite sensitivity such that the vital signals with marginal displacements can even be captured [19].

3.2   Motivation for RF-Vital Model

Let us consider the radial distance over time for a person with large motion. Because the radial distance for a moving person changes along both the GM of the body and the fluctuating depth owing to RM, $\bar{R}(t)$ can be expressed as a linear summation of the GM and RM components: $\bar{R}(t) = \bar{R}_{GM}(t) + \bar{R}_{RM}(t)$, where $\bar{R}_{GM}(t)$ and $\bar{R}_{RM}(t)$ denote the distance variations induced from the GM (i.e., body movements such as swinging, staggering, and walking) and RM (i.e., the body depth changes owing to breathing), respectively. The RM components, which are quasi-isotropic in any part of the torso and exactly coincide with the inhalation/exhalation cycles, allow human respiration to be recovered depending on the information of body depth variations, from any azimuth angle. Moreover, such chest-based sensing does not suffer from the prerequisite for continuous face tracking, and even maintains an enhanced SNR compared to the extraction from RGB face pixels.

The problem is that while the displacement of RM oscillates at the microscopic level, the radial distance caused by GM (i.e., $\bar{R}_{GM}(t)$) changes rapidly; hence, the signal strength of $\bar{R}_{RM}(t)$ present within $\alpha(t)$ and $\theta(t)$ becomes substantially trivial. For robust extraction of the RM component, it is essential to highlight the dominance of $\bar{R}_{RM}(t)$ in $\bar{R}(t)$, while suppressing the influence of $\bar{R}_{GM}(t)$. This is not a simple task because the GM and RM components are entangled in $\bar{R}(t)$ for every interval as well as the explicit separation of $\bar{R}_{GM}(t)$

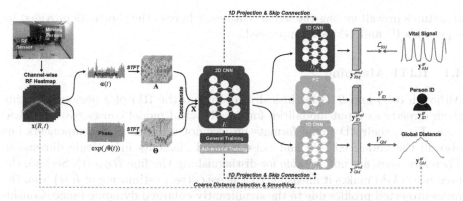

Fig. 3. Overall RF-vital model architecture. It first transforms the radio-projected profiles into RJTF map format, which is subsequently fed in to the U-Net style network [42] composed of one 2D encoder, two 1D decoders, and one discriminator. The network is trained based on the MTAL strategy. During training, the RM decoder attempts to reduce the discrepancy between the real and predicted respiration (black box), whereas the GM decoder and the ID discriminator are co-trained with the encoder in an adversarial manner (orange box), such that the features cannot preserve the signatures regarding the GM and ID of a person (Color figure online)

requires additional utilization of motion/localization sensors, which makes the overall system extremely bulky.

To tackle these challenges, we propose a novel MTAL framework (Fig. 3), which leverages the domain properties of the RF signals mentioned above: the range detections $R^{CFAR}(t)$ from the RF heatmap cannot fundamentally involve the minute displacements of RM owing to its resolution limits in hardware, but is able to coarsely track the GM of the human body. This implies that $R^{CFAR}(t)$ can act as a powerful model of $\bar{R}_{GM}(t)$. Based on this insight, we devise a network that learns the mapping from the RF inputs composed of $\boldsymbol{\alpha}(t) = \{\alpha_m(t)\}_{m=1}^4$ and $\boldsymbol{\theta}(t) = \{\theta_m(t)\}_{m=1}^4$ to the desired RM component, while simultaneously pushing out the GM component modeled from $\mathbf{R}^{CFAR}(t) = \{R_m^{CFAR}(t)\}_{m=1}^4$ in a self-supervised manner.

4   Methodology

RF-vital is a model for estimating the human respiration signal, given the channel-wise radio reflections as input. As illustrated in Fig. 3, our RF-vital pipeline consists of three main stages: 1) input transformation to convert the radio received signals into the newly proposed input modality, named RJTF maps; 2) representation encoding from the RJTF maps by leveraging 2D convolution modules; 3) decoding branches composed of two 1D convolutional decoders (for RM and GM), and an ID discriminator. During training, these modules are guided in an end-to-end manner based on the MTAL strategy such that the RM signatures prevail among the latent features, whereas the shortcuts provided by a person's ID and GM are suppressed.

4.1 RJTF Mapping

Although $\alpha(t)$ and $\theta(t)$ intrinsically encompass the RM of a person, adopting them directly as input modalities for our RF-vital model causes two complications. First, their 1D signal formats project not only the RM components but also all the undesired GM and noise-induced elements in a single dimension. Therefore, they are not suitable for distinguishing the fine $\bar{R}_{RM}(t)$. Second, the presence of GM makes it infeasible to achieve correct estimation of $\bar{R}(t)$ from the radio-projected profiles due to the significantly enlarged dynamic range. Considering these problems, we introduce the RJTF map as the input modality for our RF-vital model to further clarify $\bar{R}_{RM}(t)$ and to avoid the estimation ambiguity problem.

The RJTF map takes advantage of the Doppler characteristics of RF signals (see supplementary material for details), which can entail the information of instantaneous distance changes in radial direction [18]. Namely, instead of directly estimating $\bar{R}(t)$ from the radio-projected profiles, we rather perform short-time Fourier transform (STFT) on $\alpha(t)$ and $\exp(j\theta(t))$ to obtain joint time-frequency images $\mathbf{A}$ and Θ (Fig. 3). The additional Doppler frequency dimension in the RJTF map spans the instantaneous change in the radial distance, so is capable of tracking the human vital signs as well. Particularly, it simply scatters the distance changes of all body parts with respect to time on the 2D domain, being free from the burden for accurate distance estimation. Finally, we aggregate all the channel-wise spectrogram images in concatenated forms, resulting in the final RJTF map $\mathbf{X} \in \mathbb{R}^{8 \times T \times F}$, where T and F denote the dimensions in time and Doppler frequency, respectively.

4.2 RF-Vital Model Based on MTAL

Overall Architecture. As shown in Fig. 3, our RF-vital model adopts a 2D convolutional encoder to convert the input RJTF map $\mathbf{X}$ into high-level representations. These are subsequently fed into two parallel 1D convolutional decoders responsible for predicting the subject's respiratory signal and global body motion, respectively, and a fully-connected network responsible for identifying her/his ID. Regarding the overall encoder-decoder architecture, we leverage the modified form of a U-Net [42] architecture, where the multi-scale features produced from a series of 2D convolution layers within the encoder are averaged along the frequency dimension and skip-connected to the corresponding 1D convolution layers in each decoder network (see supplementary material for fully detailed architecture).

RM Decoder. The RM decoder $D_{RM}(\cdot)$ aims at extending the correlation with the real respiration signal from the low-dimensional RF feature. We devise the

RM decoder based on series of 1D convolution and up-convolution layers match-ing the temporal dimensions of the encoder to reconstruct a T-length respiration signal from the representations. In addition, a tanh layer is added after the last convolutional module to bound the predicted values to $[-1, 1]$. During training, the network becomes optimized based on the L_1 distance between the predicted and real respiration signals:

$$\mathcal{L}_{RM} = \left\| \mathbf{y}_{RM}^{pred} - \mathbf{y}_{RM}^{gt} \right\|_1, \tag{5}$$

where $\mathbf{y}_{RM}^{pred}$ denotes the output signals from D_{RM}, and $\mathbf{y}_{RM}^{gt}$ refers to the ground-truth respiration signals measured with the contact chest belt.

GM Decoder. A major complication in accomplishing nRRM for a moving person is the entanglement of human GM and RM within the input, which, in turn, precludes the model from the high-fidelity separation of RM. More-over, it is impossible to acquire a GM-dominant data (i.e., data affected only by the subject's GM without the RM component at all) paired with the net-work input, further complicating the disentanglement of the RM features. We address this challenge through a novel adversarial training strategy guided by range-detection-based self-supervision.

The GM decoder consists of 1D convolution and up-convolution layers identi-cal to those of the RM decoder; however, it performs a completely different role. The encoder and GM decoder are trained in an adversarial manner such that the model is encouraged to exclude the GM-dependent features. Let the encod-ing network be denoted as $E(\cdot)$ and the decoding network for GM as $D_{GM}(\cdot)$. Then, the optimization target can be defined as:

$$\min_{E} \max_{D_{GM}} V_{GM} = - \left\| \mathbf{y}_{GM}^{pred} - \mathbf{y}_{GM}^{gt} \right\|_1, \tag{6}$$

where $\mathbf{y}_{GM}^{pred}$ is the estimated GM component from the decoder, i.e., $\mathbf{y}_{GM}^{pred} = D_{GM}(E(\mathbf{X}))$, and $\mathbf{y}_{GM}^{gt}$ is the ground-truth GM-dominant data. Recall that the coarse range detection $R^{CFAR}(t)$, which is obtained from the direct detection in the RF time-range heatmap $x(R, t)$, can predominantly reflect only the human GM component owing to its range resolution limit in hardware. Based on this, we hypothesize that $R^{CFAR}(t)$ has a great potential to serve as a self-supervision for GM-dominant signals. We average $\mathbf{R}^{CFAR}(t)$ along the receiver channel domain, which is subsequently passed through the linear interpolation and smoothing filter to mitigate the influence of false detections and noise, resulting in the final T-length $\mathbf{y}_{GM}^{gt}$. From the adversarial learning between the RF encoder and GM decoder, the encoding network E can further focus on the RM-dominant signals, while eliminating the GM-dominant features.

Discriminator for Person ID. Because the input radio reflection contains unexpected subject-dependent signatures (such as gait patterns or average stay-ing positions) besides the vital signs, the person ID may provide strong shortcuts for predicting breath signals. For example, the network may learn the person ID through the gait pattern of each individual to reconstruct the subject-dependent respiration signal. Such shortcuts not only degrade the generalizability of the model for unseen subjects but also contradict our intention for the RF-based nRRM task.

To address this problem, we devise an ID discriminator that operates also in an adversarial manner during the training, similar to the case of the GM decoder. We first construct a network for ID discrimination, which consists of three fully-connected and soft-max layers to take the flattened features extracted from the encoder E as input and classify the person ID as output. Denoting this discriminator as $D_{ID}(\cdot)$, the adversarial training between D_{ID} and encoder F can be achieved using a cross-entropy loss function:

$$\min_{E} \max_{D_{ID}} V_{ID} = \sum_{n=1}^{N} \left(\mathbf{y}_{ID}^{gt} \right)_n \cdot \log \left(\left(\mathbf{y}_{ID}^{pred} \right)_n \right), \tag{7}$$

where N denotes the total number of subjects in the training data, $\mathbf{y}_{ID}^{pred}$ is the N-length output vector representing the probability for the person ID, and $\mathbf{y}_{ID}^{gt}$ is the one-hot encoded ground-truth vector. $(\cdot)_n$ represents the n-th element of an arbitrary vector.

In summary, two decoders for RM and GM, and one ID discriminator are trained together in an end-to-end manner based on MTAL. Therefore, the overall loss can be defined as:

$$\min_{\{E, D_{RM}\}} \max_{\{D_{GM}, D_{ID}\}} V = \left\| \mathbf{y}_{RM}^{pred} - \mathbf{y}_{RM}^{gt} \right\|_1$$
$$-\eta_1 \left\| \mathbf{y}_{GM}^{pred} - \mathbf{y}_{GM}^{gt} \right\|_1 + \eta_2 \sum_{n=1}^{N} \left(\mathbf{y}_{ID}^{gt} \right)_n \cdot \log \left(\left(\mathbf{y}_{ID}^{pred} \right)_n \right), \tag{8}$$

where $\eta_1 = 0.3$ and $\eta_2 = 0.2$ are the balancing factors, which have been selected empirically in our experiments. Note that the proposed MTAL strategy aims at developing a RM decomposition model in the presence of large body motions which can similarly be applied based on other input modalities (e.g. video), but it is worthwhile to adopt RF signal given that the GM-dominant self-supervision can intrinsically be provided.

5 Experimental Results

5.1 Datasets and Experimental Setup

Since there is no public dataset for the RF-based nRRM tasks, we collected two datasets for the static/moving settings. For acquiring RF data, we utilized a commercial FMCW radar (IWR1443BOOST, Texas Instruments Inc.) operating in the 77 GHz frequency band with a 1000 pulse repetition frequency. The following details the collected datasets.

RRM-Static. RRM-static dataset contains 2.4 h of synchronized RF reflected signals, uncompressed RGB videos captured at 1280×720 resolution and 30 fps through a Razer Kiyo Pro webcam, and ground-truth respiration signals recorded from the contact chest belt. The measurements were collected from 13 subjects in an indoor room, in which each individual was requested to sit in a chair and face forward, ensuring quasi-stationary settings. The participants were also asked to hold their breath periodically during the experiments to generate negative data samples.

RRM-Moving. RRM-moving dataset is obtained under conditions similar to RRM-static; however, this case was based on non-stationary, i.e., moving settings, where 13 participants were able to stand and even walk around, reflecting more challenging and realistic scenarios such as staggering, looking backward, and turning around. This dataset spans 7 h of random movements and includes some negative samples regarding walking around while holding one's breath.

Implementation Details. The overall algorithm for the RF-vital model was implemented based on 10 s of sequential frame data with a sliding window of 2.5-s intervals, resulting in 3527/10171 RF frames for RRM-static and RRM-moving, respectively. The received RF signals were transformed into RJTF maps using STFT based on a Hann window of 300 ms duration, hop length of 60 ms, and FFT size of 256. To train the network, we adopted ADAM [20] optimizer with a learning rate of 0.0001 and a batch size of 64.

Regarding the quantitative evaluation of the nRRM algorithm, we followed the protocols in [28]. That is, we measure the RRs of a person by post-processing the output signals through a band pass filter with a [0.08 Hz, 0.6 Hz] passband range, which are then compared with real RR measurements in beats per minute unit (BPM) using several standard metrics: mean absolute error (MAE), root mean square error (RMSE), standard deviation (Std), and Pearson's correlation coefficient (ρ). For train-test split, the datasets were divided into 13 folds corresponding to each participant so that the network model could be trained and tested through subject-independent 13-fold cross-validation.

5.2   Quantitative Results

We compare the proposed RF-vital model with seven state-of-the-art non-contact vital monitoring baselines (three video- [3,28,35] and four RF-based methods [14,31,45,56]). Regarding the video-based methods, we used 10-s video clips corresponding to the RF data, and center-cropped them to 400×400 pixels to focus only on the facial areas.

Considering the left side of Table 1, our RF-vital model outperforms the previous baselines under static conditions, achieving a 51.8% reduction in MAE and 57.1% in RMSE. Furthermore, the right side of Table 1 demonstrates the feasibility of realizing nRRM even in moving conditions, where the previous models completely fail because of inconsistent facial tracking induced from the erratic

Table 1. Quantitative comparison of the RF-vital and seven baseline methods based on the RRM-static and RRM-moving datasets

Method	Input	RRM-static (BPM)				RRM-moving (BPM)			
		MAE↓	RMSE↓	ρ↑	Std↓	MAE↓	RMSE↓	ρ↑	Std↓
CAN [3]	RGB	3.16	5.83	0.57	5.21				
Nowara et al. [35]	RGB	2.51	4.58	0.67	4.25				
MTTS-CAN [28]	RGB	2.65	4.13	0.69	4.04	Not applicable			
Tu et al. [45]	RF (1D)	5.46	7.31	0.19	4.86				
Mercuri et al. [31]	RF (1D)	2.52	5.64	0.54	5.47				
Zheng et al. [56]	RF (1D)	1.68	3.82	0.72	3.45				
Ha et al. [14]	RF (1D)	1.37	3.36	0.75	3.21				
RF-vital	RF (2D)	**0.66**	**1.44**	**0.88**	**1.43**	**3.67**	**7.02**	**0.32**	**6.39**

Table 2. Comparison between different input RF formats

Model input	MAE↓	RMSE↓	ρ↑	Std↓
Unwrapped phase signal	-	-	-	-
RJTFmap (phase only)	4.92	7.20	0.23	6.97
RJTFmap	**3.67**	**7.02**	**0.32**	**6.39**

Table 3. Estimation performance for different combinations of the decoding branches

Use of decoder	MAE↓	RMSE↓	ρ↑	Std↓
RM only	5.04	7.96	0.26	7.15
RM + ID	4.76	7.64	0.30	6.85
RM + GM	3.85	7.10	**0.36**	6.98
RM + GM + ID	**3.67**	**7.02**	0.32	**6.39**

and occluded face regions (for video-based approaches), or significant ambiguity for prerequisite distance estimation (for RF-based approaches). Particularly, it is remarkable that the RR estimation results of our model under moving conditions are comparable to those of Tu et al. [45] under static cases.

5.3 Ablation Study

For further in-depth analysis of the effectiveness of each component in the RF-vital model, we conduct ablation studies based on the RRM-moving dataset.

RJTF Map. To analyze the potential utility of the proposed RJTF map, we investigated the numerical performance by changing the input modality for training our RF-vital model. As candidates for the model input, we adopt unwrapped phase signals (i.e., $\theta(t)$ in Eq. (4)) widely utilized in RF-based nRRM methods

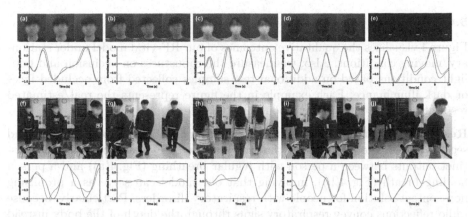

Fig. 4. Qualitative results of our RF-vital model for various realistic scenarios. The first and second rows show the reference video samples and corresponding estimation results under stationary cases. The third and fourth rows show the results under more challenging moving conditions. The ground-truth and the predicted respiration signals are indicated by blue and red lines, respectively. Note that each signal is determined to be the case of holding breath if the average absolute amplitude is less than 0.2 (Color figure online)

[5,9,14,17,31,39,44], four-channel RJTF maps based only on RF phase, and eight-channel RJTF maps based on both amplitude and phase components. As shown in Table 2, the model with the unwrapped phase signal fails entirely owing to huge unwrapping errors (i.e., distance estimation errors), generating only random jitters for the network output. This implies the inability of the conventional direct distance estimations for involving respiration signatures in the presence of GM. On the contrary, we observe that the proposed RJTF map can present a solution to resolve the estimation ambiguity problem using Doppler effect. In particular, exploiting the amplitude-based spectrograms as well with the phase spectrograms can further improve the performance, reducing the MAE by 25.4% and RMSE by 2.5% compared to the phase-only RJTF maps.

MTAL Strategy. We explore the effectiveness of the proposed MTAL strategy. Specifically, we trained the network with respect to three different combinations of decoding pipelines and evaluated the measurement performance of each model (Table 3). The comparison between the cases with and without the GM decoder clearly verifies the efficacy of the adversarial training on the GM components (23.6% and 10.8% reduction in MAE and RMSE, respectively) in encouraging the network to focus more on the desired RM components. Furthermore, considering the last row of Table 3, we observe that the proposed ID discriminator can provide an additional reduction in MAE by 4.7% and RMSE by 1.1%, demonstrating its potential to improve the model generalizability for an unseen person.

5.4 Qualitative Results

Figure 4 visualizes the qualitative outcomes of our RF-vital model under station-ary/moving conditions. Also, we measure the robustness on occlusion and poor light conditions based on additional test samples collected from occluded faces or dark illuminance. Each example in the figure represents the real/estimated respiration signal and its corresponding RGB scene.

Results for Stationary Cases. The results for a static person (the first and second rows of the figure) show that the proposed RF-vital model provides distinct outputs between a person with regular breathing (Fig. 4(a)) and a person holding breath (Fig. 4(b)), implying that our model can serve as a promising non-contact solution for people with respiratory disorders. Particularly, because radio reflections convey respiratory signs through the depth of the body instead of the exposed skin surface, it is possible to conduct stable and privacy-preserving predictions even when a person wears a mask (Fig. 4(c)) or bows her/his head (Fig. 4(d)). Furthermore, we observe that our RF-vital model maintains robustness in a dark setting (Fig. 4(e)), in which the video-based approaches are likely to suffer from significant performance degradation.

Results for Moving Cases and Limitations. The third and fourth rows in the figure demonstrate that our model still works for a moving subject. It can be noticed that the predicted outcomes reflect the respiratory signs of each individual walking toward the sensor (Fig. 4(f)) or with her/his back (Fig. 4(h)), under various spatial angles. In addition, the model can certainly factor out the unusual cases of walking around while holding one's breath (Fig. 4(g)).

However, we observed some failure cases in the RF-vital model under the scenarios with rapid movements. For example, when a person suddenly changes direction, the model generates erroneous signals as shown in (Fig. 4(i)). Moreover, the RF-vital model tends to show vulnerability to large motions in the vertical direction, such as a large faltering or falling (Fig. 4(j)). Such failures may have been affected by misalignment with the chest caused from the poor vertical resolution in our sensing system.

6 Conclusion

In this study, we present a novel RF-vital model, the first approach for implementing the nRRM task over a randomly moving individual. We propose the use of radio reflections as an input modality for the RF-vital model, based on its domain property that can capture the microscopic changes in human body depth, while preserving GM-only signals simultaneously. By leveraging the GM-dominant signals as self-supervision, we can devise a MTAL strategy that induces the network to focus more on the desired RM components, while pushing out GM components. The extensive experimental results show that the proposed RF-vital model can provide robust estimations in the presence of a moving person, occluded face, and poor illumination, demonstrating its potentiality for realizing practical vital monitoring solutions.

References

1. Ali, M., Elsayed, A., Mendez, A., Savaria, Y., Sawan, M.: Contact and remote breathing rate monitoring techniques: a review. IEEE Sens. J. **21**(13), 14569–14586 (2021)
2. Bobbia, S., Macwan, R., Benezeth, Y., Mansouri, A., Dubois, J.: Unsupervised skin tissue segmentation for remote photoplethysmography. Pattern Recognit. Lett. **124**(1), 82–90 (2019)
3. Chen, W., McDuff, D.: Deepphys: video-based physiological measurement using convolutional attention networks. In: European Conference on Computer Vision (ECCV), pp. 349–365, September 2018
4. Chintalapudi, K., Padmanabha Iyer, A., Padmanabhan, V.N.: Indoor localization without the pain. In: ACM Annual International Conference on Mobile Computing and Networking (MobiCom), pp. 173–184 (2010)
5. Choi, I.O., Kim, M., Choi, J.H., Park, J.K., Park, S.H., Kim, K.T.: Robust cardiac rate estimation of an individual. IEEE Sens. J. **21**(13), 15053–15064 (2021)
6. Choi, J.H., Kim, J.E., Jeong, N.H., Kim, K.T., Jin, S.H.: Accurate people counting based on radar: deep learning approach. In: IEEE Radar Conference (RadarConf), pp. 1–5 (2020)
7. Choi, J.H., Kim, J.E., Kim, K.T.: Deep learning approach for radar-based people counting. IEEE Internet Things J. **9**, 1–16 (2021)
8. Choi, J.H., Kim, J.E., Kim, K.T.: People counting using IR-UWB radar sensor in a wide area. IEEE Internet Things J. **8**(7), 5806–5821 (2021)
9. Ding, C., Yan, J., Zhang, L., Zhao, H., Hong, H., Zhu, X.: Noncontact multiple targets vital sign detection based on VMD algorithm. In: IEEE Radar Conference (RadarConf), pp. 0727–0730 (2017)
10. Estepp, J.R., Blackford, E.B., Meier, C.M.: Recovering pulse rate during motion artifact with a multi-imager array for non-contact imaging photoplethysmography. In: IEEE Conference on Systems, Man, and Cybernetics (SMC), pp. 1462–1469 (2014)
11. Fan, L., Li, T., Fang, R., Hristov, R., Yuan, Y., Katabi, D.: Learning longterm representations for person re-identification using radio signals. In: IEEE Conference on Computer Vision and Pattern Recognition (CVPR), pp. 10699–10709 (2020)
12. Fan, L., Li, T., Yuan, Y., Katabi, D.: In-home daily-life captioning using radio signals. In: Vedaldi, A., Bischof, H., Brox, T., Frahm, J.-M. (eds.) ECCV 2020. LNCS, vol. 12347, pp. 105–123. Springer, Cham (2020). https://doi.org/10.1007/978-3-030-58536-5_7
13. Guan, J., Madani, S., Jog, S., Gupta, S., Hassanieh, H.: Through fog high-resolution imaging using Millimeter wave radar. In: IEEE Conference on Computer Vision and Pattern Recognition (CVPR), pp. 11461–11470 (2020)
14. Ha, U., Assana, S., Adib, F.: Contactless seismocardiography via deep learning radars. In: ACM Annual International Conference on Mobile Computing and Networking (MobiCom), pp. 1–14 (2020)
15. de Haan, G., Jeanne, V.: Robust pulse rate from chrominance-based rPPG. IEEE Trans. Biomed. Eng. **60**(10), 2878–2886 (2013)
16. de Haan, G., Van Leest, A.: Improved motion robustness of remote-PPG by using the blood volume pulse signature. Physiol. Meas. **35**(9), 1913–1926 (2014)
17. He, M., Nian, Y., Liu, B.: Noncontact heart beat signal extraction based on wavelet transform. In: International Conference on Biomedical Engineering and Informatics (BMEI), pp. 209–213 (2015)

18. Iovescu, C., Rao, S.: The fundamentals of millimeter wave sensors. Texas Instrum. 1–8 (2017)
19. Jiang, C., Guo, J., He, Y., Jin, M., Li, S., Liu, Y.: mmVib: micrometer-level vibration measurement with mmWave radar. In: ACM Annual International Conference on Mobile Computing and Networking (MobiCom), pp. 1–13 (2020)
20. Kingma, D.P., Ba, J.: Adam: a method for stochastic optimization. In: International Conference on Learning Representations (ICLR), pp. 1–15 (2015)
21. Kumar, S., Gil, S., Katabi, D., Rus, D.: Accurate indoor localization with zero start-up cost. In: ACM Annual International Conference on Mobile Computing and Networking (MobiCom), pp. 483–494 (2014)
22. Lam, A., Kuno, Y.: Robust heart rate measurement from video using select random patches. In: International Conference on Computer Vision (ICCV), pp. 3640–3648 (2015)
23. Lee, E., Chen, E., Lee, C.-Y.: Meta-rPPG: remote heart rate estimation using a transductive meta-learner. In: Vedaldi, A., Bischof, H., Brox, T., Frahm, J.-M. (eds.) ECCV 2020. LNCS, vol. 12372, pp. 392–409. Springer, Cham (2020). https://doi.org/10.1007/978-3-030-58583-9_24
24. Lewandowska, M., Rumiński, J., Kocejko, T., Nowak, J.: Measuring pulse rate with a webcam - a non-contact method for evaluating cardiac activity. In: Federated Conference on Computer Science and Information Systems (FedCSIS), pp. 405–410 (2011)
25. Li, J., Stoica, P.: MIMO Radar Signal Processing. Wiley, Hoboken (2008)
26. Li, J., Liu, L., Zeng, Z., Liu, F.: Advanced signal processing for vital sign extraction with applications in UWB radar detection of trapped victims in complex environments. IEEE J. Sel. Topics Appl. Earth Observ. Remote Sens. 7(3), 783–791 (2014)
27. Li, X., Chen, J., Zhao, G., Pietikäinen, M.: Remote heart rate measurement from face videos under realistic situations. In: IEEE Conference on Computer Vision and Pattern Recognition (CVPR), pp. 4264–4271 (2014)
28. Liu, X., Fromm, J., Patel, S., McDuff, D.: Multi-task temporal shift attention networks for on-device contactless vitals measurement. In: Advances in Neural Information Processing Systems (NIPS), pp. 1–23 (2020)
29. McDuff, D.: Deep super resolution for recovering physiological information from videos. In: IEEE Conference on Computer Vision and Pattern Recognition Workshops (CVPRW), pp. 1480–1487 (2018)
30. McDuff, D.J., Sarah, G., Picard, R.W.: Improvements in remote cardiopulmonary measurement using a five band digital camera. IEEE Trans. Biomed. Eng. 61(10), 2593–2601 (2014)
31. Mercuri, M., Lorato, I., Liu, Y.H., Wieringa, F., Van Hoof, C., Torfs, T.: Vital-sign monitoring and spatial tracking of multiple people using a contactless radar-based sensor. Nat. Electron. 2, 252–262 (2019)
32. Niu, X., Han, H., Shan, S., Chen, X.: SynRhythm: learning a deep heart rate estimator from general to specific. In: International Conference on Pattern Recognition (ICPR), pp. 3580–3585 (2018)
33. Niu, X., Han, H., Shan, S., Chen, X.: VIPL-HR: a multi-modal database for pulse estimation from less-constrained face video. In: Jawahar, C.V., Li, H., Mori, G., Schindler, K. (eds.) ACCV 2018. LNCS, vol. 11365, pp. 562–576. Springer, Cham (2019). https://doi.org/10.1007/978-3-030-20873-8_36
34. Niu, X., Shan, S., Han, H., Chen, X.: RhythmNet: end-to-end heart rate estimation from face via spatial-temporal representation. IEEE Trans. Image Process. 29, 2409–2423 (2020)

35. Nowara, E.M., McDuff, D., Veeraraghavan, A.: The benefit of distraction: Denoising camera-based physiological measurements using inverse attention. In: International Conference on Computer Vision (ICCV), pp. 4955–4964 (2021)

36. Pan, J.J., Pan, S.J., Yin, J., Ni, L.M., Yang, Q.: Tracking mobile users in wireless networks via semi-supervised colocalization. IEEE Trans. Pattern Anal. Mach. Intell. **34**(3), 587–600 (2012)

37. Poh, M.Z., McDuff, D.J., Picard, R.W.: Non-contact, automated cardiac pulse measurements using video imaging and blind source separation. Opt. Express **18**(10), 10762–10774 (2010)

38. Poh, M.Z., McDuff, D.J., Picard, R.W.: Advancements in noncontact, multiparameter physiological measurements using a webcam. IEEE Trans. Biomed. Eng. **58**(1), 7–11 (2011)

39. Ren, W., et al.: Vital sign detection in any orientation using a distributed radar network via modified independent component analysis. IEEE Trans. Microw. Theory Techn. **69**(11), 4774–4790 (2021)

40. Revanur, A., Li, Z., Ciftci, U.A., Yin, L., Jeni, L.A.: The first vision for vitals (V4V) challenge for non-contact video-based physiological estimation. In: International Conference on Computer Vision Workshop (ICCVW), pp. 2760–2767 (2021)

41. Rohling, H.: Radar CFAR thresholding in clutter and multiple target situations. IEEE Trans. Aerosp. Electron. Syst. **AES-19**(4), 608–621 (1983)

42. Ronneberger, O., Fischer, P., Brox, T.: U-Net: convolutional networks for biomedical image segmentation. In: Navab, N., Hornegger, J., Wells, W.M., Frangi, A.F. (eds.) MICCAI 2015. LNCS, vol. 9351, pp. 234–241. Springer, Cham (2015). https://doi.org/10.1007/978-3-319-24574-4_28

43. Scheiner, N., et al.: Seeing around street corners: non-line-of-sight detection and tracking in-the-wild using Doppler radar. In: IEEE Conference on Computer Vision and Pattern Recognition (CVPR), pp. 2068–2077 (2020)

44. Tariq, A., Ghafouri-Shiraz, H.: Vital signs detection using Doppler radar and continuous wavelet transform. In: European Conference on Antennas and Propagation (EUCAP), pp. 285–288 (2011)

45. Tu, J., Hwang, T., Lin, J.: Respiration rate measurement under 1-D body motion using single continuous-wave doppler radar vital sign detection system. IEEE Trans. Microw. Theory Techn. **64**(6), 1937–1946 (2016)

46. Verkruysse, W., Othar Svaasand, L., Stuart Nelson, J.: Remote plethysmographic imaging using ambient light. Opt. Express **16**(26), 21434–21445 (2008)

47. Wang, W., den Brinker, A.C., Stuijk, S., de Haan, G.: Amplitude-selective filtering for remote-PPG. Biomed. Opt. Express **8**(3), 1965–1980 (2017)

48. Wang, W., den Brinker, A.C., Stuijk, S., de Haan, G.: Algorithmic principles of remote PPG. IEEE Trans. Biomed. Eng. **64**(7), 1479–1491 (2017)

49. Wang, W., Stuijk, S., de Haan, G.: Exploiting spatial redundancy of image sensor for motion robust rPPG. IEEE Trans. Biomed. Eng. **62**(2), 415–425 (2015)

50. Xiong, J., Sundaresan, K., Jamieson, K.: ToneTrack: leveraging frequency-agile radios for time-based indoor wireless localization. In: ACM Annual International Conference on Mobile Computing and Networking (MobiCom), pp. 537–549 (2015)

51. Yu, Z., Peng, W., Li, X., Hong, X., Zhao, G.: Remote heart rate measurement from highly compressed facial videos: an end-to-end deep learning solution with video enhancement. In: International Conference on Computer Vision (ICCV), pp. 151–160 (2019)

52. Zhan, Q., Wang, W., de Haan, G.: Analysis of CNN-based remote-PPG to understand limitations and sensitivities. Biomed. Opt. Express **11**(3), 1268–1283 (2020)

53. Zhao, M., et al.: Through-wall human pose estimation using radio signals. In: IEEE Conference on Computer Vision and Pattern Recognition (CVPR), pp. 7356–7365 (2018)
54. Zhao, M., et al.: Through-wall human mesh recovery using radio signals. In: International Conference on Computer Vision (ICCV), pp. 10112–10121 (2019)
55. Zhao, M., et al.: RF-based 3D skeletons. In: Conference of the ACM Special Interest Group Data Communication (SIGCOMM), pp. 267–281 (2018)
56. Zheng, T., Chen, Z., Zhang, S., Cai, C., Luo, J.: MoRe-Fi: motion-robust and fine-grained respiration monitoring via deep-learning UWB radar. In: ACM Conference on Embedded Networked Sensor Systems (SenSys), New York, NY, USA, pp. 111–124 (2021)

Camera Pose Estimation and Localization with Active Audio Sensing

Karren Yang[2], Michael Firman[1], Eric Brachmann[1(✉)], and Clément Godard[3]

[1] Niantic, London, UK
ebrachmann@nianticlabs.com
[2] MIT, Cambridge, USA
[3] Google, San Francisco, USA

Abstract. In this work, we show how to estimate a device's position and orientation indoors by echolocation, i.e., by interpreting the echoes of an audio signal that the device itself emits. Established visual localization methods rely on the device's camera and yield excellent accuracy if unique visual features are in view and depicted clearly. We argue that audio sensing can offer complementary information to vision for device localization, since audio is invariant to adverse visual conditions and can reveal scene information beyond a camera's field of view. We first propose a strategy for learning an audio representation that captures the scene geometry around a device using supervision transfer from vision. Subsequently, we leverage this audio representation to complement vision in three device localization tasks: relative pose estimation, place recognition, and absolute pose regression. Our proposed methods outperform state-of-the-art vision models on new audio-visual benchmarks for the Replica and Matterport3D datasets.

1 Introduction

Audio signals are rich with information about the scenes around us. As humans, we can often identify objects based on the sounds they make, and we can also localize objects based on the direction of their sounds. Beyond passively listening to sounds, animals such as bats and dolphins, as well as some individuals who are visually impaired, use *echolocation* (*i.e., active audio sensing*) to sense the spatial layout of their surroundings; they actively emit sounds that bounce off major surfaces, creating audio echoes that convey structural properties such as scene geometry and surface material [26,33].

A growing body of research has proposed active audio sensing for vision tasks such as room geometry estimation [26], depth estimation [24,33,65], and floor-plan estimation [68]. Inspired by these pioneering works, we ask:

K. Yang and C. Godard—Work done while at Niantic, during Karren's internship.

Supplementary Information The online version contains supplementary material available at https://doi.org/10.1007/978-3-031-19836-6_16.

Can we train a machine to "hear" where it is in an indoor scene?

Figure 1(a) illustrates the problem setting: a device consisting of a camera with a co-registered microphone emits a sound and records the echoes from the surrounding indoor scene. Our goal is to leverage these audio echoes, either alone or in conjunction with the camera's image, to perform the three classic camera localization tasks shown in Fig. 1(b): (i) relative pose estimation, (ii) place recognition, and (iii) absolute pose regression. From this point on, we refer to these tasks as *device localization* tasks, since they involve both a camera and a microphone– a reasonable assumption for most applications in AR/VR [16,101] and robotics [25,52]. See the figure caption for an overview of each task.

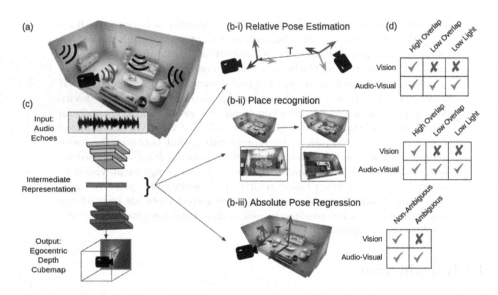

Fig. 1. Indoor device localization with active audio sensing. (a) Problem setting. A device consisting of a co-located microphone and camera generates sound (red) that bounces off major surfaces to create echoes (black). We leverage these audio echoes to perform the audio-visual device localization tasks proposed in (b). (b-i). Relative pose estimation. Audio-visual from two devices are used to estimate their relative transformation (e.g., rotation and translation). (b-ii) Place recognition. Audio-visual input from the device is used to retrieve nearby locations using a database of reference captures. (b-iii) Absolute pose regression. Audio-visual input from the device is used to estimate its global position and orientation with respect to the scene. (c) To learn audio features that capture the full geometry of the device's surroundings, we propose a pretraining task that distills an egocentric visual cube map [37] into the audio representation. (d) Audio sensing improves performance over established vision baselines. (Color figure online)

While device localization tasks are conventionally tackled with only camera images, audio offers two key advantages. First, audio echoes reflect off surfaces beyond a camera's field of view, capturing more scene information than just what can be seen in an image. Second, audio signals are invariant to adverse visual conditions such as low lighting and occlusions. Our idea is that these attributes of audio sensing can enable us to solve cases of device localization that are generally challenging for vision.

Interestingly, we find that directly optimizing models to use audio inputs for device localization is not an optimal strategy. Unlike vision, the high-dimensional input representation of audio does not explicitly depict the scene geometry around the device, which is useful for localization. To overcome this challenge, we propose a pretraining framework that distills visual information of the surroundings, represented as an egocentric depth cubemap [37], into the audio representation. As shown in Fig. 1(c), as pretraining, we task a model with reconstructing an egocentric view captured at one of six possible orientations from the microphone. In this way, we learn useful spatial audio features through the natural co-occurrence of audio-visual data [58,107], without the need for manually annotating surfaces in the scene (e.g., using a floorplan [68]).

Subsequently, we integrate these audio features into audio-visual methods for the three device localization tasks shown in Fig. 1(b). Since these tasks have not previously been done with audio sensing, we introduce new benchmarks on the Replica [85] and Matterport3D [17] datasets. Integrating our audio features with established vision baselines achieves superior results across all tasks. Importantly, audio sensing enables us to solve cases that are challenging for vision, as summarized in Fig. 1(d).

To summarize our main **contributions**: 1) We propose a pretraining framework for extracting features from audio echo recordings that are useful for device localization; 2) We introduce audio sensing to three classic visual localization tasks, that are conventionally tackled using only camera images: relative pose estimation, place recognition, and absolute pose regression, and achieve superior results on all three tasks; 3) We propose novel audio-visual benchmarks for these tasks, building on publicly available datasets and simulation platforms.

To our knowledge, our work is the first to extend classic camera localization tasks to the audio-visual domain. Our code and pretrained models are available at https://github.com/nianticlabs/audio-localization.

1.1   Related Work

Audio for Spatial Sensing. Existing research has leveraged audio to sense locations of surfaces or objects in a scene. Echolocation has previously been used to compute the shape of a convex polyhedral room [26], to predict the shape of an object around a corner [53], to predict distances to surfaces [28,84, 100], to estimate frontal depth maps [24,33,65], and to reconstruct floor plans [68]. Other prior work leverages passive rather than active audio (i.e., audio naturally emitted by sound sources in the scene) for spatial scene understanding. These generally focus on localizing the source of the object producing the sound, for example, predicting the direction of sound arrival [66], localizing multiple sound sources using SVD [93], highlighting sound sources in a video [31,40,

47,62], drawing bounding boxes around moving vehicles [32] and performing semantic object detection on street scenes [98]. Recent work in robotics even uses ambient audio in a scene to estimate distances to walls [23]. Different from all of these works, we use echolocation to estimate the surround depth of a scene in pretraining, with the ultimate goal of performing device localization.

Audio-Visual Scene Perception. Audio and visual signals often occur together in a scene and offer useful joint information for performing tasks such as action recognition [35,44,55,103,105,106] and object labeling [110]. The co-occurrence of these signals enables self-supervised representation learning [2,58,60–62,64,72,107], audio synthesis [63,83] or spatialization [34,59] corresponding to a visual scene, and navigation [18–21]. Inspired by these works, our pretraining task leverages co-occurring audio-visual signals to learn useful audio features for device localization.

Visual Place Recognition. Determining a device's location based on a captured image is a device localization problem that can be formulated as an image retrieval task, where the objective is to retrieve a database image taken from the same place as the query, rather an image that looks similar [36]. Prior works have proposed performing a nearest-neighbor search on global visual descriptors [1,3,43,94] and/or performing matching between local visual features [38,54,92,109]. Ongoing challenges in visual place recognition include the need for visual overlap between query and database images [56] as well as the need for invariance to different visual appearance conditions [36] such as lighting. Different from prior work, here we propose to augment visual place recognition with audio sensing to overcome these challenges and demonstrate our method on new audio-visual benchmarks for place recognition.

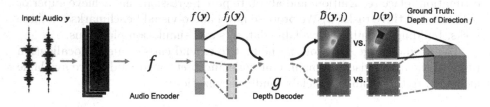

Fig. 2. Pretraining Task. We distill an egocentric visual depth map into an audio representation for downstream localization tasks. During training, we provide audio-visual samples where the camera is rotated with respect to the microphone, and we teach the model to reconstruct this egocentric view from audio. See text for details

Relative Camera Pose Estimation. Relative pose estimation is used to localize one device with respect to another by predicting the relative transformation between them, usually based on a pair of images. The most prevalent methods are feature-matching methods that use a pose solver integrated within a

RANSAC framework [69], with state-of-the-art approaches using learned methods for feature detection [6,27,71,96], matching [74,86] and robust model fitting [11,70,87,108]. Deep learning methods use convolutional neural networks to directly regress the transformation from a pair of images [29,57,67,108], including a recent work that frames regression as a classification problem [22]. An ongoing challenge in relative pose estimation is handling wide rotation cases where there is limited visual overlap between the image pair [15]. Different from prior work, here we augment relative camera pose estimation with audio sensing and demonstrate our method on new audio-visual benchmarks for relative pose estimation.

Absolute Camera Pose Estimation. Absolute pose estimation infers the camera position and orientation based on a single query frame relative to a pre-scanned environment. Traditional methods match sparse features of the query to a full 3D reconstruction of the scene, and solve for the pose [50,51,76–79,88,89]. Recent iterations of this classic formula utilize learned components for some of the steps, particularly for image retrieval, feature extraction and feature matching [42,73,75,90,91]. Scene coordinate regression dispenses with the need for discrete feature matching by regressing image-to-scene correspondences directly, via random forests [8,82,97] or neural networks [7,9,11,12]. Absolute pose regression networks predict poses in a single forward pass, and avoid any potentially costly geometric optimization altogether [13,45,46,81,102]. Finally, relative pose regression can be coupled with image retrieval to infer absolute poses [4,48,95,104,111]. One of the major challenges in absolute pose estimation is to handle scene ambiguities, such as feature-less areas or repeating structures. These are more likely to appear in larger scenes. Difficult visual conditions, such as low lighting, can also create ambiguous images. Different strategies exist to cope with ambiguities in absolute pose estimation, such as avoiding full-scale reconstructions [79], using global image context to resolve local ambiguities [10,49] or modeling uncertainty to make multi-modal predictions [14]. Orthogonal to these strategies, we demonstrate that active audio sensing effectively helps disambiguates a query by providing a surround view of the environment.

Table 1. Performance on depth pretraining task. Our framework outperforms the state-of-the-art Echo2Depth [65]; see text for details

	Frontal Camera FoV						Overall					
	RMS↓	REL↓	Log10↓	A1↑	A2↑	A3↑	RMS↓	REL↓	Log10↓	A1↑	A2↑	A3↑
Replica dataset												
Echo2Depth [65]	0.583	0.443	0.143	0.603	0.765	0.851	-	-	-	-	-	-
Ours	0.474	0.360	0.121	0.677	0.817	0.884	0.501	0.371	0.130	0.643	0.797	0.874
Matterport3D dataset												
Echo2Depth [65]	1.166	0.351	0.133	0.571	0.756	0.847	-	-	-	-	-	-
Ours	1.118	0.341	0.125	0.597	0.773	0.860	0.994	0.327	0.114	0.638	0.795	0.872

2   Spatial Audio Representation Learning Framework

The main objective of this work is to evaluate the capabilities of audio sensing for classic visual localization tasks. However, a key challenge is wrangling the high-dimensional audio input into a meaningful form. While camera images explicitly display the spatial configuration of a scene, spatial cues in audio echoes are reflected in subtler differences in signal arrival times and levels [33].

To overcome this challenge, we propose to first learn an audio representation that captures the spatial configuration of the scene around the device. Our pre-training framework exploits the natural co-occurrence between visual and audio signals to distill visual information of the device's surroundings, which we represent as an egocentric depth cubemap [37], into the audio representation. We hypothesize that such a representation will be helpful for device localization.

Method. Let $\mathbf{y}$ denote audio signal and $\mathbf{v}$ denote the visual frame. As shown in Fig. 2, we provide our model with audio-visual samples where the camera is rotated in one of six orientations with respect to the microphone. These orientations (denoted by j) correspond to the faces of an egocentric cube map. The audio encoder f extracts a feature embedding for the full scene, and the depth decoder g uses the j-th subset of this embedding to reconstruct a depth map of the camera view. We train the model by minimizing the log-loss [41,65],

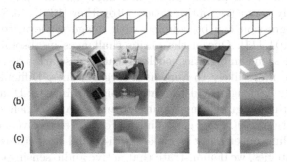

Fig. 3. Scene Geometry from Audio. Our pretraining task distills scene geometry into an audio representation. (a) Camera views corresponding to an egocentric cube-map. (b) Ground truth depth maps for these views. (c) Depth decoded from our audio representation.

$$\mathcal{L}(\mathbf{y},\mathbf{v},j) := \frac{1}{WH} \sum_{p=1}^{W} \sum_{q=1}^{H} \log(1 + |D(\mathbf{v})_{[p,q]} - g(f_j(\mathbf{y}),j)_{[p,q]}|), \qquad (1)$$

where $D(\mathbf{v})$ is the target depth map derived from visual frame $\mathbf{v}$, and (W,H) is the size of the depth map. While supervision is only provided for one face of the cube map at a time, over the course of training on many samples, the model learns to capture the full surround depth of the device's surroundings.

Dataset. We train our framework on the Replica [85] and Matterport3D [17] datasets. Replica contains 18 indoor scenes of hotels, apartments, rooms and offices. Matterport3D contains 85 indoor scenes, most of which are large, multi-room homes. Following previous work [20,33,65,68], audio-visual data for these scenes is obtained by simulating echo responses using the SoundSpaces platform [20] and rendering the corresponding camera view using the Habitat platform [80]. SoundSpaces simulates acoustics by pre-computing an impulse response (IR) for each source-receiver location pair on a dense grid with 0.5m and 1m spatial resolution for Replica and Matterport3D respectively. To simulate an echo recorded by a microphone with a specific location and orientation, the IR with both source and receiver at this grid location is selected, rotated to the desired orientation, and convolved with a 3ms audio chirp (20Hz-20kHz frequency sweep) [33]. We follow previously defined scene splits for these datasets for training, validation and testing [33,65]. Devices are placed at all possible grid locations within each scene, with random azimuth and elevation angles.

Task Performance. To assess whether our model extracts meaningful scene information from audio echoes, we compare to the SOTA Echo2Depth [65]. Table 1 shows that we significantly outperform their model across all evaluation metrics. Note that their approach only predicts the depth for the frontal camera, whereas our approach predicts omnidirectional scene geometry. Training Echos2Depth separately on six faces of the cube with the same representation size performs worse than our model, in part due to the sharing of weights in our encoder and decoder (see Supplemental Material for ablations). Figure 3 shows a qualitative result of the scene geometry captured by our audio representation.

3 Relative Pose Estimation

Having learned audio features that capture 3D scene geometry, we now show how these signals can help localize a device. We start with relative pose estimation: given inputs from two nearby devices, predict their relative transformation. Visual methods match features between two camera images, but they have difficulty handling cases with low overlap between images [22]. Audio sensing can help as it captures spatial cues beyond the camera's field of view.

3.1 Proposed Models with Audio Sensing

Let $(\mathbf{y}_1, \mathbf{v}_1)$ and $(\mathbf{y}_2, \mathbf{v}_2)$ denote the audio-visual inputs for the two devices, and let (R, t) denote their 3×3 relative rotation matrix and 3D translation vector. As in previous work, we take t to be a normalized direction without scale.

Audio Regression Model. We first propose a model that regresses relative pose directly from audio. The audio signals $\mathbf{y}_1, \mathbf{y}_2$ are passed through our pre-trained feature extractor f. We concatenate the features and pass them through a shallow multi-layer perceptron (MLP) to produce three vectors: $(\hat{r}_x, \hat{r}_y, \hat{t}_a)$. We use a partial Gram-Schmidt projection to obtain a rotation matrix $\hat{R}_a$ from $\hat{r}_x, \hat{r}_y$ [112], and train the MLP to minimize the mean-squared error between the predicted and ground truth rotation matrices [112], as well as a direction loss [22] given by the negative cosine similarity between the two translation vectors, i.e.

$$\mathcal{L}_R(\hat{R}_a, R) := ||\hat{R}_a - R||^2 \quad \text{and} \quad \mathcal{L}_t(\hat{t}_a, t) := -\frac{\hat{t}_a^T t}{||\hat{t}_a||||t||}.$$

The full loss is given by $\mathcal{L}_{audio}(\hat{R}_a, \hat{t}_a, R, t) := \beta\mathcal{L}_R(\hat{R}_a, R) + \mathcal{L}_t(\hat{t}_a, t)$, where hyperpameter $\beta > 0$ weighs the relative importance between the losses.

Audio-Visual Regression Model. Some existing visual methods tackle relative pose by regressing pose from images directly using a Siamese architecture [29,57,67,108]. We augment this approach with audio sensing. The audio signals $\mathbf{y}_1, \mathbf{y}_2$ are passed through our pretrained feature extractor f, and the images $\mathbf{v}_1, \mathbf{v}_2$ are passed through a deep residual network [39]. Similar to the audio regression model, the audio-visual features are concatenated and passed through a shallow MLP to predict pose. The model is trained to minimize $\mathcal{L}_{audio}$.

Visual Feature Matching + Audio. State-of-the-art visual methods such as Superglue [74] match local features between two images and then predict relative pose via essential matrix estimation within a RANSAC loop [30]. To incorporate audio sensing into such methods, we propose a mixture-of-experts (MoE) type model, in which a gating function decides whether to use the audio expert (audio regression model) or the visual expert (SuperGlue). An intuitive gating function to use is the output of the visual matching: if visual matching produces a pose $(\hat{R}_v, \hat{t}_v)$, then there is likely overlap between the images, and we should use this result; otherwise, we use the audio expert's prediction $(\hat{R}_a, \hat{t}_a)$.

Visual Feature Matching + Audio + (Learned) Gating. Since visual matching does not necessarily produce a better result than audio, we also propose a learned gating function that assigns an expert based on the predicted poses. Concretely, the learned gating function is a neural network that takes as input the predicted poses from both streams $(\hat{R}_a, \hat{t}_a, \hat{R}_v, \hat{t}_v)$ and outputs a vector $z \in [0,1]^4, \sum_i z_i = 1$ indicating the composition of the final prediction. Each entry of z gives the probability that one modality will outperform the other for estimating R or t. We train the gating network to minimize the cross-entropy loss between z and z^*, a one-hot vector indicating the optimal combination of expert outputs. See Fig. 4(a) for a schematic of this full model.

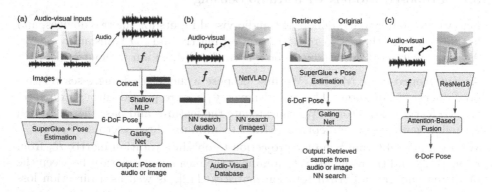

Fig. 4. Audio-visual methods for device localization. Proposed models for (a) relative pose estimation, (b) place recognition, and (c) absolute pose regression

3.2 Evaluation

Benchmarks. Since there are no datasets for relative pose estimation with audio-visual data, we introduce new benchmarks on the Replica [85] and Matterport3D [17] scenes. For training, validation, and test scenes, we use the same splits as our pretraining task. We sample audio-visual inputs from adjacent navigable points on the scene grid with random azimuth and elevation angles. We consider three evaluation scenarios: standard baseline cases (<90° rotation) that are typically studied in the vision literature where cameras have considerable visual overlap; extreme wide baseline cases (>90° rotation) where cameras have very limited visual overlap; and low-lighting cases. We evaluate methods on median angular error [22], as well as accuracy at a 20° cutoff [74].

Baselines. We compare our audio-visual models to the established vision models that they build upon. The first is a visual regression baseline that uses a Siamese architecture to regress pose from two images, as in [29,57,67,108]. The second is SuperGlue, a SOTA visual matching method for relative pose estimation [74]; we use the pretrained indoor model released by the authors. To assess the pretraining task, we compare our audio model to one trained from scratch.

Results. Table 2 shows quantitative results for all methods.

Table 2. Audio sensing improves relative pose estimation. Our best audio-visual method, which combines our audio feature representation with visual matching and a learned gating network, outperforms other methods including SOTA visual matching [74] on both the Replica and Matterport3D datasets. Audio-visual methods that outperform both visual baselines are underlined. *Visual matching fails to find a match on most test images; median values are computed from valid matches only.

		Standard Baseline (Relative Rot. <90°)			Wide Baseline (Relative Rot. >90°)			Low Lighting (Dark Image)		
		t↓	R↓	Acc.↑	t↓	R↓	Acc.↑	t↓	R↓	Acc.↑
	Replica dataset									
	Visual regression	35.0	15.0	21.0	37.4	20.0	17.3	57.3	99.1	0.7
	Visual matching [74]	34.1	12.2	39.9	55.0*	108.4*	2.0	47.6*	14.3*	1.6
Ours	Audio only (scratch)	30.2	17.9	21.9	28.8	19.5	22.3	30.2	17.9	21.9
	Audio only (pretrained)	21.6	10.5	38.1	23.0	10.9	36.8	21.6	10.5	38.1
	Audio-visual regression	33.0	14.3	24.1	35.6	18.4	19.5	58.5	91.6	0.9
	Visual matching + Audio	19.0	7.3	47.7	27.3	13.3	31.5	23.3	10.8	35.3
	Visual matching + Audio + Gating	**13.8**	**6.5**	**55.4**	**22.6**	**10.6**	**37.6**	**21.5**	**10.3**	**38.4**
	Matterport3D dataset									
	Visual regression	44.5	37.1	6.6	45.8	56.5	3.9	53.5	110.8	0.1
	Visual matching [74]	19.0	9.5	49.2	55.8*	113.09*	2.1	50.1*	31.1*	0.6
Ours	Audio only (scratch)	35.0	24.7	13.8	35.1	25.7	13.2	35.0	24.7	13.8
	Audio only (pretrained)	31.2	20.5	17.7	31.7	22.8	15.9	31.2	20.5	17.7
	Audio-visual regression	41.4	37.0	8.0	43.3	51.3	5.4	48.1	99.9	1.0
	Visual matching + Audio	13.5	7.7	52.3	36.7	30.1	14.1	32.0	20.8	17.4
	Visual matching + Audio + Gating	**11.7**	**7.2**	**54.4**	**31.2**	**22.5**	**17.2**	**31.1**	**20.3**	**18.0**

Audio-visual vs. Vision-only. Audio sensing improves the performance of both the visual regression and SOTA visual matching methods across all metrics and evaluation settings. This validates the benefit of audio for visual positioning. As expected, adding audio is most helpful to the wide-baseline and low-lighting cases, achieving large gains over the visual matching baseline.

Figure 5 shows a qualitative result of visual matching + audio + gating. In Fig. 5(a), the two devices have large relative rotation and there is low overlap between their images. As a result, visual matching performs poorly, as shown in Fig. 5(b). Our gating function chooses the audio expert to produce robust results, as shown in Fig. 5(c).

Does Pretraining Help? Our pretraining task significantly boosts the performance of the audio model over one trained from scratch. This validates our hypothesis that learning 3D scene geometry is beneficial for device localization.

Audio-Visual vs. Audio-only. In the wide-baseline and low-lighting cases, visual matching + audio does worse than the audio only model. This is due to false matches found by SuperGlue. The learned gating function correctly disambiguates many of these false matches, yielding improved scores. Interestingly, while the audio-visual regression model improves over visual regression, it does not improve over the audio only model. A different representation of the pose outputs from the visual and audio streams, e.g., using the classification framework of [22] rather than regression, may yield superior fusion results.

4   Place Recognition

Given a device capture, place recognition aims to determine its rough location by retrieving a similar capture from a reference database. Visual place recognition typically involves performing retrieval on camera inputs, but it performs poorly in situations with low overlap between query and database images [56]. Audio sensing can help by providing spatial cues beyond the camera's field of view. We let $(\mathbf{y}_q, \mathbf{v}_q)$ denote the query audio-visual input captured at position c_q.

4.1   Proposed Methods with Audio Sensing

Audio Descriptor. We first propose to learn an audio descriptor from the output of pretrained feature extractor f. We do this by appending a shallow MLP to the end of f, which we train using the triplet margin loss [5]:

$$\mathcal{L}_{\text{triplet}}(\mathbf{y}, \mathbf{y}_+, \mathbf{y}_-) := \max\{\|\mathbf{y} - \mathbf{y}_+\| - \|\mathbf{y} - \mathbf{y}_-\| + m, 0\}, \qquad (2)$$

where $\mathbf{y}$ denotes the anchor, $\mathbf{y}_+$ is a spatially-neighboring audio sample, $\mathbf{y}_-$ is a non-neighboring audio sample, and $m > 0$ represents the margin. While f captures 3D scene geometry, this additional training with triplet loss enforces that close distances in the output of the MLP reflect close distances in physical space. To perform place recognition, we compare $f^*(\mathbf{y}_q)$ to the descriptors in the reference database and perform an exact nearest neighbor search based on Euclidean distance to retrieve a sample located at $c_{\text{NN}(\mathbf{y}_q)}$.

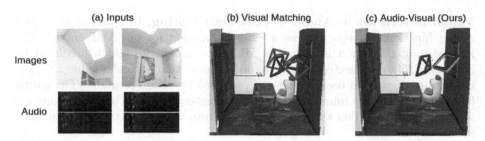

Fig. 5. Combining audio and vision for relative pose estimation. (a) Audio-visual inputs from two devices. (b) Due to the low overlap between images, visual matching preforms poorly. (c) In this case, our audio-visual chooses the pose predicted by the audio expert to make a robust prediction. Blue – ground truth. Red – visual prediction. Green – our prediction. (Color figure online)

Visual Descriptor + Audio. Visual place recognition commonly relies on state-of-the-art networks, such as NetVLAD [1], to produce visual descriptors for retrieval. To incorporate audio sensing into such methods, we propose a mixture-of-experts (MoE) type model, in which a gating function decides whether to use the audio expert (audio descriptor) or the visual expert (NetVLAD). Since our goal is to use the audio stream when the visual match between the query image and reference images is poor, we propose an intuitive gating function based on a validation step for the visual retrieval result: if local feature matching (i.e., using SuperGlue [74]) between v_q and the retrieved image $v_{NN(v_q)}$ predicts a positive result, then we use the location $c_{NN(v_q)}$ corresponding to this result; otherwise, we use the audio expert's prediction $c_{NN(y_q)}$.

Table 3. Audio sensing improves visual place recognition. Our models that combine our audio feature representation with visual descriptors outperform SOTA image retrieval with NetVLAD descriptors [1] on both the Replica and Matterport3D datasets. Audio-visual methods that outperform the visual baseline are underlined. Results are averaged over scenes; rank refers to average rank over scenes in the dataset.

		Overall All Queries			High Overlap Subset of Queries			Low Overlap Subset of Queries			Low Lighting All Queries		
		R@1	R@5	Rank	R@1	R@5	Rank	R@1	R@5	Rank	R@1	R@5	Rank
	Replica dataset												
	Visual descriptors [1]	0.59	0.76	4.0	0.91	0.98	2.3	0.38	0.61	5.0	0.18	0.34	5.0
Ours	Audio only (scratch)	0.59	0.68	4.5	0.57	0.66	5.0	0.60	0.70	1.5	0.59	0.68	4.0
	Audio only (pretrained)	0.65	0.74	2.5	0.69	0.78	4.0	0.64	0.72	1.5	0.65	0.74	1.0
	Visual descriptors + Audio	0.67	0.81	2.5	0.92	0.98	1.8	0.51	0.69	4.0	0.63	0.73	3.0
	Visual descriptors + Audio + Gating	0.71	0.83	1.5	0.92	0.98	2.0	0.58	0.73	2.5	0.64	0.74	2.0
	Matterport3D dataset												
	Visual descriptors [1]	0.44	0.66	4.3	0.90	0.97	2.4	0.39	0.63	4.3	0.12	0.26	5.0
Ours	Audio only (scratch)	0.41	0.54	4.3	0.42	0.54	4.8	0.41	0.54	4.3	0.41	0.54	3.3
	Audio only (pretrained)	0.49	0.62	3.3	0.50	0.63	4.3	0.49	0.62	3.0	0.49	0.62	2.0
	Visual descriptors + Audio	0.54	0.71	2.3	0.91	0.97	1.5	0.50	0.68	2.3	0.49	0.62	2.9
	Visual descriptors + Audio + Gating	0.55	0.71	1.0	0.90	0.97	2.1	0.51	0.69	1.3	0.49	0.62	1.9

Visual Descriptor + Audio + (Learned) Gating. In addition to a fixed gating function, we also propose a learned function for our MoE model. The learned gating function is a shallow MLP that takes the match predicted by Superglue [74], represented as relative pose, and outputs a scalar value $z \in [0, 1]$ indicating whether to use the position retrieved by vision or audio. The gating function is trained to minimize the binary cross-entropy loss between z and z^*, which indicates whether the retrieved result from vision is better than audio.

4.2   Evaluation

Benchmarks. Since there are no datasets for place recognition with audio-visual data, we introduce new benchmarks on two scenes from the Replica dataset and four scenes from the Matterport3D dataset that were held out from the pretraining task. Reference and query audio-visual data are sampled from distinct locations on the scene grid. For reference samples, we place devices within 90° and 45° of the first cardinal direction (N/0°) for Replica and Matterport3D respectively. We consider two evaluation scenarios: high overlap cases where the query devices are oriented in the same range of rotations as the reference devices; low overlap cases where query devices are oriented outside of this range; and low-lighting cases. To evaluate methods, we use the Recall@k metric [36].

Baselines. We compare our audio-visual methods to SOTA image retrieval using NetVLAD [1]. To determine the usefulness of the pretraining task, we compare our audio descriptors to those trained from scratch.

Results. Table 3 shows quantitative results for all methods.

Audio-visual vs. Vision-only. Audio-visual results that outperform vision are underlined in the table. We find that including audio sensing improves performance over NetVLAD image retrieval across almost all metrics and evaluation scenarios. This validates the benefit of audio for indoor visual place recognition. As expected, the addition of audio benefits low-overlap queries and low-lighting cases the most, bringing large gains over the visual baseline. Figure 6 shows a qualitative result of our visual descriptor + audio + gating model. Since there is no visual overlap between the query sample (blue) and the images in the reference database, NetVLAD retrieval returns an incorrect result (red). The audio-visual model chooses the audio expert to make a correct retrieval (green).

Does Pretraining Help? Our pretraining task significantly boosts the performance of the audio descriptors over those trained from scratch. This supports our hypothesis that learning 3D scene geometry from audio can help device localization.

Audio-Visual vs. Audio-only. Note that in the low-overlap cases and low-lighting cases, the visual descriptor + audio model does worse than the model with audio alone. This is because the query images have very little visual overlap with the reference, so many positive matches for these images are false matches. The learned gating function manages to correctly disambiguate many false matches,

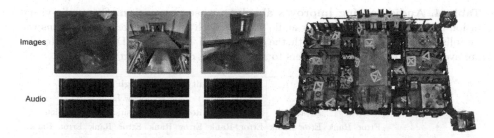

Images

Audio

Fig. 6. Combining audio and vision for place recognition. The query audio-visual sample is highlighted in blue and its position is depicted by the blue frustum. Since there is no overlap between reference frustums (subset shown in yellow) and the query, using visual descriptors results in incorrect retrieval (red). Our audio-visual method selects the audio expert to make a correct retrieval (green). Note that frustum rotations do not matter for accuracy, only its position. (Color figure online)

yielding improved scores. Audio-only shows slightly better performance on low-overlap and low-lighting queries on the smaller Replica scenes, while visual descriptor + audio + gating performs better on the larger Matterport3D scenes.

5   Absolute Pose Regression

Absolute pose estimation involves estimating the position and rotation of a device with respect to a known 3D environment. Many recent direct regression approaches [4,48,95,104,111] as well as some local feature-based approaches [42,73] combine retrieval with relative pose estimation. Our approaches for integrating audio sensing into place recognition and relative pose estimation could directly be used in those pipelines to tackle challenging cases with low visual overlap. Here, we focus instead on regression methods and use audio to tackle a separate challenge: scene ambiguities that cause images to match with different parts of the same scene. Recent work on absolute pose regression has focused on modeling distributions of poses to handle this problem [14]. As an orthogonal solution, we propose to use audio sensing to disambiguate between regions of the scene that appear visually similar.

Model. We augment an established absolute pose regression network, PoseNet [46], with our audio features. Let $(\mathbf{y}, \mathbf{v})$ denote the audio-visual capture of the device, and let (R, t) denote the device's pose. We use a deep residual network [13] to extract visual features from $\mathbf{v}$, and we use our pretrained audio feature extractor to obtain audio features from $\mathbf{y}$. The features are fused using a self-attention module [99] and a shallow MLP produces three vectors: $(\hat{r}_x, \hat{r}_y, \hat{t})$. A partial Gram-Schmidt projection is used to obtain a rotation matrix $\hat{R}$ from $\hat{r}_x, \hat{r}_y$ [112]. We train the weights of our network to minimize the mean-squared error between the predicted and ground truth poses, i.e., $\mathcal{L}_{\text{audio}}(\hat{R}, \hat{t}, R, t) := \beta||\hat{R} - R||^2 + ||\hat{t} - t||^2$, where $\beta > 0$ is a hyperparameter that weights the relative importance between the rotation and translation errors.

Table 4. Audio sensing improves absolute pose regression. Our audio-visual fusion model, which combines our audio features with visual features, outperforms the established vision baseline on both the Replica and Matterport3D datasets. Results are averaged over scenes; rank refers to average rank over scenes in the dataset

	Overall All Queries				Low Ambiguity Normal Light				High Ambiguity Low Light			
	Position		Rotation		Position		Rotation		Position		Rotation	
	Error	Rank	Error	Rank	Error	Rank	Error	Rank	Error	Rank	Error	Rank
Replica dataset												
PoseNet [46]	0.53	1.75	9.4	2.0	**0.43**	**1.25**	7.3	2.25	0.74	2.0	13.7	2.0
Audio only	2.49	4.0	27.7	4.0	2.27	4.0	27.4	4.0	2.93	4.0	28.3	3.5
Audio-Visual (scratch)	1.88	3.0	19.3	3.0	1.52	3.0	12.5	2.75	2.45	3.0	27.2	3.5
Audio-Visual	**0.52**	**1.25**	**6.9**	**1.0**	0.46	1.75	**5.4**	**1.0**	**0.64**	**1.0**	**9.9**	**1.0**
Matterport3D dataset												
PoseNet [46]	2.17	2.0	21.0	2.0	1.41	2.0	**13.5**	1.75	3.73	2.0	36.5	2.0
Audio only	9.60	4.0	74.9	4.0	9.82	4.0	76.2	4.0	9.14	4.0	72.2	3.75
Audio-Visual (scratch)	3.34	3.0	41.8	3.0	2.31	3.0	30.3	3.0	5.46	3.0	64.9	3.25
Audio-Visual	**1.86**	**1.0**	**19.4**	**1.0**	**1.31**	**1.0**	13.6	**1.25**	**3.01**	**1.0**	**31.2**	**1.0**

(The last two block groups for each dataset—Audio only, Audio-Visual (scratch), Audio-Visual—are labelled "Ours".)

5.1   Evaluation

Benchmarks. There are no datasets for absolute pose estimation with audio-visual data, so we introduce new benchmarks on two scenes from Replica [85] and four scenes from Matterport3D [17] that are held out from pretraining. Training and test samples are obtained from distinct locations on the scene grid, at random azimuth and elevation angles. To introduce more ambiguity, we reduce the brightness of specific regions (approximately 30% of the floorplan area).

Baselines. We compare our audio-visual regression network to PoseNet [46], the established visual regression approach that we build upon. To assess the usefulness of the pretraining task, we also perform an ablation of our model that trains the audio network from scratch. Note that we also experimented with DSAC* [12] and ESAC [10], state-of-the-art scene coordinate regression models. However, we found DSAC* to perform poorly on these large, ambiguous datasets, and we found ESAC to consume an unreasonable amount of training time to cover each scene with dozens of expert networks.

Results. Table 4 shows quantitative results for our approach. The audio-visual model provides a boost over the established visual baseline. This is already evident in portions of the scene with regular illumination, but particularly prominent in the portions of the scene with poor illumination (and greater visual ambiguity). Figure 7 provides a qualitative example of how audio sensing benefits the vision model for absolute pose regression in a large Matterport3D scene: the input images observe ambiguous views of the scene (blue). This result in

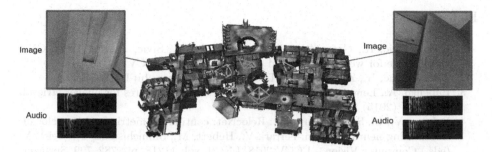

Fig. 7. Combining audio and vision for absolute pose regression. The input images observe ambiguous views of the scene (blue frustums). This result in poor performance on the part of the visual model (red frustums), whereas the audio-visual model uses audio to disambiguate the position of the device (green frustums). (Color figure online)

poor performance on the part of the visual model (red), whereas the audio-visual model uses audio to disambiguate the position of the device (green).

Does Pretraining Help? Using our pretrained audio feature extractor significantly boosts the performance of the audio-visual model. When we train the model from scratch, without our pretrained audio feature extractor, we find that it performs significantly worse– surprisingly, even worse than the vision-only model. [103] provides an explanation: multimodal models do not necessarily outperform unimodal models, since modalities trained from scratch may generalize and overfit at different rates. This further validates the use of our pretrained audio features.

6 Discussion

Overall, we present an exciting new research direction that leverages active audio sensing for classic camera localization tasks. Our experiments show that integrating our scene-aware audio features into established vision models improves performance across relative pose estimation, place recognition, and absolute pose regression. We hope that our work inspires further research in this direction, including collection of real-world audio-visual datasets of indoor scenes with ground truth poses. While we focus on improving specific vision models in this work, our insights on using audio sensing are not limited to these architectures and could be combined with other task-specific advances in the literature.

References

1. Arandjelovic, R., Gronat, P., Torii, A., Pajdla, T., Sivic, J.: NetVLAD: CNN architecture for weakly supervised place recognition. In: CVPR (2016)
2. Arandjelovic, R., Zisserman, A.: Look, listen and learn. In: ICCV (2017)
3. Babenko, A., Lempitsky, V.: Aggregating local deep features for image retrieval. In: ICCV (2015)
4. Balntas, V., Li, S., Prisacariu, V.: RelocNet: continuous metric learning relocalisation using neural nets. In: Ferrari, V., Hebert, M., Sminchisescu, C., Weiss, Y. (eds.) Computer Vision – ECCV 2018. LNCS, vol. 11218, pp. 782–799. Springer, Cham (2018). https://doi.org/10.1007/978-3-030-01264-9_46
5. Balntas, V., Riba, E., Ponsa, D., Mikolajczyk, K.: Learning local feature descriptors with triplets and shallow convolutional neural networks. In: BMVC (2016)
6. Bhowmik, A., Gumhold, S., Rother, C., Brachmann, E.: Reinforced feature points: optimizing feature detection and description for a high-level task. In: CVPR, June 2020
7. Brachmann, E., et al.: DSAC - differentiable RANSAC for camera localization. In: CVPR (2017)
8. Brachmann, E., Michel, F., Krull, A., Yang, M.Y., Gumhold, S., Rother, C.: Uncertainty-driven 6d pose estimation of objects and scenes from a single RGB image. In: CVPR (2016)
9. Brachmann, E., Rother, C.: Learning less is more - 6D camera localization via 3D surface regression. In: CVPR (2018)
10. Brachmann, E., Rother, C.: Expert sample consensus applied to camera relocalization. In: ICCV (2019)
11. Brachmann, E., Rother, C.: Neural-guided RANSAC: learning where to sample model hypotheses. In: ICCV (2019)
12. Brachmann, E., Rother, C.: Visual camera re-localization from RGB and RGB-D images using DSAC. TPAMI (2021)
13. Brahmbhatt, S., Gu, J., Kim, K., Hays, J., Kautz, J.: Geometry-aware learning of maps for camera localization. In: CVPR (2018)
14. Bui, M., et al.: 6D camera relocalization in ambiguous scenes via continuous multimodal inference. In: Vedaldi, A., Bischof, H., Brox, T., Frahm, J.-M. (eds.) ECCV 2020. LNCS, vol. 12363, pp. 139–157. Springer, Cham (2020). https://doi.org/10.1007/978-3-030-58523-5_9
15. Cai, R., Hariharan, B., Snavely, N., Averbuch-Elor, H.: Extreme rotation estimation using dense correlation volumes. In: CVPR (2021)
16. Castle, R., Klein, G., Murray, D.W.: Video-rate localization in multiple maps for wearable augmented reality. In: 2008 12th IEEE International Symposium on Wearable Computers, pp. 15–22. IEEE (2008)
17. Chang, A., et al.: Matterport3D: learning from RGB-D data in indoor environments. In: 3DV (2017)
18. Chen, C., Al-Halah, Z., Grauman, K.: Semantic audio-visual navigation. In: CVPR (2021)
19. Chen, C., et al.: Audio-visual embodied navigation. Environment 97, 103 (2019)
20. Chen, C., et al.: SoundSpaces: audio-visual navigation in 3D environments. In: Vedaldi, A., Bischof, H., Brox, T., Frahm, J.-M. (eds.) ECCV 2020. LNCS, vol. 12351, pp. 17–36. Springer, Cham (2020). https://doi.org/10.1007/978-3-030-58539-6_2

21. Chen, C., Majumder, S., Al-Halah, Z., Gao, R., Ramakrishnan, S.K., Grauman, K.: Learning to set waypoints for audio-visual navigation. arXiv preprint arXiv:2008.09622 (2020)

22. Chen, K., Snavely, N., Makadia, A.: Wide-baseline relative camera pose estimation with directional learning. In: CVPR (2021)

23. Chen, Z., Hu, X., Owens, A.: Structure from silence: learning scene structure from ambient sound. arXiv preprint arXiv:2111.05846 (2021)

24. Christensen, J.H., Hornauer, S., Stella, X.Y.: Batvision: learning to see 3D spatial layout with two ears. In: ICRA (2020)

25. Debski, A., Grajewski, W., Zaborowski, W., Turek, W.: Open-source localization device for indoor mobile robots. Procedia Comput. Sci. **76**, 139–146 (2015)

26. Dokmanić, I., Parhizkar, R., Walther, A., Lu, Y.M., Vetterli, M.: Acoustic echoes reveal room shape. Proc. Natl. Acad. Sci. **110**(30), 12186–12191 (2013)

27. Dusmanu, M., et al.: D2-net: a trainable CNN for joint detection and description of local features. arXiv preprint arXiv:1905.03561 (2019)

28. Eliakim, I., Cohen, Z., Kosa, G., Yovel, Y.: A fully autonomous terrestrial bat-like acoustic robot. PLoS Comput. Biol. **14**(9), e1006406 (2018)

29. En, S., Lechervy, A., Jurie, F.: RPNet: an end-to-end network for relative camera pose estimation. In: Leal-Taixé, L., Roth, S. (eds.) ECCV 2018. LNCS, vol. 11129, pp. 738–745. Springer, Cham (2019). https://doi.org/10.1007/978-3-030-11009-3_46

30. Fischler, M.A., Bolles, R.C.: Random sample consensus: a paradigm for model fitting with applications to image analysis and automated cartography. Commun. ACM **24**(6), 381–395 (1981)

31. Fisher III, J.W., Darrell, T., Freeman, W., Viola, P.: Learning joint statistical models for audio-visual fusion and segregation. In: NeurIPS (2000)

32. Gan, C., Zhao, H., Chen, P., Cox, D., Torralba, A.: Self-supervised moving vehicle tracking with stereo sound. In: ICCV (2019)

33. Gao, R., Chen, C., Al-Halah, Z., Schissler, C., Grauman, K.: VISUALECHOES: spatial image representation learning through echolocation. In: Vedaldi, A., Bischof, H., Brox, T., Frahm, J.-M. (eds.) ECCV 2020. LNCS, vol. 12354, pp. 658–676. Springer, Cham (2020). https://doi.org/10.1007/978-3-030-58545-7_38

34. Gao, R., Grauman, K.: 2.5D visual sound. In: CVPR (2019)

35. Gao, R., Oh, T.H., Grauman, K., Torresani, L.: Listen to look: action recognition by previewing audio. In: CVPR (2020)

36. Garg, S., Fischer, T., Milford, M.: Where is your place, visual place recognition? IJCAI (2021)

37. Greene, N.: Environment mapping and other applications of world projections. IEEE Comput. Graphics Appl. **6**(11), 21–29 (1986)

38. Hausler, S., Garg, S., Xu, M., Milford, M., Fischer, T.: Patch-NetVLAD: multiscale fusion of locally-global descriptors for place recognition. In: CVPR (2021)

39. He, K., Zhang, X., Ren, S., Sun, J.: Deep residual learning for image recognition. In: CVPR (2016)

40. Hershey, J., Movellan, J.: Audio vision: using audio-visual synchrony to locate sounds. In: NeurIPS (1999)

41. Hu, J., Ozay, M., Zhang, Y., Okatani, T.: Revisiting single image depth estimation: toward higher resolution maps with accurate object boundaries. In: WACV (2019)

42. Humenberger, M., et al.: Robust image retrieval-based visual localization using Kapture. arXiv:2007.13867 (2020)

43. Jégou, H., Douze, M., Schmid, C., Pérez, P.: Aggregating local descriptors into a compact image representation. In: CVPR (2010)
44. Kazakos, E., Nagrani, A., Zisserman, A., Damen, D.: Epic-fusion: audio-visual temporal binding for egocentric action recognition. In: ICCV (2019)
45. Kendall, A., Cipolla, R.: Geometric loss functions for camera pose regression with deep learning. In: CVPR (2017)
46. Kendall, A., Grimes, M., Cipolla, R.: PoseNet: a convolutional network for real-time 6-DOF camera relocalization. In: ICCV (2015)
47. Kidron, E., Schechner, Y.Y., Elad, M.: Pixels that sound. In: CVPR (2005)
48. Laskar, Z., Melekhov, I., Kalia, S., Kannala, J.: Camera relocalization by computing pairwise relative poses using convolutional neural network. In: ICCV Workshops (2017)
49. Li, X., Wang, S., Zhao, Y., Verbeek, J., Kannala, J.: Hierarchical scene coordinate classification and regression for visual localization. In: CVPR (2020)
50. Li, Y., Snavely, N., Huttenlocher, D.P.: Location recognition using prioritized feature matching. In: Daniilidis, K., Maragos, P., Paragios, N. (eds.) ECCV 2010. LNCS, vol. 6312, pp. 791–804. Springer, Heidelberg (2010). https://doi.org/10.1007/978-3-642-15552-9_57
51. Li, Y., Snavely, N., Huttenlocher, D., Fua, P.: Worldwide pose estimation using 3D point clouds. In: Fitzgibbon, A., Lazebnik, S., Perona, P., Sato, Y., Schmid, C. (eds.) ECCV 2012. LNCS, vol. 7572, pp. 15–29. Springer, Heidelberg (2012). https://doi.org/10.1007/978-3-642-33718-5_2
52. Lim, H., Sinha, S.N., Cohen, M.F., Uyttendaele, M.: Real-time image-based 6-dof localization in large-scale environments. In: CVPR (2012)
53. Lindell, D.B., Wetzstein, G., Koltun, V.: Acoustic non-line-of-sight imaging. In: CVPR (2019)
54. Liu, D., Cui, Y., Yan, L., Mousas, C., Yang, B., Chen, Y.: Densernet: weakly supervised visual localization using multi-scale feature aggregation. In: Proceedings of the AAAI Conference on Artificial Intelligence (2021)
55. Long, X., Gan, C., De Melo, G., Wu, J., Liu, X., Wen, S.: Attention clusters: purely attention based local feature integration for video classification. In: CVPR (2018)
56. Masone, C., Caputo, B.: A survey on deep visual place recognition. IEEE Access 9, 19516–19547 (2021)
57. Melekhov, I., Ylioinas, J., Kannala, J., Rahtu, E.: Relative camera pose estimation using convolutional neural networks. In: Blanc-Talon, J., Penne, R., Philips, W., Popescu, D., Scheunders, P. (eds.) ACIVS 2017. LNCS, vol. 10617, pp. 675–687. Springer, Cham (2017). https://doi.org/10.1007/978-3-319-70353-4_57
58. Morgado, P., Li, Y., Nvasconcelos, N.: Learning representations from audio-visual spatial alignment. In: NeurIPS, vol. 33, 4733–4744 (2020)
59. Morgado, P., Nvasconcelos, N., Langlois, T., Wang, O.: Self-supervised generation of spatial audio for 360 video. In: NeurIPS, vol. 31 (2018)
60. Morgado, P., Vasconcelos, N., Misra, I.: Audio-visual instance discrimination with cross-modal agreement. In: CVPR (2021)
61. Ngiam, J., Khosla, A., Kim, M., Nam, J., Lee, H., Ng, A.Y.: Multimodal deep learning. In: ICML (2011)
62. Owens, A., Efros, A.A.: Audio-visual scene analysis with self-supervised multi-sensory features. In: Ferrari, V., Hebert, M., Sminchisescu, C., Weiss, Y. (eds.) ECCV 2018. LNCS, vol. 11210, pp. 639–658. Springer, Cham (2018). https://doi.org/10.1007/978-3-030-01231-1_39

63. Owens, A., Isola, P., McDermott, J., Torralba, A., Adelson, E.H., Freeman, W.T.: Visually indicated sounds. In: CVPR (2016)
64. Owens, A., Wu, J., McDermott, J.H., Freeman, W.T., Torralba, A.: Ambient sound provides supervision for visual learning. In: Leibe, B., Matas, J., Sebe, N., Welling, M. (eds.) ECCV 2016. LNCS, vol. 9905, pp. 801–816. Springer, Cham (2016). https://doi.org/10.1007/978-3-319-46448-0_48
65. Parida, K.K., Srivastava, S., Sharma, G.: Beyond image to depth: improving depth prediction using echoes. In: CVPR (2021)
66. Politis, A., Mesaros, A., Adavanne, S., Heittola, T., Virtanen, T.: Overview and evaluation of sound event localization and detection in dcase 2019. IEEE/ACM Trans. Audio Speech Language Process. **29**, 684–698 (2020)
67. Poursaeed, O., et al.: Deep fundamental matrix estimation without correspondences. In: Leal-Taixé, L., Roth, S. (eds.) ECCV 2018. LNCS, vol. 11131, pp. 485–497. Springer, Cham (2019). https://doi.org/10.1007/978-3-030-11015-4_35
68. Purushwalkam, S., et al.: Audio-visual floorplan reconstruction. In: ICCV (2021)
69. Raguram, R., Frahm, J.-M., Pollefeys, M.: A comparative analysis of RANSAC techniques leading to adaptive real-time random sample consensus. In: Forsyth, D., Torr, P., Zisserman, A. (eds.) ECCV 2008. LNCS, vol. 5303, pp. 500–513. Springer, Heidelberg (2008). https://doi.org/10.1007/978-3-540-88688-4_37
70. Ranftl, R., Koltun, V.: Deep fundamental matrix estimation. In: Ferrari, V., Hebert, M., Sminchisescu, C., Weiss, Y. (eds.) ECCV 2018. LNCS, vol. 11205, pp. 292–309. Springer, Cham (2018). https://doi.org/10.1007/978-3-030-01246-5_18
71. Revaud, J., Weinzaepfel, P., de Souza, C.R., Humenberger, M.: R2D2: repeatable and reliable detector and descriptor. In: NeurIPS (2019)
72. de Sa, V.R.: Learning classification with unlabeled data. In: NeurIPS (1994)
73. Sarlin, P.E., Cadena, C., Siegwart, R., Dymczyk, M.: From coarse to fine: robust hierarchical localization at large scale. In: CVPR (2019)
74. Sarlin, P.E., DeTone, D., Malisiewicz, T., Rabinovich, A.: Superglue: learning feature matching with graph neural networks. In: CVPR (2020)
75. Sarlin, P.E., et al.: Back to the feature: learning robust camera localization from pixels to pose. In: CVPR (2021). arxiv.org/abs/2103.09213
76. Sattler, T., Havlena, M., Radenovic, F., Schindler, K., Pollefeys, M.: Hyperpoints and fine vocabularies for large-scale location recognition. In: ICCV (2015)
77. Sattler, T., Leibe, B., Kobbelt, L.: Improving image-based localization by active correspondence search. In: Fitzgibbon, A., Lazebnik, S., Perona, P., Sato, Y., Schmid, C. (eds.) ECCV 2012. LNCS, vol. 7572, pp. 752–765. Springer, Heidelberg (2012). https://doi.org/10.1007/978-3-642-33718-5_54
78. Sattler, T., Leibe, B., Kobbelt, L.: Efficient & effective prioritized matching for large-scale image-based localization. In: PAMI (2017)
79. Sattler, T., et al.: Are large-scale 3D models really necessary for accurate visual localization? In: CVPR (2017)
80. Savva, M., et al.: Habitat: a platform for embodied AI research. In: ICCV (2019)
81. Shavit, Y., Ferens, R., Keller, Y.: Learning multi-scene absolute pose regression with transformers. In: ICCV, pp. 2733–2742, October 2021
82. Shotton, J., Glocker, B., Zach, C., Izadi, S., Criminisi, A., Fitzgibbon, A.: Scene coordinate regression forests for camera relocalization in RGB-D images. In: CVPR (2013)
83. Singh, N., Mentch, J., Ng, J., Beveridge, M., Drori, I.: Image2reverb: cross-modal reverb impulse response synthesis. In: ICCV (2021)

84. Sohl-Dickstein, J., et al.: A device for human ultrasonic echolocation. IEEE Trans. Biomed. Eng. **62**(6), 1526–1534 (2015)
85. Straub, J., et al.: The replica dataset: a digital replica of indoor spaces. arXiv preprint arXiv:1906.05797 (2019)
86. Sun, J., Shen, Z., Wang, Y., Bao, H., Zhou, X.: LoFTR: detector-free local feature matching with transformers. In: CVPR (2021)
87. Sun, W., Jiang, W., Trulls, E., Tagliasacchi, A., Yi, K.M.: ACNe: attentive context normalization for robust permutation-equivariant learning. In: CVPR, June 2020
88. Svarm, L., Enqvist, O., Oskarsson, M., Kahl, F.: Accurate localization and pose estimation for large 3D models. In: CVPR (2014)
89. Svärm, L., Enqvist, O., Kahl, F., Oskarsson, M.: City-scale localization for cameras with known vertical direction. TPAMI (2017)
90. Taira, H., et aal.: InLoc: indoor visual localization with dense matching and view synthesis. In: CVPR (2018)
91. Taira, H., et al.: InLoc: indoor visual localization with dense matching and view synthesis. In: TPAMI (2021)
92. Taubner, F., Tschopp, F., Novkovic, T., Siegwart, R., Furrer, F.: LCD-line clustering and description for place recognition. In: 2020 International Conference on 3D Vision (3DV) (2020)
93. Thrun, S.: Affine structure from sound. In: NeurIPS (2005)
94. Torii, A., Arandjelovic, R., Sivic, J., Okutomi, M., Pajdla, T.: 24/7 place recognition by view synthesis. In: CVPR (2015)
95. Türkoğlu, M.Ö., Brachmann, E., Schindler, K., Brostow, G., Monszpart, A.: Visual camera re-localization using graph neural networks and relative pose supervision. In: 3DV. IEEE (2021)
96. Tyszkiewicz, M., Fua, P., Trulls, E.: Disk: learning local features with policy gradient. In: NeurIPS (2020)
97. Valentin, J., Nießner, M., Shotton, J., Fitzgibbon, A., Izadi, S., Torr, P.: Exploiting uncertainty in regression forests for accurate camera relocalization. In: CVPR (2015)
98. Vasudevan, A.B., Dai, D., Van Gool, L.: Semantic object prediction and spatial sound super-resolution with binaural sounds. In: Vedaldi, A., Bischof, H., Brox, T., Frahm, J.-M. (eds.) ECCV 2020. LNCS, vol. 12349, pp. 638–655. Springer, Cham (2020). https://doi.org/10.1007/978-3-030-58548-8_37
99. Vaswani, A., et al.: Attention is all you need. In: NeurIPS, vol. 30 (2017)
100. Villalpando, A.P., Schillaci, G., Hafner, V.V., Guzmán, B.L.: Ego-noise predictions for echolocation in wheeled robots. In: ALIFE 2019: The 2019 Conference on Artificial Life, pp. 567–573. MIT Press (2019)
101. Wagner, D., Reitmayr, G., Mulloni, A., Drummond, T., Schmalstieg, D.: Real-time detection and tracking for augmented reality on mobile phones. IEEE Trans. Visual Comput. Graphics **16**(3), 355–368 (2009)
102. Walch, F., Hazirbas, C., Leal-Taixé, L., Sattler, T., Hilsenbeck, S., Cremers, D.: Image-Based Localization Using LSTMs for Structured Feature Correlation. In: ICCV (2017)
103. Wang, W., Tran, D., Feiszli, M.: What makes training multi-modal classification networks hard? In: CVPR (2020)
104. Winkelbauer, D., Denninger, M., Triebel, R.: Learning to localize in new environments from synthetic training data. In: ICRA (2021)
105. Wu, Z., Jiang, Y.G., Wang, X., Ye, H., Xue, X.: Multi-stream multi-class fusion of deep networks for video classification. In: Proceedings of the 24th ACM international conference on Multimedia, pp. 791–800 (2016)

106. Yang, K., Lin, W.Y., Barman, M., Condessa, F., Kolter, Z.: Defending multimodal fusion models against single-source adversaries. In: CVPR (2021)
107. Yang, K., Russell, B., Salamon, J.: Telling left from right: learning spatial correspondence of sight and sound. In: CVPR (2020)
108. Yi, K.M., Trulls, E., Ono, Y., Lepetit, V., Salzmann, M., Fua, P.: Learning to find good correspondences. In: CVPR (2018)
109. Yue, H., Miao, J., Yu, Y., Chen, W., Wen, C.: Robust loop closure detection based on bag of superpoints and graph verification. In: IROS (2019)
110. Zhang, Z., et al.: Generative modeling of audible shapes for object perception. In: ICCV (2017)
111. Zhou, Q., Sattler, T., Pollefeys, M., Leal-Taixé, L.: To learn or not to learn: visual localization from essential matrices. In: ICRA (2019)
112. Zhou, Y., Barnes, C., Lu, J., Yang, J., Li, H.: On the continuity of rotation representations in neural networks. In: CVPR (2019)

PACS: A Dataset for Physical Audiovisual CommonSense Reasoning

Samuel Yu[1]([✉]) [iD], Peter Wu[2], Paul Pu Liang[1], Ruslan Salakhutdinov[1], and Louis-Philippe Morency[1]

[1] Carnegie Mellon University, Pittsburgh, USA
{samuelyu,pliang,rsalakhu,morency}@cs.cmu.edu
[2] University of California Berkeley, Berkeley, USA
peterw1@berkeley.edu

Abstract. In order for AI to be safely deployed in real-world scenarios such as hospitals, schools, and the workplace, it must be able to robustly reason about the physical world. Fundamental to this reasoning is *physical common sense*: understanding the physical properties and affordances of available objects, how they can be manipulated, and how they interact with other objects. Physical commonsense reasoning is fundamentally a multi-sensory task, since physical properties are manifested through multiple modalities - two of them being vision and acoustics. Our paper takes a step towards real-world physical commonsense reasoning by contributing PACS: the first audiovisual benchmark annotated for physical commonsense attributes. PACS contains 13,400 question-answer pairs, involving 1,377 unique physical commonsense questions and 1,526 videos. Our dataset provides new opportunities to advance the research field of physical reasoning by bringing audio as a core component of this multimodal problem. Using PACS, we evaluate multiple state-of-the-art models on our new challenging task. While some models show promising results (70% accuracy), they all fall short of human performance (95% accuracy). We conclude the paper by demonstrating the importance of multimodal reasoning and providing possible avenues for future research.

1 Introduction

To safely interact with everyday objects in the real world, AI must utilize physical commonsense knowledge about everyday objects: including their physical properties, affordances, how they can be manipulated, and how they interact with other physical objects [6,29]. Humans use *physical commonsense reasoning* in all facets of day-to-day life, whether it is to infer properties of previously unseen objects ("the water bottle over there is made of plastic, not glass"), or to solve unique problems ("I can use a puffy jacket in place of my missing pillow") [6]. This type of general understanding of object interactions is necessary

Supplementary Information The online version contains supplementary material available at https://doi.org/10.1007/978-3-031-19836-6_17.

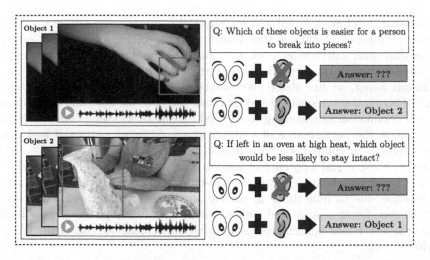

Fig. 1. PACS is the first audiovisual benchmark annotated for physical commonsense attributes, containing 13,400 question-answer pairs, 1,526 videos, and 1,377 unique questions. By benchmarking state-of-the-art unimodal and multimodal models to highlight *where* and *why* current models fail, PACS provides new opportunities to advance the research of physical reasoning through studying multimodal reasoning. This figure shows two example datapoints from PACS, with each datapoint containing a question and a pair of objects (in this figure, object 1 is a plastic lemon and object 2 is a ceramic vase). To view the video clips, please see the supplementary material.

In building robust and complete AI systems that can be safely deployed in the real world (e.g., a package delivery robot needs to treat heavier or lighter objects differently).

Physical commonsense reasoning is fundamentally a multi-sensory task, as physical properties are manifested through multiple modalities, including vision and acoustics [13,40,65]. If two objects appear similar visually, audio can provide valuable information to distinguish the physical properties between these objects. For example, in Fig. 1, instead of plastic, object 1 could be mistaken for squishy foam, and instead of ceramic, object 2 could be mistaken for painted plastic, glass, or even paper. Without the necessary audio information, this could result in the erroneous answer that object 1 is easier to break than object 2. In the real world, this misunderstanding may lead to the damaging or mishandling of an object. Therefore, to enable physical commonsense reasoning in AI, it is essential for these models to reason across both audio and visual modalities.

Recent work has explored the use of vision and/or text to understand basic physical properties [30,32,35,50,61,67], or benchmark *physical commonsense* in language [6,16]. Our work complements these previous settings by adding the acoustic modality as part of the problem formulation. Furthermore, we include not only static frames but also temporal information using videos. In these directions, our paper takes a step towards real-world physical commonsense reasoning by contributing PHYSICAL AUDIOVISUAL COMMONSENSE (PACS): the first *audiovisual* benchmark annotated for physical commonsense attributes. PACS contains a total of 13,400 question-answer pairs, involving 1,526 object-oriented videos that cover a diverse set of objects, and 1,377 unique physical commonsense questions involving a variety of physical properties.

In our paper, we first detail the construction of our new audiovisual benchmark of physical commonsense and establish the need for both the audio modality and commonsense reasoning to succeed on our task. Using this benchmark, we evaluate the performance of multiple state-of-the-art unimodal and multimodal models in comparison with human performance. We also performed an analysis of *where* and *why* current models fail, highlighting the increased difficulty of reasoning about physical commonsense, the lack of fine-grained temporal information due to limitations in current models' video and audio processing, and the need for more advanced audiovisual models. We hope our work will elicit further research into building robust multimodal representations of the physical world.[1]

2 Related Work

We cover related work in commonsense reasoning, particularly on physical understanding, which has been studied in domains spanning psychology, language, vision, robotics, and multimodal machine learning.

Psychology: Physical commonsense was first studied in humans, with psychology experiments based on naive and intuitive physics [8,17,25,28,39]. In these experiments, humans are asked to predict object motion or the result of multi-object interactions. Further research has also been conducted in general physical modeling [7] and the multisensory perception of physical properties [13,40,65]. In particular, studies on human behavior indicate that the audio modality contains valuable information about the physical properties of objects [24,40,41,57].

Language: Related work has studied physical commonsense within the text modality [6,16,32,50,67]. To our knowledge, the generalizability of their findings to other modalities is still understudied. Our dataset extends these text-based knowledge graphs and language models to multimodal settings.

Vision: Methods utilizing physical commonsense have been applied to several visual commonsense tasks, including scene understanding [12,58], activity recognition [37], and cause-effect prediction [42]. We note that these methods focus solely on the visual modality, which may bring challenges in tasks with unknown or occluded objects. Including information from other modalities such as audio and language could help mitigate these challenges.

Audio provides valuable information for one's understanding of the world [24, 57]. Currently, AI tasks studying physical properties through the lens of the audio

---

[1] For dataset download links, benchmarked models, and evaluation scripts, please visit https://github.com/samuelyu2002/PACS.

modality include navigation [10], perception [65], and generative modeling [18, 66]. We extend this research direction to higher-order reasoning through PACS.

Robotics: Comprehension of physical properties has been shown to be valuable for tool usage and object manipulation tasks [3,14,43,54,55]. Our paper provides a direction for generalizing physical commonsense reasoning utilizing both audio and visual modalities.

Multimodal: Recent work has introduced question-answering datasets with image and text inputs (e.g., VQA [5], NLVR [51], NLVR2 [52]), with some annotated for commonsense reasoning tasks (e.g., VCR [63,64], VisualCOMET [45]). There has also been the use of multimodal answer choices, such as a combination of text and image regions in VCR [63] and VisualCOMET [45]. Other works have also introduced datasets with video and text inputs to test for temporal reasoning (e.g., MovieQA [53], MovieFIB [38], TVQA [36,64]). To our knowledge, none of these approaches have explored audio and video together for physical commonsense reasoning.

3   PACS Dataset

We introduce PACS, a benchmark dataset designed to help create and evaluate a new generation of AI algorithms able to reason about physical commonsense using both audio and visual modalities. The underlying task is binary question answering, where given a question q and objects o_1, o_2, the model must pick the more appropriate object to answer the question. Each object is represented by a video v showing a human interacting with the object, the corresponding audio a, and a bounding-box b drawn around the object in the middlemost frame of v.[2] Thus, each datapoint in PACS is a tuple of values $(q, (b_1, v_1, a_1), (b_2, v_2, a_2), l)$, representing the question, two objects, and a binary label of which object is the correct answer (see Fig. 1 for an example datapoint in our dataset).

In this section, we first outline various design principles used in the creation of our dataset. Then, we give an overview of PACS statistics (see Fig. 2 for a complete overview), and finally discuss each component of our data collection and annotation process (see Fig. 3 for our complete annotation pipeline). For a more detailed overview of our data collection pipeline, please refer to section A in the appendix.

3.1   Design Principles

Through synthesis of previous work, we divide physical commonsense into two main categories based on which we designed PACS. These categories were used as guidance for annotators when creating physical commonsense questions.

---

[2] In our experiments, we usually represent the bounding box b as a red bounding box drawn directly on the middlemost frame of the video. Thus, we also interchangeably notate the bounding box as an image i.

1. **Intuitive physics, and a functional world model:** This category is inspired by previous psychology and AI experiments relating to physical commonsense, such as predicting object motion [33,34,48,59], or how objects interact with each other [28]. Questions in this category focus on predicting the result of single or multi-object interactions. Easy questions involve a single object and action, such as: *"Which object will break after being dropped on the ground?"* (*a vase, a ball of paper*). Harder questions involve multiple objects or actions, including interactions between the two objects, such as: *"Which object will become deformed if the other object is placed on top of it?"* (*a vase, a ball of paper*).
2. **Common real-world knowledge:** This category is inspired by previous commonsense datasets, which test for more concrete understandings of how and why humans or objects function in the real world [6,16,62,63]. Questions in this category ask about possible uses of an object in real-life scenarios. Importantly, these scenarios focus on less prototypical uses of an object, therefore reducing the possibility of abusing learned knowledge [6], such as *"Which object is better suited to clean up a watery mess"* (*an old t-shirt, a plastic box*). Harder questions can introduce more complicated or uncommon scenarios involving multiple objects: *"If I were to stack the two objects, which would logically go on the bottom?"* (*an old t-shirt, a plastic box*).

3.2 Dataset Statistics

This subsection presents the main object and question statistics of PACS. Each datapoint is the combination of a question, two objects, and the correct answer. Figure 2f shows the distribution of the number of questions relating to each object pair, with an average of 5.86 questions per pair.

Object Statistics: PACS contains a total of 1,526 objects, each represented by a unique video clip, with included audio and a bounding box in the middlemost frame of the video. Figure 2b shows a rough distribution of materials that the objects in our dataset are made of, as annotated in our video filtering step. Materials such as "Wax" or "Foam" occur more commonly in our dataset than in real life, due to our focus on creating a diverse set of objects. Figure 2e shows the length of each video. On average, videos in our dataset are 7.6 s long.

Question Statistics: PACS contains a total of 1,377 unique questions each used multiple times across various pairs of objects. Figure 2d shows how many times each question was used, where on average, a question was distributed to 10.8 pairs of videos. Figure 2a shows the distribution of question length in terms of the number of words. On average, a question was 16.6 words long. Figure 2c shows the distribution of physical properties that our questions relate to. Figure 2g shows the most commonly occurring words in our dataset and is also color-coded by CLIP's accuracy on datapoints conditioned on the occurrence of a specific word. We can see a variety of action words (e.g., placed, dropped, thrown, roll, rubbed, pressed, blown), each associated with different physical

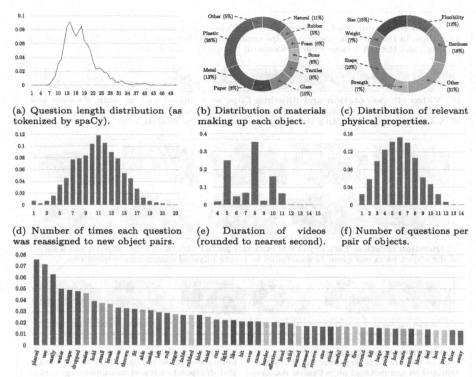

(a) Question length distribution (as tokenized by spaCy).

(b) Distribution of materials making up each object.

(c) Distribution of relevant physical properties.

(d) Number of times each question was reassigned to new object pairs.

(e) Duration of videos (rounded to nearest second).

(f) Number of questions per pair of objects.

(g) Frequency of most common words in PACS. The top 4 words (object, item, likely, better) are excluded due to their high frequency being a result of our problem formulation. The bars are colored based on the accuracy that AudioCLIP [23] achieves on them, with darker being higher accuracy.

Fig. 2. Dataset statistics for PACS. Best viewed zoomed-in and with color. Figure 2b and Fig. 2c show that the questions and objects in our dataset are diverse, involving different physical properties and materials. Figure 2g shows a variety of actions (e.g., placed, dropped, thrown, roll, rubbed, pressed, blown) covered in our diverse questions.

properties. Furthermore, we see that AudioCLIP struggles with certain physical concepts, such as having low accuracy on heat-related words (e.g., hot, fire).

3.3   Dataset Creation

In this subsection, we outline the steps used to gather and label datapoints in PACS (see Fig. 3 for a complete overview).

(a) **Video collection**: A broad set of ASMR videos were downloaded from YouTube. Specifically, we chose to use object-oriented ASMR videos, as they provide high-quality audio, and often incorporate objects that people less commonly interact with. We used a list of materials [1] to seed the search queries, which was later updated with more materials as we iterated through the first two data collection steps. For each video, we use a shot boundary detector [49] to split each video into separate scenes, and then further split each scene into roughly

(a) **Video collection**: We first downloaded YouTube videos and split them into 5-10 second long clips. In this example, the first 5 clips came from a video with the query "ASMR slime no talking", and the last 5 came from a video with the query "ASMR plastic no talking".

(b) **Video clip annotation and filtering**: Clips were filtered with an audio classifier and sparsely sampled to be sent for human filtering. Clips that passed human filtering were annotated with a bounding box (denoting the object) and added to the final dataset.

(c) **Question creation**: Each object was randomly paired with three other objects, and a subset of the object pairs was given to annotators to create physical commonsense questions.

| Q: If left in an oven, which object is more likely to melt first? | Q: Which object would make a louder noise when dropped on the ground? | Q: Which object could be manipulated to cover the entirety of the other object? |

(d) **Question reassignment**: Questions created in the previous step were randomly distributed to unannotated object pairs. Annotators removed irrelevant questions.

(e) **Quality checking**: The remaining datapoints were answered by additional annotators, and datapoints without unanimous agreement were removed.

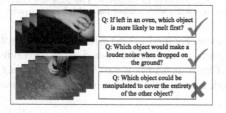

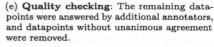

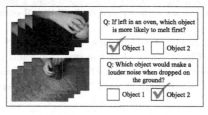

Fig. 3. Diagram of our data collection process, showing steps starting from gathering objects, to creating and checking datapoints. Best viewed zoomed-in and with color.

5–10 s long clips. Finally, an audio classifier [20] was used to remove videos with background music, talking, or silence. The remaining clips were sparsely sampled to create the candidate set of clips.

(b) Video clip annotation and filtering: When analyzing the candidate set of clips, we noticed that a large number of objects that appeared in these clips were common household objects, resulting in many repeated objects. Furthermore, common objects do not require as much multimodal understanding, as a single image and a decent knowledge base may be enough to identify the object and extract necessary physical properties. Thus, as a heuristic for how common or obvious an object is, we test to see if annotators are able to classify the materials each object is made of. If annotators are able to correctly identify an object's materials using just a single image, then this suggests that the object is likely common, and has physical properties that are easily distinguishable.

In this task, annotators were first given a single image from a candidate video clip and asked to draw a bounding box around the "object of focus", which we define as the object the person is touching in the video (if the guess is wrong, the clip is thrown away). Then, they were asked to select the materials that make up the object from a list, and to provide a confidence score from 1–5. Once they submitted their initial answer, annotators were then given access to the whole video and audio and asked to redo the task. If their confidence did not increase and their answers did not change, then the clip was removed. Otherwise, the clip and the bounding box were added to the dataset as an object, with each clip containing exactly one bounding box annotation (one object).

The final set of 1,526 objects was partitioned into train, test, and validation of 1,224, 152, and 150 videos respectively. Then, each object was paired with three other objects in the same subset, resulting in 2,289 pairs of objects.

(c) **Question creation**: From the 2,289 object pairs gathered, 242 were randomly selected to be used in this step, while the other 2,047 pairs were used in the next step. In this step, annotators were asked to write questions that require physical commonsense knowledge to answer. Annotators were given two videos, and a frame from each video containing a bounding box that specified the object. The had the option to write one or two commonsense questions related to the pair of objects, and answer with "Object 1" or "Object 2". In total, 1,377 questions were created, with each pair of videos given to 5 separate annotators.

To facilitate the process of creating high-quality questions, we provided annotators with a more detailed version of the categorization developed in Sect. 3.1 as guidance for what constitutes physical commonsense as instructions. They were also required to provide at least one relevant physical property for each question to encourage topical questions. Finally, questions were required to have a certain level of complexity, and were all quality-checked (e.g., questions that directly asked about a physical property such as *"Which object is more sticky"*, or *"Which object is larger?"* were forbidden).

(d) **Question reassignment**: We evenly redistribute the 1,377 questions created in the previous step to the remaining 2,047 object pairs. Reusing questions on new pairs of objects can create interesting scenarios, as it matches object pairs with questions that human annotators may not normally come up with [6]. The goal is to create matchings such as: *"If you absolutely needed to tie your hair up, which item would you use?"* (a plastic straw, a piece of paper). In this example, the question and object pair are not normally associated with each other, but are still answerable by humans, who have the ability to draw new connections. This puts more of the challenge on drawing relationships between physical properties, rather than directly applying past knowledge.

Specifically, in this task, each unused object pair is assigned a list of 13 questions, which is then given to annotators. Then, annotators can either mark each object-question matching as "completely irrelevant", or choose to answer the question, thus creating a new datapoint.

(e) Quality checking: To ensure the quality of final datapoints, each candidate datapoint gathered from the Question Creation and Question Reassignment stages was given to additional annotators to double-check. Every candidate was answered three times between the question annotation stages and only kept in our dataset if there was unanimous agreement.

4 Experimental Setup

In this section, we first outline the setup for testing human performance. We then list the models for checking dataset biases, and several state-of-the-art models that we tested. Finally, we outline the creation of PACS-material, a material classification subtask on our dataset.[3] Our experiments were designed to answer the following research questions:

1. How difficult is our task, as measured by the performance of human annotators and state-of-the-art models? We evaluate open-source state-of-the-art models that have high performance on comparable datasets such as VCR [63], TVQA [36], and NLVR2 [11] (Sect. 4.3), and compare these results to human performance on PACS (Sect. 4.1).
2. Are there potential biases in our dataset? While the paired binary question answering format is designed to limit bias in the language modality (correlations between questions and correct vs incorrect answers) as opposed to standard QA datasets [2,4,31,62], we explore other sources of biases in language, video, and audio in PACS (Sect. 4.2).
3. What is the importance of audio in our task, and what are the specific areas where audio is beneficial? We compare human and model performance with and without audio (with otherwise the same configurations) and analyze specific qualitative examples where including audio leads to better results (see Sect. 4.1 and Sect. 4.3 for how we set up human and model benchmarks).
4. How challenging is the level of reasoning required to capture physical commonsense? To establish this difficulty, we create an additional material classification task to compare with our physical commonsense task (Sect. 4.4).

4.1 Human Performance

To test human performance with and without audio, we randomly sampled 243 datapoints from the dataset, and give them to 10 annotators to answer. The annotators were given half of the datapoints with audio and half without, such that each datapoint would be annotated with five answers with audio, and five answers without. Consistent with other works, we compute human accuracy as a majority vote [6,63], and also report 90% confidence intervals for the results.

---

[3] For more details on experimental setups, refer to section B in the appendix.

4.2   Detecting Biases

We construct four different combinations of late-fusion models by combining state-of-the-art pre-trained image, audio, video, and text models. We used ViT [15] as the image model, AST [21] as the audio model, TDN [56] as the video model, and DeBERTa-V3 [26,27] as the text model. The specific configurations chosen for bias detection were inspired by past work studying bias on Visual Question Answering datasets [9,60,63]. We test for two main types of bias: *answer choice bias* (are there systematic biases in the answer choices that give away the correct answer without even seeing the question?), and *unimodal question-answerability* (is information from one modality enough to correctly answer the question?).

I + A + V: We study the predictability of our task given only information about the objects (no question is provided). This test demonstrates whether there is a pattern between the objects and the correct answer.

Q + I: Evaluates the usefulness of images (I) in predicting correct answers.

Q + V: Evaluates the usefulness of videos (V) in predicting correct answers.

Q + A: Evaluates the usefulness of audio (A) in predicting correct answers.

4.3   Baseline Models

Late Fusion [44]: We train a model using late fusion of all four input modalities as a simple baseline. We use SOTA image [15], audio [21], and video [56] models pretrained on large-scale classification datasets such as ImageNet21k [47], AudioSet [19], and Something-Something V2 [22], and the text [26] model is pretrained using replaced token detection. We concatenate the unimodal embeddings and use a linear layer to create multimodal embeddings for prediction.

CLIP [46] is a powerful image-text model pre-trained on a large set of images and text captions and can be used for a variety of zero-shot and finetuning tasks. CLIP embeds image and text into a shared vector space, where we can use *cosine similarity* to measure the similarity between image and text embeddings. We use CLIP to separately embed images of both objects and the question. The predicted object is the object with more similar embedding to the question embedding.

AudioCLIP [23] extends CLIP for audio inputs by training on AudioSet [19], which enables the embedding of audio inputs into the same vector space. Using this model, we extend the CLIP model mentioned above to include audio by concatenating the image and audio embedding, and using a linear layer to project them onto the same vector space as the text embedding.

UNITER [11] is an image and text model that is pre-trained using four different image-text tasks and achieves strong results on tasks such as NLVR2 [52]. We largely follow the procedure used to prepare and finetune UNITER on the NLVR2 dataset [52]. We split up both objects and generate two object-question embeddings, and finally concatenate them and use an MLP to classify the answer.

Table 1. Results on PACS test set: baseline models are reported with the mean and standard deviation of 5 runs, while human accuracy is reported with a 90% confidence interval. There is a large gap between model and human performance, with the best performing model (Merlot Reserve) lagging behind by over 25%. Models with audio also consistently outperform the corresponding models without audio, demonstrating the need for information from all modalities to succeed in our task.

Baseline model	Accuracy (%)		
	With audio	Without audio	Δ
I + A + V [44,60]	51.9 ± 1.1	–	–
Q + I [44,62]	–	51.2 ± 0.8	–
Q + A [44,62]	50.9 ± 0.6	–	–
Q + V [44,62]	–	51.5 ± 0.9	–
Late Fusion [44]	55.0 ± 1.1	52.5 ± 1.6	2.5
CLIP/AudioCLIP [23,46]	60.0 ± 0.9	56.3 ± 0.7	3.7
UNITER (Large) [11]	–	60.6 ± 2.2	–
Merlot Reserve (Base) [64]	66.5 ± 1.4	64.0 ± 0.9	2.6
Merlot Reserve (Large) [64]	70.1 ± 1.0	68.4 ± 0.7	1.8
Majority	50.4	50.4	–
Human	96.3 ± 2.1	90.5 ± 3.1	5.9

Merlot Reserve [64] uses image, audio, video, and text, achieving state-of-the-art results on VCR [63] and TVQA [36]. We follow the methods used to train Merlot Reserve on VCR and TVQA by constructing two multimodal sequences using all input modalities. Then, we separately generate confidence scores for both sequences and compare the two values as a classification output.

4.4 Material Classification

By comparing with the simpler task of classification, we can gain an understanding of the level of higher-order reasoning required in our task. In our main question-answering task, errors can come from multiple sources, either from misidentifying the properties of an object, or correctly identifying the objects, but failing to reason about the properties. Results from a material classification task using the same objects can give us an estimate on how much error stems from misidentified objects, and how much comes from the failure to exhibit higher-order reasoning.

We create a material classification task (PACS-material) formulated identically to our dataset, where a pair of objects is accompanied by a comparison question (e.g., *"Which object is more likely to be made out of glass"*). The materials used are gathered from our data-collection stage (Fig. 2b shows a distribution of material categories). We use the exact same object pairs as in the main task, and accompany each pair with comparison questions based on each object's material. In total, we created 3,460 training datapoints, 444 validation datapoints, and 445 testing datapoints. Each datapoint is a quadruplet $(o^{(1)}, o^{(2)}, q, l)$, representing the two objects, the question, and the label.

5   Results and Discussion

In this section, we assess the whether audiovisual understanding and physical commonsense reasoning are required to succeed on our dataset, and look at where current models fail. For additional results, refer to section C in the appendix.

5.1   Human and Model Performance

A summary of all model performances is shown in Table 1. Notably, all methods struggle to achieve results close to human performance, with the gap in accuracy between the best model (Merlot Reserve) and human performance being over 25%. This gap is much larger than the gap between SOTA and human performance on other datasets such as TVQA (3%) and VCR (14%) [64], demonstrating the challenging nature of our dataset.

We believe that the gap in performance comes from (1) the inherent challenge of developing physical commonsense (Sect. 5.4), and (2) the loss of information in each model. This includes the lack of video information in CLIP and UNITER, and the sparse sampling of video frames in the Merlot Reserve and Late Fusion models. Some physical information may require clear alignment between the actions displayed in the video and the audio signal to accurately understand the object, and thus require more fine-grained temporal information.

5.2   Checking for Biases in PACS

Table 1 shows the performance of our bias testing models, where we see that there is low performance among all configurations of models used. The I+A+V configuration tests for bias among the answer choices (objects), which achieves a low accuracy of 52%, demonstrating that the answer choices alone do not give away the answer. Furthermore, solely providing image, audio, or video information alongside the question yields poor performance, and it is only when all three modalities are combined that results solidly deviate from randomly guessing (55% accuracy). We believe the low results when provided with unimodal information are because all modalities play an important role. Only the image input specifies the object via a bounding box, thus making it difficult to succeed without the image. Additionally, since our dataset was curated to consist of complex objects that require video and/or audio to understand, removing such modalities also result in low performance.

5.3   Importance of Audio

In Table 1, we can see the benefit of including audio. Perhaps the most important experiment is how much audio helps humans, as the error rate decreases by more than half, with no overlap between the confidence intervals for the two values.

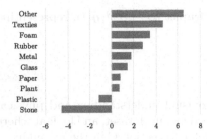 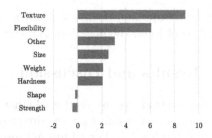

(a) Difference in accuracy with and without audio, conditioned on object materials.

(b) Difference in accuracy with and without audio, conditioned on physical properties.

Fig. 4. Comparison of results on Merlot Reserve when trained with and without audio. These results are conditioned on the material of the objects in the object pair, and on the physical properties relevant to the question (see Sect. 5.3).

When provided with audio, the models don't seem to improve as much. We theorize a few reasons for this: (1) for Merlot Reserve, the pretraining data is from a very different distribution, mostly consisting of human speech, and the input spectrograms may not be fine-grained enough to capture higher-pitched, sharper noises, such as tapping. (2) In contrast, AudioCLIP uses raw audio as an input, but the method of fusing audio and video through concatenation may be too simple.

Performance on the Most "Unique" Objects: Using the material and physical property labels gathered in the annotation steps, we can also compare results conditioned on specific materials and properties. We calculate performance with respect to a specific material (e.g., metal) by only counting datapoints where at least one of the objects is made of metal. Similarly, we calculate performance with respect to a physical property (e.g., hardness) by only counting datapoints where the question is related to the property. In Fig. 4a, we see that the biggest improvement in accuracy is on datapoints containing objects made of "Other" materials. Since our material labels cover the most common materials appearing in the dataset, this suggests that audio is especially important when reasoning about uncommon objects. From Fig. 4b, we see that properties such as texture and flexibility show the most improvement, and no category's results suffer greatly with the addition of audio.

5.4   Difficulty of Reasoning

As seen in Table 2, the material classification task on our dataset is much easier than our main task, with models achieving 10–20% higher accuracy, despite being trained using fewer datapoints (11,044 vs 3,460). Since the only other difference between PACS and PACS-material lies in the content of the questions, we believe that this gap in performance is due to the added difficulty of physical commonsense reasoning. The remaining 20–30% of misclassified datapoints on PACS-material can be attributed to both noisy labels resulting in imperfect training and evaluation, and a true failure in understanding the objects' material makeup.

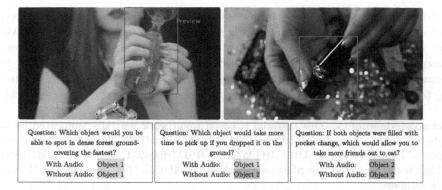

Question: Which object would you be able to spot in dense forest ground-covering the fastest?	Question: Which object would take more time to pick up if you dropped it on the ground?	Question: If both objects were filled with pocket change, which would allow you to take more friends out to eat?
With Audio: Object 1	With Audio: Object 1	With Audio: Object 2
Without Audio: Object 1	Without Audio: Object 2	Without Audio: Object 2

Fig. 5. Qualitative results showing predictions from Merlot Reserve models trained with and without audio. In this example, the first object could be mistaken as plastic and the second object could be made of plastic or metal. Thus, the model without audio doesn't realize that the glass object will shatter and takes longer to pick up off the ground. Furthermore, both models fail to answer the third question, which indirectly asks about the size and shape of both objects. This shows that models struggle on questions that are more complex, or require more implicit knowledge.

Table 2. Comparison of PACS-material and PACS. Despite PACS-material being created from relatively noisy labels, we observe that it is a far easier task, with models performing 10–20% better on it than on PACS. This suggests that our dataset requires a level of reasoning that goes beyond what is required in classification tasks.

Baseline model	Subset	Accuracy (%)		
		PACS-material	PACS	Δ
Late Fusion [44]	Val	67.8 ± 0.8	55.5 ± 0.3	12.3
	Test	67.4 ± 1.5	55.0 ± 1.1	12.4
AudioCLIP [23]	Val	81.9 ± 1.2	61.6 ± 0.9	18.8
	Test	75.9 ± 1.1	60.0 ± 0.9	15.0

5.5 Example Predictions

Finally, we analyze some specific examples to see where audio is helpful, and where both models fail. Generally, audio is helpful when models are presented with visually ambiguous or uncommon objects. In these situations, audio is necessary to clarify the physical properties of the objects (e.g., question 2 in Fig. 5). Furthermore, despite the presence of audio, both models may still fail when asked complex and/or uncommon questions that require the understanding of implicit information (e.g., question 3 in Fig. 5).

6 Conclusion

We introduced PACS, a large-scale audiovisual dataset for physical commonsense reasoning. We find that the best models still struggle to (1) fully leverage multimodal information, and (2) develop a strong understanding physical commonsense. Through experiments, we evince the multimodal nature of PACS and its usefulness in benchmarking future work in multimodal commonsense reasoning. We also provide multiple promising directions for bridging the gap between human and AI performance, which we hope provides insight in progressing towards safe and robust multimodal representations of the physical world.

Acknowledgements. This material is based upon work partially supported by the National Science Foundation (Awards #1722822 and #1750439) and National Institutes of Health (Awards #R01MH125740, #R01MH096951, and #U01MH116925). Additionally, we would also like to acknowledge NVIDIA's GPU support and Google's TPU support.

References

1. Standard list of material categories and types (2018). https://www.calrecycle.ca.gov/lgcentral/basics/standlst
2. Agrawal, A., Batra, D., Parikh, D.: Analyzing the behavior of visual question answering models. In: Proceedings of the 2016 Conference on Empirical Methods in Natural Language Processing, pp. 1955–1960 (2016)
3. Agrawal, P., Nair, A.V., Abbeel, P., Malik, J., Levine, S.: Learning to poke by poking: experiential learning of intuitive physics. In: Advances in Neural Information Processing Systems, vol. 29 (2016)
4. Anand, A., Belilovsky, E., Kastner, K., Larochelle, H., Courville, A.: Blindfold baselines for embodied QA. arXiv preprint arXiv:1811.05013 (2018)
5. Antol, S., et al.: VQA: visual question answering. In: Proceedings of the IEEE International Conference on Computer Vision, pp. 2425–2433 (2015)
6. Bisk, Y., Zellers, R., Gao, J., Choi, Y., et al.: PIQA: reasoning about physical commonsense in natural language. In: Proceedings of the AAAI Conference on Artificial Intelligence, vol. 34, pp. 7432–7439 (2020)
7. Bliss, J.: Commonsense reasoning about the physical world. Stud. Sci. Educ. **44**(2), 123–155 (2008)
8. Bobrow, D.G.: Qualitative reasoning about physical systems: an introduction. Artif. Intell. **24**(1–3), 1–5 (1984)
9. Cadene, R., Dancette, C., Cord, M., Parikh, D., et al.: Rubi: reducing unimodal biases for visual question answering. Adv. Neural. Inf. Process. Syst. **32**, 841–852 (2019)
10. Chen, C., et al.: SoundSpaces: audio-visual navigation in 3D environments. In: Vedaldi, A., Bischof, H., Brox, T., Frahm, J.-M. (eds.) ECCV 2020. LNCS, vol. 12351, pp. 17–36. Springer, Cham (2020). https://doi.org/10.1007/978-3-030-58539-6_2
11. Chen, Y.-C., et al.: UNITER: UNiversal image-TExt representation learning. In: Vedaldi, A., Bischof, H., Brox, T., Frahm, J.-M. (eds.) ECCV 2020. LNCS, vol. 12375, pp. 104–120. Springer, Cham (2020). https://doi.org/10.1007/978-3-030-58577-8_7
12. Chen, Y., Huang, S., Yuan, T., Qi, S., Zhu, Y., Zhu, S.C.: Holistic++ scene understanding: single-view 3D holistic scene parsing and human pose estimation with human-object interaction and physical commonsense. In: Proceedings of the IEEE/CVF International Conference on Computer Vision (ICCV), October 2019

13. Corlett, P.R., Powers, A.R.: Conditioned hallucinations: historic insights and future directions. World Psychiatry **17**(3), 361 (2018)
14. Coumans, E., Bai, Y.: PyBullet, a Python Module for Physics Simulation for Games, Robotics and Machine Learning (2016-2021). http://pybullet.org
15. Dosovitskiy, A., et al.: An image is worth 16x16 words: transformers for image recognition at scale. In: ICLR (2021)
16. Forbes, M., Holtzman, A., Choi, Y.: Do neural language representations learn physical commonsense? CogSci (2019)
17. Forbus, K.D.: Qualitative process theory. Artif. Intell. **24**(1–3), 85–168 (1984)
18. Gao, R., Chang, Y.Y., Mall, S., Fei-Fei, L., Wu, J.: Objectfolder: a dataset of objects with implicit visual, auditory, and tactile representations. CoRL (2021)
19. Gemmeke, J.F., et al.: Audio set: an ontology and human-labeled dataset for audio events. In: 2017 IEEE International Conference on Acoustics, Speech and Signal Processing (ICASSP), pp. 776–780 (2017). https://doi.org/10.1109/ICASSP.2017.7952261
20. Giannakopoulos, T.: pyAudioAnalysis: an open-source python library for audio signal analysis. PLoS ONE **10**(12), e0144610 (2015)
21. Gong, Y., Chung, Y.A., Glass, J.: AST: audio spectrogram transformer. In: Proceedings of Interspeech 2021, pp. 571–575 (2021). https://doi.org/10.21437/Interspeech.2021-698
22. Goyal, R., et al.: The "something something" video database for learning and evaluating visual common sense, pp. 5843–5851 (2017). https://doi.org/10.1109/ICCV.2017.622
23. Guzhov, A., Raue, F., Hees, J., Dengel, A.: Audioclip: extending clip to image, text and audio. arXiv preprint arXiv:2008.04838 (2020)
24. Handel, S.: Timbre perception and auditory object identification. Hearing **2**, 425–461 (1995)
25. Hayes, P., Nilsson, N.J.: Knowledge Representation. Morgan Kaufman, Burlington (1987)
26. He, P., Gao, J., Chen, W.: DeBERTaV3: improving DeBERTa using ELECTRA-Style pre-training with gradient-disentangled embedding sharing (2021)
27. He, P., Liu, X., Gao, J., Chen, W.: DeBERTa: decoding-enhanced BERT with disentangled attention. In: International Conference on Learning Representations (2021). https://openreview.net/forum?id=XPZIaotutsD
28. Hespos, S.J., Ferry, A., Anderson, E., Hollenbeck, E., Rips, L.J.: Five-month-old infants have general knowledge of how nonsolid substances behave and interact. Psychol. Sci. **27**, 244–256 (2016)
29. Hespos, S.J., Spelke, E.S.: Conceptual precursors to language. Nature **430**(6998), 453–456 (2004)
30. Hessel, J., Mimno, D., Lee, L.: Quantifying the visual concreteness of words and topics in multimodal datasets. In: Proceedings of NAACL-HLT, pp. 2194–2205 (2018)
31. Jabri, A., Joulin, A., van der Maaten, L.: Revisiting visual question answering baselines. In: Leibe, B., Matas, J., Sebe, N., Welling, M. (eds.) ECCV 2016. LNCS, vol. 9912, pp. 727–739. Springer, Cham (2016). https://doi.org/10.1007/978-3-319-46484-8_44
32. Jimenez, C.E.: Learning physical commonsense knowledge (2020)
33. Kaiser, M., Jonides, J., Alexander, J.: Intuitive reasoning about abstract and familiar physics problems. Mem. Cogn. **14**, 308–12 (1986). https://doi.org/10.3758/BF03202508

34. Kim, I.K., Spelke, E.S.: Perception and understanding of effects of gravity and inertia on object motion. Dev. Sci. **2**(3), 339–362 (1999). https://doi.org/10.1111/1467-7687.00080. https://onlinelibrary.wiley.com/doi/abs/10.1111/1467-7687.00080

35. Krishna, R., et al.: Visual genome: connecting language and vision using crowdsourced dense image annotations. Int. J. Comput. Vision **123**(1), 32–73 (2017)

36. Lei, J., Yu, L., Bansal, M., Berg, T.: TVQA: localized, compositional video question answering. In: Proceedings of the 2018 Conference on Empirical Methods in Natural Language Processing, pp. 1369–1379 (2018)

37. Li, Y.L., et al.: Hake: a knowledge engine foundation for human activity understanding (2022)

38. Maharaj, T., Ballas, N., Rohrbach, A., Courville, A., Pal, C.: A dataset and exploration of models for understanding video data through fill-in-the-blank question-answering. In: Proceedings of the IEEE Conference on Computer Vision and Pattern Recognition, pp. 6884–6893 (2017)

39. McCloskey, M.: Intuitive physics. Sci. Am. **248**(4), 122–131 (1983)

40. Minsky, M.: Commonsense-based interfaces. Commun. ACM **43**(8), 66–73 (2000)

41. Morrongiello, B.A., Fenwick, K.D., Chance, G.: Crossmodal learning in newborn infants: inferences about properties of auditory-visual events. Infant Behav. Dev. **21**(4), 543–553 (1998)

42. Mottaghi, R., Rastegari, M., Gupta, A., Farhadi, A.: "What happens if..." learning to predict the effect of forces in images. In: Leibe, B., Matas, J., Sebe, N., Welling, M. (eds.) ECCV 2016. LNCS, vol. 9908, pp. 269–285. Springer, Cham (2016). https://doi.org/10.1007/978-3-319-46493-0_17

43. Nair, L., Balloch, J., Chernova, S.: Tool macgyvering: tool construction using geometric reasoning. In: 2019 International Conference on Robotics and Automation (ICRA), pp. 5837–5843. IEEE (2019)

44. Pandeya, Y.R., Lee, J.: Deep learning-based late fusion of multimodal information for emotion classification of music video. Multimedia Tools Appl. **80**(2), 2887–2905 (2020). https://doi.org/10.1007/s11042-020-08836-3

45. Park, J.S., Bhagavatula, C., Mottaghi, R., Farhadi, A., Choi, Y.: VisualCOMET: reasoning about the dynamic context of a still image. In: Vedaldi, A., Bischof, H., Brox, T., Frahm, J.-M. (eds.) ECCV 2020. LNCS, vol. 12350, pp. 508–524. Springer, Cham (2020). https://doi.org/10.1007/978-3-030-58558-7_30

46. Radford, A., et al.: Learning transferable visual models from natural language supervision (2021)

47. Ridnik, T., Ben-Baruch, E., Noy, A., Zelnik-Manor, L.: ImageNet-21K pretraining for the masses (2021)

48. Smith, K.A., Battaglia, P.W., Vul, E.: Consistent physics underlying ballistic motion prediction. Cogn. Sci. **35** (2013)

49. Souček, T., Lokoč, J.: TransNet V2: an effective deep network architecture for fast shot transition detection. arXiv preprint arXiv:2008.04838 (2020)

50. Storks, S., Gao, Q., Zhang, Y., Chai, J.Y.: Tiered reasoning for intuitive physics: toward verifiable commonsense language understanding. In: EMNLP (2021)

51. Suhr, A., Lewis, M., Yeh, J., Artzi, Y.: A corpus of natural language for visual reasoning. In: Proceedings of the 55th Annual Meeting of the Association for Computational Linguistics (Volume 2: Short Papers), pp. 217–223 (2017)

52. Suhr, A., Zhou, S., Zhang, A., Zhang, I., Bai, H., Artzi, Y.: A corpus for reasoning about natural language grounded in photographs. In: Proceedings of the 57th Annual Meeting of the Association for Computational Linguistics, pp. 6418–6428 (2019)

53. Tapaswi, M., Zhu, Y., Stiefelhagen, R., Torralba, A., Urtasun, R., Fidler, S.: MovieQA: understanding stories in movies through question-answering. In: Proceedings of the IEEE Conference on Computer Vision and Pattern Recognition, pp. 4631–4640 (2016)
54. Toussaint, M.A., Allen, K.R., Smith, K.A., Tenenbaum, J.B.: Differentiable physics and stable modes for tool-use and manipulation planning (2018)
55. Tuli, S., Bansal, R., Paul, R., et al.: Tango: commonsense generalization in predicting tool interactions for mobile manipulators. arXiv preprint arXiv:2105.04556 (2021)
56. Wang, L., Tong, Z., Ji, B., Wu, G.: TDN: temporal difference networks for efficient action recognition. In: Proceedings of the IEEE/CVF Conference on Computer Vision and Pattern Recognition (CVPR), pp. 1895–1904, June 2021
57. Wilcox, T., Woods, R., Tuggy, L., Napoli, R.: Shake, rattle, and... one or two objects? Young infants' use of auditory information to individuate objects. Infancy **9**(1), 97–123 (2006)
58. Wu, J., Lu, E., Kohli, P., Freeman, B., Tenenbaum, J.: Learning to see physics via visual de-animation. In: Guyon, I., et al. (eds.) Advances in Neural Information Processing Systems. Curran Associates Inc. (2017)
59. Wu, J., Yildirim, I., Lim, J.J., Freeman, B., Tenenbaum, J.: Galileo: perceiving physical object properties by integrating a physics engine with deep learning. In: Cortes, C., Lawrence, N., Lee, D., Sugiyama, M., Garnett, R. (eds.) Advances in Neural Information Processing Systems, vol. 28. Curran Associates, Inc. (2015). https://proceedings.neurips.cc/paper/2015/file/d09bf41544a3365a46c9077ebb5e35c3-Paper.pdf
60. Yang, J., Zhu, Y., Wang, Y., Yi, R., Zadeh, A., Morency, L.P.: What gives the answer away? Question answering bias analysis on video QA datasets (2020)
61. Yatskar, M., Ordonez, V., Zettlemoyer, L., Farhadi, A.: Commonly uncommon: semantic sparsity in situation recognition. In: Proceedings of the IEEE Conference on Computer Vision and Pattern Recognition, pp. 7196–7205 (2017)
62. Zadeh, A., Chan, M., Liang, P.P., Tong, E., Morency, L.P.: Social-IQ: a question answering benchmark for artificial social intelligence. In: 2019 IEEE/CVF Conference on Computer Vision and Pattern Recognition (CVPR), pp. 8799–8809 (2019). https://doi.org/10.1109/CVPR.2019.00901
63. Zellers, R., Bisk, Y., Farhadi, A., Choi, Y.: From recognition to cognition: visual commonsense reasoning. In: The IEEE Conference on Computer Vision and Pattern Recognition (CVPR), June 2019
64. Zellers, R., et al.: Merlot reserve: multimodal neural script knowledge through vision and language and sound. arxiv (2022)
65. Zhang, Z., Li, Q., Huang, Z., Wu, J., Tenenbaum, J., Freeman, B.: Shape and material from sound. In: Guyon, I., et al. (eds.) Advances in Neural Information Processing Systems, vol. 30. Curran Associates, Inc. (2017). https://proceedings.neurips.cc/paper/2017/file/f4552671f8909587cf485ea990207f3b-Paper.pdf
66. Zhang, Z., et al.: Generative modeling of audible shapes for object perception. In: Proceedings of the IEEE International Conference on Computer Vision (ICCV), October 2017
67. Zhao, Z., Papalexakis, E., Ma, X.: Learning physical common sense as knowledge graph completion via BERT data augmentation and constrained tucker factorization. In: Proceedings of the 2020 Conference on Empirical Methods in Natural Language Processing (EMNLP), pp. 3293–3298. Association for Computational Linguistics, November 2020. https://doi.org/10.18653/v1/2020.emnlp-main.266. https://aclanthology.org/2020.emnlp-main.266

VoViT: Low Latency Graph-Based Audio-Visual Voice Separation Transformer

Juan F. Montesinos[✉], Venkatesh S. Kadandale, and Gloria Haro

Universitat Pompeu Fabra, Carrer Roc Boronat, 138, 08018 Barcelona, Spain
{juanfelipe.montesinos,venkatesh.kadandale,gloria.haro}@upf.edu

Abstract. This paper presents an audio-visual approach for voice separation which produces state-of-the-art results at a low latency in two scenarios: speech and singing voice. The model is based on a two-stage network. Motion cues are obtained with a lightweight graph convolutional network that processes face landmarks. Then, both audio and motion features are fed to an audio-visual transformer which produces a fairly good estimation of the isolated target source. In a second stage, the predominant voice is enhanced with an audio-only network. We present different ablation studies and comparison to state-of-the-art methods. Finally, we explore the transferability of models trained for speech separation in the task of singing voice separation. The demos, code, and weights are available in https://ipcv.github.io/VoViT/.

Keywords: Audio-visual · Source separation · Speech · Singing voice

1 Introduction

Human voice is usually found together with other sounds. Think of people speaking in a cafeteria or in a social gathering, a journalist reporting on the scene, or an artist singing on a stage. In these situations we can find: multiple concurrent speeches, speech with background noise or a single or multiple singing voices with music accompaniment among others. Our brain is capable of understanding and concentrating on the voice of interest [3]. This cognitive process does not only rely on the hearing. Some works have shown the sight helps to focus on the voice of interest [12] or to resolve ambiguities in a noisy environment [20]. In this paper we address the voice separation and enhancement problems from a multimodal perspective, leveraging the motion information extracted from the visual stream to guide the resolution of the problem.

We propose an audio-visual (AV) voice separation model that produces state-of-the-art results. It is based on a two-stage approach. The first stage estimates

---

Supplementary Information The online version contains supplementary material available at https://doi.org/10.1007/978-3-031-19836-6_18.

a fairly good separation by combining audio and motion features with a transformer. Motion cues are crucial when the sound mixture contains different predominant voices. We extract those cues with a graph convolutional network (CNN) that processes a sequence of face landmarks. The audio-visual features are aligned in the feature dimension and preserve the time resolution. They are processed by a multimodal spectro-temporal transformer that estimates the isolated voice corresponding to the target face landmarks. In a second stage, the predominant voice is enhanced by a small audio-only U-Net that takes as input just the pre-estimated audio. The voice of interest is predominant in the first estimation and thus an audio-only network is capable of modelling it and cancelling the sparse and mild interferences present in the pre-estimation. The paper includes an ablation study of different configurations of the multimodal transformer, its number of blocks and design of the lead voice enhancer network. The proposed method is compared to state-of-the-art methods in two different scenarios: speech and singing voice separation, showing successful results in both cases.

The contributions of this work are several: i) We propose an audio-visual network based on a transformer which performs better than current state-of-the-art models in speech and singing voice separation. ii) We show that a landmark-based approach for extracting motion information can be a lightweight competitive alternative to processing raw video frames. iii) We show how an enhancement stage based on a light network can boost the performance of AV models over larger complex models, reducing the computational cost and the required time for training. iv) We reveal that AV models trained in speech separation do not generalise good enough for the separation of singing voice because of the different voice characteristics in each case and that a dedicated training with singing voice examples clearly boosts the results. Finally, v) our method is an end-to-end gpu-powered system which is capable of isolating a target voice in real time (including the pre-processing steps).

2   Related Work

In the last years there has been a fast evolution of deep-learning-based audio-visual works for speech separation and enhancement (we refer the reader to a recent review in [23]).

Back in 2016, we can find one of the first works in exploiting visual features for speech enhancement [37]. In this work, the authors proposed a CNN to process the visual signal and a fully connected layer to process the raw waveforms. Both modalities were fused by a BiLSTM network. This network had approximately 3M parameters (M for millions), far from the 80M of the most recent work [10]. A two-tower stream for processing audio and video features and then fused with a BiLSTM module that predicted complex masks was proposed in [7].

A two-step enhancement process was proposed in [1]. In the first step, a two-tower stream processed the audio-visual information to extract a binary mask that performed separation on the magnitude spectrogram. Afterwards, the phase of the spectrogram was predicted by passing the estimated magnitude spectrogram together with the noisy phase spectrogam through a 1D-CNN. A similar idea was developed in [8], where a two-tower stream encoder generated an embedding of audio-visual features from which the enhanced speech spectrogram was recovered. On the other hand, in [17] not only the enhanced spectrogram was reconstructed but the input frames as well.

New approaches and explorations different from the two-tower CNNs appeared recently. Variational auto-encoders [28] for speech enhancement joined the scene. Concurrently, [36] developed a time-domain model for speech separation, in contrast to most of the works which usually posed the problem in the time-frequency domain. Multi-channel audio-visual speech separation was addressed in [14] in a four-tower stream fashion. The mixture spectrogram was constrained with directional features from the visual stream of the speaker. A temporal CNN extracted visual features from the lips motion. The audio and visual embeddings were concatenated together with a speaker embedding extracted from the clean audio(s). A different mechanism was used in [19, 29, 31], where the audio-visual fusion was done with an attention module; or in [38], where the system was trained in a GAN manner so that the discriminator modeled the distribution of the clean speech signals. Transformers have been used in audio-only source separation [40]. Very recently, audio-visual transformers were investigated in [32] for main speaker localization and separation of its corresponding audio. In [33] an audio-visual transformer was used for classification in order to guide an unsupervised source separation model. Finally, in [2] a transformer was used for audio-visual synchronisation.

Another interesting proposal is [4], where the authors were concerned about the extra computational cost of processing the visual features and the possible privacy problems arised from it. On the other hand, to our knowledge, there are only two works using face landmarks, instead of video frames, for source separation. In [25] they process face landmarks with fully connected layers and then use BiLSTMs to predict the masks for the target source. In [24] a U-Net conditioned by a graph convolutional network that processed face landmarks was used for audio-visual singing voice separation. The work in [22] compared different training targets and loss functions for audio-visual speech enhancement.

Most recent algorithms made use of lips motion as well as appearance information, usually implementing cross-modal losses to pull together corresponding audio-visual features [10, 21].

3 Approach

In audio-visual voice separation, given an audio-visual recording with several speaking/singing faces, and other sound sources, the goal is to recover their isolated voices by guiding the voice separation with the visual information present in the video frames. More formally, given the audio signal of each speaker, $s_i(t)$ (where t denotes time), the mixture of sounds can be defined as $x(t) = \sum_i s_i(t) + n(t)$ where $n(t)$ denotes any other sound present in the mixture, i.e. background sounds. Therefore, the task of interest can be defined as the estimation of each individual voice $\hat{s}_i(t)$. In our approach $\hat{s}_i(t) = F(x(t), v_i(t))$, where F is a function represented by a neural network. The network receives the visual information of the speaker of interest, $v_i(t)$, and estimates its isolated voice $\hat{s}_i(t)$.

3.1   The AV Voice Separation Network

Our solution comprises of a two-stage neural network that operates in the time-frequency domain. The first stage consists of an AV voice separation network which can isolate the target voice at a good quality. However, this network is the most demanding one in terms of computational cost. To alleviate this, we propose to use downsampled spectrograms in this stage. The second stage consists of a recursive lead voice enhancer network that works with full resolution spectrograms. In Sect. 5.2, we experimentally show that this two-stage design leads to a higher performance than using larger AV models. To achieve this modularity, the networks at both stages are trained independently. The whole model is presented in Fig. 1.

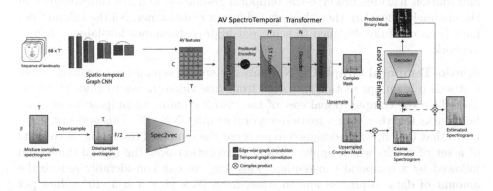

Fig. 1. Audio-visual voice separation network. Audio and video features are concatenated in the channel dimension before being fed to the transformer.

Stage 1: Audio-Visual Voice Separation. For simplicity, we seek to isolate the voice (denoted by $s(t)$ and its corresponding spectrogram $S(f, t)$) corresponding to a single face at a time. The audio waveform of the mixture, $x(t)$, is transformed into a complex spectrogram $X(f, t)$ applying the Short-Time Fourier Transform (STFT). Once the waveform is mapped to the time-frequency domain, we can define a complex mask $M(f, t)$ that allows to recover the spectrogram of the estimated source with a complex product, denoted as $*$, that is: $S(f, t) = X(f, t) * M(f, t)$ Then, the goal of the network in the first stage is to estimate the complex mask $\hat{M}(f, t)$. The optimal set of parameters of the network is found by minimising the following loss:

$$\mathcal{L}_1 = \|G \odot (M_b - \hat{M}_b)\|^2$$

where M_b and $\hat{M}_b$ are, respectively, the ground truth and estimated bounded complex masks, $\odot$ denotes the element-wise product, $\|\cdot\|$ is the $L2$-norm and G is a gradient penalty term which weights the time-frequency points of the mask according to the energy of the analogous point in the mixture spectrogram X:

$$G(f,t;X) = \max(\min(\log(1 + \|X(f,t)\|), 10), 10^{-3}). \quad (1)$$

Note that, by definition, the ground truth mask M is not bounded. In order to stabilise the training, we bound the complex masks by applying a hyperbolic tangent [35]: $M_b = \tanh M^r + i \tanh M^i$, where M^r and M^i, denote the real and imaginary parts, respectively. The audio waveform of the estimated source can be computed through the inverse STFT of the estimated spectrogram $\hat{S}(f,t) = X(f,t) * \hat{M}(f,t)$.

To solve the AV voice separation problem, we propose to leverage the face motion information present in the video frames of the target person whose voice we want to isolate. For that, we use a spatio-temporal graph neural network that processes the face landmarks to generate motion features. On the other hand, the audio features are generated by a CNN encoder, denoted as *Spec2vec*. Both audio and motion features preserve the temporal resolution and are concatenated in the channel dimension, then they are fed into a transformer. All the submodules have been carefully designed to achieve a high-performance low-latency neural network.

Spatio–Temporal Graph CNN: Many AV speech separation or enhancement methods rely on lips motion extracted from raw video frames to guide the task. To reduce the computational cost of the visual stream, we propose to use face landmarks together with a spatio-temporal graph CNN [39]. This network, similar to that in [24], was redesigned to preserve the temporal resolution. It consists of a set of blocks which apply a graph convolution over the spatial dimension followed by a temporal convolution. This way we can considerably reduce the amount of data to process and to store, from $96 \times 96 \times 3 \approx 3 \cdot 10^4$ values per frame to $68 \times 2 \approx 10^2$. This supposes a substantial reduction in the storage necessities when working with large audio-visual datasets. For example, *Voxceleb2*'s grayscale ROIs occupy 1Tb, the raw uncompressed dataset occupies several Tb while storing face landmarks only requires 70 Gb.

Spec2vec: It is well known that transformers need proper embeddings to achieve high performance. We use the audio encoder of [7] to generate embeddings without losing temporal resolution.

AV Spectro-Temporal Transformer: The traditional AV source separation methods comprise of a two-tower stream architecture. We can find two major variants: either encoder-decoder CNNs (usually with a U-Net as backbone) (e.g. [9,10,24,30,41,42]) or recurrent neural networks (RNNs), both conditioned on visual features (e.g. [7,25,37]). The major drawback of the latter is that RNNs are sequential, introducing bottlenecks in the processing pipeline. Transformers appeared as an efficient solution, reaching the same performance than RNNs and CNNs in large datasets. They are trained with a masking system allowing to process all the timesteps of a sequence in parallel. However, these architectures operate sequentially at the time of inference, like the RNNs. To overcome this issue we use an encoder-decoder transformer, which can solve the source separation problem in a single forward pass.

Transformers were originally designed to work with two unimodal signals. We study three different possible configurations for the transformer. The first proposal is to use the transformer as an auto-encoder, being fed with an audio-visual signal directly. This way we ease the task for the transformer as audio and visual features are temporally aligned by construction. Then, it just has to find relationships through the multi-head self-attention. The second proposal is to pass visual features to the encoder and audio features (from the mixture) to the decoder so that the network can find audio-visual interdependencies via multi-head attention. Nevertheless, we hypothesise the dependencies between video and audio are local as audio events mostly occur at the same time than visual events. Lastly, we feed the encoder with an audio-visual signal and the decoder with the ground-truth separated audio. Note that this model is slower than previous ones as the model runs recurrently at inference time, going from a time complexity of $\mathcal{O}(n)$ to $\mathcal{O}(n^2)$ where n is the length of the sequence. From the ablation study in Sect. 5.1 and Table 1, we conclude that the best model is the first one, i.e. the one that uses an audio-visual signal as input, we denote it as AV ST-transformer.

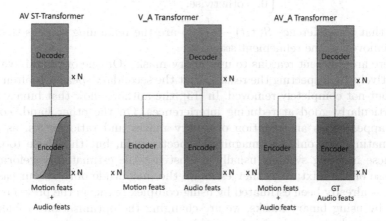

Fig. 2. Three proposed ways to feed a transformer with an audio-visual signal. Left: audio-visual signal, middle: video to the encoder and audio mixture to the decoder, right: audio-visual signal to the encoder and clean audio to the decoder.

We design our AV ST-transformer encoder upon the findings of [40]. The AV ST-transformer has 512 model features across 8 heads. We tried 256 features but it works worse. The compression layer is nothing but a fully connected layer followed by GELU [16] activation which maps the C incoming channels to the 512 channels required by the architecture. It is composed by M encoders and

M decoders. The encoder is a set of two traditional encoders in parallel, which processes the signal from a temporal and a spectral point of view [40].

Stage 2: Lead Voice Enhancer. Although lips motion is correlated with the voice signal and may help in source separation, it is not always accessible or reliable. For example, the scenarios involving a side view of the speaker or a partial occlusion of the face or an out-of-sync audio-visual pair make it challenging to incorporate the lips motion information in a useful way; all such scenarios may appear in unconstrained video recordings. In [24], the authors show that audio-only models tend to predict the predominant voice in a mixture when there is no prior information about the target speaker. Based on this idea, we hypothesise that, if the first stage of the AV voice separation network outputs a reasonable estimation of the target voice, this voice will be predominant in the estimation. Upon this idea, we use an audio-only network which identifies the predominant voice and enhances the estimation without relying on the motion, just on the pre-estimated audio. To do so, we simply use a small U-Net which takes as input the estimated magnitude spectrogram (at its original resolution) and returns a binary mask. The ground truth binary mask can be obtained from the ground truth spectrogram S and the spectogram to be refined, $\hat{S}$, which is the one estimated in the stage 1:

$$M(f,t) = \begin{cases} 1, & \text{if } \|S(f,t)\| \geq \|\hat{S}(f,t) - S(f,t)\|, \\ 0, & \text{otherwise.} \end{cases} \tag{2}$$

Notice that the difference $\hat{S}(f,t) - S(f,t)$ are the remaining sources that need to be removed in the refinement stage.

There are different reasons to use binary masks. On the one hand, we found qualitatively, by inspecting the results, that the secondary speaker is often attenuated but not completely removed. In [13], the authors show that binary masks are particularly good at reducing interferences. On the other hand, complex masks appeared as an evolution of binary masks and ratio masks, as a way of estimating, not only the magnitude spectrogram, but the phase too. Note that these masking systems usually reconstruct the estimated waveform with the phase of the mixture as they estimate the magnitude only. In our case, the phase has already been estimated by using complex masks in the previous stage. Lastly, by using binary masks, we are changing the optimisation problem and easing the task since it is simpler to take a binary decision than orienting and modulating a vector.

Note that this refinement network can run recursively, although we empirically found (see Table 2) that applying the refinement network once leads to the best results in terms of SDR and a considerable boost in SIR. Further iterations reduce the interferences (at a lesser extent) but at the cost of introducing more distortion.

Let us denote by $\hat{M}$ the binary mask estimated by the lead voice enhancer network. We trained this network to optimise a weighted binary cross entropy loss:

$$\mathcal{L}_2 = \sum_{f=1}^{F} \sum_{t=1}^{T} \frac{G(f,t;\hat{S})}{FT} \left(M(f,t) \log \|\hat{M}(f,t)\| + (1 - M(f,t))(1 - \log \|\hat{M}(f,t)\|) \right)$$

where the weights G are defined in (1).

3.2 Low-Latency Data Pre-processing

Many audio-visual works rely on expensive pipelines to pre-process data, which makes the proposed systems unusable in a real-world scenario unless a great amount of time is invested in optimisation. Pursuing the real applicability of our model, we curated an end-to-end gpu-powered system which can pre-process (from raw audio and video) and isolate the target voice of 10 s of recordings in less than 100 ms using floating-point 32 precision, and in less than 50 ms using floating-point 16 precision.

Face Landmarks: The most common approach in speech separation is to align the faces in the different frames via 2D face landmark estimation together with image warping (e.g. [10,24]). This step removes eventual head motions. In order to achieve real-time audio-visual source separation, we estimate the 3D face landmarks using an optimised version of [15] and an aligned frontal view by applying a rigid transformation, skipping the image warping step. This optimised preprocessing takes around 10 ms to process 10 s of video. Thanks to the 3D information, we can recover lips motion from side views by estimating 3D landmarks, as shown in Fig. 3. To do the registration, we use the Kabsch algorithm [18]. Finally, we drop the depth coordinate and consider just the first two spatial coordinates in the nodes of the graph.

Audio: Waveforms are re-sampled 16384 Hz. Then, we compute the STFT with a window size of 1022 and a hop length of 256. This leads to a $512 \times 64n$ complex spectrogram where n is the duration of the waveform in seconds. To reduce the computational cost of both training and inference we downsample the spectrogram in the frequency dimension by 2 in Stage 1.

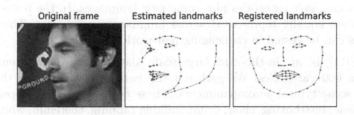

Fig. 3. Frame example from *Voxceleb2* [5] with partial occlusions. Thanks to the landmark estimation together with the registration we can estimate the unoccluded lips.

4 Datasets

Experiments are carried out in two different datasets: *Voxceleb2* [5], a dataset of celebrities speaking in a broad range of scenarios; and *Acappella* [24], a dataset of solo-singing videos. Both datasets are a collection of YouTube recordings which are publicly available. We also consider *Audioset* [11] and *MUSDB18* [27] for sampling extra audio sources that can be added to the singing voice signal as accompaniment.

Voxceleb2 contains 1 million utterances, most of them of a duration between 4 and 6 s, consisting of celebrities covering a wide range of ethnicities, professions and ages. The dataset is formed by in-the-wild videos that include several challenging scenarios, such as: different lightning, side-face views, motion blur and poor image quality. They also span across different scenarios like red carpets, stadiums, public speeches, etc. The dataset provides a test set which contains both, seen-heard and unseen-unheard speakers together. From this test set we selected the unseen-unheard samples and curated two different subsets. The first one, denoted as *unheard-unseen wild test set* consists of 1,000 samples randomly selected, reflecting the aforementioned challenges. The second one, denoted as *unheard-unseen clean test set*, is a subset of 1,000 samples, from which 500 of them have a high-quality content with the following characteristics: frontal or almost frontal point of view, low background noise and perceptual image quality above the average of the dataset. The samples were selected manually from the whole unseen-unheard test set, trying to include as many different speakers as possible. The target voice is sampled from the subset of 500 high-quality videos in the *clean set*, while the second voice is sampled from the rest of 500 videos. This way we ensure that the video content is good enough to estimate motion features from it and that the ground truth separated audio is reliable, in the sense that it does not contain background sounds that may produce unfounded performance metrics.

Acappella is a 46-hours dataset of a cappella solo singing videos. The videos are divided in four language categories: English, Spanish, Hindi and others. These videos are recorded in a frontal view with no occlussions. It also provides two test sets: the seen-heard test set and the unseen-unheard test set. The former contains videos sampled from the same singers and in the same languages than the training set, whereas the latter contains recordings sampled from new singers in the four language categories plus some new languages. In the test set all the categories are equally represented across languages and gender. This way the algorithms can be tested in challenging real-world scenarios.

Audioset [11] is an in-the-wild large-scale dataset of audio events across more than 600 categories. We gathered the categories related to the human voice and some typical accompaniments. These categories are: acappella, background music, beatboxing, choir, drum, lullaby, rapping, theremin, whistling and yodelling.

Finally, *MUSDB18* [27] is an audio-only dataset of 150 full-track songs of different styles that includes original sound sources.

5   Experiments

The experiments were carried out in a single RTX 3090 GPU. Each experiment takes around 20 days of training. We used SGD with 0.8 momentum, 10^{-5} weight decay and a learning rate of 0.01. The metrics used for comparing results are Source-to-Distortion Ratio (SDR) and Source-to-Interferences Ratio (SIR) [34].

5.1   Audio-Visual Transformer

In this experiment, we compare three different versions of the transformer (shown in Fig. 2) in the *Acappella* dataset. The goal is two-fold: i) Compare the proposed architecture against the state-of-the-art model in singing voice separation [24]; and ii) compare the performance of different transformers for the task of singing voice separation.

For the sake of comparison, we train our models the same way as in [24]. In short, we create artificial mixtures of 4 s of duration by mixing a voice sample from *Acappella* together with an accompaniment sample sourced either from *Audioset* or *MUSDB18*. Additionally, a second voice sample from *Acappella* is added 50% of the times. This results in mixtures that contain one or more voices plus musical accompaniment. For this dataset we take 4 s audio excerpts and the corresponding 100 video frames from which we extract the face landmarks.

Results shown in Table 2. From the ablation on the three versions of the transformer, we can conclude that the AV ST-transformer is the best model in terms of both performance and time complexity. Moreover, it can be observed that the three versions of the transformer greatly outperform the results of [24] in terms of SDR, while the AV ST-transformer also outperforms in SIR.

5.2   Speech Separation

In Sect. 5.1 we found the AV ST-transformer was the best model in terms of time complexity and performance. All the remaining experiments will be carried out with this model. Now we consider the task of AV speech separation and work with *Voxceleb2* dataset. We use 2 s audio excerpts which correspond to 50 video frames from which we extracted their face landmarks. In this case,

Table 1. Ablation study: performance of different ways of feeding a transformer with an audio-visual signal and comparison to Y-Net model [24]. Evaluated in *Acappella's* unseen-unheard test set. Y-Net metrics taken from *Acappella*. In this table $N = 4$ (the number of blocks in the transformers) in order to adapt the number of parameters to the size of *Acappella* dataset.

Model	Y-Net [24]	AV ST-transformer	V_A transformer	AV_A transformer
SDR ↑	6.41	**10.63 ± 5.86**	8.64 ± 5.89	9.98 ± 5.70
SIR ↑	17.38	**17.67 ± 7.73**	14.70 ± 7.88	16.11 ± 7.42

we mix two voice samples from *Voxceleb2* which are normalised with respect to their absolute maximum, so that a mixture is $x(t) = (s_1(t) + s_2(t))/2$. This normalisation aims to have two voices which are codominant in the mixture and that the waveforms of the mixtures are bounded between -1 and 1. Note that the former characteristic is not always true as *Voxceleb2* samples are sometimes accompanied by other voices or sorts of interference (clapping, music, etc.). As *Voxceleb2* is a large-scale dataset, and for the sake of comparison, we extended the size of the AV ST-transformer up to 10 encoder blocks and 10 decoder blocks so that the number of parameters of the audio subnetwork is comparable to that of Visual Voice [10]. We tested the performance of each model in the *unheard-unseen wild* test set and in the *unheard-unseen clean* test set (both described in Sect. 4). For each test set we randomly made 500 pairs out of the 1,000 samples, ensuring no sample is used more than once.

Lead Voice Enhancer. The first experiment is an ablation designed to address three main questions. i) Compare two different versions of the lead voice enhancer: the audio backbone of Y-Net [24], which is a 7M-parameter U-Net; and the audio backbone of Visual Voice [10], yet another U-Net but with 50M parameters because of a different design. ii) Evaluate the effect of recurrent iterations of the lead voice enhancer. And iii) comparing the results of the 10-block 2-stage AV ST-Transformer against a 18-block 1-stage AV ST-Transformer transformer. The details of this subnetwork are explained in Sect. 3.1. We denote our Voice-Visual Transformer as VoViT (the whole network with two stages) and VoViT-s1 the network without the second stage.

The results are shown in Table 2. As we can see, the refinement network improves the results substantially for the 10-block AV ST-Transformer. Successive iterations of the refinement module further reduce the interferences, but the best SDR is achieved with just one iteration. For the lead voice enhancer, we tried two possible audio-only U-Nets: the U-Net from the Y-Net model [24] and the larger U-Net from Visual Voice [10]. A much larger U-Net does not outperform the smaller one by a large margin. Interestingly, we can observe that adding this module performs better than using the 18-block AV ST-transformer (with around 2 times more parameters). Moreover, this subnetwork can be trained within a day, whereas the 18-block transformer required around a month to train. The reasons behind the lack of improvement of the 18-block transformer are unknown. We observed a phenomena similar to the so called "double descent" [26] while training the 10-block transformer, which may be indicative of a complex optimisation process which is worsened in the 18-block case exceeding our computational resources. In the same line, we trained a larger graph convolutional network, comparable in number of parameters to the motion subnetwork of Visual Voice, however the performance dropped. From this ablation, we can conclude that a 10-block AV ST-transformer with a small U-Net as lead voice enhancer is the best option in terms of performance-latency trade-off.

Comparison to state-of-the-Art Methods. Next we are going to compare the 10-block AV ST-Transformer to a state-of-the-art AV speech separation model and audio baselines in the *Voxceleb2* dataset. The Visual Voice network

Table 2. Ablation of different variants of the refinement stage and number of blocks in the transformer of the first stage. VoViT-s1 stands for the model with just the first stage, r stands for the number of recurrent passes in stage 2. For the stage 2 we considerered both, the Visual Voice's UNet (VV) [10] and the Y-Net's UNet (YN) [24].

		Wild test set	
		SDR ↑	SIR ↑
10-block	VoViT-s1	9.68	15.75
	VoViT (VV in stage 2, $r = 1$)	**10.05**	18.30
	VoViT (VV in stage 2, $r = 2$)	9.77	**19.38**
	VoViT (YN in stage 2, $r = 1$)	10.03	18.18
	VoViT (YN in stage 2, $r = 2$)	9.78	19.09
	18-block VoViT-s1	9.27	15.53

Table 3. Evaluation on *Voxceleb2* unheard-unseen test sets (mean ± standard deviation). VoViT stands for our model with the 10-block AV ST-Transformer with the Y-Net's UNet backbone as the lead voice enhancer. Number of parameters in millions. Results in the first block are taken from the original papers.

	# parameters		Wild Test set		Clean Test set	
	Visual Net.	Whole Net.	SDR ↑	SIR ↑	SDR ↑	SIR ↑
Visual Voice Audio-only	–	46.14	7.7	13.6	–	–
Face Filter [6]	–	–	2.53	–	–	–
The conversation [1]	–	–	8.89	14.8	–	–
Visual Voice Motion-only	9.14	55.28	9.94	17	–	–
Y-Net [24]	1.42	9.7	5.29 ± 5.06	8.45 ± 6.8	5.86 ± 4.78	9.25 ± 6.44
Visual Voice [10]	20.38	77.75	9.92 ± 3.56	16.11 ± 4.8	10.18 ± 3.36	16.49 ± 4.5
VoViT	1.42	58.2	**10.03 ± 3.35**	**18.18 ± 4.72**	**10.25 ± 2.61**	**18.65 ±3.8**

[10] is the current state of the art in speech separation. This network uses 2.55 s excerpts, the corresponding 64 video frames cropped around the lips and an image of the whole face of the target speaker. Apart from using lips motion features, it extracts cross-modal face-voice embeddings that complement the motion features and are especially useful when the motion is not reliable or when the appearance of the speakers is different. We also compare the results against Y-Net [24] as it is one of the few papers proposing face landmarks. The original work uses 4 s excerpts. As around 160 k samples for *Voxceleb2* are shorter, we just adapted the model for working with 2 s samples.

Numerical results are shown in Table 3. The 10-block VoViT outperforms all the previous AV speech separation models. Compared to Visual Voice, it achieves a much better SIR and slightly better SDR, both for the wild and clean test sets. In particular, for the clean test set, when the motion cues are more reliable, our model has a much lower standard deviation. Some aspects need to be taken into account:

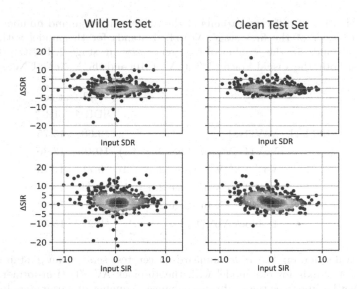

Fig. 4. Scatter plot showing the difference in SDR and SIR, ΔSDR and ΔSIR, as functions of the SDR and SIR of the input mixture in the unseen-unheard wild and clean test sets. The difference is: $\Delta SDR = SDR(\text{VoViT}) - SDR(\text{Visual Voice})$ so a positive value means VoViT outperforms Visual Voice.

- The face landmark extractor has been trained with higher quality videos than the ones in *Voxceleb2*. On the contrary, the Visual Voice video network has been trained specifically for *Voxceleb2*.
- Our visual subnetwork, the graph CNN, has 10 times less parameters than its counterpart in Visual Voice.
- Apart from motion cues, Visual Voice takes also into account speaker appearance features which are correlated with voice features, and which can be crucial in poor quality videos where lip motion is unreliable.

Figure 4 shows SDR and SIR differences between VoViT and Visual Voice in two different test sets: the *wild* and the *clean* set. Each plot is a scatter plot where each point corresponds to a 2 s long mixture. As it can be observed, our method especially outperforms Visual Voice in SIR while in SDR both methods have a comparable performance. In order to assess the significance of the results of Table 3, we calculated the p-values with respect to the Visual Voice results. Only the improvement on SIR is significant ($p < 0.05$). While the improvement from stage 1 to 2 (Table 2) is significant both in SDR and SIR. In the *wild test set* there are a few samples where our model performs worse than Visual Voice. Those correspond to samples where the audio and video are extremely unsynchronised or samples where the lip motion is mispredicted and the network separates the other speaker. In those cases, the Visual Voice model might be able to alleviate the situation either by relying on the appearance features to guide the separation or by using the motion information present in the raw video despite its poor quality (e.g. blur, compression artefacts, lack of sharpness). There are no such cases in the *clean set*, as those type of samples were filtered out. Audio-visual files with the top K worst performing examples and demos for both, Visual Voice and VoViT models, are provided in the supplementary material.

5.3 Singing Voice Separation

In this last experiment we consider the task of singing voice. We are interested in exploring how transferable models trained for speech separation are to the case of singing voice. Since speech models were trained with two voices and no extra sounds and in *Voxceleb2*, which contains mainly English, we restricted to similar types of mixtures in singing voice. In particular, we create mixtures of two singers in English from the unseen-unheard test set of *Acappella*, with no accompaniment. Table 4 compares the results of models trained directly with samples of singing voice (top block of results in Table 4) versus models trained with speech samples (bottom block). In the case of singing voice we used our model with just the first stage and a 4-block AV ST-transformer. We observe that dedicated models for singing voice perform largely better than models trained for speech. This may be explained to particular differences between a speaking and a singing voice. For example, vowels are much more sustained in singing voice, there is much less coarticulation of consonants with surrounding vowels and vibrato is not present in speech. Moreover, singing voice contains varying pitches covering a wider frequency range.

Table 4. Singing voice separation. Mixtures of two singers with no additional accompaniment from the test set unseen-unheard (only samples in English) of *Acappella*. Results in top block: models trained directly with samples of singing voice; bottom block: models trained with speech samples.

Model	SDR ↑	SIR ↑
Y-Net [24]	11.08 ± 7.51	17.18 ± 9.68
VoViT-s1 (4 blocks)	**14.85 ± 7.87**	**21.06 ± 9.69**
VoViT-s1	3.89 ± 9.28	5.89 ± 11.15
VoViT	4.04 ± 10.30	**7.21 ± 13.26**
Visual Voice [10]	**4.52 ± 8.64**	7.03 ± 7.11

6   Conclusions and Future Work

In this work we present a lightweight audio-visual source separation method which can process 10 s of recordings in less than 0.1 s in an end-to-end GPU powered manner. Besides, the method shows competitive results to the state-of-the-art in reducing distortions while clearly outperforming in reducing interferences. We show that face landmarks are computationally cheaper alternatives to raw video and help to deal with large-scale datasets. For the first time, we evaluate AV speech separation systems in singing voice, showing empirically that the characteristics of the singing voice differ substantially from the ones of speech.

As future work we would like to explore lighter and faster embedding generators for the transformer and different optimisations in its architecture which leads to a fast and powerful system.

Acknowledgments. We acknowledge support by MICINN/FEDER UE project PID2021-127643NB-I00; H2020-MSCA-RISE-2017 project 777826 NoMADS.

J.F.M. acknowledges support by FPI scholarship PRE2018-083920. We acknowledge NVIDIA Corporation for the donation of GPUs used for the experiments.

References

1. Afouras, T., Chung, J.S., Zisserman, A.: The conversation: deep audio-visual speech enhancement. In: Interspeech (2018)
2. Chen, H., Xie, W., Afouras, T., Nagrani, A., Vedaldi, A., Zisserman, A.: Audio-visual synchronisation in the wild. In: 32nd British Machine Vision Conference, BMVC (2021)
3. Cherry, E.C.: Some experiments on the recognition of speech, with one and with two ears. J. Acoust. Soc. Am. **25**(5), 975–979 (1953)
4. Chuang, S.Y., Tsao, Y., Lo, C.C., Wang, H.M.: Lite audio-visual speech enhancement. In: Proceedings of the Interspeech (2020)
5. Chung, J.S., Nagrani, A., Zisserman, A.: Voxceleb2: deep speaker recognition. In: Interspeech (2018)
6. Chung, S.W., Choe, S., Chung, J.S., Kang, H.G.: FaceFilter: audio-visual speech separation using still images. arXiv preprint arXiv:2005.07074 (2020)
7. Ephrat, A., et al.: Looking to listen at the cocktail party: a speaker-independent audio-visual model for speech separation. In: SIGGRAPH (2018)
8. Gabbay, A., Shamir, A., Peleg, S.: Visual speech enhancement. In: Interspeech, pp. 1170–1174. ISCA (2018)
9. Gao, R., Grauman, K.: Co-separating sounds of visual objects. In: Proceedings of the IEEE/CVF International Conference on Computer Vision, pp. 3879–3888 (2019)
10. Gao, R., Grauman, K.: Visualvoice: Audio-visual speech separation with cross-modal consistency. In: CVPR (2021)
11. Gemmeke, J.F., et al.: Audio set: an ontology and human-labeled dataset for audio events. In: IEEE International Conference on Acoustics, Speech and Signal Processing (2017)
12. Golumbic, E.Z., Cogan, G.B., Schroeder, C.E., Poeppel, D.: Visual input enhances selective speech envelope tracking in auditory cortex at a "cocktail party". J. Neurosci. **33**, 1417–1426 (2013)
13. Grais, E.M., Roma, G., Simpson, A.J., Plumbley, M.: Combining mask estimates for single channel audio source separation using deep neural networks. In: Interspeech (2016)
14. Gu, R., Zhang, S.X., Xu, Y., Chen, L., Zou, Y., Yu, D.: Multi-modal multi-channel target speech separation. IEEE J. Sel. Top. Sign. Process. **14**(3), 530–541 (2020)

15. Guo, J., Zhu, X., Yang, Y., Yang, F., Lei, Z., Li, S.Z.: Towards fast, accurate and stable 3D dense face alignment. In: Vedaldi, A., Bischof, H., Brox, T., Frahm, J.-M. (eds.) ECCV 2020. LNCS, vol. 12364, pp. 152–168. Springer, Cham (2020). https://doi.org/10.1007/978-3-030-58529-7_10
16. Hendrycks, D., Gimpel, K.: Gaussian error linear units (GELUs). arXiv preprint arXiv:1606.08415 (2016)
17. Hou, J.C., Wang, S.S., Lai, Y.H., Tsao, Y., Chang, H.W., Wang, H.M.: Audio-visual speech enhancement using multimodal deep convolutional neural networks. IEEE Trans. Emerg. Top. Comput. Intell. **2**(2), 117–128 (2018)
18. Kabsch, W.: A discussion of the solution for the best rotation to relate two sets of vectors. Acta Crystallogr. A **34**(5), 827–828 (1978)
19. Li, C., Qian, Y.: Deep audio-visual speech separation with attention mechanism. In: ICASSP 2020–2020 IEEE International Conference on Acoustics, Speech and Signal Processing (ICASSP), pp. 7314–7318 (2020). https://doi.org/10.1109/ICASSP40776.2020.9054180
20. Ma, W.J., Zhou, X., Ross, L.A., Foxe, J.J., Parra, L.C.: Lip-reading aids word recognition most in moderate noise: a Bayesian explanation using high-dimensional feature space. PLoS ONE **4**(3), e4638 (2009)
21. Makishima, N., Ihori, M., Takashima, A., Tanaka, T., Orihashi, S., Masumura, R.: Audio-visual speech separation using cross-modal correspondence loss. In: ICASSP 2021–2021 IEEE International Conference on Acoustics, Speech and Signal Processing (ICASSP), pp. 6673–6677. IEEE (2021)
22. Michelsanti, D., Tan, Z.H., Sigurdsson, S., Jensen, J.: On training targets and objective functions for deep-learning-based audio-visual speech enhancement. In: ICASSP 2019–2019 IEEE International Conference on Acoustics, Speech and Signal Processing (ICASSP), pp. 8077–8081. IEEE (2019)
23. Michelsanti, D., et al.: An overview of deep-learning-based audio-visual speech enhancement and separation. IEEE/ACM Trans. Audio Speech Lang. Process. **29**, 1368–1396 (2021). https://doi.org/10.1109/TASLP.2021.3066303
24. Montesinos, J.F., Kadandale, V.S., Haro, G.: A cappella: audio-visual singing voice separation. In: 32nd British Machine Vision Conference, BMVC (2021)
25. Morrone, G., Bergamaschi, S., Pasa, L., Fadiga, L., Tikhanoff, V., Badino, L.: Face landmark-based speaker-independent audio-visual speech enhancement in multi-talker environments. In: ICASSP 2019–2019 IEEE International Conference on Acoustics, Speech and Signal Processing (ICASSP), pp. 6900–6904. IEEE (2019)
26. Nakkiran, P., Kaplun, G., Bansal, Y., Yang, T., Barak, B., Sutskever, I.: Deep double descent: where bigger models and more data hurt. J. Stat. Mech: Theory Exp. **2021**(12), 124003 (2020)
27. Rafii, Z., Liutkus, A., Stöter, F.R., Mimilakis, S.I., Bittner, R.: The MUSDB18 corpus for music separation (2017). https://doi.org/10.5281/zenodo.1117372, https://doi.org/10.5281/zenodo.1117372
28. Sadeghi, M., Alameda-Pineda, X.: Mixture of inference networks for VAE-based audio-visual speech enhancement. IEEE Trans. Signal Process. **69**, 1899–1909 (2021)
29. Sato, H., Ochiai, T., Kinoshita, K., Delcroix, M., Nakatani, T., Araki, S.: Multimodal attention fusion for target speaker extraction. In: 2021 IEEE Spoken Language Technology Workshop (SLT), pp. 778–784. IEEE (2021)
30. Slizovskaia, O., Haro, G., Gómez, E.: Conditioned source separation for musical instrument performances. IEEE/ACM Trans. Audio Speech Lang. Process. **29**, 2083–2095 (2021)

31. Sun, Z., Wang, Y., Cao, L.: An attention based speaker-independent audio-visual deep learning model for speech enhancement. In: Ro, Y., et al. (eds.) MMM 2020. LNCS, vol. 11962, pp. 722–728. Springer, Cham (2020). https://doi.org/10.1007/978-3-030-37734-2_60

32. Truong, T.D., et al.: The right to talk: an audio-visual transformer approach. In: Proceedings of the IEEE/CVF International Conference on Computer Vision, pp. 1105–1114 (2021)

33. Tzinis, E., Wisdom, S., Remez, T., Hershey, J.R.: Improving on-screen sound separation for open-domain videos with audio-visual self-attention. arXiv preprint arXiv:2106.09669 (2021)

34. Vincent, E., Gribonval, R., Fevotte, C.: Performance measurement in blind audio source separation. IEEE Trans. Audio Speech Lang. Process. **14**(4), 1462–1469 (2006). https://doi.org/10.1109/TSA.2005.858005

35. Williamson, D.S., Wang, Y., Wang, D.: Complex ratio masking for monaural speech separation. IEEE/ACM Trans. Audio Speech Lang. Process. **24**(3), 483–492 (2015)

36. Wu, J., et al.: Time domain audio visual speech separation. In: 2019 IEEE Automatic Speech Recognition and Understanding Workshop (ASRU), pp. 667–673. IEEE (2019)

37. Wu, Z., Sivadas, S., Tan, Y.K., Bin, M., Goh, R.S.M.: Multi-modal hybrid deep neural network for speech enhancement. arXiv preprint arXiv:1606.04750 (2016)

38. Xu, X., et al.: VseGAN: visual speech enhancement generative adversarial network. arXiv preprint arXiv:2102.02599 (2021)

39. Yan, S., Xiong, Y., Lin, D.: Spatial temporal graph convolutional networks for skeleton-based action recognition. In: Proceedings of the AAAI Conference on Artificial Intelligence, vol. 32 (2018)

40. Zadeh, A., Ma, T., Poria, S., Morency, L.P.: Wildmix dataset and spectro-temporal transformer model for monoaural audio source separation. arXiv preprint arXiv:1911.09783 (2019)

41. Zhao, H., Gan, C., Ma, W.C., Torralba, A.: The sound of motions. In: Proceedings of the IEEE/CVF International Conference on Computer Vision, pp. 1735–1744 (2019)

42. Zhao, H., Gan, C., Rouditchenko, A., Vondrick, C., McDermott, J., Torralba, A.: The sound of pixels. In: Proceedings of the European conference on computer vision (ECCV), pp. 570–586 (2018)

Telepresence Video Quality Assessment

Zhenqiang Ying[1(✉)], Deepti Ghadiyaram[2], and Alan Bovik[1]

[1] University of Texas at Austin, Austin, USA
zqying@utexas.edu, bovik@ece.utexas.edu
[2] Facebook AI, Menlo Park, California, USA
deeptigp@fb.com

Abstract. Video conferencing, which includes both video and audio content, has contributed to dramatic increases in Internet traffic, as the COVID-19 pandemic forced millions of people to work and learn from home. Global Internet traffic of video conferencing has dramatically increased Because of this, efficient and accurate video quality tools are needed to monitor and perceptually optimize telepresence traffic streamed via Zoom, Webex, Meet, *etc.*. However, existing models are limited in their prediction capabilities on multi-modal, live streaming telepresence content. Here we address the significant challenges of Telepresence Video Quality Assessment (TVQA) in several ways. First, we mitigated the dearth of subjectively labeled data by collecting ∼2k telepresence videos from different countries, on which we crowdsourced ∼80k subjective quality labels. Using this new resource, we created a first-of-a-kind online video quality prediction framework for live streaming, using a multi-modal learning framework with separate pathways to compute visual and audio quality predictions. Our all-in-one model is able to provide accurate quality predictions at the patch, frame, clip, and audiovisual levels. Our model achieves state-of-the-art performance on both existing quality databases and our new TVQA database, at a considerably lower computational expense, making it an attractive solution for mobile and embedded systems.

Keywords: Image quality assessment · Multi-modal · Telepresence

1 Introduction

Because of restrictions on physical meetings and travel necessary to curb the spread of COVID-19, telecommuting and video conferencing are being utilized

---

The entity that conducted all of the data collection/experimentation.

Supplementary Information The online version contains supplementary material available at https://doi.org/10.1007/978-3-031-19836-6_19.

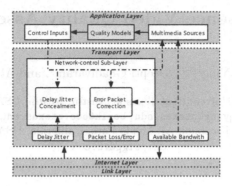

Fig. 1. System-level view of quality models in the Internet protocol suite (*c.f.* [84]). Quality prediction algorithms provide feedback to control inputs which adjust buffering and rate control strategies at the network-control sub-layer, which determines how the multimedia data are packetized and transmitted, and how the received packets are buffered and corrected, with the goal of providing network conditions that satisfy the requirements of the application layer.

at unprecedented scales. For example, the revenues of Zoom, a popular videoconferencing platform, jumped by 355% (year over year) in the 2nd quarter of 2020, after COVID-19 emerged [33]. Given the tremendous growth and continued vitality since then of telepresence videos for business, education, and interpersonal connections, being able to automatically monitor and control their perceptual quality has become quite important. Accurate and reliable quality predictors could be used to guide signal compression, transmission, reception, and display, providing perceptually optimized audio-visual conferencing experiences.

TVQA differs from other VQA/AQA problems, and presents particular challenges. To address it properly, it is necessary consider the overall telepresence workflow, including real-time requirements inherent in this type of error-prone, multi-directional live streaming. From a system-level view (*c.f.* Fig. 1), video quality algorithms serve a core purpose in the application layer, supporting tasks like acquisition, analysis, process evaluation, optimization of encoding, and stream monitoring during transmission and reception [2]. Achieving high perceptual quality of videoconferencing streams requires implementing multiple quality measurement tools under limited bandwidth constraints, to obtain analytical data that can be used to tune control inputs at run time [85]. The main challenges of TVQA include: successfully integrating multimodal signal quality models, addressing the dearth of subjectively labeled data, and efficiently modeling live-streaming content quality.

We have addressed these challenges, by learning to efficiently model multimodel features and to provide various types of quality feedback in an online manner, using our first-of-a-kind telepresence video quality dataset. We summarize the contributions we make below:

- *The first subjective database dedicated to telepresence audio-visual quality.* We gathered 2320 telepresence videos from YouTube and the Internet Archive. By comparison, the number of unique contents is fewer than 100 in any prior audiovisual quality study. We used Amazon Mechanical Turk to collect about 79K human perceptual quality judgments on the collected content from more than 500 subjects.
- *A first-of-a-kind online telepresence video quality prediction model, which we call Tele-VQA.* This new model can deliver rapid quality feedback as video streams arrive, by employing efficient backbones that extract multimodal features and integrate them into audio and visual regressors.
- *An all-in-one audio-visual quality framework that can process videos to deliver quality predictions at the patch, frame, clip, and audiovisual levels.* The image version of Tele-VQA, we call Tele-IQA, shows better performance than previous state-of-the-art models while requiring only 35% parameters.

2   Background

A/VQA Models: Video and audio quality assessment (VQA/AQA) algorithms can be classified into two main classes depending on whether reference pristine videos are available for comparison: full reference (FR) algorithms and no reference (NR) algorithms. A typical use case for NR models is the automated evaluation of user-generated content (UGC), such as videos uploaded to YouTube, Facebook, or TikTok. Unlike professional audio-visual content, UGC shared on prominent social media sites is typically acquired by novices having uncertain skills, using handheld cameras, with little or no editing. Similarly, telepresence videos are often captured by low-quality devices under imperfect conditions, and are then subjected to compression, processing, and transmission artifacts before arriving on viewers' displays. Generally, no reference signal is available, so for the TVQA problem (both visual and audio signal evaluation), we only consider NR algorithms, since pristine contents are generally unavailable.

While there has been substantial progress on the development of top-performing learned models for NR-VQA (shallow models include [3,7,34, 38,58,61,68,72,73,75,76], and deep ones include [23,37,40,45,91]) and NR-AQA [17,21,65,82,92], but relatively few NR-AVQA models [6,47,48,52] exist. Most existing AVQA models use "handcrafted" statistical features to drive shallow learners (SVMs [52], random forest ensembles [13], *etc.*.). ANNAVQA [6] was the first deep model proposed. It utilizes a pretrained convolutional neural network (CNN) model to extract A/V features from single video frames and aligned short audio segments. Thus far, all existing audio-visual QA models, whether handcrafted or deep, operate only on video frames without computing spatiotemporal video features. These models focus on modular designs, without any system-level analysis of how to apply them to live streaming content, how to handle a missing modality, or how to supply multiple levels or abstractions of audio-visual quality.

A/VQA Datasets: Representative databases are essential to learn effective VQA algorithms. A frequent misconception is that real images/videos can be characterized by one or two well-defined distortions. In reality, there are several types and severities of distortions that often coexist, interact, and create new distortions [19,66,86,87]. Early VQA databases generally comprise a small number of unique source pristine videos (typically 10–15), manually distorted by one of a few synthetic impairments (*e.g.*, Gaussian blur, compression, or transmission artifacts) [35,63,64,77–80] (Table 1). These datasets are not representative enough to capture the complex characteristics of real-world telepresence videos. More recent VQA databases have increased content diversity affected by authentic distortions [20,23,25,56,66,81,86], but none include audio signals. Although several audiovisual QA databases have been released [24,47–49,60,83], the number of unique contents and degradation types they contain is quite limited, and do not reflect real-world scenarios such as telepresence [47,51,88].

Table 1. Summary of popular audiovisual QA databases. VC: Video compression; TE: Transmission errors; AC: Audio compression;

Year	Name	# Unique contents	# Total videos	Distortion type	# Annotators	# Total ratings
2010	PLYM [22]	6	60	VC, TE	16	960
2012	VQEG-MM [60]	10	60	VC, AC	35	2100
2012	TUM [35]	5	20	VC, TE	21	420
2013	UnB-AVQ 2013 [47]	8	72	VC, AC	16	1, 152
2016	INRS [12,13]	1	160	VC, TE	30	4, 800
2016	MMSPG [59]	9	27	Display devices	20	540
2018	UnB-AVQ Exp1 [51]	60	720	VC, TE	60	43, 200
2018	UnB-AVQ Exp2 [51]	40	800	VC, TE	40	32, 000
2018	UnB-AVQ Exp3 [51]	40	800	VC, TE	40	32, 000
2018	LIVE-NFLX-II [4]	15	420	TE	65	27, 300
2020	LIVE-SJTU [53]	14	336	VC, AC	35	11, 760
2021	**Proposed database**	**2320**	**2320**	**In-the-wild**	**526**	**78, 880**

3   TVQA Dataset and Human Study

We collected 78,880 ratings (34 ratings on each video) on 2320 videos from 526 subjects. As shown in Table 1, our telepresence quality dataset is substantially larger than any previous subjective audiovisual dataset. Here we describe the new telepresence video quality dataset we constructed and the subjective quality study we conducted on it.

3.1   Data Acquisition

Data Sources: "Speaker-view" and "screen content" are the two main types of contents encountered in telepresence videos. The former can be found in widely used face analysis databases [9,10,16], but most of these are of television broadcasters, and are not affected by "in-the-wild" distortions typical of telepresence videos. Screen content video quality databases are available [8,41] but audio signals are excluded in those studies. Therefore, we decided to crawl videos online instead of using videos from existing databases. From among 6 million videos from the Internet Archive, we filtered by relevant keywords and found about 7k recorded virtual meetings and randomly sampled 1129 videos from these to avoid content redundancies. To further increase the distortion diversity, we manually searched YouTube videos uploaded from around 80 countries, using a location-based YouTube search engine [70]. In the end, we obtained 2,320 videos.

Data Processing: Each video was randomly cropped to an average duration of 7 s using ffmpeg [1]. To keep the quality intact, we did not apply re-encoding, scaling, or any further processing that could affect perceptual quality. Figure 2 shows 12 randomly selected video frames from the database. It is evident that we obtained a highly diverse TVQA dataset, representative of telepresence content (including grid-views of multiple speakers, single speaker views, slide-sharing, screen content, etc.), resolution, aspect ratios, and distortions.

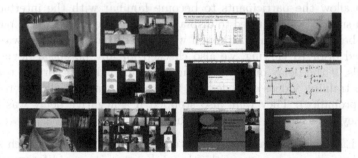

Fig. 2. Sample video frames from the proposed database, each resized to fit. The actual videos are of highly diverse sizes and resolutions. Faces are masked to ensure privacy.

3.2 Study Interface Design

We used Amazon Mechanical Turk (AMT) to collect human opinions on the collected telepresence videos, as in earlier VQA studies [19,44,66,81,87]. The human intelligence task (HIT) pipeline we designed is shown in Fig. 3. Each video was played without scaling on a black background, followed by a rating interface that prompted subjects to record scores on a rating bar. Instead of the discrete Absolute Category Rating (ACR) scale used in prior AVQA studies, we used a continuous rating scale to allow the subjects to record quality judgements with greater freedom and increased sensitivity [39]. We cached each next video while each worker was rating a current video, and ensured that each video was entirely downloaded before playback to avoid rebuffering events and/or stalling.

Next, we describe the overall study workflow in detail, including protocols we employed to identify and eliminate unreliable subjects [19,66], or those having inadequate processing or network resources.

Introduction: We showed each subject a brief task description followed by 5 sample telepresence videos exemplifying a wide range of the possible quality levels they might encounter in the study. We only accepted workers with AMT acceptance rates >75%. If a participant's browser window resolution, version, zoom, and the time taken to load videos did not meet our requirements, they were not allowed to proceed.

Checklist: We guided each subject to finish a series of setup steps to eliminate distractions, ensure their audio devices were on, adjust their seating, and wear their corrective lenses if necessary.

Instruction and Quiz: To ensure the subjects' audio devices were on and working, we displayed the instructions, then asked the subjects to reply to additional questions that were posed via audio. The subjects were allowed to participants in several tasks, each time encountering a different set of videos.

Training: A short training session was played that included 3 telepresence videos, to allow the participants to become familiar with the interface. After that, each subject was required to display and read the ethics policy page for at least 30 s before proceeding. Although we ensured that each video was entirely downloaded prior to viewing, we also checked for any potential device-related video stalls. If the delay on any training video exceeded 2 s, or the total delay over the 3 training videos exceeded 3 s, the subject was not allowed to proceed (without prejudice). They were also stopped if a negative delay was detected (*e.g.*, if they used plugins to speed up the video).

Testing: Each subject was asked to rate 90 videos. We divided each subject's participation into two sessions with a break between, to avoid fatigue. We analyzed the ratings collected halfway through each session, and also at the end of the session, to identify unreliable workers. At the middle of each subject's task, we checked for instability of the internet connection. If more than 50% of the

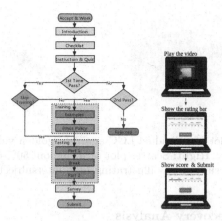

Fig. 3. Left: flowchart of the AMT workflow experienced by crowd-sourced workers when rating telepresence videos. **Right**: workflow when rating a video.

videos viewed until then had suffered from hardware stalls, the subject was disqualified, without prejudice (they could try again). We also determined whether a subject had been giving very similar quality scores to all videos.

Survey: At the end of a subject's task, several survey questions were asked to collect subject demographics and to record video and audio device specifications.

3.3 Crowdsourcing Quality Control

When conducting online crowd-sourced studies, quality control is essential to obtaining reliable quality labels. One common practice is to use repeated and/or "golden" videos for which the highly reliable subjective scores were previously obtained, which may then be used to compare with the worker's inputs.

Golden Videos: In prior VQA studies, "Gold" videos are often selected from other databases featuring similar content, to provide reliable scores that can be compared against to detect dishonest workers. Since there are no such existing databases containing reliable audiovisual telepresence contents and labels, we conducted a pilot study where we collected ratings on 90 videos, from among which we randomly selected 5 videos having a wide range of quality ratings. Those videos were inserted randomly into the first half-session videos of each AMT task, and were used to identify and eliminate unreliable subjects.

Repeated Videos: After half of the ratings were collected in each session, we systematically sampled 5 videos having diverse ratings, then inserted these randomly into the second half of the task. Based on the level of correlation of the ratings provided in the two half-sessions, we identified unreliable subjects and removed them from the study.

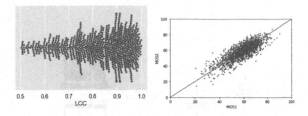

Fig. 4. Left: Swarm plot of individual LCC against "golden videos" illustrating high intrasubject consistency. **Right**: Scatter plot of a random 50% division of the human labels into two disjoint subject sets illustrating high intersubject consistency.

3.4 Subjective Recovery Analysis

Rather than applying the subjection rejection protocol BT.500 recommended by the ITU for video studies, which incorporates a number of hard coded parameters and thresholds, which may not be suitable for telepresence contents [43], we instead adopted a recent "soft" subject rejection model [42] that is designed to recover subjective quality scores from noisy measurements. To establish the internal integrity of the final set of collected subjective scores, we conducted two consistency checks on the recorded MOS, as shown in Fig. 4 and described in the following.

Inter-subject Consistency: We randomly divided the subjects into two equal and disjoint sets and computed the Spearman Rank Correlation Coefficient (**SRCC**) [36] between the two sets of MOS over 50 such random splits. We arrived at an average SRCC of **0.765**, indicating a high degree of agreement between the human subjects, implying successful testing and screening processes. A scatter plot of one of the divisions is shown in Fig. 4 (right).

Intra-subject Consistency: We also computed the Linear Correlation Coefficient (**LCC**) [62] between the collected MOS, against the original scores on the "golden" videos, obtaining a median LCC of **0.845**. These high correlations further validate the efficacy of our data collection process.

4   TVQA Modeling

TVQA algorithms should include two main modalities. As shown in Fig. 1, a quality measurement module in the application layer takes in rendered multimedia sources, providing feedback to control inputs that optimize the transport layer. This implies three requirements on the design of successful TVQA models. First, both video and audio quality need to be accurately modeled. While subjective experiments have shown that the visual component generally dominates overall audio-visual quality perception [50], audio quality is hardly insignificant (and in telepresence, is even more important), and certain types of audio distortions (such as background noise and clipping) can cause the audio component to significantly impact the overall perception of quality. Second, a TVQA algorithm should be able to handle the "missing-modality" problem, whereby if either the video or audio signal is not present during a video call, then the quality of the remaining signal is still accurately predicted. Third, a TVQA algorithm should be able to provide separate quality measurements on each modality as well as overall quality predictions. These can be useful for adjusting network traffic priorities for each modality [11]. Based on these considerations, we first designed an image model called TeleIQA to effectively predict image quality both globally and locally. Then we integrated TeleIQA to a video model called TeleVQA to perform telepresence video quality assessment.

4.1   Tele-IQA: Our Image Model

We aim to build an image model that can efficiently give accurate predictions both on the full image and on the patches. This will enable modeling the spatial non-uniformity of telepresence content and providing predictions both locally and globally. IQA models can be viewed as mapping functions from the image domain to the real set. Our Tele-IQA model is a composition of three functions: feature extraction $\mathbf{f}$, pooling $\mathbf{p}$, and regression $\mathbf{r}$. To efficiently extract patch quality predictions, we use RoIPool to estimate local predictions on extracted feature maps instead of feeding patches to the network. The RoIPool operator ($\mathbf{p}_{RoI}$) is designed to pool local feature maps from global feature maps:

$$(\mathbf{f} \circ \mathbf{p}_{RoI})(P) \approx (\mathbf{f} \circ \mathbf{p})(P_{RoI}), \tag{1}$$

where P is a picture and P_{RoI} is the local patch of P correspoding to the region of interest (RoI). Therefore, the predicted patch quality score $\widetilde{S}_{RoI}$ is close to the prediction S_{RoI} when taking the patch as input:

$$\widetilde{S}_{RoI} = (\mathbf{f} \circ \mathbf{p}_{RoI} \circ \mathbf{r})(P) \approx (\mathbf{f} \circ \mathbf{p} \circ \mathbf{r})(P_{RoI}) = S_{RoI} \tag{2}$$

4.2   Tele-VQA: Our Video Model

At each time step, Tele-VQA receives one frame (F_t), one video clip (C_t), and one audio clip (A_t), and generates timely visual ($S_t^{(v)}$), audio ($S_t^{(a)}$) and combined audio-visual quality predictions ($S_t^{(a/v)}$,). Tele-VQA involves four sequential steps: feature extraction, feature fusion, quality regression, and quality fusion (c.f. Fig. 5). First, features are extracted from patches, frames, video clips and audio clips from a video stream, capturing rich multi-modal information. The patch, frame, and clip level features are fused and then fed to the visual regressor while the audio features are fed to the audio regressor. Each regressor contain an internal state to allow information to flow from one time step to the next. Finally, the predicted visual and audio quality scores are fused to form an overall audio-visual quality prediction. We provide more details of each step below.

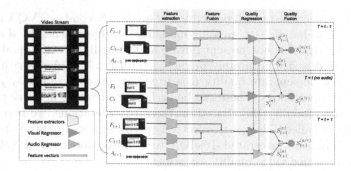

Fig. 5. Our Tele-VQA model which involves 4 sequential steps: feature extraction, feature fusion, quality regression, and quality fusion. For video conferences, the audio signal is not guaranteed to be always available. Here we describe how we handle the case of missing audio ($T = t$).

Feature Extraction. We use the frame backbone ($\mathbf{f}^{(f)}$), clip backbone ($\mathbf{f}^{(c)}$), and audio backbone ($\mathbf{f}^{(a)}$) to extract features at the frame/patch, clip, and audio levels, respectively.

1. **Frame-level features:** $\mathcal{F}_t^{(f)} = (\mathbf{f}^{(f)} \circ \mathbf{p})(F_t)$ For each incoming frame, 960 feature maps are computed using a MobileNetV3 backbone [26] pretrained on ImageNet [14] and finetuned on the LIVE-FB Dataset [87]. Adaptive Average Pooling of size 1×3 is then applied, followed by flattening, yielding a 2880-dim feature vector.

2. **Patch-level features:** Quality maps model spatial variations of distortions. To extract patch quality features, we partition the frames into a $2^d \times 2^d$ grid of RoIs ($d = 1, 2, 3, 4$) and apply RoI pooling on each RoI:

$$\mathbf{p}_i^{(M \times N)}(.) := \mathbf{p}_{RoI_i}(.), \quad i \in \{1, 2, ..., M \times N\}. \tag{3}$$

Then, the predicted quality scores for quality maps of different scales are concatenated into a vector:

$$\mathcal{F}_t^{(p)} = \bigoplus_{d=1}^{4} \bigoplus_{i=1}^{2^d \times 2^d} (\mathbf{f}^{(f)} \circ \mathbf{p}_i^{(2^d \times 2^d)} \circ \mathbf{r})(F_t), \tag{4}$$

where $\mathcal{F}_t^{(p)}$ is the extracted patch-level features on frame F_t; $\bigoplus$ is the concatenation operator. The extracted MobileNetV3 features ($960 \times 3 \times 1$) are treated as a 960-variable time series of length of 3, which is then fed to a GRU-FCN [15]. Each extracted quality map is then flattened and concatenated into a 341-dim feature vector.

3. **Clip-level features:** $\mathcal{F}_t^{(c)} = (\mathbf{f}^{(c)} \circ \mathbf{p})(C_t)$ We employ a 3D CNN to extract spatiotemporal features to model video-level distortions such as flickering, jerkiness, and edge/texture floating [74]. We modified the R(2+1)D model [71]

pre-trained on the Kinetics dataset [31] by removing the last pooling layer, to serve as the backbone for extracting spatiotemporal features. The backbone was not finetuned on quality-related tasks. As in frame and patch level features, 1×3 Adaptive Average Pooling is applied along the spatial dimension. Flattening then yields a 1536 dim feature vector.

4. **Audio-level features:** $\mathcal{F}_t^{(a)} = (\text{STFT} \circ \mathbf{f}^{(a)} \circ \mathbf{p})(A_t)$ Each 1D audio signal is transformed into a 2D spectrogram via the short-time Fourier transform (STFT). Then, 2D features are extracted from each spectrogram using YAMNet [89], which is an audio classification model that incorporates a MobileNetV1 architecture that was pre-trained on the Google AudioSet dataset [18] to predict 521 different audio events.

Feature Fusion. We use separate pathways to process the visual and audio information. For the visual branch, we concatenate frame-level, patch-level, and clip-level features. The result is a 4757-dim feature vector for the visual pathway and a 1536-dim feature vector for the audio pathway.

Quality Regression. The resulting visual and audio features are fed to two different modified GRU-FCN [15] modules to conduct quality regression. The features extracted from the entire video may be viewed as a multi-variate time series. Our online prediction model accepts a single sample point at each time step. Quality regression is formulated as a Time Series Regression (TSR) problem, which we solve using GRU-FCN, a state-of-the-art deep model often used for Time Series Classification problem. GRU-FCN includes two main building blocks. The Gated Recurrent Unit (GRU) is used to learn temporal dependencies in a step-by-step manner, while a fully convolutional network (FCN) accepts the entire time-series as input to perform feature extraction. To adapt the GRU-FCN to the online quality regression problem, we set the input for the FCN to be the current sample point instead of the entire sequence.

Quality Fusion. We refer to ITU-T Rec. P.911 [29] regarding how perceptions of audio and video quality $(S_t^{(a)}, S_t^{(v)})$ interact and how predictions of them can be combined into a single audio-visual quality prediction $(S_t^{(a+v)})$. We add a fusion layer that uses the KPN model [5] to fuse the quality predictions:

$$S_t^{(a+v)} = S_t^{(a)} \otimes S_t^{(v)} = 1.12 + 0.007 \cdot S_t^{(a)} + 0.24 \cdot S_t^{(v)} + 0.088 \cdot (S_t^{(a)} \cdot S_t^{(v)}) \quad (5)$$

We jointly trained the visual and audio pathways, and backpropagate the loss through the fusion layer, when both types of modality were available. When training Tele-VQA with a single type of modality, this fusion was not applied. To handle the "missing modality" problem during testing, Tele-VQA initializes both quality scores to 3.0 (Fair quality) and then uses the last available quality predictions $(S_{t-1}^{(a)}$ or $S_{t-1}^{(v)})$, as shown in Fig. 5.

Variants. For the unimodal version of Tele-VQA, the extracted features for modality m are fed into a TSR module $\mathbf{r}_t^{(\cdot)}[.,.]$ to obtain a predicted score $S_t^{(m)}$:

$$S_t^{(m)} = \mathbf{r}_t^{(m)}\left[\mathcal{F}_t^{(m)}, \mathbf{h}_{t-1}^{(m)}\right], \quad m \in \{f, p, c, a\}, \quad (6)$$

where $\mathbf{h}_t^{(m)}$ is the hidden state of the regressor $\mathbf{r}$ for modality m that captures historical information $(T = 1, 2, ..., t)$. The multimodal version of Tele-VQA for the video-only case is defined as:

$$S_t^{(f+c)} = \mathbf{r}_t^{(fc)} \left[\mathcal{F}_t^{(f)} \oplus \mathcal{F}_t^{(c)}, \mathbf{h}_{t-1}^{(f+c)} \right] \tag{7}$$

$$S_t^{(p+f+c)} = \mathbf{r}_t^{(p+f+c)} \left[\mathcal{F}_t^{(p)} \oplus \mathcal{F}_t^{(f)} \oplus \mathcal{F}_t^{(c)}, \mathbf{h}_{t-1}^{(p+f+c)} \right]. \tag{8}$$

Our final model considering all modalities is defined as:

$$S_t^{(p+f+c+a)} = S_t^{(p+f+c)} \otimes S_t^{(v)}. \tag{9}$$

5   Experiments

We followed the common practice of leaving out 20% for testing, while the remaining 80% contains the training and validation data (train:val:test = 6:2:2). Unlike the way most deep image networks are trained, we did not crop, resize, rotate, or otherwise process the input videos. Any such operation would introduce additional spatial and/or temporal artifacts, making comparisons to human judgments of the non-altered video quality less meaningful. Processing input videos of diverse aspect ratios, resolutions, and durations, however, makes training an end-to-end deep network impractical. Therefore, we formatted the videos which are of highly diverse sizes for efficient training, using two regularization steps which we describe next.

Spatial Regularization: First, extract video frame/clip features and audio mel spectrograms are computed and saved in a lossless compression format. The spatial dimensions of the audio spectrograms are all the same. Before training, we converted all of the frames and clips of each video to a sequence of feature vectors. In this way, we reduced the training time and also regularized the various spatial dimensions. Since frames and clips share the same spatial dimensions on each video, we fed them in batches into MobileNetV3 and R(2+1)D, respectively. We extracted features from all frames and all non-overlapping clips of 8 continuous frames in each video.

Temporal Regularization: We used a fixed number of time steps for each video/audio so that we could feed them in batches to the regressors. To trade off feature coverage with training efficiency, we set the number of time steps to be 20 for the video and 10 for the audio. If fixed sampling of the videos/frames were used, we could not use all of the extracted features. Therefore, we instead used systematic random sampling to obtain different groups of evenly-spaced videos/frames during training. We introduced this randomization as a method of data augmentation to help avoiding over-fitting, by mapping different variants of videos to the same labels.

Implementation Details: We built our code on the machine learning libraries Fast.ai2 [27] and tsai [57]. We used a batch size of 128 and employed the MSE

Table 2. Parameter efficiency on the IQA task: Performance when all models are trained and tested on the LIVE-FB dataset [87]. NIQE is not a trained model.

Model	Year	# Params	SRCC	LCC
Traditional models				
NIQE [55]	2013	–	0.094	0.131
BRISQUE [54]	2012	–	0.303	0.341
Deep models				
CNNIQA [30]	2014	0.72 M	0.259	0.242
NIMA [69]	2018	2.23 M	0.521	0.609
DB CNN [90]	2018	1.38 B	0.554	0.652
P2P-FM [87]	2020	12.24 M	0.562	0.649
HyperIQA [67]	2020	27.38 M	0.535	0.623
MUSIQ [32]	2021	27 M*	0.566	0.661
CONTRIQUE [46]	2021	27.97 M	0.580	0.641
Tele-IQA (ours)	–	9.79 M	**0.580**	**0.675**

loss when regressing the output quality scores. We trained for 60 epochs with the Adam optimizer ($\beta_1 = .9$ and $\beta_2 = .99$) and a weight decay of .01, When finetuning MobileNetV3, we first froze the backbone, and tuned the head layers over 10 epochs, then we unfroze the backbone and followed a discriminative learning approach [28] for 1 additional epoch, using a lower learning rate of $3e^{-4}$, but a higher learning rate of $3e^{-3}$ for the head layers.

5.1   Results

Image Quality: We evaluated Tele-IQA and leading IQA models, all trained on the existing LIVE-FB dataset [87], and report their parameter efficiency (Table 2). To observe whether trained models transfer well to other IQA databases, Table 3 reports cross-database validation results on two smaller, independent "in-the-wild" databases, CLIVE [19] and KonIQ [44] without any fine-tuning.

Video Quality: Audio information is optional for Tele-VQA, making it possible to evaluate it on the video-only LIVE-VQC database [66]. As shown in Table 4, Tele-VQA was able to compete very well with the other models on LIVE-VQC.

Audiovisual Quality: Table 4 compares the models' performances on our telepresence video database. Tele-VQA improved the SRCC by 9.8% as compared to the best baseline. Adding the audio information contributes an improvement of 2.4%. We also studied the contribution of the features from different modalities on the performance, by training separate models with one or two modalities excluded. As may be observed from this ablation, integrating multimodal features contributed to a significant performance boost on both telepresence videos

Table 3. Picture quality predictions: Performance of picture quality models on different databases [87]. A higher value indicates superior performance.

Model	CLIVE [19]		KonIQ [44]	
	SRCC	LCC	SRCC	LCC
NIQE [55]	0.052	0.154	0.534	0.509
BRISQUE [54]	0.495	0.494	0.641	0.596
CNNIQA [30]	0.580	0.481	0.596	0.403
NIMA [69]	0.395	0.411	0.666	0.721
P2P-FM [87]	0.756	0.783	**0.788**	**0.808**
Tele-IQA	**0.767**	**0.795**	0.772	0.800

Table 4. Video quality predictions: Performance when all models are separately trained and tested on our database and LIVE-VQC. Here p, f, c, a means patch, frame, clip, and audio features, respectively.

	Our database		LIVE-VQC [66]	
	SRCC	LCC	SRCC	LCC
IQA models				
BRISQUE [54]	0.411	0.482	0.592	0.638
TeleVQA (p)	0.476	0.488	0.621	0.603
TeleVQA (f)	0.609	0.590	0.710	0.716
VQA models				
VSFA [40]	0.601	0.655	0.773	0.795
TLVQM [38]	0.565	0.617	0.799	0.803
VIDEVAL [72]	0.536	0.560	0.752	0.751
TeleVQA (c)	0.475	0.467	0.792	0.730
TeleVQA (f+c)	0.621	0.652	0.811	0.801
TeleVQA (p+f+c)	0.633	0.672	**0.811**	**0.829**
AVQA models				
TeleVQA (a)	0.114	0.136	–	–
TeleVQA (f+a)	0.622	0.686	–	–
TeleVQA (f+c+a)	0.639	0.686	–	–
TeleVQA (p+f+c+a)	**0.663**	**0.715**	–	–

and UGC videos. Comparing unimodel Tele-VQAs, image-level features contributed more than patch-level features. Clip-level features were essential for modeling UGC videos but contributed the least to the telepresence.

Provide Local Quality Predictions: Telepresence videos often exhibit spatial non-uniformities of visual quality, *e.g.* when in grid view or slide-sharing view, where the videos are from different capture, compression and transmis-

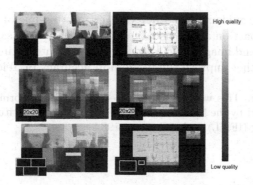

Fig. 6. Example of applying Tele-VQA on telepresence frames (top) to extract 20×20 quality maps (middle) and local quality predictions on selected regions (bottom).

sion sources. To monitor the visual quality of interested regions, we feed their coordinates of the in addition to the multi-scale grids of RoIs when extracting patch-level features. As shown in Fig. 6, Tele-VQA is able to provide multi-scale quality maps, as well as perceptual quality predictions on regions of interest. Integrating Tele-VQA into a video conferencing platform in this way can provide timely local quality feedback, which can be used to support the development of optimal strategies for processing different sources of videos and pictures.

6   Discussion and Conclusion

Videoconferencing has become much more popular in recent years, so much so that it has altered the way many people communicate. Monitoring the perceptual quality of a video conferencing session having multiple participants using different types of equipment can present many complexities. To ensure the best possible quality, standardized methods to quantify audiovisual teleconferencing quality of telemeetings are needed. Although many other studies have addressed video and audio quality, few have simultaneously addressed both, and none have in the context of video teleconferencing. This is unfortunate, since both types of sensory signals shape user-perceptions of the quality of teleconferencing sessions. To help address these challenges, we built a new dedicated telepresence quality dataset that is substantially larger, more diverse, and more representative of video conference signals than any previous audiovisual datasets. We also created an all-in-one audio-visual quality prediction model, called Tele-VQA, which integrates multimodal features to accurately infer telepresence image, video, audio and audiovisual quality. It is also able to generate predictions in an online manner, while achieving has shown state-of-the-art performance both on our new database and on other datasets.

While Tele-VQA was designed for in telepresence applications, further applications and extensions are possible. One avenue for future work is to assist visually challenged users to take better quality videos by providing timely video quality feedback as guidance. Another very interesting line of inquiry would be to consider the impact on audio-visual quality of space-time saliency (*e.g.* a current speaker voice and image) towards designing and integrating visual attention mechanisms to further improve the prediction accuracy of Tele-VQA.

Acknowledgments. This work was supported by Meta Platforms, Inc. A.C. Bovik was supported in part by the National Science Foundation AI Institute for Foundations of Machine Learning (IFML) under Grant 2019844.

References

1. FFmpeg. https://ffmpeg.org/
2. Akhtar, Z., Falk, T.H.: Audio-visual multimedia quality assessment: a comprehensive survey. IEEE Access **5**, 21090–21117 (2017)
3. Argyropoulos, S., Raake, A., Garcia, M.N., List, P.: No-reference video quality assessment for SD and HD H.264/AVC sequences based on continuous estimates of packet loss visibility. In: 2011 Third International Workshop on Quality of Multimedia Experience, pp. 31–36 (2011)
4. Bampis, C.G., Li, Z., Katsavounidis, I., Huang, T., Ekanadham, C., Bovik, A.C.: Towards perceptually optimized end-to-end adaptive video streaming. arXiv preprint arXiv:1808.03898 (2018)
5. Belmudez, B., Moeller, S., Lewcio, B., Raake, A., Mehmood, A.: Audio and video channel impact on perceived audio-visual quality in different interactive contexts. In: 2009 IEEE International Workshop on Multimedia Signal Processing, pp. 1–5. IEEE (2009)
6. Cao, Y., Min, X., Sun, W., Zhai, G.: Deep neural networks for full-reference and no-reference audio-visual quality assessment. In: 2021 IEEE International Conference on Image Processing (ICIP), pp. 1429–1433. IEEE (2021)
7. Caviedes, J.E., Oberti, F.: No-reference quality metric for degraded and enhanced video. Digit. Video Image Qual. Perceptual Coding, 305–324 (2017)
8. Cheng, S., Zeng, H., Chen, J., Hou, J., Zhu, J., Ma, K.: Screen content video quality assessment: subjective and objective study. IEEE Trans. Image Process. **29**, 8636–8651 (2020)
9. Chung, J.S., Nagrani, A., Zisserman, A.: VoxCeleb2: deep speaker recognition. arXiv preprint arXiv:1806.05622 (2018)
10. Chung, J.S., Zisserman, A.: Lip reading in the wild. In: Lai, S.-H., Lepetit, V., Nishino, K., Sato, Y. (eds.) ACCV 2016. LNCS, vol. 10112, pp. 87–103. Springer, Cham (2017). https://doi.org/10.1007/978-3-319-54184-6_6
11. Zoom Video Communications, Inc.: Using QoS DSCP marking (2021). https://support.zoom.us/hc/en-us/articles/207368756-Using-QoS-DSCP-Marking
12. Demirbilek, E., Grégoire, J.: INRS audiovisual quality dataset. In: Proceedings of the 24th ACM International Conference on Multimedia, pp. 167–171 (2016)
13. Demirbilek, E., Grégoire, J.: Towards reduced reference parametric models for estimating audiovisual quality in multimedia services. In: 2016 IEEE International Conference on Communications (ICC), pp. 1–6. IEEE (2016)
14. Deng, J., Dong, W., Socher, R., Li, L., Li, K., Li, F.: ImageNet: a large-scale hierarchical image database. In: IEEE Conference Computer Vision and Pattern Recognition, pp. 248–255, June 2009

15. Elsayed, N., Maida, A.S., Bayoumi, M.: Deep gated recurrent and convolutional network hybrid model for univariate time series classification. arXiv preprint arXiv:1812.07683 (2018)

16. Ephrat, A., et al.: Looking to listen at the cocktail party: a speaker-independent audio-visual model for speech separation. arXiv preprint arXiv:1804.03619 (2018)

17. Gamper, H., Reddy, C.K., Cutler, R., Tashev, I.J., Gehrke, J.: Intrusive and non-intrusive perceptual speech quality assessment using a convolutional neural network. In: 2019 IEEE Workshop on Applications of Signal Processing to Audio and Acoustics (WASPAA), pp. 85–89. IEEE (2019)

18. Gemmeke, J.F., et al.: Audio set: an ontology and human-labeled dataset for audio events. In: 2017 IEEE International Conference on Acoustics, Speech and Signal Processing (ICASSP), pp. 776–780. IEEE (2017)

19. Ghadiyaram, D., Bovik, A.C.: Massive online crowdsourced study of subjective and objective picture quality. IEEE Trans. Image Process. 25(1), 372–387 (2016). Jan

20. Ghadiyaram, D., Pan, J., Bovik, A.C., Moorthy, A.K., Panda, P., Yang, K.C.: In-capture mobile video distortions: a study of subjective behavior and objective algorithms. IEEE Trans. Circ. Syst. Video Tech. (2017). LIVE-Qualcomm Database. http://live.ece.utexas.edu/research/incaptureDatabase/index.html

21. Goetze, S., Albertin, E., Rennies, J., Habets, E.A., Kammeyer, K.: Speech quality assessment for listening-room compensation. In: Audio Engineering Society Conference: 38th International Conference: Sound Quality Evaluation. Audio Engineering Society (2010)

22. Goudarzi, M., Sun, L., Ifeachor, E.: Audiovisual quality estimation for video calls in wireless applications. In: 2010 IEEE Global Telecommunications Conference GLOBECOM 2010, pp. 1–5. IEEE (2010)

23. Hahn, F.G., Hosu, V., Lin, H., Saupe, D.: No-reference video quality assessment using multi-level spatially pooled features (2019)

24. Hands, D.S.: A basic multimedia quality model. IEEE Trans. Multimedia 6(6), 806–816 (2004)

25. Hosu, V., et al.: The Konstanz natural video database (KoNViD-1K). In: 2017 Ninth International Conference on Quality of Multimedia Experience (QoMEX), pp. 1–6. IEEE (2017). http://database.mmsp-kn.de/konvid-1k-database.html

26. Howard, A., et al.: Searching for MobileNetV3. In: Proceedings of the IEEE/CVF International Conference on Computer Vision, pp. 1314–1324 (2019)

27. Howard, J., Gugger, S.: Fastai: a layered API for deep learning. Information 11(2), 108 (2020)

28. Howard, J., Ruder, S.: Universal language model fine-tuning for text classification. arXiv preprint arXiv:1801.06146 (2018)

29. ITU-T Recommendation P.910: Subjective video quality assessment methods for multimedia applications. International Telecommunication Union (2021)

30. Kang, L., Ye, P., Li, Y., Doermann, D.: Convolutional neural networks for no-reference image quality assessment. In: IEEE International Conference on Computer Vision and Pattern Recognition (CVPR), pp. 1733–1740, June 2014

31. Kay, W., et al.: The Kinetics human action video dataset (2017)

32. Ke, J., Wang, Q., Wang, Y., Milanfar, P., Yang, F.: MUSIQ: multi-scale image quality transformer. In: Proceedings of the IEEE/CVF International Conference on Computer Vision, pp. 5148–5157 (2021)

33. Keegan, L.: Video conferencing statistics (all you need to know!) (2020). https://skillscouter.com/videoconferencing-statistics

34. Keimel, C., Oelbaum, T., Diepold, K.: No-reference video quality evaluation for high-definition video. In: Proceedings IEEE International Conference on Acoustics, Speech, and Signal Processing (ICASSP), pp. 1145–1148 (2009)
35. Keimel, C., Redl, A., Dieopold, K.: The TUM high definition video datasets, vol. pp. 97–102 (2012). https://doi.org/10.1109/QoMEX.2012.6263865
36. Kendall, M.G.: Rank correlation methods (1948)
37. Kim, W., Kim, J., Ahn, S., Kim, J., Lee, S.: Deep video quality assessor: from spatio-temporal visual sensitivity to a convolutional neural aggregation network. In: Ferrari, V., Hebert, M., Sminchisescu, C., Weiss, Y. (eds.) ECCV 2018. LNCS, vol. 11205, pp. 224–241. Springer, Cham (2018). https://doi.org/10.1007/978-3-030-01246-5_14
38. Korhonen, J.: Two-level approach for no-reference consumer video quality assessment. IEEE Trans. Image Process. **28**(12), 5923–5938 (2019). https://doi.org/10.1109/TIP.2019.2923051
39. Köster, F., Guse, D., Wältermann, M., Möller, S.: Comparison between the discrete ACR scale and an extended continuous scale for the quality assessment of transmitted speech. Fortschritte der Akustik, DAGA **3** (2015)
40. Li, D., Jiang, T., Jiang, M.: Quality assessment of in-the-wild videos (2019). https://doi.org/10.1145/3343031.3351028
41. Li, T., Min, X., Zhao, H., Zhai, G., Xu, Y., Zhang, W.: Subjective and objective quality assessment of compressed screen content videos. IEEE Trans. Broadcast. **67**(2), 438–449 (2020)
42. Li, Z., Bampis, C.G.: Recover subjective quality scores from noisy measurements. In: 2017 Data Compression Conference (DCC), pp. 52–61. IEEE (2017)
43. Li, Z., Bampis, C.G., Janowski, L., Katsavounidis, I.: A simple model for subject behavior in subjective experiments. Electron. Imaging **2020**(11), 131–1 (2020)
44. Lin, H., Hosu, V., Saupe, D.: KonIQ-10K: towards an ecologically valid and large-scale IQA database. arXiv preprint arXiv:1803.08489, March 2018
45. Liu, W., Duanmu, Z., Wang, Z.: End-to-end blind quality assessment of compressed videos using deep neural networks. In: Proceedings ACM Multimedia Conference (MM), pp. 546–554 (2018)
46. Madhusudana, P.C., Birkbeck, N., Wang, Y., Adsumilli, B., Bovik, A.C.: Image quality assessment using contrastive learning. arXiv preprint arXiv:2110.13266 (2021)
47. Martinez, H.B., Farias, M.C.: Full-reference audio-visual video quality metric. J. Electron. Imaging **23**(6), 061108 (2014)
48. Martinez, H.B., Farias, M.C.: A no-reference audio-visual video quality metric. In: 2014 22nd European Signal Processing Conference (EUSIPCO), pp. 2125–2129. IEEE (2014)
49. Martinez, H.A.B., Farias, M.C.Q.: Combining audio and video metrics to assess audio-visual quality. Multimedia Tools Appl. **77**(18), 23993–24012 (2018). https://doi.org/10.1007/s11042-018-5656-7
50. Martinez, H.B., Hines, A., Farias, M.C.: Perceptual quality of audio-visual content with common video and audio degradations. Appl. Sci. **11**(13), 5813 (2021)
51. Martinez, H.B., Hines, A., Farias, M.: UNB-AV: an audio-visual database for multimedia quality research. IEEE Access **8**, 56641–56649 (2020)
52. Martinez, H.B., Farias, M.C., Hines, A.: NAViDad: a no-reference audio-visual quality metric based on a deep autoencoder. In: 2019 27th European Signal Processing Conference (EUSIPCO), pp. 1–5. IEEE (2019)

53. Min, X., Zhai, G., Zhou, J., Farias, M., Bovik, A.C.: Study of subjective and objective quality assessment of audio-visual signals. IEEE Trans. Image Process. **29**, 6054–6068 (2020)
54. Mittal, A., Moorthy, A.K., Bovik, A.C.: No-reference image quality assessment in the spatial domain. IEEE Trans. Image Process. **21**(12), 4695–4708 (2012)
55. Mittal, A., Soundararajan, R., Bovik, A.C.: Making a "Completely blind" image quality analyzer. IEEE Signal Process. Lett. **20**, 209–212 (2013)
56. Nuutinen, M., Virtanen, T., Vaahteranoksa, M., Vuori, T., Oittinen, P., Häkkinen, J.: CVD2014-a database for evaluating no-reference video quality assessment algorithms. IEEE Trans. Image Process. **25**(7), 3073–3086 (2016). https://doi.org/10.1109/TIP.2016.2562513
57. Oguiza, I.: tsai - a state-of-the-art deep learning library for time series and sequential data. Github (2020). https://github.com/timeseriesAI/tsai
58. Pandremmenou, K., Shahid, M., Kondi, L.P., Lövström, B.: A no-reference bitstream-based perceptual model for video quality estimation of videos affected by coding artifacts and packet losses. In: Human Vision and Electronic Imaging XX, vol. 9394, p. 93941F (2015)
59. Perrin, A.N.M., Xu, H., Kroupi, E., Řeřábek, M., Ebrahimi, T.: Multimodal dataset for assessment of quality of experience in immersive multimedia. In: Proceedings of the 23rd ACM International Conference on Multimedia, pp. 1007–1010 (2015)
60. Pinson, M.H., et al.: The influence of subjects and environment on audiovisual subjective tests: an international study. IEEE J. Sel. Top. Sig. Process. **6**(6), 640–651 (2012)
61. Reddy Dendi, S.V., Channappayya, S.S.: No-reference video quality assessment using natural spatiotemporal scene statistics. IEEE Trans. Image Process. **29**, 5612–5624 (2020). https://doi.org/10.1109/TIP.2020.2984879
62. Rodgers, J.L., Nicewander, W.A.: Thirteen ways to look at the correlation coefficient. Am. Stat. **42**(1), 59–66 (1988). https://doi.org/10.1080/00031305.1988.10475524
63. Seshadrinathan, K., Soundararajan, R., Bovik, A.C., Cormack, L.K.: Study of subjective and objective quality assessment of video. IEEE Trans. Image Process. **19**(6), 1427–1441 (2010). https://doi.org/10.1109/TIP.2010.2042111
64. Simone, F.D., Tagliasacchi, M., Naccari, M., Tubaro, S., Ebrahimi, T.: A H.264/AVC video database for the evaluation of quality metrics. In: Proceedings IEEE International Conference on Acoustics, Speech, and Signal Processing (ICASSP), pp. 2430–2433 (2010)
65. Simou, N., Mastorakis, Y., Stefanakis, N.: Towards blind quality assessment of concert audio recordings using deep neural networks. In: ICASSP 2020–2020 IEEE International Conference on Acoustics, Speech and Signal Processing (ICASSP), pp. 3477–3481. IEEE (2020)
66. Sinno, Z., Bovik, A.: Large-scale study of perceptual video quality. IEEE Trans. Image Process. **28**(2), 612–627 (2019). LIVE VQC Database. http://live.ece.utexas.edu/research/LIVEVQC/index.html
67. Su, S., et al.: Blindly assess image quality in the wild guided by a self-adaptive hyper network. In: Proceedings of the IEEE/CVF Conference on Computer Vision and Pattern Recognition, pp. 3667–3676 (2020)
68. Søgaard, J., Forchhammer, S., Korhonen, J.: No-reference video quality assessment using codec analysis. Trans. Circuits Syst. Video Technol. **25**(10), 1637–1650 (2015)
69. Talebi, H., Milanfar, P.: NIMA: neural image assessment. IEEE Trans. Image Process. **27**(8), 3998–4011 (2018). Aug

70. YouTube Geofind: Search YouTube for geographically tagged videos by location, topic, or channel. https://mattw.io/youtube-geofind/location
71. Tran, D., Wang, H., Torresani, L., Ray, J., LeCun, Y., Paluri, M.: A closer look at spatiotemporal convolutions for action recognition. In: Proceedings of the IEEE Conference on Computer Vision and Pattern Recognition, pp. 6450–6459 (2018)
72. Tu, Z., Wang, Y., Birkbeck, N., Adsumilli, B., Bovik, A.C.: UGC-VQA: benchmarking blind video quality assessment for user generated content (2020)
73. Tu, Z., Yu, X., Wang, Y., Birkbeck, N., Adsumilli, B., Bovik, A.C.: RAPIQUE: rapid and accurate video quality prediction of user generated content. arXiv preprint arXiv:2101.10955 (2021)
74. Urban, J.: Understanding video compression artifacts, September 2017. https://blog.biamp.com/understanding-video-compression-artifacts/
75. Valenzise, G., Magni, S., Tagliasacchis, M., Tubaro, S.: No-reference pixel video quality monitoring of channel-induced distortion. IEEE Trans. Circuits Syst. Video Technol. **22**(4), 605–618 (2011)
76. Vega, M.T., Mocanu, D.C., Stavro, S., Liotta, A.: Predictive no-reference assessment of video quality. Sig. Process. Image Commun. **52**, 20–32 (2017)
77. (VQEG): VQEG HDTV phase I database. https://www.its.bldrdoc.gov/vqeg/projects/hdtv/hdtv.aspx
78. Vu, P.V., Chandler, D.M.: VIS3: an algorithm for video quality assessment via analysis of spatial and spatiotemporal slices. J. Electron. Imag. **23**(1), 013016 (2014). Feb
79. Wang, H., et al.: MCL-JCV: a JND-based H.264/AVC video quality assessment dataset. In: 2016 IEEE International Conference on Image Processing (ICIP), pp. 1509–1513 (2016). https://doi.org/10.1109/ICIP.2016.7532610
80. Wang, H., et al.: VideoSet: a large-scale compressed video quality dataset based on JND measurement (2017)
81. Wang, Y., Inguva, S., Adsumilli, B.: YouTube UGC dataset for video compression research (2019). https://doi.org/10.1109/MMSP.2019.8901772
82. Warzybok, A., et al.: Subjective speech quality and speech intelligibility evaluation of single-channel dereverberation algorithms. In: 2014 14th International Workshop on Acoustic Signal Enhancement (IWAENC), pp. 332–336. IEEE (2014)
83. Winkler, S., Faller, C.: Perceived audiovisual quality of low-bitrate multimedia content. IEEE Trans. Multimedia **8**(5), 973–980 (2006)
84. Xu, J.: Optimizing perceptual quality for online multimedia systems with fast-paced interactions. The Chinese University of Hong Kong, Hong Kong (2017)
85. Xu, J., Wah, B.W.: Optimizing the perceptual quality of real-time multimedia applications. IEEE Multimedia **22**(4), 14–28 (2015)
86. Ying, Z., Mandal, M., Ghadiyaram, D., Bovik, A.C.: Patch-VQ: 'patching up' the video quality problem. In: Proceedings of the IEEE/CVF Conference on Computer Vision and Pattern Recognition, pp. 14019–14029 (2021)
87. Ying, Z., Niu, H., Gupta, P., Mahajan, D., Ghadiyaram, D., Bovik, A.C.: From patches to pictures (PaQ-2-PiQ): mapping the perceptual space of picture quality. In: 2020 IEEE/CVF Conference on Computer Vision and Pattern Recognition (CVPR), pp. 3572–3582 (2020). https://doi.org/10.1109/CVPR42600.2020.00363
88. You, J., Reiter, U., Hannuksela, M.M., Gabbouj, M., Perkis, A.: Perceptual-based quality assessment for audio-visual services: a survey. Sig. Process. Image Commun. **25**(7), 482–501 (2010)
89. Yu, H., et al.: Yamnet (2021). https://github.com/tensorflow/models/tree/master/research/audioset/yamnet

90. Zhang, W., Ma, K., Yan, J., Deng, D., Wang, Z.: Blind image quality assessment using a deep bilinear convolutional neural network. IEEE Trans. Circuits Syst. Video Technol. **30**(1), 36–47 (2018)

91. Zhang, Y., Gao, X., He, L., Lu, W., He, R.: Blind video quality assessment with weakly supervised learning and resampling strategy. IEEE Trans. Circuits Syst. Video Technol. **29**(8), 2244–2255 (2019). https://doi.org/10.1109/TCSVT.2018. 2868063

92. Zheng, X., Zhang, C.: Towards blind audio quality assessment using a convolutional-recurrent neural network. In: 2021 13th International Conference on Quality of Multimedia Experience (QoMEX), pp. 91–96. IEEE (2021)

MultiMAE: Multi-modal Multi-task Masked Autoencoders

Roman Bachmann[✉][iD], David Mizrahi[iD], Andrei Atanov[iD], and Amir Zamir[iD]

Swiss Federal Institute of Technology Lausanne (EPFL), Lausanne, Switzerland
{roman.bachmann,david.mizrahi,andrei.atanov,amir.zamir}@epfl.ch
https://multimae.epfl.ch/

Abstract. We propose a pre-training strategy called Multi-modal Multi-task Masked Autoencoders (MultiMAE). It differs from standard Masked Autoencoding in two key aspects: **I)** it can **optionally** accept additional modalities of information in the input besides the RGB image (hence "multi-modal"), and **II)** its training objective accordingly includes predicting multiple outputs besides the RGB image (hence "multi-task"). We make use of masking (across image patches and input modalities) to make training MultiMAE **tractable** as well as to ensure **cross-modality predictive coding** is indeed learned by the network. We show this pre-training strategy leads to a flexible, simple, and efficient framework with improved transfer results to downstream tasks. In particular, the same exact pre-trained network can be flexibly used when additional information besides RGB images is available or when no information other than RGB is available - in all configurations yielding competitive to or significantly better results than the baselines. To avoid needing training datasets with multiple modalities and tasks, we train MultiMAE **entirely using pseudo labeling**, which makes the framework widely applicable to any RGB dataset.

The experiments are performed on multiple transfer tasks (image classification, semantic segmentation, depth estimation) and datasets (ImageNet, ADE20K, Taskonomy, Hypersim, NYUv2). The results show an intriguingly impressive capability by the model in cross-modal/task predictive coding and transfer. Code, pre-trained models, and interactive visualizations are available at https://multimae.epfl.ch.

Keywords: Masked autoencoders · Multi-modal learning · Multi-task learning · Transfer learning · Vision transformers

1 Introduction

Masked Autoencoders (MAEs) [28] have recently been demonstrated to be a powerful, yet conceptually simple and efficient, self-supervised pre-training strat-

R. Bachmann and D. Mizrahi—Equal contribution.

Supplementary Information The online version contains supplementary material available at https://doi.org/10.1007/978-3-031-19836-6_20.

egy for Vision Transformers [22] (ViTs). Their training objective is to mask-out a high number of patches in an input image and to predict the missing regions. To that end, only the small number of non-masked patches are first processed using a Transformer encoder [68], and then decoded with a light-weight Transformer that reconstructs the original image. To solve this task sufficiently well, it is assumed [28] that the network needs to learn representations that capture more than just low-level image statistics.

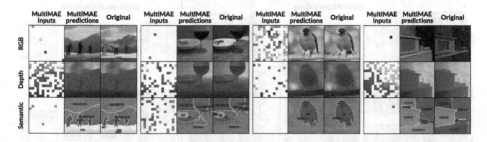

Fig. 1. MultiMAE pre-training objective. We randomly select 1/6 of all 16×16 image patches from multiple modalities and learn to reconstruct the remaining 5/6 masked patches from them. The figure shows validation examples from ImageNet, where masked inputs (left), predictions (middle), and non-masked images (right) for RGB (top), depth (middle), and semantic segmentation (bottom) are provided. Since we do not compute a loss on non-masked patches, we overlay the input patches on the predictions. More examples are shown in the supplementary and on our website. (Color figure online)

So far, however, the MAE pre-training objective has been limited to a single modality, namely RGB images, and does not make use of any other modalities that are optionally present. In practice, often more than only a single modality of information is available, either through sensing (e.g., a depth sensor) or pseudo labeling (e.g., a powerful pre-trained depth estimation network). Multi-modality is also argued to be employed by biological organisms to develop resilience and better representations [17,18,58]. As we demonstrate in our experiments, making use of such optionally present modalities has the potential to greatly improve the performance of downstream tasks, compared to using only RGB images.

Besides multi-modality (i.e., different inputs), multi-taskness (i.e., different outputs) is an important aspect, as it has been shown that there is usually no single pre-training objective that transfers best to all possible downstream tasks [43,54,79]. Instead, pre-training with a diverse set of tasks [8,66] has been observed to improve the performance on downstream tasks [26,63] and potentially learn a better representation. In general, modifying the training objectives is a powerful way to steer what representation the model will learn.

In this paper, we present Multi-modal Multi-task Masked Autoencoders (MultiMAE), a simple and effective method to make masked autoencoding include multiple modalities and tasks (see Fig. 2). In particular, in our current instantiation of this general method, we study adding dense scene depth to capture geometric information, as well as segmentation maps to include information about the semantic content of the scene. We created a multi-task dataset by pseudo labeling these tasks on ImageNet-1K [19,26]. This has the advantage that in order to train a MultiMAE, one only requires a large unstructured RGB dataset without annotations and off-the-shelf neural networks to perform the pseudo labeling.

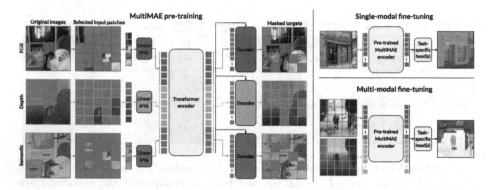

Fig. 2. (Left) MultiMAE pre-training: A small subset of randomly sampled patches from multiple modalities (e.g., RGB, depth, and semantic segmentation) is linearly projected to tokens with a fixed dimension and encoded using a Transformer. Task-specific decoders reconstruct the masked-out patches by first performing a cross-attention step from queries to the encoded tokens, followed by a shallow Transformer. The queries consist of mask tokens (in gray), with the task-specific encoded tokens added at their respective positions. **(Right) Fine-tuning**: By pre-training on multiple modalities, MultiMAE lends itself to fine-tuning on single-modal and multi-modal downstream tasks. No masking is performed at transfer time. (Color figure online)

To train MultiMAE, we randomly sample a small set of patches from different input modalities, and encode them using a Transformer encoder. MultiMAE's objective is then to reconstruct the masked-out patches of all tasks using task-specific decoders. Figure 1 shows example predictions for the multi-task masked reconstruction that MultiMAE performs. MultiMAE has to learn not only the original MAE objective (within-RGB in-painting), but also to reconstruct any task from any input modality (cross-modal prediction) all from a very sparse set of input patches. The first objective leads to learning *spatial predictive coding* while the second one leads to *cross-modal predictive coding*.

2   Related Work

Masked image prediction consists of learning useful representations by learning to reconstruct images corrupted by masking. This approach was pioneered with denoising autoencoders [69] and context encoders [48]. With the introduction of Vision Transformers (ViT) [22] and motivated by the success of BERT [20] in NLP, many recent works propose a variety of masked image prediction methods for pre-training vision models in a self-supervised way, using reconstruction targets such as pixels [5,13,22,25,28,74], discrete tokens [7,81], and (deep) features [6,70]. These methods scale very well and achieve strong results on various downstream tasks including motor control [72]. In particular, the masked autoencoder (MAE) [28] approach accelerates pre-training by using an asymmetric architecture consisting of a large encoder that operates *only* on unmasked patches followed by a lightweight decoder that reconstructs the masked patches from the latent representation and mask tokens. Our approach leverages the efficiency of the MAE approach and extends it to multi-modal and multi-task settings.

Multi-modal learning involves building models capable of relating information from multiple sources. It can either involve training separate encoders or one unified architecture (e.g., a Transformer [68]) to operate on modalities such as images and text [3,11,15,29,31–34,41,42,59,62,75], video and audio [4,30,44,46], video, text and audio [2], and depth, images and video [27]. Our work proposes a simple approach to pre-train Transformers on multiple dense visual modalities and produce strong cross-modal interaction. Unlike most prior work which assumes that all modalities are available during inference, our approach is designed to perform well on any subset of the pre-training modalities.

Related to MultiMAE are several works that perform multi-modal autoencoding [45,56,60,61,71]. Our approach differs from them in that we use a more flexible architecture and perform masked autoencoding to learn cross-modal predictive coding among optional inputs (as demonstrated in Fig. 1).

Multi-task learning consists of training models to predict multiple output domains from a single input [10,24,35]. In computer vision, the input is usually an RGB image. A common approach for multi-task learning is to use a single encoder to learn a shared representation followed by multiple task-specific decoders [26,67]. These methods differ from our approach as we use multiple tasks in both the input and the output along with masking.

In addition, many works study the importance of task diversity to improve transfer performance [26,43,54,65,79]. These works argue that learning from one task alone is insufficient and that a set of tasks can more effectively cover the many possible downstream tasks in vision. Our pre-training method operates on multiple tasks to learn more general representations capable of covering multiple downstream tasks.

Self-training is a technique to incorporate unlabeled data into a supervised learning setting [36,53,55,77]. It is one of the earliest approaches to semi-supervised learning. Self-training methods use a supervised model to generate pseudo labels on unlabeled data and then train a student model on the pseudo labeled data. These approaches have been applied to a variety of vision tasks such as image classification [49,73,76], object detection [82], and segmentation [12,82]. Most recently, multi-task self-training (MuST) [26] uses specialized teachers to create a multi-task pseudo labeled dataset and then trains a multi-task student model on this dataset to learn general feature representations. Our method also relies on pseudo labeling to produce a large-scale multi-task dataset. However, unlike prior work, pseudo labels are not only used as output targets but also as *masked* input modalities.

3 Method Description

In this Section, we describe the Multi-modal Multi-task Masked Autoencoder (MultiMAE) architecture (illustrated in Fig. 2), as well as the pre-training strategy in more detail. We first give an architectural overview of both the multi-modal encoder (Sect. 3.1) and multi-task decoders (Sect. 3.2). We then describe our multi-modal token sampling strategy (Sect. 3.3) and introduce the pseudo labeled tasks we use for pre-training (Sect. 3.4). Finally, we display the most important pre-training details (Sect. 3.5).

3.1 Multi-modal Encoder

Our multi-modal Transformer encoder is a ViT [22], but with patch projection layers for each additional input modality. Specifically, 16×16 patches of each modality are projected to tokens with the correct Transformer dimension using a different linear projection for each modality. Projected patches are concatenated into a sequence of tokens and given as input to the same Transformer encoder. We also add an additional *global* token with a learned embedding, similar to the class-token used in ViT. Due to the architectural similarities to ViT, MultiMAE pre-trained weights can directly be used in a standard single-modal ViT by loading only the desired input projection and ignoring the others.

Positional, Modality and Class Embeddings. Since all our modalities have a 2D structure, we add 2D sine-cosine positional embeddings [14,28] after the linear projection. We do not explicitly add any modality-specific embeddings, since the bias term in each linear projection can act as such. In order to perform the semantic segmentation patch projection, we first replace each class index with learned 64-dimensional class embeddings.

Low Computational Complexity. Just as in the RGB-only MAE [28], we only pass the small randomly sampled subset of all tokens to the Transformer encoder as part of the masked autoencoding objective. This is in contrast to the masked autoencoding approaches of SiT [1], BeiT [7] and SimMIM [74], that encode both the masked and visible tokens. Due to the quadratic complexity of standard self-attention as a function of the number of tokens, encoding only the random subset of visible tokens becomes increasingly important as the number of input modalities grows. Indeed, the speedup and reduction in memory are significant and crucial in enabling MultiMAE's multi-modal pre-training with three dense input modalities. A comparison of the pre-training time with and without masked tokens is given in the supplementary.

3.2 Decoders

To reconstruct the masked-out tokens from the visible tokens, we use a separate decoder for each task. The input to each decoder is the full set of visible tokens from the respective task it is reconstructing. As in MAE [28], these visible tokens are decoded jointly with a set of mask tokens, which serve as *placeholders* for the decoders to write the reconstructed patches (as shown in Fig. 2). To integrate information from the encoded tokens of other modalities, we add a single cross-attention layer in each decoder using these tokens as queries and all the encoded tokens as keys/values. Sine-cosine positional embeddings and learned modality embeddings are added to the tokens before this step. This is then followed by a small MLP and Transformer blocks. Following MAE, we compute the losses only on the masked tokens.

As each task requires its own decoder, the computational cost of decoders scales linearly with the number of tasks. To keep pre-training efficient, we use shallow decoders (a single cross-attention layer and MLP, followed by two Transformer blocks) with a low dimensionality (256 dimensional). Compared to the encoder, these decoders add little to the overall computational cost, and as He et al. [28] show, they perform similarly to deeper decoders on ImageNet-1K fine-tuning.

3.3 Multi-modal Masking Strategies

For masked autoencoding to work well, a large percentage of tokens needs to be masked-out. He et al. [28] showed that the choice of mask sampling strategy can have a large impact on transfer performance. More specifically for MultiMAE and generally learning multi-task representations, masking across different modalities ensures the model develops predictive coding across different modalities besides different spatial patches. For efficiency and simplicity, we choose a constant number of visible tokens for all our experiments, which we fix at 98. This corresponds to 1/6 of all tokens when using three modalities of dimensions 224×224 pixels and a patch size of 16×16. Adapting the MAE mask sampling strategy by selecting the visible tokens uniformly from all tokens would result in most modalities being represented to similar degrees. Cases where one or more modalities have very few or no samples would be very rare. We propose a multi-modal token sampling strategy that allows for a more diverse sampling approach. It can be broken down into two steps: First, selecting the number of tokens per modality, and second, randomly sampling the set of tokens for each modality.

Number of Tokens per Modality. We select the proportion of tokens per modality λ by sampling from a symmetric Dirichlet distribution $(\lambda_{\mathrm{RGB}}, \lambda_{\mathrm{D}}, \lambda_{\mathrm{S}}) \sim \mathrm{Dir}(\alpha)$, where $\lambda_{\mathrm{RGB}} + \lambda_{\mathrm{D}} + \lambda_{\mathrm{S}} = 1, \lambda \geq 0$. The sampling is controlled by the concentration parameter $\alpha > 0$. When $\alpha = 1$, the symmetric Dirichlet distribution is equivalent to a uniform distribution over the simplex (i.e., it is uniform over all points in its support). Smaller values ($\alpha << 1$) result in a sampling behavior where most of the tokens will be sampled from a single modality, while larger values ($\alpha \gg 1$) result in an increasingly similar number of tokens to be sampled from each modality. As a design decision, we do not bias the sampling towards certain modalities (as we use a symmetric Dirichlet), since we want to be agnostic to the choice of downstream input modalities and tasks that users might want to consider. For simplicity and better representation of any possible sampled mask, we use a concentration parameter $\alpha = 1$ for all of our experiments. Random masks sampled using $\alpha = 1$ are shown in Fig. 1, and an ablation on the choice of concentration parameter is given in the supplementary.

Sampling Tokens. From each modality, we sample the number of tokens, as specified by the above Dirichlet sampling step, uniformly at random without replacement. Uniform sampling has been shown to work well for masked autoencoders, compared to less random alternatives [28].

3.4   Pseudo Labeled Multi-task Training Dataset

We pre-train MultiMAE with three tasks that we pseudo label on ImageNet-1K [19]. Pseudo labeling has the advantage that we do not need a large multi-task dataset with aligned task images. Instead, having access to a good set of pre-trained neural networks for the tasks we want to train on can be effective. Pseudo labeling scales to RGB datasets of arbitrary size and is a one-time pre-processing step. Compared to the cost of training, this step is computationally cheap and fast if parallelized.

Taskonomy [79] demonstrated computationally that common vision tasks cluster into three main categories, namely low-level, geometric, and semantic tasks. To have a coverage over such a space of vision tasks, we choose one representative task from each of these three clusters. We note that except for object detection and classification, these are the same pseudo labeled tasks that are used in MuST [26]. In the following, we will describe them in more detail.

RGB and Per-Patch Standardized RGB. We use RGB images due to their abundance and since RGB-only masked autoencoding is shown to be a powerful pre-training task. He et al. [28] study both predicting standard RGB patches, as well as per-patch standardized RGB patches. They find that predicting standardized patches slightly improves transfer performance. Since MultiMAE is naturally a multi-task model, we add both versions as separate decoder heads to get the representational benefits of predicting standardized patches, and to get a version that we can visualize better. Note that we only add the per-patch standardized version as an output task, and not as an input modality. For both RGB versions, we follow MAE and compute the MSE loss between the ground truth and predicted pixels. In the rest of the paper, we will refer to the RGB and per-patch standardized RGB output tasks simply as RGB.

Scene Depth. Depth is a key task informative about scene geometry. As with RGB, but unlike semantic segmentation, sensors exist to capture this modality, making it possible to use depth as an optional extra input for downstream tasks. To pseudo label depth, we use a DPT-Hybrid [50] that was trained on Omnidata [23]. Since monocular depth estimation is an inherently ill-posed task due to scale and shift ambiguity, we standardize the depth values in a robust way by ignoring the top and bottom 10% of values [78]. In addition, using standardized depth values as inputs allows us to use other depth images that might have different depth ranges and scales, without needing to match them to the Omnidata depth parameterization. We use the L1 loss for depth.

Semantic Segmentation. Lastly, we use a Mask2Former [16] with a Swin-S [38] backbone trained on COCO [37] to pseudo label semantic segmentation maps on ImageNet. For that, we extract 133 semantic classes by taking the argmax of the network predictions. Unlike RGB and depth, the main purpose of this task is to improve performance on downstream tasks, rather than using it as an input modality (though we show results using pseudo labeled semantic inputs in Table 3). Since we use a network that was pre-trained on COCO, we do not evaluate semantic segmentation transfers on that dataset. For this task, we use the cross-entropy loss.

3.5   Pre-training Details

All our MultiMAE experiments use a *ViT-B* [22] with a patch size of 16×16 pixels. We pre-train the models for either 400 epochs (only for transfer ablation study in Sect. 4.4) or 1600 epochs (for best results and to be comparable to the MAE baseline) on 1.28M ImageNet images. We use the AdamW [40] optimizer with base learning rate 1e-4 and weight decay 0.05. We warm up training for 40 epochs, starting from learning rate 1e-6, and decay it to 0 over the course of training using cosine decay [39]. We set the batch size to a total of 2048 and train the models using 8 A100 GPUs with automatic mixed precision enabled. Our data augmentations are straightforward. We randomly crop the images, setting the random scale between 0.2 and 1.0 and the random aspect ratio between 0.75 and 1.33, after which we resize the crops to 224×224 pixels and apply a random horizontal flip with probability 0.5. Additional pre-training details can be found in the supplementary.

4   Experiments

Optimizing the pre-training objective of MultiMAE is successful as apparent in the various results shown in the main paper, the supplementary, and the interactive visualizations shown on our website. In this section we provide a transfer study to measure the effectiveness of MultiMAE pre-training compared to relevant baselines. This section is organized in the following manner: After introducing the downstream tasks and datasets (Sect. 4.1), we show transfer results for the case where the only available input modality is RGB (Sect. 4.2). Then, we show that MultiMAE can significantly improve downstream performance if other modalities like depth are either available as ground truth (sensor), or can be cheaply pseudo labeled (Sect. 4.3). We follow up with an ablation on the influence of pre-training tasks on the downstream performance (Sect. 4.4), and finally we visually demonstrate that MultiMAE integrates and exchanges information across modalities (Sect. 4.5).

4.1   Transfer Tasks and Datasets

We perform downstream transfers on a variety of semantic and dense regression tasks. For all transfers, we replace the pre-trained decoders by randomly initialized task-specific heads, and train them along with the pre-trained encoder. In the following, we give an overview over all tasks and datasets used in our transfer experiments. Exact training details are presented in the supplementary.

Classification. We evaluate our models and baselines by fine-tuning them on the supervised ImageNet-1K [19] 1000-way object classification task. We fine-tune our models for 100 epochs on the entire ImageNet-1K train split (1.28M images) and report the top-1 validation accuracy.

Semantic Segmentation. We further evaluate our models on semantic segmentation tasks on the ADE20K [80] (20'210 training images and 150 classes), NYUv2 [57] (795 training images and 40 classes), and Hypersim [52] (51'674 training images and 40 classes) datasets. NYUv2 and Hypersim contain ground-truth depth maps that allow us to evaluate semantic segmentation with RGB and depth as input modalities. For all datasets, we report the mean intersection over union (mIoU) metric. On ADE20K and Hypersim, we report it on the validation split, while on NYUv2, we show the test set mIoU.

Dense Regression Tasks. Finally, we study how our models transfer to geometric tasks, such as surface normals, depth and reshading, as well as tasks extracted from RGB images, such as keypoint or edge detection. For depth estimation, we use NYUv2 (795 training and 655 test images), while for all other tasks we train transfers on a subset of the Taskonomy dataset [79] (800 training images). As performance metrics, we report δ_1 on the NYUv2 test set, showing the percentage of pixels p with error $\max\{\frac{\hat{y}_p}{y_p}, \frac{y_p}{\hat{y}_p}\}$ less than 1.25 [21], while on Taskonomy we report L1 losses on the tiny-split test set.

In the tables, classification, semantic segmentation, and depth estimation are denoted by (C), (S), and (D), respectively.

4.2   Transfers with RGB-Only

In this section, we show our transfer results when fine-tuning using only the RGB modality as input.

Baselines. For this setting, we compare MultiMAE with various *ViT-B* models, namely *DeiT* [64] (without distillation) representing an ImageNet-supervised baseline, *MoCo-v3* [14], *DINO* [9], and *MAE* [28]. All these models are pre-trained on ImageNet-1K. We use the official weights for DeiT, MoCo-v3, and DINO, and reproduce MAE using the official PyTorch [47] codebase following the setting specified in [28] (i.e., decoder of depth 8 and width 512, per-patch standardized pixel loss, 1600 pre-training epochs, 75% mask ratio). In the supplementary, we compare the transfer performance of this MAE model to one with a shallower and narrower decoder (depth 2 and width 256), closer to the one used for MultiMAE.

We report the results in Table 1. We find that MultiMAE performs best on all tasks, matching MAE's performance on ImageNet-1K classification and ADE20K semantic segmentation, and outperforming it on all other tasks and datasets. These results show the effectiveness of MultiMAE as a pre-training strategy: it retains the benefits of MAE when RGB is the only fine-tuning modality but can also accept other modalities, as shown next.

Table 1. Fine-tuning with RGB-only. We report the top-1 accuracy ($\uparrow$) on ImageNet-1K (IN-1K) [19] classification (C), mIoU ($\uparrow$) on ADE20K [80] , Hypersim [52] , and NYUv2 [57] semantic segmentation (S), as well as δ_1 accuracy ($\uparrow$) on NYUv2 depth (D). Text in **bold** and <u>underline</u> indicates the first and second-best results, respectively. All methods are pre-trained on ImageNet-1K (with pseudo labels for MultiMAE)

Method	IN-1K (C)	ADE20K (S)	Hypersim (S)	NYUv2 (S)	NYUv2 (D)
Supervised [64]	81.8	45.8	33.9	50.1	80.7
DINO [9]	83.1	44.6	32.5	47.9	81.3
MoCo-v3 [14]	82.8	43.7	31.7	46.6	80.9
MAE [28]	**83.3**	**46.2**	<u>36.5</u>	<u>50.8</u>	<u>85.1</u>
MultiMAE	**83.3**	**46.2**	**37.0**	**52.0**	**86.4**

4.3 Transfers with Multiple Modalities

Since MultiMAE was pre-trained on RGB, depth, and semantic segmentation, it can optionally accept any of those modalities as input during transfer learning should they be available. In this set of experiments, we study on three semantic segmentation downstream tasks how much MultiMAE can benefit from using additional modalities during transfer. Often, ground truth depth maps are not available for a given downstream dataset and for that reason, we perform additional transfers using pseudo labeled depth. As there are several datasets that do in fact contain aligned RGB and depth images (e.g., Hypersim, NYUv2, Taskonomy, etc.) and since sensors exist that can measure depth, we consider it as a

Table 2. Fine-tuning with RGB and ground truth depth. We report semantic segmentation transfer results from combinations of RGB and depth, measured in mIoU (↑). MultiMAE can effectively leverage additional modalities such as depth, while MAE cannot. Text in gray indicates a modality that the model was not pre-trained on

Method	Hypersim (S)			NYUv2 (S)		
	RGB	D	RGB-D	RGB	D	RGB-D
MAE	36.5	32.5	36.9	50.8	23.4	49.3
MultiMAE	**37.0**	**38.5**	**47.6**	**52.0**	**41.4**	**56.0**

Table 3. Fine-tuning with RGB and pseudo labels. Semantic segmentation transfer results using *pseudo labeled* depth and semantic segmentation maps, measured in mIoU (↑). MultiMAE benefits much more than MAE from pseudo labeled modalities as input. Text in gray indicates a modality that the model was not pre-trained on

Method	ADE20K (S)					Hypersim (S)					NYUv2 (S)				
	RGB	pD	RGB-pD	RGB-pS	RGB-pD-pS	RGB	pD	RGB-pD	RGB-pS	RGB-pD-pS	RGB	pD	RGB-pD	RGB-pS	RGB-pD-pS
MAE	**46.2**	20.0	46.3	46.2	46.3	36.5	21.0	36.9	37.7	37.3	50.8	23.8	49.1	50.1	49.3
MultiMAE	**46.2**	34.4	46.8	45.7	47.1	37.0	30.6	37.9	38.4	40.1	52.0	39.9	53.6	53.5	54.0

more realistic input modality compared to semantic segmentation. Since our model was trained with semantic segmentation as an input modality, we perform additional experiments using pseudo labeled semantic segmentation maps as inputs.

All multi-modal transfers are performed by concatenating the projected patches of all modalities into a single sequence (i.e., no masking is performed here). Using more than two modalities during transfer quickly becomes computationally expensive, since without masking, our method now scales with the full number of modalities and tokens. For performing multi-modal transfers with the standard MAE, we train a new input projection for the additional modalities while fine-tuning. Further training details can be found in the supplementary.

Transfers Using Sensory Depth. First, we consider that we have access to an aligned RGB-D dataset, like NYUv2 or Hypersim. We treat depth in the exact same way as during pre-training, i.e., pre-process it by standardizing it in a robust manner [78]. Because ground-truth depth maps might contain invalid measurements, we further set all these masked-out values to 0.

Table 2 shows RGB-D transfer results on Hypersim and NYUv2. Compared to the RGB-only results in Table 1, we see a substantial increase in performance when ground truth depth is available for MultiMAE. The standard MAE on the other hand is not able to sufficiently make use of the additional depth, since it was only trained on RGB images. We observe a similar story when evaluating transfers from depth-only, in that MultiMAE works well, even when no RGB information is available, while MAE does not. On Hypersim, MultiMAE depth-only transfer is even able to surpass MultiMAE RGB-only transfer, and, as expected, RGB-D works better than either RGB or depth alone.

Transfers with Pseudo Labels. In case ground truth modalities are not available, we can pseudo label them in the same way we did for pre-training. To pseudo label depth, we use the same Omnidata DPT-Hybrid model that we used for pre-training on both ADE20K and NYUv2. On Hypersim, we use a MiDaS [51] DPT-Hybrid, since the Omnidata depth model was partially trained on this dataset. For semantic segmentation pseudo labels, we use the same COCO Mask2Former model as in pre-training.

As shown in Table 3, MultiMAE can use pseudo labeled depth or semantic segmentation to boost performance beyond the RGB-only setting, although the gain is smaller than using real depth. Moreover, performance can further be improved by adding both of these pseudo labeled modalities to the input. This setting performs the best out of all settings involving pseudo labels.

Table 4. Ablation experiments. We study the impact of additional modalities in Table 4a, and compare MultiMAE to non-masked pre-training in Table 4b. All models are pre-trained for 400 epochs. We report the top-1 accuracy ($\uparrow$) on ImageNet-1K (IN-1K) [19] classification (C), mIoU ($\uparrow$) on NYUv2 [57] semantic segmentation (S), δ_1 accuracy ($\uparrow$) on NYUv2 depth (D) and avg. rank ($\downarrow$) on Taskonomy [79]. While some specialized pre-trained models perform better at certain downstream tasks, they perform poorly at others. MultiMAE pre-trained with RGB, depth and semantic segmentation is a more generalist model that does well at transferring to a range of downstream tasks

(a) Impact of additional modalities.
Transfer results of several MultiMAE models pre-trained on different input modalities/target tasks, compared against MAE (single-modal baseline). D2 = MAE pre-trained with a decoder of depth 2 and width 256, comparable in size to the decoders of MultiMAE

Method	IN-1K (C)	NYUv2 (S)	NYUv2 (D)	Taskonomy (D)
MAE (D2)	83.0	44.0	81.3	3.8
RGB-D	82.8	45.8	83.3	2.1
RGB-S	83.2	51.6	85.5	2.6
RGB-D-S	83.0	50.6	85.4	1.5

(b) Comparison to non-masked pre-training.
We compare standard single-task and multi-task baselines pre-trained using *non-masked* RGB inputs against the RGB-D-S MultiMAE. The RGB → D-S model is conceptually similar to MuST using depth and semantic segmentation as target tasks

Method	IN-1K (C)	NYUv2 (S)	NYUv2 (D)	Taskonomy (D)
RGB→D	82.7	44.0	87.1	1.6
RGB→S	82.5	46.8	82.9	4.0
RGB→D-S	82.8	48.6	84.6	2.9
MultiMAE	83.0	50.6	85.4	1.5

4.4 Influence of Pre-training Task Choices and Masking on Transfer Performance

How does the choice of MultiMAE pre-training tasks affect downstream transfer performance? In this subsection, we aim to address this question by performing transfers from MultiMAE models that were pre-trained with RGB-D, RGB-S, or RGB-D-S. We further compare MultiMAE against MAE, single-task, and multi-task baselines.

All experiments are performed on ViT-B models that were pre-trained for 400 epochs. We transfer the pre-trained models to ImageNet, NYUv2 segmentation, as well as nine dense regression tasks on Taskonomy. On Taskonomy, we report

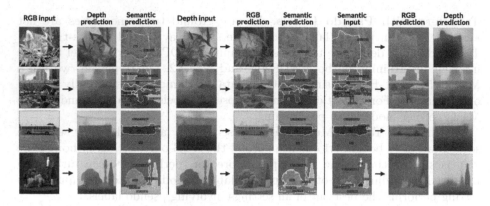

Fig. 3. Single-modal predictions. We visualize MultiMAE cross-modal predictions on ImageNet-1K validation images. Only a single, full modality is used as input. The predictions remain plausible despite the absence of input patches from other modalities.

the ranking of different pre-trained models, averaged over all nine tasks. Detailed per-task results on Taskonomy can be found in the supplementary.

Masked Multi-modal Pre-training. This experiment studies the influence that the choice of pre-training modalities has, when the input and output modalities are the same in MultiMAE pre-training. The transfer results are displayed in Table 4a. The RGB-S model performs best on ImageNet classification and NYUv2 semantic segmentation, whereas the RGB-D-S model has the best average rank on Taskonomy. The slight increase in performance of RGB-S on ImageNet and semantic segmentation compared to RGB-D-S comes at the cost of reduced flexibility, as models that were not pre-trained on depth can not as easily and effectively use it to boost performance (see Sect. 4.3).

Comparison to Non-masked Pre-training. We further compare MultiMAE against standard single-task and multi-task baselines, that were pre-trained with RGB as the only input modality and without applying any masking. Since we train on pseudo labels, the RGB→D-S multi-task model is conceptually similar to a MuST [26] model using depth and semantic segmentation targets. The transfer results are detailed in Table 4b. On nearly all categories, MultiMAE outperforms the supervised baselines.

To summarize, the results in this section show that using all modalities to pre-train a MultiMAE results in a more generalist model that does well at transferring to a range of downstream tasks. We find that there are some *specialized* pre-trained models that perform better at certain downstream tasks (e.g., models pre-trained with depth perform better at transferring to geometric tasks), but they will perform poorly at others. This is supported by previous findings [43,54,79] showing that there is usually no single visual pre-training task that transfers well to any arbitrary other task, and instead, a set is required.

4.5   Cross-Modal Exchange of Information

In this section, we explore visually how MultiMAE predicts the three pre-training tasks by changing the inputs it receives. Figure 1 already showcased how MultiMAE is able to reconstruct images from various randomly sampled input patches. Here, we will further show non-masked cross-modal predictions, and will also give examples on how MultiMAE predictions change when we change certain details about the inputs.

Single-Modal Predictions. Figure 3 displays several examples of cross-modal prediction without any masking. We show examples where, from one single modality, the two remaining ones are predicted. We note here that even though the number of patches we input to the model is 2× higher than what was seen during training, the model still predicts very reasonable results despite the distribution shift.

Demonstration of Cross-Modal Interaction. We demonstrate in Fig. 4 how MultiMAE predicts completely different but plausible RGB images when given a full depth image and three edited versions of the same two RGB input patches (no semantic segmentation maps are given as inputs). We keep one RGB patch the same, while changing the hue of another patch (part of a lizard for the first image). We can see how MultiMAE recovers all the details in the image from the full depth input, but paints the entire lizard in the colors given in the modified patch. All the while, the background does not change. This suggests an intriguingly good representation is learned by the model as it extends the colors to the right segments without any segmentation provided in the input. More interactive examples can be seen on our website.

5   Discussion

We presented Multi-modal Multi-task Masked Autoencoders (MultiMAE), an effective and simple pre-training strategy for Vision Transformers. MultiMAE encodes a small random subset of visible tokens from multiple modalities and is trained to reconstruct the missing ones. By encoding only a fixed number of non-masked tokens, we can keep the bulk of the computation in the Transformer encoder constant, while only the shallow task-specific decoders scale with the number of tasks. Masking (across image patches and input modalities) ensures the network learns to perform predictive coding across different modalities, besides across different spatial patches. The experiments showed intriguing

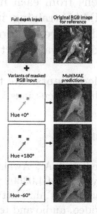

Fig. 4. Cross-modal interaction. By editing the hue of a single input token, the entire lizard's color can be changed, while keeping the background constant.

capabilities of MultiMAE at cross-modal coding and demonstrated this pre-training strategy can result in notable gains in transfer performance when additional input modalities are optionally available, either as ground truth or pseudo labels.

In the following, we briefly discuss some limitations to our approach and present exciting future directions:

Scaling Pre-training Modalities. We pre-trained MultiMAE on a set of three visual modalities, chosen to cover a large fraction of common vision problems based on prior studies [79]. It is, however, conceivable that our method can benefit from a rather straightforward inclusion of a more diverse set of modalities and tasks, such as videos, text, bounding boxes, sparse depth, feature maps, and more. In addition to providing more ways to use optional modalities as inputs, scaling up the number of pre-training modalities could have further transfer benefits by covering a larger space of useful vision problems and enabling more complex cross-modal predictive coding.

Scaling Pre-training Datasets. For pragmatic reasons and enabling comparison with prior works, we trained all of our models on pseudo labeled ImageNet-1K, but there is no reason to limit ourselves to a (classification) dataset of this size. Since we use pseudo labels, any dataset that is used for RGB-only self-supervised learning can be considered for training MultiMAE. Our method further benefits from any future improvements in model architectures, training strategy and supervised datasets that can be used to improve the quality of pseudo labels.

Masking Strategies. Lastly, we used a simple approach of sampling random tokens from each modality in an unbiased way. While this worked well for MultiMAE training, it does not have to be the optimal choice for learning a transferable representation. It will be an interesting direction to explore biasing the masking towards certain modalities and/or spatial locations.

Acknowledgments. We thank Stefan Stepanovic and Alexander Sax for their help and insightful discussions.

References

1. Ahmed, S.A.A., Awais, M., Kittler, J.: Sit: Self-supervised vision transformer. ArXiv abs/2104.03602 (2021)
2. Akbari, H., et al.: Vatt: transformers for multimodal self-supervised learning from raw video, audio and text. Adv. Neural Inf. Process. Syst. **34**, 24206–24221 (2021)
3. Alayrac, J.B.: Self-supervised multimodal versatile networks. Adv. Neural Inf. Process. Syst. **33**, 25–37 (2020)
4. Arandjelovic, R., Zisserman, A.: Look, listen and learn. In: Proceedings of the IEEE International Conference on Computer Vision, pp. 609–617 (2017)

5. Atito, S., Awais, M., Kittler, J.: Sit: self-supervised vision transformer. arXiv preprint arXiv:2104.03602 (2021)
6. Baevski, A., Hsu, W.N., Xu, Q., Babu, A., Gu, J., Auli, M.: Data2vec: a general framework for self-supervised learning in speech, vision and language. arXiv preprint arXiv:2202.03555 (2022)
7. Bao, H., Dong, L., Wei, F.: Beit: Bert pre-training of image transformers. ArXiv abs/2106.08254 (2021)
8. Baxter, J.: A model of inductive bias learning. J. Artif. Intell. Res. **12**, 149–198 (2000)
9. Caron, M., et al.: Emerging properties in self-supervised vision transformers. In: 2021 IEEE/CVF International Conference on Computer Vision (ICCV), pp. 9630–9640 (2021)
10. Caruana, R.: Multitask learning. Mach. Learn. **28**(1), 41–75 (1997). https://doi.org/10.1023/A:1007379606734. Jul
11. Castrejon, L., Aytar, Y., Vondrick, C., Pirsiavash, H., Torralba, A.: Learning aligned cross-modal representations from weakly aligned data. In: Proceedings of the IEEE Conference on Computer Vision and Pattern Recognition, pp. 2940–2949 (2016)
12. Chen, L.-C., et al.: Naive-student: leveraging semi-supervised learning in video sequences for urban scene segmentation. In: Vedaldi, A., Bischof, H., Brox, T., Frahm, J.-M. (eds.) ECCV 2020. LNCS, vol. 12354, pp. 695–714. Springer, Cham (2020). https://doi.org/10.1007/978-3-030-58545-7_40
13. Chen, M., et al.: Generative pretraining from pixels. In: Proceedings of the 37th International Conference on Machine Learning, pp. 1691–1703. PMLR (2020). iSSN: 2640-3498
14. Chen, X., Xie, S., He, K.: An empirical study of training self-supervised vision transformers. In: 2021 IEEE/CVF International Conference on Computer Vision (ICCV), pp. 9620–9629 (2021)
15. Chen, Y.-C., et al.: UNITER: UNiversal image-TExt representation learning. In: Vedaldi, A., Bischof, H., Brox, T., Frahm, J.-M. (eds.) ECCV 2020. LNCS, vol. 12375, pp. 104–120. Springer, Cham (2020). https://doi.org/10.1007/978-3-030-58577-8_7
16. Cheng, B., Misra, I., Schwing, A.G., Kirillov, A., Girdhar, R.: Masked-attention mask transformer for universal image segmentation. ArXiv abs/2112.01527 (2021)
17. De Sa, V.R.: Sensory modality segregation. In: NIPS, pp. 913–920. Citeseer (2003)
18. De Sa, V.R., Ballard, D.H.: Category learning through multimodality sensing. Neural Comput. **10**(5), 1097–1117 (1998)
19. Deng, J., Dong, W., Socher, R., Li, L.J., Li, K., Fei-Fei, L.: Imagenet: a large-scale hierarchical image database. In: CVPR (2009)
20. Devlin, J., Chang, M.W., Lee, K., Toutanova, K.: Bert: pre-training of deep bidirectional transformers for language understanding. arXiv preprint arXiv:1810.04805 (2018)
21. Doersch, C., Zisserman, A.: Multi-task self-supervised visual learning. In: Proceedings of the IEEE International Conference on Computer Vision, pp. 2051–2060 (2017)
22. Dosovitskiy, A., et al.: An image is worth 16×16 words: transformers for image recognition at scale. ArXiv abs/2010.11929 (2021)
23. Eftekhar, A., Sax, A., Bachmann, R., Malik, J., Zamir, A.R.: Omnidata: a scalable pipeline for making multi-task mid-level vision datasets from 3D scans. In: 2021 IEEE/CVF International Conference on Computer Vision (ICCV), pp. 10766–10776 (2021)

24. Eigen, D., Fergus, R.: Predicting depth, surface normals and semantic labels with a common multi-scale convolutional architecture. In: Proceedings of the IEEE International Conference on Computer Vision, pp. 2650–2658 (2015)
25. El-Nouby, A., Izacard, G., Touvron, H., Laptev, I., Jegou, H., Grave, E.: Are large-scale datasets necessary for self-supervised pre-training? arXiv preprint arXiv:2112.10740 (2021)
26. Ghiasi, G., Zoph, B., Cubuk, E.D., Le, Q.V., Lin, T.Y.: Multi-task self-training for learning general representations. In: 2021 IEEE/CVF International Conference on Computer Vision (ICCV), pp. 8836–8845 (2021)
27. Girdhar, R., Singh, M., Ravi, N., van der Maaten, L., Joulin, A., Misra, I.: Omnivore: a single model for many visual modalities. arXiv preprint arXiv:2201.08377 (2022)
28. He, K., Chen, X., Xie, S., Li, Y., Doll'ar, P., Girshick, R.B.: Masked autoencoders are scalable vision learners. ArXiv abs/2111.06377 (2021)
29. Hu, R., Singh, A.: Unit: multimodal multitask learning with a unified transformer. In: Proceedings of the IEEE/CVF International Conference on Computer Vision, pp. 1439–1449 (2021)
30. Jaegle, A., et al.: Perceiver io: a general architecture for structured inputs & outputs. arXiv preprint arXiv:2107.14795 (2021)
31. Kaiser, L., et al.: One model to learn them all. arXiv preprint arXiv:1706.05137 (2017)
32. Kamath, A., Singh, M., LeCun, Y., Synnaeve, G., Misra, I., Carion, N.: Mdetr-modulated detection for end-to-end multi-modal understanding. In: Proceedings of the IEEE/CVF International Conference on Computer Vision, pp. 1780–1790 (2021)
33. Karpathy, A., Fei-Fei, L.: Deep visual-semantic alignments for generating image descriptions. In: Proceedings of the IEEE Conference on Computer Vision and Pattern Recognition, pp. 3128–3137 (2015)
34. Kim, W., Son, B., Kim, I.: Vilt: vision-and-language transformer without convolution or region supervision. In: International Conference on Machine Learning, pp. 5583–5594. PMLR (2021)
35. Kokkinos, I.: Ubernet: training a universal convolutional neural network for low-, mid-, and high-level vision using diverse datasets and limited memory. In: Proceedings of the IEEE Conference on Computer Vision and Pattern Recognition, pp. 6129–6138 (2017)
36. Lee, D.H., et al.: Pseudo-label: the simple and efficient semi-supervised learning method for deep neural networks. In: Workshop on Challenges in Representation Learning. ICML (2013)
37. Lin, T.-Y., et al.: Microsoft COCO: common objects in context. In: Fleet, D., Pajdla, T., Schiele, B., Tuytelaars, T. (eds.) ECCV 2014. LNCS, vol. 8693, pp. 740–755. Springer, Cham (2014). https://doi.org/10.1007/978-3-319-10602-1_48
38. Liu, Z., et al.: Swin transformer: hierarchical vision transformer using shifted windows. In: Proceedings of the IEEE/CVF International Conference on Computer Vision, pp. 10012–10022 (2021)
39. Loshchilov, I., Hutter, F.: Sgdr: stochastic gradient descent with warm restarts. arXiv preprint arXiv:1608.03983 (2016)
40. Loshchilov, I., Hutter, F.: Decoupled weight decay regularization. In: ICLR (2019)
41. Lu, J., Batra, D., Parikh, D., Lee, S.: Vilbert: pretraining task-agnostic visiolinguistic representations for vision-and-language tasks. Adv. Neural Inf. Process. Syst. **32**, 1–11 (2019)

42. Lu, J., Goswami, V., Rohrbach, M., Parikh, D., Lee, S.: 12-in-1: multi-task vision and language representation learning. In: Proceedings of the IEEE/CVF Conference on Computer Vision and Pattern Recognition, pp. 10437–10446 (2020)
43. Mensink, T., Uijlings, J.R.R., Kuznetsova, A., Gygli, M., Ferrari, V.: Factors of influence for transfer learning across diverse appearance domains and task types. IEEE Trans. Pattern Anal. Mach. Intell. (2021)
44. Nagrani, A., Yang, S., Arnab, A., Jansen, A., Schmid, C., Sun, C.: Attention bottlenecks for multimodal fusion. Adv. Neural Inf. Process. Syst. **34**, 14200–14213 (2021)
45. Ngiam, J., Khosla, A., Kim, M., Nam, J., Lee, H., Ng, A.: Multimodal deep learning. In: ICML (2011)
46. Owens, A., Efros, A.A.: Audio-visual scene analysis with self-supervised multisensory features. In: Proceedings of the European Conference on Computer Vision (ECCV), pp. 631–648 (2018)
47. Paszke, A., et al.: Pytorch: an imperative style, high-performance deep learning library. In: NeurIPS (2019)
48. Pathak, D., Krahenbuhl, P., Donahue, J., Darrell, T., Efros, A.A.: Context encoders: feature learning by inpainting. In: Proceedings of the IEEE Conference on Computer Vision and Pattern Recognition, pp. 2536–2544 (2016)
49. Pham, H., Dai, Z., Xie, Q., Le, Q.V.: Meta pseudo labels. In: Proceedings of the IEEE/CVF Conference on Computer Vision and Pattern Recognition, pp. 11557–11568 (2021)
50. Ranftl, R., Bochkovskiy, A., Koltun, V.: Vision transformers for dense prediction. In: 2021 IEEE/CVF International Conference on Computer Vision (ICCV), pp. 12159–12168 (2021)
51. Ranftl, R., Lasinger, K., Hafner, D., Schindler, K., Koltun, V.: Towards robust monocular depth estimation: mixing datasets for zero-shot cross-dataset transfer. IEEE Trans. Pattern Anal. Mach. Intell. **44**, 1623–1637 (2022)
52. Roberts, M., Paczan, N.: Hypersim: a photorealistic synthetic dataset for holistic indoor scene understanding. In: 2021 IEEE/CVF International Conference on Computer Vision (ICCV), pp. 10892–10902 (2021)
53. Rosenberg, C., Hebert, M., Schneiderman, H.: Semi-supervised self-training of object detection models. In: IEEE Workshops on Applications of Computer Vision (WACV/MOTION 2005) (2005)
54. Sax, A., Emi, B., Zamir, A.R., Guibas, L.J., Savarese, S., Malik, J.: Mid-level visual representations improve generalization and sample efficiency for learning visuomotor policies. (2018)
55. Scudder, H.: Probability of error of some adaptive pattern-recognition machines. IEEE Trans. Inf. Theory **11**(3), 363–371 (1965)
56. Shi, Y., Siddharth, N., Paige, B., Torr, P.H.S.: Variational mixture-of-experts autoencoders for multi-modal deep generative models. ArXiv abs/1911.03393 (2019)
57. Silberman, N., Hoiem, D., Kohli, P., Fergus, R.: Indoor segmentation and support inference from RGBD images. In: Fitzgibbon, A., Lazebnik, S., Perona, P., Sato, Y., Schmid, C. (eds.) ECCV 2012. LNCS, vol. 7576, pp. 746–760. Springer, Heidelberg (2012). https://doi.org/10.1007/978-3-642-33715-4_54
58. Smith, L., Gasser, M.: The development of embodied cognition: six lessons from babies. Artif. Life **11**(1–2), 13–29 (2005)
59. Su, W., et al.: Vl-bert: pre-training of generic visual-linguistic representations. arXiv preprint arXiv:1908.08530 (2019)

60. Sutter, T.M., Daunhawer, I., Vogt, J.E.: Multimodal generative learning utilizing jensen-shannon-divergence. ArXiv abs/2006.08242 (2019)
61. Sutter, T.M., Daunhawer, I., Vogt, J.E.: Generalized multimodal ELBO. CoRR abs/2105.02470 (2021). https://arxiv.org/abs/2105.02470
62. Tan, H., Bansal, M.: Lxmert: learning cross-modality encoder representations from transformers. arXiv preprint arXiv:1908.07490 (2019)
63. Tian, Y., Wang, Y., Krishnan, D., Tenenbaum, J.B., Isola, P.: Rethinking few-shot image classification: a good embedding is all you need? ArXiv abs/2003.11539 (2020)
64. Touvron, H., Cord, M., Douze, M., Massa, F., Sablayrolles, A., J'egou, H.: Training data-efficient image transformers & distillation through attention. In: ICML (2021)
65. Tripuraneni, N., Jordan, M., Jin, C.: On the theory of transfer learning: the importance of task diversity. Adv. Neural Inf. Process. Syst. **33**, 7852–7862 (2020)
66. Tripuraneni, N., Jordan, M.I., Jin, C.: On the theory of transfer learning: the importance of task diversity. ArXiv abs/2006.11650 (2020)
67. Vandenhende, S., Georgoulis, S., Van Gansbeke, W., Proesmans, M., Dai, D., Van Gool, L.: Multi-task learning for dense prediction tasks: a survey. IEEE Trans. Pattern Anal. Mach. Intell. (2021)
68. Vaswani, A., et al.: Attention is all you need. ArXiv abs/1706.03762 (2017)
69. Vincent, P., Larochelle, H., Lajoie, I., Bengio, Y., Manzagol, P.A.: Stacked denoising autoencoders: learning useful representations in a deep network with a local denoising criterion. J. Mach. Learn. Res. **11**(110), 3371–3408 (2010). http://jmlr.org/papers/v11/vincent10a.html
70. Wei, C., Fan, H., Xie, S., Wu, C.Y., Yuille, A., Feichtenhofer, C.: Masked feature prediction for self-supervised visual pre-training. arXiv preprint arXiv:2112.09133 (2021)
71. Wu, M., Goodman, N.D.: Multimodal generative models for scalable weakly-supervised learning. In: NeurIPS (2018)
72. Xiao, T., Radosavovic, I., Darrell, T., Malik, J.: Masked visual pre-training for motor control. arXiv preprint arXiv:2203.06173 (2022)
73. Xie, Q., Luong, M.T., Hovy, E., Le, Q.V.: Self-training with noisy student improves imagenet classification. In: Proceedings of the IEEE/CVF Conference on Computer Vision and Pattern Recognition, pp. 10687–10698 (2020)
74. Xie, Z., et al.: Simmim: a simple framework for masked image modeling. ArXiv abs/2111.09886 (2021)
75. Xu, H., et al.: E2e-vlp: end-to-end vision-language pre-training enhanced by visual learning. arXiv preprint arXiv:2106.01804 (2021)
76. Yalniz, I.Z., Jégou, H., Chen, K., Paluri, M., Mahajan, D.: Billion-scale semi-supervised learning for image classification. arXiv preprint arXiv:1905.00546 (2019)
77. Yarowsky, D.: Unsupervised word sense disambiguation rivaling supervised methods. In: ACL (1995)
78. Yin, W., et al.: Learning to recover 3D scene shape from a single image. In: 2021 IEEE/CVF Conference on Computer Vision and Pattern Recognition (CVPR), pp. 204–213 (2021)
79. Zamir, A.R., Sax, A., Shen, W.B., Guibas, L.J., Malik, J., Savarese, S.: Taskonomy: disentangling task transfer learning. In: IEEE Conference on Computer Vision and Pattern Recognition (CVPR). IEEE (2018)
80. Zhou, B., Zhao, H., Puig, X., Fidler, S., Barriuso, A., Torralba, A.: Scene parsing through ade20k dataset. In: 2017 IEEE Conference on Computer Vision and Pattern Recognition (CVPR), pp. 5122–5130 (2017)

81. Zhou, J., et al.: ibot: image bert pre-training with online tokenizer. arXiv preprint arXiv:2111.07832 (2021)
82. Zoph, B., et al.: Rethinking pre-training and self-training. Adv. Neural Inf. Process. Syst. **33**, 3833–3845 (2020)

AudioScopeV2: Audio-Visual Attention Architectures for Calibrated Open-Domain On-Screen Sound Separation

Efthymios Tzinis[1,2], Scott Wisdom[1(✉)], Tal Remez[1], and John R. Hershey[1]

[1] Google Research, Cambridge, USA
{scottwisdom,johnhershey}@google.com
[2] University of Illinois Urbana-Champaign, Urbana, USA
etzinis2@illinois.edu

Abstract. We introduce AudioScopeV2, a state-of-the-art universal audio-visual on-screen sound separation system which is capable of learning to separate sounds and associate them with on-screen objects by looking at in-the-wild videos. We identify several limitations of previous work on audio-visual on-screen sound separation, including the coarse resolution of spatio-temporal attention, poor convergence of the audio separation model, limited variety in training and evaluation data, and failure to account for the trade off between preservation of on-screen sounds and suppression of off-screen sounds. We provide solutions to all of these issues. Our proposed cross-modal and self-attention network architectures capture audio-visual dependencies at a finer resolution over time, and we also propose efficient separable variants that are capable of scaling to longer videos without sacrificing much performance. We also find that pre-training the separation model only on audio greatly improves results. For training and evaluation, we collected new human annotations of on-screen sounds from a large database of in-the-wild videos (YFCC100M). This new dataset is more diverse and challenging. Finally, we propose a calibration procedure that allows exact tuning of on-screen reconstruction versus off-screen suppression, which greatly simplifies comparing performance between models with different operating points. Overall, our experimental results show marked improvements in on-screen separation performance under much more general conditions than previous methods with minimal additional computational complexity.

Keywords: Audio-visual sound separation · Self-attention

E. Tzinis—Work done during an internship at Google Research.

Supplementary Information The online version contains supplementary material available at https://doi.org/10.1007/978-3-031-19836-6_21.

S. Avidan et al. (Eds.): ECCV 2022, LNCS 13697, pp. 368–385, 2022.
https://doi.org/10.1007/978-3-031-19836-6_21

1 Introduction

Humans are able to effortlessly perceive sounds in a noisy scene, and associate them with any corresponding visible objects. In audio processing, a corresponding challenge is to isolate sound sources from a mixture waveform and identify the associated visual appearance of each sound source. In this paper, we target the task of *universal audio-visual on-screen sound separation*, where the goal is to recover only the sounds that originate from on-screen objects, regardless of the types of on-screen and off-screen objects as illustrated in Fig. 1a.

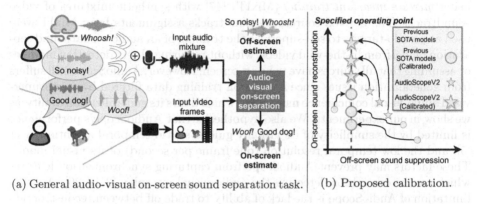

(a) General audio-visual on-screen sound separation task. | (b) Proposed calibration.

Fig. 1. Left: illustration of the task where our models make no assumptions about the existence, type, or count (up to a maximum) of on-screen and off-screen sources. Right: illustration of our proposed calibration procedure for on-screen separation models, which allows setting a specified tolerance level for off-screen sound suppression which allows more user control and easier model comparison.

This is a difficult task for numerous reasons. In stark contrast to visual objects that generally occupy distinct regions of pixels, sound sources are superimposed in the time domain. This imposes a challenge for unsupervised learning of audio-visual separation, because unlike their visual counterparts, the audio sources in a scene cannot be easily selected and aligned with video objects. Therefore, separating the constituent sources is needed, by conditioning separation on selected video objects and/or separating the audio *a priori* before associating the sounds with video objects. The *a priori* separation of the sounds, which we pursue here, has a few advantages. Thanks to recent work [47], it can be learned in an unsupervised way, and it can handle an unknown number of sounds, including those that do not appear on-screen. Also, the individual separated sounds are available to downstream processes, in addition to the on-screen estimate.

Despite remarkable progress in the field of on-screen sound separation, most of these works are constrained to isolating only a specific set of sound classes that can appear on-screen such as speech [1,10,14] or music [11,12]. Although this strategy works well under a restricted domain, where such labeled data are available, the reliance on human labels precludes scaling to large open-domain data. Recent works have started to expand beyond music and speech to a wider variety of classes, such as using visual scene graphs to model audio-visual relationships [7], but this approach still requires labeled data to train a supervised object detector. Although the seminal works in on-screen sound separation proposed models that were somewhat invariant to the types of sources [12,32], those systems were unable to be trained with real world videos mainly because they needed labeled videos in which the sources always appeared on-screen during training.

Recently, AudioScope [43] addressed several of the aforementioned problems using *mixture invariant training* (MixIT) [47] with synthetic mixtures of video soundtracks. The derived sources-to-soundtracks assignments from MixIT were used as pseudo-targets to self-supervise the training of an audio-visual sound separation model from in-the-wild videos, without requiring object detection modules or assuming that all sources have to be on-screen. However, AudioScope still suffers from generalization issues since it relies on training data filtered by an unsupervised audio-visual coincidence model [22], which limits its generalization ability, as we show in our experiments. We also hypothesize that AudioScope's performance is limited by the simplicity of its visually guided spatio-temporal attention layer [5], and the low temporal resolution (one frame per second) of its visual model. These factors may prevent AudioScope from capturing synchronization features which can be crucial for detecting the audio-visual interplay [2,19,26]. Another limitation of AudioScope is the lack of ability to trade off between reconstruction of on-screen sounds and suppression of off-screen sounds. These models achieve an arbitrary operating point during training, which makes comparing performance between different models difficult (see Fig. 1b).

We propose solutions for all of the aforementioned problems and limitations:

1. AudioScopeV2 leverages richer cross-modal and self-attention network architectures that capture audio-visual dependencies at a finer time resolution, as well as efficient separable variants that are capable of scaling to longer videos without sacrificing much performance (Sect. 3). We also find that pre-training the audio separation model using MixIT greatly improves results.
2. We provide a new dataset, for which we collected new human annotations of on-screen sounds from a large database of in-the-wild videos (YFCC100M [38]), described in Sect. 4.1. We show that our new proposed models both generalize and perform better on the more diverse and challenging evaluations sets compared to previous state-of-the-art methods.
3. We propose a novel calibration procedure (Sect. 4.4) that allows precise tuning of on-screen reconstruction versus off-screen suppression, that can also be used to greatly simplify model comparison across different models that each have their own operating point.

Dataset recipes, demos, and other supplementary material are available online google-research.github.io/sound-separation/papers/audioscope-v2.

2 Relation to Prior Work

Joint perception of audio and video modalities is not trivial, in part due to the problems of alignment between corresponding representations in each modality. Nevertheless, a variety of works have shown promising results using multimodal neural network architectures [2,6–8,13,43,48]. Audio-visual sound separation [1,10,20], and specifically separation of on-screen versus off-screen sounds [32], has enjoyed remarkable performance improvements since the initial works. Important innovations have included using localization of objects [29,48,51], forcing consistency between audio and visual representations [3,13,14,28], weakly-supervised [34] and self-supervised [2,26,35,43] approaches.

Recent work has shown that it is possible to train an open-domain audio-only universal sound separation model using a mask-based convolutional architecture regardless of the category of the sound [23,41]. A related direction is to extract sources of interest by conditioning separation networks using identity or multimodal cues. This has yielded performance improvements for speech [45] as well as universal source separation [16,24,30,31,42]. However, these experiments relied on having sufficient supervised training data and were evaluated only on test sets with similar environmental conditions and sound distributions. In order to extend the reach of this approach, methods have been proposed to train separation models with no access to ground truth clean sources by utilizing weak class labels [33], the spatial separability of the sources [9,36,40] and self-supervision in the form of MixIT [47]. These methods make it possible to learn separation of signals well outside the domains for which isolated source databases exist.

An open question in audio-visual correspondence models concerns the level of processing at which audio and video objects can be aligned. Typically audio-visual models have used high-level features at the output of neural networks to estimate correspondence between audio and video signals [7,22,26,28,39,43]. Such high-level representations may tend to focus on semantic information about the class of objects and sounds, especially when the features are computed at low video frame rates. Such methods may work well for single instances of a class of object or sound, but may struggle with identification for multiple instances of a class, or for classes not seen during training. In contrast, there may be significant information in the correspondence between lower-level features. Mutual information between low-level features was used for audio-visual localization [19], and several more recent works have shown promising results for self-supervised audio-visual learning using low-level motion [51] and optical flow [2] features. Such features may help with generalization and instance-level correspondence by detecting synchronous dynamics of the audio and video, regardless of their semantic class.

Attention mechanisms can align representations across modalities, both at the level of semantic association and in terms of low-level correspondences. An attention-based framework was recently used to modulate audio representations using motion-based visual features [51] for separation and localization. Conversely, modulating video features based on audio embeddings has also been used for speech separation [28] as well as in AudioScope's spatio-temporal attention module [43]. Other works combined self-attention layers [44] for modeling inter-modality temporal patterns, as well as cross-modal attention modules for intra-modality associations [8,48,49], for sound localization and representation learning. One issue with self-attention is that its complexity grows quadratically with the dimensionality of the input length. We therefore propose a separable variants of our proposed architectures that factorize attention across different dimensions and modalities. This strategy allows us to achieve similar performance to full self-attention with a much lower computational footprint. Other separable attention mechanisms have emerged recently [6,50], but our approach differs in that we process and capture intra-modality patterns from both audio and video features.

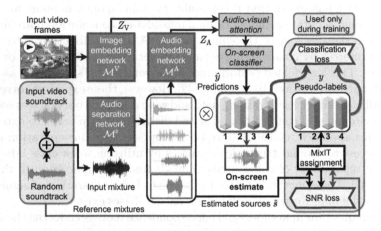

Fig. 2. Illustration of AudioScopeV2's architecture and its training procedure.

3   Model Architecture

Figure 2 illustrates the architecture and training procedure of AudioScopeV2. The run-time architecture takes as input the video frames and a mixture waveform x. The audio separation module estimates $M = 4$ sources. An audio embedding network is run on each of the estimated sources, producing audio embeddings Z_A. In parallel, an image embedding network processes each input video frame independently and produces the visual embeddings Z_V. The audio and video embeddings are fed to an audio-visual attention network, for which we propose a family of attention-based architectures. The output of the audio-visual attention network is passed to a final on-screen classifier head which produces a probability $\hat{y}_m$ corresponding to the event that the source m originates from an on-screen object. Finally, the probabilities $\hat{y}_m$ are used as weights to mix the separated sources $\hat{s}_m$ together, producing an estimate of on-screen audio. The training procedure for this model is also illustrated, where we create mixtures of mixtures (MoMs) for audio by adding the soundtrack from another random video. A MixIT SNR loss is computed by finding the best combination of estimated sources to approximate each one of the reference mixtures in terms of SNR. The assignments of these best combinations are used as pseudo-labels in the classification loss. We describe each of these components in more detail below.

3.1 Separation Module

The separation module $\mathcal{M}^S$ uses a dilated convolutional architecture [23] with learnable encoder and decoder, which was also used in [43]. This module takes as input a mixture waveform $x \in \mathbb{R}^{T'}$, estimates M masks in the encoded latent space, and outputs M estimated source waveforms $\hat{s} \in \mathbb{R}^{M \times T'}$. The latter are forced to add up to the input mixture through a mixture consistency layer [46]. However, in contrast to AudioScope [43], our separation model is not conditioned on global visual embeddings, for two reasons. First, visual conditioning was not shown to be effective [43], and second, this allows us to use MixIT to pre-train the separation module on all YFCC100M [38] audio tracks to provide a better initialization for training the audio-visual model. Thus, AudioScope* refers to our AudioScope implementation with the aforementioned source separation module.

3.2 Audio and Video Embedding Networks

Features are extracted for the M estimated sources $\hat{s}$ and the corresponding T input video frames (128×128 pixels), using a MobileNetV1 architecture [21], as in [43]. The audio encoder takes as input the log mel-scale spectrogram of the separated source waveforms $\hat{s}$, and audio features are extracted from the 23rd layer. The visual embedding network is applied to each of the T input video frames independently and extracts features with 8×8 spatial locations. Audio and video features are converted to a common depth $D = 128$ with a dense layer.

3.3 Audio-Visual Attention

We propose attention mechanisms to identify dependencies across the M estimated audio sources, space, and time between the audio features $Z_A \in \mathbb{R}^{M \times T \times D}$ and the video features $Z_V \in \mathbb{R}^{G \times T \times D}$. Our video encoder provides $G = 8^2$ spatial locations, and the time dimension T is shared across both tensors. Specifically, we propose to use *audio-visual self-attention* (SA) [44], which treats the audio sources and visual locations as a joint attention space (see Sect. 3.3), and *cross-modal attention* (CMA) layers, which perform attention between audio sources and visual locations, but avoid uni-modal attention between sources and between spatial locations (see Sect. 3.3). For both the SA and CMA attention we consider two settings: a *joint attention* setting, in which attention operates jointly over time and space/sources, and a *separable attention* setting, in which attention across time is interleaved with attention across spatial locations and sources. The joint attention scales quadratically with the product of dimensions from all of the axes which is computed over whereas the more efficient separable variation factorizes the operation across each axes individually, which makes an important difference in practice (see Sect. 5.2).

In the following formulations we use a slightly more general version of an attention layer [5] to show how attention operates across different axes of the corresponding tensors. Attention computes similarities between a packed tensor of queries $Q \in \mathbb{R}^{X_Q \times T_Q \times D}$ w.r.t. some packed keys $K \in \mathbb{R}^{X_K \times T_K \times D}$, where D is the depth dimensionality of the tensors. The similarities are computed using a generalized version of the typical tensor inner product $\langle Z_1, Z_2 \rangle_{\mathcal{A}}$, which reduces across the specified dimensions $\mathcal{A}$ of the second tensor Z_2. Note that we assume that Z_1's dimensions are a subset of Z_2's. By using a scaled tensor inner-product [44] and a softmax$_{\mathcal{A}}$ activation that averages over the dimensions specified by $\mathcal{A}$ at the output of the tensor product $\langle K, Q \rangle_{\{D\}}$, we produce the resulting similarity tensor which modulates the values $V \in \mathbb{R}^{X_V \times T_V \times D}$:

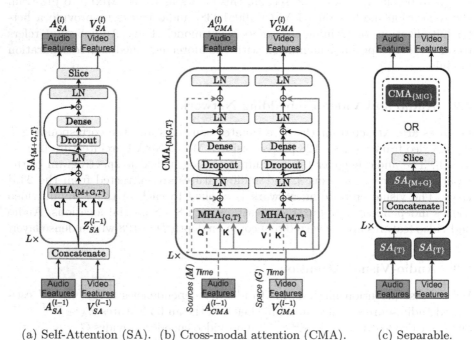

(a) Self-Attention (SA).   (b) Cross-modal attention (CMA).   (c) Separable.

Fig. 3. AudioScopeV2's attention architectures for audio-visual alignment and feature extraction. Tensors are depicted by omitting batch and depth dimensions.

$$\text{Att}_{\mathcal{A}}(Q, K, V) = \langle \alpha, f_V(V) \rangle_{\mathcal{A}}, \quad \alpha = \text{softmax}_{\mathcal{A}} \left(\frac{1}{\sqrt{D}} \langle f_K(K), f_Q(Q) \rangle_{\{D\}} \right),$$
$$(1)$$

where Q, K, V, and α are the query tensor, the key tensor, the value tensor, and the attention weight distribution tensor across the set of specified axes $\mathcal{A}$ of the value/key tensors. For example, for an input query Q of shape $X_Q \times T_Q \times D$ and value V of shape $X_V \times T_V \times D$, $\text{Att}_{\{X_V, T_V\}}(Q, V, V)$ performs attention over the first and second axes of V, yielding an output tensor of shape $X_Q \times T_Q \times D$. The dense layers f_Q, f_V, f_K are trainable and applied to the depth dimension D.

We utilize the multi-head attention (MHA) layer [44]. Each one of the H heads performs attention over some low-dimensional embeddings derived from the tensors Q and V, with the output embedding depth reduced to D/H. These independent attention heads have the capability to focus on different semantics of the input tensors. After performing attention across the specified axes $\mathcal{A}$, the final output is given by aggregating across the head outputs $o^{(h)}$:

$$
\begin{aligned}
o^{(h)} &= \text{Att}_{\mathcal{A}}(f_Q^{(h)}(Q), f_V^{(h)}(V), f_V^{(h)}(V)), \\
\text{MHA}_{\mathcal{A}}(Q, V) &= f(\text{Concat}(o_1, \ldots, o_H)),
\end{aligned}
\tag{2}
$$

where f denotes a dense layer $\mathbb{R}^{X_Q \times T_Q \times D} \to \mathbb{R}^{X_Q \times T_Q \times D}$ and the dense layers $f_Q^{(h)}$ and $f_V^{(h)}$ are linear maps $\mathbb{R}^{X_Q \times T_Q \times D} \to \mathbb{R}^{X_Q \times T_Q \times D/H}$ and $\mathbb{R}^{X_V \times T_V \times D} \to \mathbb{R}^{X_V \times T_V \times D/H}$, respectively for each one of the $h \in 1, \ldots, H$ heads, where for our purposes we always assume that the keys and values tensors are the same size. Using these definitions, we now formulate our proposed attention methods.

Self-attention (SA): First, we concatenate the audio tensor $A_{\text{SA}}^{(0)} = Z_A$ and the video $V_{\text{SA}}^{(0)} = Z_V$ tensors across the first axis to form the $(M + G) \times T \times D$ tensor $Z_{\text{SA}}^{(0)}$, the input to the first self-attention layer.

Joint SA: Attention is performed jointly across space, time, and sources (see Fig. 3a). We express the l-th layer of a joint self-attention module as follows:

$$
\begin{aligned}
b^{(l)} &= \text{MHA}_{\{M+G, T\}}(Z_{\text{SA}}^{(l-1)}, Z_{\text{SA}}^{(l-1)}) + Z_{\text{SA}}^{(l-1)}, \\
Z_{\text{SA}}^{(l)} &= \text{LN}(f^{(l)}(\text{Dropout}(b^{(l)})) + b^{(l)}),
\end{aligned}
\tag{3}
$$

where $f^{(l)}$ is a dense layer, LN is layer normalization [4] and Dropout denotes a dropout layer [37]. We define the sequence of operations in (3) as $Z_{\text{SA}}^{(l)} = \text{SA}_{\{M+G, T\}}(Z_{\text{SA}}^{(l-1)})$ where the self-attention is performed across the joint sources-and-spatial dimension M + G and the time axis T. The final representation z, after the repetition of L self-attention blocks, for all M sources, is obtained by slicing and performing attentional pooling [43] across the time axis of $\widehat{z}$:

$$
z = \text{MHA}_{\{T\}}(\textstyle\sum_t^T \widehat{z}_t, \widehat{z}) \in \mathbb{R}^{M \times D}, \quad \widehat{z} = A_{\text{SA}}^{(L)} = Z_{\text{SA}}^{(L)}[1 : M] \in \mathbb{R}^{M \times T \times D}.
\tag{4}
$$

Separable SA: The l-th separable self-attention block can be expressed using the SA module defined in (3):

$$
\begin{aligned}
a^{(l)} &= \text{SA}_{\{T\}}(Z_{\text{SA}}^{(l-1)}[1 : M]), \quad v^{(l)} = \text{SA}_{\{T\}}(Z_{\text{SA}}^{(l-1)}[M : M + G]), \\
Z_{\text{SA}}^{(l)} &= \text{SA}_{\{M+G\}}\left(\text{Concat}(a^{(l)}, v^{(l)})\right).
\end{aligned}
\tag{5}
$$

The final audio-visual representation is obtained through attentional pooling and slicing as before (see also Fig. 3c).

Cross-modal Attention (CMA). In this attention layer we keep the audio and the video modality tensors separate, and we perform queries from one modality to another. Formally, the input to the stacked CMA blocks is a pair of an audio $A_{\mathrm{CMA}}^{(0)} \in \mathbb{R}^{M \times T \times D}$ and a video $V_{\mathrm{CMA}}^{(0)} \in \mathbb{R}^{G \times T \times D}$ feature tensors.

Joint CMA: We perform a directional attention from the audio (video) modality tensor to the video (audio) tensor, attending across both sources and time (space and time) axes. Formally, at the l-th layer we have the following sequence of operations for the directional attention where we use as a query the audio modality, also illustrated in Fig. 3b:

$$a_1^{(l)} = \mathrm{MHA}_{\{G,T\}}(A_{\mathrm{CMA}}^{(l-1)}, V_{\mathrm{CMA}}^{(l-1)}), \quad a_2^{(l)} = \mathrm{LN}(a_1^{(l)} + A_{\mathrm{CMA}}^{(l-1)}),$$
$$A_{\mathrm{CMA}}^{(l)} = \mathrm{LN}(f(\mathrm{Dropout}(a_2^{(l)})) + A_{\mathrm{CMA}}^{(l-1)}). \tag{6}$$

For the other direction, we modulate the video features $v^{(l)}$ using the audio features $a^{(l)}$ by swapping A_{CMA} and V_{CMA} and attending over $\{M, T\}$ in (6). We define (6) as $A_{\mathrm{CMA}}^{(l)}, V_{\mathrm{CMA}}^{(l)} = \mathrm{CMA}_{\{M|G,T\}}(A_{\mathrm{CMA}}^{(l-1)}, V_{\mathrm{CMA}}^{(l-1)})$, where each cross-modal attention is performed across the dimension of audio sources M or spatial locations G (denoted in our notation as "M|G") and the time axis T. The output audio-visual embedding z contains information for all M sources and is obtained after the repetition of L cross-modal attention blocks via attentional pooling across time (4) on the output audio tensor $\hat{z} = A_{\mathrm{CMA}}^{(l)} \in \mathbb{R}^{M \times T \times D}$.

Separable CMA: Similar to Sect. 3.3, we can reduce the space complexity of the proposed CMA layer by first performing self-attention across the time axis for each modality separately, then performing CMA across the remaining axis (i.e. sources or spatial locations) as shown next, also illustrated in Fig. 3c:

$$a^{(l)} = \mathrm{SA}_{\{T\}}(A_{\mathrm{CMA}}^{(l-1)}), \quad v^{(l)} = \mathrm{SA}_{\{T\}}(V_{\mathrm{CMA}}^{(l-1)}),$$
$$A_{\mathrm{CMA}}^{(l)}, V_{\mathrm{CMA}}^{(l)} = \mathrm{CMA}_{\{M|G\}}(a^{(l)}, v^{(l)}). \tag{7}$$

3.4 Audio-Visual On-Screen Sound Classifier

For each estimated source $\hat{s}_m$, AudioScopeV2 predicts the probability $\hat{y}_m$ that it originates from an on-screen object. These probabilities are computed using the extracted audio-visual representation from the output z of our attention-based models for the self-attention and cross-modal attention encoders. Specifically, for each source m, we feed the audio-visual embedding $z_m \in \mathbb{R}^D$ through a dense layer f_z tied across sources to produce logits $\hat{\ell}_m$, and then apply an element-wise sigmoid activation σ to compute the audio-visual coincidence probability $\hat{y}_m$. The final on-screen waveform estimate $\hat{x}^{\mathrm{on}}$ is produced using these probabilities as soft weights and multiplied with the corresponding estimated sources:

$$\hat{\ell}_m = f_z(z_m), \quad \hat{y}_m = \sigma\left(\hat{\ell}_m\right) \in [0, 1], \quad \hat{x}^{\mathrm{on}} = \sum_{m=1}^M \hat{y}_m \hat{s}_m. \tag{8}$$

3.5   Training Procedure

To train the separation model, we use MixIT [47]. Given two reference mixtures $r_1, r_2 \in \mathbb{R}^{T'}$, M separated sources $\hat{s}$ predicted from the MoM $x = r_1 + r_2$, and a signal-level training loss $\mathcal{L}$, MixIT infers an optimal $2 \times M$ binary mixing matrix A where each column sums to one. This mixing matrix assigns each estimated source s_m to one of the reference mixtures r_1 or r_2:

$$\mathcal{L}_{\text{MixIT}}(r, \hat{s}) = \min_{A \in \mathbb{B}^{2 \times M}} \sum_{n=1}^{2} \mathcal{L}(r_n, [A\hat{s}]_n). \tag{9}$$

For $\mathcal{L}$, we use the negative thresholded SNR loss [43,47].

We use purely unsupervised training, which uses batches composed of *noisy-labeled on-screen* (NOn) examples. Each NOn example consists of the video frames and audio for a primary input 5-second video clip, where additional audio from another random 5-second video clip serves as synthetic off-screen audio that is mixed with the primary video soundtrack. These examples provide noisy pseudo-labels, because even after optimal MixIT combination, the primary soundtrack may contain off-screen background noise.

For training AudioScopeV2's audio-visual on-screen classifier with NOn examples, we use the *active combinations* loss $\mathcal{L}_{\text{AC}}$ [43] computed between the pseudo-label assignments y provided by MixIT and the predictions $\hat{y}$ of the classifier. $\mathcal{L}_{\text{AC}}$ corresponds to the minimum cross-entropy loss $\mathcal{L}_{\text{CE}}$ over all settings $\wp_{\geq 1}(\mathbb{B}^M)$ of the labels such that at least one label is 1 (equivalent to at least one source appearing on-screen):

$$\mathcal{L}_{\text{AC}}(y, \hat{y}) = \min_{\ell \in \wp_{\geq 1}(\mathbb{B}^M)} \sum_{m} \mathcal{L}_{\text{CE}}(\ell_m, \hat{y}_m). \tag{10}$$

4   Experimental Framework

4.1   Data Preparation and Labeling

For our open-domain experiments we use Flickr Creative Commons 100 Million Dataset (YFCC100M) [38] CC-BY videos respecting published train/validation/test splits [18]. Instead of using only a filtered subset of the data, as previous state-of-the-art methods suggested [43], our proposed training recipe is able to leverage unrestricted open-domain datasets by using better pre-trained separation models.

The unfiltered training data consists of ≈ 1600 hours, and we extract 5-second clips with a hop of 1 s (4.85M total clips). We also gathered human annotations for 5-second clips from unfiltered videos from the train, validation, and test splits. The count of total clips rated, unanimously-rated on-screen-only clips, and unanimously rated off-screen clips were 20000/480/4664 for training, 6500/109/1421 for validation, and 3500/43/762 for test. Notice that during training we dynamically create mixtures of pairs of these clips, so the effective number of unique examples is $\mathcal{O}(10^{13})$. We also experiment with faster video frame rate of 16 frames per second (FPS), instead of 1 FPS used by AudioScope [43].

4.2   Training Details

Both audio and visual embedding networks were pre-trained on AudioSet [15] for unsupervised coincidence prediction [22]. We also found that freezing these networks during training leads to better results. Also, instead of training the separation model from scratch, we pre-train the separation model with MixIT on unfiltered audio-only MoMs drawn from YFCC100M for 3.6M steps, which also significantly boosted the performance of our models. We use $L = 4$ stacked proposed layers of joint/separable SA/CMA (ablation studies can be found in the supplementary material). All models were trained on 32 Google Cloud TPU v3 cores with the Adam optimizer [25], batch size 128, and learning rate 10^{-4}.

4.3   Evaluation Datasets

In order to compare with the current state-of-the-art, we use the Audio-Scope dataset splits [43] provided online [17], which were drawn from a subset of YFCC100M filtered by an unsupervised coincidence model [22]. These datasets (we refer to them as *filtered off-screen background*) contain two kinds of examples: *on-screen MoMs*, where additional off-screen audio was injected into the soundtrack of a unanimously-rated on-screen-only video (i.e. input audio $x = x^{\text{on}} + x^{\text{off}}$), and *off-screen MoMs*, where additional audio was mixed into the soundtrack of a unanimously-rated off-screen-only video (input audio $x = x^{\text{off}}$).

   Similarly, we construct new evaluation sets of MoMs using videos from unfiltered validation and test splits of YFCC100M, which we call *unfiltered random background*. Instead of using off-screen-only audio, our dataset uses randomly sampled audio from all unfiltered videos as synthetic off-screen background for unanimously-rated on-screen-only or off-screen-only videos (see Sect. 4.1).

4.4   Evaluation Metrics and Calibration

For on-screen examples with input audio $x = x^{\text{on}} + x^{\text{off}}$, we report the reconstruction fidelity of on-screen estimates $\hat{x}^{\text{on}}$ (8) using *signal-to-noise ratio* (SNR) in dB. For off-screen examples with input audio $x = x^{\text{off}}$ where we know that no audio originates from on-screen objects, we measure the ability of our models to suppress off-screen sources using *off-screen suppression ratio* (OSR).

$$\text{SNR}(x^{\text{on}}, \hat{x}^{\text{on}}) = 20 \log_{10} \frac{\|x^{\text{on}}\|}{\|x^{\text{on}} - \hat{x}^{\text{on}}\|}, \text{OSR}(x, \hat{x}^{\text{on}}) = 20 \log_{10} \frac{\|x\|}{\|\hat{x}^{\text{on}}\|}. \quad (11)$$

OSR measures the power reduction of the on-screen estimate $\hat{x}^{\text{on}}$ relative to the input audio, and is only measured on examples where the input audio $x = x^{\text{off}}$ is entirely off-screen. Prior work [43] has also used scale-invariant signal-to-noise ratio (SI-SNR) [27] instead of SNR; however, this allows a model to obtain large OSR, without sacrificing SI-SNR, by scaling down its estimates.

   Both OSR and SNR are important, but there is an inherent trade-off between them, since OSR can always be increased by scaling down the output, at the expense of SNR. This makes it difficult to compare models that have different operating points in this trade-off, a problem not addressed by [43]. To illustrate this, Fig. 4 plots OSR versus SNR for the models we consider in this paper. Notice that each model achieves a different operating point. Because of these differences, SNR cannot be meaningfully compared across models without considering OSR. For example, one of our proposed models achieves a lower SNR of about 5.3 dB at 10.8 dB OSR, compared to an AudioScope* model that achieves a higher SNR of 5.5 dB at 8.9 dB OSR. It is difficult to say which model is better.

To solve this problem, we propose a novel calibration method for these on-screen separation models, where we adjust a bias in the classifiers to achieve a target average OSR. This is akin to choosing a threshold for a detector to achieve a target false positive rate. For our procedure, we define a calibrated on-screen estimate given by adding a global scalar offset θ to the on-screen logits $\hat{\ell}_{1:M}$ (8):

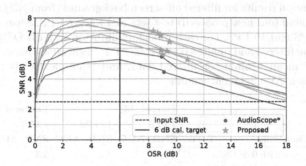

Fig. 4. OSR versus SNR curves when calibration offset θ in (12) is varied, on unfiltered random background test set for all models in Table 1 (except for AudioScope [43], which achieves 23.4 dB OSR/1.1 dB SNR for 1 FPS).

$$\tilde{x}^{\text{on}}(\theta) = \sum_m \hat{s}_m \sigma(\hat{\ell}_m + \theta). \tag{12}$$

The offset θ is tuned such that the median OSR (11) across all N_{off} off-screen examples, $\text{med}_{j=1}^{N_{\text{off}}} \text{OSR}\left[x_j, \tilde{x}_j^{\text{on}}(\theta)\right]$, is equal to a desired $\text{OSR}_{\text{target}}$. The curves in Fig. 4 illustrate the effect on OSR and SNR when θ is varied, and are akin to receiver operating characteristic (ROC) or precision-recall curves.

In practice, θ has a monotonic relationship to OSR. As θ tends towards 0 (inversely ∞), the on-screen probabilities $\hat{y}_m$ tend towards 0 (inversely 1), and thus OSR approaches ∞ (inversely 0) dB. Because of this property, optimization of θ is very simple, and can be accomplished efficiently via binary search.

For our results, we use $\text{OSR}_{\text{target}} = 6\text{dB}$, which corresponds to all off-screen sources sounding as if they are twice as far away. To choose the early stopping point, we evaluate all models on the *unfiltered random background* validation data. Running calibration on each step of model training would be prohibitively expensive. Thus, we choose the point which maximizes the minimum of SNR and OSR, favoring models which are not strongly biased towards any metric.

We also report the performance of classification using weighted area under the curve of the ROC (AUC-ROC), where the weight for each probability $\hat{y}_m$ is the normalized power of the corresponding source $\hat{s}_m$: $\|\hat{s}_m\|_2^2 / \left(\sum_{m'} \|\hat{s}_{m'}\|_2^2\right)$.

5 Results

5.1 Open-Domain On-Screen Separation

Results are shown in Table 1 for the filtered off-screen background dataset from [43], and our new and challenging unfiltered random background dataset. We include two "no processing" baselines, with the on-screen estimate equal to the input audio $\hat{x}^{on} = x$ (0 dB OSR), or half the input $\hat{x}^{on} = x/2$ (6 dB OSR).

Table 1. Evaluation results for filtered off-screen background (from [43]) and unfiltered random background (our new proposed) test sets at 1 and 16 FPS. Separate models are trained for 1 FPS and 16 FPS. For each model, calibration to 6 dB OSR is performed separately on the filtered and unfiltered test sets. "PT" indicates separation model pre-training, "Filt." means training on filtered data, and "Complexity" is the theoretical complexity of each AV-alignment module.

AV alignment		Complexity	PT	Filt.	Filtered [43]				Unfiltered (new proposed)			
					1 FPS		16 FPS		1 FPS		16 FPS	
					SNR	AUC	SNR	AUC	SNR	AUC	SNR	AUC
No processing ($\hat{x}^{on} = x$ with 0dB OSR)					4.4	–	4.4	–	2.5	–	2.5	–
No processing ($\hat{x}^{on} = x/2$ with 6dB OSR)					4.7	–	4.7	–	4.1	–	4.1	–
AudioScope [43]		$\mathcal{O}(TMG)$		✓	6.0	0.79	–	–	2.7	0.69	–	–
AudioScope*		$\mathcal{O}(TMG)$		✓	8.2	0.80	5.9	0.77	5.8	0.78	5.2	0.71
SA	Joint	$\mathcal{O}(T^2[M+G]^2)$		✓	**10.0**	0.84	9.9	**0.86**	7.2	0.82	**7.7**	0.83
	Sep.	$\mathcal{O}(T^2+[M+G]^2)$		✓	9.6	0.84	8.2	0.83	6.6	0.78	6.6	0.80
CMA	Joint	$\mathcal{O}(T^2MG)$		✓	**10.0**	**0.88**	**10.0**	0.85	**7.3**	**0.83**	**7.7**	**0.84**
	Sep.	$\mathcal{O}(T^2+MG)$		✓	9.5	0.83	9.3	0.82	6.4	0.78	7.1	0.80

On the filtered test set, our proposed models significantly outperform the previous state-of-the-art AudioScope model [43] trained on filtered data, by more than 4dB in terms of SNR and 0.09 in AUC-ROC. Training on unfiltered data, including pre-training the separation model on this data (AudioScope*), improves over the baseline AudioScope model trained on filtered data (6.0 dB → 8.2 dB).

On our newly introduced unfiltered random background dataset, AudioScope [43] trained on mismatched filtered data suffers from poor generalization, achieving only 2.7 dB SNR, which is worse than doing no processing (4.1 dB SNR). This demonstrates the limitation of training on filtered data. For our proposed models, joint CMA yields the best improvements over AudioScope* trained with matched unfiltered data (5.8 dB → 7.7 dB SNR and 0.78 → 0.84 AUC-ROC). Also, notice that the much more efficient separable versions of SA and CMA only suffer minor degradation compared to the joint versions (7.2 dB → 6.6 dB for SA, 7.3 dB → 6.4 dB for CMA). Our proposed models can perceive and leverage higher-frequency dynamics from the audio-visual scene and thus, using a higher frame rate of 16 FPS provides improvement of up to 0.7 dB SNR. On the other hand, AudioScope* seemingly cannot scale to higher frame-rates (8.2 dB → 5.9 dB for filtered and 5.8 dB → 5.2 dB for unfiltered, going from 1 FPS to 16 FPS), presumably because its audio-visual alignment is limited by only using shallow spatio-temporal attention. It is also possible that filtering with the audio-visual coincidence model [22], which averaged coincidence scores over frames at 1 FPS, may have biased towards video clips with always-visible sounding objects.

5.2 Computational Efficiency

In theory, joint SA has complexity $\mathcal{O}(T^2[M + G]^2)$, which scales poorly relative its separable version with complexity $\mathcal{O}(T^2 + [M + G]^2)$. Joint CMA has a slightly better complexity $\mathcal{O}(T^2MG)$ but still lags behind its separable counterpart $\mathcal{O}(T^2 + MG)$. However, it is important to evaluate how the computation scales in practice. The execution time versus input video length for all models is depicted in Fig. 5. The efficiency of the proposed separable self- and cross-modal attention becomes apparent for longer videos. These separable variants perform comparably to the much more complex joint CMA and joint SA models (see Table 1) but have computational requirements on par with the simpler AudioScope [43].

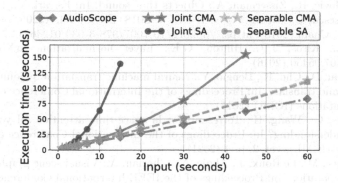

Fig. 5. Computation requirements AudioScope [43] and our proposed models with separable and joint SA and CMA for different video input lengths at 16 FPS. All measurements were taken on a machine with 16 GB of RAM and 2 Intel Xeon CPU @ 2.20 GHz cores. Input duration is increased until out-of-memory error.

6 Conclusion

We identified several issues with the previous state-of-the-art open-domain audio-visual on-screen sound separation model, AudioScope [43]. These issues include oversimplicity of shallow attention used for audio-visual alignment, lack of generalization due to filtering video data with an unsupervised audio-visual coincidence model [22], and inability to specify the trade off between on-screen reconstruction and off-screen suppression. We proposed more sophisticated self- and cross-modal attention architectures, along with more efficient separable versions, that improve performance and are able to leverage higher video frame rates. To address lack of generalization, we provide annotations for a new dataset constructed from YFCC100M [38] that is unfiltered by the audio-visual coincidence model. As a result, this dataset is more diverse and representative of in-the-wild video data. Finally, we proposed a calibration procedure that allows any on-screen separation model to be tuned for a specific level of off-screen suppression, which allows more control over model behavior and much easier comparison between different models. Using our calibration procedure, our results show that our proposed architecture is able to generalize to our more challenging test set and achieve clear improvements over the previous state-of-the-art AudioScope model [43].

References

1. Afouras, T., Chung, J.S., Zisserman, A.: The Conversation: deep audio-visual speech enhancement. In: Proceedings of the Interspeech, pp. 3244–3248 (2018)
2. Afouras, T., Owens, A., Chung, J.S., Zisserman, A.: Self-supervised learning of audio-visual objects from video. In: Vedaldi, A., Bischof, H., Brox, T., Frahm, J.-M. (eds.) ECCV 2020. Self-supervised learning of audio-visual objects from video, vol. 12363, pp. 208–224. Springer, Cham (2020). https://doi.org/10.1007/978-3-030-58523-5_13
3. Arandjelović, R., Zisserman, A.: Objects that sound. In: Ferrari, V., Hebert, M., Sminchisescu, C., Weiss, Y. (eds.) ECCV 2018. LNCS, vol. 11205, pp. 451–466. Springer, Cham (2018). https://doi.org/10.1007/978-3-030-01246-5_27
4. Ba, J.L., Kiros, J.R., Hinton, G.E.: Layer normalization. arXiv preprint arXiv:1607.06450 (2016)
5. Bahdanau, D., Cho, K., Bengio, Y.: Neural machine translation by jointly learning to align and translate. In: Proceedings of the International Conference on Learning Representations (ICLR) (2015)
6. Bertasius, G., Wang, H., Torresani, L.: Is space-time attention all you need for video understanding? In: Proceedings of the International Conference on Machine Learning (ICML), vol. 2, p. 4 (2021)
7. Chatterjee, M., Le Roux, J., Ahuja, N., Cherian, A.: Visual scene graphs for audio source separation. In: Proceedings of the IEEE International Conference on Computer Vision (ICCV), pp. 1204–1213 (2021)
8. Cheng, Y., Wang, R., Pan, Z., Feng, R., Zhang, Y.: Look, listen, and attend: Co-attention network for self-supervised audio-visual representation learning. In: ACM MM, pp. 3884–3892 (2020)
9. Drude, L., Hasenklever, D., Haeb-Umbach, R.: Unsupervised training of a deep clustering model for multichannel blind source separation. In: Proceedings of the IEEE International Conference on Acoustics, Speech, and Signal Processing (ICASSP), pp. 695–699 (2019)
10. Ephrat, A., Mosseri, I., Lang, O., Dekel, T., Wilson, K., Hassidim, A., Freeman, W.T., Rubinstein, M.: Looking to listen at the cocktail party: a speaker-independent audio-visual model for speech separation. ACM TOG 37(4), 1–11 (2018)

11. Gan, C., Huang, D., Zhao, H., Tenenbaum, J.B., Torralba, A.: Music gesture for visual sound separation. In: Proceedings of the IEEE International Conference on Computer Vision (CVPR), pp. 10478–10487 (2020)
12. Gao, R., Feris, R., Grauman, K.: Learning to separate object sounds by watching unlabeled video. In: Ferrari, V., Hebert, M., Sminchisescu, C., Weiss, Y. (eds.) ECCV 2018. LNCS, vol. 11207, pp. 36–54. Springer, Cham (2018). https://doi.org/10.1007/978-3-030-01219-9_3
13. Gao, R., Grauman, K.: Co-separating sounds of visual objects. In: Proceedings of the IEEE/CVF International Conference on Computer Vision, pp. 3879–3888 (2019)
14. Gao, R., Grauman, K.: VisualVoice: audio-visual speech separation with cross-modal consistency. In: Proceedings of the IEEE International Conference on Computer Vision (CVPR), pp. 15490–15500 (2021)
15. Gemmeke, J.F., et al.: Audio set: an ontology and human-labeled dataset for audio events. In: Proceedings of the IEEE International Conference on Acoustics, Speech, and Signal Processing (ICASSP), pp. 776–780 (2017)
16. Gfeller, B., Roblek, D., Tagliasacchi, M.: One-shot conditional audio filtering of arbitrary sounds. In: Proceedings of the IEEE International Conference on Acoustics, Speech, and Signal Processing (ICASSP), pp. 501–505 (2021)
17. Google Research Sound Separation Team: AudioScope YFCC100M clip lists (2021). https://github.com/google-research/sound-separation/tree/master/datasets/audioscope
18. Google Research Sound Separation Team: YFCC100M clip lists (2021). https://github.com/google-research/sound-separation/tree/master/datasets/yfcc100m
19. Hershey, J., Movellan, J.: Audio vision: using audio-visual synchrony to locate sounds. Adv. Neural. Inf. Process. Syst. **12**, 813–819 (1999)
20. Hershey, J.R., Casey, M.: Audio-visual sound separation via hidden Markov models. In: Advances in Neural Information Processing Systems, pp. 1173–1180 (2002)
21. Howard, A.G., et al.: Mobilenets: efficient convolutional neural networks for mobile vision applications. arXiv preprint arXiv:1704.04861 (2017)
22. Jansen, A., et al.: Coincidence, categorization, and consolidation: learning to recognize sounds with minimal supervision. In: ICASSP 2020–2020 IEEE International Conference on Acoustics, Speech and Signal Processing (ICASSP), pp. 121–125 (2020)
23. Kavalerov, I., et al.: Universal sound separation. In: Proceedings of the IEEE Workshop on Applications of Signal Processing to Audio and Acoustics (WASPAA), pp. 175–179 (2019)
24. Kilgour, K., Gfeller, B., Huang, Q., Jansen, A., Wisdom, S., Tagliasacchi, M.: Text-driven separation of arbitrary sounds. In: Proceedings of the Interspeech (2022)
25. Kingma, D.P., Ba, J.: Adam: A method for stochastic optimization. In: Proc. International Conference on Learning Representations (ICLR) (2015)
26. Korbar, B., Tran, D., Torresani, L.: Cooperative learning of audio and video models from self-supervised synchronization. In: Advances in Neural Information Processing Systems. pp. 7763–7774 (2018)
27. Le Roux, J., Wisdom, S., Erdogan, H., R. Hershey, J.: SDR-half-baked or well done? In: Proceedings of the IEEE International Conference on Acoustics, Speech, and Signal Processing (ICASSP), pp. 626–630 (2019)
28. Lee, J., Chung, S.W., Kim, S., Kang, H.G., Sohn, K.: Looking into your speech: Learning cross-modal affinity for audio-visual speech separation. In: Proceedings of the IEEE International Conference on Computer Vision (CVPR), pp. 1336–1345 (2021)

29. Lin, Y.B., Tseng, H.Y., Lee, H.Y., Lin, Y.Y., Yang, M.H.: Unsupervised sound localization via iterative contrastive learning. arXiv preprint arXiv:2104.00315 (2021)
30. Liu, X., Liu, H., Kong, Q., Mei, X., Zhao, J., Huang, Q., Plumbley, M.D., Wang, W.: Separate what you describe: language-queried audio source separation. In: Proceedings of the Interspeech (2022)
31. Ochiai, T., Delcroix, M., Koizumi, Y., Ito, H., Kinoshita, K., Araki, S.: Listen to What You Want: Neural Network-Based Universal Sound Selector. In: Proceedings of the Interspeech, pp. 1441–1445 (2020)
32. Owens, A., Efros, A.A.: Audio-visual scene analysis with self-supervised multisensory features. In: Ferrari, V., Hebert, M., Sminchisescu, C., Weiss, Y. (eds.) ECCV 2018. LNCS, vol. 11210, pp. 639–658. Springer, Cham (2018). https://doi.org/10.1007/978-3-030-01231-1_39
33. Pishdadian, F., Wichern, G., Le Roux, J.: Finding strength in weakness: learning to separate sounds with weak supervision. IEEE/ACM Trans. Audio Speech Lang. Process. **28**, 2386–2399 (2020)
34. Rahman, T., Sigal, L.: Weakly-supervised audio-visual sound source detection and separation. In: Proceedings of the IEEE International Conference on Multimedia and Expo (ICME), pp. 1–6 (2021)
35. Rouditchenko, A., Zhao, H., Gan, C., McDermott, J., Torralba, A.: Self-supervised audio-visual co-segmentation. In: ICASSP 2019–2019 IEEE International Conference on Acoustics, Speech and Signal Processing (ICASSP), pp. 2357–2361 (2019)
36. Seetharaman, P., Wichern, G., Le Roux, J., Pardo, B.: Bootstrapping single-channel source separation via unsupervised spatial clustering on stereo mixtures. In: Proceedings of the IEEE International Conference on Acoustics, Speech, and Signal Processing (ICASSP), pp. 356–360 (2019)
37. Srivastava, N., Hinton, G., Krizhevsky, A., Sutskever, I., Salakhutdinov, R.: Dropout: a simple way to prevent neural networks from overfitting. J. Mach. Learn. Res. **15**(1), 1929–1958 (2014)
38. Thomee, B., et al.: Yfcc100m: the new data in multimedia research. Commun. ACM **59**(2), 64–73 (2016)
39. Owens, A., Efros, A.A.: Audio-visual scene analysis with self-supervised multisensory features. In: Ferrari, V., Hebert, M., Sminchisescu, C., Weiss, Y. (eds.) Unified multisensory perception: Weakly-supervised audio-visual video parsing. LNCS, vol. 11210, pp. 639–658. Springer, Cham (2018). https://doi.org/10.1007/978-3-030-01231-1_39
40. Tzinis, E., Venkataramani, S., Smaragdis, P.: Unsupervised deep clustering for source separation: direct learning from mixtures using spatial information. In: Proceedings of the IEEE International Conference on Acoustics, Speech, and Signal Processing (ICASSP), pp. 81–85 (2019)
41. Tzinis, E., Venkataramani, S., Wang, Z., Subakan, C., Smaragdis, P.: Two-step sound source separation: training on learned latent targets. In: ICASSP 2020–2020 IEEE International Conference on Acoustics, Speech and Signal Processing (ICASSP), pp. 31–35 (2020)
42. Tzinis, E., Wisdom, S., Hershey, J.R., Jansen, A., Ellis, D.P.W.: Improving universal sound separation using sound classification. In: Proceedings of the IEEE International Conference on Acoustics, Speech, and Signal Processing (ICASSP), pp. 96–100 (2020)
43. Tzinis, E., et al.: Into the wild with audioscope: unsupervised audio-visual separation of on-screen sounds. In: Proceedings of the International Conference on Learning Representations (ICLR) (2021)

44. Vaswani, A., Shazeer, N., Parmar, N., Uszkoreit, J., Jones, L., Gomez, A.N., Kaiser, L, Polosukhin, I.: Attention is all you need. Adv. Neural. Inf. Process. Syst. **30**, 5998–6008 (2017)
45. Wang, Q., et al.: Voicefilter: targeted voice separation by speaker-conditioned spectrogram masking. In: Proceedings of the Interspeech, pp. 2728–2732 (2019)
46. Wisdom, S., et al.: Differentiable consistency constraints for improved deep speech enhancement. In: Proceedings of the IEEE International Conference on Acoustics, Speech, and Signal Processing (ICASSP), pp. 900–904 (2019)
47. Wisdom, S., Tzinis, E., Erdogan, H., Weiss, R.J., Wilson, K., Hershey, J.R.: Unsupervised sound separation using mixtures of mixtures. In: Advances in Neural Information Processing Systems, vol. 33, pp. 3846–3857 (2020)
48. Wu, Y., Zhu, L., Yan, Y., Yang, Y.: Dual attention matching for audio-visual event localization. In: Proceedings of the IEEE International Conference on Computer Vision (CVPR), pp. 6292–6300 (2019)
49. Yu, J., Cheng, Y., Feng, R.: Mpn: multimodal parallel network for audio-visual event localization. In: Proceedings of the IEEE International Conference on Multimedia and Expo (ICME), pp. 1–6 (2021)
50. Zhang, Y., et al.: Vidtr: video transformer without convolutions. In: Proceedings of the IEEE International Conference on Computer Vision (ICCV), pp. 13577–13587 (2021)
51. Zhu, L., Rahtu, E.: Visually guided sound source separation and localization using self-supervised motion representations. In: Proceedings of the IEEE/CVF Winter Conference on Applications of Computer Vision (WACV), pp. 1289–1299 (2022)

Audio–Visual Segmentation

Jinxing Zhou[1,2], Jianyuan Wang[2,3], Jiayi Zhang[2,4], Weixuan Sun[2,3],
Jing Zhang[3], Stan Birchfield[5], Dan Guo[1], Lingpeng Kong[6,7], Meng Wang[1(✉)],
and Yiran Zhong[2,7(✉)]

[1] Hefei University of Technology, Hefei, China
eric.mengwang@gmail.com
[2] SenseTime Research, Hangzhou, China
zhongyiran@gmail.com
[3] Australian National University, Canberra, Australia
[4] Beihang University, Beijing, China
[5] NVIDIA, Santa Clara, USA
[6] The University of Hong Kong, Pok Fu Lam, Hong Kong
[7] Shanghai Artificial Intelligence Laboratory, Shanghai, China

Abstract. We propose to explore a new problem called audio-visual segmentation (AVS), in which the goal is to output a pixel-level map of the object(s) that produce sound at the time of the image frame. To facilitate this research, we construct the first audio-visual segmentation benchmark (AVSBench), providing pixel-wise annotations for the sounding objects in audible videos. Two settings are studied with this benchmark: 1) semi-supervised audio-visual segmentation with a single sound source and 2) fully-supervised audio-visual segmentation with multiple sound sources. To deal with the AVS problem, we propose a new method that uses a temporal pixel-wise audio-visual interaction module to inject audio semantics as guidance for the visual segmentation process. We also design a regularization loss to encourage the audio-visual mapping during training. Quantitative and qualitative experiments on the AVS-Bench compare our approach to several existing methods from related tasks, demonstrating that the proposed method is promising for building a bridge between the audio and pixel-wise visual semantics. Code is available at https://github.com/OpenNLPLab/AVSBench.

Keywords: Audio-visual segmentation · Benchmarking · AVSBench

1 Introduction

A human can classify an object not only from its visual appearance but also from the sound it makes. For example, when we hear a dog bark or a siren wail,

---

J. Zhou and J. Wang—Equal contribution. This work is done when Jinxing Zhou is an intern at SenseTime Research.

Supplementary Information The online version contains supplementary material available at https://doi.org/10.1007/978-3-031-19836-6_22.

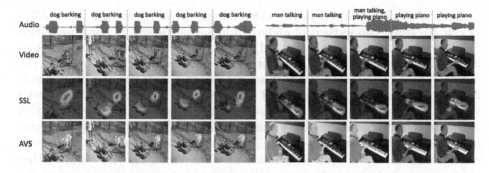

Fig. 1. Comparison of the proposed AVS task with the SSL task. Sound source localization (SSL) estimates a rough location of the sounding objects in the visual frame, at a patch level. We propose AVS to estimate pixel-wise segmentation masks for all the sounding objects, no matter the number of visible sounding objects.

we know the sound is from a dog or ambulance, respectively. Such observations confirm that the audio and visual information complement each other.

To date, researchers have approached this problem of audio-visual classification from somewhat simplified scenarios. Some researchers have investigated audio-visual correspondence (AVC) [2–4] problem, which aims to determine whether an audio signal and a visual image describe the same scene. AVC is based on the phenomenon that these two signals usually occur simultaneously, *e.g.*, a barking dog and a humming car. Others studied audio-visual event localization (AVEL) [9,20,22,30,31,38,42,44,45,51], which classifies the segments of a video into the pre-defined event labels. Similarly, some people have also explored audio-visual video parsing (AVVP) [21,37,41,46], whose goal is to divide a video into several events and classify them as audible, visible, or both. Due to a lack of pixel-level annotations, all these scenarios are restricted to the frame/temporal level, thus reducing the problem to that of audible image classification.

A related problem, known as sound source localization (SSL), aims to locate the visual regions within the frames that correspond to the sound [2,3,5,8,17,29]. Compared to AVC/AVEL/AVVP, the problem of SSL seeks patch-level scene understanding, *i.e.*, the results are usually presented by a heat map that is obtained either by visualizing the similarity matrix of the audio feature and the visual feature map, or by class activation mapping (CAM) [50]. It does not consider the actual shape of the sounding objects.

In this paper, we propose the pixel-level audio-visual segmentation (AVS) problem, which requires the network to densely predict whether each pixel corresponds to the given audio, so that a mask of the sounding object(s) is generated. Figure 1 illustrates the differences between AVS and SSL. The AVS task is more challenging than previous tasks as it requires the network to not only locate the audible frames but also delineate the shape of the sounding objects.

To facilitate this research, we propose AVSBench, the first pixel-level audio-visual segmentation benchmark that provides ground truth labels for sounding objects. We divide our AVSBench dataset into two subsets, depending on the number of sounding objects in the video (single- or multi-source). With AVS-Bench, we study two settings of audio-visual segmentation: 1) semi-supervised Single Sound Source Segmentation (S4), and 2) fully-supervised Multiple Sound Source Segmentation (MS3). For both settings, the goal is to segment the object(s) from the visual frames that are producing sounds. We test six methods from related tasks on AVSBench and provide a new AVS method as a strong baseline. The latter utilizes a standard encoder-decoder architecture but with a new temporal pixel-wise audio-visual interaction (TPAVI) module to better introduce the audio semantics for guiding visual segmentation. We also propose a loss function to utilize the correlation of audio-visual signals, which further enhances segmentation performance. We conduct extensive experiments on the AVSBench dataset to verify the benefits of considering audio signals for visual segmentation, and the effectiveness of our proposed approach.

2   Related Work

Sound Source Localization (SSL). The most related problem to ours is SSL, which aims to locate the regions in the visual frames that make sounds. Here we focus on SSL with multiple sources, which requires to accurately localize the true sound maker when there are multiple potential candidates [1,17,18,29]. As a pioneer, Hu *et al.* [17] divide the audio and visual features into multiple cluster centers and take the center distance as a supervision signal to rank the paired audio-visual information. Some methods adopt a two-stage strategy that first learn some prior knowledge of audio-visual correspondence from single sound source scenes, and then use that for multiple sound sources localization [18,29]. Rouditchenko *et al.* [33] tackle this problem by disentangling category concepts in the neural networks. This method is actually more related to the task of sound source separation [11,12,48,49] and shows sub-optimal performance regarding visual localization. It is worth noting that these SSL methods cannot clearly delineate the shape of the objects. Rather, the location map is computed by the audio-visual similarity matrix from a low resolution [2,3,5,8,28,36]. To overcome these limitations, this paper provides an audio-visual segmentation dataset with pixel-level ground truth to enable more accurate segmentation predictions.

Audio-Visual Dataset. To the best of our knowledge, there are no publicly available datasets that provide segmentation masks for the sounding visual objects with audio signals. Here we briefly introduce the popular datasets in the audio-visual community. For example, the AVE [38] and LLP [37] datasets are respectively collected for audio-visual event localization and video parsing tasks. They only have category annotations for video frames, and hence cannot be used for pixel-level segmentation. For sound source localization problem, researchers usually use the Flickr-SoundNet [36] and VGG-SS [5] datasets, where the videos are sampled from the large-scale Flickr [4] and VGGSound [6] datasets, respectively. The authors provide bounding boxes to outline the location of the target sound source, which could serve as patch-level supervision. However, this still inevitably suffers from incorrect evaluation results since the sounding objects

Table 1. AVSBench statistics. The videos are split into train/valid/test. The asterisk (*) indicates that, for Single-source training, one annotation per video is provided; all others contain 5 annotations per video. (Since there are 5 clips per video, this is 1 annotation per clip.) Together, these yield the total annotated frames.

Subset	Classes	Videos	Train/valid/test	Annotated frames
Single-source	23	4,932	3,452*/740/740	10,852
Multi-sources	23	424	296/64/64	2,120

Table 2. Existing audio-visual dataset statistics. Each benchmark is shown with the number of videos and the *annotated* frames. The final column indicates whether the frames are labeled by category, bounding boxes, or pixel-level masks.

Benchmark	Videos	Frames	Classes	Types	Annotations
AVE [38]	4,143	41,430	28	video	category
LLP [37]	11,849	11,849	25	video	category
Flickr-SoundNet [36]	5,000	5,000	50	image	bbox
VGG-SS [5]	5,158	5,158	220	image	bbox
AVSBench (ours)	5,356	12,972	23	video	pixel

are usually irregular in shape and some regions within the bounding box actually do not belong to the real sound source. This is a reason why current sound source localization methods can only roughly locate sounding objects but cannot learn their accurate shapes, which inhibits the mapping from audio signals to fine-grained visual cues.

3   The AVSBench

3.1   Dataset Statistics

AVSBench is designed for pixel-level audio-visual segmentation. We collected the videos using the techniques introduced in VGGSound [6] to ensure that the audio and visual clips correspond to the intended semantics. AVSBench contains two subsets—Single-source and Multi-sources—depending on the number of sounding objects. All videos were downloaded from YouTube with the *Creative Commons* license, and each video was trimmed to 5 seconds. The Single-source subset contains $4,932$ videos over 23 categories, covering sounds from humans, animals, vehicles, and musical instruments. We provide the category names and the video number for each category in the supplemental material. For the Multi-sources subset, we picked the videos that contain multiple sounding objects, *e.g.*, a video of baby laughing, man speaking, and then woman singing. To be specific, we randomly chose two or three category names from the Single-source subset as keywords to search for online videos, then manually filtered out videos to ensure 1) each video has multiple sound sources, 2) the sounding objects are

(a) Video examples in Single-source subset   (b) Video examples in Multiple-sources subset

Fig. 2. AVSBench samples. The AVSBench dataset contains the Single-source subset (LEFT) and Multi-sources subset (RIGHT). Each video is divided into 5 clips, as shown. Annotated clips are indicated by brown framing rectangles; the name of sounding objects is indicated by red text. Note that for Single-source training set, only the first frame of each video is annotated, whereas 5 frames are annotated for all other sets.

visible, and 3) there is no deceptive sound, *e.g.*, canned laughter. In total, this process yielded 424 videos for the Multi-sources subset, out of more than six thousand candidates. The ratio of train/validation/test split percentages are set as 70/15/15 for both subsets, as shown in Table 1. Several video examples are visualized in Fig. 2, where the red text indicates the name of sounding objects.

In addition, we make a comparison between AVSBench with other popular audio-visual benchmarks in Table 2. The AVE [38] dataset contains 4,143 videos covering 28 event categories. The LLP [37] dataset consists of 11,849 YouTube video clips spanning with 25 categories, collected from AudioSet [13]. Both the AVE and LLP datasets are labelled at a frame level, through audio-visual event boundaries. Meanwhile, the Flickr-SoundNet [36] dataset and VGG-SS [5] dataset are proposed for sound source localization (SSL), labelled at a patch level through bounding boxes. In contrast, our AVSBench contains 5,356 videos with 12,972 pixel-wise annotated frames. The benchmark is designed to facilitate the research on fine-grained audio-visual segmentation. Additionally, it provides accurate ground truth for SSL, which could help the training of SSL methods and serve as an evaluation benchmark for that problem as well.

3.2   Annotation

We divide each 5-second video into five equal 1-second clips, and we provide manual pixel-level annotations for the last frame of each clip. For this sampled frame, the ground truth label is a binary mask indicating the pixels of sounding objects, according to the audio at the corresponding time. For example, in the

Multi-sources subset, even though a dancing person shows drastic movement spatially, it would not be labelled as long as no sound was made. In clips where objects do not make sound, the object should not be masked, *e.g.*, the *piano* in the first two clips of the last row of Fig. 2b. Similarly, when more than one object emits sound, all the emitting objects are annotated, *e.g.*, the guitar and ukulele in the first row in Fig. 2b. Also, when the sounding objects in the video are dynamically changing, the difficulty is further increased, *e.g.*, the second, third, and fourth rows in Fig. 2b. Currently, for large-scale objects, we only annotate their most representative parts. For example, we label the keyboard of pianos because it is sufficiently recognizable, while the cabinet part is often too varied.

For the videos in the training split of Single-source, we only annotate the first frame (with the assumption that the information from one-shot annotation is sufficient, as the Single-source subset has a single and consistent sounding object over time). This assumption is verified by the quantitative experimental results shown in Table 3. For the more challenging Multi-sources subset, all clips are annotated for training, since the sounding objects may change over time. Note that for validation and test splits, all clips are annotated, as shown in Table 1.

3.3   Two Benchmark Settings

We provide two benchmark settings for our AVSBench: the semi-supervised Single Sound Source Segmentation (S4) and the fully supervised Multiple Sound Source Segmentation (MS3). For ease of expression, we denote the video sequence as S, which consists of T non-overlapping yet continuous clips $\{S_t^v, S_t^a\}_{t=1}^T$, where S^v and S^a are the visual and audio components, and $T = 5$. In practice, we extract the video frame at the end of each second. **Semi-supervised S4** corresponds to the Single-source subset. It is termed as semi-supervised because only part of the ground truth is given during training (*i.e.*, the first sampled frame of the videos) but all the video frames require a prediction during evaluation. We denote the pixel-wise label as $Y_{t=1}^s \in \mathbb{R}^{H \times W}$, where H and W are the frame height and width, respectively. $Y_{t=1}^s$ is a binary matrix where 1 indicates sounding objects while 0 corresponds to background or silent objects. **Fully-supervised MS3** deals with the Multi-sources subset, where the labels of all five frames of each video are available for training. The ground truth is denoted as $\{Y_t^m\}_{t=1}^T$, where $Y_t^m \in \mathbb{R}^{H \times W}$ is the binary label for the t-th video clip.

The goal for both settings is to correctly segment the sounding object(s) for each video clip with the audio and visual cues, *i.e.*, S^a and S^v. Generally, S^a is expected to indicate the target object, while S^v provides information for fine-grained segmentation. The predictions are denoted as $\{M_t\}_{t=1}^T$, $M_t \in \mathbb{R}^{H \times W}$.

4   A Baseline

We propose a new baseline method for the pixel-level audio-visual segmentation (AVS) task as shown in Fig. 3. We use the same framework in both semi- and fully-supervised settings. Following the convention of semantic segmentation methods [24,32,39,43], our method adopts an encoder–decoder architecture.

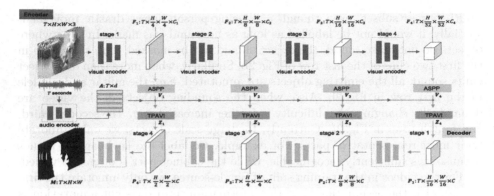

Fig. 3. Overview of the Baseline, which follows a hierarchical Encoder-Decoder pipeline. The *encoder* takes the video frames and the entire audio clip as inputs, and outputs visual and audio features, respectively denoted as F_i and A. The visual feature map F_i at each stage is further sent to the ASPP [7] module and then our TPAVI module (introduced in Sect. 4). ASPP provides different receptive fields for recognizing visual objects, while TPAVI focuses on the temporal pixel-wise audio-visual interaction. The *decoder* progressively enlarges the fused feature maps by four stages and finally generates the output mask M for sounding objects.

The Encoder: We extract audio and visual features independently. Given an audio clip S^a, we first process it to a spectrogram via the short-time Fourier transform, and then send it to a convolutional neural network, VGGish [16]. We use the weights that are pretrained on AudioSet [13] to extract audio features $A \in \mathbb{R}^{T \times d}$, where $d = 128$ is the feature dimension. For a video frame S^v, we extract visual features with popular convolution-based or vision transformer-based backbones. We try both two options in the experiments and they show similar performance trends. These backbones produce hierarchical visual feature maps during the encoding process, as shown in Fig. 3. We denote the features as $F_i \in \mathbb{R}^{T \times h_i \times w_i \times C_i}$, where $(h_i, w_i) = (H, W)/2^{i+1}$, $i = 1, \dots, n$. The number of levels is set to $n = 4$ in all experiments.

Cross-Modal Fusion: We use Atrous Spatial Pyramid Pooling (ASPP) modules [7] to further post-process the visual features F_i to $V_i \in \mathbb{R}^{T \times h_i \times w_i \times C}$, where $C = 256$. These modules employ multiple parallel filters with different rates and hence help to recognize visual objects with different receptive fields, *e.g.*, different sized moving objects.

Then, we consider introducing the audio information to build the audio-visual mapping to assist with identifying the sounding object. This is particularly essential for the MS3 setting where there are multiple dynamic sound sources. Our intuition is that, although the auditory and visual signals of the sound sources may not appear simultaneously, they usually exist in more than one video frame. Therefore, integrating the audio and visual signals of the whole video should be beneficial. Motivated by [40] that uses the non-local block to encode space-time relation, we adopt a similar module to encode the temporal pixel-wise audio-visual interaction (TPAVI). The current visual feature map V_i and the audio feature A of the entire video are sent into the TPAVI module. Specifically, the audio feature A is first transformed to a feature space with the same dimension as the visual feature V_i, by a linear layer. Then it is spatially duplicated $h_i w_i$ times and reshaped to the same size as V_i. We denote such processed audio feature as $\hat{A}$. Next, it is expected to find those pixels of visual feature map V_i that have a high response to the audio counterpart $\hat{A}$ through the entire video.

Such an audio-visual interaction can be measured by dot-product, then the updated feature maps Z_i at the i-th stage can be computed as,

$$Z_i = V_i + \mu(\alpha_i \, g(V_i)), \text{ where } \alpha_i = \frac{\theta(V_i) \, \phi(\hat{A})^{\top}}{N} \qquad (1)$$

where θ, ϕ, g, and μ are $1 \times 1 \times 1$ convolutions, $N = T \times h_i \times w_i$ is a normalization factor, α_i denotes the audio-visual similarity, and $Z_i \in \mathbb{R}^{T \times h_i \times w_i \times C}$. Each visual pixel interacts with all the audios through the TPAVI module. We provide a visualization of the audio-visual attention in TPAVI later in Fig. 6, which shows a similar "appearance" to the prediction of SSL methods because it constructs a pixel to audio mapping.

The Decoder: We adopt the decoder of Panoptic-FPN [19] in this work for its flexibility and effectiveness, though any valid decoder architecture could be used. In short, at the j-th stage, where $j = 2, 3, 4$, both the outputs from stage Z_{5-j} and the last stage Z_{6-j} of the encoder are utilized for the decoding process. The decoded features are then upsampled to the next stage. The final output of the decoder is $M \in \mathbb{R}^{T \times H \times W}$, activated by *sigmoid*.

Objective Function: Given the prediction M and the pixel-wise label Y, we adapt the binary cross entropy (BCE) loss as the main supervision function. Besides, we use an additional regularization term $\mathcal{L}_{\text{AVM}}$ to force the audio-visual mapping. Specifically, we use the KullbackLeibler (KL) divergence to ensure the masked visual features have similar distributions with the corresponding audio features. In other words, if the audio features of some frames are close in feature space, the corresponding sounding objects are expected to be close in feature space. The total objective function $\mathcal{L}$ can be computed as follows:

$$\mathcal{L} = \text{BCE}(M, Y) + \lambda \mathcal{L}_{\text{AVM}}(M, Z, A), \qquad (2)$$

$$\mathcal{L}_{\text{AVM}} = \text{KL}(avg \, (\sum_{i=1}^{n} M_i \odot Z_i), A_i), \qquad (3)$$

where λ is a balance weight, $\odot$ denotes element-wise multiplication, and avg denotes the average pooling operation. At each stage, we down-sample the prediction M to M_i via average pooling to have the same shape as Z_i. The vector A_i is a linear transformation of A that has the same feature dimension with Z_i. For the semi-supervised S4 setting, we found that the audio-visual regularization loss does not help, so we set $\lambda = 0$ in this setting.

5   Experimental Results

5.1   Implementation Details

We conduct training and evaluation on the proposed AVSBench dataset, with both convolution-based and transformer-based backbones, ResNet-50 [15] and Pyramid Vision Transformer (PVT-v2) [39]. The backbones have been pretrained on the ImageNet [34] dataset. All the video frames are resized to the shape of 224×224. The channel sizes of the four stages are $C_{1:4} = [256, 512, 1024, 2048]$ and $C_{1:4} = [64, 128, 320, 512]$ for ResNet-50 and PVT-v2, respectively. The channel size of the ASPP module is set to $C = 256$. We use the VGGish model to extract audio features, a VGG-like network [16] pretrained on the AudioSet [13] dataset. The audio signals are converted to one-second splits as the network inputs. We use the Adam optimizer with a learning rate of 1e-4 for training. The batch size is set to 4 and the number of training epochs are 15 and 30 respectively for the semi-supervised S4 and the fully-supervised MS3 settings. The λ in Eq. (2) is empirically set to 0.5.

Table 3. Comparison with methods from related tasks. Results of mIoU (%) and F-score under both S4 and MS3 settings are reported.

Metric	Setting	SSL		VOS		SOD		AVS (ours)	
		LVS [5]	MSSL [29]	3DC [26]	SST [10]	iGAN [27]	LGVT [47]	ResNet50	PVT-v2
mIoU	S4	37.94	44.89	57.10	66.29	61.59	74.94	72.79	**78.74**
	MS3	29.45	26.13	36.92	42.57	42.89	40.71	47.88	**54.00**
F-score	S4	.510	.663	.759	.801	.778	.873	.848	**.879**
	MS3	.330	.363	.503	.572	.544	.593	.578	**.645**

5.2   Comparison with Methods from Related Tasks

We compare our baseline framework with the methods from three related tasks, including sound source localization (SSL), video object segmentation (VOS), and salient object detection (SOD). For each task, we report the results of two methods on our AVSBench benchmark, i.e., LVS [5] and MSSL [29] for SSL, 3DC [26] and SST [10] for VOS, iGAN [27] and LGVT [47] for SOD. We select these methods as they are the SOTA in their fields: 1) *LVS* uses the background and the most confident regions of sounding objects to design a contrastive loss for audio-visual representation learning. The localization map is obtained by computing the audio-visual similarity. 2) *MSSL* is a two-stage method for multiple sound source localization and the localization map is obtained by Grad-CAM [35]. 3) *3DC* adopts an architecture that is fully constructed by powerful 3D convolutions to encode video frames and predict segmentation masks. 4) *SST* introduces a transformer architecture to achieve sparse attention of the features in the spatiotemporal domain. 5) *iGAN* is a ResNet-based generative model for saliency detection, considering the inherent uncertainty of saliency detection. 6) *LGVT* is a saliency detection method based on Swin transformer [23], whose long-range dependency modeling ability leads to a better global context modeling. We adopt the architecture of these methods and fit them to our semi-supervised S4 and fully-supervised MS3 settings. For a fair comparison, the backbones of these methods are all pretrained on the ImageNet [34].

Table 4. Impact of audio signal and TPAVI. Results (mIoU) of AVS with and without the TPAVI module. The middle row indicates directly adding the audio and visual features, which already improves performance under the MS3 setting. The TPAVI module further enhances the results over all settings and backbones.

AVS method	S4		MS3	
	ResNet50	PVT-v2	ResNet50	PVT-v2
Without TPAVI	70.12	77.76	43.56	48.21
With A⊕V	70.54	77.65	45.69	51.55
With TPAVI	**72.79**	**78.74**	**46.64**	**53.06**

The quantitative results are shown in Table 3, with Mean Intersection over Union (mIoU) and F-score[1] as the evaluation metrics. There is a substantial gap between the results of SSL methods and those of our baseline, mainly because the SSL methods cannot provide pixel-level prediction. Also, our baseline framework shows a consistent superiority to the VOS and SOD methods in both settings. It is worth noting that the state-of-the-art SOD method LGVT [47] slightly outperforms our ResNet50-based baseline on the Single-source set (74.94% mIoU *vs.* 72.79% mIoU), mainly because LGVT uses the strong Swin Transformer backbone [23]. However, when it comes to the Multi-sources setting, the performance of LGVT is obviously worse than that of our ResNet50-based baseline (40.71% mIoU *vs.* 47.88% mIoU). This is because the SOD method relies on the dataset prior, and cannot handle the situations where sounding objects change but visual contents remain the same (further discussed in the supplementary material). Instead, the audio signals guide our method to identify which object to segment, leading to better performance. Moreover, if also using a transformer-based backbone, our method is stronger than LGVT in both settings. Besides, we notice that although SSL methods utilize both the audio and visual signals, they cannot match the performance of VOS or SOD methods that only use visual frames. It indicates the significance of pixel-wise scene understanding. The proposed AVS baselines achieve satisfactory performance under the semi-supervised S4 setting (around 70% mIoU), which verifies that one-shot annotation is sufficient for single-source cases. Some qualitative examples are provided in our supplementary material to compare the proposed baseline with these methods.

---

[1] F-score considers both the precision and recall: $F_\beta = \frac{(1+\beta^2) \times \text{precision} \times \text{recall}}{\beta^2 \times \text{precision} + \text{recall}}$, where β^2 is set to 0.3 in our experiments.

5.3   Ablation Study

Impact of Audio Signal and TPAVI. As introduced in Sect. 4, the TPAVI module is designed to formulate the audio-visual interactions from a temporal and pixel-wise level, introducing the audio information to explore the visual segmentation. We verify its impact in Table 4. Two rows show the proposed AVS method with or without the TPAVI module, while "A⊕V" indicates directly adding the audio to visual features. It will be noticed that adding the audio features to the visual ones does not result in a clear difference under the S4 setting, but lead to a distinct gain under the MS3 setting. This is consistent with our hypothesis that audio is especially beneficial to samples with multiple sound sources, because the audio signals can guide which object(s) to segment. Furthermore, with TPAVI, each visual pixel hears the current sound and the sounds at other times, while simultaneously interacting with other pixels. The pixels with high similarity to the same sound are more likely to belong to one object. TPAVI helps further enhance the performance over various settings and backbones, e.g., 72.79% vs. 70.54% when using ResNet50 as the backbone under the S4 setting, and 53.06% vs. 51.55% if using PVT-v2 under the MS3 setting. Additionally, it is worth noting that the convolution blocks in the TPAVI module allow to project the input visual and audio features to the latent spaces that are suitable for attention computation. For instance, under the S4 setting and using ResNet50, if abandoning the four convolution blocks (θ, ϕ, g, and μ) in the TPAVI module, the mIoU will significantly drop from 72.79% to 59.21%.

We also visualize some qualitative examples to reflect the impact of TPAVI. As shown in Fig. 4, the AVS method with TPAVI depicts the shape of sounding object better, e.g., the *guitar* in the left video, while it can only segment several parts of the guitar without TPAVI. Such benefit can also be observed in MS3 setting, as shown in Fig. 5, the model enables to ignore those pixels of *human*

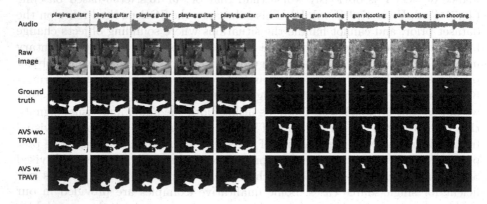

Fig. 4. Qualitative results under the semi-supervised S4 setting. Two benefits are noticed by introducing the audio signal (TPAVI): 1) learning the shape of the sounding object, e.g., *guitar* in the video (LEFT); 2) segmenting according to the correct sound source, e.g., the *gun* rather than the *man* (RIGHT).

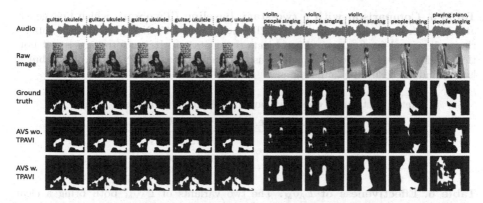

Fig. 5. Qualitative results under the fully-supervised MS3 setting. Note that AVS with TPAVI uses audio information to perform better in terms of 1) filtering out the distracting visual pixels that do not correspond to the audio, *i.e.*, the *human hands* (LEFT); 2) segmenting the correct sound source in the visual frames that matches the audio more accurately, *i.e.*, the *singing person* (RIGHT).

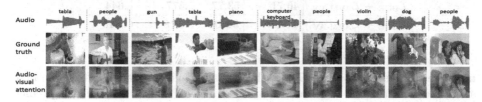

Fig. 6. Audio-Visual attention maps from the fourth stage TPAVI. A brighter color indicates a higher response. Such heatmaps are adopted as the final results for the SSL task, but just the intermediate output of the TPAVI module. TPAVI helps the model focus more on the visual regions that are semantic-corresponding to the audio.

hands with TPAVI. More importantly, with TPAVI, the model is able to segment the correct sounding object and ignore the potential sound sources which actually do not make sounds, *e.g.*, the *man* on the right of Fig. 4. Also, the "AVS w. TPAVI" has stronger ability to capture multiple sound sources. As shown on the right of Fig. 5, the *person* who is singing is mainly segmented with TPAVI but is almost lost without TPAVI.

Besides, we also visualize the audio-visual attention matrices to explore what happens in the cross-modal fusion process of TPAVI. As shown in Fig. 6, the high response area basically overlaps the region of sounding objects. The attention matrix is obtained from α_i in Eq. (1) of the fourth stage TPAVI. This is visually similar to the localization heatmap of these SSL methods, but only the intermediate result in our AVS method. It suggests that TPAVI builds a mapping from the visual pixels to the audio signals, which is semantically consistent.

Comparison with a Two-Stage Baseline. The AVS task can also be tackled by two stages. In the first stage, an off-the-shelf segmentation model extracts

Table 5. Comparison with a two-stage baseline (TwoSep), which first generates instance segmentation maps by off-the-shelf Mask R-CNN [14] and then combines the audio signal for final sounding objects segmentation. Its performance is not bottlenecked by the segmentation quality (using different Mask-RCNN backbones) but is largely influenced by the audio signal.

Metric	Setting	TwoSep wo. audio		TwoSep w. audio		Ours
		Res50	ResNeXt101	Res50	ResNeXt101	-
mIoU	S4	69.56	69.98	71.73	71.81	**78.74**
	MS3	47.25	47.40	50.32	50.22	**54.00**

Table 6. Effectiveness of $\mathcal{L}_{AVM}$. The two variants of $\mathcal{L}_{AVM}$ both bring a clear performance gain compared with only using a standard BCE loss.

Objective function	MS3 (mIoU)		MS3 (F-score)	
	ResNet50	PVT-v2	ResNet50	PVT-v2
$\mathcal{L}_{BCE}$	46.64	53.06	.558	.626
$\mathcal{L}_{BCE} + \mathcal{L}_{AVM\text{-}VV}$	46.71	53.77	.577	.644
$\mathcal{L}_{BCE} + \mathcal{L}_{AVM\text{-}AV}$	**47.88**	**54.00**	**.578**	**.645**

instance segmentation maps. Then, the maps and visual features from the first stage are concatenated with audios, and fed into a PVT-v2 structure to predict the final results. We denote this method as TwoSep, and the results are shown in Table 5. It indicates the AVS task is *Not* bottlenecked by the segmentation quality, as the final performance is almost unchanged with a much stronger Mask R-CNN (backbone from ResNet50 to powerful ResNeXt101), *e.g.*, mIoU 50.32% *vs.* 50.22% in MS3 setting. Instead, without or with audios would largely affect the performance, *e.g.*, mIoU 47.25% *vs.* 50.32%. This again reflects the positive impact of audio signals, especially in the MS3 setting.

Effectiveness of $\mathcal{L}_{AVM}$. We expect that constructing the mapping between audio and visual features will enhance the network's ability to identify the correct objects. Therefore, we propose a $\mathcal{L}_{AVM}$ loss to introduce a soft constraint. We only apply $\mathcal{L}_{AVM}$ in the fully-supervised MS3 setting because the change of sounding objects only happens there. As shown in Table 6, we explore two variants of the $\mathcal{L}_{AVM}$ loss. $\mathcal{L}_{AVM\text{-}AV}$ is the one introduced in Eq. (3). It encourages the visual features masked by the segmentation result to be consistent with the corresponding audio features in a statistical way. Alternatively, $\mathcal{L}_{AVM\text{-}VV}$ first finds the closest audio partner for each candidate audio, and then computes the KL distance of the corresponding visual features (also masked by segmentation results). This is based on the idea that if two clips share similar audio signals, the visual features of their sounding objects should also be similar. As shown in Table 6, both variants achieve a clear performance gain. For example, $\mathcal{L}_{AVM\text{-}AV}$

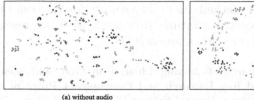
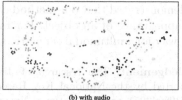

(a) without audio   (b) with audio

Fig. 7. T-SNE [25] visualization of the visual features, trained with or without audio. We divided the audio features into $K = 20$ clusters via PCA, and then assign the cluster labels to the corresponding visual features. The points with the same color share the same audio cluster labels. When training is accompanied by audio signals (right), the visual features illustrate a closer trend with the audio feature distribution, *i.e.*, points with the same colors gather together (Best viewed in color.) (Color figure online)

improves the mIoU by around 1% and F-score by about 2%. In practice, we just use $\mathcal{L}_{\text{AVM-AV}}$, since $\mathcal{L}_{\text{AVM-VV}}$ inconveniently requires a ranking operation.

Without Backbone Pre-training. We try to train the AVS framework without the pretrained backbones. As expected, we observe an obvious performance drop, *e.g.*, the mIoU decreases from 72.79% to 44.05% under S4 setting with ResNet50 as backbone. We speculate that it is difficult for the model to learn the audio and visual representation totally from scratch, especially for this challenging pixel-wise segmentation task.

T-SNE Visualization Analysis. On the test split of the Multi-sources set, we use the PVT-v2 based AVS model to obtain the visual features. Since the Multi-source set do not have category labels (its videos may contain several categories), we use the principal component analysis (PCA) to divide the audio features into $K = 20$ clusters. Then we assign the audio cluster labels to the corresponding visual features. In this case, if the audio and the visual features are correlated, the visual features should be clustered as well. We use the t-SNE visualization to verify this assumption. As shown in Fig. 7a, without audio signals, the learned visual features distribute chaotically; whereas in Fig. 7b, the visual features sharing the same audio labels tend to gather together.

6   Conclusion

We have proposed a new task called AVS, which aims to generate pixel-level binary segmentation masks for sounding objects in audible videos. To facilitate research in this area, we collected the first audio-visual segmentation benchmark (called AVSBench). We presented a new pixel-level AVS method to serve as a strong baseline, which includes a TPAVI module to encode the pixel-wise audio-visual interactions within temporal video sequences and a regularization loss to help the model learn audio-visual correlations. We compared our method with several existing state-of-the-art methods of the related tasks on AVSBench, and further demonstrated that our method can build a connection between the sound and the appearance of an object. For future work, we believe this research will pave the way for multimodal semantic segmentation.

Acknowledgement. The research of Jinxing Zhou, Dan Guo, and Meng Wang was supported by the National Key Research and Development Program of China (2018YFB0804205), and the National Natural Science Foundation of China (72188101, 61725203). Thanks to the SenseTime Research for providing access to the GPUs used for conducting experiments. The article solely reflects the opinions and conclusions of its authors but not the funding agents.

References

1. Afouras, T., Owens, A., Chung, J.S., Zisserman, A.: Self-supervised learning of audio-visual objects from video. In: Vedaldi, A., Bischof, H., Brox, T., Frahm, J.-M. (eds.) ECCV 2020. LNCS, vol. 12363, pp. 208–224. Springer, Cham (2020). https://doi.org/10.1007/978-3-030-58523-5_13
2. Arandjelovic, R., Zisserman, A.: Look, listen and learn. In: Proceedings of the IEEE International Conference on Computer Vision (ICCV), pp. 609–617 (2017)
3. Arandjelović, R., Zisserman, A.: Objects that sound. In: Ferrari, V., Hebert, M., Sminchisescu, C., Weiss, Y. (eds.) ECCV 2018. LNCS, vol. 11205, pp. 451–466. Springer, Cham (2018). https://doi.org/10.1007/978-3-030-01246-5_27
4. Aytar, Y., Vondrick, C., Torralba, A.: Soundnet: learning sound representations from unlabeled video. In: Advances in Neural Information Processing Systems 29 (2016)
5. Chen, H., Xie, W., Afouras, T., Nagrani, A., Vedaldi, A., Zisserman, A.: Localizing visual sounds the hard way. In: Proceedings of the IEEE/CVF Conference on Computer Vision and Pattern Recognition (CVPR), pp. 16867–16876 (2021)
6. Chen, H., Xie, W., Vedaldi, A., Zisserman, A.: VGGSound: a large-scale audio-visual dataset. In: IEEE International Conference on Acoustics, Speech and Signal Processing (ICASSP), pp. 721–725 (2020)
7. Chen, L.C., Papandreou, G., Kokkinos, I., Murphy, K., Yuille, A.L.: DeepLab: semantic image segmentation with deep convolutional nets, atrous convolution, and fully connected crfs. IEEE Trans. Pattern Anal. Mach. Intell. **40**(4), 834–848 (2017)
8. Cheng, Y., Wang, R., Pan, Z., Feng, R., Zhang, Y.: Look, listen, and attend: co-attention network for self-supervised audio-visual representation learning. In: Proceedings of the 28th ACM International Conference on Multimedia (ACM), pp. 3884–3892 (2020)
9. Duan, B., Tang, H., Wang, W., Zong, Z., Yang, G., Yan, Y.: Audio-visual event localization via recursive fusion by joint co-attention. In: Proceedings of the IEEE/CVF Winter Conference on Applications of Computer Vision (WACV), pp. 4013–4022 (2021)
10. Duke, B., Ahmed, A., Wolf, C., Aarabi, P., Taylor, G.W.: SSTVOS: sparse spatiotemporal transformers for video object segmentation. In: Proceedings of the IEEE/CVF Conference on Computer Vision and Pattern Recognition (CVPR), pp. 5912–5921 (2021)

11. Gao, R., Feris, R., Grauman, K.: Learning to separate object sounds by watching unlabeled video. In: Ferrari, V., Hebert, M., Sminchisescu, C., Weiss, Y. (eds.) ECCV 2018. LNCS, vol. 11207, pp. 36–54. Springer, Cham (2018). https://doi. org/10.1007/978-3-030-01219-9_3

12. Gao, R., Grauman, K.: Co-separating sounds of visual objects. In: Proceedings of the IEEE/CVF International Conference on Computer Vision (ICCV), pp. 3879–3888 (2019)

13. Gemmeke, J.F., et al.: Audio set: an ontology and human-labeled dataset for audio events. In: IEEE International Conference on Acoustics, Speech and Signal Processing (ICASSP), pp. 776–780. IEEE (2017)

14. He, K., Gkioxari, G., Dollár, P., Girshick, R.: Mask R-CNN. In: Proceedings of the IEEE International Conference on Computer Vision, pp. 2961–2969 (2017)

15. He, K., Zhang, X., Ren, S., Sun, J.: Deep residual learning for image recognition. In: Proceedings of the IEEE/CVF Conference on Computer Vision and Pattern Recognition (CVPR), pp. 770–778 (2016)

16. Hershey, S., et al.: CNN architectures for large-scale audio classification. In: IEEE International Conference on Acoustics, Speech and Signal Processing (ICASSP), pp. 131–135 (2017)

17. Hu, D., Nie, F., Li, X.: Deep multimodal clustering for unsupervised audiovisual learning. In: Proceedings of the IEEE/CVF Conference on Computer Vision and Pattern Recognition (CVPR), pp. 9248–9257 (2019)

18. Hu, D., et al.: Discriminative sounding objects localization via self-supervised audiovisual matching. In: Advances in Neural Information Processing Systems (NeurIPS) 33, pp. 10077–10087 (2020)

19. Kirillov, A., Girshick, R., He, K., Dollár, P.: Panoptic feature pyramid networks. In: Proceedings of the IEEE/CVF Conference on Computer Vision and Pattern Recognition (CVPR), pp. 6399–6408 (2019)

20. Lin, Y.B., Li, Y.J., Wang, Y.C.F.: Dual-modality seq2seq network for audio-visual event localization. In: IEEE International Conference on Acoustics, Speech and Signal Processing (ICASSP), pp. 2002–2006. IEEE (2019)

21. Lin, Y.B., Tseng, H.Y., Lee, H.Y., Lin, Y.Y., Yang, M.H.: Exploring cross-video and cross-modality signals for weakly-supervised audio-visual video parsing. In: Advances in Neural Information Processing Systems 34 (2021)

22. Lin, Y.B., Wang, Y.C.F.: Audiovisual transformer with instance attention for audio-visual event localization. In: Proceedings of the Asian Conference on Computer Vision (ACCV) (2020)

23. Liu, Z., et al.: Swin transformer: hierarchical vision transformer using shifted windows. arXiv preprint arXiv:2103.14030 (2021)

24. Long, J., Shelhamer, E., Darrell, T.: Fully convolutional networks for semantic segmentation. CoRR abs/1411.4038 (2014). http://arxiv.org/abs/1411.4038

25. Van der Maaten, L., Hinton, G.: Visualizing data using t-sne. J. Mach. Learn. Res. 9(11) (2008)

26. Mahadevan, S., Athar, A., Ošep, A., Hennen, S., Leal-Taixé, L., Leibe, B.: Making a case for 3D convolutions for object segmentation in videos. arXiv preprint arXiv:2008.11516 (2020)

27. Mao, Y., et al.: Transformer transforms salient object detection and camouflaged object detection. arXiv preprint arXiv:2104.10127 (2021)

28. Owens, A., Efros, A.A.: Audio-visual scene analysis with self-supervised multisensory features. In: Ferrari, V., Hebert, M., Sminchisescu, C., Weiss, Y. (eds.) ECCV 2018. LNCS, vol. 11210, pp. 639–658. Springer, Cham (2018). https://doi.org/10. 1007/978-3-030-01231-1_39

29. Qian, R., Hu, D., Dinkel, H., Wu, M., Xu, N., Lin, W.: Multiple sound sources localization from coarse to fine. In: Vedaldi, A., Bischof, H., Brox, T., Frahm, J.-M. (eds.) ECCV 2020. LNCS, vol. 12365, pp. 292–308. Springer, Cham (2020). https://doi.org/10.1007/978-3-030-58565-5_18

30. Ramaswamy, J.: What makes the sound?: a dual-modality interacting network for audio-visual event localization. In: IEEE International Conference on Acoustics, Speech and Signal Processing (ICASSP), pp. 4372–4376. IEEE (2020)

31. Ramaswamy, J., Das, S.: See the sound, hear the pixels. In: Proceedings of the IEEE/CVF Winter Conference on Applications of Computer Vision (WACV), pp. 2970–2979 (2020)

32. Ronneberger, O., Fischer, P., Brox, T.: U-Net: convolutional networks for biomedical image segmentation. In: Navab, N., Hornegger, J., Wells, W.M., Frangi, A.F. (eds.) MICCAI 2015. LNCS, vol. 9351, pp. 234–241. Springer, Cham (2015). https://doi.org/10.1007/978-3-319-24574-4_28

33. Rouditchenko, A., Zhao, H., Gan, C., McDermott, J., Torralba, A.: Self-supervised audio-visual co-segmentation. In: IEEE International Conference on Acoustics, Speech and Signal Processing (ICASSP), pp. 2357–2361. IEEE (2019)

34. Russakovsky, O., et al.: ImageNet large scale visual recognition challenge. Int. J. Comput. Vision 115(3), 211–252 (2015)

35. Selvaraju, R.R., Cogswell, M., Das, A., Vedantam, R., Parikh, D., Batra, D.: Gradcam: Visual explanations from deep networks via gradient-based localization. In: Proceedings of the IEEE International Conference on Computer Vision (ICCV), pp. 618–626 (2017)

36. Senocak, A., Oh, T.H., Kim, J., Yang, M.H., Kweon, I.S.: Learning to localize sound source in visual scenes. In: Proceedings of the IEEE Conference on Computer Vision and Pattern Recognition (CVPR), pp. 4358–4366 (2018)

37. Tian, Y., Li, D., Xu, C.: Unified multisensory perception: weakly-supervised audio-visual video parsing. In: Vedaldi, A., Bischof, H., Brox, T., Frahm, J.-M. (eds.) ECCV 2020. LNCS, vol. 12348, pp. 436–454. Springer, Cham (2020). https://doi.org/10.1007/978-3-030-58580-8_26

38. Tian, Y., Shi, J., Li, B., Duan, Z., Xu, C.: Audio-visual event localization in unconstrained videos. In: Ferrari, V., Hebert, M., Sminchisescu, C., Weiss, Y. (eds.) ECCV 2018. LNCS, vol. 11206, pp. 252–268. Springer, Cham (2018). https://doi.org/10.1007/978-3-030-01216-8_16

39. Wang, W., et al.: PVTv2: improved baselines with pyramid vision transformer. Comput. Visual Media 8(3), 1–10 (2022)

40. Wang, X., Girshick, R., Gupta, A., He, K.: Non-local neural networks. In: Proceedings of the IEEE/CVF Conference on Computer Vision and Pattern Recognition (CVPR), pp. 7794–7803 (2018)

41. Wu, Y., Yang, Y.: Exploring heterogeneous clues for weakly-supervised audio-visual video parsing. In: Proceedings of the IEEE/CVF Conference on Computer Vision and Pattern Recognition (CVPR), pp. 1326–1335 (2021)

42. Wu, Y., Zhu, L., Yan, Y., Yang, Y.: Dual attention matching for audio-visual event localization. In: Proceedings of the IEEE International Conference on Computer Vision (ICCV), pp. 6292–6300 (2019)

43. Xie, E., Wang, W., Yu, Z., Anandkumar, A., Alvarez, J.M., Luo, P.: Segformer: simple and efficient design for semantic segmentation with transformers. arXiv preprint arXiv:2105.15203 (2021)

44. Xu, H., Zeng, R., Wu, Q., Tan, M., Gan, C.: Cross-modal relation-aware networks for audio-visual event localization. In: Proceedings of the 28th ACM International Conference on Multimedia (ACM), pp. 3893–3901 (2020)

45. Xuan, H., Zhang, Z., Chen, S., Yang, J., Yan, Y.: Cross-modal attention network for temporal inconsistent audio-visual event localization. In: Proceedings of the AAAI Conference on Artificial Intelligence (AAAI), pp. 279–286 (2020)
46. Yu, J., Cheng, Y., Zhao, R.W., Feng, R., Zhang, Y.: MM-pyramid: multimodal pyramid attentional network for audio-visual event localization and video parsing. arXiv preprint arXiv:2111.12374 (2021)
47. Zhang, J., Xie, J., Barnes, N., Li, P.: Learning generative vision transformer with energy-based latent space for saliency prediction. Advances in Neural Information Processing Systems (NeurIPS) 34 (2021)
48. Zhao, H., Gan, C., Ma, W.C., Torralba, A.: The sound of motions. In: Proceedings of the IEEE/CVF International Conference on Computer Vision (ICCV), pp. 1735–1744 (2019)
49. Zhao, H., Gan, C., Rouditchenko, A., Vondrick, C., McDermott, J., Torralba, A.: The sound of pixels. In: Ferrari, V., Hebert, M., Sminchisescu, C., Weiss, Y. (eds.) ECCV 2018. LNCS, vol. 11205, pp. 587–604. Springer, Cham (2018). https://doi.org/10.1007/978-3-030-01246-5_35
50. Zhou, B., Khosla, A., Lapedriza, A., Oliva, A., Torralba, A.: Learning deep features for discriminative localization. In: Proceedings of the IEEE/CVF Conference on Computer Vision and Pattern Recognition (CVPR), pp. 2921–2929 (2016)
51. Zhou, J., Zheng, L., Zhong, Y., Hao, S., Wang, M.: Positive sample propagation along the audio-visual event line. In: Proceedings of the IEEE/CVF Conference on Computer Vision and Pattern Recognition (CVPR), pp. 8436–8444 (2021)

Unsupervised Night Image Enhancement: When Layer Decomposition Meets Light-Effects Suppression

Yeying Jin[1]([✉])(ID), Wenhan Yang[2](ID), and Robby T. Tan[1,3](ID)

[1] National University of Singapore, Singapore, Singapore
jinyeying@u.nus.edu, robby.tan@nus.edu.sg
[2] Nanyang Technological University, Singapore, Singapore
wenhan.yang@ntu.edu.sg
[3] Yale-NUS College, Singapore, Singapore
robby.tan@yale-nus.edu.sg

Abstract. Night images suffer not only from low light, but also from uneven distributions of light. Most existing night visibility enhancement methods focus mainly on enhancing low-light regions. This inevitably leads to over enhancement and saturation in bright regions, such as those regions affected by light effects (glare, floodlight, etc.). To address this problem, we need to suppress the light effects in bright regions while, at the same time, boosting the intensity of dark regions. With this idea in mind, we introduce an unsupervised method that integrates a layer decomposition network and a light-effects suppression network. Given a single night image as input, our decomposition network learns to decompose shading, reflectance and light-effects layers, guided by unsupervised layer-specific prior losses. Our light-effects suppression network further suppresses the light effects and, at the same time, enhances the illumination in dark regions. This light-effects suppression network exploits the estimated light-effects layer as the guidance to focus on the light-effects regions. To recover the background details and reduce hallucination/artefacts, we propose structure and high-frequency consistency losses. Our quantitative and qualitative evaluations on real images show that our method outperforms state-of-the-art methods in suppressing night light effects and boosting the intensity of dark regions.

Keywords: Night image enhancement · Low-light image · Light-effects suppression

1 Introduction

Night[1] images can contain uneven light distributions, as shown in Fig. 1, where some regions are dark and some are significantly brighter, due to the presence

---

[1] Our data and code is available at: https://github.com/jinyeying/night-enhancement.

Supplementary Information The online version contains supplementary material available at https://doi.org/10.1007/978-3-031-19836-6_23.

| Input | Our Method | Sharma [32] | EnlightenGAN [15] |

Fig. 1. An existing night light-effects suppression method [32] suffers from hallucination/artefacts and generates improper light effects, while an image enhancement method [15] is not designed to handle night light effects and incorrectly intensifies it. In contrast, our method jointly suppresses light effects and enhances dark regions.

of light effects[2]. Most existing nighttime visibility enhancement methods focus mainly on boosting the intensity of low-light regions, e.g., [7,13–15,33]. Hence, when these methods are applied to night images that contain light effects, they inevitably amplify the light effects, and impair the visibility of the images even further. Unlike these methods, our goal in this paper is to suppress the light effects while, at the same time, boosting the intensity of dark regions.

Fully-supervised learning methods could be a possible solution to achieving our goal. However, these methods would require a diverse and large collection of paired night images taken with and without light effects, which is intractable to obtain. Another possible solution would be the use of synthetic night images with rendered light effects. However, the effectiveness of methods trained on synthetic night data depends on the quality of the light-effects rendering model. To our knowledge, rendering physically correct night light effects with various background scenes and lighting conditions is still challenging [36].

In this paper, we introduce an unsupervised learning approach that integrates a decomposition network and a light-effects suppression network in a single unified framework. Our decomposition network is derived from an image-layer model and guided by our layer-specific prior losses to decompose the input image into shading, reflectance and light-effects layers (Fig. 3 shows the examples of these three layers). Subsequently, our light-effects suppression network, which is trained on unpaired images with and without light effects, provides additional unsupervised constraints. This network not only strengthens the light effects decomposition but also enhances the intensity in dark regions. The two networks, the decomposition and light-effect suppression networks, are connected.

To recover the background details behind light-effects regions, we introduce structure and high-frequency (HF) features consistency losses. We employ the structure consistency based on the VGG network and utilize the guided filter to obtain HF features. The structure and HF-features consistency losses can also reduce hallucination. In summary, our main contributions are as follows:

– To enhance the visibility of night images that suffer from low light and light effects simultaneously, we introduce a network architecture that integrates layer decomposition and light-effects suppression in one unified framework.

---

[2] Following [32], light effects in this paper refer to glare, floodlight, etc.

- To distinguish light effects from background regions, particularly when the color of the light effects is white or achromatic, we propose utilizing the estimated light-effects layer as guidance for our unsupervised light-effects suppression network.
- To restore the background details, we introduce novel unsupervised losses based on the structure and HF-features consistency. Our perceptual structure information and HF texture information are less affected by light effects. Thus, they can be employed to preserve background details, and, importantly, to suppress unwanted artefacts.

Our experiments and evaluations show that our method is effective in suppressing light-effects regions and enhancing dark regions, outperforming state-of-the-art methods both quantitatively and qualitatively.

2   Related Work

Sharma and Tan [32] introduce a method based on camera response function (CRF) estimation and HDR imaging to suppress light effects. The method is the first method that can suppress light effects and improve the dynamic range for night images. However, it suffers from artefacts and missing details as shown in Fig. 1, particularly for white (or achromatic) lights.

In the field of night image dehazing, a few methods have been proposed to suppress glow due to haze/fog particles. Li et al. [23] address glow removal on foggy nights using layer separation. Zhang et al. [44] use maximum reflectance prior for haze and glow removal. Ancuti et al. [2,3] use a fusion process and the Laplace operator to deglow and dehaze. Yan et al. [38,39] propose a semi-supervised method [37] employing a grayscale guided network. However, all these methods are designed for glow suppression in haze or foggy night, and not for removing light effects in clear night images. Moreover, unlike our method, they are also not designed for enhancing dark regions.

A number of methods have been developed to boost the brightness of low-light images without considering the presence of night light effects. A few methods are based on histogram equalization [28], inversion and dehazing [8], the retinex model (e.g. [9,21]), while more recent methods are based on deep networks [20]. Most deep-learning-based methods (e.g. [1,7,33]) adopt supervised learning to train their model and thus require a large number of pairs of low/normal-light images. A few unsupervised methods (e.g. [15]) rely on adversarial training using unpaired low/normal-light images. Semi-supervised methods (e.g. [40,41]) recompose coarse-to-fine representations towards perceptually pleasing images with the help of unpaired high-quality images. Recently, zero-shot learning methods (e.g. [13,19]) have been proposed for low-light enhancement. Most of these night image enhancement methods, however, are not designed to suppress night light effects and enhance low light regions simultaneously; therein lies the main difference with our work.

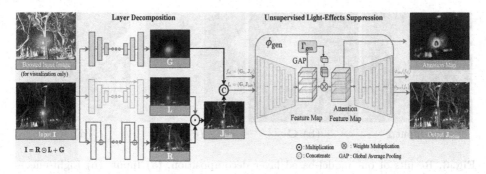

Fig. 2. The overall architecture of our proposed method. We integrate decomposition and light-effects suppression networks in one unified unsupervised framework. Given the input night image, we suppress light effects through the layer decomposition network, in which light-effects, shading, and reflectance layers are obtained (see Fig. 3). The light-effects suppression is guided by the decomposed light-effects layer **G** and based on unpaired learning (see Fig. 4) to further suppress light effects and boost dark regions.

3   Proposed Method

To suppress light effects and, at the same time, boost the intensity of dark regions, we propose an unsupervised framework by integrating a decomposition network and a light-effects suppression network. Our decomposition network is based on an image-layer model and produces three separate layers: shading, reflectance, and light-effects layers. We input these layers into our light-effects suppression network to obtain our final output, where light effects are suppressed and dark regions are boosted. This network learns from unpaired data and is guided by our estimated light-effects layer.

3.1   Model-Based Layer Decomposition Network

Our decomposition is based on the following image-layer model:

$$I = R \odot L + G,\tag{1}$$

where I represents the input night image, G represents the light-effects layer, R and L are the reflectance and shading layers, respectively. The notation $\odot$ represents element-wise multiplication. In this equation, we assume a linear gamma function. However, we do not use this equation explicitly in our method. Instead, we use it only to guide the design of our network in Fig. 2 (i.e., the layer decomposition network). When non-linear images with non-linear gamma functions are used in training, the background scenes are approximations of the physically correct values. Our decomposition goal is to obtain a background scene that is free from light effects, i.e., we want to estimate the background scene, $J_{init} = R \odot L$. Hence, even when non-linear images are used in training, applications that are less concerned about physically correct intensity values but suffer from light

| (a) Input **I** | (b) **G** | (c) **L** | (d) **R** |

Fig. 3. Results of our model-based layer decomposition. (a) Input. (b) Light-effects layer **G**. (c) Shading layer **L** and (d) Reflectance layer **R**.

effects can benefit from our method. Our model differs from the widely used intrinsic model [4,11], as the latter does not incorporate the light-effects layer.

Figure 2 shows our pipeline. The decomposition network is based on our image-layer model in Eq. (1). Given the input image (**I**), we first perform image decomposition. We use three separate networks and our novel unsupervised losses to obtain the light effects (**G**), shading (**L**), and reflectance (**R**) layers.

Learning Light Effects, Shading and Reflectance Layers. To obtain the light effects (**G**), shading (**L**), and reflectance (**R**) layers, we use three networks respectively: Light-Effects-Net (ϕ_G), Shading-Net (ϕ_L) and Reflectance-Net (ϕ_R), where $\mathbf{G} = \phi_\mathrm{G}(\mathbf{I})$, $\mathbf{L} = \phi_\mathrm{L}(\mathbf{I})$, and $\mathbf{R} = \phi_\mathrm{R}(\mathbf{I})$. The three networks are trained using unsupervised losses, which will be discussed in the subsequent paragraphs. Figure 3 shows examples of these three layers.

Light-Effects and Shading Initialization. To resolve the decomposition ambiguity problem, it is important to provide proper initial estimates of the layers. For the shading layer, we employ a shading map $\mathbf{L}_\mathrm{i}$ obtained by taking the maximum value of the three color channels, for each pixel [14]. For the light-effects layer, we use a light-effects map $\mathbf{G}_\mathrm{i}$, computed using the relative smoothness technique [22]. This is extracted using the second-order Laplacian filter from the input image, since light effects are smooth variations. We define the loss function for the initialization step as:

$$\mathcal{L}_\mathrm{init} = |\mathbf{G} - \mathbf{G}_\mathrm{i}|_1 + |\mathbf{L} - \mathbf{L}_\mathrm{i}|_1. \tag{2}$$

Gradient Exclusion Loss. The gradients of the light effects layer have a short tail distribution, similar to that of 'glow' [23]. In contrast, the gradients of the background image have a long tail distribution [22]. Hence, we employ a gradient exclusion loss to recover the uncorrelated layers $\{\mathbf{G}, \mathbf{J}_\mathrm{init}\}$, where the goal is to separate the two layers as far as possible in the gradient space. The definition of the loss follows [10,46]:

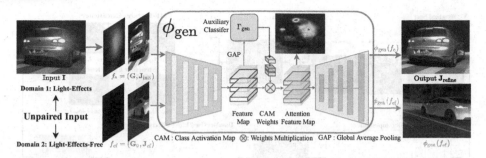

Fig. 4. Overview of our unsupervised light-effects suppression network. The network comprises a generator ϕ_{gen} and a classifier Γ_{gen}. The encoder block of our generator extracts feature maps from the input image layers. Our classifier Γ_{gen} is trained to learn the weights [49] of the feature maps. Γ_{gen} performs domain classification based on two domains, i.e., the light-effects domain $f_e = (\mathbf{G}, \mathbf{J}_{\text{init}})$ and the unpaired light-effects-free domain $f_{\text{ef}} = (\mathbf{G}_0, \mathbf{J}_{\text{ef}})$. Averaging the weighted feature maps generates an attention map that shows the network is focusing on the light-effects regions. As a result, the light effects are significantly suppressed in our output $\mathbf{J}_{\text{refine}}$.

$$\mathcal{L}_{\text{excl}} = \sum_{n=1}^{3} \left\| \tanh(\lambda_{\mathbf{G}^{\downarrow n}} |\nabla \mathbf{G}^{\downarrow n}|) \circ \tanh(\lambda_{\mathbf{J}_{\text{init}}^{\downarrow n}} |\nabla \mathbf{J}_{\text{init}}^{\downarrow n}|) \right\|_F, \qquad (3)$$

where $\|\cdot\|_F$ is the Frobenius norm, $\mathbf{G}^{\downarrow n}$ and $\mathbf{J}_{\text{init}}^{\downarrow n}$ represent $\mathbf{G}$ and $\mathbf{J}_{\text{init}}$ downsampled using the bilinear interpolation, and the parameters $\lambda_{\mathbf{G}^{\downarrow n}}$ and $\lambda_{\mathbf{J}_{\text{init}}^{\downarrow n}}$ are normalization factors.

Color Constancy Loss. To minimize any color shift in our decomposition output, inspired by the Gray World assumption [5,13,32], we use a color-constancy prior, which encourages the range of the intensity values of the three color channels in the background image $\mathbf{J}_{\text{init}}$ to be balanced:

$$\mathcal{L}_{\text{cc}} = \sum_{(c1,c2)} \left(|\mathbf{J}_{\text{init}}^{c1} - \mathbf{J}_{\text{init}}^{c2}|_1 \right), \qquad (4)$$

where $(c1, c2) \in \{(r, g), (r, b), (g, b)\}$ denotes a combination of two color channels.

Reconstruction Loss. For our decomposition task, recombining the estimated layers should give us back the original input image. Hence, we define our reconstruction loss as:

$$\mathcal{L}_{\text{recon}} = |\mathbf{I} - (\mathbf{R} \odot \mathbf{L} + \mathbf{G})|_1. \qquad (5)$$

We multiply each unsupervised loss with its respective weight, where we set λ_{init}, λ_{excl} all set to 1 since they are in the same scale. We empirically set $\lambda_{\text{recon}} = 0.1$ and employ the weight $\lambda_{\text{cc}} = 0.5$ from [13] to balance the decomposition process.

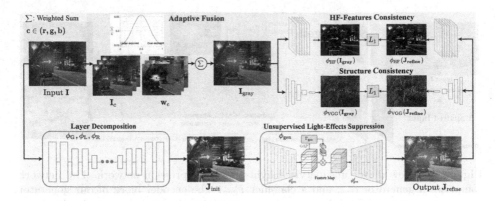

Fig. 5. Overview of our structure and HF-features consistency losses. We first use our adaptive fusion scheme to obtain a fused grayscale image $\mathbf{I}_{\text{gray}}$. Then, from $\mathbf{I}_{\text{gray}}$, we compute VGG features $\phi_{\text{VGG}}(\mathbf{I}_{\text{gray}})$ that are less affected by light effects, and HF-features $\phi_{\text{HF}}(\mathbf{I}_{\text{gray}})$ that are more robust to light effects and contain background details.

3.2   Light-Effects Suppression Network

To better suppress light effects, we integrate our decomposition network with an unpaired light-effects suppression network. We design this network to suppress light effects by using the guidance of our estimated light-effects layer, enforcing the network to focus on light-effects regions. As shown in Fig. 2, our network comprises a generator ϕ_{gen} and a classifier Γ_{gen}. It refines the initially estimated background scene ($\mathbf{J}_{\text{init}}$), and generates the final light-effects-free output ($\mathbf{J}_{\text{refine}}$). The details are as follows.

Light-Effects Layer Guidance. We employ the estimated light-effects layer $\mathbf{G}$ to guide our training process, as shown in Fig. 4. The light-effects layer is taken as part of the input of our encoder-decoder network, and is modulated with the feature maps of the network at different scales. Specifically, we concatenate $\mathbf{J}_{\text{init}}$ with the light-effects layer $\mathbf{G}$, and then we input them to our network ϕ_{gen}.

By resizing the light-effects layer, $\mathbf{G}$, to fit the size of each feature map, and multiplying it with all the intermediate feature maps, our light-effects layer can guide our network to focus more on light-effects regions. Figure 3b and Fig. 12 show some results of our light-effects layers, demonstrating that our method can successfully separate white and multi-color light effects.

Light-Effects Suppression. Besides the light-effects layer, our suppression network is also guided by an attention mechanism [15,16,18]. The basic idea is that, we input the light-effects and light-effects-free unpaired images into our encoder-decoder network. We then, use a domain classifier to judge whether the encoded features come from a certain domain, i.e., to judge whether the input is light-effects or light-effects-free. Using this domain classification, the activated feature regions can form an attention map [49] that is useful when guiding our network in suppressing light effects.

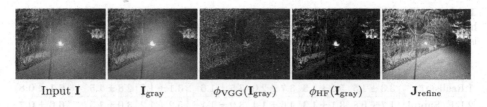

| Input $\mathbf{I}$ | $\mathbf{I}_{\text{gray}}$ | $\phi_{\text{VGG}}(\mathbf{I}_{\text{gray}})$ | $\phi_{\text{HF}}(\mathbf{I}_{\text{gray}})$ | $\mathbf{J}_{\text{refine}}$ |

Fig. 6. Examples of feature map from VGG for $\mathbf{I}_{\text{gray}}$, and a HF feature map for $\mathbf{I}_{\text{gray}}$. As one can observe, these features are less affected by light effects.

More specifically, as shown in Fig. 4, our network ϕ_{gen} contains an auxiliary classifier Γ_{gen}. One of the inputs of the network is the concatenation of $\mathbf{J}_{\text{init}}$ and $\mathbf{G}$. Another input is a light-effects-free reference image, $\mathbf{J}_{\text{ef}}$, concatenated with a dummy all zero map $\mathbf{G}_0$, which of course has no light effects. Our classifier, Γ_{gen}, then performs domain classification based on the encoded features from $f_e = (\mathbf{G}, \mathbf{J}_{\text{init}})$ or $f_{\text{ef}} = (\mathbf{G}_0, \mathbf{J}_{\text{ef}})$. To train the auxiliary classifier Γ_{gen}, we use the following attention loss:

$$\mathcal{L}_{\text{atten}} = -\big(\mathbb{E}\big[\log(\Gamma_{\text{gen}}(f_e))\big] + \mathbb{E}\big[\log(1 - \Gamma_{\text{gen}}(f_{\text{ef}}))\big]\big). \tag{6}$$

Structure and HF-Features Consistency Losses. To address hallucination/artefacts [31], and also to preserve background details, we employ two constraints: structure consistency, based on features obtained from the VGG network [17]; and HF-features consistency, based on the HF features obtained from the guided filter [35].

As shown in Fig. 5, to obtain the structure information and HF-features that are more robust to light effects, we adaptively fuse the RGB color channels of the input night image by applying: $I_{\text{gray}}(\mathbf{x}) = \sum_c \frac{1}{3}(w_c(\mathbf{x})I_c(\mathbf{x}))$ where $c \in (r, g, b)$ is a color channel, $\mathbf{x}$ is a pixel location, and the input image $\mathbf{I} = \{I_r, I_g, I_b\}$. The weight map for each color channel of the night image $I_c(\mathbf{x})$ is computed by $w_c(\mathbf{x}) = \exp\left(\frac{-(I_c(\mathbf{x})-0.5)^2}{2\sigma^2}\right)$. Note that the range of $I_c(\mathbf{x})$ is [0,1], thus 0.5 is the median of the intensity range. Our weight has a low value if a pixel in a color channel is either low (under-exposed) or high (e.g., a light-effects pixel). We define $\sigma = 0.2$, which measures how well-exposed a pixel is. This makes the resulting grayscale image I_{gray} less affected by light effects, as can be observed in Fig. 5 and Fig. 6.

Having obtained I_{gray}, we define our loss as follows:

$$\mathcal{L}_{\text{gray-feat}} = \big|\phi_{\text{HF}}(\mathbf{J}_{\text{refine}}) - \phi_{\text{HF}}(\mathbf{I}_{\text{gray}})\big|_1 + \big|\phi^l_{\text{VGG}}(\mathbf{J}_{\text{refine}}) - \phi^l_{\text{VGG}}(\mathbf{I}_{\text{gray}})\big|_1, \tag{7}$$

where $\mathbf{I}_{\text{gray}} = \{I_{\text{gray}}, I_{\text{gray}}, I_{\text{gray}}\}$. $\phi^l_{\text{VGG}}(.)$ represents the feature maps extracted from the lth layer of the VGG16 network (we set $l = 15$ in our experiments). $\phi_{\text{HF}}(.)$ represent the high-frequency feature maps obtained from the guided filter. We concatenate these HF layers to get $\phi_{\text{HF}}(\mathbf{I}_{\text{gray}})$. We use these features to better preserve the HF information in the generated refined background image $\mathbf{J}_{\text{refine}}$.

Table 1. User study evaluation on the real night data, our method obtained the highest mean and lowest standard deviation (the max score is 7), showing our method is realistic, light-effects (L.E.) suppressed, and has good visibility.

Three Aspects	EG [15]	Afifi [1]	Yan [38]	Zhang [44]	Li [23]	Sharma [32]	Ours
1.Realism↑	3.3 ± 1.5	5.5 ± 1.3	3.7 ± 2.0	3.5 ± 1.6	3.1 ± 1.8	2.8 ± 1.5	**6.1 ± 0.8**
2.L.E. Supp.↑	1.7 ± 0.8	3.1 ± 1.3	4.6 ± 1.4	3.9 ± 1.1	5.2 ± 1.2	3.0 ± 1.5	**6.6 ± 0.7**
3.Visibility↑	3.1 ± 1.6	4.2 ± 1.5	4.7 ± 1.5	3.7 ± 1.1	3.8 ± 1.5	3.0 ± 1.4	**6.4 ± 0.7**

Figure 5 shows our adaptive fusion scheme to obtain $\mathbf{I}_{\text{gray}}$ from which we compute HF-features and VGG-features. Figure 6 shows that with our loss in place, the VGG and HF features of $\mathbf{I}_{\text{gray}}$ preserve the structural information.

Adversarial and Identity Losses. Our adversarial loss for the generator and discriminator ϕ_{dis} uses its standard definition [12, 26]:

$$\mathcal{L}_{\text{adv}} = \mathbb{E}\big[\log\big(\phi_{\text{dis}}(\mathbf{J}_{\text{ef}})\big)\big] + \mathbb{E}\big[\log\big(1 - \phi_{\text{dis}}(\mathbf{J}_{\text{refine}})\big)\big]. \tag{8}$$

While our light-effects suppression network is designed to refine $\mathbf{J}_{\text{init}}$ by suppressing any remaining light effects, we also encourage it to output the same light-effects-free image when the input has no light-effects $\mathbf{J}_{\text{ef}}$. We achieve this by using the following identity loss function [51]:

$$\mathcal{L}_{\text{iden}} = \mathbb{E}\big[\|\phi_{\text{gen}}(\mathbf{J}_{\text{ef}}) - \mathbf{J}_{\text{ef}}\|_1\big]. \tag{9}$$

We multiply each loss function with its respective weight, we adjust $\lambda_{\text{gray-feat}} = 1$, $\lambda_{\text{atten}} = 0.5$ with the same scale, and employ the weights of $\lambda_{\text{adv}} = 1$ and $\lambda_{\text{iden}} = 5$ from [51]. The HF layers use smoothing kernels K, with size given by $k = 2^i$, $i = 2, 3, 4, ...$, the regularization $\epsilon = 0.04, 0.08$.

4   Experimental Results

Light-Effects Suppression on Night Data. The real night images used in our experiment are downloaded from the Internet and collected by ourselves. We use these images for our unpaired training since collecting the corresponding light-effects-free ground truth images is difficult.

For the user study, we randomly selected 210 outputs (30 per method, seven methods) and presented them to the 12 participants in random order. We asked them to rank these methods from unrealistic (1) to realistic (7); light effects still present (1) to suppressed (7); poor visibility (1) to good visibility (7). Table 1 shows the user study results. Table 2 shows the quantitative results on the night data, where our method has the highest PSNR and SSIM scores.

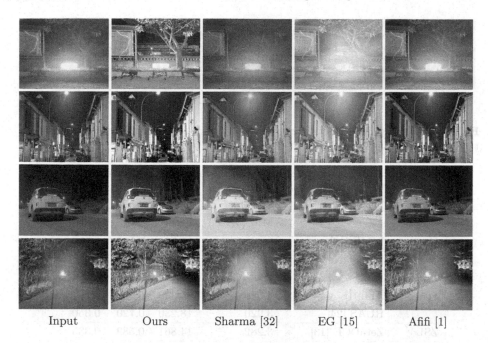

| Input | Ours | Sharma [32] | EG [15] | Afifi [1] |

Fig. 7. Comparing light-effects suppression and dark regions enhancement results on the real night images.

Table 2. Quantitative light-effects suppression comparison on the night data. In the table, UL = unsupervised learning, SL = supervised learning, SSL = semi-supervised learning, ZSL = zero-shot learning, Opti = optimization method.

Learning	-	UL	ZSL	SL	SL	SSL	Opti	Opti	SSL	UL
Datasets	Metrics	EG [15]	ZD+ [19]	RN [7]	Afifi [1]	Yan [38]	Zhang [44]	Li [23]	Sharma [32]	Ours
GTA5 [38]	PSNR↑	10.94	21.13	7.79	15.47	26.99	20.92	21.02	8.14	**29.79**
	SSIM↑	0.31	0.68	0.23	0.53	0.85	0.65	0.64	0.29	**0.88**
Syn-light-effects [27]	PSNR↑	7.38	7.84	6.39	11.31	14.88	16.30	14.66	14.00	**16.95**
	SSIM↑	0.17	0.20	0.16	0.35	0.23	0.38	0.37	0.37	**0.39**

Figure 7 shows the qualitative results on real night images, which demonstrate the superiority of our results compared to the baseline methods. Figure 8 shows the evaluation on the Dark Zurich [30] dataset. As can be observed, the light-effects suppression baseline [32] suffers from hallucination/artefacts and cannot handle white light effects. In the supplementary material, we show the results of night dehazing baselines [23,38,44], which are too dark since they are not designed to enhance dark regions; while low-light image enhancement baselines [1,7,15,19] wrongly intensify light effects, and thus degrade the visibility of the images.

| Input | Ours | Sharma [32] | EG [15] | Afifi [1] |

Fig. 8. Comparing light-effects suppression and dark regions enhancement results on the real night image from Dark Zurich [30] dataset.

Table 3. Quantitative comparisons on the LOL-test dataset [7].

Learning	Method	LOL-test			
		MSE($\times 10^3$)↓	PSNR↑	SSIM↑	LPIPS↓
Opti	LIME [14]	–	16.760	0.560	0.350
SL	RetinexNet [7]	1.651	16.774	0.462	0.474
	KinD++ [47]	1.298	17.752	0.760	**0.198**
	Afifi [1]	4.520	15.300	0.560	0.392
	RUAS [24]	3.920	18.230	0.720	0.350
ZSL	ZeroDCE [13]	3.282	14.861	0.589	0.335
SSL	DRBN [40]	2.359	15.125	0.472	0.316
UL	EnlightenGAN [15]	1.998	17.483	0.677	0.322
SSL	Sharma [32]	3.350	16.880	0.670	0.315
UL	Ours	**1.070**	**21.521**	**0.763**	0.235

Table 4. Quantitative comparisons on the *LOL-Real* dataset [42].

Learning	NA	Opti	Opti	Opti	ZSL	ZSL	ZSL	ZSL	SL
Method	Input	JED [29]	RRM [21]	SRIE [9]	RDIP [48]	MIRNet [43]	RRDNet [50]	ZD [13]	RUAS [24]
PSNR↑	9.72	17.33	17.34	17.34	11.43	12.67	14.85	20.54	15.33
SSIM↑	0.18	0.66	0.68	0.68	0.36	0.41	0.56	0.78	0.52
Learning	SL	SL	SL	SL	SL	SSL	UL	SSL	UL
Method	LLNet [25]	RN [7]	DUPE [34]	SICE [6]	Afifi [1]	DRBN [41]	EG [15]	Sharma [32]	Ours
PSNR↑	17.56	15.47	13.27	19.40	16.38	19.66	18.23	18.34	**25.53**
SSIM↑	0.54	0.56	0.45	0.69	0.53	0.76	0.61	0.64	**0.88**

Low-Light Enhancement. Besides night light-effects suppression, our method can boost the brightness of low light images with no light effects, by simply setting the light-effects layer to $\mathbf{G}_0$, which has no light-effects. For a fair comparison, we compare low-light boosting with image enhancement methods without considering the presence of light effects.

We adopt the LOL dataset [7][3], 485 training and 15 testing images, respectively. Table 3 shows quantitative results, where our method achieves better

---

[3] The LOL dataset link: https://daooshee.github.io/BMVC2018website/.

| Input | Ground Truth | Ours | Sharma [32] | EG [15] |

Fig. 9. Low-light enhancement results on the LOL-test [7], *LOL-Real* [42] datasets.

Table 5. Summary of comparisons between our method and existing night image enhancement methods. Our method can suppress light effects (including white light effects), preserve light source (L.S.) details, and boost dark regions simultaneously.

Learning	Methods	Light Effects (L.E.) Suppression			Dark Regions Boosting
		Normal L.E.	White L.E.	Details in L.S.	
UL	Ours	✓	✓	✓	✓
SSL	Sharma and Tan [32]	✓	✗	✗	✓
Opti;SSL	Night Dehazing [23,38,44]	✓	✓	✗	✗
SL;ZSL;UL	Low-light Enhancement [1,15,19]	✗			✓

performance compared with the baseline methods in terms of PSNR, SSIM, Mean Square Error (MSE) and Learned Perceptual Image Patch Similarity (LPIPS) [45]. We evaluate on *LOL-Real* [42][4], 100 testing images with more diversified scenes. We train our method on the LOL dataset and test on the *LOL-Real* test-split. The results are shown in Table 4 and Fig. 9, showing the generality of our method. Our method achieves better performance compared with the baseline methods in terms of PSNR, SSIM.

Baselines. As shown in Table 5, there is only one algorithm, i.e., Sharma and Tan [32] that suppresses night light effects and boosts the dark regions simultaneously. Yet, the method cannot handle white light effects and suffers from hallucination/artefacts. Night dehazing methods can suppress glow, but are suboptimal to enhancing low-light regions. Low-light image enhancement methods are not designed to suppress night light effects and enhance low light regions simultaneously.

Nevertheless for comprehensive comparisons, besides comparing with [32], we also compare our method with the state-of-the-art single-image low-light image enhancement methods: EnlightenGAN [15], Afifi et al. [1], etc. and the night dehazing methods: Yan et al. [38], Zhang et al. [44], Li et al. [23], etc. The codes of all the baseline methods are obtained from the authors. More baseline results are provided in the supplementary material.

Joint Light-Effects Suppression and Dark Region Boosting. As shown in Fig. 10, jointly suppressing light-effects and then boosting dark regions are more

---

[4] *LOL-Real* dataset link: https://github.com/flyywh/CVPR-2020-Semi-Low-Light/.

effective than any other possibilities (namely, (b) the light-effects suppression alone, (c) light-effects suppression followed by boosting without jointly training them, (d) boosting alone, and (e) boosting followed by light effects suppression without joint training). If we suppress light effects first, then boost the intensity without the joint training, as shown in Fig. 11c, artefacts and remaining light effects are also enhanced. If we boost the intensity first, then suppress light effects without joint training, as shown in Fig. 11e, light effects cannot be effectively suppressed since the amplified light effects cause information and detail loss.

   (a)   **(b)**   **(c)**   **(d)**   **(e)**   **(f)**

Fig. 10. Experiments on the effectiveness of joint light-effects suppression and dark regions boosting: (a) input, (b) light-effects suppression, (c) light-effects suppression followed by boosting without joint training, (d) boosting, (e) boosting followed by light-effects suppression without joint training, (f) our joint training light-effects suppression and boosting.

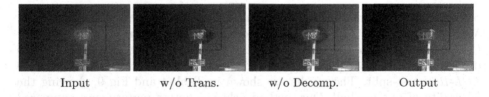

    Input   w/o Trans.   w/o Decomp.   Output

Fig. 11. Ablation studies on the framework. 'w/o Trans' denotes our method without light-effects suppression. 'w/o Decomp.' denotes our method without layer decomposition. We can observe that our framework is important for night image enhancement.

Ablation Studies. Figure 11, Fig. 12 and Fig. 13 show the effectiveness of our framework, light-effects layer guidance and structure and HF-features consistency losses used in our method, which clearly show that all the components are important for better performance.

Decomposition + Suppression. To show the effectiveness of our model-based unsupervised decomposition, we train our network without the decomposition module. We directly input the night images to the light-effects suppression network, thus there is no light-effects layer guidance and initial background results. Similarly, to show the effectiveness of our unsupervised light-effects suppression, we assume the initial background image J_{init} generated by the decomposition part is the final result without any refinement. Our final results are more effective in suppressing light effects and more natural in recovering the background.

Light-Effects Layer Guidance. We compare the results by our method with and without light-effects layer guidance. Instead of input (G, J_{init}), we input

$(\mathbf{G}_0, \mathbf{J}_{\text{init}})$ to the light-effects suppression network. That means there is no light-effects layer $\mathbf{G}$, we concatenate the initially estimated background scene with all zero maps $\mathbf{G}_0$. Figures 2–4 show the results of the light-effects layer. Figure 12 shows with light-effects layer guidance, our method can distinguish light-effects regions from background regions, focus on light-effects regions and properly suppress light effects (including white and multi-color light effects).

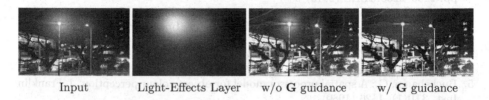

Input   Light-Effects Layer   w/o **G** guidance   w/ **G** guidance

Fig. 12. Ablation studies on light-effects layer guidance, with light-effects layer $\mathbf{G}$ guidance, our light-effects suppression network can focus on light-effects regions, separate light effects more properly.

Input   w/o $\mathcal{L}_{\text{gray-feat}}$ w/ $\mathcal{L}_{\text{gray-feat}}$ Input   w/o $\mathcal{L}_{\text{gray-feat}}$ w/ $\mathcal{L}_{\text{gray-feat}}$

Fig. 13. Ablation studies on the structure and HF-features consistency losses $\mathcal{L}_{\text{gray-feat}}$, with $\mathcal{L}_{\text{gray-feat}}$, our method suppresses artefacts, and preserves details.

Structure and HF-Features Consistency. Structure and HF-features consistency losses can suppress artefacts and restore missing details. Figure 13 compares the results by our method with and without this loss.

5 Conclusion

In this paper, we have proposed a method to suppress light effects, and at the same time, boost the intensity of dark regions, from a single night image. To achieve our goal, we cast the problem of light-effects suppression as an unsupervised decomposition problem. We proposed an integrated network consisting of layer decomposition and light-effects suppression networks. Our experiments show that our method outperforms the state-of-the-art visibility enhancement and light effects suppression methods.

Acknowledgments. This research/project is supported by the National Research Foundation, Singapore under its AI Singapore Programme (AISG Award No: AISG2-PhD/2022-01-037[T]), and partially supported by MOE2019-T2-1-130. Wenhan Yang's research is supported by Wallenberg-NTU Presidential Postdoctoral Fellowship. Robby T. Tan's work is supported by MOE2019-T2-1-130.

References

1. Afifi, M., Derpanis, K.G., Ommer, B., Brown, M.S.: Learning multi-scale photo exposure correction. In: Proceedings of the IEEE/CVF Conference on Computer Vision and Pattern Recognition, pp. 9157–9167 (2021)
2. Ancuti, C., Ancuti, C.O., De Vleeschouwer, C., Bovik, A.C.: Night-time dehazing by fusion. In: 2016 IEEE International Conference on Image Processing (ICIP), pp. 2256–2260. IEEE (2016)
3. Ancuti, C., Ancuti, C.O., De Vleeschouwer, C., Bovik, A.C.: Day and night-time dehazing by local airlight estimation. IEEE Trans. Image Process. **29**, 6264–6275 (2020)
4. Bell, S., Bala, K., Snavely, N.: Intrinsic images in the wild. ACM Trans. Graph. (TOG) **33**(4), 1–12 (2014)
5. Buchsbaum, G.: A spatial processor model for object colour perception. J. Franklin Inst. **310**(1), 1–26 (1980)
6. Cai, J., Gu, S., Zhang, L.: Learning a deep single image contrast enhancer from multi-exposure images. IEEE Trans. Image Process. **27**(4), 2049–2062 (2018)
7. Wei, C., Wang, W., Yang, W., Liu, J.: Deep retinex decomposition for low-light enhancement. In: British Machine Vision Conference. British Machine Vision Association (2018)
8. Dong, X., et al.: Fast efficient algorithm for enhancement of low lighting video. In: 2011 IEEE International Conference on Multimedia and Expo, pp. 1–6. IEEE (2011)
9. Fu, X., Zeng, D., Huang, Y., Zhang, X.P., Ding, X.: A weighted variational model for simultaneous reflectance and illumination estimation. In: Proceedings of the IEEE Conference on Computer Vision and Pattern Recognition, pp. 2782–2790 (2016)
10. Gandelsman, Y., Shocher, A., Irani, M.: "double-dip": unsupervised image decomposition via coupled deep-image-priors. In: Proceedings of the IEEE/CVF Conference on Computer Vision and Pattern Recognition, pp. 11026–11035 (2019)
11. Gehler, P., Rother, C., Kiefel, M., Zhang, L., Schölkopf, B.: Recovering intrinsic images with a global sparsity prior on reflectance. In: Advances in Neural Information Processing Systems 24, pp. 765–773. Curran Associates Inc., Red Hook (2011)
12. Goodfellow, I.J., et al.: Generative adversarial networks. arXiv preprint arXiv:1406.2661 (2014)
13. Guo, C., et al.: Zero-reference deep curve estimation for low-light image enhancement. In: Proceedings of the IEEE/CVF Conference on Computer Vision and Pattern Recognition, pp. 1780–1789 (2020)
14. Guo, X., Li, Y., Ling, H.: Lime: low-light image enhancement via illumination map estimation. IEEE Trans. Image Process. **26**(2), 982–993 (2016)
15. Jiang, Y., et al.: Enlightengan: deep light enhancement without paired supervision. IEEE Trans. Image Process. **30**, 2340–2349 (2021)
16. Jin, Y., Sharma, A., Tan, R.T.: Dc-shadownet: single-image hard and soft shadow removal using unsupervised domain-classifier guided network. In: Proceedings of the IEEE/CVF International Conference on Computer Vision, pp. 5027–5036 (2021)
17. Johnson, J., Alahi, A., Fei-Fei, L.: Perceptual losses for real-time style transfer and super-resolution. In: Leibe, B., Matas, J., Sebe, N., Welling, M. (eds.) ECCV 2016. LNCS, vol. 9906, pp. 694–711. Springer, Cham (2016). https://doi.org/10.1007/978-3-319-46475-6_43

18. Kim, J., Kim, M., Kang, H., Lee, K.: U-gat-it: unsupervised generative attentional networks with adaptive layer-instance normalization for image-to-image translation. arXiv preprint arXiv:1907.10830 (2019)

19. Li, C., Guo, C., Chen, C.L.: Learning to enhance low-light image via zero-reference deep curve estimation. IEEE Trans. Pattern Anal. Mach. Intell. (2021)

20. Li, C., et al.: Low-light image and video enhancement using deep learning: A survey. IEEE Trans. Pattern Anal. Mach. Intell. **01**, 1–1 (2021)

21. Li, M., Liu, J., Yang, W., Sun, X., Guo, Z.: Structure-revealing low-light image enhancement via robust retinex model. IEEE Trans. Image Process. **27**(6), 2828–2841 (2018)

22. Li, Y., Brown, M.S.: Single image layer separation using relative smoothness. In: Proceedings of the IEEE Conference on Computer Vision and Pattern Recognition, pp. 2752–2759 (2014)

23. Li, Y., Tan, R.T., Brown, M.S.: Nighttime haze removal with glow and multiple light colors. In: Proceedings of the IEEE International Conference on Computer Vision, pp. 226–234 (2015)

24. Liu, R., Ma, L., Zhang, J., Fan, X., Luo, Z.: Retinex-inspired unrolling with cooperative prior architecture search for low-light image enhancement. In: Proceedings of the IEEE/CVF Conference on Computer Vision and Pattern Recognition, pp. 10561–10570 (2021)

25. Lore, K.G., Akintayo, A., Sarkar, S.: Llnet: a deep autoencoder approach to natural low-light image enhancement. Pattern Recogn. **61**, 650–662 (2017)

26. Mao, X., Li, Q., Xie, H., Lau, R.Y., Wang, Z., Paul Smolley, S.: Least squares generative adversarial networks. In: Proceedings of the IEEE International Conference on Computer Vision, pp. 2794–2802 (2017)

27. Metari, S., Deschenes, F.: A new convolution kernel for atmospheric point spread function applied to computer vision. In: 2007 IEEE 11th Iinternational Conference on Computer Vision, pp. 1–8. IEEE (2007)

28. Pizer, S.M., et al.: Adaptive histogram equalization and its variations. Comput. Vision Graph. Image Process. **39**(3), 355–368 (1987)

29. Ren, X., Li, M., Cheng, W.H., Liu, J.: Joint enhancement and denoising method via sequential decomposition. In: 2018 IEEE International Symposium on Circuits and Systems (ISCAS), pp. 1–5. IEEE (2018)

30. Sakaridis, C., Dai, D., Gool, L.V.: Guided curriculum model adaptation and uncertainty-aware evaluation for semantic nighttime image segmentation. In: Proceedings of the IEEE International Conference on Computer Vision, pp. 7374–7383 (2019)

31. Sharma, A., Cheong, L.F., Heng, L., Tan, R.T.: Nighttime stereo depth estimation using joint translation-stereo learning: Light effects and uninformative regions. In: 2020 International Conference on 3D Vision (3DV), pp. 23–31. IEEE (2020)

32. Sharma, A., Tan, R.T.: Nighttime visibility enhancement by increasing the dynamic range and suppression of light effects. In: Proceedings of the IEEE/CVF Conference on Computer Vision and Pattern Recognition, pp. 11977–11986 (2021)

33. Wang, R., Zhang, Q., Fu, C.W., Shen, X., Zheng, W.S., Jia, J.: Underexposed photo enhancement using deep illumination estimation. In: Proceedings of the IEEE Conference on Computer Vision and Pattern Recognition, pp. 6849–6857 (2019)

34. Wang, R., Zhang, Q., Fu, C.W., Shen, X., Zheng, W.S., Jia, J.: Underexposed photo enhancement using deep illumination estimation. In: The IEEE Conference on Computer Vision and Pattern Recognition (CVPR), June 2019

35. Wu, H., Zheng, S., Zhang, J., Huang, K.: Fast end-to-end trainable guided filter. In: Proceedings of the IEEE Conference on Computer Vision and Pattern Recognition, pp. 1838–1847 (2018)
36. Wu, Y., et al.: How to train neural networks for flare removal. In: Proceedings of the IEEE/CVF International Conference on Computer Vision, pp. 2239–2247 (2021)
37. Yan, W., Sharma, A., Tan, R.T.: Optical flow in dense foggy scenes using semi-supervised learning. In: Proceedings of the IEEE/CVF Conference on Computer Vision and Pattern Recognition, pp. 13259–13268 (2020)
38. Yan, W., Tan, R.T., Dai, D.: Nighttime defogging using high-low frequency decomposition and grayscale-color networks. In: Vedaldi, A., Bischof, H., Brox, T., Frahm, J.-M. (eds.) ECCV 2020. LNCS, vol. 12357, pp. 473–488. Springer, Cham (2020). https://doi.org/10.1007/978-3-030-58610-2_28
39. Yan, W., Tan, R.T., Yang, W., Dai, D.: Self-aligned video deraining with transmission-depth consistency. In: Proceedings of the IEEE/CVF Conference on Computer Vision and Pattern Recognition, pp. 11966–11976 (2021)
40. Yang, W., Wang, S., Fang, Y., Wang, Y., Liu, J.: From fidelity to perceptual quality: a semi-supervised approach for low-light image enhancement. In: Proceedings of the IEEE/CVF Conference on Computer Vision and Pattern Recognition, pp. 3063–3072 (2020)
41. Yang, W., Wang, S., Fang, Y., Wang, Y., Liu, J.: Band representation-based semi-supervised low-light image enhancement: bridging the gap between signal fidelity and perceptual quality. IEEE Trans. Image Process. 30, 3461–3473 (2021)
42. Yang, W., Wang, W., Huang, H., Wang, S., Liu, J.: Sparse gradient regularized deep retinex network for robust low-light image enhancement. IEEE Trans. Image Process. 30, 2072–2086 (2021)
43. Zamir, S.W., et al.: Learning enriched features for real image restoration and enhancement. In: Vedaldi, A., Bischof, H., Brox, T., Frahm, J.-M. (eds.) ECCV 2020. LNCS, vol. 12370, pp. 492–511. Springer, Cham (2020). https://doi.org/10.1007/978-3-030-58595-2_30
44. Zhang, J., Cao, Y., Fang, S., Kang, Y., Wen Chen, C.: Fast haze removal for nighttime image using maximum reflectance prior. In: Proceedings of the IEEE Conference on Computer Vision and Pattern Recognition, pp. 7418–7426 (2017)
45. Zhang, R., Isola, P., Efros, A.A., Shechtman, E., Wang, O.: The unreasonable effectiveness of deep features as a perceptual metric. In: Proceedings of the IEEE Conference on Computer Vision and Pattern Recognition, pp. 586–595 (2018)
46. Zhang, X., Ng, R., Chen, Q.: Single image reflection separation with perceptual losses. In: Proceedings of the IEEE Conference on Computer Vision and Pattern Recognition, pp. 4786–4794 (2018)
47. Zhang, Y., Guo, X., Ma, J., Liu, W., Zhang, J.: Beyond brightening low-light images. Int. J. Comput. Vision 129(4), 1013–1037 (2021)
48. Zhao, Z., Xiong, B., Wang, L., Ou, Q., Yu, L., Kuang, F.: Retinexdip: a unified deep framework for low-light image enhancement. IEEE Trans. Circuits Syst. Video Technol. (2021)
49. Zhou, B., Khosla, A., Lapedriza, A., Oliva, A., Torralba, A.: Learning deep features for discriminative localization. In: Proceedings of the IEEE Conference on Computer Vision and Pattern Recognition, pp. 2921–2929 (2016)

50. Zhu, A., Zhang, L., Shen, Y., Ma, Y., Zhao, S., Zhou, Y.: Zero-shot restoration of underexposed images via robust retinex decomposition. In: 2020 IEEE International Conference on Multimedia and Expo (ICME). pp. 1–6. IEEE (2020)
51. Zhu, J.Y., Park, T., Isola, P., Efros, A.A.: Unpaired image-to-image translation using cycle-consistent adversarial networks. In: Proceedings of the IEEE International Conference on Computer Vision, pp. 2223–2232 (2017)

Relationformer: A Unified Framework for *Image-to-Graph* Generation

Suprosanna Shit[1,3]($\boxtimes$) (iD), Rajat Koner[2] (iD), Bastian Wittmann[1],
Johannes Paetzold[1], Ivan Ezhov[1], Hongwei Li[1], Jiazhen Pan[1],
Sahand Sharifzadeh[2], Georgios Kaissis[1], Volker Tresp[2], and Bjoern Menze[3]

[1] Technical University of Munich, Munich, Germany
suprosanna.shit@tum.de
[2] Ludwig Maximilian University of Munich, Munich, Germany
koner@dbs.ifi.lmu.de
[3] University of Zurich, Zurich, Switzerland

Abstract. A comprehensive representation of an image requires understanding objects and their mutual relationship, especially in *image-to-graph* generation, e.g., road network extraction, blood-vessel network extraction, or scene graph generation. Traditionally, *image-to-graph* generation is addressed with a two-stage approach consisting of object detection followed by a separate relation prediction, which prevents simultaneous object-relation interaction. This work proposes a unified one-stage transformer-based framework, namely Relationformer that jointly predicts objects and their relations. We leverage direct set-based object prediction and incorporate the interaction among the objects to learn an object-relation representation jointly. In addition to existing [obj]-tokens, we propose a novel learnable token, namely [rln]-token. Together with [obj]-tokens, [rln]-token exploits local and global semantic reasoning in an image through a series of mutual associations. In combination with the pair-wise [obj]-token, the [rln]-token contributes to a computationally efficient relation prediction. We achieve state-of-the-art performance on multiple, diverse and multi-domain datasets that demonstrate our approach's effectiveness and generalizability. (Code is available at https://github.com/suprosanna/relationformer).

Keywords: Image-to-graph generation · Road network extraction · Vessel graph extraction · Scene graph generation

1 Introduction

An image contains multiple layers of abstractions, from low-level features to intermediate-level objects to high-level complex semantic relations. To gain a

---

S. Shit and R. Koner—Equal contribution.

Supplementary Information The online version contains supplementary material available at https://doi.org/10.1007/978-3-031-19836-6_24.

S. Avidan et al. (Eds.): ECCV 2022, LNCS 13697, pp. 422–439, 2022.
https://doi.org/10.1007/978-3-031-19836-6_24

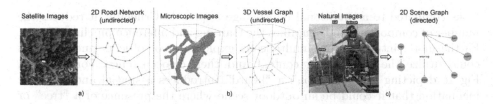

Fig. 1. Examples of relation prediction tasks. Note that the 2D road network extraction and 3D vessel graph extraction tasks have undirected relations while the scene graph generation task has directed relations.

complete visual understanding, it is essential to investigate different abstraction layers jointly. An example of such multi-abstraction problem is *image-to-graph* generation, such as road-network extraction [18], blood vessel-graph extraction [41], and scene-graph generation [55]. In all of these tasks, one needs to explore not only the objects or the *nodes*, but also their mutual dependencies or relations as *edges*.

In *spatio-structural* tasks, such as road network extraction (Fig. 1a), nodes represent road-junctions or significant turns, while edges correspond to structural connections, i.e., the road itself. The resulting spatio-structural graph construction is crucial for navigation tasks, especially with regard to autonomous vehicles. Similarly, in 3D blood vessel-graph extraction (Fig. 1b), nodes represent branching points or substantial curves, and edges correspond to structural connections, i.e., arteries, veins, and capillaries. Biological studies relying on a vascular graph representation, such as detecting collaterals [52], assessing structural robustness [21], emphasize the importance of efficient extraction thereof. In case of *spatio-semantic* graph generation, e.g. scene graph generation from natural images (Fig. 1c), the objects denote nodes and the semantic-relation denotes the edges [22]. This graphical representation of natural images is compact, interpretable, and facilitates various downstream tasks like visual question answering [19,25]. Notably, different image-to-graph tasks have been addressed separately in previous literature (see Sect. 2), and to the best of our knowledge, no unified approach has been reported so far.

Traditionally, image-to-graph generation has been studied as a complex multistage pipeline, which consist of an object detector [43], followed by a separate relation predictor [24,32]. Similarly, for spatio-structural graph generation, the usual first stage is segmentation, followed by a morphological operation on binary data. While a two-stage *object-relation* graph generation approach is modular, it is usually trained sequentially, which increases model complexity and inference time and lacks simultaneous exploration of shared object-relation representations. Additionally, mistakes in the first stage may propagate into the later stages. It should also be noted that the two-stage approach depends on multiple hand-designed features, spatial [59], or multi-modal input [8].

We argue that a single-stage image-to-graph model with joint object and relation exploration is efficient, faster, and easily extendable to multiple downstream

424   S. Shit et al.

tasks compared to a traditional multi-stage approach. Crucially, it reduces the
number of components and simplifies the training and inference pipeline (Fig. 2).
Furthermore, intuitively, a simultaneous exploration of objects and relations
could utilize the surrounding context and their co-occurrence. For example,
Fig. 1c depicting the "kid" "on" a "board" introduces a spatial and semantic
inclination that it could be an outdoor scene where the presence of a "tree" or
a "helmet", the kid might wear, is highly likely. The same notion is analogous
in a spatio-structural vessel graph. Detection of a "bifurcation point" and an
"artery" would indicate the presence of another "artery" nearby. The mutual
co-occurrence captured in joint object-relation representation overcomes individual object boundaries and leads to a more informed big picture.

Recently, there has been a surge of one-stage models in object detection
thanks to the DETR approach described in [7]. These one-stage models are
popular due to the simplicity and the elimination of reliance on hand-crafted
designs or features. DETR exploits a encoder-decoder transformer architecture
and learns object queries or [obj]-token for object representation.

To this end, we propose **Relationformer**, a *unified one-stage* framework
for end-to-end image-to-graph generation. We leverage set-based object detection of DETR and introduce a novel learnable token named [rln]-token in tandem with [obj]-tokens. The [rln]-token captures the inter-dependency and co-
occurrence of low-level objects and high-level spatio-semantic relations. Relationformer directly predicts objects from the learned [obj]-tokens and classifies
their pairwise relation from combinations of [obj-rln-obj]-tokens. In addition
to capturing pairwise object-interactions, the [rln]-token, in conjunction with
relation information, allows all relevant [obj]-tokens to be aware of the global
semantic structure. These enriched [obj]-tokens in combination with the relation
token, in turn, contributes to the relation prediction. The mutually shared representation of joint tokens serves as an excellent basis for an image-to-graph generation. Moreover, our approach significantly simplifies the underlying complex
image-to-graph pipeline by only using image features extracted by its backbone.

We evaluate Relationformer across numerous publicly available datasets,
namely Toulouse, 20 US Cities, DeepVesselNet, and Visual Genome, comprising 2D and 3D, directed- and undirected image-to-graph generation tasks. We
achieve a new state-of-the-art for one-stage methods on Visual Genome, which
is better or comparable to the two-stage approaches. We achieve state-of-the-art
results on road-network extraction on the Toulouse and 20 US Cities dataset.
To the best of our knowledge, this is the first image-to-graph approach working
directly in *3D*, which we use to extract graphs formed by blood vessels.

2   Related Work

Transformer in Vision: In recent times, transformer-based architectures have
emerged as the de-facto gold standard model for various multi-domain and multi-
modal tasks such as image classification [13], object detection [7] and even its
application of out-of-distribution detection [23]. DETR [7] proposed an end-to-
end transformer-based object detection approach with learnable object queries

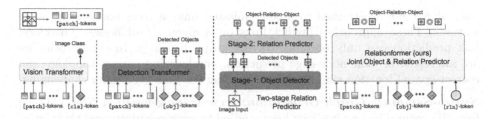

Fig. 2. This illustrates a general architectural evolution of transformers in computer vision and how Relationformer advances the concept of a task-specific learnable token one step further. The proposed Relationformer is also shown in comparison to the conventional two-stage relation predictor. The amalgamation of two separate stages not only simplifies the architectural pipeline but also co-reinforces both of the tasks.

([obj]-tokens) and direct set-based prediction. DETR eliminates burdensome object detection pipelines (e.g., anchor boxes, NMS) of traditional approaches [43] and directly predicts objects. Building on DETR, a series of object detection approaches improved DETR's slow convergence [62], adapted a pure sequence-to-sequence approach [15], and improved detector efficiency [50]. In parallel, the development of the vision transformer [13] for image classification offered a powerful alternative. Several refined idea [34,53] have advanced this breakthrough and transformer in general emerges as a cutting-edge research topic with focus on novel design principle and innovative application. Figure 2, shows a pictorial overview of transformer-based image classifier, object detector, and relation predictor including our proposed method, which we referred to as Relationformer.

Spatio-Structural Graph Generation: In a spatio-structural graph, the most important physical objects are edges, i.e., roads for a road network or arteries and veins in vessel graphs. Conventionally, spatio-structural graph extraction has only been discussed in 2D with little-to-no attention on the 3D counterpart. For 2D road network extraction, the predominant approach is to segment [4,37] followed by morphological thinning to extract the spatial graph. Only few approaches combine graph level information processing, iterative node generation [3], sequential generative modelling [9], and graph-tensor-encoding [18]. Belli et al. [5] for the first time, adopted attention mechanisms in an auto-regressive model to generate graphs conditioned on binary segmentation. Importantly, to this date, none of these 2D approaches has been shown to scale to 3D.

For 3D vessel-network extraction, segmentation of whole-brain microscopy images [39,52] has been combined with rule-based graph extraction algorithms [49]. Recently, a large-scale study [41] used the *Voreen* [38] software to extract whole-brain vascular graph from binary segmentation, which required complicated heuristics and huge computational resources. Despite recent works on 3D scene graphs [1] and temporal scene graphs [20], to this day, there exists no learning-based solution for 3D spatio-structural graph extraction.

Considering two spatio-structural image-to-graph examples of vessel-graph and road-network, one can understand the spatial relation detection task as a link prediction task. In link-prediction, graph neural networks, such as GraphSAGE

[16], SEAL [60] are trained to predict missing links among nodes using node features. These approaches predict links on a given set of nodes. Therefore, link prediction can only optimize correct graph topology. In comparison, we are interested in joint node-edge prediction, emphasizing correct topology and correct spatial location simultaneously, making the task even more challenging.

Spatio-Semantic Graph Generation: Scene graph generation (SGG) [35,55] from 2D natural images has long been studied to explore objects and their inter-dependencies in an interpretable way. Context refinement across objects [55,59], extra modality of features [35,48] or prior knowledge [46] has been used to model inter-dependencies of objects for relation prediction. RTN [24,26] was one of the first transformer approaches to explore context modeling and interactions between objects and edges for SGG. Li et al. [29] uses DETR like architecture to separately predict entity and predicate proposal followed by a graph assembly module. Later, several works [12,36] explored transformers, improving relation predictions. On the downside, such two-stage approaches increase model size, lead to high inference times, and rely on extra features such as glove vector [42] embedding or knowledge graph embedding [47], limiting their applicability. Recently, Liu et al. [33] proposed a fully convolutional one-stage SGG method. It combined a feature pyramid network [31] and a relation affinity field [40,61] for modeling a joint *object-relation* graph. However, their convolution-based architecture limits the context exploration across objects and relations. Contemporary to us [10] used transformers for the task of SGG. However, their complex pipeline for a separate subject and object further increases computational complexity. Crucially, there has been a significant performance gap between one-stage and two-stage approaches. This paper bridges this gap with simultaneous contextual exploration across objects and relations.

3   Methodology

In this section, we formally define the generalized *image-to-graph* generation problem. Each of the presented relation prediction tasks in Fig. 1 is a special instance of this generalized image-to-graph problem. Consider an image space $I \in \mathbb{R}^{D \times \#\mathrm{ch}}$, where $D = \prod_{i=1}^{d} \dim[i]$ for a d dimensional image and $\#$ch denotes the number of channels and $\dim[i]$ denotes the dimension of the ith spatial axis. Now, an image-to-graph generator $\mathcal{F}$ predicts $\mathcal{F}(I) = \mathcal{G}$ for a given image I, where $\mathcal{G} = (\mathcal{V}, \mathcal{E})$ represents a graph with vertices (or objects) $\mathcal{V}$ and edges (or relations) $\mathcal{E}$. Specifically, the ith vertex $v^i \in \mathcal{V}$ has a node or object location specified by a bounding box $v_{\mathrm{box}}^i \in \mathbb{R}^{2 \times d}$ and a node or object label $v_{\mathrm{cls}}^i \in \mathbb{Z}^C$. Similarly, each edge $e^{ij} \in \mathcal{E}$ has an edge or relation label $e_{\mathrm{rln}}^{ij} \in \mathbb{Z}^L$, where we have C number of object classes and L types of relation classes. Note that $\mathcal{G}$ can be both directed and undirected. The algorithmic complexity of predicting graph $\mathcal{G}$ depends on its size, $|\mathcal{G}| = |\mathcal{V}| + |\mathcal{E}|$ which is of order complexity $\mathcal{O}(N^2)$ for $|\mathcal{V}| = N$. It should be noted that object detection as a special case of the generalized image-to-graph generation problem, where $\mathcal{E} = \phi$. In the following, we briefly revisit a set-based object detector before expanding on our rationale and proposed architecture.

3.1   Preliminaries of Set-Based Object Detector

Carion et al. [7] proposed DETR, which shows the potential of set-based object detection, building upon an encoder-decoder transformer architecture [54]. Given an input image I, a convolutional backbone [17] is employed to extract high level and down scaled features. Next, the spatial dimensions of extracted features are reshaped into a vector to make them sequential. Afterwards, these sequential features are coupled with a sinusoidal positional encoding [6] to mark an unique position identifier. A stacked encoder layer, consisting of a multi-head self-attention and a feed-forward network, processes the sequential features. The decoder takes N number of learnable object queries ([obj]-tokens) in the input sequence and combines them with the output of the encoder via cross-attention, where N is larger than the maximum number of objects.

DETR utilizes the direct Hungarian set-based assignment for one-to-one matching between the ground truth and the predictions from N [obj]-tokens. The bipartite matching assigns a unique predicted object from the N predictions to each ground truth object. Only matched predictions are considered valid. The rest of the predictions are labeled as ∅ or 'background'. Subsequently, it computes the box regression loss solely for valid predictions. For the classification loss, all predictions, including 'background' objects, are considered.

In our work, we adopt a modified attention mechanism, namely deformable attention from deformable-DETR (def-DETR) [62] for its faster convergence and computational efficiency. In DETR, complete global attention allows each token to attend to all other tokens and hence capture the entire context in one image. However, information about the presence of an object is highly localized to a spatial position. Following the concept of deformable convolutions [11], deformable attention enables the queries to attend to a small set of spatial features determined from learned offsets of the reference points. This improves convergence and reduces the computational complexity of the attention operation.

3.2   Object-Relation Prediction as Set-Prediction and Interaction

A joint *object-relation* graph generation requires searching from a pairwise combinatorial space of the maximum number of expected nodes. Hence, a naive joint-learning for *object-relations* requires $\mathcal{O}(N^2)$ number of tokens for N number of objects. This is computationally intractable because self-attention is quadratically-complex to the number of tokens. We overcome this combinatorially challenging task with a carefully engineered inductive bias. Here it is to exploit learned pair-wise interactions among N [obj]-tokens and combine refined pair-wise [obj]-tokens with an additional $(N + 1)^{\text{th}}$ token, which we refer to as [rln]-token. One can think of the [rln]-token as a query to pair-wise object interaction.

The [rln]-token captures the additional context of pair-wise interactions among all valid predicted classes. In this process, related objects are incentivized to have a strong correlation in an embedding space of, and unrelated objects are penalized to be dissimilar. The [rln]-token attends to all N [obj]-tokens along

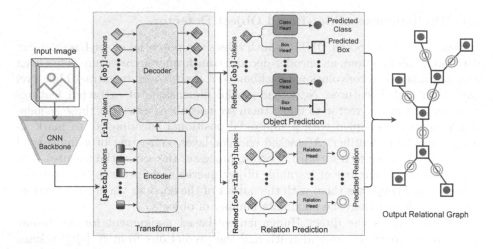

Fig. 3. Specifics of the Relationformer architecture. The image is first processed by a feature extractor, which generates [patch]-tokens for the input of the transformer encoder. Next, transformer decoder takes learnable [obj]-tokens and a [rln]-token along with output from encoder. Decoder processes them through a series of self- and cross-attention operations. The object head processes the final [obj]-tokens from the decoder to produce the bounding box and object classes. The relation head takes a tuple of the final [obj-rln-obj]-token combination and classifies their relation. Combining the output of the object and relation head yields the final graph.

with contextualized image features that enrich its local pairwise and global image reasoning. Finally, we classify a pair-wise relation by combining the pair-wise [obj]-tokens with the [rln]-token. Thus, instead of $\mathcal{O}(N^2)$ number of tokens, we only need $N + 1$ tokens in total. These consist of N [obj]-tokens and one [rln]-token. This novel formulation allows relation detection with a marginally increased cost compared to one-stage object detection.

Here, one could present a two-fold argument: 1) There is no need for an extra token as one could directly classify joint pairwise [obj]-tokens. 2) Instead of one single [rln]-token, one could use as many as all object-pairs. To answer the first question, we argue that relations can be viewed as a higher order topological entity compared to objects. Thus, to capture inter-dependencies among the relations the model requires additional expressive capacity, which can be shared among the objects. The [rln]-token reduces the burden on the [obj]-tokens by specializing exclusively on the task of relation prediction. Moreover, [obj]-tokens can also attend to the [rln]-token and exploit a global semantic reasoning. This hypothesis is confirmed in our ablation. For the second question, we argue that individual tokens for all possible object-pairs will lead to a drastic increase in the decoder complexity, which may results in computationally intractability.

3.3   Relationformer

The *Relationformer* architecture is intuitive and without any bells and whistles, see Fig. 3. We have four main components: a backbone, a transformer, an object detection head and a relation prediction head. In the following, we describe each of the components and the set-based loss formulations specific to joint *object-relation* graph generation in detail.

Backbone: Given the input image I, a convolutional backbone [17] extracts features $\boldsymbol{f}_I \in \mathbb{R}^{D_f \times \# \text{emb}}$, where D_f is the spatial dimensions of the features and $\#$ emb denotes embedding dimension. Further, this feature dimension is reduced to d_{emb}, the embedding dimension of the transformer, and flattened by its spatial size. The new sequential features coupled with the sinusoidal positional encoding [6] produce the desired sequence which is processed by the encoder.

Transformer: We use a transformer encoder-decoder architecture with deformable attention [62], which considerably speeds up the training convergence of DETR by exploiting spatial sparsity of the image features.

Encoder: Our encoder remains unchanged from [62], and uses multi-scale deformable self-attention. We use a different number of layers based on each task's requirement, which is specified in detail in the supplementary material.

Decoder: We use $N + 1$ tokens for the joint *object-relation* task as inputs to the decoder, where N represents the number of [obj]-tokens preceded by a single [rln]-token. Contextualized image features from the encoder serve as the second input of our decoder. In order to have a tractable computation and to leverage spatial sparsity, we use deformable cross-attention between the joint tokens and the image features from the encoder. The self-attention in the decoder remains unchanged. The [obj]-tokens and [rln]-token go through a series of multi-hop information exchanges with other tokens and image features, which gradually builds a hierarchical object and relational semantics. Here, [obj]-tokens learn to attend to specific spatial positions, whereas the [rln]-token learns how objects interact in the context of their semantic or global reasoning.

Object Detection Head: The object detection head has two components. The first one is a stack of fully connected network or multi layer-perceptron (MLP), which regresses the location of objects, and the second one is a single layer classification module. For each refined [obj]-token o^i, the object detection head predicts an object class $\tilde{v}_{\text{cls}}^i = \boldsymbol{W}_{\text{cls}}(o^i)$ and an object location $\tilde{\boldsymbol{v}}_{\text{box}}^i = \text{MLP}_{\text{box}}(o^i), \tilde{\boldsymbol{v}}_{\text{box}}^i \in [0,1]^{2 \times d}$ in parallel, where d represents the image dimension, $\boldsymbol{W}_{\text{cls}}$ is the classification layer, and MLP_{box} is an MLP. We use the normalized bounding box co-ordinate for scale invariant prediction. Note that for the spatio-structural graph, we create virtual objects around each node's center by assuming an uniform bounding box with a normalized width of Δx.

Relation Prediction Head: In parallel to the object detection head, the input of the relation head, given by a pair-wise [obj]-token and a shared [rln]-token, is processed as $\tilde{e}_{\text{rln}}^{ij} = \text{MLP}_{\text{rln}}(\{o^i, r, o^j\}_{i \neq j})$. Here, r represents the refined [rln]-token and MLP_{rln} a three-layer fully-connected network headed by layer normalization [2]. In the case of directional relation prediction (e.g., scene graph), the *ordering* of the object token pairs $\{o^i, r, o^j\}_{i \neq j}$ determines the direction $i \rightarrow j$.

Table 1. Brief summary of the datasets used in our experiment. For more details regarding dataset preparation, please refer to supplementary material.

Dataset	Description				Data split		
	Edge type	2D/3D	Image type	Image size	Train	Val	Test
Toulouse [5]	Undirected	2D	Binary	64×64	80k	12k	19k
20 US Cities [18]	Undirected	2D	RGB	128×128	124k	13k	25k
Synthetic vessel [51]	Undirected	3D	Grayscale	$64 \times 64 \times 64$	54k	6k	20k
Visual Genome [27]	Directed	2D	RGB	800×800	57k	5k	26k

Otherwise (e.g., road network, vessel graph), the network is trained to learn object token *order* invariance as well.

3.4 Loss Function

For object detection, we utilize a combination of loss functions. We use two standard box prediction losses, namely the ℓ_1 regression loss ($\mathcal{L}_{\text{reg}}$) and the generalized intersection over union loss ($\mathcal{L}_{\text{gIoU}}$) between the predicted $\tilde{v}_{\text{box}}$ and ground truth v_{box} box coordinates. Besides, we use the cross-entropy classification loss ($\mathcal{L}_{\text{cls}}$) between the predicted class $\tilde{v}_{\text{cls}}$ and the ground truth class v_{cls}.

Stochastic Relation Loss: In parallel to object detection, their pair-wise relations are classified with a cross-entropy loss. Particularly, we only use predicted objects that are assigned to ground truth objects by the Hungarian matcher. When two objects have a relation, we refer to their relation as a 'valid'-relation. Otherwise, the relation is categorized as 'background'. Since 'valid'-relations are highly sparse in the set of all possible permutations of objects, computing the loss for every possible pair is burdensome and will be dominated by the 'background' class, which may hurt performance. To alleviate this, we randomly sample three 'background'-relations for every 'valid'-relation. From sampled 'valid'- and 'background'-relations, we obtain a subset $\mathcal{R}$ of size M, where $\mathcal{R} \subseteq {}^N P_2$. To this end, $\mathcal{L}_{\text{rln}}$ represents a classification loss for the predicted relations in $\mathcal{R}$. The total loss for simultaneous *object-relation* graph generation is defined as:

$$\mathcal{L}_{\text{total}} = \sum_{i=1}^{N} \left[\mathbb{1}_{v_{\text{cls}}^i \notin \varnothing} (\lambda_{\text{reg}} \mathcal{L}_{\text{reg}}(v_{\text{box}}^i, \tilde{v}_{\text{box}}^i) + \lambda_{\text{gIoU}} \mathcal{L}_{\text{gIoU}}(v_{\text{box}}^i, \tilde{v}_{\text{box}}^i)) \right]$$
$$+ \quad \lambda_{\text{cls}} \sum_{i=1}^{N} \mathcal{L}_{\text{cls}}(v_{\text{cls}}^i, \tilde{v}_{\text{cls}}^i) + \lambda_{\text{rln}} \sum_{\{i,j\} \in \mathcal{R}} \mathcal{L}_{\text{rln}}(e_{\text{rln}}^{ij}, \tilde{e}_{\text{rln}}^{ij}) \quad (1)$$

where $\lambda_{\text{reg}}, \lambda_{\text{gIoU}}, \lambda_{\text{cls}}$ and λ_{rln} are the loss functions specific weights.

4   Experiments

Datasets: We conducted experiments on four public datasets for road network generation (20 US cities [18], Toulouse [5]), 3D synthetic vessel graph generation [51], and scene-graph generation (Visual Genome [27]). The road and vessel

Table 2. Quantitative comparison of Relationformer with the different baselines for undirected graph generation datasets. Relationformer achieves a near-perfect solution for the Toulouse dataset and improves the results on the 20 US Cities dataset over baseline models. Relationformer translates a similar trend in 3D and significantly outperforms the heuristic-based approach on the synthetic vessel dataset.

Dataset	Model	Graph-level metrics				Node det.		Edge det.	
		SMD ↓	Prec. ↑	Rec. ↑	F1 ↑	mAP ↑	mAR ↑	mAP ↑	mAR ↑
Toulouse (2D)	RNN [5]	0.04857	65.41	57.52	61.21	0.50	5.01	0.21	2.56
	GraphRNN [5]	0.02450	71.69	73.21	72.44	1.34	4.15	0.34	1.01
	GGT [5]	0.01649	86.95	79.88	83.26	2.94	13.31	1.62	9.75
	Relationformer	**0.00012**	**99.76**	**98.99**	**99.37**	**94.59**	**96.76**	**83.30**	**89.87**
20 US Cities (2D)	RoadTracer [3]	N.A.	78.00	57.44	66.16	N.A.	N.A.	N.A.	N.A.
	Seg-DRM [37]	N.A.	76.54	71.25	73.80	N.A.	N.A.	N.A.	N.A.
	Seg-Orientation [4]	N.A	75.83	68.90	72.20	N.A.	N.A.	N.A.	N.A.
	Sat2Graph [18]	N.A.	80.70	72.28	76.26	N.A.	N.A.	N.A.	N.A.
	Relationformer	0.04939	**85.28**	**77.75**	**81.34**	29.25	42.84	21.78	33.19
Synthetic Vessel (3D)	U-net [45]+heuristics	0.01982	N/A	N/A	N/A	18.94	29.81	17.88	27.63
	Relationformer	**0.01107**	N/A	N/A	N/A	**78.51**	**84.34**	**78.10**	**82.15**

*N.A. indicates scores are not readily available. † N/A indicates that the metric is not applicable.

graph generation datasets are spatio-structural with a binary node and edge classification task, while the scene-graph generation dataset is spatio-sematic and has 151 node classes and 51 edge classes, including 'background' class (Table 1).

Evaluation Metrics: Given the diversity of tasks at hand, we resort to widely-used task-specific metrics. Following is a brief description, while details can be found in the supplementary material. For *Spatio-Structural Graphs*, we use four different metrics to capture spatial similarity alongside the topological similarity of the predicted graphs. 1) *Street Mover Distance (SMD)* [5] computes a Wasserstein distance between predicted and ground truth edges; 2) *TOPO Score* [18] includes precision, recall, and F-1 score for topological mismatch; 3) *Node Detection* yields mean average precision (mAP) and mean average recall (mAR) for the node; and 4) *Edge Detection* yields mAP and mAR for the edges. For *Spatio-semantic Graphs*, the scene graph detection (SGDet) metric is the most challenging and appropriate for joint object-relation detection, because it does not need apriori knowledge about object location or class label. Hence, we compute recall@K, mean-recall@K, and no-graph constraint (ng)-recall@K for $K = \{20, 50, 100\}$ on the SGDet following Zellers et al. [59]. Further, we evaluate the quality of object detection using average precision, AP@50 (IoU = 0.5) [30].

4.1 Results

Spatio-Structural Graph Generation: In spatio-structural graph generation, both correct graph topology and spatial location are equally important. Note that the objects here are represented as points in 2D/3D space. For practical reasons, we put a hypothetical box of $\Delta x = 0.2$ at the points and treat the boxes as objects.

The Toulouse dataset poses the least difficulty as we predict a graph from a binary segmentation. We notice that existing methods perform poorly. Our method improves the SMD score by three orders of magnitude. All other metrics, such as TOPO-Score (prec., rec., and F–1), indicate near-optimal topological accuracy of our method. At the same time, our performance in node and edge mAP and mAR is vastly superior to all competing methods. For the more complex 20 U.S. cities dataset, we observe a similar trend. Note that due to the lack of existing scores from competing methods (SMD, mAP, and mAR), we only compare the TOPO scores, which we outperform by a significant margin. However, when compared to the results on the Toulouse dataset, Relationformer yields lower node detection scores on the 20 U.S. cities dataset, which can be attributed to the increased dataset complexity. Furthermore, the edge detection score also deteriorates. This is due to the increased proximity of edges, i.e., parallel roads.

For 3D data, such as vessels, no learning-based comparisons exist. Hence, we compare to the current best practice [49], which relies on segmentation, skeletonization, and heuristic pruning of the dense skeleta extracted from the binary segmentation [14]. The purpose of pruning is to eliminate redundant neighboring nodes, which is error-prone due to the voxelization of the connectivity, leading to poor performances. Table 2 clearly depicts how our method outperforms the current method. Importantly, we find that our method effortlessly translates from 2D to 3D without major modifications. Moreover, our 3D model is trained end-to-end from scratch without a pre-trained backbone. To summarize, we propose the first reliable learning-based 3D spatio-structural graph generation method and show how it outperforms existing 2D approaches by a considerable margin.

Scene Graph Generation: We extensively compare our method to numerous existing methods, which can be grouped based on three concepts. One-stage methods, two-stage methods utilizing only image features, and two-stage methods utilizing extra features. Importantly, Relationformer represents a one-stage method without the need for extra features. We find that Relationformer outperforms all one stage methods in Recall and ng-Recall despite using a simpler backbone. In terms of mean-Recall, a metric addressing dataset bias, we outperform [33] and our contemporary [10] @50 and perform close to [10] @20.

In terms of object detection performance, we achieve an AP@50 of 26.3, which is close to the best performing one- and two-stage methods, even though we use a simpler backbone. Note that the object detection performance varies substantially across multiple backbones and object detectors. For example, BGNN [28] uses X-101FPN, FCSGG [33] uses HRNetW48-5S-FPN, whereas Relationformer and its contemporary RelTR [10] use a simple ResNet50 [17] backbone.

Comparing our Relationformer to two-stage models, we outperform all models that use no extra features in all metrics. Moreover, we perform almost equal to the remaining two-stage models, which use powerful backbones [28], bi-label graph resampling [28], custom loss functions [32], and extra features such as word [24] or knowledge graph embeddings [8]. Therefore, we can claim that we achieve competitive performances without custom loss functions or extra features while using significantly fewer parameters. We also achieve much faster processing times, measured in frames per second (FPS) (see Table 3). For example, BGNN [28], which was the top performer in a number of metrics, requires three times more parameters and is an order of magnitude slower than our method.

Table 3. Quantitative results of Relationformer in comparison with state-of-the-art methods on the Visual Genome dataset. Relationformer achieves new one-stage state-of-the-art results and bridges the performance gap with two-stage models, while reducing model complexity and inference time significantly without the need for any extra features (e.g., glove vector, knowledge graph, etc.). Importantly, Relationformer out-performs two-stage models that previously reported mean-Recall@100 and ng-Recalls.

Method		Extra Feat.	Recall			mean-Recall			ng-Recall			AP	# param (M)↓	FPS ↑
			@20	@50	@100	@20	@50	@100	@20	@50	@100	@50		
Two-Stage	MOTIFS [59]	✓	21.4	27.2	30.5	4.2	5.7	6.6	–	30.5	35.8	20.0	240.7	6.6
	KERN [8]	✓	22.3	27.1	–	–	6.4	–	–	**30.9**	35.8	20.0	405.2	4.6
	GPS-Net [32]	✓	22.3	28.9	**33.2**	6.9	8.7	**9.8**	–	–	–	–	–	–
	BGT-Net [12]	✓	23.1	28.6	32.2	–	–	9.6	–	–	–	–	–	–
	RTN [24]	✓	22.5	29.0	33.1	–	–	–	–	–	–	–	–	–
	BGNN [28]	✓	**23.3**	**31.0**	–	**7.5**	**10.7**	–	–	–	–	**29.0**	341.9	2.3
	GB-Net [58]	✓	–	26.3	29.9	–	7.1	8.5	–	29.3	35.0	–	–	–
	IMP+ [56]	✗	14.6	20.7	24.5	2.9	3.8	4.8	–	22.0	27.4	20.0	**203.8**	10.0
	G-RCNN [57]	✗	–	11.4	13.7	–	–	–	–	28.5	**35.9**	23.0	–	–
One-Stage	FCSGG [33]	✗	16.1	21.3	–	2.7	3.6	–	16.7	23.5	29.2	**28.5**	87.1	8.3*
	RelTR [10]	✗	20.2	25.2	–	**5.8**	8.5	–	–	–	–	26.4	**63.7**	16.6
	Relationformer	✗	**22.2**	**28.4**	**31.3**	4.6	**9.3**	**10.7**	**22.9**	**31.2**	**36.8**	26.3	92.9	**18.2***

#param are taken from [10]. * Frame-per-second (FPS) is computed in Nvidia GTX 1080 GPU. Note that '-' indicates that the corresponding results are not available to us.

Figure 4 shows qualitative examples for all datasets used in our experiments. Qualitative and quantitative results from both spatio-structural and spatio-semantic graph generation demonstrate the efficiency of our approach and the importance of simultaneously leveraging [obj]-tokens and the [rln]-token. Relationformer achieves benchmark performances across a diverse set of image-to-graph generation tasks suggesting its wide applicability and scalability.

4.2   Ablation Studies

In our ablation study, we focus on two aspects. First, how the [rln]-token and relation-head guide the graph generation; second, the effect of the sample size in training transformers from scratch. We select the complex 3D synthetic vessel and Visual Genome datasets for the ablation. Further ablation experiments can be found in the supplementary material.

Table 4 (**Left**) evaluate the importance of the [rln]-token and different relation-head types. First, we train def-DETR only for object detection as proposed in [7,62], second, we evaluate Relationformer w/ and w/o [rln]-token and use a linear relation classification layer (models w/o the [rln]-token use only con-catenated pair-wise [obj]-tokens for relation classification). Third, we replace the linear relation head with an MLP and repeat the same w/ and w/o [rln]-tokens.

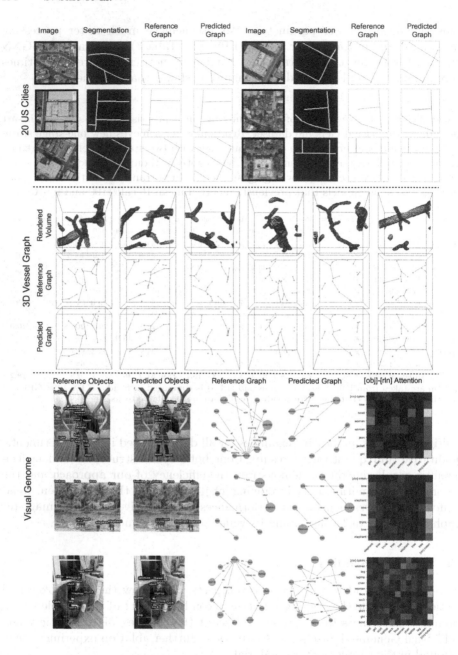

Fig. 4. Qualitative results (better viewed zoomed in) from road-network, vessel-graph, and scene-graph generation experiments. Across all datasets, we observe that Relationformer is able to produce correct results. The segmentation map is given for better interpretability of road network satellite images. For vessel-graphs, we surface-render the segmentation of corresponding greyscale voxel data. For scene graphs, we visualize the attention map between detected [obj]-tokens and [rln]-token, which shows that the [rln]-token actively attends to objects that contribute to relation formation.

Table 4. (**Left**) shows ablation on the [rln]-token and relation head type on Visual Genome. [rln]-token significantly improves relation prediction for both types of relation heads. Importantly, the improvement is larger for the linear classifier than for the MLP. (**Right**) shows ablation on the [rln]-token and train-data size on synthetic vessel. [rln]-token significantly improves both node and edge detection. Additionally, the scores improves with train-data size, suggesting further scope by training on more data.

Model	Visual Genome						Synthetic Vessel						
	[rln]-token	Rel. Head	AP	SGDet recall			[rln]-token	Train data	SMD	Node det.		Edge det.	
				@20	@50	@100				mAP	mAR	mAP	mAR
def-DETR	N/A	N/A	26.4	N/A	N/A	N/A	N/A	100%	N/A	77.5	83.5	N/A	N/A
Relationformer	✗	Linear	24.1	16.6	22.0	25.2	✗	100%	0.0129	75.5	81.6	76.3	80.4
Relationformer	✓	Linear	25.3	20.1	25.4	28.3	✓	25%	0.0138	17.0	32.1	11.5	28.3
Relationformer	✗	MLP	26.0	19.2	26.4	29.4	✓	50%	0.0124	39.2	53.5	33.3	48.9
Relationformer	✓	MLP	26.3	22.2	28.4	31.3	✓	100%	**0.0110**	**78.5**	**84.3**	**78.1**	**82.1**

We observe that a linear relation classifier w/o [rln]-token is insufficient to model the mutual relationships among objects and diminishes the object detection performance as well. In contrast, we see that the [rln]-token significantly improves performance despite using a linear relation classifier. Using an MLP instead of a linear classifier is a better strategy whereas the Relationformer w/[rln]-token shows a clear benefit. Unlike the linear layer, we hypothesize that the MLP provides a separate and adequate embedding space to model the complex semantic relationships for [obj]-tokens and our [rln]-token.

From ablation on 3D vessel (Table 4 (**Right**)), we draw the same conclusion that [rln]-token significantly improve over Relationformer w/o [rln]-token. Further, a high correlation between performance and train-data size indicates scope for improvement by increasing the sample size while training from scratch.

Limitations and Outlook: In this work, we only use bipartite object matching, and future work will investigate graph-based matching [44]. Additionally, incorporating recent transformer-based backbones, i.e., Swin-transformer [34] could further boost the performance without compromising the simplicity.

5   Conclusion

Extraction of structural- and semantic-relational graphs from images is the key for image understanding. We propose Relationformer, a unified single-stage model for direct *image-to-graph* generation. Our method is intuitive and easy to interpret because it is devoid of any hand-designed components. We show consistent performance improvement across multiple *image-to-graph* tasks using Relationformercompared to previous methods; all while being substantially faster and using fewer parameters which reduce energy consumption. Relationformer opens up new possibilities for efficient integration of a *image-to-graph* models to downstream applications in an end-to-end fashion. We believe that our method has the potential to shed light on many previously unexplored domains and can lead to new discoveries, especially in 3D.

Acknowledgement. Suprosanna Shit is supported by TRABIT (EU Grant: 765148). Rajat Koner is funded by the German Federal Ministry of Education and Research (BMBF, Grant no. 01IS18036A). Bjoern Menze gratefully acknowledges the support of the Helmut Horten Foundation.

References

1. Armeni, I., et al.: 3D scene graph: a structure for unified semantics, 3D space, and camera. In: Proceedings of the IEEE/CVF International Conference on Computer Vision, pp. 5664–5673 (2019)
2. Ba, J.L., et al.: Layer normalization. arXiv preprint arXiv:1607.06450 (2016)
3. Bastani, F., et al.: RoadTracer: automatic extraction of road networks from aerial images. In: Proceedings of the IEEE Conference on Computer Vision and Pattern Recognition, pp. 4720–4728 (2018)
4. Batra, A.: Improved road connectivity by joint learning of orientation and segmentation. In: Proceedings of the IEEE/CVF Conference on Computer Vision and Pattern Recognition, pp. 10385–10393 (2019)
5. Belli, D., Kipf, T.: Image-conditioned graph generation for road network extraction. arXiv preprint arXiv:1910.14388 (2019)
6. Bello, I., et al.: Attention augmented convolutional networks. In: Proceedings of the IEEE/CVF International Conference on Computer Vision, pp. 3286–3295 (2019)
7. Carion, N., Massa, F., Synnaeve, G., Usunier, N., Kirillov, A., Zagoruyko, S.: End-to-end object detection with transformers. In: Vedaldi, A., Bischof, H., Brox, T., Frahm, J.-M. (eds.) ECCV 2020. LNCS, vol. 12346, pp. 213–229. Springer, Cham (2020). https://doi.org/10.1007/978-3-030-58452-8_13
8. Chen, T., et al.: Knowledge-embedded routing network for scene graph generation. In: Proceedings of the IEEE/CVF Conference on Computer Vision and Pattern Recognition, pp. 6163–6171 (2019)
9. Chu, H., et al.: Neural turtle graphics for modeling city road layouts. In: Proceedings of the IEEE/CVF International Conference on Computer Vision, pp. 4522–4530 (2019)
10. Cong, Y., et al.: RelTR: relation transformer for scene graph generation. arXiv preprint arXiv:2201.11460 (2022)
11. Dai, J., et al.: Deformable convolutional networks. In: Proceedings of the IEEE International Conference on Computer Vision, pp. 764–773 (2017)
12. Dhingra, N., Ritter, F., Kunz, A.: BGT-Net: bidirectional GRU transformer network for scene graph generation. In: Proceedings of the IEEE/CVF Conference on Computer Vision and Pattern Recognition, pp. 2150–2159 (2021)
13. Dosovitskiy, A., et al.: An image is worth 16×16 words: transformers for image recognition at scale. arXiv preprint arXiv:2010.11929 (2020)
14. Drees, D., Scherzinger, A., Hägerling, R., Kiefer, F., Jiang, X.: Scalable robust graph and feature extraction for arbitrary vessel networks in large volumetric datasets. arXiv preprint arXiv:2102.03444 (2021)
15. Fang, Y., et al.: You only look at one sequence: rethinking transformer in vision through object detection. arXiv preprint arXiv:2106.00666 (2021)
16. Hamilton, W.L., et al.: Inductive representation learning on large graphs. In: Proceedings of the 31st International Conference on Neural Information Processing Systems, pp. 1025–1035 (2017)
17. He, K., et al.: Deep residual learning for image recognition. In: Proceedings of the IEEE Conference on Computer Vision and Pattern Recognition, pp. 770–778 (2016)

18. He, S., et al.: Sat2Graph: road graph extraction through graph-tensor encoding. In: Vedaldi, A., Bischof, H., Brox, T., Frahm, J.-M. (eds.) ECCV 2020. LNCS, vol. 12369, pp. 51–67. Springer, Cham (2020). https://doi.org/10.1007/978-3-030-58586-0_4

19. Hildebrandt, M., et al.: Scene graph reasoning for visual question answering. arXiv preprint arXiv:2007.01072 (2020)

20. Ji, J., et al.: Action genome: actions as compositions of spatio-temporal scene graphs. In: Proceedings of the IEEE/CVF Conference on Computer Vision and Pattern Recognition, pp. 10236–10247 (2020)

21. Ji, X., et al.: Brain microvasculature has a common topology with local differences in geometry that match metabolic load. Neuron **109**(7), 1168–1187 (2021)

22. Johnson, J., et al.: Image retrieval using scene graphs. In: Proceedings of the IEEE Conference on Computer Vision and Pattern Recognition, pp. 3668–3678 (2015)

23. Koner, R., Sinhamahapatra, P., Roscher, K., Günnemann, S., Tresp, V.: OOD-former: out-of-distribution detection transformer. arXiv preprint arXiv:2107.08976 (2021)

24. Koner, R., et al.: Relation transformer network. arXiv preprint arXiv:2004.06193 (2020)

25. Koner, R., Li, H., Hildebrandt, M., Das, D., Tresp, V., Günnemann, S.: Graphhopper: multi-hop scene graph reasoning for visual question answering. In: Hotho, A., et al. (eds.) ISWC 2021. LNCS, vol. 12922, pp. 111–127. Springer, Cham (2021). https://doi.org/10.1007/978-3-030-88361-4_7

26. Koner, R., et al.: Scenes and surroundings: scene graph generation using relation transformer. arXiv preprint arXiv:2107.05448 (2021)

27. Krishna, R., et al.: Visual genome: connecting language and vision using crowdsourced dense image annotations. arXiv preprint arXiv:1602.07332 (2016)

28. Li, R., et al.: Bipartite graph network with adaptive message passing for unbiased scene graph generation. In: Proceedings of the IEEE/CVF Conference on Computer Vision and Pattern Recognition, pp. 11109–11119 (2021)

29. Li, R., et al.: SGTR: end-to-end scene graph generation with transformer. arXiv preprint arXiv:2112.12970 (2021)

30. Lin, T.-Y., et al.: Microsoft COCO: common objects in context. In: Fleet, D., Pajdla, T., Schiele, B., Tuytelaars, T. (eds.) ECCV 2014. LNCS, vol. 8693, pp. 740–755. Springer, Cham (2014). https://doi.org/10.1007/978-3-319-10602-1_48

31. Lin, T.Y., et al.: Feature pyramid networks for object detection. In: Proceedings of the IEEE Conference on Computer Vision and Pattern Recognition, pp. 2117–2125 (2017)

32. Lin, X., et al.: GPS-Net: graph property sensing network for scene graph generation. In: Proceedings of the IEEE/CVF Conference on Computer Vision and Pattern Recognition, pp. 3746–3753 (2020)

33. Liu, H., et al.: Fully convolutional scene graph generation. In: Proceedings of the IEEE/CVF Conference on Computer Vision and Pattern Recognition, pp. 11546–11556 (2021)

34. Liu, Z., et al.: Swin transformer: hierarchical vision transformer using shifted windows. arXiv preprint arXiv:2103.14030 (2021)

35. Lu, C., Krishna, R., Bernstein, M., Fei-Fei, L.: Visual relationship detection with language priors. In: Leibe, B., Matas, J., Sebe, N., Welling, M. (eds.) ECCV 2016. LNCS, vol. 9905, pp. 852–869. Springer, Cham (2016). https://doi.org/10.1007/978-3-319-46448-0_51

36. Lu, Y., et al.: Context-aware scene graph generation with Seq2Seq transformers. In: Proceedings of the IEEE/CVF International Conference on Computer Vision, pp. 15931–15941 (2021)

37. Máttyus, G., et al.: DeepRoadMapper: extracting road topology from aerial images. In: Proceedings of the IEEE International Conference on Computer Vision, pp. 3438–3446 (2017)

38. Meyer-Spradow, J., et al.: Voreen: a rapid-prototyping environment for ray-casting-based volume visualizations. IEEE Comput. Graph. Appl. **29**(6), 6–13 (2009)

39. Miettinen, A., et al.: Micrometer-resolution reconstruction and analysis of whole mouse brain vasculature by synchrotron-based phase-contrast tomographic microscopy. BioRxiv (2021)

40. Newell, A., Deng, J.: Pixels to graphs by associative embedding. In: Advances in Neural Information Processing Systems, vol. 30 (2017)

41. Paetzold, J.C., et al.: Whole brain vessel graphs: a dataset and benchmark for graph learning and neuroscience. In: Thirty-Fifth Conference on Neural Information Processing Systems Datasets and Benchmarks Track (Round 2) (2021)

42. Pennington, J., et al.: GloVe: global vectors for word representation. In: Proceedings of the 2014 Conference on Empirical Methods in Natural Language Processing (EMNLP), pp. 1532–1543 (2014)

43. Ren, S., et al.: Faster R-CNN: towards real-time object detection with region proposal networks. In: Advances in Neural Information Processing Systems, vol. 28 (2015)

44. Rolínek, M., Swoboda, P., Zietlow, D., Paulus, A., Musil, V., Martius, G.: Deep graph matching via blackbox differentiation of combinatorial solvers. In: Vedaldi, A., Bischof, H., Brox, T., Frahm, J.-M. (eds.) ECCV 2020. LNCS, vol. 12373, pp. 407–424. Springer, Cham (2020). https://doi.org/10.1007/978-3-030-58604-1_25

45. Ronneberger, O., Fischer, P., Brox, T.: U-Net: convolutional networks for biomedical image segmentation. In: Navab, N., Hornegger, J., Wells, W.M., Frangi, A.F. (eds.) MICCAI 2015. LNCS, vol. 9351, pp. 234–241. Springer, Cham (2015). https://doi.org/10.1007/978-3-319-24574-4_28

46. Sharifzadeh, S., et al.: Classification by attention: scene graph classification with prior knowledge. In: Proceedings of the AAAI Conference on Artificial Intelligence, pp. 5025–5033 (2021)

47. Sharifzadeh, S., et al.: Improving scene graph classification by exploiting knowledge from texts. arXiv preprint arXiv:2102.04760 (2021)

48. Sharifzadeh, S., et al.: Improving visual relation detection using depth maps. In: 2020 25th International Conference on Pattern Recognition (ICPR), pp. 3597–3604. IEEE (2021)

49. Shit, S., et al.: clDice-a novel topology-preserving loss function for tubular structure segmentation. In: Proceedings of the IEEE/CVF Conference on Computer Vision and Pattern Recognition, pp. 16560–16569 (2021)

50. Song, H., et al.: ViDT: an efficient and effective fully transformer-based object detector. arXiv preprint arXiv:2110.03921 (2021)

51. Tetteh, G., et al.: DeepVesselNet: vessel segmentation, centerline prediction, and bifurcation detection in 3-D angiographic volumes. Front. Neurosci. **14**, 1285 (2020)

52. Todorov, M.I., et al.: Machine learning analysis of whole mouse brain vasculature. Nat. Methods **17**(4), 442–449 (2020)

53. Touvron, H., et al.: Training data-efficient image transformers & distillation through attention. In: International Conference on Machine Learning, pp. 10347–10357. PMLR (2021)

54. Vaswani, A., et al.: Attention is all you need. In: Advances in Neural Information Processing Systems, pp. 5998–6008 (2017)
55. Xu, D., et al.: Scene graph generation by iterative message passing. In: Computer Vision and Pattern Recognition (CVPR) (2017)
56. Xu, D., et al.: Scene graph generation by iterative message passing. In: Proceedings of the IEEE Conference on Computer Vision and Pattern Recognition, pp. 5410–5419 (2017)
57. Yang, J., Lu, J., Lee, S., Batra, D., Parikh, D.: Graph R-CNN for scene graph generation. In: Ferrari, V., Hebert, M., Sminchisescu, C., Weiss, Y. (eds.) ECCV 2018. LNCS, vol. 11205, pp. 690–706. Springer, Cham (2018). https://doi.org/10.1007/978-3-030-01246-5_41
58. Zareian, A., Karaman, S., Chang, S.-F.: Bridging knowledge graphs to generate scene graphs. In: Vedaldi, A., Bischof, H., Brox, T., Frahm, J.-M. (eds.) ECCV 2020. LNCS, vol. 12368, pp. 606–623. Springer, Cham (2020). https://doi.org/10.1007/978-3-030-58592-1_36
59. Zellers, R., et al.: Neural motifs: scene graph parsing with global context. In: Proceedings of the IEEE Conference on Computer Vision and Pattern Recognition, pp. 5831–5840 (2018)
60. Zhang, M., Chen, Y.: Link prediction based on graph neural networks (2018)
61. Zhou, X., et al.: Objects as points. arXiv preprint arXiv:1904.07850 (2019)
62. Zhu, X., et al.: Deformable DETR: deformable transformers for end-to-end object detection. arXiv preprint arXiv:2010.04159 (2020)

GAMa: Cross-View Video Geo-Localization

Shruti Vyas[✉], Chen Chen, and Mubarak Shah

Center for Research in Computer Vision, University of Central Florida,
Orlando, FL, USA
{shruti,chen.chen,shah}@crcv.ucf.edu

Abstract. The existing work in cross-view geo-localization is based on *images* where a ground panorama is matched to an aerial image. In this work, we focus on **ground videos** instead of images which provides additional contextual cues which are important for this task. There are no existing datasets for this problem, therefore we propose **GAMa dataset**, a large-scale dataset with ground videos and corresponding aerial images. We also propose a novel approach to solve this problem. At **clip-level**, a short video clip is matched with corresponding aerial image and is later used to get **video-level** geo-localization of a long video. Moreover, we propose a hierarchical approach to further improve the clip-level geo-localization. On this challenging dataset, with unaligned images and limited field of view, our proposed method achieves a Top-1 recall rate of 19.4% and 45.1% @1.0mile. Code & dataset are available at this https://github.com/svyas23/GAMa.

1 Introduction

Video geo-localization is a challenging problem with many applications such as navigation, autonomous driving, and robotics [5,11,25]. The problem to estimate geolocation of the source of a ground video is also faced by first respondents now and then. There are two main formulations to address this problem; same-view geo-localization [3,18,20] and cross-view geo-localization [13,17,36]. In same-view geo-localization, the query ground image is matched with a street view image from the reference set or gallery. Research in **videos is limited to same-view geo-localization** where a frame-by-frame approach is followed. This approach relies on availability of ground view images for all the locations which may not be possible always.

In such scenarios, cross-view geo-localization is more useful where the query image is matched with the corresponding aerial or satellite image. However, cross-view geo-localization is a more difficult problem since there is a large domain shift between ground and aerial views. The limited field-of-view in the

---

Supplementary Information The online version contains supplementary material available at https://doi.org/10.1007/978-3-031-19836-6_25.

ground view makes the problem even harder and it is sometimes difficult even for humans to identify the correct location of an image.

Fig. 1. A) Sample ground video frames and corresponding aerial image from the proposed GAMa dataset. The stars represent locations of video frames every second and mark the trajectory of the video; B) An example of larger aerial region for a video where stars represent the GPS points labeled every second and marked as $X_1, .. X_n$. The range μ is derived from the GPS points and corresponds to side of the bounding box/square. In histogram, we show frequency of number of sample videos at a given value of μ, in training set. The red dotted lines in histogram show the lower and upper threshold (i.e. 0.001 and 0.004) for selecting the videos

The existing works in cross-view geo-localization follow an image based approach where a ground image is matched with an aerial image [17,27,30]. In such an approach, the contextual information available with the video is lost. We propose to focus on the geo-localization of ground videos instead of images to take advantage of the context, i.e. how the view in one frame is related/located w.r.t. another frame. To the best of our knowledge there are no existing datasets which are publicly available and can be used for this problem. Thus, we propose a new dataset, named as *GAMa (Ground-video to Aerial-image Matching)*, which contains ground videos with GPS labels and corresponding aerial images. It consists of ∼ 1.9M aerial images and 51K ground videos where each video is around 40 s long. An example video with representative frames and corresponding aerial image is shown in Fig. 1.

We propose GAMa-Net as a benchmark method to solve this problem at *clip-level* where we match every 0.5 s (short clip), from a long video, with the corresponding aerial view. A frame-by-frame approach can be a straightforward method for video geo-localization, where a 2D convolutional network is used to get the spatial features frame-by-frame. However, as mentioned before a frame-by-frame approach ignores the rich contextual information available in a video. Thus, we propose a 3D-convolution based approach to learn the spatial-temporal features from a ground video. The proposed approach is trained using an *image-video contrastive loss* which aims to match the ground view with the aerial view. This provides a *clip-level* geo-localization which is unexplored.

Next, we propose a *hierarchical approach* which helps in improving the clip-level geo-localization performance while providing a *video-level* geo-localization with the help of clip-level predictions. Corresponding to each video, we get a set of small aerial images as matched with 0.5 s clips. We match this set of aerial images and against a larger geographical area. Therefore, we make use of the contextual information, i.e. location of smaller aerial images w.r.t. each other in a larger aerial region, to improve the geo-localization.

We evaluate the proposed approach on GAMa dataset and demonstrate its effectiveness for clip/video geo-localization. We provide an analysis and propose a set of baselines to benchmark the dataset. We make the following contributions:

- A novel problem formulation *i.e.* cross-view *video* geo-localization and a large-scale dataset, *GAMa*, with ground videos and corresponding aerial images. This is the *first* video dataset for this problem to the best of our knowledge.
- We propose *GAMa-Net*, which performs *cross-view video geo-localization* at *clip-level* by matching a ground video with aerial images using an *image-video contrastive* loss.
- We also propose a novel *hierarchical approach* which provides *video-level* geo-localization and utilizes aerial images at different *scales* to improve the clip-level geo-localization.

2   Related Works

Traditional classical features like SIFT, were earlier used for image matching in geo-localization [21,34]. As deep learning has proven successful in feature learning most of the recent studies have adopted CNN based approach for learning discriminative features for image matching [26]. The problem of image or video geo-localization is solved using either the same view, which is mostly the ground view, or cross-view. **Same-view geo-localization** makes use of the large collections of geo-tagged images available online [2,3,16,18,20,35]. The problem is approached with the assumption that there is a reference dataset consisting of geo-tagged ground images and there is an image corresponding to each query image. There is some research in video geo-localization as well which is solved at frame level and is followed by trajectory smoothing [3,6,18]. However, a more complete coverage by overhead reference data such as satellite/aerial imagery has spurred a growing interest in cross-view geo-localization.

Cross-View Geo-Localization. Most of the recent work adopt CNN based approaches. Several studies have explored CNN architectures for matching ground-level query images to overhead satellite images [8,12,27,29,30,37]. Triplet loss is mostly used optimization function [8,17]; certain studies however report better results with contrastive loss [16]. Field-of-view (FOV) also plays an important role in deciding the recall rate and ground panorama is highly accurate as compared to limited FOV [8,36]. Similarly, videos also contain more visual information as seen through the trajectory of the camera and can be expected to provide more accurate geo-localization as compared to images or frames with similar FOV.

Current works on cross-view geo-localization follow image based approach since the existing datasets only contain image pairs for ground and aerial view [9,17,19,26,32]. However, some papers do report testing their model on videos using a frame-by-frame approach [9]. Most popular datasets, Cross-View USA (CVUSA) dataset [31], CVACT [13], and Vo et al. [29] contain ground panorama aligned with corresponding aerial image. Recent publications have shown very high recall rate on these datasets while using panoramas however these values are quite low when using limited FOV and unaligned images, i.e. top@1 recall of upto 14% [23,32]. VIGOR [36] dataset also contains panorama however being unaligned it is more realistic. All these datasets use ground panorama which is not realistic from video geo-localization, as videos have limited FOV, neither do they have time series data required for such training. It is possible to get unaligned images and limited FOV from these datasets however, there is no existing dataset with ground videos and aerial image pairs to solve **cross-view** geo-localization in videos and the proposed dataset addresses this gap.

Table 1. Statistics of the proposed GAMa dataset. Note: Large aerial images are at 1792×1792 resolution whereas small aerial images or tiles are at 256×256 resolution

Parameter	Train	Test	Train (day)	Test (day)
Videos	45029	6506	21144	3103
Large aerial images	45029	6506	21144	3103
Clips	1.68M	243k	790k	116k
Centered (CN) small aerial images	1.68M	243k	790k	116k
Uncentered (UCN) small aerial images	2.21M	319k	1.04M	152k

Cross-view is also used for fine geo-localization of UAVs or robots. Camera feed (also frame-by-frame) and a known small region/map, of about a mile is used to find a more exact location in the given map [7]. Sometimes a prior is given to estimate the vehicle pose [10] or multiple modalities are used [14]. However, our focus is on coarse geo-localization where the gallery spans over multiple cities.

A frame-by-frame geo-localization of videos is also possible with the proposed GAMa dataset where 2D convolutional networks are used to extract the spatial features from each frame. However, the contextual information as available from a video is ignored with frame-by-frame processing. Fusion of features obtained from 2D-CNN is also possible however it is more memory intensive as compared to a 3D-CNN network. To address these limitations and challenges, we propose a videos based cross-view geo-localization.

3   GAMa Dataset

The proposed GAMa (**G**round-video to **A**erial-image **M**atching) dataset comprises of select videos from BDD100k [33] and aerial images from apple maps.

Ground Video Selection: Most of the videos in BDD100k dataset are 40 s long and usually have GPS label every second. The selection of videos from dataset was based on the range of latitude and longitude for a given video where we use a range parameter μ. We label the GPS points at n^{th} second as X_n (lat_n, $long_n$), where the corresponding latitude is lat_n and longitude is $long_n$ (Fig. 1B, Aerial image). Thus, for the whole video we have GPS points as $X_1(lat_1, long_1)$, $X_2(lat_2, long_2)$,.., $X_n(lat_n, long_n)$. If max latitude = lat_k and min latitude = lat_l, then Latitude range = lat_k - lat_l. Also, if max longitude = $long_p$ and min longitude = $long_q$, then Longitude range = $long_p$ - $long_q$. Range, μ = max(Latitude range, Longitude range) In order to eliminate stationary and very fast videos, we select videos with μ from 0.001 to 0.004. Figure 1B. shows the distribution of training videos with range, μ. The distribution was similar for training and test sets. This selection left us with 46596 training and 6728 testing videos which were further screened based on the availability of GPS labels.

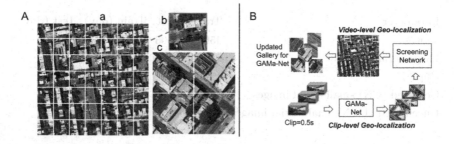

Fig. 2. A: Sample aerial images from GAMa dataset. a) A large aerial image corresponding to a video, b) Small UCN aerial image (Zoomed-in) and possible locations (stars) for a matching clip, and c) small centered (CN) aerial image as centered around the GPS label; **B**: An outline of the proposed approach. From a given ground video, clips of 0.5 s are input to GAMa-Net, one clip at a time is matched to an aerial image. The sequence of aerial images thus obtained for a video is input to the Screening network, to retrieve the large aerial region for video-level geo-localization. Top predictions of larger aerial regions provide the updated gallery for GAMa-Net

Aerial Images: For the selected videos, aerial images are downloaded as tiles from Apple maps at 19× zoom [1]. The dataset comprises of one large aerial image (1792×1792) corresponding to each video of around 40 s and 49 uncentered small aerial images (256×256) for these large aerial regions. Table 1 summarizes the dataset statistics. Since, most of the videos have a GPS label every second we divide the videos into smaller clips of 1 sec. each and for each clip we have an aerial tile. In Fig. 1A, we see an example of a large aerial region, along with the video frames at each second.

Aerial Image Centering: We have a centered (CN) and an uncentered (UCN) set of small aerial images, as reported in Table 1. As shown in Fig. 2Aa, UCN aerial images are obtained by dividing the large aerial image into smaller tiles. The GPS label in these UCN smaller aerial images can be anywhere besides the center, Fig. 2Ab. There are three labels in the figure and for each of these GPS points the same tile will be considered as the ground truth. For making a CN set, as shown in Fig. 2Ac, we take a crop centered around the corresponding GPS point however it leads to overlap among the aerial images since in some videos we have a distribution where GPS points are nearby. In the dataset, we still have a one-to-one correspondence among aerial images and short ground clips. The overlap among the aerial images increases the difficulty level for top-1 retrieval, thus we evaluate with distance thresholds.

Table 2. Comparison of GAMa dataset with existing cross-view geo-localization datasets. Note that the previous datasets do not contain ground videos

	Vo [29]	CVACT [13]	CVUSA [31]	GAMa (proposed)
Ground videos	No	No	No	51535
Panorama	450,000	128,334	44,416	No
Aerial images	450,000	128,334	44,416	1.92M
Aerial img resolution	–	1200×1200	750×750	256×256 & 1792×1792
Multiple cities	Yes	No	Yes	Yes

The ground videos in the proposed GAMa dataset are selected from BDD100k dataset [33]. They are distributed all over the US and also from middle eastern region. However, most of the videos are from four US cities; New York, Berkeley, San Francsico, and Bay area. They show different weather conditions, as well as different times of the day including day and night.

There is occlusion in videos and shadows of the skyscrapers in aerial images. Limited FOV in videos and all stated characteristics bring it closer to a realistic scenario, making it a difficult dataset for geo-localization. In Table 2, we show a comparison with existing datasets for cross-view geo-localization.

4 Method

An overview of the proposed approach which works on clip and video level is show in Fig. 2B. Ground-video to Aerial-image Matching Network (GAMa-Net) learns features for ground view clips and aerial images; and bring the matching pair closer in the feature space by applying a contrastive loss. This provides a clip-level geo-localization for a long video. In addition, we propose an hierarchical approach, where we perform video-level geo-localization and use it to update the gallery of aerial images by selecting top matched large aerial regions (Fig. 2B). The reduced gallery helps improve the clip-level geo-localization by screening out some of the visually similar however incorrect aerial images.

4.1   GAMa-Net: *Clip-Level Geo-Localization*

The proposed network takes as input a short clip from a ground video and matches it with corresponding aerial image. An overview of the proposed network is shown in Fig. 3.

Visual Encoders. In GAMa-Net, we have a video encoder i.e. Ground Video Encoder (GVE) to get features from ground video frames and an image encoder for aerial image features i.e. Aerial Image Encoder (AIE). GVE uses 3D-ResNet18 as backbone and a two layer transformer encoder. Given a ground video C, GVE provides features for a 8 frame clip C_i at the ith second of the video. There is a skip-rate of one frame so we are covering around half a second in the clip, C_i. AIE on the other hand uses 2D-ResNet18 as the backbone. It takes the corresponding aerial image, A_i as the input and learns the features to match with that of the ground video.

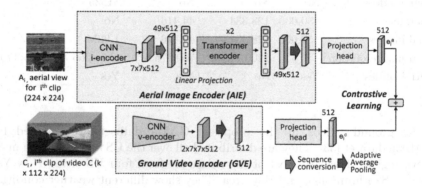

Fig. 3. Network diagram of **GAMa-Net** proposed for clip-level geo-localization. We use 3D-CNN as our base network for learning features from a ground clip (around 0.5 s). Similarly, for aerial image features, we use a 2D CNN backbone. Since only some parts of aerial images are covered by the video feed, using a transformer encoder improves the learning. Number of frames, k = 8 with skip rate = 1

Transformer Encoding: In the ground video all the visual features are not of equal importance for matching with the aerial view. This is true for aerial images as well and few features are more important when matching with ground videos. For example, the top of a building as seen from aerial images is not visible from a ground video and hence cannot be used to match the pair. To address this, we experimented with multi-headed self attention. We input the features obtained from convolutional networks to a transformer encoder framework which comprises of 4 heads and 2 layers, and uses positional encoding. A small neural network i.e. projection head is used to map the representations to the space where contrastive loss is applied. We use a MLP with one hidden layer to obtain the ground video and aerial image feature vectors e^c_i and e^a_i, respectively.

Image-Video Contrastive Loss: We utilize contrastive loss formulation, base on NT-Xent [4,15,24], to train our network. For a given ground video the corresponding aerial image is considered a positive sample and rest of the samples are considered as negatives. This is a image-video contrastive loss applied on features from two different visual modalities i.e. ground videos and aerial images. In the loss formulation, the focus is on reducing the distance between the positive pair. We have a total of $2(N)$ data points in any mini-batch with N examples. The image-video contrastive loss for a pair of positive examples is defined as,

$$l_{c,a} = -\log \frac{\exp(\text{sim}(e^c_i, e^a_i)/\tau)}{\sum_{k=1}^{N} \mathbb{1}_{[k \neq i]} \exp(\text{sim}(e^c_i, e^c_k)/\tau) + \sum_{k=1}^{N} \mathbb{1}_{[k \neq i]} \exp(\text{sim}(e^c_i, e^a_k)/\tau)}, \quad (1)$$

where e^c_i and e^a_i is a positive pair, e^c_i and (e^c_k or e^a_k) are negative pairs, $\mathbb{1}_{[k \neq i]} \in \{0,1\}$ is an indicator function with value 1 if $k \neq i$, τ is a temperature parameter, sim is the cosine similarity between a pair of features. The final loss is computed for all the positive pairs, both (e^c, e^a) and (e^a, e^c).

4.2   Hierarchical Approach

In this approach, we introduce video-level geo-localization in contrast to clip-level geo-localization which also helps in reducing the search space for GAMa-Net (Fig. 2B). The clips of a given video are temporally related and provide contextual information to help improve the geo-localization. Similarly, while looking at this problem from aerial image view point, the sequence of aerial images corresponding to clips from a given video are also related geographically and some of the correct prediction at clip-level can be used to update the gallery. Using a smaller gallery also reduces the possibility of error in feature matching.

Approach: We have four steps in this approach. In Step-1, we use GAMa-Net which takes one clip (0.5 s) at a time and matches with a small aerial image. Using multiple clips of a video, we get a sequence of aerial images for the whole video, i.e. around 40 images. In Step-2, we use predictions of aerial images and match them to the corresponding larger aerial region. We use a screening network to match the features in the same view i.e. aerial view. In Step-3, we use screening network predictions to reduce the gallery size (i.e. search space) by selecting top ranked large aerial regions corresponding to a video. These large aerial regions define our new search area for a given video. In Step-4, we use GAMa-Net i.e. the same network as in Step-1, however localize using the updated gallery. More explanation in supplementary.

Visually correct predictions from Step-1 which may not be the ground truth are used to reduce the gallery using this approach. This approach helps improve the clip-level geo-localization since the reduction of the gallery is based on the fact that all the clips of a given video are geolocated nearby. Thus, the aerial images predicted by GAMa-Net can be used to find that large aerial region where all these clips have been captured. In this case, the probability of finding all those visually correct aerial images in the same region is higher when we are searching at the correct geolocation. Hence, it is likely to match with correct large aerial region provided that meaningful and enough information is available.

Screening Network: Video-Level Geo-Localization: We use the screening network to match a sequence of smaller aerial images with the corresponding larger aerial region. The network is similar to GAMa-Net, however the sequence of aerial images is input to Small Aerial Encoder (SAE) with 2D-ResNet18 backbone and the sequence of features are later averaged to obtain a 512D feature vector (Fig. 4A). We also experimented with a 3D-ResNet18 backbone which is discussed later. The feature vector thus obtained is matched with the feature vector of corresponding large aerial image from Large Aerial Encoder (LAE). We apply contrastive loss similar to Eq. 1. The predictions from this network are used to update the gallery for GAMa-Net.

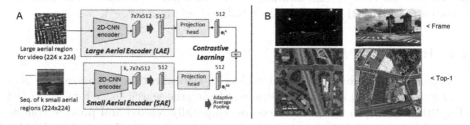

Fig. 4. A) Network diagram of the Screening network used for video-level geo-localization in our proposed Hierarchical approach. B) Predictions at video level (2 samples), where a representative frame of video (top-row) is shown along with correct matched large aerial region (bottom-row)

5   Experiments and Results

Implementation and Training Details: We implement the proposed GAMa-Net and screening network using PyTorch [15] and train the networks using Adam optimizer with a learning rate (lr) of 8e-5. We use a lr scheduler with lr decay rate of 0.1. The screening network is trained in two step; first with the actual ground truth sequences, and then finetuned with predictions from GAMa-Net. The finetuning step allows the network to adapt to noisy aerial sequences which will be used during inference. We use pre-trained weights from Kinetics-400 for 3D-ResNet18 and ImageNet weights for 2D-ResNet18. The ground videos in the proposed dataset are from different times of the day. For faster training, we used **only day** videos in our experiments unless stated otherwise.

Evaluation: We use top-k recall for clip-level and video-level matching at different values of k. Given a video query, its closest k reference neighbors in the feature space are retrieved as predictions. Similar to image based geo-localization methods we use recall rates at top-1, top-5, top-10, and top 1%. More details can be found in [8,22,29]. We have UCN and CN sets of aerial images corresponding to each clip. In UCN set there is one-to-one correspondence between the clip and aerial image. The GPS point can be anywhere within the aerial image however in the CN set there is an overlap among the aerial images. To keep the evaluation similar to UCN set it is considered a correct match if the predicted GPS is within the range of 0.05 mi of the correct location. We also report top-1@t rate where t is a distance threshold to be used for correct prediction.

Baselines: We propose several baselines for comparison. For ground image based baselines we use the center frame of the clip as an input. Image-CBn, our proposed baseline uses 2D-CNN ResNet18 model to encode the ground video frame with similar contrastive loss formulation as GAMa-Net. We use two different loss functions for video based baselines (Triplet-Bn and CBn); margin triplet loss [28] and contrastive loss [4]. In these baselines, we utilize 2D-CNN ResNet18 for aerial images and 3D-CNN ResNet18 for ground videos.

Table 3. Comparison with proposed baselines; CBn(Contrastive Baseline) & Bn(Baseline). Recall rates in parentheses() are for uncentered set. Top three rows show results with image based methods

Model	Video	R@1	R@5	R@10	R@1%
Image-CBn	✗	9.5(1.5)	18.8(5.5)	24.6(9.0)	87.7(50.7)
Shi et al. [23]	✗	9.6	18.1	26.6	71.9
L2LTR [32]	✗	11.7	20.8	28.2	87.1
Triplet-Bn	✓	< 1(< 1)	< 1(1.2)	1.1(2.4)	33.1(33.8)
CBn	✓	11.5(3.2)	21.7(10.9)	27.8(16.7)	89.2(65.0)
GAMa-Net	✓	15.2	27.2	**33.8**	**91.9**
GAMa-Net (Hierarchical)	✓	**18.3**	**27.6**	32.7	–

5.1 Results

The evaluations of GAMa-Net and a comparison with baselines is shown in Table 3. We observe a Top-1 recall rate of 18.3% and 15.2%, using GAMa-Net with and without the hierarchical approach, respectively. On UCN set, we observe poor performance as compared to CN set which was expected.

Comparison: In first row, we show results with our image-based baselines which uses a single frame from the ground video. We also compare with other image based methods using a single frame as input and observe that the proposed approach outperforms all these baselines. While training with a single image is faster we do not have the temporal information which can be perceived as relative positioning or contextual information. As the camera moves along a path or trajectory we can see the buildings or objects pass-by giving an idea of their respective location. The information of distance/relative-positioning as seen by a 3D-CNN is the additional information when we train with videos. As shown in the Table 3, using a video provides better results as compared to images.

Few studies have reported better performance with contrastive loss [16], however triplet loss is also frequently used for geo-localization [18,36]. We also observe better performance with contrastive loss as compared to triplet loss (Table 3). In GAMa-Net, we have features from two different visual modalities i.e. one from ground **videos** and other from aerial **images**, which is different from traditional contrastive loss. Similarly, training with triplet loss also use image-video features and this difference is likely responsible for the poor training with triplet loss.

Qualitative Analysis: Figure 5 show sample Top-5 predictions with different models where the leftmost is Top-1 and the rightmost is 5th. The combined model, i.e. GAMa-Net without transformer encoder, makes visually meaningful predictions. In the leftmost example, camera is passing under a fly-over and the predictions show a similar locations. The middle example is of a road without any crossings or red lights in sight, and right-most example is of a city street with crossing markings on road. The predictions by combined model match these specifications. However, in these samples, the ground truth is in top-1% but not in top-5 images. The predictions by GAMa-Net, with multi-headed self-attention improves the network performance and correct prediction moves up in the top-5.

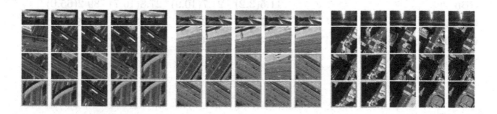

Fig. 5. Geo-localization results for three query clips, using different models. Top-row shows frames of the query clips. Second row is for combined model (Top-5 predictions), and third row is GAMa-Net. Bottom row shows predictions by GAMa-Net with Hierarchical approach (gallery reduced to 1% of larger aerial regions). Correct predictions have a green outline. Owing to close GPS labels there are multiple correct aerial images.(Color figure online)

Table 4. Screening network matches large aerial regions using a sequence of matched aerial images. In this Table, we compare 3D-CNN and 2D-CNN backbone for aerial image sequence of 8 or 32 images

Model	R@1	R@10	R@1%	R@10%
3D-CNN (seq of 8 aerial)	7.5	24.9	39.8	67.9
3D-CNN (seq of 32 aerial)	3.8	19.8	36.1	74.9
2D-CNN (seq of 8 aerial)	**12.2**	**35.3**	**49.3**	77.2
2D-CNN (seq of 32 aerial)	8.2	20.9	29.3	**83.8**

Hierarchical Approach: The predictions from the screening network are used for video-level geo-localization and to reduce the gallery for GAMa-Net. We experimented with both 2D-CNN and 3D-CNN backbone for aerial image sequence. As shown in Table 4, better results were achieved with 2D-CNN backbone likely due to better spatial features. A comparison of number of input aerial images show that 2D-CNN with 8 frames retains more ground truths at Top-1 (12.2%), Top-10 (35.3%) and Top-1% (49.3%). We do not have 32 samples in some of the samples which likely effects the performance. However, when we evaluated GAMa-Net after gallery reduction, Screening network i.e. **2D-CNN network with 32 aerial images** provided the best results. Figure 4B shows qualitative results for video-level geo-localization. It shows one frame of the video input to GAMa-Net, the predicted seq of aerial images thus obtained was used to identify the larger aerial regions. The bottom row shows the correct matched large aerial regions for video-level geo-localization. More results are in supplementary.

Table 5. Results with **GAMa-Net**, without and with the hierarchical approach

Gallery size	R@1	R@5	R@10	R@1%
Full	15.2	27.2	33.8	**91.9**
With hierarchical approach				
Top-10	16.2	22.8	25.5	–
Top-1%	**18.3**	27.6	32.7	–
Top-10%	16.6	**28.2**	**34.6**	76.6

Gallery Sizes: In Table 5, we discuss the results with GAMa-Net using various gallery sizes, i.e. Top-10, Top-1%, and Top-10% of large aerial regions, identified using screening network. We see better Top-1 results with Top-1% gallery as compared to Top-10 and Top-10%. There is a trade-off between reduced search space which improves matching and retaining the ground truth. As observed from Table 4, in Top-10 we have ground truth for only 20.9% of videos which

Table 6. Results with our best model and ablations for comparison. Here we show Top-1@threshold for comparison, with threshold values of 0.1, 0.2, 0.5 and 1.0 mi. CBn-UCN and CBn-CN, represent the contrastive baselines with uncentered and centered aerial images, respectively. Hierarchical approach uses one percent of the gallery

Model	Recall @							
	Top-1	Top-5	Top-10	Top-1%	Top-1@0.1	Top-1@0.2	Top-1@0.5	Top-1@1.0
CBn-UCN	3.2	10.9	16.7	65.0	3.6	5.9	11.3	18.6
CBn-CN	11.5	21.7	27.8	89.2	15.7	19.0	25.1	32.1
Combined	11.6	23.4	30.4	**92.4**	15.6	19.0	25.0	32.7
Video-Tx	14.1	25.4	31.8	90.8	18.7	22.1	28.1	35.7
GAMa-Net	15.2	27.2	**33.8**	91.9	19.6	23.0	28.7	36.1
Dual-Tx	14.6	26.1	32.7	91.8	19.0	22.2	28.2	35.5
Hierarchical	**18.3**	**27.6**	32.7	–	**23.5**	**27.8**	**34.9**	**43.6**

increases to 83.8% at 10% gallery. However, this percentage will be different if we consider clips since we get different number of clips from each video, as per GPS labels. We evaluated GAMa-Net, which is clip level, using a reduced gallery. Even when ground truth was not available for many samples we see a Top-10 recall rate of 25.5%. When gallery is reduced to Top-10 and Top-1% of larger aerial regions we do not have enough clips to make upto 1% of the total gallery. In Fig. 5, we show three example predictions and it is evident that results by GAMa-Net are improved with hierarchical approach.

5.2 Ablations

Combined Model: In Table 6, we observe better performance with combined model as compared to baselines, and a Top-1% recall of 92.4%. As expected, the performance improves as we increase the distance threshold. In the combined model, we have various augmentations which includes spatial and temporal centering, and random crop. Since images are not aligned in GAMa we stochastic-ally rotate the aerial view (0, 90, 180, 270°) for view-point invariance. All these augmentations have been reported to help improve geo-localization. We also include hard negatives for better training however transformer encoder is not a part of combined model.

Transformer Encoder: Similar to an aerial image, not all visual features in the ground video have the same importance for cross-view geo-localization. Thus, we implemented transformer(Tx) encoder on ground video(Video-Tx) and aerial images(Aerial-Tx), individually. In both cases, we observe an increase in recall @Top-1. The performance is better with GAMa-Net(i.e. Aerial-Tx) and we observe 15.2% Top-1 recall which is higher than 14.1% with Video-Tx (Table 6). Observing an improvement in both cases we used transformer encoder on both sides(Dual-Tx) however it did not perform better than the GAMa-Net.

Hierarchical Approach: We use hierarchical approach to improve the performance of GAMa-Net by reducing the gallery. Top-1@threshold (Table 6) shows that using the hierarchical approach makes the matching more effective by predicting the aerial images closer to the correct GPS location or ground truth. The **difference** in Top-1 recall, with and without hierarchical approach, is even higher at higher thresholds i.e. 7.5% at 1.0 mi vs 3.9% at 0.1 mi. An increase in recall to 43.6% at 1.0 mi threshold shows that the ground truth is not very far from the Top-1.

6   Discussion

Videos and Contextual Information: In videos, we have more information which can be considered as contextual information from geo-localization point of view. It enables the network to locate a given frame or view with respect to the other frames in the video. One frame may contain features to complement another and together they are likely to provide more or complete information required for geolocating. In Table 3, we have compared video based method with frame based baselines. Better recall rate with videos show that the network is able to utilize the additional information available with videos.

Centered vs Uncentered: In an UNC aerial image the corresponding GPS point can be anywhere in the tile. In cases where the GPS point is near the boundary, the visual information from the video is less likely to match the corresponding tile. As expected, after centering (CBn-CN) we observed an improvement in the recall rate as compared with the uncentered set (i.e. CBn-UCN).

Full Dataset: GAMa dataset is a large dataset which has its pros and cons. With large amount of data networks are better trained however this also increases the training time and memory requirement. Here we discuss results with models trained on full dataset (Table 7) i.e. both day and night videos. There is an improvement of 1–4% in recall at all k. Thus, using the hierarchical approach our best R@Top-1 and R@Top-1@1.0 is 19.4% and 45.1%, respectively.

Table 7. Training on full dataset and evaluation on day videos

Model	Recall @			
	Top-1	Top-1%	Top-1@0.1	Top-1@1.0
Combined	14.7	**94.8**	19.2	36.7
GAMa-Net	17.5	94.7	22.3	39.3
Hierarchical	**19.4**	–	**25.0**	**45.1**

Comparison: Our results are comparable to existing image based methods. One recent study reports **R@1=13.95% on CVUSA** when images are unaligned and have around 70% field of view (FOV) [32]. Most of the cross-view geo-localization datasets such as CVUSA report high R@k while using ground panorama and aligned aerial images; which is unrealistic since a normal camera lens has a FOV of around 72% and alignment is also not possible always. In GAMa dataset, the aerial images and ground videos are **unaligned**, and ground videos have a **limited FOV** which makes it a more realistic and difficult dataset.

Challenges: In GAMa dataset among the two sets of small aerial images, i.e. CN and UCN, the UCN set is more realistic however difficult for geo-localization. Lack of alignment increase this difficulty however, the orientation information can be extracted from the GPS information and is likely to improve the performance [13]. Also, the **ground videos** have varying lengths and in some videos GPS label is not available every second. Thus, the video length available for geo-localization is less than 40 s. Additionally, there is occlusion because of the car hood and other objects. Such cases are more likely to appear in fail cases.

Limitations: The proposed hierarchical approach performs better with longer videos (8 s. or more), however it can be used with shorter clips as well. The aim behind using a hierarchical approach is to filter out confusing samples to improve the retrieval rate. However, this sometimes leads to filtering of the ground truth from the gallery. The model is also likely to fail with indoor videos since it will not be possible to match the features with an aerial image. However, this limitation is common to all cross-view geo-localization methods.

7   Conclusions

In this work, we focus on the problem of video geo-localization via cross-view matching. We propose a new dataset for this problem which has more than 51K ground videos and 1.9 million satellite images. The dataset spans multiple cities and is a more realistic dataset, unaligned and limited FOV. We believe that this dataset will be useful for future research in cross-view video geo-localization. Our proposed GAMa-Net effectively makes use of the rich contextual information available with video. In addition, we propose a hierarchical approach which also utilize the contextual information to further improve the geo-localization.

References

1. Satellite images. https://www.apple.com/maps/. Accessed Jan 2021
2. Arandjelovic, R., Gronat, P., Torii, A., Pajdla, T., Sivic, J.: Netvlad: Cnn architecture for weakly supervised place recognition. In: Proceedings of the IEEE Conference on Computer Vision and Pattern Recognition, pp. 5297–5307 (2016)
3. Chaabane, M., Gueguen, L., Trabelsi, A., Beveridge, R., O'Hara, S.: End-to-end learning improves static object geo-localization from video. In: Proceedings of the IEEE/CVF Winter Conference on Applications of Computer Vision, pp. 2063–2072 (2021)
4. Chen, T., Kornblith, S., Norouzi, M., Hinton, G.: A simple framework for contrastive learning of visual representations. In: International Conference on Machine Learning, pp. 1597–1607. PMLR (2020)

5. Grigorescu, S., Trasnea, B., Cocias, T., Macesanu, G.: A survey of deep learning techniques for autonomous driving. J. Field Rob. **37**(3), 362–386 (2020)
6. Hakeem, A., Vezzani, R., Shah, M., Cucchiara, R.: Estimating geospatial trajectory of a moving camera. In: 18th International Conference on Pattern Recognition (ICPR 2006), vol. 2, pp. 82–87. IEEE (2006)
7. Hosseinpoor, H., Samadzadegan, F., Dadras Javan, F.: Pricise target geolocation and tracking based on uav video imagery. Int. Arch. Photogram. Remote Sens. Spatial Inf. Sci. **41** (2016)
8. Hu, S., Feng, M., Nguyen, R.M., Lee, G.H.: Cvm-net: cross-view matching network for image-based ground-to-aerial geo-localization. In: Proceedings of the IEEE Conference on Computer Vision and Pattern Recognition, pp. 7258–7267 (2018)
9. Hu, S., Lee, G.H.: Image-based geo-localization using satellite imagery. Int. J. Comput. Vision **128**(5), 1205–1219 (2020)
10. Kim, D.K., Walter, M.R.: Satellite image-based localization via learned embeddings. In: 2017 IEEE International Conference on Robotics and Automation (ICRA), pp. 2073–2080. IEEE (2017)
11. Li, A., Hu, H., Mirowski, P., Farajtabar, M.: Cross-view policy learning for street navigation. In: Proceedings of the IEEE/CVF International Conference on Computer Vision, pp. 8100–8109 (2019)
12. Lin, T.Y., Cui, Y., Belongie, S., Hays, J.: Learning deep representations for ground-to-aerial geolocalization. In: Proceedings of the IEEE Conference on Computer Vision and Pattern Recognition, pp. 5007–5015 (2015)
13. Liu, L., Li, H.: Lending orientation to neural networks for cross-view geo-localization. In: Proceedings of the IEEE/CVF Conference on Computer Vision and Pattern Recognition, pp. 5624–5633 (2019)
14. Miller, I.D., et al.: Any way you look at it: semantic crossview localization and mapping with lidar. IEEE Rob. Autom. Lett. **6**(2), 2397–2404 (2021)
15. Paszke, A., et al.: Pytorch: an imperative style, high-performance deep learning library. In: Wallach, H., Larochelle, H., Beygelzimer, A., d' Alché-Buc, F., Fox, E., Garnett, R. (eds.) Advances in Neural Information Processing Systems, vol. 32, pp. 8024–8035. Curran Associates, Inc. (2019)
16. Radenović, F., Tolias, G., Chum, O.: Fine-tuning cnn image retrieval with no human annotation. IEEE Trans. Pattern Anal. Mach. Intell. **41**(7), 1655–1668 (2018)
17. Regmi, K., Borji, A.: Cross-view image synthesis using geometry-guided conditional gans. Comput. Vision Image Underst. **187**, 102788 (2019)
18. Regmi, K., Shah, M.: Video geo-localization employing geo-temporal feature learning and gps trajectory smoothing. In: Proceedings of the IEEE/CVF International Conference on Computer Vision, pp. 12126–12135 (2021)
19. Rodrigues, R., Tani, M.: Are these from the same place? seeing the unseen in cross-view image geo-localization. In: Proceedings of the IEEE/CVF Winter Conference on Applications of Computer Vision, pp. 3753–3761 (2021)
20. Sarlin, P.E., DeTone, D., Malisiewicz, T., Rabinovich, A.: Superglue: learning feature matching with graph neural networks. In: Proceedings of the IEEE/CVF Conference on Computer Vision and Pattern Recognition, pp. 4938–4947 (2020)
21. Senlet, T., Elgammal, A.: Satellite image based precise robot localization on sidewalks. In: 2012 IEEE International Conference on Robotics and Automation, pp. 2647–2653. IEEE (2012)
22. Shi, Y., Liu, L., Yu, X., Li, H.: Spatial-aware feature aggregation for image based cross-view geo-localization. Adv. Neural Inf. Process. Syst. **32**, 10090–10100 (2019)

23. Shi, Y., Yu, X., Campbell, D., Li, H.: Where am i looking at? joint location and orientation estimation by cross-view matching. In: Proceedings of the IEEE/CVF Conference on Computer Vision and Pattern Recognition, pp. 4064–4072 (2020)
24. Sohn, K.: Improved deep metric learning with multi-class n-pair loss objective. Adv. Neural Inf. Process. Syst. **29**, 1–9 (2016)
25. Tian, X., Shao, J., Ouyang, D., Shen, H.T.: Uav-satellite view synthesis for cross-view geo-localization. IEEE Trans. Circ. Syst. Video Technol. **32**, 4804–4815 (2021)
26. Tian, Y., Chen, C., Shah, M.: Cross-view image matching for geo-localization in urban environments. In: Proceedings of the IEEE Conference on Computer Vision and Pattern Recognition, pp. 3608–3616 (2017)
27. Toker, A., Zhou, Q., Maximov, M., Leal-Taixé, L.: Coming down to earth: satellite-to-street view synthesis for geo-localization. In: Proceedings of the IEEE/CVF Conference on Computer Vision and Pattern Recognition, pp. 6488–6497 (2021)
28. Vassileios Balntas, Edgar Riba, D.P., Mikolajczyk, K.: Learning local feature descriptors with triplets and shallow convolutional neural networks. In: Richard C. Wilson, E.R.H., Smith, W.A.P. (eds.) Proceedings of the British Machine Vision Conference (BMVC), pp. 119.1-119.11. BMVA Press (2016). https://doi.org/10.5244/C.30.119
29. Vo, N.N., Hays, J.: Localizing and orienting street views using overhead imagery. In: Leibe, B., Matas, J., Sebe, N., Welling, M. (eds.) ECCV 2016. LNCS, vol. 9905, pp. 494–509. Springer, Cham (2016). https://doi.org/10.1007/978-3-319-46448-0_30
30. Wang, T., et al.: Each part matters: local patterns facilitate cross-view geo-localization. IEEE Trans. Circ. Syst. Video Technol. **32**, 867–879 (2021)
31. Workman, S., Souvenir, R., Jacobs, N.: Wide-area image geolocalization with aerial reference imagery. In: Proceedings of the IEEE International Conference on Computer Vision, pp. 3961–3969 (2015)
32. Yang, H., Lu, X., Zhu, Y.: Cross-view geo-localization with layer-to-layer transformer. Adv. Neural Inf. Process. Syst. **34**, 29009–29020 (2021)
33. Yu, F., et al.: Bdd100k: a diverse driving dataset for heterogeneous multitask learning. In: Proceedings of the IEEE/CVF Conference on Computer Vision and Pattern Recognition, pp. 2636–2645 (2020)
34. Zamir, A.R., Shah, M.: Accurate image localization based on google maps street view. In: Daniilidis, K., Maragos, P., Paragios, N. (eds.) ECCV 2010. LNCS, vol. 6314, pp. 255–268. Springer, Heidelberg (2010). https://doi.org/10.1007/978-3-642-15561-1_19
35. Zemene, E., Tesfaye, Y.T., Idrees, H., Prati, A., Pelillo, M., Shah, M.: Large-scale image geo-localization using dominant sets. IEEE Trans. Pattern Anal. Mach. Intell. **41**(1), 148–161 (2018)
36. Zhu, S., Yang, T., Chen, C.: Vigor: cross-view image geo-localization beyond one-to-one retrieval. In: Proceedings of the IEEE/CVF Conference on Computer Vision and Pattern Recognition, pp. 3640–3649 (2021)
37. Zhu, Y., Sun, B., Lu, X., Jia, S.: Geographic semantic network for cross-view image geo-localization. IEEE Trans. Geosci. Remote Sens. **60**, 1–15 (2021)

Revisiting a kNN-Based Image Classification System with High-Capacity Storage

Kengo Nakata[✉], Youyang Ng, Daisuke Miyashita, Asuka Maki,
Yu-Chieh Lin, and Jun Deguchi

Kioxia Corporation, Kawasaki, Japan
{kengo1.nakata,youyang.ng,daisuke1.miyashita,asuka.maki,yuchieh.lin,
jun.deguchi}@kioxia.com

Abstract. In existing image classification systems that use deep neural networks, the knowledge needed for image classification is implicitly stored in model parameters. If users want to update this knowledge, then they need to fine-tune the model parameters. Moreover, users cannot verify the validity of inference results or evaluate the contribution of knowledge to the results. In this paper, we investigate a system that stores knowledge for image classification, such as image feature maps, labels, and original images, not in model parameters but in external high-capacity storage. Our system refers to the storage like a database when classifying input images. To increase knowledge, our system updates the database instead of fine-tuning model parameters, which avoids catastrophic forgetting in incremental learning scenarios. We revisit a kNN (k-Nearest Neighbor) classifier and employ it in our system. By analyzing the neighborhood samples referred by the kNN algorithm, we can interpret how knowledge learned in the past is used for inference results. Our system achieves 79.8% top-1 accuracy on the ImageNet dataset without fine-tuning model parameters after pretraining, and 90.8% accuracy on the Split CIFAR-100 dataset in the task incremental learning setting.

Keywords: kNN classifier · Continual learning · Explainable AI

1 Introduction

Image classification systems using deep neural networks (DNN) have achieved superhuman recognition performance in computer vision tasks [13,15,22,30,32, 42]. On the other hand, the knowledge for image classification is implicitly stored in model parameters and is not accessible to users. For example, users cannot retrieve knowledge related to only *cats* or *dogs* from the model parameters. Training datasets may contain a small amount of inappropriate data (e.g., incorrectly

Supplementary Information The online version contains supplementary material available at https://doi.org/10.1007/978-3-031-19836-6_26.

labeled or undesirably biased images) [1,36,43]. If the model parameters are optimized using such training datasets, then the image classification systems will implicitly contain false knowledge. In existing systems, however, users cannot selectively eliminate or correct only the false knowledge in model parameters.

To update knowledge (add, delete, or modify), users need to fine-tune the model parameters. Especially, in continual or incremental learning scenarios [23,31] where new data is continually added to a training dataset, the cost for fine-tuning is incurred repeatedly as new data is added. If model parameters are fine-tuned with only newly added data in an attempt to reduce the cost, the model will acquire new knowledge for the added data while forgetting the knowledge learned in the past, which is often called catastrophic forgetting [18,31]. Although various methods have been proposed to mitigate the impact of catastrophic forgetting [4,7,27,35,39,40], as long as modifying model parameters, forgetting some knowledge is inevitable. Refs. [25,38] propose a zero-shot classifier that does not require any fine-tuning by sufficiently pretraining model parameters on large-scale datasets which contain a variety of images. Such classifier does not face the catastrophic forgetting even without fine-tuning, but it cannot additionally acquire user's desired knowledge with the user's own datasets.

Moreover, in existing systems, users cannot verify the validity of inference results or evaluate the contribution of knowledge to the results. For instance, users do not know how models utilize knowledge learned in the past to classify input images. Although we can identify unnecessary parameters through accuracy evaluation or some other parameter analyses [48,53,56], we cannot interpret why the parameters, that is, knowledge, are unnecessary (cf. explainable AI).

We investigate a system that stores image feature maps, labels, and original images of entire training datasets in external high-capacity storage as knowledge for image classification. Our image classification system refers to the external storage like a database when classifying input images. To increase knowledge, our system adds image feature maps and labels for new data to the database instead of fine-tuning model parameters using those new data. We employ a kNN (k-Nearest Neighbor) classifier [12], which is one of the most classic classification algorithms. Recently, many papers have employed kNN for the purpose of evaluating their proposed representation learning algorithms [5,33,55].

In this paper, we shed new light on the potentials of kNN classification system with high-capacity storage. A concurrent work [34] demonstrates that kNN retrieval improves long-tail recognition. Not only this, we empirically show that million scale kNN retrieval is affordable for practical image classification tasks, and that our system with kNN avoids catastrophic forgetting in continual learning scenarios and achieves better accuracy than conventional methods. Furthermore, by reviewing neighborhood samples referred by the kNN algorithm, we can verify the validity of inference results, such as whether those referred samples contain incorrectly labeled data. If those referred samples contain incorrectly labeled data, our system can correct the false knowledge and improve the accuracy by eliminating only the incorrectly labeled data from the database.

The main contributions of this paper are as follows:

- We investigate a large-scale kNN system that stores knowledge for image classification in high-capacity storage and refers to the storage when classifying images, and empirically demonstrate its effectiveness and applicability on various image classification datasets and in continual learning scenarios.
- We also show that a large-scale kNN system has a capability of verifying the validity of inference results and selectively correcting only false knowledge.

2 Related Work

2.1 Data-Driven Image Classification

DNNs, hundreds of millions to billions parameters [13,15,19,46] of which are optimized by supervised learning with labeled images, have achieved state-of-the-art results in visual understanding and image classification tasks. In recent years, unsupervised visual clustering, which does not rely on a labeled dataset for learning the feature representation and classifier, has been developed [9,10,17,20,21,47,50]. Unsupervised pretraining strategies on large-scale datasets that include unlabeled or noisily labeled images have demonstrated the potential of large-scale open-domain knowledge for improving the accuracy of closed-domain image classification tasks [15,25,38]. In addition, although the applicable dataset scale is still limited, Ref. [28] presented an architecture that utilizes an entire dataset (e.g., all training images) to classify an input image during the inference process. Data has never been more important in the quest to further improve the usability of image classification. Inspired by the data-driven approaches in classification strategies, our work focuses on the application of knowledge retrieval to image classification. We present a method that utilizes the potential of both the trained parametric representation model and the available datasets during the inference process.

2.2 Knowledge Retrieval

Knowledge retrieval has seen substantial advancement in recent years, particularly in DNN-based natural language processing (NLP). DPR [26] applied a dense representation to passage retrieval in open-domain question answering tasks and achieved better retrieval performance than traditional sparse vector space models, such as TF-IDF and BM25. KEAR [51] brought external knowledge into the predicting process of Transformer [45] to reach human parity in a challenging commonsense task [44]. RETRO [3] introduced a frozen kNN retriever into the Transformer architecture in the form of chunked cross-attention to enhance the performance of auto-regressive language models. External world knowledge has been retrieved to assist in solving various NLP tasks. Our work looks to extend the adoption of knowledge retrieval beyond the modality of NLP. We introduce an image classification architecture based on knowledge retrieval, which is a data-driven paradigm that is centralized on available large-scale data resources and is supported by a trained representation model and a kNN classifier.

2.3 Continual Learning

When new data or tasks are added continually after a training process, fine-tuning is used to update the previously trained models with new knowledge. This continual learning, also known as incremental learning, online learning, or lifelong learning [23,31], is similar to natural human learning processes and is a key challenge for achieving artificial general intelligence. However, the simple procedure of iterative fine-tuning using only new knowledge suffers from catastrophic forgetting [18,31]. To mitigate the impact of catastrophic forgetting, GEM [35] introduced episodic memory to store a subset of the previously learned data, enabling an external memory-driven continual learning strategy. ER [40], inspired by the human brain's ability to replay past experiences, introduced the experience replay of memory. Episodic memory and experience replay have seen great developments in recent years [4,6,7]. iCaRL [39] evaluated the effect of catastrophic forgetting under a class incremental learning setting, where new classes are incrementally added to classifiers, and proposed a rehearsal approach with exemplar images of old classes being stored in memory. Inspired by the aforementioned works in adopting memory and the replay mechanism, we incorporate direct knowledge retrieval to solve the catastrophic forgetting problem in continual learning scenarios. Instead of a model-based approach, we introduce a data-based approach, leveraging available datasets as knowledge sources to adapt to the incrementation of tasks and classes.

2.4 Explainable AI

DNN models have been a technological breakthrough for various computer vision tasks. However, the explainability of DNN models remains a challenge and has led to slower-than-expected deployments in critical infrastructures. Attempts [8,41,54] have been made to interpret image classification models. GradCAM [41] proposed a gradient-based localization technique for rendering attention maps on the input images. Ref. [8] went beyond attention visualization by adopting gradients and the propagation of relevancy scores. These analysis methods can visualize the areas of the input images that DNN models focus on during the inference process, but they cannot analyze how the DNN models use knowledge acquired in training when classifying the input image. For example, if a training dataset contains false data (e.g., incorrectly labeled images), then these methods will not be able to selectively retrieve knowledge related to the false data from the trained models nor evaluate the impact of the false knowledge on the classification results. Our data-driven image classification architecture visualizes how knowledge is used to classify input images and enables selective modifications to specific knowledge without fine-tuning.

3 Approach

Figure 1 provides an overview of our image classification system. Our system has three phases: pretraining, knowledge storing, and inference. The first step is to

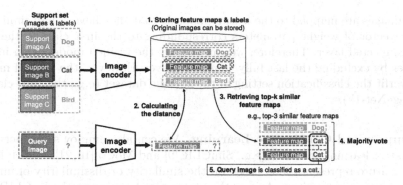

Fig. 1. Overview of our image classification system. Our system stores feature maps extracted from support images with the corresponding labels to the external storage. When classifying a query image, our system retrieves feature maps similar to the query one from the storage by calculating the distance based on cosine similarity. The query image is classified by majority vote on the labels of the top-k similar feature maps.

pretrain an image encoder model on a large-scale dataset containing a variety of images. This pretraining can use unlabeled or noisily labeled datasets. In the knowledge storing phase, the pretrained image encoder model extracts feature maps from support sets (e.g., a training dataset of a user's desired downstream task). Extracted feature maps are paired with their corresponding labels and registered in the external storage like a database. In the inference phase, the pretrained image encoder model extracts a feature map of a query image. Our system retrieves feature maps similar to the query one from the storage by calculating the distance based on cosine similarity. Then, the query image is classified by majority vote on the paired labels of the top-k similar feature maps retrieved. The following sections describe each phase in detail.

3.1 Pretraining

We pretrain an image encoder model to learn feature representations. We assume that this process is conducted on a large-scale computer system, such as a data center (not on the user side) [2]. Similarity-based retrieval in the latent space is performed in the following inference phase (see Sect. 3.3 for details). Therefore, transformations by the pretrained image encoder models should be such that semantically similar images are mapped to the neighborhood in the latent space. In this section, we describe suitability of pretraining methods that can be employed in our system.

Supervised Learning with Specific Datasets. Models trained on a specific dataset by supervised learning can be used for our system. An example is a ResNet-50 model [22] trained on the ImageNet-1k classification task [14]. If input images are classified as the first class (e.g., tench) by the trained model, those input images are mapped to the feature maps so that they have a high similarity to the vector of weight parameters corresponding to the first class in the last fully connected layer. Therefore, we can employ the trained model as an image encoder by excluding the last fully connected layer. However, the trained model can overfit the classification setting of the specific dataset (e.g., the 1000 classes of ImageNet-1k).

Self-supervised Contrastive Learning. We can also employ self-supervised contrastive learning methods (e.g., SimCLR [9] and MoCo [10,21]), which learn image feature representations based on the similarity or dissimilarity of images between two or more views. Among the contrastive learning methods, CLIP [38] and ALIGN [25] jointly learn image and text feature representations of image and text encoders using a large number of image and text pairs collected from the internet. These methods do not require hand-crafted labeling or annotation, and the number of semantic labels is much larger than the number of labels on commonly used image datasets, such as the limited 1000 labels in ImageNet-1k.

Other Self-Supervised Learning. Masked Auto Encoder [20] learns image feature representations through a task of reconstructing the original images from masked images. By fine-tuning on the labeled dataset, the encoders pretrained with Masked Auto Encoder have achieved high accuracy in the ImageNet-1k classification task. Because this pretraining method is label-independent, the pretrained model seems unlikely to overfit a specific classification setting (e.g., the 1000 classes of ImageNet-1k). However, the objective function of this pretraining method does not explicitly make the encoder model to map semantically similar images to the neighborhood in the latent space, so it is not suitable for similarity-based retrieval in our system.

Selecting Pretraining Methods. We conducted a preliminary experiment using three pretrained image encoder models: (1) a ResNet-50 model trained on the ImageNet-1k dataset with the labels by supervised learning, (2) a Vision Transformer [15] Base model with input patch sizes of 16×16 (ViT-B/16) trained by CLIP on 400 million image and text pairs collected from the internet, (3) a ViT-B/16 model trained by Masked Auto Encoder (MAE) on the ImageNet-1k dataset without the labels. We employed the three pretrained image encoders in our system, and evaluated the test accuracy on various image datasets (CIFAR-10, CIFAR-100 [29], STL-10 [11], and ImageNet-1k).

We summarize the test accuracy in Table 1. As discussed above, (1) the supervised learned model on ImageNet-1k achieves the best accuracy on ImageNet-1k, but not on the other datasets. This supervised learned model does not generalize well to unseen datasets. (3) the model pretrained by MAE shows poor performance since the objective of this pretraining method is not compatible with similarity-based retrieval in our system. On the other hand, (2) the model pretrained by CLIP achieves good accuracy on various datasets, indicating that the model is well generalized. Based on the result of this preliminary experiment, we employed image encoder models pretrained by CLIP in the experiments of Sect. 4. The exploration of better pretraining methods is our future work.

3.2 Knowledge Storing

To acquire knowledge, a pretrained image encoder model extracts feature maps from a support set, such as a training dataset of a user's desired downstream task. Given a support set of n-labeled images $\{x_{s,1}, ..., x_{s,n}\}$, the corresponding labels $\{y_1, ..., y_n\}$, and the pretrained image encoder model $f(\cdot)$, the i-th support image is mapped to the d-dimensional latent space, and the extracted feature map $z_{s,i}$ is obtained by $z_{s,i} = f(x_{s,i}), z \in \mathbb{R}^d$.

Table 1. Accuracy comparison using different pretrained image encoder models.

		ImageNet-1k	CIFAR-10	CIFAR-100	STL-10
(1)	Supervised learned on ImageNet-1k	**74.9**	85.9	64.7	96.7
(2)	CLIP [38]	74.0	**94.4**	**74.3**	**98.9**
(3)	MAE [20]	26.7	51.8	23.2	66.6

Correct classification

	Query	Top-5 similar support samples retrieved					
Original images	ILSVRC2012_val _00000796.JPEG	n02123159_ 6363.JPEG	n02123159_ 497.JPEG	n02123159_ 4362.JPEG	n02123159_ 598.JPEG	n02123159_ 5525.JPEG	Classified as
Distance	-	0.031	0.052	0.054	0.059	0.060	
Label	tiger cat (ground truth)	tiger cat	tiger cat	tiger cat	tiger cat	tiger cat	tiger cat (correct)

Misclassification due to *incorrectly labeled samples

	Query	Top-5 similar support samples retrieved					
Original images	ILSVRC2012_val _00027576.JPEG	n02129604_ 3309.JPEG	n02123159_ 3499.JPEG*	n02123159_ 3891.JPEG*	n02129604_ 3107.JPEG	n02123159_ 7344.JPEG*	Classified as
Distance	-	0.062	0.068	0.076	0.080	0.080	
Label	tiger (ground truth)	tiger	tiger cat*	tiger cat*	tiger	tiger cat*	tiger cat (wrong)

Fig. 2. Examples of query and the top-5 similar support samples retrieved. In these examples, validation and training data of ImageNet-1k are used for the query and the support set, respectively (the file names are also given in the examples). The top figure shows an example of correct classification, and the bottom figure shows one of misclassification due to *incorrectly labeled support samples. By reviewing the original images and labels, we can verify the validity of the classification results. (Color figure online)

Unlike fine-tuning, our system does not require iterative forward, backward and parameter-update operations, but it just requires one forward operation of each image in the support set for the feature extraction. Thus, the cost and effort are less than those of fine-tuning. Moreover, our system can avoid catastrophic forgetting without fine-tuning, even when the knowledge is iteratively updated in continual learning scenarios.

An extracted feature map is paired with the corresponding label such as $(z_{s,i}, y_i)$, and registered in the external storage like a database. If the original images are also registered to the database, then they can be used to verify the validity of classification results (see Fig. 2 and Sect. 3.3 for details).

3.3 Inference

Our system classifies query images (i.e., inference) by referring to image feature maps and labels registered in the database. The pretrained encoder first extracts a feature map z_q of a query image x_q as $z_q = f(x_q)$. Our system retrieves support feature maps that are similar to query one from the database by calculating the distance (D) based on cosine similarity between query and support feature maps as follows,

$$D(z_q, z_{s,i}) = 1 - \frac{z_q \cdot z_{s,i}}{||z_q|| ||z_{s,i}||}. \tag{1}$$

With $\arg\min_{i \in n} D(z_q, z_{s,i})$, we can retrieve the index of the nearest, that is, the most similar support feature map to the query one. Our system retrieves the index of top-k minimum distance, and the query image is classified based on the majority vote of the paired labels in order to mitigate the effect of outliers.

Figure 2 shows examples of query and the retrieved samples from the support set. The original images in the support set are not required for classifying query images. However, the original images registered in the database can be used for evidence or for verification of the inference results. For instance, as shown in Fig. 2, not only the labels and distance values of retrieved feature maps, but also the original images, can be listed as inference logs. By reviewing the logs, we can verify that the retrieved samples contain inappropriate data (e.g., incorrectly labeled images). The bottom figure in Fig. 2 shows an example of the misclassification of a query image due to incorrectly labeled images in the support set (using a training dataset of ImageNet-1k). If incorrectly labeled images are obtained in the logs, then we can correct false knowledge in our system by fixing the incorrect labels or eliminating such samples from the database.

The above characteristics are not present in existing image classification systems. To correct false knowledge, existing systems need to fine-tune classifier models again after fixing incorrect labels in the support set. On the other hand, our system does not require fine-tuning, thus eliminating the cost and effort for fine-tuning, and can contribute to improving the explainability of AI by visualizing and reviewing referred images and labels when classifying input images.

4   Experiments

We implemented our image classification system using the PyTorch library [37]. The setup and results for each experiment are described in detail below.

4.1   Basic Performance Evaluation

Experimental Setup. We evaluated the basic performance of our system using the CIFAR-10, CIFAR-100, STL-10, and ImageNet-1k datasets. We employed image encoder models pretrained by CLIP. We used ResNet-50 and 101 as CNN models and ViT-B/32, B/16, and L/14 as Vision Transformer models[1] for the image encoders. These pretrained models extracted feature maps from training images, and those extracted feature maps and labels were registered in the database as support sets. With the support sets, we evaluated the test accuracy of our system using test datasets as query sets. As a baseline, we employed the test accuracy of the zero-shot CLIP classifier [38]. This classifier can be applied to those classification tasks without any fine-tuning like our system.

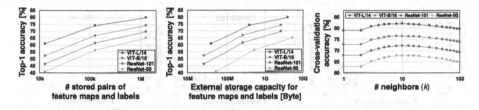

Fig. 3. Left/center: the relation between the top-1 accuracy on the ImageNet-1k dataset and the number of stored pairs of feature maps and labels/the external storage capacity for storing the pairs. **Right**: the relation between cross-validation accuracy and the number of neighbors (k) for kNN. For cross-validation, the 1.28M training images in ImageNet-1k are randomly split 9:1 into support and query sets.

In addition to the accuracy evaluation, we measured the processing time for inference of the ImageNet-1k images. We used a NVIDIA A100 GPU and measured the processing time of our system and the zero-shot CLIP classifier as a baseline. In this measurement, both the parameters of the image encoder model and the feature maps of the support set were loaded into the GPU memory from the external storage prior to the inference. We then measured the processing time for transferring query images to the GPU, encoding the query images, and calculating the distance between the query and support feature maps. The batch size was set to 1000, and the average processing time per image was calculated.

---

[1] ViT-B/32, B/16, and L/14 correspond to Vision Transformer Base, Base, and Large model, with input patch sizes of 32×32, 16×16, and 14×14, respectively.

Experimental Results. The left graph in Fig. 3 shows the relation between the top-1 accuracy on the ImageNet-1k dataset and the number of stored pairs of feature maps and labels. Here, we randomly sample images from the training dataset, adjusting the number of the stored pairs to 12.8k, 128k, and 1.28M. We set the number of neighbors (k) for kNN to 10. The more stored pairs that there are in the database, the better the accuracy will be that our system can achieve. Moreover, the larger the model size, the better the performance of the feature extractor and also the accuracy.

The center graph in Fig. 3 shows the relation between the top-1 accuracy and the external storage capacity for storing feature maps and labels. In this experiment, the maximum storage capacity is 5.3 GB to store the feature maps and labels for 1.28M samples of ImageNet-1k. As shown in the center graph, the larger the capacity, the better the accuracy.

In the right graph of Fig. 3, we evaluated the relation between the accuracy and the number of neighbors of k by cross-validation. For cross-validation, the 1.28M training images are randomly split 9:1 into support and query sets. As shown in the right graph, the best accuracy is achieved when k is set to around 10. In the following experiments, k is set to 10 unless otherwise noted.

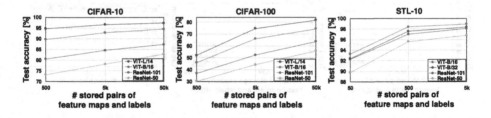

Fig. 4. Relation between the test accuracy and the number of stored pairs of feature maps and labels for various image datasets.

Table 2. Test accuracy evaluations for various image datasets. Baseline indicates the accuracy of the zero-shot CLIP classifier.

	CIFAR-10					CIFAR-100					STL-10					ImageNet-1k				
	ResNet		ViT			ResNet		ViT			ResNet		ViT			ResNet		ViT		
	50	101	B/32	B/16	L/14	50	101	B/32	B/16	L/14	50	101	B/32	B/16	L/14	50	101	B/32	B/16	L/14
Baseline	75.6	81.0	91.3	91.6	96.2	41.6	49.0	65.1	68.7	77.9	94.3	96.7	97.2	98.2	99.3	59.6	62.2	63.2	68.6	75.3
Ours	82.8	87.3	92.7	94.4	97.3	55.7	63.6	71.5	74.3	81.7	96.8	98.1	98.4	98.9	99.6	65.0	69.7	67.0	74.0	79.7
Δ	+7.2	+6.3	+1.4	+2.8	+1.1	+14.1	+14.6	+6.4	+5.6	+3.8	+2.5	+1.4	+1.2	+0.7	+0.3	+5.4	+7.5	+3.8	+5.4	+4.4

Figure 4 shows the relation between the test accuracy and the number of stored pairs of feature maps and labels on the other datasets. For all datasets, our system improves the test accuracy as the number of stored pairs increases and as the model size becomes larger.

Table 2 summarizes the test accuracy of our system. Our system can improve accuracy from the baseline (pretrained but not fine-tuned models) on the various image datasets by storing image feature maps and labels of training datasets.

Based on the experimental results in Figs. 3 and 4, we utilize a data augmentation technique to increase the number of stored pairs of feature maps and labels. Data augmentation is typically used to prevent models from overfitting during training and to improve the generalization performance. In particular, we use only horizontal flipping to augment support images (2×), and set the number of neighbors of k to 20. Table 3 summarizes the accuracy with and without data augmentation. As shown in the results for CIFAR-100 and ImageNet-1k in Table 3, our system can improve accuracy by doubling the number of pairs of stored feature maps and labels. In the results for CIFAR-10 and STL-10, data augmentation did not always improve accuracy, but the accuracy was already high enough without data augmentation (the accuracy is higher than 94%).

Figure 5 shows the processing time for inference of the ImageNet-1k images that was measured on the NVIDIA A100 GPU. The left graph shows the processing time of our system when storing 12.8k, 128k, and 1.28M pairs of feature maps and labels with different image encoder models. In this experiment, the maximum required memory capacity is 5.3 GB when using 1.28M pairs of feature maps and labels, and all the feature maps can be fully loaded into GPU memory. By exploiting massive parallel computations of GPU, we execute a linear search based on cosine distance between a query and all the feature maps calculated in Eq. (1). As shown in the left graph, as the number of stored pairs increases, the processing time becomes slightly longer (e.g., 3% in the case of ViT-L/14). The

Table 3. Accuracy comparison with and without data augmentation (DA) on the support sets.

	CIFAR-10					CIFAR-100					STL-10					ImageNet-1k				
	ResNet		ViT			ResNet		ViT			ResNet		ViT			ResNet		ViT		
	50	101	B/32	B/16	L/14	50	101	B/32	B/16	L/14	50	101	B/32	B/16	L/14	50	101	B/32	B/16	L/14
w/o DA	82.8	87.3	92.7	94.4	97.3	55.7	63.6	71.5	74.3	81.7	96.8	98.1	98.4	98.9	99.6	65.0	69.7	69.0	74.0	79.7
w/ DA	83.6	87.8	93.0	94.3	97.3	56.8	63.9	71.8	74.7	81.7	97.0	97.9	98.3	99.1	99.6	65.4	70.2	69.2	74.3	79.8
Δ	+0.8	+0.5	+0.3	-0.1	0.0	+1.1	+0.3	+0.3	+0.4	0.0	+0.2	-0.2	-0.1	+0.2	0.0	+0.4	+0.5	+0.2	+0.3	+0.1

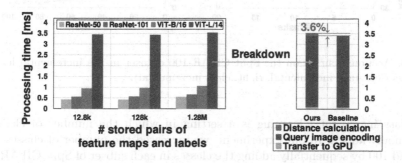

Fig. 5. Processing time for inference of the ImageNet-1k images as measured on an NVIDIA A100 GPU (left) and the breakdown comparison for ViT-L/14 with 1.28M stored pairs of feature maps and labels (right). The baseline is the processing time of the zero-shot CLIP classifier.

right graph in Fig. 5 is the breakdown of the processing time for ViT-L/14 with 1.28M stored pairs. For comparison, the right graph also includes the breakdown of the zero-shot CLIP classifier as a baseline. The processing time for query image encoding is dominant, but that for the distance calculation is short enough (about 0.1 ms). The overhead from the baseline for retrieving similar feature maps from 1.28M stored ones is as small as 3.6%.

4.2   Continual Learning

Experimental Setup. We evaluated the applicability of our system to continual learning, especially in task incremental and class incremental settings.

Task incremental learning is a setting where the number of tasks increases step by step. We used a Split CIFAR-100 dataset [7,52] in which the CIFAR-100 dataset is split into 20 disjoint subsets. Each subset consists of five randomly sampled classes without duplication from a total of 100 classes. Additionally, we applied ImageNet-100 [16,24,49] and ImageNet-1k datasets to the incremental learning setting. ImageNet-100 consists of 100 classes randomly sampled from 1000 classes in the ImageNet-1k dataset. We split the ImageNet-100 and ImageNet-1k datasets into 10 disjoint subsets, each containing 10 and 100 classes, respectively. We did not balance the number of samples in each subset. We used each subset in Split CIFAR-100, Split ImageNet-100, and Split ImageNet-1k as one task for a 5-class, 10-class, and 100-class classification, respectively.

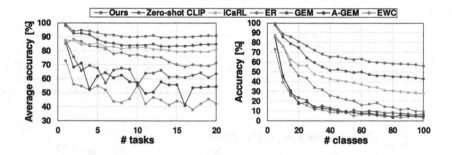

Fig. 6. Accuracy curves on the Split CIFAR-100 dataset in the incremental learning settings (left: task incremental, right: class incremental).

Class incremental learning is a setting in which the number of classes is continually added. In our experiment, we increased the number of classes by 5, 10, and 100 by sequentially adding the classes in each subset of Split CIFAR-100, Split ImageNet-100, and Split ImageNet-1k, respectively.

For each setting, we used ResNet-50, ViT-B/32, and ViT-L/14 models for the image encoder, and employed the pretrained models by CLIP as Sect. 4.1. We evaluated the accuracy of our system, the zero-shot CLIP classifier, and the conventional methods proposed for the incremental learning settings (iCaRL,

ER, GEM, A-GEM, and EWC [7,27,35,39,40]). We applied the same pretrained models to the initial values for all the methods. In iCaRL, ER, GEM, and A-GEM, a part of training data learned in the past is stored in memory, and when new data is added, the model parameters are updated along with the stored data. EWC does not store any training data learned in the past. The detailed conditions such as the hyperparameter settings are described in the supplementary materials.

Experimental Results. The left graph in Fig. 6 shows the average accuracy on the Split CIFAR-100 dataset for task incremental learning. The average accuracy is calculated by averaging the test accuracy evaluated in each task. In the conventional methods (except the zero-shot CLIP classifier), as the number of tasks increases, the average accuracy over tasks gradually drops because the models forget the knowledge for older tasks. On the other hand, our system stores extracted image feature maps and labels, so it does not require fine-tuning to acquire new knowledge. Therefore, our system avoids catastrophic forgetting and keeps the average accuracy over 90%, even when the number of tasks exceeds 15. The right graph in Fig. 6 shows the accuracy for class incremental learning. The accuracy curve of our system is higher than those of the conventional methods, even as the number of classes increases.

Table 4. Accuracy evaluations in task and class incremental learning settings.

ResNet-50 on Split CIFAR-100				ViT-B/32 on Split ImageNet-100		
Method	task	class		Method	task	class
EWC [27]	42.2	13.5		Zero-shot CLIP [38]	92.0	80.2
A-GEM [7]	54.5	15.8		**Ours**	**94.3**	**85.1**
GEM [35]	63.7	17.4				
ER [40]	71.3	29.4		ViT-L/14 on Split ImageNet-1k		
iCaRL [39]	80.9	43.9		Method	task	class
Zero-shot CLIP [38]	84.8	56.6		Zero-shot CLIP [38]	93.0	82.3
Ours	**90.8**	**67.9**		**Ours**	**94.2**	**85.5**

Table 4 summarizes the average accuracy on the Split CIFAR-100, Split ImageNet-100, and Split ImageNet-1k datasets. The accuracy of task incremental learning is the average of the accuracy evaluated on each task after all tasks have been added. The accuracy of class incremental learning is the average of the each accuracy from the first to the last class setting, which is introduced in Ref. [39] (e.g., the average of the accuracies when the number of classes is from 5 to 100 in the right figure of Fig. 6). Our system achieves better accuracy than the conventional methods, which indicates that our system is effective in incremental learning settings.

4.3 Correcting False Knowledge

Experimental Setup. Datasets used as support sets can contain incorrectly labeled images. In this section, we observe the impact of incorrectly labeled images on classification results and accuracy, and evaluate the effect of eliminating them. According to Refs. [1,36], the ImageNet-1k dataset contains a small number of incorrectly labeled images (at least 6%). Ref. [1] reassesses the label of each image in ImageNet-1k and releases an ImageNet-ReaL dataset that eliminates the incorrectly labeled images from the original ImageNet-1k dataset. We compared the accuracy before and after eliminating the incorrectly labeled images from the training dataset, namely, the support set.

Experimental Results. Figure 7 shows an example of samples retrieved with the ViT-L/14 model before and after eliminating incorrectly labeled images from the support set. Before the elimination, a query image is misclassified as a ruffed grouse (correctly as a partridge) due to the retrieval of feature maps of incorrectly labeled images. After the elimination, the incorrectly labeled samples are no longer included in the top-10 retrieved samples, and the query image is correctly classified as a partridge. These verification results of Fig. 7 can be visualized with the support images (like Fig. 2 in Sect. 3.2). In this experiment, when all the support images in the ImageNet-1k dataset are stored for the verification, the required storage capacity is 152GB.

Table 5 shows the accuracy on the ImageNet-ReaL dataset before and after the elimination. Our system can correct false knowledge and improve accuracy by simply eliminating feature maps of incorrectly labeled images. Unlike exist-

Before

Query Image		
Label (ground truth)		File name
partridge		ILSVRC2012_val_00019750.JPEG
Retrieved support samples		
Distance	Label	File name
0.000	ruffed grouse*	n01797886_6586.JPEG*
0.062	ruffed grouse*	n01797886_15633.JPEG*
0.062	partridge	n01807496_4822.JPEG
0.064	ruffed grouse*	n01797886_6603.JPEG*
0.064	partridge	n01807496_5569.JPEG
0.066	partridge	n01807496_18631.JPEG
0.066	partridge	n01807496_28384.JPEG
0.066	partridge	n01807496_15316.JPEG
0.068	ruffed grouse*	n01797886_11301.JPEG*
0.069	ruffed grouse*	n01797886_2986.JPEG*
Classified as a ruffed grouse (wrong)		

After

Query Image		
Label (ground truth)		File name
partridge		ILSVRC2012_val_00019750.JPEG
Retrieved support samples		
Distance	Label	File name
0.062	partridge	n01807496_4822.JPEG
0.064	partridge	n01807496_5569.JPEG
0.066	partridge	n01807496_18631.JPEG
0.066	partridge	n01807496_28384.JPEG
0.066	partridge	n01807496_15316.JPEG
0.069	partridge	n01807496_2534.JPEG
0.07	partridge	n01807496_6715.JPEG
0.074	partridge	n01807496_9868.JPEG
0.076	partridge	n01807496_10464.JPEG
0.076	partridge	n01807496_18094.JPEG
Classified as a partridge (correct)		

Fig. 7. Examples of query and top-10 similar support samples retrieved from ImageNet-1k before and after eliminating the incorrectly labeled samples from the support set. Before the elimination, the query image is misclassified as a ruffed grouse due to *incorrectly labeled samples. After the elimination, the query image is correctly classified as a partridge in all samples.

Table 5. Left: validation accuracy on the ImageNet-ReaL dataset before and after eliminating incorrectly labeled images from the support sets. **Right**: the details for the support and query sets.

	ResNet		ViT				Support set	Query set
	50	101	B/32	B/16	L/14	Before	1,281,167 images	46,837 images
Before	71.2	75.7	75.0	79.3	83.9		in ImageNet-1k	in ImageNet-ReaL
After	71.4	76.1	75.4	79.6	84.0	After	1,148,659 images	46,837 images
Δ	+0.2	+0.4	+0.4	+0.3	+0.1		in ImageNet-ReaL	in ImageNet-ReaL

ing image classification systems, our system does not need to fine-tune model parameters again on the modified dataset.

5 Conclusions

In this paper, we investigated a system that stores knowledge for image classification not in model parameters but in external high-capacity storage and refers to this storage like a database when classifying input images. Our system can increase knowledge by adding image feature maps and their corresponding labels to the database. Without fine-tuning the model parameters, our system avoids catastrophic forgetting in continual learning scenarios and achieves better accuracy than the conventional methods. By reviewing the neighborhood samples retrieved by the kNN classifier, we can verify the classification results. If incorrectly labeled samples are included in the classification results, then our system can correct the false knowledge and improve accuracy without fine-tuning by simply eliminating the incorrectly labeled samples from the database. In future work, we will work on scaling up our system with high-capacity storage by utilizing a large-scale fast ANN (approximate nearest neighbor) search.

References

1. Beyer, L., Hénaff, O.J., Kolesnikov, A., Zhai, X., van den Oord, A.: Are we done with ImageNet? arXiv abs/2006.07159 (2020)
2. Bommasani, R., et al.: On the opportunities and risks of foundation models. arXiv abs/2108.07258 (2021)
3. Borgeaud, S., et al.: Improving language models by retrieving from trillions of tokens. arXiv abs/2112.04426 (2021)
4. Buzzega, P., Boschini, M., Porrello, A., Calderara, S.: Rethinking experience replay: a bag of tricks for continual learning. In: ICPR (2021)
5. Caron, M., et al.: Emerging properties in self-supervised vision transformers. arXiv abs/2104.14294 (2021)
6. Chaudhry, A., Gordo, A., Dokania, P.K., Torr, P.H.S., Lopez-Paz, D.: Using hindsight to anchor past knowledge in continual learning. In: AAAI (2021)
7. Chaudhry, A., Ranzato, M., Rohrbach, M., Elhoseiny, M.: Efficient lifelong learning with A-GEM. In: ICLR (2019)

8. Chefer, H., Gur, S., Wolf, L.: Transformer interpretability beyond attention visualization. In: CVPR (2021)
9. Chen, T., Kornblith, S., Norouzi, M., Hinton, G.E.: A simple framework for contrastive learning of visual representations. arXiv abs/2002.05709 (2020)
10. Chen, X., Fan, H., Girshick, R.B., He, K.: Improved baselines with momentum contrastive learning. arXiv abs/2003.04297 (2020)
11. Coates, A., Ng, A., Lee, H.: An analysis of single-layer networks in unsupervised feature learning. In: AISTATS (2011)
12. Cunningham, P., Delany, S.J.: k-nearest neighbour classifiers: 2nd Edition (with Python examples). arXiv abs/2004.04523 (2020)
13. Dai, Z., Liu, H., Le, Q.V., Tan, M.: CoAtNet: marrying convolution and attention for all data sizes. arXiv abs/2106.04803 (2021)
14. Deng, J., Dong, W., Socher, R., Li, L.J., Li, K., Fei-Fei, L.: ImageNet: a large-scale hierarchical image database. In: CVPR (2009)
15. Dosovitskiy, A., et al.: An image is worth 16×16 words: transformers for image recognition at scale. In: ICLR (2021)
16. Douillard, A., Cord, M., Ollion, C., Robert, T., Valle, E.: PODNet: pooled outputs distillation for small-tasks incremental learning. In: Vedaldi, A., Bischof, H., Brox, T., Frahm, J.-M. (eds.) ECCV 2020. LNCS, vol. 12365, pp. 86–102. Springer, Cham (2020). https://doi.org/10.1007/978-3-030-58565-5_6
17. Dwibedi, D., Aytar, Y., Tompson, J., Sermanet, P., Zisserman, A.: With a little help from my friends: nearest-neighbor contrastive learning of visual representations. In: ICCV (2021)
18. French, R.M.: Catastrophic forgetting in connectionist networks. Trends Cogn. Sci. **3** (1999)
19. Hassani, A., Walton, S., Shah, N., Abuduweili, A., Li, J., Shi, H.: Escaping the big data paradigm with compact transformers. arXiv abs/2104.05704 (2021)
20. He, K., Chen, X., Xie, S., Li, Y., Dollár, P., Girshick, R.B.: Masked autoencoders are scalable vision learners. arXiv abs/2111.06377 (2021)
21. He, K., Fan, H., Wu, Y., Xie, S., Girshick, R.: Momentum contrast for unsupervised visual representation learning. In: CVPR (2020)
22. He, K., Zhang, X., Ren, S., Sun, J.: Deep residual learning for image recognition. In: CVPR (2016)
23. Hoi, S.C., Sahoo, D., Lu, J., Zhao, P.: Online learning: a comprehensive survey. Neurocomputing **459** (2021)
24. Hou, S., Pan, X., Loy, C.C., Wang, Z., Lin, D.: Learning a unified classifier incrementally via rebalancing. In: CVPR (2019)
25. Jia, C., et al.: Scaling up visual and vision-language representation learning with noisy text supervision. In: ICML (2021)
26. Karpukhin, V., et al.: Dense passage retrieval for open-domain question answering. In: EMNLP (2020)
27. Kirkpatrick, J., et al.: Overcoming catastrophic forgetting in neural networks. Proc. Natl. Acad. Sci. **114** (2017)
28. Kossen, J., Band, N., Lyle, C., Gomez, A., Rainforth, T., Gal, Y.: Self-attention between datapoints: going beyond individual input-output pairs in deep learning. In: NeurIPS (2021)
29. Krizhevsky, A.: Learning multiple layers of features from tiny images. Technical report (2009)
30. Krizhevsky, A., Sutskever, I., Hinton, G.E.: ImageNet classification with deep convolutional neural networks. In: NIPS (2012)

31. Lange, M.D., et al.: Continual learning: a comparative study on how to defy forgetting in classification tasks. arXiv abs/1909.08383 (2019)
32. Lecun, Y., Bottou, L., Bengio, Y., Haffner, P.: Gradient-based learning applied to document recognition. Proc. IEEE **86** (1998)
33. Li, C., et al.: Efficient self-supervised vision transformers for representation learning. In: ICLR (2022)
34. Long, A., et al.: Retrieval augmented classification for long-tail visual recognition. arXiv abs/2202.11233 (2022)
35. Lopez-Paz, D., Ranzato, M.: Gradient episodic memory for continual learning. In: NIPS (2017)
36. Northcutt, C.G., Athalye, A., Mueller, J.: Pervasive label errors in test sets destabilize machine learning benchmarks. In: NeurIPS Datasets and Benchmarks Track (2021)
37. Paszke, A., et al.: Automatic differentiation in PyTorch. In: NIPS 2017 Workshop on Autodiff (2017)
38. Radford, A., et al.: Learning transferable visual models from natural language supervision. In: ICML (2021)
39. Rebuffi, S.A., Kolesnikov, A., Sperl, G., Lampert, C.H.: iCaRL: incremental classifier and representation learning. In: CVPR (2017)
40. Rolnick, D., Ahuja, A., Schwarz, J., Lillicrap, T., Wayne, G.: Experience replay for continual learning. In: NeurIPS (2019)
41. Selvaraju, R.R., Cogswell, M., Das, A., Vedantam, R., Parikh, D., Batra, D.: Grad-CAM: visual explanations from deep networks via gradient-based localization. In: ICCV (2017)
42. Simonyan, K., Zisserman, A.: Very deep convolutional networks for large-scale image recognition. In: ICLR (2015)
43. Stock, P., Cisse, M.: ConvNets and imagenet beyond accuracy: understanding mistakes and uncovering biases. In: Ferrari, V., Hebert, M., Sminchisescu, C., Weiss, Y. (eds.) ECCV 2018. LNCS, vol. 11210, pp. 504–519. Springer, Cham (2018). https://doi.org/10.1007/978-3-030-01231-1_31
44. Talmor, A., Herzig, J., Lourie, N., Berant, J.: CommonsenseQA: a question answering challenge targeting commonsense knowledge. In: NAACL-HLT (2019)
45. Vaswani, A., et al.: Attention is all you need. In: NIPS (2017)
46. Wang, W., et al.: Pyramid vision transformer: a versatile backbone for dense prediction without convolutions. arXiv abs/2102.12122 (2021)
47. Wang, X., Liu, Z., Yu, S.X.: Unsupervised feature learning by cross-level instance-group discrimination. In: CVPR (2021)
48. Wu, D., Wang, Y.: Adversarial neuron pruning purifies backdoored deep models. In: NeurIPS (2021)
49. Wu, Y., et al.: Large scale incremental learning. In: CVPR (2019)
50. Wu, Z., Xiong, Y., Yu, S.X., Lin, D.: Unsupervised feature learning via non-parametric instance discrimination. In: CVPR (2018)
51. Xu, Y., et al.: Human parity on CommonsenseQA: augmenting self-attention with external attention. arXiv abs/2112.03254 (2021)
52. Zenke, F., Poole, B., Ganguli, S.: Continual learning through synaptic intelligence. In: ICML (2017)
53. Zhong, J., Ding, G., Guo, Y., Han, J., Wang, B.: Where to prune: using LSTM to guide end-to-end pruning. In: IJCAI (2018)
54. Zhou, B., Khosla, A., Lapedriza, À., Oliva, A., Torralba, A.: Learning deep features for discriminative localization. In: CVPR (2016)

55. Zhou, J., et al.: Image BERT pre-training with online tokenizer. In: ICLR (2022)
56. Zhou, Y., Zhang, Y., Wang, Y., Tian, Q.: Accelerate CNN via recursive bayesian pruning. In: ICCV (2019)

Geometric Representation Learning
for Document Image Rectification

Hao Feng[1], Wengang Zhou[1,2](✉), Jiajun Deng[1], Yuechen Wang[1],
and Houqiang Li[1,2](✉)

[1] CAS Key Laboratory of GIPAS, EEIS Department, University of Science and
Technology of China, Hefei, China
{fh1995,wyc9725}@mail.ustc.edu.cn, {zhwg,dengjj,lihq}@ustc.edu.cn
[2] Institute of Artificial Intelligence, Hefei Comprehensive National Science Center,
Hefei, China

Abstract. In document image rectification, there exist rich geometric
constraints between the distorted image and the ground truth one. However, such geometric constraints are largely ignored in existing advanced
solutions, which limits the rectification performance. To this end, we
present DocGeoNet for document image rectification by introducing
explicit geometric representation. Technically, two typical attributes of
the document image are involved in the proposed geometric representation learning, *i.e.*, 3D shape and textlines. Our motivation raises from
the insight that 3D shape provides global unwarping cues for rectifying a distorted document image, while overlooking the local structure.
On the other hand, textlines complementarily provide explicit geometric
constraints for local patterns. The learned geometric representation effectively bridges the distorted image and the ground truth one. Extensive
experiments show the effectiveness of our framework and demonstrate
the superiority of our DocGeoNet over state-of-the-art methods on both
the DocUNet Benchmark dataset and our proposed DIR300 test set.

Keywords: Document image rectification · Geometric constraints

1 Introduction

With the popularity of smartphones, more and more people are using them
to digitize document files. Compared to typical flatbed scanners, smartphones
provides a flexible, portable, and contactless way for document image capturing. However, due to uncontrolled physical deformations, uneven illuminations,
and various camera angles, those document images are always distorted. Such
distortions make those images invalid in many formal review occasions, and are
likely to cause the failure of the downstream applications, such as automatic text

Supplementary Information The online version contains supplementary material
available at https://doi.org/10.1007/978-3-031-19836-6_27.

recognition, analysis, retrieval, and editing. To this end, over the past few years, document image rectification has become an emerging research topic. In this work, we focus on the geometric distortion rectification for document images, aiming to rectify arbitrarily warped documents to their original planar shape.

Traditionally, document image rectification is addressed by 3D reconstruction. Generally, the 3D mesh of the warped document is estimated to flatten the document image. However, such techniques are either based on auxiliary hardware [1,3,28,46] or developed with multiview images [2,16,44,45], which are unfriendly in personal application. Some other methods assume a parametric model on the document surface and optimize the model by extracting specific representations such as shading [4], boundaries [12], textlines [17,40], or texture flow [20]. However, the oversimplified parametric models usually lead to limited performance, and the optimization process introduces non-negligible computational cost. Recently, deep learning based solutions [6,7,9,10,19,22,25] have been become a promising alternative to traditional methods. By training a network to directly predict the warping flow, a deformed document image can be rectified by resampling the pixels in the distorted image. Although these methods are reported with the state-of-the-art performance, the rich geometric constraints between distorted images and ground truth ones are largely ignored.

Generally, in a document image, the texture mainly exists in textlines. Note that there are strong geometric constraints among textlines between the distorted and ground truth image, that is, the curved textlines should be straight after rectification if they are horizontal textlines in a document. In other words, textlines provide a strong cue for the rectification. However, existing methods all just learn this prior implicitly with deep networks via the supervision on predicted warping flow, which leads to sub-optimal performance. Besides, compared to a distorted document image, the attribute of 3D shape is a more explicit representation that directly determines the unwarping process. The above two attributes bridge the distorted and ground truth image and complement each other: the distribution of textlines reflects the local deformation of a document, which serves as a complement to 3D shape on local structure detail. Based on the above motivation, we explicitly learn the geometric constraints from such attributes in a deep network to promote the rectification performance.

In this work, we present DocGeoNet, a new deep network for document image rectification. DocGeoNet bridges the distorted image and its ground truth by introducing geometric constraint representation derived from document attributes. It consists of a structure encoder, a textline extractor, and a rectification decoder. Specifically, given a distorted document image, DocGeoNet takes the structure encoder and textline extractor to model the 3D shape of the deformed document and extract its textlines, respectively. Then, to take advantage of the complementarity of such two attributes and leverage their direct constraints that link the distorted and ground truth image, we further fuse their representation and predict the rectification in the rectification decoder. During the training of DocGeoNet, the learning of 3D shape, textlines, and rectification is optimized in an end-to-end way. Besides, considering that the 3D shape is a global attribute while the textline is a local attribute, the proposed DocGeoNet adopts a hybrid network structure, which takes advantage of self-attention mechanism [36] and convolutional operation for enhanced representation learning. To evaluate our approach, extensive experiments are conducted on the Doc3D dataset [6], DocUNet Benchmark dataset [25], and our proposed challenging DIR300 Benchmark dataset. The results demonstrate the effectiveness of our method as well as its superiority over existing state-of-the-art methods.

In summary, we make three-fold contributions as follows:

- We present DocGeoNet, a new deep network that performs explicit representation learning of the geometric constraints between the distorted and target rectified image to promote the performance of document image rectification.
- We design a new pipeline to automatically annotate the textlines of the distorted document images in training set. Besides, to reflect the effectiveness of existing works, we propose a new large-scale challenge benchmark dataset.
- We conduct extensive experiments to validate the merits of DocGeoNet, and show state-of-the-art results on the prevalent and proposed benchmarks.

2   Related Work

Rectification Based on 3D Reconstruction. Early methods first estimate the 3D mesh of the deformed document and then flatten it to a planar shape. Brown and Seales [1] deploy a structured light 3D acquisition system to acquire the 3D model of a deformed document. Zhang et al. [46] use a laser range scanner and perform restoration using a physical modeling technique. Meng et al. [28] use two structured beams illuminating upon the document to recover two spatial curves of document surface. Such methods generally rely on auxiliary hardware to scan the deformed documents, which is unfriendly in daily personal use.

On the other hand, some methods make use of multiview images to reconstruct the 3D document model. Tsoi et al. [35] transform the multiple views of a document to a canonical coordinate frame based on the boundaries of the document. Koo et al. [16] build the deformed surface by registering the corresponding points in two images by SIFT [24]. Recently, You et al. [45] propose a ridge-aware surface reconstruction method based on multiview images. However, in the above works, the involvement of multiview shooting limits the further applications.

Some other methods aim to reconstruct the 3D shape from a single view. Typically, they assume a parametric model on the document surface and optimize the model by extracting specific representations, such as shading [4,37], boundaries [12], textlines [13,17,40], or texture flow [20]. Tan et al. [4] build the 3D shape of a book surface from the shading information. He et al. [12] extract a book boundary model to reconstruct the book surface. Cao et al. [13] and Meng et al. [27] represent the surface as a general cylindrical surface and extract textlines to estimate the parameter of the model.

Rectification Based on Deep Learning. For document image rectification, the first learning-based method is DocUNet [25]. By training a stacked UNet [32],

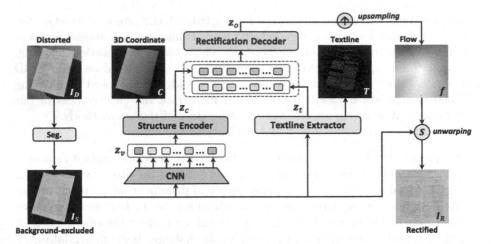

Fig. 1. An overview of our proposed DocGeoNet. It consists of three main components: (1) A preprocessing module that segments the foreground document from the clustered background. (2) A structure encoder and a textline extractor which model the 3D shape of the deformed document and extract the curved textlines, respectively. (3) A rectification decoder that estimates the warping flow for distortion rectification.

it directly regresses a pixel-wise displacement field to correct the geometric distortion. Later, Li et al. [19] propose to rectify the distorted image patches first and then stitch them for rectification. Xie et al. [42] add a smooth constraint to the learning of the pixel-wise displacement field. Recently, Amir et al. [26] propose to learn the orientation of words in a document and Das et al. [6] propose to model the 3D shape of a document with a UNet [32]. Feng et al. [9] introduce transformer [36] from natural language processing tasks to improve the feature representation. Das et al. [7] predict local deformation fields and stitch them together with global information to obtain an improved unwarping.

Different from the above methods, in this work, we approach the document image rectification by introducing the representation learning of the geometric constraints that bridge the distorted and the rectified image, which is largely overlooked by the recent state-of-the-art methods.

3   Approach

In this section, we present our Document Image Rectification Network (Doc-GeoNet) for geometric correction of distorted document images. Given a distorted document image I_D, our DocGeoNet estimates a dense displacement field $f = (f^x, f^y)$ as warping flow. Based on f, the pixel (i, j) in rectified image I_R can be obtained by sampling the pixel $(i', j') = (i + f^x(i), j + f^y(j))$ in input image I_D. As shown in Fig. 1, our framework consists of three key components: (1) preprocessing for background removal, (2) geometric constraint representation learning from two document attributes, including 3D shape and textlines,

and (3) representation fusion and geometric rectification. Here, the first preprocessing stage is trained independently, and the latter two stages are differentiable
and composed into an end-to-end trainable architecture. In the following, we
elaborate the three components separately.

3.1   Preprocessing

For the geometric rectification of document images, taking the whole distorted
image as input to the rectification network is a general operation. However,
it involves extra implicit learning to localize the foreground document besides
predicting the rectification, which limits the performance. Hence, following [9],
we adopt a preprocessing operation to remove the clustered background first,
thus the following network can focus on the rectification of the distortion.

Specifically, given a distorted RGB document image $I_D \in \mathbb{R}^{H \times W \times 3}$, a lightweight semantic segmentation network [31] is utilized to predict the confidence
map of the foreground document. Then, the confidence map is further binarized
with a threshold τ to obtain the document region mask $M_{I_D} \in \mathbb{R}^{H \times W}$. After
that, the background of I_D can be removed by element-wise matrix multiplica-
tion with broadcasting along the channels dimension of I_D, and we obtain the
background-excluded document image I_S. The preprocessing network is trained
independently with a binary cross-entropy loss [8] as follows,

$$\mathcal{L}_{seg} = -\sum_{i=1}^{N_p} [y_i \log(\hat{p}_i) + (1 - y_i) \log(1 - \hat{p}_i)], \tag{1}$$

where $N_p = H \times W$ is the number of pixels in I_D, y_i and $\hat{p}_i$ denote the ground-
truth and predicted confidence, respectively. The obtained background-excluded
document image I_S is fed into the subsequent rectification network.

3.2   Structure Encoder and Textline Extractor

In a document image, textlines are the main texture, which contain direct geometric constraints for rectification. In other words, a distorted curved textline
corresponding to a horizontal or vertical one in the ground truth should be
straight after rectification. Besides, the distribution of textlines also reflect the
deformation of a document. Therefore, textlines provide a strong cue for the
rectification. In addition, for geometric rectification, compared to a distorted
document image, the 3D shape is a more direct representation that determines
the unwarping process. Hence, we propose to model 3D shape and extract the
textlines of the deformed document in the network to leverage their geometric
constraints that bridge the distorted image and rectified image.

Specifically, as shown in Fig. 1, given a background-excluded document image
I_S, we adopt two parallel sub-networks to model 3D shape and extract the
textlines, respectively. We use a transformer-based [36] sub-network for the learning of 3D shape and a CNN-based sub-network for the learning of textlines. Such

a design is adopted based on two considerations. First, each part in a physical distorted paper is interrelated, so we introduce the self-attention mechanism [36] to capture long-distance feature dependencies. Second, whether a pixel belongs to a textline depends more on local features, so we take advantage of convolutional operations here. In the following, we elaborate the two sub-networks, *i.e.*, the structure encoder and the textline extractor.

Structure Encoder. Given a document image $I_S \in \mathbb{R}^{H \times W \times 3}$, a convolutional module consisting of 6 residual blocks [11] generates feature map $z \in \mathbb{R}^{\frac{H}{8} \times \frac{W}{8} \times C}$, where the channel dimension C is 128. Here the resolution of feature map decreases by $\frac{1}{2}$ every two blocks. Then, to adapt to the sequence input form of the subsequent transformer encoder [36], we flatten z into a sequence of tokens $z_v \in \mathbb{R}^{N_v \times C}$, where $N_v = \frac{H}{8} \times \frac{W}{8}$ is the number of tokens.

Since that transformer layer is permutation-invariant, to make it sensitive to the original 2D positions of input tokens, we utilize sinusoidal spatial position encodings as the supplementary of visual feature. Concretely, the position encodings are added with the query and key embedding at each transformer encoder layer. We stack 6 transformer encoder layers and each of the encoder layers contains a multi-head self-attention module and a feed forward network. For the ith encoder layer, the output representation is calculated as follows,

$$
\begin{aligned}
F_0 &= [z_v], \\
Q_i &= W^Q F_{i-1}, K_i = W^K F_{i-1}, V_i = W^V F_{i-1}, \\
F_i' &= LN(MA(Q_i, K_i, V_i) + F_{i-1}), \\
F_i &= LN(FFN(F_i') + F_i'),
\end{aligned}
\tag{2}
$$

where $W^Q, W^K, W^V \in \mathbb{R}^{M \times C \times C_w}$, $M = 8$ is the number of attention heads, $C_w = 256$ denotes the feature dimension in transformer, $MA(\cdot)$, $FFN(\cdot)$, $LN(\cdot)$ denote the multi-head attention, feed forward network, and layer normalization, respectively. F_i denotes the output feature of the ith encoder layer. The transformer layers conducts global vision context reasoning in parallel, and outputs the advanced visual embedding z_v', which shares the same shape as z_v.

We reshape the output feature $z_v' \in \mathbb{R}^{N_v \times C}$ to $\frac{H}{8} \times \frac{W}{8} \times C$. Finally, we upsample the reshaped feature map to match the resolution of the ground truth 3D coordinate map $C \in \mathbb{R}^{H \times W \times 3}$ based on bilinear sampling, followed by a 3 × 3 convolutional layer that reduces the channel dimension to 3. After that, we get the predicted 3D coordinate map $\hat{C} \in \mathbb{R}^{H \times W \times 3}$, in which each pixel value corresponds to 3D coordinates of the document shape.

Textline Extractor. We segment the textlines by the per-pixel binary classification on foreground document region. Given a background-excluded document image $I_S \in \mathbb{R}^{H \times W \times 3}$, a confidence map $\hat{T} \in \mathbb{R}^{H \times W}$ with values in the range of $(0, 1)$ is predicted. It contains the confidence of each pixel (text/non-text).

The textline extractor adopts a compact multi-scale CNN network. It consists of a contracting part, an expansive part and a classification part. For the contracting part, we repeat the application of two 3 × 3 convolutional layers to encode the texture features from I_S, each followed by a rectified linear unit (ReLU) and a 2×2 max pooling operation with stride 2 for downsampling. For the expansive part, after upsampling the feature map based on bilinear interpolation at each scale, we concatenate it with the corresponding feature map from the contracting path, followed by two 3×3 convolutional layers and a ReLU. In the classification part, a 1×1 convolutional layer followed by a Sigmoid function is used to generate the confidence map $\hat{T} \in \mathbb{R}^{H \times W}$.

3.3 Rectification Decoder

Hybrid Representation Learning. To take advantage of the complementarity of the two attributes and leverage their geometric constraints that bridge the distorted and target rectified image, we further fuse their representation and predict the rectification in the rectification decoder. Specifically, we first flatten the $\frac{1}{8}$ resolution representation map in expansive part of the textline extractor into a sequence of 2D features $z_t \in \mathbb{R}^{N_v \times C_t}$. Then, we concatenate it with $z_c \in \mathbb{R}^{N_v \times C}$, the output representation of the 4th transformer encoder layer of the structure encoder. The concatenated representation is feed into another 6 transformer encoder layers to obtain the fused representation $z_o \in \mathbb{R}^{N_v \times (C + C_t)}$.

Rectification Estimation. The obtained z_o is feed into a learnable module to perform upsampling and predict high-resolution rectification estimation. Specifically, we first predict a coarse resolution displacement map $\hat{f}_o \in \mathbb{R}^{(\frac{H}{8} \times \frac{W}{8}) \times 2}$ through a two-layer convolutional network. Then, in analogy to [34], we upsample $\hat{f}_o$ to full-resolution map $\hat{f} \in \mathbb{R}^{H \times W \times 2}$ by taking learnable weighted combination of the 3×3 grid of the coarse resolution neighbors of each pixel.

3.4 Training Objectives

During training, except the preprocessing module, the architecture of the proposed DocGeoNet is end-to-end optimized with the following objective as follows,

$$\mathcal{L} = \alpha \mathcal{L}_{3D} + \beta \mathcal{L}_{text} + \mathcal{L}_{flow}, \tag{3}$$

where $\mathcal{L}_{3D}$ denotes the regression loss on 3D coordinate map, $\mathcal{L}_{text}$ represents the segmentation loss of textlines, and $\mathcal{L}_{flow}$ denotes the regression loss on warping flow. α and β are the weights associated to $\mathcal{L}_{3D}$ and $\mathcal{L}_{text}$, respectively. In the following, we present the formulation of the three loss terms.

Specifically, for the learning of the 3D coordinate map, the loss $\mathcal{L}_{3D}$ is calculated as L_1 distance between the predicted 3D coordinate map $\hat{C}$ and its corresponding ground truth C_{gt} as follows,

$$\mathcal{L}_{3D} = \left\| C_{gt} - \hat{C} \right\|_1. \tag{4}$$

The segmentation loss $\mathcal{L}_{text}$ for textlines is defined as a binary cross-entropy loss [8] as follows,

$$\mathcal{L}_{text} = - \sum_{i=1}^{N_d} \left[y_i \log(\hat{p}_i) + (1 - y_i) \log(1 - \hat{p}_i) \right], \tag{5}$$

where N_d is the pixel number of the foreground document, y_i and $\hat{p}_i$ denote the ground-truth and predicted confidence, respectively. Note that here we only compute the loss on the foreground document region. One reason is that the textlines only exist in the foreground document region. The other one is that in the input background-excluded image I_S, the textline pixels have similar RGB values to the background, which would confuse the network.

The loss $\mathcal{L}_{\text{flow}}$ for warping flow is defined as the L_1 distance between the predicted warping flow $\hat{f}$ and its ground truth f_{gt} as follows,

$$\mathcal{L}_{flow} = \left\| f_{gt} - \hat{f} \right\|_1. \tag{6}$$

4   DIR300 Dataset

In this section, we present the DIR300 dataset, a new dataset for document image rectification. In the following, we first revisit the previous datasets, and then elaborate the details of the introduced one.

4.1   Revisiting Existing Datasets

The most widely adopted datasets in the field are Doc3D dataset [6] and DocUNet Benchmark dataset [25]. Doc3D dataset [6] consists of 100k synthetic distorted document images generated with the real document data and rendering software[1]. It is used for training the rectification model. For each distorted document image, there are corresponding ground truth 3D coordinate map, depth map, and warping flow. However, it does not contain the textline annotations, which we empirically demonstrate to be beneficial for rectification.

DocUNet Benchmark dataset [25] is introduced for only evaluation purpose. It contains 130 document photos captured on 65 documents, which is too small to make the evaluation results convincing. Besides, to the best of our knowledge, this is the only publicly available benchmark dataset with real image data. Thus, the introduction of a larger scale benchmark becomes an urgent demand.

Additionally, the 127th and 128th distorted images in DocUNet Benchmark dataset [25] are rotated by 180°C, which do not match the ground truth documents [10]. It is ignored by existing works [6,7,9,14,22,25,41–43]. In our experiments, we report the results on the corrected dataset. For clarity, we also report the performance with two mistaken samples.

4.2   Dataset Details

We make two-fold efforts to build the DIR300 dataset. On the one hand, we extend the synthesized Doc3D dataset [6] with textline annotations to build the training set. On the other hand, we capture 300 real document samples to build a larger test set against the DocUNet Benchmark dataset [25].

---

[1] https://www.blender.org/.

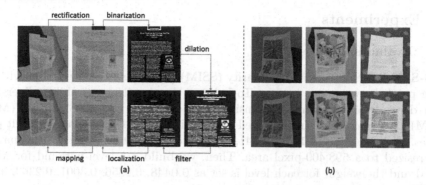

Fig. 2. An illustration of (a) the textlines annotation process, and (b) the visualization of textline annotations in corresponding distorted document images.

Training Set. Here, we describe how to generate the textline annotations on the Doc3D dataset [6] with fewer labour requirements. Typically, it is difficult to localize the textlines in a distorted document image, where the textlines take various shapes. But it is easy to achieve it in a flattened document image. Hence, we rectify all distorted images in Doc3D dataset [6] using the ground truth warping flow and then detect the horizontal textlines by the following steps.

Specifically, as shown in Fig. 2 (a), we first convert the rectified images to gray-scale and perform adaptive *binarization* based on the local Gaussian weighted sum. Next, we conduct the horizontal *dilation* in the binary image to get the connected regions and their corresponding bounding boxes. Then, we set the thresholds on the shape of bounding boxes to *filter* out non-textline connected regions. Finally, we *localize* the center and the horizontal length of the bounding boxes to generate the horizontal textlines. After *mapping* such horizontal textlines to the original distorted image using the warping flow, we obtain the curved textlines annotations. As shown in Fig. 2 (b), we visualize some textline annotation samples, where the most textlines are annotated accurately. Notably, we note that a few annotated textlines are missed when being filtered due to their size, but they are within the fault tolerance of the network.

Test Set. We build the test set of DIR300 dataset with photos captured by mobile cameras. It contains 300 real document photos from 300 documents. Compared to the DocUNet Benchmark dataset [25], the distorted document images in DIR300 involve more complex background and various illumination conditions. Besides, we also increase the deformation degree of the warped documents. The creation details are provided in the supplemental material. To the best of our knowledge, the DIR300 test set is currently the largest real data benchmark for evaluating document image rectification.

5   Experiments

5.1   Evaluation Metrics

MS-SSIM. The Structural SIMilarity (SSIM) [38] measures how similar within each patch between two images. To balance the detail perceivability diversity that depends on the sampling density, Multi-Scale Structural Similarity (MS-SSIM) [39] calculates the weighted summation of SSIM [38] across multiple scales. Following [6,7,9,14,22,25,41,42], all rectified and ground truth images are resized to a 598,400-pixel area. Then, we build a 5-level-pyramid for MS-SSIM and the weight for each level is set as 0.0448, 0.2856, 0.3001, 0.2363, and 0.1333.

Local Distortion. By computing a dense SIFT-flow [21], Local Distortion (LD) [45] matches all the pixels from the ground truth scanned image to the rectified image. Then, LD is calculated as the mean value of the L_2 distance between the matched pixels, which measures the average local deformation of the rectified image. For a fair comparison, we resize all the rectified images and the ground truth images to a 598,400-pixel area, as suggested in [6,7,9,14,22,25,41,42].

ED and CER. Edit Distance (ED) [18] and Character Error Rate (CER) [29] quantify the similarity of two strings. ED is the minimum number of operations required to transform one string into the reference string. The involved operations include deletions (d), insertions (i) and substitutions (s). Then, Character Error Rate (CER) can be computed as follows,

$$CER = (d + i + s)/N_c, \tag{7}$$

where N_c is the character number of the reference string. CER represents the percentage of characters in the reference text that was incorrectly recognized in the distorted image. The lower the CER value (with 0 being a perfect score), the better the performance of the rectification quality.

We use Tesseract (v5.0.1) [33] as the OCR engine to recognize the text in the images. Following DewarpNet [6] and DocTr [9], we select 50 and 60 images from the DocUNet Benchmark dataset [25], respectively. Besides, on the DIR300 test set, we select 90 images. In such images, the text makes up the majority of content. Since if the text is sparse in a document, the character number N_c (numerator) in Eq. (7) is a small number, leading to a large variance for CER.

5.2   Implementation Details

We implement the whole framework of DocGeoNet in Pytorch [30]. The preprocessing module and the following rectification module are trained independently on the extended Doc3D dataset [6]. We detail their training in the following.

Preprocessing Module. During training, to generalize well to real data with complex background environments, we randomly replace the background of the distorted document with the texture images from Describable Texture

Table 1. Quantitative comparisons of the existing learning-based methods in terms of image similarity, distortion metrics, OCR accuracy, and running efficiency on the **corrected** DocUNet Benchmark dataset [25]. "*" denotes that the OCR metrics could not be calculated as the rectified images or models are not publicly available. "↑" indicates the higher the better, while "↓" means the opposite.

Methods	Venue	MS-SSIM ↑	LD ↓	ED ↓	CER ↓	FPS ↑	Para.
Distorted	–	0.2459	20.51	2111.56/1552.22	0.5352/0.5089	–	–
DocUNet [25]	CVPR'18	0.4103	14.19	1933.66/1259.83	0.4632/0.3966	0.21	58.6M
AGUN [22]*	PR'18	–	–	–	–	–	–
DocProj [19]	TOG'19	0.2946	18.01	1712.48/1165.93	0.4267/0.3818	0.11	47.8M
FCN-based [42]	DAS'20	0.4477	7.84	1792.60/1031.40	0.4213/0.3156	1.49	23.6M
DewarpNet [6]	ICCV'19	0.4735	8.39	885.90/525.45	0.2373/0.2102	7.14	86.9M
PWUNet [7]	ICCV'21	0.4915	8.64	1069.28/743.32	0.2677/0.2623	–	–
DocTr [9]	MM'21	0.5105	7.76	724.84/464.83	0.1832/0.1746	7.40	26.9M
DDCP [41]	ICDAR'21	0.4729	8.99	1442.84/745.35	0.3633/0.2626	**12.38**	**13.3M**
FDRNet [43]	CVPR'22	**0.5420**	8.21	794.54/514.90	0.2010/0.1846	–	–
RDGR [14]	CVPR'22	0.4968	8.51	693.38/420.25	**0.1654**/0.1559	–	–
Ours	–	0.5040	**7.71**	**692.86/379.00**	0.1797/**0.1509**	–	24.8M

Table 2. Quantitative comparisons of the existing learning-based methods in terms of image similarity, distortion metrics, OCR accuracy on the proposed DIR300 test set. "↑" indicates the higher the better, while "↓" means the opposite.

Methods	Venue	MS-SSIM ↑	LD ↓	ED ↓	CER ↓
Distorted	–	0.3148	39.98	1512.16	0.5234
DocProj [19]	TOG'19	0.3213	31.16	1049.36	0.3984
DewarpNet [6]	ICCV'19	0.4882	14.48	1096.31	0.3626
DocTr [9]	MM'21	0.6104	7.84	741.93	0.2320
DDCP [41]	ICDAR'21	0.5484	11.44	2122.44	0.5476
Ours	–	**0.6323**	**7.07**	**706.99**	**0.2271**

Dataset [5]. We use Adam optimizer [15] with a batch size of 32. The initial learning rate is set as 1×10^{-4}, and reduced by a factor of 0.1 after 30 epochs. The network is trained for 45 epochs on two NVIDIA RTX 2080 Ti GPUs. In addition, the threshold τ for binarizing the confidence map is set as 0.5.

Rectification Module. During training, we remove the background of distorted document images using the ground truth masks of the foreground document. To generalize well to real data with various illumination conditions, we add jitter in HSV color space to magnify illumination and document color variations. We use AdamW optimizer [23] with a batch size of 12 and an initial learning rate of 1×10^{-4}. Our model is trained for 40 epochs on 4 NVIDIA GTX 1080 Ti GPUs. We set the hyperparameters $\alpha = 0.2$ and $\beta = 0.2$ (in Eq. (3)).

486   H. Feng et al.

Table 3. Ablations of the architecture settings. SE denotes the structure encoder. TE denotes the textline extracter. Here we only supervise the output warping flow.

SE	TE	MS-SSIM ↑	LD ↓	ED ↓	CER ↓
		0.4972	8.11	869.00/545.83	0.2207/0.1997
✓	✓	**0.4994**	**7.99**	**764.38/524.90**	**0.2010/0.1803**

5.3 Experiment Results

We evaluate the proposed DocGeoNet by quantitative and qualitative comparisons with recent state-of-the-art rectification methods. For quantitative evaluation, we show the comparison on distortion metrics, OCR accuracy, image similarity, and inference efficiency. The evaluations are conducted on the corrected DocUNet Benchmark dataset [25] and our proposed DIR300 test set. For clarity, in the supplementary material, we also report the performance on the DocUNet Benchmark dataset [25] with two mistaken samples described in Sect. 4.1.

Quantitative Comparisons. On the DocUNet Benchmark [25], we compare DocGeoNet with existing learning-based methods. As shown in Table 1, our DocGeoNet achieves a Local Distortion (LD) of 7.71 and a Character Error Rate (CER) of 15%, surpassing previous state-of-the-art methods DocTr [9] and RDGR [14]. In addition, we compare the parameter counts and inference time of processing a 1080P resolution image. The test is conducted on an RTX 2080Ti GPU. As shown in Table 1, the proposed DocGeoNet shows promising efficiency.

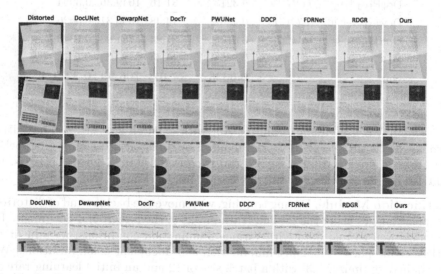

Fig. 3. Qualitative comparisons with previous methods on the DocUNet Benchmark dataset [25] in terms of the rectified images and local textline detail. For the comparisons of the rectified images, we highlight the comparisons of boundary and textlines by the yellow and red arrow, respectively. (Color figure online)

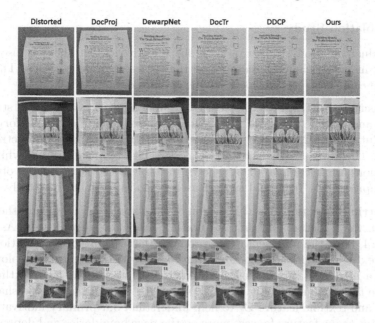

Fig. 4. Qualitative comparisons with previous methods on the proposed DIR300 test set in terms of the rectified images.

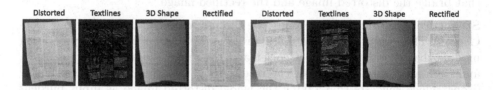

Fig. 5. Visualization of two instances on the predicted textlines and 3D coordinate map by our DocGeoNet.

On the proposed DIR300 test set, we compare DocGeoNet with typical rectification methods with model publicly available. As shown in Table 2, DocGeoNet outperforms the previous state-of-the-art method DocTr [9] on Local Distortion (LD) and OCR metrics, verifying its superior rectification ability.

Qualitative Comparisons. The qualitative comparisons are conducted on the DocUNet Benchmark [25] and DIR300 test set. To compare the local rectified detail, we also show the comparisons of cropped local rectified text. As shown in Fig. 3 and Fig. 4, the proposed DocGeoNet shows superior rectification quality. Specifically, for our method, the incomplete boundaries phenomenons existing in the previous methods are to a certain extent relieved. Besides, the rectified textlines of our method are much straighter than previous methods. More results on the both datasets are provided in the supplementary material.

5.4   Ablation Study

We conduct ablation study to verify the effectiveness of the proposed Doc-GeoNet, including the architecture and the representations to learn. The ablations are conducted on the DocUNet Benchmark dataset [25].

Architecture Setting. We first train a simple network without the structure encoder and textline extractor: the background-excluded image I_S is forward to a convolutional module and its flattened feature z_v is fed into the rectification decoder. Then, we add the structure encoder and textline extractor while their supervisions are not deployed. As shown in Table 3, the latter model obtains a slight improvement. It is used as the baseline model for following study.

Geometric Representation. Based on the baseline network, we add the supervision on the structure encoder and textline extractor, respectively. As shown in Table 4, both the representations promote the learning of rectification. Furthermore, the performance is better after both the supervisions are deployed. To provide a more specific view of the predicted 3D coordinate and textlines, we showcase two examples in Fig. 5. As shown in Fig. 6, we visualize the shape feature Z_c and textline feature Z_t to help understand our primary motivation. As we can see, shape feature focuses more on the page boundaries and depresses the inside text content, while textline feature does the opposite. The above results reveal the effectiveness of representation learning of the document attributes that bridge the distorted image and the rectified image.

Structure Modifications. Finally, we discuss some components of our Doc-GeoNet. The results are shown in Table 5. (1) We first verify the preprocessing module that is adopted in DocGeoNet and the recent state-of-the-art method, and train a network without it. The results show that the performance slightly drops, which suggests that taking the whole distorted image as input burdens

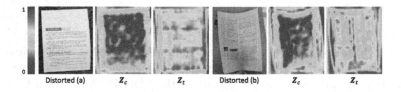

Fig. 6. Comparison of shape feature Z_c and textline feature Z_t.

Table 4. Ablations of the different representation learning settings of DocGeoNet.

3D Shape	Textlines	MS-SSIM ↑	LD ↓	ED ↓	CER ↓
		0.4994	7.99	764.38/524.90	0.2010/0.1803
✓		**0.5067**	7.83	737.56/418.53	0.1826/0.1646
	✓	0.5053	7.79	748.35/466.58	0.1873/0.1693
✓	✓	0.5040	**7.71**	**692.86/379.00**	**0.1797/0.1509**

Table 5. Ablations of the different component settings of DocGeoNet.

	MS-SSIM ↑	LD ↓	ED ↓	CER ↓
Full model	0.5040	**7.71**	**692.86/379.00**	0.1797/**0.1509**
Preprocessing → None	0.4843	8.61	786.54/514.60	0.2100/0.2003
Upsampling: Learnable → Bilinear	**0.5062**	7.77	702.83/405.21	**0.1790**/0.1523

the network with localizing the foreground document besides the rectification prediction. (2) We compare the bilinear upsampling with our learnable upsampling module. The performance is slightly better using the learnable upsampling module. We attribute this improvement to that the coarse bilinear upsampling operation is difficult to recover the small deformations.

6 Conclusion

In this work, we present a novel deep network DocGeoNet for document image rectification. It bridges the distorted and rectified image by explicitly introducing the representation learning of the geometric constraints from two document attributes, *i.e.*, 3D shape and textlines. Extensive experiments are conducted, and the results reveal that our DocGeoNet achieves state-of-the-art performance on the prevalent benchmark and proposed large-scale challenge benchmark.

Acknowledgments. This work was supported by the National Natural Science Foundation of China under Contract 61836011 and 62021001. It was also supported by the GPU cluster built by MCC Lab of Information Science and Technology Institution, USTC.

References

1. Brown, M.S., Seales, W.B.: Document restoration using 3D shape: a general deskewing algorithm for arbitrarily warped documents. In: Proceedings of the IEEE International Conference on Computer Vision, vol. 2, pp. 367–374 (2001)
2. Brown, M.S., Seales, W.B.: Image restoration of arbitrarily warped documents. IEEE Trans. Pattern Anal. Mach. Intell. **26**(10), 1295–1306 (2004)
3. Brown, M., Sun, M., Yang, R., Yun, L., Seales, W.B.: Restoring 2d content from distorted documents. IEEE Trans. Pattern Anal. Mach. Intell. **29**(11), 1904–1916 (2007)
4. Tan, C.L., Zhang, L., Zhang, Z., Xia, T.: Restoring warped document images through 3D shape modeling. IEEE Trans. Pattern Anal. Mach. Intell. **28**(2), 195–208 (2006)
5. Cimpoi, M., Maji, S., Kokkinos, I., Mohamed, S., Vedaldi, A.: Describing textures in the wild. In: Proceedings of the IEEE Conference on Computer Vision and Pattern Recognition, pp. 3606–3613 (2014)

6. Das, S., Ma, K., Shu, Z., Samaras, D., Shilkrot, R.: DewarpNet: single-image document unwarping with stacked 3D and 2D regression networks. In: Proceedings of the International Conference on Computer Vision, pp. 131–140 (2019)
7. Das, S., et al.: End-to-end piece-wise unwarping of document images. In: Proceedings of the IEEE International Conference on Computer Vision, pp. 4268–4277 (2021)
8. De Boer, P.T., Kroese, D.P., Mannor, S., Rubinstein, R.Y.: A tutorial on the cross-entropy method. Ann. Oper. Res. **134**(1), 19–67 (2005)
9. Feng, H., Wang, Y., Zhou, W., Deng, J., Li, H.: DocTr: document image transformer for geometric unwarping and illumination correction. In: Proceedings of the ACM International Conference on Multimedia, pp. 273–281 (2021)
10. Feng, H., Zhou, W., Deng, J., Tian, Q., Li, H.: DocScanner: robust document image rectification with progressive learning. arXiv preprint arXiv:2110.14968 (2021)
11. He, K., Zhang, X., Ren, S., Sun, J.: Deep residual learning for image recognition. In: Proceedings of the IEEE Conference on Computer Vision and Pattern Recognition, pp. 770–778 (2016)
12. He, Y., Pan, P., Xie, S., Sun, J., Naoi, S.: A book dewarping system by boundary-based 3D surface reconstruction. In: Proceedings of the International Conference on Document Analysis and Recognition, pp. 403–407 (2013)
13. Cao, H., Ding, X., Liu, C.: Rectifying the bound document image captured by the camera: a model based approach. In: Proceedings of the International Conference on Document Analysis and Recognition, vol. 1, pp. 71–75 (2003)
14. Jiang, X., Long, R., Xue, N., Yang, Z., Yao, C., Xia, G.S.: Revisiting document image dewarping by grid regularization. In: Proceedings of the IEEE/CVF Conference on Computer Vision and Pattern Recognition, pp. 4543–4552 (2022)
15. Kingma, D.P., Ba, J.: Adam: a method for stochastic optimization. CoRR abs/1412.6980 (2015)
16. Koo, H.I., Kim, J., Cho, N.I.: Composition of a dewarped and enhanced document image from two view images. IEEE Trans. Image Process. **18**(7), 1551–1562 (2009)
17. Lavialle, O., Molines, X., Angella, F., Baylou, P.: Active contours network to straighten distorted text lines. In: Proceedings of the International Conference on Image Processing, vol. 3, pp. 748–751 (2001)
18. Levenshtein, V.I.: Binary codes capable of correcting deletions, insertions, and reversals, vol. 10, pp. 707–710 (1966)
19. Li, X., Zhang, B., Liao, J., Sander, P.V.: Document rectification and illumination correction using a patch-based CNN. ACM Trans. Graph. **38**(6), 1–11 (2019)
20. Liang, J., DeMenthon, D., Doermann, D.: Geometric rectification of camera-captured document images. IEEE Trans. Pattern Anal. Mach. Intell. **30**(4), 591–605 (2008)
21. Liu, C., Yuen, J., Torralba, A.: SIFT flow: dense correspondence across scenes and its applications. IEEE Trans. Pattern Anal. Mach. Intell. **33**(5), 978–994 (2011)
22. Liu, X., Meng, G., Fan, B., Xiang, S., Pan, C.: Geometric rectification of document images using adversarial gated unwarping network. Pattern Recogn. **108**, 107576 (2020)
23. Loshchilov, I., Hutter, F.: Decoupled weight decay regularization. In: Proceedings of the International Conference on Learning Representations (2019)
24. Lowe, D.G.: Distinctive image features from scale-invariant keypoints. Int. J. Comput. Vis. **60**(2), 91–110 (2004)
25. Ma, K., Shu, Z., Bai, X., Wang, J., Samaras, D.: DocUNet: document image unwarping via a stacked u-net. In: Proceedings of the IEEE International Conference on Computer Vision, pp. 4700–4709 (2018)

26. Markovitz, A., Lavi, I., Perel, O., Mazor, S., Litman, R.: Can you read me now? Content aware rectification using angle supervision. In: Vedaldi, A., Bischof, H., Brox, T., Frahm, J.-M. (eds.) ECCV 2020. LNCS, vol. 12357, pp. 208–223. Springer, Cham (2020). https://doi.org/10.1007/978-3-030-58610-2_13
27. Meng, G., Pan, C., Xiang, S., Duan, J., Zheng, N.: Metric rectification of curved document images. IEEE Trans. Pattern Anal. Mach. Intell. **34**(4), 707–722 (2011)
28. Meng, G., Wang, Y., Qu, S., Xiang, S., Pan, C.: Active flattening of curved document images via two structured beams. In: Proceedings of the IEEE International Conference on Computer Vision, pp. 3890–3897 (2014)
29. Morris, A.C., Maier, V., Green, P.: From WER and RIL to MER and WIL: improved evaluation measures for connected speech recognition. In: Proceedings of the International Conference on Spoken Language Processing (2004)
30. Paszke, A., et al.: Automatic differentiation in pytorch (2017)
31. Qin, X., Zhang, Z., Huang, C., Dehghan, M., Zaiane, O.R., Jagersand, M.: U2-net: going deeper with nested u-structure for salient object detection. Pattern Recogn. **106**, 107404 (2020)
32. Ronneberger, O., Fischer, P., Brox, T.: U-net: convolutional networks for biomedical image segmentation. In: Navab, N., Hornegger, J., Wells, W.M., Frangi, A.F. (eds.) MICCAI 2015. LNCS, vol. 9351, pp. 234–241. Springer, Cham (2015). https://doi.org/10.1007/978-3-319-24574-4_28
33. Smith, R.: An overview of the tesseract OCR engine. In: Proceedings of the International Conference on Document Analysis and Recognition, vol. 2, pp. 629–633 (2007)
34. Teed, Z., Deng, J.: RAFT: recurrent all-pairs field transforms for optical flow. In: Vedaldi, A., Bischof, H., Brox, T., Frahm, J.-M. (eds.) ECCV 2020. LNCS, vol. 12347, pp. 402–419. Springer, Cham (2020). https://doi.org/10.1007/978-3-030-58536-5_24
35. Tsoi, Y.C., Brown, M.S.: Multi-view document rectification using boundary. In: Proceedings of the IEEE Conference on Computer Vision and Pattern Recognition, pp. 1–8 (2007)
36. Vaswani, A., et al.: Attention is all you need. In: Proceedings of the Neural Information Processing Systems, pp. 6000–6010 (2017)
37. Wada, T., Ukida, H., Matsuyama, T.: Shape from shading with interreflections under a proximal light source: distortion-free copying of an unfolded book. Int. J. Comput. Vision **24**(2), 125–135 (1997)
38. Wang, Z., Bovik, A.C., Sheikh, H.R., Simoncelli, E.P.: Image quality assessment: from error visibility to structural similarity. IEEE Trans. Image Process. **13**(4), 600–612 (2004)
39. Wang, Z., Simoncelli, E.P., Bovik, A.C.: Multiscale structural similarity for image quality assessment. In: Proceedings of the Asilomar Conference on Signals, Systems Computers, vol. 2, pp. 1398–1402 (2003)
40. Wu, C., Agam, G.: Document image de-warping for text/Graphics recognition. In: Caelli, T., Amin, A., Duin, R.P.W., de Ridder, D., Kamel, M. (eds.) SSPR /SPR 2002. LNCS, vol. 2396, pp. 348–357. Springer, Heidelberg (2002). https://doi.org/10.1007/3-540-70659-3_36
41. Xie, G.-W., Yin, F., Zhang, X.-Y., Liu, C.-L.: Document dewarping with control points. In: Lladós, J., Lopresti, D., Uchida, S. (eds.) ICDAR 2021. LNCS, vol. 12821, pp. 466–480. Springer, Cham (2021). https://doi.org/10.1007/978-3-030-86549-8_30

42. Xie, G.-W., Yin, F., Zhang, X.-Y., Liu, C.-L.: Dewarping document image by displacement flow estimation with fully convolutional network. In: Bai, X., Karatzas, D., Lopresti, D. (eds.) DAS 2020. LNCS, vol. 12116, pp. 131–144. Springer, Cham (2020). https://doi.org/10.1007/978-3-030-57058-3_10

43. Xue, C., Tian, Z., Zhan, F., Lu, S., Bai, S.: Fourier document restoration for robust document dewarping and recognition. In: Proceedings of the IEEE/CVF Conference on Computer Vision and Pattern Recognition, pp. 4573–4582 (2022)

44. Yamashita, A., Kawarago, A., Kaneko, T., Miura, K.T.: Shape reconstruction and image restoration for non-flat surfaces of documents with a stereo vision system. In: Proceedings of the International Conference on Pattern Recognition, vol. 1, pp. 482–485 (2004)

45. You, S., Matsushita, Y., Sinha, S., Bou, Y., Ikeuchi, K.: Multiview rectification of folded documents. IEEE Trans. Pattern Anal. Mach. Intell. 40(2), 505–511 (2018)

46. Zhang, L., Zhang, Y., Tan, C.: An improved physically-based method for geometric restoration of distorted document images. IEEE Trans. Pattern Anal. Mach. Intell. 30(4), 728–734 (2008)

S²-VER: Semi-supervised Visual Emotion Recognition

Guoli Jia⬤ and Jufeng Yang$^{(\boxtimes)}$⬤

Nankai University, Tianjin, China
exped1230@gmail.com, yangjufeng@nankai.edu.cn

Abstract. Visual emotion recognition (VER), which plays an important role in various applications, has attracted increasing attention of researchers. Due to the ambiguous characteristic of emotion, it is hard to annotate a reliable large-scale dataset in this field. An alternative solution is semi-supervised learning (SSL), which progressively selects high-confidence samples from unlabeled data to help optimize the model. However, it is challenging to directly employ existing SSL algorithms in VER task. On the one hand, compared with object recognition, in VER task, the accuracy of the produced pseudo labels for unlabeled data drops a large margin. On the other hand, the maximum probability in the prediction is difficult to reach the fixed threshold, which leads to few unlabeled samples can be leveraged. Both of them would induce the suboptimal performance of the learned model. To address these issues, we propose S²-VER, the first SSL algorithm for VER, which consists of two components. The first component, reliable emotion label learning, aims to improve the accuracy of pseudo-labels. In detail, it generates smoothing labels by computing the similarity between the maintained emotion prototypes and the embedding of the sample. The second one is ambiguity-aware adaptive threshold strategy, which is dedicated to leveraging more unlabeled samples. Specifically, our strategy uses information entropy to measure the ambiguity of the smoothing labels, then adaptively adjusts the threshold, which is adopted to select high-confidence unlabeled samples. Extensive experiments conducted on six public datasets show that our proposed S²-VER performs favorably against the state-of-the-art approaches. The code is available at *https://github.com/exped1230/S2-VER*.

1 Introduction

Visual emotion recognition (VER) aims at identifying human's emotions towards different visual stimuli [37]. With the popularization of multimedia, many people utilize images to record their feelings on social platforms, such as Instagram and Twitter. Therefore, visual emotion has drawn increasing attention from computer vision researchers [8,24,37] with its wide applications, *e.g.*, opinion mining [27,52] and image captioning [1,6]. Among them, recognizing the dominant emotion evoked by affective images is one of the most popular research directions [39,45].

© The Author(s), under exclusive license to Springer Nature Switzerland AG 2022
S. Avidan et al. (Eds.): ECCV 2022, LNCS 13697, pp. 493–509, 2022.
https://doi.org/10.1007/978-3-031-19836-6_28

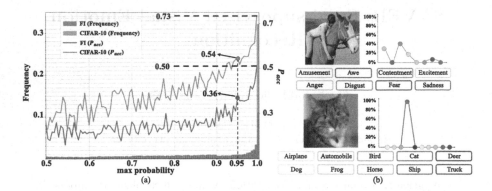

Fig. 1. Comparison between FI and CIFAR-10. (a) shows the frequency histogram and pseudo label accuracy P_{acc} when training FixMatch on FI and CIFAR-10, respectively. The maximum probability of the prediction is used to measure the confidence of the pseudo labels in SSL. FixMatch sets 0.95 as threshold to select high-confidence samples. (b) illustrates the label distribution of images from FI and CIFAR-10. The labels are represented by different colors. (Color figure online)

In the past decades, many works make considerable improvements to VER [28,39,47]. However, most of these methods train networks in fully-supervised manner, which need a large amount of labeled data. It is extremely time-consuming to construct such datasets. Besides, due to the diversity of cultural backgrounds and personalities, different viewers may have different emotions induced by the same image [52]. Furthermore, a viewer may even have multiple emotions towards an image, *i.e.*, ambiguity [42]. Therefore, compared with object recognition, it is challenging to annotate a reliable large-scale dataset for FER. In this paper, we explore leveraging pseudo-labeling based semi-supervised learning (SSL) algorithms to address this issue. On the one hand, with the help of SSL algorithm, the cost of annotation can be significantly reduced. On the other hand, the algorithms progressively adopt high-confidence samples to train the model, which alleviates the impact of unreliable samples. We believe it is a promising direction to address the difficulty of emotion annotation.

SSL aims to address the need for labeled data by designing an algorithm to utilize unlabeled data [4]. As a representative method, FixMatch [30] selects high-confidence predictions from weakly augmented unlabeled instances, and then exploits them as the pseudo labels for the strongly augmented instances. To explore the performance of FixMatch in VER, we conduct a comparison experiment on FI [44] and CIFAR-10 [15]. Specifically, on both datasets we sample 100 labeled samples and 1,000 unlabeled samples from each class to train ResNet50 [9] with the same setting. The results are shown in Fig. 1 (a), and we have two observations. First, when the maximum probability is 0.95, compared with CIFAR-10, the accuracy of pseudo labels on FI drops a large margin. During the training process, due to the challenge of VER, the accumulated mistakes of pseudo labels result in confirmation bias, which is a common hazard in SSL

[18,32]. Second, only a few samples have a high maximum probability. As shown in Fig. 1 (b), different from the one-hot description for images in CIFAR-10, the probability of dominant emotion may be limited by other existing emotions. Therefore, the number of samples reaching the threshold is small, which limits the performance of the model [35].

To address these problems, we propose S^2-VER, the first semi-supervised VER algorithm, which consists of two components. First, the reliable emotion label learning module adopts label smoothing to improve the accuracy of pseudo labels. Label smoothing has been proven to implicitly calibrate the learned models so that the confidences are more aligned with the accuracies of their predictions [22]. Inspired by this, we generate smoothing labels for affective images. Specifically, we calculate the similarity between embeddings and the emotional prototypes. To capture the associations among emotions, the smoothing labels are multiplied with a maintained emotional relation matrix. Furthermore, since the quality of smoothing labels depends on the embeddings, we introduce an continuous contrastive loss to obtain emotionally discriminative representations. Second, we propose an ambiguity-aware adaptive threshold strategy, which aims to exploit more emotionally high-confidence unlabeled samples. For each sample, the strategy measures the ambiguity of the smoothing labels by information entropy and the polarity cue of emotions. Based on this strategy, the threshold is adaptively adjusted and more high-confidence unlabeled data can be leveraged.

Our contributions are summarized as follows: 1) We address the difficulty of annotating emotion datasets by SSL. To the best of our knowledge, this is the first visual emotion work that focuses on learning in semi-supervised manner. 2) We propose S^2-VER, which can improve the accuracy of pseudo labels, and leverage more emotionally high-confidence unlabeled data for VER. 3) We conduct extensive experiments on six datasets and the results demonstrate the effectiveness of S^2-VER.

2   Related Work

2.1   Visual Emotion Recognition

The research on visual emotion recognition has developed for more than two decades [49,52]. In the early years, researchers exploit handcrafted features to recognize the dominant emotion conveyed by an affective image. Inspired by the theory of psychology and art, Machajdik et al. [20] extract features from four aspects, containing color, texture, composition, and content. It is a representative low-level handcrafted feature. Zhao et al. [48] explore the research of principles-of-art, and propose a mid-level representation of visual emotion. To understand the visual concepts that are strongly related to emotion, Borth et al. [5] automatically collect adjective-none pairs (ANP) as the high-level representation.

Recently, many methods [34,45] exploit convolutional neural network (CNN) for VER. Considering the localized information, Yang et al. [39] design a weakly supervised coupled network to integrate recognition and detection tasks. To extract various levels of related visual features, Rao *et al.* [28] construct a region-based CNN network with multi-level framework. [13,14] analyze the relation between person and context scene to extract rich information about emotional states. Furthermore, [36] proposes a novel Scene-Object network, which leverages reasoning network to mine the relations among objects and the correlation between the objects and scene. Different from previous methods, [38] proposes a stimuli-aware visual emotion model consisting of Global-Net, Semantic-Net, and Expression-Net, which extracts three aspects of emotional stimulus simultaneously. Although these methods have made great progress in VER, a fundamental weakness of these deep models is that they typically require a lot of accurately annotated data to work well [35]. However, it is still one of the main challenges for VER. Therefore, we explore SSL algorithm to address this issue.

2.2 Semi-supervised Learning

SSL trains models incorporating labeled and unlabeled samples. Many classic methods have been proposed, such as transductive models [10,11], generative models [12,29], and graph-based models [54,55]. In addition, [17] proposes to generate pseudo labels by picking up the category which has the maximum probability in the predicted distribution. ICT [33] regularizes the model based on the liner interpolation assumption.

Consistency regularization is an effective method, which is based on the smoothness theory that slight perturbations on the data points will not change the output of the network [23]. UDA [35] and ReMixMatch [3] generate targets from weakly augmented images, and then enforce consistency against strongly augmented images. In recent years, pseudo-labeling combined with strong augmentations becomes a powerful method for SSL [43]. For the pseudo-labeling methods, the network predicts pseudo labels of unlabeled samples, then trains itself with these labels. FixMatch [30] leverages a confidence-based strategy to obtain reliable pseudo labels. Considering the different learning status and difficulties of each class, FlexMatch [46] proposes a curriculum learning approach to address this issue. For VER, these SSL algorithms suffer from the low accuracy of generated pseudo labels and the lack of high-confidence unlabeled data. In this paper, we leverage the label smoothing method to improve the accuracy of pseudo labels, and adaptively adjust this threshold based on the ambiguity.

3   Methodology

3.1 Overview

Our proposed S^2-VER is illustrated in Fig. 2. Given a batch of labeled samples $\mathcal{X} = \{(x_b, q_b)\}_{b=1}^{B}$, where B is the batch size, $x_b \in \mathbb{R}^{H \times W \times 3}$ denotes a sample in the batch, $q_b \in \mathbb{R}^{1 \times 1 \times C} \in$ is one-hot label, which contains C emotions. We optimize supervised loss on the labeled samples $\mathcal{X}$ as:

$$\mathcal{L}_x = \frac{1}{B} \sum_{b=1}^{B} H\left(q_b, p(y|x_b^w)\right), \tag{1}$$

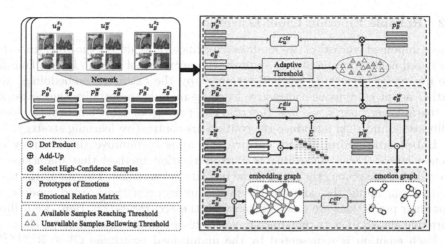

Fig. 2. Illustration of our proposed method. u_B^w, $u_B^{s_1}$, $u_B^{s_2}$ represent the weakly augmented instances and two strongly augmented instances of a batch of unlabeled samples. The three modules on the right are ambiguity-aware adaptive threshold, label smoothing based calibration, and continuous contrastive learning, respectively. For each instance, the network outputs its prediction p and low-dimensional embedding z, and e_B^w denotes the generated smoothing labels.

where p denotes the conditional probability of the sample, H is the cross-entropy between q_b and p, x_b^w means the weakly augmented instance of x_b. Let $\mathcal{U} = \{u_b\}_{b=1}^{\mu B}$, where $\mathcal{U}$ denotes a batch of unlabeled samples, μB means that the batch size of $\mathcal{U}$ is μ times of X. For each $u_b \in \mathbb{R}^{H \times W \times 3}$, we perform a weak augmentation Aug_w and two random strong augmentations Aug_s on it, obtaining the transformed instances u_b^w, $u_b^{s_1}$, $u_b^{s_2}$. The network outputs the prediction p_b and normalized embedding $z_b \in \mathbb{R}^{1 \times 1 \times D}$ of each instance, where D denotes the dimension of the embedding. Then, the unlabeled samples are optimized with losses $\mathcal{L}_u^{cls}$, $\mathcal{L}_u^{dis}$, and $\mathcal{L}_u^{ctr}$. The single label classification loss $\mathcal{L}_u^{cls}$ is defined the same as previous works [18,30,46]:

$$\mathcal{L}_u^{cls} = \frac{1}{\mu B} \sum_{b=1}^{\mu B} \mathbb{1}(q_b^w \geq \tau) H(q_b^w, p(y|u_b^{s_1})), \tag{2}$$

where $q_b^w = argmax(p_b^w)$ denotes the pseudo label from weakly augmented instance. The τ means the threshold to select high-confidence prediction. The $\mathcal{L}_u^{dis}$ and $\mathcal{L}_u^{ctr}$ are elaborated in Sect. 3.2. Let λ^{cls}, λ^{dis}, λ^{ctr} denote the weight of the three losses for unlabeled data respectively, the overall loss function can be defined as:

$$\mathcal{L} = \mathcal{L}_x + \lambda^{cls} \mathcal{L}_u^{cls} + \lambda^{dis} \mathcal{L}_u^{dis} + \lambda^{ctr} \mathcal{L}_u^{ctr}. \tag{3}$$

3.2   Reliable Emotion Label Learning

This component consists of two modules. Specifically, we design the label smoothing based calibration module to improve the accuracy of pseudo labels. Due to the quality of smoothing labels determined by the extracted embeddings, we further adopt continuous contrastive learning module to optimize the network. In the following parts, we first describe the process of label smoothing based calibration, and then introduce the continuous contrastive learning strategy.

Label smoothing based calibration aims to improve the accuracy of pseudo labels. Label smoothing is a regularization method that maintains a reasonable ratio among the logits of the incorrect classes [26]. This regularization method can implicitly calibrate the over-confidence of the learned models so that their predictions are more aligned with the accuracies [22]. Here, we utilize learnable embeddings to dynamically generate emotional smoothing labels.

Each emotion is represented by the maintained prototype $\mathcal{O}^i \in \mathbb{R}^{1 \times 1 \times D}$, $\mathcal{O} = \{\mathcal{O}^1, \mathcal{O}^2, ... \mathcal{O}^C\}$. The prototypes $\mathcal{O}$ are updated by the momentum moving average of embeddings from $\mathcal{X}$, with $\lambda = 0.9$. To be specific, the prototypes are initialized as zero-vectors, and during the training stage, the $\mathcal{O}^i$ of the i-th class is calculated as:

$$\mathcal{O}^i = \frac{\sum\limits_{b=1}^{B} z_b^w \cdot \mathbb{1}(y_b = i)}{\sum\limits_{b=1}^{B} \mathbb{1}(y_b = i)}, \tag{4}$$

where y_b is the label of the b-th labeled sample. Then, we generate initial smoothing label $\hat{d}_b^w$ by calculating the similarity between the prototypes $\mathcal{O}$ and the embedding z_b^w extracted from u_b^w. The probability of i-th class in distribution $\hat{d}_b^w$ is calculated as:

$$\hat{d}_{bi}^w = \frac{exp(z_b^w \cdot \mathcal{O}^i / t)}{\sum\limits_{i=1}^{C} exp(z_b^w \cdot \mathcal{O}^i / t)}, \tag{5}$$

where the t is a scalar which denotes the temperature. Here we use softmax to ensure $\sum\limits_{i=1}^{C} \hat{d}_{bi}^w = 1$. In addition, since the distances between emotions are different [51], we maintain an emotional relation matrix $E \in \mathbb{R}^{C \times C}$. For instance, the distance between amusement and contentment is relatively smaller than the distance between amusement and awe. In detail, the emotional relation matrix E is initialized with $\frac{1}{C}$, and updated by the distance of prototypes $\mathcal{O}$. Here we exploit L_2 distance as the metric, and the value of the i-th row and j-th column is formally defined as:

$$E^{ij} = \frac{exp(-\|(\mathcal{O}^i - \mathcal{O}^j)\|_2^2)}{\sum\limits_{k=1}^{C} exp(-\|(\mathcal{O}^i - \mathcal{O}^k)\|_2^2)}, \qquad (6)$$

The emotional relation matrix E is also updated on the moving average with the same λ. Next, the emotional distribution is adjusted by the relation matrix as $d_b^w = \hat{d}_b^w \cdot E$. In order to control the degree of smoothing, we leverage θ as the weight, and combine the model's prediction and the generated distribution as the smoothing label e_b^w. It can be formally defined as $e_b^w = (1 - \theta)p_b^w + \theta d_b^w$. Finally, the smoothing label is leveraged to calculate the Kullback-Leibler (KL) loss between two distributions e_b^w and p:

$$\mathcal{L}_u^{dis} = -\frac{1}{\mu B} \sum_{b=1}^{\mu B} \mathbb{1}(q_b^w \geq \tau) KL(e_b^w, p(y|u_b^{s_2})). \qquad (7)$$

Continuous contrastive learning aims to learn emotionally discriminative embeddings, which could improve the quality of emotional smoothing labels. Recently, many SSL algorithms exploit contrastive learning to learn better representations [2,53]. Among them, CoMatch [18] designs a graph-based contrastive algorithm, which has been proved effective for SSL. However, unlike other classification tasks, emotions are closely related to each other [37], and the distances between emotions are different. Therefore, it is suboptimal to simply identify whether the images are from the same class. Inspired by this, we introduce continuous contrastive to regularize the emotional embeddings.

Given a batch of unlabeled data U, we utilize the smoothing labels e^w to construct emotion graph $W^e \in \mathbb{R}^{B \times B}$, and utilize the embeddings z^w to construct embedding graph $W^z \in \mathbb{R}^{B \times B}$. Specifically, we use the samples as the vertex, and adopt the cosine similarity to represent the weight of the edge. In this way, the W^e and W^z can be easily obtained in each batch. Then, we adjust the emotion graph based on two priors: (i) Samples should have the same emotion with themselves, thus we set the value of the diagonal element to 1. (ii) We observe that there are many pairs with small similarities in a batch, lots of such weak associations will impact the performance, so we set the values which below T to 0. This process can be defined as:

$$W_{ij}^e = \begin{cases} 1, & i = j, \\ e_i^w \cdot e_j^w, & i \neq j, e_i^w \cdot e_j^w > T, \\ 0, & otherwise. \end{cases} \qquad (8)$$

We empirically set the T to 0.3. Note that emotion datasets usually contain few classes, such as 6 or 8. Therefore, the T with 0.3 encourages models to learn rich emotion relations. Next, both the emotion graph and embedding graph are normalized by softmax. Finally, the contrastive loss between W^e and W^z is calculated by KL loss:

$$\mathcal{L}_u^{ctr} = KL(W^e, W^z). \qquad (9)$$

3.3   Ambiguity-Aware Adaptive Threshold

Most SSL algorithms leverage the pseudo-labels exceeding the fixed threshold [18,30]. However, due to the ambiguity, an affective image may contain not only one emotion [37,41,42]. Although some unlabeled samples already have correct pseudo labels, the probability of dominant emotion of the images would be limited by other existing emotions, making it difficult to reach the threshold. Throughout the training process, the ambiguity of emotion will result in the lack of available unlabeled data. To make better use of these data, we propose a strategy to adaptively adjust the threshold. We adopt β as the lower bound of the threshold, ω controls the extent of the adjustment, the strategy can be formally defined as:

$$\tau = \beta + (1 - \beta)\omega. \tag{10}$$

Specifically, we use information entropy $\mathcal{A} = \sum_{i=1}^{C} -e_{b_i}^w \cdot lne_{b_i}^w$ to measure the ambiguity of the smoothing label. A large $\mathcal{A}$ means a low threshold is needed. However, it is difficult to distinguish whether the prediction with large $\mathcal{A}$ is caused by the ambiguity of the emotion or the poor performance of the model. As an extreme example, the $\mathcal{A}$ of distribution $[0.25, 0.25, 0.25, 0.25]$ is large, but it is more like a random prediction caused by insufficient training. Thanks to the polarity that emotions can be divided into positive and negative, we can select the ambiguous predictions in accord with the rule of emotion. Based on [41], the emotional ambiguity often exists between emotions from the same polarity. To be specific, we add the probabilities having the same polarity with the dominant emotion, which can be seen as the reliability of $\mathcal{A}$. Therefore, we can adaptively calculate the extend ω of the i-th sample as:

$$\omega = \frac{1}{(\mathcal{A} + a) \cdot \sum_{j=1}^{C} \mathbb{1}(P(j) == P(argmax_j(e_{b_i}^w))e_{b_i^j}^w}. \tag{11}$$

The constant a aims to leverage more unlabeled data, here we set a as 1 empirically. $P(j)$ means the polarity of the j-th emotion. In practice, such an algorithm is simple and effective.

4   Experiments

4.1   Datasets

We evaluate our proposed S²-VER on seven public emotion datasets, including FI [44], SE30K8 [34], FlickrLDL, TwitterLDL [42], Emotion-6 [24], UnBiasedEmo [24], and WEBEmo [24]. The images of FI are collected from Flickr and Instagram by querying Mikel's eight emotions as search keywords. A total of 225 AMT workers assess the emotions of images resulting in 23,308 images receiving at least three agreements. SE30K8 contains 33K images, which are annotated in eight emotions (anger, happiness, surprise, disgust, sadness, fear, neutral, surprise-positive, and surprise-negative). Following [44], we leave 22,866 images that receive more than half of the agreements. FlickrLDL and TwitterLDL consist of 11,150 and 10,045 images respectively, which are annotated by Mikel's emotion too. Due to the lack of manually annotated large-scale datasets, we merge these two datasets. Same as SE30K, we leave 15,816 images with high consistency. In the rest of the paper, we call it LDL dataset.

We also evaluate S^2-VER on two small-scale datasets and one large-scale dataset. Emotion-6 consists of 8,350 images, which initially collected 150K images from Google and labeled by five people. UnBiasedEmo contains 3,045 affective images from a collection of about 60,000 images. Both Emotion-6 and UnBiasedEmo are annotated by Ekman's emotion taxonomy. The WEBEmo is a large-scale web dataset searched by Parrott's hierarchical emotion model [25]. After removing duplicate images, about 268,000 stock samples are reserved.

4.2 Evaluation Settings

We first compare S^2-VER against representative VER and SSL methods on FI, SE30K8, and LDL. We report the results of four VER methods: Yang [41], RCA [40], WSCNet [39], and PDANet [50]. In particular, we make a simple transform to PDANet according to [52], making it suitable for classification. For SSL, we compare with ten representative methods, π-Model [16], Pseudo-Label [17], VAT [21], Mean-Teacher [32], MixMatch [4], ReMixMatch [3], UDA [35], Fix-Match [30], CoMatch [18], and FlexMatch [46]. Furthermore, we conduct experiments on UnBiasedEmo, Emotion-6, and WEBEmo. These experiments aim to validate the effectiveness of S^2-VER on small-scale emotion datasets with the help of large-scale unlabeled web dataset. Specifically, we compare S^2-VER with three most powerful methods FixMatch, FlexMatch, and CoMatch.

4.3 Implementation Details

To ensure fairness, we adopt ResNet-50 [9] as the backbone for all experiments. The images are resized to 256×256 followed by a center 224×224 cropping. The batch size of unlabeled data is 64, which is 4 times that of labeled data. Our network is optimized by stochastic gradient descent. The momentum and weight decay are set to 0.9 and 0.0005 respectively. The total number of epochs is 512, each epoch contains 1024 iterations. Following [30,46], the learning rate is initialized as 0.03 with a cosine learning rate decay schedule [19]. The weak augmentation is adopted as standard crop-and-flip, and the strong augmentation is implemented by the RandAugment [7] the same as [30,46]. For the experiments whose results are shown in Table 1, following [18,46], we randomly sample labeled data in a class-balanced way. Due to the lack of surprise-positive samples in SE30K8, we conduct experiments with 80, 400, and 800 labeled samples respectively. In addition, the neural is considered as a polarity different from positive and negative for ambiguity-aware adaptive threshold strategy. Same as FI, SE30K8 and LDL are randomly split into 80% training, 5% validation, and 15% testing sets. Emotion-6 and UnBiasedEmo are split into 90% training and

Table 1. Accuracy (%) of 5-folds on FI, SE30K8, and LDL datasets. We evaluate S^2-VER against four representative VER methods and ten classic SSL methods. Note that Pseu-Lab, Mean-Tea, and Remix denote Pseudo-Label, Mean-Teacher, and ReMix-Match, respectively. To ensure a fair comparison, we adopt ResNet50 as backbone for all the 15 methods.

Method	FI			SE30K8			LDL		
	80	800	1600	80	400	800	80	800	1600
Yang *et al.* [41]	19.9±0.36	25.4±0.37	30.1±0.33	19.8±0.41	22.7±0.32	26.0±0.55	21.4±0.26	26.5±0.29	32.3±0.41
RCA [40]	18.4±0.33	25.9±0.39	31.4±0.17	18.6±0.29	21.9±0.33	26.5±0.33	23.8±0.48	29.2±0.19	33.2±0.21
WSCNet [39]	20.2±0.37	27.5±0.41	31.2±0.39	18.4±0.25	23.2±0.28	27.4±0.36	22.3±0.46	29.2±0.31	35.2±0.45
PDANet [50]	21.4±0.26	26.6±0.22	33.2±0.31	20.6±0.18	23.4±0.25	27.7±0.45	23.5±0.29	30.5±0.30	33.5±0.33
π-Model [16]	22.9±0.54	28.3±0.36	31.7±0.21	22.1±1.71	23.7±0.69	26.9±0.31	24.3±0.61	31.8±0.59	34.4±0.27
Pseu-Lab [17]	22.9±0.48	31.3±0.43	33.5±0.31	23.4±1.10	25.9±0.50	27.6±0.16	24.2±0.49	32.3±0.44	35.8±0.13
VAT [21]	23.6±0.78	31.5±0.77	35.1±0.37	24.4±0.69	27.2±0.39	28.9±0.25	26.3±0.58	34.5±0.49	38.9±0.36
Mean-Tea [32]	23.8±0.51	29.3±0.48	33.9±0.33	24.3±0.67	26.7±0.53	28.2±0.22	26.6±0.54	33.8±0.42	38.6±0.20
MixMatch [4]	26.3±1.53	35.1±0.74	38.0±0.32	26.6±0.87	28.3±0.62	29.6±0.40	28.1±0.78	34.2±0.52	38.9±0.23
ReMix [3]	29.7±0.68	35.4±0.53	38.3±0.42	26.4±1.10	29.9±0.98	31.9±0.63	29.1±0.67	35.3±0.54	39.2±0.35
UDA [35]	28.5±0.87	37.7±0.56	40.3±0.38	27.3±0.89	29.6±0.64	32.2±0.37	30.7±0.76	40.9±0.58	43.4±0.47
FixMatch [30]	28.2±0.78	37.4±0.51	42.2±0.29	29.7±0.70	32.2±0.57	32.7±0.46	32.4±0.84	39.4±0.45	43.2±0.24
FlexMatch [46]	29.7±0.90	38.2±0.49	42.9±0.17	28.5±1.03	33.2±0.60	33.9±0.26	33.2±0.93	41.3±0.71	46.7±0.42
CoMatch [18]	36.7±0.87	43.5±0.39	47.9±0.26	29.9±0.65	32.5±0.47	35.3±0.26	**38.1**±0.53	42.1±0.31	45.3±0.27
S^2-VER	**39.1**±0.66	**46.9**±0.46	**51.8**±0.21	**30.1**±0.73	**33.3**±0.62	**36.2**±0.49	37.9±0.80	**43.6**±0.47	**47.4**±0.43

10% testing sets. Following previous SSL algorithms, we present the accuracy of the Exponential Moving Average (EMA) model [46].

4.4 Comparison with the State-of-the-Art Methods

We conduct extensive experiments to compare S^2-VER with the state-of-the-art methods on VER datasets. The methods include VER models and SSL algorithms. The VER models are trained using labeled samples. This comparison aims to demonstrate the effectiveness of SSL algorithms with limited labeled data. We also adopt SSL algorithms to improve the performance on small datasets. To be specific, we utilize two annotated small datasets as labeled data, large-scale WEBEmo as unlabeled data.

The comparison results are shown in Table 1. SSL algorithms are divided according to whether they use strong augmented anchors. Overall, the SSL algorithms outperform the emotion recognition models. This suggests that leveraging SSL algorithms and adopting a large amount of unlabeled data is beneficial for emotion recognition. In general, the SSL algorithms enforce the consistency between weakly augmented anchors and strongly augmented instances achieving better performance. In addition, we compare S^2-VER with the competitive approaches. S^2-VER improve about 3% on FI with different settings. On SE30K8 and LDL, S^2-VER also performs favorably against the representative methods.

For emotion analysis, many methods can be used to automatically acquire large-scale web data which has not been annotated by humans [5,24,34]. Therefore, we have an intrinsic assumption that SSL algorithms can be effective on

Table 2. Accuracy (%) on Emotion-6 and UnBiasedEmo. For both datasets, we leverage WEBEmo as unlabeled data. We compare S^2-VER with current-best SSL methods, *i.e.*,FixMatch, FlexMatch, and CoMatch.

Method	Emotion-6			UnBiasedEmo		
	20%	50%	100%	20%	50%	100%
FixMatch [30]	46.6	48.3	49.0	65.6	69.2	71.5
FlexMatch [46]	48.1	50.1	51.2	67.2	71.1	73.4
CoMatch [18]	50.2	51.2	52.4	68.5	70.8	73.8
S^2-VER	**51.7**	**53.5**	**54.0**	**70.8**	**76.7**	**78.7**

small-scale datasets with help of the large-scale web data. Inspired by this, we conduct experiments on Emotion-6, UnBiasedEmo, and WEBEmo. Specifically, we leverage WEBEmo as unlabeled data, training FixMatch, FlexMatch, CoMatch, and S^2-VER on the labeled datasets. In order to verify our assumption, we first train ResNet-50 on two small-scale datasets, the accuracy is 43.6% and 61.3% respectively. We conduct experiments with 20%, 50%, 100% data of WEBEmo, the results of SSL algorithms are reported in Table 2. As we can see, these models perform much better than the model trained only with small-scale datasets. Even though there exists bias between datasets, SSL algorithms can still improve the performance with the help of unlabeled data. Moreover, our method achieves competitive performance compared with the representative SSL algorithms.

4.5 Ablation Study

In order to prob the effectiveness of different components in S^2-VER, we display ablation results here. Note that all the experiments are conducted on FI with 1,600 labeled samples. First, we show the effect of each component in Table 3, and draw the following conclusions: 1) Since the quality of smoothing labels particularly depends on the embeddings, combining both $\mathcal{L}_u^{dis}$ and $\mathcal{L}_u^{ctr}$ surpasses only using $\mathcal{L}^{dis}$ a large margin. 2) Although leveraging $\mathcal{L}_u^{dis}$ and $\mathcal{L}_u^{ctr}$ achieves high accuracy, the performance can be further improved by optimizing $\mathcal{L}_u^{cls}$ simultaneously. 3) The model achieves the best test accuracy by utilizing all the components, which shows the complementarity of our proposed S^2-VER.

Furthermore, we conduct detailed experiments to illustrate the contribution of the proposed reliable emotion label learning and adaptive threshold strategy, respectively. We compare the M_{acc} for FixMatch, FlexMatch, CoMatch, the base model with standard label smoothing [31], and proposed label smoothing for emotion. The base model with $\mathcal{L}_u^{cls}$ downgrads to FixMatch. Since the warmup training strategy used in FlexMatch brings a large number of unreliable samples [46], we also report the results of FlexMatch without warmup. As can be seen in Table 4, label smoothing can significantly improve the M_{acc}, and our proposed label smoothing performs better for VER.

Table 3. Ablation study to prob the $\mathcal{L}_u^{cls}$, $\mathcal{L}_u^{dis}$, $\mathcal{L}_u^{ctr}$, and AT used in our S^2-VER. The $\mathcal{L}_u^{smo}$ here denotes the combination of $\mathcal{L}_u^{dis}$ and $\mathcal{L}_u^{ctr}$. Note that ✓ denotes only $\mathcal{L}_u^{dis}$ is used, ✓* denotes both $\mathcal{L}_u^{dis}$ and $\mathcal{L}_u^{ctr}$ are leveraged. AT denotes the adaptive threshold strategy.

$\mathcal{L}_u^{cls}$	$\mathcal{L}_u^{smo}$	AT	Acc
✓			42.3
	✓		41.5
	✓*		49.4
✓	✓*		50.3
✓		✓	45.1
	✓*	✓	50.7
✓	✓*	✓	**51.8**

Table 4. Evaluating the effect of the smoothing label. M_{acc} means the accuracy of pseudo labels reaching threshold. W denotes training FlexMatch with warmup strategy. S and L represent the standard label smoothing strategy [31] and our proposed label smoothing for VER, respectively. We report the M_{acc} every 150 epoch and their average.

M_{acc}	150	300	450	Avg
FixMatch	44.9	59.7	61.8	55.5
FlexMatch	36.6	44.2	47.4	42.7
FlexMatch(W)	31.4	37.4	40.6	36.5
CoMatch	48.1	67.4	66.9	60.8
Base + S	**59.8**	70.7	67.8	66.1
Base + L	58.9	**72.3**	**69.3**	**66.8**

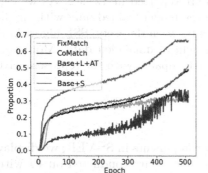

Fig. 3. Evaluating the effect of the proposed AT in detail. We show the proportion of high-confidence unlabeled samples during training.

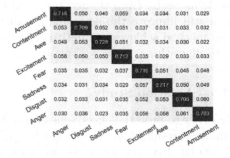

Fig. 4. The final emotional relation matrix in our model. We can find the relation between emotions from the same polarity is closer.

To evaluate the effect of the proposed adaptive threshold, we show the proportion of high-confidence unlabeled samples reaching the threshold. As shown in Fig. 3, our method using the adaptive threshold can utilize more unlabeled samples compared with other methods. Besides, we also provide the learned final emotional relation matrix in Fig. 4. The matrix is not completely symmetric. This is because we perform softmax in rows when updating the matrix at each iteration. As we can see, the values on the diagonal are large, and the emotions from the same polarity have relatively closer relations.

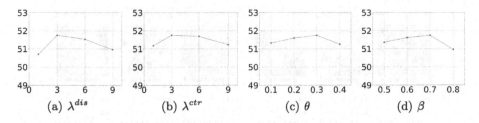

Fig. 5. Variation of accuracy with different hyperparameters. The accuracy of best settings achieves 51.8%. (a) shows the effect of λ^{dis}. (b) shows the effect of λ^{ctr}. (c) shows the effect of θ. (d) shows the effect of β.

4.6 Hyperparameter Analysis

In this section, we present experimental results to demonstrate the effect of hyperparameters. All the experiments are conducted on the FI with 1600 labeled samples. First, we explore the effect of λ^{dis} and λ^{ctr}, which denote the weights of $\mathcal{L}_u^{dis}$ and $\mathcal{L}_u^{ctr}$. With the increasing of λ^{dis}, S²-VER will first perform better. The small λ^{dis} limits the importance of the smoothing label based calibration, so the performance drops significantly. The algorithm achieves the best performance when $\lambda^{dis} = 3$. As for $\mathcal{L}_u^{ctr}$, we find S²-VER achieves highest accuracy when $\lambda^{ctr} = 3$ as well. Since the $\mathcal{L}_u^{ctr}$ is adopted to obtain more discriminative embeddings for $\mathcal{L}_u^{dis}$, it may be better to keep the λ^{ctr} consistent with the λ^{dis}.

We also present the results of θ, which denotes the weight of generated emotional smoothing label e_b^w. The larger θ would make the label more smoothing. As shown in Fig. 5(c), with the increasing of θ, the accuracy becomes higher, which demonstrates the effectiveness of smoothing label. However, the proportion of available unlabeled samples is decreasing. Our method achieves the best performance when $\theta = 0.3$. At this time, the trade off between the quality of pseudo labels and the amount of leveraged unlabeled data reaches the best balance. The results with different β are shown in Fig. 5(d). β controls the range of τ, which influences the trade off between pseudo labels and utilized unlabeled data as well. In particularly, we find that only about 55% of the samples can reach the threshold when $\beta = 0.8$, which leads to a relatively large drop in performance.

4.7 Visualization

We further present some visualization of predictions on FI. As shown in Fig. 6 (a), we show some examples that both our method and CoMatch perform well. We can find that emotions with the same polarity may have a relatively high probability, such as amusement and contentment. In (b), we show some examples that our method outperforms CoMatch. Take the middle image as an example, focusing on the emotion of the person, the model predicts it as anger. However, we can easily find the image shows an exciting competition. Training with smoothing labels can effectively alleviate over-confidence problems like

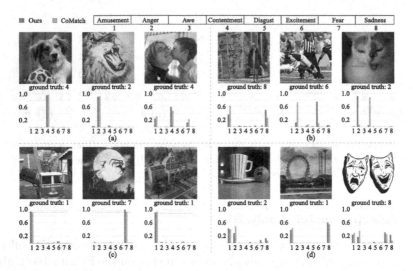

Fig. 6. Visualization of S^2-VER and CoMatch. (a) shows examples that both S^2-VER and CoMatch perform well. (b) shows examples that S^2-VER has correct predictions, while CoMatch has incorrect predictions. (c) shows examples that the predictions of S^2-VER reach the adaptive threshold, while CoMatch is below the fixed threshold. The blue and yellow line represent the threshold for S^2-VER and CoMatch, respectively. (d) shows some failure cases of our method. (Color figure online)

these examples. In (c), we present some examples showing thresholds, which are adopted to select high-confidence pseudo labels. With the ambiguity-aware adaptive threshold strategy, our method can exploit more reliable unlabeled samples. In addition, we also present some failure cases in (d). Looking at the left image, focusing on the delicate cup may bring positive emotions, but the red toy additionally shows negative emotions. Due to the complexity of emotions, cases like (d) are inevitable. Therefore, we think that it is necessary to combine more psychological knowledge to alleviate this problem in the future.

5   Conclusion

In this paper, we propose S^2-VER, which is the first work exploring visual emotion in semi-supervised setting. We design a label smoothing method in the light of the characteristic of the emotion, improving the accuracy of high-confidence pseudo labels. Then, we propose an adaptive threshold strategy. With the help of polarity, this strategy is able to leverage more unlabeled samples effectively. Extensive experiments and comparisons indicate that S^2-VER has advantages compared with the state-of-the-art methods for VER.

Acknowledgments. This work was supported by the National Key Research and Development Program of China Grant (NO. 2018AAA0100403), NSFC (NO. 61876094, U1933114), Natural Science Foundation of Tianjin, China (NO. 20JCJQJC00020).

References

1. Achlioptas, P., Ovsjanikov, M., Haydarov, K., Elhoseiny, M., Guibas, L.J.: Artemis: affective language for visual art. In: CVPR (2021)
2. Alonso, I., Sabater, A., Ferstl, D., Montesano, L., Murillo, A.C.: Semi-supervised semantic segmentation with pixel-level contrastive learning from a class-wise memory bank. In: ICCV (2021)
3. Berthelot, D., et al.: Remixmatch: semi-supervised learning with distribution alignment and augmentation anchoring. In: ICLR (2020)
4. Berthelot, D., Carlini, N., Goodfellow, I., Papernot, N., Oliver, A., Raffel, C.: Mixmatch: a holistic approach to semi-supervised learning. In: NeurIPS (2019)
5. Borth, D., Ji, R., Chen, T., Breuel, T., Chang, S.F.: Large-scale visual sentiment ontology and detectors using adjective noun pairs. In: ACM MM (2013)
6. Chen, T., et al.: "factual" or "emotional": Stylized image captioning with adaptive learning and attention. In: ECCV (2018)
7. Cubuk, E.D., Zoph, B., Shlens, J., Le, Q.V.: Randaugment: practical automated data augmentation with a reduced search space. In: CVPRW (2020)
8. Fan, S., et al.: Emotional attention: a study of image sentiment and visual attention. In: CVPR (2018)
9. He, K., Zhang, X., Ren, S., Sun, J.: Deep residual learning for image recognition. In: CVPR (2016)
10. Joachims, T.: Transductive learning via spectral graph partitioning. In: ICML (2003)
11. Joachims, T., et al.: Transductive inference for text classification using support vector machines. In: ICML (1999)
12. Kingma, D.P., Mohamed, S., Rezende, D.J., Welling, M.: Semi-supervised learning with deep generative models. In: NIPS (2014)
13. Kosti, R., Alvarez, J.M., Recasens, A., Lapedriza, A.: Emotion recognition in context. In: CVPR (2017)
14. Kosti, R., Alvarez, J.M., Recasens, A., Lapedriza, A.: Context based emotion recognition using EMOTIC dataset. IEEE Trans. Pattern Anal. Mach. Intell. 42(11), 2755–2766 (2019)
15. Krizhevsky, A., Hinton, G.: Learning multiple layers of features from tiny images. Mater's thesis, University of Toronto (2009)
16. Laine, S., Aila, T.: Temporal ensembling for semi-supervised learning. In: ICLR (2017)
17. Lee, D.H.: Pseudo-label: the simple and efficient semi-supervised learning method for deep neural networks. In: ICMLW (2013)
18. Li, J., Xiong, C., Hoi, S.C.: Comatch: semi-supervised learning with contrastive graph regularization. In: ICCV (2021)
19. Loshchilov, I., Hutter, F.: SGDR: stochastic gradient descent with warm restarts. In: ICLR (2016)
20. Machajdik, J., Hanbury, A.: Affective image classification using features inspired by psychology and art theory. In: ACM MM (2010)
21. Miyato, T., Maeda, S.I., Koyama, M., Ishii, S.: Virtual adversarial training: a regularization method for supervised and semi-supervised learning. IEEE Trans. Pattern Anal. Mach. Intell. 41(8), 1979–1993 (2018)
22. Müller, R., Kornblith, S., Hinton, G.E.: When does label smoothing help? In: NeurIPS (2019)

23. Oliver, A., Odena, A., Raffel, C., Cubuk, E.D., Goodfellow, I.J.: Realistic evaluation of deep semi-supervised learning algorithms. In: NeurIPS (2018)
24. Panda, R., Zhang, J., Li, H., Lee, J.Y., Lu, X., Roy-Chowdhury, A.K.: Contemplating visual emotions: Understanding and overcoming dataset bias. In: ECCV (2018)
25. Parrott, W.G.: Emotions in Social Psychology: Essential Readings. Psychology Press, London (2001)
26. Pereyra, G., Tucker, G., Chorowski, J., Kaiser, Ł., Hinton, G.: Regularizing neural networks by penalizing confident output distributions. In: ICLRW (2017)
27. Qian, S., Zhang, T., Xu, C.: Multi-modal multi-view topic-opinion mining for social event analysis. In: ACM MM (2016)
28. Rao, T., Li, X., Zhang, H., Xu, M.: Multi-level region-based convolutional neural network for image emotion classification. Neurocomputing **333**, 429–439 (2019)
29. Rasmus, A., Berglund, M., Honkala, M., Valpola, H., Raiko, T.: Semi-supervised learning with ladder networks. In: NIPS (2015)
30. Sohn, K., et al.: Fixmatch: simplifying semi-supervised learning with consistency and confidence. In: NeurIPS (2020)
31. Szegedy, C., Vanhoucke, V., Ioffe, S., Shlens, J., Wojna, Z.: Rethinking the inception architecture for computer vision. In: CVPR (2016)
32. Tarvainen, A., Valpola, H.: Mean teachers are better role models: Weight-averaged consistency targets improve semi-supervised deep learning results. In: NIPS (2017)
33. Verma, V., Lamb, A., Kannala, J., Bengio, Y., Lopez-Paz, D.: Interpolation consistency training for semi-supervised learning. In: IJCAI (2019)
34. Wei, Z., et al.: Learning visual emotion representations from web data. In: CVPR (2020)
35. Xie, Q., Dai, Z., Hovy, E., Luong, M.T., Le, Q.V.: Unsupervised data augmentation for consistency training. In: NeurIPS (2019)
36. Yang, J., Gao, X., Li, L., Wang, X., Ding, J.: Solver: scene-object interrelated visual emotion reasoning network. IEEE Trans. Image Process. **30**, 8686–8701 (2021)
37. Yang, J., Li, J., Li, L., Wang, X., Gao, X.: A circular-structured representation for visual emotion distribution learning. In: CVPR (2021)
38. Yang, J., Li, J., Wang, X., Ding, Y., Gao, X.: Stimuli-aware visual emotion analysis. IEEE Trans. Image Process. **30**, 7432–7445 (2021)
39. Yang, J., She, D., Lai, Y.K., Rosin, P.L., Yang, M.H.: Weakly supervised coupled networks for visual sentiment analysis. In: CVPR, pp. 7584–7592 (2018)
40. Yang, J., She, D., Lai, Y.K., Yang, M.H.: Retrieving and classifying affective images via deep metric learning. In: AAAI (2018)
41. Yang, J., She, D., Sun, M.: Joint image emotion classification and distribution learning via deep convolutional neural network. In: IJCAI (2017)
42. Yang, J., Sun, M., Sun, X.: Learning visual sentiment distributions via augmented conditional probability neural network. In: AAAI (2017)
43. Yang, X., Song, Z., King, I., Xu, Z.: A survey on deep semi-supervised learning. arXiv preprint arXiv:2103.00550 (2021)
44. You, Q., Luo, J., Jin, H., Yang, J.: Building a large scale dataset for image emotion recognition: The fine print and the benchmark. In: AAAI (2016)
45. Zhan, C., She, D., Zhao, S., Cheng, M.M., Yang, J.: Zero-shot emotion recognition via affective structural embedding. In: ICCV (2019)
46. Zhang, B., et al.: Flexmatch: boosting semi-supervised learning with curriculum pseudo labeling. In: NIPS (2021)
47. Zhang, H., Xu, M.: Weakly supervised emotion intensity prediction for recognition of emotions in images. IEEE Trans. Multimedia **23**, 2033–2044 (2020)

48. Zhao, S., Gao, Y., Jiang, X., Yao, H., Chua, T.S., Sun, X.: Exploring principles-of-art features for image emotion recognition. In: ACM MM (2014)
49. Zhao, S., Jia, G., Yang, J., Ding, G., Keutzer, K.: Emotion recognition from multiple modalities: fundamentals and methodologies. IEEE Signal Process. Mag. **38**(6), 59–73 (2021)
50. Zhao, S., Jia, Z., Chen, H., Li, L., Ding, G., Keutzer, K.: PDANet: polarity-consistent deep attention network for fine-grained visual emotion regression. In: ACM MM (2019)
51. Zhao, S., et al.: Predicting personalized emotion perceptions of social images. In: ACM MM (2016)
52. Zhao, S., et al.: Affective image content analysis: two decades review and new perspectives. IEEE Trans. Pattern Anal. Mach. Intell. **44**(10), 6729–6751 (2021)
53. Zhong, Y., Yuan, B., Wu, H., Yuan, Z., Peng, J., Wang, Y.X.: Pixel contrastive-consistent semi-supervised semantic segmentation. In: ICCV (2021)
54. Zhou, D., Bousquet, O., Lal, T.N., Weston, J., Schölkopf, B.: Learning with local and global consistency. In: NIPS (2004)
55. Zhu, X., Ghahramani, Z., Lafferty, J.D.: Semi-supervised learning using gaussian fields and harmonic functions. In: ICML (2003)

Image Coding for Machines
with Omnipotent Feature Learning

Ruoyu Feng[1], Xin Jin[2], Zongyu Guo[1], Runsen Feng[1], Yixin Gao[1], Tianyu He[3], Zhizheng Zhang[3], Simeng Sun[1], and Zhibo Chen[1(✉)]

[1] University of Science and Technology of China, Hefei, China
ustcfry@mail.ustc.edu.cn, chenzhibo@ustc.edu.cn
[2] Eastern Institute of Advanced Study, Hefei, China
jinxin@eias.ac.cn
[3] Microsoft Research Asia, Beijing, China

Abstract. Image Coding for Machines (ICM) aims to compress images for AI tasks analysis rather than meeting human perception. Learning a kind of feature that is both general (for AI tasks) and compact (for compression) is pivotal for its success. In this paper, we attempt to develop an ICM framework by learning universal features while also considering compression. We name such features as omnipotent features and the corresponding framework as Omni-ICM. Considering self-supervised learning (SSL) improves feature generalization, we integrate it with the compression task into the Omni-ICM framework to learn omnipotent features. However, it is non-trivial to coordinate semantics modeling in SSL and redundancy removing in compression, so we design a novel information filtering (IF) module between them by co-optimization of instance distinguishment and entropy minimization to adaptively drop information that is weakly related to AI tasks (*e.g.*, some texture redundancy). Different from previous task-specific solutions, Omni-ICM could directly support AI tasks analysis based on the learned omnipotent features without joint training or extra transformation. Albeit simple and intuitive, Omni-ICM significantly outperforms existing traditional and learned-based codecs on multiple fundamental vision tasks.

Keywords: Image coding for machines · Self-supervised learning · Information filtering

1 Introduction

In the big data era, massive images and videos have become an indispensable part of people's production and life. As an important industrial technology, lossy

---

R. Feng and X. Jin—Contributed equally.

Supplementary Information The online version contains supplementary material available at https://doi.org/10.1007/978-3-031-19836-6_29.

image compression aims to save storage resources and transmission bandwidth by preserving the most critical information. In the past decades, the traditional image and video coding standards such as JPEG [67], JPEG2000 [58], AVC/H.264 [68], HEVC/H.265 [64], VVC/H.266 [6] have significantly improved the coding efficiency. Recently, with the fast development of deep neural networks, learned-based image compression codecs [3,4,14,20,38,42,43,50–52,69] have achieved a great success. They have potentials to become the next-generation image compression standards due to the high performance and applicability compared to traditional hand-craft codecs. Meanwhile, deep neural networks has demonstrated their potential in various computer vision tasks, $e.g.$, object detection [45,59–61], instance segmentation [5,32,47], semantic segmentation [1,9,10,48], pose estimation [32,54]. We can anticipate that more and more data transmitting on the Internet would be consumed by machines for intelligent analysis tasks.

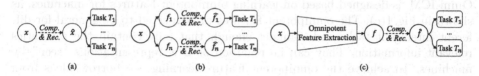

(a)   (b)   (c)

Fig. 1. Comparison of three branches for image coding for machines (ICM). They are different from each other w.r.t the object to be compressed and the characteristics of task-specific or not. (a): Codecs in this branch support downstream tasks by inputting the decompressed images. (b): One-to-one features-based ICM solution, the decompressed features of corresponding tasks are input to the task models. (c): With the proposed **omnipotent feature** f extracted and compressed first, all the downstream tasks could complete the inference based on the decompressed feature $\hat{f}$.

However, all the image compression methods mentioned above aim at saving transmitting costs while improving the reconstruction quality for human perception. When facing AI tasks analysis, existing image coding methods (even for the deep learned-based) are still questionable, regarding whether it can encode images efficiently, especially in application scenarios for big data. To facilitate the performance and efficiency in terms of high-level machine vision tasks that act on lossy compressed images, lots of research efforts have been dedicated to a new problem of image coding for machines (ICM) [26,41], which aims to compress the source image for supporting the intelligent analysis tasks. The discrepancy between human-perception oriented metric ($e.g.$, mean square error (MSE), multi-scale structured similarity (MS-SSIM)) and AI task metric ($e.g.$, classification accuracy) makes ICM particularly different from the existing compression schemes.

For ICM, there mainly exist solutions of two branches. Figure 1(a) shows the first branch that the compressed image is sent into the downstream task model for intelligent analytics. Codecs in this branch are typically designed based on a heuristic RoI (Region of Interest) bit allocation strategy [7,21,36,63] or joint optimization for image reconstruction with a task-specific constraint in an end-to-end manner [41]. This branch has two weaknesses that the image reconstruction brings more computational burden because images have to be reconstructed for subsequent intelligent analysis and there exists a new trade-off between texture fidelity and semantics integrity. The second branch is a one-to-one feature-based ICM framework [2,16,17,62]. As shown in Fig. 1(b), works of this branch tend to compress the features extracted from images for transmission efficiency. Depending on the reconstructed features, the downstream tasks could directly complete the corresponding intelligent analysis. But, such a scheme that one compressed feature can only be used to support one specific AI task lacks generalization and flexibility, thus is difficult to be applied to practical applications.

To solve the problems mentioned above, and motivated by the urgent requirements for a generalized ICM solution, in this paper, we go beyond previous pipelines and introduce a unified framework for ICM by exploring the "common knowledge" of different AI tasks. More precisely, a novel ICM framework, termed Omni-ICM, is designed based on learning omnipotent features for machines, as shown in Fig. 1(c). The omnipotent features are expected to be general for different intelligent tasks and compact enough that only contain the semantics relevant information. They can be regarded as new representations "seen" by machines. To achieve the omnipotent feature learning, we borrow ideas from the popular contrastive learning that has been proved could learn general and transferable visual representations [8,11,13,28,31], and integrate it into the image coding pipeline. However, directly compressing the features learned by contrastive objective has no obvious advantages than compressing the original images directly [15,16,18], that's because these features typically keep lots of irrelevant redundant information with no explicit constraint on information entropy.

To tackle this issue, we further design an Information Filtering (IF) module to smartly discard the redundant information for analytics before compression, so as to encourage learned representations to be sparse and compact. Basically, the IF module comprises an encoder, a decoder, and an entropy estimation model, and is optimized with contrastive loss and entropy minimization constraint. In this way, IF module learns to preserve semantic-wise information and filter out redundant ones, acting as a bridge to connect contrastive training and compression. After that, with a learned-based feature compressor, the learned omnipotent features are compressed and reconstructed in the feature latent space, enabling it to be directly input to downstream task models without pixel-level reconstruction. Moreover, compressing such omnipotent features makes it more applicable to the codec standardization, which could support for a wide range of downstream AI tasks, even for the unknown ones. Such generalization ability and flexibility are the key points of our Omni-ICM framework, which are often neglected by the existing ICM solutions.

Extensive experiments show that Omni-ICM outperforms the state-of-the-art image compression methods by significant margins w.r.t the bitstream saving and task performance, on multiple intelligent tasks, including object detection, instance/semantic/panoptic segmentation, and pose estimation.

2 Related Work

2.1 Image Compression

Traditional Codec. Traditional hand-craft image codecs typically consist of intra prediction, transformation, quantization, and entropy coder. The popular image coding standards have kept evolving, e.g., JPEG [67], JPEG2000 [58], AVC [68], HEVC/H.265 [64], VVC/H.266 [6]. However, these codecs cannot be optimized in an end-to-end manner, thus lack of flexibility and scalability to support different objectives, such as MS-SSIM and classification accuracy.

Learned-Based Codec. The success of deep learning techniques significantly promotes the development of learned-based codecs. Toderici et al. [66] apply a recurrent neural network (RNN) to end-to-end image compression, achieving a comparable performance with JPEG. Ballé et al. [3] further propose an end-to-end framework based on nonlinear transformation, generalized divisive normalization (GDN), noise-relaxed quantization, and their method outperforms JPEG 2000. Then a variational model with hyperprior is introduced to parameterize latent distribution with a Gaussian distribution in [4]. Some recent works have improved image compression from the aspects of entropy coding [20,29,39,52,53] and quantization [30,73]. However, the optimization objectives of these methods are pixel-level metrics that designed for visual fidelity, e.g., MSE, MS-SSIM. The discrepancy between pixel-level distortion and semantic-level distortion leads to the failure of above methods when tackling ICM tasks. But, they provide basic techniques to develop effective ICM solutions to handle this new problem.

Image Coding for Machine. ICM [26,34] aims to compress and transmit the source image for machines to support intelligent tasks. Based on the heuristic prior knowledge of foreground matters more for intelligent analysis, [7,36,44] merge the ROI (Region of Interest) based bit allocation strategy into the traditional codec for intelligent analytics. For learned-based codecs, Le et al. [41] propose an image compression system that jointly optimizes models for object detection and reconstruction. Codevilla et al. [22] also optimize both the intelligent task and the reconstruction task, and the difference is that the optimization of the intelligent task directly takes the latent variable features as input. However, the trade-off between semantic fidelity and pixel fidelity limits their respective performance. Thus, [35,72] introduce scalable coding to coordinate the compression for high-level information and pixel-wise texture. Singh et al. [62] explore to compress features instead of images for intelligent tasks by optimizing the task objective along with rate loss. Nevertheless, such schemes can only support a few tasks and are not general enough. The recent work of SSIC [65] structures the bitstream according to the object category and thus achieves a task-aware compression for downstream analytics. Differently, in this paper, we aim to design a unified framework for ICM by learning a kind of general and compact features and directly support a wide range of intelligent tasks.

514   R. Feng et al.

2.2   Self-supervised Representation Learning (SSL)

Self-supervised learning [37,55,57,74] is proposed to learn general representations for downstream tasks by solving various pretext tasks on large-scale unlabeled datasets. Contrastive learning is one of them and its pretext task is minimizing feature distances from the same group and maximizing feature distances from different groups with contrastive loss. Recently, the siamese network based contrastive learning methods [8,11,13,28,31] have drawn lots of attention. Among them, MOCO [31] is the first work that outperforms the supervised ImageNet pre-training on several downstream tasks, which shows its strong ability for general representations learning. More specifically, MOCO designs a dynamic queue to store negative samples features and uses a momentum update mechanism to optimize the model progressively. Inspired by that, we propose to employ SSL to learn omnipotent features for compression, so that further support heterogeneous intelligent tasks for ICM.

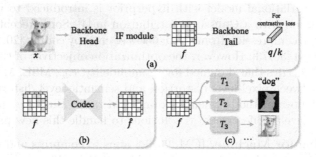

Fig. 2. Three stages in our Omni-ICM framework. (a) Omnipotent feature learning. We optimize the whole network with the contrastive loss and entropy constraint by the IF module. (b) Omnipotent feature compression. A feature compressor is trained for omnipotent feature compression, with all parameters fixed except the codec. (c) Omnipotent feature deployment. Our Omni-ICM can easily support different downstream tasks by fine-tuning the backbone tail with omnipotent features as input.

3   ICM with Omnipotent Feature Learning

3.1   Overview of Omni-ICM Pipeline

We propose a new concept of omnipotent feature learning for image coding for machines, and correspondingly design a unified framework (Omni-ICM) based on it. As shown in Fig. 2, the whole framework of Omni-ICM consists of three stages: (a) omnipotent feature learning, (b) omnipotent feature compression, and (c) omnipotent feature deployment.

For the first stage, we employ a contrastive learning pipeline while also giving consideration to compression efficiency, enabling the learned features to be

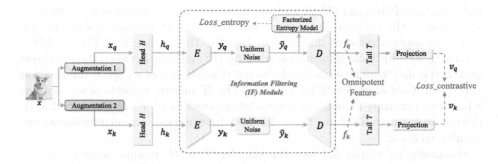

Fig. 3. Architecture of omnipotent feature learning. We use a pair of query and key for simpler illustration. By maximizing the similarity of different views of an image under entropy constraint, the network learns to discard semantic-redundant information and keep critical ones. After training, f is the omnipotent feature we need.

both semantically preserved and compact. More specifically, to coordinate the preserving of the semantics and the discarding of the semantic-irrelevant redundancy, we design an additional Information Filtering (IF) module and optimize the whole network with an instance-contrastive loss under entropy constraint.

After that, the obtained omnipotent features, which are compact and general, are "seen" by machines as an alternative for original images. To compress and transmit the omnipotent features, we additionally train a feature codec. Finally, the downstream tasks supporting are achieved by fine-tuning the backbone tail. Note that, the backbone head and the proposed IF module are fixed in this stage. We describe each stage in detail in the following subsections.

3.2 Stage 1: Omnipotent Feature Learning

Basic Network Architecture. Considering that the learned omnipotent features will be taken for a wide range of AI tasks analytics, *e.g.*, object detection [45], semantic segmentation [75], we extract the omnipotent feature f with a 4× down-sampling factor to promise the integrity of content structure and object spatial layout. Specifically, as shown in Fig. 3, a commonly used backbone (such as ResNet-50) is split into two parts, namely backbone head and backbone tail, dotted as H and T. In a ResNet-50, the backbone head comprises the stem layer and layer1, and the backbone tail comprises layer2~layer4.

Data Augmentation and Feature Extraction in Backbone Head. As illustrated in Fig. 3, at the omnipotent feature learning stage, two views of an image x_q and x_k are first generated by different augmentations. For clarity, we describe the query generation process for x_q at first. x_q is fed into the backbone head H, obtaining an 4× down-sampling feature with a size of $\frac{H_q}{4} \times \frac{W_q}{4} \times C$, where H_q, W_q are the height and width of x_q, C means the channel numbers:

$$h_q = H(x_q). \tag{1}$$

Information Filtering (IF) Module. Importantly, the representation directly generated by the backbone head is not suitable for ICM, because it still contains lots of semantic-irrelevant information (see the third column of Fig. 9). Thus, we design an additional information filtering (IF) module between the backbone head and tail, to simultaneously achieve the preservation of semantic information and the dropout of irrelevant information. The IF module consists of an encoder, a factorized entropy model, and a decoder denoted as E, F, D. To drive the IF module to learn to filter out the redundant information, an entropy constraint is enforced on it.

Formally, h_q is first fed into the encoder E of IF module with $8\times$ downsampling, obtaining a latent variable y_q with the size of $\frac{H_q}{32} \times \frac{W_q}{32} \times C_y$, C_y represents the channel numbers of y_q:

$$y_q = E(h_q). \tag{2}$$

Then, a factorized entropy model F estimates the entropy of y_q through adding an additive uniform noise [3] on it to get the derivative $\tilde{y}_q$, formulated as:

$$p_{\tilde{y}_q|\phi_o}(\tilde{y}_q|\phi_o) = \prod_i (p_{y_q|\phi_o}(\phi_o) * \mathcal{U}(-\frac{1}{2}, \frac{1}{2}))(\tilde{y}_q), \tag{3}$$

where ϕ_o represents the parameters in H and E. And, the entropy loss is:

$$\mathcal{L}_e = \mathbb{E}[-\log_2(p_{\tilde{y}_q|\phi_o}(\tilde{y}_q|\phi_o))]. \tag{4}$$

Finally, $\tilde{y}_q$ is fed into the decoder D of IF module, obtaining the feature f_q with the same size as the input of IF module, *i.e.* $\frac{H_q}{4} \times \frac{W_q}{4} \times C$.

Backbone Tail and Projection Layer. With the feature f_q generated by the IF module, the backbone tail and a projection layer are employed to map the feature to the space where contrastive loss is applied. Specifically, the projection layer is an MLP with one hidden layer. This procedure can be formulated as:

$$q = W^{(2)}\sigma(W^{(1)}(T(D(\tilde{y}_q)))), \tag{5}$$

where σ is a ReLU non-linearity transformation, $W^{(1)}$ and $W^{(2)}$ are fully connected layers, $q \in \mathbb{R}^d$.

Generation of Keys. x_k is obtained by the other augmentation from the same image. The key x_k and the query x_q together construct a positive pair. For simplicity, we use the same notation in Sect. 3.2 here. This procedure can be formulated as:

$$y_k = E(H(x_k)), \tag{6}$$
$$k_+ = W^{(2)}\sigma(W^{(1)}(T(D(\tilde{y}_k)))), \tag{7}$$

where $\tilde{y}_k$ comes from y_k by adding the additive uniform noise, and $k_+ \in \mathbb{R}^d$, denotes the positive sample. The negative samples come from different images, denoted as$\{k_-\}$, are provided by the queue coming from the previous iterations [31]. Following the setting in MOCO [31], the branch of keys is the momentum-updated one of the branch of queries.

Total Optimization Objectives. For the contrastive loss, InfoNCE [56] is employed to pull q close to k_+ while pushing it away from other negative keys:

$$\mathcal{L}_q = -\log \frac{\exp(q{\cdot}k_+/\tau)}{\exp(q{\cdot}k_+/\tau) + \sum_{k_-} \exp(q{\cdot}k_-/\tau)}, \tag{8}$$

where τ denotes a temperature hyper-parameter as in [71]. The overall optimization function is written as:

$$\mathcal{L} = \mathcal{L}_q + \alpha\mathcal{L}_e, \tag{9}$$

where a Lagrange multiplier α is a fixed value that determines the trade-off between entropy and semantic integrity. Note that, the added additive noise is only a transitional component for entropy estimation in the omnipotent feature learning stage, and is discarded in the next two steps, *i.e.* omnipotent feature compression and deployment.

3.3   Stage 2: Learned-Based Feature Compression

Similar to lossy image compression, the goal of lossy feature compression is simultaneously minimizing the size of bitstream and the distortion between f and $\hat{f}$. Such objectives can be formulated as minimizing $R + \lambda D_C$ (here we use D_C to distinguish the D in IF module), where the Lagrange multiplier λ controls the trade-off between the rate R and the distortion D_C in feature level. R denotes the rate of compressed feature and D_C represents the distortion between f and $\hat{f}$. Since quantization is non-differentiable, the additive uniform noise [3] is added to the latent variables during training for approximately rate estimation, which alters quantization to be differentiable. And, after quantization, the entropy coding is performed on latent variables y to encode it into bitstream losslessly. Entropy coding here can be Huffman coding or arithmetic coding. Finally, for the omnipotent feature reconstruction, the decoder tend to reconstruct omnipotent features from $\hat{y}$. The R-D (rate-distortion) loss function can be written as:

$$\mathcal{L}_{rd} = \mathbb{E}[-\log_2(p_{\hat{y}|\psi}(\hat{y}|\psi))] + \lambda \frac{1}{WH} \sum_{x=1}^{W} \sum_{y=1}^{H} (f_{x,y} - \hat{f}_{x,y})^2, \tag{10}$$

where W and H denotes the width and height of features.

Moreover, since the features are compressed to handle downstream tasks better, we further protect its semantic fidelity in a deeper feature level. Particularly, the omnipotent feature f and its reconstructed one $\hat{f}$ are passed through the backbone tail in the omnipotent feature learning stage, *i.e.* layer2~layer4 in a normal ResNet. And then, the Euclidean distance is calculated between those two deeper feature representations of f and $\hat{f}$ to construct this loss:

$$\mathcal{L}_f = \sum_{i=2}^{4} \lambda_i \frac{1}{W_i H_i} \sum_{x=1}^{W_i} \sum_{y=1}^{H_i} (\phi_i f_{x,y} - \phi_i \hat{f}_{x,y})^2, \tag{11}$$

where W_i and H_i are widths and heights of feature maps, ϕ_i means a differentiable function, hyperparameter λ_i controls the importances of distortions in different depths. The overall loss function of feature compression is given by:

$$\mathcal{L}_{com} = \mathcal{L}_{rd} + \mathcal{L}_f. \tag{12}$$

Practically, we design the neural network for omnipotent feature compression, which is derived from the Mean & Scale (M&S) Hyperprior model [52], and discretized Gaussian Mixture Likelihoods (GMM) entropy model [20].

Last but not least, there are two autoencoders in our pipeline, however, with different architectures, implementations, and functions. The first autoencoder in IF module is optimized with both contrastive loss and entropy constraint, without hard quantization operation in practice, acting as an information filter. The other autoencoder is used for feature compression, with hard quantization in practice. Detailed architectures are reported in **Supplementary**.

3.4   Stage 3: Feature Deployment and Task Supporting

After the omnipotent feature learning, the source data for machines has changed from images to omnipotent features. Therefore, the task models are trained with the learned omnipotent features f and are evaluated with the reconstructed omnipotent features $\hat{f}$, to finally support the AI tasks. Formally, only the backbone tail is fine-tuned for downstream tasks supporting, and the weights obtained in the omnipotent feature learning stage are used for a better initialization.

4   Experiments

4.1   Datasets

The training for both omnipotent feature learning and feature compression is conducted on the training set of the ImageNet [25] dataset, which contains ~ 1.28 million images of 1000 classes. After the training of feature extraction and compression, we evaluate the transferability of the learned omnipotent features to downstream tasks on PASCAL VOC [27], MS COCO [46] and Cityscapes [24]. PASCAL VOC and MS COCO are the widely-used datasets for dense prediction tasks, e.g., object detection, instance segmentation. Compared with PASCAL VOC, MS COCO is larger and more challenging (more complicated scenes, more objects per image, and more categories to be predicted). Cityscapes is a fundamental and challenging dataset for semantic segmentation, which contains 5000 high-quality images with the pixel-level annotations (2975, 500, and 1525 for the training, validation, and test sets respectively).

4.2   Implementation Details

Omnipotent Feature Learning. With ResNet-50 [33] as the basic architecture, the IF module takes the output of backbone head as input to obtain the omnipotent feature. In the omnipotent feature learning stage, the momentum update from one encoder to another is set to 0.999 and the dictionary size is set to 65536. Temperature in Eq. (8) is set to 0.2. The data augmentation operations and the use of MLP projection head are same as the previous contrastive learning related works [11–13,28,31]. Besides, we load the weights that pre-training 800 epochs with MOCO-v2 [31] to initialize the backbone head and backbone tail, and then keep all parameters fixed except the IF module for a stable training at the first 10 epochs. After that, all the parameters are optimized together for another 200 epochs. We adopt SGD as the optimizer with weight decay and momentum set as 10^{-4} and 0.9. The batch size is 256 and the learning rate is 10^{-3}. α in Eq. (9) is experimentally set to 0.1.

Omnipotent Feature Compression. We train the omnipotent feature compressor model for 400,000 iterations with batch size of 32. We employ the Adam [49] optimizer, where the learning rate is set to be 5×10^{-5}. Data augmentation is 256×256 random cropping. λ in Eq. (10) is set to 2048, and $\lambda_2, \lambda_3, \lambda_4$ in Eq. (11) are set to 512, 256, 128 respectively. Feature codecs with different rates are obtained by multiplying λ, λ_2, λ_3, and λ_4 by a same coefficient.

4.3   Effectiveness and Superiority of Omni-ICM

Evaluation Protocol. We evaluate the generalization of omnipotent features on different fundamental intelligent tasks by fine-tuning the backbone tail. Challenging and popular datasets are adapted for different tasks, *i.e.* VOC object detection, COCO object detection, COCO instance segmentation, COCO pose estimation, Cityscapes semantic segmentation, and Cityscapes panoptic segmentation. Experiments for Cityscapes semantic segmentation are implemented in [23] and others are implemented in [70]. To evaluate the rate-distortion performance, the rate is measured by the bits per pixel (bpp), which is calculated by dividing the size of the feature bitstream by the number of pixels in the original image, and the distortion here represents metrics of different AI tasks.

Comparison Approaches. We mainly compare our Omni-ICM with the most advanced traditional codecs (HEVC [64], VVC [6]) and a learned-based compression method [20]. To ensure the fairness of comparison, we use the pre-trained model that has trained for 800 epochs on ImageNet [12] as the initial weights and fine-tunes it on each task to get the well-trained networks for comparison, which is consistent with the operations taken by the current SOTA representation learning method, MOCO [31]. Then during evaluation of compared approaches, reconstructed images are input into these networks to obtain the final results. Our method and the compared methods follow the same training schedule for fine-tuning downstream tasks. Besides, in order to better understand the results, we provide results with uncompressed images or features performing intelligent

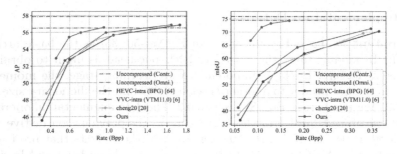

Fig. 4. Object detection mAP on PASCAL VOC (left) and semantic segmentation mIoU on Cityscapes (right) under different bitrates. We compare our method with two traditional codecs HEVC-intra [64], VVC-intra [6], and one learned-based codec [20].

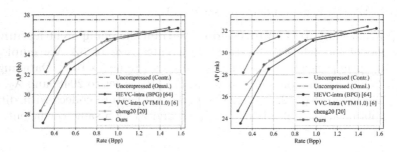

Fig. 5. Object detecion and instance segmentation on MS COCO. The metrics here include mean bounding box AP (AP^{bb}) and mask AP (AP^{mk}).

tasks, which can be seen as baselines. We also report down-stream task performances with supervised pre-training in **Supplementary**.

Object Detection on PASCAL VOC. When evaluating on VOC object detection, we follow the common protocol that fine-tuning a Faster R-CNN detector (C4-backbone) on the VOC `trainval07+12` set and testing on the VOC `test2007` set. The image scale is in [640, 800] pixels during training and is 800 at inference as default. Note that the image resolution has changed before inputting into the task model. For the fairness of comparison, we don't perform any resizing operations on the features, and we regard the original image as the source data to be compressed so that we calculate the rate by dividing the size of the bitstream file of feature by the number of pixels of the original image. Other tasks that need resizing during preprocessing all obey this setting, *i.e.* instance segmentation, pose estimation. Figure 4 (left) shows the results of detection. Our method achieves the best performance (lower rate, higher precision).

Semantic Segmentation on Cityscapes. For semantic segmentation, an FCN-based structure is used. We train task networks on the `train_fine` set

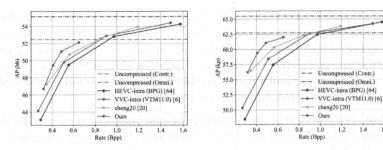

Fig. 6. Pose estimation on MS COCO. Results of person detection (AP^{bb}) and keypoint detection (AP^{kp}) are illustrated.

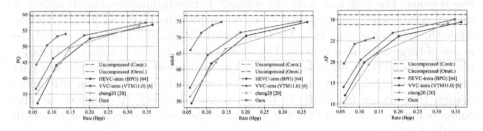

Fig. 7. Panoptic segmentation on Cityscapes. PQ, mIoU, and AP are reported. PQ is the metric of panoptic segmentation which measures the performance for both stuff and things in a uniform manner, mIoU is the metric of semantic segmentation, and AP is the metric of instance segmentation.

which consist of 2975 images for 80k iterations, and evaluate on the `val` set. Results are shown in Fig. 4 (right). Similarly, our method is also the best scheme.

Object Detection and Instance Segmentation on MS COCO. Following the setting in [31], we evaluate object detection and instance segmentation by fine-tuning a Mask R-CNN detector (C4-backbone) on COCO `train2017` split with the standard 1× schedule and evaluating on COCO `val2017` split, with BN tuned and synchronized across GPUs. The image scale is in [640, 800] pixels during training and is 800 at inference as default, same as that for PASCAL VOC. The comparison is shown in Fig. 5. Our method also achieves the best performance, and significantly outperforms the other codecs.

More Downstream Tasks. Figure 6, 7 show results on more downstream tasks:

COCO Pose Estimation: Mask R-CNN (with R50-FPN) is fine-tuned on COCO `train2017` and evaluated on `val2017`. The schedule is 1×. Results are illustrated in Fig. 6. Although Omni-ICM is better than other methods, however, there exists an obvious gap (more than 2 points in both person detection and keypoint detection) between the best performance at high bitrate. This also indicates the superiority of our method at lower bitrates.

Cityscapes Panoptic Segmentation [19,40]: Panoptic-deeplab [19] is used for this task. We train task networks on the `train_fine` set for 90k iterations, and evaluate on the `val` set. Results of PQ, mIoU, and AP are reported for panoptic segmentation in Fig. 7. The performance of mIoU is similar to Fig. 4 (right). We can observe that our method achieves the better R-D performance, which means it can use less bits to achieve higher task performance.

Discussion. For the case of image coding for machines (ICM), Omni-ICM outperforms the most advanced hand-craft traditional codecs and a learned-based codec by remarkable margins on 6 fundamental intelligent tasks. Besides, we also observe some hidden limitations. Results in Fig. 6 and Fig. 7 show the potential performance gaps at the highest bitrate. We speculate that this is caused by two reasons. The first one is the discrepancy between datasets, the ImageNet is mainly composed of images with a single conspicuous target in natural scenes, while the number of targets in MS COCO and Cityscapes is diversified, and the scales of targets are also various. The second reason is that training by instance discrimination [11,31,56] forces the model to focus more on the conspicuous part of the image, which is not conducive to the preservation of local semantic information that occurs frequently in the above two datasets. In addition, we also compare our method with SOTA ICM-related methods and report the results in **supplementary**.

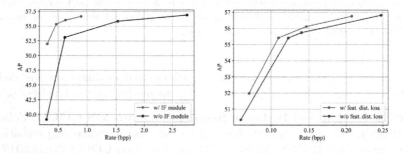

Fig. 8. Ablation studies on **IF module** (left) and **feature level distortion loss** (right), respectively.

4.4   Ablation Study

We implement ablation studies by pre-training on ImageNet and fine-tuning on VOC0712 object detection, as introduced in 4.3.

Study on IF Module. The first graph in Fig. 8 illustrates the result that validate the contribution of IF module. For the case without IF module, the features output by layer1 of the ResNet-50 network pre-trained by contrastive learning are employed for task supporting and compression. Thus, we fix parameters in stem layer and layer1, and then fine-tunes the task model on PASCAL VOC detection. A feature codec with the same architecture and training schedule as that in Sect. 3.3 is trained for feature compression. As we can see, in the absence of IF module, compressing features directly can achieve satisfying performance with low coding efficiency. However, our Omni-ICM can achieve comparable performance with much lower bitrate.

Feature Level Distortion Loss. The second graph in Fig. 8 presents the ablation study about feature-level distortion in Eq. (11). It indicates that the loss of feature level distortion helps protect semantic information.

4.5   Vision Analysis and Insights

Reconstruction Results. To better understand the functionability of the IF module, we additionally train two decoders with MSE loss to visualize the reconstruction results of features before and after IF module, *i.e.* h and f. As shown in Fig. 9, images reconstructed from h contain slight color difference, and textures are relatively complete. But images reconstructed from f suffer obvious color

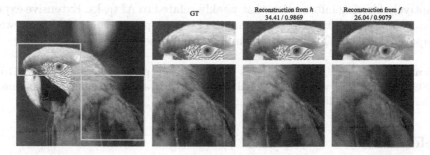

Fig. 9. Reconstruction of features before and after IF module. Numbers on the top of the crop images indicate PSNR (dB)/MS-SSIM of an entire image.

Fig. 10. Bit allocation maps in learned-based codec [20] (second line) and our IF module (third line), respectively. The first line is ground truth.

difference and texture loss. It indicates that IF module drops out some color information and texture information that has a slight influence on intelligent analytics. Details of reconstruction decoders are reported in **Supplementary**.

Bit Allocation Map. As is illustrated in Fig. 10, we also visualize the bit allocation maps in IF module and that in the learned-based codec [20] optimized with MSE loss. Learned-based codec tends to focus on areas with large, irregular, and complex textures, *e.g.*, walls, water surfaces, rocks, and eaves. But our IF module pays less attention to the texture details in the image and more attention to the objects, which is crucial for the understanding of images.

5 Conclusion

We presented a novel framework for image coding for machines (Omni-ICM) based on extracting and compressing a general and compact feature, dubbed omnipotent feature. The omnipotent feature is learned by elegantly combining the contrastive learning and entropy constraint through a new IF module, which coordinates semantics modeling and redundancy removing in our framework by adaptively filtering information that weakly related to AI tasks. Extensive experiments show an outstanding performance of our proposed Omni-ICM framework compared to the SOTA traditional and learned-based approaches.

Acknowledgement. This work was supported in part by NSFC under Grant U1908209, 62021001 and the National Key Research and Development Program of China 2018AAA0101400.

References

1. Badrinarayanan, V., Kendall, A., Cipolla, R.: Segnet: a deep convolutional encoder-decoder architecture for image segmentation. TPAMI **39**(12), 2481–2495 (2017)
2. Bajić, I.V., Lin, W., Tian, Y.: Collaborative intelligence: challenges and opportunities. In: ICASSP 2021–2021 IEEE International Conference on Acoustics, Speech and Signal Processing (ICASSP), pp. 8493–8497. IEEE (2021)
3. Ballé, J., Laparra, V., Simoncelli, E.P.: End-to-end optimized image compression. In: ICLR (2017)
4. Ballé, J., Minnen, D., Singh, S., Hwang, S.J., Johnston, N.: Variational image compression with a scale hyperprior. In: ICLR (2018)
5. Bolya, D., Zhou, C., Xiao, F., Lee, Y.J.: Yolact: real-time instance segmentation. In: ICCV, pp. 9157–9166 (2019)
6. Bross, B., et al.: Overview of the versatile video coding (VVC) standard and its applications. In: TCSVT (2021)
7. Cai, Q., Chen, Z., Wu, D., Liu, S., Li, X.: A novel video coding strategy in HEVC for object detection. In: TCSVT (2021)
8. Caron, M., Misra, I., Mairal, J., Goyal, P., Bojanowski, P., Joulin, A.: Unsupervised learning of visual features by contrasting cluster assignments. arXiv preprint arXiv:2006.09882 (2020)

9. Chen, L.C., Papandreou, G., Kokkinos, I., Murphy, K., Yuille, A.L.: DeepLab: semantic image segmentation with deep convolutional nets, atrous convolution, and fully connected CRFs. TPAMI **40**(4), 834–848 (2017)
10. Chen, L.C., Zhu, Y., Papandreou, G., Schroff, F., Adam, H.: Encoder-decoder with atrous separable convolution for semantic image segmentation. In: ECCV, pp. 801–818 (2018)
11. Chen, T., Kornblith, S., Norouzi, M., Hinton, G.: A simple framework for contrastive learning of visual representations. In: ICML, pp. 1597–1607. PMLR (2020)
12. Chen, X., Fan, H., Girshick, R., He, K.: Improved baselines with momentum contrastive learning. arXiv preprint arXiv:2003.04297 (2020)
13. Chen, X., He, K.: Exploring simple Siamese representation learning. In: CVPR, pp. 15750–15758 (2021)
14. Chen, Z., He, T., Jin, X., Wu, F.: Learning for video compression. IEEE Trans. Circuits Syst. Video Technol. **30**(2), 566–576 (2019)
15. Chen, Z., Duan, L.Y., Wang, S., Lin, W., Kot, A.C.: Data representation in hybrid coding framework for feature maps compression. In: 2020 IEEE International Conference on Image Processing (ICIP), pp. 3094–3098. IEEE (2020)
16. Chen, Z., Fan, K., Wang, S., Duan, L.Y., Lin, W., Kot, A.: Lossy intermediate deep learning feature compression and evaluation. In: ACM MM, pp. 2414–2422 (2019)
17. Chen, Z., Fan, K., Wang, S., Duan, L., Lin, W., Kot, A.C.: Toward intelligent sensing: intermediate deep feature compression. TIP **29**, 2230–2243 (2019)
18. Chen, Z., Lin, W., Wang, S., Duan, L., Kot, A.C.: Intermediate deep feature compression: the next battlefield of intelligent sensing. arXiv preprint arXiv:1809.06196 (2018)
19. Cheng, B., et al.: Panoptic-deeplab: a simple, strong, and fast baseline for bottom-up panoptic segmentation. In: CVPR, pp. 12475–12485 (2020)
20. Cheng, Z., Sun, H., Takeuchi, M., Katto, J.: Learned image compression with discretized gaussian mixture likelihoods and attention modules. In: CVPR, pp. 7939–7948 (2020)
21. Choi, H., Bajic, I.V.: High efficiency compression for object detection. In: 2018 IEEE International Conference on Acoustics, Speech and Signal Processing (ICASSP), pp. 1792–1796. IEEE (2018)
22. Codevilla, F., Simard, J.G., Goroshin, R., Pal, C.: Learned image compression for machine perception. arXiv preprint arXiv:2111.02249 (2021)
23. Contributors, M.: MMSegmentation: Openmmlab semantic segmentation toolbox and benchmark. https://github.com/open-mmlab/mmsegmentation (2020)
24. Cordts, M., et al.: The cityscapes dataset for semantic urban scene understanding. In: CVPR, pp. 3213–3223 (2016)
25. Deng, J., Dong, W., Socher, R., Li, L.J., Li, K., Fei-Fei, L.: Imagenet: a large-scale hierarchical image database. In: CVPR, pp. 248–255. IEEE (2009)
26. Duan, L., Liu, J., Yang, W., Huang, T., Gao, W.: Video coding for machines: a paradigm of collaborative compression and intelligent analytics. TIP **29**, 8680–8695 (2020)
27. Everingham, M., Van Gool, L., Williams, C.K., Winn, J., Zisserman, A.: The pascal visual object classes (VOC) challenge. IJCV **88**(2), 303–338 (2010)
28. Grill, J.B., et al.: Bootstrap your own latent: a new approach to self-supervised learning. arXiv preprint arXiv:2006.07733 (2020)
29. Guo, Z., Zhang, Z., Feng, R., Chen, Z.: Causal contextual prediction for learned image compression. IEEE Trans. Circuits Syst. Video Technol. **32**(4), 2329–2341 (2021)

30. Guo, Z., Zhang, Z., Feng, R., Chen, Z.: Soft then hard: rethinking the quantization in neural image compression. In: International Conference on Machine Learning, pp. 3920–3929. PMLR (2021)
31. He, K., Fan, H., Wu, Y., Xie, S., Girshick, R.: Momentum contrast for unsupervised visual representation learning. In: CVPR, pp. 9729–9738 (2020)
32. He, K., Gkioxari, G., Dollár, P., Girshick, R.: Mask r-cnn. In: ICCV, pp. 2961–2969 (2017)
33. He, K., Zhang, X., Ren, S., Sun, J.: Deep residual learning for image recognition. In: CVPR, pp. 770–778 (2016)
34. He, T., Sun, S., Guo, Z., Chen, Z.: Beyond coding: detection-driven image compression with semantically structured bit-stream. In: 2019 Picture Coding Symposium (PCS), pp. 1–5. IEEE (2019)
35. Hu, Y., Yang, S., Yang, W., Duan, L.Y., Liu, J.: Towards coding for human and machine vision: a scalable image coding approach. In: 2020 IEEE International Conference on Multimedia and Expo (ICME), pp. 1–6. IEEE (2020)
36. Huang, Z., Jia, C., Wang, S., Ma, S.: Visual analysis motivated rate-distortion model for image coding. In: 2021 IEEE International Conference on Multimedia and Expo (ICME), pp. 1–6. IEEE (2021)
37. Jing, L., Tian, Y.: Self-supervised visual feature learning with deep neural networks: a survey. In: TPAMI (2020)
38. Johnston, N., et al.: Improved lossy image compression with priming and spatially adaptive bit rates for recurrent networks. In: CVPR, pp. 4385–4393 (2018)
39. Kim, J.H., Heo, B., Lee, J.S.: Joint global and local hierarchical priors for learned image compression. arXiv preprint arXiv:2112.04487 (2021)
40. Kirillov, A., He, K., Girshick, R., Rother, C., Dollár, P.: Panoptic segmentation. In: CVPR, pp. 9404–9413 (2019)
41. Le, N., Zhang, H., Cricri, F., Ghaznavi-Youvalari, R., Rahtu, E.: Image coding for machines: an end-to-end learned approach. In: ICASSP 2021–2021 IEEE International Conference on Acoustics, Speech and Signal Processing (ICASSP), pp. 1590–1594. IEEE (2021)
42. Li, M., Zuo, W., Gu, S., You, J., Zhang, D.: Learning content-weighted deep image compression. In: TPAMI (2020)
43. Li, M., Zuo, W., Gu, S., Zhao, D., Zhang, D.: Learning convolutional networks for content-weighted image compression. In: CVPR, pp. 3214–3223 (2018)
44. Li, X., Shi, J., Chen, Z.: Task-driven semantic coding via reinforcement learning. arXiv preprint arXiv:2106.03511 (2021)
45. Lin, T.Y., Dollár, P., Girshick, R., He, K., Hariharan, B., Belongie, S.: Feature pyramid networks for object detection. In: CVPR, pp. 2117–2125 (2017)
46. Lin, T.-Y., et al.: Microsoft coco: common objects in context. In: Fleet, D., Pajdla, T., Schiele, B., Tuytelaars, T. (eds.) ECCV 2014. LNCS, vol. 8693, pp. 740–755. Springer, Cham (2014). https://doi.org/10.1007/978-3-319-10602-1_48
47. Liu, S., Qi, L., Qin, H., Shi, J., Jia, J.: Path aggregation network for instance segmentation. In: CVPR, pp. 8759–8768 (2018)
48. Long, J., Shelhamer, E., Darrell, T.: Fully convolutional networks for semantic segmentation. In: CVPR, pp. 3431–3440 (2015)
49. Loshchilov, I., Hutter, F.: Decoupled weight decay regularization. arXiv preprint arXiv:1711.05101 (2017)
50. Mentzer, F., Agustsson, E., Tschannen, M., Timofte, R., Van Gool, L.: Conditional probability models for deep image compression. In: CVPR, pp. 4394–4402 (2018)
51. Mentzer, F., Toderici, G.D., Tschannen, M., Agustsson, E.: High-fidelity generative image compression. NeurIPS 33, 11913–11924 (2020)

52. Minnen, D., Ballé, J., Toderici, G.: Joint autoregressive and hierarchical priors for learned image compression. In: NeurIPS (2018)
53. Minnen, D., Singh, S.: Channel-wise autoregressive entropy models for learned image compression. In: 2020 IEEE International Conference on Image Processing (ICIP), pp. 3339–3343. IEEE (2020)
54. Newell, A., Yang, K., Deng, J.: Stacked hourglass networks for human pose estimation. In: Leibe, B., Matas, J., Sebe, N., Welling, M. (eds.) ECCV 2016. LNCS, vol. 9912, pp. 483–499. Springer, Cham (2016). https://doi.org/10.1007/978-3-319-46484-8_29
55. Noroozi, M., Favaro, P.: Unsupervised learning of visual representations by solving jigsaw puzzles. In: Leibe, B., Matas, J., Sebe, N., Welling, M. (eds.) ECCV 2016. LNCS, vol. 9910, pp. 69–84. Springer, Cham (2016). https://doi.org/10.1007/978-3-319-46466-4_5
56. Oord, A.v.d., Li, Y., Vinyals, O.: Representation learning with contrastive predictive coding. arXiv preprint arXiv:1807.03748 (2018)
57. Pathak, D., Krahenbuhl, P., Donahue, J., Darrell, T., Efros, A.A.: Context encoders: Feature learning by inpainting. In: CVPR, pp. 2536–2544 (2016)
58. Rabbani, M., Joshi, R.: An overview of the jpeg 2000 still image compression standard. Signal Process. Image Commun. **17**(1), 3–48 (2002)
59. Redmon, J., Divvala, S., Girshick, R., Farhadi, A.: You only look once: Unified, real-time object detection. In: CVPR, pp. 779–788 (2016)
60. Redmon, J., Farhadi, A.: Yolo9000: better, faster, stronger. In: CVPR, pp. 7263–7271 (2017)
61. Ren, S., He, K., Girshick, R., Sun, J.: Faster r-cnn: towards real-time object detection with region proposal networks. NeurIPS **28**, 91–99 (2015)
62. Singh, S., Abu-El-Haija, S., Johnston, N., Ballé, J., Shrivastava, A., Toderici, G.: End-to-end learning of compressible features. In: 2020 IEEE International Conference on Image Processing (ICIP), pp. 3349–3353. IEEE (2020)
63. Song, M., Choi, J., Han, B.: Variable-rate deep image compression through spatially-adaptive feature transform. In: ICCV, pp. 2380–2389 (2021)
64. Sullivan, G.J., Ohm, J.R., Han, W.J., Wiegand, T.: Overview of the high efficiency video coding (HEVC) standard. TCSVT **22**(12), 1649–1668 (2012)
65. Sun, S., He, T., Chen, Z.: Semantic structured image coding framework for multiple intelligent applications. In: TCSVT (2020)
66. Toderici, G., et al.: Variable rate image compression with recurrent neural networks. arXiv preprint arXiv:1511.06085 (2015)
67. Wallace, G.K.: The jpeg still picture compression standard. IEEE Trans. Consum. Electron. **38**(1), xviii-xxxiv (1992)
68. Wiegand, T., Sullivan, G.J., Bjontegaard, G., Luthra, A.: Overview of the h.264/avc video coding standard. TCSVT **13**(7), 560–576 (2003)
69. Wu, Y., Li, X., Zhang, Z., Jin, X., Chen, Z.: Learned block-based hybrid image compression. IEEE Trans. Circuits Syst. Video Technol. **32**(6), 3978–3990 (2021)
70. Wu, Y., Kirillov, A., Massa, F., Lo, W.Y., Girshick, R.: Detectron2. https://github.com/facebookresearch/detectron2 (2019)
71. Wu, Z., Xiong, Y., Yu, S.X., Lin, D.: Unsupervised feature learning via non-parametric instance discrimination. In: CVPR, pp. 3733–3742 (2018)
72. Xia, S., Liang, K., Yang, W., Duan, L.Y., Liu, J.: An emerging coding paradigm VCM: a scalable coding approach beyond feature and signal. In: 2020 IEEE International Conference on Multimedia and Expo (ICME), pp. 1–6. IEEE (2020)
73. Yang, Y., Bamler, R., Mandt, S.: Improving inference for neural image compression. Adv. Neural Inf. Process. Syst. **33**, 573–584 (2020)

74. Zhang, R., Isola, P., Efros, A.A.: Colorful image colorization. In: Leibe, B., Matas, J., Sebe, N., Welling, M. (eds.) ECCV 2016. LNCS, vol. 9907, pp. 649–666. Springer, Cham (2016). https://doi.org/10.1007/978-3-319-46487-9_40
75. Zhao, H., Shi, J., Qi, X., Wang, X., Jia, J.: Pyramid scene parsing network. In: CVPR, pp. 2881–2890 (2017)

Feature Representation Learning for Unsupervised Cross-Domain Image Retrieval

Conghui Hu[✉] [iD] and Gim Hee Lee[iD]

Department of Computer Science, National University of Singapore,
Singapore, Singapore
{conghui,gimhee.lee}@nus.edu.sg

Abstract. Current supervised cross-domain image retrieval methods can achieve excellent performance. However, the cost of data collection and labeling imposes an intractable barrier to practical deployment in real applications. In this paper, we investigate the unsupervised cross-domain image retrieval task, where class labels and pairing annotations are no longer a prerequisite for training. This is an extremely challenging task because there is no supervision for both in-domain feature representation learning and cross-domain alignment. We address both challenges by introducing: 1) a new cluster-wise contrastive learning mechanism to help extract class semantic-aware features, and 2) a novel distance-of-distance loss to effectively measure and minimize the domain discrepancy without any external supervision. Experiments on the Office-Home and DomainNet datasets consistently show the superior image retrieval accuracies of our framework over state-of-the-art approaches. Our source code can be found at https://github.com/conghuihu/UCDIR.

Keywords: Unsupervised feature representation learning · Cross-domain alignment

1 Introduction

Cross-domain image retrieval refers to the task where the imagery data in one domain is used as query to retrieve the relevant samples in other domains. This task has many useful applications in our daily life. For example, sketch-based photo retrieval can be used in online shopping to search a product. To facilitate effective cross-domain retrieval, existing works takes the annotated class labels [24] or cross-domain pairing information [31] as supervision to train the model. However, it is always expensive and tedious to annotate labels for both domains, which severely limits the practical value of previous fully-supervised works. This

---

Supplementary Information The online version contains supplementary material available at https://doi.org/10.1007/978-3-031-19836-6_30.

S. Avidan et al. (Eds.): ECCV 2022, LNCS 13697, pp. 529–544, 2022.
https://doi.org/10.1007/978-3-031-19836-6_30

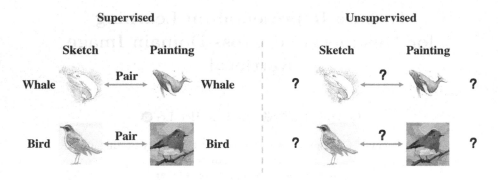

Fig. 1. Illustration of unsupervised cross-domain image retrieval. Compared with its supervised counterpart on the left, class label and pair annotation are not accessible in our unsupervised setting.

limitation motivates us to circumvent the requirement for large amounts of annotated ground truth data by investigating the task of unsupervised cross-domain image retrieval. We thus focus on the category-level unsupervised cross-domain image retrieval. Specifically, the goal is to train a network to retrieve images from the same category using the query image across a different domain without any annotated class labels and cross-domain pairing information for the training data. Two challenges must be solved to achieve the goal of category-level unsupervised cross-domain image retrieval: 1) effectively bridge the gap between an imagery input and its corresponding semantic concept without label supervision, and 2) align the data between different domains without any cross-domain pair annotation (Fig. 1).

The first challenge we faced is common in unsupervised feature representation learning [1,15,30], whose objective is to extract discriminative feature representation from pixel-level input without class annotations. Nonetheless, unsupervised feature representation learning does not consider domain shifts and thus would fail catastrophically when directly applied to our category-level unsupervised cross-domain image retrieval task due to the domain gap. The second challenge we faced is closely related to the line of works in unsupervised domain adaptation [32], where an unlabeled target domain needs to be aligned with the source domain to accurately classify the data in the target domain. However, fully [4] or partially [32] labeled source domain data are normally available for unsupervised domain adaptation. As a result, the task of unsupervised domain adaptation is easier than our category-level unsupervised cross-domain image retrieval since the labels in the source domain data can be used to learn discriminative features in the source domain and then transferred to the unlabeled target domain. Furthermore, our goal is to retrieve image of same category from the other domain, while unsupervised domain adaptation algorithms mostly focus on image classification.

In this paper, we formulate a novel end-to-end learning framework which incorporates both in-domain unsupervised representation learning and cross-domain alignment to accomplish our objective of training cross-domain image retrieval model in an unsupervised manner. We address the first challenge by introducing a new cluster-wise contrastive learning mechanism to help extract class semantic-aware features. In contrast to existing instance-wise contrastive learning loss [20] which neglects class semantic by only considering the augmented views of itself as positive samples, our cluster-wise contrastive loss is based on feature clusters that pulls samples of similar semantics closer and pushes different clusters apart. We address the second challenge by proposing a novel distance-of-distance loss which is able to effectively measure and minimize the domain discrepancy without external supervision. Specifically, we circumvent the difficulty of domain alignment due to the unknown class labels associated to the feature clusters in each domain by designing our distance-of-distance loss to be invariant to the cluster orders.

Our main contributions can be summarized as the follows:

1. We develop a novel feature representation learning algorithm for unsupervised cross-domain image retrieval.
2. To enable semantic-aware feature extraction, we propose a new cluster-wise contrastive learning loss to minimize the feature distances between semantically similar samples.
3. A novel distance-of-distance loss is carefully designed to measure domain discrepancy and help achieve cross-domain alignment.
4. Extensive experiments on the Office-Home and DomainNet datasets demonstrate the efficacy of our proposed framework.

2 Related Work

2.1 Cross-Domain Image Retrieval

Image retrieval is a long-standing research problem in computer vision. Given a query image, the objective is to retrieve images that meet certain predefined criteria from the database [26]. The criteria can be category-level or instance-level correspondence according to the granularity. All images in the database are ranked according to the distance to the query image [18]. Thus, the task boils down to effectively measure the similarity between images. It becomes more challenging when the query and images in database are from different domains, i.e., cross-domain image retrieval. For example, the query can be just a free-hand sketch with a few strokes, while images in the database are all real photographs [24]. To accurately compute the distance for images across domains, class labels are required as the supervision [24] for class semantic-aware feature extraction and cross-domain pairing annotations are leveraged to bridge the domain gap by minimizing triplet [31,33] or HOLEF loss [27]. However, the annotations used as supervision for model training are always labour-intensive to source. We are therefore motivated to investigate the unsupervised cross-domain image retrieval that shares all challenges laid out in cross-domain image retrieval but without external supervision.

2.2 Unsupervised Representation Learning

Unsupervised representation learning has been actively studied in recent years. Deep clustering related methods attempt to assign a pseudo class label for each sample by traditional clustering methods such as K-means [1] or maintain a set of trainable cluster centroids [7], and pseudo labels are continually refined during training. In contrast to deep clustering, instance discrimination [30] directly regards every sample itself as a standalone class and the training objective is to distinguish the sample from all the rest of data for the sake of extracting meaningful discriminative features. Self-supervised learning approaches facilitate the representation learning by introducing various pretext tasks like image rotation prediction [8], jigsaw puzzle solving [19] and image in-painting [22]. Supervisions for all these pretext tasks are free to obtain. Contrastive learning has been increasingly gaining popularity in unsupervised representation learning due to its effectiveness. The goal of contrastive learning algorithms is to maximize the agreement between positive pairs like two augmented views of the same images [2] or the image and its corresponding cluster centroid [15]. Nevertheless, the aforementioned unsupervised representation learning methods are originally devised for single domain data. The large gap between different domains preemptively limits their practical value.

2.3 Unsupervised Domain Adaptation

A related line of research that addresses the domain gap without full-supervision is unsupervised domain adaptation. Conventional unsupervised domain adaptation targets on transferring knowledge learned from an annotated source domain to a novel unlabeled target domain. The model can be trained to predict semantic-aware features for the source-domain data with the help of source domain label. The key challenge then becomes aligning the target domain data with their counterpart in the source domain. The domain discrepancy can be directly measured by Maximum Mean Discrepancy (MMD) [10] or Joint MMD [17], and minimized to remedy the domain gap [16,17]. [4,25] managed to search for matching data pairs across domains through Optimal Transport [29]. Moreover, Generative adversarial Networks [9] can also be utilized to break the domain barrier in either feature-level [6] or pixel-level [12]. More recently, a new domain adaptation setting with only few-shot annotated samples from source domain is introduced to further reduce the data labeling cost. [13,14] employed instance discrimination [30] for both in-domain and cross-domain to learn a shared and instance-discriminative feature space. In [32], prototypes are applied to make the feature more semantic-aware. Our unsupervised cross-domain image retrieval is different from domain adaptation in two aspects: 1) There is no requirement for labeled data. Both source and target domain are unlabeled; 2) Our task is image retrieval rather than image classification.

3 Our Method

3.1 Overview

We use domain A and domain B to denote the domain shift in images. Given a query image I_i^A of category k in domain A, category-level cross-domain image retrieval is considered successful when images of the same category k in domain B are retrieved. To accomplish the goal of cross-domain retrieval, it is required to train a valid feature extractor $f_\theta : I \mapsto \mathbf{x}$ which can project input image I from both domains to feature $\mathbf{x}$ in a common embedding space. All images $\mathcal{I}^B = \{I_j^B\}_{j=1}^M$ in domain B are then ranked by the feature distance $d(\mathbf{x}_i^A, \mathbf{x}_j^B)$ between I_j^B and the query image I_i^A in domain A. For I_i^B of category k to appear on top of the list, feature extractor f_θ needs to be capable of learning: 1) class semantic-aware features to discriminate samples among different classes; and 2) domain-agnostic features to facilitate the direct distance measurement between images in domain A and B. However, only a set of unlabeled images $\mathcal{I}^A = \{I_i^A\}_{i=1}^N$ and $\mathcal{I}^B = \{I_j^B\}_{j=1}^M$ from domain A and B are provided for training under the unsupervised cross-domain image retrieval setting. As a result, learning semantically meaningful and domain-invariant feature embeddings becomes extremely challenging. To learn feature representations that fulfill the aforementioned requirements, we design our framework according to the following two aspects: 1) In-domain representation learning which targets on learning class-discriminative features through a novel cluster-wise contrastive learning mechanism; 2) Cross-domain alignment through the distance of distance minimization as shown in Fig. 2.

3.2 In-Domain Cluster-Wise Contrastive Learning

Instance-wise contrastive learning methods take only augmented views of the same instance as positive pair, while all other samples in the dataset are regarded as the negatives. The loss function [20] is defined as:

$$\mathcal{L}_{\mathrm{IW}} = \sum_{i \in \mathbf{I}} - \log \frac{\exp(\mathbf{x}_i^\top \mathbf{x}_i'/\tau)}{\sum\limits_{a \in \mathbf{I}} \exp(\mathbf{x}_i^\top \mathbf{x}_a'/\tau)}, \tag{1}$$

where $\mathbf{x}_i$ and $\mathbf{x}_i'$ can be feature embeddings from different augmented views of instance i. $\mathbf{I}$ represents indices of all the samples in the same domain.

Although all instances are well-seperated at instance-level after training the feature extractor with $\mathcal{L}_{\mathrm{IW}}$, they are not clustered together according to their classes. However, the feature space that can encode the class semantic structure of the data is desired in the cross-domain image retrieval task. This motivates us to design the cluster-wise contrastive learning loss. Specifically, there are two steps in our cluster-wise contrastive learning: 1) image clustering and 2) contrastive learning with pseudo label. Additionally, we propose to perform cluster-wise contrastive learning separately in domain A and B. For brevity, we remove the domain notation in this section.

Image Clustering. Following MoCo [3], we maintain a momentum encoder $f_{\theta'}$ to extract features for image clustering as it yields more consistent clusters. Let $\mathbf{x}_i$ and $\mathbf{x}_i'$ be the features extracted from the trainable encoder f_θ and momentum encoder $f_{\theta'}$, respectively. We apply K-means on all image features $\{\mathbf{x}_i'\}_{i=1}^N$ in one single domain to obtain its K clusters. Each sample I_i is assigned with a pseudo label y_i according to the K-means results. All pseudo labels are updated after every epoch.

Contrastive Learning with Pseudo Label. Given the pseudo labels predicted by image clustering, we can now conduct cluster-wise contrastive learning. Samples in the same cluster as the query are used to form positive pairs. As a result, the feature extractor is trained to pull feature distances within the same cluster closer, while pushing different clusters apart. Specifically, the learning objective of cluster-wise contrastive learning is given by:

$$\mathcal{L}_{\mathrm{CW}} = \sum_{i\in\mathbf{I}} \frac{-1}{|\mathbf{P}(i)|} \sum_{p\in\mathbf{P}(i)} \log \frac{\exp(\mathbf{x}_i^\top \mathbf{x}'_p/\tau)}{\sum_{a\in\mathbf{I}} \exp(\mathbf{x}_i^\top \mathbf{x}'_a/\tau)}, \tag{2}$$

where $\mathbf{I}$ denotes indices of all the samples in the same domain and $\mathbf{P}(i)$ represents the indices for the set of samples belonging to the same cluster as I_i, i.e., $\mathbf{P}(i) = \{p \in \mathbf{I} : y_p = y_i\}$ and $|\mathbf{P}(i)|$ is its cardinality.

To encourage local smoothness and generate valid clustering results at the beginning of the training process, we also add the instance-wise contrastive loss. Therefore, our loss for in-domain feature representation learning becomes:

$$\mathcal{L}_{\text{in-domain}} = \mathcal{L}_{\mathrm{IW}} + \lambda\mathcal{L}_{\mathrm{CW}}. \tag{3}$$

Since the clustering results are not sufficient reliable at the initial learning stage, we gradually increase the weight for $\mathcal{L}_{CW}$ and set λ as:

$$\lambda = \begin{cases} 0 & ep <= T_1 \\ \alpha\frac{ep-T_1}{T_2-T_1} & T_1 < ep < T_2 \ , \\ \alpha & ep >= T_2 \end{cases} \tag{4}$$

where α is a weight hyper-parameter. ep, T_1 and T_2 are the current training epoch, the number of epoch to include $\mathcal{L}_{CW}$, the number of epoch to stop increasing the weight for $\mathcal{L}_{CW}$, respectively.

3.3 Cross-Domain Alignment

Domain-invariant is another requirement for the features in cross-domain image retrieval. However, it is difficult to effectively align feature clusters across domains when there is no class label nor correspondence annotation that can be utilized as supervision in our unsupervised setting. Furthermore, the order of the predicted cluster centroids $\{\mathbf{c}_u^A\}_{u=1}^K$ and $\{\mathbf{c}_u^B\}_{u=1}^K$ for domain A and B are not fixed since we perform K-means separately in the two domains. The unknown correspondences between the clusters across the two domains increases the challenge for cross-domain alignment. To solve this problem, we propose to measure the cross-domain distance of the in-domain distance. In other words, the Distance-of-Distance (DD) loss.

In-Domain Distance. Given an input image I_i, we calculate its clustering probabilities using the cluster centroids, $i.e.$:

$$p_i^u = \frac{\exp(\mathbf{x}_i^\top \mathbf{c}_u/\phi)}{\sum\limits_{k=1}^{K} \exp(\mathbf{x}_i^\top \mathbf{c}_k/\phi)}, \tag{5}$$

where ϕ is a temperature hyper-parameter. $\mathbf{c}_u$ represents the centroids for cluster u. The clustering probabilities for I_i is $\mathbf{p}_i = [p_i^{(1)}, p_i^{(2)} ..., p_i^{(K)}]^\top$. We leverage the centroids for domain A and B to obtain $\mathbf{p}_i^A$ and $\mathbf{p}_i^B$, respectively. The in-domain distance for domain A is defined as:

$$d_{ij}^A = \mathrm{D}(\mathbf{p}_i^A, \mathbf{p}_j^A), \quad \text{where}$$
$$\mathbf{p}_i^A = [p_i^{(A^1)}, p_i^{(A^2)} ..., p_i^{(A^K)}]^\top, \quad \mathbf{p}_j^A = [p_j^{(A^1)}, p_j^{(A^2)} ..., p_j^{(A^K)}]^\top. \tag{6}$$

Here, $\mathrm{D}(\cdot, \cdot)$ is the cosine distance. This in-domain distance measures the difference in clustering probabilities for samples.

Proposition 1. *Value of d_{ij}^A remains the same when the order of the elements in $\mathbf{p}_i^A$ and $\mathbf{p}_j^A$ are simultaneously shuffled, i.e., order of the centroids is changed.*

Proof. Suppose we randomly shuffle corresponding elements of $\mathbf{p}_i^A$ and $\mathbf{p}_j^A$ to:

$$\mathbf{p'}_i^A = [p_i^{(A^K)}, p_i^{(A^1)}, \cdots, p_i^{(A^2)}]^\top \quad \text{and} \quad \mathbf{p'}_j^A = [p_j^{(A^K)}, p_j^{(A^1)}, \cdots, p_j^{(A^2)}]^\top,$$

we get $d'_{ij}^A = \mathrm{D}(\mathbf{p'}_i^A, \mathbf{p'}_j^A) = 1 - \eta'^{-1}(p_i^{(A^K)}p_j^{(A^K)} + p_i^{(A^1)}p_j^{(A^1)} + \cdots + p_i^{(A^2)}p_j^{(A^2)}) = 1 - \eta^{-1}(p_i^{(A^1)}p_j^{(A^1)} + p_i^{(A^2)}p_j^{(A^2)} + \cdots + p_i^{(A^K)}p_j^{(A^K)}) = \mathrm{D}(\mathbf{p}_i^A, \mathbf{p}_j^A) = d_{ij}^A$, where $\eta' = \|\mathbf{p'}_i^A\|\|\mathbf{p'}_j^A\| = \|\mathbf{p}_i^A\|\|\mathbf{p}_j^A\| = \eta$ due to the commutative property of addition. $\square$

Corollary 1. *Our proposed in-domain distance has the important property of order-invariant. This order-invariant property also holds for d_{ij}^B for domain B.*

Cross-Domain Distance-of-Distance. As mentioned previously, our key challenge is to design a proper discrepancy measurement method to align the two domains while the cluster orders are unknown. Provided with the order-invariant in-domain distance, we devise a new cross-domain distance of distance:

$$dd_{ij} = \mathrm{DD}(d_{ij}^A, d_{ij}^B). \tag{7}$$

where $\mathrm{DD}(\cdot, \cdot)$ represents the distance-of-distance (DD) calculator that measures the L2 distance between two in-domain distances. As d_{ij}^A and d_{ij}^B are both order-invariant and the data samples used in the in-domain distance calculation are the

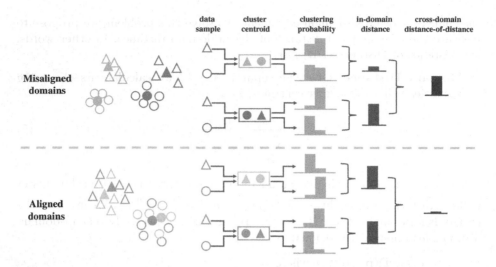

Fig. 2. Illustration of cross-domain distance-of-distance loss. Shapes and colors represent the data samples of different classes and domains, respectively.

same I_i and I_j. The value of dd_{ij} is then only related to the difference between values in the two sets of centroids $\left\{\mathbf{c}_u^A\right\}_{u=1}^{K}$ and $\left\{\mathbf{c}_u^B\right\}_{u=1}^{K}$ regardless of the order of cluster centroids. For two well-aligned domains A and B, dd_{ij} is small since the centroids for the two domains are similar. However, the corresponding centroids becomes disparate when there is a big difference between the feature distribution for domain A and B. Consequently, the value of d_{ij}^A and d_{ij}^B would differ greatly and thus lead to a large dd_{ij}. The detailed illustration can be found in Fig. 2. We thus propose our DD loss to effectively measure the discrepancy between features in two domains, where a smaller DD loss indicates better alignment. Formally, our DD loss is written as:

$$\mathcal{L}_{\mathrm{DD}} = \sum_{i \in \mathbf{R}^A} \sum_{j \in \mathbf{R}^A} dd_{ij} + \sum_{i \in \mathbf{R}^B} \sum_{j \in \mathbf{R}^B} dd_{ij}, \tag{8}$$

where $\mathbf{R}^A$ and $\mathbf{R}^B$ contains indices for domain A and domain B data in current batch. i and j are indices for instances.

Entropy Minimization. Our DD loss can also be trivially minimized when all the clustering probabilities are uniformly distributed, *i.e.*, all the elements the in $\mathbf{p}_i^A$ and $\mathbf{p}_i^B$ are the same. To prevent this trivial solution, we propose to minimize the self-entropy for all clustering probabilities:

$$\mathcal{L}_{\mathrm{SE}} = \sum_{i \in \mathbf{I}^A} (H(\mathbf{p}_i^A) + H(\mathbf{p}_i^B)) + \sum_{j \in \mathbf{I}^B} (H(\mathbf{p}_j^A) + H(\mathbf{p}_j^B)), \tag{9}$$

where $\mathbf{I}^A$ and $\mathbf{I}^B$ are the indices for all samples in domain A and B, respectively. Consequently, our training objective for cross-domain alignment is given by:

$$\mathcal{L}_{\text{cross-domain}} = \beta\mathcal{L}_{\text{DD}} + \gamma\mathcal{L}_{\text{SE}}, \tag{10}$$

where β and γ are hyper-parameters to balance the two loss terms.

3.4 Summary

To facilitate the feature extractor f_θ training for cross-domain image retrieval without any labeled data as supervision, we introduce a new cluster-wise contrastive learning loss for semantic-aware feature extraction, and propose a novel DD loss to effectively evaluate whether the two domains are aligned and train the feature extractor f_θ to minimize the DD loss. Our final training target is defined as:

$$\mathcal{L}_{\text{all}} = \mathcal{L}_{\text{in-domain}} + \mathcal{L}_{\text{cross-domain}}. \tag{11}$$

4 Experiments

4.1 Datasets and Settings

Datasets. Our proposed method is comprehensively evaluated on two datasets: 1) Office-Home [28] offers 4 domains (Art, Clipart, Product, Real) with 65 categories. 2) DomainNet [23] with six different domains (Clipart, Infograph, Painting, Quickdraw, Real and Sketch). We use all six domains and select those categories with more than 200 images in every domain for training and testing. According to this criterion, 7 categories are used in our experiments.

Implementation Details. ResNet-50 [11] is employed as the architecture for our feature extractor f_θ. Both features $\mathbf{x}_i$ and cluster centroids $\mathbf{c}_u$ are L2 normalized 128-d vectors. To make sure the whole training procedure is fully unsupervised, we use parameters from the MoCov2 [3] model trained with unlabeled ImageNet dataset [5] to initialize f_θ. The initial learning rate is 0.0002. We follow MoCov2 [3] to use the cosine learning rate schedule that gradually decreases the learning rate to 0. The total number of training epoch is 200. We adopt SGD to update the parameters in the feature extractor with momentum of 0.9 and a batch size of 64. Our framework is built with deep learning library Pytorch [21]. T_1 and T_2 are set to 20 and 100 respectively. The cluster number K is set to be the same as the number of classes in the training set, i.e., 65 for Office-Home and 7 for DomainNet.

Evaluation Metrics. To validate the retrieval performance for the Office-Home dataset, we follow [14] to calculate the precision among top 1/5/15 retrieved images as the minimum number of images for one single category is 15. As for DomainNet, we filter out those categories with fewer than 200 images. Thus, we measure the precision for top 50/100/200 retrieved image to provide a more comprehensive evaluation for retrieval accuracy in DomainNet. Since our task is

538   C. Hu and G. H. Lee

Table 1. Unsupervised cross-domain retrieval accuracy (%) on office-home.

Method	Art→Real			Real→Art			Art→Product		
	P@1	P@5	P@15	P@1	P@5	P@15	P@1	P@5	P@15
ID [30]	35.89	33.13	29.60	39.89	34.42	27.65	25.88	24.91	22.49
ProtoNCE [15]	40.50	36.39	34.00	44.53	39.26	32.99	29.54	27.89	25.75
CDS [14]	45.08	41.15	38.73	44.71	40.75	35.53	32.76	31.47	28.90
PCS [32]	41.70	38.51	36.22	44.96	39.88	33.99	33.29	31.50	29.53
Ours	**45.12**	**42.33**	**40.06**	**47.95**	**43.68**	**38.38**	**35.39**	**34.67**	**32.61**
	Product→Art			Clipart→Real			Real→Clipart		
	P@1	P@5	P@15	P@1	P@5	P@15	P@1	P@5	P@15
ID [30]	32.17	25.94	20.23	29.48	26.48	23.25	35.51	32.17	27.96
ProtoNCE [15]	35.73	30.61	24.55	25.25	22.66	20.83	41.15	37.66	31.95
CDS [14]	35.75	32.48	26.82	32.51	30.30	27.80	38.88	36.48	33.16
PCS [32]	39.24	34.77	28.77	29.07	26.06	24.00	40.60	38.11	34.06
Ours	**42.51**	**37.94**	**31.41**	**33.31**	**30.57**	**28.14**	**44.66**	**41.47**	**37.41**
	Product→Real			Real→Product			Product→Clipart		
	P@1	P@5	P@15	P@1	P@5	P@15	P@1	P@5	P@15
ID [30]	50.73	45.03	39.05	45.12	41.46	38.01	31.52	28.55	24.15
ProtoNCE [15]	53.84	48.25	42.21	47.74	44.85	41.21	36.13	33.99	28.24
CDS [14]	54.00	50.07	45.60	49.39	47.27	43.98	37.69	34.99	30.42
PCS [32]	56.45	50.78	45.37	49.90	47.11	43.73	39.51	**37.51**	32.81
Ours	**57.42**	**52.69**	**47.90**	**51.71**	**48.48**	**44.95**	**42.26**	37.42	**33.74**
	Clipart→Product			Art→Clipart			Clipart→Art		
	P@1	P@5	P@15	P@1	P@5	P@15	P@1	P@5	P@15
ID [30]	24.01	22.42	20.60	26.78	24.79	21.64	21.17	17.86	14.71
ProtoNCE [15]	21.17	20.63	20.47	28.97	26.15	22.98	21.33	17.40	14.46
CDS [14]	27.24	26.46	24.86	25.59	23.77	22.41	22.41	20.34	17.34
PCS [32]	26.39	25.86	24.92	31.23	28.74	26.11	24.51	21.27	17.54
Ours	**27.79**	**27.26**	**25.97**	**32.67**	**30.79**	**28.70**	**27.26**	**23.94**	**20.53**
Average	ID [30]			ProtoNCE [15]			CDS [14]		
	P@1	P@5	P@15	P@1	P@5	P@15	P@1	P@5	P@15
	33.18	29.76	25.78	35.49	32.15	28.30	37.17	34.63	31.30
	PCS [32]			Ours			Improvement		
	P@1	P@5	P@15	P@1	P@5	P@15	P@1	P@5	P@15
	38.07	35.01	31.42	**40.67**	**37.60**	**34.15**	**+2.60**	**+2.59**	**+2.73**

category-level cross-domain retrieval, the retrieved images with the same semantic class as the query are regarded as the correct ones.

Baselines. We use the following works as the baselines to evaluate our proposed method: 1) **ID** [30] achieves unsupervised representation learning by instance discrimination where all instance are well-separated regardless of the category.

2) **ProtoNCE** [15] is a more recent unsupervised representattion learning algorithm which proposes to use prototypes to help encode semantic structure of data and predict more aggregated feature clusters. 3) **CDS** [14] is originally designed for cross-domain self-supervised pre-training. In-domain instance discrimination and cross-domain instance matching are designed for learning a shared embedding space across domains. 4) **PCS** [32] is a cross-domain self-supervised learning approach that uses prototypical contrastive learning for in-domain feature learning and instance-prototype matching for cross-domain alignment.

4.2   Results

i) The Office-Home Dataset

Settings. Since there are four domains in the Office-Home dataset, we have altogether 6 different pairs (Art-Real, Art-Product, Clipart-Real, Product-Real, Product-Clipart, Art-Clipart) by matching any two of the four domains. Furthermore, the two domains in one pair can be both regarded as query domain to retrieve images from the other domain.

Results. From the retrieval results in Table 1 and Fig. 3, we make the following observations: 1) ID [30] and ProtoNCE [15] are designed for single domain feature representation learning. The domain gap hurts their performance when applied on cross-domain data. 2) Among all the baseline methods, PCS [32] performs the best. 3) Our proposed method outperforms nearly all the baselines for all pairs in all three evaluation metrics. This shows the effectiveness of our proposed

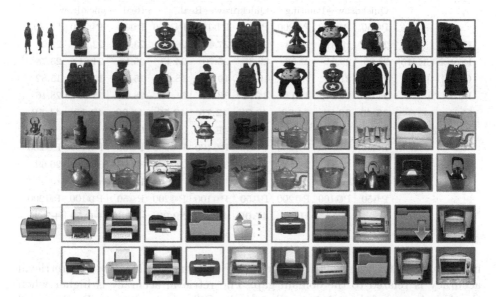

Fig. 3. Top 10 retrieval results on Office-Home. Row 1, 3, 5: Retrieval results of the best baseline method - PCS [32]; Row 2, 4, 6: Retrieval results of our framework. The green and red boxes indicate correct and incorrect retrievals, respectively.

Table 2. Unsupervised cross-domain retrieval accuracy (%) on DomainNet.

Method	Clipart→Sketch			Sketch→Clipart			Infograph→Real		
	P@50	P@100	P@200	P@50	P@100	P@200	P@50	P@100	P@200
ID [30]	49.46	46.09	40.44	54.38	47.12	37.73	28.27	27.44	26.33
ProtoNCE [15]	46.85	42.67	36.35	54.52	45.04	35.06	28.41	28.53	28.50
CDS [14]	45.84	42.37	37.16	59.13	48.83	37.40	28.51	27.92	27.48
PCS [32]	51.01	46.87	40.19	59.70	50.67	39.38	30.56	30.27	29.68
Ours	**56.31**	**52.74**	**47.38**	**63.07**	**57.26**	**48.17**	**35.52**	**35.24**	**34.35**
	Real→Infograph			Infograph→Sketch			Sketch→Infograph		
	P@50	P@100	P@200	P@50	P@100	P@200	P@50	P@100	P@200
ID [30]	39.98	31.77	24.84	30.35	29.04	26.55	42.20	34.94	27.52
ProtoNCE [15]	57.01	41.84	30.33	28.24	26.79	24.23	39.83	31.99	24.77
CDS [14]	56.69	39.76	26.38	30.55	**29.51**	**27.00**	**46.27**	36.11	27.33
PCS [32]	55.42	42.13	30.76	30.27	28.36	25.35	42.58	34.09	25.91
Ours	**57.74**	**46.69**	**35.47**	**31.29**	29.33	26.54	43.66	**36.14**	**28.12**
	Painting→Clipart			Clipart→Painting			Painting→Quickdraw		
	P@50	P@100	P@200	P@50	P@100	P@200	P@50	P@100	P@200
ID [30]	64.67	54.41	40.07	42.37	39.61	35.56	20.34	19.59	18.79
ProtoNCE [15]	55.44	43.74	32.59	39.13	35.87	32.07	21.63	21.24	20.56
CDS [14]	63.15	47.30	32.93	37.75	35.18	32.76	18.75	18.89	17.88
PCS [32]	63.47	53.21	41.68	48.83	46.21	42.10	25.12	24.65	23.80
Ours	**66.42**	**56.84**	**46.72**	**52.58**	**50.10**	**46.11**	**39.72**	**38.59**	**37.63**
	Quickdraw→Painting			Quickdraw→Real			Real→Quickdraw		
	P@50	P@100	P@200	P@50	P@100	P@200	P@50	P@100	P@200
ID [30]	21.12	19.81	18.48	28.27	27.46	26.32	23.45	22.79	22.01
ProtoNCE [15]	23.95	22.84	21.56	26.38	25.70	24.45	25.10	24.81	23.78
CDS [14]	21.37	21.44	19.46	19.28	19.14	18.67	15.36	15.57	15.82
PCS [32]	24.03	23.24	22.13	34.82	33.92	31.73	28.98	28.85	28.16
Ours	**33.45**	**33.81**	**34.29**	**42.79**	**42.75**	**42.70**	**41.90**	**42.10**	**41.59**
Average	ID [30]			ProtoNCE [15]			CDS [14]		
	P@50	P@100	P@200	P@50	P@100	P@200	P@50	P@100	P@200
	37.07	33.34	28.72	37.21	32.59	27.85	36.89	31.84	26.69
	PCS [32]			Ours			Improvement		
	P@50	P@100	P@200	P@50	P@100	P@200	P@50	P@100	P@200
	41.23	36.87	31.74	**47.09**	**43.47**	**39.09**	**+5.86**	**+6.59**	**+7.35**

in-domain cluster-wise contrastive learning and the DD loss. 4) The retrieval accuracy is related to the domain gap. The retrieval accuracy is higher when the domain gap of the pair is smaller. In the Office-home dataset, Product and Real are the two with the smallest domain gap. Thus, it can be seen that the retrieval accuracy of both Product → Real and Real → Product are higher than the others. 5) The accuracy for P@1 is always higher than P@5 and P@15, which means it is more likely to retrieve an image from a wrong category when the number of retrieved image becomes larger.

ii) The DomainNet Dataset

Settings. We report the results for 6 pairs of domains from the six domains in DomainNet dataset: Clipart-Sketch, Infograph-Real, Infograph-Sketch, Painting-Clipart, Painting-Quickdraw, Quickdraw-Real. We ensure that every domain appears twice for comprehensive evaluations in all six domains.

Results. The retrieval performance in Table 2 and Fig. 4 shows that: 1) Similar to the results from Office-Home dataset, PCS [15] is the strongest baseline in our unsupervised cross-domain image retrieval task. 2) Our framework achieves the highest retrieval accuracy for almost all the 12 retrieval tasks. 3) The Quickdraw domain in DomainNet only contain some simple strokes, which lead to the largest domain gap. All the other four baseline methods perform poorly on the Painting → Quickdraw, Quickdraw → Painting, Quickdraw → Real and Real → Quickdraw retrieval. 4) The improvement brought by our proposed method is most significant on Painting → Quickdraw retrieval. Ours is 14.60% higher in terms of P@50 when compared to the best baseline PCS. 5) Among all 12 retrieval pairs, our method performs the best for Painting → Clipart retrieval and achieves 66.42% for P@50.

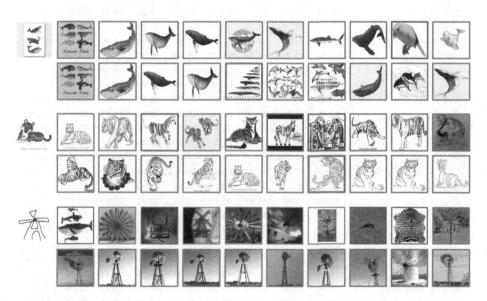

Fig. 4. Top 10 retrieval results on DomainNet. Row 1, 3, 5: Retrieval results of the best baseline method - PCS [32]; Row 2, 4, 6: Retrieval results of our framework. The green and red boxes indicate correct and incorrect retrievals, respectively.

4.3 Ablation Study

The results in Table 3 show the efficacy of different components in our framework. From the table, we can see: 1) Compared to using the instance-wise contrastive learning loss $\mathcal{L}_{IW}$ (v1), our proposed cluster-wise contrastive loss (v2) indeed helps to learn a better feature embedding for cross-domain image retrieval. All three evaluation metrics show the effectiveness of $\mathcal{L}_{CW}$. 2) In v3, we add the self-entropy loss for clustering probabilities. The improvement over v2 shows that the entropy minimization for clustering probabilities is beneficial for cross-domain feature representation learning. 3) Our full model, which employs the DD loss to minimize the discrepancy between domains, provides the best alignment and performs the best compared with all v1, v2 and v3. 4) The efficacy of the DD loss varies a lot in the experiment with different pairs. Comparing to v3 (without DD loss), our full model achieves a performance gain of only 0.66% at P@50 on Real $\rightarrow$ Infograph, but shows higher performance gain of 8.71% on Real $\rightarrow$ Quickdraw.

Table 3. Ablation Study on our model component. Cross-domain Retrieval Accuracy (%) on DomainNet.

Method	Clipart→Sketch			Sketch→Clipart			Infograph→Real		
	P@50	P@100	P@200	P@50	P@100	P@200	P@50	P@100	P@200
$\mathcal{L}_{IW}$ (v1)	48.08	43.64	37.17	56.09	47.38	37.24	30.51	30.22	29.68
$\mathcal{L}_{IW} + \mathcal{L}_{CW}$ (v2)	51.92	47.95	41.98	60.18	52.01	41.93	32.47	32.00	31.25
$\mathcal{L}_{IW} + \mathcal{L}_{CW} + \mathcal{L}_{SE}$ (v3)	53.17	49.33	43.55	60.66	52.85	42.44	33.80	33.19	32.27
Our full model	**56.31**	**52.74**	**47.38**	**63.07**	**57.26**	**48.17**	**35.52**	**35.24**	**34.35**
	Real→Infograph			Infograph→Sketch			Sketch→Infograph		
	P@50	P@100	P@200	P@50	P@100	P@200	P@50	P@100	P@200
$\mathcal{L}_{IW}$ (v1)	55.85	42.36	30.85	29.90	28.16	25.18	40.84	32.93	25.95
$\mathcal{L}_{IW} + \mathcal{L}_{CW}$ (v2)	57.30	45.51	33.80	30.98	29.21	26.38	**43.81**	35.99	27.86
$\mathcal{L}_{IW} + \mathcal{L}_{CW} + \mathcal{L}_{SE}$ (v3)	57.08	45.88	34.17	30.99	29.25	26.34	43.58	35.83	27.55
Our full model	**57.74**	**46.69**	**35.47**	**31.29**	**29.33**	**26.54**	43.66	**36.14**	**28.12**
	Painting→Clipart			Clipart→Painting			Painting→Quickdraw		
	P@50	P@100	P@200	P@50	P@100	P@200	P@50	P@100	P@200
$\mathcal{L}_{IW}$ (v1)	55.59	45.19	34.46	42.12	38.96	34.50	23.10	22.52	21.47
$\mathcal{L}_{IW} + \mathcal{L}_{CW}$ (v2)	65.00	54.08	41.81	47.66	44.59	40.82	24.09	23.45	22.48
$\mathcal{L}_{IW} + \mathcal{L}_{CW} + \mathcal{L}_{SE}$ (v3)	66.08	**57.20**	**46.88**	**52.71**	49.85	46.05	34.13	33.39	32.24
Our full model	**66.42**	56.84	46.72	52.58	**50.10**	**46.11**	**39.72**	**38.59**	**37.63**
	Quickdraw→Painting			Quickdraw→Real			Real→Quickdraw		
	P@50	P@100	P@200	P@50	P@100	P@200	P@50	P@100	P@200
$\mathcal{L}_{IW}$ (v1)	23.11	22.22	21.20	25.62	24.98	24.05	26.83	26.52	25.53
$\mathcal{L}_{IW} + \mathcal{L}_{CW}$ (v2)	24.83	23.80	22.32	32.32	31.63	30.50	28.25	27.56	26.53
$\mathcal{L}_{IW} + \mathcal{L}_{CW} + \mathcal{L}_{SE}$ (v3)	32.86	32.35	31.45	37.12	37.11	36.63	33.19	33.11	32.54
Our full model	**33.45**	**33.81**	**34.29**	**42.79**	**42.75**	**42.70**	**41.90**	**42.10**	**41.59**

Average									
$\mathcal{L}_{IW}$			$\mathcal{L}_{IW} + \mathcal{L}_{CW}$			$\mathcal{L}_{IW} + \mathcal{L}_{CW} + \mathcal{L}_{SE}$		Our full model	
P@50	P@100	P@200	P@50	P@100	P@200	P@50	P@100	P@200	P@50	P@100	P@200
38.14	33.99	29.42	41.57	37.32	32.31	44.61	40.78	36.01	**47.09**	**43.47**	**39.09**

5   Conclusion

This paper presents a novel representation learning framework for unsupervised cross-domain image retrieval which is a challenging but practically valuable task. To extract class semantic-aware feature for category-level retrieval, we propose a cluster-wise contrastive learning loss that pulls samples of similar semantics closer and pushes different clusters apart. For cross-domain alignment, a novel distance of distance loss is introduced to effectively measure the discrepancy between domains and minimized to align features in both domains. The experiment results on Office-Home and DomainNet dataset consistently illustrate the superiority of our proposed algorithm.

Acknowledgements. This research/project is supported by the National Research Foundation, Singapore under its AI Singapore Programme (AISG Award No: AISG2-RP-2021-024), and the Tier 2 grant MOE-T2EP20120-0011 from the Singapore Ministry of Education.

References

1. Caron, M., Bojanowski, P., Joulin, A., Douze, M.: Deep clustering for unsupervised learning of visual features. In: ECCV (2018)
2. Chen, T., Kornblith, S., Norouzi, M., Hinton, G.: A simple framework for contrastive learning of visual representations. In: ICML (2020)
3. Chen, X., Fan, H., Girshick, R., He, K.: Improved baselines with momentum contrastive learning. arXiv (2020)
4. Damodaran, B.B., Kellenberger, B., Flamary, R., Tuia, D., Courty, N.: Deepjdot: deep joint distribution optimal transport for unsupervised domain adaptation. In: ECCV (2018)
5. Deng, J., Dong, W., Socher, R., Li, L.J., Li, K., Fei-Fei, L.: Imagenet: a large-scale hierarchical image database. In: CVPR (2009)
6. Ganin, Y., et al.: Domain-adversarial training of neural networks. In: JMLR (2016)
7. Gao, B., Yang, Y., Gouk, H., Hospedales, T.M.: Deep clusteringwith concrete k-means. In: ICASSP (2020)
8. Gidaris, S., Singh, P., Komodakis, N.: Unsupervised representation learning by predicting image rotations. In: ICLR (2018)
9. Goodfellow, I., et al.: Generative adversarial nets. In: NeurIPS (2014)
10. Gretton, A., Borgwardt, K.M., Rasch, M.J., Schölkopf, B., Smola, A.: A kernel two-sample test. In: JMLR (2012)
11. He, K., Zhang, X., Ren, S., Sun, J.: Deep residual learning for image recognition. In: CVPR (2016)
12. Hoffman, J., et al.: Cycada: cycle-consistent adversarial domain adaptation. In: ICML (2018)
13. Kim, D., Saito, K., Oh, T.H., Plummer, B.A., Sclaroff, S., Saenko, K.: Cross-domain self-supervised learning for domain adaptation with few source labels. arXiv preprint arXiv:2003.08264 (2020)
14. Kim, D., Saito, K., Oh, T.H., Plummer, B.A., Sclaroff, S., Saenko, K.: CDS: Cross-domain self-supervised pre-training. In: ICCV (2021)

15. Li, J., Zhou, P., Xiong, C., Hoi, S.C.: Prototypical contrastive learning of unsupervised representations. In: ICLR (2020)
16. Long, M., Zhu, H., Wang, J., Jordan, M.I.: Unsupervised domain adaptation with residual transfer networks. In: NeurIPS (2016)
17. Long, M., Zhu, H., Wang, J., Jordan, M.I.: Deep transfer learning with joint adaptation networks. In: ICML (2017)
18. Müller, H., Müller, W., Squire, D.M., Marchand-Maillet, S., Pun, T.: Performance evaluation in content-based image retrieval: overview and proposals. In: PR (2001)
19. Noroozi, M., Favaro, P.: Unsupervised learning of visual representations by solving jigsaw puzzles. In: ECCV (2016)
20. Oord, A.V.D., Li, Y., Vinyals, O.: Representation learning with contrastive predictive coding. arXiv (2018)
21. Paszke, A., et al.: PyTorch: an imperative style, high-performance deep learning library. In: NeurIPS (2019)
22. Pathak, D., Krahenbuhl, P., Donahue, J., Darrell, T., Efros, A.A.: Context encoders: feature learning by inpainting. In: CVPR (2016)
23. Peng, X., Bai, Q., Xia, X., Huang, Z., Saenko, K., Wang, B.: Moment matching for multi-source domain adaptation. In: ICCV (2019)
24. Sangkloy, P., Burnell, N., Ham, C., Hays, J.: The sketchy database: learning to retrieve badly drawn bunnies. In: TOG (2016)
25. Shen, J., Qu, Y., Zhang, W., Yu, Y.: Wasserstein distance guided representation learning for domain adaptation. In: AAAI (2018)
26. Smeulders, A.W., Worring, M., Santini, S., Gupta, A., Jain, R.: Content-based image retrieval at the end of the early years. In: TPAMI (2000)
27. Song, J., Yu, Q., Song, Y.Z., Xiang, T., Hospedales, T.M.: Deep spatial-semantic attention for fine-grained sketch-based image retrieval. In: ICCV (2017)
28. Venkateswara, H., Eusebio, J., Chakraborty, S., Panchanathan, S.: Deep hashing network for unsupervised domain adaptation. In: CVPR (2017)
29. Villani, C.: Optimal transport. In: Old and New. Springer, Heidelberg (2009). https://doi.org/10.1007/978-3-540-71050-9
30. Wu, Z., Xiong, Y., Yu, S.X., Lin, D.: Unsupervised feature learning via non-parametric instance discrimination. In: CVPR (2018)
31. Yu, Q., Liu, F., Song, Y.Z., Xiang, T., Hospedales, T.M., Loy, C.C.: Sketch me that shoe. In: CVPR (2016)
32. Yue, X., et al: Prototypical cross-domain self-supervised learning for few-shot unsupervised domain adaptation. In: CVPR (2021)
33. Zhao, Y., et al.: Learning to generalize unseen domains via memory-based multi-source meta-learning for person re-identification. In: CVPR (2021)

Fashionformer: A Simple, Effective and Unified Baseline for Human Fashion Segmentation and Recognition

Shilin Xu[1,3], Xiangtai Li[1,3], Jingbo Wang[2], Guangliang Cheng[3],
Yunhai Tong[1(✉)], and Dacheng Tao[4]

[1] Key Laboratory of Machine Perception, MOE, School of Artificial Intelligence,
Peking University, Beijing, China
xushilin@stu.pku.edu.cn, {lxtpku,yhtong}@pku.edu.cn
[2] CUHK-SenseTime Joint Lab, The Chinese University of Hong Kong, Hong Kong,
Hong Kong
[3] SenseTime Research, Beijing, China
chengguangliang@sensetime.com
[4] The University of Sydney, Sydney, Australia

Abstract. Human fashion understanding is one crucial computer vision task since it has comprehensive information for real-world applications. This focus on joint human fashion segmentation and attribute recognition. Contrary to the previous works that separately model each task as a multi-head prediction problem, our insight is to bridge these two tasks with one unified model via vision transformer modeling to benefit each task. In particular, we introduce the object query for segmentation and the attribute query for attribute prediction. Both queries and their corresponding features can be linked via mask prediction. Then we adopt a two-stream query learning framework to learn the decoupled query representations. We design a novel Multi-Layer Rendering module for attribute stream to explore more fine-grained features. The decoder design shares the same spirit as DETR. Thus we name the proposed method *Fahsionformer*. Extensive experiments on three human fashion datasets illustrate the effectiveness of our approach. In particular, our method with the same backbone achieve **relative 10% improvements** than previous works in case of *a joint metric* ($AP^{\mathrm{mask}}_{\mathrm{IoU+F_1}}$) *for both segmentation and attribute recognition.* To the best of our knowledge, we are the first unified end-to-end vision transformer framework for human fashion analysis. We hope this simple yet effective method can serve as a

S. Xu and X. Li—The first two authors contribute equally.
The work was done at Sensetime Research. This research is also supported by the National Key Research and Development Program of China under Grant No.2020YFB2103402. We thank the computation resource provided by SenseTime Research.

Supplementary Information The online version contains supplementary material available at https://doi.org/10.1007/978-3-031-19836-6_31.

new flexible baseline for fashion analysis. Code will be available https://github.com/xushilin1/FashionFormer.

Keywords: Human fashion · Fine-grained attribute analysis · Segmentation · Vision transformer

1 Introduction

The capability of understanding human fashion is essential for numerous real-world applications, such as digital human modeling, AR/VR, and online business. Limited by the representation of human fashion, previous works [39,57, 58,61,69] mainly focus on fashion parts localization and ignore the fine-grained human attributes, for example, the description of clothes. To analyze such a richer context for human fashion, researchers [25] begin to categorize human fashion attributes into different aspects (*e.g.*plain, tight, normal waist) shown in Fig. 1(a). They solve this problem by extending the widely used instance segmentation framework [21] for these attributes as a multi-head prediction task, as shown in Fig. 1(b).

Although the Attribute-Mask R-CNN [25] is a strong baseline for such fashion analysis task, there are several remaining critical issues. *Firstly*, the relationship between instance segmentation and attribute recognition is not well explored and thus the fine-gained knowledge provided by these attributes for segmentation is unknown. *Secondly*, adopting single RoI (Region of Interest) representation leads to incomplete and inferior results for fine-grained attributes, causing huge gaps between segmentation results and attribute recognition. *Thirdly*, adopting box based detector limits the mask resolution and results in imprecise mask quality, which leads to uncomfortable experience for auto-segmentation when shopping. Thus, a better and unified baseline is needed for this track.

In recent years, Vision Transformers have been proven effective in feature representation learning, unification, and simplification of various downstream tasks [2,13,47,49,55]. In particular, Detection Transformer (DETR) [2] adopts *object queries* to model the detected objects. Meanwhile, several works [8,66] provide box-free segmentation solutions. Adopting query based design can naturally link segmentation and attribute recognition. More details can be obtained via corresponding masks. Moreover, as proven by ViT [13], Vision Transformers have a huge capacity, which is helpful for the shopping industry since the data is easy to obtain. These findings motivate us to formulate a new solution for fashion analysis using transformers.

In this work, we present a simple, effective and unified baseline named Fashionformer for this task. As shown in Fig. 1(c), the entire framework is an encode-decoder framework in DETR style. Our key insights are using *object queries* and *attribute queries* to encode instance-wised and attribute-wised information, respectively. Then we perform joint learning for both instance segmentation and attribute recognition. Joint learning leads to better instance segmentation results, since attribute labels constrain the scope of mask label. For example,

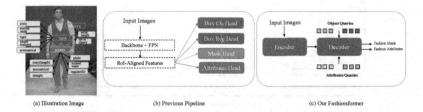

Fig. 1. Task introduction and method overview. (a) Illustration for human fashion segmentation and attribute recognition task. It requires the model to predict the masks, their labels (shown in red), and corresponding attributes (shown in yellow rectangles). (b) Overview of previous pipeline used in [25]. It contains several independent task heads and solves each task separately. (c) The proposed Fashionformer pipeline. It is an encoder-decoder framework that takes object queries and attribute queries as inputs and directly outputs masks and attributes. Best view in color and zoom in. (Color figure online)

for sleeve object, there will not exist attributes like plain or tight. In particular, we propose to match each object query into each attribute query via residual addition for implementation. This gives a good initialization of attributes and serves as the starting points for attribute recognition. Since each object query owns its corresponding mask, we name the query feature as grouped features via these corresponding masks. Then we perform updating object queries with the query features. This operation is implemented with dynamic convolution [47,66] and multi-head self-attention layers [50] between query and query features iteratively. In the experiments, surprisingly, we find *joint* learning with the object queries and attribute queries boosts the original segmentation results.

Moreover, since both attribute recognition and instance segmentation have different goals, the former needs more fine-grained and discriminative representation for multi-label classification while the latter performs mask based multi-class classification. For attribute recognition, we propose a Multi-Layer Rendering (MLR) module to generate the attributes query features. The multi-level features are grouped via corresponding predicted masks. Such a module is lightweight and bridges the gap between instance segmentation and attribute recognition. Then we perform the same procedure as object query path via dynamic convolution and self-attention layers where we use attributes query feature to re-weight the attribute query. Note that both are *independent*, which leads to a two-stream decoder.

Our framework can support both CNN backbone [22] and Transformer backbone [38] as encoder. Finally, the framework is motivated by the design of box-free architecture, and it can generate high resolution masks without box supervision or RoI-wised operation. Our framework can also adapt to previous fashion benchmarks by replacing the recognition branch with an extra classification head. Extensive experiments show that our approach achieves much better results than previous works [9,25,66]. Figure 2 (d) shows our method achieves better segmentation results when comparing to Attribute Mask-RCNN.

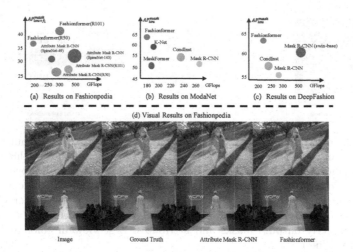

(a) Results on Fashionpedia (b) Results on ModaNet (c) Results on DeepFashion

(d) Visual Results on Fashionpedia

Image   Ground Truth   Attribute Mask R-CNN   Fashionformer

Fig. 2. Comparison Results on (a) Fashionpedia (b) ModaNet. and (c) DeepFashion. All models in (b) and (c) use ResNet50 as backbone. The GFlop is obtained via $1020 \times 1020 \times 3$ inputs. Our method achieves a significant gain with the fewer GFlops. The number of network parameters are indicated by the radius of circles. (d). Visual comparison results using ResNet-50 backbone. Best view in color. (Color figure online)

As shown in Fig. 2(a)-(c), Fashionformer achieves the new state-of-the-art results on three fashion benchmarks including Fahsionpedia [25], ModaNet [69] and Deepfashion [39] with *less computation cost and parameters*. Moreover, *The gap between attribute recognition and instance segmentation can be effectively narrowed through our approach by a significant performance margin to the state-of-the-art methods*. These results demonstrate that Fashionformer can serve as a new baseline for future research in fashion analysis. To the best of our knowledge, this is the first unified end-to-end model for this task.

2   Related Work

Instance Segmentation. This task aims to detect and segment each instance [10,20]. The two-stage pipeline Mask R-CNN like models [4,21,23,25] first generate object proposals using Region Proposal Network (RPN) [44] and then predict boxes and masks on each RoI where the advanced versions utilize more cues to enhance the mask representation. Several single-stage methods [1,3,7,48] achieve significant progress and comparable results with two-stage pipelines where they use single stage detector. SOLO [53] treats instances into grid representation and then performs instance classification and segmentation in a decoupled manner. Meanwhile, there are several bottom-up approaches [11,42] where each instance is grouped from the semantic segmentation prediction [6,29,31,71]. Several works [12,16] use object query to encode instance wised information. However, they still need object detector [47,74].

Instance Segmentation is one of the sub-task of our framework. Moreover, we show that joint learning of both segmentation and fine-grained attributes lead to better segmentation results.

Related Human Segmentation. Most works in this area focus on human part modeling, including instance part segmentation and semantic part segmentation. Several works [15,37,52,73] design specific methods for semantic part segmentation which are in category-level settings. Recent human segmentation methods focus on human instance part segmentation. There are two paradigms for this direction: *top-down* pipelines [24,28,45,59,60] and *bottom-up* pipelines [19,27,67,72]. Our framework solves the *instance level* segmentation with *fine-grained attributes recognition*, which is much more challenging.

Fine-Grained Image Recognition. Lots of works [17,68] use the localization classification subnetwork to highlight finer feature regions and then achieves better classification results. Various approaches are proposed including attention [64], extra models [63,65] and deep filters [54,56]. Meanwhile, there are several works learning the end-to-end feature encoding via specific loss [46] or high-order feature interactions [36]. Our methods adopt object query and object mask as extra spatial cues to grasp multiscale image features, which lead to better fine-grained recognition results.

Transformer in Computer Vision. There are two research directions for vision transformer. The first is to replace CNN as a feature extractor. Compared with CNN, vision transformers [13,38,49] have more advantages in modeling long-range relation among the patch features. Moreover, they show better performance and higher capacity among the downstream tasks. The second design is to use the object query representation. DETR [2] models the object detection task as a set prediction problem with object queries. The following works [8,66,74] explore the locality of the learning process to improve the performance of DETR. Meanwhile, there are also several works using object queries to solve more complex tasks [30,32,55,62,70]. Our work is inspired by these works, which also uses a transformer architecture to unify and simplify human fashion task. Thus, our main contributions lie in the second part of vision transformer. However, our method can be adapted with vision transformer backbone [38].

3 Method

In this section, we will first review the related works using object query and present our method's key insights and motivations. Then we briefly describe our Fashionformer and detail the design of our proposed two-stream query learning framework for both object query and attribute query. Finally, we describe the training and inference procedures.

3.1 Overview of Previous Work

Query based models. DETR [2] firstly introduces the concept of object query which is used as the input of transformer decoder to build one by one mapping

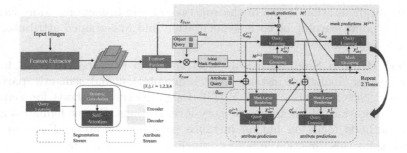

Fig. 3. Fashionformer contains three parts. (1) a feature extractor to extract multiscale features and then fuse these feature into one high resolution. (2) segmentation stream to generate segmentation masks and labels. It takes the object queries and initial mask as inputs and directly outputs refined mask and object queries interactively. (3) attribute stream to obtain the attribute predictions. It takes attribute queries, mask predictions and multiscale features as inputs and outputs the attribute prediction. (Color figure online)

on objects in the scene. Various approaches in different tasks [9,55,74] prove the effectiveness of such design including segmentation and detection. The Mask-Former [8,9] shows that the pure mask based classification can solve both semantic and instance level segmentation problems. Meanwhile, several works [47,66] show that adopting self-attention on proposal level features with their corresponding object queries can also achieve robust performance. For both aspects, the critical component is the design of object query and interaction with feature maps from backbone.

Motivation of Our Method. As stated in Sect. 1, recent works [25,39] on fashion analysis have several shortcomings. In this work, we seek a new baseline for unified fashion analysis to solve both segmentation and attribute recognition jointly. Motivated by the recent process of query based models, a natural question emerges: *can a unified model improves both instance segmentation and attribute recognition, despite the goals of these two tasks being different?* Such significant gaps between two tasks have already existed in the results of previous work [25]. Our insights are: Firstly, we add an extra attribute query with a residual like learning with object query to balance the conflicts of two tasks. Secondly, since both queries share the same instance masks, we decouple the query feature learning via designing specific modules for each task, which results in a two-stream decoder. We detail the design in the following sections.

3.2   Fashionformer as a Unified Baseline

Feature extractor. We first extract image features for each input image using a feature extractor. It contains a backbone network (Convolution Network [22] or Vision Transformer [38]) with Feature Pyramid Network [33] as neck. This results in a set of multiscale features $\{X_i, ..\}$ where $i = 1, 2, 3, 4$ are indexes of different scales. Then we sum up all the feature pyramids into one high resolution feature map X_{fuse} which follows the design of [26]. Moreover, we follow the common design of DETR-like models [2, 48, 66] to add position embeddings on the X_{fuse}. We omit this operation for simple illustration.

Meanwhile, we keep the multiscale features $\{X_i, ..\}$ for further usage. This process is shown in the gray region of Fig. 3. We denote the *object query feature* as the corresponding feature from feature extractor (shown in black line, X_{fuse}) via mask grouping, which is used in segmentation stream. We denote the *attribute query features* as corresponding feature generated by Multi-Layer Rending which is used in attribute stream. We detail the process further.

Initial Object Query. Following previous works [47, 66], the initial weights of object queries are directly obtained from the weights of initial decoder prediction. We adopt one 1×1 convolution layer to obtain the initial instance masks M_0. The kernel weights are the query weights. Such initialization shows better convergence. The object queries Q_{obj} are in $N \times d$ where N denotes the query number ($N = 100$ by default) and d is the hidden dimension ($d = 256$ by default, which is the same as DETR [2]).

Two-Stream Decoder Architecture. As shown in the yellow region of the Fig. 3, we adopt a two-stream design for both segmentation and attribute recognition. In particular, the attribute recognition module is appended to the segmentation module. Since most detection transformers [2, 9, 66] have cascaded decoder design to converge, we keep the same strategy via repeating the both modules into a cascaded decoder. In each step, the segmentation module directly outputs the binary segmentation masks and mask classification results while the recognition module outputs the attribute probability maps. We use index j to represent step number. All the results are supervised with specific loss functions during the training.

3.3   Linking Object Query and Attributes Query

Adding Extra Attribute Query. Rather than directly learning the attribute query from the object query via a multi-layer fully connected network, we present an extra attribute query design where we initialize a learnable embedding Q_{atr} with the same shape as Q_{obj}. For each step j in the two-stream decoder, we add both queries together as the new attribute query:

$$Q_{atr\_add}^{j-1} = Q_{atr}^{j-1} + Q_{obj}^{j-1}. \tag{1}$$

When $j = 1$ for the initial stage ($j \in \{1, 2, 3\}$), we denote $Q_{atr} = Q_{atr}^0$, $Q_{obj} = Q_{obj}^0$ in the following sections.

Multi-layer Rendering (MLR). This module takes previous multi-level features $\{X_i, ...\}, i = 1, 2, 3, 4$ (blue arrows in Fig. 3) and mask predictions $M^j - 1$ (red arrows in Fig. 3) from the previous stage as the inputs. It outputs a refined attribute query feature X_{atr}^j. We first resize the M^{j-1} into different scales

$(i = 1, 2, 3, 4)$ and then perform multi-level grouping with multi-level features X_i as following:

$$X_{i,atr}^{j} = \sum_{u}^{W_i} \sum_{v}^{H_i} M^{j-1}(u, v, i) \cdot X_i(u, v), i \in \{1, 2, 3, 4\}, \tag{2}$$

where j is the interaction number, W_i and H_i are the height and width of the corresponding features X_i, u and v are the spatial index of features. Then we obtain a set of features $X_{i,atr}^{j}$ with the same shape of attribute queries. Then we adopt one MLP-like to fuse these queries where it contains one fully connected layer, one Layer Norm [50] and one relu activation layer as:

$$X_{atr}^{j} = MLP(Concat(X_{atr}^{1,j}, ..X_{atr}^{i,j})), i \in \{1, 2, 3, 4\}. \tag{3}$$

This operation is shown in orange nodes in Fig. 3. The final refined attribute query feature X_{atr}^{j} will be the input of attribute stream for attribute query learning. In Sect. 4, we find this module significantly improves the attribute recognition results.

Decoupled Query Learning. For object query feature, we mainly follow the design of previous works [47,66]. The object query feature X_{obj}^{j-1} is obtained from the mask-based grouping from the previous mask prediction and feature map X_{fuse} (Mask Grouping in green nodes) where:

$$X_{obj}^{j-1} = \sum_{u}^{W} \sum_{v}^{H} M^{j-1}(u, v) \cdot X_{fuse}(u, v). \tag{4}$$

Then, following [47,48,66], we perform a Dynamic Convolution (DC) to refine input queries Q_{obj}^{j-1} with the object query features X_{obj}^{j}. The motivation of DC is to encode instance-wise features into each object query for fast convergence. This is **not** our contribution.

$$Q_{obj}^{j-1} = DC(X_{obj}^{j}, Q_{obj}^{j-1}), \tag{5}$$

where the dynamic convolution uses the query features X_{obj}^{j} to re-weight input queries Q_{obj}^{j-1}. To be more specific, $DynamicConv$ uses object query features X_{obj}^{j} to generate gating parameters via MLP and multiply back to the original query input Q_{obj}^{j-1}. For attribute branch, we adopt the same procedure:

$$Q_{atr}^{j-1} = DC(X_{atr}^{j}, Q_{atr\_add}^{j-1}), \tag{6}$$

where X_{atr}^{j} is the *attribute query feature* from the MLR. Note that both DC operations have independent parameters and learned in a separate manner. In this way, both streams are decoupled and lead to better attribute recognition results.

We adopt the same design [66] by learning gating functions to update the refined queries including both object queries and attributes queries. The DC operation is shown as follows:

$$\hat{Q}_u^{j-1} = gate_x(X_u^j)X_u^j + gate_q(X_u^j)Q_u^{j-1}, u \in \{obj, atr\}, \tag{7}$$

where $gate$ is implemented with a fully connected (FC) layers followed by Layer-Norm (LN), and a sigmoid layer. We adopt two different gate functions, including $gate_x$ and $gate_q$. The former is to weight the query features, while the latter is to weight corresponding queries. After that, one self-attention layer with feed forward layers [50,51] is used to learn the correspondence among each query. This operation leads to the full correlation among queries shown as follows:

$$Q_u^j = FFN(MHSA(\hat{Q}_u^{j-1}) + \hat{Q}_u^{j-1}), u \in \{obj, atr\}, \tag{8}$$

where $MHSA$ means Multi Head Self Attention, FFN is the Feed Forward Network that is commonly used in current vision transformers [2,13]. The output refined query sets contain Q_{obj}^j and Q_{atr}^j. Both query learning works independently, shown in blue nodes in Fig. 3. The main reason for using independent query learning is the optimization goal. The attribute query for attribute prediction is *a multi-label classification problem*, while the object query for segmentation is *a single label classification problem*.

Generating Mask and Attributes Prediction. Finally, the refined masks are obtained via dot product between the refined queries Q_{obj}^j and the input features X_{fuse}. For mask classification, we adopt two feed forward layers on Q_{obj}^j and directly output the class scores. For mask segmentation, we also adopt two feed forward layers on Q_{obj}^j and then we perform the inner product between learned queries and features X_{fuse} to generate stage i object masks. These masks will be used for the next step $j + 1$.

For attribute prediction, we also adopt several feed forward layers on Q_{atr}^j and use the outputs with a sigmoid activation function as final output. The process of these equations will be repeated several times. The iteration number is set to 3 by default. All the inter mask predictions are refined and optimized during the training.

3.4   Training and Inference

Loss Functions. We mainly follow the design of previous works [2,9,51] to use bipartite matching as a cost by considering both mask and classification results. After the bipartite matching, we apply a loss jointly considering mask prediction and classification for object queries. In particular, we apply focal loss [34] on both classification and mask prediction. We also adopt dice loss [41] on mask predictions. For attribute queries, we follow the default design of the Attirbute Mask R-CNN and the prediction is supervised in one hot format, which is the default setting of multi-label classification. It is a binary multi-label classification loss. The total loss can be written as follows:

$$\mathcal{L}_j = \lambda_{cls} \cdot \mathcal{L}_{cls} + \lambda_{mask} \cdot \mathcal{L}_{mask} + \lambda_{atr} \cdot \mathcal{L}_{atr}. \tag{9}$$

Note that the losses are applied to each stage $\mathcal{L}_{final} = \sum_j^N \mathcal{L}_j$, where N is the total stages applied to the framework. We adopt $N = 3$ and all λs are set to 1 by default.

Inference. We directly get the output masks from the corresponding queries according to their sorted scores, which are obtained from the mask classification branch. Since object queries and attribute queries are in the one-by-one mapping manner. We obtain the attribute predictions with 0.5 threshold via a sigmoid function from attribute prediction.

4 Experiment

4.1 Settings

Dataset. We carry out our experiments on Fashionpedia [25], ModaNet [69] and DeepFashion [39] dataset. Fashionpedia is a new challenging fashion dataset which contains 45,632 images for training and 1,158 images for validation. ModaNet contains 52,254 images for training. Since the online server of ModaNet is closed, we randomly sample 4,000 images from the training dataset for testing. DeepFashion datasets have 6,817 images for training and 3,112 images for testing. For both ModaNet and DeepFashion datasets, we retrain the several representative baselines [21,48,66] for fair comparison. We use the challenging Fashionpedia dataset for ablation and analysis, since it contains both segmentation and attribute labels. We only report the instance segmentation results on the two remaining datasets.

Table 1. Ablation studies and analysis on Fahsionpedia dataset set with ResNet50 as backbone. DC: Dynamic Convolution. RD: Residual Addition. MLR: Multi-Layer Rendering. N: Number of decoder layers.

RD	DC	MLR	N=1	I=3	AP^{mask}_{IoU}	$AP^{mask}_{IoU+F_1}$
✓	✓	✓	-	✓	**33.2**	**29.2**
-	✓	✓	-	✓	33.0	27.0
✓	-	✓	-	✓	32.1	27.5
✓	✓	-	-	✓	33.0	26.5
✓	✓	✓	✓	-	29.1	25.8
-	✓	-	-	✓	30.1	-

(a) Effect of each component.

Setting	AP^{mask}_{IoU}	$AP^{mask}_{IoU+F_1}$
NL=1	32.2	27.5
NL=2	33.1	28.6
NL=4	33.2	**29.2**

(b) Ablation on design of MLR. NL: number of layers in MLR.

Setting	AP^{mask}_{IoU}	$AP^{mask}_{IoU+F_1}$	Param(M)
Shared Query	33.4	27.6	36.2
Individual Query	33.3	**29.1**	37.7

(c) Decoupled query learning. The Shared Query use the same object query via a MLP to generate attribute query.

Implementation Details. We implement our models in PyTorch [43] with MMDetection toolbox [5]. We use the distributed training framework with 8 GPUs. *For Fashionpedia dataset*, we adopt similar settings as the original work. We use large scale jittering that resizes an image to a random ratio between [0.5, 2.0] of the target input image size. ResNet-50, ResNet-101 [22] and Swin-Transformer [38] are used as the backbone network and the remaining layers use Xavier [18] initialization. The optimizer is AdamW [40] with weight decay 0.0001. The training batch size is set to 16 and all models are trained with 8 GPUs. We adopt 12 epochs training (one-third of $1 \times$ schedule by default, 12 epochs in original size.) for ablation studies. We empirically found more training epochs leads to better results. All the models adopt the single scale inference. *For both ModaNet and DeepFashion dataset*, we follow the same setting from COCO [35] for fair comparison. Note that since both datasets have no attribute labels, we treat the mask classification labels as one attribute without the modification of network architecture. We present more implementation details in appendix.

Metrics. Following previous works, we adopt mask based mean average precision (AP_{IoU}^{mask}) which is the default COCO setting for instance segmentation evaluation. Moreover, we also adopt mAP that also consider F1-score ($AP_{IoU+F_1}^{mask}$) for joint evaluating segmentation and attribute recognition. This is the **main metric** for comparison. The GFlops are obtained with $3 \times 1020 \times 1020$ inputs following the original work [25]. Moreover, we also report the gap G between AP_{IoU}^{mask} and $AP_{IoU+F_1}^{mask}$ since the latter is more challenging.

4.2 Ablation Studies

Effectiveness Analysis of Each Component. In Table 1a, we explore the effectiveness of each component in our Fashsionformer. Compared with instance segmentation baseline (the last row), our method (the first row) achieves significant improvements on instance segmentation (3.1%). This indicates the effectiveness of our framework that the joint learning leads to better segmentation results. It means fine-grained attribute recognition can improve the fashion classification. Removing RD leads to inferior results on attribute recognition (about 2.0% drop) which means the mask classification conflicts with attribute recognition. Removing DC also leads to bad results since the model does not converge which is also observed in previous works [47,66]. Moreover, from the first row and the fourth row, we find that adding MLR leads to a significant improvement (2.7%) on attribute recognition *without* hurting the performance of instance segmentation. MLR explores the multi-level features to make the attribute query features. This leads to a more distinctive query representation. Decreasing the number of decoder layers leads to a significant drop (from 33.2% to 29.1 %) which means more steps are needed for the decoder. However, adding more steps in decoder will not increase performance ($I = 4$, 33.3%). Details can be found in the appendix.

Ablation on Design of MLR Module. In Table 1b, we explore the layer number that affects the final attribute recognition performance. We increase the number in a top-down manner (low resolution to high resolution). As shown in that table, we find increasing the number of layers can lead to better results. This proves that better attribute recognition needs multi-level feature representation. Moreover, it only takes *3% GFlops* increase when appending the MLR.

Ablation on Design of Decoupled Query Learning. We also explore the decoupled query learning in Eq. 5, Eq. 6 and Eq. 8. We find using independent dynamic convolution and self-attention modules can lead to better results than shared query learning where both Eq. 5 and Eq. 6 share *the same parameters*.

Table 2. Comparison with recent representative methods on Fashionpedia.

Method	backbone	AP^{mask}_{IoU}
Mask-RCNN [21]	ResNet50	30.3
CondInst [48]	ResNet50	26.6
QueryInst [16]	ResNet50	31.7
Ours	ResNet50	**33.2**

(a) Comparison on recent box based approaches.

Method	backbone	AP^{mask}_{IoU}	schedule
K-Net [66]	ResNet50	30.3	12e
MaskFormer [9]	ResNet50	31.4	12e
Our	ResNet50	**33.2**	12e
K-Net [66]	Swin-b	46.4	3×
Our	Swin-b	**49.5**	3×

(b) Comparison on recent Transformer based models. 12e means 12 epochs training.

Table 3. Benchmark results on Fashionpedia. We report AP^{mask}_{IoU} , $AP^{mask}_{IoU+F_1}$ (main metric) and their gaps G. Swin-b means Swin-base [38]. Our methods achieve significant improvement over these three metrics.

Method	Backbone	Schedule	GFlops	Params (M)	AP^{Mask}_{IoU} ↑	$AP^{Mask}_{IoU+F_1}$ ↑	G ↓
Attirbute-mask R-CNN	R50-FPN	1×	296.7	46.4	34.3	25.5	8.8
		2×			38.1	28.5	9.6
		3×			39.2	29.5	9.7
Attirbute-mask R-CNN	R101-FPN	1×	374.3	65.4	36.7	27.6	9.1
		2×			39.2	29.8	9.4
		3×			40.7	31.4	9.3
Attirbute-mask R-CNN	SpineNet-49	6×	267.2	40.8	39.6	31.4	8.2
	SpineNet-96		314.0	55.2	41.2	31.8	9.4
	SpineNet-143		498.0	79.2	43.1	33.3	9.8
Fashionformer	R50-FPN	1×	198.0	37.7	**40.3**	**36.6**	3.7
		3×			**42.5**	**39.4**	3.1
Fashionformer	R101-FPN	1×	275.7	56.6	**43.2**	**40.5**	**2.7**
		3×			**45.6**	**42.8**	**2.8**
Attirbute-Mask R-CNN	Swin-b	3×	508.3	107.3	47.5	40.6	6.9
Fashionformer	Swin-b	3×	442.5	100.6	**49.5**	**46.5**	3.0

This verifies our design of two-stream architecture and shows that both tasks need decoupled query feature learning to avoid the conflicts.

4.3 Comparison with State-of-the-Art Methods

Comparison with Box-Based Approaches on Fashionpedia. In Table 2a, we compare several representative results on Fahsionpedia dataset using 12 epochs training. Our method achieves better result than recent instance segmentation methods including dynamic convolution based [48], query based approaches [16]. This proves our query design is a better choice for fashion analysis.

Table 4. Benchmark results on ModaNet [69] (a) and DeepFashion [39] (b).

Method	backbone	AP_{IoU}^{mask}	GFlops
Mask R-CNN [21]	ResNet50	51.8	264.8
Mask R-CNN [21]	Swin-b	54.8	508.8
CondInst [48]	ResNet50	54.9	234.2
K-Net [66]	ResNet50	57.9	198.5
QueryInst [16]	ResNet50	53.6	469.2
MaskFormer [9]	ResNet50	51.5	191.5
Fashionformer	ResNet50	62.5	198.0

(a) Results on ModaNet dataset.

Method	backbone	AP_{IoU}^{mask}	GFlops
Mask R-CNN [21]	ResNet50	56.9	264.8
Mask R-CNN [21]	Swin-b	61.8	508.8
CondInst [48]	ResNet50	58.6	234.2
K-Net [66]	ResNet50	62.0	198.5
QueryInst [16]	ResNet50	61.4	469.2
Fashionformer	ResNet50	64.4	198.0

(b) Results on DeepFashion dataset.

Comparison with Transformer Based Models on Fashionpedia. We also compare several recent pure mask based approaches in Table 2b. All the methods use the same codebase with the same setting. Our method outperforms previous works [9,66] by a large margin under various settings (both ResNet and Swin Transformer).

Results on Fashionpedia Benchmark. In Table 3, we compare our model results with previous state-of-the-art approaches. Models that use the Swin Transformer are re-trained in our settings. We compare our methods with Attribute-Mask R-CNN in the different settings. In particular, using ResNet50 backbone, our method outperforms it by 6% mAP_{IoU}^{mask} and nearly 10% $mAP_{IoU+F_1}^{mask}$. The gap G is decreased nearly 50%. When adopting the ResNet101 backbone, our method still achieves nearly 4% mAP_{IoU}^{mask} gain and 10% $mAP_{IoU+F_1}^{mask}$ gain. It even outperforms the more complex backbone SpineNet [14] with more training iterations. Finally, we equip our method with the Swin-base backbone, it also outperforms the Attirbute-Mask RCNN by 5.7% mAP_{IoU}^{mask} and achieves the best performance. In the above three metrics, the improvements on $mAP_{IoU+F_1}^{mask}$ are more significant which means our model can achieve much better attribute recognition. This indicates the effectiveness of our framework including two stream decoder design and the proposed Multi-Layer Rendering module.

Results on ModaNet benchmark. We further report results on the ModaNet benchmark in Table 4a. Our Fashionformer achieves the best performance among these works with less GFlops. Note that our work with ResNet50 backbone even outperforms Mask-RCNN with Swin-base backbone [38]. This indicates the effectiveness of our approach.

Results on DeepFashion Benchmark. In Table 4b, we compare our methods with recent representative works [9,66]. Our works also achieve state-of-the-art results using ResNet50 backbone which further shows the generalization ability of our approach.

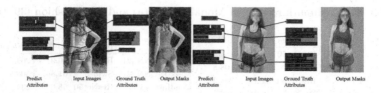

Fig. 4. Visualization results on Fashionpedia dataset. Our method obtains good segmentation results and almost right attribute predictions. Best view it on screen.

Fig. 5. Visual comparison results on ModaNet dataset. Our method has better consistent segmentation results. Best view it on screen and zoom in.

4.4   Analysis and Visualization

Results Visualization. In Fig. 4, we present several visualization examples on Fashionpedia using ResNet101 backbone. Our model can predict perfect instance segmentation masks and almost right attributes. Moreover, we compare our model on the ModaNet dataset with other methods. Our model achieves better segmentation results, including more consistent masks and correct labels. More visualization examples can be found in the appendix file (Fig. 5).

Detailed Comparison with Attribute-Mask R-CNN. In Table 5, we show the detailed comparison with Attribute-Mask R-CNN. Although our backbone is weak (ResNet101 vs. SpineNet-143), our method can achieve better results in most detailed metrics, including AP75, AP50, APl, and APm. However, our method leads to bad results on small objects. The main reason is that our work only considers the single scale feature representation with a simple fusion strategy. In the case of detailed categories, we find that our model achieves better results on "outerwear" categories because our method directly outputs masks on a high resolution feature. Moreover, for AP_{IoU+F_1}, our method achieves better results. For "part" categories, our method obtains similar results since most part objects are small. However, our method has *better* attribute recognition results for AP50 and AP75.

Table 5. Per super-category results. Result format follows [mAP$_{IoU}^{mask}$ / mAP$_{IoU+F_1}^{mask}$]. AM-RCNN means Attribute-Mask R-CNN with SpineNet-143 backbone. Our results are obtained with ResNet101 backbone. We follow the same COCO sub-metrics for overall and three super-categories for apparel objects.

Category	AP	AP50	AP75	APl	APm	APs
Overall (AM-RCNN)	43.1 / 33.3	60.3/42.3	47.6/37.6	50.0/35.4	40.2/27.0	17.3/9.4
Outerwear	64.1/40.7	77.4/49.0	72.9/46.2	67.1/43.0	44.4/29.3	19.0/4.4
Parts	19.3 / 13.4	35.5/20.8	18.4 / 14.4	28.3 / 14.5	23.9/16.4	12.5/9.8
Accessory	56.1 / –	77.9 /–	63.9 /–	57.5 /–	60.5/–	25.0/–
Overall (Fashionformer)	45.7/42.8	58.2/49.7	45.7/43.3	63.3/48.9	43.9 / 31.8	11.4 /6.5
Outerwear	72.7/52.4	78.7/56.5	73.5/53.2	76.9/55.9	48.3/31.5	8.4/2.2
Parts	19.2/20.3	31.8/30.1	17.2/19.7	42.6/29.0	29.8/26.2	8.2/7.1
Accessory	56.4/–	75.0 /–	58.6/–	73.4/–	60.9/–	18.1/–

5   Conclusion

This paper presents a new baseline named Fashionformer for joint fashion segmentation and attribute recognition. Using both object and attribute queries, we present a unified solution in the case of task association for fashion segmentation and attribute recognition. We design a two-stream query update framework in the decoder part with a novel Muti-Layer Rendering module for better attribute recognition. Extensive experiments on the Fashionpedia dataset show the reciprocal benefits on both tasks, where their gap is minimized significantly. We achieve state-of-the-art results on three datasets (Fahsionpedia, ModaNet, and Deepfashion) with fewer GFlops and parameters. Our models also show better results than the recent transformer models in various settings. We hope our method can serve as a new baseline for human fashion understanding.

References

1. Bolya, D., Zhou, C., Xiao, F., Lee, Y.J.: Yolact: Real-time instance segmentation. In: ICCV (2019)
2. Carion, N., Massa, F., Synnaeve, G., Usunier, N., Kirillov, A., Zagoruyko, S.: End-to-end object detection with transformers. In: Vedaldi, A., Bischof, H., Brox, T., Frahm, J.-M. (eds.) ECCV 2020. LNCS, vol. 12346, pp. 213–229. Springer, Cham (2020). https://doi.org/10.1007/978-3-030-58452-8_13
3. Chen, H., Sun, K., Tian, Z., Shen, C., Huang, Y., Yan, Y.: BlendMask: Top-down meets bottom-up for instance segmentation. In: CVPR (2020)
4. Chen, K., et al.: Hybrid task cascade for instance segmentation. In: CVPR (2019)
5. Chen, K., et al.: Mmdetection: Open mmlab detection toolbox and benchmark. arXiv preprint arXiv:1906.07155 (2019)
6. Chen, L.-C., Zhu, Y., Papandreou, G., Schroff, F., Adam, H.: Encoder-decoder with atrous separable convolution for semantic image segmentation. In: Ferrari, V., Hebert, M., Sminchisescu, C., Weiss, Y. (eds.) ECCV 2018. LNCS, vol. 11211, pp. 833–851. Springer, Cham (2018). https://doi.org/10.1007/978-3-030-01234-2_49

7. Chen, X., Girshick, R., He, K., Dollár, P.: Tensormask: A foundation for dense object segmentation. In: ICCV (2019)
8. Cheng, B., Misra, I., Schwing, A.G., Kirillov, A., Girdhar, R.: Masked-attention mask transformer for universal image segmentation. arXiv (2021)
9. Cheng, B., Schwing, A.G., Kirillov, A.: Per-pixel classification is not all you need for semantic segmentation. arXiv (2021)
10. Dai, J., He, K., Li, Y., Ren, S., Sun, J.: Instance-sensitive fully convolutional networks. In: Leibe, B., Matas, J., Sebe, N., Welling, M. (eds.) ECCV 2016. LNCS, vol. 9910, pp. 534–549. Springer, Cham (2016). https://doi.org/10.1007/978-3-319-46466-4_32
11. De Brabandere, B., Neven, D., Van Gool, L.: Semantic instance segmentation with a discriminative loss function. arXiv preprint arXiv:1708.02551 (2017)
12. Dong, B., Zeng, F., Wang, T., Zhang, X., Wei, Y.: Solq: Segmenting objects by learning queries. arXiv preprint arXiv:2106.02351 (2021)
13. Dosovitskiy, A., et al.: An image is worth 16×16 words: Transformers for image recognition at scale. arXiv preprint arXiv:2010.11929 (2020)
14. Du, X., et al.: Spinenet: Learning scale-permuted backbone for recognition and localization. In: CVPR, pp. 11592–11601 (2020)
15. Fang, H.S., Lu, G., Fang, X., Xie, J., Tai, Y.W., Lu, C.: Weakly and semi supervised human body part parsing via pose-guided knowledge transfer. In: CVPR (2018)
16. Fang, Y., et al.: Instances as queries. arXiv preprint arXiv:2105.01928 (2021)
17. Fu, J., Zheng, H., Mei, T.: Look closer to see better: Recurrent attention convolutional neural network for fine-grained image recognition. In: CVPR (2017)
18. Glorot, X., Bengio, Y.: Understanding the difficulty of training deep feedforward neural networks. In: Proceedings of the Thirteenth International Conference on Artificial Intelligence and Statistics, pp. 249–256. JMLR Workshop and Conference Proceedings (2010)
19. Gong, K., Liang, X., Li, Y., Chen, Y., Yang, M., Lin, L.: Instance-level human parsing via part grouping network. In: Ferrari, V., Hebert, M., Sminchisescu, C., Weiss, Y. (eds.) ECCV 2018. LNCS, vol. 11208, pp. 805–822. Springer, Cham (2018). https://doi.org/10.1007/978-3-030-01225-0_47
20. Hariharan, B., Arbeláez, P., Girshick, R., Malik, J.: Simultaneous detection and segmentation. In: Fleet, D., Pajdla, T., Schiele, B., Tuytelaars, T. (eds.) ECCV 2014. LNCS, vol. 8695, pp. 297–312. Springer, Cham (2014). https://doi.org/10.1007/978-3-319-10584-0_20
21. He, K., Gkioxari, G., Dollár, P., Girshick, R.: Mask r-cnn. In: ICCV (2017)
22. He, K., Zhang, X., Ren, S., Sun, J.: Deep residual learning for image recognition. In: CVPR (2016)
23. Huang, Z., Huang, L., Gong, Y., Huang, C., Wang, X.: Mask scoring r-cnn. In: CVPR (2019)
24. Ji, R., et al.: Learning semantic neural tree for human parsing. In: Vedaldi, A., Bischof, H., Brox, T., Frahm, J.-M. (eds.) ECCV 2020. LNCS, vol. 12358, pp. 205–221. Springer, Cham (2020). https://doi.org/10.1007/978-3-030-58601-0_13
25. Jia, M., et al.: Fashionpedia: Ontology, segmentation, and an attribute localization dataset. In: Vedaldi, A., Bischof, H., Brox, T., Frahm, J.-M. (eds.) ECCV 2020. LNCS, vol. 12346, pp. 316–332. Springer, Cham (2020). https://doi.org/10.1007/978-3-030-58452-8_19
26. Kirillov, A., Girshick, R., He, K., Dollár, P.: Panoptic feature pyramid networks. In: CVPR (2019)
27. Li, J., et al.: Multiple-human parsing in the wild. arXiv preprint arXiv:1705.07206 (2017)

28. Li, Q., Arnab, A., Torr, P.H.: Holistic, instance-level human parsing. arXiv preprint arXiv:1709.03612 (2017)
29. Li, X., et al.: Improving semantic segmentation via decoupled body and edge supervision. In: Vedaldi, A., Bischof, H., Brox, T., Frahm, J.-M. (eds.) ECCV 2020. LNCS, vol. 12362, pp. 435–452. Springer, Cham (2020). https://doi.org/10.1007/978-3-030-58520-4_26
30. Li, X., Xu, S., Yang, Y., Cheng, G., Tong, Y., Tao, D.: Panoptic-partformer: Learning a unified model for panoptic part segmentation. arxiv (2022)
31. Li, X., Zhang, L., You, A., Yang, M., Yang, K., Tong, Y.: Global aggregation then local distribution in fully convolutional networks. In: BMVC (2019)
32. Li, X., et al.: Video k-net: A simple, strong, and unified baseline for video segmentation. In: CVPR (2022)
33. Lin, T.Y., Dollár, P., Girshick, R.B., He, K., Hariharan, B., Belongie, S.J.: Feature pyramid networks for object detection. In: CVPR (2017)
34. Lin, T.Y., Goyal, P., Girshick, R., He, K., Dollár, P.: Focal loss for dense object detection. In: ICCV (2017)
35. Lin, T.-Y., et al.: Microsoft COCO: common objects in context. In: Fleet, D., Pajdla, T., Schiele, B., Tuytelaars, T. (eds.) ECCV 2014. LNCS, vol. 8693, pp. 740–755. Springer, Cham (2014). https://doi.org/10.1007/978-3-319-10602-1_48
36. Lin, T.Y., RoyChowdhury, A., Maji, S.: Bilinear cnn models for fine-grained visual recognition. In: ICCV, pp. 1449–1457 (2015)
37. Liu, S., et al.: Cross-domain human parsing via adversarial feature and label adaptation. In: AAAI (2018)
38. Liu, Z., et al.: Swin transformer: Hierarchical vision transformer using shifted windows. In: ICCV (2021)
39. Liu, Z., Luo, P., Qiu, S., Wang, X., Tang, X.: Deepfashion: Powering robust clothes recognition and retrieval with rich annotations. In: CVPR (June 2016)
40. Loshchilov, I., Hutter, F.: Decoupled weight decay regularization (2017)
41. Milletari, F., Navab, N., Ahmadi, S.: V-Net: Fully convolutional neural networks for volumetric medical image segmentation. In: 3DV (2016)
42. Neven, D., Brabandere, B.D., Proesmans, M., Gool, L.V.: Instance segmentation by jointly optimizing spatial embeddings and clustering bandwidth. In: CVPR (2019)
43. Paszke, A., et al.: Pytorch: An imperative style, high-performance deep learning library. arXiv preprint arXiv:1912.01703 (2019)
44. Ren, S., He, K., Girshick, R., Sun, J.: Faster r-cnn: Towards real-time object detection with region proposal networks. In: NeurIPS (2015)
45. Ruan, T., Liu, T., Huang, Z., Wei, Y., Wei, S., Zhao, Y.: Devil in the details: Towards accurate single and multiple human parsing. In: AAAI (2019)
46. Sun, M., Yuan, Y., Zhou, F., Ding, E.: Multi-attention multi-class constraint for fine-grained image recognition. In: Ferrari, V., Hebert, M., Sminchisescu, C., Weiss, Y. (eds.) ECCV 2018. LNCS, vol. 11220, pp. 834–850. Springer, Cham (2018). https://doi.org/10.1007/978-3-030-01270-0_49
47. Sun, P., et al.: SparseR-CNN: End-to-end object detection with learnable proposals. In: CVPR (2021)
48. Tian, Z., Shen, C., Chen, H.: Conditional convolutions for instance segmentation. arXiv preprint arXiv:2003.05664 (2020)
49. Touvron, H., Cord, M., Douze, M., Massa, F., Sablayrolles, A., Jégou, H.: Training data-efficient image transformers & distillation through attention. In: ICML. PMLR (2021)

50. Vaswani, A., et al.: Attention is all you need. arXiv preprint arXiv:1706.03762 (2017)
51. Wang, H., Zhu, Y., Adam, H., Yuille, A., Chen, L.C.: Max-deeplab: End-to-end panoptic segmentation with mask transformers. In: CVPR (2021)
52. Wang, W., Zhang, Z., Qi, S., Shen, J., Pang, Y., Shao, L.: Learning compositional neural information fusion for human parsing. In: ICCV (2019)
53. Wang, X., Kong, T., Shen, C., Jiang, Y., Li, L.: SOLO: Segmenting objects by locations. In: Vedaldi, A., Bischof, H., Brox, T., Frahm, J.-M. (eds.) ECCV 2020. LNCS, vol. 12363, pp. 649–665. Springer, Cham (2020). https://doi.org/10.1007/978-3-030-58523-5_38
54. Wang, Y., Morariu, V.I., Davis, L.S.: Learning a discriminative filter bank within a cnn for fine-grained recognition. In: CVPR, pp. 4148–4157 (2018)
55. Wang, Y., et al.: End-to-end video instance segmentation with transformers. In: CVPR (2021)
56. Xiao, T., Xu, Y., Yang, K., Zhang, J., Peng, Y., Zhang, Z.: The application of two-level attention models in deep convolutional neural network for fine-grained image classification. In: CVPR, pp. 842–850 (2015)
57. Yamaguchi, K., Kiapour, M.H., Ortiz, L.E., Berg, T.L.: Parsing clothing in fashion photographs. In: CVPR (2012)
58. Yamaguchi, K., Kiapour, M.H., Ortiz, L.E., Berg, T.L.: Retrieving similar styles to parse clothing. PAMI **37**(5), 1028–1040 (2014)
59. Yang, L., et al.: Renovating parsing R-CNN for accurate multiple human parsing. In: Vedaldi, A., Bischof, H., Brox, T., Frahm, J.-M. (eds.) ECCV 2020. LNCS, vol. 12357, pp. 421–437. Springer, Cham (2020). https://doi.org/10.1007/978-3-030-58610-2_25
60. Yang, L., Song, Q., Wang, Z., Jiang, M.: Parsing R-CNN for instance-level human analysis. In: CVPR (2019)
61. Yang, W., Luo, P., Lin, L.: Clothing co-parsing by joint image segmentation and labeling. In: CVPR, pp. 3182–3189 (2014)
62. Yuan, H., et al.: Polyphonicformer: Unified query learning for depth-aware video panoptic segmentation (2021)
63. Zhang, H., et al.: Spda-cnn: Unifying semantic part detection and abstraction for fine-grained recognition. In: CVPR, pp. 1143–1152 (2016)
64. Zhang, L., Huang, S., Liu, W., Tao, D.: Learning a mixture of granularity-specific experts for fine-grained categorization. In: ICCV, pp. 8331–8340 (2019)
65. Zhang, N., Donahue, J., Girshick, R., Darrell, T.: Part-based R-CNNs for fine-grained category detection. In: Fleet, D., Pajdla, T., Schiele, B., Tuytelaars, T. (eds.) ECCV 2014. LNCS, vol. 8689, pp. 834–849. Springer, Cham (2014). https://doi.org/10.1007/978-3-319-10590-1_54
66. Zhang, W., Pang, J., Chen, K., Loy, C.C.: K-net: Towards unified image segmentation. In: NeurIPS (2021)
67. Zhao, J., Li, J., Cheng, Y., Sim, T., Yan, S., Feng, J.: Understanding humans in crowded scenes: Deep nested adversarial learning and a new benchmark for multi-human parsing. In: MM (2018)
68. Zheng, H., Fu, J., Mei, T., Luo, J.: Learning multi-attention convolutional neural network for fine-grained image recognition. In: ICCV, pp. 5209–5217 (2017)
69. Zheng, S., Yang, F., Kiapour, M.H., Piramuthu, R.: Modanet: A large-scale street fashion dataset with polygon annotations. In: ACM Multimedia (2018)
70. Zhou, Q., et al.: Transvod: End-to-end video object detection with spatial-temporal transformers (2022)

71. Zhou, T., Wang, W., Konukoglu, E., Van Gool, L.: Rethinking semantic segmentation: A prototype view. In: CVPR (2022)
72. Zhou, T., Wang, W., Liu, S., Yang, Y., Van Gool, L.: Differentiable multi-granularity human representation learning for instance-aware human semantic parsing. In: CVPR (2021)
73. Zhou, T., Wang, W., Qi, S., Ling, H., Shen, J.: Cascaded human-object interaction recognition. In: CVPR, pp. 4263–4272 (2020)
74. Zhu, X., Su, W., Lu, L., Li, B., Wang, X., Dai, J.: Deformable detr: Deformable transformers for end-to-end object detection. In: ICLR (2020)

Semantic-Guided Multi-mask Image Harmonization

Xuqian Ren[1] and Yifan Liu[2(✉)]

[1] Beijing Institute of Technology, Beijing, China
[2] University of Adelaide, Adelaide, Australia
yifan.liu04@adelaide.edu.au

Abstract. Previous harmonization methods focus on adjusting one inharmonious region in an image based on an input mask. They may face problems when dealing with different perturbations on different semantic regions without available input masks. To deal with the problem that one image has been pasted with several foregrounds coming from different images and needs to harmonize them towards different domain directions without any mask as input, we propose a new semantic-guided multi-mask image harmonization task. Different from the previous single-mask image harmonization task, each inharmonious image is perturbed with different methods according to the semantic segmentation masks. Two challenging benchmarks, HScene and HLIP, are constructed based on 150 and 19 semantic classes, respectively. Furthermore, previous baselines focus on regressing the exact value for each pixel of the harmonized images. The generated results are in the 'black box' and cannot be edited. In this work, we propose a novel way to edit the inharmonious images by predicting a series of operator masks. The masks indicate the level and the position to apply a certain image editing operation, which could be the brightness, the saturation, and the color in a specific dimension. The operator masks provide more flexibility for users to edit the image further. Extensive experiments verify that the operator mask-based network can further improve those state-of-the-art methods which directly regress RGB images when the perturbations are structural. Experiments have been conducted on our constructed benchmarks to verify that our proposed operator mask-based framework can locate and modify the inharmonious regions in more complex scenes. Our code and models are available at https://github.com/XuqianRen/Semantic-guided-Multi-mask-Image-Harmonization.git.

Keywords: Multi-mask image harmonization · GAN · Image editing

1 Introduction

Image editing techniques play a more crucial role in our daily life. They have been widely used in advertisement propaganda, social media sharing, and digital

Supplementary Information The online version contains supplementary material available at https://doi.org/10.1007/978-3-031-19836-6_32.

entertainment. Furthermore, with the rapid expansion of electronic devices and image processing applications, such as PhotoShop and MeituPic, image composition has become a more accessible technique. However, without professional photo-editing experience, a fake composited image will have lower evaluation credibility due to its inharmonious color, texture, or illumination. Thus, image harmonization is an imperative process to improve composite image quality.

Previous image harmonization aims to improve the quality of image composition by matching the appearance between a pre-defined foreground region and background to make the whole composited image more realistic. The adjusted appearance can be color, brightness, contrast, etc. Deep-learning based methods [2,3] usually handle this task as an image-to-image translation task [8,14]. These methods have two limitations. First, these networks focus on the problem that one composite image only has one inharmonious region to change and do not consider the situation that the composite image may have multi-inharmonious regions with different kinds of perturbations but without masks to indicate. In a real application, the user may cut out the portraits from different photos and paste them on the same background. Second, the generated result is not explainable and editable, which is not flexible for users to further edit if they do not like the results generated by the automation output.

To solve these drawbacks, we propose a new setting named Semantic-guided Multi-Mask Image Harmonization(Sg-MMH), which aims to adjust the inharmonious regions according to their semantics. We construct two new benchmarks, named HScene and HLIP, which originated from public semantic segmentation datasets ADE20K [29] and LIP [5], separately. For each image, we randomly select several masks with different semantics to apply the perturbations. For the HScene, we focus on harmonizing various things and stuff in natural scenes, such as houses, lawns, and animals. And for the HLIP, we pay attention to adjusting the body parts and clothes of a person.

To realize the perturbation, we use Instagram filters, LAB perturb methods, blur perturbations to enrich disturbance scenarios, and apply different perturb functions to different regions randomly. That means the framework needs to harmonize the foreground regions towards different domains, which is a more challenging task.

Furthermore, we propose a new framework that can generate Operator Masks. Different from previous works that directly regress RGB images, we choose to generate operator masks for some pre-defined operators. These operator masks can simulate the manipulation functions in the image processing software. In this work, we define six feasible operator masks, and we multiply and add every two masks to each L, A, and B channel of inharmonious input images. Hence, each mask can be seen as an operation that can change the illumination, contrast, or color. The mask location indicates where to apply the operation, and the value of each pixel can be seen as the level each function is acted. The final generated mask is also editable and explainable, and it can locate the inharmonious region automatically. Our framework can be applied to any off-the-shelf backbones to adapt them to our task and make their output editable.

We summarize our contributions in three-fold:

- We propose a new setting that aims to simulate the situation that the foregrounds come from different images and need to be harmonized towards different domains. We propose two benchmarks, HScene and HLIP, to represent the scenery and person harmonization task separately. To enrich the training set, we perturb several foreground images with multiple semantic-guided masks on the fly.
- We propose a new framework to generate operator masks to simulate image editing operations in image processing software to harmonize images instead of generating each pixel separately in the training process. The masks indicate the level and the position to apply a certain operation, which could be the brightness, the saturation, and the color in a specific dimension.
- Quantitative and qualitative comparisons demonstrate that the proposed operator mask-based network can have a reasonable result on our multi-mask image harmonization benchmarks. It can also provide more explainable and editable outputs for further change.

2   Related Works

Image Harmonization: Traditional image harmonization methods concentrated on learning and adjusting statistical appearance between hand-crafted heuristics appearance features, such as [1,10,17,18,20–22]. Some of them have been adapted to image editing software. However, these methods are not very reliable when dealing with more complex situations. Recently several CNN networks started to use learning methods to make the harmonized image more reasonable. Zhu et al. [30] trained a discriminative model to rank the composite images according to their realism level and optimized the model by maximizing the output visual realism score. DIH [23] proposed the first end-to-end CNN network to produce harmonized images with auxiliary semantics prediction.

Since the remarkable effect of GAN in image-to-image translation [8,15,31], some GAN frameworks have also been proposed to facilitate image harmonization. S^2AM [4] considered the harmonization task as just changing the foreground appearance by keeping semantic information. So it used channel-wise and spatial-wise attention mechanisms to focus on the appearance changes in the foreground mask region. DoveNet [3] further conceived the image harmonization task as a domain transfer problem and hypothesized that the foreground and background of an inharmonious image are captured in different conditions. So, they chose to select the foreground objects in the datasets and perturbed their color or illumination to simulate an inharmonious composite, and trained the network to regress close to the original input image in a GAN framework with a domain verification discriminator. This is a good start to deeply researching harmonization tasks with a large dataset. Other methods also re-defined the image harmonization task to make this task more practical. BarginNet [2] formulated image harmonization as background-guided domain translation. They used a domain code extractor to extract foreground and background domain code and use background domain code to guide the foreground domain during translation. RainNet [13] treated image harmonization as a style transfer problem and extracted background style information, and applied it to the foreground. D-HT [6] used the strong power of Transformer to model long-range context information to perceive information for better harmonization. These methods all consider that only one foreground inharmonious region needs to be edited and directly generate and regress each pixel towards the target, which lacks interpretability. Instead, in our work, we resolve the image harmonization task using preset image editing operations to edit the inharmonious images. Specifically, we predict a series of operator masks to be applied to the inharmonious input. To tackle our proposed setting, we construct two benchmarks with semantic-guided perturbed regions that need to be adjusted in one composite image.

Photo Retouch: Photo Retouch aims to learn an automatic network to correct a raw image to a destinate expert-retouched one to enhance image quality. UEGAN [16] learned in an unsupervised fashion to realize image-to-image mapping. Deep Preset [7] realized color transfer by predicting various presets in a labeled reference photo and applied them to another image to blend and retouch a photo. Their filters are supervised and preset, however, in our framework, our filters are unsupervised and we only supervise the final harmonization output, so the filter style is not static and can be defined by users. Inspired by Deep Preset, we predict operator masks for pre-defined operations implicitly. The network can predict the position and level that each operation is applied to the picture and generate operator masks to simulate the manipulations.

3   Methods

3.1   Overview

Most image harmonization tasks try to solve the problem that a composite image comes from two pictures captured in different situations, which is a simple scene in image composition. In a more general case in our daily life, users may paste several foregrounds to one background image to make the picture meet their expectations. For example, users may cut the picture of a skirt from one picture, cut the picture of a hat from another picture, and then stick them to their portrait image. In this situation, the composite image needs to be changed in different directions to adjust the whole foreground harmonious with the background portrait. So in order to solve the problem, we propose a new setting to simulate this situation, named Semantic-guided Multi-Mask Image Harmonization(Sg-MMH) task, and construct two benchmarks, HScene and HLIP, for this task.

As shown in Fig. 1, our framework includes one generator, which contains an encoder-decoder structure and a retoucher, and a patch discriminator. First, the inharmonious image I_c is the input of our operator mask generator. I_c can

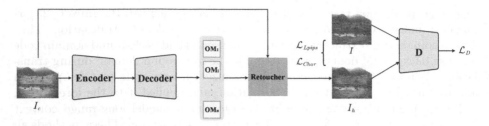

Fig. 1. This image shows the training pipeline of our framework. We first generate a composited image I_c guided by multiple semantic masks M from the original real image I, serving as the input image. The encode-decode structure generates operator masks. Then the operator masks OM will be used to retouch the composited image I_c and formulate I_h. The discriminator will compare I_h and I to make the output I_h harmonious.

be generated by perturbing selected regions according to the semantics of a natural or person image I as described in Sect. 3.2. The encoder in the generator can locate the inharmonious region automatically. The decoder aims to predict the operator masks according to the gap between the inharmonious region and natural image distributions. These two structures can be implemented by any off-the-shelf backbone used in image harmonization tasks in previous research, such as [2,3,6,13]. The output operator masks from the decoder will pass a retouch module, in which the predefined operators are applied to I_c according to the predicted locations and levels to harmonize the composited image I_c and generate a harmonious image I_h. We supervised the network by minimizing the difference between I_h and the ground truth harmonious image I. A binary regression loss ($\mathcal{L}_{Char}$) and a perceptual loss ($\mathcal{L}_{Lpips}$) will be applied to train the model and will be further introduced in Sect. 3.4. The discriminator we use is a patch discriminator. In this way, we force the discriminator to focus on some tiny objects and details.

In the following sections, we will first introduce how we construct our benchmarks and gradually illustrate the detailed structure of our framework and loss functions.

3.2   Multi-mask Image Harmonization

We define a new task called Semantic-guided Multi-mask Image Harmonization (Sg-MMH). The input is a composited image in which foregrounds are pasted from different pictures, and the background is another real image. The output is a harmonious image in which the foregrounds have been adjusted to the background.

We build two benchmarks, **HScene** and **HLIP**. And their foregrounds have been perturbed according to their semantics. The details are as follows:

HScene: The harmonized images and the semantic masks of HScene are from ADE20K Dataset. ADE20K Dataset [28, 29] consists of natural images with high accuracy pixel level human annotations. There are 150 semantic classes, such as animals, bulidings, sky, trees, etc. There are 20k/2k/30k images in the training/ validation/ testing set. Since the ground truth semantic label of the testing set is not released, we use the total images in the train set to construct our train set and use the validation set as our test set, and neglect some images with no foreground to construct HScene.

HLIP: HLIP constructed on the basis of The Look into Person(LIP) dataset, which is a large-scale dataset that focuses on the semantic understanding of a person. It contains 50462 images with elaborated pixel-wise annotations of 19 semantic human part labels, such as dress, coat, hair and face. The original training set contains 30462 images, and the validation images contain 10k pictures. Since the images contain poses, views, occlusions, appearances, and resolution variations, they can simulate real-world portrait scenarios. To construct HLIP, we also perturb the original train set as our training set, perturb the validation set as our test set, and neglect some images without proper foreground.

The statistics of training and testing images in the original datasets and our two constructed benchmarks are shown in Table 1.

Table 1. The statistics of the original datasets and our two constructed benchmarks.

Benchmark name	ADE20 K	LIP	HScene	HLIP
Training set	20210	30462	20196	30385
Testing set	2000	10000	2000	9972

Previous works often use fixed fake foregrounds during training. So in this work, we randomly select $0.2 \times len(classes) + 1$ perturb regions as the foreground and disturb them with several structural perturbations. The *classes* number depends on the total semantic regions in each image. First, we mainly use Instagram filters [19], which is a set of camera filters usually used in image-editing software. We implement them by a python API called pilgram. Here we use the total of 23 Instagram filters and randomly select one to perturb one region. Meanwhile, we superimpose a filter from pilgram.css to each region with a probability of 0.5. So in each benchmark, we apply different disturbations to multiple regions randomly. These Instagram filters can represent most of the common filters in image processing applications, and most of them can change the color, illumination, and saturation of the foreground structurally. Second, to enrich the perturbation methods, we also add some other perturb methods to add more scenarios. One is to simulate the situation that a high-resolution foreground is pasted on a low-resolution background. The blurring process is conducted by using several blur or noise methods, which are usually used in image super-resolution tasks to blur the real image I and the background of I_c, and try to regress the network to blur the foreground and make the resolution of the whole image consistent. We use Gaussian noise, Laplace noise, Poisson noise, motion blur, and jpeg compression function and randomly select one blur method if blur perturbation is chosen. The other additional perturb method is to randomly multiply a number l, a, b to each channel of the LAB version of I_c as the following equation to add more structural perturbations.

$$I_{c_i} = I_{c_i} \times i, i = (l, a, b) \tag{1}$$

Some samples of our benchmarks have been shown in Fig. 2. In this way, we want to simulate some structured perturb situation in which one region can be learned linearly in the same direction and at the same level. The reason we want to focus on this situation is that many changes in nature can be achieved by overall linear migration on a single meaningful channel, such as illumination change. So this situation is more suitable to operator masks format for they can change the appearance of one region in one direction centralized. Therefore, we have different foregrounds and perturb functions every iteration, and the network needs to regress the multi-mask region in a different direction, which adds variability and complexity to each training pair.

Fig. 2. Here we show some perturb visualization of our benchmarks. The first line shows samples from HScene, and the second line shows examples from HLIP. We can see that the foreground color, illumination, and contrast can be changed.

3.3 Framework Structure

We first use the U-Net structure from DoveNet [3] in there to illustrate our framework. It should be noted that the backbone can be replaced with any other more complex structures to boost the performance further. With our framework, the results generated in the form of operator masks are more editable and explainable. To make the fair comparison with DoveNet [3], we replace the input of the generator as I_c by removing the foreground masks, and the output of the decoder is operator masks, which its location can indicate where needs to change, and the value can represent what level needs to be changed. These operator masks could be pre-defined as certain functions and will be used to edit the inharmonious image in a Retoucher module.

Retoucher: The operator masks will be passed into a retouch module to harmonize I_c. The retouch module has some preset operations which users can define. Here we employ several simple but effective preset methods. Here we show an example. We first split I_c to L, A, and B channels. Then, we generate six operator masks: $OM_{i_{mul}}, OM_{i_{add}}, i = (l, a, b)$, and each will be multiplied or added to each L, A, B channel of the image I_c, to generate I_h, as described in the following equation,

$$I_{h_i} = I_{c_i} \odot OM_{i_{mul}} \oplus OM_{i_{add}}, i = (l, a, b) \tag{2}$$

where "$\odot$" represents the Hadamard product operation and "$\oplus$" represents the Hadamard add operation. It should be noted that other forms of retouch can also be used, and the type of the pre-defined operator can be set according to different applications or dataset volume.

Patch Discriminator: In our task, not only do the global features need to be discriminated, but accurate gradient feedback for local details also needs to be produced. Therefore, we employ a patch discriminator [8,9] in our framework, which has a fixed receptive field, and each output value of the discriminator is only related to the local fixed area. Therefore, we want the discriminator to focus on some tiny objects and local details in the image. The final loss is the average of all local losses to guarantee global consistency [9].

3.4   Loss Functions

We use four type losses in our framework:

- We apply a binary Charbonnier loss [12] to directly minimize the distance between our final output I_h and the ground truth I as:

$$\mathcal{L}_{Char} = \frac{1}{N} \sum_{i=1}^{N} \sqrt{(I_i - I_{h_i})^2 + \epsilon^2}, \tag{3}$$

where N is the batch size, ϵ is a very small constant in order to stabilize the value.
- In order to enhance the contextual details, we employ perceptual loss LPIPS [11]:

$$\mathcal{L}_{Lpips} = \text{LPIPS}(\hat{I}, I_h) \tag{4}$$

- Different from standard discriminator loss, we use a relativistic discriminator loss and try to maximize the probability that a real image is relatively more realistic than a fake one [25]. The discriminator loss is defined as:

$$\begin{aligned}
\mathcal{L}_D = & - \mathbb{E}_I \left[\log \left(D \left(I, I_h \right) \right) \right] \\
& - \mathbb{E}_{I_n} \left[\log \left(1 - D \left(I_h, I \right) \right) \right] \\
D \left(I, I_h \right) = & \sigma \left(C(I) - \mathbb{E} \left[C \left(I_h \right) \right] \right) \to 1 \\
D \left(I_h, I \right) = & \sigma \left(C \left(I_h \right) - \mathbb{E} [C(I)] \right) \to 0
\end{aligned} \tag{5}$$

σ is the sigmoid activation layer, and $C(x)$ is the output of the discriminator [25]. $\mathbb{E}_{I_h}[\cdot]$ represents the final loss is averaged on the batch-level [25].

- The adversarial loss for the generator is as following [25]:

$$\mathcal{L}_G = -\mathbb{E}_I \left[\log\left(1 - D\left(I, I_h\right)\right)\right] - \mathbb{E}_{I_h} \left[\log\left(D\left(I_h, I\right)\right)\right] \tag{6}$$

In this way, the generator benefits from the gradients from both outputs harmonized image and real image in adversarial training.

Finally, our total loss function used for the generator is :

$$\mathcal{L}_{total} = \alpha\mathcal{L}_{Char} + \beta\mathcal{L}_{\text{Lpips}} + \gamma\mathcal{L}_G, \tag{7}$$

where α, β, γ are set as 1, 1, 0.005 empirically.

4   Experiments

In this section, we introduce implementation details. Then we evaluate our proposed framework on our constructed datasets.

4.1   Implementation

As for the structure, in our framework, we first apply the backbone of an attention U-Net from DoveNet [3]. The pre-defined operator is set to the form of formula 2. So the input channel of the backbone is 3, the output channel is 6, and the number of filters in the last conv layer is 64. The number of downsamplings in U-Net is set to 8. The normalization type is instance normalization.

As for the optimization, we first trained the generator from scratch with the learning rate of 2e-4. The milestone is set as 20k, 30k, and the total iteration is 40k for the HScene benchmark. And the milestone is set as 55k, 75k, and the total iteration is 85k for the HLIP benchmark. When training the whole framework with discriminator, we loaded the pre-trained generator model and trained with another 10k for HScene and HLIP. We used the ADAM optimizer, and the batch size in each GPU is set to 64. The whole training process is on Nvidia 3090 GPUs. We implemented it based on BasicSR [24] framework. We used 256 × 256 resolution for both training and testing evaluation.

The metric we use is Mean square Error(MSE), Peak Signal-to-Noise Ration (PSNR), Structural SIMilarity (SSIM) [26] and Perceptual metrics (LPIPS) [27]. PSNR and SSIM pay more attention to the fidelity of the image rather than visual quality [9]. The larger the two metrics, the less likely the image is distorted. LPIPS mainly focuses on comparing the distance of visual features between the generated image and the real one. In this work, we use pre-trained VGG to extract image features, and the smaller the LPIPS is, the generated image is closer to the real one visually.

4.2   Comparison to Recent Works

In this section, we compare our framework with the original output, which directly regresses the RGB value of each image in both quantitative and qualitative methods. We also conduct a user study test to demonstrate the subjective effect of these algorithms.

Quantitative Comparison: We evaluate the performance of our framework on our conducted two benchmarks, HScene and HLIP. The baseline network is adjusted from Dovenet [3]. We re-implemented it on the proposed multi-mask dataset by removing the input mask. The quantitative results are shown in Table 2. The first line shows the metrics of the composited images on test datasets. When directly outputting the RGB version of the harmonious image, the result cannot be interpretable and modifiable, and the results are also sub-optimal in our setting. Our framework makes an improvement in terms of all evaluation metrics on two benchmarks.

To make a fair comparison with other SOTA methods, we also conduct experiments on previous popular single-mask benchmarks, such as iHarmony4 [3]. We train and test on iHarmony4 [3] datasets and show the results in the supplementary materials. The experiment results demonstrate that our methods can also have a reasonable effect on the single-mask image harmonization task.

Table 2. The comparison of the composite, RGB format output, and our framework output. Our framework can have a reasonable improvement on both the two benchmarks.

Method	HScene				HLIP			
Metric	MSE↓	PSNR↑	SSIM↑	LPIPS↓	MSE↓	PSNR↑	SSIM↑	LPIPS↓
Composite	271.89	27.83	0.96	0.027	111.95	30.99	0.96	0.021
Sg-MHH(RGB)	141.75	28.73	0.95	0.026	75.45	31.34	0.95	0.025
Sg-MHH(OM)	99.84	30.59	0.96	0.020	48.02	33.11	0.96	0.021
Sg-MHH(OMGAN)	**94.00**	**30.88**	**0.96**	**0.020**	**42.62**	**33.92**	**0.97**	**0.018**

Qualitative Comparison: We show visual comparison results on our proposed multi-mask harmonization datasets in Fig. 3 and show more visualization on supplementary. The first column shows the real images, and the second column shows the perturbed images. In the third to fifth columns, we show the results output in the previous version and the results output from our framework without or with a discriminator. As the perturb methods on different segmentation masks are different, our framework can deal with the situation with different adjustment directions properly. As demonstrated in the red dotted box, the methods that directly output the RGB format only adjust one inharmonious region (the results in the last line) or adjust two areas but are not in place(the results in the first line). In this way, we demonstrate that our framework has a more flexible and realistic effect and can handle more complicated scenes.

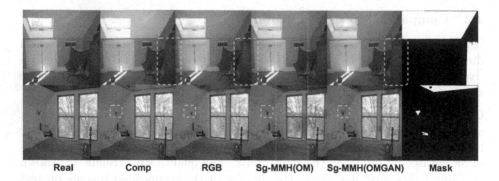

| Real | Comp | RGB | Sg-MMH(OM) | Sg-MMH(OMGAN) | Mask |

Fig. 3. Qualitative harmonization results. The first column is the real image. The second column is the composited image. The third to the fifth column is the harmonization results of a baseline RGB format and our framework with or without GAN structure. OM means *only use generator in our framework*. OMGAN represents *generate operator masks with GAN framework*.

Table 3. User study results on real composited images. We show four images to users and ask them to choose the most realistic one. The number means what percentage of subjects think the images produced by one method are more realistic.

Methods	User Study Score (%)↑
DoveNet [3]	20.6
BarginNet [2]	24.2
RainNet [13]	18.5
Sg-MMH (OMGAN)	36.7

User Study: We conduct user study to compare the results of our framework which the backbone is from DoveNet with the original DoveNet [3], BarginNet [2] and RainNet [13] methods and show the results in Table 3. We test all methods on real composited images.

We consider three realistic situations to construct real composited images. 1) Real composite images that need structured adjustment, such as only changing the illumination. 2) Real composite images that foregrounds are cut from pictures that have already been processed by Instagram filters and want to be re-processed. 3) Real composite images that the foregrounds come from two real pictures but already look realistic. Both of the composited images contain multiple regions that need to be changed. We construct 11 image pairs showing one picture of each setting in Fig. 4. Since there is no real image as reference, we cannot use evaluation like proposed in 4.1 to evaluate image quality. We asked 60 subjects, and each subject needed to independently select one image they think is the most realistic of the four images. The images from the four methods are presented randomly. From the qualitative results and user study, we can see that, when dealing with the illumination change task, our method only change

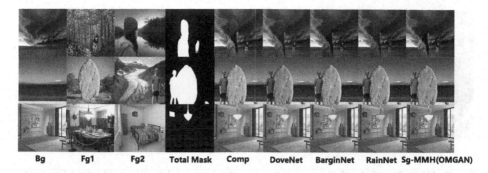

Bg   Fg1   Fg2   Total Mask   Comp   DoveNet   BarginNet   RainNet   Sg-MMH(OMGAN)

Fig. 4. Qualitative results on real composited images. We compare our method with recent state-of-the-art harmonization methods, including DoveNet, BarginNet, and RainNet. Note that they all have input masks to indicate the inharmonious regions while our method adjusts the input automatically. Our proposed framework can apply different operations for different semantic regions appropriately.

the brightness level but retain other color prosperity. This is meaningful because, in most cases, we just want to change the illumination of the foreground but keep the color of the foreground itself. When dealing with pictures such as downloading from websites which already processed by camera filters, our method can alleviate these filters and change them to a more natural appearance. This situation is also worth paying attention to because, in many cases, the landscape images posted to the Internet have already been processed with camera filters, but traditional color transfer methods cannot mimic the realistic filters. When dealing with pictures in which the foregrounds are cut from real pictures, our model mostly keeps remaining the foreground color because although the foregrounds and background are not from the same picture, the original foreground is also reasonable in the new environment. In many cases, when the foreground and background colors are not very consistent, the composite image also looks actual and sensible and does not necessarily need to be adjusted. Only when the color difference is very large and unreasonable the harmonization task needs to adjust the composite image appropriately.

4.3   Discussion

Explainable Property of Operator Masks: Our operator masks can sense the changes and respond appropriately to the corresponding operator masks. Here in Fig. 5 we visualized our operator masks effect on our datasets. For example, in the first line, the sky is perturbed to gray, and to recover it into blue, the operator mask $OM_{b_{add}}$ has a largely negative response since when the picture is in LAB format, the smaller the value of channel B, the bluer the color. In the second line, the foregrounds are disturbed in two directions, the hat is perturbed greener, and the shoes become redder, so $OM_{a_{add}}$ and $OM_{b_{add}}$ has a positive response in the hat region and has a negative response in the region of

| Real | Comp | Sg-MMH(OMGAN) | Mask | L-add | A-add | B-add |

Fig. 5. Visualization of the operator masks in our datasets. The first line is the result from the HScene dataset, and the last line is the result from the HLIP datasets. The last three columns visualize the operator masks of 'add' of L, A, and B channels.

the shoe. These pictures show that our algorithm can explain the changes the network makes for the inharmonious input.

To illustrate that our method can also explain when dealing with real images, we cut a foreground and paste it into a real background picture. Here in Fig. 6(a) show that our operator mask $OM_{l_{add}}$ has a strong negative activation, indicating that the brightness of the inharmonious region is reduced.

Editable Property of Operator Masks: Previous work often generates harmonized images directly, and the results cannot be edited if users do not like the automatic outputs. However, in our work, we locate and generate operator masks, which can be edited if users do not like the results. Here Fig. 6(b) shows the edible effect of our algorithm. Users can add or multiply a number to deepen the color or change the illumination of the foreground. This figure shows that our method can edit the harmonization results based on the automated generation.

Limitation and Future Work: Our method attempt to first realize the harmonization framework with operator masks. Although we have explored the effectiveness of operator masks and show their editable and explainable features, there are still some limitations that need further exploration. First, the training of the harmonization network may heavily depend on the perturbations. The particularity of the filters we use makes our model have many performance limitations. The performance and generalization ability of the network can be further improved if more perturbations are included in the data pre-processing. Also, without special restrictions, some filters applied in our benchmarks make some rare composited images occur. In future research, filters should be applied according to the semantics of objects, such as a green filter should not be applied to a face. Second, when dealing with the foreground color, current image harmonization methods usually choose to transform the color of the foreground to be consistent with the background, but this action is often unnecessary. Sometimes the foreground can keep its own color, and the whole composite image also looks reasonable and realistic. Future work could go further step to explore in which region the foreground color can be consistent with the background and

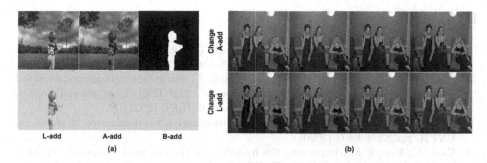

Fig. 6. Here we show the explainable and editable attributes of our operator masks. Figure 5(a) shows the **Visualization of the operator masks in real data**. First row: the composite, the harmonious result, and the ground truth foreground mask. Second row: the operator masks of 'add' operator masks in L, A, and B channels. The L channel has a strong negative activation, indicating the brightness of the inharmonious region has been reduced. Figure 5(b) shows the **Editing attribute of the operator masks**. First row: gradually enlarge the value of the 'add' operator mask in the A channel. Second row: gradually enlarge the value level of the 'add' operator mask in the L channel, which is the brightness. This figure shows that our method can edit the harmonization results based on the generated results.

give a color range, rather than just outputting one result. Third, we propose six alternative operator masks to build our retoucher. However, more complicated operators require further exploration, for example, the shadow effects, the grainy effect, or de-noise. Forth, as our operator masks are trained in an unsupervised manner, there may be coupling between different masks. The controllability can be further improved if the operator masks can be decoupled or with specific supervision.

5   Conclusion

In order to tackle the problem that one composite image has multiple foregrounds pasted from other images, we set up a new setting Sg-MMH and propose two benchmarks, HScene and HLIP, to simulate the situation. To solve the benchmarks, we propose a new framework that uses operator masks to solve the multi-mask image harmonization task. The proposed methods can simulate preset operations in the PhotoShop to edit each image channel and can be explained and edited by users. Also, the operator masks can locate the inharmonious region automatically even when the indicator masks are not given. Experiments show that our framework can handle the more complicated scenes and achieve good results. There are also some limitations for the current work, such as the design of the operator masks is easy and can not decoupled well. In the future, more parametric operator masks can be applied to this framework based on expert knowledge, which will add more control and interpretability to the image harmonization task.

References

1. Cohen-Or, D., Sorkine, O., Gal, R., Leyvand, T., Xu, Y.Q.: Color harmonization. In: ACM SIGGRAPH 2006 Papers, pp. 624–630 (2006)
2. Cong, W., Niu, L., Zhang, J., Liang, J., Zhang, L.: Bargainnet: Background-guided domain translation for image harmonization. In: 2021 IEEE International Conference on Multimedia and Expo (ICME), pp. 1–6. IEEE (2021)
3. Cong, W., et al.: Dovenet: Deep image harmonization via domain verification. In: CVPR, pp. 8394–8403 (2020)
4. Cun, X., Pun, C.M.: Improving the harmony of the composite image by spatial-separated attention module. IEEE TIP **29**, 4759–4771 (2020)
5. Gong, K., Liang, X., Zhang, D., Shen, X., Lin, L.: Look into person: Self-supervised structure-sensitive learning and a new benchmark for human parsing. In: Proceedings of the IEEE Conference on Computer Vision and Pattern Recognition, pp. 932–940 (2017)
6. Guo, Z., Guo, D., Zheng, H., Gu, Z., Zheng, B., Dong, J.: Image harmonization with transformer. In: ICCV, pp. 14870–14879 (2021)
7. Ho, M.M., Zhou, J.: Deep preset: Blending and retouching photos with color style transfer. In: ICCV, pp. 2113–2121 (2021)
8. Isola, P., Zhu, J.Y., Zhou, T., Efros, A.A.: Image-to-image translation with conditional adversarial networks. In: CVPR, pp. 1125–1134 (2017)
9. Ji, X., Cao, Y., Tai, Y., Wang, C., Li, J., Huang, F.: Real-world super-resolution via kernel estimation and noise injection. In: CVPR, pp. 466–467 (2020)
10. Jia, J., Sun, J., Tang, C.K., Shum, H.Y.: Drag-and-drop pasting. ACM TOG **25**(3), 631–637 (2006)
11. Johnson, J., Alahi, A., Fei-Fei, L.: Perceptual losses for real-time style transfer and super-resolution. In: Leibe, B., Matas, J., Sebe, N., Welling, M. (eds.) ECCV 2016. LNCS, vol. 9906, pp. 694–711. Springer, Cham (2016). https://doi.org/10.1007/978-3-319-46475-6_43
12. Lai, W.S., Huang, J.B., Ahuja, N., Yang, M.H.: Fast and accurate image super-resolution with deep laplacian pyramid networks. IEEE TPAMI **41**(11), 2599–2613 (2018)
13. Ling, J., Xue, H., Song, L., Xie, R., Gu, X.: Region-aware adaptive instance normalization for image harmonization. In: CVPR, pp. 9361–9370 (2021)
14. Liu, Y., Qin, Z., Wan, T., Luo, Z.: Auto-painter: Cartoon image generation from sketch by using conditional wasserstein generative adversarial networks. Neurocomputing **311**, 78–87 (2018)
15. Mirza, M., Osindero, S.: Conditional generative adversarial nets. arXiv preprint arXiv:1411.1784 (2014)
16. Ni, Z., Yang, W., Wang, S., Ma, L., Kwong, S.: Towards unsupervised deep image enhancement with generative adversarial network. IEEE TIP **29**, 9140–9151 (2020)
17. Pérez, P., Gangnet, M., Blake, A.: Poisson image editing. In: ACM SIGGRAPH 2003 Papers, pp. 313–318 (2003)
18. Pitie, F., Kokaram, A.C., Dahyot, R.: N-dimensional probability density function transfer and its application to color transfer. In: ICCV, vol. 2, pp. 1434–1439. IEEE (2005)
19. PyPI: pilgram. https://pypi.org/project/pilgram/
20. Reinhard, E., Adhikhmin, M., Gooch, B., Shirley, P.: Color transfer between images. IEEE Comput. Graphics Appl. **21**(5), 34–41 (2001)

21. Sunkavalli, K., Johnson, M.K., Matusik, W., Pfister, H.: Multi-scale image harmonization. ACM TOG **29**(4), 1–10 (2010)
22. Tao, M.W., Johnson, M.K., Paris, S.: Error-tolerant image compositing. In: Daniilidis, K., Maragos, P., Paragios, N. (eds.) ECCV 2010. LNCS, vol. 6311, pp. 31–44. Springer, Heidelberg (2010). https://doi.org/10.1007/978-3-642-15549-9_3
23. Tsai, Y.H., Shen, X., Lin, e.: Deep image harmonization. In: Proceedings of the IEEE Conference on Computer Vision and Pattern Recognition, pp. 3789–3797 (2017)
24. Wang, X., Yu, K., Chan, K.C., Dong, C., Loy, C.C.: BasicSR: Open source image and video restoration toolbox (2020). https://github.com/xinntao/BasicSR
25. Wang, X., et al.: ESRGAN: Enhanced super-resolution generative adversarial networks. In: Leal-Taixé, L., Roth, S. (eds.) ECCV 2018. LNCS, vol. 11133, pp. 63–79. Springer, Cham (2019). https://doi.org/10.1007/978-3-030-11021-5_5
26. Wang, Z., Bovik, A.C., Sheikh, H.R., Simoncelli, E.P.: Image quality assessment: from error visibility to structural similarity. IEEE TIP **13**(4), 600–612 (2004)
27. Zhang, R., Isola, P., Efros, A.A., Shechtman, E., Wang, O.: The unreasonable effectiveness of deep features as a perceptual metric. In: CVPR, pp. 586–595 (2018)
28. Zhou, B., Zhao, H., Puig, X., Fidler, S., Barriuso, A., Torralba, A.: Scene parsing through ade20k dataset. In: CVPR, pp. 633–641 (2017)
29. Zhou, B., et al.: Semantic understanding of scenes through the ade20k dataset, vol. 127(3), pp. 302–321 (2019)
30. Zhu, J.Y., Krahenbuhl, P., Shechtman, E., Efros, A.A.: Learning a discriminative model for the perception of realism in composite images. In: Proceedings of the IEEE International Conference on Computer Vision, pp. 3943–3951 (2015)
31. Zhu, J.Y., Park, T., Isola, P., Efros, A.A.: Unpaired image-to-image translation using cycle-consistent adversarial networks. In: ICCV, pp. 2223–2232 (2017)

Learning an Isometric Surface Parameterization for Texture Unwrapping

Sagnik Das[1](✉), Ke Ma[1,2], Zhixin Shu[3], and Dimitris Samaras[1]

[1] Stony Brook University, Stony Brook, NY 11790, USA
sadas@cs.stonybrook.edu
[2] Snap Inc., New York, USA
[3] Adobe Research, California, USA

Abstract. In this paper, we present a novel approach to learn texture mapping for an isometrically deformed 3D surface and apply it for texture unwrapping of documents or other objects. Recent work on differentiable rendering techniques for implicit surfaces has shown high-quality 3D scene reconstruction and view synthesis results. However, these methods typically learn the appearance color as a function of the surface points and lack explicit surface parameterization. Thus they do not allow texture map extraction or texture editing. We propose an efficient method to learn surface parameterization by learning a continuous bijective mapping between 3D surface positions and 2D texture-space coordinates. Our surface parameterization network can be conveniently plugged into a differentiable rendering pipeline and trained using multi-view images and rendering loss. Using the learned parameterized implicit 3D surface we demonstrate state-of-the-art document-unwrapping via texture extraction in both synthetic and real scenarios. We also show that our approach can reconstruct high-frequency textures for arbitrary objects. We further demonstrate the usefulness of our system by applying it to document and object texture editing. Code and related assets are available at: https://github.com/cvlab-stonybrook/Iso-UVField.

Keywords: Document unwrapping · Texture unwrapping · Neural rendering

1 Introduction

Reconstructing 3D shapes from images is a core problem in computer vision and graphics research. With the progress in differentiable rendering [24,27,33,44,54], recent learning-based 3D reconstruction approaches have achieved impressive results using 2D supervision from a single image [11,12,20,39,61] or multi-view images [55,66]. These methods achieve high quality 3D reconstruction using differentiable rendering with various 3D representations such as 3D meshes [61], volumetric representations [40], or implicit functions [39]. In recent neural rendering methods such as NeRF [40] and IDR [66], continuous representations

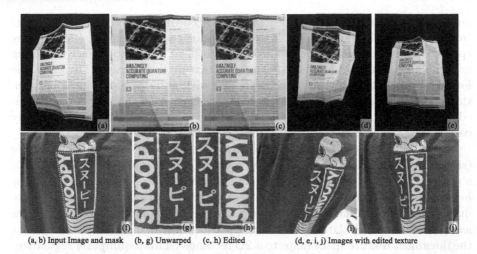

(a, b) Input Image and mask   (b, g) Unwarped   (c, h) Edited   (d, e, i, j) Images with edited texture

Fig. 1. The proposed forward-backward network can be utilized in unwrapping and editing a surface texture: the flattened texture can be edited and warped back to produce a texture edited image. In the top row we edit the unwrapped texture by overlaying a color grid. In the bottom row we edit the unwrapped texture by swapping the 'English' and 'Japanese' text. In the bottom row the desired texture mask is highlighted by a yellow dashed polygon. The warped texture is pasted at the masked region in different views. (Color figure online)

such as volume or implicit functions achieve significantly better reconstruction results than meshes or voxels because they do not discretize the 3D surface a priori. However, these continuous representations usually do not encode explicit surface parameterization, which would allow 3D shape re-texturing, editing the existing texture in the 2D texture space, or recovering 2D texture from 3D surfaces. One of the most direct applications of 2D texture unwrapping in a geometrically constrained manner, is document unwarping, i.e., the inference of a document's flatbed-scanned version from a casual photo of a potentially creased document. Moreover, 2D texture unwrapping could be equally valuable for other domains such as garments, common objects or faces. In this paper, we use the terms texture unwrapping and unwarping interchangeably.

Our novel texture mapping approach learns surface parameterization for isometrically deformed surfaces by learning continuous bijective functions between 3D surface positions and 2D texture-space coordinates. We use a signed distance function (SDF) [8] to represent the geometry and model the appearance as a function of the 2D texture coordinates. By utilizing implicit differentiable rendering (IDR), [66] we can reconstruct the 3D shape and learn the corresponding UV parameterization of the surface simultaneously. This is possible only with a per-pixel rendering loss and the appropriate geometric regularization.

We utilize two fully connected multi-layer perceptrons (MLPs) to learn a bijective mapping between 3D shapes and 2D texture space. More specifically, the *forward* MLP maps the 3D surface coordinates to 2D texture coordinates and the *backward* MLP maps the 2D texture coordinates to corresponding 3D surface coordinates. Following IDR [66], we obtain the 3D surface coordinates by sphere-tracing along the ray cast through each pixel. Our appearance rendering is formulated as a function of the 3D and the texture coordinates. Therefore, the forward and backward MLPs can be trained with a 2D pixel-wise loss between the rendered image and the given ground truth image. To the best of our knowledge, this is the first neural rendering method that can learn a geometrically constrained UV parameterization for implicit surfaces.

Thus, our method is also the first method which utilizes implicit surface (signed distance function) based neural rendering for document unwarping. It is a challenging task due to the presence of geometric and photometric distortions in a document. For this particular problem we introduce a shape-specific texture mapping prior to initialize the forward MLP (3D to 2D mapping). This prior is learned from a large dataset of UV mapped document meshes, assuming that the document texture space maps to a 2D rectangle. This assumption regularizes the forward MLP to output a high-quality texture space that avoids degenerate solutions (see Fig. 3). Moreover, we introduce a conformality constraint in the backward MLP, which is consistent with how a paper folds in the physical world, i.e., without any stretch or tear. We can directly extend our method to work on rigidly deforming objects other than paper which follow similar physical properties such as fabric, soda cans etc. We also show that our method is robust to small deviations from the assumed conformality constraint, e.g. in the case of face texture unwrapping.

The main contributions of our paper are the following: 1) We propose an efficient way to learn a texture parameterization for implicit neural representations using a differentiable rendering framework. Without 3D supervision, it only requires multi-view images as ground truth and a texture mapping prior. 2) We show that our method can be effectively used for document unwarping tasks by learning a prior for explicit texture mapping on the document shape. We show that this prior can be learned from a dataset of texture-mapped meshes. Furthermore, this prior is also suitable for other objects sharing similar geometric property as papers. 3) We show that our method is effective for document image unwarping and texture editing (see Fig. 1). We achieve a 25% relative improvement over a publicly available state-of-the-art [13] in terms of mean local distortion across 750 views from fifteen synthetic scenes. Additionally, we achieve a ~25% improvement in optical character recognition (OCR) in terms of character and word error rate. For the texture editing task, we show significant qualitative improvement over NeuTex [64].

2 Previous Work

Neural Rendering. Neural rendering generates images and videos by integrating conventional computer graphics rendering pipelines into deep neural networks [56]. It enables explicit or implicit control of scene properties, including illumination, geometry, texture, etc. Neural rendering can synthesize semantic photos [3,46], novel views [23,53], relighting [36,65], facial/body reenactment [7,63], estimate scene properties etc. Kato [24] proposed a differentiable neural renderer using an approximate gradient for rasterization. Liu [32] proposed SoftRas, which extended differentiable rasterization. Li [27] further demonstrated the feasibility of integrating ray-tracing in deep neural networks. More recently, implicit surface or volume rendering has become mainstream in neural rendering approaches such as IDR [66] and NeRF [40]. These approaches are based on multi-view surface reconstruction to associate the scene geometry to the appearance in different views. NeRF is extended to lot of variants including PixelNeRF [68], MVSNeRF [10], dynamic NeRF [29,48], GRAF [51], etc.

Texture Mapping. Texture mapping is an essential step in the computer graphics rendering pipeline. It defines a correspondence between a vertex on the 3D mesh and a pixel in the 2D texture image. To find such a mapping, FlexiStickers [58] required users to specify a sparse set of correspondences. Bi [6] proposed a patch-based texture mapping method using the 3D shape and images from multiple views. Morreale [43] used networks to represent 3D surfaces/shapes. Apart from the above general texture mapping methods, some approaches focus on a specific object categories such as faces [9,16] and human bodies [42,69]. Recently, AtlasNet [20] represented a 3D mesh as a collection of parametric surfaces showing texture mapping is trivial to obtain from a 2D parametric surface. A similar idea was adopted by Bednarik [4] where they introduced geometric constraints when learning the decomposition. More recently, NeuTex [64] aims to recover the texture of a subject using NeRF [40]. However, NeuTex uses a spherical UV domain without any geometric constraints. Therefore, the recovered texture is not smooth which is not suitable for document unwrapping. Moreover, since NeRF [40] doesn't learn an explicit geometry, NeuTex requires a coarse pointcloud to initialize the *backward* MLP. With an SDF based [66] rendering scheme, our approach does not require such an initialization routine. We can jointly learn the texture mapping and the geometry from scratch.

Document Unwrapping. Document unwrapping is a special application of texture mapping: the 3D object is usually a rectangular piecewise-developable surface and the texture is well structured, containing straight text lines (usually) rectangular text blocks and figures etc. Previous work usually adopted a two-step methodology: 1) 3D surface estimation and 2) deformed surface flattening. The 3D surface of a deformed document can be estimated from shading [60], multi-view images [59], text lines [57], local character orientations [38], document boundaries [26], and learning-based strategies [47]. Flattening the obtained 3D surface always involves an expensive optimization process under certain geometry constraints such as conformality [67] or isometries [2]. Flattening could be easier if the obtained 3D shape had a low dimensional parameterization like Generalized Cylindrical Surface (GCS) [25]. Some studies [14,30,37] proposed to unwrap each patch on the surface individually and then stitch the unwrapped patches together. In recent years, data-driven methods [13,15,17,28,34,35] have addressed document unwrapping by leveraging large-scale synthetic datasets.

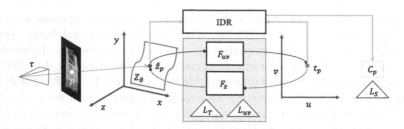

Fig. 2. Proposed surface parameterization learning using the forward (F_{uv}) and backward MLP (F_z): given camera pose τ, and a pixel p, we jointly learn the geometry represented by a SDF Z_θ, the F_{uv}, and the F_z. $\hat{z}_p$ is the ray-surface intersection point in 3D domain and t_p is the corresponding texture coordinate in UV domain. The yellow arrows denote the input and output of the IDR [66], and C_p is the predicted RGB color. Triangles denote the losses defined in Eq. 10.

These datasets contain deformed document images and their corresponding ground truth UV coordinates. Methods trained on synthetic images often suffer from generalization performance due to the domain gap between synthetic and real data. In this paper, we utilize neural rendering techniques to learn a surface parameterization of a deformed document. We simultaneously estimate both 3D shapes and UV coordinates with a cycle consistency loss and geometric constraints. By leveraging the information from multi-view images, the proposed method demonstrates better document unwarping performance compared to a previous state-of-the-art [13]. Furthermore, our method only needs multi-view images and corresponding foreground masks for training, eliminating the need of large-scale document image datasets with paired warping field ground truth.

3   Method

In Sect. 3.1 we first describe some preliminaries about surface parameterization and IDR. Then we describe the proposed approach that utilize a recent differentiable rendering method, IDR [66] for surface reconstruction and jointly learn the texture mapping of the learned implicit surface using two MLPs.

3.1   Preliminaries

Surface Parameterization. The problem of surface parameterization focuses on finding a bijective mapping F between a surface $Z \in \mathbb{R}^3$ and a polygonal domain $\Omega \in \mathbb{R}^n$. For a parametric or discrete surface representation, we can explicitly compute this mapping [58] using constrained optimization. In contrast, implicit surfaces are represented as continuous functions and cannot be readily parameterized. In this paper, we propose to learn such bijective mapping between a learned implicit surface and a 2D planar domain $\Omega \in \mathbb{R}^2$ using our proposed forward and backward MLPs. Ω is the texture space or UV space, parameterized using 2D UV coordinates $\mathbf{t} = (u, v)$. We can use any continuous parameterization function as the UV space. Since this work particularly focuses on document unwarping, we choose the UV space to be a regular 2D grid.

Implicit Differentiable Rendering. Implicit Differentiable Rendering [66] reconstructs the geometry of an object from multi-view images as the zero level set, Z_θ of an MLP S,

$$Z_\theta = \{\mathbf{z} \in \mathbb{R}^3 \mid S(\mathbf{z}; \theta) = 0\} \tag{1}$$

where θ are the learnable parameters. To render the surface Z_θ, IDR uses another MLP to model the radiance (RGB color) as a function of the surface point $(\mathbf{z}_p)$, corresponding surface normal $(\mathbf{n}_p)$, view direction $(\mathbf{v}_p)$ and a global geometry feature vector $(\mathbf{g}_p)$:

$$C_p = A(\mathbf{z}_p, \mathbf{n}_p, \mathbf{v}_p, \mathbf{g}_p) \tag{2}$$

Here, C_p denotes the predicted color at pixel p and A denotes the appearance MLP. The surface point is obtained by a sphere-tracing method [22] along the ray $r_p(\tau)$ through pixel p. $\tau \in \mathbb{R}^k$ denotes camera parameters of the scene. Additionally, IDR also presents a differentiable way to obtain a ray and geometry intersection point $(\hat{\mathbf{z}}_p)$ as a function of the camera ray. Although, the IDR can disentangle geometry and appearance, it only allows to re-render a new geometry with a learned appearance MLP, A. Editing a texture or extracting a surface texture map is not possible in a vanilla IDR framework.

3.2   Learning Surface Parameterization

To learn a meaningful parameterization of the implicit surface Z_θ, we represent the radiance at pixel p as a function of the UV space. To this end, we modify the IDR model (Eq. 2):

$$C_p = A_{uv}(\mathbf{t}_p, \mathbf{z}_p, \mathbf{n}_p, \mathbf{v}_p, \mathbf{g}_p) \tag{3}$$

The texture parameterized appearance MLP is modeled as a function of the texture coordinate $\mathbf{t}_p$ at surface point $\mathbf{z}_p$, corresponding to a pixel p. We can jointly train the surface MLP (S) and texture parameterized appearance MLP (A_{uv}) using a pixel-wise rendering loss between the predicted radiance (C_p) and ground truth radiance (C_p^{gt}) at pixel p. A schematic diagram of the proposed approach is shown in Fig. 2.

Forward and Backward Texture Parameterization. We represent the mapping between the 3D surface and 2D texture space using the *forward* function $F_{uv}: \mathbf{z} \rightarrow \mathbf{t}$. The F_{uv} is modeled as an MLP. It is trained by mapping a ray-surface intersection point $\hat{\mathbf{z}}_p$ to its corresponding texture coordinate $\mathbf{t}_p$. p denotes the pixel location. Now to establish the bijective mapping (discussed in Sect. 3.1) between the surface and texture space we utilize a *backward* function $F_z: \mathbf{t} \rightarrow \mathbf{z}$. F_z is an MLP that learns an inverse mapping between the texture and the 3D space. It is trained by mapping a texture coordinate $\mathbf{t}_p$ to its corresponding ray-surface intersection point $\hat{\mathbf{z}}_p$.

Shape Specific prior for F_{uv}.
Jointly training the forward, backward and rendering network leads to
the wrong UV mapping with local
minima (see Fig. 3) where multiple $\hat{z}_p$
map to a single texture coordinate.
To avoid such degenerate cases, we
initialize F_{uv} with a texture mapping
prior, learned from a large dataset
of UV mapped meshes. We assume
the input shape to be a isometrically

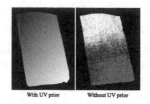

With UV prior   Without UV prior

Fig. 3. Without a prior the forward network, F_{uv} leads to degenerate cases: multiple 3D points $\hat{z}_p$ are mapped to the same
texture coordinate t_p.

deformed quadrilateral and the corresponding UV space to be a regular grid
($\in [0.0, 1.0]$). The top leftmost and the bottom rightmost 3D coordinate of the
shape maps to $(u, v) = (0, 0)$ and $(u, v) = (1, 1)$ respectively. To learn $\hat{F}_{uv}$ we
utilize a collection of UV mapped meshes from the Doc3D [13] dataset and train
an MLP with the same parameters as F_{uv}. For each scene, we use $\hat{F}_{uv}$ to initialize
the weights of F_{uv} and train jointly with S and A_{uv}. Although this learned prior
($\hat{F}_{uv}$) is designed to learn a suitable texture mapping for document unwarping,
we experimentally show this prior can be readily used for other domains as well.

Deformation Constraints for F_z. Conformal map [21] allows a 3D domain
to be mapped to a texture domain with low distortion satisfying the bijective
property between domains. We use a conformality constraint for F_z to ensure the
deformation properties mentioned above. We define the conformality constraint
in terms of the metric tensor, $\mathbf{J}^\top \mathbf{J}$ of the F_z, where $\mathbf{J}$ is the Jacobian of F_z (Eq. 4):

$$\mathbf{J} = \begin{bmatrix} \dfrac{\delta F_z}{\delta u} & \dfrac{\delta F_z}{\delta v} \end{bmatrix} = [D_u \ \ D_v] \qquad \mathbf{J}^\top \mathbf{J} = \begin{bmatrix} D_u^\top D_u & D_u^\top D_v \\ D_u^\top D_v & D_v^\top D_v \end{bmatrix} = \begin{bmatrix} E & F \\ F & G \end{bmatrix} \quad (4)$$

The conformality constraint is defined as $\mathbf{J}^\top \mathbf{J} = \beta \mathbf{I}$. Here β is a unknown
local scaling function and $\mathbf{I}$ is the identity matrix. For developable surfaces which
can be physically flattened without any stretch e.g. papers, β doesn't vary across
the parameterization space. Therefore, we consider a fixed global scale ($[\beta_u, \beta_v]$)
for the conformality constraint.

Unwarping by Sampling F_z. To unwarp the texture, we determine a foreground pixel at $p = (x, y)$ in the input image that should be projected to (u, v)
in the unwarped image. Here the unwarped image refers to the texture space.
Foreground pixel refers to a pixel within the pre-defined object mask. The coordinates (u, v) and p are associated by F_z and τ: for a (u, v) coordinate, its corresponding point in 3D is obtained by $\hat{z}_p' = F_z(u, v)$. Given the camera parameter
τ, $\hat{z}_p'$ is projected to p in the input image. Thus for each pixel in the unwarped
texture, we can find its corresponding pixel in the input image which is all we
need for unwarping (More details in supplemantary).

3.3   Loss Functions

We use the rendering losses on the predicted color, C_p, and predicted document mask M_p at pixel p to train the geometry S. Here $M_p \in \{0,1\}$ refers to whether the pixel p is occupied ($M_p = 1$) by the shape or not ($M_p = 0$). We assume masks are provided as input. Additionally, we employ appropriate regularization losses to jointly train S, A_{uv}, F_{uv} and F_z.

Loss for S. Following IDR [66], for each p we apply a sphere-tracing [22] algorithm followed by implicit differentiation to find the intersection point of the ray $r_p(\tau)$ and the surface Z_θ. Given the ground truth RGB color C_p^{gt} and the predicted RGB color C_p, the RGB loss is defined as:

$$L_{rgb} = \frac{1}{|P|} \sum_{p \in P_{in}} \left\| C_p^{gt} - C_p \right\|_1 \tag{5}$$

where P is the set of pixels in the minibatch. The pixels $P_{in} \subset P$ for which ray-surface intersection has been found and $M_p = 1$. The mask loss is defined as:

$$L_{mask} = \frac{1}{\alpha |P|} \sum_{p \in P_{out}} CE(M_p^{gt}, M_p) \tag{6}$$

Here $P_{out} = P \setminus P_{in}$, α is a tunable parameter and $CE(.)$ is the cross-entropy loss. The value of $M_p = \mathcal{M}_{p,\alpha}(\theta, \tau)$ is a differentiable function of the learned Z_θ [66]. Additionally, to force Z_θ to be a approximate signed distance function we use Eikonal Regularization [19]:

$$L_{ek} = \mathbb{E}_z(\|\nabla_z S(\mathbf{z}; \theta)\| - 1)^2 \tag{7}$$

where z denotes uniformly sampled points within a bounding box of the 3D domain.

Loss for F_{uv}. Although we initialize F_{uv} with learned prior parameters, we constrain the predicted 2D texture coordinates during training in order to avoid non-uniform mapping of the 3D and the UV domain which can squeeze or stretch the warped texture (example in supplementary). We employ a Chamfer distance between the $\mathbf{t}_p$ and uniformly sampled 2D points $\mathcal{T} \in [0,1]$ to ensure F_{uv} approximately outputs $\mathcal{U} \sim [0,1]$. This regularization term is defined as:

$$L_{uv} = CD_{p \in P_{in}}(\mathcal{T}, \mathbf{t}_p) \tag{8}$$

here $CD(.)$ denotes the Chamfer distance and t_p the predicted texture coordinates corresponding to ray-surface intersection points $\hat{\mathbf{z}}_p$.

Loss for F_z. $\hat{z}_p'$ is the output of F_z. F_z is trained with weighted regression loss between $\hat{z}_p$ and $\hat{z}_p'$:

$$L_z = \frac{1}{|P_{in}|} \sum_{p \in P_{in}} w_p(\hat{z}_p - \hat{z}_p')^2 \tag{9}$$

w_p is a pre-calculated per-pixel weight based on the document mask (M) which assigns higher value to the pixels at the boundary of the document. (More weight calculation details in supplementary).

Additionally, to constrain $F_\mathbf{z}$ to be a fixed scale conformal mapping [4]. On the elements of the metric tensor, E, F and G defined in Eq. 4, we employ the following constraints:

$$L_E = \frac{1}{|P_{in}|} \sum_{p \in P_{in}} (E_p - \tilde{E})^2 \quad L_G = \frac{1}{|P_{in}|} \sum_{p \in P_{in}} (G_p - \tilde{G})^2 \quad L_F = \frac{1}{|P_{in}|} \sum_{p \in P_{in}} (F_p)^2$$

Here $\tilde{E}$ and $\tilde{G}$ is the mean of E and G. Our combined loss function is defined as:

$$L = \underbrace{(L_{rgb} + \gamma_1 L_{mask} + \gamma_2 L_{ek})}_{L_S} + \rho L_{uv} + \underbrace{(\delta_1 L_z + \delta_2 L_E + \delta_3 L_G + \delta_4 L_F)}_{L_T} \quad (10)$$

Here γ, ρ and δ denote the hyperparameters associated with the losses.

3.4   Training Details

The surface MLP $S(\mathbf{z}, \theta)$ consists of 8 layers with a hidden layer dimension of 128, with a skip connection to the middle layer [45]. The rendering network A_{uv} has 4 layers with hidden layer dimension of 512 and uses a sine activation function [52] at each layer. F_{uv} and F_z share identical architecture with 8 layers with 512 dimensional hidden units and sine activation [52]. Following NeRF [40], we use a k dimensional Fourier mapping $(\chi_k : \mathbb{R} \to \mathbb{R}^{2k})$ to learn high frequency details in the shape, RGB and the UV space. For S, A_{uv} we follow the setting of [66], and set $k = 6$ and $k = 4$ respectively. For F_{uv} and F_z we empirically set number of Fourier bands $k = 10$. We start with an initial learning rate of 10^{-5} and train for 80K iterations by halving the learning rate twice at 16K and 24K iterations. Initially, α is set to 50 and doubled during the training at 4K, 6K and 8K iterations. We set $\gamma_1 = 100.0$, $\gamma_2 = 0.1$ and $\rho = 0.001$. δ_1 is set to 0.001 for the initial 25K iterations. Afterward, δ_1 is multiplied by a factor 3 at every 10K iterations for a maximum of 7 times. δ_2, δ_3 and δ_4, are set to zero for the initial 50 K iterations. Only L_z is sufficient to achieve a good texture to 3D mapping during the shape optimization phase. Afterwards we set $\delta_2 = \delta_3 = 0.001$ and $\delta_4 = 0.01$. The metric tensor calculation is implemented using auto-differentiation.

Initializing. S and F_z. We can start optimizing S from the standard IDR initialization (SDF of a sphere). However, we notice that a better initialization can significantly improve the training time as well as the quality of the shape reconstruction. For object specific application like document unwarping we found that initializing S with a similar object can significantly reduce the training time and converges in a half number of iterations. Furthermore, we also found that initializing F_z to produce a planar point-cloud can further reduce our training convergence time. To this end, we pre-train the F_z to produce a plane. More details are discussed in supplementary.

4 Experimental Results

First, we quantitatively compare the proposed method with a state-of-the-art document unwarping method DewarpNet [13]. Our quantitative and qualitative experiments are performed on 15 synthetic and 10 real documents. Second, we apply our method to texture editing for documents and other objects such as soda can, t-shirt, and human face. Last, we conduct ablation studies to demonstrate the effectiveness of our proposed loss functions (reported in supplementary due to space constraints).

4.1 Evaluation Dataset and Metrics

For document unwarping, the synthetic evaluation data consists of 15 scenes rendered using Blender [1] following a rendering pipeline similar to Doc3D. Each scene consists of 50 random views sampled from a 45° solid angle in the upper hemisphere. The real-world evaluation data consists of five scenes from the dataset of [67] and nine scenes captured by us. All the synthetic data and some of the real data include the document scan as the unwarping ground truth which are used for quantitative evaluation. Apart from documents we use 4 real objects for qualitative comparison. Each scene consists of 5–20 images per scene. We manually annotate the masks for each scene. To obtain camera poses for the real-world data, we use COLMAP [50]. We should note that for objects such as soda can, t-shirts, and faces, we assume a consistent foreground mask is available for all the views, designating the part of the texture to be unwrapped. For these objects, we also use the same F_{uv} learned for the document unwarping task. The learned prior from Doc3D dataset is usable as long as the surface somewhat follows the rectangular shape assumption.

We use image-based evaluation metrics for quantitative evaluation, including Local Distortion (LD) and Multi-Scale Structural Similarity (MS-SSIM). These are standard metrics used for document unwarping evaluation [13,34]. LD is based on dense SIFT flow [31] between the unwarped and scanned images. Image similarity metric MS-SSIM [62] is based on local image statistics (mean and variance) of the unwarped and scanned (ground truth) images calculated over multiple Gaussian pyramid scales. We use the same settings as [13,34] for fair comparison.

4.2 Document Unwarping

The quantitative comparison with the state-of-the-art model [13] is shown in Table 1 for the synthetic and real scenes. In terms of average performance of all the views (*all views* col. in Table 1) we improve the LD by ∼45% compared

Table 1. Quantitative comparison of DewarpNet [13] and proposed method on synthetic and real images. *All views* report the mean result of all the views across all scenes and *Frontal view* denotes the mean result of one frontal view from each scene. Frontal view can be considered as the easiest or most probable view among all the views.

Methods	Synthetic				Real			
	All views		*Frontal view*		*All views*		*Frontal view*	
	MSSIM↑	LD↓	MSSIM ↑	LD ↓	MSSIM ↑	LD ↓	MSSIM ↑	LD ↓
DewarpNet	0.5382	7.81	0.5965	5.37	0.4601	10.25	0.4724	7.85
Proposed	**0.6302**	**4.31**	**0.6405**	**4.02**	**0.4951**	**7.16**	**0.494**	**6.28**

to [13]. Since we use multi-view images for training, our results are more consistent across all the views compared to DewarpNet, which is also a key reason for the significant improvement.

We also report in a more practical evaluation scenario (*frontal view* column of Table 1) where we compare our results with DewarpNet for a frontal view unwarping of the document. This setting also shows 25% relative improvement of LD compared to DewarpNet due to the stability of the method across different views. Since DewarpNet is trained on a synthetic dataset, it's generalizability limitation is reflected through this experiment. The choice of the best unwarped result is often subjective. We conjecture that since [13] is a single image unwarping method, it should perform well on simpler deformations and frontal view images. However, it is not always the case. Qualitative comparisons on real images in Fig. 4 show DewarpNet often generates artifacts even for reasonably frontal views and simple deformations. Comparatively, our results are qualitatively superior. Similar trend is observed in synthetic scenes. We qualitatively compare the frontal view results of DewarpNet with our results across 6 scenes in Fig. 5. In Fig. 5 our results are clearly better than the DewarpNet in all cases, with straighter lines and better rectified structure. More qualitative comparisons are available in supplementary material.

The quantitative comparison for real scenes are reported in Table 1 (right). We achieve significantly better LD than DewarpNet on both the frontal view evaluation and when averaged across all views. However, we notice that the improvement in terms of MS-SSIM is not that prominent due to its sensitivity to subtle perceptually unimportant global transformations such as translation by few pixels. We also note that quantitative scores are comparatively worse for the real scenes than synthetic scenes due to the fewer available views (10–15 compared to 50). Moreover, in absence of sufficient texture and views our method may result in unsatisfactory unwarping results. Such data are a failure case of IDR since there is insufficient information to reconstruct the 3D shape. As a result of the poor 3D shape, our texture parameterization network produces an inferior unwarping result (More details are available in supplementary). We also report qualitative comparisons with [67] and [13] on additional real documents in supplementary.

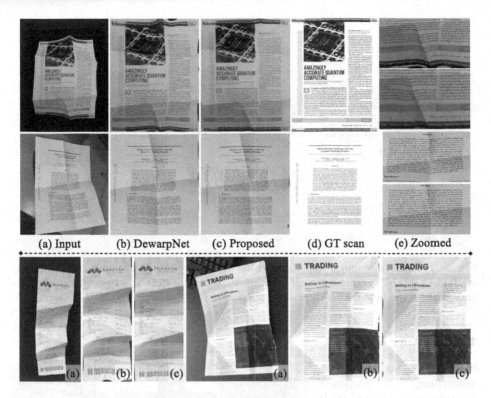

Fig. 4. Qualitative comparison with DewarpNet [13] on real images: (a) Input image (b) DewarpNet unwarping (c) Proposed unwarping (d) GT scanned image (e) enlarged regions: DewarpNet (*top*), and proposed (*bottom*). We use reasonable frontal view of the document for a fair comparison.

OCR Evaluation. We evaluated the OCR performance on 5 real scenes across 77 images in Table 2. We use Edit Distance (ED) [41], Character Error Rate (CER) and Word Error Rate (WER) as our evaluation metrics. ED is defined as the total number of substitu-

Table 2. Comparison of OCR metrics: We improve the OCR performance of [13] by ∼25% in terms of Edit Distance (ED), Character (CER), and Word Error Rate (WER).

Methods	ED↓	CER (std)↓	WER (std)↓
DewarpNet	798.30	0.2827 (0.12)	0.4646 (0.17)
Proposed	**600.78**	**0.2122 (0.10)**	**0.3568 (0.11)**

tions (s), insertions (i) and deletions (d) required to obtain the reference text, given the recognized text. The reference text is obtained by running the OCR algorithm on the scanned ground truth image of each document. CER is defined as: $(s + i + d)/N$ where N is the number of characters in the reference text. We use Tesseract 4.1.1 based LSTM OCR engine for this experiment. Our unwarped results reduce the ED, CER and WER by ∼25%. This improvement proves our unwarped results are more suitable for downstream applications like OCR.

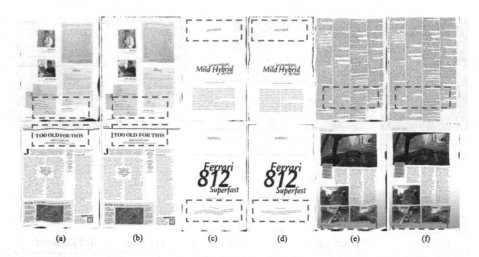

(a)   (b)   (c)   (d)   (e)   (f)

Fig. 5. Frontal view unwarping comparison of DewarpNet (a,c,e) and the proposed method (b,d,f) on synthetic images. Proposed results are clearly better with straighter lines. Follow the blue dashed boxes for discrimitative regions.

4.3   Texture Editing

In addition to document unwarping, our proposed forward and backward MLP can also be used for high quality texture editing. We show texture editing examples in Fig. 1 and Fig. 7. We use the backward MLP to unwarp the texture from the input image, then edit the texture and warp it back to image space using the learned forward MLP

(a) Input view   (b) NeuTex texture   (c) Our texture

Fig. 6. Comparison with NeuTex [64]: a prior work that aims to recover texture in a NeRF based setting, fails to recover high frequency details of the texture. Comparatively, our method clearly does a better job since we directly sample the texture from the input image.

(More details in supplementary). The proposed method can unwarp any isometrically deformed surface such as fabric or metal. It also works quite well when deformation is not exactly isometric, e.g., human faces [49]. In Fig. 6, we compare our texture editing results with NeuTex [64], a NeRF based texture unwrapping method. Compared to NeuTex [64], our results contain better details due to the forward prior and the geometric constraints.

5   Limitations and Future Work

Our proposed method for a scene can be trained in approximately 6 h for 448×448 resolution images using a single Titan Xp GPU. The current training time per scene is high compared to DewarpNet's inference time which makes

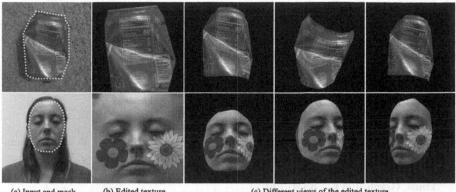

(a) Input and mask   (b) Edited texture   (c) Different views of the edited texture

Fig. 7. Examples of texture editing non-document surfaces. This demonstrates our method is flexible beyond document unwarping and can be seamlessly used for other domains [49] as long as the isometric assumption is not strongly violated. The foreground mask is shown using a yellow dashed polygon.

it unsuitable for real-time applications. However, we would like to note that in the current implementation sphere-tracing takes almost 50–60% of the running time. With a faster version of the sphere-tracing we can readily achieve a faster framework. Moreover, neural rendering is an active research field and there are multiple other works that are focusing on improving the speed and generalization abilities [5,18]. Therefore, a faster training can be achieved following any newer or faster alternatives of IDR.

In this paper, we successfully applied our method on some toy objects other than documents. However, application of our method is limited by the isometric deformation assumption. For more complex UV spaces (e.g., texture atlas), learning the prior may require decomposing the shape to multiple simple UV maps where each UV map follow the isometric assumption. The proper way to do this is beyond the scope of this paper, however we believe it's an exciting future work. Another strong assumption of our method is the learned $\hat{F}_{uv}$ prior assumes the texture to be a continuous mapping bounded in a quadrilateral. This constraint suit the rectangular paper shape and improve empirical results in a specific task. More general objects will require different constraints e.g., spherical UV domain, local scaling of the conformal map etc.

6   Conclusions

We have introduced a neural rendering based architecture that can learn texture parameterized 3D shapes from multi-view images. This is the first work to learn surface parameterization of an implicit neural representation, to the best of our knowledge. We have demonstrated the applicability of our approach on multiple synthetic and real scenes for the task of document unwarping and object texture editing. We achieve state-of-the-art texture unwrapping and editing results.

Acknowledgements. This work was done when Ke Ma was at Stony Brook University. This work was partially supported by the Partner University Fund, the SUNY2020 ITSC, the FRA project "Deep Learning for Large-Scale Rail Defect Inspection" and gifts from Adobe and Amazon.

References

1. Blender - a 3D modelling and rendering package
2. Bartoli, A., Gerard, Y., Chadebecq, F., Collins, T., Pizarro, D.: Shape-from-template. IEEE Trans. Pattern Anal. Mach. Intell. **37**(10), 2099–2118 (2015)
3. Bau, D., et al.: Semantic photo manipulation with a generative image prior. ACM Trans. Graph. (TOG) **38**(4) (2019)
4. Bednarik, J., Parashar, S., Gundogdu, E., Salzmann, M., Fua, P.: Shape reconstruction by learning differentiable surface representations. In: Proceedings of the IEEE Conference on Computer Vision and Pattern Recognition (2020)
5. Bergman, A.W., Kellnhofer, P., Wetzstein, G.: Fast training of neural lumigraph representations using meta learning (2021)
6. Bi, S., Kalantari, N.K., Ramamoorthi, R.: Patch-based optimization for image-based texture mapping. ACM Trans. Graph. (TOG) **36**(4), 1–106 (2017)
7. Chan, C., Ginosar, S., Zhou, T., Efros, A.A.: Everybody dance now. In: Proceedings of the International Conference on Computer Vision (2019)
8. Chan, T., Zhu, W.: Level set based shape prior segmentation. In: Proceedings of the IEEE Conference on Computer Vision and Pattern Recognition. IEEE (2005)
9. Chen, A., Chen, Z., Zhang, G., Mitchell, K., Yu, J.: Photo-realistic facial details synthesis from single image. In: Proceedings of the International Conference on Computer Vision (2019)
10. Chen, A., et al.: MVSNeRF: Fast generalizable radiance field reconstruction from multi-view stereo. arXiv preprint arXiv:2103.15595 (2021)
11. Chen, Z., Zhang, H.: Learning implicit fields for generative shape modeling. In: Proceedings of the IEEE/CVF Conference on Computer Vision and Pattern Recognition, pp. 5939–5948 (2019)
12. Choy, C.B., Xu, D., Gwak, J.Y., Chen, K., Savarese, S.: 3D-R2N2: A unified approach for single and multi-view 3d object reconstruction. In: Leibe, B., Matas, J., Sebe, N., Welling, M. (eds.) ECCV 2016. LNCS, vol. 9912, pp. 628–644. Springer, Cham (2016). https://doi.org/10.1007/978-3-319-46484-8_38
13. Das, S., Ma, K., Shu, Z., Samaras, D., Shilkrot, R.: DewarpNet: Single-image document unwarping with stacked 3D and 2D regression networks. In: Proceedings of the International Conference on Computer Vision (2019)
14. Das, S., Mishra, G., Sudharshana, A., Shilkrot, R.: The common fold: Utilizing the four-fold to dewarp printed documents from a single image. In: Proceedings of the 2017 ACM Symposium on Document Engineering, DocEng 2017, pp. 125–128. Association for Computing Machinery (2017). https://doi.org/10.1145/3103010.3121030
15. Das, S., et al.: End-to-end piece-wise unwarping of document images. In: Proceedings of the IEEE/CVF International Conference on Computer Vision, pp. 4268–4277 (2021)
16. Deng, J., Cheng, S., Xue, N., Zhou, Y., Zafeiriou, S.: Uv-gan: Adversarial facial uv map completion for pose-invariant face recognition. In: Proceedings of the IEEE Conference on Computer Vision and Pattern Recognition (2018)

17. Feng, H., Wang, Y., Zhou, W., Deng, J., Li, H.: Doctr: Document image transformer for geometric unwarping and illumination correction. arXiv preprint arXiv:2110.12942 (2021)
18. Garbin, S.J., Kowalski, M., Johnson, M., Shotton, J., Valentin, J.: Fastnerf: High-fidelity neural rendering at 200fps (2021)
19. Gropp, A., Yariv, L., Haim, N., Atzmon, M., Lipman, Y.: Implicit geometric regularization for learning shapes. arXiv preprint arXiv:2002.10099 (2020)
20. Groueix, T., Fisher, M., Kim, V.G., Russell, B.C., Aubry, M.: A papier-mâché approach to learning 3d surface generation. In: Proceedings of the IEEE Conference on Computer Vision and Pattern Recognition (2018)
21. Haker, S., Angenent, S., Tannenbaum, A., Kikinis, R., Sapiro, G., Halle, M.: Conformal surface parameterization for texture mapping. IEEE Trans. Visual Comput. Graphics 6(2), 181–189 (2000)
22. Hart, J.C.: Sphere tracing: A geometric method for the antialiased ray tracing of implicit surfaces. Vis. Comput. 12(10), 527–545 (1996)
23. Hedman, P., Philip, J., Price, T., Frahm, J.M., Drettakis, G., Brostow, G.: Deep blending for free-viewpoint image-based rendering. ACM Trans. Graph. (TOG) 37(6), 1–15 (2018)
24. Kato, H., Ushiku, Y., Harada, T.: Neural 3d mesh renderer. In: Proceedings of the IEEE Conference on Computer Vision and Pattern Recognition (2018)
25. Kil, T., Seo, W., Koo, H.I., Cho, N.I.: Robust Document Image Dewarping Method Using Text-Lines and Line Segments. In: Proceedings of the International Conference on Document Analysis and Recognition, Institute of Electrical and Electronics Engineers, pp. 865–870. IEEE (2017)
26. Koo, H.I., Kim, J., Cho, N.I.: Composition of a dewarped and enhanced document image from two view images. IEEE Trans. Image Process. 18(7), 1551–1562 (2009)
27. Li, T.M., Aittala, M., Durand, F., Lehtinen, J.: Differentiable monte carlo ray tracing through edge sampling. ACM Trans. Graph. (TOG) 37(6), 1–11 (2018)
28. Li, X., Zhang, B., Liao, J., Sander, P.V.: Document Rectification and Illumination Correction using a Patch-based CNN. ACM Trans. Graph. (TOG) 168, 1–11 (2019)
29. Li, Z., Niklaus, S., Snavely, N., Wang, O.: Neural scene flow fields for space-time view synthesis of dynamic scenes. arXiv preprint arXiv:2011.13084 (2020)
30. Liang, J., DeMenthon, D., Doermann, D.: Geometric rectification of camera-captured document images. IEEE Trans. Pattern Anal. Mach. Intell. 30(4), 591–605 (2008)
31. Liu, C., Yuen, J., Torralba, A.: Sift flow: Dense correspondence across scenes and its applications. IEEE Trans. Pattern Anal. Mach. Intell. 33(5), 978–994 (2011)
32. Liu, S., Li, T., Chen, W., Li, H.: Soft rasterizer: A differentiable renderer for image-based 3d reasoning. In: Proceedings of the International Conference on Computer Vision (2019)
33. Liu, S., Saito, S., Chen, W., Li, H.: Learning to infer implicit surfaces without 3d supervision. arXiv preprint arXiv:1911.00767 (2019)
34. Ma, K., Shu, Z., Bai, X., Wang, J., Samaras, D.: DocUNet: Document Image Unwarping via A Stacked U-Net. In: Proceedings of the IEEE Conference on Computer Vision and Pattern Recognition. Institute of Electrical and Electronics Engineers (2018)
35. Markovitz, A., Lavi, I., Perel, O., Mazor, S., Litman, R.: Can you read me now? Content aware rectification using angle supervision. In: Vedaldi, A., Bischof, H., Brox, T., Frahm, J.-M. (eds.) ECCV 2020. LNCS, vol. 12357, pp. 208–223. Springer, Cham (2020). https://doi.org/10.1007/978-3-030-58610-2_13

36. Meka, A., et al.: Deep reflectance fields: High-quality facial reflectance field inference from color gradient illumination. ACM Trans. Graph. (TOG) **38**(4), 1–12 (2019)
37. Meng, G., Huang, Z., Song, Y., Xiang, S., Pan, C.: Extraction of virtual baselines from distorted document images using curvilinear projection. In: Proceedings of the International Conference on Computer Vision (2015)
38. Meng, G., Su, Y., Wu, Y., Xiang, S., Pan, C.: Exploiting vector fields for geometric rectification of distorted document images. In: Ferrari, V., Hebert, M., Sminchisescu, C., Weiss, Y. (eds.) ECCV 2018. LNCS, vol. 11220, pp. 180–195. Springer, Cham (2018). https://doi.org/10.1007/978-3-030-01270-0_11
39. Mescheder, L., Oechsle, M., Niemeyer, M., Nowozin, S., Geiger, A.: Occupancy networks: Learning 3d reconstruction in function space. In: Proceedings of the IEEE/CVF Conference on Computer Vision and Pattern Recognition, pp. 4460–4470 (2019)
40. Mildenhall, B., Srinivasan, P.P., Tancik, M., Barron, J.T., Ramamoorthi, R., Ng, R.: NeRF: Representing scenes as neural radiance fields for view synthesis. In: Proceedings of the European Conference on Computer Vision (2020)
41. Miller, F.P., Vandome, A.F., McBrewster, J.: Levenshtein Distance: Information Theory, Computer Science, String (Computer Science), String Metric, Damerau?Levenshtein Distance, Spell Checker. Alpha Press, Hamming Distance (2009)
42. Mir, A., Alldieck, T., Pons-Moll, G.: Learning to transfer texture from clothing images to 3d humans. In: Proceedings of the IEEE Conference on Computer Vision and Pattern Recognition (2020)
43. Morreale, L., Aigerman, N., Kim, V., Mitra, N.J.: Neural surface maps (2021)
44. Niemeyer, M., Mescheder, L., Oechsle, M., Geiger, A.: Differentiable volumetric rendering: Learning implicit 3d representations without 3d supervision. In: Proceedings of the IEEE/CVF Conference on Computer Vision and Pattern Recognition, pp. 3504–3515 (2020)
45. Park, J.J., Florence, P., Straub, J., Newcombe, R., Lovegrove, S.: Deepsdf: Learning continuous signed distance functions for shape representation. In: Proceedings of the IEEE/CVF Conference on Computer Vision and Pattern Recognition, pp. 165–174 (2019)
46. Park, T., Liu, M.Y., Wang, T.C., Zhu, J.Y.: Semantic image synthesis with spatially-adaptive normalization. In: Proceedings of the IEEE Conference on Computer Vision and Pattern Recognition (2019)
47. Pumarola, A., Agudo, A., Porzi, L., Sanfeliu, A., Lepetit, V., Moreno-Noguer, F.: Geometry-aware network for non-rigid shape prediction from a single view. In: Proceedings of the IEEE Conference on Computer Vision and Pattern Recognition. Institute of Electrical and Electronics Engineers (2018)
48. Pumarola, A., Corona, E., Pons-Moll, G., Moreno-Noguer, F.: D-nerf: Neural radiance fields for dynamic scenes. arXiv preprint arXiv:2011.13961 (2020)
49. Ramon, E., et al.: H3d-net: Few-shot high-fidelity 3d head reconstruction. In: Proceedings of the IEEE/CVF International Conference on Computer Vision, pp. 5620–5629 (2021)
50. Schönberger, J.L., Frahm, J.M.: Structure-from-motion revisited. In: Conference on Computer Vision and Pattern Recognition (CVPR) (2016)
51. Schwarz, K., Liao, Y., Niemeyer, M., Geiger, A.: Graf: Generative radiance fields for 3d-aware image synthesis. In: Advances in Neural Information Processing Systems (2020)
52. Sitzmann, V., Martel, J.N., Bergman, A.W., Lindell, D.B., Wetzstein, G.: Implicit neural representations with periodic activation functions. arXiv (2020)

53. Sitzmann, V., Thies, J., Heide, F., Nießner, M., Wetzstein, G., Zollhofer, M.: Deep-voxels: Learning persistent 3d feature embeddings. In: Proceedings of the IEEE Conference on Computer Vision and Pattern Recognition (2019)
54. Sitzmann, V., Zollhöfer, M., Wetzstein, G.: Scene representation networks: Continuous 3d-structure-aware neural scene representations. arXiv preprint arXiv:1906.01618 (2019)
55. Tang, C., Tan, P.: Ba-net: Dense bundle adjustment network. arXiv preprint arXiv:1806.04807 (2018)
56. Tewari, A., et al.: State of the art on neural rendering. In: Computer Graphics Forum, vol. 39, pp. 701–727. Wiley Online Library (2020)
57. Tian, Y., Narasimhan, S.G.: Rectification and 3D reconstruction of curved document images. In: Proceedings of the IEEE Conference on Computer Vision and Pattern Recognition. Institute of Electrical and Electronics Engineers (2011)
58. Tzur, Y., Tal, A.: FlexiStickers: Photogrammetric texture mapping using casual images. In: Proceedings of the ACM SIGGRAPH Conference on Computer Graphics. Association for Computing Machinery (2009)
59. Ulges, A., Lampert, C.H., Breuel, T.: Document capture using stereo vision. In: Proceedings of the 2004 ACM Symposium on Document Engineering, DocEng 2004, pp. 198–200. Association for Computing Machinery (2004). https://doi.org/10.1145/1030397.1030434
60. Wada, T., Ukida, H., Matsuyama, T.: Shape from shading with interreflections under a proximal light source: Distortion-free copying of an unfolded book. Int. J. Comput. Vision **24**(2), 125–135 (1997)
61. Wang, N., Zhang, Y., Li, Z., Fu, Y., Liu, W., Jiang, Y.-G.: Pixel2Mesh: generating 3D mesh models from single RGB images. In: Ferrari, V., Hebert, M., Sminchisescu, C., Weiss, Y. (eds.) ECCV 2018. LNCS, vol. 11215, pp. 55–71. Springer, Cham (2018). https://doi.org/10.1007/978-3-030-01252-6_4
62. Wang, Z., Simoncelli, E.P., Bovik, A.C.: Multiscale structural similarity for image quality assessment. In: The Thirty-Seventh Asilomar Conference on Signals, Systems and Computers. Institute of Electrical and Electronics Engineers (2003)
63. Wei, S.E., et al.: Vr facial animation via multiview image translation. ACM Trans. Graph. (TOG) **38**(4), 1–16 (2019)
64. Xiang, F., Xu, Z., Hašan, M., Hold-Geoffroy, Y., Sunkavalli, K., Su, H.: NeuTex: Neural texture mapping for volumetric neural rendering. arXiv preprint arXiv:2103.00762 (2021)
65. Xu, Z., Sunkavalli, K., Hadap, S., Ramamoorthi, R.: Deep image-based relighting from optimal sparse samples. ACM Trans. Graph. (TOG) **37**(4), 1–13 (2018)
66. Yariv, L., Kasten, Y., Moran, D., Galun, M., Atzmon, M., Ronen, B., Lipman, Y.: Multiview neural surface reconstruction by disentangling geometry and appearance. In: Advances in Neural Information Processing Systems, vol. 33 (2020)
67. You, S., Matsushita, Y., Sinha, S., Bou, Y., Ikeuchi, K.: Multiview rectification of folded documents. IEEE Trans. Pattern Anal. Mach. Intell. **40**, 505–511 (2017)
68. Yu, A., Ye, V., Tancik, M., Kanazawa, A.: pixelNeRF: Neural radiance fields from one or few images. arXiv preprint arXiv:2012.02190 (2020)
69. Zhao, F., Liao, S., Zhang, K., Shao, L.: Human parsing based texture transfer from single image to 3D human via cross-view consistency. In: Advances in Neural Information Processing Systems (2020)

Towards Regression-Free Neural Networks for Diverse Compute Platforms

Rahul Duggal, Hao Zhou, Shuo Yang, Jun Fang$^{(\boxtimes)}$, Yuanjun Xiong, and Wei Xia

AWS/Amazon AI, Seattle, USA
rduggal7@gatech.edu, {zhouho,shuoy,junfa,yuanjx,wxia}@amazon.com

Abstract. Our work tackles the emergent problem of reducing predictive inconsistencies arising as negative flips: test samples that are correctly predicted by a less accurate model, but incorrectly by a more accurate one. We introduce **REG**ression constrained **N**eural **A**rchitecture **S**earch (REG-NAS) to design a family of highly accurate models that engender fewer negative flips. REG-NAS consists of two components: (1) A novel architecture constraint that enables a larger model to contain all the weights of the smaller one thus maximizing weight sharing. This idea stems from our observation that larger weight sharing among networks leads to similar sample-wise predictions and results in fewer negative flips; (2) A novel search reward that incorporates both Top-1 accuracy and negative flips in the architecture search metric. We demonstrate that REG-NAS can successfully find desirable architectures with few negative flips in three popular architecture search spaces. Compared to the existing state-of-the-art approach [35], REG-NAS enables 33–48% relative reduction of negative flips.

1 Introduction

Consider a manufacturer that uses deep learning to detect defective products on their assembly line. To improve throughput, they use a small, low-latency, on-device model to quickly detect potentially defective products which later undergo a secondary examination by a large, and more accurate model deployed on the cloud. If there are many cases where the on-device model correctly identifies a defective product which, on second inspection the on-cloud model incorrectly believes to be qualified, the defective product may end up entering the market and damaging the reputation of the manufacturer (See Fig. 1a).

R. Duggal—Currently at Georgia Tech. Work conducted during an internship with AWS AI.

Supplementary Information The online version contains supplementary material available at https://doi.org/10.1007/978-3-031-19836-6_34.

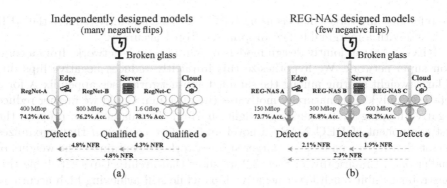

Fig. 1. Regression arises when samples that are correctly predicted by a less accurate model are *negatively flipped* or incorrectly predicted by a more accurate one. (a) Three models from the popular RegNet [23] family trained on ImageNet suffer from 4.3 − 4.8% pairwise negative flip rate (NFR); (b) Models designed via REG-NAS achieve 1.9 − 2.3% NFR with similar Top-1 accuracy.

Such samples, which one model predicts correctly while the other predicts incorrectly, are called negative flips. The fraction of negative flips over the dataset size is called the negative flip rate (NFR) [35] and is used to measure regression between two models[1]. In this work, we aim to design a family of models for diverse compute budgets (*e.g.* deployed on edge, server, and cloud) that maximize Top-1 accuracy and minimizes the pairwise negative flip rate (See Fig. 1b).

Positive congruent training [35] is the first work to tackle negative flips. They propose the Focal Distillation (FD) loss, which enforces congruence with the reference model by giving more weights to samples that were correctly classified by the reference model. While [35] aims at reducing flips along the *temporal* axis, *i.e.* between different model versions trained on growing datasets, we tackle regression along the *spatial* axis, *i.e.* between models deployed on diverse compute platforms. The key difference being that the temporal setting constrains the model design to necessarily be *sequential* since the past model is fixed while the current model is designed and the future model is unknown. In contrast, the spatial setting enjoys larger flexibility wherein all models can be *jointly* adapted towards minimizing negative flips.

To quantify the difference between sequential and joint design strategies, Fig. 2a presents the case of designing a small (reference) and a large (target) model. Independently training a MobileNet-v3 reference and an EfficientNet-B1 target model using cross entropy loss achieves 73.6% and 77.08% Top-1 accuracies with more than 4.25% negative flip rate. Training the target model *sequentially* against the fixed reference model via focal distillation loss [35] reduces the NFR to 3.25% with a 0.8% drop in Top-1 accuracy. However, *jointly* designing

---

[1] Please note this definition of regression is different from the traditional one which pertains to predicting the outcome of continuous variables.

the reference and target models using REG-NAS significantly reduces the NFR to 2.16% with a marginal 0.25% drop in the Top-1 accuracy.

REG-NAS can jointly design models by sampling sub-networks from a common super-network. We hypothesize this implicitly reduces negative flips due to large weight sharing among the sampled sub-networks (see appendix A for a detailed study). This naturally motivates the question: Could we further reduce negative flipping by maximizing weight sharing? To this end, we propose the first component of REG-NAS—a novel *architecture constraint* that maximizes weight-sharing by enabling the larger sub-networks to contain all the weights of smaller ones. Empirically, in Sect. 3.2 we show that architectures satisfying this constraint exhibit much lower negative flips while still achieving high accuracy.

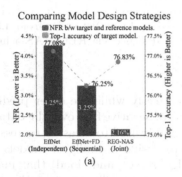
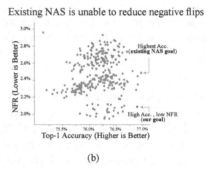

(a)   (b)

Fig. 2. (a) Independently training a MobileNet-V3 and EfficientNet-B1 as reference and target models leads to 73.6%, 77.08% Top-1 accuracies with 4.25% negative flip rate (NFR). Sequentially training the target against the reference model with the Focal Distillation loss [35] reduces NFR to the detriment of target model's accuracy. Jointly designing the reference and the target models via REG-NAS leads to lowest NFR with negligible drop in accuracy. (b) Plotting the Top-1 accuracy and NFR (measured against a common reference model) for 300 randomly sampled architectures. Observe that the NFR and Top-1 accuracy are uncorrelated which means existing NAS that maximizes Top-1 accuracy may fail to find models with the lowest negative flip rate.

While weight sharing implicitly helps reduce negative flips, it is not sufficient. Figure 2b shows that among architectures that maximally share weights by satisfying the architecture constraint, there is a significant variance in NFR and Top-1 accuracy. Importantly, the Top-1 accuracy and NFR are *uncorrelated*. This means that existing architecture search methods that solely optimize for higher Top-1 accuracy may fail to find models with low NFR. To search for highly accurate architectures that minimize regression, in Sect. 3.3 we propose the second component of REG-NAS—a novel *search reward* that includes both Top-1 accuracy and NFR as the architecture search metric.

Together, our proposed architecture constraint and novel search reward enable REG-NAS to reduce negative flips by 33 − 48% over the existing state-of-the-art FD loss [35]. We also show that REG-NAS can find low NFR sub-networks from popular architecture search spaces, demonstrating its strong generalization ability. Additionally, the models searched via REG-NAS are transitive under the NFR metric, enabling the search for N ($\geq$ 2) models across diverse compute budgets. To summarize, our contributions are:

1. We extend the search for regression-free models from the temporal to the spatial setting. This support scenarios that simultaneously deploy a family of models across diverse compute budgets.
2. We propose two novel ideas to minimize negative flips while achieving high Top-1 accuracy: an architecture constraint that maximizes weight sharing thereby inducing similar sample-wise behavior; and a novel architecture search reward to explicitly include NFR in the architecture search metric.
3. We comprehensively evaluate our search method on ImageNet and demonstrate its generalization on three popular architecture search spaces.

2   Related Work and Background

Minimizing regression between different models has previously been explored in the temporal setting where different model versions arise during model updates [26,27]. Generally, this task closely relates to research in continual learning [5,16,21], incremental learning [1,3,33] and model compatibility [13,26,35]. However, the main difference lies in how regression is measured. Traditionally, regression or forgetting was measured via the error rate [4,17,20], however, Yan *et.al.* [35] observe that two models having the similar error rates may still suffer from a high negative flip rate. Moreover, the methods that proposed to alleviate catastrophic forgetting are insufficient at reducing NFR. Different from these works, our work tackles NFR in the spatial setting wherein different models arise due to a diversity in deployment targets (*e.g.* edge, server, cloud). The spatial setting is fundamentally different from the temporal one since it enjoys the additional flexibility of jointly designing all architectures that can benefit from weight sharing that ultimately leads to similar sample-wise behavior and lower NFR. This key distinction calls for new methods that can leverage the flexibility of joint architecture design.

Neural architecture search (NAS) is a popular tool for automated design of neural architectures. Earlier NAS methods based on reinforcement learning [18,29,38], evolutionary algorithms [24,25,28,34], and Bayesian optimization [15] find highly accurate networks but are notoriously computational heavy due to the independent evaluation of candidate networks. Recently One-Shot NAS approaches [19,22,36] successfully adopt weight sharing to alleviate the compute burden. The main innovation in this area is a super-network [2,7,14,30–32,37] that can encode and jointly train all candidate sub-networks in an architecture space. Typically, One-Shot NAS algorithms have the following two phases:

[P1] Super-network Pre-training: The goal of which is to jointly optimize all sub-networks through a weight sharing super-network. The optimization process typically samples and minimizes the loss on many individual sub-networks during training. Recent methods innovate on the sampling strategy [2,7,31,32,37] or the loss formulation [30].

[P2] Sub-network Searching: The goal of this phase is to find the best sub-network from the well-trained super-network under some compute measure such as flops or latency. This search is typically implemented via an evolutionary algorithm [2,30,31] with Top-1 accuracy as the reward function.

Our work leverages a super-network for an entirely new benefit– for reducing negative flips between networks optimized for diverse compute platforms. This is yet an unexplored problem that we believe will become increasingly important in the era of on-device AI powered by hardware optimized neural networks.

3   Regression Constrained Neural Architecture Search

Our REG-NAS algorithm relates to the super-network searching phase (**P2**) and generally works with any super-network obtained via the recent pre-training strategies (**P1**) [2,30,31]. We modify the search optimization of **P2** along two directions: We propose a novel architecture constraint that maximizes weight sharing among sub-networks which is discussed in Sect. 3.2. We propose a novel search reward that incorporates both Top-1 accuracy and the NFR metric as described in Sect. 3.3. Finally, we integrate these two ideas into our REG-NAS algorithm as discussed in Sect. 3.4.

3.1   Measuring Regression

We use the negative flip rate (NFR) [35] as the metric to measure the regression between two models. Given a dataset $\mathcal{D}$ that contains image and label pairs (x_i, y_i), $i \in \{1, ..., N\}$, the output of two deep CNNs ϕ_1, ϕ_2 on an input image x_i are denoted by y_i^1 and y_i^2. The NFR between ϕ_1, ϕ_2 is defined as:

$$\text{NFR}(\phi_1, \phi_2; \mathcal{D}) = \frac{1}{N} \sum_{i=1}^{N} \mathbb{1}(y_i^1 = y_i, y_i^2 \neq y_i), \tag{1}$$

where $\mathbb{1}$ is an indicator function. The NFR measures the fraction of samples that are predicted correctly by ϕ_1 and incorrectly by ϕ_2. Note that NFR is asymmetric, so $\text{NFR}(\phi_1, \phi_2) \neq \text{NFR}(\phi_2, \phi_1)$. We select ϕ_1 as the model with a lower Top-1 accuracy and ϕ_2 as the one with the higher Top-1 accuracy. As a result, $\text{NFR}(\phi_1, \phi_2) \in [0, 1]$.

3.2 Architecture Constraint to Reduce Negative Flips

We hypothesize that sub-networks sampled from a super-network share a lot of weights, which induces similar sample-wise behavior and results in less negative flips. A natural extension of this hypothesis prompts the question: can we further reduce negative flips by maximizing weight-sharing between sub-networks? In what follows, we describe the architecture constraint that answers this question.

Consider a reference model with architecture a_r that inherits weights $W^*_{a_r}$ from a super-network. We aim to search for a target architecture a_t with weights $W^*_{a_t}$ such that the weight sharing between a_r and a_t is maximized, $i.e.$:

$$a_t = \arg\max_{a \in \mathcal{A}} \mathcal{N}(W^*_a \cap W^*_{a_r}),$$

$$\text{s.t.} \ \ C(a) < \tau, \tag{2}$$

where $\mathcal{N}$ counts the number of weights, $\cap$ represents the intersection of weights between two architectures, C represents a performance constraint such as flops or latency and $\mathcal{A}$ represents the search space defined by the super-network. Equation 2 specifies the architecture constraint and we refer to the process of solving it as **constrained architecture search (CAS)**.

Observe that $N(W^*_a \cap W^*_{a_r})$ is upper bounded by $N(W^*_{a_r})$, with the supremum occurring when a contains all the weights of a_r. This means Eq. 2 partitions the architecture space $\mathcal{A}$ to a space $\mathcal{A}_t$ of constrained architectures:

$$\mathcal{A}_t = \{a : W^*_{a_r} \subseteq W^*_a, \forall a \in \mathcal{A}\}, \tag{3}$$

and its complementary space $\mathcal{A}_c = \mathcal{A} - \mathcal{A}_t$ that includes target architectures that do not contain *all* the weights of the reference model. To visualize the two architecture spaces, we plot NFR $v.s.$ Top-1 accuracy for 300 randomly sampled architectures from $\mathcal{A}_t$ and $\mathcal{A}_c$ in Fig. 4a. Observe that the architectures in space $\mathcal{A}_t$ generally have lower NFR and higher Top-1 accuracy compared to those in $\mathcal{A}_c$. As a result, it is easier to find architectures with lower NFR and higher Top-1 accuracy in space $\mathcal{A}_t$ than in the complete space $\mathcal{A}$ as demonstrated empirically in Sect. 4.3.

Note that, not all super-networks allow for partitioning the search space according to Eq. 3. For example DARTS [6,19] implements different operators ($e.g.$ 3×3 and 5×5 conv) using a completely non-overlapping set of weights. In such search spaces, enforcing the architecture constraint trivially leads to the same architecture for the reference and target model. On the other hand, recent works [2,30,31] implement different operators using an overlapping set of weights $e.g.$ the innermost 3×3 weights of the 5×5 kernel implements a 3×3 kernel. To enable the architecture constraint for such works, we propose the CAS recipe which specifies three rules for searching a candidate architecture a_t against a reference model a_r:

1. Add new layers within blocks of a_r (Fig. 3a).
2. Add additional channels to filters in a_r (Fig. 3b).
3. Extend kernel size for filters in a_r (Fig. 3c).

Operations permitted by CAS

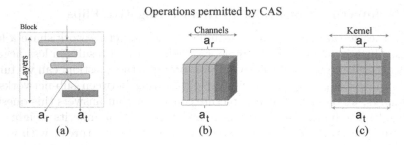

Fig. 3. Constrained Architecture Search (CAS) recipe specifies three operations for searching a target model a_t given a reference model a_r: (a) Adding new layers within an existing block of a_r; (b) Adding new channels to existing filters in a_r; (c) Extending the kernel size beyond the existing one in a_r.

3.3   Search Reward to Reduce NFR

While the architecture constraint implicitly helps reduce NFR through weight sharing, it is not sufficient. To illustrate this, we plot the Top-1 accuracy and the NFR of 300 randomly sampled sub-networks from $\mathcal{A}_t$ against a fixed reference model in Fig. 2b. Observe that the model with highest Top-1 accuracy has a NFR around 2.5% which is higher than many of the sampled architectures. This means that optimizing solely for the Top-1 accuracy as in existing NAS methods will not lead to architectures with small NFR. Consequently, to optimize for architectures with low NFR it is essential to include NFR in the search reward.

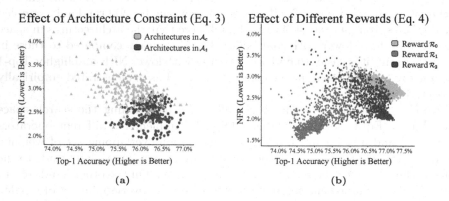

Fig. 4. Through random sampling architectures from the MobileNet-V3 search space $\mathcal{A}$ of OFA [2], we show: (a) The architecture constraint partitions $\mathcal{A}$ into A_t and A_c wherein the architectures in A_t tend to have lower NFR; (b) An evolutionary search fitted with rewards $(\mathcal{R}_0, \mathcal{R}_1, \mathcal{R}_2)$ explores different regions of the architecture space. Specifically, $\mathcal{R}_0$ leads to architectures with high Top-1 and NFR, $\mathcal{R}_1$ leads to architectures with low Top-1 and NFR while $\mathcal{R}_2$ achieves the best of both–high Top-1 accuracy and low NFR.

The observations of Fig. 2b naturally motivate the inclusion of NFR in the search reward $\mathcal{R}$ as below:

$$\mathcal{R}\left(W_{a_t}^*; W_{a_r}^*, \mathcal{D}^{val}\right) = \lambda_1 * \text{Top-1}(W_{a_t}^*; \mathcal{D}^{val})$$
$$- \lambda_2 * \text{NFR}(W_{a_t}^*, W_{a_r}^*; \mathcal{D}^{val}), \qquad (4)$$

where $W_{a_r}^*, W_{a_t}^*$ represents the weights of the reference and target models while λ_1, λ_2 balance the trade off between Top-1 accuracy and NFR respectively. To illustrate the extreme effect of the two terms, we consider three different rewards obtained by setting the following values of λ_1 and λ_2.

$\mathcal{R}_0$ ($\lambda_1 = 1, \lambda_2 = 0$): reward used by existing NAS methods that solely optimizes for high Top-1 accuracy.

$\mathcal{R}_1$ ($\lambda_1 = 0, \lambda_2 = 1$): reward that solely optimizes for low NFR.

$\mathcal{R}_2$ ($\lambda_1 = 1, \lambda_2 = 1$): reward that optimizes for high accuracy and low NFR.

We find that the rewards $\mathcal{R}_0$, $\mathcal{R}_1$ and $\mathcal{R}_2$ can guide evolutionary search to different regions of the architecture search space. Figure 4b illustrates this by plotting the Top-1 accuracy and NFR of all architectures sampled during an evolutionary search fitted with the three rewards. The plot clearly shows that $\mathcal{R}_2$ guides the search to architectures with high Top-1 and low NFR. We consider $\mathcal{R}_2$ as the default choice for REG-NAS since it equally balances the Top-1 accuracy and NFR. Please refer to appendix B for a complete ablation on λ_1, λ_2.

3.4   REG-NAS: Regression Constrained Neural Architecture Search

To search for sub-networks that achieve the highest Top-1 accuracy with the minimum negative flips, we integrate the novel architecture constraint of Eq. 3 with the novel reward of Eq. 5 to propose REG-NAS, which solves the following optimization.

$$a_t = \arg\max_{a \in \mathcal{A}} \mathcal{R}\left(W_a^*; W_{a_r}^*, \mathcal{D}^{val}\right),$$
$$\text{s.t. } W_{a_r}^* \subseteq W_a^*, \text{and } C(a) < \tau \qquad (5)$$

We solve the above optimization using a standard evolutionary based NAS algorithm with two modifications: the random sampling and mutate operations can only perform the operations specified by the CAS in Sect. 3.2; and the search reward uses the reward formulation of Sect. 3.3 with $\lambda_1 = 1, \lambda_2 = 1$.

4   Experiments

We begin by comparing REG-NAS against the state-of-the-art method [35] designed to reduce NFR. To understand the effectiveness of REG-NAS, we dissect the performance gains due to the novel architecture constraint and search reward. We then extend the proposed method to search for an entire family of architectures. Finally, we test the generalization of REG-NAS across: different flop budgets, super-networks, and latency constraints on diverse platforms.

4.1 Dataset, Metrics and Implementation Details

We implement our methods using Pytorch on a system containing 8 V100 GPUs. Other details are as follows:

Dataset. We present all results on ImageNet [8]. We carve out a sub-training set of 20,000 images from the original training set to evaluate the rewards and update batchnorm statistics for each sub-network [2]. The final results are presented on the original ImageNet validation set.

Evolutionary Search. To search for a sub-network, we run the evolutionary search with the following hyper-parameters: 20 generations, 100 population size, 0.1 mutate probability, 0.5 mutation ratio and 25% Top-K architectures moving into the next generation. Overall, our search evaluates 1,525 architectures in each super-network. Following the setting of the original work, for MobileNet-V3 and ResNet-50 search spaces of OFA [2], the rewards are computed on the sampled sub-training set, while for FBNet-V3 super-network of AttentiveNAS [31] and AlphaNet [30], the search is performed on the ImageNet validation set as suggested by [30,31].

Notation. We refer to different models following the consistent notation AA-BB-CC. The first initial "AA" refer to the super-network, the middle initial "BB" refers to the search reward and the final initial "CC" refers to the performance constraint such as flops or latency. We use CAS to represent constrained architecture search discussed in Sect. 3.2.

4.2 Regression Constrained Search

Given a small reference model, we aim to find a larger target model that, under a fixed compute budget, maximizes the Top-1 accuracy while minimizing NFR. Table 1 illustrates this task with comparative results from the MobileNet-V3 and ResNet-50 search spaces of OFA [2].

We first search for the best reference model under 150 mega flops constraint (MB-$\mathcal{R}_0$-150) using the $\mathcal{R}_0$ reward which maximizes Top-1 accuracy. Then, we establish a baseline by training an off-the-shelf EfficientNet-B0 model[2] using vanilla cross entropy. This model improves Top-1 accuracy to 77%, but suffers from 4.25% negative flips. A stronger baseline can be achieved by training the EfficientNet using Focal Distillation [35] which is the current state-of-the-art method to reduce negative flips. It reduces the NFR to 3.25% with a 0.8% drop in Top-1 accuracy. Another strong weight sharing baseline can be obtained via searching a sub-network from the same super-network as the reference model

---

[2] We choose EfficientNet-B0 since it has similar Top-1 accuracy with sub-networks searched from MobileNet-V3 in OFA [2].

Table 1. Comparing different model design strategies. We present results for MobileNet-V3 (MB) and ResNet-50 (RN) search spaces of OFA [2]. EffNet and RN101 represents EfficientNet-B0 and ResNet-101 trained with cross entropy loss, while EffNet+FD and RN101+FD are trained with state-of-the-art focal distillation loss [35]. Results of weight sharing and our proposed method are averaged from three runs with different random seeds.

	Model	Flops	Top-1 $\uparrow$(%)	NFR $\downarrow$ (%)
ref	MB-$\mathcal{R}_0$-150 [2]	149	73.70	–
baseline	EffNet	385	77.08	4.25
PCT	EffNet+FD [35]	385	76.25	3.25
wt. share	MB-$\mathcal{R}_0$-300 [2]	298	77.11	2.51
REG-NAS	MB-($\mathcal{R}_2$+CAS)-300	294	76.83	2.16

(a) MobileNet-V3 search space of OFA

	Model	Flops	Top-1 $\uparrow$(%)	NFR $\downarrow$ (%)
ref	RN-$\mathcal{R}_0$-2000 [2]	1973	78.25	–
baseline	RN101	7598	79.21	4.83
PCT	RN101+FD [35]	7598	79.90	3.06
wt. share	RN-$\mathcal{R}_0$-3000 [2]	2941	78.78	2.04
REG-NAS	RN-($\mathcal{R}_2$+CAS)-3000	2915	78.80	1.57

(b) ResNet search space of OFA

using $\mathcal{R}_0$ reward. This leads to an NFR of 2.51% with 77.11% Top-1 accuracy. Compared to all of these, the networks obtained via REG-NAS *i.e.* (MB-($\mathcal{R}_2$+CAS)-300) achieves the lowest NFR of 2.16% with less than 0.3% drop in Top-1 accuracy compared with MB-$\mathcal{R}_0$-300. This constitutes a 50% and 33% relative reduction of NFR with respect to the baseline and existing state-of-the-art method with less than 1% change in accuracy (see appendix C). The strong performance of REG-NAS clearly demonstrates the benefits of the search reward and architecture constraint. Similar results can be observed for the ResNet-50 search space of OFA [2] in Table 1b.

Table 2. Comparing different search rewards using the MobileNet-V3 (MB) and ResNet-50 (RN) search spaces of OFA [2]. Results (except ref) are averaged from three runs with different seeds.

	Model	Flops	Top-1 $\uparrow$ (%)	NFR $\downarrow$ (%)
ref	MB-$\mathcal{R}_0$-150	149	73.70	–
paragon Top-1	MB-$\mathcal{R}_0$-300	298	77.11	2.51
paragon NFR	MB-$\mathcal{R}_1$-300	279	76.20	2.07
	MB-$\mathcal{R}_2$-300	292	76.90	2.25
REG-NAS	MB-($\mathcal{R}_2$+CAS)-300	294	76.83	2.16

(a) MobileNet-V3 search space of OFA

	Model	Flops	Top-1 $\uparrow$(%)	NFR $\downarrow$ (%)
ref	RN-$\mathcal{R}_0$-2000	1973	78.25	–
paragon Top-1	RN-$\mathcal{R}_0$-3000	2941	78.78	2.04
paragon NFR	RN-$\mathcal{R}_1$-3000	2537	78.57	1.28
	RN-$\mathcal{R}_2$-3000	2972	78.87	1.76
REG-NAS	RN-($\mathcal{R}_2$+CAS)-3000	2915	78.80	1.57

(b) ResNet search space of OFA

4.3 Dissecting the Performance of REG-NAS

In this subsection, we study the contribution of different components of REG-NAS—the search reward and the constrained architecture search, in reducing NFR. Table 2 presents the performance of architectures searched via $\mathcal{R}_0$, $\mathcal{R}_1$, $\mathcal{R}_2$ and $\mathcal{R}_2$+CAS. We observe that since $\mathcal{R}_0$ only includes Top-1 accuracy in its formulation, the optimal architecture searched via it achieves the best accuracy, which we treat as the paragon for Top-1 accuracy. However, this same architecture also suffers from the highest NFR. On the other hand, $\mathcal{R}_1$, which only includes the NFR in its formulation, leads to a model with the lowest NFR, and also lowest Top-1 accuracy. We treat this model as the paragon for NFR.

Effect of Reward $\mathcal{R}_2$. By including both the Top-1 accuracy and NFR in its formulation, reward $\mathcal{R}_2$ leads to models that lie closer to the paragon of both metrics. The best results, however, are achieved by including the architecture constraint which further brings the models closer to the respective paragons. In the case of MobileNet-V3, architecture searched by $\mathcal{R}_2$+CAS is within 0.09% of the paragon of NFR and within 0.28% of the paragon of Top-1 accuracy, which demonstrates the effectiveness of the proposed method.

Effect of Architecture Constraint. Besides reducing NFR, we find that CAS also help search for an architecture with low NFR much faster compared with $\mathcal{R}_2$ as shown in Fig. 5a. This is because CAS partitions the overall architecture space into a subspace containing well performing architectures that achieve low NFR and high Top-1 accuracy as described in Sect. 3.2.

Effect of Model Size. It is natural to ask if a smaller gap in Top-1 accuracy would imply a smaller NFR? The answer is provided in Fig. 5b which plots the accuracy and NFR for 9 target models (from 175 to 600 Mflops) searched against a common 150 Mflop reference model with 73.7% Top-1 accuracy. Observe that with $\mathcal{R}_0$, even for the smallest model with similar accuracy as the reference, the NFR is consistently high ($\approx 2.5\%$). This suggests that accuracy gap between reference and target has little impact on the NFR. Additionally, we see that the search with $\mathcal{R}_2 + CAS$ outperforms $\mathcal{R}_0$ across all model sizes.

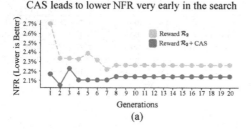
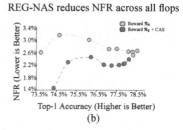

CAS leads to lower NFR very early in the search

Generations

(a)

REG-NAS reduces NFR across all flops

Top-1 Accuracy (Higher is Better)

(b)

Fig. 5. (a) NFR of the optimal architecture in each generation of the evolutionary search. Observe that CAS leads to lower NFR early and throughout the search. (b) Top-1 accuracy and NFR for 9 models (175–500 mflops) searched against a common reference (150 mflops). Observe that a smaller accuracy gap doesn't imply a smaller NFR. Also $\mathcal{R}_2 + CAS$ outperforms $\mathcal{R}_0$ for all sizes.

4.4 Supercharging REG-NAS with PCT

We study if fine-tuning with FD loss proposed in [35] can help further reduce the NFR for architectures searched via REG-NAS. Table 3 compares two loss functions: vanilla cross entropy (CE) and FD[3] for fine-tuning the target sub-networks obtained via REG-NAS.

We observe that fine tuning with CE generally results in a higher NFR. This is expected because CE optimizes the weights for higher Top-1 accuracy, which may push the weights of the target model away from those of the reference. In contrast, FD loss promotes similar sample-wise behavior by penalizing negative flips and leads to a lower NFR. This study demonstrates that FD loss can work in tandem with REG-NAS to further reduce NFR. However, even without fine tuning, the architectures searched by REG-NAS already enjoy a very low NFR, even outperforming the MB-$\mathcal{R}_0$-300 architecture with fine tuning. Considering the large time cost of fine tuning, we avoid it in the following discussion.

Table 3. Comparing fine-tuning strategies post inheriting the weights from a super-network. "–" denotes no fine tuning, CE denotes cross entropy, and FD denotes focal distillation [35]. Results averaged across three random seeds.

Super-networks	Model	Fine tune	Top-1 ↑(%)	NFR ↓ (%)
MobileNet-V3	MB-$\mathcal{R}_0$-150	–	73.70	–
	MB-$\mathcal{R}_0$-300	–	77.11	2.51
		CE	77.37	2.53
		FD [35]	76.94	2.20
	MB-($\mathcal{R}_2$+CAS)-300	–	76.83	2.16
		CE	77.05	2.37
		FD [35]	76.70	2.12
ResNet	RN-$\mathcal{R}_0$-2000	–	78.25	–
	RN-$\mathcal{R}_0$-3000	–	78.78	2.04
		CE	78.68	2.47
		FD [35]	78.37	1.33
	RN-($\mathcal{R}_2$+CAS)-3000	–	78.79	1.57
		CE	78.63	2.16
		FD [35]	78.47	0.96

4.5 Additional Properties of REG-NAS

In this section, we study two key properties of REG-NAS: *transitivity*, as it enables the search for models at diverse flop budgets and the *search direction*.

---

[3] We use FD-KD from [35] since it outperforms FD-LM in our setting.

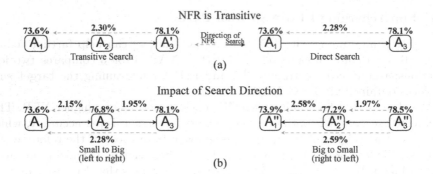

Fig. 6. Using the MobileNet-V3 search space of OFA [2] we illustrate two key properties of NFR (a) **transitivity**: (left) A 600 Mflops model A'_3 searched against a 300 Mflops model A_2 that was previously searched against a 150 Mflops one A_1, automatically achieves a similar NFR as directly searching A_3 against A_1 (right). (b) **Effect of search direction**: small to big search (left) leads to lower NFR compared to the opposite direction (right).

Transitivity of NFR. Transitivity is measured through the following experiment. Given a reference model A_1, we first search for a model A_2 having low NFR using REG-NAS. Then we study whether the model A_3 searched using A_2 as reference model can lead to a low NFR between A_3 and A_1. Figure 6a illustrates this property using the MobileNet-V3 search space of OFA [2]. We can search for a 600 Mflops model in two ways: (1) Transitively search a 600 Mflops model A'_3 against a 300 Mflops A_2 that was previously searched the 150 Mflops reference A_1. (2) Directly search a 600 Mflops model A_3 against the 150 Mflops reference A_1; Observe that the two models A'_3, A_3 so obtained achieve a similar NFR with respect to A_1, demonstrating that NFR among architectures searched via REG-NAS is transitive. Based on transitivity property, when searching for a series of architectures, the ith one can be searched against the $i - 1^{th}$ one thereby ensuring a low NFR between the ith and $i - 2^{th}$ ones.

Search Direction. Until now we have focused on a setting in which given a *small* reference model, we search for a *larger* target model. We call this the small → large setting. Figure 6b compares the opposite setting *i.e.* large → small. We observe that the small → large setting benefits in reducing NFR for all subnets whereas the opposite direction leads to higher Top-1 accuracy at the cost of higher NFR. Since we aim to minimize NFR, we follow the small → large setting for all experiments.

4.6   Generalization Performance of REG-NAS

In this subsection, we investigate the performance of REG-NAS for searching a family of models; from different super-networks and search spaces; with latency constraints on different platforms.

REG-NAS for Searching a Family of Models. By leveraging transitive search as discussed in Sect. 4.5, we can use REG-NAS to search for a family of models suited for different devices (*e.g.* phone, laptop, cloud). We demonstrate this by searching for three different models A1, A2, A3 with different flop budgets in Table 4 where we present the NFR between each pair of models. Compared to vanilla NAS that optimizes for Top-1 accuracy using $\mathcal{R}_0$ reward, REG-NAS can consistently reduce the NFR metric. In some scenarios, the benefit is quite large *e.g.* between models A2, A3 searched in the MobileNet-V3 and ResNet-50 based super-networks of OFA [2]. Please see appendix D for results on four models.

Table 4. Testing generalization of REG-NAS for searching multiple models with diverse super-networks. Model size increases from A_1 to A_3. NFR is indicated in green and Top-1 accuracy in orange. REG-NAS successfully reduces NFR in all scenarios.

Supernet	Method	Results
MB-V3	OFA [2]	$A_1(73.7\%)\xleftarrow{2.51\%}A_2(77.1\%)\xleftarrow{2.41\%}A_3(78.5\%)$; 2.63%
	REG-NAS	$A_1(73.7\%)\xleftarrow{2.16\%}A_2(76.8\%)\xleftarrow{1.95\%}A_3(78.2\%)$; 2.30%
RN-50	OFA [2]	$A_1(78.2\%)\xleftarrow{2.04\%}A_2(78.8\%)\xleftarrow{1.53\%}A_3(79.2\%)$; 1.90%
	REG-NAS	$A_1(78.2\%)\xleftarrow{1.57\%}A_2(78.8\%)\xleftarrow{0.83\%}A_3(79.0\%)$; 1.74%
FBNet-V3	Att-NAS [31]	$A_1(76.5\%)\xleftarrow{2.39\%}A_2(79.7\%)\xleftarrow{2.03\%}A_3(80.9\%)$; 2.31%
	REG-NAS	$A_1(76.5\%)\xleftarrow{2.26\%}A_2(79.5\%)\xleftarrow{1.84\%}A_3(80.7\%)$; 2.30%
FBNet-V3	α-Net [30]	$A_1(76.9\%)\xleftarrow{2.10\%}A_2(80.0\%)\xleftarrow{1.84\%}A_3(80.9\%)$; 2.07%
	REG-NAS	$A_1(76.9\%)\xleftarrow{1.97\%}A_2(79.9\%)\xleftarrow{1.32\%}A_3(80.7\%)$; 1.96%

REG-NAS with Different Supernetworks. One-shot NAS is an actively evolving research area, with many recent innovations in super-network pre-training. To demonstrate that REG-NAS can generalize to different super-networks, we apply REG-NAS on two state-of-the-art FBNet-V3 based super-networks: AttentiveNAS [31] that uses attentive sampling to improve sub-network accuracy and AlphaNet [30] that uses alpha divergence to improve knowledge transfer from larger to small sub-networks. Table 4 shows that REG-NAS consistently reduces the NFR for all pairs of models, with particularly large reduction between models A_2 and A_3 in the case of AlphaNet.

Table 5. Testing generalization of REG-NAS under latency constraints. We use a model with 15 ms latency on a Samsung Note 10 as the reference to search a target model with 30 ms latency on an Nvidia 1080ti GPU. REG-NAS successfully reduces NFR.

Target device	Model	Latency (ms)	Top-1 ↑(%)	NFR (%) ↓(%)
Note10	MB-$\mathcal{R}_0$-15	14.83	73.34	–
	MB-$\mathcal{R}_0$-30	29.40	77.30	2.72
1080ti	MB-($\mathcal{R}_2$+CAS)-30	29.88	77.07	2.22

REG-NAS with Latency Constraints. We test whether REG-NAS can find low NFR sub-networks using latency (instead of flops) as the compute metric. For this experiment, we search for two models: a reference model with 15 ms latency deployed on a Samsung Note 10 phone and a target model with 30 ms latency running on an Nvidia 1080ti GPU. We measure latency via latency lookup tables built on each device following OFA [2]. The results in Table 5 show that REG-NAS can indeed find a target model with considerably low NFR without a large drop in Top-1 accuracy while using latency as the compute metric.

5 Discussion

In this paper, we tackle the problem of regression (measure via NFR) between models deployed on diverse compute platforms. We observe that architectures sampled from the same One-Shot NAS super-network naturally share a lot of weights and lead to a low NFR. Inspired by this finding, we propose a novel architecture constraint that maximizes weight sharing and a novel search reward function which further reduces the NFR. There are two limitations of our work: First, the impact of different supernet pre-training strategies on the NFR needs to be investigated. Our preliminary experiments show that the same super-network (FBNet-V3) obtained via different pre-training strategies (AlphaNet [30] and AttentiveNAS [31]) lead to different NFRs, indicating a measurable impact of super-network pre-training on NFR. Second, REG-NAS samples sub-networks from the same super-network which itself may not span the entire range of compute budgets of different platforms e.g. tiny embedded platforms to large data-centers. A future direction may investigate sampling from many different super-networks. Additionally, designing regression-free models via filter pruning [11,12] and early-exiting [9,10] are interesting future directions. Overall, we believe this paper only scratches the surface for an emerging problem—designing regression-free neural networks for diverse compute platforms—that will become more prominent in the era of on-device deep learning.

References

1. Belouadah, E., Popescu, A.: Il2m: Class incremental learning with dual memory. In: ICCV (2019)
2. Cai, H., Gan, C., Wang, T., Zhang, Z., Han, S.: Once for all: train one network and specialize it for efficient deployment. In: ICLR (2020)
3. Castro, F.M., Marín-Jiménez, M.J., Guil, N., Schmid, C., Alahari, K.: End-to-end incremental learning. In: Ferrari, V., Hebert, M., Sminchisescu, C., Weiss, Y. (eds.) ECCV 2018. LNCS, vol. 11216, pp. 241–257. Springer, Cham (2018). https://doi.org/10.1007/978-3-030-01258-8_15
4. Chaudhry, A., Dokania, P.K., Ajanthan, T., Torr, P.H.S.: Riemannian walk for incremental learning: understanding forgetting and intransigence. In: Ferrari, V., Hebert, M., Sminchisescu, C., Weiss, Y. (eds.) ECCV 2018. LNCS, vol. 11215, pp. 556–572. Springer, Cham (2018). https://doi.org/10.1007/978-3-030-01252-6_33
5. Chen, Z., Liu, B.: Lifelong machine learning. Synth. Lect. Artif. Intell. Mach. Learn. **12**(3), 1–207 (2018)
6. Chu, X., Zhou, T., Zhang, B., Li, J.: Fair DARTS: eliminating unfair advantages in differentiable architecture search. In: Vedaldi, A., Bischof, H., Brox, T., Frahm, J.-M. (eds.) ECCV 2020. LNCS, vol. 12360, pp. 465–480. Springer, Cham (2020). https://doi.org/10.1007/978-3-030-58555-6_28
7. Dai, X., et al.: Fbnetv3: joint architecture-recipe search using predictor pretraining. In: CVPR (2021)
8. Deng, J., Dong, W., Socher, R., Li, L.J., Li, K., Fei-Fei, L.: Imagenet: a large-scale hierarchical image database. In: CVPR (2009)
9. Duggal, R., Freitas, S., Dhamnani, S., Chau, D.H., Sun, J.: Elf: an early-exiting framework for long-tailed classification. arXiv preprint arXiv:2006.11979 (2020)
10. Duggal, R., Freitas, S., Dhamnani, S., Chau, D.H., Sun, J.: Har: hardness aware reweighting for imbalanced datasets. In: BigData (2021)
11. Duggal, R., Freitas, S., Xiao, C., Chau, D.H., Sun, J.: Rest: robust and efficient neural networks for sleep monitoring in the wild. In: Proceedings of The Web Conference 2020 (2020)
12. Duggal, R., Xiao, C., Vuduc, R., Chau, D.H., Sun, J.: Cup: cluster pruning for compressing deep neural networks. In: BigData (2021)
13. Duggal, R., et al.: Compatibility-aware heterogeneous visual search. In: CVPR (2021)
14. Guo, Z., et al.: Single path one-shot neural architecture search with uniform sampling. In: Vedaldi, A., Bischof, H., Brox, T., Frahm, J.-M. (eds.) ECCV 2020. LNCS, vol. 12361, pp. 544–560. Springer, Cham (2020). https://doi.org/10.1007/978-3-030-58517-4_32
15. Kandasamy, K., Neiswanger, W., Schneider, J., Poczos, B., Xing, E.: Neural architecture search with bayesian optimisation and optimal transport. arXiv preprint arXiv:1802.07191 (2018)
16. Kirkpatrick, J., et al.: Overcoming catastrophic forgetting in neural networks. Proc. Natl. Acad. Sci. **114**(13), 3521–3526 (2017)
17. Li, Z., Hoiem, D.: Learning without forgetting. IEEE Trans. PAMI **40**(12), 2935–2947 (2017)
18. Liu, H., Simonyan, K., Vinyals, O., Fernando, C., Kavukcuoglu, K.: Hierarchical representations for efficient architecture search. arXiv preprint arXiv:1711.00436 (2017)

19. Liu, H., Simonyan, K., Yang, Y.: Darts: differentiable architecture search. arXiv preprint arXiv:1806.09055 (2018)
20. Lopez-Paz, D., Ranzato, M.: Gradient episodic memory for continual learning. In: NeurIPS (2017)
21. Parisi, G.I., Kemker, R., Part, J.L., Kanan, C., Wermter, S.: Continual lifelong learning with neural networks: a review. Neural Netw. **113**, 54–71 (2019)
22. Pham, H., Guan, M., Zoph, B., Le, Q., Dean, J.: Efficient neural architecture search via parameters sharing. In: ICML (2018)
23. Radosavovic, I., Kosaraju, R.P., Girshick, R., He, K., Dollár, P.: Designing network design spaces. In: CVPR (2020)
24. Real, E., Aggarwal, A., Huang, Y., Le, Q.V.: Regularized evolution for image classifier architecture search. In: AAAI (2019)
25. Real, E., et al.: Large-scale evolution of image classifiers. In: ICML (2017)
26. Shen, Y., Xiong, Y., Xia, W., Soatto, S.: Towards backward-compatible representation learning. In: CVPR (2020)
27. Srivastava, M., Nushi, B., Kamar, E., Shah, S., Horvitz, E.: An empirical analysis of backward compatibility in machine learning systems. In: ACM SIGKDD (2020)
28. Suganuma, M., Ozay, M., Okatani, T.: Exploiting the potential of standard convolutional autoencoders for image restoration by evolutionary search. In: ICML (2018)
29. Tan, M., et al.: Mnasnet: platform-aware neural architecture search for mobile. In: CVPR (2019)
30. Wang, D., Gong, C., Li, M., Liu, Q., Chandra, V.: Alphanet: improved training of supernet with alpha-divergence. In: ICML (2021)
31. Wang, D., Li, M., Gong, C., Chandra, V.: Attentivenas: improving neural architecture search via attentive sampling. In: CVPR (2021)
32. Wu, B., et al.: Fbnetv5: neural architecture search for multiple tasks in one run. arXiv preprint arXiv:2111.10007 (2021)
33. Wu, Y., et al.: Large scale incremental learning. In: CVPR (2019)
34. Xie, L., Yuille, A.: Genetic cnn. In: ICCV (2017)
35. Yan, S., et al.: Positive-congruent training: towards regression-free model updates. In: CVPR (2021)
36. Yu, J., Huang, T.: Autoslim: towards one-shot architecture search for channel numbers. arXiv preprint arXiv:1903.11728 (2019)
37. Yu, J., et al.: BigNAS: scaling up neural architecture search with big single-stage models. In: Vedaldi, A., Bischof, H., Brox, T., Frahm, J.-M. (eds.) ECCV 2020. LNCS, vol. 12352, pp. 702–717. Springer, Cham (2020). https://doi.org/10.1007/978-3-030-58571-6_41
38. Zoph, B., Le, Q.V.: Neural architecture search with reinforcement learning. arXiv preprint arXiv:1611.01578 (2016)

Relationship Spatialization for Depth Estimation

Xiaoyu Xu[1], Jiayan Qiu[1(✉)], Xinchao Wang[2], and Zhou Wang[1]

[1] University of Waterloo, Waterloo, Canada
{x423xu,zhou.wang}@uwaterloo.ca, jiayan.qiu.1991@outlook.com
[2] National University of Singapore, Singapore, Singapore
xinchao@nus.edu.sg

Abstract. Considering the role played by the inter-object relationships in monocular depth estimation (MDE), it is easy to tell that relationships, such as *in front of* and *behind*, provide explicit spatial priors. However, it is hard to answer the questions that which relationships contain useful spatial priors for depth estimation, and how much do their spatial priors contribute to the depth estimation? In this paper, we term the task of answering these two questions as 'Relationship Spatialization' for Depth Estimation. To this end, we strive to spatialize the relationships by devising a novel learning-based framework. Specifically, given a scene image, its image representations and relationship representations are first extracted. Then, the relationship representations are modified by spatially aligned into the visual space and redundancy elimination. Finally, the modified relationship representations are adaptively weighted to concatenate with the image ones for depth estimation, thus accomplishing the relationship spatialization. Experiments on KITTI, NYU v2, and ICL-NUIM datasets show the effectiveness of the relationship spatialization on MDE. Moreover, adopting our relationship spatialization framework to the current state-of-the-art MDE models leads to marginal improvement on most evaluation metrics.

1 Introduction

Having a look at Fig. 1, it can be found that the depth estimation benefits from cooperating with the relationships in the scene. For example, the woman is closer to us than the screen because it is *in front of* the screen, which provides explicit spatial prior. The table is farther than the bag, although the spatial prior of *under* is implicit, the bag is with smaller depth in the imaging coordinate because it is closer to the image center compared with the table. More interestingly, although *wear* seems with no spatial priors intuitively, it certainly contributes to the depth estimation, since it constrains that the depth of the shirt should be aligned with

Supplementary Information The online version contains supplementary material available at https://doi.org/10.1007/978-3-031-19836-6_35.

Fig. 1. Given a scene image (a), relationships contribute to depth estimation, as shown left to right in (b–d). Compared with the explicit spatial information from *in front of* (a), the implicit spatial information from *under* (b) also benefits the depth estimation. More interestingly, *wear* (c), which is intuitively non-spatial, in reality contributes significantly to depth estimation.

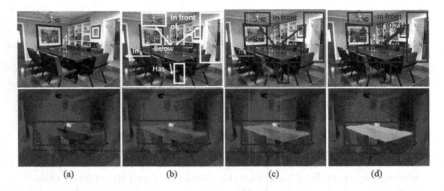

Fig. 2. Depth error decreases during our relationship spatialization process in the red boxed Table area (a–d). Only the visual understanding is utilized in (a); all Table-related in-image relationships are added in (b); only the effective relationships are identified and then equally added in (c); the identified relationships are contribution-accordingly weighted and then added(d). (Color figure online)

the depth of the man. Hence, it can be seen that the inter-object relationships provide a huge amount of spatial priors for depth estimation.

Despite the relationships come with lots of spatial priors, before we claim their effects on MDE, there are two questions that require explorations. Firstly, which kinds of relationships are effective for MDE? Some of the relationships always come with spatial priors, such as *behind*, while others, like *has*, may not. Thus, it is important to learn to find effective relationships for each object. Secondly, how much do the effective ones contribute to MDE? Even human observers can easily find out which relationships provide the cues for the object's depth, it is indeed hard to tell their relative importance. Therefore, in order to reveal the embedded spatial priors in the relationships, it is important to quantify their contribution to MDE. In this paper, we term the task of answering these two questions as *Relationship Spatialization for Depth Estimation*.

Towards solving the proposed Relationship Spatialization task, we propose a novel framework that combines both visual understanding and relationship understanding for depth estimation. Different from the simple combination of information, the relationship representations are automatically and adaptively weighted, thus are learned to be effectiveness-identified and contribution-quantified. Thus, the relationships are spatialized for depth estimation.

Specifically, given a scene image, we firstly feed it into an image representation extractor module, which can be any deep learning MDE model, to obtain the image representations. Meanwhile, the objects in the image are detected to construct the corresponding scene graph, where nodes denote the objects and edges denote the inter-object relationships. Then, the scene graph is processed by the relationship recognition module to predict the inter-object relationships and extract their corresponding representation. Secondly, the relationship representations from the scene graph space are modified by spatially aligning into the visual space and redundancy elimination. Finally, the modified relationship representations are fed into an attention layer for representation weighting, which is the respective contribution quantification. Then, the concatenation of the weighted relationship representations and the image ones is fed into the depth predictor for depth estimation. Through this process, the relationships are spatialized for enhancing the depth estimation, as shown in Fig. 2.

Our contribution is therefore a novel framework that, for the first time, tries to spatialize the relationships for depth estimation, during which the spatial priors from relationships are mined automatically, identified effectively, and quantified adaptively. Moreover, our proposed framework can be implemented on any deep learning-based MDE method for performance boosting. Experiments on all datasets show encouraging and promising results.

2   Related Work

In this section, we briefly review the prior works related to ours, including depth estimation, relationship recognition and graph neural network.

Depth Estimation. Early works of depth estimation [21,22,87] focus on utilizing the geometry-based information, such as the points correspondence among different views. With the development of deep learning techniques, the CNN based depth methods [5,7,17,18,24,48] show high-performance on depth estimation tasks. Some of them try to improve the performance by avoiding using the ground-truth information from the real world [2,13,23,25,26,29,32,63,82,85, 93,117–119], which reduce the demand for expensive annotations. Other works aim to increase the methods' generalizability and work in the wild [11,12,58,71, 98,99,121] thus saving the heavy training cost. The most related works to ours are the multi-task ones [10,17,38,41,42,47,53,60,61,68,76,85,95,100,115,116], where information from other tasks are used in depth estimation. However, none of them try to utilize the spatial priors in inter-object relationships.

Relationship Recognition. The handful of visual relationships are categorized into three types: the inter-object ones [16], the property ones [34] and the activity ones [106]. In this work, we focus on the inter-object relationships, where the early works focus on the visual phrase recognition [19,55,57]. Then, thanks to the boosting performance brought by deep learning, the DNN based methods show promise performance due to their high representation capability [14,45,56, 62,64,67,75,111,113,120]. The most related works to ours are the ones that try to detect the relationship in scene graphs as one of the attributes [8,20,40,57,59]. However, none of these works explore the spatial priors in the relationships and their enhancement on depth estimation.

Graph Neural Network. Earlier works on graph-related tasks usually require pre-defined node and edge features [49,69,70,77,78,96,97], or aggregating the node and edge features in an iterative manner, which is computation expensive and time consuming [27,33,86,89]. Recently, graph neural networks have been proposed to learn the features. Specifically, the spectral-based networks implement the spectral theory for graph convolution design [6,15,37,44,52,54], and spatial-based ones utilize the mutual dependency by designing the information aggregation manner [1,3,4,9,28,31,35,39,51,65,66,72,73,79,80,84,91,92, 94,102–105,108,109,112,114]. More recently, the hierarchical GCN [107] with high representation capability is proposed and shows promising performance.

3 Method

In this section, we explain the proposed framework in detail. As depicted in Fig. 3, our framework comprises three stages. In Stage 1, the image representations of the input image are extracted from a deep learning-based MDE model. Meanwhile, a detection module is utilized on the input image to detect the objects in the scene, which constructs the scene graph. Afterward, the relationship representations are extracted from the scene graph by implementing a relationship recognition module. In Stage 2, we first spatially align the relationship representations from the graph space with the image representations from the visual space. Then, the aligned relationship representations are modified by eliminating their redundancies compared with the image representations. In Stage 3, the concatenation of the modified relationship representation and the image representation is fed into the depth predictor the depth estimation, during which the attention is implemented on the modified relationship representations. The attention scores are automatically learned and used for identifying the effective relationships and quantifying their respective contributions on MDE.

3.1 Stage 1: Representation Extraction

Image Representation Extraction. The image representation extractor is implemented to obtain understanding from appearance cues, such as edges and shapes while eliminating the interference from surface textures. As shown in Fig. 4, a U-Net encode-decoder network is adopted as our image representation extractor, where different resolution representations are combined by BiFPN

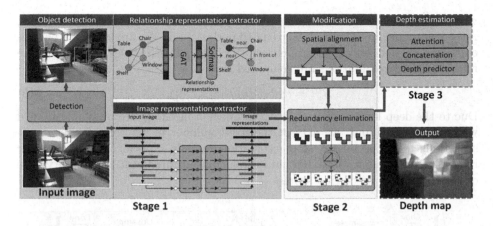

Fig. 3. The framework of the proposed model. An input image is firstly sent to an image feature extractor to generate image representations. The input image is also fed to relationship recognition module to generate relationship representations. then, the relationship ones are aligned to the image ones and being eliminated with redundancy. Finally, the effective relationship representations are quantified and concatenated with image features to estimate depth.

[90] to preserve both the high-level understanding and visual details. Then, the image representation is:

$$R_I = f_{image}(I), \tag{1}$$

where I denotes the input image and f_{image} denotes the image representation extractor.

Relationship Representation Extraction. We first adopt an offline detector model [83] to detect the objects in the scene image so as to derive object-level understanding and their spatial position:

$$z_i, M_i = Detector(I), i = 1, .., N, \tag{2}$$

where N denotes the number of the detected objects and z_i denotes the object-level understanding of the i-th detected object. M_i denotes the object mask, 1 for the object area. Then, the graph-rcnn [101] is adopted as the relationship recognition module. Specifically, the object-level understanding $(z_1, z_2, \cdots, z_N)$ of the N detected objects are treated as nodes features of the scene graph G. The $N \times N$ edges in the G correspond to $N \times N < subject, object >$ relationships. Then, the node features are aggregated as:

$$z_i^{(l+1)} = \sigma \left(z_i^{(l)} + \sum_{i \in N(i)} a_{ij} W z_j^{(l)} \right), \tag{3}$$

$$a_{ij} = softmax(\sigma(W_a[z_i^{(l)}, z_j^{(l)}])), \tag{4}$$

where $z_i^{(l)}$ denotes the i-th node at l-th iteration, σ denotes activation function, $N(i)$ denotes neighboring nodes of the i-th node, W and W_a are learnable parameters, and a_{ij} denotes attention between the i-th and j-th nodes. Afterward, the relationship representations are computed as:

$$R_r^{i,j} = embedding([z_i^{(l)} . z_j^{(l)}]). \tag{5}$$

Due to the deep learning based depth estimation methods are only able to deal with fixed sized input, we extract the fixed number of N_r relationship representations from the relationship recognition module. Specifically, we feed the relationship representations $R_r^{i,j}$ into a relationship predictor and preserve the ones with top-N_r prediction scores.

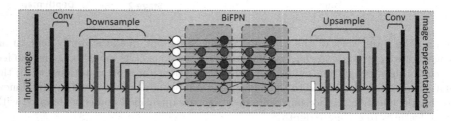

Fig. 4. Image representation extractor.

3.2   Stage 2: Representation Modification

After obtaining the image representations R_I and relationship representations R_r^n, where $n \in [1, N_r]$, we modify the relationship ones according to the image ones by first spatial alignment and followed by the redundancy elimination.

Spatial Alignment. Since the image representations, R_I are in the visual space and the relationship representations R_r^n are in the graph space, spatial alignment is implemented to translate the relationship ones into the visual space for depth estimation. Specifically, given the relationship representation $R_r^n \in \mathbb{R}^d$, where d denotes the representation dimension of R_r^n, and its corresponding object masks M_i and M_j, we first project the relationship representation upon a zero-initialized feature set:

$$F^n(x, y, :) = R_r^n(M_i(x, y)||M_j(x, y)), x = [1, ..., I_w], y = [1, ..., I_h], \tag{6}$$

where $F^n \in \mathbb{R}^{I_w \times I_h \times d}$, I_w and I_h denote the width and height of the input image I, and $||$ denotes the logic operation or. Then, a single output channel convolutional layer is implemented on the feature set F to obtain the visually aligned relationship representation:

$$VA\_R^n = Conv(F^n), n = 1, ..., N_r, \tag{7}$$

where $VA\_R^n \in \mathbb{R}^{I_w \times I_h}$ denotes the visually aligned single channel feature map of each relationship representation.

Redundancy Elimination. After obtaining the visually aligned feature maps of relationship representations, we eliminate their redundancy information according to the image representations, since the overlap information between them may lead to overlook the distinguished spatial information contained in the relationships. In detail, the overlaps between the relationship representation and the image representation are eliminated by (Fig. 5):

$$M_R^c = G(M_R^{c-1}, R_I^{c-1}), c = 1, ..., N_I, \tag{8}$$

$$G(M_R^{c-1}, R_I^{c-1}) = M_R^{c-1} - \frac{< M_R^{c-1}, R_I^{c-1} >}{< R_I^{c-1}, R_I^{c-1} >} R_I^{c-1}, \tag{9}$$

$$M_R^0 = V A\_R, \tag{10}$$

where M_R denotes the modified relationship representation, N_I denotes the number of feature maps in the image representation R_I and $< \cdot, \cdot >$ denotes inner product. At the end of this stage, we obtain the modified relationship representation M_R.

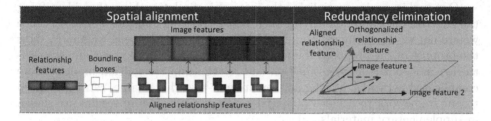

Fig. 5. Representation modification is composed of spatial alignment and redundancy elimination. Firstly, relationship representations are spatially aligned towards image representations with bounding boxes. Secondly, the aligned relationship are orthogonalized against image representations to eliminate information redundancy.

3.3 Stage 3: Depth Estimation and Contribution Quantification

Once the modified relationship representations M_R are obtained, we feed them into an attention layer for learning to identify their effectiveness and quantify their respective contributions:

$$\alpha^n = Attn(M_R^n), n = 1, ..., N_r, \tag{11}$$

where the attention scores α^n are used as the effectiveness identification and contribution quantification of the relationships. Then, we concatenate the image representations and the weighted relationship representations, feed it in the depth estimator for depth estimation:

$$y = Predictor(Concat(R_I, \alpha^n M_R^n)), n = 1, ..., N_r. \tag{12}$$

Then we impose the scale invariant loss [5], who focus on minimizing the ratio of the depth error, rather than the absolutely scaled depth:

$$\mathbf{L}_{depth} = var([\log(y) - \log(\tilde{y})]) + \lambda[\frac{1}{N}\sum_{i=1}^{N}[\log(y) - \log(\tilde{y})]]^2, \qquad (13)$$

where $var()$ denotes variance computation, $\tilde{y}$ denotes the ground-truth depth and λ denotes the balancing weight.

4   Experiments

In this section, we provide our experimental setups and show the results. Specifically, for the experiments, we first evaluate the performance of our framework on three MDE datasets. Then analysis the effectiveness of relationship spatialization, effective spatialized relationship identification and the respective contribution quantification are explained in detail. Finally, ablation study is conducted for measuring the necessary of the redundancy elimination operation.

Our goal is, again, spatializing the inter-object relationships, then identifying the effective ones and quantifying their respective contributions on MDE. Since we are not aware of any existing work that performs same task, we aim to show the promise of the proposed framework, rather than trying to beat any state-of-the-art monocular depth estimation and relationship recognition models. More complicated networks, as long as they are end-to-end trainable, can be adopted to our framework to achieve potentially better results. More results are shown in supplementary materials.

4.1   Datasets and Implementation Details

We adopt three datasets for depth estimation, KITTI [30], NYU Depth v2 [88], and ICL-NUIM [36] to validate the proposed framework. Since there is no dataset that provides both the ground-truth annotated depth and inter-object relationship, we evaluate our framework by the MDE performance. As for the relationship recognition, we pretrain a model on Visual Genome dataset [46], and adopt it directly in our framework. User studies are designed for evaluating the performance of the adopted relationship recognition module on the three depth estimation datasets.

KITTI [30]. It is a dataset of outdoor scene images with the corresponding 3D laser scans captured by moving vehicles. All the scene categories are used as our training/test sets. Following the split manner in [18], we use 26k images for training and 697 images for the test, with the image resolution of 1241 × 376. For a fair comparison, all compared MDE methods are retrained and evaluated on the adopted training/test sets in our experiments.

NYU Depth v2 [88]. It is a dataset of indoor scene images with the corresponding depth maps captured by Microsoft Kinect. Following the previous work, we use 50k images from 249 scenes for training and the 654-images set for the test, with the image resolution of 640×480. Different from the existing MDE methods like [5] that training only on cropped parts of the image, which may lead to the loss of relationship information, we perform the training on the entire image.

ICL-NUIM [36]. It is a smaller size dataset of an indoor scene, which comprises of 1500 images with their corresponding depth maps. Due to its limited amount of images, we adopt this dataset for verifying the generalizability of the model trained on NYU Depth v2.

Implementation. In the experiment, our framework is implemented with *Pytorch* [74] and with 4 NVIDIA P100 Pascal GPUs. We optimize with Adam [43], setting the learning rate $l = 5e - 4$, $\beta_1 = 0.9$, and $\beta_2 = 0.99$. Our framework is trained with batch size 16 for 25 epochs.

4.2 Performance Evaluation

In this part, we evaluate the performance of our proposed relationship spatialization framework on MDE. In order to show the effect of the learned relationship spatialization, we conduct the evaluations with our baseline framework and frameworks that implement the commonly used MDE networks as the image representation extractor. In the experiment, the state-of-the-art MDE methods, Adabins [5], Midas [81] and Bts [50], are adopted. We use Baseline, Adabins, Midas, and Bts to denote the MDE-only frameworks; and use Baseline+, Adabins+, Midas+ and Bts+ to denote the frameworks with relationship spatialization. For a fair comparison, all frameworks in the experiment are trained from the scratch.

Table 1. Results of monocular depth estimation on KITTI dataset. ↑: the higher is better. ↓: the lower is better.

Metrics		Adabins	Adabins+	Midas	Midas+	Bts	Bts+	Baseline	Baseline+
↑	δ_1	0.9292	**0.9483**	0.9483	**0.9486**	0.8832	**0.9161**	0.9113	**0.9260**
	δ_2	0.9883	**0.9911**	0.9912	**0.9927**	0.9746	**0.9837**	0.9852	**0.9884**
	δ_3	0.9973	**0.9981**	0.9980	**0.9984**	0.9937	**0.9960**	0.9972	**0.9977**
↓	*abs_rel*	0.0775	**0.0758**	0.0655	**0.0652**	0.1195	**0.0831**	0.0917	**0.0789**
	rmse	3.4291	**2.9441**	2.8099	2.8747	4.4126	**3.4930**	3.6264	**3.2560**
	log_10	0.0348	**0.0339**	0.0291	**0.0289**	0.0486	**0.0368**	0.0399	**0.0342**
	rmse_log	0.1196	**0.1104**	0.1026	**0.1025**	0.1567	**0.1297**	0.1327	**0.1191**
	silog	10.6605	**9.5903**	9.3816	**9.3112**	11.8858	**11.8858**	13.5749	12.3885	**11.0609**
	sq_rel	0.3406	**0.2875**	0.2660	**0.2603**	0.4026	**0.4026**	0.4042	**0.3554**

Table 2. Results of monocular depth estimation on NYU Depth v2 dataset.

Metrics	Adabins	Adabins+	Midas	Midas+	Bts	Bts+	Baseline	Baseline+
δ_1	0.7971	**0.8603**	0.8173	**0.8519**	0.6936	**0.7715**	0.8293	**0.8889**
δ_2	0.9486	**0.9704**	0.9519	**0.9655**	0.9214	**0.9493**	0.9522	**0.9597**
δ_3	0.9840	**0.9928**	0.9858	**0.9901**	0.9803	**0.9852**	0.9791	**0.9894**
abs_rel	0.1537	**0.1203**	0.1437	**0.1282**	0.1772	**0.1557**	0.1488	**0.1432**
$rmse$	0.5318	**0.4469**	0.5016	**0.4717**	0.6652	**0.5847**	0.7632	**0.5342**
log_10	0.0629	**0.0515**	0.0596	**0.0544**	0.0806	**0.0703**	0.0596	0.0646
$rmse\_log$	0.1900	**0.1588**	0.1822	**0.1779**	0.2327	**0.2245**	0.2015	**0.1924**
$silog$	15.9615	**13.9534**	15.4977	**15.4224**	18.5223	21.9191	17.9495	**15.8711**
sq_rel	0.1234	**0.0803**	0.1116	**0.0896**	0.1542	**0.1233**	0.1979	**0.1032**

KITTI. It can be seen from Table 1 that, for all chosen frameworks on KITTI dataset, relationship spatialization brings performance gain on almost every MDE evaluation metric, which shows that our proposed framework is able to learn to find the effective relationship spatialization for the outdoor scenes. Moreover, it is worth noting that the framework Bts+ performs obviously poor than Bts on the $silog$ metric. Since the $silog$ reflects the variation of scale error (calculated by dividing predicted depth with ground truth depth), the $rmse\_log$ reflects the mean value of the scale error, the BTS+ model focuses more on reducing mean error in relationship related areas and neglects areas without relationship enhancement, thus bringing in variation increment. So the BTS+ gets the greatest progress in $rmse\_log$ and does not outperform in $silog$.

NYU Depth v2. The results on NYU Depth v2 dataset are shown in Table 2, where the frameworks with the relationship spatialization outperform the original ones on almost all of the evaluation metrics. It shows that our proposed

Table 3. Results of frameworks trained on NYU Depth v2 dataset and evaluated on ICL_NUIM dataset.

Metrics	Adabins	Adabins+	Midas	Midas+	Bts	Bts+	Baseline	Baseline+
δ_1	0.9160	**0.9521**	**0.8432**	0.7903	0.6735	**0.7758**	0.7344	**0.8446**
δ_2	0.9993	**1.0000**	0.9446	**0.9566**	0.9112	**0.9539**	0.9438	**0.9744**
δ_3	1.0000	**1.0000**	**1.0000**	0.9890	0.9783	**0.9882**	0.9902	**0.9943**
abs_rel	0.1048	**0.0758**	0.1878	**0.1521**	0.2075	**0.1634**	0.1732	**0.1297**
$rmse$	0.3283	**0.2584**	0.5462	**0.3492**	0.4727	**0.3726**	0.4158	**0.3141**
log_10	0.0438	**0.0319**	0.0761	**0.0637**	0.0843	**0.0694**	0.0709	**0.0545**
$rmse\_log$	0.1276	**0.0959**	0.2059	**0.1936**	0.2417	**0.2373**	0.2076	**0.1681**
$silog$	12.6962	**8.5677**	20.8457	**19.2291**	24.0221	**23.6079**	20.5816	**16.7161**
sq_rel	0.0438	**0.0261**	0.1273	**0.0770**	0.1456	**0.0827**	0.1026	**0.0578**

Table 4. The model added with relationship representations (+R) outperforms baseline model only using image representations (B) both on KITTI and NYU datasets.

Models		δ_1	δ_2	δ_3	abs_rel	rmse	log_10	rmse_log	silog	sq_rel
KITTI	B	0.9292	0.9883	0.9973	0.0775	3.4291	0.0348	0.1196	10.6605	0.3406
	+R	**0.9446**	**0.9910**	**0.9981**	**0.0738**	**2.9988**	**0.0331**	**0.1098**	**9.5838**	**0.2892**
NYU	B	0.8237	0.9597	0.9895	0.1390	0.5006	0.0581	0.1770	15.0716	0.1042
	+R	**0.8608**	**0.9715**	**0.9932**	**0.1295**	**0.4487**	**0.0519**	**0.1576**	**13.2523**	**0.0796**

framework is able to learn to find the effective relationship spatialization of the indoor scenes. It is worth noting that, again, the Bts outperforms the Bts+ in the *silog* metric due to the same reason on KITTI.

ICL_NUIM. Due to its limited amount of training data, ICL_NUIM dataset is utilized for measuring the generalizability of our proposed framework. Specifically, we pre-train all frameworks on NYU Depth v2 dataset and evaluate them on ICL_NUIM dataset. As can be seen from Table 3, the frameworks with relationship spatialization outperform the original ones on all evaluation metrics, which shows the promising generalizability of our framework.

4.3   Effect of Relationship Representation

In this part, we evaluate the effect of relationship representations on MDE by performance comparison, correlation evaluation, related area evaluation, and framework derivation visualization.

Performance Comparison. To illustrate the effect of relationship representation for depth estimation, here we compare the performance of framework with only image representation and framework with both the image and relationship one. Note that, the attention layer in the predictor of our proposed framework is not implemented in this part, which means that all the relationship representations are equally treated. As shown in Table 4, the framework with relationship representations outperforms the original one, which shows the relationship representations benefit the depth estimation.

Correlation Evaluation. In this experiment, we evaluate the correlation between the MDE performance and the relationship recognition accuracy. Specifically, we adopt relationship recognition modules with different pre-trained accuracy into our framework and then observe the difference in the MDE performance. As can be seen from Table 5, we MDE performance increase with the pre-trained relationship recognition accuracy, which shows that correctly predicted relationships benefit the depth estimation.

Table 5. The MDE performance increases with the relationship recognition accuracy. *Recall* is used as the evaluation metric of the pre-trained relationship recognition module, *User_Acc* is used as the metric for user-oriented accuracy and *rmse* is used as the metric for MDE.

Relationship		Depth estimation								
Recall	User_Acc	Adabins+		Midas+		Bts+		Baseline+		
	KITTI	NYU	KITTI	NYU	KITTI	NYU	KITTI	NYU	KITTI	NYU
10.5	79.62	78.58	2.9988	0.5318	3.0122	0.5134	7.8685	0.7915	4.5427	0.7463
12.5	81.27	83.01	2.9441	0.4654	2.9671	0.5016	7.5241	0.6246	4.1325	0.6824
16.7	84.53	83.27	2.8803	0.4487	2.9035	0.4925	7.1373	0.5874	3.9776	0.6596
18.3	88.17	86.31	2.8742	0.4456	2.8747	0.4791	6.5481	0.5831	3.8212	0.5342
18.8	89.33	87.25	**2.8652**	**0.4392**	**2.8099**	**0.4717**	**6.0439**	**0.5058**	**3.2560**	**0.5209**

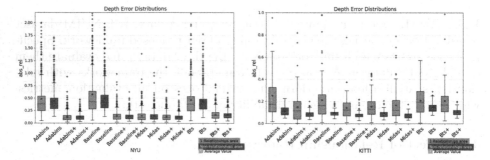

Fig. 6. Distribution of depth errors on relationship-related areas and non-related areas. The yellow boxes denote the *abs_rel* on the relationship-related areas, the blue boxes denote the *abs_rel* on the non-related areas, the in-box red line denotes median value, and the star symbol denotes the mean value. (Color figure online)

Moreover, since there are no ground-truth annotated relationships in the MDE datasets, a subjective user study is designed for evaluating the accuracy of the pre-trained relationship recognition module on the MDE datasets. Specifically, we involve 107 users and send each user 200 randomly selected relationships, which are used in our framework. Then, we ask the user whether each relationship is correctly recognized, according to which calculate the user-oriented relationship recognition accuracy. The user-oriented accuracy is close to the ground-truth one while covering only part of the used relationships. The user-oriented accuracy is shown in the second column in Table 5, it increases with the pre-trained accuracy.

Related Area Evaluation. Since the representations of the spatialized relationship are spatially aligned into the visual space, the majority of its spatial priors should have effects on the relationship-related areas. Although the performance on the entire image shows improvement, it is hard to fully reveal the effect of relationship spatialization for MDE. In this experiment, we compare the MDE performance on relationship-related areas and the non-related ones, the *abs_rel* metric is chosen for clear visualization. As can be seen from the box plots in Fig. 6, the introduction of the relationship, firstly, improves both the MDE performance on the relationship-related areas and non-related areas. More importantly, the overall depth error reduction on the relationship-related areas highly outperforms that on the non-related areas, which shows the large benefits from relationship spatialization on MDE.

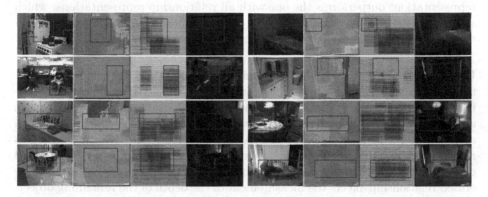

Fig. 7. Framework derivation visualization. The first column of each group shows the input scene image, the second column shows the framework derivation map, the third column shows the relationship representation map, the fourth column shows the depth error map, and the bounding box denotes the relationship area.

Framework Derivation Visualization. In this experiment, we calculate and show the framework derivation map in Fig. 7. It can be seen that, after introducing the relationship representations, the derivation values are larger on the relationship areas than that on other areas, which means the relationship areas contribute more to depth estimation, thus more important. It is worth noting that, excluding the relationship areas, the sudden texture changing areas are with the highest derivation scores, which shows the fact that image representation-based methods abstract the spatial information from edge areas. Then, the introduction of our relationship spatialization helps to extract the spatial information from object surface areas, complement with the image representation-based MDE methods, thus improving the MDE performance.

4.4   Effective Spatialized-Relationship Identification

In this part, we evaluate the identified effective relationships from our framework by performance comparison and user study.

628   X. Xu et al.

Performance Evaluation. In order to evaluate whether the identified effective relationships are meaningful for MDE, here we compare the performance of the framework with all relationship representations and the one with only the identified effective relationship representations. Specifically, a binary feature channel mask is learned from the relationship representations and used for effective relationship representations identification. Then, all identified effective relationship representations are equally treated to concatenate with the image ones for depth estimation. As shown in Table 6, the framework with only effective relationship representations outperforms the one with all relationship representations, which shows that the effective relationships for MDE are preserved and the noisy information from the non-effective relationships is eliminated.

User Study. Due to the lack of ground-truth annotations of the effective relationships in MDE, a user study is designed and performed to evaluate the identified effective relationships from our framework. Specifically, we involve 107 users and send each user 100 randomly selected relationship sets shown in Fig. 8. Each relationship set includes the input image and 4 images that each randomly gets rid of one of our identified effective relationships, where one of the two related objects is erased with an inpainting model [110]. Then, we ask the user if the erased relationship affects the measurement of the depth of the remaining object, then evaluate if we correctly identify the effective relationships. Our identified effective relationships finally achieve 89.33% accuracy, which is highly aligned with human recognition.

Table 6. The model added with effective relationship representations (+ER) outperforms the model with equally treated relationship representations (+R) both on KITTI and NYU datasets.

Models		δ_1	δ_2	δ_3	abs_rel	$rmse$	log_10	$rmse\_log$	$silog$	sq_rel
KITTI	+R	0.9446	0.9910	0.9981	0.0738	2.9988	0.0331	0.1098	9.5838	0.2892
	+ER	**0.9512**	**0.9913**	**0.9981**	**0.0725**	**2.8574**	**0.0215**	**0.0905**	**9.4273**	**0.2138**
NYU	+R	0.8608	0.9715	0.9932	0.1295	0.4487	0.0519	0.1576	13.2523	0.0796
	+ER	**0.8752**	**0.9833**	**0.9932**	**0.1107**	**0.3583**	**0.0462**	**0.1113**	**12.4264**	**0.0686**

Fig. 8. In each image, one target object of the identified effective relationships is erased. Then, users' judgments on whether the erased object is effective in depth estimation are recorded.

4.5 Respective Contributions Quantification

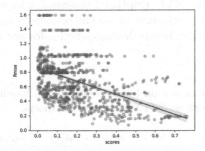

Fig. 9. Correlation between the depth error and its quantified respective contribution on relationship areas.

In this part, we evaluate the quantified respective relationship contributions from our framework by performance comparison, correlation evaluation, and user study.

Performance Evaluation. To evaluate whether the quantified respective contributions from our framework are accurate, here we compare the performance of the framework that equally treats all relationship representations and the one that weights relationship representations according to their quantified respective contributions, which is our proposed framework. As shown in Table 7, the framework with quantified respective contributions outperforms the one with equal contributions, which shows that our respective contribution quantification spatialized the relationship adaptively.

Table 7. The model added with quantified relationship representations (+QR) outperforms the model only using effective relationship representations (+ER) both on KITTI and NYU datasets.

Models		δ_1	δ_2	δ_3	abs_rel	$rmse$	log_10	$rmse\_log$	$silog$	sq_rel
KITTI	+ER	0.9512	0.9913	0.9981	0.0725	2.8574	0.0215	0.0905	9.4273	0.2138
	+QR	**0.9549**	**0.9914**	**0.9981**	**0.0690**	**2.8541**	**0.0208**	**0.0856**	**9.3253**	**0.1838**
NYU	+ER	0.8752	0.9833	0.9932	0.1107	0.3583	0.0462	0.1113	12.4264	0.0686
	+QR	**0.8820**	**0.9833**	**0.9932**	**0.1071**	**0.3552**	**0.0413**	**0.1004**	**12.1541**	**0.0666**

Correlation Evaluation. In this experiment, we evaluate the correlation between the depth error and our quantified respective contribution on the relationship-related areas. As can be seen from Fig. 9, the relationship area depth error decrease when its quantified respective contribution increase, which shows that our respective contribution quantification accurately rank and spatialized the relationship for depth estimation.

4.6 Ablation Study

In this experiment, we verify the effectiveness of our redundancy elimination operation by comparing the framework with and without it. As can be seen from Table 8, the redundancy elimination operation leads to a marginal performance improvement on both the KITTI and NYU Depth v2 datasets, which is because it reduces the affection of redundancy information on the respective contribution quantification, thus increasing the focus on distinguished information from relationship spatialization.

Table 8. The model added with redundancy elimination (+RE) outperforms baseline model only using image representations (B) both on KITTI and NYU datasets.

Models		δ_1	δ_2	δ_3	abs_rel	$rmse$	log_10	$rmse\_log$	$silog$	sq_rel
KITTI	B	0.9292	0.9883	0.9973	0.0775	3.4291	0.0348	0.1196	10.6605	0.3406
	+RE	**0.9433**	**0.9884**	**0.9973**	**0.0640**	**3.2055**	**0.0338**	**0.0982**	**9.5324**	**0.2760**
NYU	B	0.8237	0.9597	0.9895	0.1390	0.5006	0.0581	0.1770	15.0716	0.1042
	+RE	**0.8634**	**0.9722**	**0.9933**	**0.1205**	**0.4383**	**0.0509**	**0.1556**	**13.1205**	**0.0790**

5 Conclusion

In this paper, we propose a novel framework to dig out spatial priors, which are embedded in relationships in a scene image, to enhance depth estimation. We strive to answer two questions: (1) which relationships contain useful spatial priors? (2) How much do the spatial priors contribute to the depth estimation? Several modules including 'Spatial alignment', 'Orthogonalization' and 'Attention' are designed to solve the questions. Subsequently, extensive objective and subjective experiments are conducted which strongly proves the proposed model successfully captures spatial priors in relationships. Besides, other complicated MDE models can be inserted to our framework to enhance performance.

Acknowledgement. This work is in part supported by Natural Sciences and Engineering Research Council of Canada, Canada Research Chair program, NRF Centre for Advanced Robotics Technology Innovation (CARTIN) of Singapore, and AI Singapore (Award No.: AISG2-RP-2021-023).

References

1. Abu-El-Haija, S., Perozzi, B., Al-Rfou, R., Alemi, A.A.: Watch your step: learning node embeddings via graph attention. Adv. Neural Inf. Process. Syst. **31**, 9180–9190 (2018)
2. Atapour-Abarghouei, A., Breckon, T.P.: Real-time monocular depth estimation using synthetic data with domain adaptation via image style transfer. In: Proceedings of the IEEE Conference on Computer Vision and Pattern Recognition, pp. 2800–2810 (2018)
3. Atwood, J., Towsley, D.: Diffusion-convolutional neural networks. Adv. Neural Inf. Process. Syst. **29**, 1993–2001 (2016)

4. Bacciu, D., Errica, F., Micheli, A.: Contextual graph markov model: a deep and generative approach to graph processing. In: ICML (2018)
5. Bhat, S.F., Alhashim, I., Wonka, P.: Adabins: depth estimation using adaptive bins. In: Proceedings of the IEEE/CVF Conference on Computer Vision and Pattern Recognition, pp. 4009–4018 (2021)
6. Bruna, J., Zaremba, W., Szlam, A., LeCun, Y.: Spectral networks and locally connected networks on graphs. arXiv preprint arXiv:1312.6203 (2013)
7. Cao, Y., Wu, Z., Shen, C.: Estimating depth from monocular images as classification using deep fully convolutional residual networks. IEEE Trans. Circ. Syst. Video Technol. **28**(11), 3174–3182 (2017)
8. Chang, A., Savva, M., Manning, C.D.: Learning spatial knowledge for text to 3D scene generation. In: Proceedings of the 2014 Conference on Empirical Methods in Natural Language Processing (EMNLP), pp. 2028–2038 (2014)
9. Chen, J., Zhu, J., Song, L.: Stochastic training of graph convolutional networks with variance reduction. arXiv preprint arXiv:1710.10568 (2017)
10. Chen, P.Y., Liu, A.H., Liu, Y.C., Wang, Y.C.F.: Towards scene understanding: unsupervised monocular depth estimation with semantic-aware representation. In: Proceedings of the IEEE/CVF Conference on Computer Vision and Pattern Recognition, pp. 2624–2632 (2019)
11. Chen, W., Fu, Z., Yang, D., Deng, J.: Single-image depth perception in the wild. Adv. Neural Inf. Process. Syst. **29**, 1–9 (2016)
12. Chen, W., Qian, S., Deng, J.: Learning single-image depth from videos using quality assessment networks. In: Proceedings of the IEEE/CVF Conference on Computer Vision and Pattern Recognition, pp. 5604–5613 (2019)
13. Chen, Y.C., Lin, Y.Y., Yang, M.H., Huang, J.B.: Crdoco: pixel-level domain transfer with cross-domain consistency. In: Proceedings of the IEEE/CVF Conference on Computer Vision and Pattern Recognition, pp. 1791–1800 (2019)
14. Dai, B., Zhang, Y., Lin, D.: Detecting visual relationships with deep relational networks. In: Proceedings of the IEEE Conference on Computer Vision and Pattern Recognition, pp. 3076–3086 (2017)
15. Defferrard, M., Bresson, X., Vandergheynst, P.: Convolutional neural networks on graphs with fast localized spectral filtering. Adv. Neural Inf. Process. Syst. **29**, 3844–3852 (2016)
16. Desai, C., Ramanan, D., Fowlkes, C.C.: Discriminative models for multi-class object layout. Int. J. Comput. Vision **95**(1), 1–12 (2011)
17. Eigen, D., Fergus, R.: Predicting depth, surface normals and semantic labels with a common multi-scale convolutional architecture. In: Proceedings of the IEEE International Conference on Computer Vision, pp. 2650–2658 (2015)
18. Eigen, D., Puhrsch, C., Fergus, R.: Depth map prediction from a single image using a multi-scale deep network. arXiv preprint arXiv:1406.2283 (2014)
19. Farhadi, A., Sadeghi, M.A.: Phrasal recognition. IEEE Trans. Pattern Anal. Mach. Intell. **35**(12), 2854–2865 (2013)
20. Fisher, M., Savva, M., Hanrahan, P.: Characterizing structural relationships in scenes using graph kernels. In: ACM SIGGRAPH 2011 Papers, pp. 1–12 (2011)
21. Flynn, J., Neulander, I., Philbin, J., Snavely, N.: Deepstereo: learning to predict new views from the world's imagery. In: Proceedings of the IEEE Conference on Computer Vision and Pattern Recognition, pp. 5515–5524 (2016)
22. Forsyth, D., Ponce, J.: Computer Vision: A Modern Approach. Prentice hall, Upper Saddle River (2011)

23. Fu, H., et al.: 3D-front: 3D furnished rooms with layouts and semantics. In: Proceedings of the IEEE/CVF International Conference on Computer Vision, pp. 10933–10942 (2021)
24. Fu, H., Gong, M., Wang, C., Batmanghelich, K., Tao, D.: Deep ordinal regression network for monocular depth estimation. In: Proceedings of the IEEE Conference on Computer Vision and Pattern Recognition, pp. 2002–2011 (2018)
25. Fu, H., Gong, M., Wang, C., Batmanghelich, K., Zhang, K., Tao, D.: Geometry-consistent generative adversarial networks for one-sided unsupervised domain mapping. In: Proceedings of the IEEE/CVF Conference on Computer Vision and Pattern Recognition, pp. 2427–2436 (2019)
26. Fu, H., Li, S., Jia, R., Gong, M., Zhao, B., Tao, D.: Hard example generation by texture synthesis for cross-domain shape similarity learning. Adv. Neural Inf. Process. Syst. **33**, 14675–14687 (2020)
27. Gallicchio, C., Micheli, A.: Graph echo state networks. In: The 2010 International Joint Conference on Neural Networks (IJCNN), pp. 1–8. IEEE (2010)
28. Gao, H., Wang, Z., Ji, S.: Large-scale learnable graph convolutional networks. In: Proceedings of the 24th ACM SIGKDD International Conference on Knowledge Discovery & Data Mining, pp. 1416–1424. ACM (2018)
29. Garg, R., B.G., V.K., Carneiro, G., Reid, I.: Unsupervised CNN for single view depth estimation: geometry to the rescue. In: Leibe, B., Matas, J., Sebe, N., Welling, M. (eds.) ECCV 2016. LNCS, vol. 9912, pp. 740–756. Springer, Cham (2016). https://doi.org/10.1007/978-3-319-46484-8_45
30. Geiger, A., Lenz, P., Stiller, C., Urtasun, R.: Vision meets robotics: the kitti dataset. Int. J. Rob. Res. **32**(11), 1231–1237 (2013)
31. Gilmer, J., Schoenholz, S.S., Riley, P.F., Vinyals, O., Dahl, G.E.: Neural message passing for quantum chemistry. In: Proceedings of the 34th International Conference on Machine Learning, vol. 70, pp. 1263–1272. JMLR. org (2017)
32. Godard, C., Mac Aodha, O., Brostow, G.J.: Unsupervised monocular depth estimation with left-right consistency. In: Proceedings of the IEEE Conference on Computer Vision and Pattern Recognition, pp. 270–279 (2017)
33. Gori, M., Monfardini, G., Scarselli, F.: A new model for learning in graph domains. In: Proceedings. 2005 IEEE International Joint Conference on Neural Networks, vol. 2, pp. 729–734. IEEE (2005)
34. Gupta, A., Davis, L.S.: Beyond nouns: exploiting prepositions and comparative adjectives for learning visual classifiers. In: Forsyth, D., Torr, P., Zisserman, A. (eds.) ECCV 2008. LNCS, vol. 5302, pp. 16–29. Springer, Heidelberg (2008). https://doi.org/10.1007/978-3-540-88682-2_3
35. Hamilton, W., Ying, Z., Leskovec, J.: Inductive representation learning on large graphs. Adv. Neural Inf. Process. Syst. **30**, 1024–1034 (2017)
36. Handa, A., Whelan, T., McDonald, J., Davison, A.: A benchmark for RGB-D visual odometry, 3D reconstruction and SLAM. In: IEEE International Conference on Robotics and Automation, ICRA, Hong Kong, China (2014)
37. Henaff, M., Bruna, J., LeCun, Y.: Deep convolutional networks on graph-structured data. arXiv preprint arXiv:1506.05163 (2015)
38. Hoiem, D., Efros, A.A., Hebert, M.: Closing the loop in scene interpretation. In: 2008 IEEE Conference on Computer Vision and Pattern Recognition, pp. 1–8. IEEE (2008)
39. Huang, W., Zhang, T., Rong, Y., Huang, J.: Adaptive sampling towards fast graph representation learning. Adv. Neural Inf. Process. Syst. **31**, 4558–4567 (2018)

40. Johnson, J., et al.: Image retrieval using scene graphs. In: Proceedings of the IEEE Conference on Computer Vision and Pattern Recognition, pp. 3668–3678 (2015)
41. Karsch, K., Liu, C., Kang, S.B.: Depth transfer: depth extraction from video using non-parametric sampling. IEEE Trans. Pattern Anal. Mach. Intell. **36**(11), 2144–2158 (2014)
42. Kim, S., Park, K., Sohn, K., Lin, S.: Unified depth prediction and intrinsic image decomposition from a single image via joint convolutional neural fields. In: Leibe, B., Matas, J., Sebe, N., Welling, M. (eds.) ECCV 2016. LNCS, vol. 9912, pp. 143–159. Springer, Cham (2016). https://doi.org/10.1007/978-3-319-46484-8_9
43. Kingma, D.P., Ba, J.: Adam: a method for stochastic optimization. arXiv preprint arXiv:1412.6980 (2014)
44. Kipf, T.N., Welling, M.: Semi-supervised classification with graph convolutional networks. arXiv preprint arXiv:1609.02907 (2016)
45. Krishna, R., Chami, I., Bernstein, M., Fei-Fei, L.: Referring relationships. In: Proceedings of the IEEE Conference on Computer Vision and Pattern Recognition, pp. 6867–6876 (2018)
46. Krishna, R.: Visual genome: connecting language and vision using crowdsourced dense image annotations. Int. J. Comput. vision **123**(1), 32–73 (2017)
47. Ladicky, L., Shi, J., Pollefeys, M.: Pulling things out of perspective. In: Proceedings of the IEEE Conference on Computer Vision and Pattern Recognition, pp. 89–96 (2014)
48. Laina, I., Rupprecht, C., Belagiannis, V., Tombari, F., Navab, N.: Deeper depth prediction with fully convolutional residual networks. In: 2016 Fourth International Conference on 3D Vision (3DV), pp. 239–248. IEEE (2016)
49. Lan, L., Wang, X., Zhang, S., Tao, D., Gao, W., Huang, T.S.: Interacting tracklets for multi-object tracking. IEEE Trans. Image Process. **27**(9), 4585–4597 (2018)
50. Lee, J.H., Han, M.K., Ko, D.W., Suh, I.H.: From big to small: multi-scale local planar guidance for monocular depth estimation. arXiv preprint arXiv:1907.10326 (2019)
51. Lee, J.B., Rossi, R., Kong, X.: Graph classification using structural attention. In: Proceedings of the 24th ACM SIGKDD International Conference on Knowledge Discovery & Data Mining, pp. 1666–1674. ACM (2018)
52. Levie, R., Monti, F., Bresson, X., Bronstein, M.M.: Cayleynets: graph convolutional neural networks with complex rational spectral filters. IEEE Trans. Signal Process. **67**(1), 97–109 (2018)
53. Li, B., Shen, C., Dai, Y., Van Den Hengel, A., He, M.: Depth and surface normal estimation from monocular images using regression on deep features and hierarchical crfs. In: Proceedings of the IEEE Conference on Computer Vision and Pattern Recognition, pp. 1119–1127 (2015)
54. Li, R., Wang, S., Zhu, F., Huang, J.: Adaptive graph convolutional neural networks. In: Thirty-Second AAAI Conference on Artificial Intelligence (2018)
55. Li, Y., Ouyang, W., Wang, X., Tang, X.: Vip-cnn: visual phrase guided convolutional neural network. In: Proceedings of the IEEE Conference on Computer Vision and Pattern Recognition, pp. 1347–1356 (2017)
56. Liang, K., Guo, Y., Chang, H., Chen, X.: Visual relationship detection with deep structural ranking. In: Thirty-Second AAAI Conference on Artificial Intelligence (2018)
57. Liang, X., Lee, L., Xing, E.P.: Deep variation-structured reinforcement learning for visual relationship and attribute detection. In: Proceedings of the IEEE Conference on Computer Vision and Pattern Recognition, pp. 848–857 (2017)

58. Lienen, J., Hullermeier, E., Ewerth, R., Nommensen, N.: Monocular depth estimation via listwise ranking using the plackett-luce model. In: Proceedings of the IEEE/CVF Conference on Computer Vision and Pattern Recognition, pp. 14595–14604 (2021)
59. Lin, X., Ding, C., Zeng, J., Tao, D.: Gps-net: graph property sensing network for scene graph generation. In: Proceedings of the IEEE/CVF Conference on Computer Vision and Pattern Recognition, pp. 3746–3753 (2020)
60. Liu, B., Gould, S., Koller, D.: Single image depth estimation from predicted semantic labels. In: 2010 IEEE Computer Society Conference on Computer Vision and Pattern Recognition, pp. 1253–1260. IEEE (2010)
61. Liu, B., Dong, Q., Hu, Z.: Zero-shot learning from adversarial feature residual to compact visual feature. In: AAAI, pp. 11547–11554 (2020)
62. Liu, B., Dong, Q., Hu, Z.: Hardness sampling for self-training based transductive zero-shot learning. In: IEEE Conference Computer Vision Pattern Recognition, pp. 16499–16508 (2021)
63. Liu, B., Dong, Q., Hu, Z.: Semantic-diversity transfer network for generalized zero-shot learning via inner disagreement based ood detector. Knowl.-Based Syst. **229**, 107337 (2021)
64. Liu, B., Hu, L., Hu, Z., Dong, Q.: Hardboost: boosting zero-shot learning with hard classes. arXiv preprint arXiv:2201.05479 (2022)
65. Liu, H., Yang, Y., Wang, X.: Overcoming catastrophic forgetting in graph neural networks. In: Proceedings of the AAAI Conference on Artificial Intelligence (2021)
66. Liu, Z., et al.: Geniepath: graph neural networks with adaptive receptive paths. In: Proceedings of the AAAI Conference on Artificial Intelligence, vol. 33, pp. 4424–4431 (2019)
67. Lu, C., Krishna, R., Bernstein, M., Fei-Fei, L.: Visual relationship detection with language priors. In: Leibe, B., Matas, J., Sebe, N., Welling, M. (eds.) ECCV 2016. LNCS, vol. 9905, pp. 852–869. Springer, Cham (2016). https://doi.org/10.1007/978-3-319-46448-0_51
68. Lu, Y., et al.: Taskology: utilizing task relations at scale. In: Proceedings of the IEEE/CVF Conference on Computer Vision and Pattern Recognition, pp. 8700–8709 (2021)
69. Maksai, A., Wang, X., Fleuret, F., Fua, P.: Non-markovian globally consistent multi-object tracking. In: The IEEE International Conference on Computer Vision (ICCV) (2017)
70. Maksai, A., Wang, X., Fua, P.: What players do with the ball: a physically constrained interaction modeling. In: The IEEE Conference on Computer Vision and Pattern Recognition (CVPR) (2016)
71. Mertan, A., Sahin, Y.H., Duff, D.J., Unal, G.: A new distributional ranking loss with uncertainty: illustrated in relative depth estimation. In: 2020 International Conference on 3D Vision (3DV), pp. 1079–1088. IEEE (2020)
72. Monti, F., Boscaini, D., Masci, J., Rodola, E., Svoboda, J., Bronstein, M.M.: Geometric deep learning on graphs and manifolds using mixture model cnns. In: Proceedings of the IEEE Conference on Computer Vision and Pattern Recognition, pp. 5115–5124 (2017)
73. Niepert, M., Ahmed, M., Kutzkov, K.: Learning convolutional neural networks for graphs. In: International Conference on Machine Learning, pp. 2014–2023 (2016)
74. Paszke, A., et al.: Pytorch: an imperative style, high-performance deep learning library. Adv. Neural Inf. Process. Syst. **32**, 8026–8037 (2019)

75. Plummer, B.A., Mallya, A., Cervantes, C.M., Hockenmaier, J., Lazebnik, S.: Phrase localization and visual relationship detection with comprehensive image-language cues. In: Proceedings of the IEEE International Conference on Computer Vision, pp. 1928–1937 (2017)
76. Qi, X., Liao, R., Liu, Z., Urtasun, R., Jia, J.: Geonet: geometric neural network for joint depth and surface normal estimation. In: Proceedings of the IEEE Conference on Computer Vision and Pattern Recognition. pp. 283–291 (2018)
77. Qiu, J., Wang, X., Fua, P., Tao, D.: Matching seqlets: an unsupervised approach for locality preserving sequence matching. IEEE Trans. Pattern Anal. Mach. Intell. 43, 745–752 (2019)
78. Qiu, J., Wang, X., Maybank, S.J., Tao, D.: World from blur. In: Proceedings of the IEEE/CVF Conference on Computer Vision and Pattern Recognition, pp. 8493–8504 (2019)
79. Qiu, J., Yang, Y., Wang, X., Tao, D.: Hallucinating visual instances in total absentia. In: Vedaldi, A., Bischof, H., Brox, T., Frahm, J.-M. (eds.) ECCV 2020. LNCS, vol. 12350, pp. 264–282. Springer, Cham (2020). https://doi.org/10.1007/978-3-030-58558-7_16
80. Qiu, J., Yang, Y., Wang, X., Tao, D.: Scene essence. In: Proceedings of the IEEE/CVF Conference on Computer Vision and Pattern Recognition, pp. 8322–8333 (2021)
81. Ranftl, R., Lasinger, K., Hafner, D., Schindler, K., Koltun, V.: Towards robust monocular depth estimation: mixing datasets for zero-shot cross-dataset transfer. arXiv preprint arXiv:1907.01341 (2019)
82. Ranjan, A., et al.: Competitive collaboration: joint unsupervised learning of depth, camera motion, optical flow and motion segmentation. In: Proceedings of the IEEE/CVF Conference on Computer Vision and Pattern Recognition, pp. 12240–12249 (2019)
83. Ren, S., He, K., Girshick, R., Sun, J.: Faster r-cnn: towards real-time object detection with region proposal networks (2016)
84. Ren, S., Zhou, D., He, S., Feng, J., Wang, X.: Shunted self-attention via multi-scale token aggregation. In: Proceedings of the IEEE/CVF Conference on Computer Vision and Pattern Recognition (2022)
85. Ren, Z., Lee, Y.J.: Cross-domain self-supervised multi-task feature learning using synthetic imagery. In: Proceedings of the IEEE Conference on Computer Vision and Pattern Recognition, pp. 762–771 (2018)
86. Scarselli, F., Gori, M., Tsoi, A.C., Hagenbuchner, M., Monfardini, G.: The graph neural network model. IEEE Trans. Neural Netw. 20(1), 61–80 (2008)
87. Scharstein, D., Szeliski, R.: A taxonomy and evaluation of dense two-frame stereo correspondence algorithms. Int. J. Comput. Vision 47(1), 7–42 (2002)
88. Silberman, N., Hoiem, D., Kohli, P., Fergus, R.: Indoor segmentation and support inference from RGBD images. In: Fitzgibbon, A., Lazebnik, S., Perona, P., Sato, Y., Schmid, C. (eds.) ECCV 2012. LNCS, vol. 7576, pp. 746–760. Springer, Heidelberg (2012). https://doi.org/10.1007/978-3-642-33715-4_54
89. Sperduti, A., Starita, A.: Supervised neural networks for the classification of structures. IEEE Trans. Neural Netw. 8(3), 714–735 (1997)
90. Tan, M., Pang, R., Le, Q.V.: Efficientdet: scalable and efficient object detection. In: Proceedings of the IEEE/CVF Conference on Computer Vision and Pattern Recognition, pp. 10781–10790 (2020)
91. Veličković, P., Cucurull, G., Casanova, A., Romero, A., Lio, P., Bengio, Y.: Graph attention networks. arXiv preprint arXiv:1710.10903 (2017)

92. Veličković, P., Fedus, W., Hamilton, W.L., Liò, P., Bengio, Y., Hjelm, R.D.: Deep graph infomax. arXiv preprint arXiv:1809.10341 (2018)
93. Wang, C., Buenaposada, J.M., Zhu, R., Lucey, S.: Learning depth from monocular videos using direct methods. In: Proceedings of the IEEE Conference on Computer Vision and Pattern Recognition, pp. 2022–2030 (2018)
94. Wang, C., Wang, C., Xu, C., Tao, D.: Tag disentangled generative adversarial networks for object image re-rendering. In: International Joint Conference on Artificial Intelligence (IJCAI) (2017)
95. Wang, P., Shen, X., Lin, Z., Cohen, S., Price, B., Yuille, A.L.: Towards unified depth and semantic prediction from a single image. In: Proceedings of the IEEE Conference on Computer Vision and Pattern Recognition, pp. 2800–2809 (2015)
96. Wang, X., Türetken, E., Fleuret, F., Fua, P.: Tracking interacting objects optimally using integer programming. In: Fleet, D., Pajdla, T., Schiele, B., Tuytelaars, T. (eds.) ECCV 2014. LNCS, vol. 8689, pp. 17–32. Springer, Cham (2014). https://doi.org/10.1007/978-3-319-10590-1_2
97. Wang, X., Turetken, E., Fleuret, F., Fua, P.: Tracking interacting objects using intertwined flows. IEEE Trans. Pattern Anal. Mach. Intell. **38**(11), 2312–2326 (2016)
98. Xian, K., et al.: Monocular relative depth perception with web stereo data supervision. In: Proceedings of the IEEE Conference on Computer Vision and Pattern Recognition, pp. 311–320 (2018)
99. Xian, K., Zhang, J., Wang, O., Mai, L., Lin, Z., Cao, Z.: Structure-guided ranking loss for single image depth prediction. In: Proceedings of the IEEE/CVF Conference on Computer Vision and Pattern Recognition, pp. 611–620 (2020)
100. Xu, D., Ouyang, W., Wang, X., Sebe, N.: Pad-net: multi-tasks guided prediction-and-distillation network for simultaneous depth estimation and scene parsing. In: Proceedings of the IEEE Conference on Computer Vision and Pattern Recognition, pp. 675–684 (2018)
101. Yang, J., Lu, J., Lee, S., Batra, D., Parikh, D.: Graph r-cnn for scene graph generation. In: Proceedings of the European Conference on Computer Vision (ECCV), pp. 670–685 (2018)
102. Yang, Y., Feng, Z., Song, M., Wang, X.: Factorizable graph convolutional networks. In: Neural Information Processing Systems (NeurIPS) (2020)
103. Yang, Y., Qiu, J., Song, M., Tao, D., Wang, X.: Distilling knowledge from graph convolutional networks. In: IEEE Conference on Computer Vision and Pattern Recognition (CVPR) (2020)
104. Yang, Y., Wang, X., Song, M., Yuan, J., Tao, D.: SPAGAN: shortest path graph attention network. In: International Joint Conference on Artificial Intelligence (IJCAI) (2019)
105. Yang, Z., Liu, D., Wang, C., Yang, J., Tao, D.: Modeling image composition for complex scene generation. In: Proceedings of the IEEE/CVF Conference on Computer Vision and Pattern Recognition, pp. 7764–7773 (2022)
106. Yao, B., Fei-Fei, L.: Modeling mutual context of object and human pose in human-object interaction activities. In: 2010 IEEE Computer Society Conference on Computer Vision and Pattern Recognition, pp. 17–24. IEEE (2010)
107. Ying, Z., You, J., Morris, C., Ren, X., Hamilton, W., Leskovec, J.: Hierarchical graph representation learning with differentiable pooling. Adv. Neural Inf. Process. Syst. **31**, 4800–4810 (2018)
108. Yu, B., Liu, T., Gong, M., Ding, C., Tao, D.: Correcting the triplet selection bias for triplet loss. In: Proceedings of the European Conference on Computer Vision (ECCV), pp. 71–87 (2018)

109. Yu, B., Tao, D.: Deep metric learning with tuplet margin loss. In: Proceedings of the IEEE/CVF International Conference on Computer Vision, pp. 6490–6499 (2019)
110. Yu, J., Lin, Z., Yang, J., Shen, X., Lu, X., Huang, T.S.: Free-form image inpainting with gated convolution. In: Proceedings of the IEEE International Conference on Computer Vision, pp. 4471–4480 (2019)
111. Yu, R., Li, A., Morariu, V.I., Davis, L.S.: Visual relationship detection with internal and external linguistic knowledge distillation. In: Proceedings of the IEEE International Conference on Computer Vision, pp. 1974–1982 (2017)
112. Yu, W., et al.: Metaformer is actually what you need for vision. In: Proceedings of the IEEE/CVF Conference on Computer Vision and Pattern Recognition (2022)
113. Zhang, H., Kyaw, Z., Chang, S.F., Chua, T.S.: Visual translation embedding network for visual relation detection. In: Proceedings of the IEEE Conference on Computer Vision and Pattern Recognition, pp. 5532–5540 (2017)
114. Zhang, J., Shi, X., Xie, J., Ma, H., King, I., Yeung, D.Y.: Gaan: gated attention networks for learning on large and spatiotemporal graphs. arXiv preprint arXiv:1803.07294 (2018)
115. Zhang, Z., Cui, Z., Xu, C., Jie, Z., Li, X., Yang, J.: Joint task-recursive learning for semantic segmentation and depth estimation. In: Proceedings of the European Conference on Computer Vision (ECCV), pp. 235–251 (2018)
116. Zhang, Z., Cui, Z., Xu, C., Yan, Y., Sebe, N., Yang, J.: Pattern-affinitive propagation across depth, surface normal and semantic segmentation. In: Proceedings of the IEEE/CVF Conference on Computer Vision and Pattern Recognition, pp. 4106–4115 (2019)
117. Zhao, S., Fu, H., Gong, M., Tao, D.: Geometry-aware symmetric domain adaptation for monocular depth estimation. In: Proceedings of the IEEE/CVF Conference on Computer Vision and Pattern Recognition, pp. 9788–9798 (2019)
118. Zheng, C., Cham, T.J., Cai, J.: T2net: synthetic-to-realistic translation for solving single-image depth estimation tasks. In: Proceedings of the European Conference on Computer Vision (ECCV), pp. 767–783 (2018)
119. Zhou, T., Brown, M., Snavely, N., Lowe, D.G.: Unsupervised learning of depth and ego-motion from video. In: Proceedings of the IEEE Conference on Computer Vision and Pattern Recognition, pp. 1851–1858 (2017)
120. Zhuang, B., Liu, L., Shen, C., Reid, I.: Towards context-aware interaction recognition for visual relationship detection. In: Proceedings of the IEEE International Conference on Computer Vision, pp. 589–598 (2017)
121. Zoran, D., Isola, P., Krishnan, D., Freeman, W.T.: Learning ordinal relationships for mid-level vision. In: Proceedings of the IEEE International Conference on Computer Vision, pp. 388–396 (2015)

Image2Point: 3D Point-Cloud Understanding with 2D Image Pretrained Models

Chenfeng Xu[1], Shijia Yang[1], Tomer Galanti[2], Bichen Wu[3]([⊠]),
Xiangyu Yue[1], Bohan Zhai[1], Wei Zhan[1], Peter Vajda[3], Kurt Keutzer[1],
and Masayoshi Tomizuka[1]

[1] University of California, Berkeley, Berkeley, USA
[2] Massachusetts Institute of Technology, Cambridge, USA
[3] Meta Reality Labs, Menlo Park, USA
wbc@fb.com

Abstract. 3D point-clouds and 2D images are different visual representations of the physical world. While human vision can understand both representations, computer vision models designed for 2D image and 3D point-cloud understanding are quite different. Our paper explores the potential of transferring 2D model architectures and weights to understand 3D point-clouds, by empirically investigating the feasibility of the transfer, the benefits of the transfer, and shedding light on why the transfer works. We discover that we can indeed use the same architecture and pretrained weights of a neural net model to understand both images and point-clouds. Specifically, we transfer the image-pretrained model to a point-cloud model by copying or inflating the weights. We find that finetuning the transformed image-pretrained models (FIP) with minimal efforts—only on input, output, and normalization layers—can achieve competitive performance on 3D point-cloud classification, beating a wide range of point-cloud models that adopt task-specific architectures and use a variety of tricks. When finetuning the whole model, the performance gets further improved. Meanwhile, FIP improves data efficiency, reaching up to 10.0 top-1 accuracy percent on few-shot classification. It also speeds up the training of point-cloud models by up to 11.1x for a target accuracy (e.g., 90% accuracy). Lastly, we provide an explanation of the image to point-cloud transfer from the aspect of *neural collapse*. The code is available at: https://github.com/chenfengxu714/image2point.

Keywords: Point-cloud · Pre-training · Finetuning · Neural collapse

---

C. Xu and S. Yang—Equal contribution.

Supplementary Information The online version contains supplementary material available at https://doi.org/10.1007/978-3-031-19836-6_36.

S. Avidan et al. (Eds.): ECCV 2022, LNCS 13697, pp. 638–656, 2022.
https://doi.org/10.1007/978-3-031-19836-6_36

1 Introduction

Point-cloud is an important visual representation for 3D computer vision. It is widely used in a variety of applications, including autonomous driving [3,6,81], robotics [1,53,76], augmented and virtual reality [61,62,72], *etc*. However, a point-cloud represents visual information in a significantly different way from a 2D image. Specifically, a point-cloud consists of a set of unordered points lying on the object's surface, with each point encoding its spatial x, y, z coordinates and potentially other features such as intensity. In contrast, a 2D image organizes visual features as a dense 2D RGB pixel array.

Due to the representation differences, 2D image and 3D point-cloud understanding are treated as two separate problems. 2D image models and point-cloud models are designed to have different architectures and are trained on different types of data. No efforts have tried to directly transfer models from images to point-clouds.

Intuitively, both 3D point-clouds and 2D images are visual representations of the physical world. Their low-level representations are drastically different, but they can represent the same underlying visual concept. Furthermore, human vision has no problem understanding both representations. To connect images and point-clouds, previous works attempted to generate pseudo point-clouds by estimating the depth of mono/stereo images [24,67,80]. However, depth estimation from a single image is a challenging problem in computer vision, which requires large-scale dense depth labels [58]. Estimating depth from stereo images is easier but requires strict calibrated and synchronized stereo cameras, which limits the data scale. Therefore, it is interesting to ask whether we could use large-scale image models that were pretrained using supervised classification datasets (*e.g., ImageNet1K/ImageNet21K* classification) for point-cloud understanding.

Remarkably, the answer to the question above is positive. As we show in this work, 2D image models trained on image datasets can be transferred to understand 3D point-clouds with minimal effort. As illustrated in Fig. 1, given the commonly-used image-pretrained models, such as 2D ConvNets [27] and vision transformers [17], we can easily convert them into various kinds of point-cloud models. In particular, a pretrained 2D ConvNet or vision transformer can be easily extended into a projection-based, voxel-based, or transformer-based point-cloud model via copying weights or inflating weights [9].

In this paper, we primarily focus on 3D ConvNets inflated from 2D pretrained models. With the transformed point-cloud model (*e.g.*, inflated 3D ConvNets), we add linear input and output layers to the network; and on a target point-cloud dataset, we only finetune the input and output layers, and batch normalization layers, while keeping the pretrained model weights untouched. We call such partially-finetuned-image-pretrained models as *FIP-IO+BN* (finetuning input, output, and BN layers). As we show, FIP-IO+BN can achieve competitive performance up to 90.8% top-1 accuracy on the ModelNet 3D Warehouse dataset, on top of ResNet50, outperforming previous point-cloud models that adopt task-specific model architectures and tricks.

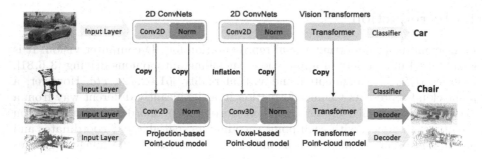

Fig. 1. We investigate the feasibility of pretrained 2D image models transferring to 3D point-cloud models. For example, with filter inflation and finetuning the input, output (classifier for classification task and decoder for semantic segmentation task), and normalization layers, the transformed 2D ConvNets are capable of dealing with point-cloud classification, indoor, and driving scene segmentation.

Even though incorporating pretrained models is useful for tackling downstream tasks, point-cloud models are typically trained from scratch. Based on our discovery, we further investigate fully-finetuned-image-pretrained models (termed as *FIP-ALL*). We observe that FIP-ALL brings significant improvement on top of different kinds of point-cloud models transformed from image-pretrained models. Besides, we also find that it generalizes to PointNet++ [55] which is pre-trained on images by ourselves. Specifically, FIP-ALL outperforms the training-from-scratch by a large margin on top of PointNet++, SimpleView, ViT-B-16, and ViT-L-16, respectively. In addition to the performance gain, FIP-ALL exhibits superior data efficiency with up to 10.0% accuracy improvement in few-shot classification on the ModelNet 3D Warehouse dataset. Compared with training-from-scratch, FIP-ALL also dramatically speeds up the training by using 11.1 times fewer epochs to reach the same validation accuracy (*e.g.*, 90% accuracy).

Finally, we theoretically explore the relationship between transferring knowledge between tasks of different modalities and neural collapse to shed light on why the transfer works. The analysis is based on extending the framework proposed in [19] and is provided in Appendix.

2   Related Work

2.1   Point-Cloud Processing Models

In this section, we list the most prominent approaches for processing point-clouds.

The **3D convolution-based method** is one of the mainstream point-cloud processing approaches which efficiently processes point-clouds based on voxelization. In this approach, voxelization is used to rasterize point-clouds into regular grids (called voxels). Then, we can apply 3D convolutions to the processed point-cloud. However, enamors empty voxels make lots of unnecessary computations. Sparse convolution is proposed to apply on the non-empty voxels [13,18,64,66,78,85], largely improving the efficiency of 3D convolutions.

The **projection-based method** attempts to project a 3D point-cloud to a 2D plane and uses 2D convolution to extract features [5,38,63,69–71,75]. Specifically, bird-eye-view projection [37,79] and spherical projection [50,70,71,75] have made great progress in outdoor point-cloud tasks.

Another approach is the **point-based method**, which directly processes the point-cloud data. The most classic methods, PointNet [54] and PointNet++ [55], consume points by sampling the center points, group the nearby points, and aggregate the local features. Many works further develop advanced local-feature aggregation operators that mimic the 3D convolution operation to structured data [32,36,40–42,44,66,76].

2.2 Pretraining in 2D and 3D Computer Vision

Pretraining in 2D Computer Vision. is an effective approach using supervised [17,21], self-supervised [23,33], and contrastive learning [2,8,10,12,26,29]. After pretraining on a large amount of data, a 2D model requires less computational and data resources for finetuning in order to obtain competitive performance on downstream tasks [7,11,28,34].

Pretraining in 3D Computer Vision. has been studied similarly as pretraining in 2D vision: both self-supervised and contrastive pretraining [31,65,73] show promising results. 3D point-clouds are difficult to annotate, and there is no large-scale annotated dataset available. To address this, previous works have tried to use model pretraining to improve data efficiency [77]. Recent works [30,83] explored using contrastive learning on point-clouds. Our work does not rely on long-time pretraining. Instead, we can directly take large amounts of open-sourced image-pretrained models for a variety of point-cloud tasks.

2.3 Cross-Modal Transfer Learning

Cross-Modal Transfer Learning. takes advantage of data from various modalities [15,45,47,52,74]. For example, [43] proposed pixel-to-point knowledge transfer (PPKT) from 2D to 3D which uses aligned RGB and RGB-D images during pretraining. Our work does not rely on joint image-point-cloud pretraining. Instead, we directly transfer an image-pretrained model to a point-cloud model with the simplest pretraining-finetuning scheme.

Some of the previous works for video and medical images [9,60] have adopted the method of simply extending a pretrained 2D convolutional filter along time or depth direction for transferring to 3D models. However, the domain gaps between point-clouds and images are much more than that of videos/medical images and images. Between language and image modalities, transfer learning with minimal finetuning also shows a competitive performance [46,57].

2.4   Neural Collapse

Neural collapse (NC) [25,51] is a recently discovered phenomenon in deep learning. It has been observed that during the training of deep overparameterized neural networks for standard classification tasks, the penultimate layer's features associated with training samples belonging to the same class concentrate around their class means. Essentially, [51] observed that the ratio of the within-class variances and the distances between the class means converge to zero. In addition to that, it has also been observed that asymptotically the class means (centered at their global mean) are not only linearly separable, but are also maximally distant and located on a sphere centered at the origin up to scaling, and furthermore, that the behavior of the last-layer classifier (operating on the features) converges to that of the nearest-class-mean decision rule.

Recently, [19] studied the relationship between **neural collapse and transfer learning**. They studied a transfer learning setting, where we intend to solve a target (classification) task, where only a limited amount of samples is available, so a model is pretrained and transferred from a source (classification) task. They showed that neural collapse extends beyond training and generalizes also to unseen test samples and new classes. In addition, it was shown that in the presence of neural collapse in the new classes, training a linear classifier on top of the learned penultimate layer requires only a few samples to generalize well. However, their empirical and theoretical analysis assumes that the source and target classes are i.i.d. samples (*e.g.*, a random split of the classes in ImageNet). This implies that the two tasks share the same modality. Therefore, we suggest training an adaptor (*e.g.*, a linear layer) along with retraining the normalization parameters as part of the transfer process. Intuitively, the adaptor takes samples of the second modality and translates them to representations that are interpretable by the pretrained model, such that it produces feature embeddings that are clustered into classes. In Appendix B, we extend the framework in [19] to the case where the source and target tasks are of different modalities and theoretically analyze it.

3   Converting a 2D Image Model to a 3D Point-Cloud Model

In this paper, we primarily focus on the 3D sparse-convolution-based method to process point-clouds, since it can be extended to a wide range of point-cloud tasks. The other point-cloud models we use in this paper are byproducts of copying the weights of 2D image models, for example, 2D ConvNets [27] or vision transformers [17]. In this section, we provide an in-depth introduction to how we transform the 2D ConvNets into 3D sparse ConvNets by inflation [9].

Inflating a 2D ConvNet into a 3D sparse ConvNet. As discussed in Sect. 2.1, we consider a set of points, where each point is represented by its 3D coordinates and additional features such as its intensity and RGB. We then voxelize/quantize these points into voxels according to their 3D space coordinates, following [13]. A voxel's feature is inherited from the point that lies within the voxel. If there are multiple points associated with the same voxel, we average all points' features and assign the mean to the voxel. If there is no point in the voxel, then we simply set the voxel's feature to 0. With sparse convolution, the computation on empty voxels can be skipped.

Given a pretrained 2D ConvNet, we convert it to a 3D ConvNet that takes 3D voxels as input. The key element of this procedure is to convert 2D convolution filters to 3D, *i.e.*, constructing 3D filters with the weights directly inherited from 2D filters. A 2D convolutional filter can be represented with a 4D tensor of shape $[M, N, K, K]$, representing output dimension, input dimension, and two spatial kernel sizes, respectively. A 3D convolutional filter has an extra dimension, and its shape is $[M, N, K, K, K]$. To better illustrate, we ignore the output and input dimensions and only consider a spatial slice of the 2D filter with shape $[K, K]$. The simplest way to convert this 2D filter to 3D is to repeat the 2D filter K times along a third dimension. This operation is the same as the *inflation* technique used by [9] to initialize a video model with a pretrained 2D ConvNet.

Besides convolution, other operations such as downsampling, BN, and non-linear activation can be easily migrated to 3D. Our 3D model inherits the architecture of the original 2D ConvNet, but we also add a linear layer as the input layer and an output layer depending on the target task. For classification, we use a global average pooling layer followed by one fully connected layer to get the final prediction. For semantic segmentation, the output layer is a U-Net style decoder [59]. The architecture of the input/output layers is described in more detail in Appendix B.7.

A note on image-to-video transfer. It is noteworthy to mention that although inflation is commonly used in video domains, image-to-point-cloud transfer is fundamentally different. Even though videos and point-clouds are both 3D data, they are represented with completely different visual modalities with different distributions. Intrinsically, 3D point-clouds are represented as a sparse set of points lying on object surfaces and parameterized by xyz-coordinates, while videos are dense RGB arrays, where the two spatial arrays represent RGB images and the temporal array reflects how images evolve through time. Point-clouds are translation and rotation invariant or equi-variant, while for videos, the spatial and temporal dimensions are not interchangeable. In this paper, we surprisingly find that with simple operations such as inflation, the image-pretrained models can be directly used for point-cloud understanding under the situation that image and point-cloud are drastically different. The detailed experiments showing the feasibility and utility, and the discussion of why it works from the aspect of neural collapse are illustrated in Sect. 4 and Sect. 5, respectively.

4   Empirical Evaluation

To explore the image to point-cloud transfer, we study three settings: , **(1)** fine-tuning input, output, and batch normalization layers (FIP-IO+BN), **(2)** fine-tuning the whole pretrained network (FIP-ALL), and optionally (3) partially-finetuned-image-pretrained model, only finetuning input and output layers (FIP-IO). Under the three settings, we extensively explore the feasibility of transferring the image-pretrained model for point-cloud understanding and its benefits. The entire empirical evaluation is organized as four questions: (1) Can we transfer pretrained-image models to recognize point-clouds? (Sect. 4.1) (2) Can image-pretraining benefit the performance of point-cloud recognition? (Sect. 4.2) (3) Can image-pretrained models improve the data efficiency on point-cloud recognition? (Sect. 4.3) (4) Can image-pretrained models accelerate training point-cloud models? (Sect. 4.4).

Datasets. We evaluate the transferred models on ModelNet 3D Warehouse classification [72], S3DIS indoor segmentation [1], and SemanticKITTI outdoor segmentation [3] tasks. ModelNet 3D Warehouse is a CAD model classification dataset that consists of point-clouds with 40 categories, and CAD models come from 3D Warehouse [62]. In this benchmark, we only utilize x, y, z coordinates as features. S3DIS is a dataset collected from real-world indoor scenes and includes 3D scans of Matterport Scanners from 6 areas. It provides point-wise annotations for indoor objects like chair, table, and bookshelf, *etc.* SemanticKITTI dataset from KITTI Vision Odometry [20] is a driving scene dataset. It provides dense point-wise annotations for the complete $360°C$ field-of-view of the deployed automotive lidar, which is currently one of the most challenging datasets.

ResNet [27] series is used mostly throughout our experiments. Depending on the experiments, ResNets are pretrained on Tiny-ImageNet, ImageNet-1K, ImageNet-21K [16], and Fractal database (FractalDB) [34]. Our pretrained models are directly downloaded from various sources, with detailed links provided in the Appendix. To study the benefits of using pretrained image models, we also utilize PointNet++ [55], ViT [17], and SimpleView [22] as our baselines.

4.1 Can We Transfer Pretrained-Image Models to Recognize Point-Clouds?

To evaluate the feasibility of transferring pretrained 2D image models to 3D point-cloud tasks, we conduct experiments on top of the ResNet series since there are abundant open-source pretrained ResNet available. In particular, we convert 2D ConvNets into 3D ConvNets using the procedure described in Sect. 3. We hypothesize that, if a pretrained 2D image model is capable of understanding point-clouds directly, we can see a non-trivial performance by only finetuning input and output layers of the transferred model. Further, as we gradually relax the frozen parameters, finetuning BN parameters as well, the transferred model can achieve better performance, even surpassing training-from-scratch.

We conduct two groups of experiments with FIP-IO and FIP-IO+BN, with the results shown in Fig. 2. The first is to evaluate the performance as the trainable parameters gradually increase. As shown in Fig. 2 (a), training **no more than 0.3 % (345.5 x fewer)** of the whole parameters, the image pretraining even beats the training-from-scratch (100 % trainable parameters). Specifically,

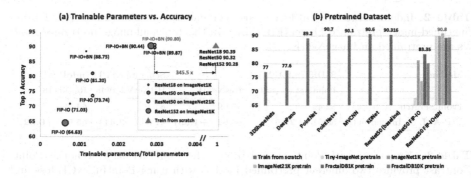

Fig. 2. a) the left figure shows the trainable parameters ratio *w.r.t* top-1 accuracy on ModelNet 3D Warehouse dataset. **b)** the right figure shows the performance of FIP-IO and FIP-IO+BN on top of **ResNet50** pretrained on different datasets.

Table 1. ModelNet 3D Warehouse classification results (top-1 accuracy %) of fully-finetuned-image-pretrained models (FIP-ALL) based on different pretrained models. We include 2021 SOTAs, such as RSMix [39], Point Transformer (Point-Trans) [84], DRNet [56], and PointCutMix [82], for comparison.

Method	ResNet18	ResNet50	ResNet152	ResNet101×2
From Scratch	90.39	90.32	90.28	90.03
FIP-ALL on ImageNet1K	90.52 (**+0.13**)	90.92 (**+0.60**)	91.09 (**+0.81**)	90.52 (**+0.49**)
FIP-ALL on ImageNet21K	–	91.05 (**+0.73**)	–	–
Method	PointNet++(SSG)	ViT-B-16	ViT-L-16	SimpleView
From Scratch	90.34	84.27	83.48	93.3
FIP-ALL on ImageNet1K	91.22 (**+0.88**)	–	–	93.8 (**+0.50**)
FIP-ALL on ImageNet21K	–	87.77 (**+3.50**)	87.66 (**+4.18**)	–
Method	RSMix	Point-Trans	DRNet	PointCutMix
From Scratch	93.5	93.7	93.1	93.4

ResNet152 FIP-IO+BN with ImageNet1K pretraining improves training-from-scratch by 0.16 points, and ResNet50 FIP-IO+BN with ImageNet21K pretraining improves 0.48 points. Meanwhile, FIP-IO reaches a non-trivial performance. ResNet50 FIP-IO pretrained on ImageNet1K achieves 81.20 % top-1 accuracy, only 9.12 points worse than training-from-scratch with approximately 0.1 % trainable parameters.

Furthermore, to investigate the effect of different datasets, as shown in the right figure of Fig. 2, we inflate ResNet50 pretrained from different image datasets, including Tiny-ImageNet, ImageNet1K, ImageNet21K, FractalDB1K, and FractalDB10K, then evaluate on the ModelNet 3D Warehouse.

We discover that, even if we only finetune the input and output layers while keeping the image-pretrained weights frozen, the FIP-IO pretrained from ImageNet1K, FractalDB1K, and FractalDB10K achieves competitive performance. Specifically, ResNet50 FIP-IO with ImageNet1K pretraining outperforms 3D

Table 2. Indoor scene and outdoor scene segmentation results (mIoU %) of fully-finetuned-image-pretrained Model (FIP-ALL). In this table, all image-pretrained models are pretrained on ImageNet1K.

Method	S3DIS (mIoU %)		SemanticKITTI (mIoU %)	
	PointNet++(SSG)	ResNet18	HRNetV2-W48	ResNet18
From Scratch	52.45	55.09	44.12	64.75
FIP-ALL on ImageNet1K	55.01 (**+2.56**)	56.62 (**+1.53**)	47.53 (**+3.41**)	65.57 (**+0.82**)

Table 3. Comparison with PointContrast [73] on the ModelNet 3D Warehouse. Point-Contrast provides two different pretrained models with using PointInfoNCE loss and Hardest Contrastive loss, respectively.

From scratch	PointInfoNCE	Hardest contrastive	ImageNet1K pretrain (Ours)
89.95	90.24 (**+0.29**)	90.15 (**+0.20**)	90.88 (**+0.93**)

ShapeNet [72] and DeepPano [61], which were the state-of-the-arts in 2015, by 4.2 and 3.6 points respectively in top-1 accuracy on ModelNet 3D Warehouse. More importantly, with ImageNet21K pretrained model, ResNet50 FIP-IO+BN surpasses training-from-scratch by 0.48 points, even beating a variety of well-known methods including PointNet [54], MVCNN [63], *etc.*.

Notably, we find out the answer to "Can we transfer pretrained-image models to recognize point-clouds?": Yes. The pretrained 2D image models can be directly used for recognizing point-clouds. Surprisingly, the pretraining dataset is not restricted to natural but also synthetic images like those in FractalDB1K/10K.

4.2   Can Image-Pretraining Benefit Point-Cloud Recognition?

From the previous subsection, we find unexpectedly that the image-pretrained model can be directly used for point-cloud understanding. In this subsection, we investigate whether the image-pretrained model is helpful to improve the performance of point-cloud tasks. We use different baselines, including voxelization-based method (simply ResNet), point-based method (PointNet++ [55]), projection-based method (SimpleView [22]), and current popular transformer-based method (ViT-B-16 and ViT-L-16 [17]), and fully finetune them on three point-cloud datasets: classification on ModelNet 3D Warehouse, scene segmentation on S3DIS and SemanticKITTI, as shown in Table 1 and Table 2.

For PointNet++, we use ImageNet1K to pretrain: we break each image into pixels and regard it as a point-cloud. For ViT, we directly use the open-source pretrained model and finetune it on ModelNet 3D Warehouse. All the implementation details are illustrated in Appendix A.

Table 1 presents performance on ModelNet 3D Warehouse dataset. We observe that FIP-ALL improves all baselines steadily and significantly. Besides, pretraining brings more improvements to deeper models. For example, ResNet18 can only be improved by 0.13% top-1 accuracy, but pretraining on ImageNet1K leads to 0.81 points top-1 accuracy improvement on top of ResNet152. Moreover, larger pretrained datasets also lead to better performance. Specifically, ResNet50 FIP-ALL from ImageNet21K can reach 91.05% top-1 acc, with 0.73 points improvement over training-from-scratch. Such FIP-ALL significantly outperforms a series of well-known methods such as [35,40,54,55,63,68].

We also explore FIP-ALL on different architectures, as shown in the second group of Table 1. In particular, FIP-ALL on top of PointNet++, ViT-B-16, ViT-L-16, and SimpleView with image dataset pretraining improve the training-from-scratch by 0.88, 3.50, 4.18, 0.50 points, respectively. Especially for the current superior baseline in image recognition, ViT-B-16 and ViT-L-16, the improved performance is quite significant, revealing the huge potential of using image-pretrained models for point cloud recognition.

For the challenging indoor and outdoor scene segmentation, using ImageNet1K pretrained models (FIP-ALL on ImageNet1K) also improve the training-from-scratch consistently, as shown in Table 2. PointNet++ (resp. ResNet18) pretrained on ImageNet1K outperforms the training-from-scratch by 2.56 points (resp. 1.53 points) mIoU on S3DIS dataset. For SemanticKITTI, we utilize the commonly used projection-based method with 2D ConvNet HRNet. With ImageNet1K pretraining, we observe 3.41 points mIoU improvement, a large margin in such a challenging task. Since HRNetV2-W48 has rich pretrained models, we finetune Cityscapes pretrained HRNetV2-W48 and observe this enhances more (5.25% mIoU improvement over training from scratch). Even for the ResNet18 with a high from-scratch performance of 64.75% mIoU, the ImageNet1K pretraining can also bring 0.82 points mIoU improvement.

Finally, we compare the performance gain with the well-known point-cloud self-supervised method PointContrast [73], as presented in Table 3. We use the same model architecture and finetuning recipe, and the only difference is the pretraining weights. Note that the model architecture used in PointContrast does not have corresponding open-sourced image-pretrained weights, so we pretrain it by ourselves on ImageNet1K, with the standard ImageNet training recipe provided by Pytorch. We can observe that image-pretraining on ImageNet1K significantly boosts the training-from-scratch by 0.93 points, surpassing the Point-Contrast by at least 0.64 points.

Therefore, the answer to "Can image-pretraining benefit point-cloud recognition" is: Yes. Image-pretraining can indeed improve point-cloud recognition, generalize to a wide range of backbones, and benefit multiple challenging tasks.

4.3 Can Image-Pretrained Models Improve the Data Efficiency on Point-Cloud Recognition?

Data efficiency is essential in point-cloud understanding due to the huge labor of collecting and annotating point-cloud data. In this subsection, we investigate whether the image-pretrained model can help to improve the data efficiency by conducting few-shot setting experiments, including 1-shot, 5-shot, and 10-shot.

Table 4. Few-shot experiments on top of different ResNets on the ModelNet 3D Warehouse dataset. We conduct 3 trials for each setting and results are as mean ± std.

Few-shot	ResNet18 (from scratch/FIP-ALL)	ResNet50	ResNet152
10-shot	72.2±0.8/73.2±0.6 (+1.0)	71.7±0.7/74.1±0.8 (+2.4)	69.8±1.1/73.9±0.4 (+4.1)
5-shot	63.7±1.6/66.6±0.8 (+2.9)	62.4±1.1/66.0±2.2 (+3.6)	59.4±0.8/66.5±0.9 (+7.1)
1-shot	26.8±4.4/36.8±0.6 (+10.0)	28.1±0.4/34.1±0.2 (+6.0)	23.3±4.3/33.2±1.3 (+9.9)

Table 5. Semi-supervised distillation experiments on top of ResNet34 on the ModelNet 3D Warehouse dataset.

Few-shot	From scratch	PointInfoNCE	Hardest contrastive	ImageNet1K pretrain (Ours)
10-shot	72.2	74.6 (+2.4)	74.6 (+2.4)	74.9 (+2.7)
5-shot	61.9	65.1 (+3.2)	65.9 (+4.0)	66.0 (+4.1)
1-shot	29.2	39.0 (+9.8)	37.2 (+8.0)	41.1 (+11.9)

In detail, for each class (ModelNet 3D Warehouse involves 40 classes), we randomly choose a few point-clouds as training data and still evaluate on the whole test set. We compare the results between training-from-scratch and FIP-ALL pretrained on the ImageNet1K dataset. The experimental results are shown in Table 4. We observe that FIP-ALL dramatically surpasses training-from-scratch on the low data regime (1-shot): pretraining on ImageNet1K brings 10.0, 6.0, and 9.9 points top-1 accuracy improvement for ResNet18, ResNet50, and ResNet152, respectively. For 5-shot and 10-shot settings, using ImageNet1K pretraining can still consistently improve the performance.

Furthermore, inspired by previous work [11] which proposed *big self-supervised models are strong semi-supervised learners* in 2D image recognition, we borrow the idea and propose *an image-pretrained model is also a strong semi-supervised learner in point-cloud recognition*. We also compared the image-pretrained model with the self-supervised pretrained model in this experiment. Specifically, we first take pretrained models from the previous self-supervised pretraining method PointContrast [73]. PointContrast provides two ScanNet [14] pretrained models of architecture ResNet34 trained with hardest-contrastive loss and PointInfoNCE loss. Then, we finetune PointContrast on 1/5/10 shot of the labeled ModelNet 3D Warehouse dataset and regard it as a teacher model. Finally, we distill the teacher model to a randomly initialized student model. In detail, we pass in the rest of unlabeled ModelNet 3D Warehouse dataset and 1/5/10 shot of the labeled dataset into the teacher model to generate pseudo labels. We use softmax MSE loss as consistency loss between student model outputs and pseudo labels. When the data instance is labeled, we add an additional cross entropy loss as a class criterion between student output and the label.

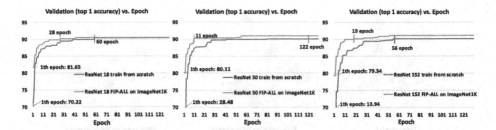

Fig. 3. The curves of validation accuracy w.r.t training epoch. We compare the results between training-from-scratch and FIP-ALL on the ImageNet1K, on top of ResNet18, ResNet50, and ResNet152, respectively.

To show the effectiveness of the image-pretrained model, we repeat the above experiment, only replacing self-supervised pretrained models with ResNet34 ImageNet1K pretrained models. Results are reported in Table 5. We observe that image-pretrained ResNet34 consistently outperforms PointContrast, and improves the baseline by a large margin with 11.9, 4.1, and 2.7 points on 1-shot, 5-shot, and 10-shot, respectively. The results in Table 5 show that an image-pretrained model is indeed a strong semi-supervised learner in point-cloud recognition.

However, in both Table 4 and Table 5, we observe that as the amount of training data increases, the performance increases. Therefore, our answer to"Can image-pretrained models improve the data efficiency on point-cloud recognition?" is: Yes. Image-pretrained models can improve the data efficiency on point-cloud recognition, especially on low data regime. Although when the training data increases, performance gain becomes marginal.

4.4 Can Image-Pretrained Models Accelerate Point-Cloud Training?

We also investigate whether the image-pretrained model can accelerate training on the point-clouds. The results are shown in Fig. 3.

We discover that, after training only one epoch on ModelNet 3D Warehouse dataset, FIP-ALL pretrained on ImageNet1K achieves very impressive performance, yet the performance of training-from-scratch is still low. For instance, after the first epoch, ResNet50 (resp. ResNet152) with training from scratch achieves 28.48% (resp. 13.94%) top-1 accuracy while ResNet50 (resp. ResNet152) with ImageNet1K pretraining reaches 80.11% (resp. 79.34%) top-1 accuracy. Moreover, to reach 90% top-1 accuracy, a non-trivial performance, FIP-ALL significantly accelerates the training by 2.14x (28 vs. 60 epoch), 11.1x (11 vs. 122 epoch), 2.95x (19 vs. 56 epoch) over training-from-scratch, on top of ResNet18, ResNet50, and ResNet152, respectively.

Therefore, our answer to "Can image-pretrained models accelerate point-cloud training?" is still positive. The image-pretrained models can significantly accelerate the training speed of point-cloud tasks.

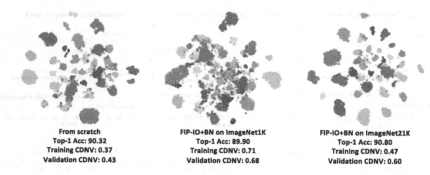

From scratch
Top-1 Acc: 90.32
Training CDNV: 0.37
Validation CDNV: 0.43

FIP-IO+BN on ImageNet1K
Top-1 Acc: 89.90
Training CDNV: 0.71
Validation CDNV: 0.68

FIP-IO+BN on ImageNet21K
Top-1 Acc: 90.80
Training CDNV: 0.47
Validation CDNV: 0.60

Fig. 4. tSNE visualization and class-distance normalized variance of fine-tuned models on train and validation split of ModelNet 3D Wharehouse dataset. FIP-IO+BN on ImageNet1K/21K are the same models in Fig. 2.

5   Neural Collapse in Cross-Modal Transfer

In this section, we provide an explanation of why the image to point-cloud transfer works based on the recently observed phenomenon called neural collapse [25,51]. [19] in depth studied the relationship between neural collapse and transfer learning between two classification tasks of the same modality (image domain). Similar to this work, we focus on transferring pretrained models between domains of different modalities, *i.e.*, from images to point-clouds.

As illustrated in Sect. 4, we can transfer image-pretrained models to the point-cloud domain. This motivates us to question whether the phenomenon of neural collapse generalization [19] (see Sect. 2.4) is also evident in our case. Following [19], we explore the relationships between neural collapse and image-to-point transfer by calculating the class-distance normalized variance (CDNV). Informally, the CDNV measures the ratio between the within-class variances of the embeddings and the squared distance of their means (see Appendix B.6 for details). We measure the CDNV of the fine-tuned model on both train and test data of the point-cloud domain. Since neural collapse is essentially a clustering property of features learned by neural networks, we further examine the neural collapse using tSNE visualizations. The results are summarized in Fig. 4.

We observe that with finetuning much fewer (345.5x fewer) parameters in ResNet50 pretrained on ImageNet1K, both class-distance-normalized-variance and the clustering of tSNE are worse than training-from-scratch, but still show relatively obvious clustering phenomenon. However, when we use the ResNet50 pretrained on ImageNet21K, the top-1 accuracy, and CDNV are significantly improved. More importantly, CDNV of ImageNet1K pretrained ResNet50 and ImageNet21K pretrained ResNet50 is lower than 1. This observation indicates although the image domain and point-cloud domain are quite different, the phenomenon of neural collapse generalization [19] still exists in their transfer. More results and analysis are illustrated in Appendix B.6.

Moreover, the interesting discovery pushes us to think about the reason of cross-modal transfer having neural collapse. Inspired by [19], we briefly explain below. More detailed theoretical proof is presented in Appendix C.

Theoretical idea. In this work, we focused on the problem of transferring knowledge between two tasks (source and target) consisting of two different modalities with different classes. Therefore, in the theoretical analysis, we have two separate modes of generalization: *between classes* and *between modalities*. In order to model this problem, we assume that the target and source tasks are decomposed of i.i.d. classes that are samples of two different distributions $\mathcal{D}_1$ and $\mathcal{D}_2$ (each stands for a different domain/modality). Each class is defined by a distribution over samples (e.g., samples of dog images). Given a target task (consisting of a set of randomly selected classes $P_1, \ldots, P_k \sim \mathcal{D}_1$), the pretrained model is evaluated after training an adaptor and a linear classifier on top of it. Its overall performance is measured in expectation over the selection of target tasks.

To capture the similarity between the two domains, we assume there exists an invertible mapping F between the classes that preserves the density of the two distributions, namely, $\hat{P}_c = F(P_c) \sim \mathcal{D}_2$ for $P_c \sim \mathcal{D}_1$. To characterize the similarity between the classes coming from $\mathcal{D}_1$ and $\mathcal{D}_2$, we further assume that the classes P_c and $\hat{P}_c$ share a 'mutual representation space' from which the class label can be recovered. The shared space is given by two simple functions g^* and $\tilde{g}^*$ for which the distance between $g^* \circ P_c$ and $\tilde{g}^* \circ \hat{P}_c$ is small (in expectation over $P_c \sim \mathcal{D}_1$). By utilizing tools from the theory of Unsupervised Domain Adaptation [4,48,49], we translate the performance of a pretrained model on randomly selected target tasks into its expected error on randomly selected tasks with classes from $\mathcal{D}_2$. Then, in order to bound this error, we use Proposition 5 in [19] that relates the error and the degree of neural collapse of the pretrained model on randomly selected classes from $\mathcal{D}_2$. Finally, according to Propositions 1 and 2 in [19], this quantity can be upper bounded by the degree of neural collapse of the pretrained model on the source train data.

6 Conclusions

In this work, we use finetuned-image-pretrained models (FIP) to explore the feasibility of transferring image-pretrained models for point-cloud understanding and the benefits of using image-pretrained models on point-cloud tasks. We surprisingly discover that, with simply transforming a 2D pretrained ConvNet and minimal finetuning—input, output, and batch normalization layer (FIP-IO or FIP-IO+BN), FIP can achieve very competitive performance on 3D point-cloud classification, beating a wide range of point-cloud models that adopt a variety of tricks. Moreover, we find that when finetuning all the parameters of the pretrained models (FIP-ALL), the performance can be significantly improved on point-cloud classification, indoor and outdoor scene segmentation. Fully finetuned models generalize to most of the popular point-cloud methods. We also find that FIP-ALL can improve the data efficiency on few-shot learning and accelerate the training speed by a large margin. Additionally, we explore the relationships between neural collapse and cross modal transferring for our case, and shed light on why it works based on neural collapse. Compared with previous works that seek improvements from designing architectures and pretraining only on point-cloud modality, our work is not limited by the architecture design and the small-scale point-cloud dataset. We believe that image pretraining is one of the solutions to the bottleneck of point-cloud understanding and hope this direction can inspire the research community.

Acknowledgements. Co-authors from UC Berkeley were sponsored by Berkeley Deep Drive (BDD). Tomer Galanti's contribution was supported by the Center for Minds, Brains and Machines (CBMM), funded by NSF STC award CCF-1231216.

References

1. Armeni, I., Sax, S., Zamir, A.R., Savarese, S.: Joint 2d–3d-semantic data for indoor scene understanding. arXiv preprint arXiv:1702.01105 (2017)
2. Bachman, P., Hjelm, R.D., Buchwalter, W.: Learning representations by maximizing mutual information across views. arXiv preprint arXiv:1906.00910 (2019)
3. Behley, J., Garbade, M., Milioto, A., Quenzel, J., Behnke, S., Stachniss, C., Gall, J.: SemanticKITTI: A Dataset for Semantic Scene Understanding of LiDAR Sequences. In: Proceedings of the IEEE/CVF International Conference on Computer Vision (ICCV) (2019)
4. Ben-david, S., Blitzer, J., Crammer, K., Pereira, F.: Analysis of representations for domain adaptation. In: Advances in Neural Information Processing Systems 19, pp. 137–144. Curran Associates, Inc. (2006)
5. Boulch, A., Le Saux, B., Audebert, N.: Unstructured point cloud semantic labeling using deep segmentation networks. 3DOR 2, 7 (2017)
6. Caesar, H.,et al.: A multimodal dataset for autonomous driving. In: Proceedings of the IEEE/CVF conference on computer vision and pattern recognition, pp. 11621–11631 (2020)
7. Caron, M., Bojanowski, P., Mairal, J., Joulin, A.: Unsupervised pre-training of image features on non-curated data. In: Proceedings of the IEEE/CVF International Conference on Computer Vision, pp. 2959–2968 (2019)
8. Caron, M., Misra, I., Mairal, J., Goyal, P., Bojanowski, P., Joulin, A.: Unsupervised learning of visual features by contrasting cluster assignments. arXiv preprint arXiv:2006.09882 (2020)
9. Carreira, J., Zisserman, A.: Quo vadis, action recognition? a new model and the kinetics dataset. In: proceedings of the IEEE Conference on Computer Vision and Pattern Recognition, pp. 6299–6308 (2017)
10. Chen, T., Kornblith, S., Norouzi, M., Hinton, G.: A simple framework for contrastive learning of visual representations. In: International conference on machine learning, pp. 1597–1607. PMLR (2020)
11. Chen, T., Kornblith, S., Swersky, K., Norouzi, M., Hinton, G.: Big self-supervised models are strong semi-supervised learners. arXiv preprint arXiv:2006.10029 (2020)
12. Chen, X., Fan, H., Girshick, R., He, K.: Improved baselines with momentum contrastive learning. arXiv preprint arXiv:2003.04297 (2020)

13. Choy, C., Gwak, J., Savarese, S.: 4d spatio-temporal convnets: Minkowski convolutional neural networks. In: Proceedings of the IEEE Conference on Computer Vision and Pattern Recognition, pp. 3075–3084 (2019)
14. Dai, A., Chang, A.X., Savva, M., Halber, M., Funkhouser, T., Nießner, M.: Scannet: Richly-annotated 3d reconstructions of indoor scenes. In: Proceedings of the Computer Vision and Pattern Recognition (CVPR), IEEE (2017)
15. Dai, A., Nießner, M.: 3dmv: Joint 3d-multi-view prediction for 3d semantic scene segmentation. In: Proceedings of the European Conference on Computer Vision (ECCV), pp. 452–468 (2018)
16. Deng, J., Dong, W., Socher, R., Li, L.J., Li, K., Fei-Fei, L.: Imagenet: A large-scale hierarchical image database. In: 2009 IEEE conference on computer vision and pattern recognition, pp. 248–255. IEEE (2009)
17. Dosovitskiy, A., et al.: An image is worth 16x16 words: Transformers for image recognition at scale. arXiv preprint arXiv:2010.11929 (2020)
18. Feng, D., Zhou, Y., Xu, C., Tomizuka, M., Zhan, W.: A simple and efficient multi-task network for 3d object detection and road understanding. arXiv preprint arXiv:2103.04056 (2021)
19. Galanti, T., György, A., Hutter, M.: On the role of neural collapse in transfer learning. In: International Conference on Learning Representations (2022), https://openreview.net/forum?id=SwIp410B6aQ
20. Geiger, A., Lenz, P., Urtasun, R.: Are we ready for Autonomous Driving? The KITTI Vision Benchmark Suite. In: Proc. of the IEEE Conference on Computer Vision and Pattern Recognition (CVPR), pp. 3354–3361 (2012)
21. Girshick, R., Donahue, J., Darrell, T., Malik, J.: Rich feature hierarchies for accurate object detection and semantic segmentation. In: Proceedings of the IEEE conference on computer vision and pattern recognition, pp. 580–587 (2014)
22. Goyal, A., Law, H., Liu, B., Newell, A., Deng, J.: Revisiting point cloud shape classification with a simple and effective baseline. arXiv preprint arXiv:2106.05304 (2021)
23. Goyal, P., et al.: Self-supervised pretraining of visual features in the wild. arXiv preprint arXiv:2103.01988 (2021)
24. Gur, S., Wolf, L.: Single image depth estimation trained via depth from defocus cues. In: Proceedings of the IEEE/CVF Conference on Computer Vision and Pattern Recognition, pp. 7683–7692 (2019)
25. Han, X.Y., Papyan, V., Donoho, D.L.: Neural collapse under mse loss: Proximity to and dynamics on the central path (2021)
26. He, K., Fan, H., Wu, Y., Xie, S., Girshick, R.: Momentum contrast for unsupervised visual representation learning. In: Proceedings of the IEEE/CVF Conference on Computer Vision and Pattern Recognition, pp. 9729–9738 (2020)
27. He, K., Zhang, X., Ren, S., Sun, J.: Deep residual learning for image recognition. In: Proceedings of the IEEE conference on computer vision and pattern recognition, pp. 770–778 (2016)
28. Henaff, O.: Data-efficient image recognition with contrastive predictive coding. In: International Conference on Machine Learning, pp. 4182–4192. PMLR (2020)
29. Hjelm, R.D., et al.: Learning deep representations by mutual information estimation and maximization. arXiv preprint arXiv:1808.06670 (2018)
30. Hou, J., Graham, B., Nießner, M., Xie, S.: Exploring data-efficient 3d scene understanding with contrastive scene contexts. arXiv preprint arXiv:2012.09165 (2020)
31. Hou, J., Graham, B., Nießner, M., Xie, S.: Exploring data-efficient 3D scene understanding with contrastive scene contexts. In: Proceedings of the IEEE/CVF Conference on Computer Vision and Pattern Recognition, pp. 15587–15597 (2021)

32. Hua, B.S., Tran, M.K., Yeung, S.K.: Pointwise convolutional neural networks. In: Proceedings of the IEEE Conference on Computer Vision and Pattern Recognition, pp. 984–993 (2018)
33. Jing, L., Tian, Y.: Self-supervised visual feature learning with deep neural networks: A survey. IEEE Transactions on Pattern Analysis and Machine Intelligence (2020)
34. Kataoka, H., et al.: Pre-training without natural images. In: Proceedings of the Asian Conference on Computer Vision (2020)
35. Klokov, R., Lempitsky, V.: Escape from cells: Deep kd-networks for the recognition of 3d point cloud models. In: Proceedings of the IEEE International Conference on Computer Vision, pp. 863–872 (2017)
36. Komarichev, A., Zhong, Z., Hua, J.: A-cnn: Annularly convolutional neural networks on point clouds. In: Proceedings of the IEEE/CVF Conference on Computer Vision and Pattern Recognition, pp. 7421–7430 (2019)
37. Lang, A.H., Vora, S., Caesar, H., Zhou, L., Yang, J., Beijbom, O.: Pointpillars: Fast encoders for object detection from point clouds. In: Proceedings of the IEEE/CVF Conference on Computer Vision and Pattern Recognition, pp. 12697–12705 (2019)
38. Lawin, F.J., Danelljan, M., Tosteberg, P., Bhat, G., Khan, F.S., Felsberg, M.: Deep projective 3D semantic segmentation. In: Felsberg, M., Heyden, A., Krüger, N. (eds.) CAIP 2017. LNCS, vol. 10424, pp. 95–107. Springer, Cham (2017). https://doi.org/10.1007/978-3-319-64689-3_8
39. Lee, D., et al.: Regularization strategy for point cloud via rigidly mixed sample. In: Proceedings of the IEEE/CVF Conference on Computer Vision and Pattern Recognition, pp. 15900–15909 (2021)
40. Li, J., Chen, B.M., Lee, G.H.: So-net: Self-organizing network for point cloud analysis. In: Proceedings of the IEEE conference on computer vision and pattern recognition, pp. 9397–9406 (2018)
41. Li, Y., Bu, R., Sun, M., Wu, W., Di, X., Chen, B.: Pointcnn: Convolution on χ-transformed points. In: Proceedings of the 32nd International Conference on Neural Information Processing Systems. pp. 828–838 (2018)
42. Liu, Y., Fan, B., Meng, G., Lu, J., Xiang, S., Pan, C.: Densepoint: Learning densely contextual representation for efficient point cloud processing. In: Proceedings of the IEEE/CVF International Conference on Computer Vision, pp. 5239–5248 (2019)
43. Liu, Y.C., et al.: Learning from 2d: Pixel-to-point knowledge transfer for 3d pre-training. arXiv preprint arXiv:2104.04687 (2021)
44. Liu, Z., Hu, H., Cao, Y., Zhang, Z., Tong, X.: A closer look at local aggregation operators in point cloud analysis. In: Vedaldi, A., Bischof, H., Brox, T., Frahm, J.-M. (eds.) ECCV 2020. LNCS, vol. 12368, pp. 326–342. Springer, Cham (2020). https://doi.org/10.1007/978-3-030-58592-1_20
45. Liu, Z., Qi, X., Fu, C.W.: 3d-to-2d distillation for indoor scene parsing. arXiv preprint arXiv:2104.02243 (2021)
46. Lu, K., Grover, A., Abbeel, P., Mordatch, I.: Pretrained transformers as universal computation engines. arXiv preprint arXiv:2103.05247 (2021)
47. Lu, Y., et al.: Open-vocabulary 3d detection via image-level class and debiased cross-modal contrastive learning. arXiv preprint arXiv:2207.01987 (2022)
48. Mansour, Y.: Learning and domain adaptation. In: Algorithmic Learning Theory, 20th International Conference, ALT, pp. 4–6 (2009)
49. Mansour, Y., Mohri, M., Rostamizadeh, A.: Domain adaptation: Learning bounds and algorithms. In: COLT - The 22nd Conference on Learning Theory (2009)

50. Milioto, A., Vizzo, I., Behley, J., Stachniss, C.: Rangenet++: Fast and accurate lidar semantic segmentation. In: 2019 IEEE/RSJ International Conference on Intelligent Robots and Systems (IROS), pp. 4213–4220. IEEE (2019)

51. Papyan, V., Han, X.Y., Donoho, D.L.: Prevalence of neural collapse during the terminal phase of deep learning training. Proc. Natl. Acad. Sci. 117(40), 24652–24663 (2020)

52. Park, J., Xu, C., Zhou, Y., Tomizuka, M., Zhan, W.: Detmatch: Two teachers are better than one for joint 2d and 3d semi-supervised object detection. arXiv preprint arXiv:2203.09510 (2022)

53. Pomerleau, F., Colas, F., Siegwart, R.: A review of point cloud registration algorithms for mobile robotics. Foundations Trends Robot. 4(1), 1–104 (2015)

54. Qi, C.R., Su, H., Mo, K., Guibas, L.J.: Pointnet: Deep learning on point sets for 3d classification and segmentation (2016). arxiv:1612.00593

55. Qi, C.R., Yi, L., Su, H., Guibas, L.J.: Pointnet++: Deep hierarchical feature learning on point sets in a metric space. arXiv preprint arXiv:1706.02413 (2017)

56. Qiu, S., Anwar, S., Barnes, N.: Dense-resolution network for point cloud classification and segmentation. In: Proceedings of the IEEE/CVF Winter Conference on Applications of Computer Vision, pp. 3813–3822 (2021)

57. Radford, A., et al.: Learning transferable visual models from natural language supervision. In: International Conference on Machine Learning, pp. 8748–8763. PMLR (2021)

58. Ranftl, R., Lasinger, K., Hafner, D., Schindler, K., Koltun, V.: Towards robust monocular depth estimation: Mixing datasets for zero-shot cross-dataset transfer. IEEE Transactions on Pattern Analysis and Machine Intelligence (TPAMI) (2020)

59. Ronneberger, O., Fischer, P., Brox, T.: U-Net: convolutional networks for biomedical image segmentation. In: Navab, N., Hornegger, J., Wells, W.M., Frangi, A.F. (eds.) MICCAI 2015. LNCS, vol. 9351, pp. 234–241. Springer, Cham (2015). https://doi.org/10.1007/978-3-319-24574-4_28

60. Shan, H., Zhang, Y., Yang, Q., Kruger, U., Kalra, M.K., Sun, L., Cong, W., Wang, G.: 3-D convolutional encoder-decoder network for low-dose ct via transfer learning from a 2-d trained network. IEEE Trans. Med. Imaging 37(6), 1522–1534 (2018)

61. Shi, B., Bai, S., Zhou, Z., Bai, X.: Deeppano: deep panoramic representation for 3-D shape recognition. IEEE Signal Process. Lett. 22(12), 2339–2343 (2015). https://doi.org/10.1109/LSP.2015.2480802

62. Sketchup: 3d modeling online free—3d warehouse models. https://3dwarehouse.sketchup.com (2021)

63. Su, H., Maji, S., Kalogerakis, E., Learned-Miller, E.: Multi-view convolutional neural networks for 3d shape recognition. In: Proceedings of the IEEE international conference on computer vision, pp. 945–953 (2015)

64. Tang, H., et al.: Searching efficient 3d architectures with sparse point-voxel convolution. In: European Conference on Computer Vision (2020)

65. Wang, H., Liu, Q., Yue, X., Lasenby, J., Kusner, M.J.: Unsupervised point cloud pre-training via view-point occlusion, completion. arXiv preprint arXiv:2010.01089 (2020)

66. Wang, P.S., Liu, Y., Guo, Y.X., Sun, C.Y., Tong, X.: O-cnn: Octree-based convolutional neural networks for 3d shape analysis. ACM Trans. Graph. (TOG) 36(4), 1–11 (2017)

67. Wang, Y., Chao, W.L., Garg, D., Hariharan, B., Campbell, M., Weinberger, K.: Pseudo-lidar from visual depth estimation: Bridging the gap in 3D object detection for autonomous driving. In: CVPR (2019)

68. Wang, Y., Sun, Y., Liu, Z., Sarma, S.E., Bronstein, M.M., Solomon, J.M.: Dynamic graph cnn for learning on point clouds. Acm Trans. Graph. (tog) **38**(5), 1–12 (2019)
69. Wang, Z., Zhan, W., Tomizuka, M.: Fusing bird's eye view lidar point cloud and front view camera image for 3D object detection. In: 2018 IEEE Intelligent Vehicles Symposium (IV), pp. 1–6. IEEE (2018)
70. Wu, B., Wan, A., Yue, X., Keutzer, K.: Squeezeseg: Convolutional neural nets with recurrent crf for real-time road-object segmentation from 3D lidar point cloud. In: ICRA (2018)
71. Wu, B., Zhou, X., Zhao, S., Yue, X., Keutzer, K.: Squeezesegv 2: Improved model structure and unsupervised domain adaptation for road-object segmentation from a lidar point cloud. In: ICRA (2019)
72. Wu, Z., Song, S., Khosla, A., Yu, F., Zhang, L., Tang, X., Xiao, J.: 3d shapenets: A deep representation for volumetric shapes. In: Proceedings of the IEEE Conference on Computer Vision and Pattern Recognition (CVPR) (2015)
73. Xie, S., Gu, J., Guo, D., Qi, C.R., Guibas, L., Litany, O.: PointContrast: unsupervised pre-training for 3D point cloud understanding. In: Vedaldi, A., Bischof, H., Brox, T., Frahm, J.-M. (eds.) ECCV 2020. LNCS, vol. 12348, pp. 574–591. Springer, Cham (2020). https://doi.org/10.1007/978-3-030-58580-8_34
74. Xu, C., et al.: Pretram: Self-supervised pre-training via connecting trajectory and map. arXiv preprint arXiv:2204.10435 (2022)
75. Xu, C.: SqueezeSegV3: spatially-adaptive convolution for efficient point-cloud segmentation. In: Vedaldi, A., Bischof, H., Brox, T., Frahm, J.-M. (eds.) ECCV 2020. LNCS, vol. 12373, pp. 1–19. Springer, Cham (2020). https://doi.org/10.1007/978-3-030-58604-1_1
76. Xu, C., et al.: You only group once: Efficient point-cloud processing with token representation and relation inference module. arXiv preprint arXiv:2103.09975 (2021)
77. Xu, X., Lee, G.H.: Weakly supervised semantic point cloud segmentation: Towards 10x fewer labels. In: Proceedings of the IEEE/CVF Conference on Computer Vision and Pattern Recognition, pp. 13706–13715 (2020)
78. Yan, Y., Mao, Y., Li, B.: Second: sparsely embedded convolutional detection. Sensors **18**(10), 3337 (2018)
79. Yang, B., Luo, W., Urtasun, R.: Pixor: Real-time 3D object detection from point clouds. In: Proceedings of the IEEE conference on Computer Vision and Pattern Recognition, pp. 7652–7660 (2018)
80. Yin, W., Liu, Y., Shen, C.: Virtual normal: Enforcing geometric constraints for accurate and robust depth prediction. IEEE Transactions on Pattern Analysis and Machine Intelligence (2021)
81. Yue, X., Wu, B., Seshia, S.A., Keutzer, K., Sangiovanni-Vincentelli, A.L.: A lidar point cloud generator: from a virtual world to autonomous driving. In: Proceedings of the 2018 ACM on International Conference on Multimedia Retrieval, pp. 458–464 (2018)
82. Zhang, J., et al.: Pointcutmix: Regularization strategy for point cloud classification. arXiv preprint arXiv:2101.01461 (2021)
83. Zhang, Z., Girdhar, R., Joulin, A., Misra, I.: Self-supervised pretraining of 3d features on any point-cloud. arXiv preprint arXiv:2101.02691 (2021)
84. Zhao, H., Jiang, L., Jia, J., Torr, P.H., Koltun, V.: Point transformer. In: Proceedings of the IEEE/CVF International Conference on Computer Vision, pp. 16259–16268 (2021)
85. Zhou, H., et al.: Cylinder3d: An effective 3d framework for driving-scene lidar semantic segmentation. arXiv preprint arXiv:2008.01550 (2020)

FAR: Fourier Aerial Video Recognition

Divya Kothandaraman[1](✉)(iD), Tianrui Guan[1](iD), Xijun Wang[1], Shuowen Hu[2],
Ming Lin[1](iD), and Dinesh Manocha[1](iD)

[1] University of Maryland, College Park, USA
dkr@umd.edu
[2] DEVCOM Army Research Laboratory, Adelphi, USA
https://gamma.umd.edu/far

Abstract. We present an algorithm, Fourier Activity Recognition
(FAR), for UAV video activity recognition. Our formulation uses a novel
Fourier object disentanglement method to innately separate out the
human agent (which is typically small) from the background. Our disentanglement technique operates in the frequency domain to characterize
the extent of temporal change of spatial pixels, and exploits convolution-
multiplication properties of Fourier transform to map this representation to the corresponding object-background entangled features obtained
from the network. To encapsulate contextual information and long-range
space-time dependencies, we present a novel Fourier Attention algorithm,
which emulates the benefits of self-attention by modeling the weighted
outer product in the frequency domain. Our Fourier attention formulation uses much fewer computations than self-attention. We have evaluated our approach on multiple UAV datasets including UAV Human
RGB, UAV Human Night, Drone Action, and NEC Drone. We demonstrate a relative improvement of **8.02%–38.69%** in top-1 accuracy and
up to **3** times faster over prior works.

1 Introduction

Deep learning techniques have been widely used for activity recognition [5,7,21].
Video analysis of scenes captured using UAV cameras [43,52] is much harder than
activity recognition in ground-camera datasets [7,63]. In these UAV videos, the
object of interest, *i.e.* the human actor (any individual appearing in the video
performing scripted or non-scripted actions), is typically much smaller in terms
of number of pixels or the area than the corresponding background, and thus
provides less knowledge than a front view capture. Moreover, it is harder to
capture and label UAV videos. Overall, there are fewer and smaller labeled

---

The second and third authors contributed equally.

Supplementary Information The online version contains supplementary material
available at https://doi.org/10.1007/978-3-031-19836-6_37.

datasets of aerial videos, as compared to ground videos. For instance, ground-camera datasets like Kinetics-400 [7] contain $306,245$ videos while the recent UAV-Human [43] database has $22,476$ videos.

Given that the size of the human actor in UAV videos is much smaller than the corresponding background, a neural network trained on these datasets may learn to infer more from the background [41] than the human actor. While both background and context are important [12], the network must learn to first identify the human actor and the corresponding action, and then deduce relations of the human actor with the surroundings in a judicious manner. In the absence of annotated detection boxes that can demarcate the human actor, the network needs to be able to differentiate the moving human actor from the background in an intrinsic manner. One approach is to detect the object of interest via object detection [57]. However, action recognition models that heavily rely on localization of the human actor require near to perfect object detection accuracy [82]. While it is practically not feasible to annotate all datasets for object detection, object detectors trained on ground camera datasets will not generalize well UAV videos due to domain gap issues [4,8,70]. Domain adaptation solutions do not lead to perfect generalization yet.

On the other hand, traditional optical flow [3] techniques require hundreds of optimization iterations each frame, and split the network into RGB and motion streams which increases computation and model parameters [54]. Low computation alternatives such as deep learning based optical flow [16,33,58], motion feature networks [39] and ActionFlowNet [50] are inferior in performance compared to optical flow. Techniques such as background subtraction [53] and motion segmentation [77] are not very promising either [19,60]. Thus, the network needs to learn to automatically *disentangle* [18,81] object feature representations from the corresponding entangled state containing both the object and background information.

In addition to object-background separation, it is important for the network to acquire knowledge [5] about the context, relationships between the object, and background and intra-pixels correspondences as well. Self-attention [69,78] can model this information by capturing long-range dependencies within an image/video. Prior work on attention based video activity recognition [1,5,44] has seen two classes of self attention networks by either directly applying self-attention on convolutional layers or using self-attention as the building block. Mathematically, the core step in the computation of self-attention is matrix multiplication, which makes it computationally expensive.

1.1 Main Contributions

We present a novel method, FAR , for UAV video action recognition. The design of FAR in the frequency domain is motivated by the fact that frequency spectrums contain knowledge about a signals' characteristics that are not easily interpretable in the time domain. Our novel components include:

- We propose a novel Fourier Object Disentanglement method (FO) to bestow the network with the ability to *intrinsically* recognize the moving human actor

from the background. FO operates in the frequency domain dictated by the spectrum of the Fourier transform corresponding to the temporal dimensions of the video. It characterizes the motion of the human actor based on the magnitude and rate of temporal change of feature maps that encode information about the spatial pixels of the video. The amplitudes at each spatial-temporal location of the feature maps are innately representative of dynamic salient, static salient, dynamic non-salient and static non-salient regions, in the same order of relevance. This also empowers the network to handle videos with moving background pixels and dynamic cameras.
- We present Fourier Attention (FA) to encapsulate context and long range space-time dependencies within a video. Fourier attention works in the frequency domain corresponding to the space-time dimensions of the video, and emulates the benefits of self-attention. The time complexity of FA is $O(n^2 log n)$ as opposed to $O(n^3)$ for traditional self-attention, and the accuracy of Fourier-attention approximates that of self-attention.

Moreover, such a representation promotes global mixing. FAR has multiple benefits. (i) It elegantly exploits the mathematical properties of Fourier transform to achieve the desired objectives of object background separation and context encoding by performing fewer computations than traditional methods. (ii) It is parameter-less, i.e., it does not have any learnable layers/ parameters. (iii) FAR can be embedded within any 3D action recognition network such as I3D [7,21] to achieve state-of-the-art performance. (iv) FAR converges faster than the corresponding 3D action recognition backbone.

We experimentally demonstrate that FAR outperforms prior work by 8.02%−38.69% performance across multiple UAV datasets including UAV Human RGB [43], UAV Human Night [43], Drone Action [52], and NEC Drone [13]. We compare with the state-of-the-art Fourier method, efficient attention method and self-attention based transformer methods and demonstrate accuracy, computation and memory benefits.

2 Related Work

Action Recognition: Action recognition is a well studied topic in computer vision. The emergence of large-scale ground-camera videos datasets [7,49,63] has led to development of deep learning techniques for action recognition. We refer the reader to [11] for a survey on action recognition. Broadly speaking, three classes of network architectures have been proposed for action recognition. The first [23,26,30,64,73] builds on the two-stream theory in cognition to model space and time separately. The second [5,7,21,22,32,67] models space and time jointly via 3D CNNs. The third class includes transformer-based architectures [5,27,46,55,72]. These transformer-based solutions are built on self-attention [69,78] and have high computational complexity. In the interest of optimizing GPU memory, frame sampling strategies [28,29,37,80] for video action recognition have been proposed. The above solutions are focused on challenges pertaining to action recognition in ground-camera videos. However, UAV video action recognition is much more difficult.

UAV Action Recognition: UAV video databases [2,13,43,52] have been used to develop solutions [15,51,65,68] for UAV action recognition. However, these solutions are directly based off techniques designed for ground-camera datasets [7,49], where the size of the object is comparable to the background. Moreover, for ground camera videos, an auxilliary guidance factor based on object detection [57] is a viable option. However, these assumptions do not hold true in UAV videos [17,48].

FFT and Deep Learning. FFT has been immensely used in traditional image [6,56] and video processing [14,79] applications. Fast Fourier Transform (FFT) has been recently used in deep learning methods. One of its first applications was to accelerate convolution operations [38]. Incorporating FFT between NN layers [10,66,75] instead of CNNs to transform the feature space to the frequency domain, and aid global mixing of knowledge, has been used to improve accuracy for image classification, detection and ground-camera action recognition. An interesting application of FFT includes image stylization [76] as a guiding factor for domain adaptation. Most recently, FFT was used to naively replace self-attention layers [69] for NLP applications.

Efficient Attention. Methods to improve memory efficiency of transformers include modifications in matrix multiplication [61], low rank approximations [71], kernel modifications [35] for linear time complexity [36,42,59,74]. While most of these solutions are focused on NLP and image-based computer vision tasks, EA [61] demonstrates results on temporal action localization and STAR [62] performs skeleton action recognition. The former can be regarded as a localization task w.r.t. the temporal dimension while the latter uses pose information making the task of classification easier. None of these solutions are customized to UAV action recognition which brings forth different challenges.

3   Fourier Disentangled Space Time Attention

In this section, we describe our approach. We design two novel methods to decipher the human actor performing action, and encode context. Fourier Object Disentanglement (FO) disentangles the object from the background in an automatic manner. Fourier Space-Time Attention (FA) imbibes the properties of self-attention to capture long range space-time relationships at a lower computational cost. These modules can be embedded within any state-of-the-art 3D video recognition backbone such as I3D [7] or X3D [21] for improved action recognition. We now describe the methods in detail.

3.1   Fourier Object Disentanglement

We present a Fourier Object Disentanglement (FO) method to automatically separate the human actor from the background. Movement of the human actor

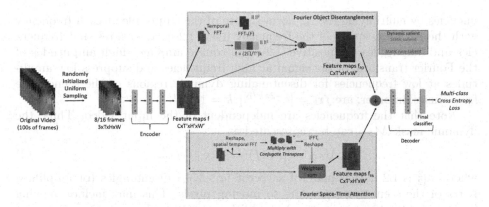

Fig. 1. Fourier object disentanglement (FO) and Space-time Fourier attention (FA): FO empowers the network to intrinsically separate out the moving human agent from the background, without the need for any annotated object detection bounding boxes. This enables our network to explicitly focus on the low resolution human agent performing action, and not just learn from background cues. FO inherently characterizes salient and non-salient, and static and dynamic regions of the scene via the amplitudes of the feature maps it computes. FA elegantly exploits the mathematical properties of the Fourier transform to imbibe the properties of self-attention and capture contextual knowledge and long-range space-time dependencies at a much lower computational complexity.

in the scene can be characterised by temporal change of feature maps encoding spatial pixels (across space dimensions $H \times W$) in the video frames. The rate and magnitude of change of a signal can be quantified by amplitude of a signal at different frequencies. Thus, to identify the movement, we first transform the feature maps to a temporal frequency space. We perform this computation using 1D Fourier transform along the temporal dimension. Specifically, let $f(c, t, h, w) \in C \times T' \times H' \times W'$ denote the feature maps on which FO is applied, where C is the number of channels and T' and $(H' \times W')$ denote the temporal and spatial dimensions of the feature maps, respectively. The amplitude of the temporal Fourier transform at the frequency $-2\pi k/N$ is:

$$\mathcal{F}_T(f)(k) = \sum_{n=0}^{n=T'} f(c, t, h, w) \times e^{-2\pi kn/N}, \tag{1}$$

which can be computed efficiently using the FFT algorithm [24]. $\mathcal{F}_T(f)(k)$ mathematically represents the amplitude of the temporal signal at every spatial and channel location of the feature map f, at various frequencies. Intuitively, high frequency in the temporal dimension corresponds to the movement, and low frequency represents static regions of the scene. Therefore, regions corresponding to the moving human actor should have higher amplitude of Fourier transform at high frequencies. To infer the presence of the moving human actor at various spatial locations, we encapsulate the relationships between amplitudes and frequencies by multiplying the L2-norm-square of the amplitude at each frequency with the L2-norm-square of the frequency itself. L2-norm ensures that frequencies and amplitudes are positive. L2-norm-square amplifies high amplitudes of the Fourier transform of the signal at high frequencies and suppress low amplitudes at low frequencies for disentangling dynamic regions of the scene. The frequencies, in order, are: $fr_k = [e^{-2\pi k/N}], k = 1....T'$.

Note that the frequencies are independent of the input video. Thus, the dynamic mask $\mathcal{M}_{FO}$ can be represented as

$$M_{FO} = \|F_T(f)(k)\|_2^2 \times \|fr_k\|_2^2, \tag{2}$$

where $|a|_2^2$ is L2 norm-square of a vector $|a|$. M_{FO} disentangles (or amplifies) parts of the scene corresponding to moving pixels. This may include moving background (and camera motion) in addition to moving human actor. Our next task is to use M_{FO} to demarcate moving object pixels from **moving background pixels**.

To further separate out only the moving actor, we capitalize on the activation maps f computed by the model. While not perfect, the activations at salient regions of the scene are higher than those at the non-salient regions. Hence, the final object disentangled representations can be represented as a dot product of M_{FO} and network features f, which amplifies dynamic, salient regions of the scene. Mathematically,

$$F_{FO} = f \odot M_{FO}. \tag{3}$$

According to this formulation, dynamic salient regions are amplified the most, and static non-salient regions are heavily suppressed. The amplitude at static salient regions and dynamic non-salient regions is lower than the amplitude at dynamic salient regions. Due to the $l2$ operation in the computation of M_{FO} and linear application of f in Eq. 3, static salient regions have a higher amplitude than the dynamic non-salient regions. Thus, the ordering of amplitudes that is formed as: dynamic-salient > static-salient > dynamic-non-salient > static-non-salient, in concordance with the relevance for decision making for action recognition. Thus, static as well as dynamic background regions have lower amplitudes than static and dynamic regions of the object executing action.

Time Complexity: The time complexity of FO depends on the time complexity of 1D FFT, which is $nlog(n)$, for an n-element input vector. Consider the classical case [31] where the temporal and spatial dimensions at the mid level feature representations is half and one-fourth of the number of frames sampled and spatial dimensions of the image respectively. The number of FFTs that need to be computed is $C \times (H/8) \times (W/8)$ where C, H, W correspond to the number of channels at the mid-level, and spatial dimensions of the image. Therefore, the total time complexity is $C \times (H/8) \times (W/8) \times (T/2)log(T/2)$.

3.2   Space-Time Fourier Attention

Consider a scene that depicts a human actor swimming in a swimming pool. Here, it is important to decipher the relationship between the human actor and the pool. While explicit modeling of correspondences between different pixels illustrating pose, orientation, and joint movements may not be necessary, it is crucial for the neural network to inherently capture this knowledge. Space-time self-attention for video action recognition [1,5,44] is capable for extracting this knowledge, but comes at the cost for expensive matrix multiplications.

We propose Fourier Space-Time Attention (FA) for acquiring knowledge about the long-range space-time relations within a video. Fourier attention approximates self-attention in an elegant fashion at a reduced computational cost. To understand the mechanics of Fourier attention, we first succinctly present self-attention [78]. The inputs to self-attention are key, query and value vectors which are representations obtained by 1×1 convolutions using a common input feature map. Vaswani et al. [69] describe the computation of self-attention as "a weighted sum of the values, where the weight (or sub-attention) assigned to each value is computed by a compatibility function of the query with the corresponding key." Key, query and value are 1×1 convolution layers transforming the input feature maps. Mathematically, with x representing the input feature maps, and $\odot$ denoting matrix multiplication,

$$\text{Attention} = \text{Value(x)} \odot [\text{Query(x)}^T \odot \text{Key(x)}]^T \tag{4}$$

Our space-time Fourier attention method proceeds as follows. The first step is to obtain a representation equivalent to the key-query computation, termed *Fourier sub-attention*. Fouurier sub-attention is motivated by autocorrelaton, which is the correlation coefficient between different parts of the same signal. We define *Fourier sub-attention* as the element-wise product of the Fourier transform of feature maps with the conjugate transpose of the Fourier transform of these feature maps (Eq. 6). To compute this space-time Fourier sub-attention, we reshape the video feature maps f to a 3D representation $C \times T' \times (HW)$, which are transformed to the frequency domain via 2D Fourier transform along the space and time axes as follows:

$$\mathcal{F}_{ST}(f)(m,n) = \sum_{h,w} f(c,t,h,w)e^{-2\pi mh/M}e^{-2\pi nw/N}. \tag{5}$$

computed efficiently using the FFT algorithm [24]. FFT is a representation of the signal as a whole at a wide spectrum of frequencies, and enables inherent and exhaustive global mixing between various spatial and temporal regions of the video. The space-time Fourier sub-attention $\mathcal{A}_{ST}$ in the Fourier domain is simply the element wise multiplication between $\mathcal{F}_{ST}$ and its complex conjugate $\mathcal{F}_{ST}^*$:

$$\mathcal{A}_{ST} = \mathcal{F}_{ST} \times \mathcal{F}_{ST}^* \tag{6}$$

Next, we compute the inverse FFT ($\mathcal{IF}$) of $\mathcal{A}_{ST}$ to obtain the correlations in the time domain, and reshape to $C \times T' \times H' \times W'$. These sub-attention "weights" are then used in a dot product (or element wise multiplication) with the input feature maps f to compute the final space-time Fourier attention maps f_{FA}.

A scaling factor λ_{FA}, chosen empirically to be 0.01, scales these Fourier attention maps, which are then sum-fused with the input feature maps. Mathematically,

$$f_{FA} = F + \lambda_{FA} \times \mathcal{IF}(\mathcal{A}_{ST}), \tag{7}$$

Time complexity: Traditional self-attention [69] requires the model to perform two matrix multiplications. In the first matrix multiplication of self attention, we multiply the query matrix $(THW \times C)$ with the key matrix $(C \times THW)$. The time complexity is $O(C \times THW \times THW)$. In the second matrix multiplication, we multiply the value matrix $(C \times HWT)$ with the attention matrix $(HWT \times HWT)$. The complexity of this stage is $O(C \times HWT \times HWT)$. Hence, the overall time complexity of space-time self-attention [5] is $O(HWT \times HWT \times C)$.

In contrast, our Fourier attention solves the problem via one 2D FFT and one 2D iFFT. 2D FFT is computed on a matrix of dimensions $HW \times T$. The number of 2D FFTs that need to be computed is equal to the number of channels (C). Hence, the complexity is $O(C \times HWTlog(HWT))$. The complexity of 2D FFT and 2D iFFT are the same. Therefore, the overall time complexity of Fourier attention is $O(C \times HWTog(HWT))$. Clearly, Fourier attention is much more efficient than self attention. In terms of accuracy, space-time Fourier attention is comparable to space-time self-attention [5].

3.3   Mathematical Analysis

Lemma 1. *Given an input matrix A, Fourier attention as well self-attention [5, 69] encapsulate long-range relationships for global mixing by computing outer products.*

Proof. We refer the reader to the supplementary material for the detailed proof. We present a concise version here. Without loss of generality, let $[a_{ij}]$ denote the elements of a square matrix A (with dimensions N) in 2D. f, g, h represent 1×1 convolutions for key, query, value computations in self-attention. The self-attention matrix S_{mn} is:

$$S_{mn} = \sum_{l=1}^{N} ha_{ml} \sum_{k=1}^{N} [ga_{lk} \times fa_{kn}] \tag{8}$$

Fourier attention F_{mn} is:

$$F_{mn} = \sum_{b=1}^{N}\sum_{c=1}^{N} \overbrace{\exp(-2\pi mc/N)\exp(-2\pi nb/N)}^{h_{mn}(b,c)} a_{mn} \times$$

$$\{\sum_{j=1}^{N}\sum_{i=1}^{N} \underbrace{\exp(-2\pi j(b-c)/N)}_{f_{mn}(b,c)} a_{ij} \times \underbrace{\exp(-2\pi i(c-b)/N)}_{g_{mn}(b,c)} a_{ij}\} \tag{9}$$

f, g, h in Eq. 8 are 1×1 convolutions, and that the exponential terms span the entire spectrum of frequencies lets us define f, g, h for Fourier attention as shown in Eq. 9. Thus, the equation for Fourier attention can be simplified as:

$$F_{mn} = \sum_{b=1}^{N} \sum_{c=1}^{N} h_{mn}(b,c)a_{mn} \times \{\sum_{j=1}^{N} \sum_{i=1}^{N} f_{mn}(b,c)a_{ij} \times g_{mn}(b,c)a_{ij}\}$$

In self-attention, f,g,h are learnable. In contrast, in Fourier attention, f,g,h are pre-defined by the Fourier spectrum. Nonetheless, they exhaustively cover the Fourier spectrum. Moreover, the terms involved and the structure of computations (multiplications followed by summation) in Eqs. 8 and 10 are similar, both promote global mixing and encapsulate long-range relationships. □

4   FAR: Activity Recognition in UAVs

We present FAR, a network for video action recognition in UAVs (Fig. 1). FAR samples 8–16 frames from the input video by using randomly initialized uniform sampling, described in Sect. 4.1. These frames are passed through the first few layers of the 3D backbone network (or encoder) to generate feature maps f. These features contain entangled object and background information along the space-time dimensions. The choice of this intermediate layer in the backbone network that extracts feature maps f is a careful trade-off between the spatial-temporal resolutions needed for FAR to work well and the amount of knowledge contained in the networks' layers. We describe this choice in detail in this section, as well as present ablation experiments in Sect. 5.3 to justify our choice.

The *Fourier Object Disentanglement* module (Sect. 3.1), and the *Fourier Space-Time Attention* module (Sect. 3.2) act on f, in parallel, to generate f_{FO} and f_{FA}, respectively. f_{FO} and f_{FA} are sum fused and passed through the remaining layers of the neural network to generate the final action classification probability distribution, used in a multi-class cross entropy loss term with the ground-truth label for back-propagation.

Incorporating FO within the 3D Backbone: Typically, to encapsulate temporal movement at each spatial location, we need to ensure that the spatial temporal dimensions of the feature map is not too small. Thus, it is useful to perform this operation using mid-level features (output from the middle layer of the network, as shown in Fig. 1) that strike a fine balance between generic features that capture context, and focused high level features (at output layer).

Incorporating FA within the 3D Backbone: After FO, the network does not contain any background signal. Hence, Fourier attention needs to be applied either before FO or in parallel with FO. FO is applied on mid-level features. Applying FA at a high level is not very effective because the extracted features do not have sufficient information. Hence we apply FA on the mid-level features as well, in parallel with the Fourier object disentanglement module.

4.1   Randomly Initialized Uniform Sampling

It is computationally expensive to use all the frames in a video. In traditional uniform sampling, T frames are sampled at uniform intervals. The standard way of uniform sampling under-utilizes [37,80] the knowledge that can be gained from the original video, which adds to the pre-existing issue of limited data. We use a variation of uniform sampling to improve the variance of the network and hence boost accuracy. First, we compute the step size as the ratio of total number of frames in the video and number of frames that we desire to sample. Next, we generate a random number between 0 and step size, and correspondingly designate the first frame to be sampled. This is followed by uniformly sampling video frames at step size intervals from the designated first frame.

5   Experiments and Results

We will make all code and trained models publicly available.

5.1   Datasets

In this section, we briefly describe the UAV datasets used for evaluating FAR. **UAV Human RGB** [43] is the largest UAV-based human behavior understanding dataset. Split 1 contains 15172 and 5556 images for training and testing respectively captured under various adversities including illumination, time of day, weathers, etc. **UAV Human Night Camera** [43] contains videos similar to UAV Human RGB captured using a night-vision camera. The night vision camera captures videos in color mode in the daytime, and grey-scale mode in the nighttime. **Drone Action** [52] is an outdoor drone video dataset captured using a free flying drone. It has 240 HD RGB videos across 13 human actions. **NEC Drone** [13] is an indoor UAV video dataset with 16 human actions, performed by human subjects in an unconstrained manner.

5.2   Implementation Details

Backbone Network Architecture: We benchmark our models using two state-of-the-art video recognition backbone architectures (i) I3D [7] (CVPR 2017) (ii) X3D-M [21] (CVPR 2020). For both X3D and I3D, we extract mid-level features after the second layer.

Training Details: Our models were trained using NVIDIA GeForce 1080 Ti GPUs, and NVIDIA RTX A5000 GPUs. Initial learning rates were {0.01, and 0.001} across datasets. We use the Stochastic Gradient Descent (SGD) optimizer with weight decay of 0.0005 and momentum of 0.9, and cosine/ poly annealing for learning rate decay. The final softmax predictions of all our models were constrained using multi-class cross entropy loss.

Table 1. Results on UAV Human RGB. Table (a): FAR can be embedded within any 3D action recognition backbone to achieve state-of-the-art performance. Pretraining with Kinetics boosts performance, and large input sizes work better since FA and FO are designed to capture global, as well as local knowledge. FAR imparts improvements of 2.20%-38.69% over 3D action recognition backbones across training configurations. **Table (b) - Ablation experiments:** We demonstrate that each component of FAR imparts substantial improvement in top-1 accuracy by upto **8%**.

Backbone	FAR	Frames	Input Size	Init.	Top-1	Top-5
(i) I3D	✗	8	540 × 960	Kinetics	21.06	40.81
(ii) I3D	✓	8	540 × 960	Kinetics	29.21	50.27
(iii) X3D-M	✗	16	224 × 224	None	27.0	44.2
(iv) X3D-M	✓	16	224 × 224	None	27.6	44.1
(v) X3D-M	✗	16	224 × 224	Kinetics	30.6	50.3
(vi) X3D-M	✓	16	224 × 224	Kinetics	31.9	50.3
(vii) X3D-M	✗	8	540 × 540	Kinetics	36.6	57.1
(viii) X3D-M	✓	8	540 × 540	Kinetics	38.6	59.2

(a)

FO	FA	Sampling	Top-1
✗	✗	✗	21.06
✓	✗	✗	25.89
✗	✓	✗	24.15
✓	✓	✗	27.00
✓	✓	✓	29.21

(b)

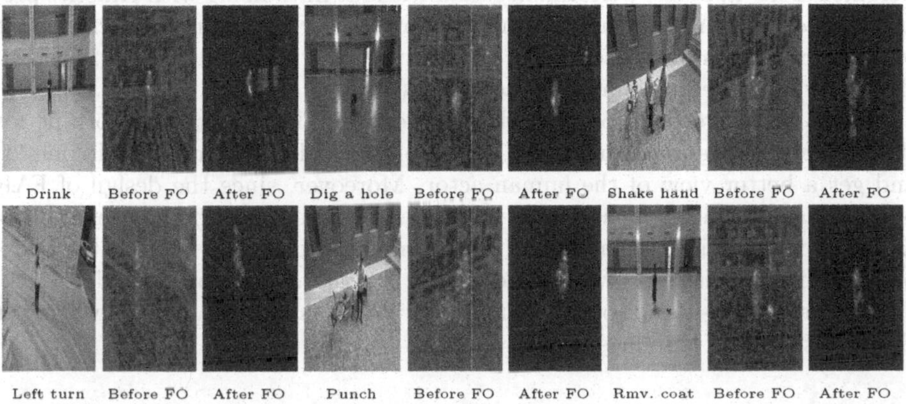

Fig. 2. Qualitative results on UAV human RGB. We show the effect of our Fourier Object Disentanglement (FO) method. In each sample, the images, in order, correspond to a frame from the video, feature representation before disentanglement and the feature representation after disentanglement respectively. Notice the effectiveness of FO in scenes with light noise (Row 1 Image 2, Row 2 Image 3), dim light (Row 1 Image 2), dynamic camera and dynamic background (Row 1 Image 1). Regions of the scene corresponding to moving human actor (or salient dynamic) are amplified most (solid yellow). Static background is completely suppressed (solid purple). Static salient regions are slightly amplified (e.g. lower body of human actor in Row 2 Image 3 - yellow), and dynamic backgrounds are suppressed to a great extent (pale yellow in Row 1 Image 1). We show more results in the supplementary material. (Color figure online)

Evaluation: We report top-1 and top-5 accuracies.

5.3 Main Results: UAV Human RGB

Benchmarking FAR. *FAR can be embedded within any 3D action recognition backbone to achieve state-of-the-art performance.* In Table 1a, we show results on UAVHuman RGB at different frame rates, input sizes, backbone network architectures and pre-trained weights initialization. In experiment (i) and (ii), we use the I3D backbone, and initialize the network with pretrained Kinetics weights. Spatially, we downsample the input video by a factor of 2, and sample 8 frames per video. This configuration gives the network full access to the spatial portions of the video at every stage of training and testing. FAR imparts a relative improvement of **38.69%** and **23.18%** in top-1 and top-5 accuracy, respectively.

In the subsequent experiments, we use X3D-M, as the backbone. Many vision-based papers crop the original video into small patches of resolution 224 × 224. We explore this in experiments (iii)-(vi) under two settings: without initializing with Kinetics pretrained weights, and by initializing with Kinetics pretrained weights. Concurrent with our intuition, initializing with Kinetics pretrained weights results in better performance than without initializing with Kinetics pretrained weights. In both cases, with small crop siz, FAR improves performance over the corresponding baselines by 2.2%−4.24%. At a resolution of 224 × 224, there is a slight decrease in Top-5 accuracy (0.1%).

Video action recognition is a global level task. Hence, it is important for the network to see a larger spatial region of the video to understand context, and get a better view of the human actor. Moreover, since the design of FAR is specifically inspired of challenges pertaining to object background separation, and context encoding, the margin of improvement imparted by FAR to the backbone architecture is larger when the crop size is higher. At a crop size of 540×540, FAR improves top-1 and top-5 accuracies by 5.46% and 3.67% respectively, over the corresponding baselines.

Ablation Experiments FAR ablations. We present ablation experiments on the components of FAR in Table 1b. We use the I3D backbone [7], and sample

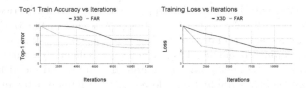

Fig. 3. FAR converges much faster than the state-of-the-art action recognition method X3D-M [21]. In the left curve, we show the top-1 train accuracy as a function of the networks' training iterations. In the right figure, we plot the training loss curve. We demonstrate that FAR imparts convergence benefits over prior work, under the same hyperparameter and GPU configurations.

Table 2. Comparisons with state-of-the-art self-attention based transformer methods on UAV Human. We initialize all our models with Kinetics pre-trained weights. We observe higher accuracy and computational benefits (up to **3x**) with FAR.

Method	Param M	Top-1 %	FLOPs GFlops/video	GPU GB/video	Inference Time (sec)/video
I. Baseline non-attention models					
X3D-M	3.8	36.6	14.39	3	0.08
I3D-M	12	21.06	346.55	10	0.1
II. Comparisons with the state-of-the-art Fourier-based method					
I3D + FNet [40] (2021)	12	24.39	346.56	10	0.1
I3D + FAR (Ours)	12	29.21	346.6	10	0.2
III. Comparison with the state-of-the-art efficient-attention method					
I3D + Efficient Attention [61] (WACV 2021)	12	21.13	462	13.3	0.12
I3D + Fourier Attention (Ours)	12	24.15	346.57	10	0.19
IV. Comparisons with the state-of-the-art self-attention based transformer methods					
ViT-B-TimeSformer (ICML 2021) [5]	121.4	33.9	2380	32	0.27
MVIT (ICCV 2021) [20]	36.6	24.3	70.8	9	0.16
X3D-M + FAR (Ours)	3.8	38.6	14.41	3	0.09

8 frames per video. We initialize with Kinetics pretrained weights, and spatially downsample (and then feed in the entire frame) the video by a factor of 2. In the first four experiments, we uniformly sample 8 frames from frame 0. The first row is the baseline experiment with neither Fourier object disentanglement nor Fourier attention. We observe in the experiment corresponding to Row 2 that object disentanglement improves performance by 22.9% over the baseline. FO is a high pass filter (L2). The usage of a linear (L1) high pass filter results in an accuracy of 25.56%. Thus, we used the L2 high-pass filter as it results in a higher accuracy. Next, we determine the importance of context and long-range space-time relationships by using only Fourier attention, and demonstrate an improvement of 14.67% in Row 3.

FO and FA complement each other - the former disentangles object from the background, while the latter decodes contextual information and inter-pixel, inter-frame relations. Using FO and FA in parallel, and sum-fusing the resultant feature maps cumulatively improves performance by 28.2% over the baseline. Finally, we incorporate the sampling scheme, vis-a-vis, randomly initialized uniform sampling along with FO and FA. This results in a final accuracy of 29.21%, 38.69% over the baseline.

FA Ablations. We conduct ablation experiments on our proposed Fourier Attention (FA). We use the I3D backbone, and a video resolution of $540 \times 960 \times 8$. In all these experiments, FO is applied on level 2. In the first experiment, we extend FA to channels [25] in addition to space-time, at level 2, the accuracy is 26.48. In the second experiment, we apply channel FA at level 4 [25] while retaining space-time FA at level 2, the accuracy further degrades to 25.77. In contrast, the accuracy with space-time Fourier attention is 27.00. Thus, we find that global mixing at channel level does not contribute to improvement in performance.

Next, we explore the notion of multi-level FA, where FA is applied at multiple levels and not just level 2, the accuracy is 29.16. In contrast, FAR's accuracy is 29.21. Our conclusion is that FA extracts knowledge prerequisite to learning long-range space-time relationships at level 2, to its maximum capacity, and applying it at more layers is redundant.

State-of-the-Art Comparisons. We report state-of-the-art comparisons in Table 2. For all our experiments, we set the temporal and spatial resolutions at 8 frames and upto 540 (short side) respectively. We establish the baseline accuracies using non-attention networks vis-a-vis, I3D [7] and X3D [21], in experiment I.

Comparisons with FNet. In Table 2 experiment II, we report the accuracy using FNet, which is the state-of-the-art Fourier transform based self-attention method. FNet naively replaces every self-attention layer with the Fourier transform of the feature maps at that level. The motivation is to "mix" different parts of the feature representation and thus gain global information. Originally designed for NLP, it achieves 92−97% of the accuracy of BERT counterparts on the GLUE counterparts. However, when applied to video activity recognition on UAV Human RGB with the I3D backbone, we find that the accuracy is just 24.39%. In contrast, with the same backbone and hyperparameter settings, we demonstrate that FAR achieves 29.21%, an improvement of 19.76%.

Comparisons with Efficient Attention Methods. We compare with the current state-of-the-art efficient attention method [61] in experiment III. For fair comparisons, we use the I3D backbone in both cases, at a video resolution of $540 \times 960 \times 8$. We demonstrate better accuracies with our Fourier Attention formulation at lower FLOPs and GPU memory.

Comparisons with Transformer/Self-attention Methods. We compare against self-attention based transformer methods in Table 2. Specifically, we compare against (i) TimesFormer [5] (ICML 2021) - a self-attention video recognition method based on joint space-time self attention, and (ii) MViT (ICCV 2021) - a transformer based method that combines multi-scale feature hierarchies. We demonstrate much better performance at lower number of FLOPs, GPU memory and inference time. Another benefit is that FAR does not add any new parameters to the neural network and uses the same number of parameters as its backbone network. In contrast, MVIT and TimeSformer use much higher number of parameters.

Table 3. Results on more UAV datasets. We demonstrate that FAR improves the state-of-the-art accuracy by **8.02%–17.61%** across popular UAV datasets.

Method	Frames	Input Size	Init.	Top-1
(i) Dataset: UAV Human Night [43]				
I3D [7]	8	480 × 640	Kinetics	28.72
FAR	8	480 × 640	Kinetics	33.78
(ii) Dataset: Drone Action [52]				
HLPF [34]	All	1920 × 1080	None	64.36
PCNN [9]	-	1920 × 1080	None	75.92
X3D-M [21]	16	224 × 224	Kinetics	83.4
FAR	16	224 × 224	Kinetics	92.7
(iii) NEC Drone [13]				
X3D-M [21]	8	960 × 540	Kinetics	66.15
FAR	8	960 × 540	Kinetics	71.46

5.4   Results: More UAV Datasets

We demonstrate the effectiveness of FAR on multiple UAV benchmarks in Table 3. We demonstrate that FAR outperforms prior work by **17.61%, 11.15%** and **8.02%** on UAV Human Night, Drone Action, and NEC Drone respectively.

6   Conclusions, Limitations and Future Work

We present a new method for UAV Video Action Recognition. Our method exploits the mathematical properties of Fourier transform to automatically disentangle object from the background, and to encode long-range space-time relationships in a computationally efficient manner. We demonstrate benefits in terms of accuracy, computational complexity and training time on multiple UAV datasets. Our method has a few limitations. The sampling strategy based on randomly initialization is a naive method to span all video frames. It might be interesting to explore the usage of better video sampling strategies [37,80]. Next, we assume that the input videos contain only one human agent performing action. Multi-action videos could be a potential extension of our method. Moreover, we believe that FAR can be extended to other tasks such as video object segmentation and video generation, front-camera action recognition, graphics and rendering [45,47].

Acknowledgements. We thank Rohan Chandra for reviewing the paper. This research has been supported by ARO Grants W911NF1910069, W911NF2110026 and Army Cooperative Agreement W911NF2120076.

References

1. Arnab, A., Dehghani, M., Heigold, G., Sun, C., Lučić, M., Schmid, C.: Vivit: A video vision transformer. arXiv preprint arXiv:2103.15691 (2021)
2. Barekatain, M., et al.: Okutama-action: An aerial view video dataset for concurrent human action detection. In: Proceedings of the IEEE conference on computer vision and pattern recognition workshops, pp. 28–35 (2017)
3. Beauchemin, S.S., Barron, J.L.: The computation of optical flow. ACM Comput. Surveys (CSUR) 27(3), 433–466 (1995)
4. Benjdira, B., Bazi, Y., Koubaa, A., Ouni, K.: Unsupervised domain adaptation using generative adversarial networks for semantic segmentation of aerial images. Remote Sensing 11(11), 1369 (2019)
5. Bertasius, G., Wang, H., Torresani, L.: Is space-time attention all you need for video understanding? arXiv preprint arXiv:2102.05095 (2021)
6. Buijs, H., Pomerleau, A., Fournier, M., Tam, W.: Implementation of a fast fourier transform (fft) for image processing applications. IEEE Trans. Acoust. Speech Signal Process. 22(6), 420–424 (1974)
7. Carreira, J., Zisserman, A.: Quo vadis, action recognition? a new model and the kinetics dataset. In: proceedings of the IEEE Conference on Computer Vision and Pattern Recognition, pp. 6299–6308 (2017)
8. Chen, Y., Li, W., Sakaridis, C., Dai, D., Van Gool, L.: Domain adaptive faster r-cnn for object detection in the wild. In: Proceedings of the IEEE conference on computer vision and pattern recognition, pp. 3339–3348 (2018)
9. Chéron, G., Laptev, I., Schmid, C.: P-cnn: Pose-based cnn features for action recognition. In: Proceedings of the IEEE international conference on computer vision, pp. 3218–3226 (2015)
10. Chi, L., Jiang, B., Mu, Y.: Fast fourier convolution. In: Larochelle, H., Ranzato, M., Hadsell, R., Balcan, M.F., Lin, H. (eds.) Advances in Neural Information Processing Systems, vol. 33, pp. 4479–4488. Curran Associates, Inc. (2020), https://proceedings.neurips.cc/paper/2020/file/2fd5d41ec6cfab47e32164d5624269b1-Paper.pdf
11. Choi, J.: Action recognition list of papers. In: https://github.com/jinwchoi/awesome-action-recognition
12. Choi, J., Gao, C., Messou, J.C., Huang, J.B.: Why can't i dance in the mall? learning to mitigate scene bias in action recognition. arXiv preprint arXiv:1912.05534 (2019)
13. Choi, J., Sharma, G., Chandraker, M., Huang, J.B.: Unsupervised and semi-supervised domain adaptation for action recognition from drones. In: Proceedings of the IEEE/CVF Winter Conference on Applications of Computer Vision, pp. 1717–1726 (2020)
14. Chun, B.T., Bae, Y., Kim, T.Y.: Automatic text extraction in digital videos using fft and neural network. In: FUZZ-IEEE'99. 1999 IEEE International Fuzzy Systems. Conference Proceedings (Cat. No. 99CH36315), vol. 2, pp. 1112–1115. IEEE (1999)
15. Ding, M., Li, N., Song, Z., Zhang, R., Zhang, X., Zhou, H.: A lightweight action recognition method for unmanned-aerial-vehicle video. In: 2020 IEEE 3rd International Conference on Electronics and Communication Engineering (ICECE), pp. 181–185. IEEE (2020)
16. Dosovitskiy, A., et al.: Flownet: Learning optical flow with convolutional networks. In: Proceedings of the IEEE international conference on computer vision, pp. 2758–2766 (2015)

17. Du, D., et al.: The unmanned aerial vehicle benchmark: Object detection and tracking. In: Proceedings of the European Conference on Computer Vision (ECCV), pp. 370–386 (2018)
18. Dundar, A., Shih, K.J., Garg, A., Pottorf, R., Tao, A., Catanzaro, B.: Unsupervised disentanglement of pose, appearance and background from images and videos. arXiv preprint arXiv:2001.09518 (2020)
19. Ellenfeld, M., Moosbauer, S., Cardenes, R., Klauck, U., Teutsch, M.: Deep fusion of appearance and frame differencing for motion segmentation. In: Proceedings of the IEEE/CVF Conference on Computer Vision and Pattern Recognition, pp. 4339–4349 (2021)
20. Fan, H., Xiong, B., Mangalam, K., Li, Y., Yan, Z., Malik, J., Feichtenhofer, C.: Multiscale vision transformers. In: Proceedings of the IEEE/CVF International Conference on Computer Vision, pp. 6824–6835 (2021)
21. Feichtenhofer, C.: X3d: Expanding architectures for efficient video recognition. In: Proceedings of the IEEE/CVF Conference on Computer Vision and Pattern Recognition, pp. 203–213 (2020)
22. Feichtenhofer, C., Fan, H., Malik, J., He, K.: Slowfast networks for video recognition. In: Proceedings of the IEEE/CVF international conference on computer vision, pp. 6202–6211 (2019)
23. Feichtenhofer, C., Pinz, A., Zisserman, A.: Convolutional two-stream network fusion for video action recognition. In: Proceedings of the IEEE conference on computer vision and pattern recognition., pp. 1933–1941 (2016)
24. Frigo, M., Johnson, S.G.: Fftw: An adaptive software architecture for the fft. In: Proceedings of the 1998 IEEE International Conference on Acoustics, Speech and Signal Processing, ICASSP'98 (Cat. No. 98CH36181). vol. 3, pp. 1381–1384. IEEE (1998)
25. Fu, J., et al.: Dual attention network for scene segmentation. In: Proceedings of the IEEE/CVF Conference on Computer Vision and Pattern Recognition, pp. 3146–3154 (2019)
26. Gammulle, H., Denman, S., Sridharan, S., Fookes, C.: Two stream lstm: A deep fusion framework for human action recognition. In: 2017 IEEE Winter Conference on Applications of Computer Vision (WACV), pp. 177–186. IEEE (2017)
27. Girdhar, R., Carreira, J., Doersch, C., Zisserman, A.: Video action transformer network. In: Proceedings of the IEEE/CVF Conference on Computer Vision and Pattern Recognition, pp. 244–253 (2019)
28. Gowda, S.N., Rohrbach, M., Sevilla-Lara, L.: Smart frame selection for action recognition. arXiv preprint arXiv:2012.10671 (2020)
29. Griffin, B.A., Corso, J.J.: Bubblenets: Learning to select the guidance frame in video object segmentation by deep sorting frames. In: Proceedings of the IEEE/CVF Conference on Computer Vision and Pattern Recognition, pp. 8914–8923 (2019)
30. Hara, K., Kataoka, H., Satoh, Y.: Can spatiotemporal 3D cnns retrace the history of 2d cnns and imagenet? In: Proceedings of the IEEE conference on Computer Vision and Pattern Recognition, pp. 6546–6555 (2018)
31. He, K., Zhang, X., Ren, S., Sun, J.: Deep residual learning for image recognition. In: Proceedings of the IEEE conference on computer vision and pattern recognition, pp. 770–778 (2016)
32. Hussein, N., Gavves, E., Smeulders, A.W.: Timeception for complex action recognition. In: Proceedings of the IEEE/CVF Conference on Computer Vision and Pattern Recognition, pp. 254–263 (2019)

33. Ilg, E., Mayer, N., Saikia, T., Keuper, M., Dosovitskiy, A., Brox, T.: Flownet 2.0: Evolution of optical flow estimation with deep networks. In: Proceedings of the IEEE conference on computer vision and pattern recognition, pp. 2462–2470 (2017)
34. Jhuang, H., Gall, J., Zuffi, S., Schmid, C., Black, M.J.: Towards understanding action recognition. In: Proceedings of the IEEE international conference on computer vision, pp. 3192–3199 (2013)
35. Katharopoulos, A., Vyas, A., Pappas, N., Fleuret, F.: Transformers are rnns: Fast autoregressive transformers with linear attention. In: International Conference on Machine Learning, pp. 5156–5165. PMLR (2020)
36. Kim, Y.J., Awadalla, H.H.: Fastformers: Highly efficient transformer models for natural language understanding. arXiv preprint arXiv:2010.13382 (2020)
37. Korbar, B., Tran, D., Torresani, L.: Scsampler: Sampling salient clips from video for efficient action recognition. In: Proceedings of the IEEE/CVF International Conference on Computer Vision, pp. 6232–6242 (2019)
38. Lavin, A., Gray, S.: Fast algorithms for convolutional neural networks. In: 2016 IEEE Conference on Computer Vision and Pattern Recognition (CVPR). pp. 4013–4021. IEEE Computer Society, Los Alamitos, CA, USA (jun 2016). https://doi.org/10.1109/CVPR.2016.435
39. Lee, M., Lee, S., Son, S., Park, G., Kwak, N.: Motion feature network: fixed motion filter for action recognition. In: Ferrari, V., Hebert, M., Sminchisescu, C., Weiss, Y. (eds.) ECCV 2018. LNCS, vol. 11214, pp. 392–408. Springer, Cham (2018). https://doi.org/10.1007/978-3-030-01249-6_24
40. Lee-Thorp, J., Ainslie, J., Eckstein, I., Ontanon, S.: Fnet: Mixing tokens with fourier transforms (2021)
41. Li, K., Wu, Z., Peng, K.C., Ernst, J., Fu, Y.: Tell me where to look: Guided attention inference network. In: Proceedings of the IEEE Conference on Computer Vision and Pattern Recognition, pp. 9215–9223 (2018)
42. Li, R., Su, J., Duan, C., Zheng, S.: Linear attention mechanism: An efficient attention for semantic segmentation. arXiv preprint arXiv:2007.14902 (2020)
43. Li, T., Liu, J., Zhang, W., Ni, Y., Wang, W., Li, Z.: Uav-human: A large benchmark for human behavior understanding with unmanned aerial vehicles. In: Proceedings of the IEEE/CVF Conference on Computer Vision and Pattern Recognition, pp. 16266–16275 (2021)
44. Liu, Z., et al.: Video swin transformer. arXiv preprint arXiv:2106.13230 (2021)
45. Lloyd, D.B., Govindaraju, N.K., Quammen, C., Molnar, S.E., Manocha, D.: Logarithmic perspective shadow maps. ACM Trans. Graph. (TOG) 27(4), 1–32 (2008)
46. Mazzia, V., Angarano, S., Salvetti, F., Angelini, F., Chiaberge, M.: Action transformer: A self-attention model for short-time human action recognition. arXiv preprint arXiv:2107.00606 (2021)
47. Mitchell, D.P., Netravali, A.N.: Reconstruction filters in computer-graphics. ACM Siggraph Comput. Graph. 22(4), 221–228 (1988)
48. Mittal, P., Singh, R., Sharma, A.: Deep learning-based object detection in low-altitude uav datasets: a survey. Image Vis. Comput. 104, 104046 (2020)
49. Monfort, M., et al.: Moments in time dataset: one million videos for event understanding. IEEE Trans. Pattern Anal. Mach. Intell. 42(2), 502–508 (2019)
50. Ng, J.Y.H., Choi, J., Neumann, J., Davis, L.S.: Actionflownet: Learning motion representation for action recognition. In: 2018 IEEE Winter Conference on Applications of Computer Vision (WACV), pp. 1616–1624. IEEE (2018)

51. Peng, H., Razi, A.: Fully autonomous UAV-based action recognition system using aerial imagery. In: Bebis, G. (ed.) ISVC 2020. LNCS, vol. 12509, pp. 276–290. Springer, Cham (2020). https://doi.org/10.1007/978-3-030-64556-4_22
52. Perera, A.G., Law, Y.W., Chahl, J.: Drone-action: an outdoor recorded drone video dataset for action recognition. Drones 3(4), 82 (2019)
53. Piccardi, M.: Background subtraction techniques: a review. In: 2004 IEEE International Conference on Systems, Man and Cybernetics (IEEE Cat. No. 04CH37583). vol. 4, pp. 3099–3104. IEEE (2004)
54. Piergiovanni, A., Ryoo, M.S.: Representation flow for action recognition. In: Proceedings of the IEEE/CVF Conference on Computer Vision and Pattern Recognition, pp. 9945–9953 (2019)
55. Plizzari, C., Cannici, M., Matteucci, M.: Spatial temporal transformer network for skeleton-based action recognition. arXiv preprint arXiv:2012.06399 (2020)
56. Reddy, B.S., Chatterji, B.N.: An fft-based technique for translation, rotation, and scale-invariant image registration. IEEE Trans. Image Process. 5(8), 1266–1271 (1996)
57. Ren, S., He, K., Girshick, R., Sun, J.: Faster r-cnn: Towards real-time object detection with region proposal networks. Adv. Neural. Inf. Process. Syst. 28, 91–99 (2015)
58. Ren, Z., Yan, J., Ni, B., Liu, B., Yang, X., Zha, H.: Unsupervised deep learning for optical flow estimation. In: Thirty-First AAAI Conference on Artificial Intelligence (2017)
59. Schlag, I., Irie, K., Schmidhuber, J.: Linear transformers are secretly fast weight programmers. In: International Conference on Machine Learning, pp. 9355–9366. PMLR (2021)
60. Sengupta, S., Jayaram, V., Curless, B., Seitz, S.M., Kemelmacher-Shlizerman, I.: Background matting: The world is your green screen. In: Proceedings of the IEEE/CVF Conference on Computer Vision and Pattern Recognition, pp. 2291–2300 (2020)
61. Shen, Z., Zhang, M., Zhao, H., Yi, S., Li, H.: Efficient attention: Attention with linear complexities. In: Proceedings of the IEEE/CVF Winter Conference on Applications of Computer Vision, pp. 3531–3539 (2021)
62. Shi, F., et al.: Star: Sparse transformer-based action recognition. arXiv preprint arXiv:2107.07089 (2021)
63. Sigurdsson, G.A., Gupta, A., Schmid, C., Farhadi, A., Alahari, K.: Charades-ego: A large-scale dataset of paired third and first person videos. arXiv preprint arXiv:1804.09626 (2018)
64. Simonyan, K., Zisserman, A.: Two-stream convolutional networks for action recognition in videos. arXiv preprint arXiv:1406.2199 (2014)
65. Sultani, W., Shah, M.: Human action recognition in drone videos using a few aerial training examples. Comput. Vis. Image Underst. 206, 103186 (2021)
66. Tancik, M., et al.: Fourier features let networks learn high frequency functions in low dimensional domains. In: Larochelle, H., Ranzato, M., Hadsell, R., Balcan, M.F., Lin, H. (eds.) In: Advances in Neural Information Processing Systems. vol. 33, pp. 7537–7547. Curran Associates, Inc. (2020), https://proceedings.neurips.cc/paper/2020/file/55053683268957697aa39fba6f231c68-Paper.pdf
67. Tran, D., Wang, H., Torresani, L., Feiszli, M.: Video classification with channel-separated convolutional networks. In: Proceedings of the IEEE/CVF International Conference on Computer Vision, pp. 5552–5561 (2019)

68. Ulhaq, A., Yin, X., Zhang, Y., Gondal, I.: Action-02MCF: A robust space-time correlation filter for action recognition in clutter and adverse lighting conditions. In: Blanc-Talon, J., Distante, C., Philips, W., Popescu, D., Scheunders, P. (eds.) ACIVS 2016. LNCS, vol. 10016, pp. 465–476. Springer, Cham (2016). https://doi.org/10.1007/978-3-319-48680-2_41

69. Vaswani, A., et al.: Attention is all you need. In: Advances in neural information processing systems, pp. 5998–6008 (2017)

70. Wang, M., Deng, W.: Deep visual domain adaptation: a survey. Neurocomputing **312**, 135–153 (2018)

71. Wang, S.e.a.: Linformer: Self-attention with linear complexity. arXiv:2006.04768 (2020)

72. Wang, X., Girshick, R., Gupta, A., He, K.: Non-local neural networks. In: Proceedings of the IEEE conference on computer vision and pattern recognition, pp. 7794–7803 (2018)

73. Wang, X., Jabri, A., Efros, A.A.: Learning correspondence from the cycle-consistency of time. In: Proceedings of the IEEE/CVF Conference on Computer Vision and Pattern Recognition, pp. 2566–2576 (2019)

74. Xiong, Y., et al.: Nyströmformer: A nyştöm-based algorithm for approximating self-attention. In: Proceedings of the. AAAI Conference on Artificial Intelligence. In: AAAI Conference on Artificial Intelligence. vol. 35, p. 14138. NIH Public Access (2021)

75. Xu, K., Qin, M., Sun, F., Wang, Y., Chen, Y., Ren, F.: Learning in the frequency domain. In: 2020 IEEE/CVF Conference on Computer Vision and Pattern Recognition (CVPR), pp. 1737–1746. IEEE Computer Society, Los Alamitos, CA, USA (2020). https://doi.org/10.1109/CVPR42600.2020.00181

76. Yang, Y., Soatto, S.: Fda: Fourier domain adaptation for semantic segmentation. 2020 IEEE/CVF Conference on Computer Vision and Pattern Recognition (CVPR), pp. 4084–4094 (2020)

77. Zappella, L., Lladó, X., Salvi, J.: Motion segmentation: A review. Artificial Intelligence Research and Development, pp. 398–407 (2008)

78. Zhang, H., Goodfellow, I., Metaxas, D., Odena, A.: Self-attention generative adversarial networks. In: International conference on machine learning, pp. 7354–7363. PMLR (2019)

79. Zhang, Z., Zhao, J., Zhang, D., Qu, C., Ke, Y., Cai, B.: Contour based forest fire detection using fft and wavelet. In: 2008 International Conference on Computer Science and Software Engineering, vol. 1, pp. 760–763. IEEE (2008)

80. Zhi, Y., Tong, Z., Wang, L., Wu, G.: Mgsampler: An explainable sampling strategy for video action recognition. arXiv preprint arXiv:2104.09952 (2021)

81. Zhu, Y., Deng, C., Cao, H., Wang, H.: Object and background disentanglement for unsupervised cross-domain person re-identification. Neurocomputing **403**, 88–97 (2020)

82. Zou, Z., Shi, Z., Guo, Y., Ye, J.: Object detection in 20 years: A survey. arXiv preprint arXiv:1905.05055 (2019)

Translating a Visual LEGO Manual to a Machine-Executable Plan

Ruocheng Wang[1]([✉]), Yunzhi Zhang[1], Jiayuan Mao[2], Chin-Yi Cheng[3], and Jiajun Wu[1]

[1] Stanford University, Stanford, USA
rcwang@stanford.edu
[2] Massachusetts Institute of Technology, Cambridge, USA
[3] Google Research, Mountain View, USA

Abstract. We study the problem of translating an image-based, step-by-step assembly manual created by human designers into machine-interpretable instructions. We formulate this problem as a sequential prediction task: at each step, our model reads the manual, locates the components to be added to the current shape, and infers their 3D poses. This task poses the challenge of establishing a 2D-3D correspondence between the manual image and the real 3D object, and 3D pose estimation for unseen 3D objects, since a new component to be added in a step can be an object built from previous steps. To address these two challenges, we present a novel learning-based framework, the Manual-to-Executable-Plan Network (MEPNet), which reconstructs the assembly steps from a sequence of manual images. The key idea is to integrate neural 2D keypoint detection modules and 2D-3D projection algorithms for high-precision prediction and strong generalization to unseen components. The MEPNet outperforms existing methods on three newly collected LEGO manual datasets and a Minecraft house dataset.

1 Introduction

As a community, we would like to build machines that can assist humans in constructing and assembling complex objects, such as block worlds [7], LEGO models [9], and furniture [35]. The assembly task involves a sequence of actions that move different 3D parts to desired poses. Tackling such a long-horizon task with machines requires significant engineering effort [35]. On the other hand, humans usually rely on visual manuals to guide assembly procedures. These manuals are built by expert designers to decompose the task into a sequence of short steps that can be executed smoothly and efficiently. In this paper, we aim

---

C.-Y. Cheng—Work done when working at Autodesk AI Lab.

Supplementary Information The online version contains supplementary material available at https://doi.org/10.1007/978-3-031-19836-6_38.

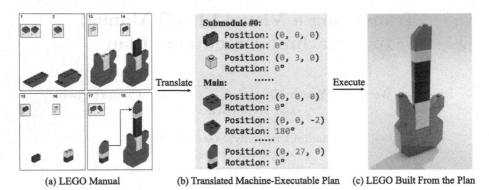

(a) LEGO Manual   (b) Translated Machine-Executable Plan   (c) LEGO Built From the Plan

Fig. 1. We study the problem of translating a LEGO manual to a machine-executable plan that can be executed to build the target shape. (a) Screenshots from an original LEGO manual. (b) A machine-executable plan generated by our model MEPNet. (c) LEGO built by executing the generated plan.

to facilitate the assembly tasks for machines by building a model that translates manuals into machine-interpretable plans. Figure 1a shows an example of LEGO manuals that guides the user to build a guitar. Each step in the manual involves multiple building components presented in 2D images, and our goal is to extract the pose of each component in order to inform a downstream autonomous agent to execute the step to build the target object.

We identify two key challenges of interpreting visual manuals. First, it requires identifying the correspondence between a 2D manual image and the 3D geometric shapes of the building components. Since each manual image is the 2D projections of the desired 3D shape, understanding manuals requires machines to reason about the 3D orientations and alignments of components, possibly with the presence of occlusions.

The second challenge is the rich library of assembly components. Taking LEGO as an example, while most LEGO shapes can be built from a finite set of primitives, these primitives can be flexibly composed into more complex sub-parts that are added to the main body as a whole (e.g., the head of the guitar in Fig. 1) in a step. The compositionality of primitive bricks greatly increases the diversity of LEGO components, and as a result increases the difficulty for machines to interpret LEGO manuals: it requires inferring 3D poses of *unseen* objects composed of seen primitives.

In this work, we develop a method that tackles this challenging problem. Concretely, we formulate the problem of translating manuals into machine-executable plans as a sequential task. For each step, the inputs consist of 1) a set of primitive bricks and parts that have been built in previous steps represented in 3D, and 2) a target 2D image showing how components should be connected to each other. The expected output is the (relative) poses of all components involved in this step, as shown in Fig. 1b.

There are roughly two groups of solutions to parsing a single step of a manual. The first group is search-based methods (i.e., "analysis-by-synthesis") [3,45]. These methods make use of a given forward synthesis model, i.e., the underlying manual image renderer, for pose inference. They search over possible 3D poses of new components, render manual images based on the candidate poses, and select the pose that maximizes the matching score between the input and the rendered images. This approach is simple and accurate but assumes a given renderer. It is also computationally expensive as we need to search for the 3D poses of multiple components jointly in a single assembly step. The second group is learning-based, using end-to-end neural networks that predict the 3D pose of each component. This approach does not require an image renderer and is fast, but typically suffers from poor generalization to unseen 3D shapes.

Inspired by these observations, we propose the Manual-to-Executable-Plan Network (MEPNet), a hybrid approach that combines the best of both worlds. The MEPNet has two stages. In the first stage, a convolutional neural network takes as input the current 3D LEGO shape, the 3D model of new components, and the 2D manual image of the target shape. It predicts a set of 2D keypoints and masks for each new component. In the second stage, 2D keypoints predicted in the first stage are back-projected to 3D by finding possible connections between the base shape and the new components. It also refines component orientation predictions by a local search. Our approach does not require the groundtruth image renderer during training or inference. Experiments show that our proposed approach maintains the efficiency of learning-based models, and generalizes better to unseen 3D components compared to end-to-end learning-based approaches.

We evaluate MEPNet on two benchmarks: one in the LEGO domain and another in a Minecraft-style house crafting domain [8]. Our results show that MEPNet enables more accurate pose estimation and, more importantly, generalizes better to unseen novel 3D components compared with several baselines. Most notably, we demonstrate that MEPNet is capable of generalizing to real-world LEGO manuals by training solely on synthetically generated manuals. We will release all code and data for full reproducibility.

2   Related Work

Parsing Human-Designed Diagrams. A diagram is a fundamental and commonly-used tool for humans to communicate concepts and information [1]. There have been a number of works on parsing different types of diagrams like engineering drawings [13], cartographic road maps [26] and sewing patterns [2] into machine-understandable data. We focus on the task of parsing assembly manuals into instructions that can be executed by machines. Shao et al. [34] proposes a technique to parse assembly instructions into executable plans, but focuses manuals in vector-graphic formats, while we work on LEGO manuals in RGB image format with no known visual primitives like edges and polygons. Li et al. [23] proposes a method to parse the 3D poses of parts from a single

RGB image, while our work focuses on sequentially inferring 3D poses from a series of manual images.

Inverse 3D Modeling. Inferring the geometry procedures that reconstruct a 3D shape is useful in many domains like robotic assembly [19,35], shape synthesis [6,12,21] and computer-aided design [20,40]. A line of research focuses on using different geometry operations like poses of 3D primitive parts [37], shape programs [18,36], constructive solid geometry [10] and CAD operations [44]. Different kinds of information are studied to guide the inverse inference process: final 3D shape [16,27], single image [23,30] or multi-view images [9,15]. When it comes to image-guided inverse modeling, previous works often assume access to images of the final 3D shape, where the inverse problem is inherently ambiguous. To tackle this issue, a shape prior is learned from a corpse of 3D shapes like ShapeNet [5], which can not be directly transferred to distribution different from the training data. Our work focuses on recovering the poses of LEGO bricks from a series of manual images that progressively specify building operations, which are intended to guide the assembly of diverse shapes of objects.

Pose Estimation. To parse the information from manual images, we need to infer the poses of primitive parts to be assembled. Estimating the 3D poses of objects is a fundamental problem in 3D vision. A line of research uses convolutional neural networks to directly localize objects in a scene and regress their 6D poses [4,22,38,41]. Other works adopt a two-stage approach where 2D keypoints of objects are first extracted and then poses are inferred from them [31–33]. Most works focus on detecting objects from the same category of the training objects, while our work aims to build models that can estimate the pose of known primitives as well as novel shapes composed from them. Xiao et al. [42,43] proposes a CNN architecture to estimate the pose of a single object in the image with a known 3D model. On the other hand, assembly manuals often require estimating poses of multiple objects. Furthermore, to understand manuals, models need to ignore the parts that are assembled in previous steps and only detect parts of interest, which is not addressed in previous works.

3   Problem Formulation

Throughout the paper, we will be using LEGO manuals as our example, although many of the ideas generalize to other types of assembly manuals such as Minecraft and furniture. A LEGO manual is composed of a sequence of images. The images specify a step-by-step instruction sequence of adding new components to an existing LEGO shape (called the *base shape*, which is typically the target shape in the previous step). Each new component is either a primitive brick with specified type and quantities, (in which case the image will specify the type and the number of new bricks) or a pre-built component (called a *submodule*, such as the guitar head shown in Fig. 1). The main diagram in each

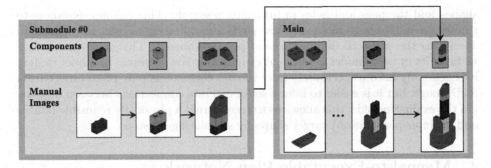

Fig. 2. Our factorized representation of LEGO manuals, which is a tree-structured plan specified by manual images. Each component is either a primitive brick or a submodule, and each submodule is recursively constructed from a sequence of manual images with corresponding components.

image will specify the poses of the new components w.r.t.the *base shape*, by showing a 2D view of the target shape at this step.

Sequential Manual Parsing. We formulate the task as a sequential prediction task of T steps. At each step, a manual parser receives the following inputs.

1. A 3D representation of the *base shape* at this step. In this paper, we focus on a voxel-based representation V_i^{cur}. It might be an empty voxel grid when we start building a new shape. In LEGO manuals, this usually comes from the target shape of the previous step.
2. A set of components to be added at this step, where each component is either a primitive brick or a pre-built shape composed of multiple primitive bricks. In either cases, their shape will be represented as a set of 3D voxels V_{ij}^{new}, where $j = 1, 2, \cdots, C_i$ and C_i is the number of components for step i. In a LEGO manual image, these are usually specified in a small diagram at a corner as shown in Fig. 1a.
3. A 2D image I_i specifying the target shape after we compose all components at step i. In LEGO manuals, this corresponds to the main diagram of a manual image.

Our goal is to predict the 3D translation and rotation w.r.t.V_i^{cur} for each added component $\{(t_{ij}, r_{ij})\}_{j=1}^{C_i}$ for each step i, where $t_{ij} \in \mathbb{R}^3, r_{ij} \in \mathbb{R}^{3\times3}$.

Once we have a model that predicts 3D poses of components at each step, they serve as a plan that can be executed by machines to assemble a complete object (called a LEGO *set*) in an iterative manner. In general, the dependency between steps is a tree because of *submodules* in assembly—a step may depend on the resulting shapes from multiple previous steps, as shown in Fig. 2.

The Connection Constraint. An important feature of object assembly is the inherent connection constraints among object parts, such as the studs in LEGO shapes and the pegs and holes in furniture assembly. This enables designers to simply use a 2D image to specify how parts should be connected, in contrast to specifying the exact 3D dimensions and poses of objects. This constraint brings us benefits in both model design and evaluation. For example, in model design, it is generally hard to accurately infer the 3D continuous pose of an object from a 2D image, but it is easier to infer a set of discrete connections between objects. On the evaluation side, this allows us to reconstruct a physically plausible (stable and no inter-penetration) target shape by simulating all steps.

4   Manual-to-Executable-Plan Network

In this section, we will be focusing on developing a learning-based method for solving the one-step prediction task. It can be applied iteratively to each assembly step to reconstruct the full 3D shape. Recall that the input to our model is the base shape at this step V^{cur}, a set of new components, $\{V_j^{new}\}$, and a 2D image I (omitting the step index i for all variables for clarity). Our goal is to infer the 3D poses of all components $\{V_j^{new}\}$.

Our model, the Manual-to-Executable-Plan Network (MEPNet), consists of two stages. In the first stage, we use a neural pose estimation model to predict the

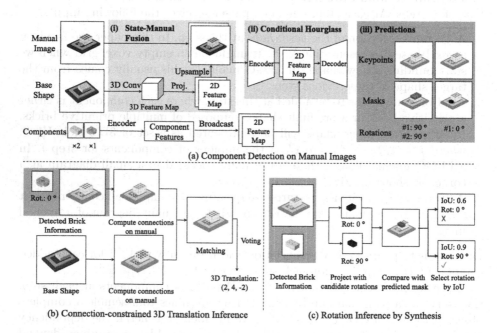

Fig. 3. MEPNet consists of two stages. (a) In the first stage, the model detects the 2D center keypoints, the masks, and the rotations for all added components on the manual. (b) and (c): We use a connection-constrained inference subroutine and an inference-by-synthesis subroutine to recover 3D poses of components from 2D information predicted in the first stage.

2D keypoint (corresponding to the center of the object), mask, and rotation for each new component to be added. In the second stage, we use two deterministic algorithms to infer the 3D poses of new components by fusing the predictions from the first stage.

Our two-stage approach is primarily motivated by the difficulty of directly estimating 3D poses from 2D images, especially considering the generalization to unseen components. Here, we leverage the connection constraint between components and the idea of analysis-by-synthesis to design post-processing algorithms that refine the raw prediction made by neural networks. In the experiment section, we will compare our two-stage approach with other alternatives, including a single-stage neural network baseline and an analysis-by-synthesis baseline based on mask predictions.

4.1 Neural Pose Estimation

Our neural module for estimating component poses follows an encoder-fusion-decoder pipeline. It combines convolution-based 3D shape encoders and a 2D Hourglass network—a state-of-the-art model for 2D keypoint and mask prediction. We will use separate 2D and 3D encoders to extract features for V^{cur}, V_j^{new}, and I, fuse the latent representations, and predict the center keypoint, mask, and rotation for each individual V_j^{new}.

Our first module, shown in Fig. 3a (i) is a state-manual encoder, which fuses the information of V^{cur} and the image I representing the target shape. Specifically, the state-manual encoder takes the voxel representation of V^{cur} as input, and extracts a 3D representation with two 3D Convolution-BatchNorm-ReLU modules. Let f_{3d} denote the output tensor of shape $\mathbb{R}^{C_1 \times H \times W \times D}$, where (H, W, D) is the 3D dimension of the input voxel and C_1 is the number of channels. Then, we use the camera parameters of the manual image to transform this voxel to the camera frame. This is computed by a differentiable spatial transformation based on [17]. Next, we project this voxel to the camera plane by rasterization, that is, for each pixel on the sensor plane, select the first non-empty voxel hit by a ray shooting from the sensor pixel towards the camera center. This gives us a 2D feature map $f^{2d} \in \mathbb{R}^{C_1 \times H \times W}$. Then the feature map is upsampled with bilinear interpolation to have the same resolution as the manual image I. Then we concatenate this feature map and the image along the feature channel to generate an "augmented" image representation, i.e., $I^a \in \mathbb{R}^{(C_1+3) \times H_{img} \times W_{img}}$.

Our second module, shown in Fig. 3a (ii) is a component-conditioned Hourglass model for predicting the center keypoint, mask, and rotation for each component. Specifically, for each new component V_j^{new}, also represented as a 3D voxel, we use five 3D Convolution-BatchNorm-ReLU layers, followed by an average pooling layer to extract the corresponding feature, denoted as $f_j^{new} \in \mathbb{R}^{C_2}$. Note that, for multiple components that have the same shape (w.r.t.$SO(3)$), we only encode one of them. We order all components based on their order in the input manual and get an sequence of component feature embeddings $\{f_j^{new}\}$. We concatenate all embeddings along the channel dimension into a vector f^{new*}, whose number of channels is $K \times C_2$, where K is the total number of distinct-shaped components, which we call "*component types*". We pad this vector by adding 0's into a vector of length $K_{max} \times C_2$, where $K_{max} = 5$ is the maximum number of distinct components considered in MEPNet.

Given the state-aware manual image I^a and component features $\{f_j^{new}\}$, we predict the 3D poses of the added components using an adapted implementation of stacked Hourglass Networks [29,46]. We first use a top-down network to process the I^a into a low-resolution 2D feature map I^{aenc} of resolution $(H_{img}/32, W_{img}/32)$. Next, we tile the concatenated component embeddings f^{new*} along spatial dimensions into a 2D feature map of resolution $(H_{img}/32, W_{img}/32)$, and concatenate this feature map to I^{aenc}. Then we use a bottom-up decoder network to output a high-resolution feature map of resolution $(H_{img}/4, W_{img}/4)$.

Then we use three separate small fully-convolutional neural networks to extract the center keypoint, mask, and rotation for each input component based on the feature map output by the Hourglass decoder.

1. For the center keypoint, we employ the structure of CenterNet [46]. For each component type, the model output is a tuple of three 1D feature maps: (h, dx, dy). h is a heatmap of centers, and dx and dy form a two-dimensional offset prediction which is the difference between the actual center of an object and the pixel location of the heatmap. This helps mitigate the discretization error caused by downsampling.
2. For the component mask, we employ the structure of Associative Embedding [28]. For each component type, the output is a tuple of two feature maps (m, emb), where m is a segmentation mask of the component type and emb is a 2D feature map where each pixel is associated with a vector embedding (called the "associative embeddings"). The L2 distance between pixels associated with different instances should be large, while the distance between pixels of the same instance should be small. To get the instance-level segmentation, we perform a pixel clustering based on emb.
3. For the rotation, our model output is a 4-dimensional vector, with a Softmax nonlinearity[1], since the component will only have rotations chosen from ($0°$, $90°$, $180°$, $270°$) around the vertical axis in the LEGO problem we considered.

It is important to note that since we have merged components of the same shape into one component type, there will be multiple instances detected for each component type. For example, shown in Fig. 3a, the center keypoint heatmap for the first component type has two peaks, corresponding to two instances of this component type.

Training and Losses. We train MEPNet with full supervision on a synthetically generated dataset where we have the groundtruth keypoint, mask, and

---

[1] In the implementation we used a slightly more complex scheme to handle symmetries. Details are included in the supplementary material.

rotation information. The entire neural network module is trained end-to-end with gradient descent. Our objective function is computed by

$$\mathcal{L} = \alpha \cdot \mathcal{L}_{keypoint} + \beta \cdot \mathcal{L}_{mask} + \gamma \cdot \mathcal{L}_{rotation}.$$

We adopt the keypoint loss adapted from [46]: $\mathcal{L}_{keypoint} = \mathcal{L}_{heatmap} + \mathcal{L}_{offset}$, where $\mathcal{L}_{heatmap}$ is a focal loss [24] computed based on the predicted heatmap and a groundtruth heatmap generated by Gaussian kernels. $\mathcal{L}_{offset}$ is an L1 loss for the regression task of dx and dy (the offsets). The mask loss is adapted from [28]: $\mathcal{L}_{mask} = \mathcal{L}_{semantic} + \mathcal{L}_{pull} + \mathcal{L}_{push}$, where $\mathcal{L}_{semantic}$ is a cross-entropy loss applied to the predicted mask, and $\mathcal{L}_{pull} + \mathcal{L}_{push}$ is the contrastive loss for learning the associative embeddings. Finally, we use a cross-entropy loss to train the rotation prediction module. More details are in the supplementary material.

4.2   3D Pose Inference

Based on the 2D predictions from the first stage, we infer 3D poses for each component. Here, we will exploit two important ideas: the connection constraint in assembly domains, and the idea of analysis-by-synthesis.

Connection-Constrained 3D Translation Inference. Given the center keypoint of each component, our goal is to find the 3D XYZ position of the component. Here, we will rely on the connection constraints, that is, there should be at least one position where the new component is attached to another existing brick. In LEGO, the attachment is achieved by inserting a "stud" of the existing brick into an "anti-stud" of the new component. As illustrated in Fig. 3b, our inference has three steps. First, given the center keypoint of the new component, we infer the 2D location of all anti-studs of the new component (this process is deterministic and does not require any depth information because images in LEGO manuals are orthographically projected, see a detailed proof in the supplementary material). Next, we also project all studs in the base shape V^{cur} onto the same 2D plane. Finally, we perform a matching between all possible studs and anti-studs followed by a majority voting. Then we can predict the 3D position of the new component based on the 3D position of existing studs, which is known.

Rotation Inference by Synthesis. We empirically found that directly predicting the rotation of a *submodule* is hard. Thus, instead of using the rotation predicted from Sect. 4.1, we employ an analysis-by-synthesis process to estimate the rotation. Illustrated in Fig. 3c, for each *submodule*, we compute all possible translations for each of the 4 rotations based on connection constraints. Then for each rotation-translation candidate (r, t), we project the component with pose (r, t) to the image, obtain a mask and compute its Intersection-over-Union (IoU) with the predicted mask from Sect. 4.1. We select the pose (r, t) with the highest IoU score as the final pose prediction.

4.3 Implementation Details

LEGO Discretization. To enable flexible attachments between different LEGO bricks, most LEGO bricks have sizes that are the multiples of the smallest $1 \times 1 \times 1$ brick and thus are inherently voxelized. In this work, we voxelize the basic $1 \times 1 \times 1$ LEGO brick as a $2 \times 2 \times 2$ voxel grid. We double the resolution of the voxel grid because the 3D translation of a brick can be half the size of the brick.

Center Keypoint. We observe that although the components of interest can be severely occluded in a manual image, their top faces often remain visible. This is a consistent design pattern across many LEGO manuals [14]. Thus, the center keypoint of a primitive brick is defined as the center of the top surface of a LEGO brick, as illustrated in Fig. 3a (iii). For submodules, we define the center keypoint to be the center keypoint of the topmost primitive brick in the submodule. If there are multiple topmost primitive bricks, we use a randomly selected brick during training and use a modified 3D pose inference algorithm during evaluation. Details are in supplementary materials.

Camera Projection. Same as the real-world LEGO manuals, we model the camera projection as a weak perspective (scaled orthographic) transformation. Thus, the camera is parameterized by scale $s \in \mathbb{R}$, translation $t \in \mathbb{R}^2$, and rotation r represented by three Euler angles. In this paper, we assume known camera parameters for all methods including baselines. The camera parameters are predicted by a pretrained pose estimation model [43] which takes the input base shape and manual image as input. Details are in supplementary materials.

5 Experiments

We evaluate MEPNet in two assembly domains: LEGO and 3D-Craft [7].

5.1 Setup

Baselines. We compare MEPNet with two baselines.

PartAssembly [23] is a two-stage method designed for inferring object part poses from a single image. It first predicts the masks for individual components. Then, it encodes the feature for each component and predicts the pose. We have made the following adaptations to it for our sequential prediction setting. First, to incorporate information about the current object state, we replaced the input image with the state-augmented manual image I^a using the same encoder as MEPNet. Second, we add CoordConv [25] to the model to enhance its prediction about 3D positions. Third, we add a post-processing procedure to the model prediction that quantizes the prediction based on the connection constraints. Finally, we also replaced their original point cloud encoder with our voxel-based encoder. More details can be found in the supplementary materials.

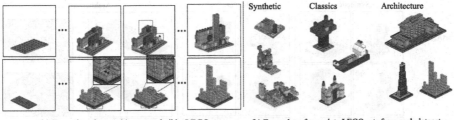

(a) Examples of manual images to build a LEGO set.   (b) Examples of complete LEGO sets from each dataset.

Fig. 4. Example manual images and shapes in our LEGO datasets.

Direct3D, the second baseline, is an ablative variant of MEPNet, in which we directly predict the 3D translation and rotation for each instance (instead of predicting keypoints, masks, and rotations). We also use CoordConv and prediction quantization with connection constraints in this model.

Metrics. We evaluate MEPNet and baselines at three different levels of granularity: componentwise, stepwise and setwise. In the componentwise and the stepwise case, the input to each model is the ground truth voxel grid V^{cur} and submodules (if any). We evaluate the *3D pose accuracy* (correct or incorrect because we have quantized the model predictions using the connection constraint) and the *Chamfer distance* [11]. To account for the rotation symmetry of components, we restricted the set of possible rotations based on component shapes. For stepwise pose accuracy, we say a step is correct if the predictions for all components in this step are correct. To compute Chamfer distance, following [39], we uniformly sample 10000 points from their meshes. For stepwise Chamfer distance, we compute the metric between the union of all components in a step.

In the setwise case, each model will be run on all manual images sequentially, and auto-regressively. That is, the predicted target shape from the first step will be the input for the second step. Submodules will be built by models as well. We compute two metrics: the Chamfer distance between the ground truth final shape and the shape output by each model. We also compute a normalized *Mistakes to Complete (MTC)* score, proposed in [7]. MTC computes the average percentage of steps where a model gives wrong poses predictions. In this case, the model will be fed with the ground truth V^{cur} and submodules.

5.2   Results on LEGO

Dataset. Our first dataset is a synthetic LEGO dataset that is procedurally generated based on 72 types of primitive bricks, and rendered using a standard LEGO manual renderer[2]. Our data generation pipeline encapsulates two features

___
[2] https://trevorsandy.github.io/lpub3d/.

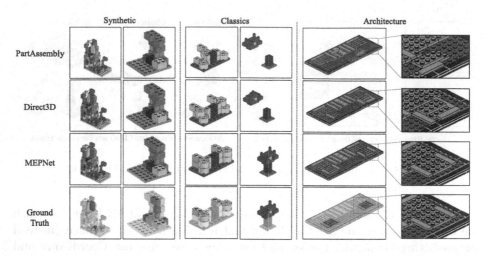

Fig. 5. Qualitative Results on the LEGO datasets. Each column contains the ground truth and the predictions from models for a single step. Components added in the step are highlighted in the manual images. To have a straightforward comparison between different models, we render their predictions in the same way as rendering the target manual.

Table 1. Quantitative results of models on the three LEGO datasets. Chamfer distance metrics are multiplied by a factor of 10^5. MEPNet outperforms baselines in all metrics on the three datasets.

		Componentwise		Stepwise		Setwise	
		Pose Acc ↑ (%)	CD ↓	Pose Acc ↑ (%)	CD ↓	CD ↓	MTC ↓ (%)
Synthetic	PartAssembly [23]	63.74	393.21	47.05	226.48	321.91	52.72
	Direct3D	88.51	32.60	77.39	5.08	9.18	25.62
	MEPNet	**96.96**	**11.60**	**93.41**	**1.93**	**4.74**	**8.63**
Classics	PartAssembly [23]	2.26	1171.57	0.00	296.82	775.29	100.00
	Direct3D	34.84	303.56	24.27	3.00	67.75	80.77
	MEPNet	**88.69**	**72.79**	**90.29**	**0.10**	**15.52**	**13.97**
Architecture	PartAssembly [23]	5.12	1964.31	3.24	858.58	719.88	96.13
	Direct3D	13.71	936.77	23.17	227.41	191.28	87.79
	MEPNet	**83.47**	**136.40**	**82.23**	**15.35**	**107.95**	**16.00**

of real-world LEGO manuals: 1) using submodules to assemble two components that have been built separately, and 2) stacking or tiling multiple bricks of the same shape at one step to form structures such as walls and floors. Examples of generated LEGO objects are shown in Fig. 4(b). Details of the generation pipeline, attribution of assets and their license can be found in the supplementary materials. We generate 8000 manuals for training, 10 sets for validation, and 20 sets for testing. In sum, there are 200 K individual steps in training, 300 for the validation split, and 600 for the test split.

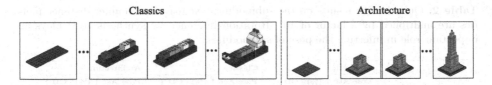

Fig. 6. Qualitative Results of MEPNet building LEGOs from scratch. We visualize several intermediate steps and final results by rendering them in the same way as the manual images. MEPNet can successfully parse manuals into executable plans with diverse target shapes.

We have also collected two datasets from real-world LEGO manuals. We select 11 sets from LEGO's Classics theme, which contains simple objects designed for children older than 4, and 5 sets from LEGO's Architecture theme, which contains more complex building-shaped LEGOs for kids older than 10. There are around 200 individual steps in each dataset. We manually exclude or replace bricks that are not in our primitive brick set, and re-render the LEGO manuals with the factorized representation. Examples of our datasets are shown in Fig. 4.

Results on the Synthetic Dataset. Quantitative results on the synthetic dataset are summarized in Table 1. MEPNet outperforms baseline models in all metrics considered. From visualizations in Fig. 5, we can see MEPNet is able to accurately predict 3D poses of both primitive bricks and submodules, even in cases with significant occlusions. Baseline models tend to either have a small deviation in 3D translation, or fail to infer the orientation of submodules. We also find that PartAssembly fails to predict accurate masks for target components, which are critical in its pose estimation.

Generalization to the Classics and the Architecture Datasets. We directly apply models trained on our synthetically generated datasets on the Classics and the Architecture datasets. Illustrated in Table 1, there is a large performance drop for PartAssembly and Direct3D due to the distribution mismatch between these two datasets and our synthetic training dataset, while MEPNet maintains high accuracy. We found that the Direct3D model can still predict accurate keypoints on these two datasets, but fails to accurately predict their 3D poses. This shows the effectiveness of our two-stage inference procedure. Noticeably, MEPNet can successfully build sets with diverse shapes guided by manuals as illustrated in Fig. 6, although they look drastically different from the synthetic dataset and contain submodules of unseen shapes. We present several examples of the full assembly process in the supplementary materials.

The architecture dataset is the most challenging one because it contains a large number of primitive bricks and severe occlusion. MEPNet still achieves a decent prediction accuracy while both baselines fail significantly.

Table 2. Quantitative results on the submodules exclusively. Chamfer distance metrics are multiplied by a factor of 10^5. Rotation inference by synthesis (RS) plays an important role in inferring the pose of submodules.

	Synthetic		Classics		Architecture	
	Pose Acc ↑ (%)	CD ↓	Pose Acc ↑ (%)	CD ↓	Pose Acc ↑ (%)	CD ↓
PartAssembly [23]	0.00	1754.64	0.00	2107.11	0.00	4816.21
Direct3D	22.75	161.59	10.00	180.86	0.00	1539.04
MEPNet (w.o. RS)	22.27	192.93	20.00	25.17	23.08	**256.55**
MEPNet	**75.83**	**23.27**	**90.00**	**0.25**	**38.46**	271.35

Table 3. Comparison with an ablation model based purely on analysis-by-synthesis. We show the component pose accuracy and the average inference time per step (which may include multiple components). TLE (Time-Limit-Exceeded) measures the percentage of components whose prediction cannot terminate in 1 min.

	Classics			Architecture		
	Pose Acc ↑ (%)	Time ↓ (s)	TLE ↓ (%)	Pose Acc ↑ (%)	Time ↓ (s)	TLE ↓ (%)
Direct3D	34.84	**0.233**	0	13.71	**0.320**	0
MEPNet (a-by-s)	48.42	10.94	0.9	34.14	70.77	11.65
MEPNet	**88.69**	0.311	0	**83.47**	0.406	0

Ablation: Submodules. We perform an ablation study comparing how different models handle submodules, as shown in Table 2. Specifically, we evaluate the componentwise pose prediction accuracy and Chamfer distance across all steps that involve submodules. The table indicates the challenge of 3D pose inference for submodules. Our rotation-inference-by-synthesis (RS) consistently improves the results across all three datasets.

Ablation: Pure Analysis-by-Synthesis. We also perform an ablation study of the second stage algorithm by replacing it with an algorithm that is entirely based on analysis-by-synthesis, for both primitive bricks and submodules. In contrast, our full model MEPNet only applies analysis-by-synthesis for the rotation inference of submodules. Since we do not assume access to the underlying image renderer, we will perform analysis-by-synthesis based on the 2D mask of the manual image.

Specifically, we use the mask prediction from our Hourglass model. Our goal is to set the 3D pose for new components to maximize the matching score between detected 2D masks and the 2D projections of these new components. To avoid the exponential scaling with respect to the number of components, we employed a sequential greedy algorithm. Given the current shape and a set of new components to be added, we iteratively search the pose for each new component. For each component, we enumerate all possible poses, and select the pose that minimizes the IoU between the projected mask and segmentation mask of that component type predicted by the Hourglass model. We set the maximum searching time for each component to 1 min.

The accuracy and runtime of different models are summarized in Table 3. Direct3D is the fastest because 3D poses are directly predicted by the Hourglass model, but the performance is significantly worse than other methods. The analysis-by-synthesis baseline outperforms the Direct3D method, but it runs significantly slower. Our full model, MEPNet, performs the best. We empirically attribute the inferior performance of the analysis-by-synthesis variant to the imprecise prediction of component masks, especially for small primitive bricks.

5.3 Results on 3D-Craft

We also evaluate MEPNet on building Minecraft houses from 3D-Craft [7].

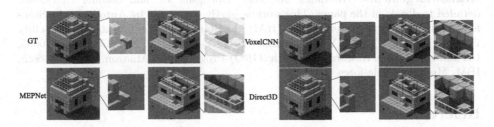

Fig. 7. Qualitative results on the 3D-Craft dataset. Ground truth and predictions of new bricks are zoomed in. Predictions of baseline models often lie in a small neighborhood of the ground truth positions, while our model is more accurate.

Data. The original 3D-Craft contains houses built with equally-sized bricks from crowdworkers in the format of building operation sequence. We leverage this sequence information to generate manuals. Each step in the manuals contains only one new brick. And our goal is to predict the 3D translation of the new brick in each manual image. We select 80 houses (20k steps) for training, 5 (1.5k steps) for validation, and 5 (1.5k steps) for testing. As the original dataset has a heavily imbalanced distribution of brick types, we select 5 frequently-used types in the dataset. In general houses in 3D-Craft contains more bricks than LEGO, and the appearance of bricks will be affected by lighting.

Setup. To migrate MEPNet to this setting, we use one-hot embedding to encode different types of bricks occupying each voxel. Because there is no rotation involved, we also remove the rotation prediction modules for all methods. Finally, we modify the 2D-to-3D algorithm according to Minecraft's connection constraints. Details are in the supplementary material.

Results. MEPNet achieves translation accuracy of 86.3% on the 3D-Craft dataset, while VoxelCNN and Direct3D only achieve 49.8% and 75.8%. Based on the visualizations shown in Fig. 7, we can also see that MEPNet can yield more accurate results across all different lighting conditions.

6 Discussion

We study the problem of translating an image-based, step-by-step assembly manual created by human designers into machine-interpretable instructions. We propose Manual-to-Executable-Plan Network (MEPNet), a model that reconstructs the assembly steps from a sequence of manual images. The key idea behind our model is to combine learning-based methods and inference-by-synthesis algorithms to wire in the connection constraints in assembly domains. Results show that our model outperforms existing methods on three newly collected LEGO manual datasets and a Minecraft house dataset.

Acknowldegements. We thank Joy Hsu, Chengshu Li, and Samuel Clarke for detailed feedback on the paper. This work is partly supported by Autodesk, the Stanford Institute for Human Centered AI (HAI), the Stanford Center for Integrated Facility Engineering (CIFE), ARMY MURI grant W911NF-15-1-0479, NSF CCRI #2120095, the Samsung Global Research Outreach (GRO) Program, and Amazon, Analog, Bosch, IBM, Meta, and Salesforce.

References

1. Agrawala, M., Li, W., Berthouzoz, F.: Design principles for visual communication. Commun. ACM **54**(4), 60–69 (2011)
2. Berthouzoz, F., Garg, A., Kaufman, D.M., Grinspun, E., Agrawala, M.: Parsing sewing patterns into 3d garments. ACM TOG **32**(4), 1–12 (2013)
3. Bever, T.G., Poeppel, D.: Analysis by synthesis: a (re-) emerging program of research for language and vision. Biolinguistics **4**(2–3), 174–200 (2010)
4. Brachmann, E., Krull, A., Michel, F., Gumhold, S., Shotton, J., Rother, C.: Learning 6D object pose estimation using 3D object coordinates. In: Fleet, D., Pajdla, T., Schiele, B., Tuytelaars, T. (eds.) ECCV 2014. LNCS, vol. 8690, pp. 536–551. Springer, Cham (2014). https://doi.org/10.1007/978-3-319-10605-2_35
5. Chang, A.X., et al.: Shapenet: An information-rich 3D model repository. arXiv:1512.03012 (2015)
6. Chaudhuri, S., Kalogerakis, E., Guibas, L., Koltun, V.: Probabilistic reasoning for assembly-based 3D modeling. ACM TOG **30**(4), 35 (2011)
7. Chen, Z., et al.: Order-aware generative modeling using the 3d-craft dataset. In: ICCV (2019)
8. Chu, H., Wang, S., Urtasun, R., Fidler, S.: Housecraft: Building houses from rental ads and street views. In: ECCV (2016)
9. Chung, H., et al.: Brick-by-brick: Combinatorial construction with deep reinforcement learning. In: NeurIPS (2021)
10. Du, T.: Inversecsg: automatic conversion of 3D models to csg trees. ACM TOG **37**(6), 1–16 (2018)
11. Fan, H., Su, H., Guibas, L.: A point set generation network for 3D object reconstruction from a single image. In: CVPR (2017)
12. Funkhouser, T., et al.: Modeling by example. ACM TOG **23**(3), 652–663 (2004)
13. Haralick, R.M., Queeney, D.: Understanding engineering drawings. Comput. Graphics Image Process. **20**(3), 244–258 (1982)

14. Heiser, J., Phan, D., Agrawala, M., Tversky, B., Hanrahan, P.: Identification and validation of cognitive design principles for automated generation of assembly instructions. In: Proceedings of the working conference on Advanced Visual Interfaces, pp. 311–319 (2004)
15. van den Hengel, A., Russell, C., Dick, A., Bastian, J., Pooley, D., Fleming, L., Agapito, L.: Part-based modelling of compound scenes from images. In: CVPR (2015)
16. Huang, J., et al.: Generative 3d part assembly via dynamic graph learning. In: NeurIPS (2020)
17. Jaderberg, M., Simonyan, K., Zisserman, A.: Spatial transformer networks. In: NeurIPS (2015)
18. Jones, R.K., Barton, T., Xu, X., Wang, K., Jiang, E., Guerrero, P., Mitra, N.J., Ritchie, D.: Shapeassembly: Learning to generate programs for 3d shape structure synthesis. ACM TOG **39**(6), 1–20 (2020)
19. Lee, Y., Hu, E.S., Lim, J.J.: Ikea furniture assembly environment for long-horizon complex manipulation tasks. In: ICRA (2021)
20. Li, C., Pan, H., Bousseau, A., Mitra, N.J.: Sketch2cad: Sequential cad modeling by sketching in context. ACM TOG **39**(6), 1–14 (2020)
21. Li, J., Xu, K., Chaudhuri, S., Yumer, E., Zhang, H., Guibas, L.: Grass: Generative recursive autoencoders for shape structures. In: SIGGRAPH (2017)
22. Li, Y., Wang, G., Ji, X., Xiang, Y., Fox, D.: Deepim: Deep iterative matching for 6d pose estimation. In: ECCV (2018)
23. Li, Y., Mo, K., Shao, L., Sung, M., Guibas, L.: Learning 3d part assembly from a single image. In: ECCV (2020)
24. Lin, T.Y., Goyal, P., Girshick, R., He, K., Dollár, P.: Focal loss for dense object detection. In: ICCV (2017)
25. Liu, R., et al.: An intriguing failing of convolutional neural networks and the coord-conv solution. arXiv:1807.03247 (2018)
26. Mena, J.B.: State of the art on automatic road extraction for gis update: a novel classification. Pattern Recogn. Lett. **24**(16), 3037–3058 (2003)
27. Mo, K.: Structurenet: hierarchical graph networks for 3D shape generation. ACM TOG **38**(6), 1–19 (2019)
28. Newell, A., Huang, Z., Deng, J.: Associative embedding: End-to-end learning for joint detection and grouping. In: NeurIPS (2017)
29. Newell, A., Yang, K., Deng, J.: Stacked hourglass networks for human pose estimation. In: Leibe, B., Matas, J., Sebe, N., Welling, M. (eds.) ECCV 2016. LNCS, vol. 9912, pp. 483–499. Springer, Cham (2016). https://doi.org/10.1007/978-3-319-46484-8_29
30. Niu, C., Li, J., Xu, K.: Im2struct: Recovering 3d shape structure from a single rgb image. In: CVPR (2018)
31. Oberweger, M., Rad, M., Lepetit, V.: Making deep heatmaps robust to partial occlusions for 3d object pose estimation. In: ECCV (2018)
32. Peng, S., Liu, Y., Huang, Q., Zhou, X., Bao, H.: Pvnet: Pixel-wise voting network for 6dof pose estimation. In: CVPR (2019)
33. Rad, M., Lepetit, V.: Bb8: A scalable, accurate, robust to partial occlusion method for predicting the 3d poses of challenging objects without using depth. In: CVPR (2017)
34. Shao, T., Li, D., Rong, Y., Zheng, C., Zhou, K.: Dynamic furniture modeling through assembly instructions. In: ACM TOG. vol. 35. Association for Computing Machinery (2016)

35. Suárez-Ruiz, F., Zhou, X., Pham, Q.C.: Can robots assemble an ikea chair? Science Robotics **3**(17) 6385 (2018)
36. Tian, Y., Luo, A., Sun, X., Ellis, K., Freeman, W.T., Tenenbaum, J.B., Wu, J.: Learning to infer and execute 3d shape programs. In: International Conference on Learning Representations (2018)
37. Tulsiani, S., Su, H., Guibas, L.J., Efros, A.A., Malik, J.: Learning shape abstractions by assembling volumetric primitives. In: CVPR (2017)
38. Wang, C., et al.: Densefusion: 6d object pose estimation by iterative dense fusion. In: CVPR (2019)
39. Wang, N., Zhang, Y., Li, Z., Fu, Y., Liu, W., Jiang, Y.G.: Pixel2mesh: Generating 3d mesh models from single rgb images. arXiv:1804.01654 (2018)
40. Willis, K.D., et al.: Fusion 360 gallery: a dataset and environment for programmatic cad construction from human design sequences. ACM TOG **40**(4), 1–24 (2021)
41. Xiang, Y., Schmidt, T., Narayanan, V., Fox, D.: Posecnn: A convolutional neural network for 6d object pose estimation in cluttered scenes. In: RSS (2018)
42. Xiao, Y., Marlet, R.: Few-shot object detection and viewpoint estimation for objects in the wild. In: Vedaldi, A., Bischof, H., Brox, T., Frahm, J.-M. (eds.) ECCV 2020. LNCS, vol. 12362, pp. 192–210. Springer, Cham (2020). https://doi.org/10.1007/978-3-030-58520-4_12
43. Xiao, Y., Qiu, X., Langlois, P.A., Aubry, M., Marlet, R.: Pose from shape: Deep pose estimation for arbitrary 3d objects. In: BMVC (2019)
44. Xu, X., Peng, W., Cheng, C.Y., Willis, K.D., Ritchie, D.: Inferring cad modeling sequences using zone graphs. In: CVPR (2021)
45. Yuille, A., Kersten, D.: Vision as bayesian inference: analysis by synthesis? TiCS **10**(7), 301–308 (2006)
46. Zhou, X., Wang, D., Krähenbühl, P.: Objects as points. arXiv preprint arXiv:1904.07850 (2019)

Fabric Material Recovery from Video Using Multi-scale Geometric Auto-Encoder

Junbang Liang[1(✉)] and Ming Lin[2]

[1] Amazon, Seattle, USA
liangjb@cs.unc.edu
[2] University of Maryland, College Park, USA

Abstract. Fabric materials are central to recreating realistic appearance of avatars in a virtual world and many VR applications, ranging from virtual try-on, teleconferencing, to character animation. We propose an end-to-end network model that uses video input to estimate the fabric materials of the garment worn by a human or an avatar in a virtual world. To achieve the high accuracy, we jointly learn human body and the garment geometry as *conditions to material prediction*. Due to the highly dynamic and deformable nature of cloth, general data-driven garment modeling remains a challenge. To address this problem, we propose a two-level auto-encoder to account for both *global* and *local* features of any garment geometry that would directly affect material perception. Using this network, we can also achieve smooth geometry transitioning between different garment topologies. During the estimation, we use a closed-loop optimization structure to share information between tasks and feed the learned garment features for temporal estimation of garment materials. Experiments show that our proposed network structures greatly improve the material classification accuracy by 1.5x, with applicability to unseen input. It also runs at least *three orders of magnitude* faster than the state-of-the-art [59,61]. We demonstrate the recovered fabric materials on virtual try-on, where we recreate the entire avatar appearance, including body shape and pose, garment geometry and materials from only a single video.

Keywords: Fabric material estimation · Synthetic dataset

1 Introduction

Human appearance reconstruction is one of the key techniques for building a vivid, interactive virtual world. However, especially for fabric material estimation, has been under-explored due to the complexity and the diversity of cloth dynamics and coupled interaction with an avatar body. Image features are often sparse, containing many noisy signals regarding the fabric materials worn on the body. An effective way to amplify useful signals is to estimate garment geometry

© The Author(s), under exclusive license to Springer Nature Switzerland AG 2022
S. Avidan et al. (Eds.): ECCV 2022, LNCS 13697, pp. 695–714, 2022.
https://doi.org/10.1007/978-3-031-19836-6_39

from images as a by-product. However, this is an open challenge due to several reasons. First, garments have highly dynamical geometry that is not easy to capture and model. Previous works on garment modeling [21,40,55] and estimation [6,16,39] often propose solutions on one single type of garment, mostly t-shirts. Although the methods are also applicable to other garments, lack of generalization in capturing different garment geometries presents a considerable barrier for virtual try-on applications: users can only choose one of few pre-trained garment types and are not able to import new ones easily. Second, accurate estimation is often hindered by view projection, body occlusion, and limited availability of 3D scanning. For example, the human-body estimation network may disagree with the garment reconstruction network in skeleton orientation due to the projection ambiguity (*e.g.* an arm is posed forward vs. backward), resulting in prediction misalignment. Thus, without a general garment representation and an accurate geometry estimation, it is very difficult to regress the fabric materials solely from images.

In this paper, we introduce a learning model that addresses these issues, achieving both garment geometry and fabric material estimation simultaneously from commonly available video inputs for virtual try-on. To handle the dynamic geometry and different topologies of the garments and to provide a unified parametric model for the garments, we propose a two-level auto-encoder network. The key observation is that classical point cloud encoders such as PointNet [42] are great for capturing global shapes, but not suitable for encoding the local details. Multi-scale feature extraction decomposes the problem into smaller partitions and also decouples global and local features to enable larger coverage on local shape learning and capturing local topology transitions. During the estimation, we couple the human body inference with the garment recovery to maximize the estimation accuracy of the two correlated tasks. Other than traditional multi-tasking, we further introduce a closed-loop structure so that the garment features of different scales can guide the body estimation to improve the accuracy for both. Based on the temporal change of garment features, we can perform accurate material classification accordingly. Our key contributions include:

- The first neural network for fabric material recovery of a garment from a RGB video (Sect. 3);
- A novel two-level auto-encoder for learning the latent space of garments through multi-scale feature coupling, resulting in higher accuracy for material parameter estimation (Sect. 4);
- Joint estimation of human body and apparels through a close-loop iterative optimization that can account for arbitrary topologies of garments and ensure geometric consistency (Sect. 5);
- A large dataset of garment motion sequences with wide variations of human body, fabric materials, textures, and lightings for virtual try-on.

Our experiments show that the proposed network structure effectively increases the performance and accuracy of the virtual fabric material estimation. By using only a few frames of a person wearing a garment, our model can faithfully reconstruct the garment fabric material(s), using the recovered shape and motion of both the garment and the avatar body as the conditioning in virtual fabric material estimation.

2   Related Work

Fabric Material Estimation. Researchers have been tackling different inverse problems, including inverse cloth design [13], combinatorial material design [9], BRDF parameter capturing [53], weaving pattern reconstruction [20], human material perception [7,8], and frictional coefficient estimation [38,44]. Cloth material estimation is among the most challenging due to cloth's highly dynamic motions. Previous works study the task in a simplified and constrained scenario, and recover the materials using statistical observation [10,15], optimization [37,59], or learning [5,60]. In contrast, our method learns fabric materials from videos of a human wearing garments in more general and widely applicable framework, assuming commonly available inputs like image sequences and videos. More importantly, *our method makes use of the estimated multi-scale garment latent codes as input signal that is shown to be more effective in recovering overall garment geometry with local details than merely image features.*

Garment Modeling and Estimation. Garment geometry capturing or recovery has been widely studied: non-learning methods using symmetry and user input [65], optimization [25,59,61], or binocular data [11]. Recently, methods using deep learning have been proposed for faster speed and more convenient usage [3,6,14,16,21,22,24,26,39,62,67]. In addition, direct garment modeling methods have also been proposed using spherical parameterization [40] for estimation or displacement map [51] for retargetting.

Different from displacement-based cloth representation [6], PCA-based models [55], and mesh-CNN-based methods [21], our garment model is universal to all topologies, applicable to those not homotopic to human surfaces (*e.g.* long dresses), enabling semantic interpolation between different garments. Compared with [40], our model generates a stand-alone garment mesh that is easy to export and retarget. Our method is the *first network that jointly estimates the garment material and geometry* for virtual try-on. Our method is substantially different from most garment capturing or generation methods [30,47,62] regarding model input, output, and assumptions. *It does not required 3D scanning, which is often not easily available, but only videos that can be easily captured using mobile devices.*

Point Cloud Encoder and Decoder. PointNet [42] was among the first network model for encoding an unordered point set. Follow-on improvements include spatial partition [28,31,43], edge convolution [56], local region filtering [41,66], and analogous convolutional operators [32]. Although these recent works have utilized hierarchical structure to some extent, their methods are not sufficient for auto-encoding the garment geometry or topology. The key difference between garment auto-encoding and rigid gadgets auto-encoding is that there are a large number of local details (*e.g.*wrinkles) due to cloth's highly deformable and dynamical nature. As a result, latent codes for local details are necessary.

Recently, [35,63] use similar ideas on point-based garment geometry modeling. The main differences between these methods and ours include (1) our garment latent code is independent and does not need a body point-cloud to morph on, (2) their latent code is randomly assigned before training, which is not ideal for learning a compact latent space for smooth interpolation, and could result in noisy estimation results when applied to downstream task, and (3) their local and global patches depend heavily on human body surface, which makes it difficult for the resulting point cloud to represent loose dresses.

Human Reconstruction from Images. Human estimation using RGB images has been a popular research topic in deep learning for its importance in virtual reality and computer animation. While early works propose network models for only 2D/3D body skeletons [12,36,57], more recent works introduce techniques to regress the entire human body – either using a parametric human model [2,27] or voxel-based representation [45,52,64]. Given the fact that the annotations in most real-world datasets contain only joint positions, the learning process has been refined in various ways [1,29,33,48,58].

In order to estimate the fabric material, we need to recover the garment shape on the human body, which is an important problem rarely addressed in avatar reconstruction. In our pipeline, we use state-of-the-art human body predictions *as a strong prior* for the garment estimation module. Given the focus of this paper, we assume to use video input for only garment material recovery. We refer the interested readers to a recent survey [19] for comprehensive review on video-based pose estimation instead.

3   Method Overview

We first give the formal problem definition. Given a video clip showing a person moving (*e.g.*walking, jumping, bending, etc.), we estimate the fabric materials of the garment worn by the person. We assume that the garment worn is made of the same material. By *fabric materials*, we refer to the physical material parameters used in cloth simulation. We adopt the same material parameter definition introduced in [54], which consists of 24 parameters for stretching stiffness and 15 parameters for bending stiffness.

Given the fact that the differences of the material parameter values do not intuitively reflect the human visual perception, we follow the previous work [60] to discretize the material parameter space based on the amount of deformations due to external forces. Using sensitivity analysis [46], the stretching stiffness is split into 6 classes and 9 for the bending. Combining both dimensions will yield 54 different material classes. As confirmed by [60], these 54 classes cover most of the common materials, including polyester, cotton, nylon, rayon, and their combinations. For example, one type of materials named *'white-swim-solid'* consisting of 87% nylon and 13% spandex, as measured by [54], fits in the discrete classification model with the stretching label of 2 and the bending label of 3.

In this paper, we introduce a deep neural network (Fig. 1) for simultaneously estimating the garment geometry and its material type(s), along with the human body. Our key idea is that image features are not sufficient for inferring garment materials; it is necessary to extract the garment geometry as well for a more accurate estimation. To support different topologies of garments, we choose point clouds for its geometry representation. To better account for the highly dynamic garment surfaces, we train a two-level point cloud auto-encoder (Sect. 4) so that it can learn the global shapes and local features of the garment to reduce the total number of degrees of freedom. We use the SMPL model (see [34] for its rigorous math definition) to represent the human pose and shape.

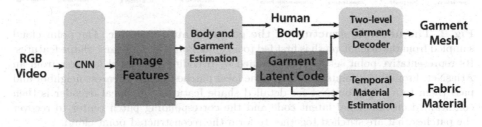

Fig. 1. Overall network structure. Given an RGB video, we extract its image features and estimate the body and garment shape frame by frame (Sect. 5.1). The latter is decoded to obtain a garment mesh (Sect. 4). The temporal sequences of image and garment are fed to an LSTM for material classification (Sect. 5.2).

We divide the estimation pipeline into two phases. First, we estimate the human body and the cloth geometry in a frame-by-frame manner (Sect. 5.1). A closed-loop optimization structure is used to improve the estimation accuracy of these two correlated tasks. The garment geometry prediction module is conditioned on the human body parameters, and at the same time provides corrective feedback to the human body prediction module. We then feed the features of the image and the garment geometry from each frame together to a temporal neural network for the garment material estimation (Sect. 5.2). By sharing common features, providing corrective feedback, and conditioning on outputs of closely-related tasks, our network model can achieve higher estimation accuracy on all three tasks than independent estimation baselines.

4 Garment Auto-Encoder

We first set up an auto-encoder for the cloth model. Since the model is designed not to assume fixed garment topology, we choose to use point clouds as the underlying representation. Other representations, such as graph-based [49] or displacement-based [6,39], rely on either fixed graph structure, or fixed human surface, thus not applicable for generalization to different garments. The use of auto-encoder here is necessary because the degrees of freedom (DoF) for point clouds are too high for estimation. An encoder-decoder structure can effectively reduce the DoF and retain only the essential information, such as the global shape and the local details. More importantly, it clusters similar shapes to similar latent codes, which is beneficial to the estimation module. As later shown in the Appendix, our model provides smooth transitioning between different topologies by using simple interpolation between latent codes. We discuss details on recovery methods from point cloud to mesh in the Appendix.

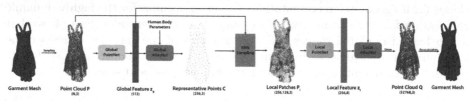

Fig. 2. The network structure of the garment auto-encoder. The point cloud sampled from the original mesh is first fed to a global PointNet for coarse shape features. Its representative point set is then obtained by decoding the global features from an AtlasNet. From those points, we sample the local patches using K-nearest neighbor and pass them to a local PointNet for detailed shape features. The local decoder is then conditioned on the global latent code and the corresponding patch center to recover the patches that are stitched together to form the reconstructed point cloud.

4.1   Two-Level Encoder-Decoder Structure

Previous point cloud auto-encoders such as AtlasNet [17] use Multi Layer Perceptron (MLP) to transform a 2D patch to a set of 3D points in the space. Their method performs well in point cloud datasets that include rigid objects, such as airplanes or chairs, since the deformations presented in those objects are simple and regular. However, it cannot be directly applied to learn garment point clouds, since garments have a much larger variance in point cloud distribution due to its dynamic nature. For example, a simple dress can create different wrinkle structures under different external forces. As a result, one global auto-encoder cannot account for all detailed structures, resulting in overly smoothed point clouds. Recently, [4] proposes a method to resolve patch overlapping and collapsing occurred in AtlasNet, but it still cannot account for arbitrary topologies and detailed wrinkles.

We propose a two-level auto-encoder for learning the latent space of the cloth. As shown in Fig. 2, we use a set of representative points $\mathbf{C}$ to express the global shape of the garment, and sample around them to form local patches, which are encoded independently to account for local shapes. Specifically, given a point cloud $\mathbf{P}$, we first pass it through a global auto-encoder to form a representative point cloud:

$$\mathbf{C} = D_g(E_g(\mathbf{P}), \theta) \qquad (1)$$

where E_g and D_g are the global encoder and decoder, and θ is the human body parameter. Next, we use K-nearest-neighbor to sample points around the representative ones:

$$\mathbf{P}_i = KNN(\mathbf{P}, \mathbf{c}_i) \qquad (2)$$

where c_i is the i-th element in $\mathbf{C}$, and $\mathbf{P}_i$ is the i-th patch. This step forms local patches around the representative points. Finally, we pass each patch to the shared local auto-encoder, and do a union operation to obtain the reconstructed point cloud:

$$\mathbf{Q}_i = D_l(E_l(\mathbf{P}_i), \mathbf{z}_g, \mathbf{c}_i) \tag{3}$$

$$\mathbf{Q} = \bigcup_i \mathbf{Q}_i \tag{4}$$

where $\mathbf{Q}_i$ and $\mathbf{Q}$ are the reconstructed patches and point cloud, D_l and E_l are the local decoder and encoder, and $\mathbf{z}_g = E_g(\mathbf{P})$ is the global latent code.

4.2 Representative Point Set Extraction

Note that Eq. 3 and 4 imply that the representative points $\mathbf{C}$ have to be in the same order as the local latent codes $\mathbf{z}_l$. This is the key reason why traditional methods such as farthest point sampling [43] do not work: its ordering is very sensitive to the input, resulting in an unknown mapping between reconstructed patch centers $\mathbf{C}$ and the local patches $\mathbf{P}_i$ (thus the local latent code $\mathbf{z}_{l_i}$).

To resolve this issue, we encode the entire point cloud and compute the representative points using the decoder itself. Due to the continuous nature of the auto-encoder network, the continuity and consistency regarding similar point clouds are guaranteed, thus ensuring $\mathbf{c}_i$ to be exactly matched with $\mathbf{P}_i$.

4.3 Training Losses

During training, we use Chamfer Distance between two point clouds as the loss:

$$d(\mathbf{P}, \mathbf{Q}) = \frac{1}{|\mathbf{P}|} \sum_{\mathbf{p} \in \mathbf{P}} \min_{\mathbf{q} \in \mathbf{Q}} \|\mathbf{p} - \mathbf{q}\| + \frac{1}{|\mathbf{Q}|} \sum_{\mathbf{q} \in \mathbf{Q}} \min_{\mathbf{p} \in \mathbf{P}} \|\mathbf{q} - \mathbf{p}\| \tag{5}$$

In Eq. 6, we apply the Chamfer Distance loss between the representative point set and the point cloud to learn the global shape (first term), and the one between the recovered and the original point clouds, both patch-wisely (second term) and globally (third term) to capture the local details:

$$\mathcal{L}_{AE} = d(\mathbf{P}, \mathbf{C}) + \frac{1}{n} \sum_{i=1}^{n} d(\mathbf{P}_i, \mathbf{Q}_i) + d(\mathbf{P}, \mathbf{Q}) \tag{6}$$

5   Material Estimation

With the garment auto-encoder (Sect. 4) at hand, garment material estimation becomes tractable. We design our overall pipeline as shown in Fig. 3. Given the sequence of image frames, we first feed them one by one to a model for estimating the human body and cloth geometry. By predicting the latent vector instead of the exact positions of the point cloud, the single-frame estimation network avoids severe overfitting or producing irrational results, due to the reduction of the degree of freedom by the auto-encoder.

Next, we combine the image features as well as the estimated garment latent code as the temporal signals, which go through a canonical temporal network module (*i.e.* LSTM [23]) to predict the final material type. Since the latent space preserves similarity (*i.e.* positive correlation between distances of latent vectors and distances between the original point clouds), the motion of the estimated latent vector becomes a better indicator of garment motion than image features, which is beneficial to garment material learning. We do not include body features here because the garment material is directly related to the garment motion, which has already taken the human body as the condition (Sect. 5.1). We discuss more details of the network in the following sections.

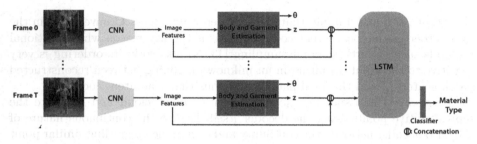

Fig. 3. Our estimation pipeline. Each video frame is first processed to obtain the image feature, the human body, and the garment shape. Then the image features are concatenated with the garment latent code as input to LSTM for material recovery.

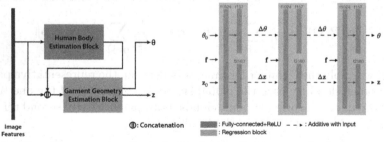

(a) Closed loop structure for body & garment estimation

(b) Detailed structure in the garment estimation block

Fig. 4. The network structure for body and garment estimation in each frame. (a) The garment shape estimation block takes the human body parameters as a prior, but also provides a feedback correction. (b) The garment estimation module consists of three identical, shared-weight blocks, each of which takes image features f and current predictions of the human body θ_0 and garment z_0, and outputs the corrective values.

5.1 Single Frame Closed-Loop Estimation

As shown in Fig. 4, we train a model to estimate the human body and cloth geometry given one single frame. Formally, in each frame, we are given the image features $\mathbf{f}$. We first go through a state-of-the-art body estimation block [29], HB, to get a first-hand body estimation, $\hat{\theta} = HB(\mathbf{f})$, where $\hat{\theta} = [\theta, \beta]$ are the human body parameters including pose and shape. In the garment estimation block, we take as input $\mathbf{f}$ together with $\hat{\theta}$ and regress the garment latent code $\mathbf{z}$, consisting of both $\mathbf{z}_g$ and $\mathbf{z}_l$, and body parameters θ. Inside the garment estimation block, we use three shared-parameter small regression blocks, RB, to iteratively provide the correction, given the current estimation:

$$\theta_0 = \hat{\theta} \quad \mathbf{z}_0 = \mathbf{0} \tag{7}$$
$$\Delta\theta_i, \Delta\mathbf{z}_i = RB(\theta_{i-1}, \mathbf{z}_{i-1}) \tag{8}$$
$$\theta_i = \theta_{i-1} + \Delta\theta_i \quad \mathbf{z}_i = \mathbf{z}_{i-1} + \Delta\mathbf{z}_i \tag{9}$$

Overall, the garment estimation block forms a closed-loop structure, in which the human body parameters are required to predict the garment, and are later corrected back by the garment prediction as well.

The key insight of our module design is that the human body and garment shape are highly correlated at different scales and should be jointly learned using shared information. On the global scale, the detailed features of the garments restrict the variance of the human body and reduce ambiguity due to camera projection. On the local scale, the body pose and shape largely defines the valid distribution of the garment wrinkle positions. Our proposed structure is also analogous to iterative optimization and feedback control in other areas, where two objectives serve as prior knowledge of each other and are improved iteratively. This work is the first to introduce this idea for the human and garment joint estimation task.

The loss function for the single-frame estimation is defined as:

$$\mathcal{L}_s = \mathcal{L}_{body} + \mathcal{L}_{AE} \tag{10}$$
$$\mathcal{L}_{body} = \mathcal{L}_{2D} + \mathcal{L}_{3D} + \mathcal{L}_{SMPL} \tag{11}$$

where $\mathcal{L}_{2D}$, $\mathcal{L}_{3D}$, and $\mathcal{L}_{SMPL}$ represent the 2D joint loss, the 3D joint loss, and the body parameter loss defined to supervise the human body estimation [33], and $\mathcal{L}_{AE}$ is the Chamfer distance defined in Eq. 6 to supervise the garment estimation.

5.2 Temporal Estimation for Garment Material

Garment material estimation is challenging since the visual difference of different materials is subtle and can easily be overwhelmed by disturbance, e.g. various directions or magnitudes of external forces. To tackle this problem, previous works often assume fixed environment settings and cloth shapes [59,60]. While we follow a similar principle when training the material estimation module, we go one step further that we only assume common human motion for driving the garment instead of the whole external force field. While previous works [59,60] can only handle videos of a piece of cloth hanging and dragged by the wind, our method possesses a wider applicability regarding the diversity of the garment shapes, sizes and human motions in the input video, which for the first time enables practical usages for garment material cloning.

As shown in Fig. 3, we collect and concatenate the image features and the estimated garment latent vector of each frame as the input signal, and feed the sequence of the signals to LSTM to produce a summary feature. Finally, we pass the summary feature to a fully-connected layer for material type classification. We use the cross-entropy loss for supervision.

Training the entire pipeline from scratch is not ideal because the system is too large and the training could be unstable. Instead, we first trained the single frame body and garment estimation module using single view images. After the convergence on the single frame module, we fixed its parameters and applied it to train the material estimation network. Our experiments demonstrated in Sect. 6 indicate that the multi-scale garment features are not merely useful for detecting the fabric materials; they are the dominant features during the estimation and can boost the test accuracy compared to methods that only use the image features.

6   Results

We demonstrate the performance of our model as follows. (1) We compare our work with with the baselines and SOTA methods *quantitatively* (Sect. 6.1) and *qualitatively* (Sect. 6.2). (2) Ablation studies are presented in Sect. 6.2 on the improvements by our network design. (3) A user study on material perception using this work and the similarity between the measurements of real-world fabrics from lab experiments vs. our predicted garment materials from videos is presented in Sect. 6.4, with detail in Appendix. (4) We compare ours with other related learning-based methods (Sect. 6.5) and show application to virtual try-on, with detail in Appendix. (5) Additional latent code interpolation between garments, training data and perceptual study examples can be found in both Appendices and the supplementary video.

Training Process. We first trained the auto-encoder alone. Next, we trained the single-frame estimation module, with the fixed decoder attached at the end. Finally, we trained the material estimation with other parts fixed. See Appendix for more training details.

6.1   Quantitative Analysis

Ours vs. Image-Only [60]. Due to the difference regarding the input distribution (dressed garment on a human body in our method vs. hanging cloth in theirs), we re-train their model on our datasets for a fair comparison. We study the contribution of image-only features vs. garment-only features, as well as CNN vs. LSTM (that exploits the temporal coherence). Finally, we compare the overall performance difference between ours and [60]. The test classification accuracy is reported in Table 1.

Findings: (1) While all three models have learned the relationship between motion and materials and all three outperform random guess, *the garment feature signals are shown to be much more important than the image features.* This finding is not surprising, since the garment shape is directly affected by the material. (2) Combining the two features, as our model does, further improves the test accuracy. A possible reason is that an overall capturing of the garment shape (*e.g.*width and length of the entire piece), which is difficult to retrieve using garment latent codes, could be more easily extracted using image features. (3) By exploiting temporal coherence, unsurprisingly all three versions of the model achieve better accuracy than only using 1 image.

Table 1. Comparison on material estimation: our method achieves ∼1.5x higher accuracy (45.27% vs. 70.14%) in material identification than [60].

Method	Mean accuracy	Temporal gain	Garment features gain
Random guess	1.85%	-	-
Image only, CNN	5.11%	40.16%	–
Image only, LSTM [60]	45.27%		–
Garment only, CNN	11.85%	53.31%	6.74%
Garment only, LSTM	65.16%		19.89%
Image + Garment, CNN	12.62%	**57.52%**	7.51%
Image + Garment, LSTM *(ours)*	**70.14%**		**24.87%**

Ours vs. Optimization-Based [59,61]: An optimization-simulation framework to obtain the fabric material parameters using wrinkle density of the garment in a single image was proposed in [59,61]. In contrast, our method extracts both static image features and spatio-temporal *garment features* across frames. We generate the same set of test scenes as shown in the Appendix. Our model is tested on these sequences under varying lighting and visibility conditions (Appendix); the average accuracy is reported in Table 2. In this challenging case where the lighting condition and the textures are not seen in the training distribution, our method still achieves comparable accuracy with previous method [59,61], but it runs **more than 1,000x faster**. *Ours is the first learning-based method to predict fabric materials directly from a video of garments worn on a human body.*

6.2 Qualitative Results

We compare ours with the most relevant work of [59] for joint estimation of garment shapes and materials, as shown in Fig. 5. Our method achieves similar reconstruction accuracy and visual quality as [59,61]. But, [59,61] uses semantic segmentation, thus suffering from tedious manual processing and long inference time. In contrast, our learning-based method is fully automatic and can compute the prediction in real time. Moreover, our method does not assume the sewing patterns as a prior.

Table 2. Quantitative comparison with [59,61]. Our method achieves comparable or higher accuracy, but runs at least *three orders of magnitude* faster than the state-of-the-art [59,61].

Method	Accuracy (%)						Speed
	Mid-day			Sunset			
	T-shirt	Pants	Skirt	T-shirt	Pants	Skirt	
[59,61]	80.2	80.2	**83.3**	81.6	79.9	**80.7**	4–6 h
Ours	**86.5**	**91.6**	81.6	**82.4**	**91.6**	79.6	**8.7 s**

(a) Input image (b) Results from [61] (c) Our results

Fig. 5. Qualitative comparison with [59,61]: Ours is easier to use and achieves visually comparable reconstruction much faster without priors on garment patterns and topology.

We further compare with several learning methods [6,22] in the Appendices for reference. Many often use additional information (*e.g.*mesh templates or known garment types) as priors, so direct visual comparison is not meaningful. Nonetheless, our model successfully generalizes to unseen real-world images/videos with comparable visual results, as shown in Appendices. During these experiments, our method is directly applied without any fine-tuning or post-optimization. Although trained using synthetic datasets, our model correctly identifies people and the garments from real-world images, and achieves similar visual results in all examples, when compared with previous works. The network is also capable of the predicting correct sizes of garments relative to the body, due to multiscale auto-encoders.

Material Cloning for Virtual Try-On: We show three application scenarios of our method. In Fig. 6, given an RGB video of a person wearing garments of different fabric materials, our method can identify the underlying material and *clone* it onto other garment models using cloth simulation. Our method is the first to achieve fast and accurate material extraction from videos of dressed garments on a body. We further show the ability of our method to reconstruct the entire human appearance from the input video using one single network. We first estimate the body and the garment geometry frame by frame, and use the temporal information to infer the material. The three parts are combined using cloth simulation to generate the final output. Figure 7 shows the reconstruction results (also see the supplement video). Our reconstructed garment shapes and wrinkles match those in the input video frames.

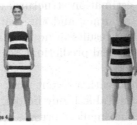

Input video | Reconstructed Avatar wearing the same garment

Fig. 6. Material transfer between videos. Our method can take videos of a person wearing any garments and clone the underlying fabric materials onto a virtual avatar wearing the same garment with the same fabric.

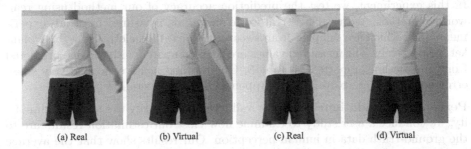

(a) Real   (b) Virtual   (c) Real   (d) Virtual

Fig. 7. Qualitative results: our method faithfully recovers the T-shirt materials (a, c) in video so that the wrinkles around the simulated t-shirt sleeves (b, d) appear similar under different poses.

Table 3. Ablation study for different parts of our proposed network. CD stands for errors in Chamfer Distance; SD stands for Sinkhorn Divergence [18]; and MPJPE stands for Mean Per Joint Position Error – all in millimeters (mm). *Separate* predicts the body and the garment separately in parallel branches. Our method results in notably smaller errors (in CD, SD, MPJPE) than all baselines in reconstruction and material prediction, with 30% to 40% higher accuracy.

Method	CD	SD	Accuracy	Method	MPJPE	CD	Accuracy
AtlasNet [17]	0.31	8.05	54.20%	Separate	80.89	1.55	49.15%
Ours	**0.12**	**1.03**	**70.14%**	Ours	**55.20**	**0.88**	**70.14%**
	(a) Auto-encoder				(b) Human and garment estimation		

6.3 Ablation Study

We verify the effectiveness of our network model in the following ablation studies reported in Table 3. We compare our method with baselines that replaces (a) the two-level auto-encoder with AtlasNet [17], and (b) the joint body-garment estimation block with a parallel estimation structure, respectively. The metrics include both the reconstruction accuracy and the material classification accuracy in the final stage. Our method results in notably smaller errors than both baselines in reconstruction and material prediction. See Appendix on the details of this ablation study.

We further compare our method with a recent work [6] since their task is the most relevant to ours. As shown in Table 4, our model, without any fine-tuning or domain adaptation, achieves the smallest error – whether the ground-truth human body model is provided or not during reconstruction. Since our model is trained on a wider range of body poses and garment types than theirs while achieving better accuracy, it has shown to offer good generality to unseen inputs. See Appendix for more detail.

6.4 Lab Experiments and User Study

In this experiment, we test the prediction accuracy of our method using real-world materials. We used five real-world materials measured from lab experiments [54], which are sampled from sweater, t-shirt, tablecloth, jeans, and blanket, respectively. The measured values are then compared with the one predicted from our method, reported in Table 5. Our method achieves a relatively small error between 9.5% to 16.7%. See Appendix for more detail.

Perceptual Validation: To further validate and quantify the material similarity, we conduct a user study to examine how close our estimation results are to the ground-truth data in human perception. Our results show that the average similarity ratings for five tested materials vs. the ground-truth data are all larger than 5, ranging from 5.7 to 8.5, with an overall mean value of 7.1. These indicate that our method indeed can recover fabric materials with only minor perceptible differences to the real-world materials. Furthermore, we also conducted on material perceptions under different environmental conditions. Please see Appendix for details on these perceptual studies.

Table 4. Test errors on the Multi-Garment Net datasets [1,6]. Our method achieves the lowest errors (by up to **3x–4x**) across all garment types, without any fine-tuning or reference body.

Methods	[1]	[6]		Ours	
	GT Pose	GT Pose	Full Pred.	GT Pose	Full Pred.
Pants (mm)	5.44	5.57	10.16	**1.58**	**3.08**
Short Pants (mm)	8.23	5.97	10.00	**4.92**	**5.69**
T-shirt (mm)	5.80	5.63	11.97	**1.67**	**3.08**
Shirt (mm)	5.71	6.33	9.05	**2.29**	**3.75**
Coat (mm)	5.85	5.66	9.09	**2.84**	**3.65**

Table 5. Lab experiment results. Our material estimation achieves relatively small errors compared to lab measurements on all real-world materials tested.

Material name [54]	Stretching ratio (GT/Prediction)	Bending ratio (GT/Prediction)	Mean relative Error
Gray-interlock	1.01/1	1.6/2	10.5%
Navy-sparkle-sweat	0.56/0.5	1.7/2	12.8%
White-dots-on-blk	15.8/20	3.5/4	16.7%
11oz-black-denim	3.6/3	3.0/3	8.3%
Pink-ribbon-brown	2.93/3	12/10	9.5%

Table 6. Comparison with previous works. Our method can handle the largest set of garments, using the fewest possible information (*i.e.* widely available RGB images only), in one stand-alone network.

Method	Input	Dependencies	Generality	Dresses support	Separate mesh	Material estimation
MGN [6]	Semantic seg. + 2D joints	Garment correspondences	One model per garment	No	Yes	No
DeepCap [22]	Foreground seg	Template mesh	One model per garment	Yes (w/ known template)	No	No
[59]	Semantic seg	Template mesh	One model per garment	Yes (w/ known template)	Yes	Yes
DeepFashion3D [67]	RGB frame (garment only)	None	One model for all	Yes (limited topologies)	Yes	No
Tailornet [39]	Body parameters	Garment correspondences	One model per garment	Yes (limited topologies)	Yes	No
BCNet [26]	RGB frame	Garment correspondences	One model per garment	Yes (limited topologies)	Yes	No
SIZER [51]	Body scan	Garment labels	One model per garment	No	Yes	No
ARCH [24]	RGB frame (foreground only)	None	One model for all	Yes (water-tight)	No	No
Ours	RGB frame	None	One model for all	Yes	Yes	Yes

6.5 More Comparison with Previous Works

In Table 6, we extensively compare our work with previous ones regarding different assumptions, functionalities, and abilities. We define 'one model per garment' in 'generality' as that the method needs to create extra templates or registrations to the body, or need to retrain part of the network in order to predict a different garment type. Although DeepFashion3D [67] and ARCH [24] also have generality to different topologies to some extent, there are still limitations in their pipeline. The output from DeepFashion3D has to be continuous in one body part, meaning that they cannot support all topologies (*e.g.* dresses with holes). ARCH does support different garments on the body, but the output is a water-tight mesh together with the body, which is not always convenient for certain applications like virtual try-on. In contrast, our method naturally supports all kinds of topologies, and predicts the body and the garment in separate

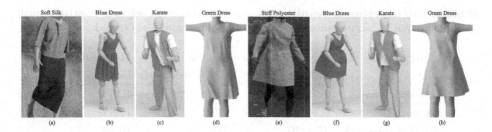

Fig. 8. Material transfer examples. Our method can accurately estimate the material parameters from input videos (a, e) and replicate the same 'feel' in other animations (b, c, d) and (f, g, h), respectively, creating significantly different visual effects for the same pose.

meshes. Additional comparison results with DeepCap [22] and MGN [6] can be found in the Appendix.

Virtual Try-on: Visual results of our work on application to virtual try-on are shown in Fig. 8. More animations are shown in the supplementary video.

7   Conclusion

In this paper, we introduced a learning model for garment material estimation using RGB videos. We do not assume other inputs (e.g. segmentation, 3D scans, multi-views, etc.) or any prior knowledge on the garment shape/topology, design patterns/templates, or correspondences. We extract the multi-scale features to effectively represent the dynamic geometry structure of garments, which can be combined with image features to estimate fabric materials by learning their temporal patterns, while improving the human body reconstruction using a feedback loop. This approach is perhaps the first to introduce a unified parametric model for all garment types, and it can thereby support garments of different topologies without the need to retrain different models. Experiments show that our method achieves much higher accuracy up to 70.14% in estimating fabric materials than prior works, while offering capabilities in recovering garment types and topologies with generality and simplicity for an unification of multiple correlated tasks.

Limitations: We assume that garment motion is captured as videos of adequate image resolution under sufficient lighting to show fabric movement, wrinkles and folds. The current implementation does not support multi-layer, folded garments, or detection of different materials at once. These issues can likely be addressed by adding more structural prior to encode multi-layer clothing, introduction of curvature representation for multi-fold features, and a point cloud segmentation module. The accuracy of fabric material estimation perhaps can probably be further enhanced by integrating neural rendering [50] with this work.

References

1. Alldieck, T., Magnor, M.A., Bhatnagar, B.L., Theobalt, C., Pons-Moll, G.: Learning to reconstruct people in clothing from a single RGB camera. In: IEEE Conference on Computer Vision and Pattern Recognition, CVPR 2019, Long Beach, CA, USA, 16–20 June 2019, pp. 1175–1186. Computer Vision Foundation/IEEE (2019). https://doi.org/10.1109/CVPR.2019.00127, http://openaccess. thecvf.com/content_CVPR_2019/html/Alldieck_Learning_to_Reconstruct_People_in_Clothing_From_a_Single_RGB_CVPR_2019_paper.html

2. Alldieck, T., Magnor, M.A., Xu, W., Theobalt, C., Pons-Moll, G.: Video based reconstruction of 3d people models. In: 2018 IEEE Conference on Computer Vision and Pattern Recognition, CVPR 2018, Salt Lake City, UT, USA, 18–22 June 2018, pp. 8387–8397. IEEE Computer Society (2018). https://doi.org/10.1109/CVPR.2018.00875, http://openaccess.thecvf.com/content_cvpr_2018/html/Alldieck_Video_Based_Reconstruction_CVPR_2018_paper.html

3. Alldieck, T., Pons-Moll, G., Theobalt, C., Magnor, M.A.: Tex2shape: detailed full human body geometry from a single image. In: 2019 IEEE/CVF International Conference on Computer Vision, ICCV 2019, Seoul, Korea (South), October 27–November 2, 2019, pp. 2293–2303. IEEE (2019). https://doi.org/10.1109/ICCV.2019.00238

4. Bednarik, J., Parashar, S., Gundogdu, E., Salzmann, M., Fua, P.: Shape reconstruction by learning differentiable surface representations. In: Proceedings of the IEEE/CVF Conference on Computer Vision and Pattern Recognition, pp. 4716–4725 (2020)

5. Bhat, K.S., Twigg, C.D., Hodgins, J.K., Khosla, P., Popovic, Z., Seitz, S.M.: Estimating cloth simulation parameters from video (2003)

6. Bhatnagar, B.L., Tiwari, G., Theobalt, C., Pons-Moll, G.: Multi-garment net: learning to dress 3d people from images. In: 2019 IEEE/CVF International Conference on Computer Vision, ICCV 2019, Seoul, Korea (South), October 27–November 2, 2019, pp. 5419–5429. IEEE (2019). https://doi.org/10.1109/ICCV.2019.00552

7. Bi, W., Jin, P., Nienborg, H., Xiao, B.: Estimating mechanical properties of cloth from videos using dense motion trajectories: Human psychophysics and machine learning. J. Vision 18(5), 12–12 (2018)

8. Bi, W., Xiao, B.: Perceptual constancy of mechanical properties of cloth under variation of external forces. In: Proceedings of the ACM Symposium on Applied Perception, pp. 19–23 (2016)

9. Bickel, B., et al.: Design and fabrication of materials with desired deformation behavior. ACM Trans. Graph. (TOG) 29(4), 1–10 (2010)

10. Bouman, K.L., Xiao, B., Battaglia, P., Freeman, W.T.: Estimating the material properties of fabric from video. In: Proceedings of the IEEE International Conference on Computer Vision, pp. 1984–1991 (2013)

11. Bradley, D., Popa, T., Sheffer, A., Heidrich, W., Boubekeur, T.: Markerless garment capture. In: ACM SIGGRAPH 2008 papers, pp. 1–9 (2008)

12. Cao, Z., Simon, T., Wei, S.E., Sheikh, Y.: Realtime multi-person 2d pose estimation using part affinity fields. In: Proceedings of the IEEE Conference on Computer Vision and Pattern Recognition, pp. 7291–7299 (2017)

13. Casati, R., Daviet, G., Bertails-Descoubes, F.: Inverse elastic cloth design with contact and friction. Ph.D. thesis, Inria Grenoble Rhône-Alpes, Université de Grenoble (2016)

14. Chen, X., Zhou, B., Lu, F.X., Wang, L., Bi, L., Tan, P.: Garment modeling with a depth camera. ACM Trans. Graph. **34**(6), 203–1 (2015)
15. Clyde, D., Teran, J., Tamstorf, R.: Modeling and data-driven parameter estimation for woven fabrics. In: Proceedings of the ACM SIGGRAPH/Eurographics Symposium on Computer Animation, pp. 1–11 (2017)
16. Daněřek, R., Dibra, E., Öztireli, C., Ziegler, R., Gross, M.: Deepgarment: 3d garment shape estimation from a single image. In: Computer Graphics Forum, vol. 36, pp. 269–280. Wiley Online Library (2017)
17. Deprelle, T., Groueix, T., Fisher, M., Kim, V., Russell, B., Aubry, M.: Learning elementary structures for 3d shape generation and matching. In: Advances in Neural Information Processing Systems, pp. 7433–7443 (2019)
18. Feydy, J., Séjourné, T., Vialard, F.X., Amari, S.I., Trouvé, A., Peyré, G.: Interpolating between optimal transport and mmd using sinkhorn divergences. arXiv preprint arXiv:1810.08278 (2018)
19. Gong, W., et al.: Human pose estimation from monocular images: a comprehensive survey. Sensors **16**(12), 1966 (2016)
20. Guarnera, G.C., Hall, P., Chesnais, A., Glencross, M.: Woven fabric model creation from a single image. ACM Trans. Graph. (TOG) **36**(5), 1–13 (2017)
21. Gundogdu, E., Constantin, V., Seifoddini, A., Dang, M., Salzmann, M., Fua, P.: Garnet: a two-stream network for fast and accurate 3d cloth draping. In: Proceedings of the IEEE International Conference on Computer Vision, pp. 8739–8748 (2019)
22. Habermann, M., Xu, W., Zollhoefer, M., Pons-Moll, G., Theobalt, C.: Deepcap: monocular human performance capture using weak supervision. In: IEEE Conference on Computer Vision and Pattern Recognition (CVPR), IEEE, June 2020
23. Hochreiter, S., Schmidhuber, J.: Long short-term memory. Neural Comput. **9**(8), 1735–1780 (1997)
24. Huang, Z., Xu, Y., Lassner, C., Li, H., Tung, T.: Arch: animatable reconstruction of clothed humans. In: Proceedings of the IEEE/CVF Conference on Computer Vision and Pattern Recognition, pp. 3093–3102 (2020)
25. Jeong, M.H., Han, D.H., Ko, H.S.: Garment capture from a photograph. Comput. Animation Virtual Worlds **26**(3–4), 291–300 (2015)
26. Jiang, B., Zhang, J., Hong, Y., Luo, J., Liu, L., Bao, H.: Bcnet: learning body and cloth shape from a single image. arXiv preprint arXiv:2004.00214 (2020)
27. Kanazawa, A., Black, M.J., Jacobs, D.W., Malik, J.: End-to-end recovery of human shape and pose. In: Proceedings of the IEEE Conference on Computer Vision and Pattern Recognition, pp. 7122–7131 (2018)
28. Klokov, R., Lempitsky, V.: Escape from cells: Deep KD-networks for the recognition of 3d point cloud models. In: The IEEE International Conference on Computer Vision (ICCV), October 2017
29. Kolotouros, N., Pavlakos, G., Black, M.J., Daniilidis, K.: Learning to reconstruct 3d human pose and shape via model-fitting in the loop. In: Proceedings of the IEEE International Conference on Computer Vision, pp. 2252–2261 (2019)
30. Lahner, Z., Cremers, D., Tung, T.: Deepwrinkles: accurate and realistic clothing modeling. In: Proceedings of the European Conference on Computer Vision (ECCV), pp. 667–684 (2018)
31. Li, J., Chen, B.M., Hee Lee, G.: So-net: self-organizing network for point cloud analysis. In: The IEEE Conference on Computer Vision and Pattern Recognition (CVPR), June 2018

32. Li, Y., Bu, R., Sun, M., Wu, W., Di, X., Chen, B.: PointCNN: convolution on x-transformed points. In: Advances in Neural Information Processing Systems, pp. 820–830 (2018)
33. Liang, J., Lin, M.C.: Shape-aware human pose and shape reconstruction using multi-view images. In: Proceedings of the IEEE International Conference on Computer Vision, pp. 4352–4362 (2019)
34. Loper, M., Mahmood, N., Romero, J., Pons-Moll, G., Black, M.J.: SMPL: a skinned multi-person linear model. ACM Trans. Graph. (TOG) 34(6), 1–16 (2015)
35. Ma, Q., Saito, S., Yang, J., Tang, S., Black, M.J.: Scale: modeling clothed humans with a surface codec of articulated local elements. In: Proceedings of the IEEE/CVF Conference on Computer Vision and Pattern Recognition, pp. 16082–16093 (2021)
36. Mehta, D., et al.: VNect: real-time 3d human pose estimation with a single RGB camera. ACM Trans. Graph. (TOG) 36(4), 1–14 (2017)
37. Miguel, E., et al.: Data-driven estimation of cloth simulation models. In: Computer Graphics Forum, vol. 31, pp. 519–528. Wiley Online Library (2012)
38. Miguel, E., et al.: Modeling and estimation of internal friction in cloth. ACM Trans. Graph. (TOG) 32(6), 1–10 (2013)
39. Patel, C., Liao, Z., Pons-Moll, G.: TailorNet: predicting clothing in 3d as a function of human pose, shape and garment style. In: IEEE Conference on Computer Vision and Pattern Recognition (CVPR), IEEE, June 2020
40. Pumarola, A., Sanchez-Riera, J., Choi, G., Sanfeliu, A., Moreno-Noguer, F.: 3dpeople: Modeling the geometry of dressed humans. In: Proceedings of the IEEE International Conference on Computer Vision, pp. 2242–2251 (2019)
41. Qi, C.R., Liu, W., Wu, C., Su, H., Guibas, L.J.: Frustum pointnets for 3d object detection from RGB-d data. In: The IEEE Conference on Computer Vision and Pattern Recognition (CVPR), June 2018
42. Qi, C.R., Su, H., Mo, K., Guibas, L.J.: Pointnet: deep learning on point sets for 3d classification and segmentation. In: Proceedings of the IEEE Conference on Computer Vision and Pattern Recognition, pp. 652–660 (2017)
43. Qi, C.R., Yi, L., Su, H., Guibas, L.J.: Pointnet++: deep hierarchical feature learning on point sets in a metric space. In: Advances in Neural Information Processing Systems, pp. 5099–5108 (2017)
44. Rasheed, A.H., Romero, V., Bertails-Descoubes, F., Wuhrer, S., Franco, J.S., Lazarus, A.: Learning to measure the static friction coefficient in cloth contact. In: Proceedings of the IEEE/CVF Conference on Computer Vision and Pattern Recognition, pp. 9912–9921 (2020)
45. Saito, S., Huang, Z., Natsume, R., Morishima, S., Kanazawa, A., Li, H.: PIFu: Pixel-aligned implicit function for high-resolution clothed human digitization. In: Proceedings of the IEEE International Conference on Computer Vision, pp. 2304–2314 (2019)
46. Saltelli, A.: Sensitivity analysis for importance assessment. Risk Anal. 22(3), 579–590 (2002)
47. Santesteban, I., Otaduy, M.A., Casas, D.: Learning-based animation of clothing for virtual try-on. In: Computer Graphics Forum, vol. 38, pp. 355–366. Wiley Online Library (2019)
48. Smith, D., Loper, M., Hu, X., Mavroidis, P., Romero, J.: Facsimile: fast and accurate scans from an image in less than a second. In: Proceedings of the IEEE International Conference on Computer Vision, pp. 5330–5339 (2019)

49. Tan, Q., Pan, Z., Gao, L., Manocha, D.: Realtime simulation of thin-shell deformable materials using CNN-based mesh embedding. IEEE Robot. Autom. Lett. **5**(2), 2325–2332 (2020)
50. Thies, J., Zollhöfer, M., Nießner, M.: Deferred neural rendering: image synthesis using neural textures. ACM Trans. Graph. (TOG) **38**(4), 1–12 (2019)
51. Tiwari, G., Bhatnagar, B.L., Tung, T., Pons-Moll, G.: Sizer: a dataset and model for parsing 3d clothing and learning size sensitive 3d clothing. arXiv preprint arXiv:2007.11610 (2020)
52. Varol, G., et al.: Bodynet: Volumetric inference of 3d human body shapes. In: Proceedings of the European Conference on Computer Vision (ECCV), pp. 20–36 (2018)
53. Vidaurre, R., Casas, D., Garces, E., Lopez-Moreno, J.: BRDF estimation of complex materials with nested learning. In: 2019 IEEE Winter Conference on Applications of Computer Vision (WACV), pp. 1347–1356. IEEE (2019)
54. Wang, H., O'Brien, J.F., Ramamoorthi, R.: Data-driven elastic models for cloth: modeling and measurement. ACM Trans. Graph. (TOG) **30**(4), 1–12 (2011)
55. Wang, T.Y., Ceylan, D., Popovic, J., Mitra, N.J.: Learning a shared shape space for multimodal garment design. arXiv preprint arXiv:1806.11335 (2018)
56. Wang, Y., Sun, Y., Liu, Z., Sarma, S.E., Bronstein, M.M., Solomon, J.M.: Dynamic graph CNN for learning on point clouds. ACM Trans. Graph. (TOG) **38**(5), 1–12 (2019)
57. Wei, S.E., Ramakrishna, V., Kanade, T., Sheikh, Y.: Convolutional pose machines. In: Proceedings of the IEEE Conference on Computer Vision and Pattern Recognition, pp. 4724–4732 (2016)
58. Xu, Y., Zhu, S.C., Tung, T.: DenseRaC: joint 3d pose and shape estimation by dense render-and-compare. In: Proceedings of the IEEE International Conference on Computer Vision, pp. 7760–7770 (2019)
59. Yang, S., et al.: Detailed garment recovery from a single-view image. arXiv preprint arXiv:1608.01250 (2016)
60. Yang, S., Liang, J., Lin, M.C.: Learning-based cloth material recovery from video. In: Proceedings of the IEEE International Conference on Computer Vision, pp. 4383–4393 (2017)
61. Yang, S., et al.: Physics-inspired garment recovery from a single-view image. ACM Trans. Graph. (TOG) **37**(5), 1–14 (2018)
62. Yu, T., et al.: SimulCap: Single-view human performance capture with cloth simulation. In: 2019 IEEE/CVF Conference on Computer Vision and Pattern Recognition (CVPR), pp. 5499–5509. IEEE (2019)
63. Zakharkin, I., Mazur, K., Grigorev, A., Lempitsky, V.: Point-based modeling of human clothing. In: Proceedings of the IEEE/CVF International Conference on Computer Vision, pp. 14718–14727 (2021)
64. Zheng, Z., Yu, T., Wei, Y., Dai, Q., Liu, Y.: DeepHuman: 3d human reconstruction from a single image. In: Proceedings of the IEEE International Conference on Computer Vision, pp. 7739–7749 (2019)
65. Zhou, B., Chen, X., Fu, Q., Guo, K., Tan, P.: Garment modeling from a single image. In: Computer Graphics Forum, vol. 32, pp. 85–91. Wiley Online Library (2013)
66. Zhou, Y., Tuzel, O.: VoxelNet: End-to-end learning for point cloud based 3d object detection. In: The IEEE Conference on Computer Vision and Pattern Recognition (CVPR), June 2018
67. Zhu, H., et al.: Deep fashion3d: a dataset and benchmark for 3d garment reconstruction from single images. arXiv preprint arXiv:2003.12753 (2020)

MegBA: A GPU-Based Distributed Library for Large-Scale Bundle Adjustment

Jie Ren[1,2] , Wenteng Liang[1] , Ran Yan[1(✉)] , Luo Mai[2] , Shiwen Liu[1] ,
and Xiao Liu[1]

[1] Megvii Inc., Beijing, China
yanran2012@gmail.com
[2] The University of Edinburgh, Edinburgh, UK

Abstract. Large-scale Bundle Adjustment (BA) requires massive memory and computation resources which are difficult to be fulfilled by existing BA libraries. In this paper, we propose MegBA, a GPU-based distributed BA library. MegBA can provide massive aggregated memory by automatically partitioning large BA problems, and assigning the solvers of sub-problems to parallel nodes. The parallel solvers adopt distributed Precondition Conjugate Gradient and distributed Schur Elimination, so that an effective solution, which can match the precision of those computed by a single node, can be efficiently computed. To accelerate BA computation, we implement end-to-end BA computation using high-performance primitives available on commodity GPUs. MegBA exposes easy-to-use APIs that are compatible with existing popular BA libraries. Experiments show that MegBA can significantly outperform state-of-the-art BA libraries: Ceres (41.45×), RootBA (64.576×) and DeepLM (6.769×) in several large-scale BA benchmarks. The code of MegBA is available at: https://github.com/MegviiRobot/MegBA.

1 Introduction

Bundle Adjustment (BA) is the foundation for many real-world 3D vision applications [20,31], including structure-from-motion and simultaneous-localization-and-mapping. A BA problem minimises the re-projection error between camera poses and map points. The error is a non-linear square function, and it is minimised through iterative methods, such as Gauss-Newton (GN) [34], Leverberg-Marquardt (LM) [25] and Dog-Leg [29]. In each iteration, a BA library differentiates the errors with respect to solving states and constructs a linear system

---

J. Ren and W. Liang—Equal contribution, work was done during their internship in Megvii Inc.

Supplementary Information The online version contains supplementary material available at https://doi.org/10.1007/978-3-031-19836-6_40.

which is solved by optimisation algorithms, such as Cholesky decomposition [4] and Precondition Conjugate Gradient (PCG) [9].

Large-scale BA is increasingly important given the recent rise of city-level high-definition maps for autonomous driving [3,21,22,24] and indoor maps for augmentation reality [28,33,38]. A structure-from-motion application, for example, can produce massive images [2,15], resulting in billions of points and observations to be adjusted. Such a BA problem is orders of magnitude larger than those in conventional vision applications [32,39].

Existing BA libraries (e.g., g2o [12] and Ceres [1]) however provide insufficient support for large-scale BA. We observe several reasons: (i) Existing libraries focus on single-node execution, and they lack algorithms to distribute computation. They thus cannot provide massive aggregated memory that is the key for large-scale BA. Even though there are algorithms, such as RPBA [26], DPBA [6] and STBA [39], which explore distributed BA. These algorithms adopt *approximation* which can adversely affect the precision of found solutions. (ii) Existing BA libraries are designed for CPU architectures, and they under-utilise GPUs which is particularly useful for large-scale BA. Even though there are systems, such as PBA [36], to accelerate BA with GPUs. They leave key BA operations un-accelerated (e.g., error differentiation and linear system construction). DeepLM [16] offloads error differentiation into GPUs through PyTorch, but the performance is often sub-optimised.

In this paper, we propose MegBA, a novel GPU-optimised distributed library for large-scale BA. The design of MegBA makes several contributions:

(1) **Distributed BA algorithms**. MegBA provides a large amount of aggregated memory by distributing BA computation to multiple nodes. To this end, we propose a generic BA problem partitioning method. This method leverages a key observation in BA problems: BA problems are often expressed as graphs where nodes represent points/cameras, and edges represent the associations between cameras and points. MegBA can thus automatically partition the graphs based on edges, and ensure each sub-graph has an equal number of edges (with an aim of achieving load balancing). MegBA further assigns sub-graphs to distributed nodes and merges the local solutions to sub-graphs. To ensure that distributed BA can offer the precision as those computed by single-node BA libraries, we propose the distributed PCG algorithm and the distributed Schur elimination algorithm. These two algorithms synchronise the states of solvers on parallel nodes, and the synchronisation is realised using NCCL.

(2) **GPU-Optimised BA computation**. MegBA thoroughly optimise BA computation for GPUs, thus providing massive computation power for large-scale BA. Computation-intensive operators (e.g., inverse, inner project, etc.) are implemented as Single-Instruction-Multiple-Data (SIMD) operators. MegBA store data in *JetVector*, a data structure that stores BA data in SIMD-friendly vectors, and JetVector minimises data serialisation cost between CPUs and GPUs. To minimise data movement cost which could block GPU execution, MegBA has algorithms that can predict the GPU memory usage of BA, thus pre-fetching BA data if possible. It exposes easy-to-use APIs that are compatible with g2o and Ceres. Ceres and g2o applications can be thus easily ported to MegBA.

We evaluate the performance of MegBA on servers and each server has 8 NVIDIA V100 GPUs. Experiments with public large BA datasets (i.e., Final-13682 [2]) show that MegBA can out-perform Ceres by up to 41.45×, and RootBA [7] by up to 64.576×, indicating the benefits of optimising BA computation for GPUs. We further compare MegBA with DeepLM [16], a GPU-based BA library. MegBA out-performs DeepLM by 5.213× on 4 GPUs. With 8 GPUs, MegBA out-performs DeepLM by 6.769×, making MegBA the state-of-the-art BA library on GPUs.

To evaluate the scalability of MegBA, we construct an extremely large synthetic BA dataset which is modelled after by the BA problems we have in real-world applications. This dataset contains 80 million observations, 2.76× larger than Final-13682. DeepLM and RootBA incur out-of-memory error and cannot handle such a dataset. On the contrary, MegBA can solve this BA problem in 216.26 s by distributing BA computation to 8 GPUs, which is 23.54× faster than Ceres.

2   Related Work

This section describes the related work of MegBA. g2o [12] and Ceres [1] are **exact BA libraries** that can compute high-accuracy solutions to BA problems. These libraries are designed for using parallel CPU cores, and they cannot use GPUs. These libraries also fail to provide distributed execution, which makes them suffer from out-of-memory issues in solving large-scale BA problems.

Approximated BA algorithms can substantially speed up BA, though often come with a compromise in the quality of BA solutions. PBA [36] is limited to run on a single device. $\sqrt{BA}$ [8] replaced Schur Complement with a memory-efficient nullspace projection of Jacobian, thus improving its performance with single-precision float numbers. iSAM [18] and iSAM2 [17] exploit states ordering; while ICE-BA [23] exploits the states in temporal orders. Though fast in speed, approximated BA algorithms modify the original BA problems, which adversely affect the quality of BA solutions. As a result, commercial 3D vision software, such as PIX4D[1] usually avoid any form of approximation and adopt exact BA libraries if possible.[1]

Distributed BA libraries have been recently designed for large-scale BA. Anders Eriksson et al. [10] present consensus-based optimisation which leverages proximal splitting. Runze Zhang et al. [37] purpose an Alternating Direction Method of Multipliers to distribute the optimisation problem. Later RPBA [26], DPBA [6], STBA [39] partition the BA problems based on ADMM. These ADMM-based systems incur massive redundant computation on distributed devices, making them sometimes under-perform single-node libraries. Further, their users must manually partition BA problems, resulting in sub-optimal distributed performance. BA-Net [30] and DeepLM [16] leverages GPUs to speed up BA. They however rely on PyTorch to use GPU, which incurs non-trivial performance overheads when using GPU and extra memory copies. Decentralised SLAM libraries, such as DEDV-SLAM [5], often solve approximated BA problems on distributed robots, then they merge local solutions. However, the merged solution is not equivalent to the original global BA problem.

---

[1] https://www.pix4d.com/.

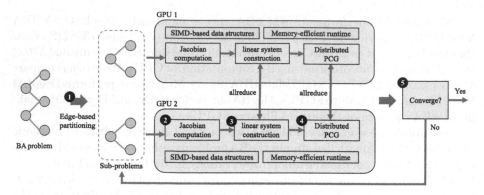

Fig. 1. MegBA overview. ❶ *MegBA partitions a BA problem based on edges. BA sub-problems are in the same size, and they are dispatched to distributed GPUs. Each GPU computes Jacobians* ❷*, constructs a linear system* ❸*, and solve the linear system using the distributed PCG algorithm* ❹*. The communication involved in linear system construction and distributed PCG is implemented using allreduce operations. Step* ❷*,* ❸*, and* ❹ *are executed iteratively until* ❺ *convergence criteria has been met.*

Custom hardware and algorithms are useful in accelerating BA [14]. GBP [27] uses a neural processing unit (i.e., GraphCore IPU) to speed up BA; but the limited availability of IPU makes GBP difficult to be used as a general solution. Practitioners also propose an approximated BA solver tailored for facial capture [11], and this solver cannot be used for arbitrary BA problems such as structure-from-motion.

3   Preliminaries

This section introduces the preliminaries of MegBA. A BA problem can be expressed as a graph, and its solving is realised an iterative process which minimises a non-linear square error objective function:

$$x^* = \arg\min_x \sum e_{i,j}^\top \Sigma_{i,j} e_{i,j}, \tag{1}$$

where $e_{i,j}$ is the constraint (i.e. error or graph edge) between state (i.e. parameters or graph nodes) x_i and x_j, $\Sigma_{i,j}$ is an information matrix.

Solving Eq. 1 is equivalent to iteratively updating the incremental amount Δx, given by the linear system $H\Delta x = g$, upon the current state x until convergence. The Hessian matrix $H = J^T \Sigma J$ for GN method and $H = J^T \Sigma J + \lambda I$ for LM method, the residual vector g equals to $-J^T \Sigma r$, J is the Jacobian of the error e with respect to current state x.

To solve BA problems, BA libraries can use Schur Complement (SC):

$$\begin{bmatrix} B & E \\ E^T & C \end{bmatrix} \begin{bmatrix} \Delta x_c \\ \Delta x_p \end{bmatrix} = \begin{bmatrix} v \\ w \end{bmatrix} \tag{2}$$

where B and C are block diagonal and they are related to camera-camera and point-point edges, respectively. E refers to edges between camera and point. v and w refer to the residual vectors for camera and point states.

Solving $H\Delta x = g$ is equivalent to compute the incremental update for states related to cameras Δx_c by solving an alternative linear system, called Reduced Camera System (RCS)

$$[B - EC^{-1}E^T]\Delta x_c = v - EC^{-1}w, \tag{3}$$

and followed by a substitution Δx_c into

$$\Delta x_p = C^{-1}\left(w - E^T \Delta x_c\right), \tag{4}$$

to get the update for 3D map points.

BA libraries solve linear systems using either direct methods or iterative methods. Direct methods, such as Gaussian-Elimination, LU, QR, and Cholesky Decomposition, return optimised solution of x in one pass. They however suffer from $O(n^3)$ time and $O(n^2)$ space complexity, making them only suitable for small-scale BA problems. On the contrary, iterative methods, such as PCG [31], are suitable for large-scale BA problems. Specifically, PCG replaces the explicit computation of $EC^{-1}E^T$ with multiple iterative sparse matrix-vector operations. It reduces the space complexity to $O(n)$, thus saving memory.

4   MegBA Design

This section introduces the design of MegBA. A key design goal of MegBA is to transparently distribute the solving of a given BA problem to multiple nodes, thus addressing the memory wall of a single node.

Figure 1 presents an overview of the distributed execution of MegBA. A MegBA user declares a BA problem as a graph. MegBA can automatically partition the BA problem based on edges with an aim of each BA sub-problem to have an even number of edges ❶. Specifically, each GPU first ❷ computes the Jacobian (i.e. differentiation of the edge for the node), and then ❸ construct the linear system, and finally, ❹ apply PCG to compute the update for adjusting the current BA sub-problem. The PCG intermediate state is synchronised so that MegBA can eventually solve the shared global BA problem. The BA update step is iteratively performed until a user-defined convergence criterion is met ❺. Notably, the BA computation on each GPU is implemented as SIMD operations which can best utilise GPUs (The details of SIMD-friendly data structure and the memory-efficient runtime are given in Sect. 5)

4.1   Edge-Based Partitioning Method

We focus on partitioning the Hessian matrix produced in BA. For example, in a BA dataset with 80M edges, a Hessian matrix H consume over 50G memory, leading to over 99.9% storage to be allocated to E and E^T. We want to have a generic method that partitions the Hessian matrix in a BA problem. This method needs to assign each parallel device with a part of the matrix E and E^T, preferably in equal sizes. The partitioning needs to guarantee that the global solution merged from local solutions is *equivalent* to the one computed using a single node. This equivalence property is the key to ensuring a high-precision solution found by MegBA.

At the high level, MegBA achieves distributed BA using two major components: (i) a method that can divide a BA problem into sub-problems, and (ii) an algorithm that can coordinate distributed PCG algorithms to solve sub-problems in parallel. Our partitioning method is based on a key observation in BA problems: the non-zero blocks in E and E^T are corresponding with edges, i.e., the i-th row j-th column non-zero block in E is computed by $e_{i,j}$, we can partition edges based on the number of available GPUs, and each GPU only store part of these non-zero blocks (We provide an example to illustrate the partitioning process in the supplementary materials).

Assume there are K GPUs, given a BA problem, we tile edges to a vector $e = [\ldots e_{i,j} \ldots]^T$, then we partition it to several blocks $e = [e_1^T \, e_2^T \ldots e_K^T]^T$. The Jacobian J could be partitioned into several blocks:

$$J = \frac{de}{dx} = \left[\frac{de_1}{dx}^T \, \frac{de_2}{dx}^T \, \ldots \, \frac{de_K}{dx}^T \right]^T = \left[J_1^T \, J_2^T \ldots J_K^T \right]^T. \tag{5}$$

Assuming identity information matrix is given here, Hessian H can be partitioned:

$$H = J^T J \;= \sum_{k=1}^{K} J_k^T J_k = \sum_{k=1}^{K} H_k. \tag{6}$$

To perform Schur elimination, we represented H_k as sub-blocks:

$$H_k = \begin{bmatrix} B_k & E_k \\ E_k^T & C_k \end{bmatrix}. \tag{7}$$

Matrix blocks in Eq. 2 have the following equivalent forms in the edge-based partition setting: $B = \sum_{k=1}^{K} B_k$, $E = \sum_{k=1}^{K} E_k$, $E^T = \sum_{k=1}^{K} E_k^T$, and $C = \sum_{k=1}^{K} C_k$. The number of non-zero parameter blocks in E or E^T equals the number of edges. Notably, the sub-matrices B_k and C_k have the same number of non-zero elements as B and C, respectively. Since we store matrices in the Compressed Sparse Row (CSR) format, each GPU only stores $\frac{1}{K}$ non-zero blocks in E and E^T. The blocking strategy greatly alleviates the problem that E and E^T are too large to be stored on a single device.

By applying the above partition method for Eq. 2, an equivalent distributed version can be formulated as follow:

$$g = -J^T r = -[J_1^T \, J_2^T \ldots J_K^T][r_1^T \, r_2^T \ldots r_K^T]^T = -\sum_{k=1}^{K} J_k^T r. \tag{8}$$

Algorithm 1. Distributed BA

Input: BA initial state $x = [\,x_c^T \; x_p^T\,]^T$, vector of edges e_k, and local GPU rank k
Output: Optimised state x
1: **while** *BA Convergence Criteria* not satisfied **do**
2:    $r_k = e_k(x), J_k = de_k(x)/dx$ /* *Residual and Jacobian* */
3:    $\begin{bmatrix} B_k \; E_k \\ E_k^T \; C_k \end{bmatrix} = J_k^T J_k, [\,v_k \; w_k\,] = -J_k^T r_k$ /* *Hessian and Constant vector* */
4:    $B = allreduce(B_k)$, $C = allreduce(C_k)$,
     $v = allreduce(v_k)$, $w = allreduce(w_k)$
             /* $B = \sum_{i=1}^{K} B_i$, $C = \sum_{i=1}^{K} C_i$, $v = \sum_{i=1}^{K} v_i$, $w = \sum_{i=1}^{K} w_i$ */
5:    $\alpha_k = E_k C^{-1} w$
6:    $\alpha = allreduce(\alpha_k)$ /* $\sum_{i=1}^{K} \alpha_i$ */
7:    $g = v - \alpha$ /* *Constant vector in Equation 3* */
8:    $\Delta x_c = \texttt{DPCG}(0, B, E_k, E_k^T, C, g, k)$ /* *Update x_c using Algorithm 2* */
9:    $\beta_k = E_k^T \Delta x_c$
10:   $\beta = allreduce(\beta_k)$ /* $\sum_{i=1}^{K} \beta_i$ */
11:   $\Delta x_p = C^{-1}(w - \beta)$ /* *Increment of x_p* */
12:   $x_c = x_c + \Delta x_c$, $x_p = x_p + \Delta x_p$ /* *Update state* */
13: **end while**
14: **return** $x = [\,x_c^T \; x_p^T\,]^T$

4.2   Distributed BA Algorithm

By far we have partitioned a BA problem and assigned sub-problems to all GPUs. In the following, we will discuss how does MegBA coordinates the solving of sub-problems in a distributed manner.

Algorithm 1 introduces the overall distributed BA algorithm in MegBA. The distributed BA algorithm takes as initial state and partitioned edges as described in Sect. 4.1. We use *JecVector* to compute the Jacobian and residual (Line 2). *JetVector* is a novel data structure to represent BA data in a SIMD format, it can make full use of the hardware characteristics of GPU (e.g. coalesced memory loading) to do auto-differentiation over millions of edges in parallel. We give a more detailed illustration in Sect. 5.1. Then we build a linear system (Line 3). We perform allreduce on diagonal-blocks and constant vector (Line 4) before solving the linear system because the size of diagonal-blocks and constant vector is small and they would be used several times in the following procedures.

We then compute constant vector in Eq. 3 (Line 5–7) and solve the linear system by using a distributed PCG (DPCG) algorithm (Line 8). Notably, we do necessary allreduce in the DPCG algorithm to guarantee DPCG output the same result as non-distributed PCG solver does in solving Eq. 3, further implementation details will be shown in Sect. 4.3. After solving the linear system in Eq. 3, we compute the increment of x_p following Eq. 4 (Line 9–11). Once we have computed the increment Δx_c and Δx_p, we update the state x_c and x_p (Line 12). If it doesn't satisfy the convergence criteria we will start another loop; otherwise, we will return the optimised state x.

Algorithm 2. Distributed PCG (DPCG)

Input: Initial state x^0, matrix block B, E_k, E_k^T, C of H_k, constant vector b, and local GPU rank k

Output: Solution x for linear system $[B - EC^{-1}E^T]x = b$, where $E = \sum_{i=1}^{K} E_i$ and $E^T = \sum_{i=1}^{K} E_i$

1: $r^0 = b - \text{DSE}(x^0, B, E_k, E_k^T, C^{-1}, k)$ /* Algorithm 3 */
2: $n = 0$
3: **while** *Convergence Criteria* not satisfied **do**
4:     $z^n = B^{-1}r^n$
5:     $\rho^n = r^{nT}z^n$
6:     **if** $n > 1$ **then**
7:         $\beta^n = \rho^n/\rho^{n-1}$
8:         $p^n = z^n + \beta^n p^n$
9:     **else**
10:         $p^n = z^n$
11:     **end if**
12:     $q^n = \text{DSE}(p^n, B, E_k, E_k^T, C^{-1}, k)$ /* Algorithm 3 */
13:     $\alpha^n = \rho^n/p^{nT}q^n$
14:     $x^{n+1} = x^n + \alpha^n p^n$
15:     $r^{n+1} = r^n - \alpha^n q^{n-1}$
16:     $n = n + 1$
17: **end while**
18: **return** x^n

Algorithm 3. Distributed Schur Elimination (DSE)

Input: Vector x, matrix B, E_k, E_k^T, C^{-1}, and local GPU rank k

Output: Schur elimination result $[B - EC^{-1}E]x$, where $E = \sum_{i=1}^{K} E_i, E^T = \sum_{i=1}^{K} E_i^T$

1: $a_k = E_k^T x$
2: $a = allreduce(a_k)$ /* $\sum_{i=1}^{K} a_i$ */
3: $b = C^{-1}a$
4: $c_k = E_k b$
5: $c = allreduce(c_k)$ /* $\sum_{i=1}^{K} c_i$ */
6: $d = Bx$
7: **return** $d - c$

4.3   Distributed PCG

We then discuss how to distribute the PCG algorithm in BA, shown in Algorithm 1. This algorithm first constructs a linear system defined in Eq. 2. It then solves Eq. 3 and computes increment following Eq. 4. It finally uses the increments update state x, and tested if a convergence criterion has been met. To guarantee that the distributed BA algorithm achieves the convergence performance, we make Algorithm 1, named DPCG, return the same result as the non-distributed linear solver.

In the following, we describe the execution of DPCG. DPCG takes BA initial state x^0, matrix block B, E_k, E_k^T, C of H_k, constant vector b as input and output solution x for linear system $[B - EC^{-1}E^T]x = b$, where $E = \sum_{k=1}^{K} E_k$ and $E^T = \sum_{k=1}^{K} E_k$. The procedures of DPCG using Schur elimination is similar to single-node PCG. Notably, the coefficient matrix of the linear system to be solved is Schur complement. The matrix-vector multiplication operations (Line 1, 12 in Algorithm 2) is thus the multiplication between Schur complement and vector. The difference between distributed compared with non-distributed setting is that DPCG only assign E_k and E_k^T rather than the complete matrices E and E^T to GPU k, so we need to guarantee operations that use E_k and E_k^T have the same output compared with using E and E^T, these operations happen when doing Schur elimination (Line 1, 12).

Our key idea of computing Schur elimination in a distributed manner is that: the summation of matrix-vector multiplication is the same as the result matrix summation multiplies vector, i.e., $\sum_{k=1}^{K}(E_k v) = \sum_{k=1}^{K}(E_k)v$. We compute an intermediate vector (Line 1) and reduce it (Line 2), then we compute intermediate vectors sequentially (Line 3, 4). We perform all-reduce operation over the intermediate vector (Line 5) and compute another intermediate vector (Line 6. After those procedures, we do subtraction to the last two intermediate vectors and output the final result. The result would be the same as computing the complete Schur complement $[B - EC^{-1}E]$ then multiplying it with vector x.

4.4   Complexity Analysis

In the end, we present the complexity analysis of MegBA. Assume that MegBA is given m cameras, n points, and k observations and we often have $k \gg m, n$, the time complexity for building the linear system is $\mathcal{O}(m+n+k)$ and the time complexity for each iteration of the conjugate gradient is $\mathcal{O}(m+n+k)$. Assume we distribute the problem to K GPUs, on each GPU, the time complexity for building the linear system is $\mathcal{O}(m + n + k/K)$ and the time complexity for each iteration of the conjugate gradient is $\mathcal{O}(m + n + k/K)$. The ring all-reduce communication time complexity of each conjugate gradient iteration is $\mathcal{O}(m+n)$. In summary, the total complexity of MegBA is $\mathcal{O}(m + n + k/K)$.

5   MegBA Implementation

This section describes the implementation of MegBA. There are several goals of our implementation: (i) We want to use as many SIMD operations as possible because both computation and memory operations on GPU are essentially SIMD-friendly. (ii) We want to optimise the memory efficiency of MegBA, thus avoiding memory allocation and deallocation; (iii) We want to implement the APIs of MegBA that are fully compatible with existing popular BA libraries: g2o and Ceres. In the following, we highlight how MegBA achieves these implementation goals.

5.1 SIMD-Friendly Data Structures

JetVector is a novel data structure to perform auto-differentiation over millions of edges. Compared to conventional BA data structure: *Jet* implemented in Ceres, *JetVector* represents a list of Jets (i.e., Array-of-Structure) as a single data object where Jet's data fields: *data* and *grad* across all items are represented as single arrays (i.e., Array-within-Structure). When we perform mathematical operations on *JetVector*, we will start as many GPU threads as the elements in it, every GPU thread process one element. Because *data* and *grad* are stored in the structure of Array-within-Structure, the memory transactions are coalesced and make it easy to reach a high memory throughput. The detailed structure layout of *JecVector* could be found in supplementary materials.

Besides *JetVector*, other parts of MegBA are also implemented as SIMD-friendly data structures. The construction of linear system (Line 3 in Algorithm 1) uses L1 cache on GPU to store Jacobian blocks in a SIMD manner. The DPCG algorithm includes a lot of matrix/vector operations which also be benefited from the SIMD structure. A full list of SIMD operations implemented in MegBA can be found in supplementary materials.

5.2 Memory-Efficient Runtime

BA computation involves massive objects to be allocated in GPU memory. To avoid expensive memory allocation [19], we leverage a key observation in BA computation: The automatic differentiation works on GPU buffers that are in the same size across BA iterations. By monitoring the sizes of GPU buffers used in the forward pass of differentiating the BA errors, we can predict the sizes of all memory buffers involved in future BA iterations. Based on this observation, we can pre-allocate these memory buffers in a memory pool, thus avoiding calling the CUDA driver to allocate memory during runtime.

5.3 Easy-to-Use APIs

The APIs of MegBA comprises of two major components:
(i) Declaring BA problems. Following the API convention of g2o and Ceres, a BA problem in MegBA is declared a graph that contains nodes and edges. The MegBA nodes describe the 3D coordinates or the poses of cameras and these nodes can be directly imported from g2o and Ceres applications. The MegBA edges are error functions that can be written using the Eigen library [13], identical to Ceres. A MegBA user can build a large BA problem by adding BA nodes and edges (using the g2o-equivalent *addEdge* and *addNode* functions).
(ii) Choosing BA solvers. MegBA also support users to choose solvers given the characteristics of their BA problems. The default solver is the SIMD-optimised DPCG which can automatically use multiple GPUs. Given a small-scale BA problem where intrinsic parallelism is not sufficient, MegBA provides users with the CPU-optimised CHOLMOD solver [4].

6   Experimental Evaluation

We conduct a comprehensive evaluation with MegBA. The evaluation comprises of BAL [2], 1DSfM [35], and a large synthetic dataset modelled after a city-scale BA application we have in production. The dataset statistic is shown in Table 1. Due to the page limit, this section only presents the results with BAL [2], and we put the results of 1DSfM and the synthetic dataset in the supplementary materials.

We compare MegBA with four baselines: (i) Ceres [1] (version 2.0) is the most popular BA library that can efficiently use massive CPU cores, (ii) g2o [12] is a lightweight CPU-based BA library, (iii) RootBA [7] is a recent CPU-based BA library that uses Nullspace-Marginalization in place of Schur Complement, and (iv) DeepLM [16] is the state-of-the-art GPU-based BA library (2021), and it was shown to out-perform other popular BA libraries: STBA [39] and PBA [36] (We provide comparison results between PBA and MegBA in the supplementary materials).

Table 1. Dataset statistics.

Benchmark	Dataset	#Points	#Observations
BAL	Trafalgar-257	65132	225911
	Ladybug-1723	156502	678718
	Dubrovnik-356	226730	1255268
	Venice-1778	993923	5001946
	Final-13682	4456117	28987644
Synthesised	Synthesised-20000	80000	80000000
1DSfM	Alamo-577	140080	816891
	Ellis_Island-233	9210	20500
	Gendarmenmarkt-704	76964	268747
	Madrid_Metropolis-347	44479	195660
	Montreal_Notre_Dame-459	151876	811757
	Notre_Dame-548	224153	1172145
	NYC_Library-334	54757	211614
	Piazza_del_Popolo-336	29731	150161
	Piccadilly-2292	184475	798085
	Roman_Forum-1067	223844	1031760
	Tower_of_London-484	126648	596690
	Trafalgar-5052	327920	1266102
	Union_Square-816	26430	90668
	Vienna_Cathedral-846	154394	495940
	Yorkminster-429	100426	376980

We run experiments on a server that has 80 Intel Xeon 2.5 GHz CPU cores, 8 Nvidia V100 GPUs and 320GB memory. The GPUs are inter-connected using NVLink 2.0. We use 64-bit floating points (FP64) unless otherwise specified.

6.1 Overall Performance

We first evaluate the overall performance of MegBA, Ceres, g2o, RootBA, and DeepLM. MegBA uses from 1 to 8 GPUs, and CPU-based algorithms use 16 threads. We measure the Mean Squared Error (MSE) in pixels over time.

Figure 2 shows the evaluation results. In the Venice-1778 dataset (Fig. 2(a)), MegBA achieves the best performance with 8 GPUs, while DeepLM can only use a single GPU. MegBA completes with 3.34 s while Ceres, RootBA, g2o uses 319.0, 73.94, and 890.6 s, respectively. It shows the substantial speed-up (95.5×, 22.1×, and 266.6×), which indicates the benefits of fully exploiting GPUs to accelerate BA computation. For GPU-based BA libraries, MegBA can complete with 11.96 s while DeepLM spent 24.44 s, showing the effectiveness of implementing full vectorisation for BA on a single GPU. With more GPUs, MegBA out-performs DeepLM by 7.316×, which reflects the necessity of adopting multiple GPUs.

Thanks to the vectorisation and distributed BA designs, MegBA becomes the state-of-the-art in the large BA dataset (i.e., Final-13682). As shown in Fig. 2(b),

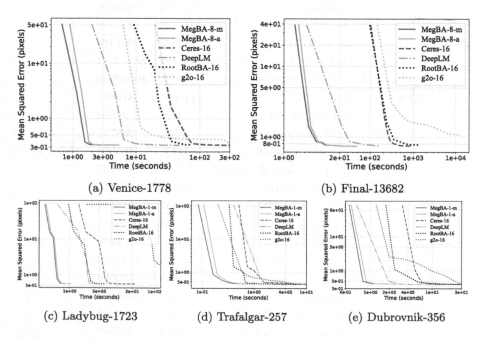

(a) Venice-1778   (b) Final-13682

(c) Ladybug-1723   (d) Trafalgar-257   (e) Dubrovnik-356

Fig. 2. Mean Squared Error over Time. *MegBA-X-Y refers to X GPUs while* **-a** *refers to auto-differentiation Jacobian and* **-m** *refers to analytical differentiation Jacobian. Ceres/RootBA/g2o-X refers to X CPU threads.*

Table 2. Small-scale experiments *We only report the results of MegBA with a GPU because the datasets in this table are small. MSE is the final Mean Squared Error (pixels), Time is BA duration, and Mem is the memory in GB.*

	Trafalgar-257			Ladybug-1723			Dubrovnik-356		
	MSE	Time	Mem	MSE	Time	Mem	MSE	Time	Mem
Ceres-16	0.434	8.160	1.659	0.562	34.50	2.093	0.393	116.0	2.550
DeepLM	0.434	3.820	1.445	0.573	3.930	2.144	0.396	6.119	2.693
g2o-16	0.434	21.69	1.358	1.961	140.7	1.866	0.394	94.39	2.308
RootBA-16	**0.433**	3.307	1.468	0.562	7.050	2.423	0.393	78.16	3.942
MegBA-1-a	0.438	1.364	1.270	0.560	0.932	2.450	0.411	3.640	3.940
MegBA-1-m	0.438	**1.148**	1.010	**0.560**	**0.774**	1.660	0.411	**3.263**	2.480

Table 3. Large-scale experiments.

	Venice-1778			Final-13682		
	MSE	Time	Mem	MSE	Time	Mem
Ceres-16	0.334	319.0	5.983	0.749	916.0	26.08
DeepLM	0.333	24.44	6.256	0.751	149.6	14.89
g2o-16	0.335	890.6	5.999	1.061	13161	36.89
RootBA-16	0.337	73.94	14.14	0.773	1,427	263.2
MegBA-1-a	0.333	11.96	13.68	OOM	OOM	OOM
MegBA-2-a	0.333	7.133	14.51	OOM	OOM	OOM
MegBA-4-a	0.333	4.767	16.76	0.748	28.70	81.03
MegBA-8-a	0.333	3.340	22.61	0.748	22.10	89.74
MegBA-1-m	0.333	10.92	7.870	OOM	OOM	OOM
MegBA-2-m	0.333	6.618	8.693	0.748	50.57	43.60
MegBA-4-m	0.333	4.617	10.95	0.748	26.46	47.33
MegBA-8-m	**0.333**	**3.014**	16.79	**0.748**	**20.68**	56.06

MegBA completes in 22.10 s, while DeepLM uses 149.6 s (6.769× speed-up), Ceres uses 916 s (41.45× speed-up), g2o uses 13161 s (595.5× speed-up), and RootBA uses 1427 s seconds (64.57× speed-up). In other datasets (Fig. 2(c)-(e)), we observe similar speed-up achieved by MegBA, indicating the general effectiveness of our proposed approaches. We omit the discussion of these datasets, and their results are reported in Table 2.

6.2   Scalability

Table 3 further provides the detailed experimental results to show the scalability of MegBA, Ceres and DeepLM. In the Venice-1778 dataset, MegBA can consistently improve its performance by adding GPUs (from 11.96 s to 3.34 s if we increase the number of GPUs from 1 to 8). In addition, the large dataset (Final-

Table 4. Performance with 32-bit and 64-bit floating points.

	Venice-1778			Final-13682		
	MSE	Time	Mem	MSE	Time	Mem
MegBA-1-a(FP32)	0.334	2.620	8.300	OOM	OOM	OOM
MegBA-1-a(FP64)	0.333	11.96	13.68	OOM	OOM	OOM
MegBA-1-m(FP32)	0.333	2.065	4.821	0.750	11.82	24.51
MegBA-1-m(FP64)	0.333	10.92	7.870	OOM	OOM	OOM
MegBA-2-a(FP32)	0.333	1.903	8.447	0.750	11.04	42.48
MegBA-2-a(FP64)	0.333	7.133	14.51	OOM	OOM	OOM
MegBA-2-m(FP32)	0.333	1.353	5.541	0.750	5.133	25.63
MegBA-2-m(FP64)	0.333	6.618	8.693	0.748	50.57	43.60
MegBA-4-a(FP32)	0.333	1.680	10.50	0.749	4.804	45.28
MegBA-4-a(FP64)	0.333	4.767	16.76	0.748	28.70	81.03
MegBA-4-m(FP32)	0.334	1.274	7.598	0.748	**4.279**	28.43
MegBA-4-m(FP64)	0.333	4.617	10.95	0.748	26.46	47.33
MegBA-8-a(FP32)	0.334	1.622	16.02	0.748	8.973	52.15
MegBA-8-a(FP64)	0.333	3.340	22.60	0.748	22.10	89.74
MegBA-8-m(FP32)	**0.333**	**1.271**	12.99	**0.747**	7.582	35.31
MegBA-8-m(FP64)	0.333	3.014	16.79	0.748	20.68	56.06

13682) can better show the scalability of MegBA. By increasing the number of GPUs from 4 to 8, the time can be reduced to 22.10 s.

6.3 Floating Point Precision

The accuracy of solving a BA problem is sensitive to the choice of floating point precision (i.e., 32-bit vs. 64-bit floating points). We further evaluate MegBA in all datasets with 32-bit and 64-bit floating points, and we report the results of Venice-1778 and Final-13682 in Table 4. Other datasets show consistent results and we omit them here. In the dataset of Final-13682, with 4 GPUs, MegBA (FP32) can complete in 4.804 s and MegBA (FP64) can complete in 28.70 s, while both of them are reaching the same MSE. This shows the exactness of the distributed BA algorithm in MegBA. Even with lower precision, MegBA can reach the same MSE as double-precision; but offering 5.97× speed up, making MegBA (FP32) be the state-of-the-art in Final-13682.

7   Conclusion

We present MegBA, a novel GPU-based distributed BA library. MegBA has a set of algorithms that enables automatically distributing BA computation to parallel GPUs. It has a group of SIMD-optimised data structures, and a memory-efficient runtime, making MegBA capable of fully utilising a GPU. MegBA has high-level and compatible APIs, making it quickly become a popular open-sourced BA library. Experimental results show that MegBA can out-perform SOTA BA libraries by orders of magnitudes in several large-scale BA benchmarks.

Acknowledgement. We would like to thank our colleagues at Megvii Inc., Dikai Fan, Shuxue Peng, Yijia He, Zheng Chai, Haotian Zhang and Can Huang for their invaluable inputs. Also, we thank Qingtian Zhu at Peking University and Xingxing Zuo at Technical University of Munich to help with proof reading.

References

1. Agarwal, S., Mierle, K., Others: Ceres solver. http://ceres-solver.org
2. Agarwal, S., Snavely, N., Seitz, S.M., Szeliski, R.: Bundle adjustment in the large. In: European Conference on Computer Vision (2010)
3. Chen, X., Ma, H., Wan, J., Li, B., Xia, T.: Multi-view 3d object detection network for autonomous driving. In: IEEE conference on Computer Vision and Pattern Recognition (2017)
4. Chen, Y., Davis, T.A., Hager, W.W., Rajamanickam, S.: Algorithm 887: CHOLMOD, supernodal sparse cholesky factorization and update/downdate. ACM Trans. Math. Softw. (TOMS) **35**(3), 1–14 (2008)
5. Cieslewski, T., Choudhary, S., Scaramuzza, D.: Data-efficient decentralized visual slam. In: IEEE International Conference on Robotics and Automation (2018)
6. Demmel, N., Gao, M., Laude, E., Wu, T., Cremers, D.: Distributed photometric bundle adjustment. In: IEEE International Conference on 3D Vision (2020)
7. Demmel, N., Sommer, C., Cremers, D., Usenko, V.: Square root bundle adjustment for large-scale reconstruction. In: IEEE Conference on Computer Vision and Pattern Recognition (2021)
8. Demmel, N., Sommer, C., Cremers, D., Usenko, V.: Square root bundle adjustment for large-scale reconstruction. In: IEEE/CVF Conference on Computer Vision and Pattern Recognition (2021)
9. Eisenstat, S.C.: Efficient implementation of a class of preconditioned conjugate gradient methods. SIAM J. Sci. Stat. Comput. **2**(1), 1–4 (1981)
10. Eriksson, A., Bastian, J., Chin, T.J., Isaksson, M.: A consensus-based framework for distributed bundle adjustment. In: IEEE Conference on Computer Vision and Pattern Recognition (2016)
11. Fratarcangeli, M., Bradley, D., Gruber, A., Zoss, G., Beeler, T.: Fast nonlinear least squares optimization of large-scale semi-sparse problems. In: Computer Graphics Forum (2020)
12. Grisetti, G., Kümmerle, R., Strasdat, H., Konolige, K.: g2o: a general framework for (hyper) graph optimization. In: IEEE International Conference on Robotics and Automation (2011)
13. Guennebaud, G., Jacob, B., et al.: Eigen v3. http://eigen.tuxfamily.org (2010)
14. Guo, Y., Liu, J., Li, G., Mai, L., Dong, H.: Fast and flexible human pose estimation with hyperpose. In: Proceedings of the 29th ACM International Conference on Multimedia (2021)
15. Hackel, T., Savinov, N., Ladicky, L., Wegner, J.D., Schindler, K., Pollefeys, M.: Semantic3d. net: a new large-scale point cloud classification benchmark. arXiv preprint arXiv:1704.03847 (2017)

16. Huang, J., Huang, S., Sun, M.: DeepLM: large-scale nonlinear least squares on deep learning frameworks using stochastic domain decomposition. In: IEEE/CVF Conference on Computer Vision and Pattern Recognition (2021)
17. Kaess, M., Johannsson, H., Roberts, R., Ila, V., Leonard, J.J., Dellaert, F.: iSAM2: incremental smoothing and mapping using the bayes tree. Int. J. Robot. Res. **31**(2), 216–235 (2012)
18. Kaess, M., Ranganathan, A., Dellaert, F.: iSAM: incremental smoothing and mapping. IEEE Trans. Robot. **24**(6), 1365–1378 (2008)
19. Koliousis, A., Watcharapichat, P., Weidlich, M., Mai, L., Costa, P., Pietzuch, P.: Crossbow: scaling deep learning with small batch sizes on multi-GPU servers. In: Proceedings of the VLDB Endowment (2019)
20. Konolige, K., Agrawal, M.: FrameSLAM: from bundle adjustment to real-time visual mapping. IEEE Trans. Robot. **24**(5), 1066–1077 (2008)
21. Levinson, J., et al.: Towards fully autonomous driving: systems and algorithms. In: IEEE Intelligent Vehicles Symposium (2011)
22. Li, P., Chen, X., Shen, S.: Stereo r-cnn based 3d object detection for autonomous driving. In: IEEE/CVF Conference on Computer Vision and Pattern Recognition (2019)
23. Liu, H., Chen, M., Zhang, G., Bao, H., Bao, Y.: ICE-BA: Incremental, consistent and efficient bundle adjustment for visual-inertial slam. In: IEEE Conference on Computer Vision and Pattern Recognition (2018)
24. Ma, X., Wang, Z., Li, H., Zhang, P., Ouyang, W., Fan, X.: Accurate monocular 3d object detection via color-embedded 3d reconstruction for autonomous driving. In: IEEE/CVF International Conference on Computer Vision (2019)
25. Marquardt, D.W.: An algorithm for least-squares estimation of nonlinear parameters. J. Soc. Ind. Appl. Math. **11**(2), 431–441 (1963)
26. Mayer, H.: RPBA - robust parallel bundle adjustment based on covariance information (2019)
27. Ortiz, J., Pupilli, M., Leutenegger, S., Davison, A.J.: Bundle adjustment on a graph processor. In: IEEE/CVF Conference on Computer Vision and Pattern Recognition (2020)
28. Park, Y., Lepetit, V., Woo, W.: Multiple 3d object tracking for augmented reality. In: IEEE/ACM International Symposium on Mixed and Augmented Reality (2008)
29. Powell, M.J.: A hybrid method for nonlinear equations. numerical methods for nonlinear algebraic equations (1970)
30. Tang, C., Tan, P.: Ba-net: dense bundle adjustment network. arXiv preprint arXiv:1806.04807 (2018)
31. Triggs, B., McLauchlan, P.F., Hartley, R.I., Fitzgibbon, A.W.: Bundle adjustment-a modern synthesis. In: International workshop on vision algorithms (1999)
32. Vo, M., Narasimhan, S.G., Sheikh, Y.: Spatiotemporal bundle adjustment for dynamic 3d reconstruction. In: IEEE Conference on Computer Vision and Pattern Recognition (2016)
33. Wang, H.-R., Lei, J., Li, A., Wu, Y.-H.: A geometry-based point cloud reduction method for mobile augmented reality system. J. Comput. Sci. Technol. **33**(6), 1164–1177 (2018). https://doi.org/10.1007/s11390-018-1879-3
34. Wedderburn, R.W.: Quasi-likelihood functions, generalized linear models, and the gauss-newton method. Biometrika **61**(3), 439–447 (1974)
35. Wilson, K., Snavely, N.: Robust global translations with 1dsfm. In: Proceedings of the European Conference on Computer Vision (2014)
36. Wu, C., Agarwal, S., Curless, B., Seitz, S.M.: Multicore bundle adjustment. In: IEEE Conference on Computer Vision and Pattern Recognition (2011)

37. Zhang, R., Zhu, S., Fang, T., Quan, L.: Distributed very large scale bundle adjustment by global camera consensus. In: 2017 IEEE International Conference on Computer Vision (2017)
38. Zhao, Y., Guo, T.: Pointar: Efficient lighting estimation for mobile augmented reality. In: European Conference on Computer Vision (2020)
39. Zhou, L., et al.: Stochastic bundle adjustment for efficient and scalable 3d reconstruction. In: European Conference on Computer Vision (2020)

The One Where They Reconstructed 3D Humans and Environments in TV Shows

Georgios Pavlakos[✉], Ethan Weber, Matthew Tancik, and Angjoo Kanazawa

University of California, Berkeley, USA
pavlakos@berkeley.edu

Abstract. TV shows depict a wide variety of human behaviors and have been studied extensively for their potential to be a rich source of data for many applications. However, the majority of the existing work focuses on 2D recognition tasks. In this paper, we make the observation that there is a certain persistence in TV shows, *i.e.*, repetition of the environments and the humans, which makes possible the 3D reconstruction of this content. Building on this insight, we propose an automatic approach that operates on an entire season of a TV show and aggregates information in 3D; we build a 3D model of the environment, compute camera information, static 3D scene structure and body scale information. Then, we demonstrate how this information acts as *rich 3D context* that can guide and improve the recovery of 3D human pose and position in these environments. Moreover, we show that reasoning about humans and their environment in 3D enables a broad range of downstream applications: re-identification, gaze estimation, cinematography and image editing. We apply our approach on environments from seven iconic TV shows and perform an extensive evaluation of the proposed system.

1 Introduction

Remember that time when you binge-watched an entire season of your favorite TV show, *e.g.*, "Friends", over a weekend? After that experience, you would know the layout of the rooms, the locations of the furniture, and even the relative height of the characters as they interact closely on screen. As a result, for any frame, you could tell where the room is viewed from, where the characters are situated, and how they relate to the rest of the scene, even the parts of the scene outside the frame. Essentially, as viewers, we aggregate all the visual information into a dynamic 3D world where the new observations are aligned to.

In this paper, we propose a method that can similarly aggregate 3D information over video collections and use it to perceive accurate 3D human pose and

---

G. Pavlakos and E. Weber—Equal contribution.

Supplementary Information The online version contains supplementary material available at https://doi.org/10.1007/978-3-031-19836-6_41.

S. Avidan et al. (Eds.): ECCV 2022, LNCS 13697, pp. 732–749, 2022.
https://doi.org/10.1007/978-3-031-19836-6_41

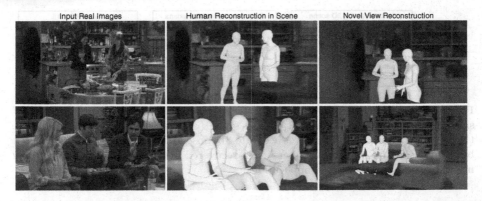

Input Real Images   Human Reconstruction in Scene   Novel View Reconstruction

Fig. 1. Reconstruction of humans in TV show environments. Given images across the whole season of a TV show, we present an approach that recovers the 3D scene context, which enables accurate estimation of every actor's 3D pose and location. We show the input (left), the mesh reconstructions of the actors in the camera view (center) and in a novel view (right). Human meshes are visualized against the reconstructed scene, which is represented by a Neural Radiance Field (NeRF). To appreciate the correct 3D localization of people, notice the position in the novel view and the occlusions. Readers are encouraged to watch video results in the project page: http://ethanweber.me/sitcoms3D/.

location of the actors. Although reconstruction of dynamic scenes is challenging from a single video clip, our insight is that in the context of TV shows, across many episodes, there are many video clips that *depict the same scene and people many times.* The repeated observations provide a strong multi-view signal of the underlying scene, enabling reconstruction of the camera and the dense structure. These serve as context to accurately recover the 3D pose and location of the people in the 3D environment. A representative result is shown in Fig. 1. Although we demonstrate our method & results on TV shows, our insight is also applicable to other domains with repetition in the environment and the people, *e.g.*, sports [20,47,71], late night shows [15,40] and movies [45].

We operationalize our insight by focusing on an entire season from TV shows and collecting the sequences that correspond to a specific environment. These sequences are organized in shots [3], which are typically captured by different cameras. To collect a diverse set of images, we sample frames at the shot boundaries (cuts between cameras). This ensures a wide variety of viewpoints, while avoiding redundancy, making it practical to apply a structure-from-motion pipeline [53] to estimate the intrinsic and extrinsic camera parameters (calibration). Then we use a neural radiance field (NeRF-W [36]) to disentangle the static and transient components and obtain a dense 3D reconstruction (Fig. 2, first block).

The 3D scene reconstruction offers rich 3D context - cameras and scene structure - enabling an in-depth study of humans (Fig. 2, second block). First, for frames on the shot boundaries, the viewpoints from the two different shots act

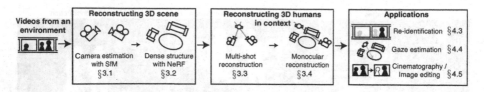

Fig. 2. Overview of our workflow. First, we use a collection of videos from a TV show environment and reconstruct the 3D scene (cameras and dense structure). We then use this information to recover accurate 3D pose and location of people over shot boundaries and on monocular frames. The recovered 3D information is immediately useful for various downstream applications.

as effective multi-view (or multi-shot) information for human reconstruction [45]. We use the calibrated cameras and propose a multi-shot human reconstruction method, which jointly solves for body pose, body shape, identity and location. In this **calibrated multi-shot** method, camera information enables triangulation of people, which removes ambiguity and provides significant improvement upon the equivalent uncalibrated baseline [45]. Next, human reconstructions on the shot boundary inform us of the scale of each person relative to the scene. This is additional 3D context that is complementary to the cameras and scene structure. Since most frames are not on shot boundaries, we also formulate a monocular human reconstruction method that is explicitly guided by the extracted 3D context (camera, structure, body scale). The successful integration of the 3D context in our **contextual monocular** method leads to improvements over the state-of-the-art monocular baselines.

Our proposed "3Dification" of TV shows opens the door to many immediate applications (Fig. 2, third block). First, our human reconstruction on the shot boundaries associates person detections, by incorporating geometric and anthropometric constraints. We show that this form of **re-identification** consistently outperforms traditional image-based baselines [12,22,23]. In parallel, from our reconstructed humans we can extract reliable **gaze information**, which can outperform specialized gaze estimation [46]. Moreover, our results provide estimates of the camera-to-person distance, which is relevant for **cinematography** applications [50,51]. Finally, we illustrate the potential use in **image editing** applications, like object insertion or human deletion.

In summary, our contributions can be summarized as follows:

- We identify the significant amount of 3D context (cameras, structure and body shape) in domains with repetition in the environment and the people, *e.g.*, TV shows, and propose a method to aggregate it from video sequences.
- We propose a formulation that integrates this context in 3D human estimation methods, which improves human reconstruction.
- We demonstrate how the aggregated 3D information can help a wide variety of downstream tasks: re-ID, gaze estimation, cinematography, image editing.
- We perform extensive qualitative and quantitative evaluation to validate the quality of our recovered 3D results.

2   Related Work

2.1   Perceiving TV Shows

The computer vision community has a long history of works on perceiving TV shows/movies. One of the most common tasks in this setting is studying the show characters with emphasis in face/character identification [2,9,39,43,57,58], where different cues have also been explored, e.g., body, voice or gaze [6,8,34,35]. TV show data has been used extensively to study human behavior. Ferrari *et al.* study 2D pose estimation [10] and perform pose-based analysis [11]. Patron *et al.* [44] and Hoai *et al.* [19] focus on human interactions, while Recasens *et al.* [46] and Marín-Jiménez *et al.* [34] use this data to study gaze. Vondrick *et al.* [60] use sequences from TV shows to learn activity forecasting, while Wang *et al.* [61] leverage it for affordance learning. Despite this attention, all the above methods reason in 2D, with only a few exceptions. Everingham and Zisserman [9] use a 3D head model for re-identification. Here, we demonstrate how 3D location information can significantly simplify the re-ID problem. Pavlakos *et al.* [45] reconstruct humans from videos with multiple shots. However, they operate without camera calibration, while we show the importance of recovering reliable cameras.

2.2   Scene Reconstruction

Reconstruction of 3D scenes is a well studied problem, e.g., [1,21, 53,54], however, most methods assume static scenes. Related work focuses on dynamic reconstruction [4,38], but requires capture from multiple wide-baseline synchronized cameras. Luo *et al.* [33] and Kopf *et al.* [29] present pipelines for recovering depth in monocular videos that include humans, but

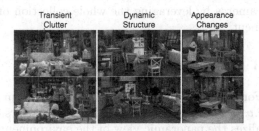

Fig. 3. Reconstruction challenges of TV shows include transient and dynamic objects as well as appearance changes.

they assume that the underlying scene is static. View synthesis approaches like NeRF [37] and follow-ups [41,66] can be used to solve multi-view stereo, however these also assume static scenes. Other extensions of NeRF focus on reconstructing 3D motion in the scene [13,30,42], but are often limited when handling changes in appearances and transient objects. NeRF in the wild [36] is the most relevant approach for the type of data we use (Fig. 3), since it can deal with appearance and transient changes. In this paper, we find that when our data is properly curated we can use NeRF-W to recover dense 3D structure. We then show that this structure can be used to guide consistent 3D human reconstruction.

2.3   Humans in 3D Scenes

Most works that reconstruct humans in context with the scene assume a static, pre-captured 3D environment. Savva *et al.* [52] is one of the first works that explore 3D human-scene interactions from RGB-D video, while Hassan *et al.* [17] study the recovery of 3D humans in context with their environment from monocular images. Many works incorporate environmental constraints for motion estimation from videos [48,49,55,56,63,67,69], by assuming known floor or contact points. Recently, Guzon *et al.* [16] proposed a system for localizing a person in a known environment and estimating their 3D pose. Again, the environment is reconstructed *a priori* and the approach also requires an egocentric sensor and IMUs for pose estimation. Liu *et al.* [31] propose a method that reconstructs the scene and the people together using egocentric video captured in static outdoor scenes. In this work, we reconstruct structure from much more challenging dynamic scenes, by aggregating 3D information over video content.

Some works [62,68] have studied human reconstruction from single images, while also recovering aspects of the environment. PHOSA [68] recovers humans interacting with objects from in-the-wild images, and is followed by [62,64] in other settings. While they focus on visible human-object interactions, we consider cases where the scene might not be fully visible. Knowing camera parameters is an integral part of scene perception. SPEC [27] regresses camera parameters from a single image. In contrast, we can recover more reliable context for cameras by leveraging the whole collection of images from a TV show environment.

3   Technical Approach

For the following discussion, we use the term *environment* to refer to a location, *i.e.*, a room, kitchen, cafe, etc., that appears often in a TV show. Figure 4 visualizes the panoramic view of the environments we reconstruct in this paper. We use the term *shot* for an uninterrupted sequence captured by a camera. Shots are organized in *scenes*, which are typically captured in the same environment. Multiple scenes comprise an *episode* and multiple episodes are organized into a *season*. In this work we collect videos across the whole season of a TV show.

3.1   Camera Estimation

For the first step of our workflow, we need to register the cameras in a common coordinate frame (*i.e.*, computing intrinsics and extrinsics) for each environment. This amounts to hundreds of thousands of frames across the season. To keep the number of frames at a practical scale for Structure-from-Motion (SfM) pipelines, we sample frames at shot boundaries, which are automatically detected [23]. This helps to increase the variety of viewpoints - we only use two frames per shot, and inter-shot variety is typically larger than intra-shot variety.

On this reduced set of frames, we use DISK [59] to find correspondences. Since our data includes dynamic actors, we run Mask R-CNN [18] to detect human

Fig. 4. Panoramic views of the reconstructed TV show environments. We obtain and render the static structure using NeRF-W [36]. The environments represent seven TV shows: "The Big Bang Theory", "Frasier", "Everybody Loves Raymond", "Friends", "Two And A Half Men", "Seinfeld" and "How I Met Your Mother".

masks, and we reject correspondences on these regions. We use COLMAP [53] on the remaining feature matches and estimate the sparse 3D reconstruction and camera registration. We use a simple pinhole camera model, and allow each camera to have different focal length. For each frame t we get estimates of camera intrinsics $K_t \in \mathbb{R}^{3 \times 3}$ and extrinsics $R_t^{CW} \in \mathbb{R}^{3 \times 3}, T_t^{CW} \in \mathbb{R}^3$, where CW denotes camera to world transformation. This sparse reconstruction is used to register other frames (non shot-boundary images). Since we do not have access to 3D ground truth for TV show environments, the quality of our cameras is evaluated implicitly by the effect it has on the human reconstruction (see also Sup. Mat.).

3.2 Dense Structure

Besides the camera registration returned from SfM, we also estimate the dense structure of the environment to help with human position estimation. Traditional dense reconstruction methods assume static scenes, but these assumptions are not satisfied in TV show environments which contain many images of extreme diversity (Fig. 3). Instead, we use a NeRF-W network [36] for dense structure estimation. NeRF-W extends NeRF [37], to account for varying appearances and transient occluders. For efficiency, instead of training NeRF-W with all images, we use an automatic selection method to maximize viewpoint variety. We cluster the images based on camera location and viewing direction. For each cluster we select the image with least percent of Mask R-CNN human pixels to use for training (i.e., maximum number of scene rays). After training, NeRF-W returns a volumetric 3D representation of the static structure of the scene.

Fig. 5. Calibrated cameras for scale estimation and identity association. Given calibrated cameras, we can use frames at a shot change to solve for the actors' pose, location, relative scale and association. The four overlapping regions (left) indicate possible locations triangulated by the cameras. Circles indicate correct matches after Hungarian matching. Reconstructed humans are visualized in a NeRF (right).

3.3 Calibrated Multi-shot Human Reconstruction

In movies and TV shows, scenes are filmed in consecutive shots. The shot changes within a scene correspond to consecutive time frames seen by different viewpoints. This serves as *effective multi-view* information, providing signal to recover the 3D location and pose of the actors [45]. However, doing so requires knowledge of the identity of the actors across the shot changes. Prior work utilizes a pre-trained recognition-based re-ID model to establish these correspondences, but this is not always reliable, for example when only the back of the character is visible. We make an observation that when camera information is available, the association can be solved jointly with the 3D human pose, shape, and location. We refer to this approach as *calibrated multi-shot optimization*.

Let us assume there are M actors in frame t, N actors in frame $t + 1$, and a shot change happens from frame t to $t+1$. We need to solve a matching problem to associate the two sets of actors. We propose to use the objective of SMPLify fitting [5] to model the cost for this matching.

Formally, let us consider a detection of a person at time instance t, with detected 2D keypoints $J_{est,t}$ [7]. We denote with θ_t the pose parameters and with β_t the shape parameters of the person in the SMPL format [32]. We use J_t for the joints and T_t^C for the translation of the body in the *camera frame*. Moreover, from SfM, we have access to the transformations R_t^{CW}, T_t^{CW} from the camera frame to the world frame at time t. Given all of the above, we minimize the objective function with respect to $\{\theta_t, \theta_{t+1}, \beta_t, \beta_{t+1}, T_t^C, T_{t+1}^C\}$:

$$E = \underbrace{E_{J_t} + E_{J_{t+1}}}_{\text{2D reprojection}} + \underbrace{E_{\text{priors}_t} + E_{\text{priors}_{t+1}}}_{\text{anthropometric constraints}} + \underbrace{E_{\text{glob}_{t,t+1}}}_{\text{3D consistency}} \quad (1)$$

Here, $E_{J_t} = E_{J_t}(\beta_t, \theta_t, K_t, J_{est,t})$ is the joints reprojection term and E_{priors} are anthropometric priors similar to [5]. The key constraint is multi-shot consistency, which encourages the estimated bodies to be similar in the global frame:

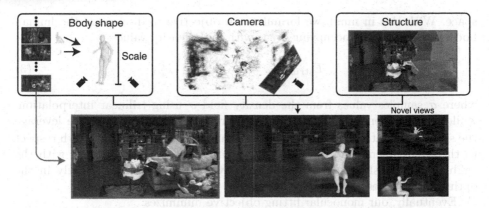

Fig. 6. Contextual monocular human reconstruction. For an input frame, we can leverage (a) the body shape (scale) of the person from a neighboring shot change, (b) the camera registration, and (c) the static **structure** of the environment. This enables monocular reconstruction of the person in context with their environment.

$$E_{\text{glob}_{t,t+1}} = \|(R_t^{CW} J_t^C + T_t^{CW}) - (R_{t+1}^{CW} J_{t+1}^C + T_{t+1}^{CW})\|^2. \qquad (2)$$

In contrast to prior work, we do not need to solve for the camera as we have access to reliable extrinsics and intrinsics (prior works [25,45,68] use a heuristic for focal lengths). This leads to more accurate human placement and constraints that allow for solving associations. Using this fitting cost E, we solve association by Hungarian matching. See Fig. 5 for an illustration of this optimization.

3.4   Contextual Monocular Human Reconstruction

Although shot changes provide effective multi-view information for free, the majority of the frames in the video only have monocular observations. Monocular human reconstruction is challenging, particularly so for TV shows with many close-up shots; however, in our case, we can capitalize on the contextual information we have recovered. In this subsection, we explain how we can make use of this 3D context in an effective way. We demonstrate this using a single-frame optimization approach, SMPLify [5], but other methods could also benefit from our context, *e.g.*, we show representative results for HuMoR [48] in the Sup. Mat.

A high-level overview of this step is presented in Fig. 6. First, given the sparse reconstruction of the environment, we can register the camera for a new frame. This gives us both extrinsics R_t^{CW}, T_t^{CW} and intrinsics K_t for the camera via solving PnP with COLMAP [53]. We leverage these parameters for accurate projection. Moreover, we can employ the structure captured by our NeRF-W network. In general, it is not trivial to extract the structure from NeRF [41,66]. The native representation used by NeRF is in the form of densities for each point. Here, we propose to use this density as a proxy for occupancy of the 3D space. With this in mind, we formulate an objective to discourage the human body vertices V from occupying areas with high density values:

$$E_{\text{structure}} = \rho\Big(\sum_{v \in V} \tilde{\sigma}(v)\Big), \tag{3}$$

where $\tilde{\sigma}$ samples values from the density field σ using trilinear interpolation, while ρ is the Geman-McClure robust error function [14]. Finally, we leverage the shape parameters $\hat{\beta}$ that capture the relative scale of the person with respect to the environment, and are recovered from the nearest shot change with the calibrated multi-shot reconstruction. This value can be used explicitly in the optimization to resolve the scale ambiguity.

Eventually, our monocular fitting objective minimizes:

$$E_J(\beta = \hat{\beta}, \theta, K = \hat{K}, J_{est}) + E_{\text{priors}} + E_{\text{structure}}, \tag{4}$$

with respect to θ_t, T_t^C, where we employ the camera information and the body shape parameters of the person during the fitting, while also discouraging the body mesh from penetrating the static **structure** of the scene.

3.5   Applications

An important argument in favor of 3D reconstruction for people in TV show environments is that it can simplify many reasoning tasks in this domain. For example, the calibrated multi-shot optimization explicitly reasons about the identity of the detected humans, as part of the Hungarian matching. This enables reliable *re-identification* in the challenging case of shot changes where the viewpoint can change significantly (Sect. 4.3). Moreover, one can extract *gaze information* from our 3D humans by considering the 3D pose of the face/head. With knowledge of camera pose, we can easily estimate the gaze direction in the global space, and thus compute gaze across the shot change (Sect. 4.4). Finally, we perform an analysis of our data which could be useful for *cinematography* applications, and highlight the potential of *image editing* using our results (Sect. 4.5).

4   Experiments

In this section, we present the quantitative and qualitative evaluation of our approach. We use seven popular TV shows (Fig. 4) and one season from each. We follow the procedure described in Sect. 3 to collect the images we use. Each environment has 1k-5k frames from shot changes. For evaluation, we select per TV show a set of 50 person identities present on these shot changes. We use these frames as a test set to evaluate our method qualitatively with a crowd-sourced perceptual evaluation on AMT and curate it with the information we require for quantitative evaluation, *i.e.*, human-human associations, body keypoints, top-down location of the pelvis in the scene and gaze target across the shot change.

Input Shot Changes   Results   Novel View Results

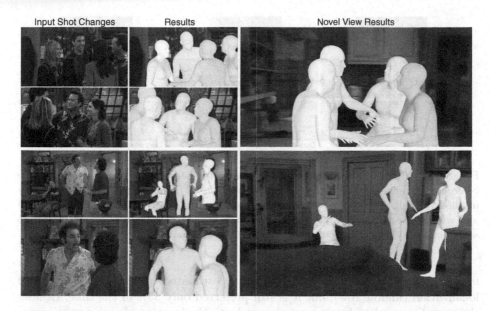

Fig. 7. Calibrated multi-shot and re-ID results. Using input shot changes (left), we perform our calibrated multi-shot optimization which jointly solves for pose, shape, location and association (middle). Note that identity, illustrated with colors, is not available a priori, but is estimated jointly with the 3D reconstruction. The recovered humans can be rendered in novel views using the NeRF of the environment (right).

4.1   Calibrated Multi-shot Human Reconstruction

For a proof of concept, we first evaluate our proposed calibrated multi-shot optimization in a controlled setting, with the Human3.6M dataset [24], where we have accurate 3D ground truth for pose. Since our focus is on the effect of having access to camera parameters, we compare with the equivalent uncalibrated baseline, which is similar to [45]. The results are presented in Table 1. The significant improvement when having access to camera information further motivates the importance of our calibrated multi-shot algorithm.

For our data from TV shows, we do not have access to 3D ground truth for humans, so we perform two evaluations for the human reconstructions. First, we perform a system evaluation by Amazon Mechanical Turk (AMT) workers. For each 3D human reconstruction, we task the annotators to select the rendered result video (our method vs. a baseline) where the human reconstruction is more accurate and consistent with the scene and shot boundary images. Each result video is 10 s and provides multiple viewpoints of the person in the scene. We test on our test set, resulting in 2100 human labels from 48 participants who went through quality control (please see Sup. Mat. for more details). We report the percent of choices where our method is preferred over the baselines in Table 1. The uncalibrated baseline (first row; without intrinsics or extrinsics) is very rarely preferred over our calibrated baseline (last row; with estimated

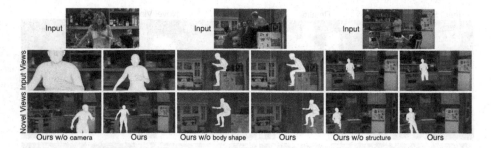

Fig. 8. Results for the contextual monocular reconstruction. We ablate the basic components of the contextual reconstruction to demonstrate their effects. Our method uses all three forms of context. Without our estimated camera intrinsics (left) and without body shape (middle), the person is incorrectly placed in the scene due to scale ambiguity. Using structure (right) avoids interpenetration with the environment.

intrinsics and extrinsics). Having access to estimated intrinsics can help with localization (middle row), but it is still preferred only 35% of the time. Besides the crowd-sourced evaluation, we also evaluate the location of each person quantitatively. In this case, we compute the mean metric distance error for the pelvis joint in the top-down projection, which is reported in Table 1. The conclusions are consistent with the AMT evaluation, highlighting the importance of camera information. Some representative results of our calibrated multi-shot optimization are presented in Fig. 7, where we also indicate the estimated identity association (which we evaluate in more detail in Sect. 4.3).

4.2   Monocular Contextual Human Reconstruction

Next, we investigate our proposed contextual monocular reconstruction. For this evaluation, we study the effect of each component separately – knowledge of the cameras, access to the person's body shape, and finally scene **structure** information. We present the results of this ablation in Table 2, where we report

Table 1. Evaluation of the proposed calibrated multi-shot optimization. We ablate the effect of camera information in multi-shot optimization. On Human3.6M, we report results on the standard 3D pose metrics in mm [70]. On our TV show data, we perform a system evaluation on AMT and provide quantitative results based on the spatial localization of the reconstructed person in the scene.

Method	Camera information		Human3.6M		TV shows	
Multi-shot optimization	Intrinsics	Extrinsics	MPJPE	PA-MPJPE	% preferred vs. Ours ↑	Distance error ↓
Uncalibrated [45]	✗	✗	131.9	56.9	4%	889 cm
Partial Calibration	✓	✗	123.8	56.3	35%	59 cm
Calibrated	✓	✓	**65.8**	**47.1**	—	**38 cm**

Table 2. Ablation of the main components of our contextual reconstruction.
Cross-shot PCK @ $\alpha = 0.5$ is reported. Knowledge of the camera focal length is very
important to get a good 3D location for the human. Information about body shape
can have significant improvements, as it resolves the scale ambiguity. Structure helps
to avoid the incoherent interpenetrations with the scene.

Method	Cross-shot PCK
No context: ProHMR [28]	14.7%
No context: PARE [26]	14.2%
No context: SMPLify [5]	16.5%
Context w/o camera (intrinsics)	16.0%
Context w/o body shape (scale)	65.9%
Context w/o structure	87.5%
Context (full)	**88.7%**

cross-shot PCK @ $\alpha = 0.5$ [45]. Effectively, we project the person to the view
across the shot boundary and measure localization accuracy for the joints in
that space (more details in the Sup. Mat.). First, we see that state-of-the-art
monocular methods without context [5,26,28] perform similarly on this data.
Then, we examine the effect of context, using the optimization baseline [5] as our
starting point (third row). Access to camera intrinsics is important to estimate
a rough location of the person, and without it the method performs as the
baseline without context. Knowledge of the body scale of the person, can make
our estimate even more accurate. Finally, structure gives a smaller quantitative
improvement but has a more pronounced qualitative effect by placing the person
coherently in the environment. See Fig. 8 for qualitative results.

Table 3. Re-ID results for actors in shot boundary frames. We use different
methods to estimate matching costs for detections and we run Hungarian matching
to establish associations. A geometric baseline using the reprojection error from person keypoint triangulation improves upon SOTA image-based baselines [12,22,23], but
using our multi-shot fitting cost performs better because it also includes anthropometric constraints, i.e., the triangulated points should respect the human body priors.

Matching costs	Re-ID F1 ↑
Fu et al. [12] (Appearance)	0.78
Huang et al. [22] (Appearance)	0.79
Huang et al. [23] (Appearance)	0.80
Keypoint triangulation (Geometry)	0.86
Ours (Geometry + Anthropometric)	**0.91**

4.3   Re-identification

For the re-ID evaluation, we examine the challenging case of person association after a shot change. For our case, re-ID is directly estimated from our calibrated multi-shot optimization. We compare this result with two types of baselines for computing affinities/costs between instances for Hungarian matching. The first type is image-based re-ID networks for affinity estimation, where [12] achieves SOTA on standard re-ID benchmarks, while [22,23] are trained on movies, a source of data similar to TV shows. The second type is a geometric baseline that uses our recovered cameras and is based on human keypoint triangulation, where the reprojection error is used as the cost for the Hungarian algorithm. Notice, that unlike SMPL fitting, this does not incorporate anthropometric constraints, *i.e.*, it considers every keypoint match independently, without using human body shape priors or measuring the holistic result. We report re-ID F1 scores in Table 3 using the visible pairs of actors before/after the shot change. Based on the results, our re-identification can consistently outperform these baselines.

4.4   Gaze Estimation

For gaze estimation, we compare with the method of [46] that estimates the gaze target after the shot change. We evaluate the angular error in the gaze direction projected on the image plane. We report the Percentage of Correct Gaze Directions (similar to PCK [65]), using $\alpha = 20^o$ as threshold. Please see Sup. Mat. for details.

Results are reported in Table 4. Since [46] relies on face detection, we report results on our whole test set (column "all") and on the subset

Table 4. Gaze following results. We report the Percentage of Correct Gaze Directions (see text for description). Our approach outperforms the baseline of [46].Gaze following results. We report the Percentage of Correct Gaze Directions (see text for description). Our approach outperforms the baseline of [46].

Method	PCGD ($\alpha = 20^o$) ↑	
	All	w/ face
Recasens *et al.* [46]	16%	32%
Ours	**62%**	**67%**

where face detection is successful (column "w/ face"). Our approach outperforms [46] in both cases. Since we rely on body detection, we are more robust even when the face is occluded. Moreover, our extracted camera poses allow us to follow gaze across shots in a more accurate way. Further improvements are expected by modeling eye pose and saliency estimation to detect the gaze target, similarly to [46].

4.5   Cinematography/Image Editing Applications

We provide an initial analysis of our results in Fig. 9, and present an extended study in the Sup. Mat. First, we visualize the *distribution of the estimated field of view for the cameras*. Here we can see the long-tail distribution for the views with a large field of view, *i.e.*, more informative viewpoints for 3D reconstruction. This justifies our insight to process data across the whole season, since the large majority of the views is typically close-ups. Moreover, we visualize the *locations of the cameras and the human actors*. The camera data could be useful for cinematography analysis [51], and the person data for behavior or affordance analysis [61]. Finally, we illustrate potential editing applications enabled by the reconstruction of humans and the environment: *person removal and object insertion*. More editing options are possible, given the 3D nature of our processing.

(a) Camera FOV Distribution (b) Camera Pose Distribution (c) Person Location Distribution

(d) Person Removal (e) The Big Bunny Insertion

Fig. 9. Cinematography applications/Image editing. We present analysis of our processed data, including distribution of field of view, camera pose distribution and person location distribution for Friends (top). Moreover, we present editing options after our processing, including person removal and object insertion (bottom).

5 Discussion

Conclusion: To the best of our knowledge, we are the first to reconstruct the people and the environment in TV shows and reason about them in 3D. We start with multi-shot video sequences associated with a specific environment and recover the camera, structure and relative human scale. We use this information as context to reconstruct humans even from a single frame, in a way that is consistent with their environment. We demonstrate our approach on seven different TV shows and present qualitative and quantitative results, as well as a wide variety of applications and analysis of the reconstructed data.

Future Directions: Our work has only scratched the surface of this extremely challenging and in-depth problem. Currently, we do not reconstruct the transient objects or dynamic objects that humans interact with (*e.g.*, chairs that move around, fridge opening). Also, the recovered pose of the humans is completely dependent on the quality of the 2D keypoint detections. It would be an interesting direction to incorporate appearance models for pose fitting.

Acknowledgements. This research was supported by the DARPA Machine Common Sense program as well as BAIR/BDD sponsors. Matthew Tancik is supported by the NSF GRFP.

References

1. Agarwal, S., et al.: Building Rome in a day. In: ICCV (2009)
2. Arandjelovic, O., Zisserman, A.: Automatic face recognition for film character retrieval in feature-length films. In: CVPR (2005)
3. Arijon, D.: Grammar of the Film Language. Hastings House, New York (1976)
4. Ballan, L., Brostow, G.J., Puwein, J., Pollefeys, M.: Unstructured video-based rendering: interactive exploration of casually captured videos. ACM Trans. Graph. (TOG) **29**(4), 1–11 (2010)
5. Bogo, F., Kanazawa, A., Lassner, C., Gehler, P., Romero, J., Black, M.J.: Keep it SMPL: automatic estimation of 3D human pose and shape from a single image. In: ECCV (2016)
6. Brown, A., Kalogeiton, V., Zisserman, A.: Face, body, voice: video person-clustering with multiple modalities. In: ICCVW (2021)
7. Cao, Z., Hidalgo, G., Simon, T., Wei, S.E., Sheikh, Y.: OpenPose: realtime multi-person 2D pose estimation using part affinity fields. In: PAMI (2019)
8. Everingham, M., Sivic, J., Zisserman, A.: "Hello! My name is... Buffy" - automatic naming of characters in TV video. In: BMVC (2006)
9. Everingham, M., Zisserman, A.: Identifying individuals in video by combining generative and discriminative head models. In: ICCV (2005)
10. Ferrari, V., Marín-Jiménez, M., Zisserman, A.: Progressive search space reduction for human pose estimation. In: CVPR (2008)
11. Ferrari, V., Marín-Jiménez, M., Zisserman, A.: Pose search: retrieving people using their pose. In: CVPR (2009)
12. Fu, D., et al.: Unsupervised pre-training for person re-identification. In: CVPR (2021)
13. Gao, C., Saraf, A., Kopf, J., Huang, J.B.: Dynamic view synthesis from dynamic monocular video. In: ICCV (2021)
14. Geman, S., McClure, D.E.: Statistical methods for tomographic image reconstruction. Bull. Int. Stat. Inst. **4**, 5–21 (1987)
15. Ginosar, S., Bar, A., Kohavi, G., Chan, C., Owens, A., Malik, J.: Learning individual styles of conversational gesture. In: CVPR (2019)
16. Guzov, V., Mir, A., Sattler, T., Pons-Moll, G.: Human POSEitioning system (HPS): 3D human pose estimation and self-localization in large scenes from body-mounted sensors. In: CVPR (2021)
17. Hassan, M., Choutas, V., Tzionas, D., Black, M.J.: Resolving 3D human pose ambiguities with 3D scene constraints. In: ICCV (2019)
18. He, K., Gkioxari, G., Dollár, P., Girshick, R.: Mask R-CNN. In: ICCV (2017)
19. Hoai, M., Zisserman, A.: Talking heads: detecting humans and recognizing their interactions. In: CVPR (2014)

20. Homayounfar, N., Fidler, S., Urtasun, R.: Sports field localization via deep structured models. In: CVPR (2017)
21. Huang, P.H., Matzen, K., Kopf, J., Ahuja, N., Huang, J.B.: DeepMVS: learning multi-view stereopsis. In: CVPR (2018)
22. Huang, Q., Liu, W., Lin, D.: Person search in videos with one portrait through visual and temporal links. In: ECCV (2018)
23. Huang, Q., Xiong, Y., Rao, A., Wang, J., Lin, D.: MovieNet: a holistic dataset for movie understanding. In: ECCV (2020)
24. Ionescu, C., Papava, D., Olaru, V., Sminchisescu, C.: Human3.6M: large scale datasets and predictive methods for 3D human sensing in natural environments. In: PAMI (2013)
25. Jiang, W., Kolotouros, N., Pavlakos, G., Zhou, X., Daniilidis, K.: Coherent reconstruction of multiple humans from a single image. In: CVPR (2020)
26. Kocabas, M., Huang, C.H.P., Hilliges, O., Black, M.J.: PARE: part attention regressor for 3D human body estimation. In: ICCV (2021)
27. Kocabas, M., Huang, C.H.P., Tesch, J., Muller, L., Hilliges, O., Black, M.J.: SPEC: seeing people in the wild with an estimated camera. In: ICCV (2021)
28. Kolotouros, N., Pavlakos, G., Jayaraman, D., Daniilidis, K.: Probabilistic modeling for human mesh recovery. In: ICCV (2021)
29. Kopf, J., Rong, X., Huang, J.B.: Robust consistent video depth estimation. In: CVPR (2021)
30. Li, Z., Niklaus, S., Snavely, N., Wang, O.: Neural scene flow fields for space-time view synthesis of dynamic scenes. In: CVPR (2021)
31. Liu, M., Yang, D., Zhang, Y., Cui, Z., Rehg, J.M., Tang, S.: 4D human body capture from egocentric video via 3D scene grounding. In: 3DV (2021)
32. Loper, M., Mahmood, N., Romero, J., Pons-Moll, G., Black, M.J.: SMPL: a skinned multi-person linear model. ACM Trans. Graph. (TOG) 34(6), 1–16 (2015)
33. Luo, X., Huang, J.B., Szeliski, R., Matzen, K., Kopf, J.: Consistent video depth estimation. ACM Trans. Graph. (TOG) 39(4), 71-1 (2020)
34. Marín-Jiménez, M.J., Kalogeiton, V., Medina-Suárez, P., Zisserman, A.: LAEO-Net++: revisiting people looking at each other in videos. In: PAMI (2021)
35. Marín-Jiménez, M.J., Zisserman, A., Eichner, M., Ferrari, V.: Detecting people looking at each other in videos. In: IJCV (2014)
36. Martin-Brualla, R., Radwan, N., Sajjadi, M.S., Barron, J.T., Dosovitskiy, A., Duckworth, D.: NeRF in the wild: neural radiance fields for unconstrained photo collections. In: CVPR (2021)
37. Mildenhall, B., Srinivasan, P.P., Tancik, M., Barron, J.T., Ramamoorthi, R., Ng, R.: NeRF: representing scenes as neural radiance fields for view synthesis. In: ECCV (2020)
38. Mustafa, A., Volino, M., Kim, H., Guillemaut, J.Y., Hilton, A.: Temporally coherent general dynamic scene reconstruction. In: IJCV (2021)
39. Nagrani, A., Zisserman, A.: From benedict Cumberbatch to Sherlock Holmes: character identification in TV series without a script. In: BMVC (2017)
40. Ng, E., Ginosar, S., Darrell, T., Joo, H.: Body2Hands: learning to infer 3D hands from conversational gesture body dynamics. In: CVPR (2021)
41. Oechsle, M., Peng, S., Geiger, A.: UNISURF: unifying neural implicit surfaces and radiance fields for multi-view reconstruction. In: ICCV (2021)
42. Park, K., et al.: Nerfies: deformable neural radiance fields. In: ICCV (2021)
43. Parkhi, O.M., Rahtu, E., Cao, Q., Zisserman, A.: Automated video face labelling for films and TV material. In: PAMI (2018)

44. Patron-Perez, A., Marszalek, M., Reid, I., Zisserman, A.: Structured learning of human interactions in TV shows. In: PAMI (2012)
45. Pavlakos, G., Malik, J., Kanazawa, A.: Human mesh recovery from multiple shots. In: CVPR (2022)
46. Recasens, A., Vondrick, C., Khosla, A., Torralba, A.: Following gaze in video. In: ICCV (2017)
47. Rematas, K., Kemelmacher-Shlizerman, I., Curless, B., Seitz, S.: Soccer on your tabletop. In: CVPR (2018)
48. Rempe, D., Birdal, T., Hertzmann, A., Yang, J., Sridhar, S., Guibas, L.J.: HuMoR: 3d human motion model for robust pose estimation. In: ICCV (2021)
49. Rempe, D., Guibas, L.J., Hertzmann, A., Russell, B., Villegas, R., Yang, J.: Contact and human dynamics from monocular video. In: ECCV (2020)
50. Savardi, M., Kovács, A.B., Signoroni, A., Benini, S.: CineScale: a dataset of cinematic shot scale in movies. Data Brief **36**, 107002 (2021)
51. Savardi, M., Signoroni, A., Migliorati, P., Benini, S.: Shot scale analysis in movies by convolutional neural networks. In: ICIP (2018)
52. Savva, M., Chang, A.X., Hanrahan, P., Fisher, M., Nießner, M.: PiGraphs: learning interaction snapshots from observations. ACM Trans. Graph. (TOG) **35**(4), 1–12 (2016)
53. Schönberger, J.L., Frahm, J.M.: Structure-from-motion revisited. In: CVPR (2016)
54. Schönberger, J.L., Zheng, E., Frahm, J.M., Pollefeys, M.: Pixelwise view selection for unstructured multi-view stereo. In: ECCV (2016)
55. Shimada, S., Golyanik, V., Xu, W., Pérez, P., Theobalt, C.: Neural monocular 3D human motion capture with physical awareness. ACM Trans. Graph. (TOG) **40**(4), 1–15 (2021)
56. Shimada, S., Golyanik, V., Xu, W., Theobalt, C.: PhysCap: physically plausible monocular 3D motion capture in real time. ACM Trans. Graph. (TOG) **39**(6), 1–16 (2020)
57. Sivic, J., Everingham, M., Zisserman, A.: "Who are you?" - Learning person specific classifiers from video. In: CVPR (2009)
58. Tapaswi, M., Law, M.T., Fidler, S.: Video face clustering with unknown number of clusters. In: ICCV (2019)
59. Tyszkiewicz, M.J., Fua, P., Trulls, E.: DISK: learning local features with policy gradient. In: NeurIPS (2020)
60. Vondrick, C., Pirsiavash, H., Torralba, A.: Anticipating visual representations from unlabeled video. In: CVPR (2016)
61. Wang, X., Girdhar, R., Gupta, A.: Binge watching: Scaling affordance learning from sitcoms. In: CVPR (2017)
62. Weng, Z., Yeung, S.: Holistic 3D human and scene mesh estimation from single view images. In: CVPR (2021)
63. Xie, K., Wang, T., Iqbal, U., Guo, Y., Fidler, S., Shkurti, F.: Physics-based human motion estimation and synthesis from videos. In: ICCV (2021)
64. Xu, X., Joo, H., Mori, G., Savva, M.: D3D-HOI: dynamic 3d human-object interactions from videos. arXiv preprint arXiv:2108.08420 (2021)
65. Yang, Y., Ramanan, D.: Articulated human detection with flexible mixtures of parts. In: PAMI (2012)
66. Yariv, L., Gu, J., Kasten, Y., Lipman, Y.: Volume rendering of neural implicit surfaces. In: NeurIPS (2021)
67. Yuan, Y., Wei, S.E., Simon, T., Kitani, K., Saragih, J.: SimPoE: simulated character control for 3D human pose estimation. In: CVPR (2021)

68. Zhang, J.Y., Pepose, S., Joo, H., Ramanan, D., Malik, J., Kanazawa, A.: Perceiving 3D human-object spatial arrangements from a single image in the wild. In: ECCV (2020)
69. Zhang, S., Zhang, Y., Bogo, F., Pollefeys, M., Tang, S.: Learning motion priors for 4D human body capture in 3D scenes. In: ICCV (2021)
70. Zhou, X., Zhu, M., Pavlakos, G., Leonardos, S., Derpanis, K.G., Daniilidis, K.: MonoCap: monocular human motion capture using a CNN coupled with a geometric prior. In: PAMI (2018)
71. Zhu, L., Rematas, K., Curless, B., Seitz, S.M., Kemelmacher-Shlizerman, I.: Reconstructing NBA players. In: ECCV (2020)

Author Index

Printed in the United States
by Baker & Taylor Publisher Services